FEMINIST WRITERS

FEMINIST WRITERS

Foreword by

HORTENSE SPILLERS

Editor

PAMELA KESTER-SHELTON

ST. JAMES PRESS
AN IMPRINT OF GALE

DETROIT • NEW YORK • TORONTO • LONDON

Pamela Kester-Shelton, *Editor*
Ashley A. Shelton, *Associate Editor*

Margaret Mazurkiewicz, *Project Editor*

Laura Standley Berger, Peg Bessette, Joann Cerrito, David Collins, Miranda H. Ferrara,
Janice Jorgensen, Michael J. Tyrkus, *Contributing Editors*
Peter M. Gareffa, *Managing Editor, St. James Press*

Mary Beth Trimper, *Production Director*
Shanna Heilveil, *Production Assistant*
Cynthia Baldwin, *Art Director*

Victoria B. Cariappa, *Research Manager*
Julia Daniel, Jennifer Lund, *Research Specialists*

∞™ The paper used in this publication meets the minimum requirements of American National Standard for Information Sciences—Permanence Paper for Printed Library Materials, ANSI Z39.48-1984.

Feminist writers / editor, Pamela Kester-Shelton ; with an introductory forward [sic] by Hortense Spillers.
p. cm.
Includes bibliographical references and indexes.
ISBN 1-55862-217-9
1. Authors—Bio-bibliography. 2. Feminists—Bio-bibliography. 3. Feminism and literature—Bio-bibliography. 4. Feminism in literature—Bio-bibliography. I. Kester-Shelton, Pamela, 1957-
Z5304.A8F46 1996
[PN451]
016.30542—dc20 96-25679
CIP

Printed in the United States of America
Published simultaneously in the United Kingdom

St. James Press is an imprint of Gale

10 9 8 7 6 5 4 3 2 1

CONTENTS

FOREWORD

Feminist Writings: At Century's End

I. Feminist Writings: A Framework

Strictly speaking, "feminist writings" as an extension of "feminism" could only have come about in the 20th century, if historian Nancy Cott is right. In the introduction to *The Grounding of Modern Feminism,* she argues that the word *feminism* gained currency in the United States during the 1910s and that its coinage marked "a new phase in the debate and agitation about women's rights and freedoms that had flared for hundreds of years." The 19th century's *woman movement,* stretching over several decades, came to focus on a set of struggles regarding "civic rights, social freedoms, higher education, remunerative occupations, and the ballot." But at a precise moment in the new century—Cott believes that it occurred at the beginning of the second decade, during "the height of the suffrage campaign"—the older movement reached a point of crisis. The unity symbolized by the singular "woman" was no longer tenable. *Feminism,* as an ideological marker, both carried forward the aims of the woman movement and articulated a cluster of new ambitions that we would recognize today as the goals of the *Women's Movement*—the 1960's women's revolt that sought what Cott proposes, after Nietzsche, as a "'transvaluation of values.'"

Let us assume for the moment that "feminist writing" pertains to readily definable social and political ends regarding the life of women in culture and society; such writings that precede our century would be retrospectively claimed, as Cott argues, by "the vocabulary of feminism ... grafted onto the history of women's rights." This tactical maneuver works quite well in the abstract, until we get down to cases and contradictions: What happens to that assumption when we encounter propositions like the ones put forward by Alice Jardine in *Gynesis,* or Teresa De Lauretis in *Technologies of Gender*? Jardine suggests, on the one hand, that "feminist writing" (*une écriture féminine*) can be carried out by male subjects when it is a matter of engagement with certain tropologies of the feminine. On the other hand, Lauretis entertains the possibility that the subject "woman" in itself, a position in discourse, incurs an overlapping split between the "subject of history" in feminism and empirical women subjects in history. Both of these works appeared during the 1980s and well after the facts of feminism and the women's movement had become established points of reference in contemporary life. But more than that, both texts join a plethora of others in signalling the degrees of complexity, sophistication, and diversity that distinguish this period—1963 to the present—of feminist writings as the most prolific moment, perhaps, of cultural production by women in the fields of the humanities, the social sciences, and the literary art in this entire century. When we think of feminism(s) today—pluralized since the late 1980s when African American women's social and culture critique and post-colonial women's theorizations, among others, revealed yet one more fault line in the new movement—we think the impossible: a political activism concurrent with the Vietnam War protest, the Black Power Movement, surging activity on the radical left, and the global fruition of anti-colonial struggle gradually transformed into a *writing* and a new epistemology. Between the 14th century's Christine de Pisan and the 20th century's Virginia Woolf and Toni Morrison more than six centuries' passage is implied, and for sure, a summary of the time line is never a simple task to fulfill. We are well aware that both this introduction and the anthology that compels it are a sampling of a human and social movement whose cross-generic origins are virtually irrecoverable, try as we might.

In the final analysis, "feminist writing" might only embody the visible tip of an iceberg, almost quite literally speaking, if we think of the historic movement of women as the official name of something we will never exhaustively gauge: the longings and aspirations of communities of women, since time immemorial, towards fully human status and recognition. Early on in the first half of her impressive work, *Food in History,* Reay Tannahill provocatively speculates:

> There are still many mysteries about the 7000 years that pitch-forked humanity from a Stone Age existence into a state of civilization. One is that, beforehand, women and men appear to have been more or less equal politically, whereas by the time society emerged from the Neolithic mists into the full light of recorded history, most institutions, most inventions and all power were the prerogatives of the male.

Alice Walker's unwieldy and otherworldly 1989 fiction, *The Temple of My Familiar,* attempts to imagine what those days might have been like through the fantasies of a character (of many avatars) named Lizzie. The outcome is rather remote, in my view, and not always successful, insamuch as the novel form itself, with its vehicle firmly planted in the modern world, seems to be directed in the forward position and cannot go back so easily because language stops it. Did Tannahill's Neolithic woman "talk" in accents that we might recognize now as human speech? It is well within our experience to imagine that not only might she have done so, but may have done so for reasons with which we could empathize as well: and *his* name is "Fred Flinstone," not improbably hamfisted. The Neolithic first family would have miles and miles to go before its progenies invented script, and by the time they arrived at *that* momentous occasion there may have been a few things that the women had to say.... It is lovely to think that there must have been a "feminist writing" in the beginning.

II. Mapping the Territory

Actually, the character of prehistoric communities and the role of women and the feminine in light of them might be thought of as one of the opening conceptual gambits of the new women's movement. In one of the classic essays of the period—Adrienne Rich's "The Antifeminist Woman"—we are provided with a brief sketch of research in the field of anthropology that attempted to trace a pre-patriarchal family order back to a matriarchal provenance. We are reminded that Engel's *Family, Private Property, and the State* "had earlier connected the advent of the patriarchal family with the beginnings of property-hunger, slavery, war as acquisitive pillage, and ultimately the State itself with its sanction and encouragement of human exploitation." Well after Engels, Elizabeth Gould Davis, in *The First Sex,* attempted to locate primacy in the matriarchal by bringing to bear evidence drawn from anthropology, archaeology, mythology, and history. Before Davis's work of the 1970s, however, Mary Beard's 1945 *Woman as Force in History* extended research on the matriarchal nexus that had been the subject of sporadic forays onto the territory over several decades, by, among other researchers, J. J. Bachofen (*Das mutterrecht*) and Robert Briffault (*The Mothers*).

Of this research protocol, perhaps none has been more controversial than Mary Daly's *Gyn/Ecology,* which played a key role in the feminist revision of patriarchal scholarship in the field of theology. With its studies trained on the concept of the maternal divinity, Daly's work became one of the central texts of the women's studies itinerary of the late 1970s. The importance of Daly's project might also be measured in another way: no less significant a figure in the U.S. women's movement than late poet/activist Audre Lorde took exception to *Gyn/Ecology because* it presumed to explore issues in "myth, legend, religion for the true nature of old female power." In an "open letter" to the author, Lorde sounded one of the relentlessly worrisome and unresolved problems of the women's movement: its perennial unease with non-European and non-European-American women's communities as well as in critical inquiry concerning their varied historic pasts. Specifically addressing Daly's failure to deal with the African elements of a mythical and mythic background, Lorde commenced the essay/letter with neither euphemism nor indirection:

> The history of white women who are unable to hear Black women's words, or to maintain dialogue with use, is long and discouraging. But for me to assume that you will not hear me represents not only history, perhaps, but an old pattern of relating, sometimes protective and sometimes dysfunctional, which we, as women shaping our future, are in the process of shattering and passing beyond, I hope.

While it is tempting to succumb to a decade-by-decade reading of the new movement (as if its character shifted precisely on the decennial mark), we can descry, with some justification nevertheless, certain trends and emphases that capture the early *collective* aspirations of the 1960s movement. The closing phrase of Lorde's letter—"women shaping our future ... I hope."—is reminiscent of comparable words from Adrienne Rich, whose formidable career as poet and writer embodies within itself one of the most powerful and persistently eloquent interventions against the ravages of patriarchal institutions in this survey of writings. Having "made it" long before in a "man's world," Rich might be regarded as a kind of omnibus figure, whose energies as writer/teacher/theorist provide a cross-section of the movement. A successful woman of New England background and the upper middle class, who might have every reason *not* to have become a feminist, Rich weaves her testimony of transformational consciousness throughout the body of her work. Toward the end of "The Antifeminist Woman," which essay inspired the germinal *Of Woman Born,* Rich explains:

I am a feminist because I feel endangered, psychically and physically, by this society, and because I believe that the women's movement is saying that we have come to an edge of history when men—insofar as they are embodiments of the patriarchal idea—have become dangerous to children and other living things, themselves included; and that we can no longer afford to keep the female principle enclosed within the confines of the tight little postindustrial family, or within any male-induced notion of when the female principle is valid and where it is not.

The recipient of the 1974 National Book Award for the poetry collection *Diving into Wreck,* Rich turned the award down as a mark of her personal achievement, but did accept it in company with two other nominees for that year's literary prize, Audre Lorde and Alice Walker, "in the name of all women." The award statement was written by the trio of winners. As far as I know, a "first" in the National Book Award annals, this joint gesture, which attempted to reclaim an ethical sense of a feminist practice, seems quite a lot closer to the notion of the power of sisterhood, as the title of Robin Morgan's anthology suggests, and feminism as a space of personal transformation *for* political change, than the movement would appear to be headed a few years later, as it moved closer to its current postmodernist postures. But again, a hard and fast rule would only rigidly apply. Nonetheless, these three writers are not, by accident, key figures in our notion of both the vocation of feminist writing—Walker has added filmmaking to her contingent of interests—and egalitarian in their political vision—Rich, with fellow poet Michelle Cliff, edited the journal *Sinister Wisdom* for several years. Separately and together, they have helped to advance investigations into patriarchal institutions, lesbian sexuality, race theory, "compulsory heterosexuality," and the homophobic impulse as a powerful thematic cluster within feminist inquiries.

Rich and Walker, in particular, have rethreaded the genre of the personal essay and witness as an especially dense scene of feminist writing possibilities. Walker's *In Search of Our Mother's Gardens,* with its exquisite intergenerational interrogations, movingly invokes the buried and forgotten literary foremother Zora Neale Hurston as an act of personal courage and insistence, and as a genealogical gesture of revisionist biography as well. By recovering Hurston's Florida gravesite Walker literally reopens the books on a sort of "rendezvous with destiny," as Hurston becomes the "found" and capital subject of a new literary history and practice for black American women. Working off the trope of the "garden" as an undervalued field of artistic labor (as woman-work) and as a mnemic trace "thinking" its way back through the mothers, Walker lines up in temporal perspective with what is past and what is to come, her daughter Rebecca the subject of "One Child of One's Own" in the same volume of essays. In poem after poem, story after story, in the essays and in the novels, especially the controversial *The Color Purple* (for which she was roundly excoriated by black male critics), Walker has worked consistently over the decades to spell out in fine print the problematics of *articulation*—what it means for a female subject to overcome the haltings and stutterings of a private speech; Celie of *The Color Purple,* for instance, learning to lift the ban on the critical "I am."

Twentieth-century American women's poetry, fiction, criticism, drama, autobiography, essays, and even personal correspondence are topics of enormity all their own, of course, and we cannot do them justice in these pages; but a gesture of gratitude for this cross-cultural visionary company must at least be attempted: starting with Gertrude Stein, on the front end of what has been called the "American century," and moving on down the line with Edith Wharton, Willa Cather, Amy Lowell, Mourning Dove, Caroline Gordon, Nella Larsen, H.D., Jesse Fauset, Ann Petry, Flannery O'Connor, Eudora Welty, Mary McCarthy, Lillian Hellman, Lorraine Hansberry, Gwendolyn Brooks, Mari Evans, Margaret Walker, Maya Angelou, Nikki Giovanni, Alison Lurie, Anne Tyler, May Sarton, Joyce Carol Oates, Sylvia Plath, Anne Sexton, Denise Levertov, Tillie Olsen, Grace Paley, Adrienne Kennedy, Toni Cade Bambara, Paule Marshall, Elizabeth Bishop, Louise Glück, Leslie Silko, Rita Dove, Octavia Butler, Maxine Hong Kingston, Amy Tan, and Sandra Cisneros, to name only some of the crucial players. American readers have just about seen all than counts in an embarrassment of riches, veins running back through the blood-red of the national past. No one need argue any longer that the context of these writing and, often enough, the products themselves, will attest to other than a complicated, often fierce, struggle between communities of social subjects and institutions in the formation of a national identity, even at this late date still passionately, richly contested. And it will never be different. There is no "tradition" of American women's writings unless its name is plural. As if we had come to the end of a long, involuted period, the Nobel Prize committee awarded Toni Morrison its highest laurels for literature during the fall of 1993 for *Beloved* and other work.

It is at once mysterious and not all a surprise that writing seems to beget its like. We would probably guess correctly that the cross-cultural bonanza of 20th-century writings by women yielded the harvest prepared in the preceding century by that "damn mob of scribbling females," about whom Nina Baym and Jane Tompkins have capably written. We now know that Emily Dickinson and Harriet Beecher Stowe, for example, were not the isolated figures that they once appeared, but were themselves among the most eminent practitioners of literary work by women in their century and before. It is just as clear that the mature tradition of English women writers—in fact, the novel form gained one of its most powerful impulses from women's writings of the 18th and 19th centuries—played its part in engendering the writing discipline among women. It would be difficult to claim that women's writing in English over the decades have all been feminist, or that we might require them to be, if by that we mean a carefully circumscribed (and predictable) repertoire of poetics, narratologies, argument, and politics. But if, in this instance, we might speak broadly, after the inimitable example laid down by Virginia Woolf in *A Room of One's Own,* of the conditions of history, biography, economics, and the pressures of culture under which women's communities live and work, then "feminist writing" appropriately engages a general transhistorical observation.

In precisely that way, certain women writers have not evolved a practice that easily fits a rubric of "feminist writings," but whose projects nonetheless have captured the imagination of what Woolf once described as a highly intelligent "common reader" because of a particular stroke of boldness on the writers' part, perhaps even a dash of the unique. Certain women intellectuals of the New York/Boston axis in the 1960s and beyond come to mind—Elizabeth Hardwick's work in literary criticism and review and Susan Sontag's peripatetic prolificality, if I might say so much, cut lapidary figures in this regard, as well as Sisela Bok's unusual protocols in subjects of perennial (though hidden) interest—lying and secrets. Patricia Spack's study of literary gossip completes this triumvirate of topics around certain stratagems of intimacy.

We do not normally think of the work of women journalists as an elaboration of feminist writing, especially in today's media markets, in their overwhelmed response to the grinding engines of late capital, but the newspaper columns of Anna Quindlen, for instance, whose editorial presence at the *New York Times* helped to humanize that great ambiguous male organ, of Ellen Goodman at the *Boston Globe,* of Katha Pollitt, Susan Faludi, and Patricia Williams (in her editorialist's hat), all at the *Nation*—among other women working this field in both mainstream and alternative print media—inscribe noteworthy instances of an all-too-rare journalist sanity.

Even for an owner of a relatively small library inventory, the women's book shelves have demanded that she call the carpenter more than once—make mo' room!

III. The Academic Mission

No one could have predicted 30 years ago, when there was still time to read the crystal ball on these matters, that Betty Friedan's *The Feminist Mystique,* Mary Ellman's *Thinking about Women,* and Kate Millett's *Sexual Politics* were leading a procession of prose documents that, in their steady unfolding, would literally transform the face of humanistic and social science studies in the United States and Great Britain. Some of that work lends this volume its *raison d'être.* But if I understand the work of "epistemology"—an inquiry into and meditation on the grounds or basis of knowledge—then I would say that these feminist writings in scholarship have not simply offered a spectacle of one book after another supplementing the traditional knowledge already in place. Taken together, these works have transformed our understanding of how we presume to know and the conditions under which we learn what we know. In short, feminist writings over the last three decades have driven to the forefront of our intellectual recognition at least two crucial presuppositions: 1) the concept of standpoint—that the investigator's sense of his/her work is inextricably tied to his/her historical and social situatedness—and 2) that knowledge itself is a product of human and historic agency—it does not come in with the tides, neither is it divinely ordained, nor naturally irrefutable. If that is the case then the world is presented to the subject in a new light—we can alter its human and social arrangements, its historical and institutional configurations, its tensions and pressures on the subject-effects of individuals and communities *for the better.* It seems to me that it is no longer tenable, in light of theories of standpoint and human agency, to execute scholarship, or any writing that gestures toward it, as if its outcome and conclusion were a matter of self-evidentiary "truth." It is not that there is no such thing as the latter, but that we arrive at it through processes of negotiation, the commitment to close reading, and a respect for comparative recall, all engendered in the *orders of knowledge.* (In other words, "common sense," even for the experiential feminists—not as sharply divided from the conceptualists as we should like to think—is not all that interesting here, and certainly feminists were not aiming to convince anybody by its lights, and they still aren't.) I believe, then, that we owe this change of perspective—most certainly its reinforcement—to feminist writings and their exhaustive interventions on the closed circuits of knowledge production in the West. I think that this current phase of the movement in fact distinguishes itself from the earlier social formations as a shift in the alignment of postulates that enable the way we do the business of knowledge. Feminist writers are looking for ways to establish women and their productions in time and space as the *subject* of investigation, rather than its objects and mute facticity.

Now, I have just summoned a gigantic feast here, but the "meal" that I want to bring to the table has been in the making for a long time—well before this century—as numerous women historians have attempted to show. From that point of view, the 1960s movement and the writings that it has generated might be read as the fruition of 1) women's political activity since the Jacksonian era of U.S. politics during the third decade of the 19th century, and as an outcome of 2) the bloom of affluence, among other factors, that broke over society as a result of the military-industrial complex put in place by a U.S. war machinery (World War I, the Korean Conflict, the Vietnam War) and its imperialist interests defined as the "Cold War."

But from another angle, the 1960s movement inscribed its own cultural property because higher education became one of its principal ambitions. More precisely, it aimed to change curricula and the itineraries of learning, and I believe that it has succeeded to an impressive extent inasmuch as the "target" was the woman herself—first as a student, then as a teacher, in many cases. The backlash against feminist writings (as Adrienne Rich observed quite a while ago) is fundamentally shallow because it has caught their breeze, not their substance. To say this differently, the backlash has failed in a spectacular way to do the intellectual "heavy lifting" of *sustained investigation and reading* that became early on, it seems to me, one of the primary signatures of the new women's scholarship; indeed, it is the hallmark of *any* scholarship. Parasitic on the positive energies of feminist writing in their most creative and progressive instances, these "political correctness" eruptions, I would call them—or more exactly, *émissions,* as the French might say—have only operated at the level of surface and excitement, at the instigation of a borrowed animus. This naive, bullying, loud-mouthed obscenity—like so much else in the society now—seems to wish to sell itself as the next new order, and perhaps such a desire reveals its true nature: it is little more than a strategy/anxiety for the attraction of *market share.* But contrastively, the feminist writing, just as it also wants to situate itself in the marketplace as successfully as possible, wishes to interrogate the very logic of market—Nancy Hartsock's *Money, Sex, and Power* for example—and seeks, then, a *conversation* with its wealth of conceptual and experiential precedents in order to demonstrate their fault lines, gaps, inconsistencies, incompletions, blindnesses, and insights. The new subjects of social order, consequently, are engendered in the interstices, and not in all the old familiar places. To purloin a "beautiful idea" from the late Elizabeth Bruss, I would say that feminist writings of the period, from their early emphases on "consciousness-raising" and women's respect and affection for other women, or a mid-century version of a rhetoric of "conversion," to their current wrestlings with the full panoply of modernist-postmodernist protocols, have engaged with the notion of making "beautiful theories." Along the way, many of the feminist writers, I suspect, have seriously wanted to change the world in which we find ourselves. Their way of doing it is the *writing,* and even though we will find much to criticize here, and perhaps, from time to time, a few things that we do not like very much at all, I believe that it would be wrong to misjudge the passion and anguish of a dogged and unmistakable idealism, at least on the part of some. It seems to me that in the end, the latter must also enter the standard of measure. The works are varied, and their outcome, still unfolding, is quite uneven, but after all this time I know no colleague who calls herself "feminist" who disrespects and discredits the labor-intensive work of writing, of trying to *find out.* And *that* really is something.

In an effort to make a quantitatively daunting task somewhat possible to approach, I made a list of the epistemic, or curricular, clusters on which feminist writings are at work; within minutes I came up with about 20 categories, non-stop, and not counting the institutional arrangements that have run concurrent with them (i.e., certain of the journals—*Signs, Feminist Studies, The Women's Review of Books, Tulsa Studies, Sage, The Women's Studies Newsletter, Ms.,* among others, and a feminist current running through a number of other mainstream journals and presses—the series editions at many of the major presses, for example: the circuit of conferences, symposia/fora, and fellowship support—i.e., the Bunting Institute and Harvard/Radcliffe; the "Feminist and Scholar" forum at Barnard College; the National Women's Studies Association; the Berkshire Conference, affectionately known among academics as "the Berks"; the Ford and the Rockefeller Foundations' programs for minorities; certain of the women's presses, i.e., the Feminist Press, Persephone, Kitchen Table, to name a few of them, and the network of Women's Studies programs and centers on college and university campuses across the country). Even though a quantitative countdown of feminist writings might not offer the best procedure—Toril Moi's study of conceptual trends as a way to define the problem may suggest a superior strategy—some sense, however, of the terrain covered yields a collective picture of solid achievement. The breakout would include 1) retrieval work in women's history and literature; 2) literary criticism and theory; 3) women's history; 4) Marxist and materialist feminisms; women, work, labor-relations, and the new economic order of transglobal capitalism; 5) anthologies of literary criticism and feminist theory; 6) anthologies of literature by women writers; 7) psychoanalytic feminist criticism and feminist work in psychology; 8) deconstructive feminist theory and criticism; 9) feminist work in religious studies, the sciences, the social sciences, law, and critical legal theory; 10) feminist work on the "seven arts," including painting, music, and dance; 11) new historicist feminist work; 12) American cultural and literary studies from a feminist/gender angle; 13) work in semiotics and philosophy; 14) postmodernist feminist work; 15) poststructuralist feminist readings; 16) postcolonial feminist work; 17) African American women's literary, social, and culture critique; 18) Diasporic African and Asian studies from a feminist point of view; 19) Subsaharan African women's literatures and cultures; 20) Caribbean women's literatures and cultures; 21) histories of slavery, colonization, women, and the institutions of motherhood and childrearing; 22) Hispanic women's studies and communities; 23) Chicana cultural and literary studies; 24) film studies; 25) sexuality and gender studies—gay, lesbian, and bisexual postmodernities; 26) cultural studies from a feminist perspective on a range of issues, i.e., Rap, video, T.V. studies; 27) the fashion/hair/dressing industries and the body image; 28) "minority discourse" theory on the multiculturalisms; 29) cybernetic properties and their translation as subject-trope; 30) Asian-American women's studies; 31) women on line—technologies, machines, and the Internet; ... quite likely, there are several that I have inadvertently left out.

I would say, then, that we would do well to call this era of writing *classical* new feminisms, 1965-200; most of the news here is good, but the very best of it is that the period has generated a configuration of authors and propositions too numerous to simply add up. I would even go so far as to say that this intellectual movement is greater than the sum of its parts. If I were convoking an assembly of such figures, I would need a good long time to come up with an exhaustive list, but it would most certainly include: Elizabeth Abel, Janet Adleman, Jacqui Alexander, Gloria Anzaldua, Bettina Aptheker, Nina Auerbach, and Michelle Barrett, Gillian Beer, Seyla Benhabib, Jessica Benjamin, Shari Benstock, Carole Boyce-Davies, Teresa Brennan, Mary Lynn Broe, Judith Butler, Carolyn Bynum, and Hazel Carby, Cynthia Chase, King-Kok Cheung, Nancy Chodorow, Barbara Christian, Kim Crenshaw, and Deidre English, Angela Davis, Thadious Davis, Dorothy Dinnerstein, Ann Douglass, Mary Douglass, Ann duCille, Rachel Blau DuPlessis, Andrea Dworkin, and Zilla Eisenstein, Shoshana Felman, Moira Ferguson, Judith Fetterley, Dianna Fuss, and Jane Gallop, Marjorie Garber, Paula Giddings, Sandra Gilbert, Carol Gilligan, Germaine Greer, Susan Gubar, and Donna Haraway, Sandra Harding, Barbara Harlow, Carolyn Heilbrun, Mae Henderson,

Marianne Hirsch, Jean Howard, Florence Howe, Gloria Hull, and Mary Jacobus, Myra Jehlen, Barbara Johnson, Jacqueline Jones, and E. Ann Kaplan, Elaine Kim, Annette Kolodny, and Donna Landry, Gerda Lerner, Wahneema Lubiano, and Jane Marcus, Jackie McClendon, Deborah McDowell, Nellie McKay, Catharine McKinnon, Ellen Messer-Davidow, Nancy Miller, Trinh T. Minha, Juliet Mitchell, Ellen Moers, Chandra Mohanty, Cherrie Moraga, Laura Mulvey, Lindoa Nicholson, and Nell Painter, Ruth Perry, Carolyn Porter, Marjoire Pryse, and Lillian Robinson, Phyllis Rose, and Eve Sedgwick, Susan Rubin Suleiman, Elaine Scarry, Naomi Schor, Jenny Sharpe, Beverly Guy-Sheftall, Elaine Showalter, Barbara Smith, Barbara Hernnstein Smith, Carroll Smith-Rosenberg, Ann Snitow, Gayatri Spivak, Madalon Sprengnether, Domna Stanton, Catharine Stimpson, Susan Stuard, and Claudia Tate, Paula Treichler, and Carol Vance, and Judith Walkowitz, Cheryl Wall, Michele Wallace, Mary Helen Washington, Gloria Watkins, Susan Willis, Amy Wong, Pat Yaeger, Jean Fagin Yellin, Iris Young, and Bonnie Zimmerman.

IV. Breaking out of the Unseen

When a well-informed, generously intended intellectual history of women's work in our era can finally be written (and the time is nigh), the investigator(s) will need to break down these veritable flows of production, category by category, text by text, writer by writer; obviously we cannot perform this imperative here and now, but I wish to try to touch on some of the highlights in the space remaining, apologizing in advance for the incompletions.

The notion that women's histories of achievement were a matter of restoring texts and of setting the record straight was not only an early source of inspiration for academic feminist, but in one way or another, remains the impetus behind the pluralizing of "feminism" as a term deployed to describe a set of social practices. In other words, no single community of women, no matter how visible and prominently placed, could claim to speak for women in a transhistorical way. Starting with the early 1980s, roughly, the women's movement, at least in its academic and conceptual phase, began to reflect those undeniable differences set in motion by history and politics that, for all intents and purposes, fractured an idealized and romanticized women's community into particular cultural and historic orders. While it would be difficult to say what the net gain has been, it seems clear that from a certain perspective the movement has been enriched by fragmentation, or more precisely, the reach of its discourses expanded in order to account for the complex weave of human, social, and institutional relations engendered by history's vast differentials of power. But perhaps it is just as accurate to say that academic feminism gained, early on, a "center of gravity" resistant to efforts to displace it. There is a tendency here toward a scholarship and writing that valorize western culture (though it is hardly clear what else it might do) and that adopt their paradigms of reading and interpretation—a repertoire of argumentative and expository strategies and devices—from traditional methods of discourse, while at the same time making it virtually impossible for such discursive tradition to be executed again according to custom. In other words, feminist writings have inscribed women subjects in western value in ways, perhaps, unprecedented before now.

Because of so much of feminists' scholarly energies were tied, by definition, to the historiographical project, one way or another, feminist historians may be said to have constituted a first line of defense not only in the designation of a feminist objective of investigation, but also in the delineating of a narrative pattern of inquiry, intent on the retrieval and elaboration of lost and/or muted moments of women's work over the centuries. Joan Wallach Scott's *Gender and the Politics of History* and Joan Kelly's *Women, History and Theory* offer examples of a mature feminist historiography that seemed to follow, quite appropriately, on the heels of a powerful polemical intervention forged by Kate Millett's *Sexual Politics,* Shulamith Firestone's *Dialectic of Sex,* and Susan Brownmiller's *Against Our Will: Men, Women and Rape,* among other works that had helped to spell out a feminist program. But a work like *Our Bodies, Ourselves,* put out by the Boston Women's Health Collective, went far to claim the contemporary movement for a *collective* political end. Authored by several women, with special thanks to editor Alice Mayhew, the second edition of the book acknowledges multiples of men and women for "information, advice, and support." Perhaps it could be said that the urge toward anonymity and the egalitarian principle distinguishes one of the aims of the contemporary women's movement as an antidote to what is perceived to be the hierarchical tendencies of a masculinist culture, with its ego-driven emphasis on "great men" and "history" as a record of their deeds. But we might also regard the posture of anonymity as an ironical and contradictory feature of the movement, inasmuch as breaking out of the unseen is as crucial a mandate for women's communities and women subjects as are the goals of cooperative movement. In any event, we must acknowledge that academic feminism, as we currently understand its premises and practices and as we now perform it, has extended the mythos of individualism as a positive cultural value. The movement has not succeeded in overturning the individualistic presumption, nor has it gone far to undermine its profound claims on the attention and our allegiance to it. In other words, not only do we essentially know the work of feminisms by way of texts and authors, but understand their impulses as an *embodiment* of willful personalities, defining desire, in part, as a *writing,* rather than as ideas primarily. The difference intended here is too sharply stated, inasmuch as "ideas" can only be known and transmitted as the concrete embodiment of a "voice" and a positionality, but the point that I mean to make here must stand as something of the hyperbole that it is—feminist writers no more signal "the death of the author" than their male counterparts, nor is it clear that their *not* doing so is a bad or undesirable outcome.

In a very real sense, feminist writing, as a modernist/postmodernist form, is inconceivable without Simone de Beauvoir's *The Second Sex.* Having set out to establish the "woman question" as a situation for philosophical inquiry, Beauvoir succeeds in driving the issues hard and fast onto the forbidden terrain of epistemology. Toril Moi is quite right, it seems to me, to project Beauvoir as the "founder" of a line of thought that might be called, for lack of a better term, "French feminisms," the name given to an important collection of writings edited by Elaine Marks and Isabelle de Courtivron, as well to as a *style* of work that opposes the ideology of empiricism and what Louis Althusser, in *Reading Capital,* describes as the religious "myth of reading." Opposition in this case is true and not the strategically enabling postulate that parodies the other fellow's argument—in other words, the perennial "straw woman" of inadvertent caricature. If we aligned all feminist writings since the mid-1960s against these major critico-theoretical tendencies—Anglo-American feminist writing postures, on the one hand, and French feminist postures on the other—we would not exaggerate by much and might even go so far as to say that these "attitudes" of writing may be said to regard one another with mutual suspicion, if not actual hostility, as it is just as accurate to note that both have had their successes, as both, together, have, in my view, helped to define the last three decades of writing as a new era of women.

What I am describing here as a writing "posture" or "attitude" is not only meant to designate different sightings on an object of investigation, but quite likely demarcates, as a result, contrary ways of working. In the case of the Anglo-American style, dictated by traditions of discourse that belong to the cultures in question, the investigator seems to project the issue at hand as a puzzle open to closure. The process of reaching an end (or the closed loop) is less interesting within itself than its systematic pacings and punctualities that lead, step by step, to some point that appears to have already been constituted—"hidden" more precisely—before the researcher revealed its whereabouts. The steps along, which accumulate like so many clues in a labyrinthine construction, are sequential and progressive. While respective works within this style of presuppositions will vary widely according to discipline, subject matter, the categories of alignment that decide emphases, etc., I believe that I am observing their *trend line* with a fair degree of accuracy. To say that this way of working projects a kind of conceptual narrative that imitates the classic plot sequence—roughly, beginnings, middles, and ends—appears plausible as well to what I am describing.

By contrast, the work that belongs to the discursive traditions of "French feminisms" as a general (and not entirely accurate) stipulated function, articulates *process* as puzzle; the object of investigation appears to shift ground, as it can only be designated—"caught," let us say—as a vanishing point on the researcher's horizon. This writing remains within the maze, having entered it, as its clues are constituted in the very act of statement. It seems fair to say that within this repertory of presuppositions and procedures, sequence flattens out into a meditation on, or perhaps we could say that it is displaced onto, the complexities and irritations of *form.* I run an incredible risk here by suggesting that the style of work under this rubric offers a postmodernist version of modernism, but by that, I mean what Ortega y Gasset described decades ago as the self-conscious pursuit of the laws of formal behavior. I will place that morsel on the table in closing, fully award that as titillation to the palate, it is not nearly enough within itself. It seems to me, however, that we might offer it as an appetizer to the fine and moveable feast of feminist writings at century's end.

—Hortense J. Spillers

EDITOR'S NOTE

Scope

Designed to meet the needs of both students and the general public seeking information on feminist topics, *Feminist Writers* provides biographical/bibliographical/critical entries focusing on almost 300 novelists, authors in other fictional genres, and writers of works of nonfiction espousing a feminist viewpoint.

International in scope, inclusion in *Feminist Writers* is based upon the feminist content of the writer's work, the degree to which that work is studied, and the availability of such works in English-language versions. The diversity of feminist thought and expression is reflected by entries representing a wide range of nationalities and cultures; rather than dealing with works written exclusively by women, it concentrates upon those containing an overt feminist theme relative to the era in which they were written.

Feminist Writers provides an introduction to the works of men and women writing on a variety of feminist topics in a variety of historical epochs. While the preponderance of writers featured are English-language authors who have written in the 20th century, significant foreign-language authors whose works are available in English translation are also featured. In addition, authors of written works that can be considered precursors of the 20th-century feminist movement in its many facets have also been included. The selection of writers is based on the recommendations of the advisors listed on page xvii.

Entry Format

The entry for each writer consists of biographical data, a complete list of published works arranged by genre, a list of works about the author, including published biographies, interviews, and criticism, and a critical essay focusing on the author's works relating to the feminist movement and discussing their historical/political implications. Living authors were invited to provide a commentary on their work.

Original editions of all works have been listed, in addition to first U.S. and British editions if translated from a language other than English.

Indexes and Other Highlights

Feminist Writers contains three indexes: a **Title Index** providing an alphabetical listing of English-language titles; a **Nationality Index** listing authors by country of origin; and a **Genre and Subject Index,** useful in resourcing authors through literary genres and subject areas relevant to the study of feminism.

Sources for More Information on Feminist Writers details further resources—bibliographies, dictionaries, indexes, critical overviews, and period anthologies that should prove useful to the student of the international feminist movement as reflected through its literature. **Additional Resources for the Study of Feminist Writing** highlights other resources, including libraries, feminist periodicals and presses, and avenues for online research.

Also of note is the alphabetical listing, **Additional Feminist Writers Not Covered in This Work.** Limited space has not allowed us to include the full spectrum of writers on feminist topics; in this section additional authors of broad interest are listed, along with relevant dates and a brief description of their contribution to the international feminist movement. **Notes on Advisors and Contributors** contains information on the many scholars who have contributed to this volume.

ACKNOWLEDGEMENTS

I would like to extend my sincere appreciation to all the advisors and contributors who gave of their time and their expertise during the course of this project. Special thanks are due J. J. Wilson for her marvelous enthusiasm, Tom Wiloch for his encouragement, and David Null for his invaluable aid in compiling the volume's appendices. Many thanks also go out to Margaret Mazurkiewicz, who kept the project on track; to Peter Gareffa, to Laura Standley Berger, and to the rest of the St. James Staff, who provided invaluable assistance in the completion of *Feminist Writers.* I would like to dedicate the results of all these efforts to my family: particularly to my grandmother, Anne, who endured; my mother, Rose-Marie, who rebelled; and my children, Ashley and Stephen, whose lives will continue to be impacted by the writers represented in this volume.

I hope that *Feminist Writers* is found to be a useful reference work. Comments or suggestions regarding this work are welcome; please send them to: The Editor, *Feminist Writers,* St. James Press, 835 Penobscot Building, Detroit, MI 48226-4094.

—Pamela Kester-Shelton
Editor

ADVISERS

Rosemary Keefe Curb
Barbara Godard
Ellen Greenblatt
Marie J. Kuda
Jacquelyn Y. McLendon
David Null
Jane Schaberg
Annette White-Parks
J. J. Wilson

CONTRIBUTORS

Frances Akins
Ellen Arnold
R. Edward Ball
Naomi M. Barry
Debra Beilke
Sandia Belgrade
Edith J. Benkov
Cynthia Bily
Benay Blend
Christina Boufis
Jennifer Brantley
Eileen Bresnahan
Siobhan Craft Brownson
Amy Caiazza
Caroline Lockett Cherry
Nancy Chick
Monica Chiu
Tracy Clark
Helena Antolin Cochrane
Katharine Cockin
Ann Mauger Colbert
Rebecca Copeland
Sarah Cornell
Rosemary Keefe Curb
Renee R. Curry
Phyllis Surrency Dallas
Maria M. Davidis
Stacey Donohue
Kathleen Drowne
Patricia Duncan
P. A. Duffy
Helen-May Eaton
Kimberly Engdahl
Deborah Evans
Melissa Evans
Keith Louise Fulton
Sarah Gamble
Kathleen E. Garay
Janet E. Gardner
Mahnaz Ghaznavi
Edvige Giunta
Barbara Godard
Amy S. Green
Ann E. Green
Gurleen Grewal
Jeanne Grinnan
Pamela Haag
Janet V. Haedicke
Jae-Nam Han
Judith E. Harper
Jennifer Henderson
Martha Henn
Karin U. Herrmann
Mary Hess
Kate Lynn Hibbard
Susanna Hoeness-Krupsaw
Jane Hoogestraat
Meredith Hyde
Heidi L. M. Jacobs
Sophie Anna Jensen
Nancy Jesser
Darlene Jushka
Dalia Kandiyoti
Janet E. Kaufman
Ivy Kennelly
Allison Kimmich
Jennifer Kohout
Stacie J. Koochek
Jeraldine R. Kraver
Tomoko Kuribayashi
Jeannelle Laillou Savona
Victoria Larimore
Julie Linden
Devoney Looser
Lisa Loutzenheiser
Teresa Lyle
Lynn MacGregor
Jacqueline Marie
Theresa A. Martinez
Suchitra Mathur
Gita May
Vivian May
Barbara Lesch McCaffrey
Jacquelyn McClendon

Jennifer Davis McDaid
Nancy McHugh
Aorewa Pohutukawa McLeod
Laura McLeod
Gerri McNenny
Deborah T. Meem
Joya Misra
Janet J. Montelaro
Bonnie Morris
Lucy Morrison
Jonathan Morrow
Norma C. Noonan
Kathleen A. O'Grady
Anne Osler
Linda Rohrer Paige
Yiota Papadopoulos
Sandra Peacock
Marilyn Elizabeth Perry
Annmarie Pinarski
Judith Poxon
Maria Pramaggiore
Eric Prenowitz
Gönül Pultar
Maria Elena Raymond
Elizabeth Renfro
Daniel Robinson
Kate Robinson
John Roche
Lori Rogers
Sara Romeyn
Beth Carole Rosenberg
Victoria Rosner
Hazel Rowley
Lori Saint-Martin
Sonita Sarker
Sabine Schmidt
Leslie-Anne Skolnik
Megan Simpson
James R. Simmons
Michelle A. Spinelli
Staci L. Stone
Nora Foster Stovel
Barbara Stretchberry
Nancy Rae Tarcher
Valerie Taylor
Helen Thompson
Annette Van Dyke
Nina Van Gessel
Melissa Walker
Stephanie Kirkwood Walker
Amy Jo-Lan Wan
Lori Williamson
Richard Williamson
Denise Wiloch
J. J. Wilson
Bronwyn Winter
Elizabeth V. Young

FEMINIST WRITERS

LIST OF ENTRANTS

Edith Abbott
Fleur Adcock
Jane Addams
Etel Adnan
Ama Ata Aidoo
Louisa May Alcott
Meena Alexander
Paula Gunn Allen
Isabel Allende
Dorothy Allison
Nawal al'Sadaawi
Susan B. Anthony
Gloria Anzaldúa
June Arnold
Harriette Simpson Arnow
Mary Astell
Margaret Atwood
Mary Austin
Marilou Awiakta

Enid Bagnold
Sandra Bartky
Dorothea Beale
Mary Ritter Beard
August Bebel
Patricia Beer
Aphra Behn
Jessie Bernard
Marie-Claire Blais
Harriot Stanton Blatch
Karen Blixen
Eavan Boland
Elizabeth Bowen
Marion Zimmer Bradley
Anne Bradstreet
Beth Brant
Vera Brittain
Nicole Brossard
Charles Brockden Brown
Rita Mae Brown
Susan Brownmiller
Dorothy Bryant
Charlotte Bunch
Katharine Burdekin
Judith P. Butler

Marie Cardinal
Emily Carr
Rachel Carson
Angela Carter
Rosario Castellanos
Ana Castillo
Carrie Chapman Catt
Denise Chávez
Phyllis Chesler
Nancy Chodorow
Kate Chopin
Barbara T. Christian
Christine de Pisan
Caryl Churchill
Sandra Cisneros
Hélène Cixous
Michelle Cliff
Frances Power Cobbe
Colette
Patricia Hill Collins
Anna Julia Haywood Cooper
Nancy F. Cott
Maria Rosa Cutrufelli

Caroline Wells Healey Dall
Mary Daly
Kamala Das
Angela Davis
Rebecca Harding Davis
Simone de Beauvoir
Marie le Jars de Gournay
Barbara Deming
Anita Desai
Ding Ling
Frederick Douglass
Margaret Drabble
Maureen Duffy
Alice Moore Dunbar-Nelson
Andrea Dworkin

Maria Edgeworth
Barbara Ehrenreich
Buchi Emecheta
Carol Emshwiller
Fumiko Enchi
Marian Engel

Lillian Faderman
Emily Faithfull
Oriana Fallaci
Susan Faludi
Jessie Redmon Fauset
Eva Figes
Shulamith Firestone
Elizabeth Fox-Genovese
Miles Franklin
Mary E. Wilkins Freeman
Marilyn French
Betty Friedan
Marilyn Frye
Margaret Fuller

Matilda Joslyn Gage
Sally Miller Gearhart
Pam Gems
Sandra M. Gilbert and Susan Gubar

Michèle Roberts
Mary Robinson
Sheila Rowbotham
Rosemary Radford Ruether
Muriel Rukeyser
Jane Rule
Joanna Russ

George Sand
Margaret Sanger
Sappho
May Sarton
Olive Schreiner
Elisabeth Schüssler Fiorenza
Anne Sexton
Ntozake Shange
Ann Allen Shockley
Elaine Showalter
Alix Kates Shulman
Bapsi Sidhwa
Agnes Smedley
Barbara Smith
Lillian Smith
Dame Ethel Mary Smyth
Christina Hoff Sommers
Cathy Song
Sophia
Muriel Spark
Catherine Helen Spence
Dale Spender
Gayatri Chakravorty Spivak
Charlene Spretnak
Germaine de Staël
Elizabeth Cady Stanton
Starhawk
Christina Stead
Verena Stefan
Gloria Steinem
Merlin Stone
Marie Stopes
Sui Sin Far

Amy Tan
Ngahuia Te Awekotuku
Martha Carey Thomas
Dorothy Thompson
Marta Traba
Phyllis Trible
Trinh T. Min-Ha
Flora Tristan
Sojourner Truth
Tsushima Yūko
Katharine Tynan

Sigrid Undset

Luisa Valenzuela

Alice Walker
Margaret Walker
Rebecca Walker
Michele Wallace
Sylvia Townsend Warner
Wendy Wasserstein
Beatrice Webb
Mary Webb
Simone Weil
Fay Weldon
Rebecca West
Emma Hart Willard
Patricia J. Williams
Barbara Wilson
Jeanette Winterson
Monique Wittig
Christa Wolf
Naomi Wolf
Mary Wollstonecraft
Virginia Woolf

Anzia Yezierska

Clara Zetkin

A

ABBOTT, Edith

Nationality: American. **Born:** Grand Island, Nebraska, 26 September 1876; sister of social reformer Grace Abbott. **Education:** University of Nebraska, B.A. 1901, University of Chicago, Ph.D. in economics (with honors) 1905. **Career:** Taught high school in Grand Island and Lincoln, Nebraska, beginning 1893; secretary, Women's Trade Union League, Boston, Massachusetts, 1905-06; received Carnegie fellowship to study at London School of Economics, where she met Beatrice and Sydney Webb, 1906; joined sister, Grace Abbott, at Jane Addams's Hull House, Chicago, 1908-20; teacher at Wellesley College, 1907-08; codirector, with Sophonisba Breckinridge, Chicago School of Civics and Philanthropy, 1908-42 (merged with University of Chicago, 1920); activist for social reform, beginning 1920; professor of social economy, then dean, 1924-42, School of Social Service Administration, University of Chicago; cofounder and editor, with Breckinridge, *Social Service Review,* 1927-53, and University of Chicago Social Service monograph series. Contributor of articles to *New Republic* and *Nation.* **Died:** Grand Island, Nebraska, 28 July 1957.

PUBLICATIONS

Political/Social Theory

The Delinquent Child and the Home, with Sophonisba P. Breckinridge. Chicago, n.p., 1912; New York, Arno Press, 1970.

The Real Jail Problem. N.p., 1915.

The Wage-Earning Woman and the State, with Sophonisba P. Breckinridge. Boston, Boston Equal Suffrage Association for Good Government, n.d.

The One Hundred and One County Jails of Illinois and Why They Ought to Be Abolished. N.p., 1916.

Truancy and Non-Attendance in the Chicago Schools: A Study of the Social Aspects of the Compulsory Education and Child Labor Legislation of Illinois, with Sophonisba P. Breckinridge. Chicago, University of Chicago Press, 1917.

The Administration of the Aid-to-Mothers Law in Illinois, with Sophonisba P. Breckinridge. Washington, D.C., United States Children's Bureau, 1921; in *The Family and Social Services in the 1920s,* New York, Arno Press, 1972.

Report on Crime and the Foreign Born. Chicago, University of Chicago Press, 1931.

Social Welfare and Professional Education. Chicago, University of Chicago Press, 1931; revised and enlarged, 1942.

Public Assistance. Chicago, University of Chicago Press, 1940.

From Relief to Social Security: The Development of the New Public Welfare Services. N.p., 1941.

History

The Wages of Unskilled Labor in the United States, 1850-1900 (thesis). Chicago, University of Chicago Press, 1905.

Women in Industry: A Study in American Economic History. New York and London, Appleton, 1910.

The Tenements of Chicago, 1908-1935, with Sophonisba P. Breckinridge and others. Chicago, University of Chicago Press, 1936.

Other

Twenty-one Years of University Education for Social Service. N.p., 1942.

"Grace Abbott: A Sister's Memories," in *Social Service Review,* September 1939.

Editor, *Immigration: Select Documents and Case Records.* Chicago, University of Chicago Press, 1924.

Editor, *Historical Aspects of the Immigration Problem: Select Documents.* Chicago, University of Chicago Press, 1926.

Editor, *Some American Pioneers in Social Welfare: Selected Documents.* Chicago, University of Chicago Press, 1937.

Editor, *From Relief to Social Security,* by Grace Abbott. N.p., 1941.

*

Bibliography: "The Published Writings of Edith Abbott: A Bibliography" by Rachel Marks, in *Social Service Review,* March 1958.

Manuscript Collections: Joseph Regenstein Library, University of Chicago; Archives of Social Welfare History, University of Minnesota; Nebraska State Historical Association.

Critical Studies: "Three against Time: Edith and Grace Abbott and Sophonisba P. Breckinridge" by Helen Wright, in *Social Service Review,* March 1954; "Edith Abbott's Contributions to Social Work Education" by Elizabeth Wisner, in *Social Service Review,* March 1958; *Seedtime of Reform: American Social Service and Social Action, 1918-1933* by C.A. Chambers, n.p., 1963; *Two Sisters for Social Justice: A Biography of Grace and Edith Abbott* by Lela B. Costin, Urbana, University of Illinois Press, 1983.

* * *

While Edith Abbott's important contributions as a social reformer opened up new opportunities for women to become social workers, her accomplishments were often eclipsed by the more famous women around her. Much of her dedication stemmed from the influence of her mother, Elizabeth Griffin Abbott, who had taught both Edith and her sister Grace the values of independence, pacificism, and woman's suffrage. Although they differed, both sisters dedicated themselves to improving the situation of working women and labored throughout their lifetimes to further this cause.

Abbott received her doctorate in economics in 1905 from the University of Chicago. During her studies she had co-authored a statistical analysis of women employed in mills and factories with Sophonisba Breckinridge. Following her studies in Chicago, Abbott left for Boston to become the secretary of the Women's Trade

Union League and to do a research assignment on wages and employment of women for the Carnegie Institution. In the process of this research her interest in women's work as it related to economic history heightened, eventually becoming the impetus for her book *Women in Industry.* Within a year of research Abbott had accumulated enough data to begin the book—a lengthy, detailed historical volume—that was published in 1910. *Women in Industry* depicted the lives and conditions of women in industries, recorded the first women's labor movements, and polled 1909 public opinion. Beginning in 1906, portions of the book would regularly appear in the *Journal of Political Economy.*

After traveling to England, where she studied at the London School of Economics under noted Fabian economists Beatrice and Sidney Webb, Abbott returned to Chicago where she joined Grace and Breckinridge at Hull House. At the settlement residence Abbott became familiar with the problems of immigrants. It was there that her social work training would begin, as she tried to improve the lot of immigrant women. The rights of women workers were of special concern to her and she sought legislation for a ten-hour working day, worked toward bringing women into labor unions, and attempted to help immigrants find better living quarters and secure them their rights. By 1924 Abbott was employed with the University of Chicago's School of Social Service Administration and became its first woman dean in 1924.

Over her long career, Abbott wrote over 100 books and articles covering many topics. As a scholar she relied on factual evidence to lay the foundation for concrete solutions to the problems of women and children working long hours and living in poor conditions—a situation that grew to be of particular concern during the Great Depression. With friend and collaborator Breckinridge, Abbott established the *Social Service Review* in 1927 and began a well-respected monograph series for the University of Chicago that included such documents as *Immigration: Select Documents and Case Records* and *Historical Aspects of the Immigration Problem: Select Documents.*

Over the years, the once-shy Abbott blossomed into a woman of action, but, following her sister's death in 1939, she became more withdrawn and increasingly more demanding of her students. Resolute in her belief that women were intellectually equal to their male counterparts and therefore equally deserving of an education, Abbott served as a major influence both in the formation of guidelines for the research and study of social work and in creating unique opportunities for women to contribute to each other's success in the field.

—Marilyn Elizabeth Perry

ADAMS, Mary. *See* **PHELPS (WARD), Elizabeth Stuart.**

ADCOCK, Fleur

Nationality: British. **Born:** Kareen Fleur Adcock, in Papakura, New Zealand, 10 February 1934; immigrated to the United Kingdom in 1963. **Education:** Studied in England, 1939-47; Wellington Girls' College and Victoria University of Wellington, M.A. (honors) in classics 1956. **Family:** Married Alistair Campbell in 1952 (divorced 1957), two sons. **Career:** Assistant lecturer in classics, University of Otago, Dunedin, New Zealand, 1958. Held library posts at the University of Otago, 1959-61, Alexander Turnbull Library, Wellington, New Zealand, 1962, and Foreign and Commonwealth Office, London, England, 1963-79. Arts Council Creative Writing Fellow, Charlotte Mason College of Education, Ambleside, Cumbria, 1977-78; Northern Arts Fellow, Universities of Newcastle upon Tyne and Durham, 1979-81; Eastern Arts Fellow, University of East Anglia, Norwich, 1984; currently freelance writer. **Awards:** Festival of Wellington prize, 1961; New Zealand State Literary Fund award, 1964; Buckland Awards, 1967, 1979; Jessie MacKay award, 1968, 1972; Cholmondeley Award, 1976; New Zealand National Book Award, 1984; Arts Council Writer's Award, 1988. **Address:** 14 Lincoln Rd., London N2 9DL, England.

Publications

Poetry

The Eye of the Hurricane. Wellington, Reed, 1964.
Tigers. Oxford, Oxford University Press, 1967.
High Tide in the Garden. Oxford, Oxford University Press, 1971.
The Scenic Route. Oxford, Oxford University Press, 1974.
The Inner Harbour. London and New York, Oxford University Press, 1979.
Below Loughrigg. Newcastle upon Tyne, Bloodaxe, 1979.
Selected Poems. Oxford, Oxford University Press, 1983; revised edition, 1991.
4-Pack 1: Four from Northern Women, with Maura Dooley, S.J. Litherland, and Jill Maugham. Newcastle upon Tyne, Bloodaxe, 1986.
Hotspur, music by Gillian Whitehead. Newcastle upon Tyne, Bloodaxe, 1986.
The Incident Book. Oxford, Oxford University Press, 1986.
Meeting the Comet. Newcastle upon Tyne, Bloodaxe, 1988.
Time-Zones. Oxford, Oxford University Press, 1991.

Other

Editor, with Anthony Thwaite, *New Poetry 4.* London, Hutchinson, 1978.
Editor, *The Oxford Book of Contemporary New Zealand Poetry.* Oxford, Oxford University Press, 1982.
Editor, *The Faber Book of 20th-Century Women's Poetry.* London, Faber, 1987.
Editor and translator, *Hugh Primas and the Archpoet.* Cambridge, Cambridge University Press, 1994.
Editor, with Jacqueline Simms, *The Oxford Book of Creatures.* Oxford, Oxford University Press, 1995.

Translator, *The Virgin and the Nightingale: Medieval Latin Poems.* Newcastle upon Tyne, Bloodaxe, 1983.
Translator, *Orient Express: Poems,* by Grete Tartler. Oxford, Oxford University Press, 1989.
Translator, *Letters from Darkness,* by Daniela Crasnaru. Oxford, Oxford University Press, 1991.

*

Critical Studies: Introduction by Dannie Abse to *Corgi Modern Poets in Focus 5,* London, Corgi, 1973; *Penguin Book of Contemporary New Zealand Poetry* edited by Miriama Evans, London, Penguin, 1989; *Fleur Adcock in Context: From Movement to Martians* by Julian Stannart, Lampeter, Wales, Edwin Mellen Press, 1996.

Fleur Adcock comments:

I no longer feel inclined to make comments on my own work, which I feel should speak for itself.

As for my relationship with the feminist movement, I will only say that I was a rather late convert to its enriching influence—it was during the 1980s, when I was working on my anthology of women's poetry, that my eyes were fully opened; and although I have never been an active member of any feminist group, I am grateful for what I have learnt. It is enormously heartening to see so many women poets, in particular, writing so well and being so well received.

* * *

Fleur Adcock is in the curious position of being praised as one of the foremost poets of one country (New Zealand), while having lived in another (Britain) for over 30 years. Being a perennial expatriate has influenced not only the recurrent themes of her poetry, but helped shape her idea of what poetry is and should be. Her definition of poetic method, which she describes as "an attitude," sounds as if it is her personal creed, a response to her experience of dislocation, "Poetry is a search for ways of communication; it must be conducted with openness, flexibility, and a constant readiness to listen."

The splitting of her life between two countries that are on opposite sides of the globe began in Adcock's childhood, and has continued, emotionally and physically, ever since. Born in New Zealand in 1934, she was educated both in Britain and New Zealand, graduating from the University of Wellington in 1956 with a degree in classics. She started as an assistant lecturer in classics at the University of Otago in 1958, and worked as a librarian there and in Wellington. She has two sons, whom she left in New Zealand when she emigrated to Britain in 1963. Her first volume of poetry, *The Eye of the Hurricane,* was published in 1964. While publishing volumes such as *Tigers* (1967), *High Tide in the Garden* (1971), and *The Scenic Route* (1974) she worked as a librarian in the Foreign and Commonwealth Office, leaving in 1979. Adcock has held various fellowships since, working as an editor and translator of poetry while continuing to publish works that include 1979's *The Inner Harbour,* 1983's *Selected Poems,* and 1986's *The Incident Book.* She currently lives in North London.

Adcock says that she writes "primarily for the printed page, not for performance (regarding poetry readings as the trailer, not the movie)." Her dismissal of the latter again suggests that she keeps a deliberate distance between herself and her reader, preferring to communicate through the written word, as would be necessary from half a world away. Her isolation and sense of disjunction seems purposefully cultivated; in "Gas" she speaks of her ability to perform an "amoeba's trick," and begins "Against Coupling": "I write in praise of the solitary act:/of not feeling a trespassing tongue/forced into one's mouth.... /Pyramus and Thisbe are dead, but/the hole in the wall can still be troublesome./I advise you, then, to embrace it without encumbrance." The conscious detachment is, in part, a defense against the constant awareness of the missing in her life: "Invocation for Gregory" pleads for gentleness towards the son she has left behind, and "Voices" describes "a chronic convalescence from hope deferred."

One of the most important ways Adcock achieves this distancing is through her characteristically British use of irony and acerbic humor. In her introduction to *The Faber Book of 20th-Century Women's Poetry* Adcock says she admires "the odd or the unexpected ... the kind of detail which throws new and startling light," something which she feels is "related to another quality I admire: wit." Her approach to even the most emotional of subjects is undercut by humor, her light touch highlighting the emotions expressed: "I'd write with more conviction about death/if it were clutching at my every breath./And now we've come to it. The subject's out:/The ineluctable, the all-pervasive .../and if so far I've seemed a bit evasive/it's not from cowardice or phoney tact—/it's simply that I can't believe the fact." Much of the strength of her poetry comes from what is deliberately not said; in "The Soho Hospital for Women" a cancer patient explains "Doctor, I am not afraid of a word./But neither do I wish to embrace that visitor."

Though Adcock's approach to her subject is personal, domestic, and familiar, the actual subject matter is not confessional. "The content of my poems derives largely from those parts of my life which are directly experienced," she explains, "relationships with people or places; images and insights which have presented themselves sharply from whatever source, conscious or subconscious; ideas triggered off by language itself." In "Remarks on Sernyl," for instance, the impetus is the memory of "a static, sunny, twenty-year old moment." The awareness of the split in her life makes Adcock concentrate on the present, leading to rich description and clear imagery. She often focuses on particular places, immediate and concrete, to suggest that which is missing, using the present landscape as a backdrop for the "receding pictures" it emotionally evokes. The fact that she is a traveler means that, as a tourist, she views places as a series of details, collecting images like "a suitcase full of stones," constantly aware of what is present but also nostalgically conscious of the absent.

Adcock's need for control is reflected in her poetic form, which is, as she herself describes it, "relatively traditional ([though] traditions alter)," with its crafted, complex sentence structure and lyrical form. Adcock notes that she has "moved away from strict classical patterns in the direction of greater freedom—as is usual with most artists learning a trade" but adds that "It takes courage, however, to leave all props behind, to cast oneself, like Matisse, upon pure space. I still await that confidence." However, she says, "words, not their shape on the page, are what matter. If one is fortunate their destination, like their origin, will be as voices speaking in the mind."

In her poem suggestively titled "An Epigraph," Adcock writes: "I could stand rejection—/so grand, 'the stone the builders rejected ...'—/but not acceptance. 'Alas,' I said/(a word I use), 'alas, I am taken/up, or in, or out of myself:/Shall I never be solitary?'/Acceptance fell on me like a sandbag./My bones crack .../ Ah, acceptance! Leave me under this stone."

—Meredith E. Hyde

ADDAMS, Jane

Nationality: American. **Born:** Cedarville, Illinois, 6 September 1860. **Education:** Rockford Female Seminary, A.B. 1882; briefly attended the Woman's Medical College of Pennsylvania. **Career:** Visited England and toured Toynbee Hall, London; cofounder, with Ellen Starr, Hull House (settlement house), 19th Ward, Chicago, 1889; cofounder, National Women's Trade Union League, 1903; founder and president, National Federation of Settlements, 1911-35; coorganizer, Women's Peace Party, 1915; cofounder, American Civil Liberties Union, 1920. **Awards:** Nobel Peace Prize, 1931. **Member:** National American Women Suffrage Association (vice-president, 1911-14), National Conference of Social Work (president 1910), Women's International League for Peace and Freedom (president 1919-35). **Died:** 21 May 1935.

PUBLICATIONS

Political/Social Theory

Philanthropy and Social Progress. New York, T. Crowell, 1893.
Hull-House Maps and Papers. New York, T. Crowell, 1895.
Democracy and Social Ethics. New York, Macmillan, 1902; edited by Anne Firor Scott, Cambridge, Harvard University Press, 1964.
Newer Ideals of Peace. New York, The Chautaugua Press, 1907.
The Spirit of Youth and the City Streets. New York, Macmillan, 1909.
A New Conscience and an Ancient Evil. New York, Macmillan, 1912.
The Long Road of Woman's Memory. New York, Macmillan, 1916.
Peace and Bread in Time of War. New York, Macmillan, 1922; introduction by John Dewey, New York, King's Crown Press, 1945.
My Friend, Julia Lathrop. New York, Macmillan, 1935.

Autobiography

Twenty Years at Hull-House, with Autobiographical Notes. New York, Macmillan, 1910.
The Second Twenty Years at Hull-House. New York, Macmillan, 1930.

*

Bibliography: *A Preliminary Checklist for a Bibliography on Jane Addams* by M. Helen Perkins, n.p., 1960.

Manuscript Collections: Swarthmore College Peace Collection, Swarthmore College, Swarthmore, Pennsylvania; Sophia Smith Collection, Smith College, Northampton, Massachusetts.

Critical Studies: *Jane Addams, a Biography* by James Weber Lin, New York, D. Appleton-Century, 1935; "Jane Addams: An American Heroine" by Jill Conway, in *Daedalus,* spring 1964; *Beloved Lady: A History of Jane Addams' Ideas on Reform and Peace* by John C. Farrell, n.p., 1964; *American Heroine: The Life and Legend of Jane Addams* by Allen F. Davis, New York, Oxford University Press, 1973, and his *Spearheads for Reform: The Social Settlements and the Progressive Movement, 1890-1914,* New Brunswick, New Jersey, Rutgers University Press, 1984; "The Historical Value and Historiographic Significance of Jane Addams' Autobiographies *Twenty Years at Hull-House* and *Second Twenty Years at Hull-House*" by Ursula Lehmkuhl, in *Reconstructing American Literary and Historical Studies,* edited by Gunter H. Lenz, Hartmut Keil, and Sabine Brock-Sallah, n.p., 1990; "A Feminist American Success Myth: Jane Addams' *Twenty Years at Hull-House*" by Lois Rudnick, in *Tradition and the Talents of Women,* edited by Florence Howe, Urbana, University of Illinois Press, 1991.

* * *

Jane Addams challenged many Americans to rethink their vision of democracy. More than just a system of government, democracy—as Addams understood it—meant collective responsibility for the social welfare of a nation. Implicit in her vision was the feminist belief that women have an active role in the evolution of democratic society, a belief she promoted through her own actions. A prolific writer and frequent lecturer, Addams authored numerous books and essays on the subject of democratic responsibility and ultimately achieved worldwide recognition for her work on behalf of American social reform.

Born on the brink of the American Civil War, Addams came of age at a time when the very tenets of American democracy were being tested. Questions concerning citizenship, voting rights, and federal power were at the forefront of political debates. Addams' father, an Illinois state senator and abolitionist, impressed upon his daughter a sense of social responsibility. That sense, urgent in nature, dictated the direction her life's work would take.

In 1877 Addams enrolled at Rockford Female Seminary, where she studied the writings of some of the world's most prominent social theorists. The works of Thomas Carlyle and John Ruskin inspired her to flesh out her own nascent ideas, and her idealistic beliefs began to acquire an intellectual foundation. Profiting from the sense of female solidarity she experienced at Rockford, Addams received her degree in 1882 and joined the ranks of the first generation of U.S. female college graduates.

In the years immediately following graduation, Addams's urgent sense of social duty clashed head on with late 19th-century society's expectations of acceptable female conduct. Educated women were expected to return home after college and resume prescribed family duties. Addams, wanting desperately to find an outlet for her yet unclear ambitions, found few opportunities besides teaching and mission work. She enrolled in medical school but dropped out due to illness. She became enmeshed in what she would later describe in *Twenty Years at Hull-House* as the "family claim": like many women in her circumstances, a sense of familial obligation psychologically constrained her from creating a full and independent life for herself outside of the home.

By the fall of 1889 Addams could no longer ignore her social calling. Finding the courage necessary to leave her family she embarked upon an experiment that would engage her for the rest of her life. With Ellen Gates Starr, whom she knew from Rockford, Addams opened Hull House in one of Chicago's immigrant neighborhoods. One of the first "settlement" houses to open in the United States, Hull House was the physical embodiment of the spirit of democracy that Addams envisioned. Settlement workers—mostly white, middle-class women who rejected geographic and social boundaries based on class, gender, and ethnicity—moved into immigrant neighborhoods and organized social programs for industrial workers and their families. Indeed, women would provide the driving force, not only behind Hull House but behind the settlement movement at large. At Hull House, Addams surrounded herself with such able, intelligent women as Mary Rozet Smith, who would become her lifelong companion.

Addams viewed the settlement house as a first step in the social development of democracy. In *Democracy and Social Ethics,* published in 1902, she spelled out her democratic ideal: that the ultimate mission of any democracy was to give voice to the opinions of common working people. Therefore, she maintained, common people should hold a valued place in American society. Settlement houses provided a vehicle by which middle-class men and women could aid in that end: by living among immigrant neighbors they could share their cultural and educational privilege, thereby combating class isolationism and working to temper the ethos of individualism so prevalent at the time.

Within just a few years Hull House achieved remarkable success. Programs included a day nursery, social clubs for women and children, a kindergarten, and a labor history museum. Addams commanded celebrity status, and a national settlement movement had found its leader. By 1910 there were over 400 settlements in the United States. Thanks in large part to the inspiration and example of Addams, women made up the majority of America's settlement workers. Addams would chronicle her experiences at Hull House in two collections of autobiographical essays, *Twenty Years at Hull House* and *The Second 20 Years at Hull-House,* both of which illuminate Hull House as a working model for her vision of democracy.

Success at Hull House thrust Addams into the public and political arena. In 1912 she seconded the Progressive Party's presidential nomination of Theodore Roosevelt. An active campaigner for women's rights, she served as vice-president of the National American Woman Suffrage Association (NAWSA) from 1911 until 1914. Addams believed that the evolution of democracy demanded women's full and equal participation in the political sphere.

In addition to her work for social reform, Addams championed the cause of peace. She published books and essays on the subject, including *Newer Ideals of Peace,* which was published in 1907. Inspired by what she witnessed in the neighborhoods surrounding Hull House, Addams wrote about the impact of foreign wars on American immigrants. She observed that conflicts abroad could violently divide immigrant populations in America. In 1915 Addams would be elected chairman of the Woman's Peace Party.

Despite public disapproval, Addams agitated for peace throughout the period of U.S. involvement in World War I and in 1919 was elected president of the Women's International League of Peace and Freedom. As she wrote in *Peace and Bread in Time of War,* "During war it is impossible for the pacifist to obtain an open hearing." Understanding dissent as one of the fundamental aspects of a democracy, Addams continued her campaign for peace despite the accusations of treason that were often levelled against her. In the years following World War I, she survived "Red Scare" intimidation and regained her status as an American hero. Addams received the Nobel Peace Prize in 1931.

Jane Addams envisioned a democracy empowered by women and imbued with a social code of ethics. Her influence is still being felt today—in social welfare legislation, professional social work, and expanded career opportunities for women.

—Michelle A. Spinelli

ADNAN, Etel

Nationality: Lebanese. **Born:** Beirut, 24 February 1925; resident of the United States since 1955; naturalized U.S. citizen, 1986. **Education:** Attended French convent schools in Beirut; attended L'Ecole Supèrieure des Lettres de Beyrouth; Sorbonne, Diplôme d'Etudes Supèrieures de Philosophie 1950; postgraduate studies in philosophy at the University of California, Berkeley, 1955-57, and Harvard University, Cambridge, Massachusetts, 1957-58. **Career:** Worked for the Bureau de la Presse, Beirut, 1941-45; high school teacher of French literature, Al-Ahliya School for Girls, Beirut, 1947-49; professor of philosophy, Dominican College, San Rafael, California, 1958-72; literary editor for Lebanese French-language newspapers *al-SAFA,* then *L'Orient-Le Jour*, Beirut, 1972-75; moved to France after outbreak of Lebanese civil war, 1977; reestablished home in Sausalito, California, 1979; also maintains home in Paris. Author of two television documentaries on the war in Lebanon, 1976; commissioned to write French part of *Civil warS* (multi-language opera) by American stage creator Robert Wilson, 1984; author, with French actress Delphine Seyrig, of film scenario based on life of Calamity Jane, 1985-90. Internationally recognized painter, with works in museums including Tunis Modern Art Museum, Royal Jordanian Museum, British Museum, Musée de L'Institut du Monde Arabe, Paris, and National Museum of Women in the Arts, Washington, D.C.; tapestry designs on file in Contemporary Crafts Museums, New York and Los Angeles. Participated in over 20 one-person shows and over 50 group shows in Belgium, England, France, Italy, Germany, Japan, Kuwait, Lebanon, Morocco, Saudi Arabia, Tunisia, the United States, and West Germany. **Address:** 35 Marie Street, Sausalito, California 94965, U.S.A; 29 Rue Madame, Paris, 75006 France.

Publications

Poetry

Moonshots. Beirut, n.p., 1966.
Five Senses for One Death. New York, The Smith, 1971.
"Jebu" [and] "l'Express Beyrouth—Enfer." Paris, P. J. Oswald, 1973.
L' Apocalypse Arabe (illuminated verse, in French). Paris, Editions Papyrus, 1980.
From A to Z. Sausalito, California, Post-Apollo Press, 1982.
Pablo Neruda Is a Banana Tree. Lisbon, Da Almeida, 1982.
The Indian Never Had a Horse & Other Poems. Sausalito, California, Post-Apollo Press, 1985.
The Arab Apocalypse (illuminated verse, translated from the French by the author). Sausalito, California, Post-Apollo Press, 1989.
The Spring Flowers Own & The Manifestations of the Voyage. Sausalito, California, Post-Apollo Press, 1990.
Kitab Al Bahr [The Book of the Sea] (translated into Arabic from unpublished French manuscript). Beirut, n.p., 1994.
There (prose poem). Sausalito, California, Post-Apollo Press, 1996.

Uncollected Poetry

"Jebu," "Five Senses for One Death," "The Beirut-Hell Express," and "Love Poems," in *Women of the Fertile Crescent,* edited by Kamal Boullata. Washington, D.C., Three Continents Press, 1978.

Novel

Sitt Marie Rose. Paris, Editions Des Femmes, 1978; translated by Georgina Kleege, Sausalito, California, Post-Apollo-Press, 1982.

Short Stories

Al Confini Della Luna (translated into Italian). Rome, n.p., 1995.

"My Friend Kate," in *2000 and What?,* edited by Karl Roeseler and David Gilbert. San Francisco, Trip Street, 1996.

Uncollected Essays

"In the Heart of the Heart of Another Country," in *Mundus Artium: A Journal of International Literature and the Arts,* 10(1), 1977.

"In the Sea Mirror: A 'Memoir' of Margaret Yourcenar" in *Poetry Flash,* February 1988.

Autobiography

"Growing Up to Be a Woman Writer in Lebanon," in *Opening the Gates,* edited by Margot Badran and Miriam Cooke. Bloomington and Indianapolis, Indiana University Press, 1990.

Other

Journey to Mt. Tamalpais (illuminated essay). Sausalito, California, Post-Apollo Press, 1986.

Paris, When It's Naked (essay). Sausalito, California, Post-Apollo Press, 1993.

Of Cities and Women (Letters to Fawwaz). Sausalito, California, Post-Apollo Press, 1993.

*

Media Adaptations: Poem set to music by Tania Leon, produced New York, 1990; *The Adnan Songbook* (eight poems set to music by Gavin Bryars), broadcast on BBC-Radio, 1995.

Theatrical Activities: Narrator, *A funeral march for the first cosmonaut,* music by Eugene Stewart, produced Dominican College, 1968.

Critical Studies: *Women of the Fertile Crescent,* edited by Kamal Boullata, Washington, D.C., Three Continents Press, 1978; interview with Hilary Kilpatrick in *Unheard Words,* edited by Mineke Schipper, London and New York, Allison & Busby, 1985; "Life after Lebanon (October, 1984)" by June Jordan, in *On Call: Political Essays,* Boston, South End, 1985; review of *The Indian Never Had a Horse & Other Poems* by Barbara Lesch McCaffry, in *NWSA Perspectives* IV(1), winter 1986; "Toward the Heights with Etel Adnan" by David Volpendesta, in *Poetry Flash,* November 1987; *Opening the Gates,* edited by Margot Badran and Miriam Cooke, Bloomington and Indianapolis, Indiana University Press, 1990; "Our Memory Has No Future" by Ammeil Alcalay, in *The Nation,* 7 March 1994; "Cities of Oppression, Circles of Repression: Etel Adnan's *Sitt Marie Rose*" by Thomas Foster, in *PMLA,* LX(1), January 1995.

Etel Adnan comments:

It seems to me that I was a feminist in an instinctive way since my childhood. I rebelled in the French convent school to which I was sent in Beirut, against the excessive regulations imposed by the nuns and was reminded that my behavior was not befitting little girls! Later I discovered discrimination against girls in my own family. My mother raised a nephew of hers in our home and subordinated my own interests to his: I was taken out of school at age 16 with the pretext that being a girl I didn't need further education, the more so, it was argued, that we were broke, while my little cousin went to private schools and had private lessons to help him keep up with his classes.

At age 16 I went to work and was paid much less, for years, than the lowest-paid men in the office. I put myself to school and managed with evening classes and then scholarships to pursue my studies. When I declared that I wanted to become an architect my mother reacted with disgust: "You want a man's job," she exclaimed, "Shame on you!"

I realized, though, in those years, that work was a liberation: I learned more in the office during the last years of World War II than in any school, and the working hours were a time freed of my mother's gaze upon me. I learned by experience the meaning of personal freedom and the self-confidence that earning money meant for a woman.

It is much later that I took notice of the vast international movement for the liberation of women. I read avidly works by feminists and became a part of that intellectual community, which included Americans such as Adrienne Rich with European or Asian women, as well as activists and thinkers from Egypt such as Nawal Al-Sa'dawi and other African sisters.

The feminist battle has just begun, it is far from being won. The battle should rage on many fronts. Everyone finds her own concerns, specialty, her own voice. The battle against the practices of sexual mutilation in countries such as Egypt, Sudan, or others is as urgent as the battle against violence in the U.S. or elsewhere, or against the degrading aspects of the pornographic industry. Feminism as expressed in poetry, fiction, political action, social work, etc. ... comes from that side of the feminine heart (and the masculine as well) where generosity and solidarity are still alive in our commitment to human dignity.

* * *

Etel Adnan is a significant Arab and Arab-American poet and painter who writes in both French and English. Her subjects range from the political to the poetic to the philosophic. She is a lightening rod for all the senses and images that surround her, which she then reflects and refracts in her works, both written and visual. Several of Adnan's texts have fused the written word with images, especially her long essay on creativity, *Journey to Mount Tamalpais,* in which she includes numerous illustrations of the mountain visibly from the balcony of her home just north of San Francisco. Adnan has published an enormous range of works: from *Sitt Marie Rose,* the internationally recognized novel about the Lebanese Civil War, to volumes of poetry such as *The Indian Never Had a Horse & Other Poems,* to essays that include *Paris, When It's Naked,* to a collection of letters entitled *Of Cities and Women.* She has even translated her own work from French into English—for example, *The Arab Apocalypse*—and from English into French—*Journey to Mount Tamalpais.*

Adnan's father, a Syrian from Damascus, was a general staff officer and commander of the Ottoman Empire in Smyrna during the First World War. Although already married and the father of three children who lived with his first wife in Damascus, he nonetheless married Adnan's mother, a Greek from Smyrna who was 18 years his junior. At the end of the war the family moved to Beirut where Adnan was born in 1925. In the household of her childhood, both Greek and Turkish were spoken. As Lebanon was a newly created French colony, all of the schools were run by the French Catholic Church. When she began school at the age of five, Adnan learned French and "grew up thinking that the world was French." As the only child of mixed background in her school—her mother was a Christian and her father a Muslim—Adnan had a very unique upbringing, with frequent visits to Damascus. "Thus," she explains, "I got used to standing between situations, to being a bit marginal and still a native, to getting acquainted with notions of truth which were relative and changed like the hours of the days and the passing of the seasons."

Adnan has admitted that she has "always regretted not writing in Arabic, and therefore running the risk of not actually being accepted as an Arab writer." She initially began writing in French at the age of eight and wrote her first major poem, "The Book of the Sea," at the age of 22. It only as a result of her activity in the American anti-Vietnam movement that Adnan would start to write in English. Although she never learned Arabic well enough to write in it, when she began to paint in 1960, she heard herself "say out loud, 'I paint in Arabic!' At that moment my soul was at peace, as if I'd been given the answer to an important problem."

Most readers have discovered Adnan through her powerful anti-war novel, *Sitt Marie Rose.* Set in Beirut during the mid-1970s, the work explores the dimensions of violence and shows characters caught between opposing forces. For Adnan, the conflict in her homeland represents the extreme of tribal mentality where respect for individuals and for humane values are lost to tribal urges. The novel is based on an incident that took place early in the Lebanese Civil War. However, *Sitt Marie Rose* was not Adnan's first political work. In three earlier poems—"Jebu," "L'Express Beyrouth—Enfer," and *L'Apocalypse Arabe*—she had already begun to explore the situation of the Palestinians within her homeland. During a discussion with Adnan in 1988, she indicated that when she began to write, her intentions were not those of a pacifist, but as a supporter of the cause of the Palestinians. It was not until civil war broke out in Beirut that she began to realize that "solving passionate conflicts with violence" would lead to the destruction of the planet and its inhabitants. The strength of Adnan's novel is that it does not put its primary focus on the various warring factions, but shows, instead, how the conflict sweeps even ordinary individuals into its midst.

Although Adnan wrote about women within the Arab context against the background of the Lebanese Civil War in *Sitt Marie Rose,* her poetry shows a concern with broader issues, such as peace and the preservation of the earth. In *The Indian Never Had a Horse & Other Poems,* she speaks eloquently of the destruction of the planet and the fate of the original inhabitants of the United States. For the plight of the Native American people is not unlike that which faces the inhabitants of the Middle East unless there is an end to warfare. In "Spreading Clouds ...," which is dedicated to poet June Jordan, Adnan draws perceptive analogies between situations in the United States and in her homeland. For her, Native American culture exemplifies an understanding of the precious connection between humankind and the earth: "Indian nations we need the wisdom / which descends into your daily visions / look what we did to our common / mother Earth! / God is woman if God is to be / creator / But we are all part and agent / of a continuous creation...." Adnan's motivation in writing is not just to exhibit a facility with words, a lyrical montage that hits the reader and washes into and over her. Her purpose is, in great part, to awaken others to the potential for destruction inherent in all of our cultures.

Adnan's most overtly feminist work, *Of Cities and Women (Letters to Fawwaz),* was written to a friend in lieu of a letter on feminism for a special issue on Arab women to be published in the magazine *Zawaya.* The collection of letters, written from June of 1990 to August 1992, includes impressions from eight cities: Aix-en-Provence (France), Amsterdam, Barcelona, Berlin, Beirut, Murcia (Spain), Rome, and Skopelos (Greece). Adnan explores each city and the women who inhabit it against the current political panorama: "In Barcelona, the women, when in the street, don't seem to consciously play a role, or live an exception: they are part of humanity, of a place, of a climate, of a country." In the section written from Aix-en-Provence, she says: "I tell myself: art is the search for the feminine, and, in turn, art feminizes the world. Hence its indispensable value to society, and its powers of subversion." Her words from Beirut after a 12-year absence are especially insightful: "I feel that I haven't settled anywhere, really, that I'm rather living in the world, all over.... The books I'm writing are houses that I build for myself." And it is the global scope of her vision and the specific attachment to place that makes many of her works soar. Also published in 1993, the essays in *Paris, When It's Naked* are an evocation of place, a philosophical rumination across time, and an analysis of Paris and its place in the world of politics, poetry, and ideas.

Adnan's writing often staggers us with its enormous scope, while at the same time pointing to the smallest of details. The eye of the painter and the craft of the poet combine to reveal comparable concerns both for the fate of indigenous peoples and for the survival of the planet. On first encountering her works, one is stunned by the power of the connections between them, and by her uniquely feminist voice. It is a perception that grows as one rereads her words. Etel Adnan's audience is composed of those concerned with peace and the preservation of the planet, as well as those who are moved by literature of the highest lyrical value. But it is especially those for whom the revelation of self in poetic or narrative form inspires action—be it political, social, artistic, or literary—who will discover a personal resonance in her writing.

—Barbara Lesch McCaffry

AIDOO, Ama Ata

Nationality: Ghanaian. **Born:** Abeadzi Kyiakor, 23 March 1942. **Education:** University of Ghana, Legon, B.A. in English 1964. **Family:** Married; one daughter. **Career:** Lecturer in English, University of Cape Coast, Ghana, 1970-83; consulting professor, Phelps-Stokes Fund Ethnic Studies program, 1974-75; Minister for Education, Ghana, 1982-83; currently a full-time writer. **Member:** Zimbabwe Women Writers Group (chair). **Address:** Harare, Zimbabwe.

Publications

Novels

Our Sister Killjoy; or, Reflections from a Black-eyed Squint. Harlow, Longmans, 1970; New York, NOK, 1979.

Changes: A Love Story. London, Women's Press, 1991.

Short Stories

No Sweetness Here. Harlow, Longmans, 1970; Garden City, New York, Doubleday, 1971.

Literary Criticism

"The African Poet, His Critics and His Future," in *Legonite,* 1964.
"No Saviours," in *African Writers on African Writing,* edited by G.D. Killam. New York, Africana, 1973.
"Unwelcome Pals and Decorative Slaves—or Glimpses of Women as Writers and Characters in Contemporary African Literature," in *Medium and Message,* edited by Ernest Emenyonu. Calabar, Nigeria, University of Calabar Press, 1981.
"GHANA: To Be a Woman," in *Creative Women in Changing Societies: A Quest for Alternatives.* Dobbs Ferry, New York, Transnational Publishers, Inc., 1982; in *Sisterhood Is Global,* edited by Robin Morgan, Garden City, New York, Doubleday, 1984.
"Literature, Feminism, and the African Woman Today," in *Reconstructing Womanhood, Reconstructing Feminism,* edited by Delia Jarrett-Macauly. London and New York, Routledge, 1996.

Poetry

Someone Talking to Sometime. Harare, Zimbabwe, College Press, 1985.

Plays

The Dilemma of a Ghost (produced Legon, Ghana, 1964). Harlow and Accra, Longmans, 1965; New York, Collier, 1971.
Anowa (produced England, 1991). Harlow, Longmans, 1970; Washington, DC, Three Continents, 1980.

For Children

The Eagle and the Chickens and Other Stories. Enugu, Nigeria, Tana, 1986.
Birds and Other Poems. Harare, Zimbabwe, College Press, 1987.

*

Critical Studies: "Women in African Literature" by G.C.M. Mutiso, in *East African Journal,* 8(3), 1971; "Ama Ata Aidoo: The Art of the Short Story and Sexual Roles in Africa" by Lloyd Brown, in *World Literature Written in English,* 13, November 1974; "Womanism: The Dynamics of the Contemporary Black Female Novel in English" by Chikwenye O. Ogunyemi, in *Signs,* 11, autumn 1985; "The Feminist Impulse and Social Realism in Ama Ata Aidoo's *No Sweetness Here* and *Our Sister Killjoy"* by Chimalum Nwankwo, in *Ngambika: Studies of Women in African Literature,* edited by Carole Boyce Davies and Anne Adams Graves, Trenton, New Jersey, African World, 1986; "The Afro-American-West African Marriage Question: Its Literary and Historical Contexts" by Brenda Berrian, in *African Literature Today,* 15, 1987; "Canons under Siege: Blackness, Femaleness and Ama Ata Aidoo's *Our Sister Killjoy"* by Kofi Owusu, in *Callaloo,* 13, spring 1990; "'A New Tail to an Old Tale': An Interview with Ama Ata Aidoo" by Rosemary Marangoly George and Helen Scott, in *Novel: A Forum on Fiction,* spring 1993; *The Art of Ama Ata Aidoo: Polylectics and Reading against Neocolonialism* by Vincent O. Odamtten, Gainsville, University of Florida Press, 1994.

* * *

The feminist insight of Ama Ata Aidoo is inflected by an acute awareness of the racist ideologies that underpin the economic exploitation of the African continent and its people. Born into a royal household in March of 1942 at Abeadzi Kyiakor in Ghana's central region, Aidoo went on to attend Wesley Girls' School in Cape Coast. She graduate with a degree in English from the University of Ghana at Legon in 1964. The same year witnessed the stage debut of her play *The Dilemma of a Ghost,* performed by the Legon Students' Theater. Published a year after its performance, the play established its 23-year-old author as an emerging voice on the world literary horizon. Aidoo has since published a number of essays, novels, poems, reviews, plays, and short fiction. She has taught English literature at the University of Cape Coast, presented lectures at universities across the African and North American continents, and held a post as Secretary of Education in Ghana.

In her literary and critical reflections Aidoo explores the formations of African female identity foregrounding the ways in which African women view themselves and are viewed by others. This subject is rendered inseparable from a past of British imperialist rule and contemporary neo-colonial rule over present-day Ghana by an indigenous elite. Different phases and aspects of this history constitute the subject matter of Aidoo's literary enterprise. The disintegration of marital bonds between the title character of *Anowa* and Kofi on the eve of colonization is intimately linked to the disruptive effects of British intervention in 19th-century West Africa. The legacy of slavery, the historical dimension of which is addressed in *Anowa,* also appears in *The Dilemma of a Ghost.* The culture clash between Eulalie Rush, the African American bride of Ato Yawson, and Ato's family when he brings her for the first time to his homeland of Ghana in *The Dilemma of a Ghost* is due in no small part to the stereotypical and distorted first world images of the "dark continent" that Eulalie brings with her. The persistence of colonial ideology in the era after the nominal end of European rule, a theme of *Our Sister Killjoy,* is also interrogated in the collection of short stories *No Sweetness Here* from a multiplicity of perspectives. From those displaced male and female migrants in search of wage work ("Certain Winds from the South," "In the Cutting of a Drink") to those of Ghana's educated classes' subservience to Western norms of beauty ("Everything Counts") and behavior ("For Whom Things Did Not Change") Aidoo's characters make visible the complexity of social relations in the contemporary world.

"It has become common [by some in Africa] to dismiss feminism as a foreign ideology, imported into Africa with crusading zeal to ruin good African women and stultify intellectual debate," asserts Aidoo in her essay "Literature, Feminism, and the African Woman Today." The marginalization of educated African women's perspectives, a theme she explores in other essays (for example, "GHANA: To Be a Woman") and fiction (*Our Sister Killjoy*), is linked to a sexist legacy inherent not to African cultures but rather inherited from the colonizer. She goes on in "Literature, Feminism, and the African Woman Today" to address the pernicious effects of first world feminism's insistence on a racist and essentialist view of African culture as inherently sexist. Aidoo is weary of this type of analysis on the grounds that it blatantly refuses to acknowledge the part first world women (and men), as heirs to the racist legacy of colonialism and as consumers participating in a global economy of neocolonialism, play in the oppression of African women. In this piece, as in all of her writing, she contests the construction of feminist consciousness and female activism as somehow irrelevant to or outside of Africa's past, present, or future.

Though female experience may have been far from perfect in the pre-colonial history of the continent, along with other African feminists (for example Nigeria's Molara Ogundipe-Leslie) Aidoo asserts that it was European colonial rule that introduced severe limitations and burdens to the balance of social relations, including those between men and women on the continent. Unduly discredited by some critics for her flat representations of male characters and by other for her pointed representations of the West, Aidoo's work instead reflects a feminist consciousness that is based upon accountability and connection. As she remarks throughout her writings, because African women must contend with a double burden of racism and sexism their perspectives, experiences, and analyses contest feminist paradigms that wish away cultural distinctions in order to press falsely universalizing claims for female solidarity.

—Mahnaz Ghaznavi

ALCOTT, Louisa May

Pseudonyms: A. M. Barnard; Flora Fairfield. **Nationality:** American. **Born:** Germantown, Pennsylvania, 29 November 1832. **Education:** Home-schooled until the age of sixteen; studied botany with Henry David Thoreau, student of Ralph Waldo Emerson. **Military Service:** Nurse at Union Hospital, Georgetown, District of Columbia, 1862-63. **Career:** Worked as a teacher, seamstress, and domestic servant; editor of *Merry's Museum* (children's magazine), 1867. **Died:** Roxbury, Massachusetts, 6 March 1888.

PUBLICATIONS

Novels

Moods. N.p., A. K. Loring, 1865; revised edition, Boston, Roberts Bros., 1882.

V.V.; or, Plots and Counterplots (as A. M. Barnard). Boston, Thomes & Talbot, 1870.

Work: A Story of Experience. Boston, Roberts Bros., and London, Low, 2 vols., 1873.

A Modern Mephistopheles (published anonymously). Boston, Roberts Bros., 1877; with *A Whisper in the Dark,* Boston, Roberts Bros., and London, Low, 1889.

A Long Fatal Love Chase. New York, Random House, 1995.

Short Stories

Morning-Glories, and Other Stories. Boston, H. B. Fuller, 1868.

Something to Do (contains *Proverb Stories).* London, Ward Lock & Tyler, 1873.

Silver Pitchers [and] *Independence, a Centennial Love Story.* Boston, Roberts Bros., and London, Low, 1876.

Meadow Blossoms. New York, Crowell, 1879.

Water Cresses. New York, Crowell, 1879.

Sparkles for Bright Eyes. New York, Crowell, 1879.

Spinning Wheel Stories. Boston, Roberts Bros., and London, Low, 1884.

A Round Dozen: Stories, edited by Anne Thayer Eaton. New York, Viking, 1963.

Glimpses of Louisa: A Centennial Sampling of the Best Short Stories by Louisa May Alcott, edited by Cornelia Meigs. Boston, Little Brown, 1968.

Behind a Mask: The Unknown Thrillers of Louisa May Alcott, edited by Madeleine B. Stern. New York, Morrow, 1975.

Plots and Counter Plots: More Unknown Thrillers of Louisa May Alcott, edited by Madeleine B. Stern. New York, Morrow, 1976.

Diana And Persis, edited by Sarah Elbert. New York, Arno, 1978.

Transcendental Wild Oats. Boston, Harvard Common Press, 1981.

Alternative Alcott, edited by Elaine Showalter. New Brunswick, New Jersey, Rutgers University Press, 1988.

A Double Life: Newly Discovered Thrillers of Louisa May Alcott, edited by Madeleine B. Stern, Joel Myerson, and Daniel Shealy. Boston, Little Brown, 1988.

Freaks of Genius: Unknown Thrillers of Louisa May Alcott, edited by Daniel Shealy, Madeleine B. Stern, and Joel Myerson. New York, Greenwood Press, 1991.

From Jo March's Attic: Stories of Intrigue and Suspense, edited by Madeleine B. Stern and Daniel Shealy. Boston, Northeastern University Press, 1993.

Plays

Comic Tragedies Written by "Jo" and "Meg" and Acted by the Little Women. Boston, Roberts Bros., and London, Low, 1893.

Essays

Hospital Sketches. Boston, James Redpath, 1863; with *Camp and Fireside Stories,* Boston, Roberts Bros., 1869.

On Picket Duty, and Other Tales. Boston, James Redpath, 1864.

For Children

Flower Fables. Boston, George W. Briggs, 1855.

The Rose Family: A Fairy Tale. Boston, James Redpath, 1864.

Kitty's Class Day. Boston, A. K. Loring, 1868.

Aunt Kipp. Boston, A. K. Loring, 1868.

Psyche's Art. Boston, A. K. Loring, 1868.

Little Women; or, Meg, Jo, Beth, and Amy [Part Second]. Boston, Roberts Bros., and London, Low, 2 vols., 1868-69; vol. 2 as *Little Women Wedded,* London, Low, 1872, as *Little Women Married,* London, Routledge, 1873, as *Nice Wives,* London, Weldon, 1875; revised edition, 1 vol., 1880; as *Little Women and Good Wives,* London, Nisbet, 1895.

Louisa M. Alcott's Proverb Stories (contains *Kitty's Class Day, Aunt Kipp,* and *Psyche's Art).* Boston, A. K. Loring, 1868.

Will's Wonder Book. Boston, H. B. Fuller, 1870.

An Old-Fashioned Girl. Boston, Roberts Bros., and London, Low, 1870.

Little Men: Life at Plumfield with Jo's Boys. Boston, Roberts Bros., and London, Low, 1871.

Aunt Jo's Scrap-Bag. Boston, Roberts Bros., and London, Low, 6 vols., 1872-82.

Eight Cousins; or, The Aunt-Hill. Boston, Roberts Bros., and London, Low, 1875.

Rose in Bloom: A Sequel to "Eight Cousins." Boston, Roberts Bros., and London, Low, 1876.

Under the Lilacs. Boston, Roberts Bros., and London, Low Marston, 1878.

Jack and Jill: A Village Story. Boston, Roberts Bros., and London, Low, 1880.

Jo's Boys, and How They Turned Out: A Sequel to "Little Men." Boston, Roberts Bros., and London, Low, 1886.

A Garland for Girls. Boston, Roberts Bros., and London, Blackie, 1887.

Louisa's Wonder Book: An Unknown Alcott Juvenile, edited by Madeleine B. Stern. Central Michigan University/Clark Historical Library, 1975.

Autobiography

Louisa May Alcott: Her Life, Letters and Journals, edited by Ednah D. Cheney. Boston, Roberts Bros., 1889.

The Journals of Louisa May Alcott, edited by Joel Myerson and Daniel Shealy. Boston, Little Brown, 1989.

Other

Nelly's Hospital. Washington, D.C., U.S. Sanitation Commission, 1865.

The Mysterious Key, and What It Opened. Boston, Elliott Thomes & Talbot, 1867.

Lulu's Library:

A Christmas Dream. Boston, Roberts Bros., and London, Low, 1886.

The Frost King. Boston, Roberts Bros., 1887.

Recollections. Boston, Roberts Bros., 1889; as *Recollections of My Childhood Days,* London, Low, 1884.

The Selected Letters of Louisa May Alcott, edited by Joel Myerson and Daniel Shealy. Boston, Little Brown, 1987.

*

Media Adaptations: *Little Women* (film), Lasky Corp, 1919, RKO, 1933, Metro-Goldwyn-Meyer, 1949; Columbia Pictures, 1995; *Little Men,* Mascott, 1934, RKO, 1940; *An Old-Fashioned Girl,* Pathé, 1949.

Bibliography: *Louisa May Alcott: A Reference Guide* by Alma J. Payne, Boston, G.K. Hall, 1980.

Manuscript Collections: Houghton Library, Harvard University, Boston, Massachusetts.

Critical Studies: *Louisa May Alcott* by Katharine S. Anthony, New York, Knopf, 1938; *Louisa May Alcott* by Madeleine B. Stern, University of Oklahoma Press, 1950; *We Alcotts: The Story of Louisa May Alcott's Family as Seen through the Eyes of "Marmee," Mother of Little Women* by Aileen Fisher and Olive Rabe, New York, Atheneum, 1968; *Louisa May: A Modern Biography of Louisa May Alcott* by Martha Saxton, Boston, Houghton Mifflin, 1977; *Communities of Women* by Nina Auerbach, Cambridge, Harvard University Press, 1978; *Louisa May Alcott and the Woman Problem* by Sarah Elbert, Boston, Little Brown, 1978; *The Alcotts: Biography of a Family* by Madelon Bedell, New York, Clarkson N. Potter, 1980; *Louisa May Alcott* by Ruth K. MacDonald, Boston, Twayne, 1983; *Critical Essays on Louisa May Alcott* edited by Madeleine B. Stern, Boston, G. K. Hall, 1984; *A Hunger for Home: Louisa May Alcott's Place in American Culture* by Sarah Elbert, New Brunswick, New Jersey, Rutgers University Press, 1988; *Sister's Choice: Traditions and Change in American Women's Writing* by Elaine Showalter, Oxford, Clarendon Press, 1991.

* * *

"Don't shut yourself up in a bandbox because you are a woman, but understand what is going on, and educate yourself to take your part in the world's work, for it all affects you and yours," Marmee tells Meg in the best-loved of Louisa May Alcott's novel, *Little Women,* a novel read and loved by girls and women since its publication in 1868-69. Feminists from Simone de Beauvoir to Gertrude Stein and Joyce Carol Oates have praised Alcott's most-known work, and women writers have a history of identifying with the "Topsy Turvey" scribbling woman, Jo March. What is less known are Alcott's other strong woman characters, her consistent advocacy of women's careers outside the home, and her progressive stance on education. Her heroines are often complicated women searching for ways to uphold both 19th-century values of "true womanhood" and transcendentalist goals of self-actualization. In both her children's books and her recently discovered sensational fiction, Alcott portrays women's struggle toward self-fulfillment. While feminist and progressive, Alcott also advocated more traditional notions of women's roles; in much of her work, heroines like Jo March must learn "plain cooking" and other household tasks in order to fulfill Alcott's complicated ideas of a woman's loyalty to home and family. For Alcott, women's roles included, and extended from, the home.

The second daughter of Abigail May Alcott and transcendentalist philosopher, Amos Bronson Alcott, Alcott lived most of her life in Concord, Massachusetts. She never attended school, but was educated according to her father's progressive ideas, reading widely in neighbor Ralph Waldo Emerson's library and studying botany with Henry David Thoreau. Like other members of her family, Alcott supported women's rights, women's suffrage, and abolition. Bronson Alcott continuously tried to curb his daughter's will while promoting her intellectual growth. During her childhood and adolescence, Alcott kept a journal that was read and commented on by both her parents. While journals were often shared among family members during the 19th century, Bronson used Alcott's journal as a way to track her moral development and felt that Alcott wrote too much about herself in her journal.

While other transcendentalists, including Emerson, considered him brilliant, Bronson Alcott was incapable of financially supporting his family; his continuous financial failures lead Alcott to begin writing for money early in her life. *Flower Fables,* a book of stories and poems written for Emerson's daughter, was published in 1855. Meanwhile, in an attempt to create a transcendental utopian community, Bronson Alcott moved his entire family to "Fruitlands," a failed experiment in farming and communal living. Later Alcott was able to recast the hunger and cold she experienced at Fruitlands into the humorous, autobiographical short story "Transcendental Wild Oats." This story exemplifies the conflicts between women's roles and transcendentalist notions of independence, conflicts that Alcott further explored in her first novel, *Moods.*

Although well known for her children's fiction, Alcott wrote in a variety of genres, from sensational fiction and adult novels to children's stories. In her first commercial success, *Hospital Sketches,* she described the difficulty of nursing during the Civil War. Based on letters she wrote during her brief stint as a Civil War nurse, *Hospital Sketches* drew on its author's wry sense of humor, but still managed to convey the horrible conditions experienced by Union casualties and recently freed slaves. After its success, Alcott was able to find a publisher for *Moods.*

In *Moods,* first published in 1865, Alcott's heroine Sylvia Yule marries Geoffrey Moor, only to discover that she has chosen the wrong man. Sylvia recognizes too late that she is in love with Moor's best friend, Adam Warwick, and considers divorce and social ostracism in order to achieve her desire. At the end of *Moods,* Sylvia dies, still married to Geoffrey; the only socially acceptable ending Alcott could imagine for Sylvia was death. Alcott argues that a woman needs freedom to explore her own consciousness before marriage: If Sylvia had time to be self-reflective, she would have been better able to negotiate the choices she made about her life. Sylvia also suffered because of her parents' loveless marriage and her mother's early death. Unlike the March sisters, Sylvia Yule did not have a mother to guide her decisions and journey to self-actualization. Interestingly, after the success of *Little Women,* Alcott revised *Moods* according to some of the reviews she had received 18 years previously. These revisions, according to Alcott critic Sarah Elbert, made the 1882 edition "tidier" and more "formulaic," but less interesting. The revised *Moods* has a less controversial ending: Sylvia lives and accepts her marriage to Geoffrey.

Little Women was an overnight success. Alcott originally resisted the idea of writing a book for girls, but in *Little Women* she revolutionized the genre of children's writing, creating four independent, thoughtful, and complicated young women who struggled with issues in ways that still interest us today. Based partly on her childhood, the story of the March family established Alcott as a writer for children and stereotyped her work for the rest of her life. Although she continued to write in other genres occasionally, Alcott's writing for children became her main source of income.

Like much of Alcott's other writing, *Little Women* portrayed sisterhood positively and women's education for careers as important. It is the positive portrayal of sisterhood that makes much of Alcott's other writing interesting, particularly *Work,* another of Alcott's autobiographical fictions. In *Work,* Alcott's heroine Christie Devon journeys from occupation to occupation, from servant to actress to governess, in an exploration of women's financial independence and in a search for women's place in male-dominated culture. In the imaginative world that Alcott creates, Christie marries, but then is widowed, allowing her the freedom to establish her own utopian community of women across race and class lines. As *Work* closes, women unite, holding hands around a table. Alcott again shows the power of female friendship, and its necessity for 19th-century women's survival. By creating strong roles for women within her fiction, Louisa May Alcott revealed a host of new possibilities that could be available for women, thereby influencing diverse generations of readers.

—Ann E. Green

ALEXANDER, Meena

Nationality: American. **Born:** Allahabad, India, 17 February 1951; immigrated to the United States in 1979. **Education:** University of Khartoum, B.A. (honors) 1969; University of Nottingham, Ph.D. in English 1973. **Family:** Married David Lelyveld in 1979; one son and one daughter. **Career:** Tutor in English, University of Khartoum, 1969; lecturer in English, University of Delhi, 1974, and Central Institute of English and Foreign Language, Hyderabad, 1975-77; CSIR Fellow, Jawaharlal Nehru University, New Delhi, 1975; lecturer, 1977-79, and reader in English, 1979, University of Hyderabad; assistant professor of English, Fordham University, Bronx, New York, 1980-87; assistant professor, 1987-89, associate professor, 1989-91, and professor of English and women's studies beginning 1992, Hunter College and the Graduate Center, City University of New York. Visiting assistant professor, University of Minnesota, Minneapolis, 1981; lecturer in poetry, Columbia University, New York, beginning 1990. Visiting fellow, Centre de Recherches en Litterature et Civilization Nord-Americaines, Sorbonne, University of Paris, 1979; writer-in-residence, Center for American Culture Studies, Columbia University, 1988; MacDowell Colony fellow, 1993; poet-in-residence, American College, Madurai, Indian, 1994; International Writer-in-Residence, Arts Council of England, 1995; Lila Wallace Writer-in-Residence, Asian American Renaissance, 1995. **Agent:** Anne Dubuisson, Ellen Levine Agency, 15 East 26th Street, Suite 1801, New York, New York 10010, U.S.A. **Address:** English Department, Hunter College, City University of New York, 695 Park Avenue, New York, New York 10021, U.S.A.

Publications

Poetry

The Bird's Bright Ring. Calcutta, Writers Workshop, 1976.
I Root My Name. Calcutta, United Writers, 1977.
Without Place. Calcutta, Writers Workshop, 1978.
Stone Roots. New Delhi, Arnold Heinemann, 1980.
House of a Thousand Doors. Washington, D.C., Three Continents Press, 1988.
The Storm: A Poem in Five Parts. New York, Red Dust, 1989.
Night-Scene, the Garden. New York, Red Dust, 1992.
River and Bridge. New Delhi, Rupa, 1995; Toronto, TSAR Press, 1996.

Novels

Nampally Road. San Francisco, Mercury House, 1991.
Manhattan Music. San Francisco, Mercury House, 1997.

Play

In the Middle Earth (one-act). New Delhi, Enact, 1977.

Autobiography

Fault Lines. New York, Feminist Press, 1993.

Other

The Poetic Self: Towards a Phenomenology of Romanticism. New Delhi, Arnold Heinemann, 1979; Atlantic Highlands, New Jersey, Humanities Press, 1980.

Women in Romanticism: Mary Wollstonecraft, Dorothy Wordsworth and Mary Shelley. London, Macmillan, 1989.

The Shock of Arrival: Reflections on Postcolonial Experience. Boston, South End Press, 1996.

*

Critical Studies: "Exiled by a Woman's Body: Substantial Phenomena in the Poetry of Meena Alexander" by John Oliver Perry, in *Journal of South Asian Literature* (East Lansing, Michigan), 21(1), winter/spring 1986, and his "The Inward Body: Meena Alexander's Feminist Strategies of Poetry," in *Feminism and Literature,* edited by K. Radha, Trivandrum University of Kerala, 1987; "Poetry, Language and Feminism: The Writings of Meena Alexander" by K. Raveendran, in *Kala Gomati* (Kerala), October 1987; "Living in a Pregnant Time: Meena Alexander Discusses Feminism, Literature, Decolonization" by Chitra Divakaruni, in *India Currents,* May 1991; "On Writing and Contemporary Issues: Interview with Meena Alexander" by Ayisha Abraham, in *Toronto South Asian Review,* winter 1993; "The Doors to Home and History: Post-Colonial Identities in Meena Alexander and Bharati Mukherjee" by Shilpa Dave, in *Amerasia Journal,* 19(3), 1993; "The Poetry of Multiple Migrations" by Hema Nair, in *Ms.,* January/February 1994.

Meena Alexander comments:

While I do not think I consciously write as woman, I have little doubt that some of my deepest emotions and insights spring from having been born into a female body, learning to grow up as a woman in both a traditional Indian culture—South Indian, Syrian Christian, Malayalam speaking—and as part of the complex, shifting South Asian diaspora. How odd the "having been born" part sounds, yet what else can I say? It is my embodiment I am trying to speak of, the seat of my knowledge. My art flows from that source. I think that feminism has allowed me to give voice to these thoughts. A feminism complicated by issues of race and dislocation, yet enriched by the immigrant world I am now part of. Voices of women haunt my work, other women, many selves inside me.

* * *

The daughter of a diplomat and member of a socially prominent Indian family, Meena Alexander was born in Allahabad, India, raised in the Sudan, educated in England, and now lives in America. Her many travels, and her heritage as a Syrian Christian living among a variety of ethnic and religious groups, has made Alexander acutely aware of the differences among peoples and the contradictions embodied within herself. Her writings—poetry, novels, nonfiction, and a memoir—explore the multicultural aspects of her life, and she ponders the proper role for an educated woman from the Third World who now enjoys the luxuries found in the West. Through her writing, especially her poetry, Alexander seeks to unify the disparate aspects of her heritage into a consistent whole, and in the process overcome cultural displacement.

In her verse, Alexander creates female narrators who speak of their painful personal histories in an attempt to create some order from the formlessness of their lives. The poem "After the Wedding," published in *I Root My Name,* for example, tells of a young bride who feels suicidal on the day of her wedding. "A Mirror's Grace," published in *Without Place,* is a retelling of the Cleopatra story, this time from the context of a woman trapped by the limitations of a patriarchal language. In *The Storm: A Poem in Five Parts,* Alexander attempts to use poetic ritual to clarify and redeem her memories of childhood, creating a tension between the fragments of memory and the order of the narrative. The collection *Night-Scene, the Garden* again focuses on Alexander's early memories, this time memories of her family members, especially her mother. This mother-daughter relationship forms a part of the matrilineal society of Alexander's native Southern India, one link in a chain of family relations. Women are prominent characters in all of Alexander's poems. Mothers, grandmothers, aunts and friends appear, while the more rhetorical poetic moments find Alexander addressing such larger groups as the "Women of Delhi." Present too in these poems is the idea of Alexander creating her own sense of identity as she writes her poetry, the writing process being a kind of psychological process in which she analyzes, rejects, accepts, and orders the elements that compose her personality.

In her novel *Nampally Road,* Alexander tells the autobiographical story of Mira Kannadical, a young woman who returns to her home in India after four years of schooling in England. She hopes to write a book covering the tumultuous history she has lived through, putting it into a literary order in much the same way as Wordsworth did, whom she has studied in college. But Mira becomes caught up in events in India as violence breaks out among the competing groups there. In addition, the young woman resists her mother's attempts at an arranged marriage and develops a relationship with Ramu, a leftist intellectual fighting the government. In the end, Mira is torn between writing her story or involving herself in the political violence surrounding her. She wonders if the literary order she dreamed of creating has anything to do with the disorderly and violent world of India. Literature's relationship to life, and the role of women in healing society, are questions raised by Mira's plight. Much of the novel's action is set in Little Mother's clinic, where Mira's landlady administers to the sick and needy. Like Little Mother, Mira had hoped to bring some kind of order to a suffering world, but the two women find that their efforts, in fact, can do very little to alleviate the pain around them.

Alexander turns to autobiography in *Fault Lines,* a memoir of her life. In the process of recounting the many places she has lived and the many languages she speaks, Alexander draws a portrait of herself as a woman of many disparate parts who is searching for a solid self and a personal voice. Although the forces that shaped her are sometimes conflicting or wildly divergent, she finds that they do have one thing in common: the denial of the value of women. This denial is a central part of her life, something that Alexander believes she must counter and struggle against in her writing. But the disruptions in her life, the conflicting forces at work within her, are, Alexander makes clear, the reason she is compelled to write. *Fault Lines* uses a poetic style to recount not only the story of Alexander's life but those of her grandfather, with whom she was close, and those of the many women in her family as well. As such, it goes well beyond autobiography to present a sensitive picture of family life among the Indian elite.

—Denise Wiloch

ALLEN, Paula Gunn

Nationality: American. **Born:** Albuquerque, New Mexico, in 1939. **Education:** Holder of B.A., M.F.A., degrees; University of New Mexico, Ph.D. in American studies. **Career:** Lecturer, San Francisco State University, University of New Mexico, Albuquerque, and Fort Lewis College, Durango, California; professor of ethnic and Native American studies, then professor of English, University of California, Berkeley; currently professor of English, University of California, Los Angeles. **Awards:** National Endowment for the Arts award; Ford Foundation grant; American Book Award, 1990, for *Spider Woman's Granddaughters.* **Address:** c/o Fawcett Books, 201 East 50th Street, New York, New York 10022, U.S.A.

Publications

Novel

The Woman Who Owned the Shadows. San Francisco, Spinsters/Aunt Lute Books, 1983.

Poetry

The Blind Lion. Berkeley, California, Thorp Springs Press, 1974.
Coyote's Daylight Trip. Albuquerque, New Mexico, La Confluencia, 1978.
A Cannon between My Knees. New York, Strawberry Hill Press, 1981.
Star Child. Marvin, South Dakota, Blue Cloud Quarterly, 1981.
Shadow Country. Los Angeles, University of California Indian Studies Center, 1982.
Wyrds. San Francisco, Taurean Horn, 1987.
Skins and Bones. Albuquerque, New Mexico, West End, 1988.

Essays

The Sacred Hoop: Recovering the Feminine in American Indian Traditions (includes "Hwame, Koshkalaka, and the Rest: Lesbians in American Indian Cultures" and "How the West Was Really Won"). Boston, Beacon Press, 1986; portion published as "Lesbians in American Indian Cultures," in *Hidden from History: Reclaiming the Gay and Lesbian Past,* edited by Martin Bauml Duberman, Martha Vicinus, and George Chauncey Jr., New York, New American Library, 1989.

Other

Sipapu: A Cultural Perspective. Albuquerque, New Mexico, University of New Mexico Press, 1975.
Grandmothers of the Light: A Medicine Woman's Sourcebook. Boston, Beacon Press, 1991.
Indian Perspectives. N.p., Southwest Parks and Monuments Association, 1992.

Editor, *From the Center: A Folio: Native American Art and Poetry.* New York, Strawberry Hill Press, 1981.
Editor, *Studies in American Indian Literature: Critical Essays and Course Design.* New York, Modern Language Association, 1983.
Editor, *Spider Woman's Granddaughters: Traditional Tales and Contemporary Writing By Native American Women.* New York, Fawcett, 1990.
Editor, *Voice of the Turtle: American Indian Literature, 1900-1970.* New York, Ballantine, 1994.

*

Critical Studies: "Paula Gunn Allen (Laguna-Sioux-Lebanese)" by John R. Milton, in *Four Indian Poets,* Vermillion, South Dakota, n.p., 1974; "A Laddered, Rain-bearing Rug: Paula Gunn Allen's Poetry" by Elaine Jahner, in *Women and Western Literature,* edited by Helen Winter Stauffer and Susan Rosowski, Troy, New York, Whitston, 1982; "A MELUS Interview: Paula Gunn Allen" by Franchot Ballinger and Brian Swann, in *MELUS,* 10(2), summer 1983; "Paula Gunn Allen and Joy Harjo: Closing the Distance between Personal and Mythic Space" by James Ruppert, in *American Indian Quarterly,* 7(1), 1983; "I Climb the Mesas in My Dreams: An Interview with Paula Gunn Allen" in *Survival This Way: Interviews with American Indian Poets* by Joseph Bruchac, Tucson, Sun Tracks/University of Arizona Press, 1987; "Paula Gunn Allen, 'The Autobiography of a Confluence'" in *I Tell You Now: Autobiographical Essays by Native American Writers,* edited by Brian Swann and Arnold Krupat, Lincoln, University of Nebraska Press, 1987; "Native American Literature" by Patricia Holt, in *San Francisco Chronicle,* 2 July 1989; *Paula Gunn Allen* by Elizabeth I. Hanson, Boise, Idaho, Boise State University Press, 1990; "The Journey Back to Female Roots: A Laguna Pueblo Model" by Annette Van Dyke, in *Lesbian Texts and Contexts: Radical Revisions,* edited by Karla Jay and Joanne Glasgow, New York, New York University Press, 1990; "Despite Successes, Scholars Express Ambivalence about Place of Minority Literature in Academe" by Ellen K. Coughlin, in *Chronicle of Higher Education,* 10 January 1990; *Winged Words: American Indian Writers Speak* by Laura Coltelli, Lincoln, University of Nebraska Press, 1990; "Curing Ceremonies: The Novels of Leslie Marmon Silko and Paula Gunn Allen" by Van Dyke, in her *The Search for a Woman-Centered Spirituality,* New York, New York University Press, 1992.

* * *

In the field of contemporary Native American literature, lesbian-feminist Paula Gunn Allen is at the forefront, not only as a writer, but as a scholar, educator, and literary critic as well. Allen refers to herself as a "multicultural event," pointing to her Pueblo/Sioux/Lebanese/Scotch-American heritage. However, she writes as a Native American woman. Born in Albuquerque, New Mexico, she grew up in Cubero, New Mexico, a Spanish-Mexican land-grant village next to the Laguna and Acoma reservations and bordering the Cibola National Forest. She attended mission schools until she was sent to a Catholic boarding school in Albuquerque, from which she graduated. Allen has both her B.A. in English and

M.F.A. in creative writing from the University of Oregon. She also has a Ph.D. in American Studies with an emphasis on Native American literature from the University of New Mexico. She is related to two other writers from Laguna Pueblo: her sister Carol Lee Sanchez and Leslie Marmon Silko, a cousin.

The traditional Laguna Pueblo culture from which Allen writes is woman-centered: Women own the houses; descent is reckoned through the female line; the major deities are female. A major theme in Allen's writing is to restore this woman-centered perspective and to illustrate to Euro-American culture that all women are not weak and that cultures existed in which women's power was equal to men's. Although Allen admits that she has received the most support from feminists and that they are her best audience, she has some ambivalence about the feminist movement because of a Euro-American cultural chauvinism and the misrepresentation of Native American women as fitting the "weak" stereotype. In her own family, woman-centered traditions have been so strong that her grandfather wanted to name her Susan B. Anthony.

In addition to serving as the major focus of her collected essays, 1986's *The Sacred Hoop: Recovering the Feminine in American Indian Traditions,* the role and power of Native American women also is the focus of the essay, "Who Is Your Mother: Red Roots of White Feminism," first published in *Sinister Wisdom* in 1984 and subsequently included in *Sacred Hoop.* In this original essay, Allen points out Native American women's contributions both to democracy and feminism. Her 1983 novel, *The Woman Who Owned the Shadows,* draws on Allen's multicultural background to trace the journey of the protagonist through varied cultural influences back to her woman-centered roots and to a role as ceremonial lesbian or medicine woman.

In addition to advocating for women in her work, Allen also focuses on the place of Native American lesbians and gays in traditional cultures. In her ground-breaking essay in an 1981 edition of *Conditions,* "Beloved Women: Lesbians in American Indian Cultures"—revised for *Sacred Hoop*—Allen explains the role of gay and lesbian Native Americans as spiritual, working for the good of the community by bridging the worlds of men and women.

An edited collection, *Spider Woman's Granddaughters: Traditional Tales and Contemporary Writings by Native American Women,* is an attempt to restore stories by Native American women to the usually predominantly male collections. Allen extends her interest in the ritual experience of women as exhibited in the traditional stories in 1991's *Grandmother of the Light: A Medicine Woman's Sourcebook.* These stories, and Allen's commentary, illustrate spiritual pathways for women and the mythic dimensions of women's relationship to the sacred.

A basis of much of Allen's work is her belief in the power of the oral tradition now embodied in Native American literature to effect healing, survival, and continuance of the community. Indeed, her 1975 essay "The Sacred Hoop: A Contemporary Perspective" was the first work to point out the ritual and mythic function of Native American literature. Through her editorship of the 1994 collection, *Voice of the Turtle: American Indian Literature 1900-1970,* Allen attempts to show how story, through the oral tradition, shapes Native American life and, in turn, is shaped by it. In 1983, Allen edited an important work on teaching Native American literature, entitled *Studies in American Indian Literature.* This work contains an extensive bibliography as well as suggested course outlines.

In addition to her scholarly works, Allen is well known as a poet, having received an honorable mention from the 1982 National Book Award Before Columbus Foundation for *Shadow Country.* Her poetry draws on the varying structures and rhythms from her background: Pueblo corn dances, Catholic masses, and Arabic chanting. Allen has cited as influential to her work as a poet writers as diverse as Gertrude Stein; the Romantic poets Keats and Shelley; Beat poet Allen Ginsberg; and, more recently, Judy Grah, Adrienne Rich, and Audre Lord. Her finely detailed poetry resonates with a sense of place: urban, the reservation, or interior. In addition to bringing a unique dimension to her verse, Paula Gunn Allen's multicultural perspective will continue to enrich her work in Native American literature and feminism.

—Annette Van Dyke

ALLENDE, Isabel

Nationality: Chilean. **Born:** Lima, Peru, 2 August 1942; niece of assassinated Chilean President Salvador Allende. **Education:** Graduated from a private high school in Santiago, Chile, at age 16. **Family:** Married 1) Miguel Frias in 1962 (divorced 1987); 2) William Gordon in 1988; one daughter and two sons. **Career:** Secretary, United Nations Food and Agricultural Organization, Santiago, 1959-65; journalist, editor, and advice columnist, *Paula* magazine, Santiago, 1967-74; journalist, *Mampato* magazine, Santiago, 1969-74; television interviewer for Canal 13/Canal 7, 1970-75; worked on movie newsreels, 1973-75; administrator, Colegio Marroco, Caracas, Venezuela, 1979-82. Guest teacher at Montclair State College, New Jersey, 1985, and University of Virginia, 1988; Gildersleeve Lecturer, Barnard College, 1988; teacher of creative writing, University of California, Berkeley, 1989. **Awards:** Quality Paperback Book Club New Voice Award nomination, 1986, for *The House of the Spirits; Los Angeles Times* Book Prize nomination, 1987, for *Of Love and Shadows; Eva Luna* was named one of *Library Journal*'s Best Books of 1988. **Agent:** Carmen Balcells, Diagonal 580, Barcelona 21, Spain. **Address:** 15 Nightingale Lane, San Rafael, California 94901, U.S.A.

Publications

Novels

La casa de los espíritus. Barcelona, Plaza y Janés, 1982; translated by Magda Bogin as *The House of the Spirits,* New York, Knopf, and London, Cape, 1985.

De amor y de sombra. Barcelona, Plaza y Janés, 1984; translated by Margaret Sayers Peden as *Of Love and Shadows,* New York, Knopf, and London, Cape, 1987.

Eva Luna. Barcelona, Plaza y Janés, 1987; translated by Margaret Sayers Peden, New York, Knopf, 1988; London, Hamish Hamilton 1989.

Los cuentos de Eva Luna. Buenos Aires, Editorial Sudamericana, 1990; translated by Margaret Sayers Peden as *The Stories of Eva Luna,* New York, Atheneum, and London, Hamish Hamilton, 1991.

El plan infinito. Buenos Aires, Editorial Sudamericana, 1990; translated by Margaret Sayers Peden as *The Infinite Plan,* New York and London, HarperCollins, 1993.

Other

Civilice a su troglodita: Los impertinentes de Isabel Allende (humor). Santiago, Lord Cochran, 1974.
La gorda de porcelana (for children). Madrid, Alfaguara, 1984.
Paula. New York, HarperLibros, 1995; translated by Margaret Sayers Peden, New York, HarperCollins, 1995.

*

Media Adaptations: *House of the Spirits* (film), 1994.

Critical Studies: *Los libros tienen sus propios espiritus: Estudios sobre Isabel Allende* edited by Marcelio Coddou, Universidad Veracruzana, 1986; review of *De amor y de sombra* by Maria Ines Lagos-Pope, in *Latin American Literary Review,* 15(29), January-June 1987; "Isabel Allende on Love and Shadow" by Ambrose Gordon, and "Literature as Survival: Allende's 'The House of the Spirits'" by Peter G. Earle, both in *Contemporary Literature,* 28(4), winter 1987; "Exile and the Female Condition in Isabel Allende's 'De amor y de sombra'" by Doris Meyer, in *International Fiction Review,* 15(2), summer 1988; "Isabel Allende's *La casa de los espíritus* and the Literature of Matrilineage" by Mary Gómez Parham, in *Discurso Literario* (Stillwater, Oklahoma), 6(1), 1988; "La desconstrucción y la crítica feminista: Lecturas posibles de *Cien años de soledad* y *La casa de los espiritus"* by Lyana María Amaya and Aura María Fernández, in *Nuevo Texto Crítico,* 2(4), 1989; "A Life like a Dimestore Romance" by Eleanor J. Bader, in *Belles Lettres,* 4(2), winter 1989; "A Passage to Androgyny: Isabel Allende's *La casa de los espíritus*" by Linda Gould Levine, in *In the Feminine Mode: Essays on Hispanic Women Writers,* Lewisburg, Pennsylvania, Bucknell University Press, 1990; "'Parenting the Text': Female Creativity and Dialogic Relationships in Isabel Allende's 'La casa de los espíritus'" by Doris Meyer, in *Hispania,* 73, May 1990; *Critical Approaches to Isabel Allende's Novels* edited by Sonia Riquelme Rojas and Edna Aguirre Rehbein, New York, Lang, 1991; "Two Modes of Writing the Female Self: Isabel Allende's *The House of the Spirits* and Clarice Lispector's *The Stream of Life* by Flora H. Schiminovich, in *Redefining Autobiography in 20th-Century Women's Fiction,* New York, Garland Press, 1991.

* * *

Isabel Allende's private life has never been without a political dimension. Allende's father was a Chilean diplomat in Lima, Peru, when she was born there in 1942. Although she resided for much of her childhood in Santiago, Chile, her adolescence was spent traveling after her parents' divorce her mother remarried another diplomat who brought the family to Bolivia, Europe, and regions of the Middle East. Salvador Gossens Allende, Isabel's beloved uncle and godfather, participated in the organization of Chile's Socialist Party in 1933 and was elected to the Chilean legislature in 1937. In 1970 he became the first democratically elected Marxist to preside in Chile and in a Western nation. Shortly after President Allende's assassination in 1973 by right-wing military leaders who, with the help of CIA operatives and the U.S. State Department, violently toppled his socialist reform government, Isabel Allende, active in her opposition to the new dictatorship, was forced to flee Chile with her husband and children for fear of reprisal. In exile in Caracas, Venezuela, Allende began her career as a novelist.

During her exile in Venezuela, Allende did not immediately envision herself pursuing a literary career. Until this time her professional writing had been limited to television journalism and magazine features. For a short time she also translated popular romance fiction into Spanish. But her narrative gifts were fostered since childhood by her mother's storytelling, her early reading, and a passion for language that endeared her to writing. After fleeing Chile in 1974, Allende recalls a number of years when she could find no work as a journalist and therefore experienced an inner silence that was as much a result of the loneliness of exile as it was her search for a new means of communication. She broke through this period of silence in 1981 by composing a long letter to her grandfather that included memories of her family history. Her grandfather had always preached that one lived after death only in the memories of loved ones. Allende gradually became cognizant of the fact that this letter to her grandfather was only a pretext for writing what was to become her first novel, *The House of the Spirits.*

The publication of *The House of the Spirits,* Allende's most important work, was met with almost instant international acclaim. Readers were quick to detect her indebtedness to another Latin American novelist, Gabriel García Márquez, whose *One Hundred Years of Solitude* shares many stylistic similarities with Allende's novel, especially the use of magic realism, a technique that blends supernatural elements into the otherwise mundane events of everyday life. But just as many readers noted that *The House of the Spirits* is no mere tribute to Allende's famed Colombian predecessor; they argue that Allende's narrative sets a precedent by positing a female consciousness and asserting a feminine voice and historical vision in an otherwise masculine dominated Latin American literary tradition.

The House of the Spirits comprises the histories of four generations of Chilean women (some who are based on Allende's relatives) and is narrated largely from these multiple feminine perspectives. Their stories are told against the backdrop of Chile's emerging socialist movement, the election of the Marxist president Salvador Allende, and the coup d'état by military leaders that began a repressive dictatorship under General Augusto Pinochet Ugarte. *The House of the Spirits* begins near the turn of the century with the early lives of Clara (a clairvoyant) and Rosa (a remarkable green-haired beauty), daughters of the upper class del Valle family. Their mother, Nivea del Valle, is an ardent feminist and social activist, while her husband, Severo del Valle, is an aspiring progressive politician. Rosa, engaged to be married to Esteban Trueba (a middle-class man seeking his fortune in mining), suffers an untimely death by drinking from a decanter given to her father as a gift celebrating his candidacy for Congress. Clara, traumatized after secretly witnessing the embalming and violation of her sister's body by a doctor's assistant, becomes mute for the next nine years. The narration of Clara's life is filled with instances of magic realism as her strange powers of clairvoyance and levitation are described as normal occurrences in the life of the del Valle family. At the age of 19, Clara breaks her silence upon the arrival of her sister's fiancé Esteban Trueba when she announces that she will marry him.

The House of the Spirits continues with the successive generations of female descendants of the Trueba family on their estate, *Tres Marías.* Clara's daughter Blanca falls in love with a peasant, Pedro Tercero García, a folk singer and political organizer of farm workers. Esteban Trueba, angered by Pedro Tercero's political ideology, severs three of the young man's fingers with an axe before chasing him off the estate. The lovers reunite periodically until

Pedro is forced to save his life by going into hiding, and Esteban succeeds in forcing the pregnant Blanca to marry the perverse and wealthy Jean de Satigny. Blanca, unable to endure her husband, returns to her family where she gives birth to Alba. As a young woman, Alba becomes a political activist for the socialist cause in Chile, and by the time of the military coup, she becomes one of thousands of political prisoners who were victimized by the dictatorship's reign of terror and massive human rights violations. Locked in a cramped prison cell and having undergone rape and torture, Alba is awakened by the apparition of her grandmother Clara, who urges her to survive and keep the memory of her family alive through writing. The reader is left with the realization at the end of the story that the first-person narrative voice emerging at intervals during the novel belongs to Alba, who is authoring the text, that is, reconstructing the family history with the help of her grandfather Esteban and her grandmother Clara's notebooks.

The House of the Spirits is a complex narrative with both a spiritual and political agenda. Allende has often remarked that writing the novel helped her overcome the painful paralysis of hatred and anger over the injustices of the military dictatorship toward her family and the people of her country. Although Allende relies on the technique of magic realism for much of Clara's history, social realism gains more prominence over magical elements in the narrative as the harsher political realities of the novel emerge. Allende's matrilineal text charts not only a family's growth from innocence to a more sober maturity, but a country's development as well, from the idealist vision of shared wealth (Allende's democratic socialism) to confrontation with the harsher political realities of the dictatorship which favor corporate ownership and free enterprise to the benefit of Chile's elite. If *The House of the Spirits* represents a female historical perspective that is new to the Latin American literary tradition, perhaps this vision insists on the connection between a country's people and the life of its culture, a spiritual fabric woven by individuals and families whose lives are irrevocably affected by brute historical forces.

Allende's second novel, *Of Love and Shadows,* is situated during the time of Chile's military junta under General Pinochet's rule. Although the country and its leaders are not named specifically, Allende's indirect references to the military's abuse of power leave little doubt that the time frame of the novel directly follows where the action of *The House of the Spirits* ends. Critics have remarked that *Of Love and Shadows* is more firmly situated in social realism than *The House of the Spirits,* but that both novels, despite their stylistic differences, are effective forms of social criticism. Irene Beltrán, a magazine journalist, and Francisco Leal, a photographer, develop a friendship as they investigate a story about a young peasant girl, Evangelina Ranquileo, who purportedly enters a mystical trance each day at noon. When the two arrive at the Ranquileo home, they witness Evangelina's trance, which is interrupted by the arrival of soldiers who attempt to break up the crowd and discredit the "miracle." Unexpectedly, Evangelina arises from her bed, lifts the soldier in charge off his feet, and casts him to the ground. The humiliated soldiers later return and abduct Evangelina, whose parents fear the worst for her fate. Driven by disbelief and outrage, Irene and Francisco continue their investigation until they discover a cave filled with the decomposing bodies (including Evangelina's) of people who have "disappeared" under the repressive regime. Irene and Francisco, who have become lovers over the course of events, are forced to flee their country for fear of retribution. Allende has acknowledged that this compelling story is based in fact, and like *The House of the Spirits,* she is again working to bring to light the abuses of human rights that her country's people have endured.

Allende's third novel, *Eva Luna,* represents a return to the genre of magic realism. Eva Luna, the heroine, is an illegitimate child who later becomes orphaned. She works at menial jobs, suffers deprivation and homelessness, but eventually finds success as a television scriptwriter. The novel becomes a story about the act of storytelling since Eva Luna, through the resourcefulness of her imagination, continually reinvents the world as she would like it to be for herself and others. Allende chose as an epigraph for this novel a passage from *A Thousand and One Tales of the Arabian Nights:* "Then he said to Scheherazade: 'Sister, for the sake of Allah, tell us a story that will help pass the night.'" Although many readers have complained that *Eva Luna* has too many characters whose destinies are left unresolved and that the entire plot of the novel is implausible, few would dispute that this novel lacks the fine verbal crafting of Allende's previous works.

Allende revives Eva Luna's persona in a series of short fiction that purports to tell many of Eva's stories that were only alluded to in the previous novel. *The Stories of Eva Luna* opens with Eva lying in the arms of her lover Rolf Carlé (introduced in *Eva Luna*), a German refugee who is haunted by his father's Nazi past. Rolf asks Eva, "Tell me a story you have never told anyone before. Make it up for me." With this request, Allende's Eva tells 23 stories, which complete the narrative begun in *Eva Luna.*

The Infinite Plan, Allende's most recent work of fiction, has been a surprising novel for readers grown used to her magic realism and Latin American settings. Set in America at the end of the Depression, the novel traces the life of Gregory Reeves, the son of an itinerant preacher who claims to have received knowledge of "the infinite plan" through a mystical experience. After the death of his father, Reeves, with his sister and mother, are given hospitality by the Morales family in an East Los Angeles barrio. Gregory befriends Juan José Morales, and later these two young men share a tour of duty in Vietnam, where Juan José is killed. Gregory returns to the States where he becomes an entrepreneur, is married twice, and is consumed with making money. Although the plot seems pointless at times and the prose lacks the richness of her previous work, Allende is certainly experimenting with new materials and techniques in *The Infinite Plan.*

In 1991, after the publication of the Spanish version of *The Infinite Plan,* Allende's daughter Paula contracted porphyria and lapsed into a coma. Paula was hospitalized in Madrid where she fell ill, and Allende remained by her daughter's bedside for almost a year until Paula's death. During that time, Allende wrote an autobiographical work which she titled *Paula,* a multi-layered family history as well as a record of her daughter's progressively worsening condition. *Paula* shares many similarities with *The House of the Spirits* in that both works are inspired to preserve family memories as well as to produce a restorative effect on the storyteller. One of the pleasures of reading *Paula* is the recognition of many characters and events in Allende's past that went into the creation of *The House of the Spirits.* Allende weaves into this history her agonizing and soul-searching conversations with her unconscious daughter, who Allende hopes will benefit from the narrative, easing her journey toward death. This autobiography refuses to become morbid; instead, it is often humorous, sensitive, and compelling, offering the reader new insights into Allende's personality and writing. Indeed, *Paula* only hints at how much more Isabel Allende has to offer her reading public.

—Janet J. Montelaro

ALLISON, Dorothy (E.)

Nationality: American. **Born:** Greenville, South Carolina, 11 April 1949. **Education:** Florida Presbyterian College, St. Petersburg, B.A. 1971; New School of Social Research, M.A. in anthropology. **Family:** Companion of Alix Layman since 1987; one son. *Awards:* Lambda Literary awards, 1988, for *Trash;* National Book Award nomination and Bay Area Book Reviewers Association prize for fiction, both 1992, both for *Bastard out of Carolina.* **Agent:** Frances Goldin, 305 East 11th Street, New York, New York 10003, U.S.A.

Publications

Novels

Bastard out of Carolina. New York and London, Flamingo, 1993.
Cavedweller. New York, Dutton, forthcoming.

Short Stories

Trash. Ithaca, New York, Firebrand Books, 1988; as *Trash: Stories and Poems,* London, Flamingo, 1995.
"A Lesbian Appetite," in *Women on Women,* edited by Joan Nestle and Naomi Holoch. New York, Dutton, 1990.
"Private Rituals," in *High Risk,* edited by Amy Shoulder and Ira Silverberg. New York, Dutton, 1991.
"Her Body, Mine, and His," in *Leatherfolk: Radical Sex, People, Politics, and Practice,* edited by Mark Thompson. Boston, Alyson, 1991.

Poetry

The Women Who Hate Me. Brooklyn, New York, Long Haul Press, 1983; as *The Women Who Hate Me: Poetry, 1980-1990,* Ithaca, New York, Firebrand Books, 1991.

Essays

Skin: Talking about Sex, Class and Literature. Ithaca, New York, Firebrand Books, 1994.

Uncollected Essays

"I Am Working on My Charm," in *Conditions: Six* (Lincoln, Nebraska), 1980.
"The Billie Jean King Thing," in *New York Native* (New York), 18(31), May 1981.
"Confrontation: Black/White," in *Building Feminist Theory: Essays from "Quest,"* edited by Charlotte Bunch and others. New York, Longman, 1981.

Autobiography

Two or Three Things I Know for Sure. New York, Dutton, 1995.

*

Media Adaptations: *Bastard out of Carolina* (audiocassette), New York, Penguin/HighBridge, 1993; *Bastard out of Carolina* has been optioned for film.

Critical Studies: "Dorothy Allison" by Lisa Moore, in *Contemporary Lesbian Writers of the United States: A Bio-Bibliographical Critical Sourcebook,* edited by Sandra Pollack and Denise Knight, Westport, Connecticut, Greenwood Press, 1993; "The Roseanne of Literature" by Alexis Jetter, in *New York Times Magazine,* December 17, 1995.

* * *

The life and writing of Dorothy Allison illustrate her firm commitment to the two "outlaw" cultures with which she identifies: her "white trash" South Carolina family, and her sexually daring (and non-PC) lesbian activist associates. Allison's poetry, essays, and fiction explore the terrible violence and beauty of both these cultures; indeed, she says, "writing is the only way I know to make sure of my ongoing decision to live."

Born in 1949, Allison grew up in Greenville, South Carolina, in a hardscrabble "trash" family where the women died of cancer and the men of knife wounds or cirrhosis long before they were old enough to qualify for Social Security. Her stepfather abused her sexually from the time she was five until she was eleven years old. The memory of this abuse, and of her mother's inability to protect her from it, represent the core of much of Allison's writing. Several of the stories in her 1988 collection *Trash* attempt to make sense of her painful and impoverished childhood. In 1992 Allison's first full-length novel, *Bastard out of Carolina,* introduced Bone, a semi-autobiographical title character. Bone's life—from her illegitimate birth through young adulthood—is described in raw detail and with painful love. *Bastard out of Carolina* was a finalist for the National Book Award; Allison had transformed her vision of her painful roots into a nationwide bestseller. She would follow up this success with a nonfiction meditation on her family, entitled *Two or Three Things I Know for Sure* (1995). In this memoir Allison includes stories, personal memories, and photographs of family members who would otherwise be forgotten; "The bottom line," she says, "is I'm writing to save the dead."

Others of Allison's writings focus on her life as a lesbian activist. Here again she writes from the margins, describing not only her involvement in lesbian-feminist communal life in the early 1970s, but also her status as a sexual outlaw during the so-called "Lesbian Sex Wars" of the 1980s. Allison's 1983 poetry collection entitled *The Women Who Hate Me* outraged mainstream feminists by praising sexual promiscuity, sadomasochism, and butch-femme lesbian roles. Some of the stories in *Trash* also push the PC envelope, as does Allison's 1994 essay collection *Skin: Talking about Sex, Class, and Literature.* On the one hand, Allison says that her involvement in vanilla-sex "[f]eminism saved my life." On the other hand, however, at night she would "sneak out of the collective to date a butch women my house mates thought retrograde and sexist." Even in the aggressively countercultural world of lesbian feminism, Allison was a maverick.

For Allison, writing is a dramatic, life-affirming act in a world which consistently threatens death. A storyteller since childhood, Allison chronicles her discovery how telling even her most terrible stories out loud confines them to the realm of the "ironic and playful," but writing them down gives her power over the experiences she describes. "Putting those stories down on paper," she writes, enables her "to shape my life outside my terrors and helplessness, to make it visible and real in a tangible way." Rather than whitewashing unpleasant experience, Allison's writing opens the way into healthy truth-telling. Herein lies the connection between her writing and her lesbian identity and politics. For Allison, telling the truth about growing up "trash" is part of a politics of disclosure: "It is only as the child of my class and my unique family background that I have been able to ... regain a sense of why I believe in activism, why self-revelation is so important for lesbians." Her queer writing seeks to portray the world as "a place where the truth would be hallowed, not held on contempt, where silence would be impossible." In short, in a world where Silence = Death, Allison insists on the counter-equation Self-revelation = Life = Survival.

This philosophy plays itself out repeatedly in her writing. A frequent theme is how a female character journeys from an oral to a "literate" culture, a journey which leads the young woman away from silence towards voice, from lies towards truth, from death towards life. In *Bastard out of Carolina,* for instance, Bone learns that both her orality-based "trash" culture and academic "book-learning" are helpless to prevent the violence that threatens to engulf her—poverty, sickness, beatings, rape, death. Sensing that survival is linked to telling stories, Bone learns to lie. With engaging bravado she enthralls neighbor children with her tales, and dreams of spinning spellbinding sermons in revival tents. But behind the dreams lay only silence where the truth should have been. Only after Bone breaks the conspiracy of silence surrounding her stepfather's abuse can the healing begin. Similarly, author Allison's books emerge from her desire "to be real in the world, without lies or evasions or sweet-talking nonsense." For her, books—fiction—represent a kind of reality that "real" experience lacks. She uses literature to communicate the "dreams I dare not speak" but can write. Such written dreams form part of a literary, cultural, and political project that Allison sees as "vital to organizing your own survival."

—Deborah T. Meem

al'SADAAWI, Nawal

Also known as Nawal el-Sadaawi. **Nationality:** Egyptian. **Born:** Kafr Tahla, 27 October 1931. **Education:** Cairo University, M.D. 1955; Columbia University, New York, M.P.H., 1966; attended Ain Shams University, 1973-75. **Family:** Married 1) Ahmed Halmy in 1955 (divorced 1956); one daughter; 2) a lawyer (divorced); 3) the writer Sherif Hetata in 1964; one son. **Career:** Physician, University of Cairo, 1955-56, and Rural Health Center, Tahla, Egypt, 1956-58; director of health education, Ministry of Health, Cairo, 1958-72 (dismissed after publication of *Al-mar'a wa-al-jins;* writer, High Institute of Literature and Science, Cairo, 1973-78; director of African Training and Research Center for Women, United Nations (UN) Economic Commission for Africa, Addis Ababa, Ethiopia, 1978-80; editor-in-chief, *Health* magazine, 1968-72; advisor for women's programs, UN Economic Commission for West Asia, Beirut, Lebanon, 1978-80; practicing psychiatrist, beginning 1980; arrested under "Law for the Protection of Values from Shame" and imprisoned for three months, 1981. Founder, *Confrontation* magazine, and Pan-Arab women's organization, 1982; co-founder, African Women's Association for Research and Development, 1977. Books banned in Egypt and several other Arab countries. **Awards:** High Assembly for Literature short story award, 1975, for *Al'khait wa'al jidār;* Franco-Arab Association Literary France-Arab Friendship Award, 1982, for *Emra'a 'inda nuqṭat al'ṣifr;* Kalil Gobran Literary Award (Australia), 1987; Decoration of the First Degree of Libya, 1989. **Member:** Egyptian Medical Syndicate, Egyptian Writers Union, Arab Women Solidarity Association (co-founder and president). **Agent:** Michael Shaw, Curtis Brown Ltd., 162-168 Regent St., London W1R 5TB, England.

Publications

Political/Social Theory

Al'mar'a wa'al'jins [Woman and Sex]. Cairo, Al Shaab, 1971; Beirut, Al'Mu'assasah al-'Arabiyyah lil'Tahrīr wa'al-Nashr, 1972.

Al'rajul wa'al'jins [Man and Sex]. Beirut, Al'Mu'assasah al-'Arabiyyah lil-Tahrīr wa'al-Nashr, 1973.

Al'mar'a hiy al'asl [The Essentiality of the Woman]. Beirut, Al'Mu'assasah al-'Arabiyyah lil-Tahrīr wa'al-Nashr, 1975.

Al mar'a wal sirā' al'nafsī [Woman and Psychological Conflict]. Beirut, Al'Mu'assasah al-'Arabiyyah lil-Tahrīr wa'al-Nashr, 1976.

Al-wajh al-'ārā lil-mar'ah al-'Arabiyyah. Beirut, Al'Mu'assasah al-'Arabiyyah lil-Tahrīr wa'al-Nashr, 1977; translated by Sherif Hetata as *The Hidden Face of Eve: Women in the Arab World,* London, Zed, 1980; Boston, Beacon Press, 1982.

Dirāsāt 'an al-mar'ah wa-al-rajul fi al'mujtama' al-'Ārabi [Studies on the Arabic Woman and Man in the Arab Society]. Beirut, Al'Mu'assasah al-'Arabiyyah lil-Tahrīr wa'al-Nashr, 1986.

Autobiography

Muzakkirāti fi sijn al-nisa'. Cairo, Dar al'Mustaqbal al-Ārabi, 1983; translated by Marilyn Booth as *Memoirs from the Women's Prison,* London, Women's Press, 1986; Berkeley and Los Angeles, University of California Press, 1993.

Rihlati hawla al-'ālam. Cairo, Dar al-Hilāl, 1986; translated by Shirley Eber as *My Travels around the World,* London, Methuen, 1991.

"An Overview of My Life," in *Contemporary Authors Autobiography Series,* vol. 11. Detroit, Gale, 1990.

Novels

Możakkerat ṭabība. Cairo, Dār al Ma'āref, 1958; Beirut, Dār āl-Ādāb, 1979; translated by Catherine Cobham as *Memoirs of a Woman Doctor,* London, Al'Saqi, 1988; San Francisco, City Lights, 1989.

Al ghayib [The Absent]. Cairo, Al Kitāb al Zahabi, 1965; Beirut, Dār āl-Ādāb, 1976.

Imra'atān fi imra'ah. Cairo, Dār al Kitāb, 1968; Beirut, Dār āl-Ādāb, 1973; as *Al- bahitha 'an al-hub* [The Searcher for Love], Cairo, Al Haya al Misriya al-'Ama Lilkitāb, 1974; translated by Osman Nusari and Jana Gough as *Two Women in One,* London, Al'Saqui, 1985; Seattle, Washington, Seal Press, 1986.

Al Ghaeb. N.p., Hayat al-Kitāb, 1968; translated as *Searching,* London, Zed, 1989.

Emra'a 'inda nuqṭat al'-ṣifr. Beirut, Dār āl-Ādāb, 1975; translated by Sherif Hetata as *Woman at Point Zero,* London, Zed, 1983.

Mawt al-rajul al-wahīd 'ala al-ard [The Death of the Only Man on Earth]. Beirut, Dār āl-Ādāb, 1976; translated by Sherif Hetata as *God Dies by the Nile,* London, Zed, 1985.

Ughniyat al-alfāl al dā' iriyah. Beirut, Dār āl-Ādāb, 1977; translated by Marilyn Booth as *The Circling Song,* London, Zed, 1989.

Şuqūṭ al-Imam. Cairo, Dar al-Mustaqbal al-'Ārabi, 1987; translated by Sherif Hetata as *The Fall of the Imam,* London, Methuen, 1988.

Ganah wa iblīs. Beirut, Dār āl-Ādāb, 1992; translated as *The Innocence of the Devil,* London, Methuen, 1993.

Al-hob fī zamān 'al-naft [Love in the Kingdom of Oil]. Cairo, Maktabet Madbouli, 1993.

Short Stories

Ta'lamt al-hub [I Learned to Love]. Cairo, Maktabet al Nahda, 1958; Beirut, Dār āl-Ādāb, 1980.

Hanān qalīl [Little Sympathy]. Cairo, Al Kitāb al Zahabi, 1959; Beirut, Dār āl-Ādāb, 1980.

Lahdhat ṣidq [A Moment of Truth]. Cairo, Al Kitāb al Zahabi, 1962; Beirut, Dār āl-Ādāb, 1980.

Al-khait wa-al jidār [The Thread and the Wall]. Cairo, Al Shaab, 1972.

Al-khait wa'ayn al-hayāt [The Thread and the Wall of Life]. Cairo, Al Shaab, 1972.

Kānat hiya al-ad'af [She Was the Weaker]. Cairo, Al Shaab, 1972; Beirut, Dār āl-Ādāb, 1980; translated by Shirley Eber as *She Has No Place in Paradise,* London, Methuen, 1987.

Mawt ma'āli al wazīr sābiqan. Beirut, Dār āl-Ādāb, 1979; translated by Shirley Eber as *Death of an Ex-Minister,* London, Methuen, 1987.

Plays

Al-insān [The Human Being] (two-act). Cairo, Maktabet Madbouli, 1983; as *Ethna ashra Imra' a fī zinzanah* [Twelve Women in One Cell], London, Methuen, 1983.

Izis [Isis]. Cairo, Dār al-Mustaqbal al-'Ārabi, 1986.

Other

The Spring of Life. London, Methuen, 1992.

*

Critical Studies: *Untha did al-untha* by Georges Tarabishi, translated as *Woman against Her Sex: A Critique of Nawal el-Sadaawi, with a Reply by Nawal el-Sadaawi,* London, Al'Saqi, 1988; *Nawal al-Sa'adawi and Modern Egyptian Feminist Writings* (dissertation) by Heong-Dung Park, Ann Arbor, University of Michigan, 1988; "Reflections of a Feminist: An Interview with Nawal al-Saadawi" by Fedwa Malti-Douglas and Alan Douglas, in *Opening the Gates: A Century of Arab Feminist Writing,* edited by Margot Badran and Miriam Cooke, Bloomington, Indiana University Press, 1990; "Feminism and an Arab Humanism: An Interview with Nawal el-Saadawi and Sherif Hetata" by Gaurev Desai and David Chioni Moore, in *SAPINA: A Bulletin of the Society for African Philosophy in North America,* 1, January/June 1993; "Living the Struggle: Nawal el Saadawi Talks about Writing and Resistance" with Sherif Hetata and Peter Hitchcock, in *Transition* (Kampala, Uganda), 61, 1993.

* * *

Nawal al'Sadaawi is one of the best known Egyptian writers in the West. Her writing ranges from political and social analysis (*The Hidden Face of Eve: Women in the Arab World*) to autobiography (*Memoirs from the Women's Prison*) to fiction (*Women at Point Zero*). Her works, which are written in Arabic, have been translated into more than 20 languages, and a significant number are currently available in English. al'Sadaawi's commitment to changing the status of women in her region of the world, coupled with her resistance to colonization and other inappropriate forms of authority, mark her as a significant feminist and political voice, as one who has influenced people across the globe. As al'Sadaawi writes in *My Travels around the World,* she does "not separate the liberation of women from the liberation of people or from the oppression of local and international patriarchal class systems."

Born in the village of Kafr Tahla in 1931, al'Sadaawi was the second of nine children (including an older brother, two younger brothers, and five sisters). Both of her parents were well educated; her father was a university graduate and a provincial controller of education and her mother had been taught in French schools. Although she rebelled against the injustice of the privileges that her older brother was granted by her parents because of his gender, her own education was unusual for an Egyptian girl growing up in the 1940s. She attended elementary school in her village and when she graduated there was pressure from her father's relatives to marry her to a wealthy peasant in her village. She resisted the arranged marriage and threatened to commit suicide. Eventually her father relented and allowed her to enroll in a girl's secondary school: first as a day student at a school in Cairo and then at the Halwan boarding school. al'Sadaawi was an outstanding student of Arabic literature, but in her final year she enrolled in science courses. The practice in Egypt at that time was for the most gifted students, regardless of gender, to enroll in medical school upon graduation from secondary school. While in medical school she continued to write and sometimes published her work in the university's journal. "I used to see myself as a free wirer who obeys only her mind," al'Sadaawi later explained in "An Overview of My Life." "I did not dream of being a wife, nor of being a physician." In addition, she also continued her political activity in opposition to the British occupation. Thus, the roles of writer and activist were merged from very early on in her adult life.

After practicing medicine for several years in poor rural villages, al'Sadaawi realized that "writing was a stronger weapon than medicine in the fight against poverty and ignorance.... Writing was a release for my anger. What angered me most was oppression: oppression of women and oppression of the poor." It was in the early '70s, at the same time that the international feminist movement was gaining recognition, that she began to write a series of books on sexuality and on the status of women in the Arab world.

The most widely translated of these works is *The Hidden Face of Eve,* published in 1977. The book opens with a recollection of lying in bed at age six, halfway "between wakefulness and sleep, with the rosy dreams of childhood flitting by, like gentle fairies in quick succession" only to be carried to the bathroom by a group of women, including her mother, where rather than cutting her throat, "the sharp metallic edge seemed to drop between my thighs and there cut off a piece of flesh from my body." Her younger sister, who was also subjected that night to this form of female circumcision (or removal of the clitoris), exchanged a terrified glance with her that seemed to al'Sadaawi to say "We were born of a special sex, the female sex. We are destined to advance to taste of misery."

As a physician she learned that her own experience, which continued to haunt her, was not unlike that of women in many other Arab countries, many of whom suffered more profound physical and psychological scars. However, once she began to write on social and political issues, she found that her status in her own country was in jeopardy: in 1972 she was fired from a position with the Ministry of Health, her works were banned in Egypt, and in 1981 she was imprisoned for three months by Egyptian president Anwar Sadat. *Memoirs from the Women's Prison* is a testament to the resistance of women behind bars. In the afterward written in 1994 for the book's U.S. edition, al'Sadaawi says: "Writing: such has been my crime ever since I was a small child. To this day writing remains my crime. Now, although I am out of prison, I continue to live inside a prison of another sort, one without steel bars. For the technology of oppression and might without justice has become more advanced, and the fetters imposed on mind and body have become invisible."

For al'Sadaawi, the fact that she is a physician and a psychiatrist is integrally connected to her role as a writer of fiction, be it novels, short stories, or plays. She does not "see any contradiction between studying the body, its anatomy and physiology, psychology, politics, religion, and literature. This inter-relation is needed for an artist because artists cannot write novels in a vacuum." Although each of her novels has a different style according to the topic, all are focused on the status of women in patriarchal societies. Her first published novel was *Memoirs of a Woman Doctor,* which she acknowledges as partly autobiographical. In the introduction to the British edition she refers to it as "a simple, spontaneous novel in which there is a lot of anger against the oppression of women in my country, but also a great deal of hope for change."

The heroines in her novels, especially Firdaus in *Woman at Point Zero,* display a courage and a commitment to themselves that transcends concerns for their own survival. That novel, based on her interviews with a prostitute sentenced to die for killing her pimp, ends with the voice of Firdaus vibrating in the ears of the narrator "shaking everything, spreading fear wherever it went, the fear of the truth which kills, the power of truth, as savage, and as simple, and as awesome as death, yet as simple and as gentle as the child that has not yet learned to lie."

After the publication of *The Fall of the Imam* in Egypt in 1987, al'Sadaawi once more found herself under the cloud of suspicion from her government, and armed guards were posted in front of her home for more than a year. The novel, which records the dreamlike story of the illegitimate daughter (Bint Allah, or daughter of God) of the religious leader (the Imam), has been seen by many as a political allegory about the Sadat regime.

The one thread that runs through all of al'Sadaawi's works is that of courage: of the courage of the writer to explore sensitive topics and of the characters in her fictional works to resist easy answers. Hers is a voice of resistance and while she is honored throughout much of the Western world, her voice in her own region is still muffled by censorship. By 1944 she was unable to continue to live in Egypt. Her own words in *Memoirs from the Women's Prison* are haunting: "Futilely I seek a place free of the structures of patriarchy and class. I search for true justice, true peace, but to no avail.... Danger has been a part of my life ever since I picked up a pen and wrote.... Nothing is more perilous than truth in a world that lies." al'Sadaawi continues to be a beacon for justice and peace in that world.

—Barbara Lesch McCaffry

ALTON, Delia. *See* **H.D.**

ANDREZEL, Pierre. *See* **BLIXEN, Karen (Christentze Dinesen).**

ANTHONY, Susan B(rownell)

Nationality: American. **Born:** Adams, Massachusetts, 15 February 1820. **Education:** Attended school run by father, Daniel Anthony; attended Friends' seminary, Philadelphia. **Career:** Moved, with family, to Battenville, New York, 1826; teacher, Canajoharie Academy, New York, c. 1839-49; active in temperance movement until 1852; campaigned for abolition of slavery, 1852-63; active in women's suffrage movement beginning 1863; cofounder, with Elizabeth Cady Stanton, National Woman's Loyal League, 1869; cofounder, with Parker Pillsbury and Stanton, *The Revolution* (suffragist newspaper), 1868; founder, International Council of Women, 1888, and International Woman Suffrage Alliance, Berlin, Germany, 1904. **Died:** Rochester, New York, 13 March 1906.

Publications

History

A History of Woman Suffrage, Vols. 1-3 with Matilda Joslyn Gage and Elizabeth Cady Stanton, Vol. 4 with Ida Husted Harper. New York, Fowler & Welles, 3 vols., 1881-88; vol. 4, 1903.

Other

Elizabeth Cady Stanton, Susan B. Anthony: Correspondence, Writings, Speeches, edited by Ellen Carol Dubois. New York, Schocken, 1981; revised, Boston, New England University Press, 1992.

Failure Is Impossible: Susan B. Anthony in Her Own Words, edited by Lynne Sherr. New York, Times, 1995.

*

Manuscript Collections: Library of Congress, Washington, D.C.; Schlesinger Library, Radcliffe College; Susan B. Anthony Memorial Library, Rochester, New York.

Critical Studies: *The Life and Work of Susan B. Anthony* by Ida Husted Harper, Hollenbeck Press, 3 vols., 1898-1908; *Susan B. Anthony: The Woman Who Changed the Mind of a Nation* by Rhetta Louise Dorr, New York, F. Stokes, 1928; *The Story of a Pioneer* by Anna Howard Shaw, New York and London, Harper, 1915; *Susan B. Anthony: Her Personal History and Her Era* by Katharine Anthony, New York, Doubleday, 1954; *Susan B. Anthony: Rebel, Crusader, Humanitarian* by Alma Lutz, Boston, Beacon Press, 1959; *Susan B. Anthony: A Biography of a Singular Feminist* by Kathleen Barry, New York, Ballantine, 1988; *Sowing Good Seeds: The Northwestern Suffrage Campaign of Susan B. Anthony* by G. Thomas Edwards, Portland, Oregon History Association Press, 1990.

* * *

Susan Brownell Anthony, the woman given credit for much of the early impetus behind the long fight for woman suffrage in the United States, spent her childhood in a fairly unconventional home. Born in Addams, Massachusetts, the Anthonys moved to Battenville, New York, when Susan was six. The second of eight children, Anthony received an introduction to independent thought and action from both her parents. Her mother, Lucy Read, had agreed to marry Daniel Anthony, a birthright Quaker, if he would allow her to spend one last night dancing; according to family tradition, the bridegroom-to-be spent until early in the morning watching his betrothed change partners and dance. Daniel Anthony was independent and freethinking as well; he was actively involved in social movements that included temperance, abolitionism, and women's rights. In fact, both Susan's parents and her younger sister, Mary, would attend the Seneca Falls women's rights gathering in 1848.

Although Daniel Anthony speculated perhaps too freely, he would remain undaunted by a series of business failures in the textile trade and eventually build a successful insurance practice. One of the life-altering incidents from Susan Anthony's early life was an auction in which all her family's belongings were sold to pay debts made and accumulated by her father. Everything except a few personal clothing items was auctioned; although her mother's brother was there to bid and retrieve ownership of some of the housekeeping, furniture, and personal items, the fact that women's property could be taken to pay debts accrued by a husband was one Anthony remembered and campaigned against all her life. In fact, she is said to have refused marriage offers, deciding instead to devote her energies to fighting for reform, especially women's property and political rights.

Anthony's parents insisted that all their children receive the best available education: she was educated in a home school set up by her father, at district schools, and at a Philadelphia Friends' seminary run by Deborah Moulson. Anthony, who followed an older sister to the seminary, had some personality conflicts with Miss Moulson, but the education she received there prepared her to teach and begin to build her independent life.

Through Amelia Bloomer, editor of *Lily,* a temperance journal in Seneca Falls, Anthony met Elizabeth Cady Stanton, who would introduce her to the fledgling woman's rights movement. In addition to creating a legendary partnership, the two women would become lifelong friends. Although Anthony is said to have been drawn to feminist work, her greater commitment in the early 1850s was to the temperance movement. But, like others, she became outraged that the women who attended an 1853 world temperance convention were not allowed to be seated as delegates; thereafter she began to focus on women's rights.

Anthony is generally credited with outstanding organizational abilities, demonstrated by her efforts assisting with the behind-the-scenes work of arranging speakers and holding women's rights conventions. After six years of working for women's property rights, Anthony saw them secured through a married woman's property law passed by the New York Legislature in 1860. She spent much of her later life arranging lectures and taking tours herself, despite possessing what have been described as less than dynamic speaking abilities; listeners forgave Anthony her reported monotone because of her intelligence and earnestness.

Despite her commitment to women's rights, Anthony continued to work for the abolition of slavery and assumed that the "universal suffrage" they demanded for African Americans would also extend to women. At the end of the Civil War, she and other women's rights activists were shocked that politicians were ready to extend the vote to males, irrespective of color, but continue to deny it to females. Women were told that this was the "Negro's Hour," that they would have to wait.

After the war Anthony spent some time in Kansas with her brother Daniel's family. He was a newspaper publisher; here she would gain experience that would prove useful three years later, when a wealthy eccentric named George Francis Train offered to finance a woman suffrage paper to be published by Anthony and edited by Stanton and Parker Pillsbury. The new weekly, called *The Revolution,* was radical in that it opposed the 14th and 15th amendments and urged, instead, an educated suffrage regardless of sex or color. The new journal also promoted equal pay for the sexes and additional employment opportunities for women. Unfortunately for Stanton and Anthony, the journal also carried columns by Train, who advocated the boycott of foreign goods and greenback currency and was increasingly openly racist. His support for the newspaper venture was soon withdrawn; he went on to other projects, and the women found that the financial requirements of the paper were too great. The paper was ultimately sold to Laura Curtis Bullard, leaving Anthony with a $10,000 debt.

Spurred by her need to pay off creditors of *The Revolution,* Anthony began a series of lectures through western circuits that found her facing travel through all kinds of weather, enduring living arrangements in shoddy hotels with poor food, and sometimes leaving her without travel connections between towns. Traveling by every possible form of conveyance, Anthony's efforts not only raised the money needed to pay back the debts, but also created new friends for woman suffrage. Indeed, when she finally succeeded—just prior to a suffrage anniversary in 1876—her achievement was national news: "Susan B. Anthony has paid her debts like a man, even better than most men" editorialized the papers. That same year she plotted with other suffragists to present an officially denied declaration of rights at the centennial of the declaration of independence in Philadelphia.

One of the lingering and unfortunate results of Anthony's acceptance of the help of Train and her insistence on a federal solution to the woman suffrage issue was the splitting of U.S. suffragists into two organizations—the National Woman Suffrage Association (NWSA), which was the philosophic home of Anthony and Stanton, and the American Woman Suffrage Association (AWSA), founded by Lucy Stone and Julia Ward Howe, which favored a state-by-state approach to changes in voting laws. These organizations were to remain separate for almost three decades: While efforts towards reconciliation began in 1887, they did not officially come together until 1890, when the efforts of a new generation of woman suffrage workers prevailed. This new organization, the National American Woman Suffrage Association, would work toward both state and national franchise legislation.

Meanwhile, several western states had begun to consider woman suffrage and women in Wyoming and Utah did receive the franchise in 1871. Anthony had spoken in these territories and hoped to see a similar success in California, as well. Unfortunately, California would not follow the lead of the others, perhaps because, as some historians note, the state's liquor lobby interests began to actively campaign against woman suffrage at this time.

Two major suffrage campaigns at the federal level would also prove unsuccessful. Congressman George W. Julian of Indiana introduced the first woman suffrage amendment in 1868; ten years later, Senator Aaron Sargent of California introduced a woman suffrage amendment to the wording of the 15th Amendment. Neither of these efforts was successful, although Anthony campaigned for both. While she continued to believe in a federal solution and made sure that the annual NWSA national convention was held in Washington, D.C., between 1877 and 1883 she traveled throughout the country to speak and campaign locally for woman suffrage.

In the late 1870s Anthony also began to compile a chronicle of the women's rights movement. With the help of Stanton and Matilda Joslyn Gage, the first volume of what was to become a massive six-volume work was published in 1881. Anthony herself was the primary contributor to the first three volumes; the fourth volume, published in 1902, was edited by Ida Husted Harper, who was also Anthony's choice for a biographer. An Indiana native, Harper had worked for labor leader Eugene Debs and was a seasoned columnist and worker for reform causes. Along with long-time friend Reverend Anna Howard Shaw, she was a member of Anthony's household when volume four was released to good reviews. The last two volumes of the massive history would not be published in 1922, two years after the 19th amendment was finally ratified by Congress on August 26, 1920. Although once arrested and fined for casting a vote in Rochester, New York, Anthony never reaped the reward of her efforts on behalf of gaining women the legal opportunity to vote. She died in 1906.

Although Susan B. Anthony is remembered for her activism on behalf of woman suffrage—indeed, the 19th amendment carried her name—she was also a major contributor to feminist thought and was the catalyst behind the published history of the U.S. suffrage movement that documented the first 50 years of political women's rights activity. While Stanton is conceded to have been a more facile writer, Anthony's continuous work and her experience as a newspaper writer and publisher made possible a considerable body of literature. Her work has longstanding relevance and importance to both women and students of political history, as well as to those wishing to understand women's activism in various reform movements.

—Ann Mauger Colbert

ANZALDÚA, Gloria (Evanjelina)

Nationality: American. **Born:** Jesus Maria of the Valley, South Texas, 26 September 1942. **Education:** Pan-American University, Edinburg, Texas, B.A. 1969; University of Texas at Austin, M.A. 1973; studied at University of California at Santa Cruz. **Career:** Has taught high school English and in migrant, adult, and bilingual programs in Texas. Has taught creative writing, women's studies, and Chicano studies at University of Texas at Austin, Vermont College of Norwich University, San Francisco State University, and University of California at Santa Cruz. Writer-in-residence at the Loft in Minneapolis, Minnesota; artist-in-residence at Pomona College, California. Contributing editor of *Sinister Wisdom.* Has given lectures, panels, and workshops throughout the United States, Canada, and Mexico. **Awards:** MacDowell Artist Colony fellowship, 1982; National Endowment of the Arts award for fiction, 1991; Astraea National Lesbian Action Foundation Lesbian Writers Fund Sappho Award of Distinction, 1992. **Address:** c/o Literature Board, University of California, Santa Cruz, California 95064, U.S.A.

Publications

Poetry

"Reincarnation (for Julie)," "Birth," "Abstractions (for H. Michaux)," "Now Let Us Go (Tinuique)," "The Visitor," and "El pecado," in *Tejidos* (Austin, Texas), fall 1976.

"Woman," "Temple," "Guitarrera," "Helpless," and "Pesadilla," in *Tejidos* (Austin, Texas), spring 1977.

"Holy Relics," in *Conditions: Six* (Lincoln, Nebraska), summer 1980.

"Tres mujeres en el gabinete/Three Women in the Closet," in *Lesbian Poetry Anthology,* edited by Elly Bulkin and Joan Larkin. Watertown, Massachusetts, Persephone Press, 1981.

"A Woman Lies Buried under Me," in *Sinister Wisdom* (Lincoln, Nebraska), spring 1982.

"Shadow," "Tres pajaros perdidos," and "Never, Momma," in *Third Woman* (Bloomington, Indiana), 2(1), 1984.

"In the Name of All the Mothers Who Have Lost Children in the War/En el nombre de todas las madres que han perdido hijos en la guerra," in *Ikon: Creativity and Change,* second series (New York), winter/summer 1985.

This Way Daybreak Comes, with Annie Cheatham and Mary Clare Powell. N.p., 1986.

"De las otras," in *Companera: Latina Lesbians: An Anthology,* edited by Juanita Ramos. New York, Latina Lesbian History Project, 1987.

Borderlands—La Frontera: The New Mestiza (prose and poetry; English and Spanish). San Francisco, Spinsters Book Company, 1987.

"Nightvoice" and "Old Loyalties," in *Chicana Lesbians: The Girls Our Mothers Warned Us About.* Berkeley, California, Third Woman Press, 1991.

Short Stories

"El Paisano Is a Bird of Good Omen," in *Cuentos: Stories by Latinas,* edited by Alma Gomez, Cherríe Moraga, and Mariana

Romo-Carmona. New York, Kitchen Table Women of Color Press, 1983.
"Life Line," in *Lesbian Love Stories,* edited by Irene Zahava. Freedom, California, Crossing Press, 1989.
"Ms. Right, My Soul Mate," in *Lesbian Love Stories,* Volume 2, edited by Irene Zahava. Freedom, California, Crossing Press, 1991.
"A Tale," in *Word of Mouth: Short-Short Stories by Women Writers,* edited by Irene Zahava. Freedom, California, Crossing Press, 1991.

Essays

"The Homeland, Aztlán/El otro Mexico," in *Aztlán: Essays on the Chicano Homeland,* edited by Rudolfo A. Anaya and Francisco A. Lomeli. Albuquerque, New Mexico, Academia/El Norte, 1989.
"Bridge, Drawbridge, Sandbar or Island: Lesbians-of-Color Hacienda Alianzas," in *Bridges of Power: Women's Multicultural Alliances,* edited by Lisa Albrecht and Rose M. Brewer. Philadelphia, New Society Publishers, 1990.
"Metaphors in the Tradition of the Shaman," in *Conversant Essays: Contemporary Poets on Poetry,* edited by James McCorkle. Detroit, Wayne State University Press, 1990.

For Children

Prietita Has a Friend—Prietita tiene un amigo. San Francisco, Children's Book Press, 1991.
Friends from the Other Side—Amigos del otra lado. San Francisco, Children's Book Press, 1993.

Other

"La historia de una marimacho," in *Third Woman* (Bloomington, Indiana), 4, 1989.
"Border Crossings," in *Trivia: A Journal of Ideas* (North Amherst, Massachusetts), spring 1989.
"People Should Not Die in June in South Texas," in *Daughters and Fathers,* edited by Irene Zahava. Freedom, California, Crossing Press, 1990.
"To(o) Queer the Writer—Loca, Escritora y Chicana," in *InVersions: Writing by Dykes, Queers, and Lesbians,* edited by Betsy Warland. Vancouver, Press Gang Publishers, 1991.
Lloronas, Women Who Howl: Autohistorias-Teorias and the Production of Writing, Knowledge and Identity. San Francisco, Aunt Lute Books, forthcoming.

Editor, with Cherríe Moraga, *This Bridge Called My Back: Writings by Radical Women of Color.* Watertown, Massachusetts, Persephone Press, 1981.
Editor, *Making Face, Making Soul—Hacienda Caras: Creative and Critical Perspectives by Feminists of Color.* San Francisco, Aunt Lute Books, 1990.

*

Media Adaptations: *This Bridge Called My Back: Writings by Women of Color* (recording), 1983.

Critical Studies: "Dare to Write: Virginia Woolf, Tillie Olsen, Gloria Anzaldúa" by Carolyn Woodward, in *Changing Our Power: An Introduction to Women's Studies,* edited by Jo Whitehorse Cochran and others, Dubuque, Iowa, Kendall/Hunt Publishing, 1988; "Reading along the Dyke" by Valerie Miner, in *Out/Look* (San Francisco), spring 1988; "Algo Secretamente Amado" by Cherríe Moraga, in *Third Woman* (Bloomington, Indiana), 4, 1989; "Living on the Borderland: The Poetic Prose of Gloria Anzaldúa and Susan Griffin" by Diane P. Freedman, in *Women and Language* (Urbana, Illinois), spring 1989; "The Borderlands of Culture: Writing by W. E. B. Du Bois, James Agee, Tillie Olsen, and Gloria Anzaldúa" by Shelley Fisher Fishkin, in *Literary Journalism in the 20th Century,* edited by Norman Sims, New York, Oxford University Press, 1990; "The Limits of Cultural Studies" by Jose David Saldivar, in *American Literary History* (New York), summer 1990; "Politics, Representation and the Emergence of a Chicana Aesthetic" by Alvina E. Quintana, in *Cultural Studies* (London), October 1990; "The Construction of Self in U.S. Latina Autobiographies" by Lourdes Torres, in *Third World Women and the Politics of Feminism,* edited by Chandra Talpade Mohanty, Ann Russo, and Lourdes Torres, Bloomington, Indiana University Press, 1991; *Criticism in the Borderlands: Studies in Chicano Literature, Culture, and Ideology* edited by Hector Calderon and Jose David Saldivar, Durham, North Carolina, Duke University Press, 1991; "On Borderlands/La frontera: An Interpretive Essay" by Maria Lugones, in *Hypatia* (North Amherst, Massachusetts), fall 1992; "Making Face, Making Soul-Haciendo-Caras" by Denise A. Segura and Beatriz M. Pesquera, in *Gender & Society* (Newbury Park, California), September 1992.

* * *

One's first impressions upon meeting Gloria Anzaldúa are of a keen intellect, a straightforward attitude, and an unfailing warmth. Anzaldúa is a writer whose work has challenged generations of white feminist thinkers, while also introducing and inspiring generations of women of color whose voices had been distorted, quieted, or completely silenced in both public and academic discourse.

Anzaldúa characterizes her work and her life with the symbolism of the "Borderlands." By this she means a crossroads, a meeting place, a nexus where ways, times, and people of various backgrounds meet. She suggests that it is in the Borderlands, that old worlds merge and collide, that we can reach new relationships and new means of understanding each other. The Borderlands are significant, especially, in a world of boundaries and rifts, where people have split apart over differences in race, class, gender, and sexuality.

It is in writing of the Borderlands in *Borderlands/La Frontera: The New Mestiza,* that Anzaldúa reaches her most poignant. It is here, also, that she develops key her themes about a conscious oppositional culture. Anzaldúa's work reflects such a culture in that it brings to light the experience of oppression along the lines of race, class, gender and sexuality, while also acting to empower both reader and community. In both prose and poetry, she seeks the reader's aid in the struggle to resist oppression, whether on the battlefields of institutional discrimination, sexism, or heterosexism. Anzaldúa's work, then, is a social critique but also a message of empowerment. Herein lies her wisdom, the wisdom of the storyteller.

The history that Anzaldúa reveals in *Borderlands*—a visceral recreation of longstanding institutional discrimination and oppression of the Chicano/a people—rings with her strident clarification. She journeys back to the 1800s and the land of the Alamo and recreates in prose and poetry the legal chicanery that led Mexico to lose much of its land to whites. She portrays the legendary battle at the Alamo, as well as others fought during the U.S.-Mexican War, as imperialist provocations leading to the Treaty of Guadalupe-Hidalgo, designed to wrest land away from her people. The land belonging to Mexicans "annexed by conquest along with the land ... was soon swindled away from its owners," Anzaldúa writes. "The Gringo, locked into the fiction of white superiority, seized complete political power," she continues, "stripping Indians and Mexicans of their land while their feet were still rooted in it." Within this glaring indictment of institutional discrimination, Anzaldúa relates how her own grandmother was a victim of this swindle, recalling how her mother told her: "A smart *gabacho* [white] lawyer took the land away mamá had not paid taxes. *No hablaba inglés,* she didn't know how to ask for time to raise the money." Later, agribusiness would buy out her family's remaining land. "To make a living my father became a sharecropper," Anzaldúa writes.

Within her history, Anzaldúa describes the act of tribal thinking itself, both in kinship ties and artistic expression, as an act of cultural resistance, strengthening that culture in opposition to this legacy of oppression. She contends that Western cultures treat works of art differently than tribal cultures, housing their art in ornate and architecturally elite buildings and guarding it for the enjoyment of the upper classes. Tribal cultures, on the other hand, "keep art works in honored and sacred places in the home and elsewhere ... The works are treated not just as objects, but also as persons. The 'witness' is a participant in the enactment of the work in a ritual, and not a member of the privileged classes." While calling Western art "a conquered thing, a dead 'thing' separated from nature and, therefore, its power," she describes tribal art as a living, breathing performance art. There is no separation between art, life, and the artists' and "witnesses'" power. Art is empowering in and of itself. And this empowerment works to succor and nurture those who honor it as part of their culture.

In Anzaldúa's prose and poetry, she discusses oppression along the lines of race, class, gender, and sexual orientation. In the poem, "We Call Them Greasers," she gives voice to the Texan filibuster. In the deep, male voice of the poem's narrator is heard the pronounced contempt of the Anglos who came to this territory, how they "waved" a frayed piece of paper at families to convince them that they hadn't paid taxes and were required to leave—more legal trickery. The white Texan voice jeers at those Mexicans who went to court to fight the frayed piece of paper. The story then takes on a ruthless twist; the Texan decides that those who won't "budge" deserve more intense convincing. Singling out a particular couple who refused to "budge" from their land, the narrator recounts in graphic language the violence he visited upon them: raping the woman and ordering her husband lynched. The defiled, terrorized woman is an object of contempt—a dirty Mexican; an object of scorn—a poor woman unable to speak English; and a mere object—a woman—to be violently raped. She is at once her race, her class, and her gender.

In *Borderlands*, Anzaldúa also examines the Chicano/a culture. She marks the patriarchal and homophobic responses of her own community: a community in which she both revels and suffers; a community where she both fully belongs and is the ultimate rebel; a community where she fears "going home." Anzaldúa stresses that a "lesbian of color" faces ultimate rejection within the Chicano/a community, while also being constrained by even greater oppression from the dominant culture. Chicano/a culture rejects her because she should conform to its criteria: straight, Catholic, and non-sexual (except in monogamous marital union and that guardedly). As a lesbian, she is not only "unacceptable" within Catholic dogma, but is also perceived as a threat by virtue of being doubly sexual—she is an overtly sexual being, with a "faulty" sexuality at that. For the lesbian of color there is, indeed, a "fear of going home"—a fear of ultimate rejection by the community, the mother, *la Raza,* for this multiple "rebellion."

The culmination of Anzaldúa's work is what she terms "a new *mestiza* consciousness." It is a consciousness that comes from being a *mestiza*—of mixed Spanish and Indian heritage—and from living and surviving in the Borderlands: both the concrete border between the United States and Mexico and the psychic borderlands between races, classes, cultures, genders, and sexual orientations. The Borderlands serve as a bridge between the worlds of the Chicano/a and *gabacho/a*; the straight and the "queer"; the male and the female, that essentially breaks down "either/or" dichotomous thinking. The *mestiza* consciousness, then, is a "tolerance for ambiguity," a standpoint that is both flexible and inclusive, a synthesis of colliding parts, opening its arms to all and excluding none, serving as a "crossroads" between cultures, genders, and paradigms. It is born out of oppression and in conscious struggle against it, both a site of great struggle and the source of great strength. Ultimately, the *mestiza* consciousness is Anzaldúa's personal, self-defined standpoint, a standpoint that empowers. For her, a *mestiza* consciousness has emerged both from being *mestiza* and from engaging in life in the Borderlands.

More than simply being of mixed racial heritage, being *mestiza* takes on more significant ramifications in Anzaldúa's work. It means to be mixed, period: a blend, an amalgam of cultures, sexual orientations, colors, and ideas. Moreover it means learning to cope with and find ways to survive within this amalgam. At the same time, while the Borderlands can refer to Aztlán, the historical/mythical homeland of the Chicano/a people, it also represents the psychic boundary between all worlds, and all dichotomies. Where Western thought creates such either/or thinking—light/dark, man/woman, parent/child, strong/weak—living in the Borderlands creates a *mestiza* consciousness, a consciousness that breaks such thinking thinking down. Living in the Borderlands means accepting a collision of cultures, an atmosphere of multiple tongues, revealing paradigms, and new ways of knowing. Such an atmosphere leaves little room for rigid, static dichotomies.

For Anzaldúa, this breakdown of dichotomous thinking—the birth of a *mestiza* consciousness—that emerges from life in the Borderlands, is heralded by a "tolerance for ambiguity" and a certain flexibility. She writes in *Borderlands*, that the *mestiza* "copes by developing a tolerance for contradictions, a tolerance for ambiguity ... nothing is thrust out, the good the bad and the ugly, nothing rejected, nothing abandoned." The Borderlands emerge as a crossroads of sorts, where all roads meet and converge. More importantly, this crossroads, this site of the *mestiza* consciousness where "nothing is rejected, nothing abandoned," means that divergent cultures, paradigms, and worlds meet as non-combatants to be healed rather than as dichotomous opposites that have no tolerance of each other.

But for the *mestiza,* the Borderlands also holds a paradox. This place, this free space of consciousness, while the site of her worst battles with racism, sexism, classism, and heterosexism, is also the place of her greatest strength. Where cultures collide, struggle is inevitable. It forces the *mestiza* consciousness—through psychic rebirthing and synthesis—into existence as a juncture, a crossroads, a consciousness of multiple voices and paradigms. It is within such a *mestiza* consciousness—this new mode of coping that has been created in the Borderlands—that oppositional culture is both born and reaches fruition. Taking inventory, the *mestiza* consciousness then takes issue with racist, sexist, classist, and homophobic elements in both the dominant society and the Chicano/a community. As Anzaldúa states in *Borderlands*, the *mestiza* consciousness makes a "conscious rupture with all oppressive traditions ... communicates that rupture, documents the struggle ... adopts new perspectives toward the darkskinned, women and queers." Essentially, the new *mestiza* consciousness is Anzaldúa's personal viewpoint and source of empowerment. It is the space where she lives that affirms both her own humanity as well as the humanity of all others. It is a consciousness of resistance, an oppositional consciousness. Storytelling is Gloria Anzaldúa's method of knowing, of coping, of resistance. As well, is it her way of drawing others to the Borderlands.

—Theresa A. Martinez

ARNOLD, June (Davis)

Pseudonym: Carpenter. **Nationality:** American. **Born:** Greenville, South Carolina, 27 October 1926. **Education:** Vassar College, 1943-44; Rice University, B.A. 1948, M.A. 1958; attended New School, New York City. **Family:** Married (divorced), four children; companion of Parke Bowman. **Career:** Cofounder and publisher, Daughters Inc. (lesbian press), Plainfield, Vermont, beginning 1972. **Died:** 11 March 1982.

Publications

Novels

Applesauce. New York, McGraw-Hill, 1967.

The Cook and the Carpenter (as Carpenter). Plainfield, Vermont, Daughters, Inc., 1973.

Sister Gin (portion originally published in *Amazon Quarterly* [Somerville, Massachusetts], 3[2], 1975). Plainfield, Vermont, Daughters Inc., 1975; with afterword by Jane Marcus, New York, Feminist Press at the City University of New York, 1989.

Baby Houston, introduction by Beverly Lowry. Austin, Texas Monthly Press, 1987.

Uncollected Essay

"Feminist Presses and Feminist Politics," in *Quest: A Feminist Quarterly* (Washington, D.C.), summer 1976.

*

Critical Studies: "Daughters Inc.: A Publishing House Is Born" by Marilyn Webb, in *Ms.,* June 1974; "The Politics of Publishing and the Lesbian Community" by Jan Clausen, in *Sinister Wisdom,* 1(2), fall 1976; "Creating a Woman's World" by Lois Gould, in *New York Times Magazine,* 2 January 1977; "Retrieved from Silence: My Life and Times with Daughters Inc." by Harriet Desmoines, in *Sinister Wisdom,* 5, winter 1978; "Exiting from Patriarchy" by Bonnie Zimmerman, in *The Voyage In: Fictions of Female Development,* edited by Elizabeth Abel, Marianne Hirsh, and Elizabeth Langland, Hanover, New Hampshire, University Press of New England, 1983; *My Mama's Dead Squirrel: Lesbian Essays on Southern Culture* by Mab Seacrest, Ithaca, New York, Firebrand Books, 1985; *The Safe Sea of Women: Lesbian Fiction 1969-1989* by Bonnie Zimmerman, Boston, Beacon Press, 1990; "Mother Wit: American Women's Literary Humor" by Barbara Monroe (dissertation), University of Texas, 1991; *Odd Girls and Twilight Lovers* by Lillian Faderman, New York, Columbia University Press, 1991.

* * *

As a publisher of lesbian novels in the 1970s, as well as a novelist herself, June Arnold holds a special place in lesbian literary history. With her life partner, Parke Bowman, she founded Daughters Inc., in 1972—a press that would publish the works of Arnold and such notables as Rita Mae Brown, Bertha Harris, Elana Nachman, and Monique Wittig. Arnold believed in establishing a woman's publishing network and urged feminists not to publish with mainstream presses. Highly successful, Daughters was able to publish eighteen novels and an anthology during the 1970s. The press' writers were paid fees comparable to or better than those offered by the mainstream presses of the day.

Politically active, Arnold was a member of the New York Women's Liberation Movement, a group that took over an empty building in the lower East Side of Manhattan for 13 days in an attempt to establish a woman's building. In 1976 she organized a Women in Print conference. During that same year, Arnold was also a speaker for the Modern Language Association's Lesbian Caucus and the New York City Lesbian Conference. She would address the Southeastern Gay and Lesbian Conference in 1977.

Arnold was born into a prominent Southern family, moving from Greenville, South Carolina, to Houston, Texas, with her mother and older sister after her father's death. In Houston she attended private schools and even made her social debut. Following her graduation from Rice University in 1948, Arnold married and had four children. After her marriage failed a few years later, she went back to school, earning an M.A. in literature, also from Rice.

After graduation, Arnold took her children to Greenwich Village and became one of the first to live there in a loft. After taking writing classes at the New School for Social Research, she wrote her first novel, *Applesauce,* which was published in 1967 by McGraw-Hill. Although it was widely reviewed, the critical reception was mixed because of Arnold's experimental style. While it features a male protagonist, *Applesauce* also contains several of the themes that would characterize its author's later works: exploration of relationships, playfulness with gender constructions and perceptions of reality, and the role of alcohol as a coping mechanism.

Her next two novels, 1973's *The Cook and the Carpenter* and *Sister Gin,* released two years later, were published by Arnold's own press, Daughters Inc., and were explicitly lesbian. Through these works, Arnold attempts to portray each character as a real person, complete with all their flaws, despite pressure to paint her lesbian characters as exemplary. *The Cook and the Carpenter* also attempts to get rid of gendered pronouns, using "na" and the plural "nan" instead. In *Sister Gin* Arnold covers topics seldom portrayed in the literature of the time, such as menopause and violent lesbian relationships. Both novels were generally well received in the feminist community, but were taken little note of by the mainstream press.

Arnold returned to Houston a few years before her death to work on what would be her final novel, *Baby Houston,* which was published posthumously in 1987. The novel is an autobiography of Arnold's mother, written by the daughter in her mother's voice; in this way it is similar to Gertrude Stein's *Autobiography of Alice B. Toklas.* Praised by some critics for its depiction of the mother-daughter relationship, *Baby Houston* was condemned by others as pathological. Few critics other than those from the feminist press noticed the lesbian content of the work, or mentioned that Arnold was a lesbian. June Arnold was claimed by cancer on 11 March 1982, but her contributions as activist, publisher, and novelist will not be forgotten.

—Annette Van Dyke

ARNOW, Harriette Simpson

Also wrote as Harriette Simpson. **Nationality:** American. **Born:** Wayne County, Kentucky, 7 July 1908. **Education:** Berea College, 1924-26; University of Louisville, B.S. 1930. **Family:** Married Harold Arnow in 1939; one daughter and one son. **Career:** Worked as a teacher, 1930-32; moved to Cincinnati, Ohio, 1934; worked for the Federal Writers' Project; moved to Detroit, Michigan, 1944. **Awards:** *Saturday Review* best novel citations, 1949, for *Hunter's Horn,* and 1954, for *The Dollmaker;* National Book Award runner-up, 1954, for *The Dollmaker.* **Died:** 1986.

Publications

Novels

Mountain Path (as Harriet Simpson). New York, Covici-Friede, 1936.
Hunter's Horn. New York, Macmillan, 1949; London, Collins, 1950.
The Dollmaker. New York, Macmillan, 1954; London, Heinemann, 1955.
The Weedkiller's Daughter. New York, Knopf, 1970.
The Kentucky Trace: A Novel of the American Revolution. New York, Knopf, 1974.

Uncollected Short Stories

"Marigolds and Mules," in *Kosmos,* February/March 1935.
"A Mess of Pork," in *New Talent,* October/December 1935.
"The Washerwoman's Day," in *Southern Review,* winter 1936.
"The Two Hunters," in *Esquire,* July 1942.
"The Hunter," in *Atlantic Monthly,* November 1944.
"Love?" in *Twigs,* fall 1971.
"Fra Lippi and Me," in *Georgia Review,* winter 1979.

History

Seedtime on the Cumberland. New York, Macmillan, and London, Collier-Macmillan, 1960.
Flowering of the Cumberland. New York, Macmillan, and London, Collier-Macmillan, 1963.

Uncollected Essays

"Language—The Key that Unlocks All the Boxes," in *Wilson Library Bulletin,* May 1956.
"Reading without a Purpose," in *American Library Association,* November 1959.
"Progress Reached Our Valley," in *Nation,* 3 August 1970.
"Gray Woman of Appalachia," in *Nation,* 28 December 1970.
"No Rats in the Mines," in *Nation,* 25 October 1971.

Autobiography

Old Burnside. Lexington, University Press of Kentucky, 1977.
"Personal Recollections," in *Appalachian Heritage,* fall 1973.

*

Manuscript Collections: University of Kentucky, Lexington.

Critical Studies: "Joyce Carol Oates on Harriette Arnow's *The Dollmaker*" in *Rediscoveries,* edited by David Madden, New York, Crown, 1971, reprinted as "The Nightmare of Naturalism" in Oates's *New Heaven, New Earth: Visionary Experiences in Literature,* New York, Vanguard, 1974, London, Gollancz, 1976; *Harriette Arnow* by Wilton Eckley, New York, Twayne, 1974; "A Portrait of the Artist as Mother: Harriette Arnow and *The Dollmaker*" by Glenda Hobbs, in *Georgia Review,* winter 1979; "'Beholden to No Man': Artistry and Community in Harriette Arnow's *The Dollmaker*" by Kristina Groover, in *The Kentucky Review,* 1996.

* * *

In 1971 Harriette Arnow's *The Dollmaker* would be praised by Joyce Carol Oates as "our most unpretentious American masterpiece." Yet this critical acclaim was long overdue, coming nearly 15 years after the novel's initial publication in 1954. Even today, literary biographers maintain that Arnow's contributions to both fiction and nonfiction have largely been overlooked by scholars and the general public alike.

Some suggest that Arnow never gained recognition because of a writing style that was perceived by her contemporaries to be outdated. Arnow was a regionalist writer; her precise renderings of Kentucky's hill country and her portraits of highlander folk scratching a living from the land, while picturesque, did not seem innovative in a literary era marked by radical experimentation with narrative form.

Arnow has also been labeled a writer in the naturalist school, another literary genre that was then out of fashion. Inspired by the powerful example of Emile Zola, Arnow herself masterfully revealed the social and economic forces that mercilessly destroyed both individuals and individual within modern rural and urban landscapes alike.

While her work was influenced by both genres—regionalism and naturalism—Arnow was never beholden to a specific literary code, statement, or style. She created worlds—-the Little Smokey Creek country of Kentucky in *Hunter's Horn* (1949), and Detroit's Merry Hill housing project in *The Dollmaker* (1954)—in which ordinary people unreflectively live out the human predicament of suffering, compassion, confusion, innocence, and evil. The central characters who inhabit these worlds are exquisitely drawn, and preponderantly female. As Arnow-biographer Wilton Eckley has written, "of Arnow's characters, the women stand out as the strongest and most fully developed."

And here, perhaps, is the most compelling answer to the problem of Arnow's latent fame. She created a gallery of strong female characters during a period in American history (the decades of the 1940s and 1950s) when feminine nonconformity was particularly suspect. Her writing parallelled her life: while her family insisted she become a schoolteacher, Arnow chose to be a writer instead; she was determined to shape her own destiny.

Born in Wayne County, Kentucky, in 1908, Arnow grew up on a wooded hill overlooking Burnside, a lumber-town that was a central axis-point for commerce along the Cumberland River and the Southern Railroad. From her vantage point atop this 30-acre hill, Arnow developed two perspectives: the land on which she stood, the lonely and unhurried world of nature, served as a powerful anchor to home, family, and self; below the hill was the continuous thrum of commerce, which stimulated her imagination with thoughts of steamboat and railroad rides to cities like Cincinnati and New Orleans. Raised in a narrowly pious family, Arnow was forbidden to explore the world below; her family deemed urban forms of entertainment—movies, baseball, the circus—unholy activities. Arnow's childhood pastimes were limited to baking special treats, riding the mules, and strolling through the woods. When she reached young adulthood she expressed an interest in writing, but this too was forbidden as frivolous and impractical. At her family's insistence Arnow prepared for a career as a schoolteacher.

Unable to sustain any passion for this vocation, Arnow quit teaching after a few years and scandalized her family by making a solo journey to Cincinnati. Here she found a furnished room to rent and libraries by the dozen to feed her thirst for literary creativity. To support herself, she worked as a waitress and wrote historical vignettes about Cincinnati for the Federal Writers' Project. Within a widening social circle of intellectuals and artists, Arnow began to write short stories, culminating with "Washerwoman's Day," which the prestigious *Southern Review* published in 1936. It is from this story that we can trace Arnow's development as a female writer; as well, her decision to explore the lives and dilemmas of women emanates from this tale.

"Washerwoman's Day" tells the story of Laurie Mae, the daughter of a dirt-poor domestic worker, on the day of her mother's funeral. Laurie Mae understands full well that the town had never shown anything but disdain for her mother. When the Ladies Aid Society offers her six roses—and keeps the remaining dozen and a half for their sewing circle—she is not deceived by this uncharitable form of charity. Laurie Mae discards the flowers along the roadside, barely concealing them under a layer of mud.

"Washerwoman's Day" established many of the themes that would pulse through Arnow's uncontested masterpiece, *The Dollmaker.* This novel is about the struggle for self-determination in a world whose rules are often not of one's making—rules set by men, by the larger society, and by the wealthy classes upon whom the poor are hellishly dependent.

At the center of this novel is Gertie Nevels, a woman of Amazonian stature who impresses us from the start. In the opening scene, Gertie—with hardly more than a knife and poplar bough at her disposal—performs a crude tracheotomy to save her dying son. In her hometown of Bellew, Kentucky, Gertie is a master of her world—an adept healer, an unstudied artist who carves beautiful dolls, but whose only dream is to buy the Tipton farm and live her days working the land. However, playing the role of the dutiful wife, Gertie moves with her husband Clovis to Detroit, where he finds work in a World War II industrial plant.

Prevented from living out her dream, Gertie watches helplessly while her family is crushed under the weight of urban-industrial life. The Nevels are despised by other city dwellers as backward "hillbillies," and tragically impoverished by job insecurity and the vicious cycle of buying on credit. Even the children are lost to Gertie, swallowed up by the juvenile anarchy of the streets.

Still, Gertie is neither a static nor tragic character. Her embittered yearning for the healing power of the land begins to dissolve as she realizes that salvation now lies not in nature but in other people, particularly the women who inhabit the pathetic housing project of Merry Hill. Gertie's adaptation is not surrender, but a willingness to live under less-than-ideal circumstances.

From her first semi-autobiographical novel, 1936's *Mountain Path,* to her final novel, *The Weedkiller's Daughter,* published in 1970, Harriette Arnow created a unique and unforgettable cast of female characters. Slowly, these works have begun to achieve literary recognition. What have still gone unnoticed almost entirely are two major works of nonfiction—1960's *Seedtime on the Cumberland* and *Flowering of the Cumberland,* published in 1963. With scholarly deftness, Arnow wrote the history of the Cumberland region during its early years of settlement. Presaging the work of "new western" historians, she ignored the great events and legends of the "old frontier" and reconstructed the details of everyday life—family, work, and gender relations. Arnow must be celebrated, then, not just for her literary accomplishments but her contributions to social and women's history as well.

—Amy Green

ASTELL, Mary

Pseudonyms: Tom Single; Mr. Wooton. **Nationality:** British. **Born:** Newcastle upon Tyne, 1666. **Education:** Tutored by her uncle Ralph Astell. **Career:** Author; began correspondence with John Norris, 1693; proposed Anglican sisterhood, 1694; gained patronage of Lady Catharine Jones. **Died:** 28 May 1731.

Publications

Religion/Spirituality

Letters concerning the Love of God, Between the Author of the Proposal to the Ladies and Mr. John Norris. Wherein his late Discourse shewing that it ought to be intire and exclusive of all other Loves, is further cleared and justified. London, Samuel Manship & Richard Wilkin, 1695.

The Christian Religion, as Profess'd by a Daughter of the Church of England. London, Richard Wilkin, 1705; New York, St. Mark's Library, 1992.

Essays

A Serious Proposal to the Ladies for the Advancement of Their True and Greatest Interest. By a Lover of Her Sex. London, Richard Wilkin, 1694.

A Serious Proposal to the Ladies, Part II. Wherein a Method Is Offer'd for the Improvement of Their Minds. London, Richard Wilkin, 1697.

Some Reflections upon Marriage, Occasion'd by the Duke and Dutchess of Mazarine's Case. London, John Nutt, 1700; 3rd edition, 1706; New York, Source Book Press, 1970.

An Impartial Inquiry into the Causes of Rebellion and Civil War in This Kingdom: In an Examination of Dr. Kennett's Sermon, January 31, 1703/4. London, Richard Wilkin, 1704.

A Fair Way with the Dissenters and Their Patrons. Not Writ by Mr. L—-y, or any Other Furious Jacobite Whether Clergyman or Layman; But By a Very Moderate Person and Dutiful Subject to the Queen. London, Richard Wilkin, 1704.

Moderation Truly Stated: or, A Review of a Late Pamphlet Entitl'd, Moderation a Vertue. With a Prefatory Discourse to Dr. D. Avenant, concerning His Late Essays on Peace and War (as Tom Single). London, Richard Wilkin, 1704.

*Bart'lemy Fair: or, An Enquiry after Wit; In Which Due Respect Is Had to a Letter concerning Enthusiasm, To My Lord** * * (as Mr. Wooton). London, Richard Wilkin, 1709.

An Enquiry after Wit: Wherein the Trifling Arguing and Impious Railery of the Late Earl of Shaftsbury, in His Letter concerning Enthusiasm, and Other Profane Writers, Are Fully Answer'd and Justly Exposed. London, John Bateman, 1722.

Poetry

A Collection of Poems Humbly Presented and Dedicated TO the Most Reverend Father in GOD WILLIAM by Divine Providence Lord Archbishop of Canterbury (Rawlinson Manuscript, Bodleian Library, Oxford). N.p., 1689.

Other

The First English Feminist: Reflections upon Marriage and Other Writings, edited by Bridget Hill. Aldershot, Gower, and New York, St. Martin's Press, 1986.

*

Manuscript Collections: Bodleian Library, Oxford, England (letters); Newberry Library, Chicago, Illinois; Henry E. Huntington Library, San Marino, California; Folger Shakespeare Library, Washington, D.C.; Beinecke Library and Yale Divinity School, Yale University, New Haven, Connecticut; University of North Carolina, Chapel Hill.

Critical Studies: *Mary Astell* by Florence M. Smith, New York, Columbia University Press, 1916; *Women and the Enlightenment* by Margaret Hunt, New York, Haworth Press/Institute for Research in History, 1984; *The Celebrated Mary Astell: An Early English Feminist* by Ruth Perry, Chicago and London, University of Chicago Press, 1986; "De-ciphering Women and De-Scribing Authority: The Writings of Mary Astell" by Catherine Sharrock, in *Women, Writing, History: 1640-1740,* edited by Isobel Grundy and Susan Wiseman, Athens, University of Georgia Press, 1992; "Mary Astell: Reclaiming Rhetorica in the 17th Century" by Christine Mason Sutherland, in *Reclaiming Rhetorica: Women in the Rhetorical Tradition,* edited by Andrea A. Lunsford, Pittsburgh, University of Pittsburgh Press, 1995.

* * *

Born in 1666 in the coal-mining town of Newcastle, Mary Astell was raised in the Church of England as the daughter of a devout Anglican father and a converted Catholic mother. While she never received a formal education, she obtained instruction from her uncle, Ralph Astell, curator of St. Nicholas Church and a strong loyalist, whose Neoplatonist creed would later influence her own political beliefs. After her uncle's death, Mary pursued an independent course of study, reading widely in French and philosophy. When Astell was 12, her father died, leaving her in the care of her mother and aunt. It was among this community of women that Astell found a sheltering feminine environment, one she later advocated for women.

When Astell was 22 she moved to London and settled in the burgeoning district of Chelsea, known for its artist population and as a refuge for wealthy Londoners seeking a rural retreat. Though she had no assured income and was forced to live modestly, Astell soon cultivated a close group of friends whose wealth, influence, and patronage helped the aspiring young writer establish a reputation for herself. Among her closest friends were Lady Catherine Jones, Lady Elizabeth Hastings, and Lady Ann Coventry. However, Astell did not limit herself to this circle; for example, she began a correspondence with the Reverend John Norris, one of the last Cambridge Platonists, who later published their exchange as *Letters concerning the Love of God* (1695). These letters reveal not only Astell's deeply felt religious beliefs but also her maturity as a writer. Moreover, despite the sustained humility topos throughout the letters, Astell must have had confidence in her intellectual skills to have begun the exchange with a man of Norris's position.

Born into an era that was especially ambivalent towards women's writing and intellectual achievements, Astell created a new role—the learned lady—for herself and the women around her. The preceding generation had experienced the English Civil War, had survived the commonwealth, and had restored the monarchy; yet little had changed for women. Into this atmosphere, Astell emerged as a leading advocate of women's rights. While she never overtly defied masculine authority, she vigorously challenged the prevailing attitude that claimed women's inferiority and irrationality. According to biographer Florence Smith, "Mary Astell belongs more to this century than to her own, and would find today the support she lacked in her own time."

Although she publicly participated in the political and philosophical debates of her time, often questioning leading thinkers such as John Locke, the works Astell is most recognized for today are the explicitly feminist essays *A Serious Proposal to the Ladies for the Advancement of their True and Greatest Interest* (1694) and *Some Reflections upon Marriage* (1700). In *A Serious Proposal to the Ladies,* Astell proposed a religious community for women, "a Type and Antepast of Heav'n." She argued that a tradition of inadequate education had created a cycle that kept women ignorant, a tradition that likened women to "Tulips in a Garden, to make a fine show and [to] be good for nothing," and while Astell was not the first writer to advocate education for women—Bathsua Makin had written *An Essay to Revive the Ancient Education of Gentlewomen, in Religion, Manners, Arts, and Tongues* in 1673—part of the originality of her message lay in its specific address to an audience of women. Astell encouraged women to improve their minds in order to be better wives, Christians, and friends. Although this first book was immensely popular, particularly among its intended female audience, Astell's planned religious refuge never materialized, though in 1729 she helped open a school for poor daughters of veterans at the Chelsea Hospital.

In her next explicitly feminist work, *Some Reflections upon Marriage,* a tract that, like its predecessor, articulates liberation strategies for women, Astell argued that a good education is necessary if women are to marry wisely. As she defiantly proclaimed: "A Woman has no mighty Obligations to the Man who makes Love to her; she has no Reason to be fond of being a Wife, or to reckon it a Piece of Preferment when she is taken to be a Man's Upper-Servant; it is no Advantage to her in this World; if rightly managed it may prove one as to the next."

Clearly, Astell recognized the disparity of the marriage contract and concluded that generally necessity rather than reason caused a woman to submit to such an overtly antagonistic alliance. A woman's only hope to pass beyond her subordination in the home was education. In 1706 Astell would add a lengthy polemical preface to *Some Reflections upon Marriage* in which she addressed specific charges against her early edition and further encouraged all women to aspire beyond the roles reserved for them: "Let us learn to pride ourselves in something more excellent than the invention of a Fashion, and not entertain such a degrading thought of our own worth as to imagine that our Souls were given us only for the service of our Bodies, and that the best improvement we can make of these is to attract the Eyes of men." In Astell's ideal narrative of conjugal relations, friendship—not beauty, money, or station alone—should be the basis of marriage. Without a genuine fondness between the husband and wife, only tyranny was possible. Astell refused the "tyranny" of marriage for herself and championed other women's right to follow her example.

After a long and prolific career as a writer, Mary Astell died of cancer in 1731. An obituary in the 29 May issue of *The Daily Journal* observed that Astell's works showed "the Traces of an elevated Mind, display'd in an excellent Manner of Reasoning and a Turn of Genius above what is usual in her own Sex, and not unworthy of the most distinguish'd Writers of the other." Undoubtedly, Astell attracted the attention of commanding intellectual forces of the late 17th and early 18th century, but she also captured the imagination of a newly emergent class of female readers who increasingly questioned the basis of their subordination and found in Astell's message a blueprint for change.

—Teresa Lyle

ASTREA. *See* **BEHN, Aphra.**

ATWOOD, Margaret

Nationality: Canadian. **Born:** Ottawa, Ontario, 18 November 1939. **Education:** Victoria College, University of Toronto, 1957-61; B.A. 1961; Radcliffe College, Cambridge, Massachusetts, A.M. 1962; Harvard University, Cambridge, Massachusetts 1962-63, 1965-67. **Family:** One daughter. **Career:** Lecturer in English, University of British Columbia, Vancouver, 1964-65; instructor in English, Sir George Williams University, Montreal, 1967-68; teacher of creative writing, University of Alberta, Edmonton, 1969-70; assistant professor of English, York University, Toronto, 1971-72. Writer-in-residence, University of Toronto, 1972-73, University of Alabama, Tuscaloosa, 1985, Macquarie University, North Ryde, New South Wales, Australia, 1987, and Trinity University, San Antonio, Texas, 1989; Berg Visiting Professor of English, New York University, 1986. Editor and member of the board of directors, House of Anansi Press, Toronto, 1971-73. Contributor of articles, reviews, and short fiction to periodicals. **Awards:** E.J. Pratt Medal, 1961; University of Western Ontario President's Medal, 1965; Governor-General's award, 1966, 1986; Centennial Commission prize, 1967; Union League Civic and Arts Foundation prize, 1969, and Bess Hokin prize (*Poetry,* Chicago), 1974; City of Toronto award, 1976; St. Lawrence award, 1978; Radcliffe Medal, 1980; Companion, Order of Canada, 1981; Molson award, 1981; Guggenheim fellowship, 1981; Welsh Arts Council International Writers prize, 1982; Ida Nudel Humanitarian award, 1986; *Los Angeles Times* Book Award, 1986; Arthur C. Clarke Science-Fiction award, 1987; Royal Society of Canada fellow, 1987; Commonwealth Writer's prize (regional), 1987, 1994; Humanist of the Year award, 1987; Canadian Bookseller's Association Author of the Year award, 1988; City of Toronto Book Award, 1989; Order of Ontario, 1990; Harvard University Centennial Medal, 1990; Trillium Award, 1992, 1994; Canadian Authors Association award, 1993, Commonwealth Writers' Prize for Canadian and Caribbean Region and Sunday *Times* (London) award, both 1994, and Swedish Humour Association award, 1995, all for *The Robber Bride;* Chevalier dans l'Ordre des Arts et des Lettres (France), 1994. D.Litt.: Trent University, Peterborough, Ontario, 1973; Concordia University, Montreal, 1980; Smith College, Northampton, Massachusetts, 1982; University of Toronto, 1983; Mount Holyoke College, South Hadley, Massachusetts, 1985; University of Waterloo, Ontario, 1985; University of Guelph, Ontario, 1985; Victoria College, 1987; L.L.D.: Queen's University, Kingston, Ontario, 1974; University of Leeds, Ontario, 1994.**Member:** American Academy of Arts and Sciences (honorary member), 1988. **Agent:** Phoebe Larimore, 228 Main Street, Venice, California 90291, U.S.A. **Address:** c/o McClelland & Stewart, 481 University Ave, #900, Toronto, Ontario, Canada M5G 2E9.

Publications

Novels

The Edible Woman. Toronto, McClelland & Stewart, and London, Deutsch, 1969; Boston, Little Brown, 1970.
Surfacing. Toronto, McClelland & Stewart, 1972; London, Deutsch, and New York, Simon & Schuster, 1973.
Lady Oracle. Toronto, McClelland & Stewart, and New York, Simon & Schuster, 1976; London, Deutsch, 1977.
Life before Man. Toronto, McClelland & Stewart, 1979; New York, Simon & Schuster, and London, Cape, 1980.
Bodily Harm. Toronto, McClelland & Stewart, 1981; New York, Simon & Schuster, and London, Cape, 1982.
The Handmaid's Tale. Toronto, McClelland & Stewart, 1985; Boston, Houghton Mifflin, and London, Cape, 1986.

Cat's Eye. Toronto, McClelland & Stewart, 1988; New York, Doubleday, and London, Bloomsbury, 1989.
The Robber Bride. Toronto, McClelland & Stewart, New York, Doubleday, and London, Bloomsbury, 1993.
Alias Grace. Toronto, McClelland & Stewart, 1996.

Short Stories

Dancing Girls and Other Stories. Toronto, McClelland & Stewart, 1977; New York, Simon & Schuster, and London, Cape, 1982.
Encounters with the Element Man. Concord, New Hampshire, Ewert, 1982.
Murder in the Dark: Short Fictions and Prose Poems. Toronto, Coach House Press, 1983; London, Cape, 1984.
Bluebeard's Egg and Other Stories. Toronto, McClelland & Stewart, 1983; Boston, Houghton Mifflin, 1986; London, Cape, 1987.
Unearthing Suite. Toronto, Grand Union Press, 1983.
Wilderness Tips. Toronto, McClelland & Stewart, London, Bloomsbury, and New York, Doubleday, 1991.
Good Bones. Toronto, Coach House, and London, Bloomsbury, 1992; as *Good Bones and Simple Murders,* New York, Doubleday, 1994; as *Bones and Murder,* London, Virago, 1995.

Poetry

Double Persephone. Toronto, Hawkshead Press, 1961.
The Circle Game. Bloomfield Hills, Michigan, Cranbrook Academy of Art, 1964.
Talismans for Children. Bloomfield Hills, Michigan, Cranbrook Academy of Art, 1965.
Kaleidoscopes: Baroque. Bloomfield Hills, Michigan, Cranbrook Academy of Art, 1965.
Speeches for Doctor Frankenstein. Bloomfield Hills, Michigan, Cranbrook Academy of Art, 1966.
The Circle Game (collection). Toronto, Contact Press, 1966.
Expeditions. Bloomfield Hills, Michigan, Cranbrook Academy of Art, 1966.
The Animals in That County. Toronto, Oxford University Press, 1968; Boston, Little Brown, 1969.
Who Was in the Garden. Santa Barbara, California, Unicorn, 1969.
The Journals of Susanna Moodie. Toronto, Oxford University Press, 1970.
Procedures for Underground. Toronto, Oxford University Press, and Boston, Little Brown, 1970.
Power Politics. Toronto, Anansi, 1971; New York, Harper, 1973.
You Are Happy. Toronto, Oxford University Press, and New York, Harper, 1974.
Selected Poems. Toronto, Oxford University Press, 1976; New York, Simon & Schuster, 1978.
Marsh, Hawk. Toronto, Dreadnaught, 1977.
Two-Headed Poems. Toronto, Oxford University Press, 1978; New York, Simon & Schuster, 1981.
True Stories. Toronto, Oxford University Press, 1981; New York, Simon & Schuster, and London, Cape, 1982.
Notes towards a Poem That Can Never Be Written. Toronto, Salamander Press, 1981.
Snake Poems. Toronto, Salamander Press, 1983.
Interlunar. Toronto, Oxford University Press, 1984; London, Cape, 1988.
Selected Poems II: Poems Selected and New, 1976-1986. Toronto, Oxford University Press, 1986; Boston, Houghton Mifflin, 1987.
Selected Poems 1966-1984. Toronto, Oxford University Press, 1990.
Margaret Atwood's Poems 1965-1975. London, Virago, 1991.
Morning in the Burned House. Toronto, McClelland & Stewart, London, Virago, and Boston, Houghton Mifflin, 1995.

Plays

Radio Play: *The Trumpets of Summer,* 1964.

Television Plays: *The Servant Girl,* 1974; *Snowbird,* 1981; *Heaven on Earth,* with Peter Pearson, 1986; *Road to Heaven,* 1987.

For Children

Up in the Tree. Toronto, McClelland & Stewart, 1978.
Anna's Pet, with Joyce Barkhouse. Toronto, Lorimer, 1980.
For the Birds. Vancouver, Douglas & McIntyre, 1990.
Princess Prunella and the Purple Peanut. Toronto, Key Porter, and New York, Workman Publishing, 1995.

Other

Survival: A Thematic Guide to Canadian Literature. Toronto, Anansi, 1972.
Days of the Rebels 1815-1840. Toronto, Natural Science of Canada, 1977.
Second Words: Selected Critical Prose. Toronto, Anansi, 1982; Boston, Beacon Press, 1984.
Margaret Atwood: Conversations, edited by E. Ingersoll. Princeton, New Jersey, Ontario Review Press, 1990; London, Virago, 1992.
Strange Things: The Malevolent North in Canadian Literature. Oxford, Oxford University Press, 1995.

Editor, *The New Oxford Book of Canadian Verse in English.* Toronto, New York, and Oxford, Oxford University Press, 1982.
Editor, with Robert Weaver, *The Oxford Book of Canadian Short Stories in English.* Toronto, Oxford, and New York, Oxford University Press, 1986; revised, 1995.
Editor, *The Canlit Food Book.* Toronto, Totem, 1987.
Editor, with Shannon Ravenel, *The Best American Short Stories 1989.* Boston, Houghton Mifflin, 1989.
Editor, with Robert Weaver, *The New Oxford Book of Canadian Short Stories in English.* Toronto, Oxford, and New York, Oxford University Press, 1995.

Recordings: *Oratorio for Sasquatch, Man, and Two Androids: Poems for Voices.* Toronto, Canadian Broadcasting Corporation, 1970; *The Poetry and Voice of Margaret Atwood,* Caedmon, 1977; *Margaret Atwood Reads* Unearthing Suites, American Audio Prose Library, 1985; *Margaret Atwood Reads from A Handmaid's Tale,* Caedmon, n.d.

*

Media Adaptation: *A Handmaid's Tale* (film), 1990.

Bibliography: "Margaret Atwood: An Annotated Bibliography" by Alan J. Horne, in *The Annotated Bibliography of Canada's Major Authors 1-2,* edited by Robert Lecker and Jack David,

Downsview, Ontario, ECW Press, 2 vols., 1979-80; *Margaret Atwood: A Reference Guide* by Judith McCombs and Carole L. Palmer, Boston, G.K. Hall, 1991.

Manuscript Collection: Fisher Library, University of Toronto.

Critical Studies: *Margaret Atwood: A Symposium* edited by Linda Sandler, Victoria, British Columbia, University of Victoria, 1977; *A Violent Duality* by Sherrill Grace, Montréal, Véhicule Press, 1979, and *Margaret Atwood: Language, Text, and System* edited by Grace and Lorraine Weir, Vancouver, University of British Columbia Press, 1983; *The Art of Margaret Atwood: Essays in Criticism* edited by Arnold E. and Cathy N. Davidson, Toronto, Anansi, 1980; *Margaret Atwood* by Jerome H. Rosenberg, Boston, Twayne, 1984; *Margaret Atwood: A Feminist Poetics* by Frank Davey, Vancouver, Talonbooks, 1984; *Margaret Atwood* by Barbara Hill Rigney, London, Macmillan, 1987; *Critical Essays on Margaret Atwood* edited by Judith McCombs, Boston, G.K. Hall, 1988; *Margaret Atwood: Vision and Forms* edited by Kathryn van Spanckeren and Jan Garden Castro, Carbondale, Southern Illinois University Press, 1988; *The Other Side of the Story: Structures and Strategies of Contemporary Feminist Narrative* by Molly Hite, Ithaca, New York, Cornell University Press, 1989; *Margaret Atwood's Power: Mirrors, Reflections, and Images in Select Fiction and Poetry* by Shannon Hengen, St. Paul, Minnesota, Second Story Press, 1993; *Brutal Choreographies: Oppositional Strategies and Narrative Design in the Novels of Margaret Atwood* by J. Brooks Bouson, Amherst, University of Massachusetts Press, 1993; *Collecting Clues: Margaret Atwood's Bodily Harm* by Lorna Irvine, Toronto, ECW Press, 1993; *Strategies for Identity: The Fiction of Margaret Atwood* by Eleonora Rao, New York, P. Lang, 1993; *Margaret Atwood's Fairy-Tale Sexual Politics* by Sharon Rose Wilson, Jackson, University Press of Mississippi, 1993; *Margaret Atwood: Writing and Subjectivity: New Critical Essays* edited by Colin Nicholson, New York, St. Martin's Press, 1994; *Textual Escap(e)ades: Mobility, Maternity, and Textuality in Contemporary Fiction by Women* by Lindsay Tucker, Westport, Greenwood Press, 1994; "Maternity and the Ideology of Sexual Difference in *The Handmaid's Tale*" by Janet J. Montelaro, in *LIT: Literature, Interpretation, and Theory,* 6, fall 1995; *Margaret Atwood's Novels: A Study of Narrative Discourse* by Hilda Staels, Tübingen, Francke Verlag, 1995; *Various Atwoods: Essays on the Later Poems, Short Fiction, and Novels,* edited by Lorraine M. York, Toronto, Anansi, 1995.

* * *

Margaret Atwood, a varied and prolific writer, has been recognized for her terse, evocative and intellectually probing poetry and dazzling comic invention in fiction. One of Canada's major contemporary authors on the international scene, her novels have been twice short-listed for the Booker Prize and her work translated into more than 22 languages.

Readers are hooked by the seductive but deceptive subjectivity of first-person narrators into an exploration of psychic states in writing characterized by an intensity of focus, through which Atwood engages in a challenging scrutiny of modern life. Questions of subjectivity, identity, and power are addressed on a number of fronts. While international readers and critics are increasingly interested in her subtle allegories of gender relations as constituting power struggles, Canadian readers take additional pleasure in her brilliant satires of contemporary Canadian life, which are enfolded in biting critiques of allegories of empire.

There is a certain irony in Atwood's immense popularity in the United States, for her early writing took fire from the cultural nationalism of the 1960s, animated both by opposition to American imperialism in a virulent phase during the Viet Nam War and by the fervour surrounding celebration of the Canadian centenary in 1967 with its accompanying burgeoning of the creative arts. Atwood was an active leader in this emerging national literary scene as editor for the House of Anansi Press (1971-73) and as an editor and political cartoonist for the left-wing *This Magazine.* Drawing on her teaching in various Canadian universities, she published a pioneering work of Canadian literature criticism, *Survival: A Thematic Guide to Canadian Literature* (1972). In this work she argued for the uniqueness of Canadian literature in its depiction of the struggle with the wilderness through four different developmental phases climaxing with a refusal of victimhood or subordination. These themes informed Atwood's creative writing during the same years. *The Journals of Susanna Moodie* (1970) is a reworking in poetry of the autobiographical sketches of a reluctant pioneer Ontario writer of the 1830s, whose fear of the implacable wilderness ultimately is transformed into love. Moodie's final verses are prayers from the grave against the urban civilization her sacrifice has created. *Surfacing* (1972) exhibits equally complex irony as it explores, through the narrative of a canoe journey into northern Quebec, the convoluted power relations between Anglophobe and Francophone Canadians in an era of intense Quebec separatist activity and between descendants of European immigrants and the culture of the aboriginal inhabitants they have displaced, both complicated by the invasion of American technology. The title sequence in *Two-Headed Poems* (1978) returns to these anti-imperialist struggles to proffer an allegorical emblem of the troubled nation as Siamese twins joined at the head, each desperate to be an individual, but caught in the other's identity.

While the saliency of Atwood's political analysis is a major strength of her works, these are not tracts or manifestos but carefully crafted texts that engage in a critical refashioning of literary genres in a spirit of post-modern parody. Much of her appeal to international readers is her work on cliché, stereotype, and convention: she evokes contemporary popular culture and reworks it through ironic displacement, a double whammy for those who follow her subtle irony to wink at its critique of these dominant cultural codes and of the very nationalism and feminism that would oppose them. Both Atwood's familiarity with conventions and her strategy of displacement are the legacy of another important force shaping her work: the archetypal theory of Northrop Frye and of Jay MacPherson, who taught her at Victoria College, University of Toronto. Atwood's own critical approach follows Frygean "thematic criticism" to read Canadian culture through literary texts as exemplifications of the dilemma of a "garrison mentality" in its colonialist self-alienation and paralysis of the imagination. Her understanding of literary texts as displacements of mythic archetypes was heightened not only by Frye's theory of romance as "secular scripture," but by her own research into 19th-century metaphysical romances in the course of graduate studies at Harvard University. Consequently, it is not just the trajectory of liberation struggles against imperialist oppression, but also the descent plots of romance quests with their motifs of confinement, burial, and procedures for escape that constitute Atwood's texts' characteristic structural pattern of "jailbreak and recreation." This shapes Atwood's early poetry collections: *The Circle Game*

(1966), winner of the Governor General's Award, explores metaphors of confinement, as does *Power Politics* (1971), which introduces her second overarching concern, the unreliability of representation, here in the form of the duplicity of language. *Procedures for Underground* (1970) takes up these themes of difficulty engaging with the irrational to stage the persona's attempt at breakout by plunging into the elements in more universal terms than Moodie's immolation and resurrection. The title evokes the mythical plot of Atwood's first book, *Double Persephone* (1961), where the constraining power was not just the inherited weight of the past but an explicitly gendered one that forcibly abducted the female speaker. Mythic rape transmutes into gothic horror in the confinement of burial alive. But, as Atwood's first novel *The Edible Woman* (1969) demonstrates, escapes are not easy for the women personas in her books who have lost their sense of self and of place. Masculinity, technology, and representation may be the external forms of power enfolded in the constraining social gaze (Marian flees her fiancé Peter's attempt to photograph her in the novel, running from the horror of domestic enclosure), but their force has produced the split feminine/colonial subject, the leaky abjected feminine unable to separate or to act, caught in the vicious circle. The women characters cannot find themselves in the reflecting surfaces around them. Paradoxically, the surfaces are more than reflectors. Screens are also skins, membranes connecting, separating, concealing. What can't be seen in the mirror may be lurking under ground, under water, behind the looking glass. A shift in positions changes the angle of vision and the relations of force. Still, the endings of Atwood's texts are hyperreal or cryptic, as in Moodie's ghostly return, or the *Surfacing* narrator's isolated reemergence from the bush, or Marian's incorporation of her own image formed in the cake she consumes. This ambiguity or double-voiced discourse, a characteristic duality noted by early critics of Atwood's work, does not endear her to feminist readers seeking positive representations for women, nor to humanist Marxists seeking Utopian solutions for social injustice. Writing to defamiliarize the "natural" existence of any fixed position, her work has the moral function of unease. The political issues Atwood addresses require solutions she refuses to provide, lingering instead on a critique of complicity in power structures. Indeed, such complicitous modes as parody and irony are her stock in trade as she challenges structures of containment through gothic excess. While critiquing in *Survival* the land-as-woman/woman-as-land metaphor dominant in Canadian literature that has produced so many "ice women" of thwarted creativity, Atwood uses it extensively in her own writing in the metaphor "Canada-is-a-woman" to interrogate the function of gender inequality in the service of national and imperial projects.

Throughout the 1970s Atwood's work focused more on gendered oppression and increasingly appeared in fictional form, though she experimented with a number of genres and mediums, writing TV scripts ("The Servant Girl"), Canadian history (*Days of the Rebels: 1815-1840*), and a children's book, *Up in the Tree,* which she also illustrated. *You Are Happy* (1974), a poetry collection including a reworking of *The Odyssey* from Circe's perspective, points to her continued interest in revising classical myth for feminist critique. During these years, Atwood produced some of the first feminist literary criticism in Canada: in "Paradoxes and Dilemmas: On Being a 'Woman Writer'" (1976) she denounced the phallic criticism that neglected women's writing to focus on stereotypical representations of their lives, possibly in response to charges about the negativity of her acerbic wit in *Lady Oracle* (1976), a parodic reworking of fairy tales and gothic romances. While her irony was considered cruel, that of a male novelist would be taken as evidence of toughmindedness, Atwood replied to critics. A self-reflexive fiction, *Lady Oracle* develops the labyrinthine situation of a writer whose life has become complicated by fame and the staleness of her creative activity. She stages a fake suicide to escape from the trap, only to find herself caught up in yet another game of disguise that is as intolerably convoluted as the old. The mask of writer is only the most recent of the narrator's masquerades in this fiction which probes both the games of representation and narrative for stringing a line and the manifold performances of femininity.

Atwood shifts from nature-as-monster to focus on the feminine-as-excess in *Lady Oracle,* and develops this further in the short stories about the problematic status of women collected in *Dancing Girls* (1977). And in *Life before Man* (1979), a more traditional novel than the earlier fiction, she develops a series of love triangles that centre around an Alice regressing to dinosaurland in the Royal Ontario Museum through exposition rather than image; it is a fiction that exposes the absurdities of ordering. *Bluebeard's Egg* (1983), a second collection of short stories, further polishes Atwood's fictional devices of intricate embedding, surprise escape, fairy-tale conventions rewritten to expose their misogyny and violence. These were reworked into self-reflexive prose poems in *Murder in the Dark* (1984) that expose the gendered violence of literary conventions to biting critique. Her reviews and criticism were collected in *Second Words* (1982).

Although Atwood continued to work in familiar modes at the beginning of the 1980s, producing another TV script and a second children's book, her social vision demanded a larger fresco in this decade as increasingly, in response to her political work in such positions as vice-chair of the Writers' Union of Canada (1980), president of PEN International's Anglo-Canadian branch (1984-86), and member of Amnesty International, she was involved in struggles against totalitarian power and censorship on the international scene. This influenced her subject matter in *True Stories,* a book of poems, and *Bodily Harm,* a novel set during an uprising on a Caribbean island. Both deal with imprisonment and torture, "bearing witness" and so breaking down a distinction Atwood herself makes between poetry (at the heart of her relationship with language) and fiction (her moral vision of the world). The gendered difference of such abuses of power is examined in *The Handmaid's Tale* (1985), her most celebrated novel, a chilling dystopia set in a right-wing nuclear wasteland in a landscape evocative of Boston, which practices censorship and state control of reproduction. The violence to women's bodies and identity under extreme conditions where writing is outlawed and women reduced to nameless reproductive machines is framed by a meditation on the gender biases of historiography where men's words are taken for the real and work to confuse rather than expose "the truth." This persistent concern with the instability of meaning and identity takes a different form in *Cat's Eye* (1988), a fictional autobiography of a woman artist that probes questions of subjectivity and creativity. It explores the differing modes of figuration of temporality in science and the visual arts as the narrator summons up the ghosts of her childhood and organizes an exhibition of her surreal canvases in a Toronto gallery. The narrating "I" becomes an eye turned lovingly and caustically on this city in another ghost story of burial and recreation. Atwood's growing international renown through this period may be charted in the many compilations of her poems: *Selected Poems* (1976) and *Interlunar* (1984), a collection of new poems, were followed by *Selected Poems II: Poems Selected and New, 1976-1986* (1986), *Selected Poems 1966-1984* (1990) and *Margaret Atwood Poems 1965-1975* (1991). Her eminence among Canadian writers of her generation was confirmed with editorship of *The New Oxford Book of Canadian Verse in English* (1982), *The Oxford Book of Canadian Short Stories in English* (1986, revised 1995) and co-editorship of *The Best American Short Stories* (1989). During this busy period she wrote the script for *Road to Heaven* (1987), a TV film about the Barnardo children in Canada, and *The Festival of Missed Crass* (1987), a fantastic and satiric story for children transformed into a musical. Other works for children followed: *For the Birds* (1990) and *Princess Prunella and the Purple Peanut* (1995) exhibited her love of word play.

Through the 1990s, Atwood has continued to publish prize-winning fiction. *Wilderness Tips* (1991), a collection of short stories with gothic overtones about women facing middle age mixed with narratives about girls' immolations in the pseudo-wilderness of summer camp country, was followed by *Good Bones* (1992), brief texts about female body parts and social constraints with all the mordant wit of the earlier prose poems. Longer, though equally trenchant in its examination of Toronto lifestyles and women's friendships in a mode reminiscent of *Cat's Eye, The Robber Bride* (1993) involves three women and a contemporary, female vampire, whose ghostly returns incite the others to defensive warlike maneuvers in a critique of commonplaces about women's innate benevolence. Nonetheless, a darker shading is characteristic of Atwood's recent work. *Morning in the Burned House* (1995), her first collection of new poems in a decade, with its title sequence of elegiac poems demonstrated a new emotional range in her work. So too, in *Strange Things: The Malevolent North in Canadian Literature* (1996), essays delivered as the Clarendon lectures in English literature at Oxford University (1991), Atwood pursues her obsession with the wilderness theme and the failed sacrifice in the Canadian imagination to examine desperate images connected with the Canadian north, beginning with the image of cannibalism and the doomed Franklin expedition. This is no longer the playful cannibalism of *The Edible Woman* nor the adaptable survivor's testimonial of *The Journals of Susanna Moodie* of 25 years earlier, but a much starker perspective on a world where death holds fort. It is to the life of one of Moodie's darker characters, the imprisoned murderess Grace Marks, that Atwood returns in her latest novel *Alias Grace* (1996).

Oxford is not the only place where Atwood has lectured. Indeed, her large international readership has been increased by her many readings and guest lectureships in such dispersed universities as York, Alabama, New York, Berlin, Macquarie (Sydney). Audiences continue to respond strongly to the precision of language and striking images that give resonance and authority to Atwood's exploration of the issues of our time: through hyperbole and laughter she would bring us to our senses and curb monstrosities against women and other creatures.

—Barbara Godard

AUSTIN, Mary (Hunter)

Pseudonym: Gordon Stairs. **Nationality:** American. **Born:** Carlinville, Illinois, 9 September 1868. **Education:** Blackburn College, B.A. 1888. **Family:** Married Stafford Wallace Austin in 1891 (separated 1905, divorced 1914); one daughter. **Career:** With family, homesteaded to California, 1888; worked as a teacher; lived in artists' communities in New York and London, c. 1905-11; worked for social reforms for women; after a breakdown, settled in Santa Fe, New Mexico, 1923; became involved in Native American rights movement. **Died:** Santa Fe, New Mexico, 13 August 1934.

Publications

Novels

Isidro. Boston and New York, Houghton Mifflin, and London, Constable, 1905.
Santa Lucia. New York and London, Harper, 1908.
Outland, as Gordon Stairs. London, Murray, 1910; as Austin, New York, Boni & Liveright, 1910.
A Woman of Genius. Garden City, New York, Doubleday Page, 1912; revised, Boston, Houghton Mifflin, 1917.
The Lovely Lady. Garden City, New York, Doubleday, 1913.
The Green Bough. N.p., 1913.
The Ford. Boston and New York, Houghton Mifflin, 1917.
A Study Oak: A Composite Novel by 14 American Authors, with others. N.p., 1917.
No. 26 Jayne St. Boston and New York, Houghton Mifflin, 1920.
Starry Adventure. Boston and New York, Houghton Mifflin, 1931.
Cactus Thorn. N.p., 1987.

Short Stories

Lost Borders. New York and London, Harper, 1909.
One-Smoke Stories. Boston and New York, Houghton Mifflin, 1934.
Stories from the Country of Lost Borders, edited by Marjorie Pryse. 1987.
A Mary Austin Reader. N.p., 1996.
Western Trails, edited by Melody Graulich. N.p., 1987.

Plays

The Arrow Maker (three-act; produced New York, 1910). New York, Duffield, 1911; revised, Boston and New York, Houghton Mifflin, 1915.
Fire (produced Carmel, California, 1912).
The Man Who Didn't Believe in Christmas (produced New York, 1916).

Essays

One Hundred Miles on Horseback. N.p., 1889.
The Land of Little Rain (originally published in *Atlantic Monthly*). Boston and New York, Houghton Mifflin, 1903.
The Flock. Boston and New York, Houghton Mifflin, and London, Constable, 1906.
California: The Land of the Sun, illustrated by Palmer Sutton. New York, Macmillan, and London, A.C. Black, 1914; revised as *The Lands of the Sun,* Boston and New York, Houghton Mifflin, 1925.
The American Rhythm. New York, Harcourt Brace, 1923; enlarged as *The American Rhythm: Studies and Reexpressions of Amerindian Songs,* Boston and New York, Houghton Mifflin, 1930.

The Land of Journey's Ending. New York and London, Century, 1924.
Everyman's Genius. Indianapolis, Bobbs-Merrill, 1925.
Experiences Facing Death. Indianapolis, Bobbs Merrill, and London, Rider, 1931.
Can Prayer Be Answered? New York, Farrar & Rinehart, 1934.

For Children

The Basket Woman: A Book of Fanciful Tales for Children. Boston and New York, Houghton Mifflin, 1904.
The Trail Book. Boston and New York, Houghton Mifflin, 1918.

Autobiography

Earth Horizon. Boston and New York, Houghton Mifflin, 1932.

Other

Christ in Italy: Being the Adventures of a Maverick among Masterpieces. New York, Duffield, 1912.
Love and the Soul Maker. New York and London, Appleton, 1914.
The Young Woman Citizen. New York, Woman's Press, 1918.
The Man Jesus: Being a Brief Account of the Life and Teaching of the Prophet of Nazareth. New York and London, Harper, 1915; revised as *A Small Town Man,* 1925.
The Children Sing in the Far West. Boston and New York, Houghton Mifflin, 1928.
Taos Pueblo, photographs by Ansel Adams. San Francisco, Grabhorn Press, 1930.
Indian Pottery of the Rio Grande. N.p., 1934.
Literary America, 1903-1934: The Mary Austin Letters, edited by T.M. Pearce. Westport, Connecticut, and London, Greenwood Press, 1979.

*

Bibliography: "Mary Austin, Bibliography and Biographical Data" in *California Literary Research Project Digest* (Berkeley), 11(1), 1934.

Manuscript Collections: Huntington Library, San Marino, California; University of New Mexico Library, Special Collections Division, Albuquerque.

Critical Studies: "The American Rhythm: Mary Austin's Poetic Principle" by T. W. Ford, in *Western American Literature,* 5, n.d.; "American Rhythm: Mary Austin" by Carl Van Doren, in his *Many Minds,* New York, Knopf, 1924; *Woman of Genius* by Helen McKnight Doyle, New York, Gotham House, 1939; *A Critical Study of the Writings of Mary Hunter Austin* (dissertation) by D. Wynn, n.p., 1941; *Mary Austin: A Memorial* edited by William Hoagland, Santa Fe, The Laboratory of Anthropology, 1944; *Mary Hunter Austin* by T.M. Pearce, New York, Twayne, 1965; *These Modern Women: Autobiographical Essays from the Twenties* edited by Elaine Showalter, Old Westbury, New York, Feminist Press, 1978; *I—Mary: A Biography of Mary Austin* by Augusta Fink, Tucson, University of Arizona Press, 1983; "Mary Austin: Nature and Nurturance" by David Wyatt, in *The Fall into Eden,* Cambridge, Cambridge University Press, 1986; "Re-Naming the Land: Anglo Expatriate Women in the Southwest" by Lois Rudnick, in *The Desert Is No Lady,* edited by Vera Norwood and Janice Monk, New Haven, Yale University Press, 1987; *Mary Austin: Song of a Maverick* by Lanigan Stineman, n.p., 1989; "Mary Austin and the Western Conservation Movement" by Benay Blend, in *Journal of the Southwest,* spring 1988; "Heroines of Nature: Four Women Respond to the American Landscape" by Vera Norwood, in *Environmental Review,* 8; "Mary Austin, Woman Alone" by Dudley Wynn, in *Virginia Quarterly Review,* 13.

* * *

Writer Mary Austin has undergone academic scrutiny almost exclusively in terms of her contributions to the literature of the American Southwest. The author of over 30 books in a number of genres and of some 250 articles in periodicals, she is increasingly being recognized as an early feminist. In fact, one of Austin's major themes is women's subordination by men in her society; even her nature works—*The Land of Little Rain, Lost Borders,* and *Cactus Thorn*—explore ways in which patriarchal Western culture subjects both women and the natural world to both male domination and exploitation. Austin's more overtly political work received little attention until the resurgent women's movement of the 1970s, when reprints of her 1912 feminist novel, *A Woman of Genius,* brought her new readers and renewed acclaim.

Austin's life was characterized by a failure to fit into roles appropriate to her time and her gender. Born in 1868, in Carlinville, Illinois, she grew up in a social climate more concerned with appearances than with intellectual achievement. As she recalls her youth in the autobiography *Earth Horizon* (1932), and as her biographers have amply documented, Austin's was a traumatic, unhappy childhood. Her lifelong love of words sprang from early deprivation, for her piercing intellect and passionate independence made her an outsider in her own family. She persisted in this rebellion when she moved with her family to homestead in Southern California in 1888. There she was mocked for efforts to understand the region's meaning: spending time alone in the desert night; talking to others outside the norm of conventional society—Native Americans, shepherds, Chinese laborers—who broadened her experience and provided her with diverse points of view. Eventually Austin would leave her home and join artist communities in Los Angeles, Carmel, and Greenwich Village. During those years she was introduced to leading writers, artists, and intellectuals, including Charlotte Perkins Gilman, Emma Goldman, and Margaret Sanger, who introduced her to the suffrage and labor movements. In 1924 Austin moved permanently to Santa Fe, New Mexico.

Austin never doubted her talent as a writer, despite her conviction that her family's indifference, her restrictive Midwestern upbringing, her marriage to an irresponsible and unresponsive dreamer, the birth of an autistic daughter, and the patriarchal culture in which she lived had all converged to hinder her career. Much of her work focused on independent and aspiring women who struggled to merge marriage with work outside the home. In her 1908 novel *Santa Lucia,* written as Austin's own marriage was failing, she develops a critique, including arguing against conventions that forced mismatched couples to remain together; restrictions on married women working outside the home; and assumptions that husbands should handle financial matters even when their wives were more responsible.

A Woman of Genius, which explores many of Austin's feminist ideals, is drawn from her own experiences and her observations of society's attitudes towards gender. As in several of her other novels—*Starry Adventure* and *No. 26 Jayne Street*—Austin tried to imagine the foundations for an egalitarian marriage, something earlier writers such as Louisa May Alcott, Elizabeth Stuart Phelps, and Sarah Orne Jewett had failed to do. When Olivia's suitor refuses to make concessions that would make room for her career, Austin's protagonist telegraphs her answer: that she would marry him only if he marries her work. Olivia channels her emotion into art, but eventually finds personal fulfillment in marriage to a long-time friend.

Austin explored the difficulties of ambitious women in other works as well. In the short story "Frustrate," the narrator, a middle-aged woman unhappy with her marriage, seeks self-fulfillment in an artist's colony. There she meets an independent woman writer whose path implies that a successful woman artist inevitably lives alone. In other early stories that pair two women, including "The Coyote-Spirit and the Weaving Woman" (in *Lost Borders,* 1909) and her 1910 play *The Arrow-Maker,* Austin examines further how these doubles represent conflicts she saw within herself.

While Austin would repudiate what Virginia Woolf called the "Angel," she spent a lifetime negotiating between her self-definition as "feminine" and "womanly" and the way she lived her life as an independent writer. During her years in New York, she became a preeminent theorist of the woman question, explicating what would later become major feminist concerns: in particular, her views on marriage and women's culture. Austin transformed thought into action for various women's causes: suffrage, birth control, and social programs such as communal kitchens to help conserve food and free women workers during World War I. Yet she eventually grew disillusioned with organized reform agendas. An egotist, Austin preferred to base her feminism on a sisterhood of one and to see herself as far ahead of others of her time.

Austin's writing places her in the middle of an ongoing debate among feminist theorists concerning how to weigh the relative values of biological difference against socially constructed gender roles. In connecting patriarchal oppression of women and nature and in asserting that the liberation of women would also serve the cause of nature—as she does most clearly in her novel *Cactus Thorn*—Austin articulated what today is at the core of ecofeminism, a modern movement that draws on insights of ecology, feminism, and socialism in order to analyze connections between domination both of women and of nature. She also raised questions that continue to plague the modern feminist movement. Austin herself was often ambivalent about what she called the "homecentric" tradition, finding value in women's culture but realizing the difficulties of merging a traditional lifestyle with meaningful work outside the home.

Feminist critics continue this debate, questioning whether the woman/nature connection is potentially liberating or whether, given the cultural baggage that it carries with it in Western society, it perpetuates the implication that women's nature is to nurture, condemning them to be sole care takers of other human beings as well as Mother Earth. While Austin struggled in her own life with these issues, her sensitivity to emerging women's issues foreshadowed concerns that would be picked up by a later generation of women working within the ecofeminist and women's movements.

—Benay Blend

AWIAKTA, Marilou

Nationality: American. **Born:** Marilou Awiakta Bonham, in Knoxville, Tennessee, 24 January 1936. **Education:** University of Tennessee, B.A.(magna cum laude) in English and French 1958. **Family:** Married Paul Thompson in 1957; two daughters and one son. **Career:** Poet and author active in environmental, Native American, and women's issues. Lecturer at various institutions, including Brandeis University, Tufts University, and New Mexico University. Civilian liaison officer and interpreter for U.S. Air Force, Laon Air Force Base, France, 1964-67; consultant for *The Good Mind* (film), 1982, and Aaron Copeland festival; cofounder, 1982, ambassador-at-large, 1986-90, Far-away Cherokee Association (now Native American Inter-Tribal Association); member of literary panel, 1982-89, chair, 1987-89, Tennessee Arts Commission; commissioner, Mayor's International Heritage Commission, Memphis, 1987-89. Contributor to periodicals, including *Callaloo, Greenfield Review, Ms., Parabola, Southern Exposure, Southern Style, Who Cares?* and *Women of Power.* **Awards:** Nashville "Homecoming '86" Literary Festival honor, 1986; Women of Achievement Woman of Vision award, 1988; Smokey Mountain Writers' Conference distinguished Tennessee Writer award, 1989; Appalachian Writers Association award, 1991; National Conference of Christians and Jews Women's Rights Leadership award; National Organization for Women Person of Quality award; Grammy Award nomination, 1995, for audio version of *Selu: Seeking the Corn Mother's Wisdom.* **Member:** National Conference of Christians and Jews (board member, 1984-90), Network of Girl Scouts of America, Leadership Memphis, Women's Foundation of Greater Memphis (board member beginning 1995). **Address:** c/o Fulcrum Publishing, 350 Indiana St., Suite 350, Golden, Colorado 80401, U.S.A.

Publications

Poetry

Abiding Appalachia: Where Mountain and Atom Meet. Memphis, Tennessee, St. Luke's Press, 1978; 8th edition, Binghamton, New York, Iris Press, 1995.

For Children

Rising Fawn and the Fire Mystery: A Story of Heritage, Family, and Courage, 1833, illustrated by Beverly Pringle. Memphis, Tennessee, St. Luke's Press, 1983.

Philosophy

Selu: Seeking the Corn-Mother's Wisdom, illustrations by Mary Adair, foreword by Wilma Mankiller. Golden, Colorado, Fulcrum, 1993.

Recording: *Selu: Seeking the Corn-Mother's Wisdom* (audiocassette; music by Jo Harjo and Poetic Justice), Audio Literature, 1995.

Essays

"Seed Corn Must Not Be Ground," in *Confessing Conscience: Churched Women on Abortion,* edited by Phyllis Tickle. Nashville, Abingdon Press, 1990.

"A Bridge is a Gift to the People," in *Keepers of Life,* by Michael J. Caduto and Joseph Bruchac. Golden, Colorado, Fulcrum, 1994.

"Grandmothers," in *Oxford Companion to Women's Writing in the United States,* edited by Cathy N. Davidson and Linda Wagner-Martin. New York, Oxford University Press, 1995.

"Southern Women," and "Southwestern Indian Women," in *The Reader's Companion to U.S. Women's History,* edited by Wilma Mankiller, Gwendolyn Mink, Marysa Navarro, Barbara Smith, and Gloria Steinem. Boston, Houghton Mifflin, 1996.

Plays

Focus on Conservation (conservation education package). Lexington, Kentucky Educational Television, 1991.

Television Plays: "Telling Tale," "Little Deer and Mother Earth," and "Rising Fawn and the Fire Mystery," in *Focus on Conservation,* PBS, 1991.

*

Critical Studies: "A Woman of Substance" (interview) by Marilyn Sadler, in *Memphis,* 19(6), September 1994; "Nuclear Visions" by Jane Caputi, in *American Quarterly,* 47(1), March 1995; article by Giney Carney in *Journal of Appalachian Studies,* 7, 1995; review of *Selu* by Jerold Savory, in *Southern Humanities Review,* 29(2), spring 1995; review of *Selu* by M. Rupert Cutler, in *Now & Then,* spring 1995; *Women Reshaping Human Rights* by Marguerite Bouvard, Wilmington, Delaware, Scholarly Resources, 1996.

Marilou Awiakta comments:

In my life and work, I take up the ancient "Song of the Grandmothers," sing it in the key of my own voice and times, and pass it on. This is the song:

I am Cherokee.

My people believe in the Spirit that unites all things.

I am woman. I am life force. My word has great value.

The Beloved Woman is one of our principle chiefs. Through her the Spirit often speaks to the people. In the Great Council at the capital, she is a powerful voice. Concerning the fate of hostages, her word is absolute.

Women share in all of life. We lead sacred dances. In the Council we debate freely with men until an agreement is reached. When the nation considers war, we have a say, for we bear the warriors.

Sometimes I go into battle. I also plant and harvest.

I carry my own name and the name of my clan. If I accept a mate, he and our children take the name of my clan. If there is deep trouble between us, I am as free to tell him to go as he is to leave. Our children and our dwelling stay with me. As long as I am treated with dignity, I am steadfast.

I love to work and sing.
I listen to the spirit.
In all things I speak my mind.
I walk without fear.
I am Cherokee.

This song is from "Amazons in Appalachia" in *Selu.*

* * *

The story of Awiakta's names suggests the outlines of her rich heritage: Bonham from her Scottish ancestors who settled in the mountains of East Tennessee seven generations ago and Awiakta, meaning "eye of the deer" in Cherokee. The Cherokee and Appalachian "component cultures"—*not* sub-cultures, as Awiakta is quick to remind us—combine in her very veins the indigenous and Celtic traditions of storytelling and spiritual connections to the land. Her father worked at Oak Ridge, Tennessee, one of the first nuclear research communities, and Awiakta has always sought the relationship between science and traditional Cherokee philosophy, feeling at home with the language of science and the atom. As if all these languages were not enough (a writer can never have too many), Awiakta lived in France from 1964-67, serving as interpreter and civilian liaison officer at a U.S. Air Force base where her husband was stationed. Rather than being "lost in translation," she has found herself in the confluence of all these cultures. As she tells us in her retrospective and forward-looking book, *Selu,* "Living in France made me think deeply about who I was, about the value of my heritages, and about the necessity of working out harmonies with peoples from different cultures. By the time I returned to America, I knew I was a Cherokee/Appalachian poet. I was determined to sing my song."

This demanding calling brought with it burdens as well as joy, for the late-1960s was a time of strife in the United States (when is it not?). In the aftermath of the civil rights movement, before the women's movement, Awiakta's path was difficult and lonely. But her "song"—her work—gradually attracted supporters such as Phyllis Tickle of St. Luke's Press (who commissioned Awiakta's first book, *Abiding Appalachia: Where Mountain and Atom Meet,* in 1978) and mentors such as Cherokee chief Wilma Mankiller and Joseph Bruchac (an Abenaki), Rene Parks Lanier, and African American writers Alice Walker and the late Etheridge Knight. Paula Gunn Allen and Leslie Silko were also significant literary influences, as was Virginia Woolf.

It was around 1982 that she decided to use her middle name, Awiakta. "Traditionally, it is a Native American custom to have several names during one's lifetime," she say of this decision. "In childhood and youth, I was called 'Marilou.' When my spirit had deepened and I had reached a new level of understanding and creativity, it was time to move to the name that expressed my more mature state of being." Five years before, while visiting Oak Ridge's Museum of Science and Energy, Awiakta had a profound visionary experience with the white deer sacred to the Cherokee: the story of *Awi Usdi,* or Little Deer, teaches the law of respect. "With my whole being I made a quantum leap and connected Little Deer to the web of my life—at the center.... That night, I drew what I'd seen: a white stag leaping at the heart of three atopic orbits." This unique image of so much in her past, present, and future, has become her personal logo. "To me it signifies the hope that if we have respect for everything—down to the atom—we can restore harmony and balance to our world."

Awiakta also identifies with what she terms the "new tribes": the women's movement and environmental groups, which she hopes will help make modern society more permeable to the Cherokee traditions of women holding leadership positions. In response to critics who claim that women's judgement might be impaired by their menstrual cycles, Awiakta answers with lively feminist wit and impeccable logic: "If that's the case, looking at history and all the wars through the ages, men must have been having a continual period!"

On a more serious note, she recalls the words of her mother: "When I was young and said 'I want to be a poet,' my mother would always say, 'That's good. And what will you do for the people?'" Awiakta accepts the full consequences of the Cherokee belief that "true art is for Life's sake, as well as for individual expression." She has taken her fusion of science and Cherokee/Appalachian philosophy "wherever people asked me to come": to festivals, schools, conservation conferences, prisons, women's groups, and hospitals. Through her poetry and her presence, Awiakta has inspired countless gatherings, from a tender talk she gave to some young women graduating *cum laude* from their high school to a keynote address at a National Colloquium on Nuclear Waste Disposal.

These many conversations and writings, ranging from matters of public policy to personal philosophy, culminated in what Jane Caputi calls an "extraordinarily beautiful, complex, persuasive meditation on the powers of corn as a sacred tradition." *Selu: Seeking the Corn-Mother's Wisdom,* a ground- and genre-breaking compendium of Awiakta's work, celebrates, at its center, Selu the Corn-Mother (*not* a Goddess, but a living spirit to Native Americans), whose story teaches survival wisdoms of strength, respect, balance, adaptability, and cooperation. Awiakta applies these common-sense teachings to contemporary concerns: the environment, gender issues, cultural diversity, and government. What emerges from this fusion is a transfusion of new-old ideas and images, what Jerold Savory has praised as "required reading for all of us who are ready to be informed, inspired, and shaped by the native roots of our national heritage." Since its publication in 1993 *Selu* has been adopted by universities spanning the United States for courses ranging from sociology and women's studies to literature. It has been compared to such works as Vine Deloria's flagship book on Native spirituality, *God Is Red,* and Rachel Carson's *Silent Spring.*

Important to *Selu*'s unique effect is its double-woven basket form. "Reading will be easy if you keep the weaving mode in mind: Over ... under ... over," writes Awiakta. "A round basket never runs 'straight-on.'" This form reflects the author's perspective, for Native realities are cyclical experiences of interrelationship and renewal.

While *Selu* encompasses such painful issues as the flooding of the historic heartland of the Cherokee in the Tellicoe Dam scam, it also dares to be humorous, as in "Selu and the Sex Expert." And Awiakta's all-pervasive feminist perspective "busts out" in such poems as "Song of Grandmothers," "When Earth Becomes an 'It'," "Mother Nature Send a Pink Slip," and "On Being a Female Phoenix," where she protests "Not only do I rise/from my own ashes,/I have to carry them out!" In her longer poem "Anorexia Bulimia Speaks from the Grave" comes the following advice: "Listen young women,/the Grandmothers and Anorexia Bulimia/are talkin' to you—Feed your body./Feed your soul./Feed your dream./BUST OUT!!!"

Also contained in *Selu*'s flexible basket structure are essays that had appeared earlier, such as "Amazons in Appalachia," "Living in the Round: What Maria's Bowl Teaches Me," and "Baring the Atoms' Mother Heart," which Gloria Steinem heralded as a "groundbreaking" piece. "Awiakta is one of the rare writers whose words help readers see the world in a different way," noted Steinem. "Her weaving of essays, stories and poems in *Selu* creates the sense of an ancient knowledge being brought to bear on modern problems. For the majority culture of this country, she brings an inkling of the wisdom it has done its best to destroy, and the generosity of spirit that continues giving that wisdom as gift."

Awiakta is imbued with that same generosity of spirit and will continue giving and developing in her work. The paradoxical terms *continuity* and *growth,* along with Little Deer's leap and balance, may help describe why Awiakta remains such an interesting writer to watch. As Paula Gunn Allen has said: "Thank you Grandmother Corn, Selu, for Awiakta."

—J. J. Wilson

B

BAGNOLD, Enid

Pseudonym: A Lady of Quality. **Nationality:** British. **Born:** Rochester, England, 27 October, 1889. **Education:** Attended Priors Field School, Godalming, England, and schools in France, Switzerland, and Germany; studied drawing and painting with Walter Sickert. **Military Service:** Served in English hospitals, 1917-18; served as driver attached to French Army until end of World War I. **Family:** Married Sir Roderick Jones in 1920 (died 1962); one daughter and three sons. **Career:** Journalist and writer. **Awards:** Arts Theatre Prize, 1951, for *Poor Judas;* American Academy of Arts and Letters Award of Merit Medal and prize, 1956, for *The Chalk Garden;* named Commander of the British Empire. **Died:** In London, 31 March 1981.

Publications

Novels

The Girl's Journey. Garden City, New York, Doubleday, 1954.
The Happy Foreigner. Century, 1920.
The Door of Life. New York, Morrow, 1938; as *The Squire,* London, Heinemann, 1940.
Serena Blandish: or, The Difficulty of Getting Married (as A Lady of Quality). London, Heinemann, 1924.
The Loved and Envied. Garden City, New York, Doubleday, 1951.

Essays

A Diary without Dates. London, Heinemann, 1918.

Poetry

The Sailing Ship and Other Poems. London, Heinemann, 1918.
Poems of Enid Bagnold. Cheltenham, Gloucester, Whittington Press, 1979.
Early Poems of Enid Bagnold. Cheltenham, Gloucester, Whittington Press, 1987.

Plays

Lottie Dundass (produced Santa Barbara, California, 1942; produced London, 1943). London, Heinemann, 1941. In *Two Plays,* 1951.
National Velvet (three-act; adapted from her novel; produced London, 1945). New York, Dramatists Play Service, 1961.
Poor Judas (produced London, 1951). In *Two Plays,* 1951.
Two Plays (contains *Lottie Dundass* and *Poor Judas*). Garden City, New York, Doubleday, 1951.
Gertie (produced New York, 1952; as *Little Idiot,* produced London, 1953).
The Chalk Garden (produced New York, 1955). New York, Random House, 1956; in *Four Plays,* London, Heinemann, 1970.
The Last Joke (produced London, 1960). In *Four Plays,* 1970.
The Chinese Prime Minister (three-act; produced New York, 1965; produced London, 1965). Garden City, New York, Doubleday, 1964; in *Four Plays,* London, Heinemann, 1970.
Call Me Jacky (produced Oxford, 1967; revised as *A Matter of Gravity,* produced Washington, D.C., 1975), in *Four Plays.* 1970.
Four Plays (contains *The Chalk Garden, The Last Joke, The Chinese Prime Minister,* and *Call Me Jacky*). London, Heinemann, 1970; Boston, Little Brown, 1971.

For Children

Alice and Thomas and Jane, illustrated by daughter, Laurienne Jones. London, Heinemann, 1930; New York, Knopf, 1931.
National Velvet, illustrated by Laurienne Jones. London, Heinemann, and New York, Morrow, 1935.

Autobiography

Enid Bagnold's Autobiography: From 1889. London, Heinemann, 1969; Boston, Little Brown, 1970.

Other

Translator, *Alexander of Asia,* by Princess Marthe Bibesco. London, Heinemann, 1935.

*

Media Adaptations: "Serena Blandish," in *Three Plays* by S. H. Behrman (stage play), 1929; *Alice, Thomas, and Jane* (two-act stage play), S. French, 1934; *National Velvet* (film), Metro-Goldwyn-Mayer, 1944, radio play, 1950, television series, NBC-TV, 1960-62; *Lottie Dundass* (radio play), 1950; *The Chalk Garden,* Universal, 1964; *International Velvet,* Universal, 1978.

Critical Studies: "Enid Bagnold" by Richard B. Gidez, in *Dictionary of Literary Biography,* Vol. 13: *British Dramatists since World War II,* Detroit, Gale Research, 1982; *Enid Bagnold* by Lenemaja Friedman, Boston, Twayne, 1986.

* * *

Enid Bagnold, like many of her early 20th-century female contemporaries, took advantage of her new-found freedom and lived independently for a while before marrying relatively late. Her husband supported her writing but also expected her to fulfill the conventional roles—a "double life of the greatest pressure," but a challenge Bagnold met. This combined independence and tradition led her to portray many underlying feministic aspects of traditional female life: a mother's nurturing of a daughter's ambitions, retaining one's identity and self-reliance in relationships, hidden sides of childbearing and aging, and how to move forward in life. Her novels and plays feature strong female protagonists—adolescents, mysterious loners, and matriarchs—and are flavored with entertaining dialogue, sharp observations, and a love of life.

Bagnold's most popular novel, *National Velvet* (1935), is about a girl who rides her horse in the Grand National steeplechase disguised as a boy. Velvet Brown's mother exemplifies Bagnold's strong matriarchs, "an enormous woman who had once swum the Channel." Velvet's more traditional father declares, "You girls have got your faces for your fortunes," but Mrs. Brown nurtures their inner selves: "She valued and appraised each daughter, she knew what each daughter could do.... She was glad too that her daughters were not boys because she could not understand the courage of men." However, Mrs. Brown does value the men who brought out her potential, like her swimming trainer, and the doctor during her pregnancies: "He knew what she was made of.... Nobody else, ever." She uses her gold prize money from the Channel to pay Velvet's entry fee for the race. "If Mrs. Brown had been asked what her hope and expectancy in life was for Velvet, she ... would have answered 'guts.'" Afterward, she feels that Velvet's accomplishments are not passing: "She's got more to come ... a child that can do that can more when she's grown."

Bagnold is also well known for her comi-serious play about difficult aspects of the mother-daughter relationship: 1955's *The Chalk Garden.* The plot involves a beautiful, mysterious governess attempting to manage an unruly girl, Laurel, who lives with her grandmother. The girl's mother has remarried and seemingly abandoned her. In reality Laurel's grandmother has thwarted her mother from reclaiming her, because she carries a grudge over their own past mother-daughter problems. The governess sees that this pattern is harming the girl, and she too knows the dangers of being unloved and unbelieved—having nothing to lose she is able to take a risk to help heal the relationships around her. Her future is uncertain, but she will "continue to explore the astonishment of living."

Bagnold's first novel was *A Diary without Dates* (1918), written when she was working in a wartime hospital. A frank portrayal of what she saw there, it caused her immediate dismissal. Her wartime ambulance-driving experience appears in another early novel, *The Happy Foreigner,* in which a young woman, Fanny, is a driver for the French army. Fanny's refuses "to surrender to the emotional dependence expected of her sex.... They too could display what was considered to be fortitude in the face of often gruelling situations." She also learns, through an affair with a married man there, that true happiness comes mainly from within; once she knows that, she is "half out of reach of pain."

The novel *Serena Blandish; or, The Difficulty of Getting Married* (1924) satirizes the machinations required to land a husband, and how women's fortunes are so vulnerably tied to marriage. Serena is befriended by a countess, who thinks the beautiful, unspoiled girl will marry brilliantly. However, though it is not known, Serena has been promiscuous. But she has no moral code and therefore feels pure—"And since what seems to be is—I am a virgin." Dismayed by Serena's lack of success, the countess coaches her that "nothing must be given away." Serena's frankness is also a problem: When a bachelor inquires about her greatest desire in life and she answers "To marry you," he recoils in horror. Bagnold's father insisted that the book be published under a pen name.

Bagnold once commented, "If a man had a child and he was also a writer we should have heard a lot about it." Her *The Squire* (1938) would be one of the first books to treat the hushed topics of childbearing and breast feeding. A man on an extended business trip has left his pregnant wife, "the squire," in charge of the household. But she feels secure: "In a strange way these absences suit nature.... I miss him, but I have time to put on my humanity again." Her life is centered on motherhood—"I look at those other creatures, my own.... I shiver and *I love.* No young man ever came near that." In contrast, her single friend Caroline discusses new conquests. The "squire" too used to be "strutting about life for spoil," but is now "occupied with ... her knot of human lives ... what was left standing at the core was the rock of neutral human stuff, neither male nor female." The squire feels that a new name might be needed for women like herself: "Wumen ... hard-working, faulty, honest female males." Critic Rosemary Benet called this book "Feminism at its best."

Bagnold's later works include an excellent autobiography and many plays. *The Chinese Prime Minister* (1965) is about a 70-year-old actress, "She," she is badgered into retirement and must deal with her ex-husband and her sons' wives. Still seeking her identity, she decides to take time for herself: "I wish there was another adventure for me and, good God, there may be! But not while I am pulled down by the pressure on me of what you think I am!" She has "brought pleasure to men. And brought up boys ... But there is a Me in me that I have never conquered!"

—Leslie-Anne Skolnik

BARNARD, A. M. *See* **ALCOTT, Louisa May.**

BARTKY, Sandra (Lee)

Nationality: American. **Born:** Evanston, Illinois, 5 May 1935. **Education:** University of Illinois, Urbana, B.A. 1955, M.A. 1959, Ph.D. in philosophy 1963. **Career:** Associate professor of philosophy, beginning 1970, and chairman of women's studies program, University of Illinois, Chicago Circle. **Awards:** National Endowment for the Humanities fellow, 1968-69. **Member:** American Philosophy Association, Society for Women in Philosophy. **Address:** Department of Philosophy, University of Illinois at Chicago, 601 South Morgan Street, Chicago, Illinois 60607-7100, U.S.A.

Publications

Philosophy

Philosophy and Feminism. Totowa, New Jersey, Littlefield, 1977; as *Philosophy and Women,* Belmont, California, Wadsworth, 1979.

Femininity and Domination: Studies in the Phenomenology of Oppression. New York and London, Routledge, 1990.

Uncollected Essays

"Seinsverlassenheit in the Later Philosophy of Heidegger," in *Inquiry* (Chicago, Illinois), 10.

"Heidegger's Philosophy of Art," in *British Journal of Aesthetics,* November 1969.

"Originative Thought in the Later Philosophy of Heidegger," in *Philosophic and Phenomenologic Research,* 10.

"Toward a Phenomenology of Feminist Consciousness," in *Social Theory and Practice,* 3(4), 1976.

"Heidegger and the Modes of World-Disclosure," in *Philosophic and Phenomenologic Research,* December 1979.

Other

Editor, with Nancy Fraser, *Revaluing French Feminism: Critical Essays on Difference, Agency, and Culture.* Bloomington, Indiana University Press, 1992.

*

Critical Studies: Special "Bartky" issue of *Hypatia,* 8(1), winter 1993.

* * *

Sandra Bartky has been a pivotal figure in feminist philosophy, not only as one of the earliest members of the Society for Women in Philosophy, but also for her role in forming a feminist theory grounded in Phenomenology and Marxist ideology. Her early, pre-feminist work focused on the German phenomenologist Martin Heidegger and encompassed both his Aesthetics and Metaphysics.

In the introduction to her 1990 work, *Femininity and Domination: Studies in the Phenomenology of Oppression,* Bartky writes of the first meeting of Society for Women in Philosophy in Chicago in 1971 as a life-changing experience in which many women philosophers who had never encountered another female in their field—either as a professor or as a student—were able to come "together in joy and solidarity. We stared at one another and even touched each other, as if we were fabulous beasts." This conference served as the occasion for forging an explicitly feminist philosophy, as well as for the presentation of Bartky's first paper on feminist philosophy, *Toward a Phenomenology of Feminist Consciousness.* This essay would later be published in 1976 in the journal *Social Theory and Practice* and again in her collection *Femininity and Domination.* Bartky states that she "was impelled to write [*Toward a Phenomenology of Feminist Consciousness*] not only in order to make sense of what was happening in my own life but because of practical urgency." This work served to present several of the various areas of feminist theory, as well as arguing for the need for a feminist philosophy.

Bartky brings her training in Phenomenology to bring to bear on the experience of women's oppression, while at the same time calling for a feminist consciousness based on this lived experience. Her goal has been to eradicate women's oppression. While most feminists have focused on gender or class as the sole locus of oppression, Bartky problematizes the notion of oppression under these terms and has been one of the first feminist theorists to recognize that all the structural conditions—among which are race, gender, class, sexual orientation, and age—of a woman's life affect the means through which she is oppressed.

This would be a significant development for feminist theory. Early second-wave feminist theory grounded itself in the perceived shared experiences of women, fearing that differences among women would serve to create a lack of unity, common cause, and strength. Many feminist theorists during this time were educated white women; such "shared experiences" served only to represent *their* experiences of oppression, not the experiences of many less privileged, non-white women. Bartky, in her acknowledgment of this problem, served as an early springboard for the understanding of the multiplicity of women's experiences, an issue that is still of current interest.

Bartky is most well known for her formulation of femininity constructed as primarily a mode of domination. Encompassed in this understanding is a rich and thought-provoking philosophy of the body in which many bodily practices—such as dieting, makeup, and clothing—are put under scrutiny to question their potential as elements of the oppression of women. She uses a Marxist approach to analyze women's emotional care-giving as a mode of domination and alienation similar to the type of domination and alienation of workers in a capitalistic society. Bartky also draws on the work of the French thinker Michel Foucault to argue that the policing gaze of society becomes internalized by women, who then, in turn, begin to self-police. She argues that when women internalize this gaze they begin to become obedient to the patriarchal society and accept its norms for their bodies. They thus try to achieve these norms through diet, exercise, makeup, fashion, etc., and continue to monitor themselves to ascertain their success in living up to or within these norms.

Bartky's other essays on feminist theory include "On Psychological Oppression: Narcissism, Femininity, and Alienation," "Femininity, and the Politics of Personal Transformation," and "Foucault, Femininity, and the Modernization of Patriarchal Power," all previously published. Along with "Toward a Phenomenology of Feminist Consciousness," "Shame and Gender," and "Feeding Egos and Tending Wounds: Deference and Disaffection in Women's Emotional Labor," are included in *Femininity and Domination.*

Her book received so much reaction that a symposium was held by the American Philosophical Association in the year following its 1990 publication. The panel presented papers in which they applauded Bartky's contribution to the understanding of women's oppression; panelists also attempted to draw further conclusions from her work, such as how it might be used to inspire activism as a means to eradicate women's oppression. These papers also served to critique her work. The papers presented during that conference were later collected and published in the feminist philosophy journal *Hypatia.*

Sandra Bartky continues to be an important and active figure in philosophy. Unlike many theorists, she has not lost faith in Marxism's emancipatory and explanatory power. She continues to use Marxist modes of analysis which these modes can be salvaged to further societal reform and enhance feminist theory.

—Nancy McHugh

BEALE, Dorothea

Nationality: British. **Born:** London, 1831. **Education:** Educated at home; attended school in Shalford, Essex; attended lectures at Gresham College; briefly attended finishing school, Paris, France; attended Queen's College, Harley Street. **Career:** Teacher of mathematics, then senior teacher, Queen's College, Harley Street, 1849-57; briefly, headmistress, Clergy Daughters' School, Casterton,

Westmoreland, 1857; principal, Cheltenham Ladies College, 1858-1906; established St. Hilda's College, Cheltenham, 1885, and St. Hilda's Hall, Oxford, 1893; president, Headmistresses' Association, 1875-77; active in women's suffrage movement. **Died:** 1906.

Publications

Political/Social Theory

A Report on the Education of Girls. London, Bell & Daldy, 1866.
Work and Play in Girls' Schools, with Lucy H. M. Sousby and Jane Francis Dove. London and New York, Longmans, 1898.

Literary Criticism

Literary Studies of Poems, New and Old. London, G. Bell & Son, 1902.

Essays

Addresses to Teachers. London and New York, Longmans, 1909.

Other

The Student's Text-book of English and General History. London, Bell & Daldy, 1858; revised edition, 1862.
History of the Cheltenham Ladies' College, 1853-1901. Cheltenham, Cheltenham Ladies' College, 1904.

*

Critical Studies: *Dorothea Beale of Cheltenham* by Elizabeth Raikes, London, A. Constable, 1908; *In the Days of Miss Beale: A Study of Her Work and Influence* by F. Cecily Steadman, London, E. J. Burrows, 1931; *How Different from Us: A Biography of Miss Buss and Miss Beale* by Josephine Kamm, London, Bodley Head, 1958.

* * *

When Dorothea Beale was born in 1831, women's education in England was in a deplorable state. In addition to the widely held belief that it was unnecessary and unwomanly to educate girls, few formal schools existed. Most middle-class girls were taught, if at all, by governesses who were themselves too poorly educated and underpaid to impart much useful knowledge. Rote memorization of facts was the preferred instructional method, and finishing schools for the upper classes did little to prepare girls to be other than useless ornaments. This was all to change during the course of Beale's lifetime. By the time she died in 1906, there had been a revolution in young women's education and Beale stands out as one of the leaders of this movement.

Born into a religious and bookish family, Beale received little formal education herself, but was strongly encouraged to study at home. Largely self-educated, she was a serious, determined, and devout student who even studied Euclid on her own. With the opening of Queen's College in 1848 (begun as a series of lectures intended primarily for governesses), Beale found her calling. After receiving six subject certificates—women could not yet receive degrees—she became a tutor of mathematics and Latin. Staunchly believing in teaching as "divine ministry," she undertook a position first at a Clergy Daughter's School, then as Lady Principal of Cheltenham Ladies' College, where she would remain "married" to the school for the rest of her life.

Unlike her famous contemporary, Frances Mary Buss, it was the education of girls from her own upper-middle class that Beale worked tirelessly to improve. Though she founded two additional teacher training colleges—St. Hilda's College, Cheltenham, and St. Hilda's Hall, Oxford—and later became active in women's suffrage, Beale always thought of women's position in terms of duties rather than rights. Yet judging by the standards of her day, she was a feminist: more conservative that other pioneers in women's education and following patriarchal religious beliefs to the core—teaching Scripture was her favorite subject—she nevertheless strongly believed that girls deserved to be taught to develop their minds to their fullest potential, despite the "subordinate part" she thought they ultimately would play. Her writings are addressed primarily to teachers, and are part of the reform to standardize women's education, but the devoutly serious tone is Dorothea Beale's: her "mission" is evident in every word.

—Christina Boufis

BEARD, Mary Ritter

Nationality: American. **Born:** Indianapolis, Indiana, 5 August 1876. **Education:** De Pauw University, B.A. 1897; studied at Columbia University, 1904. **Family:** Married Charles Austin Beard in 1900 (died 1948), one son and one daughter. **Career:** Taught German in public schools until 1900; organizer for National Women's Trade Union League, 1907; editor, *The Woman Voter,* 1910-12; member of National Woman's Party led by Alice Paul, 1913-19. **Died:** 14 August 1958.

Publications

Nonfiction

Women's Work in Municipalities. New York and London, Appleton, 1915.
A Short History of the American Labor Movement. New York, Harcourt Brace, 1920; as *The American Labor Movement,* New York, Arno Press, 1969.
The Rise of American Civilization, with Charles A. Beard. New York, Macmillan, 1930; revised, 1949; revised and enlarged, 1956.
On Understanding Women. New York and London, Longmans, 1931.
Laughing Their Way: Women's Humor in America, with Martha B. Bruère. N.p., 1934.
America in Midpassage, with Charles A. Beard. New York, Macmillan, 1939.
A Basic History of the United States, with Charles A. Beard. New York, Doubleday, 1944; revised by William Beard, 1968.
Woman as Force in History: A Study in Traditions and Realities. New York, Macmillan, 1946.
The Force of Women in Japanese History. Washington, D.C., Public Affairs Press, 1953.

The Making of Charles A. Beard: An Interpretation, with others. New York, Exposition Press, 1955.

The American Spirit: A Study of the Idea of Civilization in the United States, with Charles A. Beard. New York, Collier, 1962.

Other

A Woman Making History: Mary Ritter Beard through Her Letters, edited by Nancy F. Cott. New Haven, Connecticut, and London, Yale University Press, 1991.

Editor, *America through Women's Eyes.* New York, Macmillan, 1933.

*

Manuscript Collections: Schlesinger Library, Radcliffe College; Smith College, Northampton, Massachusetts.

Critical Studies: *Mary Beard as Force in History* by Barbara K. Turoff, Dayton, Ohio, Wright State University, 1979; *Mary Ritter Beard: A Source Book* by Ann J. Lane, Boston, Northeastern University Press, 1978, 2nd edition, 1988.

* * *

One of the first to actively define and promote "women's history," Mary Ritter Beard had a fairly conventional childhood in a comfortable home in what was then suburban Indianapolis. Her father was a Methodist minister and her well-educated mother had taught school. Beard was 16 when she enrolled at DePauw (then Asbury) University, in nearby Greencastle, where her father had attended college. She would meet her future husband, Charles Austin Beard, at Asbury, where she was an exceptional student and concentrated on political science, languages, and literature.

Graduating in 1897, Beard taught high school German until her marriage in March of 1900. The couple left immediately for England, where Charles was enrolled at Oxford and helping to form a workingmen's branch of the university. Beard, too, became involved in social movements during her stay in England, particularly women's suffrage and women's trade unions.

The Beards had a daughter and returned in 1902 to New York, where a second child, a son, would be born five years later. During the time her children were small, Beard remained socially active: she was involved with protesting the city's infamous Triangle factory fire and helped to organize a women's shirtwaistmakers' strike. She also edited a suffrage newspaper, *The Woman Voter,* from 1910-12 and became involved with a younger, more radical group of women suffragists under the leadership of the radical suffragist Alice Paul.

In 1915 Beard published her first book, *Woman's Work in Municipalities,* followed five years later by her second, *A Short History of the American Labor Movement.* Although both of these volumes were well received, she and her husband are best known for their highly praised and collaborative work in history, *The Rise of American Civilization.* According to historian Nancy Cott, the Beard's work was more attentive to women's roles and contributions than any comparable historical writing. Cott also notes that although it is impossible to separate their individual contributions, most of the credit has traditionally gone to Charles. Despite that, the thesis central to much of his wife's later writing—that women were, in fact, the architects of civilization through their creation of the arts of life and origination of thought about culture—appears in its early form in this work.

In addition to the couple's collaborative work, Beard continued her work into women's roles throughout history. She published work on women's humor, on "understanding" women; indeed, her first full-length argument that woman is the "elemental force" in the rise of civilization was called *On Understanding Women,* published when she was 55 years old. She also spent much time trying to help organize a women's archive, but found herself again disappointed at the reaction of some female university administrators. Beard's belief that women's highest education came from outside the university—that college stifled the imagination—was controversial; in her *Mary Ritter Beard: A Source Book* Ann J. Lane writes that Beard "detested and fought the trap of imitation" which women in colleges seemed to accept.

Beard's most famous—and most criticized—work, *Woman as Force in History,* repeated her contention that women created civilization and argued against the accepted wisdom that women were a subject class as a result of limited political rights. By her work and her life, Mary Ritter Beard was a model for women who wanted a new kind of lifestyle and a more equitable marriage. Although criticized for some of her philosophic stands regarding women's power, she nevertheless refused to accept male-defined standards of success as her guidepost, arguing, instead, that woman-defined standards could be formed when women understood and accepted the realities of their past.

—Ann Mauger Colbert

BEAUCHAMP, Kathleen Mansfield. *See* **MANSFIELD, Katherine.**

BEBEL, (Ferdinand) August

Nationality: German. **Born:** Cologne, 1840. **Education:** Attended school for poor boys, Wetzlar, Prussia. **Career:** Worked as a master turner in Leipsig, c. 1860; joined Industrial Educational Association (radical group); became Marxist socialist; cofounder, with Wilhelm Liebknecht, Saxon People's Party, 1866; elected to Constituent Reichstag of North German Confederation, beginning 1867; cofounder, with Liebknecht, and chief spokesperson for Social Democratic Party, Eisenach, beginning 1869; elected to German Reichstag, beginning 1871; imprisoned twice. Editor, with Liebknecht, of *Vorwärts.* **Died:** Passugg, Switzerland, 1913.

PUBLICATIONS

Political/Social Theory

Der deutsche bauerkrieg mit berücksichtigung der hauptsälichsten sozialen bewegungen des mittelalters. Braunschweig, W. Bracke Jr., 1876.

Die Frau und der Sozialismus. Zürich-Hottingen, Volksbuchhandlung, 1879; 66th edition, Berlin, Deitz, 1990; translated as *Woman in the Past, Present, and Future,* London, Modern Press, 1885; New York, J.W. Lovell, 1886; as *Woman under Socialism,* New York, New York Labor News Press, 1904; as *Woman and Socialism,* 50th Jubilee edition, New York, Socialist Literature Co., 1910; as *Woman: Past, Present, and Future,* New York, Boni & Liveright, 1918; selections published as *Frau und der Sozialismus: Selections,* Moscow, Progress Publishers, 1971.

Charles Fourier, sein leben und seine theorien. Stuttgart, J.H.W. Dietz, 1888; 3rd edition, 1907.

Zur lage der arbeiter in den bäckereien. Stuttgart, J.H.W. Dietz, 1890.

Die sozialdemokratie und das allgemeine stimmrecht. Mit besonderer berüchksichtigung des frauen-stimmrechts und proportional-wahlsystems. Berlin, T. Glocke, 1895.

Speeches of August Bebel. Berlin, n.p., 1926; translated, New York, International Publishers, 1928.

Autobiography

Aus meinem Leben. Stuttgart, J.H.W. Dietz, 3 vols., 1910-14; translated as *Bebel's Reminiscences,* New York, Socialist Literature Company, 1911; abridged as *My Life,* London and Leipzig, T.F. Unwin, 2 vols., 1912.

Other

August Bebels briefwechsel mit Friedrich Engles (letters), edited by Werner Blumenberg. The Hague, Mouton, 1965.

*

Bibliography: In *August Bebel, 1840-1913: ein biographischer Essay* by Dieter Fricke, Jenna, Freidrich-Schiller-Universität, 1989.

Critical Studies: *From Bassermann to Bebel: The Grand Bloc's Quest for Reform in the Kaiserreich, 1900-1914* by Beverly Heckart, New Haven, Yale University Press, 1975; *Women in the German Democratic Republic: On the 100th Anniversary of the Publication of August Bebel's Book "Women and Socialism,"* Dresden, Verlag Zeit im Bild, 1978; *August Bebel, Shadow Emperor of the German Workers* by William Harvey Maehl, Philadelphia, American Philosophical Society, 1980; *Thoughts on Women and Society* by Eleanor Marx-Aveling and Edward Aveling, edited by Joachim Müller and Edith Schotte, New York, International Publishers, 1986.

* * *

A key figure in the German Socialist movement, August Bebel rose from a childhood of poverty to become one of the most influential thinkers of his day. A cofounder, with Wilhelm Liebknecht, of the German Social Democratic Party, Bebel's oratorical gifts made him a political figurehead amid the rising tide of Marxism that swept the unified German states after the Austro-Prussian war of 1866.

Born in Cologne in 1840, Bebel was the son of a Prussian petty officer who died when August was a young boy. After obtaining a rudimentary education at a school for impoverished boys in Wetzlar, he apprenticed as a turner, a vocation that ultimately led him to settle in Leipsig in 1860. Living in the hub of German political activity, Bebel quickly became involved in politics, joining the radical Gewerblicher Bildungsverein (Industrial Educational Association, or IEA) and becoming immersed in the study of European political, social, and economic history. He also studied the works of Lassalle and, with the encouragement of fellow IEA member Liebknecht, those of Karl Marx and Friederich Engels. Marx, particularly, would be a major influence on Bebel's growing socialist beliefs.

A commanding speaker, Bebel attained prominence as a leader in labor circles, and later, in the realm of politics. From his election to the North German Constituent Reichstag in 1867 as a representative of his own Saxon People's Party, he would go on to represent Dresden and, later, Hamburg, in the German Reichstag. A founder, with Liebknecht, of the German Social Democratic Party and instrumental in aligning it with other social reform factions, Bebel, by the time of his death in 1913, had become a cornerstone of the growing Social Democratic movement.

As a social democrat, Bebel believed that the social change he viewed as necessary could best be achieved through the reform of existing social and political structures, rather than by the revolutionary tactics that would later be advocated by Lenin. *Woman and Socialism,* published as *Die Frau und der Sozialismus* in 1879, was an outgrowth of such beliefs, an attempt to mobilize an existing women's movement under the banner of socialism.

Basing his work on the central tenet of Marxism—that political and social structures are determined by the economic conditions of *all* people—Bebel maintained that the antagonisms between women of different social classes were diminished due to more pressing common interests; that both laboring women and the well-heeled wives of the bourgeois class, although they might "march in separate armies ... may strike a united blow" in their fight for social, economic, and political equality. The aims of the bourgeois suffrage movement—gaining a "complete civic equality" that focused on higher education, professional careers, and the right to hold public office—would do nothing to ameliorate the underlying cause of women's historic inequality: a social order institutionalizing a "wage slavery" that forced proletarian women to endure "physical and mental degeneration" and the "sex slavery" that masquerades under the name of marriage.

For Bebel, of course, the cause of female equality was secondary to the class struggle; indeed, *Women and Socialism* can be viewed as a shrewd piece of political propaganda aimed at a female audience. The "duty of the proletarian woman to join the men of her class in the struggle for a thorough-going transformation of society, to bring about an order that by its social institutions will enable both sexes to enjoy complete economic and intellectual independence"—in other words, to work with men towards the abolishment of capitalism—overshadows the work.

Gaining additional popularity after the formation of the Second International in Paris in 1889, August Bebel's tract has been widely read throughout Western Europe and in the United States. It has undergone numerous translations and has been reprinted countless times; although the inclusion of now-outdated statistical data has rendered portions of the work obsolete, abridged versions of *Women and Socialism* are still read and studied by those seeking to abolish, as Bebel would note, "all barriers that make one human being dependent upon another."

—Pamela Kester-Shelton

BEER, Patricia

Nationality: British. **Born:** Exmouth, Devonshire, 4 November 1924. **Education:** Attended University of Exeter; University of London, B.A. (with honors); St. Hugh's College, Oxford, B.Litt. **Family:** Married the architect John Damien Parsons in 1964. **Career:** Lecturer in English at University of Padua, Italy, 1946-48, British Institute, Rome, 1948, and Ministero Aeronautica, Rome, 1950; senior lecturer, University of London, Goldmith's College, 1962-68; poet and writer, beginning 1968. Contributor to periodicals, including *Listener, London Review of Books, New Statesman, Sunday Times* (London), and *Time & Tide.* **Address:** 1 Oak Hill Park, London NW3, England; Tiphayes, Up Ottery, Near Honiton, Devon, England.

Publications

Novel

Moon's Ottery. London, Hutchinson, 1978.

Literary Criticism

An Introduction to the Metaphysical Poets. London, Rowman & Littlefield, 1972.

Reader, I Married Him: A Study of the Woman Characters of Jane Austen, Charlotte Brontë, Elizabeth Gaskell, and George Eliot. New York, Barnes & Noble, 1974.

Poetry

Loss of the Magyar and Other Poems. London, Longmans Green, 1959.

The Surviviors. London, Longmans Green, 1963.

Just like the Resurrection. London, Macmillan, and Chester Springs, Pennsylvania, Dufour, 1967.

The Postilion Has Been Struck by Lightening. London, Macmillan, 1967.

The Estuary. London, Macmillan, 1971.

Spanish Balcony. London, Poem-of-the-Month Club, 1973.

Driving West. London, Gollancz, 1975.

Selected Poems. London, Hutchinson, 1975.

The Lie of the Land. London, Hutchinson, 1983.

Collected Poems. Manchester, Carcanet, 1988.

Friend of Heraclitus. Manchester, Carcanet, 1993.

Plays

The Enterprise of England (produced Up Ottery, Devon, 1979).

Radio Play: *Pride, Prejudice, and the Woman Question,* 1975.

Autobiography

Mrs. Beer's House. London, Macmillan, 1968.

Other

Editor, with Ted Hughes and Vernon Scannell, *New Poems 1962: A PEN Anthology of Contemporary Poetry.* London, Hutchinson, and New York, Transatlantic, 1962.

Editor, *New Poems 1975: A PEN Anthology of Contemporary Poetry,* London, Hutchinson, 1975.

Editor, with Kevin Crossley-Holland, *New Poetry 2: An Anthology.* London, Arts Council of Great Britain, 1976.

Recordings: *Patricia Beer Reading Her Poems with Comment,* 1983.

*

Critical Studies: *British Poetry Since 1960: A Critical Survey,* edited by Michael Schmidt and Grevel Lindop, Chatham, W. & J. Mackay, 1972; *British Poetry 1964 to 1984: Driving through the Barricades* by Martin Booth, London, Routledge & Kegan Paul, 1985; "Patricia Beer" by Caroline L. Cherry, in *Dictionary of Literary Biography,* Vol. 40: *Poets of Great Britain and Ireland since 1960,* Detroit, Gale, 1985.

* * *

Patricia Beer, a consistently productive writer since the 1950s in several genres—primarily poetry—does not fit neatly under any label, including feminist. However, her concerns center on aspects of the human condition fundamental to women as well as men, and her major book of criticism is a sensible assessment of feminist issues in four 19th-century women novelists.

Although apolitical, Beer's work resonates with the female literary tradition. The details of home and family often form a vehicle for her perceptions; as in such typical titles as "Kitchen Calendar," "The Cat in the Tree," and "Farmhouse Time." Running through these is a desire for belonging, for rootedness in the land, in relationships, and in a spiritual dimension; she sees home in its many senses as a basic human need. Dependable love is another such need; it appears in her writing both in its absence and presence. Beer has dedicated several of her volumes to her husband, whom she married in 1964.

This element has occasionally led critics to regard her work as tame. Martin Booth, for instance, notes in her poetry the "security that chauvinists might say is typical of women who are happy and safe in a home, a marriage and a round of life in which they know themselves." Beer's tone, however, is not cozy but ranges from the pithily insightful to the fierce: "The Witch," a creature reminiscent of Sylvia Plath's fury, threatens:

> I shall see justice done
> Whenever the homeward bound
> Mistake their true home....
> Never shall bogus love—
> Habit, duty or weakness—
> Win any mercy from me.

The dominant themes of Beer's poetry include death, time, loss, and the persistence of existence after death. She traces these themes in daily life, in nature, and in history and literature. An unsentimental nostalgia tinges many of her poems, an awareness of the discrepancy between how things are and how they were or might have been. Balancing this is her rootedness in the value of ordinary experience, in relationships and the attachments that tie us to this world. Her stance is often ironic or whimsical; she sees humor in life and death, and is fascinated by the eerie, the supernatural, and the magical. These qualities combine to form a quirkily mordant view sometimes compared with that of her friend Stevie Smith. For example, the title of Beer's third volume of poetry alludes to the well-dressed attenders of a church concert who have wandered into the graveyard and stand among the tombstones looking "just like the resurrection."

Her voice is generally restrained, though both terror and a desire for "a hailstorm of grace" ("Poem Found in a Modern Church," in *Friend of Heraclitus*) lurk beneath the surface calm. In "Mighty, Mighty Witches. Salem. Mass.," the witches suggest a feminist image of the disruptive power of resistance and inspiration:

For recently I saw them flying in
Over the ocean, beautiful as saints,
Coming to me, not just to everyone.
Yes, witches, and yes, mighty more than once.

Much of Beer's material is colored by her childhood in Exmouth and Torquay, Devonshire, particularly her family situation, her religious upbringing, and the rural landscape and customs. In her autobiography, she describes her parents' sometimes tense marriage and her mother's sudden death when Beer was 14; her awareness of family and her relationship with her frustrated, ambitious mother, in life and in death, has touched her work. In "The Lost Woman" (*The Lie of the Land*), "The ivy-mother turned into a tree/That still hops away like a rainbow down/The avenue as I approach./My tendrils are the ones that clutch." All poets have "a lost woman to haunt the home,"

But my lost woman evermore snaps
From somewhere else: 'You did not love me.
I sacrificed too much perhaps,
I showed you the way to rise above me
And you took it. You are the ghost
With the bat-voice, my dear. I am not lost.'

Her mother's firmly held religious tradition was Plymouth Brethren, a fundamentalist group stressing salvation through the blood of Christ and separation from the world, with a marked disdain for non-believers, useless education, and worldly pleasures. The enclosed fellowship of this group provided much of the social life and worldview of Beer's childhood; she began to question them only in her teens. The influence of this religious fellowship persisted in many forms; their vivid accounts of Hell, for instance, perhaps fed into her later poetry of the afterlife, while their comforting certainty of salvation lurks behind the poet's adult need to find an acceptance and certainty in which she can believe.

Another influence was education. Beer's mother, a former schoolteacher, had a high regard for education as a means of advancement, and although contemporary literature was almost unknown in their world, her father respected such traditional giants as Shakespeare and Milton. Beer excelled in academics, eventually obtaining a B.Litt. from Oxford and becoming a teacher, first in Italy (which gave her, among other things, an objective sense of the English language as she taught it to others) and later at Goldsmith's College in London. Her immersion in literary tradition produced not only *Reader, I Married Him*, her critical study of "how women and their situation were depicted in certain English novels of the past," but has also provided material for poetry, evident in such titles as "Jane Austen at the Window," "Transvestitism and the Novels of Charlotte Brontë," and in her tribute to Dorothy Wordsworth walking with her brother and Coleridge in "The Woods near Alfoxden": "All three noticed the same leaf, and they/Wrote several lines about it. She wrote one."

Beer's work is characterized by a taut economy of words, a keen visual perception, and a strong sense of form; her prosody includes traditional meters, syllabics, and free verse. Critics have sometimes found in her analogies with Emily Dickinson and Marianne Moore, and have placed her in the company of her respected contemporaries Elizabeth Jennings and Fleur Adcock, but in general, she says, "I have never been accused of imitating any particular poet." In 1970 she remarked that the poets she most admired were Yeats, Robert Lowell, and Ted Hughes.

Beer's interest in history, her insight into women, and her love of her native Devonshire are brought together in her novel *Moon's Ottery* (1968), set in a Devon village in 1557-1559, against the backdrop of the passing of the Armada and the Spanish threat. The protagonist is a literarily inclined farmer's daughter who, like Beer herself, is exiled prematurely from the security of childhood by the sudden death of her "young and spirited" but acerbic mother. A pair of white witches, a jovial squire's wife, and a beautiful sister enrich the picture of women in Elizabethan times.

Beer's writing has been consistently well-received since 1958, when she won a prize at the Cheltenham Festival of Art and Literature for "The Loss of the Magyar." In the 1960s she was added to the list of "Macmillan Poets" by one of the most prominent British presses supporting contemporary poetry. In 1968 she retired from teaching to write full time. The dominant critical reception has consistently recognized the strength of her vision and the discipline of her technique; Patricia Beer's place in 20th-century British literature seems assured.

—Caroline Lockett Cherry

BEHN, Aphra

Pseudonym: Astrea. **Nationality:** British. **Born:** Wye, Kent, 1640. **Family:** Married the merchant Behn c. 1664 (died c. 1670). **Career:** Raised in Surinam; returned to England, 1663; political spy for the King of England, Antwerp, 1666; imprisoned for debt upon return to England, 1667; full-time writer and translator of works from French and Latin, beginning 1669. **Died:** 1689; buried in Westminster Abbey.

Publications

Novels

Love Letters between a Nobleman and His Sister. London, R. Taylor, 1684; sections published as *The Amours of Philander and Silvia,* London, n.p., 1687; as *Loveletters from a Nobleman to His Sister,* edited by M. Duffy, London, Virago, 1987.

La Montre; or, The Lover's Watch. London, W. Canning, 1686.

The Fair Jilt. 1688; with *The Royal Slave* as *Two Tales,* London, Folio Society, 1953.

Oroonoko; or, The Royal Slave. London, W. Canning, 1688; as *The History of Oroonoko,* 1759; expanded and edited by Montague Summers as *Oroonoko and Other Prose Narratives,* New York, B. Blom, 1967.

The Lucky Mistake. London, R. Bentley, 1689.
The Lady's Looking-Glass, to Dress Herself By; or, The Whole Art of Charming. London, S. Briscoe, 1697.
The Novels of Mrs. Aphra Behn. London, Routledge and Sons, 1905; New York, Dutton, 1913.
Oroonoko and Other Stories, edited by Maureen Duffy. London, Methuen, 1986.

Poetry

Poems on Several Occasions, with A Voyage to the Island of Love. London, J. Tonson, 1684.
Miscellany, with others. London, J. Hindmarsh, 1685.
A Pindarick on the Death of Our Late Sovereign. London, H. Playford, 1685.
A Pindarick Poem on the Happy Coronation of His ... Majesty James II and His Illustrious Consort Queen Mary. London, J. Playford, 1685.
A Poem Humbly Dedicated to the Great Patern of Piety and Virtue Catherine Queen Dowager, on the Death of Her Dear Lord ... King Charles II. London, J. Playford, 1685.
Two Congratulatory Poems to Their Most Sacred Majesties. The First, Occasioned on the Universal Hopes of All Loyal Persons for a Prince of Wales. The Second, on the Happy Birth of the Prince. London, W. Canning, 1688.
Lycidus; or, The Lover in Fashion, with others. London, J. Knight and F. Saunders, 1688.
A Congratulatory Poem to Her Sacred Majesty Queen Mary, upon Her Arrival in England. London, W. Canning, 1689.
A Pindarick Poem to the Reverend Doctor Burnett, on the Honor He Did Me of Enquiring After Me and My Muse. London, R. Bentley, 1689.
The Uncollected Verse of Aphra Behn, edited by Germaine Greer. Stump Cross, Essex, Stump Cross Books, 1989.
Selected Poems, edited by Malcolm Hicks. Manchester, England, Fyfield, 1993.

Plays

The Forc'd Marriage; or, The Jealous Bridegroom (produced London, 1670). London, J. Knapton, 1688.
The Amorous Prince, or, The Curious Husband (produced London, 1671). London, T. Dring, 1671.
The Dutch Lover (produced London, 1673). London, T. Dring, 1673.
Abdelazar, or The Moor's Revenge (produced London, 1676). London, J. Magnes and R. Bentley, 1677.
The Town Fop; or, Sir Timothy Tawdrey (produced London, 1676). London, J. Tonson, 1677.
The Rover; or, The Banish't Cavaliers (produced London, 1677). London, J. Amery, 1677; edited by Frederick M. Link, Lincoln, University of Nebraska Press, 1967; edited by Jane Spencer, Oxford, Oxford University Press, 1995.
Sir Patient Fancy (produced London, 1678). London, J. Tonson, 1678.
The Feign'd Curtizans; or, A Night's Intrigue (produced London, 1678). London, J. Tonson, 1679.
The Second Part of The Rover (produced London, 1681). London, J. Tonson, 1681; edited by Frederick M. Link, Nebraska University Press, 1967.
The False Count; or, A New Way to Play an Old Game (produced London, 1682). London, J. Tonson, 1682.
The Roundheads; or, The Good Old Cause (produced London, 1682). London, D. Brown, 1682.
The City Heiress; or, Sir Timothy Treat-all (produced London, 1682). London, D. Brown, 1682; as *A Critical Old-spelling Edition of Aphra Behn's The City Heiress,* New York, Garland, 1987.
The Young King; or, The Mistake (produced London, 1683). London, D. Brown, 1683.
The Lucky Chance; or, An Alderman's Bargain (produced London, 1686). London, W. Canning, 1687; critical edition by Jean A. Coakley, New York, Garland, 1987.
The Emperor of the Moon (produced London, 1687). London, J. Knight and F. Saunders, 1688.
The Fair Jilt; or, The History of Prince Tarquin and Miranda (produced London, 1688). London, Will. Canning, 1688.
The Widow Ranter; or, The History of Bacon in Virginia (produced London, 1689). London, J. Knapton, 1690; critical edition edited by Aaron R. Walden, New York and London, Garland, 1993.
The History of the Nun; or, The Fair Vow-breaker. London, A. Baskervile, 1689.
The Younger Brother; or, The Amorous Jilt (produced London, 1695). London, J. Harris, 1696.
Five Plays, edited by Maureen Duffy. London, Methuen Drama, 1990.

Other

All the Histories and Novels Written by the Late Ingenious Mrs. Behn. London, S. Briscoe, 1696; 8th edition as *The Plays, Histories, and Novels of the Ingenious Mrs. Aphra Behn,* London, J. Pearson, 1871.
The Works of Aphra Behn, edited by Montague Summers. London, Heinemann, 6 vols., 1915; New York, Phaeton Press, 1967.
The Complete Works of Aphra Behn, edited by Janet Todd. Columbus, Ohio State University, and London, Pickering and Chatto, 7 vols., 1992-95.
Oroonoko and Other Writings, edited by Paul Salzman. Oxford and New York, Oxford University Press, 1994.

Translator, *Aesop's Fables: in English, French and Latin.* London, n.p., 1687.
Translator, *Agnes de Castro; or, The Force of Generous Love,* from the French by J. B. de Brilhac. London, n.p., 1688.
Translator, *A Discovery of New Worlds,* from the French of Bernard le Bovier de Fontenell. London, 1688.
Translator, *The History of Oracles,* from the French of Bernard le Bovier de Fontenell. London, 1688; as *The History of Oracles and the Chests of the Pagan Priests,* 1699.
Translator, with others, *The Works of Mr. Abraham Cowley.* London, n.p., 1693.
Translator, with others, *A Week's Conversation on the Plurality of Worlds,* from the French of Bernard le Bovier de Fontenell. London, n.p., 1737.

*

Media Adaptations: *Abdelazer; or, The Moor's Revenge* (suite for strings) by Henry Purcell; *An Adaptation of the Rovers* (revised for Royal Shakespeare Company), London, Methuen, 1986; *Aphra Behn: Dispatch'd from Athole: The Journal of Aphra Behn's Secret Mission to Scotland in 1689* (novel) by Ross Laidlaw, Nairn, Scotland, Balnain, 1992.

Bibliography: *Aphra Behn: An Annotated Bibliography of Primary and Secondary Sources* by Mary Ann O'Donnell, New York, Garland, 1986.

Critical Studies: *Aphra Behn, the Incomparable Astrea* by Vita Sackville-West, New York, Russell and Russell, 1927; *Aphra Behn* by Frederick M. Link, New York, Twayne, 1968; *The Passionate Shepherdess: Aphra Behn 1640-89* by Maureen Duffy, New York, Discus, and London, Cape, 1977; *Reconstructing Aphra: A Social Biography of Aphra Behn* by Angeline Goreau, Oxford, Oxford University Press, and New York, Dial Press, 1980; *Women of Ideas and What Men Have Done to Them: From Aphra Behn to Adrienne Rich* by Dale Spender, London, Routledge and Kegen Paul, 1982; *Four Restoration Playwrights: A Reference Guide to Thomas Shadwell, Aphra Behn, Nathaniel Lee, and Thomas Otway* by J. M. Armistead, Boston, G. K. Hall, 1984; *The Rise of the Woman Novelist: From Aphra Behn to Jane Austen* by Jane Spencer, New York, Blackwell, 1986; *The Mental World of Stuart Women: Three Studies* by Sara Heller Mendelson, Amherst, University of Massachusetts Press, 1987; *The New Eighteenth Century: Theory, Politics, English Literature* edited by Laura Brown and Felicity Nussbaum, New York, Methuen, 1987; *The Prostituted Muse: Images of Women and Women Dramatists, 1642-1737* by Jacqueline Pearson, New York, St. Martin's Press, 1988; *The Sign of Angellica: Women, Writing, and Fiction, 1660-1800* by Janet Todd, New York, Columbia University Press, 1989; "Women Becoming Poets: Katherine Philips, Aphra Behn, Anne Finch" by Dorothy Mermin, *in English Literary History* 57(2), summer 1990; "Aphra Behn and the Genealogy of the Man of Feeling" by G. A. Starr, in *Modern Philology* 87(4), May 1990; "The Political Possibilities of Desire: Teaching the Erotic Poems of Behn" by Carol Barash, in *Teaching 18th-Century Poetry*, edited by Christopher Fox, New York, AMS, 1990; "Gender and Narrative in the Fiction of Aphra Behn, I and II" by Jacqueline Pearson, in *Review of English Studies* 42(165-66), February and May 1991; "'That Which I Dare Not Name': Aphra Behn's 'The Willing Mistress'" by Bernard Duylhuizen, in *English Literary History,* 58(1), spring 1991; "Reworking Male Models: Aphra Behn's *Fair Vow-Breaker,* Eliza Haywood's *Pantomina,* and Charlotte Lennox's *Female Quixote*" by Catherine A. Craft, in *The Modern Language Review,* 86(4), October 1991; *Curtain Calls: British and American Women and the Theater, 1660-1820* edited by Mary Anne Schofield and Cecilia Macheski, Athens, Ohio University Press, 1991; "A Verse Miscellany of Aphra Behn: Bodleian Library MS Firth c. 18" by Mary Ann O'Donnell, in *English Manuscript Studies, 1100-1700,* 2, 1992; "Seizing the Means of Seduction: Fiction and Feminine Identity in Aphra Behn and Delarivier Manley" by Ros Ballaster, in *Women, Writing, History 1640-1740,* edited by Isobel Grundy and Susan Wiseman, Athens, University of Georgia Press, 1992; "Oroonoko: Birth of a Paradigm" by Moira Ferguson, in *New Literary History* 23(2), spring 1992; "New Hystericism: Aphra Behn's *Oroonoko:* The Body, the Text and the Feminist Critic" by Ballaster, in *New Feminist Discourses: Critical Essays on Theories and Texts*, edited by Isobel Armstrong, London, Routledge, 1992; "'Once a Whore and Ever?': Whore and Virgin in *The Rover* and Its Antecedents" by Nancy Copeland, in *Restoration* 18(1), spring 1992; "Aphra Behn, Gender, and Pastoral" by Elizabeth V. Young, in *Studies in English Literature*, 33(3), summer 1993; "Mrs. A. Behn and the Myth of Oroonoko-Imoinda" by Robert A. Erickson, in *18th-Century Fiction*, 5(3), 1993; *Rereading Aphra Behn: History, Theory and Criticism* edited by Holly Hutner, Charlotte, University Press of Virginia, 1993; "'Night Mares of the Commonwealth'"; Royalist Passion and Female Ambition in Aphra Behn's *The Roundheads*" by Elizabeth Bennett Kubek, in *Restoration* 17(2), fall 1993; "Oroonoko's Gendered Economics of Honor/Horror: Reframing Colonial Discourse Studies in the Americas" by Stephanie Athey and Daniel Cooper Alarcon, in *American Literature* 65(3), September 1993.

* * *

Aphra Behn, the first female professional writer in England, wrote plays, fiction, and poems. To each genre she brought a new female-centered perspective and used new rhetorical strategies to express that point of view. Her many contributions to feminist thought center on her literary portrayal of autonomous women who think, feel, plan, act, and talk for themselves. At a time when women were conventionally depicted as two-dimensional props for men, Behn's female characters exhibited complex personalities and lives of their own, and reflected Behn's own interests in women working together to better their lives.

Behn's plays were written to be performed in the London theatre in the 1670s and 1680s. The English theatre had reopened in 1660, with women playing parts for the first time. Behn's many contributions to the development of the remarkable drama of the period include writing large and central roles for the actresses in the theatre companies, and for making them more than pretty faces. Among her most famous and enduring comedies, *The Rover*—which is still performed in repertory today—presents women who use their wits, social standing, and sex appeal to contend with the social restrictions regarding their marital status, their economic and moral values, and their place and involvement in the world.

Revealing four different levels of female autonomy in *The Rover*—aristocratic and obedient Florinda, her sister the feisty Hellena, the proud but poor courtesan Angellica, and the desperate, depraved prostitute Lucetta—Behn shows the complex relationship among such factors as social networks and economic class, intellect, self-confidence, and self-control in women's lives. Both Hellena and Angellica recognize the limitations in their lives and strive to manipulate their circumstances to improve their chances of happiness and security. Hellena disparages a traditional "good" or economically profitable marriage: "[the husband] expects you in his foul sheets; and ere you can get yourself undressed, calls you with a snore or two.... And this you must submit to for threescore years, and all for a jointure," and then later defines how her marriage will and won't operate by vowing that she will "find out all your haunts, to rail at you to all that love you, till I have made you love only me in your own defense, because nobody else will love you." Angellica determines her own value in economic terms, only to lose herself emotionally:

> Oh, name not such mean trifles [as 500 crowns]! Had I given
> Him all my youth has earned from sin,
> I had not lost a thought or sigh upon't.
> But I have given him my eternal rest,
> My whole repose, my future joys, my heart!
> My virgin heart!

Behn's fiction, written approximately 30 years before the so-called first English novel, Defoe's *Robinson Crusoe*, follows many of the conventions of French romances, but Behn's female characters are, again, fleshed out and placed in more central and complex roles. Thus in *Oroonoko*, her novella about an enslaved African prince Oroonoko and his wife, Imoinda, Behn establishes the nexus of race, class, and gender: Imoinda is initially acted upon by men and colonists, then creates her own identity and meaning as a warrior and a martyr. Behn's female narrator, a colonial Englishwoman, is both observer-recorder and participant in the action: a seemingly confusing but structurally important role that highlights the conflicts among race (black African, white colonists, aboriginal Indians), class (enslaved prince), and gender (warrior woman, writing woman, helpless male slave).

In her lengthy epistolary novel, *Love Letters between a Nobleman and His Sister*, Behn explores further the power in categories such as class and gender. At one level a complicated political allegory about the Exclusion Crisis, the novel is also an examination of the relationship between female virtue and female power. The main character, Sylvia, degenerates in the course of the novel from a socially noble woman to a liar, thief, prostitute, and male impersonator; she wields power in a corrupt society. The female heroine, Calista, resists temptation and corruption, but has no earthly power beyond her virtue. The novel emphasizes the danger of false appearances and deceit, and in so doing advocates a reassessment of women's roles: women can be honest, Behn argues, and they ought to be rewarded for honesty and penalized for deception.

Behn's poems focus largely on the need for women to resist the patriarchal authority that defines female virtue. In "The Golden Age," Behn shows how the construct of feminine honor or sexual purity, serves to repress women and reinforce men's control of sexual activity. In "The Disappointment," irony underscores the injustice of men's assumed sexual supremacy. In her pastoral poems and elegies, Behn asserts her own authority as a writer and defines poetry as communication rather than the traditional male model of competition. In her poetic translations, Behn retells classical stories and subtly revises the perspective by making the speaker either androgynous or female.

In all her writing, Aphra Behn establishes a clear and powerful female voice—a remarkable achievement for the first woman to make her living by her pen. And in creating a strong female voice, Behn is able to reveal and develop the multiple, complex, and essential roles that women have always performed at home, in the local community and for the larger culture.

—Elizabeth V. Young

BERAN, J. *See* **H.D.**

BERNARD, Jessie

Nationality: American. **Born:** Jessie Shirley Ravich, Minneapolis, Minnesota, 8 June 1903. **Education:** University of Minnesota, B.A. 1923, M.A. 1924; Washington University, Ph.D. 1935. **Family:** Married Luther Lee Bernard in 1925 (died 1951); three children. **Career:** Statistical analyst, 1938-40; professor of sociology, Lindenwood College, St. Charles, Missouri, 1940-47; professor of sociology, 1947-64, honorary research scholar since 1964, Pennsylvania State University. Visiting professor, Princeton University; visited Europe, 1951; delegate, White House Conference on Youth, 1971; visiting research scholar, National Institute for Education, U.S. Department of Health, Education, and Welfare, 1974-75; scholar-in-residence, U.S. Commission on Civil Rights, 1975-76; member of advisory board, International Institute of Womens Studies. **Awards:** Pennsylvania State University Press for Academic Women award, 1964; Eastern Sociological Society Merit award, 1971; National Council on Family Relations' E.W. Burgess Research Award, 1972; Society for Psychological Study of Social Studies' Kurt Lewin Award, 1976; American Association of University Women Outstanding Achievement award, 1976. Distinguished alumni awards: Washington University, 1966; University of Minnesota, 1972; Pennsylvania State University, 1976. **Member:** American Sociological Society, Eastern Sociological Society, Sociologists for Women in Society, Sigma Xi, Phi Beta Kappa, Pi Gamma Mu, Alpha Kappa Delta. **Address:** 4200 Cathedral Ave N.W., Washington, D.C., 20016, U.S.A.

Publications

Political/Social Theory

Sociology and the Study of International Relations, with Luther Lee Bernard. Washington University Studies, 1934.

American Family Behavior. New York and London, Harper, 1942.

Origins of American Sociology, with Luther Lee Bernard. New York, Russell & Russell, 1943.

American Community Behavior: An Analysis of Problems Confronting American Communities Today. New York, Dryden Press, 1949; revised, New York, Holt Rinehart, 1962.

Remarriage: A Study of Marriage. New York, Dryden Press, 1956.

Social Problems at Midcentury: Role, Status, and Stress in a Context of Abundance. New York, Dryden Press, 1957.

Academic Women. University Park, Pennsylvania State University Press, 1964.

Marriage and Family among Negroes. Englewood Cliffs, New Jersey, Prentice-Hall, 1966.

Dating, Mating, and Marriage: A Documentary-Case Approach, with Helen E. Buchanan and William M. Smith Jr. Cleveland, Ohio, H. Allen, 1958; second edition, New York, Arco, 1959.

An Introduction to Sociology and Social Problems, with Lida Thompson. St. Louis, Missouri, Mosby, and London, Kimpton, n.d.; ninth edition as *Sociology: Nurses and Their Patients in a Modern Society*, 1966.

The Sex Game. Englewood Cliffs, New Jersey, Prentice-Hall, 1968; London, Frewin, 1969.

Women and the Public Interest: An Essay on Policy and Protest. Chicago, Aldine, 1971.

The Future of Marriage. New York, World, 1972; London, Souvenir Press, 1973; second edition, New Haven, Connecticut, and London, Yale University Press, 1982.

The Sociology of Community. Glenview, Illinois, Scott Foresman, 1973.

The Future of Motherhood. New York, Dial Press, 1974; as *The Future of Parenthood*, London, Calder & Boyars, 1975.

Women, Wives, Mothers: Values and Options. Chicago, Aldine, 1975.

The Female World. New York, Free Press, and London, Collier Macmillan, 1981.

The Female World from a Global Perspective. Bloomington, Indiana University Press, 1987.

Other

Self-Portrait of a Family: Letters by Jessie, Dorothy Lee, Claude, and David Bernard. Boston, Beacon Press, 1978.

Editor, with Carlfred B. Broderick, *The Individual, Sex and Society.* Baltimore, Johns Hopkins Press, 1969.

Editor, with Jean Lipman-Blumen, *Sex Roles and Social Policy: A Complex Social Science Equation.* Beverly Hills and London, Sage, 1979.

*

Critical Studies: "Jessie Bernard: An Appreciation" by Muriel G. Cantor, in *Gender and Society,* 2(3), September 1988; *Jessie Bernard: The Making of a Feminist* by Robert C. Bannister, Rutgers University Press, 1991; "Jessie Bernard: The Unfolding of the Female World" by Harriet Howe and M.G. Cantor, in *Sociological Inquiry* (Austin, Texas), 64(1), February 1994.

* * *

Jessie Bernard's influential career in sociology has spanned more than 60 years. Surprisingly, her significant feminist writings did not occur until well after her 60th birthday. While always interested in issues surrounding family and motherhood, her career began as a traditional social scientist who migrated from positivist to functionalist, only to embrace a feminist position well into her seventh decade.

Bernard was born to Rumanian-Jewish immigrant parents in Minneapolis. She entered the University of Minnesota at the age of 16 to study sociology and economics. She became a research assistant for Luther Lee Bernard, a sociology professor. They were married five years later. After completing her Ph.D. at Washington University in St. Louis, she co-authored *Sociology and the Study of International Relations* (1934) and *Origins of American Sociology* (1943) with her husband.

Bernard began her career-long interest in the study of marriage, motherhood, family and work with the publication of *American Family Behavior* (1942). Although this and other works through out the '40s and '50s were traditional in scope and method, as early as *American Family Behavior* Bernard began exploring the position of women within families and marriage. For example, she was among the first researchers to discuss the ways in which role expectations for women might cause distress among housewives due to isolation. This "role strain," and the desire to resist it brought women into conflict with themselves and their husbands.

Academic Women (1964), a study of women's marginal position within academia, was one of the first works to openly document the differences in pay, advancement, and working conditions for men and women. It is also the book that marked the beginning of Bernard's move toward a feminist model. Nevertheless, *Academic Women* was criticized for failing to confront the issue of discrimination directly. In *Self-Portrait of a Family,* Bernard's volume of letters between her children and herself, she describes the "intellectual shakedown" that occurred soon after *Academic Women* was published:

> As an inhabitant of what came derisively to be know as the "sociological ghetto" relegated to women—the study of marriage, family, community—I had spent considerable amount of time studying women in their institutional relationships. But I had never seen them from the newly emerging feminist perspective. I had accepted the male-delineated perspective of my colleagues. Although *Academic Women* had dealt with discrimination against women it had not probed deeply enough.

The ramifications of this shakedown are evident in *Women and the Public Interest: An Essay on Policy and Protest* (1971), where Bernard asserts that not only is discrimination present and widespread but also that it poses a threat to the public interest.

Her continued movement toward feminism is evident in each of her succeeding works. In *The Future of Marriage* (1973) Bernard clearly argues that, within each marriage, two "marriages" are present simultaneously: one for the man and another for the woman. In their 1994 review of Bernard's works for *Sociological Inquiry,* Harriet Howe and Muriel Cantor contend that *Future of a Marriage* "clarified and precipitated alterations in attitudes by presenting an entirely new way of looking at marriage." In her study, Bernard found that marriage was a positive experience for men. Compared to their single counterparts, married men lived longer and had greater feelings of well-being. The opposite was true for women; the single woman had an increased sense of well-being than her married sisters. She analyzes women's perceptions of marriage as distinct and separate from the male or husband realm. In a similar manner, Bernard went on to explore perceptions of motherhood in *The Future of Motherhood* (1974). Yet, as with much of the feminist literature of the time, Bernard universalizes all women from the experience of white women, leaving the impression that this experience the only one, or at the very least the only one that should be documented.

By the time Bernard published the now classic *The Female World* in 1981, her writing was quite explicit concerning a female outlook distinct from the universalized male experience, the role of power in women's lives, and how this affected public and social policy. Her policy solutions lean toward the more moderate; she advocates equal protection and opportunity for women, increased sharing of housework and better child care. Bernard's latest book, *The Female World from a Global Perspective* (1987) moves the theories of *The Female World* forward in an attempt to apply them outside of Western feminism.

Not only have Jesse Bernard's writings contributed to the field of sociology, she has also served on the boards of community groups such as the Urban Institute, and played a leading role in the development of Sociologists for Women in Society. Two generations of academics and others speak of the countless hours Bernard has spent during her long career, acting as a personal mentor and role model to many. In the introduction to the special issue of *Gender and Society* dedicated to Bernard and her work, Muriel Cantor relates how upon meeting Bernard she asked Jesse if she would speak to her class. "When she said yes, it was the beginning for me of both personal and professional change.... The support I received from Jesse enabled me to change my self-concept.... Not only was I introduced to the ideas that were to influence my work on popular culture... I [also] had the advantages of her insights and advice about the politics of academic life and the importance of continuing one's own work regardless of the slings and arrows from one's associates. Because of her," writes Cantor, "I became enlightened about the feminist revolution in progress."

—Lisa W. Loutzenheiser

BINGZHI. *See* **DING LING.**

BLAIS, Marie-Claire

Nationality: Canadian. **Born:** Quebec City, Québec, 5 October 1939. **Education:** Couvent Saint-Roch de Québec, until 1956; attended secretarial school; studied French literature at Université Laval, Quebec. **Career:** Writer; worked a variety of secretarial jobs, 1956-59; lived in the United States, 1963-74. **Awards:** L'Academie française Prix de la langue française, 1961; Guggenheim fellowships, 1963, 1964; Prix France-Québec, 1966; Prix Médicis (France), 1966; Prix du Gouverneur-général du Canada, 1969, 1979; Ordre du Canada, 1975; Prix Belgique-Canada, 1976; Calgary University honorary professor, 1978; Prix Athanase-David, 1982, for body of work; Prix de l'Academie française, 1983; Nessim Habif prize (Belgium), 1991. Honorary degrees: York University, Toronto, 1975; Victoria University. **Agent:** John C. Goodwin & Associates, 839, Sherbrooke Est., suite 2, Montréal, Québec H2L 1K6, Canada. **Address:** 448, chemin Sims, Kingsbury, Québec J0B 1X0, Canada.

Publications

Novels

La belle bête. Québec, Institut Littéraire, 1959; translated as *Mad Shadows,* Toronto, McClelland & Stewart, Boston, Little Brown, and London, Cape, 1960.

Tête blanche. Québec, Institut Littéraire, 1960; translated as *White Head,* Toronto, McClelland & Stewart, and Boston, Little Brown, 1961; London, Cape, 1962.

Une saison dans la vie d'Emmanuel. Montréal, Éditions du Jour, 1965; translated as *A Season in the Life of Emmanuel,* New York, Farrar Straus, 1966; London, Cape, 1967.

L'insoumise. Montréal, Éditions du Jour, 1966; translated as *The Fugitive,* Ottawa, Oberon, 1978.

David Sterne. Montréal, Éditions du Jour, 1967; translated, Toronto, McClelland & Stewart, 1973.

The Manuscripts of Pauline Archange. New York, Farrar Straus, 1970; Toronto, McClelland & Stewart, 1982.

Manuscrits de Pauline Archange. Montréal, Éditions du Jour, 1978.

Vivre! Vivre! Montréal, Éditions du Jour, 1969.

Les apparences. Montréal, Éditions du Jour, 1970; translated as *Dürer's Angel,* Vancouver, Talonbooks, 1976.

Le loup. Montréal, Éditions du Jour, 1972; translated as *The Wolf,* Toronto, McClelland & Stewart, 1974.

Un joualonais, sa joualonie. Montréal, Éditions du Jour, 1973; translated as *St. Lawrence Blues,* New York, Farrar Straus, 1974; London, Harrap, 1975.

Une affaire parisienne. Montréal, Stanké/Quinze, 1975; translated as *A Literary Affair,* Toronto, McClelland & Stewart, 1979.

Les nuits de l'Underground. Montréal, Stanké, 1978; as *Nights in the Underground,* Don Mills, Ontario, Musson, 1979; New York, Beaufort, 1983.

Le sourd dans la ville. Montréal, Stanké, 1979; translated as *Deaf to the City,* Toronto, Lester Orphen & Dennys, 1980; Woodstock, New York, Overlook, 1987.

Visions d'Anna ou le vertige. Montréal, Stanké, 1982; translated as *Anna's World,* Toronto, Lester Orphen & Dennys, 1985.

Pierre ou la guerre du printemps 1981. Montréal, Primeur, 1984; translated as *Pierre, or The Spring War,* n.p., 1991.

L'ange de la solitude. Montréal, VLB Editeur, 1989.

Soifs. Montréal, Boréal, 1995; translated as *Thirsts,* Toronto, Anansi Press, 1997.

Short Stories

Le jour est noir. Montréal, Éditions du Jour, 1962; translated with *Les voyageurs sacrés* as *The Day Is Dark and Three Travelers: Two Novellas,* New York, Farrar Straus, 1967.

Les voyageurs sacrés. Montréal, HMH, 1969; translated with *Le jour est noir* as *The Day Is Dark and Three Travelers: Two Novellas,* New York, Farrar Straus, 1967.

L'exilé. Montréal, Leméac, 1992.

Poetry

Pays voilés. Québec, Garneau, 1963; translated with *Existences* as *Veiled Countries/Lives,* Montréal, Vehicule, 1984.

Existences. Québec, Garneau, 1964; translated with *Pays voilés* as *Veiled Countries/Lives,* Montréal, Vehicule, 1984.

Plays

La roulotte aux poupées (produced Québec, 1960); translated as *The Puppet Caravan* (televised 1967).

Eléonor (produced Québec, 1960).

L'exécution (produced Montréal, 1968). Montréal, Éditions du Jour, 1968; translated as *The Execution,* Vancouver, Talonbooks, 1976.

Fièvre, et autres textes dramatiques. Montréal, Éditions du Jour, 1974.

La nef des sorcières (produced Montréal, 1976), with Nicole Brossard, Marthe Blackburn, Luce Guilbeault, France Théoret, Odette Gagnon, and Pol Pelletier. Montréal, Quinze, 1976; translated as *A Clash of Symbols,* Toronto, Coach House Press, 1979.

L'océan, suive de Murmures. Montréal, Quinze, 1977; *L'océan* translated as *The Ocean,* Toronto, Exile, 1977; *Murmures* translated in *Canadian Drama/L'Art Dramatique Canadien,* 5, fall 1979.

Sommeil d'hiver. Montréal, Éditions de la Pleine Lune, 1984.

L'île (produced Montréal, 1991). Montréal, VLB Editeur, 1988; translated as *The Island,* Ottawa, Oberon, 1991.

Un jardin dans la tempête (broadcast 1990); translated as *A Garden in the Snow.*

Television Plays: *L'Ocean,* 1976; *Journal en images froides, Scénario,* 1978; *L'exil, L'escale,* 1979.

Radio Plays: *Le disparu,* 1971; *L'envahisseur,* 1972; *Deux destins,* 1973; *Fièvre,* 1973; *Une autre vie,* 1974; *Un couple,* 1975; *Une femme et les autres,* 1976; *L'enfant-video,* 1977; *Murmures,* 1977; *Le fantôme d'une voix,* 1980.

Other

Voies de pères, voix de filles. Saint-Laurent, Québec, Lacombe, 1988.

Parcours d'un écrivain. Notes américaines. Montréal, VLB, 1993; translated as *A Writer's Passage: Notes on America,* Vancouver, Talonbooks, 1997.

*

Bibliography: "Bibliographie de Marie-Claire Blais" by Aurélien Boivin and others, in *Voix et Images,* 8, winter 1983.

Manuscript Collections: National Library of Canada, Ottawa.

Critical Studies: *Marie-Claire Blais* by Philip Stratford, Toronto, Forum House, 1971; "Fiction as Autobiography in Québec: Notes on Pierre Vallière and Marie-Claire Blais" by James Kraft, in *Novel,* 6, autumn 1972; "*Mad Shadows* as Psychological Fiction" by Joan Caldwell, and "The Shattered Glass: Mirror and Illusion in *Mad Shadows*" by Douglas H. Parker, both in *Journal of Canadian Fiction* (Montréal), 2(4), 1973; *Lily Brisco: A Self-Portrait* by Mary Meigs, Vancouver, Talonbooks, 1981; "The Censored Word and the Body Politic: Reconsidering the Fiction of Marie-Claire Blais" by Karen Gould, in *Journal of Popular Culture* (Bowling Green, Ohio), winter 1981; "From Shattered Reflections to Female Bonding: Mirroring in Marie-Claire Blais' *Visions d'Anna*" by Paula Gilbert Lewis, in *Québec Studies,* 2, 1984; "Redefining the Maternal: Women's Relationships in the Fiction of Marie-Claire Blais" by Mary Jean Green, in *Traditionalism, Nationalism and Feminism: Women Writers of Quebec,* edited by Paula Gilbert Lewis, Westport, Connecticut, Greenwood Press, 1985; "The Question of Lesbian Identity in Marie-Claire Blais' Work" by Janine Ricouart, in *Redefining Autobiography in 20th-Century Women's Fiction,* edited by Janice Morgan and Colette T. Hall, New York, Garland, 1991.

* * *

Since publishing her first novel in 1959, when she was barely 20, Marie-Claire Blais has enjoyed a long and productive literary career. Although her works include some early poems and theatrical writing, she is known mainly as a novelist. Essentially self-taught (she left school at 15), she has developed friendships with many writers and artists, as her recent *Parcours d'un écrivain* reveals, has travelled widely, and lived for long periods in the United States (she winters in Key West). The winner of the most prestigious literary awards of Québec, Canada, and the French-speaking world, she has rarely appeared in public or granted interviews (except for her latest novel, *Soifs*). Of all the openly lesbian writers in Quebec, Blais is arguably the best-known and the most widely read; however, she has received considerably less critical attention from academic feminists than more hermetic lesbian authors such as Nicole Brossard.

Although a few of Blais's novels have been the subject of feminist analyses, her body of work is so diverse that it is difficult to describe the whole from a feminist viewpoint. While she is clearly committed to gay and lesbian rights and, through that struggle, to feminism, only a handful of her works deal specifically with those subjects, or with women's issues as such. One of the most striking features of her novels is the way she interweaves a critical perspective on the major social issues of our time (poverty and violence, ecology, and exploitation of the Third World, particularly through tourism) and an in-depth exploration of the human soul: her recent writing is realistic in content through its portrayal of the class and sex wars of North American life, but poetic in its prose style and romantic in its emphasis on inwardness, suffering, tenderness, passion, and creativity. Violence and poetry are in fact the enduring hallmarks of Blais's work. She is the novelist of the rebellious, the lost, the panic-stricken, the dispossessed. In her works, young drug addicts or gang members are never condemned as juvenile delinquents; rather, they are poets gone wrong, fallen angels, tortured souls whose agony she explores, with rare compassion, from within. In her later novels, such as *L'ange de la solitude,* Blais has her characters proposing humane solutions to social problems: one of them points out that government-funded shelters for the homeless cost five times less than prisons. Several of her works, including *Visions d'Anna* and *Pierre ou la guerre du printemps 1981,* focus on young people, often from upper- or middle-class liberal families, who reject the comfort and the hypocrisy of the adult world in a desperate search for more authentic values. Sometimes cruel inquisitors, sometimes well-meaning obstacles in their children's path, parents are occasional allies whose love can ultimately rescue and reclaim their progeny.

Over time, Blais' prose style has become increasingly challenging. The brief poetic sentences of *La belle Bête* and the finely crafted Proustian phrasing of *Manuscrits de Pauline Archange* have given way to increasingly longer sentences, to detailed and lengthy focus on characters' thought processes, and to denser narrative segments (*Soifs*, her latest novel, contains a single paragraph of 300 pages). The effect is sometimes overwhelming. While Blais's long blocks of text seem stifling, almost unreadable, it could be argued that they are an attempt to break prose free of conventional narrative structures and bring it closer to the human voice, breath, thought, and experience. Certainly Blais's writing is an experiment without precedent or parallel in the contemporary Québec novel.

Blais's commitment to feminism and to gay and lesbian rights has emerged only progressively in her novels, appearing in her earlier works as subtexts. Her first novel, *La belle bête,* explores the psychic life of Isabelle-Marie, an ugly young woman who ultimately murders the beloved mother who has rejected her in favor of her handsome idiot brother. *Une saison dans la vie d'Emmanuel* is a nightmarish parody of Québec rural life in the early 20th century and of the "novel of the land," a literary genre that idealized the traditional Québec lifestyle and urged readers to adopt it. While novels of the land offer a sanitized, conflict-free version of rural life that reinforces male power as exemplified in fathers, Church, and State, *Une saison dans la vie d'Emmanuel* demolishes that false idyll. It features an abusive and ignorant father, a mother worn out by constant childbearing (she has so many children that some, like Number Seven, are named according to their order of birth), a priest-rapist of young boys, a tubercular poet, and an ex-nun turned prostitute in search of human kindness. Only the puritanical but loving grandmother and the infant Emmanuel seem to offer a ray of hope in this novel, written in a hallucinatory prose closer to the visionary French poet Rimbaud than to Ringuet (the master of the traditional Quebec novel of the land Blais parodies). Although present to some extent, feminist concerns are peripheral in this, perhaps Blais's most famous novel.

Unlike many feminist writers who concentrate almost exclusively on female characters and women's experience, Blais has often featured male protagonists and their sometimes misogynistic view of women. The aspiring writer of *Une saison dans la vie d'Emmanuel* is a young man, as are most of the artistic figures (writers, painters, composers) Blais's characters reverently refer to throughout her work. *L'insoumise* (literally "The Rebellious Woman"), which begins as the story of a middle-class wife and mother who gradually rejects the conventions of a traditional woman's life, soon shifts thematic and narrative focus to deal with her homosexual son's accidental death and his father's grief. *Une affaire parisienne,* an uncharacteristic, almost Jamesian portrait of New World innocence destroyed by European charm and corruption, is told from the standpoint of two men brought to the brink of financial and emotional ruin by the beautiful but greedy and heartless Madame d'Argenti, whose point of view is never given. *Pierre ou la guerre du printemps 1981* is the story of a 16-year-old boy who explicitly rejects "the transparent, feminine universe of love" to become "a soldier, a god", through his association with a motorcycle gang and the torture of a young women, Stone. The troubling misogyny of this novel can be read as an attempt to account for and come to terms with male violence against women.

In addition to works exploring homosexual love or male violence, Blais has written a number of novels highlighting feminist and lesbian issues. The semi-autobiographic trilogy *Manuscrits de Pauline Archange, Vivre! Vivre!* and *Les apparences* sensitively relate a young girl's efforts to emerge from poverty and ignorance to become a writer. Pauline's complex relationship to her mother is particularly important: in order to escape her mother's fate—exhaustion and illness caused by poverty, overwork, and too-frequent childbirth—Pauline must suppress her feelings of love and pity for the older woman in whom she reluctantly recognizes a spirit similar to her own, broken by life's trials. "Marcelle," Blais's monologue in the collective feminist play *La nef des sorcières,* movingly expresses tender love between women, a key theme of several novels of the 1980s and 1990s. *Les nuits de l'Underground* exemplifies this vein in Blais's work. It is the story both of a love affair between Geneviève Aurès, a Québec sculptor, and Lali Dorman, a European-born physician tortured by her memories of World War II, and of a group of women who congregate in the bar of the novel's title to celebrate their love for one another. The Underground is a world within a world, a haven where women can protect themselves and each other, while the streets outside threaten to destroy them (one of the characters, an anti-racist activist, is raped by a black man on her way home from the bar). Both these novels play on gender boundaries: Lali is as slim and austere as a young boy, and several female characters bear men's names, including Gérard and Johnie, who is named for her passion for Radclyffe Hall. Without idealizing lesbian relationships—she portrays the quarrels, conflicts and betrayals all love affairs harbor—Blais sees friendship and passion between women as empowering forces in a hostile world. Narrative focus broadens here to consider the group as well as the individual, as it does even more dramatically in *L'ange de la solitude,* the story of a number of women artists united by their lives in a commune and their struggle against homophobia. This novel, more pessimistic than *Les nuits de l'Underground,* reminds the reader that despite their loyalty to one other, the lives of lesbians and gays are continually threatened, whether by the "pink star" pinned on homosexuals sent to the crematoria of Nazi Germany and the prisons of Siberia or by the new "pink star," AIDS, which is no longer pinned on the outside of the body but attacks from within, condemning the blood, the veins, the tears and sperm of its victims.

Over the years the Gothic imagination of Blais's dreamlike early works has given way to a hallucinatory portrait of the violence of modern life from the standpoint of the disenfranchised: children, mothers, gays, and lesbians. But Blais also insists on life's pleasures, small and great, on all the passions that redeem: love, friendship, and beauty in all its forms, whether it be a landscape, a face, a piece of music, or a painting. Although fragile and constantly threatened, art is the way into the deepest inner life of human beings, but also the way out, the surest path towards beauty, truth, and, ultimately, freedom. Certainly Marie-Claire Blais herself is an example of lifelong devotion to writing. Her work reveals a lesbian feminist perspective that is at once lucid and poetic, tender and uncompromising.

—Lori Saint-Martin

BLATCH, Harriot Stanton

Nationality: American. **Born:** Seneca Falls, New York, 1856; daughter of Elizabeth Cady Stanton. **Education:** Vassar College, B.A. in mathematics 1878, M.A. 1894; attended Boston School of Oratory, c. 1879. **Military Service:** Member, Food Administration and Women's Land Army during World War I. **Family:** Married William Blatch in 1882; two children. **Career:** Lived in Hampshire, England, 1882-1902; joined Fabian Society and met Beatrice and Sidney Webb, George Bernard Shaw, and Ramsay Macdonald; returned to the United States and founded the Equality League of Self-Supporting Women, c. 1907 (changed name to Women's Political Union, 1908, merged with Alice Paul's Congressional Union, 1915; led first suffrage parade in New York, 1910; visited England, 1915; nominated by Socialist party as comptroller of the City of New York, 1921. **Died:** 1940.

Publications

Political/Social Theory

A Woman's Point of View: Some Roads to Peace. New York, The Womans Press, 1920.

History

A History of Woman Suffrage, Volume 2, with Susan B. Anthony, Matilda Joslyn Gage, and Elizabeth Cady Stanton. New York, Fowler & Welles, 1881.

Essays

Mobilizing Woman-Power, foreword by Theodore Roosevelt. New York, The Womans Press, 1918.

Autobiography

Challenging Years: The Memoirs of Harriot Stanton Blatch, with Alma Lutz. New York, G.P. Putnam, 1940.

Other

Village Life in England, with Charles Booth. London, n.p., c. 1894.

Editor, *Two Speeches by Industrial Women (Mary Duffy, Clara Silver).* New York, n.p., 1907.
Editor, with Theodore Stanton, *Elizabeth Cady Stanton, as Revealed in Her Letters, Diary, and Reminiscences.* New York and London, Harper Bros., 2 vols., 1922.

*

Manuscript Collection: Library of Congress, Washington, D.C.

Critical Sources: *Women as a Force in History* by Mary Ritter Beard, New York, Macmillan, 1946.

* * *

As the daughter of woman's rights leader Elizabeth Cady Stanton and abolitionist Henry Brewster Stanton, Harriot Eaton Stanton was born into a politically active family. Eight years before her birth in 1856, her parents had been central organizers of the Seneca Falls woman's rights convention. She was sixth of seven children and attended private schools in Seneca Falls, New York City, Englewood, New Jersey, eventually enrolling at Vassar College. She graduated from Vassar with honors and then spent a year at the Boston School of Oratory. A statistical study of villages in Great Britain resulted in her being awarded an M.A. degree from Vassar in 1894, even though she was living in England at the time.

Blatch's first major contribution to the woman suffrage movement was her insistence that Volume 2 of *A History of Woman Suffrage* include the work of the American Woman Suffrage Association, as both her mother and Susan B. Anthony had written their history from the point of view of their own National Woman Suffrage Association. As a result, Blatch was the author of that part the history; indeed, this work is credited with aiding the reconciliation of these two major woman suffrage organizations.

After marrying Englishman William Henry Blatch in 1882, she lived for 20 years west of London in Basingstoke. The couple had two children, and Blatch became involved with a number of social movements, including the Fabian Society. When she and her family moved to the United States in 1902, Blatch was disturbed by the lethargy exhibited by the American suffrage movement. Accordingly, she organized working women and in 1907 was founder of the Equality League of Self-Supporting Women, an organization that would eventually become the Women's Political Union and, in 1916, merge with the Congressional Union under Alice Paul.

Historian Mary Ritter Beard has written that Harriot Blatch was one of the most important strategists of woman suffrage and that her contributions to various reforms have not been fully appreciated. Among Blatch's many active concerns was an attempt to develop ways to positively apply the lessons learned during World War I. Her understanding of international politics was keen and she is credited with attempting to organize social thought toward understanding the war's devastation. She encouraged the examination and elimination of national hatreds and believed that women could do much to change the warlike nature of governments.

Blatch fought against protective legislation for women workers, a stand which put her in conflict with several other reform organizations. She remained active in labor causes and supported many liberal causes as an organizer and writer. Blatch passed away in 1940, her last months spent in a nursing home after she had fractured a hip.

—Ann Mauger Colbert

BLIGHT, Rose. *See* **GREER, Germaine.**

BLIXEN, Karen (Christentze Dinesen)

Pseudonyms: Pierre Andrezel; Isak Dinesen; Osceola. **Nationality:** Danish. **Born:** Rungsted, 17 April 1885. **Family:** Married Baron Bror Blixen-Finecke in 1914 (divorced 1921). **Education:** Oxford University, 1904; studied painting at Royal Academy in Copenhagen, in Paris, 1910, and in Rome. **Career:** Managed a coffee plantation in British East Africa (now Nairobi, Kenya), 1913-31; commissioned by three Scandinavian newspapers to write articles on wartime Berlin, Paris, and London, 1940. **Member:** American Academy of Arts and Letters (honorary member), National Institute of Arts and Letters (honorary member), Bayerische Akademie der Schoenen Kuenste (corresponding member), Danish Academy (founding member), Cosmopolitan Club (New York). **Awards:** Ingenio et Arti Medal, 1950; Golden Laurels award, 1952; Hans Christian Andersen Prize, 1955; Danish Critics' Prize, 1957; Henri Nathansen Memorial Fund award, 1957. **Died:** Rungsted Kyst, Denmark, of emaciation, 7 September 1962.

PUBLICATIONS

Novels

The Angelic Avengers (as Pierre Andrezel). New York, Random House, 1946.

Short Stories

Seven Gothic Tales. N.p., Smith & Haas, 1934.
Winter's Tales. New York, Random House, 1942.

Om revtskrivning 23-24 marts 1938. Copenhagen, Gyldendal, 1949.
Farah. Copenhagen, Wivel, 1950.
Babette's Feast (originally appeared in *Ladies' Home Journal*), in *Anecdotes of Destiny.* New York, Random House, 1958; as *Babette's Feast and Other Anecdotes of Destiny,* edited by Martha Levin, New York, Vintage, 1988.
Omkring den Nye Lov om Dyreforsög. Copenhagen, Politikens, 1952.
Kardinalens tredie Historie. Copenhagen, Gyldendal, 1952.
En Baaltale med 14 Aars Forsinkelse. Copenhagen, Berlingske, 1953.
Spögelseshestene. Fremad, 1955.
Last Tales. New York, Random House, 1957.
Osceola (collection of early stories and poems). Copenhagen, Gyldendal, 1962.
Ehrengard. New York, Random House, 1963.
Efterladte Fortällinger. Copenhagen, Gyldendal, 1975.
Carnival: Entertainments and Posthumous Tales, Danish portions translated by P.M. Mitchell and W.D. Paden. Chicago, University of Chicago Press, 1977.
"Det drömmende barn" og andre fortällinger. Copenhagen, Gyldendal, 1979.
Karyatiderne en ufuldendt historie, edited by Sonia Brandes. Copenhagen, Gyldendal, 1993.

Play

Sandhedens Hävn (produced Copenhagen, 1936). In *Tilskueren,* 1926; Copenhagen, Gyldendal, 1960.

Essays

Daguerreotypier (radio talks). Copenhagen, Gyldendal, 1951; in *Daguerreotypes and Other Essays,* translated by P.M. Mitchell and W.D. Paden, Chicago, University of Chicago Press, 1979.
"On Mottoes of My Life," in *Proceedings of The American Academy of Arts and Letters and The National Institute of Arts and Letters,* Second Series, 10, 1960.
Skygger paa Grässet. Copenhagen, Gyldendal, 1960; as *Shadows on the Grass,* New York, Random House, 1961.
Essays. Copenhagen, Gyldendal, 1965; expanded edition as *Mitlivs Mottoer og Andre Essays,* 1978.
Modern ägteskab og Andre Betragtninger. Copenhagen, Gyldendal, 1981; as *On Modern Marriage: And Other Observations,* New York, St. Martin's Press, 1986.
Samlede essays. Copenhagen, Gyldendal, 1985.

Autobiography

Out of Africa. London, Putnam, 1937; New York, Random House, 1938; as *The Illustrated Out of Africa,* London, Cresset Press, 1989.

Other

Breve fra Afrika, 1914-1924 [1925-1931]. Copenhagen, Gyldendal, 2 vols., 1978; translated by Anne Born as *Letters from Africa, 1914-1931,* edited by Frans Lasson, Chicago, University of Chicago Press, 1981.

*

Media Adaptations: *The Immortal Story* (film), Altura, 1969; *Out of Africa* (film), Universal, 1985; *Babette's Feast* (film), Orion Pictures, 1987.

Bibliography: *Isak Dinesen: A Bibliography* by Liselette Henricksen, University of Chicago Press, 1977.

Critical Studies: *The World of Isak Dinesen* by Eric O. Johannesson, University of Washington Press, 1961; *The Gayety of Vision: A Study of Isak Dinesen's Art* by Robert Langbaum, Chicago, University of Chicago Press, 1964; *Titania: The Biography of Isak Dinesen* by Permenia Migel, New York, Random House, 1967; *The Life and Destiny of Isak Dinesen,* edited by C. Svendsen, New York, Random House, 1970; *"Isak Dinesen" and Karen Blixen: The Mask and the Reality* by Donald Hannah, New York, Putnam, 1971; *Isak Dinesen's Aesthetics* by Thomas R. Whissen, Port Washington, New York, Kennikat Press, 1973; *The Pact: My Friendship with Isak Dinesen* by Thorkild Bjornvig, Louisiana State University Press, 1974; *My Sister, Isak Dinesen* by Thomas Dinesen, translated by Joan Tate, London, M. Joseph, 1975; "'The Blank Page' and Issues of Female Creativity" by Susan Gubar, in *Critical Inquiry* 8, winter 1981; *Isak Dinesen: The Life of a Storyteller* by Judith Thurman, New York, St. Martin's Press, 1982; *Isak Dinesen; Karen Blixen: The Work and the Life* by Aage Henriksen, translated by William Mishler, New York, St. Martin's Press, 1988; *The Witch and the Goddess in the Stories of Isak Dinesen: A Feminist Reading* by Sara Stambaugh, Ann Arbor, Michigan, UMI Research Press, 1988; *Isak Dinesen and the Engendering of Narrative* by Susan Hardy Aiken, Chicago, University of Chicago Press, 1990; *Isak Dinesen: The Life and Imagination of a Seducer* by Olga Pelensky, Athens, Ohio University Press, 1991, and her edited *Isak Dinesen: Critical Views,* Athens, Ohio University Press, 1993; *Out of Isak Dinesen in Africa: The Untold Story* by Linda Conelson, Iowa City, Coulsong List, 1995; *Difficult Women, Artful Lives: Olive Schreiner and Isak Dinesen, in and out of Africa* by Susan R. Horton, Baltimore, Johns Hopkins University Press, 1995.

* * *

In a 1934 interview in *Politiken,* Karen Blixen explained that she chose to write under a pseudonym and to set her tales in the past because, "Only in that way did I become completely free." This insistence on a human being's right to freedom of expression and choice informs Blixen's writing, particularly her short stories, in a way perhaps unfamiliar to those who know the Danish author solely through her popular memoir, *Out of Africa.*

Blixen was born into a well-to-to Danish family and, despite toying with storywriting in the early 1900s, expended most of her youthful artistic energies in studying painting. Her writing after her marriage to Bror Blixen consisted mainly of her letters from their coffee plantation in Kenya, a business she ultimately managed by herself after she separated from her husband; this correspondence was posthumously collected in *Letters from Africa.* Blixen's feminist viewpoint can be found in many of these letters. She wrote to her Aunt Bess in 1926, for example, that feminism was the "most significant movement of the nineteenth century" and that the feminist movement consisted of women desiring and striving "to be human beings with a direct relationship with life in the same way as men have done and do this." About this time, Blixen also composed the essay "On Modern Marriage and Other

Considerations," in which she discussed her belief that in an ideal marriage, the partners jointly commit to a philosophy of kinship, family, or divinity, rather than to one another.

Blixen developed her fiction-writing sensibilities through the oral tradition of storytelling. During evenings on the plantation spent with her lover, Denys Finch Hatton, she told story after story; she remarked in *Out of Africa* that during these sessions, she was "like Scheherezade herself." When Blixen knew she would be forced to sell her failing farm and leave Africa, she began to write down some of these tales. After her arrival back in Denmark, she wrote to alleviate both her loneliness and her precarious financial situation, delaying poverty with her storytelling just as she had delayed Finch Hatton's departures in Africa. *Seven Gothic Tales,* her first book, came out when she was 48; the collection was an immediate critical and commercial success. While contemporary critics noted the exotic nature of the stories, as well as Blixen's skillful reshaping of the 19th-century Gothic form, later critics have commented on the feminist themes expressed in them. Sara Stambaugh draws attention, for instance, to Blixen's exploration of the "false image which men project upon women and which women in turn contort themselves to embody." Blixen's play with notions of identity in these stories reflects her insistence on freedom as the hallmark of woman's choice, as well—women disguise themselves as men, a woman turns into a monkey, a mirror reflects both fictional and real selves, and the gulf between life and death becomes mere tissue. Finally, Blixen emphasizes the importance of woman's role as storyteller, the person of Scheherezade in which she would cast herself in *Out of Africa,* the storyteller who cheats death through words, and who achieves power with her ability to cast a spell over her audience.

Though critics have tended to label *Seven Gothic Tales, Out of Africa,* and *Winter's Tales,* her second volume of short stories, her most significant work, feminist scholars have recently devoted special attention to Blixen's penultimate collection, *Last Tales,* particularly the story "The Blank Page." Susan Gubar believes the story illustrates how "women's limited options ... have shaped the art they create." In this brilliant and uncharacteristically brief tale, Blixen develops many of the feminist themes of her early fiction: the power of the female storyteller, the recursive nature of oral and print forms and of stories passed down from one woman to another, and the capacity of woman to create myths and bind her audience to herself through imagination. "The Blank Page" concerns a gallery in a convent of Carmelite nuns in Portugal where hangs the framed evidences of a royal virgin's wedding night—a spot of blood on the snow-white linen bridal sheet. The narrator, an old woman "who made her living by telling stories," catechizes the woman and man listening to her: "Who then ... tells a finer tale than any of us? Silence does. And where does one read a deeper tale than upon the most perfectly printed page of the most precious book? Upon the blank page." In the midst of the gallery there hangs an unspotted square of linen; underneath it, an uninscribed nameplate. Yet it is this silent square, this blank page, that commands the most attention of any in the hall. This anonymous woman's story has the breadth and depth of infinity. Blixen forces the issue of the contradictory demands placed upon women by society and by their desire to choose their destinies freely. Whether the unknown princess refused to consummate the marriage or chose an unmandated sexual experience, her unconventional story speaks the most insistently to the audience.

Blixen ends "The Poet," the final story in *Seven Gothic Tales,* with the image of an echo. The protagonist, Fransine, has just murdered the satanic Councilor because he is a poet, a liar. As he dies, he hears, "like an echo in the engulfing darkness, winding and rolling in long caverns, her last word ... repeated again and again." Fransine's action renders impotent the Councilor's lies; the recursive nature of her echo as it repeats the word "poet" underscores the veracity of her cry. Blixen insisted on the literal and figurative power of woman's voice in society and culture; her writing continues to demand that her audience pay attention to the truth inherent in that voice.

—Siobhan Craft Brownson

BOLAND, Eavan

Nationality: Irish. **Born:** Dublin, 24 September 1944. **Education:** Attended convent schools in London, New York, and Killiney, County Dublin, until 1962; Trinity College, Dublin, B.A. in English 1967. **Family:** Married the novelist Kevin Casey; two daughters. **Career:** Worked as a housekeeper at Dublin's Gresham Hotel, c. 1962; junior lecturer, Trinity College, Dublin, 1967-68; lecturer, School of Irish Studies, Dublin, beginning 1968. Contributor to periodicals, including *Irish Times* and *P.N. Review.* **Awards:** Macaulay fellowship in poetry, 1968; Jacobs Awards for Broadcasting, 1977; Irish American Cultural Award, 1983; American Ireland Fund Literary Award, 1994.

Publications

Essays

A Kind of Scar: The Woman Poet in a National Tradition. Dublin, Attic Press, 1989.

Object Lessons: The Life of the Woman and the Poet in Our Time. New York, Norton, 1995.

Poetry

23 Poems. Dublin, Gallagher Press, 1962.

New Territory. Dublin, Allen Figgis, 1967.

The War Horse. London, Gollancz, 1975; Dublin, Arlen House, 1980.

In Her Own Image. Dublin, Arlen House, 1980.

Introducing Eavan Boland. Princeton, Ontario Review Press, 1981.

Night Feed. Dublin, Arlen House, and London and Boston, Marion Boyars, 1982.

The Journey. Dublin, Gallery Press, and Deerfield, Massachusetts, Deerfield Press, 1983.

The Journey and Other Poems. London, Carcanet, and New York, Carcanet, 1987.

Outside History: Selected Poems, 1980-1990. Manchester, Carcanet, and New York, Norton, 1990.

In a Time of Violence. Manchester, Carcanet, and New York, Norton, 1994.

Collected Poems. Manchester, Carcanet, 1995.

Other

W.B. Yeats and His World, with Micheal MacLiammoir. London, Thames & Hudson, 1970; New York, Viking, 1972.

*

Critical Studies: "Nationalism and Obsession in Contemporary Irish Poetry" (interview) by Adrian Frazier, in *Literary Review,* 22, winter 1979; "Eavan Boland" by Caroline Walsh in *Irish Times,* 8 October 1983; "Contemporary Irish Women Poets: The Privatization of Myth" by Clair Wills in *Diverse Voices,* edited by Harriet Devine Jump, New York, St. Martin's Press, 1991; "An Interview with Eavan Boland" by Patty O'Connell, in *Poets & Writers,* 22, November/December 1994; *Women Creating Women: Contemporary Irish Women Poets* by Patricia Boyle Haberstroh, Syracuse, New York, Syracuse University Press, 1995.

* * *

Eavan Boland is one of the most important women poets writing in Ireland in the 1980s and 1990s, and certainly the most widely read outside her own country. With other women poets of her generation, including Medbh McGuckian, Nuala Ní Dhomhnaill, and Eiléan Ní Chuilleanáin, she has reinvented the Irish poem, using some traditional forms but opening them to accept new imagery and ideas that reflect the lives and thoughts of women.

Boland was born in Dublin in 1944. Her mother was the artist Frances Kelly; her father was Frederick H. Boland, a diplomat. During Boland's childhood her father was Irish Ambassador to England, and the family lived in a splendid home in London. Later her father became Ambassador to the United Nations, and Boland would spend her adolescence in New York. Living in these two cities broadened Boland's education, certainly, but also solidified for her a sense of her own Irishness. In an essential way, Ireland was home. When she was 14 the family returned to Dublin, where Boland enrolled in a boarding school and then Trinity College. She has lived in or near Dublin ever since.

Boland read poetry throughout her teens, and studied English at Trinity. By 19 she knew that she was—or would be—a poet. But, as she has often recounted, it was not until some years later that she became aware that, although she was developing the poet's ability to see and understand, the poetry she was reading and writing was distant from her, it was not *hers.* The work of most young artists is somewhat derivative; as they mature, artists stop echoing their models and find their own way. But for Boland and, she believes, for all Irish women poets, the problem is deeper.

Ireland is a country with a strong poetic tradition. It has embraced and honored its poets, and it has produced many fine ones, including W.B. Yeats and Nobel Prize-winner Seamus Heaney. However, much Irish poetry is grounded in issues of history and nationalism and with the traditional image of the homeland as motherland. This feminine image has been an icon, not a real women; the woman who stands for Ireland is deathless, and therefore emotionless and lifeless. Most of the poetry has been written by men. As Boland explains it, this has meant that women have traditionally been the *objects* of the Irish poem. Her challenge was to find a way to write poems about her own experiences as a women, a wife, and a mother living in suburban Dublin, and to write about history as it is experienced by women—to write poems with women as their *subjects.*

Boland's commitment to feminism but not separatism, to finding a way for women to operate within tradition, has shaped both her poetry and her essays and reviews, which examine Irish writing and Irish women writers, and which have appeared regularly in the *Irish Times.* She has dealt in her poetry with the traditionally "masculine" themes of war, violence, and nationalism, but has used the stories and experiences of women (including her own ancestors) to illuminate these themes. Her third volume, *The War Horse,* includes poems dealing with the conflicts between the Irish Republic and Northern Ireland, new treatments of figures from Irish folklore, as well as poems such as "Ode to Suburbia." *Outside History,* Boland's first volume published in the United States, delves into how women's stories have somehow been excluded from conventional notions of "history." Her eighth volume, *In a Time of Violence,* deals with Irish history, geography, and cartography. Several poems from *In a Time of Violence* also explore the devastation caused by the famines of the mid-19th century, especially their effects on women and children.

Another important focus of Boland's poetry, and of her concept of women's poetry, is on the everyday lives of women, which she maintains are every bit as valuable and profound as the "great deeds" of men. Her fourth book of verse, the illustrated *In Her Own Image,* pleased many of her readers (and shocked a few critics) with its treatment of domestic violence, eating disorders, breast cancer, and other subjects deemed inappropriate for Irish art at the time. Beginning with this book, published in 1980, reviewers debated, at the appearance of each new volume, whether Boland's poetry was "too feminist." Her next two volumes, *Night Feed* and *The Journey and Other Poems,* focus on motherhood and the home. All of her volumes contain images of steaming tea kettles and bicycles and children, the stuff of her somewhat ordinary—but not unimportant—life as a wife and mother in a Dublin suburb.

In two prose works, Boland has explained and explored the thesis that over the past few generations Irish women have moved from being the objects of poems to the subjects and creators of them. 1989's *A Kind of Scar: The Woman Poet in a National Tradition* introduces the idea and examines the icon of woman in Irish literature and the challenges facing Irish women writers. *Object Lessons,* a collection of ten essays exploring how the ideas of *woman* and *poet* could come together, is more autobiographical, using Boland's own life and the lives of women in her family to show how women's status in Ireland, and how Boland's image of herself as poet, have evolved.

In addition to 11 volumes of poetry and two of essays, Eavan Boland has published many reviews and pieces of literary journalism. She has taught creative writing and literature in Ireland, Europe, and the United States, and formerly hosted a poetry program on Irish radio.

—Cynthia A. Bily

BOWEN, Elizabeth Dorothea Cole

Nationality: Anglo-Irish. **Born:** Dublin, Ireland, 7 June 1899. **Education:** Downe House, Downe, Kent, 1914-17; London County Council School of Art, 1918. **Military Service:** Worked briefly in a shell-shock hospital near Dublin in World War I; worked for Ministry of Information and as an air-raid warden in London during World War II. **Family:** Married Alan Charles Cameron in 1923 (died 1952). **Career:** Novelist and short story writer; associate editor, *London Magazine,* in the 1950s. **Awards:** Named to Irish Academy of Letters, 1937; Commander, Order of the British Empire, 1948; named a Royal Society of Literature Companion of Literature, 1965; James Tait Black Memorial Prize, 1970. D.Litt.: Trinity College, 1949; Oxford University, 1956. **Died:** 22 February 1973.

Publications

Novels

The Hotel. London, Constable, 1927, and New York, L. MacVeagh/Dial Press, 1928.
The Last September. London, Constable, and New York, L. MacVeagh/Dial Press, 1929; with preface by Bowen, New York, Knopf, 1952.
Friends and Relations. London, Constable, and New York, L. MacVeagh/Dial Press, 1931.
To the North. London, Gollancz, 1932; New York, Knopf, 1933.
The House in Paris. London, Gollancz, 1935; New York, Knopf, 1936.
The Death of the Heart. London, Gollancz, 1938; New York, Knopf, 1939.
The Heat of the Day. London, J. Cape, and New York, Knopf, 1949.
A World of Love. London, J. Cape, and New York, Knopf, 1955.
The Little Girls. London, J. Cape, and New York, Knopf, 1964.
Eva Trout, or Changing Scenes. New York, Knopf, 1968; London, J. Cape, 1969.

Short Stories

Encounters: Stories. London, Sidgwick & Jackson, and New York, Boni & Liveright, 1923.
Ann Lee's, and Other Stories. London, Sidgwick & Jackson, and New York, Boni & Liveright, 1926.
Joining Charles and Other Stories. London, Constable, and New York, L MacVeagh/Dial Press, 1929.
The Cat Jumps and Other Stories. London, Gollancz, 1934.
Look at All Those Roses: Short Stories. London, Gollancz, and New York, Knopf, 1941.
The Demon Lover and Other Stories. London, J. Cape, 1945; as *Ivy Gripped the Steps and Other Stories,* New York, Knopf, 1946.
Selected Stories. Dublin and London, M. Fridberg, 1946.
Early Stories: Encounters and Ann Lee's. New York, Knopf, 1951.
Stories. New York, Vintage, 1959.
A Day in the Dark and Other Stories. London, J. Cape, 1965.
Elizabeth Bowen's Irish Stories. Dublin, Poolbeg Press, 1978.
The Collected Stories of Elizabeth Bowen, introduction by Angus Wilson. New York, Knopf, 1981.

Plays

Nativity Play: A Christmas Musical. Chicago, Dramatic Publishing, 1974.

Literary Criticism

English Novelists. London, W. Collins, 1942; New York, Hastings House, n.d.
Anthony Trollope: A New Judgement. London and New York, Oxford University Press, 1946.

Essays

Collected Impressions. London, Longmans Green, and New York, Knopf, 1950.
Afterthought: Pieces about Writing. London, Longmans, 1962; as *Seven Winters: Memories of a Dublin Childhood & Afterthoughts: Pieces on Writing,* New York, Knopf, 1962.

Autobiography

Bowen's Court. London, Longmans Green, and New York, Knopf, 1942.
Seven Winters. Dublin, Cuala Press, 1942; as *Seven Winters: Memories of a Dublin Childhood,* London and New York, Longmans Green, 1943.
Pictures and Conversations. New York, Knopf, and London, Allen Lane, 1975.

For Children

The Good Tiger, illustrated by M. Nebel. New York, Knopf, 1965; illustrated by Quentin Blake, London, J. Cape, 1965.

Other

Why Do I Write?: An Exchange of Views between Elizabeth Bowen, Graham Greene & V.S. Pritchett. London, P. Marshall, 1948; Folcroft, Pennsylvania, Folcroft Library, 1948.
The Shelbourne Hotel. New York, Knopf, 1951; as *The Shelbourne: A Centre in Dublin Life for More than a Century,* London, G.C. Harrap, 1951.
A Time in Rome. London, Longmans, and New York, Knopf, 1960.
The Mulberry Tree: Writings of Elizabeth Bowen, edited by Hermione Lee. London, Virago, and San Diego, Harcourt Brace, 1986.

Recordings: *Dramatic Highlights from The House in Paris* (sound recording), Living Literature, 1969; *Dramatic Highlights from The Death of the Heart* (sound recording), Living Literature, 1969;

Editor, *The Faber Book of Modern Stories.* London, Faber & Faber, 1937.
Editor, *Thirty-four Short Stories,* by Katherine Mansfield. London, Collins, 1957.
Editor, *Doctor Thorne,* by Anthony Trollope. Boston, Houghton Mifflin, 1959.

*

Media Adaptations: *The House in Paris* (television film), 1977; *The Death of the Heart* (television film), 1977; *The Heat of the Day* (stage play; adapted by Harold Pinter) 1989, (television play; adapted by Pinter), 1991; *Rosemary Harris as Elizabeth Bowen:*

Rosemary Harris Performs the Works of the Anglo-Irish Writer Elizabeth Bowen (sound recording), 1995.

Manuscript Collections: Berg Collection, New York Public Library; Ransom Humanities Research Center, University of Texas at Austin; Houghton Library, Harvard University; Trinity College Library, Dublin.

Bibliography: *Elizabeth Bowen: A Descriptive Bibliography* by J'nan M. Sellery, Austin, Texas University Press, 1977; *Elizabeth Bowen: A Bibliography* by J'nan M. Sellery and William O. Harris, Austin, The Humanities Research Center of the University of Texas, 1981.

Critical Studies: *Elizabeth Bowen* by Jocelyn Brooke, London and New York, Longmans Green, 1952; *Elizabeth Bowen: An Introduction to Her Novels* by William W. Heath, Madison, University of Wisconsin Press, 1961; *Elizabeth Bowen* by Allan E. Austin, Boston, Twayne, 1971, revised 1989; *Elizabeth Bowen* by Edwin J. Kenney, Lewisburg, Pennsylvania, Bucknell University Press, 1974; *Patterns of Reality: Elizabeth Bowen's Novels* by Harriet Blodgett, The Hague, Mouton, 1975; *Elizabeth Bowen: Portrait of a Writer* by Victoria Glendinning, London, Weidenfeld & Nicolson, 1977, New York, Knopf, 1978; *Elizabeth Bowen: An Estimation* by Hermione Lee, London, Vision Press, 1981; *Elizabeth Bowen* by Patricia Craig, London, Penguin, 1986; *Elizabeth Bowen* edited by Harold Bloom, New York, Chelsea House, 1987; *Elizabeth Bowen* by Phyllis Lassner, Savage, Maryland, Barnes & Noble, 1989, and her *Elizabeth Bowen: A Study of the Short Fiction,* New York, Twayne, 1991; *How Will the Heart Endure: Elizabeth Bowen and the Landscape of War* by Heather Bryant Jordan, Ann Arbor, University of Michigan Press, 1992; *Elizabeth Bowen and the Dissolution of the Novel: Still Lives* by Andrew Bennet and Nicholas Royle, New York, St. Martin's Press, 1994; *Elizabeth Bowen: A Reputation in Writing* by Renée C. Hoogland, New York, New York University Press, 1994.

* * *

Elizabeth Bowen was born Anglo-Irish, a distinction that put her in a curious position both in Ireland and in England, and one that affected her life and writing in profound ways. Her family was Protestant and landed gentry, and being a Protestant to the manor born in Ireland means she occupied a class position that put her at odds with most of her fellow Irish. Her father, Henry Cole Bowen, had rebelled against his own father by opting for a career rather than full-time management of Bowen's Court, the family estate and ancestral home in Ireland. Bowen's grandfather Robert left the home to his son Henry, but without the surrounding lands to support it. Consequently, Henry Bowen struggled greatly to support and maintain Bowen's Court. His constant hard work meant that he was often away or unavailable to Bowen as she grew up. When she was five, her father suffered a severe mental breakdown, and eventually Elizabeth's mother, Florence Colley Bowen, was advised to leave Ireland and move with her daughter to the English coast, where she had family. Bowen and her mother spent the next several years living at Hythe and Folkstone in England, and all of Bowen's formal education took place in England.

The separation from her father was hard on Bowen, but her relationship with him had been distant in any case. Bowen felt that both her father and mother were distracted and lived in their own worlds, from which she felt somewhat excluded. Although Bowen was close to her mother during their years in England, she felt at a distance from her mother and looked back on her childhood as an unhappy time, marked by silence. The difficulty of her childhood was heightened by the fact that Florence Colley Bowen developed cancer and died when Bowen was only 13. A series of aunts assumed guardianship of Elizabeth and supervised her education. Her father sufficiently recovered in 1912 and eventually remarried, so Bowen was able to spend summers at Bowen's Court and returned to live there briefly once her education at Downe House was complete. During this time in Ireland, she was again exposed to the political difficulties of Anglo-Irish life in Ireland. Her novel *The Last September* reflects her awareness of these difficulties. Although Bowen Court was not destroyed, several Anglo-Irish big houses nearby were destroyed during Irish political unrest, and the house in *The Last September* is destroyed as its owner watches.

Bowen returned to England in 1918 to study art, but her artistic pursuits were abandoned in favor of a career in writing. Phyllis Lassner argues that "[w]riting overcame the silence which characterized her life while dramatizing its crippling effect on fictive characters." Indeed, many Bowen novels and stories feature adolescent characters whose own family stability has been destroyed and who are left foundering, as adults around them hide truths and offer no real comfort or love. Her stories met with rejection at first, until the writer Rose Macaulay took an interest in Bowen and helped to promote her. Her first collection of stories was published in 1923, and shortly thereafter, Bowen met and married Alan Cameron, who worked first as an educational administrator and later for the BBC. Their marriage, while not particularly passionate, was a haven for each and endured despite the many affairs Bowen had, some perhaps with women, and despite Cameron's health problems and tendencies to abuse alcohol. As Bowen's literary reputation grew, she became a favorite in certain literary and intellectual circles. Cameron was never directly a part of such circles but was tolerated and even liked by most of the young writers who flocked to his wife.

Bowen's novels and short stories focus mainly on female characters, often young women, often women in intense and significant relation to each other. Her 1928 novel *The Hotel* describes one such significant attachment between a young woman, Sydney Warren, and the older, widowed Mrs. Kerr. Critics Jane Rule and Renee Hoogland argue convincingly that Bowen's fiction grew increasingly concerned with lesbian themes and should be read as part of a lesbian literary heritage. Her fiction generally is concerned with themes of identity: national, gendered, and sexual. Though the attachments between women in her novels are not usually overtly sexual or lesbian, the intensely passional connections between her women characters are surely homoerotic. Bowen also wrote several stories that are supernatural in theme and qualify as ghost or horror stories.

In her novels, Bowen is an acute observer of social pretensions and, without being nostalgic or falsely sentimental, can express great sympathy for young people, especially young women coming of age without appropriate guidance or honest, caring adult role models. Her novel *The Death of the Heart* traces the life of Portia Quayne, an orphaned teenager who is sent to live with an older half-brother and his wife. Their home offers no real refuge for Portia, who is the offspring of a scandalous second marriage, and she is left alone to try to make her way through a confusing maze of class expectations and budding sexuality.

Bowen believed that fiction is rooted in the experiences of the author's life, but at the same time she rejected the overtly autobiographical or confessional impulse. Her private life was marked by passionate affairs and unconventional behaviors, but publicly her life was governed by social conventions and traditions. At age 31 she inherited Bowen's Court upon her father's death, and she and Cameron spent much of their time there, entertaining grandly and playing the role of heirs to the aristocracy. Bowen struggled to maintain Bowen's Court even after her husband's death in 1952, but finally in 1960 she conceded that it was too much of a financial and emotional strain and sold the estate. Elizabeth Bowen died in 1973 of lung cancer but was a writer to the end, working on the autobiographical *Pictures and Conversations* at the time of her death.

—Martha Henn

BRADLEY, Marion Zimmer

Pseudonyms: Lee Chapman; John Dexter; Miriam Gardner; Valerie Graves; Morgan Ives. **Nationality:** American. **Born:** Albany, New York, 3 June 1930. **Education:** New York State College for Teachers, 1946-48; Hardin-Simmons University, Abilene, Texas, B.A. in English, Spanish, psychology 1964; University of California, Berkeley. **Family:** Married 1) Robert A. Bradley in 1949 (divorced 1964), one son; 2) Walter Henry Breen in 1964 (divorced 1990), one son and one daughter. **Career:** Editor, *Marion Zimmer Bradley's Fantasy Magazine,* Berkeley, California, since 1988. Singer and writer. **Awards:** *Locus* Award, 1984. **Address:** P.O. Box 72, Berkeley, California 94701-0072, U.S.A. **Online Address:** (web site) http://www.well.com/user/mzbfm.

Publications

Novels

The Door through Space. New York, Ace, 1961; London, Arrow, 1979.

Seven from the Stars. New York, Ace, 1962.

The Planet Savers. New York, Ace, 1962; London, Arrow, 1979; expanded edition, Ace, 1976.

The Sword of Aldones. New York, Ace, 1962; London, Arrow, 1979; revised as *Sharra's Exile,* New York, DAW, 1981; London, Arrow, 1983.

Spare Her Heaven (as Morgan Ives). Derby, Connecticut, Monarch, 1963; abridged edition, as *Anything Goes,* Sydney, Stag, 1964.

The Bloody Sun. New York, Ace, 1964; London, Arrow, 1978; revised edition, New York, Ace, 1979.

Falcons of Narabedla. New York, Ace, and London, Arrow, 1984.

Star of Danger. New York, Ace, 1965; London, Arrow, 1978.

Castle Terror. New York, Lancer, 1965; Sutton, Surrey, Severn House, 1994.

Knives of Desire (as Morgan Ives). San Diego, Corinth, 1966.

No Adam for Eve (as John Dexter). San Diego, Corinth, 1966.

Souvenir of Monique. New York, Ace, 1967.

Bluebeard's Daughter. New York, Lancer, 1968.

The Brass Dragon. New York, Ace, 1969; London, Methuen, 1978.

The Winds of Darkover. New York, Ace, 1970; London, Arrow, 1978.

The World Wreckers. New York, Ace, 1971; London, Arrow, 1979.

Dark Satanic. New York, Berkley, 1972; Sutton, Surrey, Severn House, 1991.

Darkover Landfall. New York, DAW, 1972; London, Arrow, 1978.

Witch Hill (as Valerie Graves). San Diego, Greenleaf, 1972; as Bradley, Sutton, Surrey, Severn House, 1992.

In the Steps of the Master (novelization of TV play). New York, Tempo, 1973.

Hunters of the Red Moon. New York, DAW, 1973; London, Arrow, 1979; bylined with Paul Edwin Zimmer, New York, DAW, 1992.

The Spell Sword. New York, DAW, 1974; London, Arrow, 1978.

Endless Voyage. New York, Ace, 1975; expanded edition, as *Endless Universe,* 1979.

The Heritage of Hastur. New York, DAW, 1975; London, Arrow, 1979.

Can Ellen Be Saved? (novelization of TV play). New York, Grosset & Dunlap, 1975.

Drums of Darkness: An Astrological Gothic Novel: Leo. New York, Ballantine, 1976.

The Shattered Chain. New York, DAW, 1976; London, Arrow, 1978.

The Forbidden Tower. New York, DAW, 1977; London, Prior, 1979.

Stormqueen! New York, DAW, 1978; London, Arrow, 1980.

The Ruins of Isis. Norfolk, Virginia, Donning, 1978; London, Arrow, 1980.

The Catch Trap. New York, Ballantine, 1979; London, Sphere, 1986.

The Survivors, with Paul E. Zimmer. New York, DAW, 1979; London, Arrow, 1985.

The House between the Worlds. Garden City, New York, Doubleday, 1980; expanded edition, New York, Ballantine, 1981.

Two to Conquer. New York, DAW, 1980; London, Arrow, 1982.

Survey Ship. New York, Ace, 1980.

Hawkmistress! New York, DAW, 1982; London, Arrow, 1985.

The Mists of Avalon. New York, Knopf, 1982; London, Joseph, 1983.

Web of Light. Norfolk, Virginia, Donning, 1983.

Thendara House. New York, DAW, 1983; London, Arrow, 1985, revised, Sutton, Surrey, Severn House, 1995.

Oath of the Renuciates (includes *The Shattered Chain* and *Thendara House*). Garden City, New York, Doubleday, 1984.

Web of Darkness. New York, Pocket Books, 1984; with *Web of Light,* Glasgow, Drew, 1985; as *The Fall of Atlantis,* New York, Baen, 1987.

The Inheritor. New York, Tor, 1984; Wallington, Surrey, Severn House, 1992.

City of Sorcery. New York, DAW, 1984; London, Arrow, 1986.

Night's Daughter. New York, Ballantine, and London, Inner Circle, 1985.

Warrior Woman. New York, DAW, 1985; London, Arrow, 1987.

The Firebrand. New York, Simon and Schuster, 1987; London, Joseph, 1988.

The Heirs of Hammerfell. New York, DAW, 1989; London, Legend, 1991.

Black Trillium, with Julian May and Andre Norton. New York, Doubleday, 1990; London, Grafton, 1991.
Witch Hill. New York, Tor, 1990; Wallington, Surrey, Severn House, 1992.
Rediscovery, with Mercedes Lackey. New York, DAW, 1993.
The Forest House. London, Joseph, 1993; New York, Viking, 1994.
Lady of the Trillium. New York, Bantam, 1995.
Ghostlight. New York, Tor, 1995.
Tiger Burning Bright, with Andre Norton and Mercedes Lackey. New York, Morrow, 1995.

Novels as Miriam Gardner

The Strange Women. Derby, Connecticut, Monarch, 1962.
My Sister, My Love. Derby, Connecticut, Monarch, 1963.
Twilight Lovers. Derby, Connecticut, Monarch, 1964.

Short Stories

The Dark Intruder and Other Stories. New York, Ace, 1964.
The Parting of Arwen. Baltimore, T-K Graphics, 1974.
Lythande. New York, DAW, 1986; London, Sphere, 1988.
The Best of Marion Zimmer Bradley, edited by Martin H. Greenberg. Chicago, Academy Chicago, 1985; abridged edition, New York, DAW, 1988; London, Orbit, 1990; original version expanded as *Jamie and Other Stories: The Best of Marion Zimmer Bradley,* Chicago, Academy Chicago, 1993.
Marion Zimmer Bradley's Darkover. New York, DAW, 1993.
That Way Lies Camelot. New York, HarperCollins, 1996.

For Children

The Colors of Space. Derby, Connecticut, Monarch, 1963; expanded edition, Norfolk, Virginia, Donning, 1983; as *The Colours of Space,* London, Lightning, 1989.

Other

Songs from Rivendell. N.p., 1959.
A Complete, Cumulative Checklist of Lesbian, Variant, and Homosexual Fiction. N.p., 1960.
Of Men, Halflings, and Hero-Worship. Rochester, Texas, Fantasy Amateur Press Association, 1961.
I am a Lesbian (as Lee Chapman). Derby, Connecticut, Monarch, 1962.
The Necessity for Beauty: Robert W. Chambers and the Romantic Tradition. Baltimore, T-K Graphics, 1974.
The Jewel of Arwen. Baltimore, T-K Graphics, 1974.
Fandom: Its Value to the Professional," in *Inside Outer Space: Science Fiction Professionals Look at Their Craft,* edited by Sharon Jarvis. New York, F. Ungar, 1985.

Editor, *The Keeper's Price and Other Stories.* New York, DAW, 1980.
Editor, *Sword of Chaos and Other Stories.* New York, DAW, 1982.
Editor, *Greyhaven: An Anthology of Fantasy.* New York, DAW, 1983.
Editor, *Sword and Sorceress 1-12.* New York, DAW, 1984-95; vol. 1 published London, Headline, 1988.
Editor, *Free Amazons of Darkover.* New York, DAW, 1985.
Editor, *Other Side of the Mirror.* New York, DAW, 1987.
Editor, *Red Sun of Darkover.* New York, DAW, 1987.
Editor, *Four Moons of Darkover.* New York, DAW, 1988.
Editor, *The Spells of Wonder.* New York, DAW, 1989.
Editor, *Domain of Darkover.* New York, DAW, 1990.
Editor, *Renunciates of Darkover.* New York, DAW, 1991.
Editor, *Leroni of Darkover.* New York, DAW, 1991.
Editor, *Towers of Darkover.* New York, DAW, 1993.
Editor, *Snows of Darkover.* New York, DAW, 1994.
Editor, *The Best of Marion Zimmer Bradley's Fantasy Magazine.* New York, Warner, 2 vols., 1994-95.

Translator, *El Villano in su Ricon,* by Lope de Vega. N.p., 1971.

*

Bibliography: *Leigh Brackett, Marion Zimmer Bradley, Anne McCaffrey: A Primary and Secondary Bibliography* by Rosemarie Arbur, Boston, Hall, 1982.

Manuscript Collection: Boston University.

Critical Studies: *The Gemini Problem: A Study in Darkover* by Walter Breen, Baltimore, T-K Graphics, 1975; *The Darkover Dilemma: Problems of the Darkover Series* by S. Wise, Baltimore, T-K Graphics, 1976; "Marion Zimmer Bradley's Ethic of Freedom" by Susan M. Shwartz, in *The Feminine Eye,* edited by Tom Staicar, New York, F. Ungar, 1982; "Why Write Fantasy? A Mythopoeic Conference XIV Panel" (interview), in *Mythlore* (Whittier, California), 10(4), spring 1984; "Heterosexual Plots and Lesbian Subtexts: Toward a Theory of Lesbian Narrative Space" by Marilyn R. Farwell, in *Lesbian Texts and Contexts: Radical Revisions,* edited by Karla Jay and Joanne Glasgow, New York, New York University Press, 1990; "Why Change the Arthur Story? Marion Zimmer Bradley's *The Mists of Avalon*" by Lee Ann Tobin, in *Extrapolation* (Kent, Ohio), 34(2), summer 1993.

* * *

When Marion Zimmer Bradley was asked the question "Why write fantasy?" she answered "I write Fantasy because it is the only way I can tell the absolute, unvarnished truth." In a career that began in the 1950s, Bradley has pioneered a space for women writers of science fiction, broadening the role of independent female heroines as early as her 1954 short story "Centaurus Changeling." In more than 50 novels and short story collections, and as editor of the *Marion Zimmer Bradley's Fantasy Magazine,* she has written about and encouraged writing about gender roles, human relationships, and sexuality in a variety of fantastic, mythic, and realistic circumstances. However, Bradley herself has remained on the margins of literary acclaim: she has won neither a Hugo or Nebula award, and none of her "Darkover" books have been honored with a coveted review in the *New York Times.* Among all her novels only *The Mists of Avalon,* a re-telling of the Arthurian romance, has received notice from mainstream reviewers, while also attracting the modicum of scholarly attention that has focused on her work. Recently however, Bradley's science fiction has received increased academic interest as one of the early manifestations of proto-feminist science fiction.

Throughout her career Bradley has maintained a steady following among female readers—traditionally a minority in the sci-fi genre. In her essay "Fandom: Its Value to the Professional," she describes how she herself rose from the ranks of fans and amateurs: Her stories were "published in the letter columns of the old pulp magazines; later, in the pages of ... fanzines published by other young science fiction or fantasy fiction enthusiasts." Bradley's relationship to her own "fandom" has been ongoing and productive for both herself and those who follow her work. She has served as mentor and advocate for several writers—including Diane Paxson—who first appeared in fan publications before going professional. Besides giving writers and fans of fantasy a place to experience "a very strong sense of togetherness," and besides giving Bradley herself "feedback," fanzines and fandom offer readers a place, Darkover, where "it is easier, and safer ... to talk about women's rights, homosexuality, unusual approaches to religion, gender roles in society, and extrasensory perception." Bradley frequently counters the stereotype of science fiction/fantasy fans as mindless escapists. Instead, she would argue, they are politically and intellectually engaged.

Bradley uses fantasies based on myths and scientific speculation to explore the very down-to-earth journeys of protagonists who struggle with physical, societal, or psychological limitations. Her characters often face making choices between conflicting cultures, each offering different fulfillments and constraints. Many of her characters find themselves unable to reconcile their places in either culture. For instance, Lew Alton, protagonist of *The Sword of Aldones* and its revision, *Sharra's Exile* (the first Darkover novel), is the son of a Darkovan father and a Terran mother. Often such characters find themselves moving between two conflicting cultures, comfortable in neither and isolated from both. Throughout her novels, whether they take place in the England of Camelot or on distant planets, Bradley's characters journey toward maturity and acceptance of their complex selves and conflicting social obligations.

The Darkover series—which is exemplified by the revision of 1962's *The Sword of Aldones* into the psychologically more complex *Sharra's Exile,* released by DAW in 1981—is the heart of Bradley's work. The series loosely chronicles the history of Planet Darkover, from its colonization by Terrans, its isolation and development as a distinct culture, and its subsequent rediscovery by and conflicts with the Terran Empire. Darkovan resistance to Terran technology and culture, development and control of psychic powers (*laran*), and the struggle of women in a feudal and patriarchal culture rooted in the Colonists' own Anglo/Celtic background form the basis of this series, which encompasses 18 novels. While each can be read as a self-contained story, some characters develop and come to self-knowledge across several novels.

Feminist scholars have been most interested in the three Darkover novels that concern the Free Amazons/Renunciate sisterhood. In *The Shattered Chain* (1976), *Thendara House* (1983), and *City of Sorcery* (1984), Bradley shows how women on Darkover resist the patriarchal and rigidly hierarchical social system. Tradition mandates that women of the aristocratic class, the Comyn, be controlled, protected, and married off by male "protectors" to preserve the genes and psychic powers of the aristocracy. All women, with the exception of Renunciates, are therefore subject to male control. The Renunciates, a sisterhood that requires an oath to renounce all protections and obligations to men and the patriarchal family, forms an alternative "family" for women. Most have joined seeking freedom from particularly abusive men or from experiences of male violence such as battering or rape. In the opening novel of the trilogy, *The Shattered Chain,* the aristocratic Rohana disguises herself as a Free Amazon to accomplish the rescue of her relative, Melora, and Melora's daughter. Melora had been kidnapped and forced into concubinage/marriage by a despot who lived in the Dry Towns, where women are literally chained. Because the Dry Towns were outside their Domain, Melora's male relatives had refused to attempt a rescue. Melora is finally rescued, only to die giving birth to her son. But her adolescent daughter, Jaelle, is saved from life as a chained woman. Hating male domination, she chooses to join the Renunciates.

Jaelle figures largely in the next novel, *Thendara House,* in which a female-accomplished rescue mission/quest forms the plot. Magdalen Lorne, a Darkovan-reared Terran, attempts to rescue her ex-husband, who has been kidnapped by bandits. In order to travel freely in the Domains, she disguises herself as a Renunciate. When she is discovered by Jaelle and a traveling group of Free Amazons, Magdalen is forced to take their oath. She decides to honor the oath, even though it was taken under duress, and becomes oath-bound to the women who live in the "guild house" at Thendara.

Bradley's Renunciate stories, with their plots of female adventure and questing, are frequently complicated by the conflicting desires of their protagonists. For instance, Jaelle finds herself in love with Peter Haldane, a Terran whom she and Magdalen have rescued. This complicates the relationship between the two women; what appears as jealousy over male affection will later resolve itself when Jaelle and Magdalen become lovers and then freemates (an alternative form of marriage). Prior to this, however, Jaelle marries Haldane and lives as a Terran wife, although her marriage will prove to be a failure and she will return to the Renunciate sisterhood. But Magdalen is one who has understood the sacrifices and made an informed choice between two conflicting forms of fulfillment—marriage and self-determination. The purpose of the Renunciate sisterhood on Darkover is to give women a choice to live outside the patriarchal rules and protections of Darkovan society. Never easy, such choices require renouncing pleasures and following the rough path forged by women in a man's world. According to Susan Shwartz in *The Feminine Eye,* Bradley depicts the choices of women as "pain-filled," and restricted by their roles. In *The Shattered Chain,* Shwartz argues, "The Amazons (or Renunciates) became a metaphor for female and human conditions on Darkover and elsewhere of being bound by old choices, refusing to remain so, and—through enduring the pain of choice—arriving at new solutions and restored integrity."

In novels outside the Darkover series Bradley explores the possibilities of matriarchal rule—*The Ruins of Isis* (1978)—and a nonsexist, non-reproduction-based culture—*Endless Universe* (1979). In *The Ruins of Isis,* Bradley shows her condemnation of the flip side of male domination. The matriarchal society of the Planet Isis, in order to eliminate war, has subjugated men to the role of pet/slave. The protagonist, the anthropologist Cendri, accompanies her husband Dal, an archeologist, to the planet Isis. They come from Unity, a federation/empire that is supposedly egalitarian. While on the female-dominated planet, Cendri must treat her husband as the women on Isis treat their men: with contempt and brutality. Cendri, who is secretly studying the planet's culture, learns not only that oppression is wrong no matter who's on top, but also about the subtle ways in which her own world—and her own marriage—is less egalitarian than she had realized. Both she and Isis undergo a transformation. The matriarchy on Isis collapses after a rebellion by the men, emerging at novel's end as a fledgling nonsexist culture; Cendri learns to value female relationships, including lesbian love, and becomes a more equal partner in her marriage.

In *Endless Universe* Bradley explores androgyny among a group of space travelers called Explorers. Because of their exposure to radiation, Explorers have been stripped of all skin-color variations and have lost the ability to reproduce—forcing them to buy unwanted children to rear. Whether their lack of sex roles is the result of, or the cause of, their lack of reproductive capability, the society on board ship is one without sexual discrimination of any kind. Bradley uses *Endless Voyage* as a vehicle to comment on race and racism as culturally constructed, though, by in large, her work focuses on European, Anglo-based cultures and deals with non-European culture only occasionally.

The Mists of Avalon, published in 1982, allows Bradley to bring to bear her concerns about gender and sexuality through the retelling and revising of the King Arthur legend. According to Lee Ann Tobin in "Why Change the Arthur Story?" Bradley rewrites the medieval tale in a way that de-centers Christianity and the chivalric tradition. In its place the author repositions the witch Morgaine le Fay as a "powerful heroine," and Gwenhyfar as a woman who emerges from an "unnatural, self-hating upbringing" to find comfort in a Goddess-focused and female-oriented spirituality "more fulfilling than life in the patriarchal world of the chivalric kingdom." Marilyn R. Farwell also notes that in this "basically heterosexual text," Bradley has written in "strong lesbian overtones." Indeed, Bradley has not turned to the Arthurian romance nostalgically, but rather to rewrite it with women as complex heroines rather than heroines fatally cast amid the tragic fall of Camelot.

A self-proclaimed "high-output" writer, the prolific Bradley has written numerous science fiction and fantasy novels set on worlds other than Darkover, as well as several lesbian romances (under pseudonyms), *The Catch Trap* (a novel set in the 1940s about two male circus performers who fall in love), and bibliographies of gay and lesbian fiction. Her productivity and her loyalty to her fans have made her a difficult author for the academic establishment to take seriously. Bradley's books, while they engage with serious societal and political issues, also indulge in fantasies about feudal, aristocratic worlds where horses and swords abound and sorceresses wield amazing powers both terrifying and healing. While she claims her readers are "not looking for vicarious experience of life," her novels bring to vivid life an oppressive class system, patriarchy, and a relatively homogenous European culture within which independent, powerful heroines move. In Marion Zimmer Bradley's fantastic worlds characters often must choose whether to marry the lord and have a family, or climb mountains, fight with swords, and join a sisterhood. There is neither absolute freedom nor absolute fulfillment. What *is* important for Bradley's female protagonists is the choice: how they will balance freedom with obligations.

—Nancy Jesser

BRADSTREET, Anne (Dudley)

Nationality: American. **Born:** Northampton, England, 1612(?). **Education:** Educated at home. **Family:** Married Simon Bradstreet in 1628; eight children. **Career:** Sailed to New England with John Winthrop, 1630; settled in Ipswich, Massachusetts, 1635-45; settled in North Andover, Massachusetts, 1645. **Died:** 16 September 1672.

Publications

Poetry

Several Poems Compiled with a Great Variety of Wit and Learning. Boston, n.p., 1640; as *The Tenth Muse Lately Sprung Up in America ...,* introduced by John Woodbridge, London, Stephen Bowtell, 1650; second, enlarged, edition, under original title, Boston, John Foster, 1678; as *The Works of Anne Bradstreet in Prose and Verse,* edited by John Harvard Ellis, Charleston, Massachusetts, A. E. Cutter, 1867.

The Works of Anne Bradstreet, edited by Jeannine Hensley, forward by Adrienne Rich. Cambridge, Massachusetts, Harvard University Press, and Oxford, Oxford University Press, 1967.

The Complete Works of Anne Bradstreet, edited by Joseph R. McElrath, Jr. Boston, Twayne, 1981.

A Woman's Inner World: Selected Poetry and Prose of Anne Bradstreet, edited by Adelaide P. Amore. Lanham, Maryland, University Press of America, 1982.

New England Meditative Poetry: Anne Bradstreet and Edward Taylor, edited by Charles E. Hambrick-Stowe, New York, Paulist Press, 1988.

*

Media Adaptations: *Portrait of Anne Bradstreet: A Cantata for Soprano Voice* (musical scores) by Dorothy L. Crawford, Hannacroix, New York, Loux Music, 1987.

Bibliography: *Anne Bradstreet: A Reference Guide* by Raymond F. Dolle, Boston, G. K. Hall, 1990.

Critical Studies: *Anne Bradstreet* by Josephine K. Piercy, New York, Twayne, 1965; *Anne Bradstreet, "The Tenth Muse"* by Elizabeth Wade White, New York, Oxford University Press, 1971; *Critical Essays on Anne Bradstreet* edited by Pattie Cowell and Ann Stanford, Boston, G. K. Hall, 1983; *An American Triptych: Anne Bradstreet, Emily Dickinson, Adrienne Rich* by Wendy Martin, Chapel Hill, University of North Carolina Press, 1983; *Anne Bradstreet Revisited* by Rosamond Rosenmeier, Boston, Twayne, 1991; *Sinful Self, Saintly Self: The Puritan Experience of Poetry* by Jeffrey A. Hammond, Athens, University of Georgia Press, 1993; *Gender Roles, Literary Authority, and Three American Women Writers* by Theresa Freda Nicolay, New York, P. Lang, 1995.

* * *

In 1640, Anne Bradstreet became the first person in British North America to have a volume of poetry published when her *Several Poems Compiled with a Great Variety of Wit and Learning* was printed in Boston, Massachusetts. Most famous now for her lyric poetry, Bradstreet also wrote several long poems and a series of religious meditations in prose. A Puritan, her writing reveals a struggle between her religious faith and the harsh experiences of living in colonial Massachusetts during the mid-17th century.

Bradstreet's first volume of poetry was published without her permission in London in 1650 under the title *The Tenth Muse Lately Sprung Up in America....* Her brother-in-law, John Woodbridge, had secretly arranged for her poetry to be printed and sold. While the volume received significant acclaim, the poet herself had a mixed reaction to the publication. While it was gratifying to see her work in print, the poems were published with errors and weak spots she would liked to have corrected. In addition, the Puritan society in which she lived would have little sympathy for such poetry because its purpose was other than to serve God. Bradstreet's brother-in-law, however, had taken care to protect her from literary and Puritan criticism; in his introduction Woodbridge notes that "these Poems are the fruit but of some few houres, curtailed from her sleep."

When the second edition of Bradstreet's poems was published posthumously in 1678, under the volume's original title, the poet had corrected the first British edition and added poems, including "The Author to Her Book," in which she confronts her roles as poetic and Puritan mother. Bradstreet describes *The Tenth Muse* as an "ill-form'd offspring" and speaks of her poetry with embarrassment and attachment: "At thy return my blushing was not small, / My rambling brat (in print) should mother call /.... Yet being mine own, at length affection would / Thy blemishes amend, if so I could." The organizing principle of Bradstreet's verse is connection, especially between her own roles as poet, Puritan, wife, and mother.

The subjects of Bradstreet's earliest poems are vast, including the nature of man, and the history of the world. In her "Prologue" to these works, Bradstreet acknowledges her traditionally masculine scope: "Let *Greeks* be *Greeks,* and Women what they are, / Men have precedency, and still excell, / It is but vaine, unjustly to wage war, / Men can doe best, and Women know it well; / Preheminence in each, and all is yours, / Yet grant some small acknowledgement of ours." Bradstreet's voice seems to be that of a humble woman feebly trying to imitate great men, yet she is also ironic in saying that men are better than women at waging war: the poet, detailing historical wars in gory detail, does not think war-making an admirable activity. Rather, the "small" effort for which she requests acknowledgment—writing poems—is the area in which she desires to be preeminent. So while she imitates men in the poems, Bradstreet is careful to distinguish the ways in which she, a woman, is superior.

Similarly, Bradstreet refines and tailors the role of Puritan to herself. Thus in her dialogue "The Flesh and the Spirit," she presents the Puritan struggle between sensual flesh and God-serving spirit. She makes the flesh and the spirit remarkably similar: both seek beauty and riches, but in different incarnations. The Flesh wants material wealth, beauty, and fame; the Spirit seeks spiritual riches and salvation. Thus Bradstreet reconciles the tension between the immediate experiences of life on earth with the Puritan ethic of preparation for the next world. The Spirit persuades the reader that she will have all that the Flesh offers, and more: "If I of Heaven may have my fill, / Take thou the world, and all that will." Bradstreet, rather than simply silencing the desires of the Flesh with sheer willpower, addresses earthly desires with the offer of heavenly gratification, again emphasizing connection as an ideal relationship.

In her more mature poems, included 1678's *Several Poems,* Bradstreet continues to find connections and balance between her different roles. In the poem "Before the Birth of one of her Children," the poet fears her own potential death and desires to be remembered by her husband: "... when that knot's unty'd that made us one, / I may seem thine, who in effect am none." And later in the same poem, she jealously worries about her children with a stepmother: "Look to my little babes my dear remains. / And if thou love thy self, or loved'st me. / These O protect from step Dames injury." In another poem she misses her absent husband: "Tell him here's worse then a confused matter, / His little world's a fathom under water, / Nought but the fervor of his ardent beams / Hath power to dry the torrent of these streams." Bradstreet expresses her emotional anguish over loss in part by focusing on the whole: her husband and she complement or complete each other. In some poems the completeness of their love ensures their connection with God, as in "To my Dear and loving Husband": "Then while we live, in love lets so persever, / That when we live no more, we may live ever." And in others, her relationship with her husband becomes a symbol of her relationship with God, as in the lines about the "torrent of these streams" quoted above, his return and their renewed connection will mark the salvation after the Flood.

Bradstreet resolves the conflict in her experience as a wife by making her marriage a figure of divine completion. But in poems mourning the deaths of grandchildren, she finds it more difficult to accept the God that she, as a Puritan, must love and obey: she writes with bitter irony about a God who kills children in order to test adults. The elegy for her grandchild Elizabeth Bradstreet ends with the poet making a rote observation of God's power; later, mourning her grandson Simon Bradstreet, the word "say" is chillingly ironic: "Such was [God's] will, but why, let's not dispute, / With humble hearts and mouths put in the dust, / Let's say he's merciful, as well as just." Here Bradstreet cannot connect her roles of grandmother and Puritan; she can only go through the gesture—write the poem in which she tries to trust God—of reconciling her personal experience with her religious faith.

From a feminist perspective, Anne Bradstreet's effort to unify her socially circumscribed roles with her role as published poet in the New World clears ground upon which later women writers would build: she establishes that a woman can be wife, mother, Puritan, and poet without sacrificing any aspect of her life. She shows that reconciling those disparate roles requires a feminine identity made up of many connected and changing parts, rather than one hierarchically and rigidly structured.

—Elizabeth V. Young

BRAMBLE, Tabitha. *See* **ROBINSON, Mary (Darby).**

BRANT, Beth (E.)

Also known as Degonwadonti. **Nationality:** Mohawk. **Born:** Melvindale, Michigan, 6 May 1941. **Family:** Married (divorced), three daughters; companion of Denise Dorsz since 1976. **Career:**

Writer. Part-time teacher and lecturer on creative writing and Native American women's writing. Writer-in-residence, University of British Columbia, 1989, 1990, Pitzer College, Claremont, California, 1991, Trent University, 1992, Ka:nhiote Library, Tyendinaga Mohawk Territory, 1993, and Native Women's Resource Centre, Toronto, 1995. Contributor of short fiction, poems, and essays to periodicals, including *Aboriginal Voices, Canadian Woman Studies, Kenyon Review, Off Our Backs, Signs,* and *Sinister Wisdom.* **Awards:** Michigan Council for the Arts Creative Writing Awards, 1984 and 1986; Ontario Arts Council Creative Fiction Award, 1989; National Endowment for the Arts Literature fellowship, 1991; Canada Council Creative Writing Award, 1992; Affirmations Community Heritage Award (Detroit), 1995. **Member:** National Writers Union (United States and Canada), Native Circle of Writers of the Americas, North American Indian Association, Lesbians and Gays of the First Nations, Turtle Clan. **Address:** 18890 Reed, Melvindale, Michigan 48122, U.S.A.

Publications

Short Stories

Mohawk Trail. Ithaca, New York, Firebrand Books, 1985; Toronto, Women's Press, 1988.
Food & Spirits: Stories. Ithaca, New York, Firebrand Books, and Vancouver, Press Gang, 1991.

Uncollected Short Stories

"Songs from the Earth on Turtle's Back: Contemporary American Indian Poetry, edited by Joseph Bruchac. Greenfield Review Press, 1984.
"Indigenous Acts," in *Early Ripening: Poetry by Women,* edited by Marge Piercy. London and New York, Pandora Press, 1987.
"Native Origin," in *New Voices from the Longhouse: Contemporary Iroquois Writing,* edited by Joseph Bruchac. Greenfield, New York, Greenfield Review Press, 1989.
"Swimming Upstream," in *Talking Leaves: Contemporary Native American Short Stories,* edited by Craig Lesley. New York, Dell, 1991.
"Turtle Gal," in *Making Face, Making Soul/Haciendo Caras: Creative and Critical Perspectives by Women of Colour,* edited by Gloria Anzaldúa. San Francisco, Aunt Lute Press, 1990.
"Her Name Is Helen," in *An Intimate Wilderness: Lesbian Writers on Sexuality,* edited by Judith Barrington. Portland, Oregon, Eighth Mountain Press, 1991.
"Coyote Learns a New Trick," in *Getting Wet: Lesbian Tales of Seduction.* London, Women's Press, 1992.

Essays

"To Be or Not to Be Has Never Been the Question," in *Inversions,* edited by Betsy Warland. Vancouver, Press Gang, 1991.
"Giveaway: Native Lesbian Writers," in *Signs* (Durham, North Carolina), 18, summer 1993.
"Good Red Road: Native Women's Journey of Writing," in *And Still We Rise: Canadian Feminists Organizing for Change,* edited by Linda Carty. Toronto, Women's Press, 1993.
Writing as Witness: Essays and Talk. Toronto, Women's Press, 1994.

Other

Editor, *A Gathering of Spirit: A Collection by North American Indian Women.* Lincoln, Nebraska, Sinister Wisdom, 1984; expanded edition, Ithaca, New York, Firebrand, and Toronto, Women's Press, 1988.
Editor, *I'll Sing 'til the Day I Die: Conversations with Tyendinaga Elders.* Toronto, McGilligan, 1995.

*

Critical Studies: "Beth Brant: Telling the Truth for Each Other" by Kerrie Charmley in *Kinesis,* September 1989; "The Making of *A Gathering of Spirit*" by Cora Hoover, master's thesis, Yale University, 1991; "Disobedience (in Language) in Texts by Lesbian Native Americans" by Janice Gould in *Ariel* (Calgary, Alberta), 25, 1994; "Beth Brant: Writer and Poet, Visionary and Prophet" (interview) by Julie R. Enszer, *Between the Lines* (Ann Arbor, Michigan), April 1995.

* * *

The multiple voices in Beth Brant's stories reflect her varying experiences as a lesbian, grandmother, mother, and Native American raised to be a working-class woman in Detroit, Michigan. Brant writes for those who have been silenced. Her stories often explore disturbing topics that other less brave authors have failed to cover, such as incest, rape, and AIDS. Brant did not begin writing until the age of 40, when an eagle appeared to her as she was driving across the country. She interpreted its message as telling her to write for her people, whom she sees as equally Native Americans and lesbians.

Brant's powerful writing is both lyrical and blunt. Her working-class characters speak in language that makes the reader both see and feel them. Brant's first collection, *Mohawk Trail,* published in 1990, is centered in her experience of growing up in the industrial city of Detroit, but is framed by more traditional stories from her Native American origin. Her second collection, 1991's *Food and Spirits,* continues in this vein, adding stories set either on the reservation or in the country. Brant is able to portray convincingly male characters as well as female; many of her stories have sympathetic male protagonists, some of whom are African American. Both Brant's collection have been reviewed in the feminist press, but have received little attention from mainstream critics.

Seeking a better life for their children, Brant's grandparents moved from Ontario's Tyendinaga Mohawk Territory south to Detroit, where all of their children would married non-Native Americans. Although Brant has a mixed heritage, she considers herself a woman of the Mohawk turtle clan of the Bay of Quinte (Canada). She never finished high school, dropping out when she was 17 to marry and raise her three daughters.

In 1981 Brant sent her first short stories to the lesbian-feminist journal *Sinister Wisdom.* The editors, Adrienne Rich and Michelle Cliff, asked Brant to edit a special edition of the journal on Native American women, which eventually became *A Gathering of Spirit: A Collection by North American Indian Women,* published in 1984. Well received, *Gathering* was reprinted by Firebrand Books in 1988.

Beth Brant continues to advocate for lesbians and Native American women through the lectures and readings she gives not only locally but throughout the United States and Canada. Actively involved in numerous organizations and workshops, she also co-founded Turtle Grandmother Books, an archive and library of information about North American Indian women and a clearinghouse for Native American women's manuscripts, which continued from 1982 until 1987. Her gift—bringing to life the stories of those who have been silenced—continues to enrich us all.

—Annette Van Dyke

BRENT, Linda. *See* **JACOBS, Harriet Ann.**

BRENT OF BIN BIN. *See* **FRANKLIN, (Stella Marian Sarah) Miles.**

BRIDGET. *See* **ROBINSON, Mary (Darby).**

BRITTAIN, Vera

Nationality: British. **Born:** Newcastle under Lyme, Staffordshire, in 1893. **Education:** Somerville College, Oxford, B.A. 1921, M.A. 1925. **Military Service:** Voluntary Aid Detachment, nurse in London, Malta, and France, 1915-19; chairman, Food Relief Campaign, England, 1941-44. **Family:** Married the philosopher George Edward Gordon Catlin in 1925; one son, two daughters. **Career:** Author and journalist; lectured in United States and Canada, 1934-59, Holland, 1936, Scandinavia, 1945, Germany, 1947, India, 1949-50 and 1963, and South Africa, 1960. Chairman emeritus, *Peace News;* contributor to periodicals, including *Author, Books, This Week,* and *Week-end* (Canada). **Awards:** D.Litt., Mills College, 1950. **Member:** International League for Peace and Freedom (vice-president, 1945-70), Royal Society of Literature (fellow), Royal Commonwealth Society, Society of Women Writers and Journalists (honorary life member; president, 1965-70), National Peace Council, National Arts Theatre Club, Married Women's Association (president, 1962). **Died:** 29 March 1970.

PUBLICATIONS

Novels

The Dark Tide. Grant Richards, 1923.
Not without Honour. Grant Richards, 1924.
Honorable Estate. London, Macmillan, 1936.
Account Rendered. London, Macmillan, 1945.
Born 1925: A Novel of Youth. London, Macmillan, 1948.

Political/Social Theory

Women's Work in Modern England. Noel Douglas, 1928.
Halcyon, or the Future of Monogamy. London, Kegan Paul, 1929.

History

The Story of St. Martin's: An Epic of London. London, St. Martin-in-the-Fields, 1951.
Lady into Woman: A History of Women from Victoria to Elizabeth II. London, Dakers, 1953.
The Women at Oxford. London, Harrap, 1960.
The Pictorial History of St. Martin-in-the-Fields. London, Pitkin Pictorials, 1962.

Poetry

Verses of a V.A.D. Erskine Macdonald, 1918.
Poems of the War and After. London, Macmillan, 1934.

Essays

England's Hour. London, Macmillan, 1941.
On Becoming a Writer. London, Hutchinson, 1947; as *On Being an Author,* New York, Macmillan, 1948.
Radclyffe Hall: A Case of Obscenity? Femina, 1968; San Diego, A. S. Barnes, 1969.
Massacre by Bombing. Revisionist Press, 1981.

Autobiography

Testament of Youth. London, Macmillan, 1933.
Testament of Friendship: The Story of Winifred Holtby. London, Macmillan, 1940; with introduction by Carolyn Heilbrun, New York, Wideview Books, 1981.
Testament of Experience. London, Macmillan, 1957.
Chronicle of Friendship: Diary of the Thirties, 1932-1939. London, Gollancz, 1986.
Diary 1939-1945: Wartime Chronicle, edited by Alan Bishop and Y. Aleksandra Bennett. London, Gollancz, 1990.

Other

Thrice a Stranger (travel). London, Macmillan, 1938.
Humiliation with Honour. London, Dakers, 1942; New York, Friendship, 1945.
Seed of Chaos. New Vision, 1944.
In the Steps of John Bunyan. London, Rich & Cowan; as *Valiant Pilgrim,* New York, Macmillan, 1950.
Search after Sunrise: A Traveller's Story. London, Macmillan, 1951.
Long Shadows, with G. E. W. Sizer. London, A. Brown, 1958.
Selected Letters of Winifred Holtby and Vera Brittain. London, A. Brown, 1960.
Pethick-Lawrence: A Portrait. London, Allen & Unwin, 1963.
The Rebel Passion: A Short History of Some Pioneer Peace-making. Fellowship Publications, 1964.

Envoy Extraordinary: A Study of Vijaya Lakshmni Pandit and Her Contribution to Modern India. London, Allen & Unwin, 1965; San Diego, A. S. Barnes, 1966.
Testament of a Generation: The Journalism of Vera Brittain and Winifred Holtby, edited by Paul Berry and Allen Bishop. London, Virago, 1985.

Editor, with George Catlin and Sheila Hodges, *Above All Nations.* London, Gollancz, 1945; New York, Harper, 1949.
Editor, *Pavements at Anderby: Tales of 'South Riding' and Other Regions,* by Winifred Holtby. London, Collins, 1937.

*

Critical Studies: *Vera Brittain* by Hilary Bailey, London, Penguin, 1987; *Vera Brittain and Winifred Holtby: A Working Partnership* by Jean E. Kennard, Hanover, New Hampshire, University Press of New England, 1989.

* * *

From the beginning of her writing career, which spanned over half a century, Vera Brittain elicited powerful responses from readers, critics, and the subjects of her scrutiny. In fact, her first novel, *The Dark Tide*—though it received lukewarm reviews from critics at the time of its publication in 1923—created a stir among Oxford denizens because it exposed unsavory conditions for women in the college. Brittain's own alma mater, Somerville College, banned the novel outright.

Brittain is probably best known for her autobiography *Testament of Youth,* which chronicles her fervent desire to be educated—chiefly influenced by South African writer Olive Schreiner's *Women and Labour,* which Brittain read when she was 16—and the many obstacles she encountered along the way to such higher education. Of her own chronicle, Brittain herself would probably have suggested that *Testament of Youth* is more about her personal coming of age as a woman against the backdrop of World War I than it is a feminist tract. Indeed, the work focuses on her experiences in London, Malta, and the Western Front in France. Brittain's views at the beginning of the war reflected those of most people: it was an inconvenience more than anything else. She begins *Testament of Youth* by stating, "When the Great War broke out, it came to me not as a superlative tragedy, but as an interruption of the most exasperating kind to my personal plans." Little did she realize that, by the time the war ended over four years later, she would lose nearly everyone who was closest to her, including her fiance, Roland Leighton, and her beloved younger brother, Edward. Little did the rest of Europe know that it would lose a tremendous portion of its younger generation in a war to which there was then no comparison, either in firepower or lives lost or shattered; Gertrude Stein would later refer to that age group as the "Lost Generation." After the war, Brittain would return to Oxford—but Oxford was a much different place than the school she had left in 1915. *Testament of Youth* is at once historical reminisce and feminist awakening: "As a generation of women we were now sophisticated to an extent which was revolutionary when compared to the romantic ignorance of 1914."

While at Oxford for the second time, Brittain met Winifred Holtby, a fellow student who would become her confidante and the subject of her 1940 book, *Testament of Friendship: The Story of Winifred Holtby.* First meetings between the two women were inauspicious ones, as Holtby's popularity and Brittain's depression made for an awkward tension between them. "We did not, to begin with, like each other at all," Brittain states tersely in *Testament of Friendship.* But their common service during the war eventually brought the two together and they became friends. After receiving seconds at Oxford, Brittain and Holtby lived together while they each pursued literary and journalistic careers. Even after Brittain married George Catlin in 1925, she and Holtby were constant companions, especially since Catlin was away from home more than he was there. Holtby would die in 1935 at the age of 37; *Testament of Friendship* was Brittain's effort to memorialize both a promising young novelist and a true friend.

Brittain's *Testament of Experience* covers the years 1925-1950, during which she married the political scientist and philosopher George Catlin, had three children, lost Holtby to chronic kidney disease, and lived through another world war and its aftermath. Her diary entry for 4 September 1939, as recorded in this book, reads, "As I write this date, I think to myself incredulously that before long it will be as familiar as August 4, 1914, and stand for as great significance—but what significance? More misery? A longer or shorter period of terror? Victory or defeat or revolution?" Brittain's words are more prophetic than she, or anyone, could have known. The difference this time would be the number of civilians who were killed, not by invading soldiers fighting for strategic position but by a regime bent on racial and religious monopoly.

Immediately after the war began Brittain received a summons from the Ministry of Information imploring her to use her writing skills toward creating war propaganda. She declined, stating that she wanted to work toward peace with the then-neutral United States. In 1941, after the Japanese attack on Pearl Harbor signalled the United States' entry into the war, Brittain worked as the chairman of the Food Relief Campaign until the Allied invasion of France three years later. When the war ended, she continued her work to feed the war's ravaged survivors. The final pages of *Testament of Experience* chronicle Brittain's trip to India in 1948; she was instrumental in helping to improve relations between England and its former colony after India's independence.

In 1960 Brittain published *The Women at Oxford,* an overview of the history of women's involvement with England's prestigious Oxford University. Brittain discusses the 12 female students who, in 1879, were the first to enter this then-exclusively male bastion of higher education. Although enrolled in Somerville College, female students were not allowed to receive degrees until 1919; it would be another 40 years before the women's colleges would obtain equal status with the men's. Despite Brittain's personal ties to Oxford University and any residual feelings regarding her alma mater's treatment of her first novel, the approach of *The Women at Oxford* was generally considered to be even-handed, and its author includes some fascinating appendices detailing the post-graduation lives and careers of select female Oxford students.

Radclyffe Hall: A Case of Obscenity? appeared in 1968, forty years after controversy surrounded one of that author's novels. *The Well of Loneliness,* which Hall published in 1928, was immediately banned under the Obscene Libel Act because of its positively portrayed lesbian content. Brittain retraces the path of the book, beginning with Hall's life prior to *Well*'s creation. She continues with a discussion of lesbianism, both in literature at large and in Hall's book and personal life in particular—thus setting up the rest of her book, which concerns the legal actions undertaken in both England and the United States that involved charges of obscenity. In concluding, Brittain contends that the courts do not fall under the same kind of public scrutiny as do British and American legislatures and should; the view of lawyers is short-sighted and should not be used to "legislate" or determine "current moral opinion." Brittain's interest in the case was more than intellectual; she had been asked to testify for the defense in 1928.

In both her writing and her life, during which she lectured throughout the world in support of pacifism and other social causes, Vera Brittain strove to rise beyond the traditional expectations of her sex. A wife and mother, she also managed to combine a natural talent for writing with her determination to acquire an education and her resolute personal convictions, thereby contributing, up until her death in 1970, to the betterment of a wartorn society.

—Tracy Clark

BROSSARD, Nicole

Nationality: Canadian. **Born:** Montréal, 27 November 1943. **Education:** University of Montréal, Licence ès Lettres 1968, B.A., 1971, Scolarité de Maîtrise, 1972. **Career:** Founder and editor, *La Barre du Jour* (then *La Nouvelle Barre du Jour*), beginning 1965; performance coordinator, Pavillon de la Jeuness, Expo '67, Montréal, 1967; member, Cultural Congress, Havana, Cuba, 1968; imprisoned under War Measures Act, 1970; cofounder, *Les Têtes de pioche* magazine; coproducer, *Some American Feminists* (film), 1976; president, 3rd International Feminist Book Fair, Montréal, 1988. Visiting professor at Queens University, Kingston, Ontario, 1982, 1984, and Westword School of Writing for Women, Vancouver, 1987; scholar-in-residence, Bucknell University, 1990; Princeton University, 1991. Speaker at feminist writers conferences and poetry festivals in Canada, Argentina, Australia, England, France, Holland, Italy, Norway, Spain, the United States, and Yugoslavia. Contributor to periodicals, including *La Barre du Jour, Revue de l'Université Laurentienne,* and *Etudes françaises.* **Awards:** Governor General award, 1974, for *Mécanique jongleuse,* and 1984, for *Double Impression;* Therafields Foundation Chapbook award, 1987, for *Sous la langue/Under Tongue;* Fondation Les Forges Grand Prize for poetry, 1989, for *Installations;* Prix Athanase-David du Québec, 1991. **Agent:** Union des Ecrivains Québécois (member, executive board).

Publications

Novels

Un Livre. Montréal, Éditions du Jour, 1970; translated as *A Book,* Toronto, Coach House Press, 1976.

Sold-Out (étreinte/illustration). Montréal, Éditions du Jour, 1973; translated as *Turn of a Pang,* Toronto, Coach House Press, 1976; translated as *A Pang's Progress,* 1986.

French Kiss (étreinte-exploration). Montréal, Éditions du Jour, 1974; translated, Toronto, Coach House Press, 1986.

L'Amèr; ou, Le Chapitre effrité (fiction théorique). Montréal, Quinze, 1977; translated by Barbara Godard as *These Our Mothers; or, The Disintegrating Chapter,* Toronto, Coach House Press, 1983.

Le Sens apparent. Paris, Flammarion, 1980; translated as *Surface of Sense,* Toronto, Coach House Press, 1989.

Picture Theory. Montréal, Nouvelle Optique, 1982; translated by Barbara Godard, Montréal, Guernica Press, and New York, Roof Press, 1990.

Journal intime; ou, Voilà donc un manuscrit. Montréal, Les Herbes rouges, 1984.

Le Désert Mauve. Montréal, L'Hexagone, 1987; translated as *Mauve Desert,* Toronto, Coach House Press, 1990.

Baroque d'aube [Baroque Dawn]. Montréal, L'Hexagone, 1995.

Poetry

"Aube à la saison" [Dawn in Season], in *Trois,* with Michel Beaulieu and Micheline de Jordy. Montréal, A.G.E.U.M., 1965.

Mordre en sa chair [To Bite the Flesh]. Montréal, Esterel, 1966.

L'Echo bouge beau. Montréal, Esterel, 1968.

Suite logique. Montréal, L'Hexagone, 1970.

Le Centre blanc. Montréal, Orphée, 1970; translated as *The White Centre,* Toronto, n.p., 1980.

Mécanique jongleuse. Colombes, France, Génération, 1973; with her *Masculin grammaticale,* Montréal, L'Hexagone, 1974; translated as *Daydream Mechanics,* Toronto, Coach House Press, 1980.

La Partie pour le tout. Montréal, L'aurore, 1975.

Le Centre blanc: poèmes 1965-1975. Montréal, L'Hexagone, 1978.

D'Arc de cycle la derive, illustrated by Francine Simonin. Saint-Jacques-le-Mineur, La Maison, 1979.

Amantes. Montréal, Quinze, 1980; translated by Barbara Godard as *Lovhers,* Montréal, Guernica Press, 1986.

Double Impression. Montréal, L'Hexagone, 1984.

L'Aviva. Montréal, Nouvelle Barre du Jour, 1985.

Domaine d'écriture. Montréal, Nouvelle Barre du Jour, 1985.

Mauve, with Daphne Marlatt. NBJ/ Kootenay School of Writing, 1985.

Character/Jeu de lettres, NBJ/ Kootenay School of Writing, with Daphne Marlatt. 1986.

Sous la langue/Under Tongue, English translation by Susanne de Lotbinière-Harwood. Montréal, Ragweed Press, 1987.

Installations. Paris, Les Ecrits des Forges, 1989.

A tout regard. Montréal, NBJ/BQ, 1989.

Typhon gru. Paris, Générations, 1990.

Langues obscures [Obscure Tongues]. Montréal, L'Hexagone, 1992.

Plays

"L'Ecrivain," in *La Nef des sorcières,* with Marie-Claire Blais, Marthe Blackburn, Luce Guilbeault, France Théoret, Odette Gagnon, and Pol Pelletier (produced Montréal, 1976). Montréal, Quinze, 1976; translated as *A Clash of Symbols,* Toronto, Coach House Press, 1979.

Radio Plays: *Narratuer et Personnages,* 1971; *Une Impression de fiction dans le retrovisur,* 1978; *La falaise,* 1985; *Souvenirs d'enfance et de jeuness,* 1986; *Correspondance,* with Michèle Causse, 1987.

Essays

La Lettre aérienne. Montréal, Remu-Ménage, 1985; translated as *The Aerial Letter,* Toronto, Women's Press, 1988.

"Poetic Politics," in *The Politics of Poetic Form,* edited by Charles Bernstein. New York, Roof Press, 1990.

Other

Editor, *Les Stratégies du réel/The Story So Far 6.* Toronto, Coach House Press, 1979.

*

Critical Studies: "The Novels of Nicole Brossard: An Active Voice" by Louise Forsyth, in *Room of One's Own,* 4(1-2), 1978, her "L'Ecriture au féminine," in *Journal of Canadian Fiction,* 25/26, 1979, and her *Traditionalism, Nationalism and Feminism: Women Writers of Québec,* n.p.; "The Avant-Garde in Canada: *Open Letter* and *La Barre du Jour*" by Barbara Godard, in *Ellipse,* 4(23), 1979.

* * *

Nicole Brossard's preeminent role among the generation of writers who, from 1965-70, made the exploration of gender and language central to Québec poetics, was recognized for the totality of her work in 1991 by the Athanase-David Prize of Québec. Brossard's international reputation as a feminist theorist has grown as her works have been translated into English, German, Italian, and Spanish.

This acknowledgement is ironic, for Brossard's writing has developed in the margins—in the avant-garde—as a critique of received practices and of the text as commodity. Working from the materialist theories of culture as praxis, as well as post-structuralist theories about the way language inscribes power relations in constructing our world, Brossard has made writing resistance, transforming literary and social institutions first in the name of Québec nationalism and then in the name of feminism. Self-reflexively drawing attention to the established conventions of reading and writing—especially to rules of syntax and plot—Brossard disrupts habitual knowledge relations under the name of the father with women's desire for women in excess of this phallic law. Through play on the textual surface—neologisms and typographical variations—she reveals the constructedness of texts and undermines the referential power of language and the mimetic aspect of literature in a textual practice that demands an active reader in order to make sense. Formulating writing as research, Brossard considers fiction as a hypothesis-generating rather than a reality-representing activity. Ordering relationships among entities, such fictions are taken for reality and establish truth-claims that organize social relations. In its interrogative mode, its preoccupation with hyperreality and textual surfaces, Brossard's poetic is postmodernist. Her fictions work to displace the dominant, masculine, imaginary ordering of the real that normally would exclude, as "fictive," such women's "realities" as harassment. Through a strategic deployment of fiction, she aims to produce visibility for women.

Brossard's works can be divided into three periods. In poetry written during the 1960s, she was influenced by surrealism, exploring sexuality as a mode of consciousness in an associative flux of images with surprising juxtapositions. Focusing on the desiring female body, *Mordre en sa chair* challenges the poetry, then dominant, that celebrated a Québec national homeland in a metaphor of land-as-woman, producing a self-division for a woman poet as speaking subject. Brossard attempted to undermine this symbolic Woman by examining women's desires while retaining the prevalent view of avant-garde art forms as revolutionary political activity. Poetic language needed renewing: Not by writing in *joual,* a popular urban dialect, but by disrupting the formal elements of language—the subject-verb-complement rule of syntax (also the grammar of narrative) and French gender rules (masculine takes precedence over feminine)—and so challenging textual decorum and all notions of the "proper," especially those of fixed identity. Transgression, Brossard advances after Michel Foucault, is the assertion of a subject whose desire realigns power relations.

Brossard's work went through a formalist phase during the 1970s, stimulated by both French post-structuralism and the work of Roland Barthes, who developed the semiotics of Fernand de Saussure to theorize the text as a system of differences. This freed Brossard from the constraints of capturing the life of her body in words, allowing her to combine verbal signs in multiple networks capable of producing an infinity of arrangements. She explored these possibilities of language around the paradox of absence/presence, white space/black marks, and through puns on *personne* as both "person" and "nobody" in poetic forms such as *Le centre blanc* (The White Centre). She also began writing works that interrogated the conventions of the novel. *Un livre* (*A Book*) uses names such as *Or* (Now) and *Dominique* for both a male and female character as a means of examining how "characters" are verbal fabrications—word beings—that function as points of connection for other words. Anecdotes are incomplete. The text insists on its lack of "depth": its only "reality" is words that take place on the surface, accessible through the activities of writing and reading. In *Sold-Out,* written after she had been imprisoned under the War Measures Act during the October Crisis (1970), Brossard explores how words can do ideological work: When *inscrire* means both to inscribe and to conscript, it has power as a political slogan or a sexual putdown. Brossard critiques the hegemony of masculinist language in a poetic text in *Masculin grammaticale* and posits a different order of signs within relations of female desire in *French Kiss,* a fictional text published in 1974. Here an automobile moving through the city establishes an allegory of women's desire circulating in the public space in the utopian mode of Brossard's major feminist fictions. The lesbian kiss displaces the conventional fictional economy to constitute a "sapphic semantic chain" of transgressive sexualities where the erotic centre of the body is no longer the site of reproduction but of creative energies.

In its third phase, Brossard's writing pursues this call to "make the difference" and develops a poetics and politics of sexual difference. Her involvement in feminist politics led her away from the influential avant-garde periodical *La barre du jour,* of which she was founding co-editor, to help found a feminist collective *Les Têtes de pioche* (Axeheads) and to make a film about feminist theory, *Some American Feminists.* Subsequently, she combined her experimental writing with feminist theories and returned to *La Nouvelle barre du jour* to make it an influential site for avant-garde feminist writing, the most important field within Quebec literature from the late '70s through the '80s. Influenced by French feminists such as Luce Irigaray and Hélène Cixous, Brossard developed a mode of writing she calls fiction/theory: fiction as hypothesis-forming and critique. *L'Amèr; ou, Le Chapitre effrité* (*These Our Mothers; or, The Disintegrating Chapter*), the first volume in her lesbian triptych, is an exercise in self-defense in a patriarchal society where women are limited to the role of symbolic mother, their only product—the child—appropriated by the father's name/language. In a discontinuous text ordered around forms ranging from lyric to prose poem to analytic essay, Brossard exposes the contradictions of the patriarchal mother in order to posit relationships among women figured in the embrace of three generations of women and in the lesbian embrace. The text works to inscribe women in the trajectory of the species by writing them into history. With its articulation of difference as radical alterity and indeterminacy, *L'Amér* has been an influential work of feminist theory as well as of experimental fiction. *Le sens apparent* (*Surfaces of Sense*), the second text in the series, centers on the thought of emotion while articulating the sensation of emotion and thought in its emphasis on textual surfaces as the skin of culture. A narrative that constantly digresses, a manifesto that refuses clarity: the text circles around the work of lesbian writers that include Gertrude Stein and Adrienne Rich in the "spiral pattern of books written by women," in the activity of reading women writing. A model for the superimposition of texts, it informs 1980's *Amantes* (*Lovhers*), a poetic suite that explores the vertigo of lesbian lovemaking in New York and celebrates the emotion of thought.

Picture Theory, Brossard's major work to date, reworks these motifs in a complex theoretical fiction based on Wittgenstein's statement that a "proposition is a picture of reality." A superimposition of Monique Wittig's Amazonian island on anecdotes of the family of "Dérive Stein" (Stein Derivative, Stein Adrift) and Djuna Barnes's *Nightwood,* it rewrites the latter as lightwood to counter the great modernist books of the night, especially the works of James Joyce. Anecdote and plot are again displaced by networks of metonymies around *peau/écran/écrit/cri* (skin/screen/scream) in another mode of notating emotion. In developing the text as combinations of different permutations of these words, Brossard draws on contemporary science and a "mathematics of the imaginary" to construct a text as hologram that can enable a reader incited by desire to produce, from these fragments, a virtual woman. It offers a model for the text as a process of transformation, something central to Brossard's aesthetic.

Brossard has elaborated such concepts in *La lettre aérienne* (*The Aerial Letter*), which contains theoretical essays focusing on the problem of representation for women. Women's writing must inevitably be fiction—feigning, visionary, self-conscious artifice—to avoid the trap of naturalization, of claiming to be reality, that has made traditional literature an extension of the patriarchal symbolic and party to the subjugation of women and reality. Fiction is the way to fight such constraining fictions: exposing their fictionality and opening a space for alternate fictions animated by an economy of women's desire. The possibilities for a lesbian aesthetic are further developed in essays in *Double Impression;* questions of representation and narrative are addressed in *Journal intime,* a diary and yet not one in that it refuses both the sequential temporality and the confessional convention of life-writing genres, questioning the feminist formulation of the "personal is political" by exposing the way a life is constructed within social conventions by language. Similar concerns with the constitution of subjectivity are addressed in poetic texts such as *Langues obscures,* which explores the adventures of the subjective pronoun "I," a shifter, "pure marvel" of transformation, and through which is carried out the work of relating a speaker with an other, with a world.

Brossard's work on language and social codes also examines translation as both a textual practice and a metaphor for transcoding, in a transformative rather than mimetic practice, through the proliferation of chains of signification across languages. Introducing words from other languages into her French texts, Brossard imagines how reality would be shaped by another language. In *L'Aviva* and *Picture Theory* she also experiments with homolinguistic or intralingual translation to explore the recombinant possibilities of syllables. French-English translation of texts by poet Daphne Marlatt in *Mauve* and *Jeu de lettres/Character* was followed by *Le Désert Mauve* (*Mauve Desert*) a fiction about a translator's work on a text from French to French that links a violent murder of a lesbian in the Arizona desert to atomic explosions. Through her customary motif of reading as de-siring from the French pun on *délire* as "delerium" and "unreading," this fiction develops in three parts: a translator's discovery of another woman's text, her meditation on the processes of transformative reading to transfer the text into a different cultural network of signification, and the "translated" text, a reworking of the first section, recombinant work such as the shift from *Laure* Angestelle, author, to Maude *Laure*, translator-author. Translation remains an important metaphor in the Québec literary scene standing midway between Paris and New York, an important axis and a productive crossover for French feminist theory. The pertinence of its subject, as well as its less fragmented narrative, have made *Le Désert Mauve* the most accessible and popular of Brossard's novels.

Similar structural features mark Brossard's 1995 novel, *Baroque d'aube,* which infolds, in a return to the topos of her first publication, *Aube à la saison,* the erotic centre of the body lived now within a different economy of desire. More referential than her earlier fictions, *Baroque d'aube* opens with a scene of lesbian lovemaking that contrasts to the middle section, "Dark Future," where women in a heterosexual economy serve as experimental subjects for the pornographic gaze within virtual reality. Still, this fiction about the sexism and violence of American culture plays with the shifting boundary between art and life via the perspective of Cybil Noland, an English novelist who remembers a conversation with another "English" novelist, Nicole Brossard, and comments at a conference on autobiography about the absurdity of "wanting to enter into the world of fiction while remaining oneself." The vertiginous perspectival play between the virtual and the actual—between the character Brossard, who is English, and the author Brossard, a Québécois—stages the author's continuing interest in the transformation produced by a shift in the angle of vision. Reading, like writing, from the perspective of a woman makes a difference. While the opening words of the novel recall *Aube à la saison*—"Dawn came first. Then the woman reached orgasm"—they return with a difference, that of lesbian pleasure. Like all Brossard's texts, *Baroque d'aube* focuses self-reflexively on the work of writing, of ordering words and worlds, where gender makes a difference.

—Barbara Godard

BROWN, Charles Brockden

Nationality: American. **Born:** Philadelphia, Pennsylvania, 17 January 1771. **Education:** Tutored by the historian Robert Proud, until age 16. **Family:** Married Elizabeth Linn in 1804; four children. **Career:** Read for the bar; moved to New York, c. 1795; editor, *Monthly Magazine & American Review,* until 1800; founder, *Ameri-*

can Review & Literary Magazine, and *American Register,* Philadelphia, beginning 1803; as America's first professional author, contributed essays to numerous periodicals, including *Columbus Magazine* and *Weekly Magazine.* **Died:** 2 February 1810.

Publications

Novels

Wieland; or, The Transformation. New York, T. & J. Swords for H. Caritat, 1798; London, n.p., 1811; with a memoir by the author, Philadelphia, M. Polock, 1857; with *Memoirs of Carwin the Biloquist,* edited by Jay Fliegelman, New York and London, Penguin, 1991.
Ormund; or, The Secret Witness. New York, G. Foreman for H. Caritat, 1799.
Arthur Mervyn; or, Memoirs of the Year 1793. Philadelphia, H. Maxwell, 2 vols., 1799-80.
Edgar Huntley; or, Memoirs of a Sleep-Walker. Philadelphia, H. Maxwell, 1799; London, H. Colburn, 1831.
Jane Talbot. Philadelphia, J. Conrad, 1801.
Clara Howard; or, The Enthusiasms of Love. N.p. 1801; as *Philip Stanley; or, The Enthusiasms of Love,* London, Lane Norman, 1807.

Short Stories

Carwen, the Biloquist, and Other American Tales and Pieces. London, H. Colburn, 1822.
Somnambulism and Other Stories, edited by Alfred Weber. Frankfurt am Main, P. Lang, 1987.

Essays

Alcuin; A Dialogue, parts 1-2. New York, T. & J. Swords, 1798; parts 3-4 published in *Life of Brown,* by Dunlap, Philadelphia, n.p., 1815.
An Address to Congress on the Cession of Louisiana to the French. Philadelphia, J. Conrad, 1803.
An Address to Congress on the Utility and Justice of Restrictions on Foreign Commerce. Philadelphia, J. Conrad, 1804.
Literary Essays and Reviews, edited by Alfred Weber and Wolfgang Schäfer, Frankfurt am Main, P. Lang, 1992.

Other

The Rhapsodist and Other Uncollected Writings, edited by Harry R. Warfel. New York, Scholars' Facsimiles & Reprints, 1943.

Translator, *Travels in the U.S.,* by Constantin François Volney. N.p., 1804.

*

Bibliography: *Charles Brockden Brown: A Reference Guide* by Patricia L. Parker, Boston, G.K. Hall, 1980.

Critical Studies: *Charles Brockden Brown and the Rights of Women* (bulletin) by David Lee Clark, Austin, University of Texas, 1922; *Critical Essays on Charles Brockden Brown* edited by Bernard Rosenthal, Boston, G. K. Hall, 1981; *Charles Brockden Brown: An American Tale* by Alan Axelrod, Austin, University of Texas Press, 1983; *A Right View of the Subject: Feminism in the Works of Charles Brockden Brown and John Neal* by Fritz Fleishmann, Erlangen, Palm & Enke, 1983; *Dialogue in Utopia: Manners, Purpose, and Structure in Three Feminist Works of the 1790s* by Liana Borghi, Pisa, ETS, 1984; *The Romance of Real Life: Charles Brockden Brown and the Origins of American Culture* by Steven Watts, Baltimore, Johns Hopkins University Press, 1994.

* * *

Charles Brockden Brown, the first American author to attempt to make his living by writing, devoted his first major work to an exploration of the status of women in the early republic. Although literary critics disagree about Brown's receptivity to feminism, his *Alcuin,* first published in 1798, presented an outline of the arguments promoted by early women's rights advocates.

The youngest son of Elijah and Mary Brown, Charles was a sickly child who loved books. The Browns, a well-to-do Quaker family, sent their son to the Friends' Latin School in Philadelphia. By age ten, Brown had begun composing poetry and by the time he left the Friends' Latin School he had planned three epic poems on the discovery, exploration, and conquest of the New World. While Brown's parents had encouraged the intellectual development and emerging literary talent of their son, they insisted that he be trained in a profession. Consequently, in 1789, Brown was apprenticed to Alexander Wilcocks and began studying law.

Although the law and literary pursuits were presumed to be entirely compatible, Brown was unhappy as a lawyer and abandoned that career in 1793, against the wishes of his family. For the next eight years he shuttled between his native Philadelphia and New York, devoting himself to a life of reading and writing. Brown established himself as a writer during this period, publishing all seven of his major works between 1789 and 1801. His novels earned him little money, however, and after *The Monthly Magazine & American Review*—the literary magazine he edited—folded at the end of 1800, he returned to Philadelphia and became a business partner with his brothers. The family business had failed by 1806; Brown, now married with children, became an independent merchant. Although he would continue to write for and edit various literary magazines, Brown's career as a full-time author was over.

Beginning in the early 1790s, Brown began exploring the condition and status of women, writing a positive review of Mary Wollstonecraft's *A Vindication of the Rights of Women* in 1792 and focusing his first published work, *Alcuin; A Dialogue,* on this topic six years later. Constructed as a dialogue between Alcuin, a Philadelphia schoolmaster, and Mrs. Carter, a moderate advocate of women's rights, the book examined the status of women at the close of the American Revolution. Although by no means a radical treatment of this subject, Brown considered his handling of it to be so controversial that he published only the first half during his lifetime. The second half remained unpublished until 1815, five years after his death.

While *Alcuin* demonstrates Brown's interest in the question of women's status in the early years of the American republic, the book does not clearly define his position on women's rights. In the first half of the work, Mrs. Carter outlines the discrepancy between the ideals of the recently completed political revolution and the legal and social status of women. The institution of marriage, Mrs. Carter points out, provided but the most glaring example of women's exclusion from the liberty promised by the Revolution, for with marriage women lost all property rights and became legally subject to the will of their husbands. Alcuin admits that women were indeed barred from countless opportunities, but he maintains that innate gender differences determined the distribution of responsibilities and tasks. Subscribing to the "heart/head" dichotomy, which posited that women's strength lay in matters of the heart while men were masters of the intellect, or "head," Brown nevertheless credited women as morally superior to men.

In the second half of the work, Alcuin and Mrs. Carter change positions. Alcuin, who claims to have visited a utopia featuring absolute equality between the sexes, begins advocating an end to marriage and all gender divisions of labor. Yet these suggestions horrify Mrs. Carter, who now suggests a fondness for traditional gender roles and rejects any "speculative systems" of absolute gender equality. Mrs. Carter's distaste for the gender utopia described by Alcuin that makes Brown's views on women's rights difficult to discern. While he aired the grievances of many of his female contemporaries, he may well have harbored ambivalence about the potential effects of a women's rights movement. Indeed, after completing *Alcuin,* Charles Brockden Brown would take up a very different sort of writing, composing gothic novels that featured psychologically tortured characters. He never returned to further discussions of women's rights.

—Anne Lewis Osler

BROWN, Rita Mae

Nationality: American. **Born:** Hanover, Pennsylvania, 28 November 1944. **Education:** Broward Junior College, A.A. 1965; University of Florida; New York University, B.A. in English and classics 1968; New York School of Visual Arts, Manhattan, cinematography certificate 1968; Institute for Policy Studies, Washington, DC, Ph.D. 1973. **Career:** With others, founded Student Homophile League at New York University, and opened the first women's center in New York City. Photo editor, Sterling Publishing, New York, 1969-70; cofounder, Lavender Menace (lesbian feminist group), 1970; lecturer in sociology, Federal City College, Washington, DC, 1970-71; cofounder, with Charlotte Bunche, The Furies (radical lesbian collective), 1971; visiting member of faculty in feminist studies, Goddard College, Plainfield, Vermont, 1973; president, American Artists, Inc., Charlottesville, Virginia, beginning 1980, visitn instructor in writing University of Virginia, Charlottesville, 1992. Former member of National Gay Task Force and National Women's Political Caucus; member of board of directors of Human Rights Campaign Fund, New York, 1986. **Awards:** Writers Guild of America award, 1983; Emmy award nominations, 1983, for *I Love Liberty,* and 1985, for *Long Hot Summer;* New York Public Library Literary Lion award, 1986; named Charlottesville's favorite author, 1990; H.H.D., Wilson College, 1992. **Agent:** Julian Bach Literary Agency, Inc., 747 Third Avenue, New York, New York 10017, U.S.A. **Address:** Wendy Weil, Wendy Weil Literary Agency, 232 Madison Ave, Ste. 1300, New York, NY 10016, U.S.A.

Publications

Novels

Rubyfruit Jungle. Plainfield, Vermont, Daughters Inc., 1973.
In Her Day. Plainfield, Vermont, Daughters Inc., 1976.
Six of One. New York, Harper, 1978.
Southern Discomfort. New York, Harper, 1982.
Sudden Death. New York, Bantam, 1983.
High Hearts. New York, Bantam, 1986.
Bingo. New York, Bantam, 1988.
Wish You Were Here, with Sneaky Pie Brown. New York, Bantam, 1990.
Rest in Pieces, with Sneaky Pie Brown. New York, Bantam, 1992.
Venus Envy. New York, Bantam, 1993.
Dolley: A Novel of Dolley Madison in Love and War. New York, Bantam, 1994.
Murder at Monticello, or, Old Sins, with Sneaky Pie Brown. New York, Bantam, 1994.
Pay Dirt;, or Adventures at Ash Lawn, with Sneaky Pie Brown. New York, Bantam, 1996.
Riding Shotgun. New York, Bantam, 1996.

Poetry

The Hand that Cradles the Rock. New York University Press, 1971.
Songs to a Handsome Woman. Baltimore, Diana Press, 1973.
The Poems of Rita Mae Brown. Freedom, California, Crossing Press, 1987.

Plays

Screenplays: *Slumber Party Massacre,* 1982; *Rubyfruit Jungle; Cahoots.*

Television Plays: *I Love Liberty,* 1982; *Long Hot Summer* (remake of 1958 film based on *The Hamlet* by William Faulkner), 1985; *My Two Loves,* 1986; *The Alice Marble Story,* 1986; *The Mists of Table Dancing,* 1987; *The Girls of Summer,* 1989; *Selma, Lord, Selma,* 1989; *Rich Men, Single Women,* 1989; *Sweet Surrender,* 1989; *Southern Exposure,* 1990; *The 39-Year Itch,* 1990; *Home, Sweet, Home,* 1990; *Passing Through,* 1993; *The Nat Turner Story,* 1994; *The Wall,* 1994; *A Family Again,* 1995.

Essays

A Plain Brown Rapper. Baltimore, Diana Press, 1976.

Uncollected Essays

"Take a Lesbian to Lunch" and "Hanoi to Hoboken, a Round-Trip Ticket," in *Out of the Closets: Voices of Gay Liberation,* edited by Karla Jay and Allen Young. New York, Douglas, 1972.
"The Last Straw," in *Class and Feminism: A Collection of Essays from The Furies,* edited by Charlotte Bunch and Nancy Myron. Baltimore, Diana Press, 1974.
"Living with Other Women" and "The Shape of Things To Come," in *Lesbianism and the Women's Movement,* edited by Nancy Myron and Charlotte Bunch. Baltimore, Diana Press 1975.

"Queen for a Day: A Stranger in Paradise," in *Lavender Culture,* edited by Karla Jay and Allen Young. New York, Jove/HBJ, 1978.

Other

Starting from Scratch: A Different Kind of Writer's Manual. New York, Bantam, 1988.

Translator, *Hrotsvitra: Six Medieval Latin Plays.* New York University Press, 1971.

*

Critical Studies: "The Woman-Identified Woman" by Radicalesbians, in *Radical Feminism,* edited by A. Koedt, E. Levine, and A. Rapone, New York, Quadrangle, 1973; "Zero Degree Deviancy: The Lesbian Novel in English" by Catharine Stimpson, in *Writing and Sexual Difference,* edited by E. Abel, Chicago, University of Chicago Press, 1982; "Rita Mae Brown: Feminist Theorist and Southern Novelist" by Martha Chew, in *Women Writers of the Contemporary South,* edited by Peggy Whitman Prenshaw, Jackson, University Press of Mississippi, 1984; "*Rubyfruit Jungle:* Lesbianism, Feminism, and Narcissism" by Leslie Fishbein, in *International Journal of Women's Studies* (Montréal, Québec), March/April 1984; "Questions of Genre and Gender: Contemporary American Versions of the Feminine Picaresque" by James Mandrell, in *Novel: A Forum on Fiction,* 20(2), winter 1987; "Toward a Definition of the Lesbian Literary Imagination" by Marilyn R. Farwell, in *Signs,* 14, 1988; "Uses of Classical Mythology in Rita Mae Brown's *Southern Discomfort*" by Daniel B. Levine, in *Classical and Modern Literature* (Terre Haute, Indiana), fall 1989; *Daring to Be Bad: Radical Feminism in American 1967-1975* by Alice Echols, Minneapolis, University of Minnesota Press, 1989; *The Safe Sea of Women: Lesbian Fiction, 1969-1989* by Bonnie Zimmerman, Boston, Beacon Press, 1990; "Contemporary Lesbian Feminist Fiction: Texts for Everywoman" by Paulina Palmer, in *Plotting Change: Contemporary Women's Fiction,* edited by L. Anderson, London, E. Arnold, 1990; *Rita Mae Brown* by Carol M. Ward, New York, Twayne, 1993.

Rita Mae Brown comments:

Any woman whose I.Q. hovers above her body temperature must be a feminist.

* * *

Rita Mae Brown was born in Hanover, Pennsylvania, just north of the Maryland border, in 1944. Adopted by Ralph and Julia Ellen Brown, she lived in Hanover until the family moved to Fort Lauderdale, Florida eleven years later. A fine student and athlete, Brown would earn a scholarship to the University of Florida, where, in addition to being a student, she also became a civil rights activist. As a result of these activities, she was expelled from the university. She then hitchhiked north, arriving friendless and penniless in New York City, where she encountered an established, yet diverse, lesbian community. Menial jobs and a scholarship allowed Brown to attend New York University; she graduated with a B.A. in English and classics in 1968.

In New York Brown joined the embryonic gay rights movement. One of few gay activists willing to use her real name, she cofounded the New York University Student Homophile League. Increasingly disillusioned with male sexism within gay organizations, Brown gradually transferred her energies to women's liberation. She joined the National Organization for Women and became editor of NOW's New York newsletter. But in the late 1960s the women's liberation movement was suspicious of lesbians, not wishing to alienate mainstream America. In 1969 NOW president Betty Friedan referred to growing lesbian visibility as a "lavender menace"; Brown was relived of her duties as newsletter editor. Stung, Brown denounced NOW's homophobia and resigned from the organization, vowing to form a lesbian-feminist movement. She cofounded Lavender Menace, which pushed the lesbian agenda within women's liberation, and which published (under the name Radicalesbians) the influential position paper "The Women-Identified Women" in 1970. Later that year Radicalesbians disintegrated and Brown moved to Washington D.C., drawn both by the Institute for Policy Studies (IPS), a leftist think tank, and by the lure of a lesbian-feminist commune. Together with activist and IPS associate Charlotte Bunch, in early 1971 Brown started a "lesbian come-out c-r [conscious-raising] group" which evolved into the Furies collective. The Furies were perhaps the most influential of the lesbian-feminist cells in the early 1970s because their revolutionary fervor ignited the lesbian movement and positioned their particular brand of lesbianism as the locus of meaningful change for women. The Furies disbanded after one turbulent year (1971-72); nevertheless, that year crystallized Brown's thinking about the role of class and enabled her to produce "The Last Straw," a perceptive analysis of class dynamics within the feminist movement. During this period Brown also wrote *The Hand that Cradles the Rock, Songs to a Handsome Women,* and *The Plain Brown Rapper.* She maintained her link with the IPS, working as a research fellow there until 1973, and eventually earning her Ph.D. in political science.

Despite her academic and political work, Brown had always wanted to write fiction; in 1973 she completed *Rubyfruit Jungle,* her first full-length novel. Originally published by the feminist press Daughters, Inc., *Rubyfruit Jungle* achieved considerable notoriety among alternative readers. In 1977 Bantam reissued it as a mass-market paperback, and the response was overwhelming: The novel sold over a million copies and catapulted Brown into the position of unofficial spokeswoman for American lesbians.

Rubyfruit Jungle, like several of Brown's other novels, is semiautobiographical. It traces the childhood and young adulthood of symbolically named Molly Bolt—a molly-bolt, available in any hardware store, is a fastener which, when inserted through wood into an empty space beyond, opens and anchors itself to the wood's away side. Molly, like her author, is born out of wedlock and adopted, and spends her early childhood in Southern Pennsylvania. A sexual outlaw even as a young girl, she has her first lesbian experience before her family moves to Florida. The novel follows her through high school, expulsion from college for lesbianism, discovery of the New York lesbian scene, and graduation from college with a degree in film.

Molly Bolt is a kind of female Tom Jones, romping through a series of humorous sexual escapades; *Rubyfruit* is a *Bildungsroman* with a picaresque heroine. Never afflicted with self-doubt, Molly faces repeated rejections with her sense of identity intact. Naturally, such a novel as *Rubyfruit Jungle* represented an astonishing validation of lesbian existence: Molly Bolt's boundless self-confidence contrasts mightily with angst-ridden Stephen Gordon, heroine of Radclyffe Hall's *The Well of Loneliness* (1928), the only earlier lesbian novel to gain a wide mainstream readership. Like

Well, Rubyfruit awakened the general public to the existence of lesbianism; but unlike *Well,* it featured a well-adjusted, empowerED lesbian woman.

After the phenomenal success of *Rubyfruit Jungle,* Brown's second novel, *In Her Day* (1976), was a failure. It takes up many compelling issues central to the radical feminism of the time, but the humorless, preachy tone is not Brown's natural voice. As a result *In Her Day* is heavy going. Fortunately, two years later Brown rediscovered her buoyant, breezy style; in *Six of One* Brown creates the fictional towns of North and South Runnymeade, invents a history for them, and populates them with eccentric and amusing people. Some of these people—like Julia Ellen ("Juts") and her adopted lesbian daughter Nickel, who just happens to have been born on the author's birthday—bear a striking resemblance to Brown and her family. *Six of One* rambles and lacks conflict, but Runnymeade and its citizens come to life.

By contrast, Brown's next novel, *Southern Discomfort,* definitely has conflict. Set in Alabama, it explores the intersecting oppressions of racism, classism, and sexism. Even more powerfully than in *Rubyfruit Jungle, Southern Discomfort* takes up the question of being publicly true to oneself, even when one's life violates society's accepted code of conduct. 1983's *Sudden Death* explores this same theme, but this time the setting is the women's professional tennis tour. The plot revolves around whether or not the tennis star will admit her lesbianism, but the real interest of *Sudden Death* lies in its description of the behind-the-scenes workings of top-rank women's tennis. *Sudden Death* is an intriguing *roman a clef;* readers cannot help but try to identify the real people behind the fictional characters.

Released in 1986, *High Hearts* is the Civil War novel Brown had always wanted to write. The book has an air of authenticity about it, largely due to Brown's painstaking preliminary research. On the surface, the plots and subplots are typical of historical romance; the novel's depth rests in its questioning of the nature of gender. Brown later revisits the theme of women and war in 1995's *Dolley: A Novel of Dolley Madison in Love and War.*

Starting From Scratch, a fiction writer's manual written in 1988, represented a new direction for Brown. The book opens with a personal statement outlining Brown's beliefs about writing, specifically that it takes great faith to write in a "postliterate world." It then discusses strategies for writing, from navigating tricky publishing procedures to self-promotion, dealing with fame, branching out, and reaching flagging creativity.

Also in 1988 appeared *Bingo,* which revisits Runnymeade and the cast of characters from *Six Of One.* It reintroduces us to now-elderly Juts and her sister Louise, but the primary focus is Nickel, who faces several midlife challenges: how to live as a lesbian in a small town; how to handle her attraction to a man; how to deal with an unexpected pregnancy.

Wish You Were Here (1990) was "coauthored" by Brown's cat, Sneaky Pie Brown, and signalled its authors' entry into the rapidly expanding area of mystery novels featuring women detectives. It has been followed by *Rest in Pieces* (1992), *Murder at Monticello* (1994), and *Pay Dirt* (1996). Brown's 1993 novel, *Venus Envy,* takes up another intriguing idea. The central character, believing she is terminally ill, writes letters to her closest friends and family revealing her lesbianism; she must then deal with the repercussions when she recovers. *Venus Envy* begins as a "grown-up coming out story" but ultimately wanders off into fantasy; one reviewer has seen this thematic unsteadiness as a sign of a literary "identity crisis" for Brown.

Since the late 1960s, Brown has battled for women's rights, for lesbian visibility, and for literary acceptance. Her early essays and novels profoundly inspired a generation of women who sought validation for their identity as lesbians. Her later writing deemphasizes lesbian consciousness in favor of historical romance, mystery, and Southern regionalism. In fact, Brown has stated that she is offended when others refer to her as a lesbian writer; it is enough that she is a writer, and female, and southern. This irrepressible attitude is vintage Brown—impudent, iconoclastic, individualistic, egotistical. Refusing labels, Rita Mae Brown insists on her right to set her own literary, political, and personal agenda. Over the years, her participation in social change organizations has followed a pattern; she quit the civil rights movement, the Gay Liberation Front, NOW, and many lesbian-feminist groups when their dogma conflicted with her ideological independence. And this independence informs every piece of her writing.

—Deborah T. Meem

BROWNMILLER, Susan

Nationality: American. **Born:** Brooklyn, New York, 15 February 1935. **Education:** Cornell University, 1952-55; attended Jefferson School of Social Sciences. **Career:** Editorial assistant, *Coronet,* New York, 1959-60; editor, *Albany Report,* Albany, New York, 1961-62; staff writer, *Village Voice,* New York, 1965; reporter, NBC-TV, Philadelphia, 1965; network newswriter, ABC-TV, New York, New York, 1966-68; freelance journalist and writer, beginning 1968. **Awards:** Alicia Patterson Foundation grant; Louis M. Rabinowitz Foundation grant; named among 12 Women of the Year, *Time,* 1975. **Office:** c/o Grove Weidenfeld, 841 Broadway, New York, New York 10003-4793, U.S.A.

Publications

Novel

Waverly Place. New York, Grove Press, and London, Hamilton, 1989.

Political/Social Theory

Against Our Will: Men, Women, and Rape. New York, Simon & Schuster, and London, Secker & Warburg, 1975.

Femininity. New York, Simon & Schuster, and London, Hamilton, 1984.

Nonfiction

Seeing Vietnam: Encounters of the Road and Heart. New York, HarperCollins, 1994.

For Children

Shirley Chisholm: A Biography. Garden City, New York, Doubleday, 1970.

Other

Recordings: *Against Our Will,* Los Angeles, Pacifica Radio Archive, 1983.

*

Critical Studies: Review of *Against Our Will* by M.J. Sobran Jr., in *National Review,* 5 March 1976; *Rape, Racism, and the White Women's Movement: An Answer to Susan Brownmiller* by Alison Edwards, Chicago, Sojourner Truth Organization, 198?; review of *Waverly Place* by Christopher Lehmann-Haupt, in *New York Times,* 2 February 1989; "Out to Make Killings: Crime Pays" by Stefan Kanver, in *Time,* 133(8), 23 February 1989.

* * *

Journalist Susan Brownmiller has been researching, lecturing, and writing about women's issues since the 1960s. In 1968 Brownmiller joined other New York City activists to form the New York Radical Feminists; she would later co-organize Women against Pornography. Her activism has also included staging protests on such feminist issues as the portrayal of women in traditional women's magazines (e.g., *Ladies Home Journal*), pornography, and violence against women.

Brownmiller's first book-length work, *Shirley Chisholm: A Biography,* describes for young readers the strength and tenacity of the first African-American U.S. Congresswomen. Although neither as forcefully feminist nor as controversial as some of Brownmiller's later work, the biography emphasizes the difficulties Chisholm faced in politics as a minority woman and the high moral courage she models for all woman.

Brownmiller's second and best-known work, *Against Our Will: Men, Women, and Rape* (1975), was prompted by conversations with friends during which Brownmiller says she staunchly argued that "[r]ape wasn't a feminist issue." Through her four years of research Brownmiller's views changed completely, and in the book she asserts: "From prehistoric times to the present, I believe, rape has played a critical function. It is nothing more or less than a conscious process of intimidation by which all men keep all women in a state of fear." Indeed, "[w]omen are trained to be rape victims. To simply learn the word 'rape' is to take instruction in the power relationship between males and females." As participants in this patriarchal rule, all men benefit from and thus implicitly support what Adrienne Rich terms the "culture of rape."

Against Our Will received reviews ranging from extravagant praise for its depth and insight to condemnation for being "not scholarship but henpecking," according to M.J. Sobran Jr. in the *National Review.* Other criticism came from many feminists of color who charged that Brownmiller spoke, as did the feminist movement itself, solely from the point of view of middle-class white women, ignoring the role class and race have in issues of oppression. Brownmiller wrote from "a position of isolation, and appalling racism and anti-communism," charged Alison Edwards in her *Rape, Racism, and the White Women's Movement.*

Despite such criticism, *Against Our Will* was a bestseller. Brownmiller was named one of *Time*'s Women of the Year in 1975, and she traveled the lecture circuit, calling on women to fight back "to redress the imbalance and rid ourselves and men of the ideology of rape."

Brownmiller's second feminist analysis, *Femininity,* appeared in 1984. In it, she explores femininity as a "powerful esthetic that is built upon a recognition of powerlessness." "Appearance, not accomplishment," she states, "is the feminine demonstration of desirability and worth."

Brownmiller catalogues and critiques the components of femininity, including breasts ("a thoroughly colonized province of masculine sexuality"), dieting and looks ("the chief physical weapon in female-against-female competition"), and hair (a mark of both sexual and racial superiority, e.g., blondness being privileged). She analyzes the purpose and effect of traditional women's clothing in comparison with men's: "Feminine clothing has never been designed to be functional, for that would be a contradiction in terms. Functional clothing is a masculine privilege and practicality is a masculine virtue." Emotional traits traditionally ascribed to women, Brownmiller finds, "[run] counter to clinical descriptions of maturity and mental health."

Some feminist reviewers objected to what they perceived as Brownmiller's lack of feminist revisioning in *Femininity.* Brownmiller herself acknowledges that she has not written "a manual of how-not-to, nor a wholesale damnation," but rather has attempted to "invite examination ... in the effort to illuminate the restrictions on free choice." Further, she notes, "[c]oming down hard on certain familiar aspects while admitting a fond tolerance for some others has been unavoidable in my attempt to give an honest appraisal of the feminine strategies as I have myself practiced or discarded them."

Still committed to awakening the public to the ongoing problem violence presents to women and children, Brownmiller tried to reach audiences through a different writing style in *Waverly Place* (1989). A novelistic treatment of the Joel Steinberg case, the book would receive varied reviews. In recreating the story of domestic abuse that ended in the death of a couple's illegally adopted daughter, Brownmiller attempts to explore how people whom she "*might* have known"—the actual incident occurred only blocks from Brownmiller's own home—became the protagonists in a "nightmare ... [that] seemed to be a paradigm for a thousand case histories and clinical studies of family violence." Christopher Lehmann-Haunt praised the novel in *New York Times* for its author's attempt to " fill the emotional void created by any incomprehensible human act." Although Brownmiller's hope, she asserted, was to have "a subversive affect, reaching people who would not read a 400-page nonfiction history of a crime and theoretical discussion of child abuse," critics such as Stefan Kanfer took aim at *Waverly Place* and excoriated Brownmiller herself for presenting "elaborate rationales for [her] exploitation of human misery."

In *Seeing Vietnam: Encounters of the Road and Heart* (1994), Brownmiller shifts her focus to exploring a country about which she wrote network news reports during the mid-1960s. After her visit to Vietnam, she wrote several articles, primarily for travel magazines, and the book itself generally carries the breezy, informational tone of a travel vignette, detailing open-air markets, hotels, and exotic foods, occasionally to the point of sounding callous or ethnocentric. Nonetheless, there are passages of social and feminist critique, such as her memories of the Buddhist monks who self-emolated to protest the U.S. presence during the Vietnam War, and her discovery that "prostitution [is] one of the growth industries in the new Vietnam," in part because "[d]uring the war, the U.S. military, abetted by local officials, had fostered" it.

—Elizabeth Renfro

BRYANT, Dorothy

Nationality: American. **Born:** San Francisco, 1930. **Education:** San Francisco State University, B.A. in music 1950; teaching credential 1952; M.A. in creative writing 1964. **Family:** Married Robert Bryant in 1968; one son, one daughter. **Career:** Teacher of music and English in local high schools, two-year colleges, and universities; writer, beginning 1978; founder and publisher, Ata Books, Berkeley, beginning 1978. Radio host for "Morning Reading," KPFA, Berkeley, 1980-94. **Awards:** Joseph Henry Jackson award, 1964; Bay Area Book Reviewer's Association award for publishing, 1986; Before Columbus Foundation American Book Award, 1987, for *Confessions of Madame Psyche;* Bay Area Critics Circle Best New Play award, and *Drama-Logue* Best New Play award, both 1991, both for *Dear Master.* **Address:** c/o Ata Books, 1928 Stuart Street, Berkeley, California 94793, U.S.A.

Publications

Novels

Ella Price's Journal. New York, Lippincott, 1972.
The Kin of Ata Are Waiting for You. New York, Moon Books, 1976.
Miss Giardino. Berkeley, Ata Books, 1978.
The Garden of Eros. Berkeley, Ata Books, 1979.
Prisoners. Berkeley, Ata Books, 1979.
Killing Wonder. Berkeley, Ata Books, 1981; London, Women's Press, 1986.
A Day in San Francisco. Berkeley, Ata Books, 1983.
Confessions of Madame Psyche. Berkeley, Ata Books, 1986; London, Women's Press, 1988.
The Test. Berkeley, Ata Books, 1991.
Anita, Anita. Berkeley, Ata Books, 1993.

Nonfiction

Writing a Novel. Berkeley, Ata Books, 1979.

Essays

Myths to Lie By. Berkeley, Ata Books, 1984.

Plays

Delilah. N.p., 1973.
Dear Master (produced Berkeley, 1991). Berkeley, Ata Books, 1991.
Tea with Mrs. Hardy. (produced Berkeley, 1992). Berkeley, Ata Books, 1992.
The Panel (produced Berkeley, 1996).
The Trial of Cornelia Connelly (work in progress).

*

Critical Studies: "Breaking an Unsound Barrier: Two Women Speak to Us All—Tillie Olsen and Dorothy Bryant" by Rochelle Gatlin, in *San Francisco Bay Guardian,* 5 October, 1978; "Interview with Patricia Holt, in *Publishers Weekly,* 5 September 1980; "The Demoralization Paper" by Nan Bauer Maglin, in *College English,* 44(6), October 1982; "Retrospective: Books that Changed Our Lives" by J.J. Wilson, in *Women's Studies Quarterly,* fall/winter 1991; "Prophetic Day in the Life of a Writer" by Joanne Greenberg, in *Washington Times,* 12 June 1994.

Dorothy Bryant comments:

"Italian-American writer" is one of several labels that, at one time or another, are attached to me, like "woman writer," "feminist writer," "Bay-area writer," "California writer," "working class writer," and so on. I am all of these things when I draw on experience denoted by them, and none of these things when anyone attempts to confine me with a label.

* * *

As Dorothy Bryant says, she finds labels confining. As applied to writers, or any other individuals, labels can be simplistic, misleading, and, perhaps the greatest sin, boring, because using them too often signals a stop in the actual critical thinking that Bryant sees as essential to a democratic society. For the last 20 years, in her novels Bryant has cast her cool eye on such hot topics as homosexuality, race, feminism, immigration, philistinism, psychic phenomena, and the Church. Even such apparently bland topics as English grammar, the driver's test, adult education, childbirth, corresponding with prisoners, and women writers have, under this author's thoughtful scrutiny, become controversial.

And yet Bryant's tone, in interviews as well as in her writing, is mild, reasonable, determinedly fair-minded, her politics and practice irreproachable. Somehow that very rationality and moderation could be the key to what makes her books so controversial in a society as tendentious and extreme as ours, but is also that her issues are always in advance. With an almost eerie far-sightedness and by applying her clear intelligence, Bryant manages to put her finger on some of society's sore spots in each novel. As early as her 1973 play, *Delilah,* she recognized the possible negative reception likely for such clear vision, having the messenger in the play admit that "in the present climate my message will be unpopular."

Fortunately for the more open-minded reading audience—those who like their novels thoughtful, surprising, and eminently readable at all levels of sophistication—Bryant has not allowed negative responses from the publishing world to discourage her from writing her books as she wants to. As she says in her encouraging "how to" book, *Writing a Novel,* she "quit quitting." Together with her husband, Bob Bryant, "who makes everything work," Dorothy has developed self-publishing into a respectable and effective alternative to the selling out of the self. Since 1978 Ata Books has been keeping Bryant's books in circulation. Her oft-reprinted essay, "My Publisher/Myself," collected in *Myths to Lie By,* describes the price of that decision, the hard work, and the satisfaction of seeing her works with their controversial topics and plain style find their own way into the right hands.

The first hint of Bryant's miraculous ability to prevail over the philistines can be found in the strange publishing history of her most often reprinted book, *The Kin of Ata Are Waiting for You* (after which her publishing house is named). *Kin of Ata* was the first of her books which Bryant and her husband published themselves. When it was republished—thanks to an editor of Moon Books, the feminist arm of Random House—*The Kin of Ata* once again demonstrated the unpredictability of the book market. Try to imagine the possible markets in the mid-'70s for an allegory where a macho murderer is redeemed by a low-key guru who happens to be a black woman! No wonder Alice Walker describes it as "one of my favorite books in all the world"; and of course the book, now in its 18th printing, has gone on to become a favorite of Jungians, feminists, teachers, and all who take their own spiritual quests seriously. While Bryant has never written another book like it, she doesn't disavow this utopian fantasy, although she does worry that people may misread it as a "feel good" fantasy rather than a "get to work on yourself" exemplum.

An earlier book, which has also won Bryant many readers, *Ella Price's Journal* is written in a much more realistic mode, but is just as much a quest and request for transformation as *The Kin of Ata.* Notice Bryant's choice of form here: that self-actualizing journal form so popular since the 1960s, which is especially apt in this novel as it gives Ella herself the microphone. We hear from the inside what it feels like to go back to school as an adult, thrilling to all those bright new ideas that sometimes show up the shoddiness of the former-life situation. This book was published with no fanfare by Lippincott in 1972 and again the miracle is that it did not sink like a stone into the remainder sea. To its credit, *Redbook,* a women's magazine, picked up the novel in its fiction section, which led Signet to reprint it in paper (with an appallingly misleading erotic cover). The *Redbook* readers' responses were upfront and personal, and Bryant still cherishes the letters she received from women all over the country recognizing themselves in Ella, and, alas, all too often their husbands in Joe....

Unfortunately, Bryant's next novel on the public and private life of a "hatchet-faced, old maid" English teacher (a too-often maligned species, in Bryant's view) was impossible to get published. Her belief in *Miss Giardino* pushed her into self-publication, where at least she could choose her own covers! Much of Anna Giardino's childhood is based on Bryant's own mother's stories, and the novel is an example of what Virginia Woolf called in *A Room of One's Own,* "thinking back through our mothers." This brave and unusual book is also a thinking forward about the changes in inner-city schools, changes that are still evoking public policy debates. Personalized in the unforgettable Miss Giardino, the issues in this novel have made it a beacon for many teachers trying, like the young teacher Maria in the book, to find their own ways through all the different trends in educational theory and practice.

Bryant's next unlikely heroine is a blind woman going though childbirth in the wilds of Northern California. She wrote *The Garden of Eros* to illustrate that giving birth was the heroic risk for women equivalent to that taken by men in battle. The form is again ingeniously suited to the topic, being written in stream-of-consciousness flashbacks between the ever-quickening birth contractions. It is a *tour de force.*

A Day in San Francisco contains the most painfully prophetic writings, and aside from *The Test,* the most personal, that Bryant has done. In an as-yet-unpublished account, she describes the anguished process she went through with this book, many times considering not publishing it even after the manuscript was completed. The novel springs from her relationship with her own gay son who, at age 30, went back to living in the Castro district of San Francisco. Once again the forms she chose are ingenious and apt. Bryant decided to have her "fictional" liberal mother, Clara, be from Mendocino, four hours north of San Francisco, so that her reaction to what she saw during her "day in San Francisco"—Gay Freedom Day 1980—would therefore be more fresh and vivid. I had almost become convinced that her dawning concern would be more credible if she lived far away," Bryant notes, "for it seemed to me more and more incredible that we liberals in the Bay area—gay and straight, young and old—lived in a state of denial approaching delusion and silence approaching lies."

In the climate of the times, this message was decidedly unpopular, of course, and Bryant received along with negative reviews, much hate mail and boycotts of her books by some bookstores and libraries because of what they perceived incorrectly as a homophobic attitude. Due to Bryant's understandable unwillingness to drag her son into the fray, her defense of her point of view was necessarily muted, but soon thereafter she and her son, reconciled and working together to raise consciousness as to the possible consequences of unsafe sex, read together over KPFA radio in Berkeley excerpts from this tender and telling novel. This memorable program is all the more treasured because in 1994 John died of AIDS, one of the many talented people lost to that terrible epidemic. What a toll this whole process must have taken on Dorothy Bryant, who probably felt more like Cassandra than Delilah at this point in her prophetic career. As she has the protagonist Clara ask toward the end of *A Day in San Francisco,* "Can't a mother ever be right?" Bryant goes on to posit that the answer to this question, in most 20th-century literature, is "No."

As you might expect, this ordeal did not stop Bryant from writing. Her next book, *The Test,* which grew out of *A Day in San Francisco,* treats another mothers' issue, the caretaking of the older generation, as her heroine sees herself and her aging father through the curious American ritual of the driving test. Many readers identify with this family story, which, characteristic of Bryant's work, leads readers to reconsider some public policy issues as well. What can be done to make growing old in this "driven" society a more dignified and natural process for all involved?

Her big next novel, *Confessions of Madame Psyche,* because of the amount and accuracy of the historical detail, convinced some readers that it was a "real story," despite the careful designation: "this is a work of fiction." Mei-li is one of Bryant's most amazing fictional heroines yet, managing in good picaresque style to have nearly every experience available to a female protagonist in the 20th century. (*Anita, Anita* uses an actual historical figure, Anita de Duarte, who was the heroic companion to Italian revolutionary leader Garibaldi.) The myth "to lie by," which underlies the story, is, of course, that of Psyche; as with Psyche all mistakes that Mei-li makes are "doors opening. All her punishments were tests that transformed her and the gods as well." This book has won may accolades, including being one of the 35 novels recommended to "help us deal with the real-world conflicts of ordinary people who must struggle to achieve genuine freedom and justice, equality and opportunity, individuality and community, sanity and human connection," according to Arthur Blaustein in his much-reprinted article "Values Added," first published in the *Brown University Alumni Monthly,* October 1995.

Lately, Bryant has chosen to write in an entirely different form: the bio-historical play. Or is it so different? What better vehicle for the dialectic than *stichmythia,* the dialogue in alternating lines employed in sharp disputes in classical drama?

In *Dear Master,* for example, the two voices of George Sand and Gustave Flaubert, combined ingeniously and convincingly from their own words as researched by Bryant in biographies and letters, play back and forth in an argument that lasted a lifetime. The play becomes a lesson in how to argue with respect, and provides a intellectually challenging experience. Even more of a tour de force of argument, *The Panel* sets up four "experts" on the

French Jewish metaphysician, Simone Weil. With the freedom of imaginative literature, the spirit of the late Simone Weil walks among these proponents of differing views of her significance, answering back and reacting, by far the most relaxed of them all. It is a thought-provoking meditation upon the after effects of a kind of saint, with a surprising amount of humor.

Will the next play be as funny? It seems unlikely, but perhaps Bryant will manage to inject some humor into the remarkable story of another saint-in-the-making, Cornelia Connelly, who leads a life almost as contrary and full of incident as Madame Psyche, except that she is a real historical figure. This play was, in 1996, a work in progress, being in the phase of public readings that Bryant finds "a necessary part of development and revision."

Who knows what Dorothy Bryant will come up with next? Whatever it is, it will almost certainly be beyond labeling, commercially unmarketable on the face of it, and timely. While Bryant herself rightly eschews labels, her work and approach to life is indelibly identified with the best of feminism, that is the rigorous, fair-minded, critical thinking imaginatively cast so that we can live through the characters' arguments with others and with themselves and feel our own standards rising to match those of the "old-fashioned" teacher, Miss Giardino. It seems, therefore, particularly appropriate that Bryant was recently asked by publisher Florence Howe of The Feminist Press to include her works on their distinguished list.

—J. J. Wilson

BUNCH, Charlotte

Also writes as Charlotte Bunch-Weeks. **Nationality:** American. **Born:** West Jefferson, North Carolina, 13 October 1944. **Education:** Attended University of California, Berkeley, 1965; Duke University, B.A. (magnum cum laude) in history and political science 1966; attended Institute for Policy Studies, 1967-68. **Family:** Married James L. Weeks in 1967 (divorced 1971). **Career:** Cofounder and national president, 1966-67, consultant to college campuses, 1967-68, University Christian Movement, New York City; member of campus ministry, Case Western Reserve University, Cleveland, Ohio, 1968-69; visiting fellow, 1969-70, resident fellow, 1971-75, tenured fellow, 1975-77, Institute for Policy Studies, Washington, D.C.; cofounder and editor, *The Furies,* 1972-73, and *Quest: A Feminist Quarterly,* 1974-81; consultant to Daughters, Inc. (publishing company), Plainfield, Vermont, 1976-78; founder and director, Public Resource Center, Washington, D.C., 1977-81; founder, director, and consultant to organizations, Interfem Consultants, New York City, 1979-87; Laurie New Jersey chair in women's studies, 1987-89, director of Women's Global Leadership, Douglas College, beginning 1989, and professor in urban studies, Bloustein School of Planning and Public Policy, beginning 1991, Rutgers University, New Brunswick, New Jersey, 1987-89. Guest lecturer at numerous colleges and universities; involved in conferences, workshops, and seminars in several countries, including Australia, Canada, Chile, Denmark, Ethiopia, Finland, India, Japan, Kenya, Mexico, the Netherlands, New Zealand, Peru, the Philippines, Sri Lanka, Switzerland, Tanzania, Thailand, and the United States. Author of pamphlets on feminist topics and contributor to numerous periodicals, including *Broadsheet, Christianity & Crisis, Christopher Street, Heresies, IKON, Interact, Isis, Ms., Nouvelles questions féministes, New Student, Response, Sings, Sinister Wisdom, Sojourner, Student World,* and *Women's World.* **Awards:** Community service awards, Lambda Legal Defense Fund, 1982, and National Lesbian and Gay Health Foundation, 1986; Resourceful Woman award, 1992; Feminist Majority Foundation Feminist of the Year award, 1993. **Member:** Isis International (associate beginning 1985), National Organization for Women (NOW), National Gay and Lesbian Task Force (member, board of directors, 1974-81; member, executive committee, 1976-78), National Women's Studies Association, National Women's Conference Committee, American Friends Service Committee, Women's Liberation Movement (cofounder, Washington, DC, branch, 1968), Women's Institute for Freedom of the Press (associate, 1978-86), New York Feminist Art Institute (member, advisory board beginning 1979), New York City Commission on the Status of Women (chair, United Nations Decade committee, 1982-86). **Address:** Center for Womens' Global Leadership, 27 Clifton Ave., Rutgers University, New Brunswick, New Jersey 08903, U.S.A. **Online Address:** cwgl@lgc.apc.org.

Publications

Political/Social Theory

A Broom of One's Own (as Charlotte Bunch-Weeks). Washington, DC, Women's Liberation Movement, 1970.

Passionate Politics: Feminist Theory in Action: Essays, 1968-1986. New York, St. Martin's Press, 1987.

Demanding Accountability: The Global Campaign and Vienna Tribunal for Women's Human Rights, with Niamh Reilly. New York, UNIFEM, 1994.

Essays

"Feminist Perspectives on Women in Development," with Roxanna Carrillo, in *Persistent Inequalities: Women and World Development,* edited by Irene Tinker. New York, Oxford University Press, 1989.

"Women's Rights as Human Rights: Towards a Re-Vision of Human Rights," in *Human Rights Quarterly,* 12(4), November 1990.

"Feminist Visions of Human Rights in the 21st Century," in *Human Rights in the 21st Century: A Global Challenge,* edited by Kathleen and Paul Mahoney. N.p., Caswell, 1992.

"Organizing for Women's Human Rights Globally," in *Ours by Right: Women's Rights as Human Rights,* edited by Joanna Kerr. N.p., Zed Press, 1993.

"Global Violence against Women: The Challenge to Human Rights and Development," with Roxanna Carrillo, in *World Security: Challenges for a New Century,* edited by Michael T. Klare and Daniel C. Thomas. New York, St. Martin's Press, 1994.

Other

Editor (as Charlotte Bunch-Weeks), with Joanne Cooke and Robin Morgan, *The New Women: A Motive Anthology on Women's Liberation.* New York, Bobbs-Merrill, 1970.

Editor, with Nancy Myron, *Class and Feminism: A Collection of Essays from The Furies.* Oakland, California, Diana Press, 1974.

Editor, with Nancy Myron, *Women Remembered: A Collection of Biographies from The Furies.* Oakland, California, Diana Press, 1974.

Editor, with Nancy Myron, *Lesbianism and the Women's Movement.* Oakland, California, Diana Press, 1975.
Editor, with others, *Building Feminist Theory, Essays from Quest.* New York, Longman, 1981.
Editor, with Sandra Pollack, *Learning Our Way: Essays in Feminist Education.* Plainfield, Vermont, Daughters, 1977; Freedom, California, Crossing Press, 1983.
Editor, with Kathleen Barry and Shirley Castley, *International Feminism: Networking against Female Sexual Slavery.* International Women's Tribune Centre, 1984.

*

Critical Studies: Interview with Gloria Steinem in *Ms.*, April 1977; interview with Karla Dobinski in *Feminist Connection,* March 1983; interview with Torie Osborne in *Commonground,* April 1983; article in *Signs,* winter 1987.

* * *

In addition to being one of the most highly regarded feminist theorists of the 20th-century women's movement, Charlotte Bunch has been one of global feminism's chief proponents. Whether speaking before groups around the world, mobilizing women through such books as *Passionate Politics: Feminist Theory in Action* (1987), or serving an instrumental role in one of the many feminist organizations to which she has devoted her time, Bunch has dedicated her adult life to promoting a gender-based perception of human rights on both a national and international level.

It was as an undergraduate student at Duke University in the early 1960s that Bunch first began to involve herself in social activism, first on behalf of civil rights and then for student Christian organizations. After earning her bachelor's degree in 1966 she cofounded the University Christian Movement. As the group's national president Bunch joined the campus ministry staff of Case Western Reserve from 1968-69. The religious aspect of her job were not what inspired her, the social aspects were: promoting love, equality, and justice within a fragmenting modern society.

By the early 1970s the women's movement had begun to take hold of the consciousness of many women of Bunch's generation; for her it would cause great personal and intellectual transformation. In 1971, after four years of marriage, she came out to her friends and family as a lesbian. "It was like coming out in a fishbowl," Bunch would later remark to Torie Osborne. "Some friends were especially shocked because I had an 'ideal marriage' to a man who was very supportive of me and of feminism.... Other friends revealed to me that *they* were lesbians, and still others began to deal with lesbianism as at least a political possibility for other women, if not for themselves." To Bunch, lesbianism was the ultimate, and indeed necessary, expression of her feminist beliefs.

To promote the "political possibility" of a lesbian feminist lifestyle—which she viewed as an explicit statement challenging patriarchy rather than merely a personal choice—Bunch founded The Furies, a Washington, D.C.-based collective that published an influential magazine during the three years of its existence. In 1974 she helped to found *Quest: A Feminist Quarterly,* through which she was able to voice her opinions and inform her readers of the progress in the arena of women's and lesbian's rights. When separatist factions began to form within the women's movement—most significantly between lesbian and heterosexual feminists—Bunch's diplomacy helped lesbian feminists gain acceptance for the need to "keep a base outside" the system, as she told Gloria Steinem in 1977. "We need a place to create ourselves."

However, Bunch soon saw feminist concerns as more global in nature, and during a national women's conference in 1975 she spoke on integrating lesbian feminist concerns within the larger, global, feminist struggle. Fortunately, women—both straight and lesbian—listened and the growing rift was healed. While the U.S. feminist movement seemed to get mired down in rhetoric and what she compared to her own "activist mid-life crisis," Bunch has been encouraged by the growing interest in third world and international feminism over the past decade. Indeed, it is an interest that she herself has fostered, through both her writing and her work with The Center for Women's Global Leadership. As the organization's founder, Bunch has been a major force in bringing world attention to bear on the human rights of women. As well, she has awakened women to the understanding that they need to demand from their respective governments a political and social equality on par with men.

"I see feminism as a movement of people working for a change across and despite national boundaries, not of representatives of nation-states or national governments," Bunch explained to Karla Dobinski. "We must be global, recognizing that the oppression of women in one part of the world is often affected by what happens in another, and that no woman is free until the conditions of oppression of women are eliminated everywhere." In 1989, before a meeting of Amnesty International, Bunch reiterated those same beliefs, marking a turning point in that organization's platform as it accepted the commitment to address gender-specific human rights issues. Throughout her 30-year career as an activist, Charlotte Bunch has been, and continues to be, a catalyst for social change.

—Lynn MacGregor

BUNCH-WEEKS, Charlotte. *See* **BUNCH, Charlotte.**

BURDEKIN, Katharine

Also wrote as Kay Burdekin. **Pseudonym:** Murray Constantine. **Nationality:** British. **Born:** Katharine Penelope Cade, Derbyshire, England, 23 July 1896. **Education:** Attended Cheltenham Ladies' College, 1907-13. **Military Service:** Army nurse, Voluntary Aid Detachment, Cheltenham, during World War I. **Family:** Married Beaufort Burdekin in 1915 (separated 1921); two daughters. **Career:** Worked in a shoe factory, a printer's shop, and a flour mill. **Died:** 10 August 1963.

Publications

Novels

Anna Colquhoun. London, J. Lane, 1922.

The Reasonable Hope. London, J. Lane, 1924.
The Burning Ring (as Kay Burdekin). London, Butterworth, 1927; New York, Morrow, 1929.
The Children's Country (as Kay Burdekin). New York, Morrow, 1929.
The Rebel Passion (as Kay Burdekin). London, Butterworth, and New York, Morrow, 1929.
Quiet Ways. London, Butterworth, 1930.
Proud Man (as Murray Constantine). London, Boriswood, 1934; (as Katharine Burdekin) New York, Feminist Press, 1993.
The Devil, Poor Devil! (as Murray Constantine). London, Boriswood, 1934; New York, Arno, 1978.
Swastika Night (as Murray Constantine). London, Gollancz, 1937; (as Katharine Burdekin), introduction by Daphne Patai, New York, Feminist Press, and London, Lawrence & Wishart, 1985.
Venus in Scorpio: A Romance of Versailles 1770-1793 (as Murray Constantine), with Margaret Leland Goldsmith. London, J. Lane, 1940.
The End of This Day's Business, afterword by Daphne Patai. Old Westbury, New York, Feminist Press, 1990.

*

Critical Studies: "Orwell's Despair, Burdekin's Hope: Gender and Power in Dystopia" by Daphne Patai, *Women's Studies International Forum,* 7(2), 1984; *The Orwell Mystique: A Study in Male Ideology,* by Daphne Paul, Amherst, University of Massachusetts Press, 1984; "Worlds without End Foisted upon the Future" by Andy Croft, in *Inside the Myth: Orwell, Views from the Left,* edited by Christopher Norris, London, Lawrence & Wishart, 1984; "Dystopian Nights" by Robert Crossley, in *Science-Fiction Studies* (Greencastle, Indiana), 14(41), 1987; "In the Year of Our Lord Hitler 720: Katharine Burdekin's *Swastika Night*" by Carlo Pagetti, translated by Clara Mucci and Maria R. Philmus, in *Science-Fiction Studies,* 17(3), 1990; "The Loss of the Feminine Principle in Charlotte Haldane's *Man's World* and Katharine Burdekin's *Swastika Night*" by Elizabeth Russell, in *Where No Man Has Gone Before: Women and Science Fiction,* edited by Lucie Armitt, London, Routledge, 1991; "Imagining Reality: The Utopian Fiction of Katharine Burdekin" by Daphne Patai, in *Rediscovering Forgotten Radicals,* edited by Patai and Ingram, Chapel Hill, University of North Carolina Press, 1993; "Metapropaganda: Self-Reading Dystopian Fiction: Burdekin's *Swastika Night* and Orwell's *Nineteen Eighty-Four*" by George McKay, in *Science-Fiction Studies,* 21(3), 1994.

* * *

Katharine Burdekin explored gender roles and social issues in a score of novels, as well as plays, poetry, and short fiction. Although ten of these novels were published between 1922 and 1940, this influential utopian/dystopian writer was largely forgotten, or remembered only by her male pseudonym, Murray Constantine, until the early 1980s, when scholar Daphne Patai confirmed suspicions that Burdekin and Constantine were the same person. Contacting publishers and relatives, including Burdekin's longtime female companion, Patai reestablished the facts about the author, and, in collaboration with the Feminist Press, undertook the project of publishing the unpublished, and republishing the out-of-print, novels.

Burdekin was born Katharine Penelope Cade in 1896 to an upper-middle-class family in the English village of Spondon, was educated at Cheltenham Ladies' College, and married Beaufort Burdekin in 1915. She served locally as an Army nurse during World War I; then, in 1920, she moved to Australia with her husband and two daughters. There she began writing and soon produced her first novel, *Anna Colquhoun,* which was published in 1922. That same year her marriage ended, and she returned to England with the children, settling in Cornwall to be near her mother and sister Rowena Cade (designer and director of the open-air Minack Theatre). In 1926 she met the woman who was to be her lifetime companion; they moved to Suffolk, where they remained until Burdekin's death in 1963. As well as writing prolifically for many years, Burdekin worked on and off at a shoe factory (during World War II), printer's shop, and flour mill. Despite her rural isolation she did take trips to London to meet publishers and writers, and conducted correspondences with writers like H.D., Laura Riding, Virginia Woolf, Bertrand and Dora Russell, Margaret Goldsmith, and Norah James.

Notable among Burdekin's published works is *The Children's Country* (1929), illustrated by Beth Krebs Morris, which Patai calls "a 'nonsexist children's book,' long before there was such a category." Also noteworthy are *The Rebel Passion* (1929), which Burdekin felt was her first mature work, her pacifist novel, *Quiet Ways* (1930), and the historical novel *Venus in Scorpio* (1940). The first of her books to be republished was *The Devil, Poor Devil!* in 1978 by Arno Press (but the author was still listed as Murray Constantine). So far, the Feminist Press has published three novels by Burdekin, with accompanying essays by Patai. These include *Swastika Night* (1985), *The End of This Day's Business* (1990), and *Proud Man* (1993).

Swastika Night was originally published in 1937 by Victor Gollancz (also Orwell's publisher). The novel can alternately be viewed as anti-Nazi propaganda, as a prescient view of the horrors soon to besiege Europe, or as a more wide-ranging indictment of the violence and self-deceit at the core of all patriarchal societies. Reissued as a Left Book Club selection in 1940, which sold 17,000 copies, it is likely to have influenced Orwell's *Nineteen Eighty-Four.* In Burdekin's scenario, the Nazis have conquered Europe and much of the world, and have ruled for 700 years, during which time they have exterminated the Jews, reduced Christianity to a despised and persecuted sect, and established a state religion worshipping "Our Lord Hitler" and his father, "God the Thunderer." A feudal world has been created, ruled by a hereditary Fuehrer and his Knights, who embody "pride," "brutality," "ruthlessness," and "all other soldierly and heroic virtues." In order to render more effective control over the conquered populations, they have abolished books and the historical memory they represent. The worst treatment is reserved for women, who, having been reduced to the value of beasts, are caged, beaten, and raped at will. Illiterate, with heads shaved, dressed in ill-fitting, ugly uniforms, women are objects of scorn and ridicule. Men mate with them reluctantly, for purposes of procreation, but reserve romantic feelings for their own gender. Against this bleak backdrop the author projects a conspiracy by an apostate Knight and an Englishman to preserve a secret book that reveals the history the Nazis have suppressed.

The End of This Day's Business forms, in many respects, a mirror image of *Swastika Night.* Here it is women who rule society and define culture, while men are kept in a seemingly benign subjugation, free to play sports and do physical labor, but restricted from education or leadership. Nearly all traces of male literature and culture have been obliterated. One female elder, Grania, challenges this arrangement, as the knight in *Swastika Night,* Von Hess, had challenged his society. Both are aided in their cause by young disciples from the subject populations. In this novel, Burdekin creates a world which is in many respects a utopia. As Grania says, "The world under women has been well ruled." Yet the author rejects any society, no matter how well intentioned, that stifles individual freedom and human potential.

Proud Man relies on a narrator from an advanced future society to satirize male dominance and other contemporary faults. "The Person," as the narrator is known, dreams of a world of "subhumans," which, in Swiftian fashion, turns out to be the world we recognize as our own, full of war, injustice, superstition, and misogyny. Taking, in turn, female and male forms, the narrator engages in dialogues with an old priest, a woman writer, and a serial child-murderer, to learn more of the subhumans.

The recent appearance of these novels and the reestablishment of Burdekin's literary reputation are welcome developments, indeed. Yet the previous submergence of such a talented and prolific writer raises fascinating and disturbing questions. She shared the fate of many left-wing writers of the 1930s; much of the utopian, anti-fascist, and feminist literature of her generation has been neglected, and much still deserves redress. In her case, moreover, the use of a male pseudonym, though it may have helped her works to be taken seriously and may have protected her from fascist reprisals, confused readers and scholars for years. If Burdekin is emblematic of the lost woman writer, she is also, thankfully, emblematic of the "real find" that determined scholarship and publishing can uncover. Her legacy should continue to grow as more of her novels are made available, and subsequently, as the critical literature accumulates.

—John F. Riche

BURDEKIN, Kay. *See* **BURDEKIN, Katharine.**

BUTLER, Judith P.

Nationality: American. **Education:** Yale University, B.A. 1978, M.Phil., Ph.D. in philosophy 1984. **Family:** Companion of Wendy Brown; one son. **Career:** Professor of rhetoric and comparative literature, University of California, Berkeley. **Address:** Department of Rhetoric, University of California, Berkeley, 2125 Dwinelle Hall, Berkeley, California 94720-0001, U.S.A.

Publications

Political/Social Theory

Subjects of Desire: Hegelian Reflections in 20th-Century France. New York and Guildford, Columbia University Press, 1987.

Gender Trouble: Feminism and the Subversion of Identity. New York and London, Routledge, 1990.

Bodies That Matter: On the Discursive Limits of "Sex". New York and London, Routledge, 1993.

Subjection. Stanford, California, Stanford University Press, 1996.

Other

Editor, with Joan Wallach Scott, *Feminists Theorize the Political.* New York and London, Routledge, 1992.

Editor, with Linda Singer and Maureen MacGrogan, *Erotic Welfare: Sexual Theory and Politics in the Age of Epidemic.* New York, Routledge, 1993.

* * *

Philosopher Judith Butler has written several books that attempt to reevaluate and rearticulate issues of sex and gender, thereby disenforcing the power of patriarchy and compulsory heterosexual behavior. This she attempts to do through two major works: *Gender Trouble: Feminism and the Subversion of Identity* (1990) and *Bodies That Matter: On the Discursive Limits of Sex* (1993).

In *Gender Trouble: Feminism and the Subversion of Identity,* Butler addresses the issue of gender as a social construct. Responding to the work of such critics as Simone de Beauvoir, Luce Irigaray, and Monique Wittig, she argues that "women" and, for that matter, "men," do not exist outside of or prior to their construction within a cultural context. There is no "natural state" of being a woman, as De Beauvoir postulated in *The Second Sex.* Nor are there gendered "inner selves," with sexual characteristics that can be enhanced or suppressed as society dictates. According to Butler, sex and gender categories exist as a result of an individual's acceptance of and adherence to a narrowly defined set of characteristics attributed to each category; hence, one who can successfully pass for what our culture defines as "woman"—whether it be procreative, possessing the appropriate physical attributes, or exhibiting the appropriate sexual behaviors—is indeed a woman, even if in possession of male anatomy. The process of being "gendered," therefore, remains an ongoing one, for it is dependent upon an individual's continued action in conformity to specific characteristics.

To Butler, homosexual culture uses the same sex-gender categories as does its heterosexual counterpart, thereby reinforcing a heterosexual framework: "The terms *queens, butches, femmes, girls,* even the parodic reappropriation of *dyke, queer,* and *fag* redeploy and destabilize the categories of sex and the originally derogatory categories for homosexual identity," she explains. "All of these terms might be understood as symptomatic of the 'straight mind,' modes of identifying with the oppressor's version of the identity of the oppressed." Butler disagrees with Wittig's assertion that heterosexual supremacy can be disempowered by violating the coerced heterosexual "contract," maintaining that such an assertion assumes that the contract is upheld through individual choice. Rather, she states, "power-relations can be understood ... as constraining and constituting the very possibilities of volition"—power can deployed but not withdrawn. Rejecting the heterosexual contract merely reinforces it, thus perpetuating the very power one is attempting to usurp.

What, then, is one to do to join heterosexual and homosexual women in a solution to the subversion of feminine identity? The answer lies in the book's title: "Trouble." Butler's solution requires that we make "trouble" in the form of what she calls "a radical proliferation of gender" in the hope that "[c]ultural configurations of sex and gender might then proliferate or, rather, their present proliferation might then become articulable within the discourses that establish intelligible life, confounding the very binarism of sex and exposing its fundamental unnaturalness." In other words, each individual strays outside the cultural confines of what is deemed appropriately—characteristically—homosexual or appropriately—characteristically—heterosexual; this deviance from the sex-gender "norms," this "redeployment of the categories of identity themselves," will make such categories increasingly problematic.

Butler expands upon this reasoning in *Bodies That Matter* by confronting the physical "realities" of sex and gender and then showing them as constructs of the very discourses—the coerced heterosexual contracts—that define them. In an earlier work, *Subjects of Desire: Hegelian Reflections in 20th-Century France,* which she wrote in 1987, she analyses the works of several contemporary French philosophers in their relationship to both desire and the subject of desire. Using Hegel's *Phenomenology of Spirit* as a starting point, she contrasts the existentialism of Sartre and the poststructuralism of Derrida, Lacan, and Foucault, among others.

—Lynn MacGregor

C

CARDINAL, Marie

Nationality: French; immigrated to Québec, Canada. **Born:** Algeria, 9 March 1929. **Education:** Université d'Alger, Algeria, 1947-53, licence and diplôme d'études supérieures in philosophy. **Family:** Married Jean-Pierre Ronfard in 1953; three children. **Awards:** Prix International du Premier Roman, 1962, for *Ecoutez la mer;* Prix Littré, 1976, for *Les Mots pour le dire.*

Publications

Novels

Ecoutez la mer [Listen to the Sea]. Paris, Julliard, 1962.
La Mule de corbillard [The Hearse Mule]. Paris, Julliard, 1963.
Guide junior de Paris, with Christiane Cardinal. Paris, Julliard, 1964.
La Souricière [The Mousetrap]. Paris, Julliard, 1965.
Cet Eté-lá [That Summer], published with *Deux ou trois choses que je sais d'elle,* by Jean-Luc Godard. Paris, Gallimard, 1970.
Mao, with Lucien Bodard. Paris, Gallimard, 1970.
La Clé sur la porte [The Key in the Door]. Paris, Grasset, 1972.
Les Mots pour le dire. Paris, Grasset, 1975; translated as *The Words to Say It,* Cambridge, Massachusetts, VanVactor & Goodheart, 1983.
A pays de mes racines [In the Country of My Roots], published with *Au pays de Moussia,* by Bénédicte Ronfard. Paris, Grasset, 1980.
Une Vie pour deux [One Life for Two]. Paris, Grasset, 1983.
Le Passé empieté [The Past Encroached]. Paris, Grasset, 1983.
Les Grands Désordres. Paris, Grasset, 1987; translated as *Devotion and Disorder,* London, Women's Press, 1990.
Comme si de rien n'était [As If It Were Nothing]. Paris, Grasset, 1990.
Les Jeudis de Charles et de Lula [The Thursdays of Charles and Lula]. Paris, Grasset, 1993.

Political/Social Theory

La Cause des Femmes, with Gisèle Halimi. Paris, Grasset, 1973; translated as *The Right to Choose,* St. Lucia, Australia, University of Queensland Press, 1977.
Autrement Dit, with Annie LeClerc. Paris, Grasset, 1977; translated as *In Other Words,* postscript by LeClerc, Bloomington, Indiana University Press, 1995.
Les Pieds-Noirs [The Algerian-French]. Tours, Belfond, 1988.

Other

Translator, *La Médée d'Euripide.* Montréal, Editions Victor Lévy Beaulieu, 1986; Paris, Grasset, 1987.
Translator, *Peer Gynt,* by Henrik Ibsen. Montréal, Lemeac, 1991.
Translator, *Les Troyennes,* by Euripides. Montréal, Lemeac, 1993.

*

Media Adaptations: *Les Mots pour le dire* (film), 1983;

Bibliography: *French Feminist Criticism: Women, Language, and Literature* by Elissa D. Gelfand and Virginia Thorndike Hules, New York, Garland, 1985.

Critical Studies: "Mother and Motherland: The Daughter's Quest for Origins" by Marguerite Le Clézio, in *Stanford French Review,* winter 1981; "Mothers, Madness, and the Middle Class in *The Bell Jar* and *Les Mots pour le dire"* by Elaine Martin, in *French-American Review,* 5, spring 1981; "Feminism and Formalism: Dialectical Structures in Marie Cardinal's *Une Vie pour deux"* by Carolyn A. Durham, in *Tulsa Studies in Women's Literature,* 4, spring 1985; *Maternity, Morality, and the Literature of Madness* by Marilyn Yalom, University Park and London, Pennsylvania State University Press, 1985; "Patterns of Influence: Simone de Beauvoir and Marie Cardinal" by Durham, in *French Review,* 60, February 1987; "In the Eye of Abjection: Marie Cardinal's *The Words to Say It"* by Patricia Elliot, in *Mosaic,* 20(4), fall 1987; "*L'Ecriture féminine* and the Search for the Mother in the Works of Violette Leduc and Marie Cardinal" by Colette Hall, in *Women in French Literature,* edited by Michel Guggenheim, Stanford, Stanford University Press, 1988; "Métissage, Emancipation, and Female Textuality in Two Francophone Writers" by Françoise Lionnet, in *Life/Lines: Theorizing Women's Autobiography,* edited by Bella Brodzki and Celeste Schenck, Ithaca, Cornell University Press, 1988; "Reading for Pleasure: Marie Cardinal's *Les Mots pour le dire* and the Text as (Re)Play of Oedipal Configurations" by Phil Powrie, in *Contemporary French Fiction by Women: Feminist Perspectives,* edited by Powrie and Margaret Atack, Manchester, Manchester University Press, 1990; *The Contexture of Feminism: Marie Cardinal and Multicultural Literacy* by Durham, Urbana and Chicago, University of Illinois Press, 1992; *Marie Cardinal: Motherhood and Creativity* by Lucille Cairns, Glasgow, University of Glasgow French and German Publications, 1992; "Marie Cardinal's *Comme si de rien n'était:* Language and Violence" by David J. Bond, in *International Fiction Review,* 21(1-2), 1994; "Between Irigaray and Cardinal: Reinventing Maternal Genealogies" by Samantha Haigh, in *Modern Language Review,* 89(1), 1994.

* * *

That relatively few of Marie Cardinal's works have been translated into English belies her popularity as a best-selling novelist in France. Her works have been translated into 18 languages, and she is a popular feminist media figure, appearing frequently on both television and radio and attending numerous meetings, debates, and conferences. Though criticized for the lack of formal innovation in her novels, Cardinal's more traditional style has allowed her to bring feminist ideas to a far broader audience than more radical writers are able. Her work is intensely personal, even autobiographical, yet she strikes emotional chords that resonate for a range of readers, and especially for women. "In my books I think that readers meet a woman who lives in France today, and who basically resembles all women," she writes in *In Other Words.* "That is who I am."

Cardinal was born and raised in French-occupied Algeria, where she lived until the age of 24, when she moved to France (she has since emigrated to Québec). Her parents divorced in the year of her birth, and she was raised by a strict mother in an atmosphere of colonial wealth. Her works, which frequently draw on the landscapes of her childhood, are pervaded by feelings of homelessness and exile, as well as guilt over her own family's role in the Algerian conflict. Other frequently occurring themes in her work include the mother-daughter relationship, psychoanalysis, and women's relation to language. Such ideas have often been treated in complex theoretical terms, but Cardinal's writing is always both accessible and moving.

Les Mots pour le dire/The Words to Say It (1975) is Cardinal's best known work; it has sold several million copies in Europe alone and was released as a film in 1983. Its popularity is particularly remarkable given its seemingly unprepossessing subject matter—a seven-year-long psychoanalysis. A genre-crossing work that contains elements of autobiography, novel, and case history, *The Words to Say It* tells the story of its heroine's journey from crippling anxiety, physically expressed by constant menstrual bleeding, to writing and self-acceptance. Though chiefly a tale of the transformation wrought by psychoanalysis, *The Words to Say It* is intercut with evocations of the political context of the Algerian revolution and violent decolonization. Unfortunately, the English edition, with a preface and afterword by psychologist Bruno Bettelheim, deemphasizes this crucial aspect. Though Bettelheim calls *The Words to Say It* "the best account of psychoanalysis as seen and experienced by the patient," Cardinal's book is much more than that: it is also a meditation on the inextricable connections between personal and political violence. Though the narrator struggles to come to terms with her flesh-and-blood mother, she also must wrangle with her connection to what she perceives as the larger maternal presence of the motherland; she writes, "For Algeria was my real mother." The final chapter of the book, consisting of exactly one sentence, is omitted in the English translation, but it epitomizes this conflation of the individual and the historical. "Quelques jours plus tard c'était Mai 68"—"A few days later it was May '68." Invoking the revolutionary politics of that time, Cardinal implies that the psychoanalytic voyage inwards is only half the battle, and must be matched with an external politics of commitment.

Since publishing *The Words to Say It,* Cardinal has received an overwhelming tide of letters from women affected by the book. By way of response she wrote *In Other Words* with Annie Leclerc, and indeed, this work is largely concerned with women's relation to writing and language. Cardinal believes that "Men hermetically sealed ... words, imprisoned women within them. Women must open them if they want to survive. She urges women to find words to express themselves, while resisting the masculinism built into language. Her words seem to call for an *écriture féminine*, the French feminist concept of "feminine writing" that suggests women must reinvent language to write their bodily differences. But Cardinal rejects the idea of a separate language for women, urging rather that women find ways "to express the unexpressed and to use the French vocabulary as it is, directly, without cleaning it up. It will thus become evident and clear that there are things we can't translate into words." As women write about themselves, language will have to expand to encompass their differences; language itself will become richer and more diverse.

The challenge for women to express themselves within language also plays a major role in *Devotion and Disorder,* Cardinal's only novel thus far translated into English. Like *The Words to Say It, Devotion and Disorder* is a tale of recovery: it tells the story of a mother/psychologist (Elsa Labbé) and her attempt to cure her daughter's heroin addiction. The recovery story is interspersed with the mother's recollections of the past, and is further complicated by the framing narration of a male ghostwriter, whom she has hired to write about the experience. In the end, despite Elsa's best efforts, she finds that her daughter can only kick the habit with the help of another addict, leaving Elsa to face her own personal problems.

Though the mother-daughter bond is the crux of *Devotion and Disorder,* the book ends with the possibility of love between Elsa and the unnamed male ghostwriter. Cardinal has been criticized for her female protagonists' seemingly unquestioning acceptance of the conventions of heterosexuality and marriage, but her comments in *In Other Words* clarify her views: "I think that the traditional couple is living through its final death pangs, for women are beginning to understand that they don't only exist as 'women' but also simply as human beings, and human beings who have volumes to say."

—Victoria Rosner

CARMICHAEL, Marie. *See* **STOPES, Marie (Charlotte).**

CARPENTER. *See* **ARNOLD, June (Davis).**

CARR, Emily

Nationality: Canadian. **Born:** Victoria, British Columbia, 13 December 1871. **Education:** Studied art at California School of Design, San Francisco, 1891-93; in England at Westminister School of Art, London, with Julius Olsson and Algernon Talmage in Cornwall and with John Whitely in Hertfordshire, 1899-1904; in France at Académie Colarossi and with John Duncan Fergusson in Paris, with Henry Phelan Gibb at Crécy-en-Brie near Paris, and in Brittany with Gibb and Frances Hodgkins, 1910-11; studied short story writing by correspondence with the Palmer Institute of Authorship, Hollywood, California, in 1926-27; and in Victoria during the summer and autumn, 1934. **Career:** Studio artist, taught art classes and travelled within British Columbia to document native heritage, 1893-1913; produced pottery and rugs, raised dogs and managed her apartment house, 1914-27; work exhibited at National Gallery, Ottawa, 1927; subsequently widely exhibited, both alone and with groups such as the British Columbia Society of Fine Arts, the Group of Seven, and the Canadian Group of Painters; stories broadcast on the Canadian Broadcasting Corporation in 1940. **Awards:** Governor General's Award, 1941, for *Klee Wyck.* **Died:** 2 March 1945.

Publications

Short Stories

Klee Wyck [Laughing One]. Toronto and New York, Oxford University Press, 1941.
The Book of Small. Toronto, Oxford University Press, 1942; London and New York, Oxford University Press, 1943.
The House of All Sorts. Toronto and London, Oxford University Press, 1944.
The Heart of a Peacock, edited by Ira Dilworth. Toronto, Oxford University Press, 1953.
Pause: A Sketch Book. Toronto, Clarke Irwin, 1953.

Autobiography

Growing Pains: The Autobiography of Emily Carr. Toronto, Oxford University Press, 1946.
Hundreds and Thousands: The Journals of Emily Carr. Toronto, Clarke Irwin, 1966.
"Letters from Emily Carr" edited by Ruth Humphrey in *University of Toronto Quarterly,* 41(2), winter 1972.
Dear Nan: Letters of Emily Carr, Nan Cheney, and Humphrey Toms, edited by Doreen Walker. Vancouver, University of British Columbia Press, 1990.

Other

Fresh Seeing: Two Addresses by Emily Carr. Toronto, Clarke, Irwin, 1972.

*

Bibliography: *The Life and Work of Emily Carr (1871-1945): A Selected Bibliography* by Marguerite Turpin, Vancouver, University of British Columbia School of Librarianship, 1965.

Manuscript Collections: British Columbia Archives & Records Service, Victoria.

Critical Studies: *Emily Carr: The Untold Story* by E. Hembroff-Schleicher, Saanichton, British Columbia, Hancock House, 1978; *The Art of Emily Carr* by Doris Shadbolt, Toronto, Clarke Irwin, 1979; *Emily Carr: A Biography* by Maria Tippett, Toronto, Macmillan, 1979; "Literary Versions of Emily Carr" by Eva-Marie Kröller, in *Canadian Literature,* 109, summer 1986; *The Life of Emily Carr* by Paula Blanchard, Seattle, University of Washington Press, 1987; "Emily Carr and the Language of Small" in *Everyday Magic: Child Languages in Canadian Literature* by Laurie Ricou, Vancouver, University of British Columbia Press, 1987; "'Paint above Paint': Telling Li(v)es in Emily Carr's Literary Self-Portraits" by Timothy Dow Adams, in *Journal of Canadian Studies,* 27(2), summer 1992.

* * *

Since her death in 1945, regard for Emily Carr's art and writing has grown and her life has become a frequent subject for biographers, poets, and playwrights. Eccentric by many accounts, oddly dressed, and customarily surrounded by small animals, she dwells in imaginations as a bold modernist inspired by the natural world and the heritage of aboriginal peoples, a tough pragmatist able to manage through hard times, a visionary painter, and a writer who set down her life in crafted, faceted prose.

The fifth of six children, Carr enjoyed a childhood permeated by British tradition, carefree privilege, and surrounded by the striking landscape of Canada's west coast in Victoria, British Columbia. Following the death of both parents during her teens, she determined to become an artist and took steps to study art trends in North America and Europe. That process, lengthy and arduous, required separate trips to San Francisco, London, and Paris between 1890 and 1911. In Europe urban life created serious health problems for Carr; forced to retreat to the countryside, she applied her new skills to landscape painting. In her 40s when she decided to establish a permanent studio in Victoria, Carr intended to support herself with rents from an apartment house. Unfortunately, a weak economy thwarted her scheme and during a hiatus that lasted until her mid-50s, she made rugs and pottery to sell, raised dogs, and did very little for her art.

In 1927, when some of her paintings were included in a show of native and modern west coast art at the National Gallery in Ottawa, Carr travelled east and met the Group of Seven, kindred artists whose innovative paintings, like hers, focused on Canadian landscape. Their effect upon her work and her spirit was cataclysmic. One of the group, Lawren Harris, offered Carr much needed encouragement and introduced her to Theosophy. Carr's journal, published as *Hundreds and Thousands* two decades after her death, begins with this trip. In her entry on 17 November 1927 she described the terrain in the Group's landscapes in prose whose rhythms have become her hallmark:

> a world stripped of earthiness, shorn of fretting details, purged, purified, a naked soul, pure and unashamed; lovely spaces filled with wonderful serenity. What language do they speak, those silent, awe-filled spaces?

In this journal, over the next 14 years, she explored her spiritual life, her work, and the world around her in a fluid prose that epitomizes the *fresh seeing* she recommended.

For the rest of her life Carr would continue to paint and, as her declining health made sketching trips more and more difficult, do increasingly more writing. Unlike her painting, which can be periodized by her focus on aboriginal themes, the deep forest, and finally, light-filled landscapes, Carr's writing was done late in her life and is marked by differing autobiographical styles. Her carefully crafted stories, based on her own experience, reached a wide audience when they were first read on Canadian radio in 1940. *Klee Wyck,* her first published collection, was released the following year. Focusing on Carr's travels to native settlements, *Klee Wyck,* which means "Laughing One," won the Canadian Governor General's Award for non-fiction in 1941. Two other volumes would appear before Carr's death in 1945: reminiscences of her childhood in 1942's *The Book of Small* and the adventures and hardships of landladying in *The House of All Sorts,* published in 1944. A miscellaneous selection of stories entitled *Heart of a Peacock* and *Pause,* which drew on Carr's life in an English sanatorium, were published in the 1950s. Taken together, Carr's collections of short stories present a determined, observant, and humorous author whose sense of regional life added another layer of meaning to the indelible images in her paintings.

In her own time Carr had only a peripheral awareness of feminist concerns. That she has become an exemplary figure in the intervening years may be due to the choices she made and the examined sense of her own life that suffuses her writing. Her formal autobiography, *Growing Pains,* published shortly after her death, charts the course of her art education, especially her sojourns in San Francisco and England. The inadequacy of institutions of art to address her situation reveals Carr's powers of self-invention and the sustaining strength of ties to her friends and her sisters. The less formal account in *Hundreds and Thousands,* published in 1966—just as interest in women's lives was escalating—added a compelling spiritual level to the emerging sense of her creative genius. Exhibitions of Carr's paintings, and major studies of her life and art in the late 1970s by Edythe Hembroff-Schleicher, Maria Tippett, and Doris Shadbolt, yielded so captivating a portrait that they generated a range of creative interpretations by others. Carr's predicament has called forth cultural questions around her life as a female artist, her relations with aboriginal peoples, her vision of the natural world, and the dimensions of her religious life.

More recently Carr's autobiographical writing has been augmented by a major collection of her letters, *Dear Nan: Letters of Emily Carr, Nan Cheney, and Humphrey Toms,* published in 1990. This remarkably intimate record blends together the complexities of friendship, daily life, her work, and her health; it adds yet another version of Carr's voice to the existing record of her life. Notions of writing the female self, measured against this woman who continues to inspire and to resist simple classification, are grounded by a journal entry on 5 March 1940 in which she avowed, with characteristic directness, that "writing is a splendid sorter of your good and bad feelings, better even than paint. The whole thing of life is trying to crack the nut and get at the bitter-sweetness of the kernel." Emily Carr seldom veered from that task, whether at work with words or visual images.

—Stephanie Kirkwood Walker

CARSON, Rachel

Nationality: American. **Born:** Springdale, Pennsylvania, 27 May 1907. **Education:** Pennsylvania College for Women, A.B. in biology 1929; Johns Hopkins University, A.M. 1932; studied at Marine Biological Laboratory, Woods Hole, Massachusetts. **Career:** Member of zoology staff, University of Maryland, College Park, 1931-36; marine biologist, beginning 1936, editor-in-chief of publications, 1949-52, U.S. Bureau of Fisheries (now the Fish and Wildlife Service), Washington, DC; part-time instructor, Johns Hopkins University, 1930-36. **Awards:** Eugene Saxon Memorial fellowship, 1949; George Westinghouse Science Writing Award, 1950; National Book Award, 1951, for *The Sea around Us;* Guggenheim fellowship, 1951-52; John Burroughs Medal, 1952; Henry G. Bryant Gold Medal, 1952; Page-One Award, 1952; Frances K. Hutchinson Medal, 1952; Limited Editions Club Silver Jubilee Medal 1954; National Council of Women in the United States Book award, 1956; American Association of University Women achievement award, 1956; Animal Welfare Institute Schweitzer Medal, 1962; Women's National Book Association Constance Lindsay Skinner Award, 1963; New England Outdoor Writers Association Award, 1963; National Wildlife Federation Conservationist of the Year award, 1963; Einstein College of Medicine achievement award, 1963; New York Zoological Society Gold Medal; special citations: Garden Clubs of America, Pennsylvania Federation of Women's Clubs, Izaak Walton League of America, 1963; D.Sc.: Oberlin College, 1952; D.Litt.: Pennsylvania College for Women, 1952; Drexel Institute of Technology, 1952; Smith College, 1953. **Member:** American Ornithologists' Union, National Institute of Arts and Letters, Royal Society of Literature (fellow), Audubon Society (director), Society of Women Geographers. **Died:** Of cancer, in Silver Springs, Maryland, 14 April 1964.

Publications

Nonfiction

Under the Sea-Wind: A Naturalist's Picture of Ocean Life. New York, Simon & Schuster, 1941; revised, New York and Oxford, Oxford University Press, 1952.
Food from the Sea: Fish and Shellfish of New England. Washington, DC, U.S. Government Printing Office, 1943.
Food from Home Waters: Fishes of the Middle West. Washington, DC, U.S. Government Printing Office, 1943.
Fish and Shellfish of the South Atlantic and Gulf Coasts. Washington, DC, U.S. Government Printing Office, 1944.
Fish and Shellfish of the Middle Atlantic Coast. Washington, DC, U.S. Government Printing Office, 1943.
The Sea around Us. New York and Oxford, Oxford University Press, 1951; revised edition, New York, Watts, 1966.
The Edge of the Sea. Boston, Houghton Mifflin, 1955.
Silent Spring, illustrated by Lois and Louis Darling. Boston, Houghton, 1962.
The Sense of Wonder. New York, Harper, 1965; selections published as *Life under the Sea,* New York, Golden Press, 1968.
The Rocky Coast. New York, Macmillan, 1971.
Silent Spring Revisited. N.p., American Chemical Society, 1987.

Other

The House of Life: Rachel Carson at Work, edited by Paul Brooks. Boston, Houghton Mifflin, 1972.

*

Manuscript Collection: Yale University Library, New Haven, Connecticut.

Critical Studies: *Since Silent Spring* by Frank Graham Jr., Boston, Houghton, 1970; *Rachel Carson Who Loved the Sea* by Jean L. Latham, Easton, Maryland, Garrard, 1973; *Sea and Earth, The Life of Rachel Carson* by Philip Sterling, New York, Crowell, 1970; *The Recurring Silent Spring* by H. Patricia Hynes, n.p., 1989.

* * *

Perhaps more than any other women of this century, Rachel Carson has impacted our world. Upon its publication in 1962, *Silent Spring,* Carson's pioneering polemic on the harm caused by industrial technology, made Americans and the world gain a new awareness of their environment. Fostered by a concern over the diminishing numbers of New England songbirds, Carson's work on behalf of biological preservation served as the foundation for the environmental movement of the last half of the 20th century.

As early as age ten Carson was writing about the world of nature in essays she submitted to *St. Nicholas Magazine,* a love inspired by her mother, Maria McLean Carson. Born and raised on a farm near Springdale, Pennsylvania, Carson, who considered herself "a solitary child," learned to appreciate the forces of balance in the natural world; later, as a student of genetics at Johns Hopkins University she furthered that appreciation by obtaining her M.A. in biology in 1932. After the tragic death of her father and younger sister, Carson rejoined her mother; together the two women moved to Silver Spring, Maryland, in 1936 to raise her sister's orphaned daughters. While there, Carson combined her knowledge of biology with her skill as a writer and began working for the U.S. Bureau of Fisheries (now the Fish and Wildlife Service) as an aquatic biologist, compiling informational pamphlets on shellfish of the various Atlantic Ocean regions. By 1949 she had become editor-in-chief of their bureau of publication, a position she would hold until 1952.

Carson never lost her dream of becoming a writer and her increasing fascination with the ocean world provided her with an unending source of inspiration and material. In 1941 she published *Under the Sea-Wind: A Naturalist's Picture of Ocean Life,* followed, in 1951, by *The Sea around Us.* Both books captured the ebb and flow of ocean life in their discussion of the many unusual forms of undersea creatures—arthropods, echinoderms, coelenterates, and the like—and their importance to the planet's ecology. Carson's love of her subject was infectious; her second book quickly became a bestseller and received the 1951 National Book Award.

Carson was now nationally known as an expert on biology, prompting Olga Huckins, a journalist working for the *Boston Post,* to ask for her help. As Huckins explained to Carson, the bird population across the state of Massachusetts had dramatically declined in recent years; Huckins believed it was a direct result of the state's widespread use of aerial insecticides intended to control the mosquito population. By 1958 Carson was hard at work researching Huckins's theories, and the results of her work were released to the world three years later. *Silent Spring* hit the American conscience like a thunderbolt.

While vehemently denounced by the U.S. chemical industry, Carson's study of the effects of insecticides such as DDT (dichlorodiphenyltrichloroethane) was hailed by scientists and—translated into over thirty languages—devoured by readers world wide. Arguing that residue from such chemical compounds remains in the ecosystem long after its initial use, working its way down the food chain where it results in deformity and death to many vertebrates, *Silent Spring* ended on a note of hope: that through perseverance and understanding of the chain of life on earth such damage could yet be undone.

In the years after publication of *Silent Spring,* Carson retired from her job and devoted much of her time to her family. Her last book, *The Sense of Wonder,* was written to share her love of nature with her grand-nephew Roger; she died of cancer in 1964 before it could be completed. Tragically, Rachel Carson also died before she saw the true fruits of her labor: in November 1968, after years of bureaucratic wrangling, the federal government finally banned the use of DDT in the United States.

—Pamela Kester-Shelton

CARTER, Angela (Olive)

Nationality: British. **Born:** Eastbourne, Sussex, 7 May 1940. **Education:** University of Bristol, 1962-65, B.A. in English 1965. **Family:** Married Paul Carter in 1960 (divorced 1972). **Career:** Journalist, Croydon, Surrey, 1958-61. Arts Council fellow in creative writing, University of Sheffield, 1976-78; visiting professor of creative writing, Brown University, Providence, Rhode Island, 1980-81; writer-in-residence, University of Adelaide, 1984. **Awards:** John Llewellyn Rhys Memorial prize, 1968, for *The Magic Toyshop;* Somerset Maugham award, 1969, for *Several Perceptions;* Cheltenham Festival prize, 1979; Kurt Maschler award, for children's book, 1982; James Tait Black Memorial prize, 1985. **Died:** 1992.

Publications

Novels

Shadow Dance. London, Heinemann, 1966; as *Honeybuzzard,* New York, Simon & Schuster, 1967.

The Magic Toyshop. London, Heinemann, 1967; New York, Simon & Schuster, 1968.

Several Perceptions. London, Heinemann, 1968; New York, Simon & Schuster, 1969.

Heroes and Villains. London, Heinemann, 1969; New York, Simon & Schuster, 1970.

Love. London, Hart-Davis, 1971; revised edition, London, Chatto & Windus, 1987; New York, Penguin, 1988.

The Infernal Desire Machines of Dr. Hoffman, London, Hart-Davis, 1972; as *The War of Dreams,* New York, Harcourt Brace, 1974.

The Passion of New Eve. London, Gollancz, and New York, Harcourt Brace, 1977.

Nights at the Circus. London, Chatto & Windus, 1984; New York, Viking Press, 1985.

Wise Children. London, Chatto & Windus, 1991; New York, Farrar Strauss, 1992.

Short Stories

Fireworks: Nine Profane Pieces. London, Quartet, 1974; New York, Harper, 1981; revised edition, London, Virago, 1987.

The Bloody Chamber and Other Stories. London, Gollancz, 1979; New York, Harper, 1980.

Black Venus's Tale. London, Next-Faber, 1980.

Black Venus. London, Chatto & Windus, 1985; as *Saints and Strangers,* New York, Viking, 1986.

Artificial Fire (includes *Fireworks* and *Love*). Toronto, McClelland & Stewart, 1988.

Expletives Deleted: Selected Writings. London, Chatto & Windus, 1992.

American Ghosts and Old World Wonders. London, Chatto & Windus, 1993.

Burning Your Boat, introduction by Salman Rushdie. London, Chatto & Windus, 1995.

Plays

Vampirella (broadcast 1976; produced London, 1986). Included in *Come unto These Yellow Sands,* 1984.

Come unto These Yellow Sands (includes *The Company of Wolves, Vampirella, Puss in Boots).* Newcastle upon Tyne, Bloodaxe, 1984.
Curious Room: Collected Dramatic Works. London, Chatto & Windus, 1996.

Screenplays: *The Company of Wolves,* with Neil Jordan, 1984; *The Magic Toyshop,* 1987.

Radio Plays: *Vampirella,* 1976; *Come unto These Yellow Sands,* 1979; *The Company of Wolves* (from her own story), 1980; *Puss in Boots,* 1982; *A Self-Made Man* (on Ronald Firbank), 1984.

Poetry

Unicorn, Leeds, Location Press, 1966.

For Children

Miss Z, The Dark Young Lady. London, Heinemann, and New York, Simon & Schuster, 1970.
The Donkey Prince. New York, Simon & Schuster, 1970.
Moonshadow. London, Gollancz, 1982.
Sleeping Beauty and Other Favourite Fairy Tales. London, Gollancz, 1982; New York, Schocken, 1984.

Other

Comic and Curious Cats, illustrated by Martin Leman. London, Gollancz, and New York, Crown, 1979.
The Sadeian Woman: An Exercise in Cultural History. London, Virago, 1979; as *The Sadeian Woman and the Ideology of Pornography,* New York, Pantheon, 1979.
Nothing Sacred: Selected Writings. London, Virago, 1982.

Editor, *Wayward Girls and Wicked Women: An Anthology of Stories.* London, Virago Press, 1986; New York, Penguin, 1989.
Editor, *The Virago Book of Fairy Tales.* London, Virago Press, 1990; as *The Old Wives' Fairy Tale Book,* New York, Pantheon, 1990.
Editor, *The Second Virago Book of Fairy Tales.* London, Virago, 1992; as *Strange Things Sometimes Still Happen: Fairy Tales from around the World,* Boston, Faber, 1993.

Translator, *The Fairy Tales of Charles Perrault.* London, Gollancz, 1977; New York, Avon, 1978.

*

Critical Studies: "Through the Looking Glass: When Women Tell Fairy Tales" by Ellen Cronan Rose, in *The Voyage In: Fictions of Female Development,* edited by Elizabeth Able, Marianne Hirsch, and Elizabeth Langland, Hanover, New Hampshire, University Press of New England, 1983; "Re-Imagining the Fairy Tales: Angela Carter's Bloody Chambers" by Patricia Duncker, in *Literature and History,* 10(1), spring 1984; "Wayward Girls but Wicked Women?: Female Sexuality in Angela Carter's 'The Bloody Chamber'" by Avis Lewallen, in *Perspectives on Pornography: Sexuality in Film and Literature,* edited by Gary Day and Clive Bloom, New York, Macmillan, 1988; "Lolita Meets the Werewolf: 'The Company of Wolves'" by Maggie Anwell, in *The Female Gaze: Women as Viewers of Popular Culture,* edited by Lorraine Gamman and Margaret Marshment, Women's Press Limited, 1988; "Each Other: Images of Otherness in the Short Fiction of Doris Lessing, Jean Rhys, and Angela Carter" by Clare Hanson, in *Journal of the Short Story in English,* 10, spring 1988; "Reconstructing Oedipus through 'Beauty and the Beast'" by Sylvia Bryant, in *Criticism,* XXXI(4), fall 1989; "Blonde, Black, and Hottentot Venus: Context and Critique in Angela Carter's 'Black Venus'" by Jill Matus, in *Studies in Short Fiction,* 28(4), fall 1991.

* * *

Angela Carter was a prominent British fantasist who employed the traditional themes of fairy tales and Gothic literature to satirize patriarchy, explore sexual relations, and criticize the values and power structure of free-market capitalism. Often featuring characters and situations drawn from traditional literary sources or from Western history, Carter's fiction, although presenting a feminist perspective, is often concerned with the grotesque or erotic and is written in a vivid, richly layered prose. In addition to her fiction, Carter also wrote the study *The Sadeian Woman and the Ideology of Pornography* and edited two collections of fairy tales. Although sometimes criticized for putting her talent for fiction to mere ideological purpose, Carter is noted for her Baroque, luxurious prose style, and her ability to update familiar stereotypes in entertaining ways.

Carter's early novels set Gothic characters and situations against the counterculture England of the 1960s. Her first novel, *Shadow Dance,* published in the United States as *Honeybuzzard,* concerns a slum-dwelling scavenger who mutilates his girlfriend's face with a knife before his final descent into murder and madness. The primary character in *The Magic Toyshop* is a 15-year-old girl who, when she is orphaned, must live with her eccentric aunt and uncle who run a strange toyshop in London. The novel is essentially a coming-of-age tale set within a grotesque atmosphere of isolation, fear, and sexual danger. *The Infernal Desire Machines of Dr. Hoffman,* published in the United States as *The War of Dreams,* updates the stereotype of the mad scientist. In this story the crazed Dr. Hoffman has invented a machine that uses erotic energies to replace reality with images drawn from the subconscious mind. The hero Desiderio is called upon to save the normal world, choosing the stable and reasonable over the fantastic and anarchic. These early novels, drawing heavily on the themes of such Gothic writers as Edgar Allan Poe and the colorful prose of the surrealists, established Carter as a modern fantasist successfully updating the Gothic genre for a sophisticated, contemporary audience.

With the novels *The Passion of New Eve* and *Nights at the Circus,* Carter turned her Gothic fiction to feminist concerns. *The Passion of New Eve* is set in America's Southwest, where an Englishman who has heartlessly abandoned his pregnant girlfriend is set upon and captured by a band of Amazons. Because of his treatment of his girlfriend, the Amazons surgically transform him into a woman so he might experience the brutalization of rape for himself. In the 1984 novel *Nights at the Circus,* winner of the James Tait Black Memorial Prize, Carter tells the story of a turn-of-the-century traveling sideshow which stars the six-foot-tall winged woman, Fevvers. As the show travels around the world, it is followed by the journalist Walser who suspects that Fevvers is a fraud. Their relationship leads to love, however, as he comes to understand and accept the reality of her condition.

In her short fiction, especially those stories gathered in *Fireworks: Nine Profane Pieces* and *The Bloody Chamber and Other*

Stories, Carter took motifs from traditional fairy tales and rewrote them from a feminist viewpoint. The story "The Lady of the House of Love," for example, is Carter's revision of the Sleeping Beauty tale. It tells of the queen of the vampires who lives in an isolated castle, whiling away the cursed centuries until a young soldier arrives to kiss her and, by this action, release her to death. The rose she gives to him in return, however, leads to a generation's bloodshed on the battlefields of World War I. In the story "The Snow Child," Carter's version of Snow White, the evil mother hands over her maturing young daughter to the father's lust, which destroys the girl, rather than try to compete with her for his affection.

Carter's interest in the relationship between violence and sexuality led her to write the nonfiction study *The Sadeian Woman,* in which she examines the two feminine stereotypes of pornographic literature: the dangerous temptress and the innocent victim. In this work she argues that the writing of the Marquis de Sade, whose characters Justine and Juliette embodied these familiar stereotypes, can be read as feminist satire of the sexual roles men create for women. But ultimately Carter finds de Sade's quest for the limits of acceptable behavior a failure, believing that he ultimately succumbed to an acceptance of traditional sexual roles.

In the collections of fairy tales she edited—*The Old Wives' Fairy Tale Book* and *Strange Things Sometimes Still Happen*—Carter gathered together examples of traditional stories featuring the many stock female characters typical of the genre. These stock characters include witches, the resourceful and therefore "bad" girl, and the passive and therefore "good" girl. Her introduction to each story provided an overview of how these stereotypes had been used in fairy tales.

Explaining why she saw the Gothic genre as the best vehicle for her enduring concerns, Carter wrote in the 1974 afterword to her collection *Fireworks: Nine Profane Pieces:* "We live in Gothic times." Perhaps this statement best sums up her continuing appeal to a contemporary audience.

—Denise Wiloch

CASTELLANOS, Rosario

Nationality: Mexican. **Born:** Comitán, Chiapas, 25 May 1925. **Education:** Attended Universidad Nacional Autonoma (UNAM), Mexico City and received a fellowship to study in Madrid. **Family:** Divorced; one son. **Career:** Professor of literature, Universidad Nacional Autonoma Mexico, Mexico City; lecturer at universities throughout the United States and at Hebrew University, Jerusalem, 1971-74; served as ambassador to Israel, beginning 1971. **Awards:** Named Mexican Woman of the Year, 1967; Sourasky Prize for literature, 1971. **Died:** Tel Aviv, Israel, 7 August 1974.

PUBLICATIONS

Novels

Balún-Canán. Mexico City, Fondo de Cultura Económica, 1957; as *The Nine Guardians,* London, Faber & Faber, 1959; New York, Vanguard, 1960.

Oficio de tinieblas. Mexico City, Mortiz, 1962; as *Tenebrae Service,* 1961.

Album de familia. Mexico City, Joaquin Mortiz, 1971; 3rd edition, 1977.

Short Stories

Ciudad Real [Royal City]. Jalapa, Mexico, Universidad Veracruzana, 1960; 3rd edition, 1986.

Los convidados de agosto. Mexico City, Ediciones Era, 1964; 5th edition, 1979.

Essays

Sobre Cultura femenina [On Feminine Culture]. Mexico City, América, 1950.

Juicios sumarios [Summary Judgements]. Jalapa, Mexico, Universidad Veracruzana, 1966.

Mujer que sabe latín... [A Woman Who Knows Latin...]. Mexico City, SEP-Setentas/Educación Pública, 1973.

El mar y sus pescaditos [The Sea and Its Little Fishes]. Mexico City, SEP-Setentas/Educación Pública, 1975.

El eterno femenino. Mexico City, Fondo de Cultura Económica, 1975.

Meditación en el umbral. Mexico City, Fondo de Cultura Económica, 1985; as *Meditation on the Threshold,* Tempe, Arizona, Bilingual Press, 1988.

Poetry

Trayectoria del polvo. N.p., 1948.

Apuntes para una declaración de fe. Mexico City, América/Educación Pública, 1948.

Poemas : 1953-1955. Mexico City, Metáfora, 1957.

Poesía no eres tú; Obra poética: 1948-1971. Mexico City, Fondo de Cultura Económica, 1972; bilingual edition as *Selected Poems,* St. Paul, Minnesota, Graywolf, 1988.

Bella dama sin piedad y otros poemas. Mexico City, Fondo de Cultura Económica, 1984.

Plays

El eterno femenino: Farsa [The Eternal Feminine]. Mexico City, Fondo de Cultura Economica, 1957.

Other

De la vigilia estéril. Mexico City, América, 1950.

El rescate del mundo. N.p., 1952.

Tablero de damas: Pieza en un acto. Mexico City, América, 1952.

Al pie de la letra. Jalapa, Mexico, Universidad Veracruzana, 1959.

Salomé Y Judith. Mexico City, Jus, 1959.

Lívida luz. Mexico City, UNAM, 1960.

La constitución. Mexico City, Instituto Nacional Indigenista, 1960.

Les Etoiles d'herbe. Paris, Gallimard, 1962.

Teatro Petul. Mexico City, Instituto Nacional Indigenista, 1962.

La novela mexicana contemporánea y su valor testimonial. Mexico City, Juventud Mexicana, 1964.

Materia memorable. Mexico City, UNAM, 1969.

El uso de la palabra. Mexico City, Excélsior, 1974.

El verso, la palabra y el recuerdo. Mexico City, Instituto Cultural Mexicano-Israeli/Costa-Amic, 1984.

A Rosario Castellanos Reader, edited by Maureen Ahern. Austin, University of Texas Press, 1988.

Another Way to Be: Selected Works, translated and edited by Myralyn F. Allgood. Athens, University of Georgia Press, 1990.

*

Critical Studies: "Images of Women in Rosario Castellanos' Prose" by Phyllis Rodríguez-Peralta, *Latin American Literary Review,* 6, fall/winter 1977; "Female Characterization and Contexts in Rosario Castellanos' *Album de familia*" by Beth Miller, in *American Hispanist,* 32-33, January/February 1979; *Homenaje a Rosario Castellanos* edited by Maureen Ahern and Mary Seale Vásquez, Valencia, Albatros, 1980; "Rosario Castellanos and the Structures of Power" by Helene. M. Anderson, in *Contemporary Women Authors of Latin America,* edited by Doris Meyer and Margarite Fernandez Olmos, Brooklyn, Brooklyn College Press, 1983; "Women's Expression and Narrative Technique in Rosario Castellanos's *In Darkness*" by Naomi Lindstrom, in *Modern Language Studies,* 13, summer 1983; "Conformity and Resistance to Enclosure: Female Voices in Rosario Castellanos' *Oficio de tinieblas* (*The Dark Service*)" by Stacey Schlau, in *Latin American Literary Review,* 12, spring/summer 1984; Marriage in the Short Stories of Rosario Castellanos" by Hanna Geldrich-Leffman, in *Chasqui—Revista de literatura latinoamericana,* 21(1), May 1992.

* * *

Rosario Castellanos's haunting portrait of life in rural Chiapas, Mexico, during the 1930s, during the "ejido" land reform programs of Mexican president Lázaro Cardenas, features aspects of her philosophy of life and her objection to the oppression of women and Indians by the dominant Hispano-European Mexican society. *Balún Canán* (1957), translated as *The Nine Guardians,* is both a very personal recollection and an historical reconstruction of a period that would radically alter her own existence—as it ultimately did that of many other "Ladino" families—while also offering a glimmer of hope to the long-oppressed Indians of the region. In *Balún Canán* Castellanos recounts incidents from the perspective of a seven-year-old girl; by doing so, she allows very little clarification of complex issues of justice, fairness, ethnic fear, and misunderstanding.

Such issues would receive a less lyrical, more analytical treatment in Castellanos's numerous essays on social justice and feminine equality. Her belief that social enlightenment and the ability to become active in one's community would lead to self-respect and dignity underlay much of her writing, itself a reflection of the difficult and often very painful life that she led. She encouraged her countrywomen, in particular, to cease their complicity in their own oppression: intellectual and emotional enfranchisement must be embraced rather than the self-sacrificing image dictated by Mexican society. Castellanos's *Sobre Cultura femenina* [On Feminine Culture], published in 1950, and her collection of essays entitled *Mujer que sabe latin...* [A Woman Who Knows Latin...] are credited with being two of the cornerstones of Latin feminist literature.

Castellanos was born in 1925, in the mountainous state of Chiapas, remote from the capital city of Mexico, where her family owned large tracts of land farmed by Indian tenants in the production of sugar and coffee. She was older than her brother Benjamin; after his death at the age of six she remained as the only child in a family whose wealth and social position were slipping away due to land reform implemented by Mexico's post-revolutionary government. Benjamin had been the apple of his parents' eye; as a male he would have inherited their wealth and position. Castellanos, on the other hand, was overly protected and smothered by parents whose hope it was that she receive an education sufficient for her to become a pharmacist, that she marry and have children for them to fuss over. Feeling the stigma of belonging to the "less worthy sex," Castellanos strove to overcome her feelings of inadequacy and, at the same time, sought a more intellectual education than the one chosen for her.

When she was still a teenager, the Castellanos family left the provincial capital and took up residence in Mexico City, where Rosario finished her secondary education and began studying at the Universidad Nacional Autonoma Mexico (UNAM) while living at home, as is typical for Mexican students. In 1948 both parents died suddenly, within a month of one another. Castellanos finally achieved freedom, though it was spoiled by her overwhelming sense of loneliness and guilt as a survivor. She saw further involvement in University life as an available remedy for each, and studied towards a doctoral degree in humanities and sociology. Upon completion of her formal education, she returned to Chiapas, where she sought to relieve the social ills—unemployment, illiteracy, undermedication and poor general health, and superstition—that plagued the local Indian population. In addition to working towards social reform, her participation in the Instituto Indigenista San Cristobal de las Casas in 1956-57 would be Castellanos's first foray into socially instructive theater.

The plight of the Indians of Chiapas weaves its way intricately into much of the fiction of Castellanos. The novels and short stories that deal with the lives of the Indians in relation to the "ladino", the white men, is known as her "Chiapas Cycle." In novels such as *Oficio de tinieblas,* translated as *Tenebrae Service* (1961), she includes in this fabric of Mexican oppression of its people, the difficulty of women as well as Indians in a society that values masculinity and European Hispanicity. Castellanos's service among the Indians lasted only two years, and then she returned to Mexico City where she became an extraordinarily popular professor of literature at the UNAM.

She was married for a brief time to a professor of philosophy; after several miscarriages the couple bore a son, Gabriel, in 1961. Castellanos's marriage would dissolve during Gabriel's childhood, and this failure added to her already deep-seated feelings of loneliness, though it did not diminish her inordinate productivity as a poet and commentator on Mexican life, or as a novelist.

When *Balún Canán* was published in 1957 it was the recipient of critical acclaim, as was her poetry and subsequent short fiction. The most unique aspect of Castellanos's portrayal of Indian life was her refusal to create an idealized portrait of the noble savage. Instead, her treatment of all literary characters as complete people and round characters lent fullness to their stories. Even with their flaws exposed, the Indians could be seen as having been treated unjustly.

Castellanos's incorporation of the lyrical and mythical language of the Tzeltzal-Tzotzil peoples creates texts that are haunting and mysterious, as though she were at times transcribing the experience of the Indians from their own tongue. Myralyn Allgood describes her writing as a counterpoint of abstract/concrete, lyric/narrative, image/idea, and this structure pervades much of the Chiapanecan, as well as other periods of her literary production. In several of her commentaries on the condition of women in

Mexico, the tone is markedly different, however, with an ironic playfulness that derides the machista tendency toward domination. Specifically, her farsical play *El eterno femenino* (1957) deals with the role assigned young women in Mexican society. It includes numerous historical figures, such as Sor Juana Ines de la Cruz and La Malinche, who decry the notion that women lose their attractiveness and their value as people just as soon as they are married. Castellanos's depiction of a young woman at the beauty parlor on the eve of her wedding day is peppered with clever insights about the historical, social, and economic issues that trouble women of Mexico and prevent them from achieving an equal footing with men in their society.

Despite the self-deprecating tone often seen in her essays and her poetry—"I'm rather ugly. It all depends on/the hand that applies the make-up" she writes in "Self-portrait" in *Poesía no eres tu* (1972)—Castellanos was one of Mexico's most highly acclaimed writers, and certainly the first woman since Sor Juana Ines de la Cruz in the 1600s to achieve such a wide readership. In 1967 she was named "Woman of the Year" in Mexico, and in 1971, she won the prestigious Sourasky Prize for literature, the same year she was appointed as Mexican ambassador to Israel. In addition to her diplomatic duties, Castellanos lectured on Latin American literature in Israel.

Tragically, Castellanos' life was cut short in August of 1974, when she was accidentally electrocuted in her apartment in Tel Aviv. Had she lived longer, Rosario Castellanos would surely have continued to occupy her prestigious place in Mexican letters, and she would have continued to advocate women's and Indian's rights in Mexico.

—Helena Antolin Cochrane

CASTILLO, Ana

Nationality: American **Born:** Chicago, Illinois, 15 June 1953. **Education:** Northern Illinois University, B.A. 1975; University of Chicago, M.A. in Latin-American and Caribbean studies, 1979; University of Bremen, Ph.D. in American studies, 1991. **Family:** One son. **Career:** Has taught and lectured at numerous colleges and universities, including Northwestern Illinois University, San Francisco State University, Sonoma State University, Mill College, and Mount Holyoke College; dissertation fellow, University of California, Santa Barbara, 1989-90. German Association of Americanist reading tour of Europe, 1987; writer-in-residence, Illinois Arts Council. Contributor to periodicals, including *Essence, Frontiers, Heresies, Letras Femininas, Los Angeles Times, Nation, Prairie Schooner, Revista Chicano-Riqueña, San Francisco Chronicle, Spoon River Quarterly,* and *Washington Post.* **Awards:** Before Columbus Foundation American Book Award, 1987, for *The Mixquiahuala Letters;* Women's Foundation of San Francisco award, 1988; California Arts fellowship for fiction, 1989; National Endowment for the Arts fellowship, 1990, 1995; New Mexico Arts Commission grant, 1991; Carl Sandburg Literary Award, 1993, for *So Far from God;* Gustaves Myers Award, 1995, for *Massacre of the Dreamers.* **Agent:** Susan Bergholz, 17 West 10th St., #5, New York, New York 10011, U.S.A. **Address:** 701 Southwest 62nd Blvd., # J-67, Gainesville, Florida 32607-6012, U.S.A.

Publications

Novels

The Mixquiahuala Letters. Tempe, Arizona, Bilingual Press, 1986.
Sapogonia (An Anti-Romance in 3/4 Meter). Tempe, Arizona, Bilingual Press, 1990.
So Far from God. New York, Norton, 1993.

Short Stories

Loverboys. New York, Norton, 1996.

Poetry

Otro Canto. Chicago, Alternative Publication, 1977.
The Invitation. Chicago, 1979; revised, San Francisco, La Raza, 1986.
Pajaros enganosos. Cross Cultural Communications, 1983.
Women Are Not Roses. Houston, Arte Público, 1984.
My Father Was a Toltec. New York, West End, 1988; enlarged as *My Father Was a Toltec and Selected Poems,* New York, Norton, 1995.

Essays

"La macha: Toward a Beautiful Whole Self" and "What Only Lovers," in *Chicana Lesbians: The Girls Our Mothers Warned Us About,* edited by Marta A. Navaro. Berkeley, California, Third Woman Press, 1991.
Massacre of the Dreamers: Essays on Xicanisma. Albuquerque, University of New Mexico Press, 1994.

Play

Clark Street Counts (produced 1983).

Other

Editor and translator, with others, *Esta Puente, Mi Espalda.* San Francisco, ISM Press, 1988.
Editor, with Heiner Bus, *Chicago Poetry.* University of Bamberg, 1994.
Editor, *Goddess of the Americas.* New York, Putnam, 1996.

Translator, with Daniel Fogel and Cathy Mahoney, *On the Edge of a Countryless Weariness/Al filo de un cansancio apatricia,* by Victoria Miranda and Camilo Feñini. San Francisco, ISM Press, 1986.

*

Media Adaptations: *The Invitation* (musical score), 1982.

Manuscript Collection: University of California, Santa Barbara.

Critical Studies: Interview in *Contemporary Chicano Poetry II/ Partial Autobiographies,* edited by Wolfganger Binder, West Germany, Palm & Enke Erlander, 1985; "The Sardonic Powers of the Erotic in the Work of Ana Castillo" by Norma Alarcón, in *Break-*

ing Boundaries: Latina Writings and Critical Readings, edited by Asuncion Horno-Delgado, Eliana Ortega, Nini M. Scott, and Nancy Saporta-Sternbach, Amherst, University of Massachusetts Press, 1989; "Entrevista a Ana Castillo" (interview) by Jacqueline Mitchell, Silvia Pellarolo, Javier Rangel, Xochitl Shuru, and Leticia Torres, in *Mester,* 20(2), fall 1991; "The Multiple Subject in the Writing of Ana Castillo" by Yvonne Yarbro-Bejarano, in *The Americas Review,* 20(1), 1992; "Debunking Myths: The Hero's Role in Ana Castillo's *Sapogonia*" by Ibis Gómez-Vega, in *The Americas Review,* spring/summer 1994; "Claiming the Present: Ana Castillo" by Rafael Pérez-Torres in *Movements in Chicano Poetry,* Cambridge and New York, Cambridge University Press, 1995.

* * *

Poet, novelist, essay writer, Ana Castillo is one of the most original voices in Chicana and contemporary American feminist literatures. In her work, she has created a complex and multifaceted world in which she explores issues relating to multiculturalism and feminism from the position of a Chicana feminist and, even more specifically, as she points out in an interview published in *Mester,* a Chicana from Chicago, with a history quite different from that of Chicanas in Texas and California. For Castillo, it is essential to bring to the forefront of literary debates questions relating to the condition of women of color in the United States; to examine the relationship between Latin American and Chicana women; and to call attention to the fact that Chicana women face a form of racism comparable to, if historically different from, that suffered by African American women. Castillo always includes in her work, fictional and theoretical, a consideration of how gender and sexuality intersect with racism and cultural marginalization, generating "multiple oppression," as Castillo argues in *Mester.* This author's work, however, cannot be described solely in terms of her political commitment. Castillo's political ideals inform and are informed by the exquisite craftsmanship that characterizes her opus.

In response to a culture that is largely unwilling to legitimize difference, Castillo forges a language that enacts her cultural specificity. In her book of poems, *My Father Was a Toltec* (enlarged and reprinted as *My Father Was a Toltec and Selected Poems*), biculturalism is articulated through a different kind of bilingualism, juxtaposing poems in English and Spanish without translation. The four sections into which the book is divided touch upon issues of female and lesbian identity and outline the journey towards self-creation that women must undertake in order to understand their place in culture and re-invent a world free of prejudice and racism. Castillo's early poetry, published in chapbooks (*Otro Canto* and *The Invitation*), exhibits a greater concern with rooting her identity in Mexican traditions and mythologies than her later poetry, in which she broadens and complicates her political vision. In "The Toltec," the opening poem of *My Father Was a Toltec,* the word "Toltec" serves, as Rafael Pérez-Torres explains, as "an ultimately diminished evocation of the lost world of Meso-American indigenous populations." In "In My Country," the last poem in *Toltec,* Castillo claims the need not only for social changes but aesthetic changes as well: "so these are not poems/i readily admit,/as i grapple with non-existence,/making scratches with stolen pen .../Rape is not a poem./Incest does not rhyme." Castillo wants to extricate her art from the trappings of a Western tradition that has historically ignored or misrepresented people of color, especially women.

Castillo's first novel, *The Mixquiahuala Letters,* relies on an epistolary narrative to present the history of the friendship between two women, Teresa and Alicia. The epistolary narrative, which includes only Teresa's letters, authorizes female artistry by simultaneously asserting and breaching the privacy of the domestic space. Castillo combines the choice of a genre that is both literary and rooted in the quotidian with experimental narrative strategies. This postmodern novel challenges traditional notions of reading from the very beginning, proposing three different orders for reading the letters: for the conformist, the cynic, and the quixotic, none of which includes the totality of the letters. The author does not fail to pay tribute to the Argentinean writer Julio Cortázar who, in *Hopscotch* (1963), had similarly demanded that the reader take an active part in the reading process by choosing between one of two possible readings. *The Mixquiahuala Letters,* like Castillo's poetry, retains a fascination with the visual that Castillo traces back to her beginnings as a painter.

Sapogonia (An Anti-Romance in 3/4 Meter), published in 1990, though completed five years earlier, has been described by Yvonne Yarbro-Bejarano as a "project of negotiation with and translation of male narrative form and male point of view." Ibis Gómez-Vega rejects Yarbro-Bejarano's reading, claiming that in order "to make a political statement," the critic misreads the novel. To be sure, *Sapogonia* does not lend itself to unidirectional readings and, like Castillo's other novels, raises questions more than it provides answers. Castillo's third novel, *So Far From God,* published in 1994 and described by Sandra Cisneros as a "Spanish *telenovela,*" is a parodic text in the post-modern tradition, permeated by a distinctly Chicana flavor. Through the preposterous stories of Sofi and her four daughters, Castillo transports the reader into a surreal and poetical world reminiscent of Gabriel García Márquez's *One Hundred Years of Solitude,* but with a clearly Chicana feminist slant.

While Castillo believes that a certain kind of nationalism was necessary in the beginnings of the Chicano movement in the 1970s and still argues for the recognition of one's own ethnic/racial roots, she dismisses facile nostalgia for traditions and customs that oppress women as well as exclusionary forms of nationalism. Thus in her 1991 interview in *Mester* she claimed: "I'm looking for a broader vision for us as a humanity and part of that means breaking down nationalism and understanding what nationalism means.... I don't go for nationalism.... I'm a poet and a visionary, so I'm not always very practical. And in my dream of what I would like to see would be that we could move on as a humanity. And it's not about assimilation, it's really about looking for ways for us to survive as people." In the ten essays of her latest book, *Massacre of the Dreamers: Essays on Xicanisma,* Castillo provocatively outlines the situation of women of color in the United States and claims that as a Chicana she has "much more in common with an Algerian woman" than with a Mexican man. Coining the term "Xicanisma" (which replaces Chicana feminism), Castillo argues for the need for political "*conscientización*" as well for a poetics of "*conscientización*" for the self-empowerment of Mexic Amerindian women. Dreamers, like the dreamers massacred by Moteuczoma, are at risk in a society that fears their visionary powers. In the concluding essay, "The Resurrection of the Dreamers," Castillo prophetically announces the awakening of the dreamers and encourages the awakening of all Xicanas: "Let us be alchemists for our culture and our lives and use this conditioning as our raw material to convert it into a driving force pure as gold." *Massacre of the Dreamers* is a text to be added to the list of key-texts of Chicana theoretical and political feminist thought, which includes Gloria Anzaldúa's *Borderlands/La Frontera: The New Mestiza,* Cherríe Moraga's *Loving in the War Years: Lo que nunca pasó por sus labios,* and *This Bridge Called My Back: Writings by Radical Women of Color,* edited by Moraga and Anzaldúa and translated into Spanish by Castillo and Norma Alarcón.

—Edvige Giunta

CATT, Carrie (Clinton) Chapman

Nationality: American. **Born:** Carrie Lane in Ripon, Wisconsin, 9 January 1859. **Education:** Iowa State College, B.S. 1880. **Family:** Married Leo Chapman in 1885 (died 1886); married George W. Catt in 1890 (died 1905). **Career:** Principal, Mason City High School, Mason City, Iowa, 1881-83; superintendent of schools, Mason City, 1883-85; coeditor, *Republican*, Mason City, 1885-86; moved to San Francisco, California, and worked as a reporter, 1886-87; returned to Iowa as a public lecturer; organizer and lecturer, Iowa Woman's Suffrage Association, 1887-90; organizer and lecturer, then president, 1900-1904, 1915-47, National American Woman Suffrage Association; president, International Woman Suffrage Alliance, 1904-23; travelled to Europe and made world tour, 1911-12; chairwoman, Empire State Campaign Committee, 1915; cofounder, with Jane Addams and others, Women's Peace Party, 1915; received inheritance of $1 million from Miriam Leslie, wife of publisher of *Leslie's Illustrated Newspaper,* 1917; cofounder, National League of Women Voters, 1919; honored by parade in New York City after ratification of 19th Amendment, 1920; attended Pan American Women's Conference, Baltimore, Maryland, 1922; founder, Protest Committee of Non-Jewish Women against the Persecution of Jews in Germany, 1933; publisher, *Women Citizen;* founder, Committee on the Causes and Cures of War, 1925-32. **Awards:** Pictoral Review Prize, 1930, for services to women's suffrage, human rights, and peace; American Hebrew Medal, 1933; Turkish government postage stamp, 1935; citation of honor from President Franklin D. Roosevelt, 1936; Order of White Rose (Finland), 1942. **Died:** New Rochelle, New York, 9 March 1947.

Publications

Political/Social Theory

Woman Suffrage and Politics, with Nettie Rogers Shuler. N.p., 1893; expanded as *Woman Suffrage and Politics: The Inner Story of the Suffrage Movement,* New York, Scribners's Sons, 1923.

Other

Compiler, *The Ballot and the Bullet.* Philadelphia, A. J. Ferris for the National-American Woman Suffrage Association, 1897.

*

Critical Sources: *Carrie Chapman Catt* by Mary Gray Peck, New York, H.W. Wilson, 1944; *Carrie Catt: Feminist Politician* by Robert Booth Fowler, Boston, Northeastern University Press, 1986; *Carrie Chapman Catt: A Public Life* by Jacqueline Van Voris, New York, Feminist Press, 1987.

* * *

Carrie Chapman Catt, president of the National American Woman Suffrage Association (NAWSA) from 1900 to 1904 and again from 1915 to 1920, led supporters of woman suffrage to victory by transforming them into an "army" that lobbied Congress and the states for the passage of a federal amendment granting women the right to vote. Catt recognized that winning the vote depended on organization and under her leadership the NAWSA developed the strategy and mechanisms necessary for success.

Born in Wisconsin in 1859 to Lucius and Maria Lane, Carrie Catt displayed resourcefulness in overcoming gender discrimination even as a young woman. When her father refused to allow her to attend college, she worked as a teacher for a year to earn the money to go to Iowa State University, where she entered as a sophomore in 1877. Although she originally planned to go to law school and worked in a law office after graduating from Iowa State in 1880, Catt soon began a career in education. In 1881 she worked as the principal of the high school in Mason City, Iowa, where, two years later, she was named superintendent of schools. Catt would leave her position as superintendent when she married Leo Chapman in 1885, becoming an assistant editor of the Mason City Republican, the paper her husband edited. After her husband's death in 1886, Catt spent a year working on a newspaper in San Francisco.

Catt's return to Iowa in 1887 marked the beginning of her involvement in the woman suffrage movement. She joined the Iowa Woman Suffrage Association while embarking on a new career as a lecturer. Her marriage to George Catt in 1890 posed no threat to her growing interest in agitating for votes for women. Supported in her reform activities by her husband, she remained active in the suffrage movement, serving as a member of the Iowa delegation to the NAWSA's annual convention the year they were married. Catt's introduction to the NAWSA occurred at a critical juncture in the history of the fight for woman suffrage. Shortly after the Civil War, supporters of woman suffrage had split into two wings, divided in their response to the 15th Amendment which, while it allowed black men the right to vote, continued the exclusion of all women, white and black. The convention that Catt attended in 1890 reunited the two factions into one organization, the NAWSA.

Catt rose rapidly through the leadership ranks of the NASWA, winning the recognition and respect of the organization's national leaders in 1893 when she successfully headed the fight for woman suffrage in Colorado. Her previous job experience awakened her to the lack of coordination that plagued the NAWSA's efforts and in 1895 she proposed the formation of a National Organization Committee. As chair of this committee, Catt oversaw campaigns for suffrage on the state level. Her effectiveness in this position led Susan B. Anthony to support Catt as her successor when she stepped down from the presidency of the NAWSA in 1900.

The NAWSA grew during Catt's first presidency, although progress on expanding suffrage remained stalled. Membership increased between 1900 and 1904 and Catt proved an able fundraiser, securing a stable financial foundation for the organization. But campaigns for suffrage on the state and federal levels met with no further success. In 1904, citing her husband's health problems, Catt stepped down from her position as president. A year later, George Catt's death spurred his wife to once again take up agitation for the vote: she headed the effort in New York state and devoted herself to the newly formed International Woman Suffrage Alliance (IWSA).

Divided by the defection of Alice Paul and her followers—who advocated more radical protest tactics—and lacking any overall strategy for winning the vote, the NAWSA again turned to Catt for leadership in 1915. Although she initially resisted resuming the presidency, pressure from her peers combined with Mrs. Frank Leslie's bequest of almost one million dollars to Catt to use for the fight for suffrage convinced her to take the post. The crisis in the NAWSA provided Catt with an opportunity to re-direct the organization. At an emergency meeting in 1916, she presented what became known as the "Winning Plan." To win the vote, Catt argued, the NAWSA must become a single-issue group, pursuing suffrage to the exclusion of all other reforms. Its former piecemeal, state-by-state approach must be abandoned and all efforts must be focussed on winning the passage of a federal suffrage amendment. While state-level agitation was still crucial—the approval of three fourths of the states was needed for passage of an amendment—Catt's "Winning Plan" emphasizing the passage of a federal amendment provided the NAWSA with its first coherent strategy for securing the vote.

Although the NAWSA endorsed Catt's plan, critics arose from several quarters. Those associated with the early woman's rights movement, for example, disagreed with the single-issue focus and argued that the NAWSA should fight for women's rights on a variety of fronts. U.S. entry into World War I further complicated the "Winning Plan." Catt refused to suspend the fight for suffrage during the war, even though her stand subjected her to charges of harboring pro-German sentiments. In fact, Catt used the war to buttress the suffrage movement by arguing that women's patriotism and sacrifice should be rewarded with the vote. Catt's willingness to support the war effort, serving on the Women's Committee of the Council of National Defense, offers a measure of her commitment to the suffrage movement. Although she personally detested war and devoted herself to eradicating war after 1920, she sacrificed such personal views to advance the cause of woman suffrage.

In the space of four years Catt's "Winning Plan" succeeded. By June 1919 Congress had passed the Anthony amendment; 14 months later, with Tennessee's acceptance of the amendment, women gained the right to vote. Her goal of 30 years accomplished, Catt resigned from the NAWSA presidency in 1920. However, the completion of the suffrage campaign did not signal the end of Catt's activism. She continued her work on an international level with the IWSA, serving as president until 1923. She devoted most of her energy, however, to calling for an end to war. Under her direction, the Committee on the Causes and Cures of War met annually from 1925 to 1939 to discuss ways of eliminating armed conflict.

Although she took no active role in the League of Women Voters, the successor organization to the NAWSA, Carrie Chapman Catt continued to participate in national debates about women's status. Most significantly, in the 1920s she became a vocal critic of the Equal Rights Amendment (ERA) supported by Alice Paul and her radical National Woman's Party. Catt clearly believed in women's equality, but she opposed the ERA because she feared it would harm working women, whose numbers were steadily increasing in the post-war years. Passage of the ERA would render any legislation regulating the hours and conditions of women's work unconstitutional; the actual complex circumstances of women's lives, Catt maintained, should be more highly prized than adherence to abstract principles of equality.

—Anne Lewis Osler

CAYER, D. M. *See* **DUFFY, Maureen (Patricia).**

CHAPMAN, Lee. *See* **BRADLEY, Marion Zimmer.**

CHÁVEZ, Denise (Elia)

Nationality: American. **Born:** Las Cruces, New Mexico, 15 August 1948. **Education:** New Mexico State University, B.A. in drama 1971; Trinity University, San Antonio, Texas, M.A. 1974; University of New Mexico, M.A. in creative writing 1984. **Family:** Married the photographer Daniel C. Zolinsky in 1984. **Career:** Artist in the schools, New Mexico Arts Division, 1977-83; instructor in play writing, College of Santa Fe, Santa Fe, New Mexico; instructor in drama, English literature, and composition, Northern New Mexico Community College, Espanola, 1975-77; visiting professor, then assistant professor of drama, University of Houston, 1988-91; visiting professor of creative writing, New Mexico State University, beginning 1993. Worked in the Dallas Theatre Center, c. 1973; playwright for La Compania de Teatro de Albuquerque and Theatre-in-the-Red, Santa Fe. Organizes workshops for elementary and secondary schools; former director, Senior Citizens' Arts Project, Las Cruces, New Mexico. **Awards:** New Mexico State University Best Play award, 1970; New Mexico State University Steele Jones Fiction Award, 1986; University of Houston visiting scholar grant, 1987; City of Houston Creative Artist Award, 1990; Premio Aztlán award, American Book award, and Mesilla Valley Author of the Year award, all 1995, all for *Face of an Angel;* New Mexico Governor's Award in literature, and *El Paso Herald Post* Writers of the Pass distinction, both 1995. **Member:** Author's Guild, New Mexico Street Theatre. **Address:** 480 La Colonia, Las Cruces, New Mexico 88005, U.S.A.

PUBLICATIONS

Novel

Face of an Angel. New York, Farrar Straus, 1994.

Short Stories

The Last of the Menu Girls. Houston, Arte Público, 1986.

Plays

Novitiates (produced Dallas, 1973).
The Mask of November (produced Espanola, New Mexico, 1975).
The Flying Tortilla Man (produced Espanola, New Mexico, 1975).
Elevators (produced Santa Fe, New Mexico, 1977).
The Adobe Rabbit (produced Taos, New Mexico, 1980).
Nacimiento (produced Albuquerque, New Mexico, 1980).
Santa Fe Charm (produced Santa Fe, New Mexico, 1980).
An Evening of Theatre (produced Santa Fe, New Mexico, 1981).
How Junior Got Throwed in the Joint (produced Santa Fe, State Penitentiary of New Mexico, 1981).
Sí, Hay Posada (produced Albuquerque, New Mexico, 1981).
El Santero de Cordova (produced Albuquerque, New Mexico, 1981).
The Green Madonna (produced Santa Fe, New Mexico, 1982).
Hecho en México, with Nita Luna (produced Albuquerque, New Mexico, 1983).
La Morenita (produced Las Cruces, New Mexico, 1983).
Francis! (produced Las Cruces, New Mexico, 1983).
Plaza (produced Albuquerque, New Mexico, New York, then Edinburgh, Scotland, 1984).
Plague-Time (produced Albuquerque, New Mexico, 1985).
Novena Narrativas (toured New Mexico, 1987).
The Step (produced Houston, 1987).
Language of Vision (produced Albuquerque, New Mexico, 1988).
Women in the State of Grace (produced Grinnell, Iowa, 1989).

For Children

The Woman Who Knew the Language of Animals/La Mujer que sabía el idioma de los animales. Boston, Houghton, 1992.

Other

"Heat and Rain (Testimonio)," in *Breaking Boundaries: Latina Writing and Critical Readings,* edited by Asunción Horno-Delgado, Eliana Ortega, Nina M. Scott, and Nancy Saporta Sternbach. Amherst, University of Massachusetts Press, 1989.

*

Theatrical Activities: Solo performer in her *Women in the State of Grace* throughout the United States.

Critical Studies: "Playwright Sees through Eyes of Mexican Workers" by Beita Budd, in *Performance,* 6, 1983; "The Theatre of Denise Chávez: Interior Landscapes with *Sabor Nuevomexicano"* by Martha E. Heard, in *Americas Review* (Houston, Texas), 16(2), 1988; interview by Annie O. Eysturoy in *This Is about Vision: Interviews with Southwestern Writers,* Albuquerque, University of New Mexico Press, 1989; *Criticism in the Borderlands: Studies in Chicano Literature, Culture, and Ideology,* edited by Hector Calderón and José David Saldivar, Durham, Duke University Press, 1991.

Denise Chávez comments:

I grew up with mostly women. My parents were divorced when I was very young, and although I often missed my father and his influence, I was happy to live with women. I recall giving my mother gifts for "Fathers Day." It was she, a single woman, a teacher for 42 years, a women with bad varicose legs, she who stood all her life, who taught me the meaning of work. She was ahead of her time, and somehow made me realize that I could do whatever I set my mind to. I didn't have the sense to realize in high school that I couldn't write a full-length play, it just never occurred to me that I needed to study. Why not just try my hand at it? This was my philosophy, and it has helped me throughout my life. I have been brave enough or foolish enough to try so many things. I have written plays, poetry, short stories and the novel form. I am an actress, director, playwright, and teacher. No one thing holds me; I am a writer who performs/a performance writer and a community activist. Early on, I knew that I was the person who would detail women's lives. It is very natural to me, and I hold it as a responsibility, and as my salvation. As a Chicana writer, I am deeply committed to bringing to American and world literature voices unheard and stories dismissed. I write to heal, empower, enlighten, and with all my work I would hope that the fragile beauty of life would hold mercy for all.

* * *

"Perhaps I am just a transmitter," Chicana playwright and actress Denise Chávez tells interviewer Annie Eysturoy. "I see myself as somebody who has been given a gift, something I never asked for. I am here to have this stuff move through me, and it is a responsibility and a commitment." In an interview with Eysturoy published in *This Is about Vision: Interviews with Southwestern Writers,* Chávez speaks of her dedication to the people around her and to their lives. Understanding that her own voice has been created by those surrounding her, she hopes to present their struggles, joys, and realities with admiration and respect. Indeed, Chávez's very motivation stems from the lives of the women, relatives, Latinos, neighbors, indeed all the human beings encountered throughout her life; with that, her writing, in whatever form, contends with the truthful representation of soul and grace.

Born in Las Cruces, New Mexico in 1948, Chávez came into the world with a characteristic dramatic flair. She was born at home, in the room that was later to become her own bedroom, to a Tex-Mex family. Her mother moved to New Mexico from West Texas, met a young man whose family had emigrated from Socorro, Mexico, and married him; the couple would ultimately divorce after their third child was born. Chávez's mother, a teacher, greatly influenced her daughter's life and career. "She was such a strong woman...," Chávez remarks, "There was always a yearning for education and improvement in the family, so my mother instilled this into us." In considering the roots of her writing today, Chávez credits growing up in a household of women with the inspiration for much of her work. Moreover, her grandparents and many other relatives played active roles in the young girl's life. Chávez recalls not only their care, but their storytelling as seeds for her literary calling.

The origins of Chávez's writing began with a diary. Always willing to share her work, she provides us with some entries in "Heat and Rain," a personal testimonial included in *Breaking Boundaries: Latina Writing and Critical Readings.* In a short letter written 1 January 1958, a ten-year-old Chávez exclaims "Today is New Year and the old year is gone and the new one here. Today schools starts. I can't wait to go." From these humble beginnings, Chávez continued her commitment to creative pursuits, majoring in drama in high school. Winning a theater scholarship secured her entrance into college, where, as a senior, she took a playwrighting class, won a prize in a New Mexico State literary contest with her first play, and was on her way.

Chávez credits much of her work to the role models present in her early life. In "Heat and Rain" she explains again that growing up in a house of women fostered "writ(ing) about women, women who are without men." Enlivened by the experiences of her mother, the nuns in the Catholic schools she attended, compadres in the neighborhood, and housekeepers from Mexico, Chávez writes about common people and their universal experiences. Understanding her task as a responsibility, she feels "that if you have something you should give it to people." Most often, this commitment gives a voices to the lives of those historically silenced. "Our grandmothers did not have voices. My mother's voice was a cry, perhaps, a moan; it was a sad voice." Chávez respects this call for help and acts as a cultural liberator for many women.

Indeed, the essence of Chávez's theatrical characters embodies these hopes. In an article about her work for the theatre, Martha Heard notes that "the dramatic action in many of Chávez's plays centers around the unmasking of the character." Illuminating space and legitimacy for historical understanding, Chávez demonstrates the social boundaries limiting life's possibilities, the path to personal acceptance, and the triumphs realized. From 1973 to 1984, she wrote over 21 theatrical pieces. Included in these works are children's plays, modern tragedy, a plethora of characters, various themes, and a wide range of production successes.

The year 1986 marked the unveiling of her first published book of short stories, *The Last of the Menu Girls.* In its introduction, Chicano literary master Rudolfo Anaya offers his opinion of the text and of its importance in the Chicano literary tradition: Readers "will savor the poignant experiences and dreams of Rocío," he writes of the book's young protagonist, whose growth into womanhood provides a framework for Chávez's stories. "Rocío cries out against the traditional serving roles which society has prescribed for women and she opts for the life of the artist. By the novels end she has found her calling, and that is to give meaning to the emotionally turbulent lives of the people she has known."

Chávez's aspirations for transformation and inner peace seem to have been construed effectively. In locating strength from various women's pasts, the protagonist Rocío is able to self-identify more fully and fairly. Like Chávez herself, Rocío engages in the "healing process" of writing. Both the character and the author thereby offer an escape from the "psychological girdle" harnessing women.

In addition to her career as a writer, Chávez teaches and lectures throughout the country. Currently a visiting professor at New Mexico State University, she inspires her students to confront their own histories. In addition, Chávez published her first novel, *Face of an Angel,* in 1995. Other ongoing activities for the talented writer include books tours, classroom presentations, organizing book festivals, and performing her touring one-woman show, *Women in the State of Grace.* Chávez's hard work has paid off not only spiritually but with some prestigious awards. *Face of an Angel* received the American Book Award, the Premio Aztlán award for a Chicana/Chicano book, the New Mexico Governor's Award in Literature, and numerous local awards. Despite her national presence and demanding lifestyle, Chávez remains committed to honoring the lives of women; crediting her personal success to the struggles of those who came before her, she comments that, as a result, "our voices are hopefully stronger, and we can sing our stories and other women's stories as well." Inspiring others through her role as a transmitter, Denise Chávez builds bridges that continue to transcend and reinvent the place of women.

—Naomi Barry

CHESLER, Phyllis

Nationality: American. **Born:** Brooklyn, New York, 1 October 1940. **Education:** Bard College, B.A. 1962; New School for Social Research, M.A. 1967, Ph.D. 1969; New York Medical College, 1968-69. **Family:** Married 2) Nachmy Bronstein in 1973; one daughter. **Career:** Clinical research associate, Metropolitan Hospital, New York, 1968-69; assistant professor of psychology, beginning 1969, College of Staten Island of the City University of New York. Lecturer at institutions, including Institute for Developmental Studies and New School for Social Research, City University of New York; psychotherapist in private practice. Founder, Association for Women in Psychology, 1970; founder, National Women's Health Network, 1976. Member of board of directors, Women's Action Alliance and Adele Cohen Foundation, beginning 1972; member, New York State Council of the Arts, and Women's History Research Center. Contributor to periodicals, including *Aphra, Journal of Marriage and the Family, Mademoiselle, Ms., New York Magazine, Psychology Today, Radical Therapist, Science, Village Voice,* and *Women's Studies.* **Member:** American Association for the Abolition of Involuntary Mental Hospitalization, American Association for the Advancement of Science, American Psychological Association, American Organization of University Professors, National Organization for Women, Eastern Psychological Association, New York State Psychological Association. **Address:** Department of Psychology, College of Staten Island of the City University of New York, Staten Island, New York 10301, U.S.A.

Publications

Political/Social Theory

Women and Madness. Garden City, New York, Doubleday, 1972; London, Allen Lane, 1974.

Women, Money and Power, with Emily Jane Goodman. New York, Morrow, 1976.

About Men. New York, Simon & Schuster, and London, Women's Press, 1978.

Mothers on Trial: The Battle for Children and Custody. New York, McGraw-Hill, 1986.

Sacred Bond: The Legacy of Baby M. New York, Times Books, 1988; as *Sacred Bond: Motherhood under Siege,* introduction by Ann Oakley, London, Virago, 1990.

Patriarchy: Notes of an Expert Witness. Monroe, Maine, Common Courage Press, 1994.

Autobiography

With Child: A Diary of Motherhood. New York, Crowell, 1979.

*

Critical Studies: "On Maternal Splitting: A Propos of Mary Gordon's *Men and Angels*" by Susan Rubin Suleiman, in *Signs: Journal of Women and Culture in Society,* 14(1), 1988.

* * *

Phyllis Chesler has been an articulate and consistent critic of American culture for over 25 years. As an author she has broken new ground by exposing the unequal treatment of women in the health care system, and her book *Women and Madness* (1972) was instrumental in initiating reforms in the mental health establishment. Chesler has continued to ask difficult questions of the women's movement, insisting on a fair and all-encompassing global sisterhood. Her work has often focused on motherhood and the shifting attitudes of society towards mothers and children. Her candor and incisive prose style have made her a reputation as one of America's most articulate and thoughtful feminist writers, while her activism in representing women who are marginalized by illness, poverty, and exploitation has not diminished despite personal hardship. Never afraid to examine an unpopular issue, Chesler spoke out and wrote in defense of Mary Beth Whitehead, the surrogate mother in the Baby M Case and Aileen Wuronos, the media-styled "first female serial killer."

Chesler's unapologetic defense of women and children's rights have made her a controversial figure. Her account of her 1977 pregnancy, *With Child: A Diary of Motherhood,* is as represented: "An Intimate Account of Pregnancy, Childbirth, and Mothering." In that book she examines her own fears about motherhood—at 37, she confronts the possibility that her child might have Down Syndrome, connects with other women as mothers in a new way, and experiences the discomfort of some of her friends who are either envious or disapproving of her pregnancy. Like many feminists before her, her integrity as a reformer is called into question because of her choice to bear a child. As a new mother, Chesler confronts the dilemma of a professional woman who loves her child but fears losing her work to the demands of childrearing. In a revealing incident, she and her mother discuss her concerns and find common ground: "I'm hearing her talk about her religion: motherhood. Not my religion, but worthy of my respect."

Chesler describes the facts of her own life without restraint and with great honesty, although her primary attention as an author is not autobiographical but rather as a researcher and a passionate advocate for her subjects. Born in Brooklyn, New York in 1940, the eldest child of a Polish immigrant Jewish father, her relationship to her father was strong and affectionate while she experienced difficulty with her mother, who was a traditional wife who favored her two sons. Chesler pursued a career in psychology, attending first Bard College and then earning a Ph.D. at the New School for Social Research in 1970. She married an Israeli, Nachmy Bronstein, in 1973, after meeting him on a visit to Israel in 1972. Her academic experience has been one characteristic of a radical feminist in academia—she was given tenure in the mid-1970s and was promoted to full professor in 1990 after a class-action lawsuit. She is a committed feminist teacher who expressed frustration with having been denied the opportunity to mentor graduate students and transmit the legacy of her generation of activists.

Chesler's career in psychology and as a best-selling author made her a controversial figure, beginning with her talk at the American Psychological Association (APA) in 1970. Recalling it as a watershed moment in her career in *Patriarchy: Notes of an Expert Witness,* Chesler shocked the audience with her call for a million dollars in reparations "for those women who had never been helped by the mental health professions but who had, in fact, been further abused." Dismissed as "crazy" herself by the conservative and largely male psychological establishment, Chesler continued her research into the history of women's lives, presenting powerful arguments shaped by her exhaustive inquiries into history, both medical case studies and the everyday lives of women, famous and obscure. Her personal experiences have often dictated a new line of inquiry: just as *Women and Madness* was generated from her experience at the APA, *Mothers on Trial* began during her pregnancy in 1977 when she decided to explore the assault on custody rights for women. She is often approached by women seeking her advocacy, as she was by numerous mothers whose experiences as both traditional and non-traditional mothers were challenged on the basis of their fitness as caregivers and as a result of the non-custodial parent claiming rights to the child. Whenever possible, she uses oral histories to grant silenced women their own voice, believing strongly in their power to persuade the reader. She is well-known as a speaker and as a journalist—the majority of essays in her 1994 collection *Patriarchy* were first lectures or published in the feminist political magazine *On the Issues.* As a journalist, Chesler has published widely: from *Radical Therapist* to *New York Magazine* and *Ms.,* among many others.

In the forward to *Mothers on Trial* Chesler notes that in 1982, during the preparation of that book, she was involved in a serious car accident and experienced a great deal of personal and financial hardship as a result. In 1991 she was diagnosed with Chronic Fatigue Immune Dysfunction Syndrome, which characteristically has given her a new perspective on her subject and inspired the essay "Feminism and Illness." She calls on the feminist community to help each other in crisis and notes that "being ill and temporarily disabled made me more outraged by the contempt and indifference with which most sick and disabled/differently abled people are treated in our country." She is at work at present on a new book, *Male Psychology in the 20th Century.*

—Mary A. Hess

CHODOROW, Nancy

Nationality: American. **Born:** New York, New York, 20 January 1944. **Education:** Radcliffe College, New York, A.B. (summa cum laude) 1966; London School of Economics and Political Science, 1966-67; Harvard University, 1967-68; Brandeis University, M.A. 1972, Ph.D. in sociology 1975; psychoanalytic training at San Francisco Psychoanalytic Institute, 1985-93. **Family:** Married Michael Reich in 1977; one daughter, one son. **Career:** Instructor in women's studies, Wellesley College, Wellesley, Massachusetts, 1973-74; lecturer, 1974-76, then assistant professor, 1976-79, associate professor, 1979-86, University of California, Santa Cruz; associate research sociologist, Institute for Personality Assessment and Research, University of California, Berkeley, 1981-83; associate professor, then professor of sociology, University of California, Berkeley, beginning 1986. Member of faculty, San Francisco Psychoanalytic Institute, beginning 1984; psychoanalyst in private practice. Consulting editor for *Feminist Studies;* member, editorial board for *Signs.* **Awards:** Brandeis University fellowship, 1966-68; National Institute for Mental Health fellowship, 1966-

68, 1972-73; National Science Foundation fellowship, 1970-72; American Sociological Association Jessie Bernard Award, 1979, for *The Reproduction of Mothering;* Center for Advanced Study in the Behavioral Sciences fellow, 1980-81; Russell Sage Foundation grant, 1981-86; National Endowment for the Humanities grant, 1982-85, 1986, and fellowship, 1995-96; Editions Iichiko prize (Tokyo), 1991; American Council of Learned Societies fellowship, 1991-92; Guggenheim fellowship, 1995-96. **Member:** International Psychoanalytic Association, American Sociological Association, American Psychoanalytic Association, National Women's Studies Association, Phi Beta Kappa. **Address:** Department of Sociology, University of California, Berkeley, 410 Barrows Hall, Berkeley, California 94720-0001, U.S.A.

Publications

Nonfiction

The Reproduction of Mothering: Psychoanalysis and the Sociology of Gender. Berkeley, University of California Press, 1978.

Feminism and Psychoanalytic Theory. Cambridge, England, Polity Press, and New Haven, Connecticut, Yale University Press, 1991.

Femininities, Masculinities, Sexualities: Freud and Beyond. London, Free Association Books, and Lexington, University Press of Kentucky, 1994.

Essays

"Mothering, Object-Relations, and the Female Oedipal Configuration," in *Feminist Studies,* 4(1), February 1978.

"Feminism, Femininity, and Freud," in *Advances in Psychoanalytic Sociology,* edited by Jerome Rabow, Gerald M. Platt, and Marion S. Goldman. Malabar, Florida, Krieger, 1987.

"Feminism and Difference: Gender, Relation, and Difference in Psychoanalytic Perspective," in *The Psychology of Women: Ongoing Debates,* edited by Mary Roth Walsh. New Haven, Connecticut, Yale University Press, 1987.

"Gender, Relation, and Difference in Psychoanalytic Perspective," in *Essential Papers on the Psychology of Women,* edited by Claudia Zanardi. New York, New York University Press, 1990.

"What Is the Relation between Psychoanalytic Feminism and the Psychoanalytic Psychology of Women?" (originally appeared in *Annual of Psychoanalysis,* 17, 1989), in *Theoretical Perspectives on Sexual Difference,* edited by Deborah L. Rhode. New Haven, Connecticut, Yale University Press, 1990.

"Freud on Women," in *Cambridge Companion to Freud,* edited by Jerome Neu. New York, Cambridge University Press, 1991.

"Where Have All the Eminent Women Psychoanalysts Gone? Like Bubbles in Champagne, They Rose to the Top and Disappeared," in *Social Roles and Social Institutions: Essays in Honor of Rose Laub Coser,* edited by Judith R. Blau and Norman Goodman. Boulder, Westview Press, 1991.

"Heterosexuality as a Compromise Formation: Reflections on the Psychoanalytic Theory of Sexual Development," in *Psychoanalysis and Contemporary Thought,* 15(3), 1992.

"Perspectives on the Use of Case Studies: All It Takes Is One," in *Family, Self, and Society: Toward a New Agenda for Family Research,* edited by Philip A. Cowan and others. Hillsdale, New Jersey, Lawrence Erlbaum Associates, 1993.

"Gender as a Personal and Cultural Construction," in *Signs,* 20(3), spring 1995.

"Becoming a Feminist Foremother," in *Women and Therapy,* 17(1-2), 1995.

*

Critical Studies: *From Klein to Kristeva: Psychoanalytic Feminism and the Search for the "Good Enough" Mother* by Janice L. Doane and Devon L. Hodges, Ann Arbor, University of Michigan Press, 1992; "Nancy J. Chodorow," in *Feminism in Psychoanalysis: A Critical Dictionary,* edited by D. Chisholm, J. F. MacCannell, and M. Whitford, Oxford, Blackwell, 1992; "Gender, Patriarchy, and Women's Mental Health: Psychoanalytic Perspectives" by Sharna Olfman, in *Journal of the American Academy of Psychoanalysis,* 22(2), summer 1994; "Multiplicities and Uncertainties of Gender: 'Analysis of a Case of Transsexualism': Reply to Chodorow" by Ruth Stein, in *Psychoanalytic Dialogues,* 5(2), 1995.

* * *

Sociologist, psychoanalyst, and educator Nancy Chodorow is best known for her pioneering work on the central role that mothers play in childrearing, as well as for her emphasis on the family as the primary location for gender socialization. In her influential book, *The Reproduction of Mothering: Psychoanalysis and the Sociology of Gender* (1978), Chodorow argues that gender identity formation—that is, how a girl or boy forms a concept of what is properly a feminine or masculine identity in their society—is primarily shaped within the family structure and process, in particular through the child's early experiences of mothering—performed almost exclusively by women.

Drawing on object-relations theory and the work of Talcott Parsons and the Frankfurt school, Chodorow contends that gender identity formation is largely a result of the dynamics of family relationships, and that "family structure and process, in particular the asymmetrical organization of parenting, affect unconscious psychic structure and process." In the "preoedipal" stage, Chodorow points out, the infant experiences a "primary identification" with the mother and forms a primary love for the mother that makes no differentiation between the child's needs and desires and the ability of the mother to fulfill them. Gradually the child goes on to establish a sense of self through an expanded awareness of its own physical being. It begins to differentiate from the mother as it becomes less dependant upon her. Freud argues that once a girl forms an attachment to her father—in the "oedipal" stage—her relationship to her mother diminishes and is replaced by hostility for her as a rival; her love is wholly transferred to her father. Chodorow refutes this, arguing that, instead, the girl's preoedipal attachment to her mother continues alongside this newly formed fascination for her father. To establish her gender identity, a girl need not dissociate herself from the mother as radically as a boy does; a boy must establish his gender identity in contradistinction to his mother. Chodorow emphasizes the impact of same-gendered mothering on the psychosocial development of girls as well as boys:

> Because of their mothering by women, girls come to experience themselves as less separate than boys, as having more permeable ego boundaries. Girls come to define

themselves more in relation to others. Their internalized object-relational structure becomes more complex, with more ongoing issues.

Equally important is Chodorow's critique of Freudian psychoanalytic theory. She argues that psychoanalysis cannot make universal claims concerning psychological development; they must take into account the cultural and historical conditions of the time, including the awareness of the fact that the nuclear family is the model from which most hypotheses and theories about psychological development are constructed. Psychoanalytic accounts must be drawn from the "real subject [of study]: a socially and historically specific mother-child relationship of a particular intensity and exclusivity and a particular infantile development that this relationship produces." Instead, Chodorow notes, "Freud was only sometimes describing how women develop in a patriarchal society." She characterizes his work as "making unsupported assertions" or "statements about how women (and men) ought to be." Instead of arising out of clinical observation, such theories emerge from "unexamined patriarchal cultural assumptions." Moreover, "Freud defines gender and sexual differentiation as presence or absence of masculinity and the male genital rather than two different processes" in which a woman's psychosexual development is understood as a satisfying experience in its own right and not simply a state of deficiency. This position has been echoed by many other feminists.

Chodorow, now at the University of California at Berkeley, continues her work with the sometimes contradictory theories that psychoanalysis and feminism have generated. Her own contributions, especially her reappraisal of the ways in which the psychological dynamics of the sex-gender system is systematically reproduced and subject to historical change and development, are uniformly acknowledged as significant contributions to feminist theory.

—Gerri McNenny

CHOPIN, Kate

Nationality: American. **Born:** Katherine O'Flaherty, St. Louis, Missouri, 8 February 1850. **Education:** Graduated from Academy of the Sacred Heart, St. Louis, Missouri, 1868. **Family:** Married Oscar Chopin in 1870 (died 1883); five sons, one daughter. **Career:** With husband, moved to New Orleans, 1870; family underwent severe financial losses and moved to Cloutierville, Louisiana, 1879; moved, with children, to St. Louis home of her grandmother, 1884; had nervous breakdown for which doctor prescribed writing, 1888; opened regular salon in St. Louis. Contributor of articles, short stories, and translations to periodicals, including *Atlantic Monthly, Criterion, Harper's Young People, St. Louis Dispatch,* and *Vogue.* **Died:** 22 August 1904.

Publications

Novels

At Fault. Nixon-Jones Printing Co., 1890.

The Awakening. Chicago, Herbert S. Stone, 1899; 2nd critical edition edited by Margo Culley, New York and London, Norton, 1994.

Short Stories

Bayou Folk. Boston, Houghton, 1894; with introduction by Warner Berthoff, Garrett Press, 1970.

A Night in Acadie. Way & Williams, 1897.

The Storm and Other Stories, with The Awakening (includes "Wiser than God," "A Point at Issue," and "The Story of an Hour"), edited by Per Seyersted. Old Westbury, New York, Feminist Press, 1974.

A Vocation and A Voice, edited by Emily Toth. New York, Penguin, 1991.

Other

The Complete Works of Kate Chopin, edited by Per Seyersted. Baton Rouge, Louisiana State University Press, 2 vols., 1969.

A Kate Chopin Miscellany, edited by Per Seyersted. Natchitoches, Northwestern State University Press, 1979.

Kate Chopin's The Awakening, and Selected Stories, edited by Sandra M. Gilbert. New York, Penguin, 1984.

*

Media Adaptations: *The End of August* (film adaptation of *The Awakening*), 1982; *The Story of an Hour* (film), 1982.

Bibliography: *Edith Wharton and Kate Chopin: A Reference Guide* edited by Marlene Springer, Boston, G.K. Hall, 1976.

Manuscript Collections: Missouri Historical Society, St. Louis; Cammie G. Henry Research Center, Eugene Watson Memorial Library, Northwestern State University, Natchitoches.

Critical Studies: *Kate Chopin and Her Creole Stories* by Daniel S. Rankin, Philadelphia, University of Pennsylvania Press, 1932; *Kate Chopin: A Critical Biography* by Per Seyersted, Baton Rouge, Louisiana State University Press, 1969; *The Authority of Experience: Essays in Feminist Criticism* by Arlyn Diamond and Lee R. Edwards, Amherst, University of Massachusetts Press, 1977; *Diving Deep and Surfacing: Women Writers on Spiritual Quest* by Carol P. Christ, Boston, Beacon Press, 1980; *Tomorrow Is Another Day: The Woman Writer in the South, 1859-1936* by Ann Goodwyn Jones, Baton Rouge, Louisiana State University Press, 1981; "Kate Chopin" in *Dictionary of Literary Biography,* Volume 12: *American Realists and Naturalists,* Detroit, Gale, 1982; *Kate Chopin* edited by Harold Bloom, New York, Chelsea House, 1987; *New Essays on The Awakening* edited by Wendy Martin, Cambridge, Cambridge University Press, 1988; *Women on the Color Line: Evolving Stereotypes and the Writings of George Washington Cable, Grace King, Kate Chopin* by Shannon Elfenbein, Charlottesville, University of Virginia, 1989; *Gender, Race, and Region in the Writings of Grace King, Ruth McEnery Stuart, and Kate Chopin* by Helen Taylor, Baton Rouge, Louisiana State University Press, 1989; *Verging on the Abyss: The Social Fiction of Kate Chopin and Edith Wharton* by Mary E. Papke, New York, Greenwood Press, 1990; *Kate Chopin* by Emily Toth, New York, Morrow, 1990; *Sister's Choice: Traditions and Change in Ameri-*

can Women's Writing by Elaine Showalter, Oxford, Clarendon Press, 1991; *Kate Chopin Reconsidered: Beyond the Bayou* edited by Lynda S. Boren and Sara D. Davis, Baton Rouge, Louisiana University Press, 1992.

* * *

Considered one of the foremost Southern regionalist writers, Kate Chopin's fiction details the social and sexual subtleties of the Cajun and Creole culture in which she lived during her childhood and marriage. In works such as *Bayou Folk, A Night in Acadie,* and *The Awakening,* she presents ironic and even daring treatments of the sexual, racial, and moral underpinnings of polite southern Louisiana society. The most well-known of her works, *The Awakening* has become required reading for any student of the history of women's cultural oppression.

Although born and raised in a St. Louis devastated by the Civil War, Katherine O'Flaherty Chopin became the storyteller of a sultry and sometimes dangerous south Louisiana. In June of 1970 she married Oscar Chopin, a French businessman, and moved to New Orleans; nine years, after her husband's business failed and the family faced economic hardship, the Chopins and their five sons moved to the small village of Cloutierville, in Natchitoches Parish, where the flamboyant Chopin soon developed a reputation for her urban ways. It was while living in Cloutierville, that Chopin would collect much of the raw material for her later short stories, novels, and poems.

Oscar died in 1882, leaving his young widow with five children and $12,000 in debt. A strong, resourceful, and outspoken woman, she continued to run the family business until 1884. During this time, she had an affair with a married man, Albert Sampite, a hard-living, passionate Louisiana farmer. This experience and others fueled her later writing, which often involved illicit passions in the heat-sodden world of the swamps.

One of Chopin's better-known short stories, "The Storm," is a vignette exploring female desires that cannot be fulfilled in marriage, a common theme for Chopin. In "The Storm," Calixta is married to Bobinot, who is away for the afternoon with their son. As Calixta is sewing, a great storm arrives and with the storm comes Alcee Laballiere, a man from her life before marriage. During the raging of the storm in nature, these two have their own storm of passion. Afterwards, Alcee rides away and writes a loving letter to his absent wife. Calixta's husband comes home, bringing shrimp, and life goes on quite happily; in fact, happier than before for Calixta. Unlike much other 19th- and early 20th-century fiction, the adulterous woman is not punished, but is instead, now more satisfied in her marriage.

Chopin is best known, however, for her novel, *The Awakening,* published in 1899. After its publication, *The Awakening* created such an uproar that its author was alienated from certain social circles in St. Louis. The novel also contributed to rejections of Chopin's later stories, and the heavy criticism for the book that she endured hindered her writing. The patriarchal publishing world was simply not ready for such an honest exploration of female independence, a frank cataloguing of a woman's desires and her search for fulfillment outside marriage.

Edna Pontellier, the main character in *The Awakening,* is a wife and mother, but more importantly, she is an artist in search of female freedom, sexuality, and creativity. At the end of the novel Edna commits suicide by walking out, naked, into the ocean, realizing that "for the first time in her life she stood naked in the open air, at the mercy of the sun, the breeze that beat upon her, and the waves that invited her." She thinks: "How strange and awful it seemed to stand naked under the sky! how delicious! She felt like some new-born creature, opening its eyes in a familiar world it had never known." This act of suicide is a positive embracing of freedom, an act of re-birth.

Like her protagonist Edna Pontellier, upon the publication of *The Awakening* Chopin herself stood naked in her exploration of female creativity and sexuality. She, too, must have opened her 19th-century female readers' eyes to "a familiar world [they] had never known." Although never officially banned, the novel was heavily criticized and then ignored for decades. Chopin died in 1904, never knowing that her novel of female liberation was reprinted in the 1960s, paralleling a resurgence in the women's movement; *The Awakening* is now a major American novel.

—Jennifer Brantley

CHRISTIAN, Barbara T.

Nationality: American. **Born:** St. Thomas, Virgin Islands, 12 December 1943. **Education:** Marquette University, Milwaukee, Wisconsin, A.B. (cum laude) 1963; Columbia University, New York, M.A. 1964, Ph.D. (with distinction) 1970. **Family:** Divorced; one daughter. **Career:** instructor in English, College of the Virgin Islands, 1963, then Hunter College, New York, 1963-64; lecturer, SEEK program and department of English, City College of New York, 1964-71; lecturer in English, 1971-72, assistant professor, 1972-78, associate professor, 1978-86, then professor of African American studies and president, Women's Studies Board, University of California, Berkeley. Co-editor, *Feminist Studies,* 1984-92; *Black American Literature Forum,* 1985-90; *Sage,* 1987-89; and *Contentions,* beginning 1990. Contributor of essays and reviews to numerous journals. **Awards:** Afro-American Society Hall of Fame award, 1980; American Women's Educators Association award, 1982, for *In Search of Our Past;* Before Columbus American Book Award, 1983, for *Black Women Novelists;* University of California, Berkeley, Feminist Institute grant, 1987; Louise Patterson African American Studies Award, 1992, 1995; City of Berkeley Icon award for community service, 1994; Modern Language Association *MELUS* award for contribution to ethnic studies and African American scholarship, 1994; Gwendolyn Brooks Center award, 1995. **Member:** Women's Studies Board (Berkeley). **Address:** Department of Afro-American Studies, University of California at Berkeley, 3335 Dwinelle Hall, Berkeley, California 94720-0001, U.S.A.

Publications

Literary Criticism

Black Women Novelists: The Development of a Tradition, 1892-1976. Westport, Connecticut, Greenwood Press, 1980.

Black Feminist Criticism: Perspectives on Black Women Writers. New York, Pergamon Press, 1985.

From the Inside Out: Afro-American Women's Literary Tradition and the State. Minneapolis, University of Minnesota Center for Humanistic Studies, 1987.

Uncollected Essays

"Black, Female, and Foreign-Born: A Statement," in *Female Immigrants to the U.S.: A Caribbean, Latin American, and African Experience,* edited by Bryce La Porte. Washington, DC, Smithsonian Institute, 1982.
"Alternate Visions of the Gendered Past: African American Writers vs. Ivan Illich," in *Feminist Issues,* spring 1983.
"Alice Walker: The Black Woman Artist as Wayward," in *Black Women Writers, 1950-1980,* edited by Mari Evans. Garden City, New York, Doubleday, 1984.
"No More Buried Lives: The Theme of Lesbianism in Lorde, Naylor, Shange, Walker," in *Feminist Issues,* spring 1985.
"The Race for Theory," in *Cultural Critique,* 6, spring 1987; in *Gender and Theory: Dialogues on Feminist Criticism,* edited by Linda Kauffman, Oxford, Blackwell, 1989.
"But What Do We Think We're Doing Anyway: The State of Black Feminist Criticism(s), or My Version of a Little Bit of History," in *Changing Our Own Words: Essays on Criticism, Theory and Writing by Black Women,* edited by Cheryl Wall. Rutgers, New Jersey, Rutgers University Press, 1989.
"The Highs and the Lows of Black Feminist Criticism: A Speak Peace," in *Reading Black, Reading Feminist,* edited by Henry Louis Gates. New York, Meridian, 1990.
"Your Silence Will Not Protect You: Tribute to Audre Lorde," in *Crossroads,* 28, February 1993.

Other

Teaching Guide to "Black Foremothers" by Dorothy Sterling. New York, Feminist Press, 1980; revised, 1988.

Editor, *"Everyday Use"; Alice Walker: A Casebook.* New Brunswick, New Jersey, Rutgers University Press, 1994.
Editor, with Elizabeth Abel and Helen Moglen, *Female Subjects in Black and White.* Berkeley, University of California Press, 1996.

*

Critical Studies: "Kinship and Resemblances: Women on Women" by Hortense J. Spillers, in *Feminist Studies,* 11(1), spring 1985.

* * *

A professor of African American studies at the University of California, Berkeley, Barbara Christian is noted for her insights into the development of a unique African American female literary tradition. In addition to numerous essays on topics of relevance to that tradition, as well as to the field of women's studies in general, she is the author of *Black Women Novelists: The Development of a Tradition, 1872-1976* (1980) and *Black Feminist Criticism: Perspectives on Black Women Writers* (1985).

Black Women Novelists is, as Christian writes in her introduction, "an attempt to describe [the tradition of those few Black women able to get their works into print], to articulate its existence, to examine its origins, and to trace the development of stereotypical images imposed on black women and assess how these images have affected the works of black women artists." Combining an historical survey, Christian then embarks upon a humanist critical evaluation of the works of Paule Marshall, Toni Morrison, and Alice Walker, focusing on the process of each writer's path to self-discovery through her fiction.

In the collection of 17 essays entitled *Black Feminist Criticism* Christian first explains, and then demonstrates the process of why she, and why black women in general, write. It is, as she notes, "a process that delineates their continual pushing beyond a previously held idea, refining it, changing it—a process that illuminates the movement of their thought." Within these essays, written between 1975 and 1984, Christian examines, from a black feminist perspective, such issues as the importance of motherhood and the mother-child relationship within both the works of both African American and Native African writers; 19th-century black women novelists' efforts to transcend the prevailing racial and sexual stereotypes of their age; and the attempts by such writers as Paule Marshall to destroy the image of the domineering black matriarch—the "superwoman," if you will, in modern African American literature. While the book's chronological organization tends to fragment the examination of certain writers, who are discussed in essays separated by several years, on the whole *Black Feminist Criticism* has been praised for its well-written, thoughtful analysis, and for Christian's own efforts to, as she would later note in her essay 1987 "The Race for Theory": "respon[d] to the writer to whom there is often no response, to folk who need the writing as much as they need anything. I know, from literary history, that writing disappears unless there is a response to it. Because I write about writers who are now writing, I hope to help ensure that their tradition has continuity and survives."

—Nancy Raye Tarcher

CHRISTINE de PISAN

Also known as Christine de Pizan. **Nationality:** Italian/French. **Born:** Venice, Italy, c. 1364. **Education:** Educated by her father, a scholar and astronomer. **Family:** Married courtier Étienne du Castel in 1380 (died 1389); three children. **Career:** Joined father in Paris, 1369; wrote under the patronage of the Earl of Salisbury and Philip of Burgundy, beginning 1389; supervised the copying and illuminating of her own texts; founder, Order of the Rose; retreated to a convent in Poissy, c. 1415. **Died:** c. 1431.

PUBLICATIONS

Political/Social Theory

Livre du trésor de la cité de Dames. [Paris], n.p., 1405; as *Le livre des trois vertus,* [Paris], n.d.; translated as *The Treasure of the City of Ladies, or, The Book of the Three Virtues,* Harmondsworth, Penguin, 1985.
Livre du chemin du long éstude. Paris, Etienne Groulleau, 1549.
Livre du corps de policie. [Paris], n.d.; translated as *The Book of the Body Politic,* Cambridge, Cambridge University Press, 1994.
Epistre de la prison de vie humaine [The Epistle of the Prison of Human Life]. [Paris], n.d.; in *Letters,* 1984.

History

Livre de la mutacion de fortune. [Paris], n.p., 1403.
Livre de la cité des dames. Paris, n.p., 1405; translated as *The City of Ladies,* London, Wynkyn de Word, n.d.; translated as *The Book of the Ladies,* London, n.p., 1521; translated by Earl Jeffrey Richards, n.p., 1982.
Le livre de Duc des vrais amants. [Paris], n.p., 1407; translated as *The Book of the Duke of True Lovers,* London, New Medieval Library, 1908.
Le cent histoires de troyo. Paris, P. Pigouchet, c. 1500.

Literary Criticism

Epistre au dieu d'amours. [Paris], n.p., 1399; translated in *La Querell de la Rose: Letters and Documents,* edited by Joseph L. Baird and John R. Kane, n.p., 1978.
Epistres du débat sur le Roman de la Rose [Letters on the Debate of the *Romance of the Rose*]. [Paris], n.p., 1401-03.

Poetry

Epître au dieu d'amour. [Paris], n.p., 1399.
Cent ballades, Virelays, Rondeaux. Paris, n.p., c. 1404.
Oeuvres poétiques. Paris, Société de Anciens Textes Français, 3 vols., 1886-96.
Le livre de la paix. [Paris], n.d.
Ditié en l'honneur de Jehanne d'Arc, chronique rimée (song in honor of Joan of Arc). Paris, n.p., 1429; translated by Angus Kennedy and Kenneth Varty, n.p., 1977.

Autobiography

Avision—Christine. [Paris], n.p., 1405; translated as *Christine's Vision,* London and New York, Garland, 1993.

Other

Le livre des faicts et bonnes meurs du sage Roi Charles V [The Book of the Deeds and Morals of the Wise King Charles V]. Paris, n.p., 1404.
Proverbes. [Paris], n.p.; translated by John Saxon, Earl of Rivers, as *Morall Proverbes of Christyne,* London, W. Caxton, 1478.
The Fayettes of Arms. London, William Caxton, 1489.
Letters, edited and translated by Josette A. Wisman. London and New York, Garland, 1984.

*

Bibliography: "Manuscrits et éditions des oeuvres de Christine de Pisan" by Josette A. Wisman, in *Manuscripta,* 21, 1977; *Christine de Pizan: A Bibliographical Guide* by Angus Kennedy, London, Grant & Cutler, 1994.

Critical Studies: *Les Idées féministes de Christine de Pisan* by Rose Rigaud, n.p., 1911; *The Order of the Rose: The Life and Ideal of Christine de Pisan* by E. McCleod, n.p., 1976; *Christine de Pizan: The First French Woman of Letters* by Charity Cannon Willard, n.p., 1982; *Christine de Pizan: Her Life and Works* by Charity Cannon Willard, New York, Persea, 1984; *The Mythographic Art: Classical Fable and the Rise of the Vernacular in Early France and England* edited by Jane Chance, Talahasse, University of Florida Press, 1990; *The Reception of Christine de Pisan from the 15th through the 19th Centuries* edited by Glenda K. McLeod, Lewiston, Maine, E. Mellen Press, 1991; *Reinterpreting Christine de Pizan* edited by Earl Jeffrey Richards, London and Athens, University of Georgia Press, 1992; *Ideals for Women in the Works of Christine de Pizan* by Diane Bornstein, n.p., n.d.

* * *

One of the most notable Italian intellectuals of the later medieval period, Christine de Pisan was a stalwart defender of the rights of women to education and a more respected role in society. A historian, poet, and philosopher whose written works were popular during her own lifetime and widely translated throughout the centuries since her death, Pisan's most enduring legacy remains her essays on behalf of women: *La cité de dames/ The Book of the Ladies* was one of the first written works to devote full attention to the lives of notable women from the past.

Born in Venice in 1364, Christine de Pisan was the daughter of Tommaso di Benvenuto da Pizzano, a learned man who served as court astrologer to Charles V of France (1337-1380); in her father's library in Paris Christine was exposed to the literature, science, and intellectual debates of the period. At 15 she married Étienne du Castel, notary and secretary to the French king and a man who valued his wife's obvious intellectual gifts. Referring to her husband as one "whom no other could surpass in kindness, peacefulness, loyalty, and true love," Christine was devastated—both emotionally and financially—when Castel became a victim of the bubonic plague nine years later. The widowed Christine was left with her husband's debts, as well as three children, a niece, and an elderly mother (Tommaso had died in 1386, leaving the family in debt) to support. She would later describe this period of hardships in the *Avision;* meanwhile, she quickly decided to make use of her wits, her intellect, and her writing, becoming what many consider the first professional writer.

Finding patronage from nobles such as the Earl of Salisbury and Philip, Duke of Burgundy, Christine produced several volumes of history, verses inspired by both politics and her personal feelings of loneliness and loss, and a laudatory biography of Charles V. While many of her shorter works were completed in the first years of her writing career—many of her ballads reflect her devastation at the loss of her beloved husband—later poetic compositions would find Christine exploring lyrical and thematic innovations. Modeled on the works of Latin writers like the Roman poet Virgil, Christine de Pisan's prose is stylistically complex and varied, while her works in the traditional genres of history, biography, and political treatise are often held up as exemplary in their technical proficiency.

It was Christine's *Epistre au dieu d'amour,* published in 1399, that first openly expressed her dissatisfaction with the station of women within medieval European society. An attack on the openly misogynistic works of such widely read authors as Ovid and Jean de Meun, Christine's vehement opposition to the latter's sequel to the classic *Roman de la Rose* would be more fully set forth in *Epistres du débat sur le Roman de la Rose,* in which she rebelled against the traditional role of women as foils for literary and social satire. In *Le livre des trois vertus* Pisan defended the right of women to an education that would allow them to make good use of their natural abilities, and maintained that the female mind was so well constituted as to be less susceptible to the greed and corruption exhibited by male politicians. "If it were customary to send little girls to school and to teach them the same subjects that are taught to boys, they would learn just as fully and would understand the subtleties of all arts and sciences," she contended in her prologue. "Indeed, maybe they would understand them better ... for just as women's bodies are softer than men's, so their understanding is sharper."

La cité des dames/The Book of the City of Ladies (1405) is significant not only as a rare historical record of the lives of notable women, but for its groundbreaking stature as what some have called the first feminist treatise. Widely translated from the 15th century onward, Christine de Pisan's scripturally based work would be used to fuel the arguments for women's social and political equality made by later feminists in both Europe and England. Interestingly, after its author's death *La cité* would be disparaged by critics who claimed that the work was simply a disguised translation of an earlier work, *De claris mulieribus,* by Italian writer Giovanni Boccaccio; such charges have since been proven to be without merit. Pisan's *Le livre du trésor de la cité de dames/The Treasure of the City of Ladies* advanced her own feminist arguments still further. Outlining the realities of the status and conditions of women's lives, *Le trésor* offers advice to what Pisan establishes as the three basic classes of women: ladies of the aristocracy and the nobility; women, like herself, of the lesser nobility and those residing at court; and female members of the rising bourgeois class. While Christine also includes common women in this latter classification, their lack of literacy would seem to make them a doubtful audience for her advice.

In 1415, following the French defeat by English troops at the Battle of Agincourt, a disillusioned Christine de Pisan retreated from the futility and continuing folly of the Hundred Years' War and entered a convent at Poissy, France, where she died in 1431 at the age of 96. A tireless intellectual to the end, her final work, a song in praise of the heroism of Joan of Arc, was published in 1429, breaking her self-imposed 11-year silence. Enduring the inequalities that plagued the life of women in the Medieval period, Christine channelled her fortuitous education and written skill to aid in the plight of others less educated than herself. And she did so with wit; in her *Avision,* she recounts an occassion when a man attempted to insult her by saying that a woman possessing an education was unattractive because so few existed. An ignorant man, Christine de Pisan replied, was, to her eyes, even more unattractive because they existed in such great numbers.

—Lynn MacGregor

CHURCHILL, Caryl

Nationality: British. **Born:** London, 3 September 1938. **Education:** Attended school in Montréal; Lady Margaret Hall, Oxford, B.A. in English 1960. **Family:** Married the barrister David Harter in 1961; three sons. **Career:** Resident dramatist, Royal Court Theatre, London, 1974-75; tutor for Young Writers' Group. **Awards:** Richard Hillary Memorial Prize, 1961; Obie Award, 1982-83, for *Top Girls;* Susan Smith Blackburn Prize, 1984, for *Fen;* Olivier Award and *London Evening Standard* Award, 1987, both for *Serious Money; Time Out* Award, 1987. **Agent:** Casarotto Ramsay Ltd., National House, 60-66 Wardour St., London W1V 3HP, England. **Address:** 12 Thornhill Square, London N1, England.

Publications

Plays

Downstairs (produced Oxford, 1958).
Having a Wonderful Time (produced London, 1960).
Easy Death (produced Oxford, 1962).
Schreber's Nervous Illness (produced London, 1972). In *Churchill: Shorts,* 1990.
Owners (produced London, 1972). London, Eyre Methuen, 1973.
Objections to Sex and Violence (produced London, 1975).
Moving Clocks Go Slow (produced London, 1975).
Light Shining in Buckinghamshire (produced Edinburgh, 1976). London, Pluto Press, 1978.
Vinegar Tom (produced Hull, 1976). London, TQ Publications, 1978.
Floorshow, with David Bradford, Bryony Lavery, and Michelene Wandor (produced London, 1977).
Traps (produced London, 1977). London, Pluto Press, 1978.
Cloud Nine (produced London, 1979). London, Pluto Press, 1979.
Three More Sleepless Nights (produced London, 1980). In *Churchill: Shorts,* 1990.
Top Girls (produced London, 1982). London, Methuen, and New York, French, 1982; revised edition, London, Methuen, 1984.
Fen (produced London, 1983). London, Methuen, 1983; New York, French, 1984.
Softcops (produced London, 1984). London, Methuen, 1984.
Midday Sun, with Geraldine Pilgrim, Pete Brooks, and John Ashford (produced London, 1984).
Churchill: Plays One (collection). London, Methuen, 1985.
A Mouthful of Birds, with David Lan (produced London, 1986). London, Heinemann Educational, 1987.
Serious Money (produced London, 1987). London, Heinemann Educational, 1987.
Ice Cream with Hot Fudge, London, Samuel French, 1990.
  Ice Cream (produced London, 1989).
  Hot Fudge (produced New York, 1990).
Churchill: Shorts (includes *The Judge's Wife, The Ants, The After Dinner Joke, Identical Twins,* and *Not ... Not ... Not ... Not Enough Oxygen*). London, Nick Hern, 1990.
Churchill: Plays Two (collection). London, Methuen, 1990.
Mad Forest: A Play from Romania (produced London, 1990). London, Samuel French, 1990.
Lives of the Great Poisoners, with Orlando Gough and Ian Spink (produced Bristol, 1991). London, Methuen, 1993.
The Skriker (produced London, 1994). London, Nick Hern, 1994.

Television Plays: *The Judge's Wife,* 1972; *Turkish Delight,* 1974; *The After Dinner Joke,* 1978; *The Legion Hall Bombing,* 1978; *Crimes,* 1981; Fugue (with Ian Spink), 1987.

Radio Plays: *You've No Need to Be Frightened,* 1961; *The Ants,* 1962; *Lovesick,* 1967; *Identical Twins,* 1968; *Abortive,* 1971; *Not ... Not ... Not ... Not ... Not Enough Oxygen,* 1971; *Henry's Past,* 1972; *Schreber's Nervous Illness,* 1972; *Perfect Happiness,* 1973.

*

Critical Studies: "Caryl Churchill" in *Stages in the Revolution: Political Theatre in Britain since 1968* by Catherine Itzin, London, Methuen, 1980; "The Dramas of Caryl Churchill: The Politics of Possibility" by Helene Keysar, in *Massachusetts Review* 24, 1983; "Caryl Churchill" in *Interviews with Contemporary Women Playwrights* by Kathleen Betsko and Rachel Koenig, New York, Beech Tree, 1987; *Churchill: The Playwright* by Geraldine Cousin, London, Methuen, 1989; *File on Churchill* by Linda Fitzsimmons, London, Methuen, 1989; *The Plays of Caryl Churchill: Theatre of Empowerment* by Ameila Howe Kritzer, New York, St. Martin's 1991; "Caryl Churchill: Theatre as a Model for Change" in *Modern British Drama 1890-1990* by Christopher Innes, Cambridge, Cambridge University Press, 1992; "Mirrors of Utopia: Caryl Churchill and Joint Stock" by Frances Gray, in *British and Irish Drama since 1960* edited by James Acheson, New York, St. Martin's Press, 1993.

* * *

Since the mid-1970s, Caryl Churchill has ranked among the best-known political playwrights in England, indeed among the most popular playwrights of any sort. "Of course socialism and feminist aren't synonymous," she told an interviewer in 1984, "but I feel strongly about both and wouldn't be interested in a form of one that didn't include the other." Her work deals with a variety of issues, many of them strongly politically charged, yet she has managed to reach audiences from across the political spectrum. Not only do political critics find much to admire in her work, ordinary playgoers also find a consistently good night of theater.

In 1958, while she was earning her degree in English literature at Oxford, Churchill's first play, *Downstairs,* was produced by the Oriel College Dramatic Society. In the 1960s and early 1970s, she honed her craft by writing short plays, mostly for radio and television broadcast, while living in London and caring for her young children. The plays from this period frequently focus on male characters and are often about family and psychological themes—for instance, in *The Ants* (BBC radio, 1962) a confused young boy must choose between his parents, and *Schreber's Nervous Illness* (BBC radio, 1972) is based on a memoir chronicling the mental breakdown of a 19th-century judge (an early example of Churchill's lasting interest in history). But this is not to suggest that Churchill was uninterested in politics at this time. *Not ... Not ... Not ... Not ... Not Enough Oxygen* (BBC radio, 1971) is a frightening look at a future London destroyed by ecological disasters, and *The Judge's Wife* (BBC television, 1972) concerns the widow of a man executed by revolutionaries.

Churchill's first major theatrical break came in 1972, when the Royal Court Theatre in London produced *Owners.* It is the story of Marion, a driven property owner who evicts her tenants and harasses her husband just to demonstrate her control over them. The play addresses issues of social class and power structures, and Marion may be seen as a prototype for later Churchill characters who ask the audience to question women's relationship to social hierarchies. Through the 1970s, Churchill continued to write for radio and television, but she devoted more of her time to the stage. During this period, her work increasingly focused on women characters and the political content of her plays was on the rise.

In 1976 Churchill wrote *Vinegar Tom* for the feminist theater collective Monstrous Regiment. The author has suggested that this was a turning point for her, that by working with an overtly political company she became more aware of the power of her work to teach audiences. She also engaged in close collaboration for the first time, an act which she considers vital to her feminist aesthetic. *Vinegar Tom* is a story about witch hunting in 17th-century England. In the play, various women are accused of black magic; the audience, however, knows that their only crime is having transgressed social norms. These women are victims of a system that criminalizes their aspirations and their sexuality. Sexual politics was also the focus of *Cloud Nine,* which enjoyed a successful run at the Royal Court in 1979 and later transferred to New York, giving Churchill her first international hit. Set half in colonial Africa in the 19th century and half in contemporary London, it follows one family's struggles with their own social and sexual desires and with changing norms for sexual behavior. A bold play, both deeply serious and seriously comic, it includes cross-gender and -racial casting and a 100-year time, shift during which the characters age only 25 years. *Cloud Nine* secured Churchill's reputation for theatrical experimentation, as well as giving her popular success.

Though she was already well established by this time, the 1980s brought the playwright's most successful period. Curiously, while the social and political climate in England was becoming increasingly conservative under then-Prime Minister Margaret Thatcher, Churchill's feminist and socialist plays continued to please audiences and critics alike. *Top Girls* (1982), perhaps her most obviously "feminist" work, was a hit in both England and America; since its debut, the play has been frequently revived and is taught in college courses on both sides of the Atlantic. Staging the social and financial rise of a woman executive, the play asks audiences to define what "feminism" means and examine the price women often pay for success in the traditionally male work world. It reminds us that, while women *can* achieve career success, the world might be better if success for both women and men were measured by a more humane standard than income. Churchill's next play, *Fen* (1983), is also about work, but it moves to the other end of the class spectrum, examining the bleak lives of agricultural laborers in England's fen country. Women here, the author reminds us, often do the most backbreaking labor by day yet still remain responsible for the care of their families after hours. But men, and even children, are not immune from the deadening routine of work with little reward and less chance of escape. While these were popular plays among critics and audiences, Churchill's biggest commercial success in England was *Serious Money* (1987). An exuberant romp written in jangling verse, this exposé of corruption and greed in the world of high finance extended *Top Girls's* critique of success to consider the ethically hollow world of stock traders, both female and male.

In the late 1980s and early 1990s, Churchill continued to experiment with form, and much of her work began to take on a rather dreamlike quality. Both *A Mouthful of Birds* (1986, with David Lan) and *Lives of the Great Poisoners* (1991, with Orlando Gough and Ian Spink) integrate dance, mime, and song with Churchill's text; in them she demonstrates her continued commitment to a collaborative creative process. *The Skriker* (1994) uses elements of ancient British folklore as well as choreographed movement to tell a tale of contemporary London. While such experimental work has proved less popularly successful than some of her earlier plays, Caryl Churchill remains a model of mainstream success for a feminist playwright.

—Janet E. Gardner

CISNEROS, Sandra

Nationality: American. **Born:** Chicago, Illinois, 1954. **Career:** Writer. Guest lecturer, California State University, Chico. Contributor to periodicals, including *Imagine, Contact II,* and *Revista Chicano-Riqueña.* **Awards:** Before Columbus Foundation American Book Award, 1985, for *The House on Mango Street;* Library Journal Best Book designation, 1992, for *Woman Hollering Creek.* **Address:** c/o Susan Bergholz Literary Services, 340 West 72nd Street, 4-B, New York, New York 10023, U.S.A.

Publications

Poetry

Bad Boys. Mango Publications, 1980.
The Rodrigo Poems. Third Woman Press, 1985.
My Wicked, Wicked Ways. Third Woman Press, 1987.
Loose Woman. New York, Knopf, 1994.

Short Stories

Woman Hollering Creek and Other Stories. New York, Random House, 1991; London, Bloomsbury, 1993.

For Children

The House on Mango Street. Houston, Arte Público, 1983; London, Bloomsbury, 1992.
Hairs = Pelitos. New York, Knopf, 1994.

Other

Recordings: *Woman Hollering Creek* [and] *The House on Mango Street* (cassette), 1992; *Nina Cassian and Sandra Cisneros Reading Their Poems,* 1995.

*

Critical Studies: "Claiming the Bittersweet Matrix: Alice Walker, Sandra Cisneros, and Adrienne Rich" by Nancy Corson Carter, in *Critique,* 35(4), summer 1994.

* * *

Sandra Cisneros is a writer, a poet, of grace, simplicity, and power. From her earliest work in *The House on Mango Street,* to the more mature vision of *Woman Hollering Creek,* to the deeply lyrical *My Wicked, Wicked Ways,* Cisneros explores life, love, pain, and struggle with ever more richly variegated tints.

Cisneros begins a life journey in literature with *The House on Mango Street.* It is here that we are introduced to an all but childlike character in the form of Esperanza—the girl who will not take a back seat to anyone. She is ready, hips poised, "like a new Buick with the keys in the ignition." The vignettes in *The House on Mango Street* take us onto a playground, where we take a carnival-like tour through life with young Esperanza as she explores neighbors, friendships, funny people, myopic people, prejudiced people, sexist people, and prejudged people.

"The Family of Little Feet" is sometimes humorous, always precocious, and inevitably jarring. In the story, Cisneros describes a family of which the narrator, Esperanza, is a part. The funny descriptions of family feet leave the reader—like a child—open and guileless to the story as it ensues. The mother gives the narrator a bag of old shoes—significantly, high-heeled shoes in various colors—to keep if she likes. They are a treasure trove that she shares with her girlfriends. The young girls love to wear and try on the pretty high-heeled shoes, "one pair of lemon shoes and one red and one pair of dancing shoes that used to be white but were now pale blue." The game kindles the girls' interest, as well as that of the reader, who can not fail to notice, as the girls do, that their entire look is transformed by the shoes: "We have legs. Skinny and spotted with satin scars where scabs were picked, but legs, all our own, good to look at, and long." The intensity of the story escalates as the girls, with shoes on, leave the house and test out their newly discovered look on a walk down to the corner, "where the men can't take their eyes of us. We must be Christmas." The story has turned a corner too, where innocence is confronted by one man in particular, a "bum man," who tries to lure one of the girls away from her friends. One of the girlfriends, Rachel, engages the bum man in a conversation that the narrator and her other girlfriends immediately distrust. While Rachel is enthralled—"She is young and dizzy to hear so many sweet things in one day, even if it is a bum man's whiskey words"—the narrator and her other girlfriends are instinctively wary. "But we don't like it. We got to go, Lucy says." They take Rachel's hand and run "fast and far away," deciding to take off the false "magic" of the shoes, which are eventually thrown away. "But no one complains." The high-heels are a spurious "all that glitters" gendered ethic that is ultimately rejected by the girlfriends, who decide that "[they] are tired of being beautiful."

Cisneros's *Woman Hollering Creek* is a continuation of the vignette motif with added spice and complexity. There are girlchildren here, as in the story "Eleven," but the voice of a more mature narrator begins to be heard in stories like "Woman Hollering Creek." Cisneros weaves her way through a tapestry of characters and lifestyles that sometimes jar but always move.

Like *The House on Mango Street,* "Eleven" takes us into a child's standpoint as the young narrator recounts an incident on her eleventh birthday. This is a particularly distressing birthday because the girl is humiliated by her teacher in front of her classmates. The chilling moment of humiliation centers around a red sweater that the teacher literally forces the little girl to put on despite the child's obvious discomfort. At this same moment the girl of eleven realizes that you carry with you all the years that you have lived inside yourself. In this way, she squeezes a tiny three-year-old out of her eyes, in the face of this harrowing moment in time, as a way of coping with a moment not soon to be forgotten. Cisneros is piquant and tragic in this tale of childhood tragedy that smacks of remembered pain as well as spontaneously lived experience.

In the title story, "Woman Hollering Creek," Cisneros invites the reader into the nightmare world of spouse abuse endured by a young Mexican bride who has come north to live with her husband across the border in Texas. Cleófilas's view of gender relations comes to her from watching the *telenovelas,* or soap operas, where all of life—and certainly all of a woman's life—is centered around giving, nurturing, and loving without counting the cost. But there is a cost in her real life drama: her own physical and psychological health, as Juan Pedro, her new husband, proceeds to beat her and go out with his friends for a rendezvous with the bottle. Cleófilas attempts to rationalize her existence, to remove any possible dissonance that might threaten hearth and home—"She has to remind herself why she loves him," writes Cisneros. Yet her existence becomes increasingly unbearable as the *telenovela* of her life gets "sadder and sadder."

Remembering the words of her father—"I will never abandon you"—the young bride enlists the help of Felice, a woman from town, who is appalled at Cleófilas's circumstances and wants to help her return to her family in Mexico. Felice is a marvel to Cleófilas: "when Cleófilas asked if [the pickup] was her husband's, she said she didn't have a husband. The pickup was hers. She herself had chosen it. She herself was paying for it." Together the two women ride over *la gritona*—the "woman hollering creek"—where Felice lets out a yell "as loud as any mariachi." Felice confides that she always hollers when she crosses the creek because it is the only thing named after a woman, "[u]nless she's a Virgin." Both Felice and the creek become a fresh way of understanding freedom, as a "long ribbon of laughter" emerges from Cleófilas's own throat.

My Wicked, Wicked Ways is a collection of verse that Cisneros introduces with poems reminiscent of the girlchild, Esperanza, but through the voice of the mature poet, whose growth is tied to family as in the works "Six Brothers" and "The Poet Reflects on Her Solitary Fate." Still further on in the volume, the poet stretches her arms to encompass far lands, and loves are met and lost in both sensual and sad poems like "Postcard to the Lace Man—the Old Market, Antibes," "One Last Poem for Richard," and "14 de Julio." The narrator of these works is fearful and shy, as well as powerful and commanding. She is a girl/woman of many shades and textures, light and dark, "good" and "bad." The lines are blurred as Cisneros, like Gloria Anzaldúa before her, debunks the dichotomous thinking so characteristic of the modern era.

In "Six Brothers," Cisneros's narrator is keeping time to the Grimm's fairy tale "The Six Swans," as a girl takes a vow of silence to save her brothers. The narrator insists that the family "likes to keep silence," although muted uncles and cousins keep making appearances nonetheless. The father has a "master plan" for his children—all tidy and smartly pressed—because "[a]ppearances are everything." The mold, the way things should be, is somehow hard for the narrator. Unlike the rest of her family, her voice is not so silent, "I've got the bad blood in me I think, the mad uncle, the bit of the bullet." Her brothers, she insists, are angelic, swanlike, and cloud travelers, while she is "earthbound," decidedly down-to-earth, and finding it hard to "keep the good name clean."

"The Poet Reflects on Her Solitary Fate" is a poem about the paradox of loneliness and growth. Like Anzaldúa's poet-self in *Borderlands/La Frontera: The New Mestiza*, Cisneros's narrator finds herself alone out of her own ultimate need to create. Abandonment works two ways, as she leaves others alone and they, in turn, leave her "to her own device." Loneliness is brooding and sometimes resentful of "the stray lovers" who "have gone home" away from the cold house. Not even the TV offers a reprieve. Yet this is only a temporarily gloomy state, a false self-pity, for what emerges is the creative soul, the poet, "She must write poems." Poetry—both painful and miraculous—emerges from a lonely and sometimes isolated self who is, at the same time, truly her core being, a woman who is well worth knowing for her own sake.

The tea is Persian, the photos are from Tangiers, and the eyes are Catalán at the Museé Picasso in "Postcard to the Lace Man—the Old Market, Antibes." The feel of the poem is exotic and quixotic as the narrator rejects the allure of a married man. "One Last Poem for Richard" is a wave goodbye at the door to a long-time lover. The narrator is alone on Christmas Eve, drinking and remembering the relationship just past, the relationship that didn't work, though "sometimes there were good times." On this night symbolic of family and togetherness, the bitterness is clear—"[t]here should be stars for great wars like ours ... all the years of degradation"—but just palatable enough to accept and regret the end of two dreams—"I'm willing to admit a part of me ... loves still."

In "14 de Julio" the words of the poem evoke a deep empathy for the narrator. Essentially, the action of the poem is a kiss between "a man and a woman in the rain." But something more, it is the narrator's idiosyncratic view of the kiss through the less than happy lens of her own life. It is not just a man who wants to kiss a woman but a man who wants to kiss a woman even though it is Friday, even though Church and State might oppose it, even though the taxi-cabs pass by, and even though the tourists might stare. This simple act is a "miracle" in the eyes of the narrator who is "envious of that simply affirmation." She has, sadly, lived in the shadow of a "half-dark" and secret relationship, taking and giving "timidly ... you who never admitted a public grace."

Through both her vignettes of childhood and her verse, Cisneros informs our view of women of color in a postmodern age. Her works bring to sharp, poignant relief those who are living the traditional world of *familia* and *cultura,* juggling memories of shame and prejudice, eventually living, breathing, and learning to grow amid struggles to become true to their inner self and honest with their all-knowing soul.

—Theresa A. Martinez

CIXOUS, Hélène

Nationality: French. **Born:** Oran, Algeria, 5 June 1937. **Education:** Received Agrégation in English 1959; Doctorat d'état in English literature 1968. **Family:** Married in 1955 (divorced 1964); one daughter and one son. **Career:** Assistante, University of Bordeaux, 1962-65; maître assistante, the Sorbonne, Paris, 1965-67; maître de conférence, University of Paris X, Nanterre, 1967-68; co-founder of experimental University of Paris VIII, Vincennes, 1968; since 1968 professor of English literature, and since 1974 founder and director of Centre de Recherches en Études Féminines, University of Paris VIII, Saint Denis. Founder, with Tzvetan Todorov and Gérard Genette, of the journal *Poétique,* 1968. Visiting professor and lecturer at Northwestern University, Cornell University, Irvine University (Wellek Library Lectures), Dartmouth College, New York University, State Universities of New York at Binghampton and Buffalo, University of Wisconsin at Madison (Hill Lectures), Yale University, Kings' College, Cambridge University, Oxford University (Amnesty International Lectures), and other colleges and universities in the United States, Great Britain, Canada, Germany, Austria, Denmark, The Netherlands, Norway, Greece and Spain, among others. Contributor to periodicals, including *Boundary, L'Herne, Le Monde, New Literary History, Poétique,* and *Signs.* **Awards:** Prix Médicis, 1969, for *Dedans;* Southern Cross of Brazil, 1989; Légion d'Honneur, 1994;

Prix des Critiques for best theatrical work, 1994, for *La Ville parjure ou le réveil des Erinyes.* Doctor honoris causa: Queen's University, Kingston, Ontario, 1991; Edmonton University, Alberta, Canada, 1992; York University, England, 1993; Georgetown University, 1995; Northwestern University, 1996. **Member:** Conseil Scientifique, Fondation de France. **Address:** Université de Paris VIII, 2 rue de la Liberté, 93526 Saint Denis Cedex 02, France.

Selected Publications

Fiction

Le Prénom de Dieu. Paris, Grasset, 1967.
Dedans. Paris, Grasset, 1969, Des femmes, 1986; translated by Carol Barko as *Inside,* New York, Shocken, 1986.
Le Troisième Corps. Paris, Grasset, 1970.
Les Commencements. Paris, Grasset, 1970.
Un vrai jardin. Paris, l'Herne, 1971.
Neutre. Paris, Grasset, 1972; translated by Lorene M. Birden as "Making English Clairielle: An Introduction and Translation for Hélène Cixous' 'Neutre,'" Amherst, University of Massachusetts Press, 1988.
Tombe. Paris, Seuil, 1973.
Portrait du soleil. Paris, Denoël, 1974.
Révolutions pour plus d'un Faust. Paris, Seuil, 1975.
Souffles. Paris, Des femmes, 1975.
La. Paris, Gallimard, 1976, Des femmes, 1979.
Partie. Paris, Des femmes, 1976.
Angst. Paris, Des femmes, 1977; translated by Jo Levy, London, Calder, and New York, Riverrun Press, 1985.
Préparatifs de noces au delà de l'abîme. Paris, Des femmes, 1978.
Vivre l'orange: To Live the Orange (bilingual; English translation by Ann Liddle and Sarah Cornell). Paris, Des femmes, 1979.
Anankè. Paris, Des femmes, 1979.
Illa. Paris, Des femmes, 1980.
With; ou L'Art de l'innocence. Paris, Des femmes, 1981.
Limonade tout était si infini. Paris, Des femmes, 1982.
Le Livre de Promethea. Paris, Gallimard, 1983; translated by Betsy Wing as *The Book of Promethea,* Lincoln, University of Nebraska Press, 1991.
La Bataille d'Arcachon. Laval, Québec, Editions Trois, 1986.
Manne aux Mandelstams aux Mandelas. Paris, Des femmes, 1988; translated by Catherine A.F. MacGillivray as *Manna: For the Mandelstams for the Mandelas,* Minneapolis, University of Minnesota Press, 1993.
Jours de l'an. Paris, Des femmes, 1990; translated by Catherine MacGillivray as *First Days of the Year,* Minneapolis, University of Minnesota, 1996.
L'Ange au secret. Paris, Des femmes, 1991.
Déluge. Paris, Des femmes, 1992.
Beethoven à jamais ou l'existence de Dieu. Paris, Des femmes, 1993.
La Fiancée juive ou de la tentation. Paris, Des femmes, 1995.
Messie. Paris, Des femmes, 1996.

Plays

La Pupille. Paris, Cahiers Renault-Barrault, Gallimard, 1971.
Portrait de Dora (produced Paris, 1976). Paris, Des femmes, 1976; translated by Anita Barros as *The Portrait of Dora* in *Benmussa Directs,* London, Calder, and Dallas, Riverrun Press, 1979; translated by Sarah Burd in *Diacritics* (Baltimore), spring, 1983.
Le Nom d'Oedipe, Chant du corps interdit (libretto; produced Avignon, 1978), music by André Boucourechliev. Paris, Des femmes, 1978; translated by Christiane Makward and Judith Miller as *The Name of Oedipus* in *Out of Bounds: Women's Theater in French,* Ann Arbor, University of Michigan Press, 1991.
La Prise de l'école de Madhubaï (produced Paris, 1983). Paris, Avant-Scène, 1984; translated by Deborah Carpenter as *The Conquest of the School at Madhubaï* in *Women and Performance,* 3, 1986.
L'Histoire terrible mais inachevée de Norodom Sihanouk, roi du Cambodge (produced Paris, 1985). Paris, Editions du Théâtre du Soleil, 1985; translated by Juliet Flower MacCannell, Judith Pike, and Lollie Groth as *The Terrible but Unfinished Story of Norodom Sihanouk, King of Cambodia,* Lincoln and London, University of Nebraska Press, 1994.
Théâtre (collection). Paris, Des femmes, 1986.
L'Indiade ou L'Inde de leurs rêves (produced Paris, 1987). Paris, Editions du Théâtre du Soleil, 1987.
On ne part pas, on ne revient pas. Paris, Des femmes, 1991.
Translator, *Les Euménides d'Eschyle* (produced Paris, 1992). Paris, Editions du Théâtre du Soleil, 1992.
L'Histoire (qu'on ne connaîtra jamais) (produced Paris, 1994). Paris, Des femmes, 1994.
La Ville parjure ou le réveil des Erinyes (produced Paris, 1994). Paris, Editions du Théâtre du Soleil, 1994.
Voile Noire Voile Blanche/Black Sail White Sail (bilingual; English translation by Catherine A.F. MacGillivray; produced London, 1994), in *New Literary History* (Minneapolis) 25(2), 1994.

Television Play: *La Nuit miraculeuse,* with Ariane Mnouchkine, 1989.

Radio Play: *Amour d'une délicatesse,* 1982.

Literary Criticism

L'heure de Clarice Lispector. Paris, Des Femmes, 1989; translated by Verena Andermatt Conley as *Reading with Clarice Lispector,* Minneapolis, University of Minnesota Press, and London, Harvester, 1990.
Readings: The Poetics of Blanchot, Joyce, Kafka, Kleist, Lispector, and Tsvetayeva, edited and translated by Verana Andermatt Conley. Minneapolis, University of Minnesota Press, 1991; London, Harvester, 1992.
Three Steps on the Ladder of Writing (lectures), translated by Sarah Cornell and Susan Sellers. New York and Chichester, Columbia University Press, 1993.

Essays

L'Exil de James Joyce ou L'Art du remplacement (doctoral thesis). Paris, Grasset, 1968; translated by Sally A.J. Purcell and David Lewis as *The Exile of James Joyce,* New York, Lewis, 1972; London, Calder, 1976.
Prénoms de personne. Paris, Seuil, 1974.
Un K incompréhensible : Pierre Goldman. Paris, Christian Bourgois, 1975.
La Jeune Née, with Catherine Clément. Paris, Union Générale d'Editions, 1975; translated by Betsy Wing as *The Newly Born*

Woman, with introduction by Sandra M. Gilbert, Minneapolis, University of Minnesota Press, and Manchester, Manchester University Press, 1986.

La Venue à l'écriture, with Madeleine Gagnon and Annie Leclerc. Paris, Union Générale d'Editions, 1977.

"Le Rire de la méduse." in *L'Arc* (Paris), 1975; translated by Keith and Paula Cohen as "The Laugh of the Medusa," in *New French Feminisms: An Anthology* edited by Elaine Marks and Isabelle de Courtivron. Amherst, University of Massachusetts Press, 1980.

"Poésie, e(s)t Politique?" in *des femmes en mouvements hebdo,* 4, November 1979; translated as "Poetry Is/and the Political" in *Bread and Roses,* 2-1, 1980,

Entre l'écriture. Paris, Des femmes, 1986.

"De la Scène de l'inconscient à la scène de l'histoire," in *Hélène Cixous, Chemins d'une écriture,* edited by Françoise Van Rossum-Guyon and Myriam Diaz-Diocaretz. Paris, PUV/ Rodopi, 1988; translated by Deborah Carpenter as "From the Scene of the Unconscious to the Scene of History," in *The Future of Literary History,* edited by Ralph Cohen, New York and London, Routledge, 1988.

"Incarnation," in *Qui Parle,* (Berkeley), 3(1), 1989.

Coming to Writing and Other Essays, edited by Deborah Jenson, translated by Sarah Cornell, Deborah Jenson, Ann Liddle, and Susan Sellers. Cambridge, Massachusetts, and London, Harvard University Press, 1991.

Hélène Cixous, Photos de racines, with Mireille Calle-Gruber. Paris, Des femmes, 1994; translated by Eric Prenowitz as *Hélène Cixous, Rootprints,* London and New York, Routledge, 1996.

Other

The Hélène Cixous Reader edited and translated by Susan Sellers, foreword by Jacques Derrida. London and New York, Routledge, 1994.

*

Bibliography: *French Feminist Theory: Luce Irigaray and Hélène Cixous: A Bibliography* by Joan Nordquist, Santa Cruz, Reference & Research Services, 1990.

Critical Studies: *New French Feminisms: An Anthology* edited by Elaine Marks and Isabelle de Courtivron, Amherst, University of Massachusetts Press, 1980; "Writing and Body: Toward an Understanding of L'écriture féminine" by Ann Rosalind Jones, in *French Studies* (Oxford), summer 1981; "Introduction to Hélène Cixous's 'Castration or Decapitation?'" by Annette Kuhn, in *Signs* (Durham, North Carolina), autumn 1981; "Amazons and Mothers? Monique Wittig, Hélène Cixous and Theories of Women's Writing" by Diane Griffin Crowder, in *Contemporary Literature* (Madison, Wisconsin), summer 1983; *Writing the Feminine* by Verena Andermatt Conley, Lincoln, University of Nebraska Press, 1984, expanded, 1991; "I Want Vulva! Cixous and the Poetics of the Body" by Vivian Kogan, in *Esprit Créateur* (Baton Rouge, Louisiana), summer 1985; *French Feminist Criticism: Women, Language, and Literature* edited by Elissa Gelfland and Virginia Hules, New York, Garland, 1985; "Cixous: An Imaginary Utopia" by Toril Moi, in her *Sexual/Textual Politics: Feminist Literary Theory,* London, Methuen, 1985; "Difference on Trial: A Critique of the Maternal Metaphor in Cixous, Irigaray, and Kristeva" by Dommna C. Stanton, in *The Poetics of Gender,* edited by Nancy K. Miller and Carolyn G. Heilbrun, New York, Columbia University Press, 1986; *Writing Differences: Readings from the Seminar of Hélène Cixous* edited by Susan Sellers, Milton Keynes, Open University Press, and New York, St. Martin's Press, 1988; "The Mystic Aspect of *l'écriture féminine:* Hélène Cixous' *Vivre l'Orange*" by Anu Aneja, in *Qui Parle* (Berkeley, California), spring 1989; "In Search of a Feminist Theatre: Portrait of Dora" by Jeannette Laillou Savona, in *Feminist Focus: The New Women Playwrights,* Oxford, Oxford University Press, 1989; *The Body and the Text: Hélène Cixous, Reading and Teaching* edited by Helen Wilcox and others, New York, St. Martin's Press, 1990; *Hélène Cixous: A Politics of Writing* by Morag Shiach, London, Routledge, 1991; *Hélène Cixous* by Verena Andermatt Conley, Toronto, University of Toronto Press, 1992; *Transfigurations: Theology and the French Feminists* by C.W. Maggie Kim, Susan M. St. Ville, and Susan M. Simonaitis, Minneapolis, Fortress Press, 1993.

* * *

Hélène Cixous has published nearly 40 major fictional and theatrical texts, as well as a myriad of shorter fictional pieces, university lectures, and theoretical essays interweaving philosophy and literary criticism. Praised and admired, controversial and sometimes misunderstood, Cixous has often thrown critics off balance by the diversity and extent of her work, which is impossible to classify within the limited confines of canonical academic categories. In the words of noted philosopher Jacques Derrida, "Cixous is, in my view, the greatest writer in what I will call my language, the French language if you like. And I am weighing my words as I say this. For a great writer must be a poet-thinker, very much a poet and a very thinking poet."

Born in Oran, Algeria, in 1937, Cixous's mother's family was of Ashkenazic Germanic and Austro-Czechoslovakian descent while her father's was of Sephardic Spanish origin. Early on, she developed a musical poetic ear for language, growing up in a polyglot environment with German and French spoken at home and Arabic and Spanish spoken in the streets. "We must remember that [Cixous], this great-French-Jewish-woman-writer-from-Sephardic-Algeria, who reinvents, among others, her father's language, *her (his)* French language, an unheard-of French language, is *also* a German-Ashkenazic-Jewish-woman-writer through her 'mother tongue,'" explains Derrida in his *Le Monolinguisime de l'autre.*

The crossroads of her family background and the historico-political upheavals that took place during her childhood have remained as determinant engendering factors in Cixous's writing and thought. From her earliest years in Algeria, Cixous lived the violent consequences of racism, repression, and exclusion as both a woman and as a Jew. Her mother fled the rise of Nazism in Germany in 1933. Subsequently, the anti-Semitic laws of the French colonial Vichy government banned her father from his medical practice in Algeria during World War II.

Enclosed within an Algerian society marked by overt sexism and dominated by French colonialism, Cixous was immersed in the turbulences of a multi-faceted system of racism: oppression of Arabic Algerians by the French, anti-Semitism, racism mirrored between formerly Algerian Jews (now so-called "French" Jews) and the Arabic Algerians. Her father, a doctor, and her mother, a mid-wife, worked amongst the most impoverished members of the Algerian population. However, there was no place for allies from the "outside" in the anti-colonialist logic that came to dominate Algerian society in the necessary struggle for independence. The Cixous family could not avoid being associated with the French colonists.

Leaving Algeria in 1955, Cixous arrived in France where she sought a non-national identification in the homeland of literature and writing. Ever since, the relationship between the political and the poetical has been essential to Cixous's approach to writing, which she sees as a necessarily liberational practice. She writes in "Poetry Is/and the Political":

> What about poems in these times of repression? What does a certain relationship to life and death mean for us? Us: women "struggling" in writing, research or the movement? For example: what did poetry and music mean in the Warsaw ghetto? In Auschwitz, how could one think? Up to what point can one remain human? Starting from what moment does one absolutely lose poetry? (literary genre)? Why poems in these times of repression? Songs, when women are silenced?

The question of the use or the need for poetry (to be understood in a broad sense) is seen here in relation to the issue of repression, in particular the marginalization and silencing of women in society, and this leads to a consideration of extreme situations, near the edge of life and death, situations in which one might think poetry would have little importance. On the contrary, poetic writing in a Cixousian sense constitutes a symbolic space of great power, a vital necessity in the forging of human destinies.

In the 1960s, Cixous was a university scholar; she was noted in particular for her study of Joyce's works in her doctoral thesis: *The Exile of James Joyce or the Art of Replacement.* In 1969 she was awarded the prestigious Prix Médicis for her first extended fictional text, *Dedans.*

In English-speaking countries, Cixous's early feminist positions have often overshadowed the importance of her inventive poetical writing which, due to its intensely playful use of language, is extremely difficult to translate. In 1975 with the publication of "The Laugh of the Medusa" and "The Newly Born Woman," Cixous introduced the pioneering notion of "feminine writing." These two essays, situated in the historical context of the women's movement in the 1970s, represented a conscious effort to make a militant and pedagogical gesture. However, as she wrote in *The Newly Born Woman,* she did not envision "feminine writing" as a simple theoretical concept:

> At the present time, *defining* a feminine practice of writing is impossible with an impossibility that will continue; for this practice will never be able to be *theorized*, enclosed, coded, which does not mean it does not exist. But it will always exceed the discourse governing the phallocentric system... But one can begin to speak. Begin to point out some effects, some elements of unconscious drives, some relations of the feminine Imaginary to the Real, to writing.

Far from being a sort of biological essentialism, the theoretical use of the term "feminine" stems in large part from Freud's study of the child's originary bisexual potential and of libidinal economy, which is the economy of desire and of sexual life. Drawing thus on Freud but going beyond his theoretical systematization and rejecting in particular his approach to feminine sexuality, Cixous elaborated the idea of two decipherable libidinal economies: "feminine" and "masculine" are not fixed essences, but rather the terms of a constant play of sexual difference. They are not related in a rigid way to social roles or cultural connotations, nor do they refer to human anatomy. However the translated traces of these libidinal economies, passing through the unconscious, the body and sexual pleasure can find their inscription in the poetic text. In the deconstructionist sense of her thought, Cixous speaks affirmatively of sexual difference without implying any hierarchical or binary opposition between the sexes.

As part of the same political strategy, Cixous created the Centre de Recherches en Études Féminines at the University of Paris VIII in 1974. Based on innovative interdisciplinary research, the center offers the only doctoral program in Women's Studies in France. In an overtly misogynous move, the right-wing French government eliminated the doctoral program in 1980; however the newly elected Socialists reinstated it in 1981. In 1995 and 1996 the right-wing Education Ministry aggressively threatened once again to shut down the program. After a fierce ideological battle, the ministerial authorities backed down in the face of a massive international campaign supporting the Center.

Cixous's seminar at the Center is entitled "The Poetics of Sexual Difference" and takes place at the Collège International de Philosophie in Paris. The syllabus includes a far-ranging scope of literary, philosophical, and psychoanalytical texts: Clarice Lispector, Ingeborg Bachmannn, Paul Celan, Tsvetaeva, Akhmatova, Mandelstam, Kafka, Rilke, Hesse, Shakespeare, Genet, Dostoevsky, Stendhal, Balzac, Proust, Freud, Mélanie Klein, Derrida, and Heideigger are among many other authors of diverse languages and cultures who are included. Examining with great care and precision this broad spectrum of texts, she focuses on strong examples of "feminine writing," writing combining philosophical rigor with a generous, overflowing quality that is neither calculating nor entirely calculable. "Some years ago, at the height of the feminist campaigns, a number of women came to the seminar who asked me why there were texts on the annual program by men," Cixous explained in *Writing Differences.* "These women had been expecting an exclusively 'feminist' program with texts only by women. There has never been in the seminar opposition to or exclusion of one genre by another, one sex by the other. We work on the mystery of human being, including the fact that humans are sexed beings, that there is sexual difference, and that these differences manifest themselves, write themselves in texts."

In the French feminist movement during the mid-1900s, Cixous became a political ally of Antoinette Fouque, leader of the group Psych et Po/MLF. Linked to her militant activity and her politico-analytical thought in the women's movement, Fouque founded the Des femmes publishing house in 1974. Since then, in a marked political choice of solidarity, Cixous has published nearly 30 books with Des femmes.

Over the years, Cixous has increasingly written for the theater, although she has not abandoned poetic fiction. Certain theatrical texts incorporate important contemporary women figures such as her feminist re-reading of Freud's well-known case study, "Dora: An Analysis of a Case of Hysteria" (*Portrait of Dora,* 1976); or the staging of the story of Phoolan Devi, the rebellious Indian outlaw who has since become an important political leader (*The Conquest of the School at Madhubaï,* 1984); or the Russian poetess, Anna Akhmatova, victim of Stalinist repression (*Black Sail White Sail,* 1994).

However, her theatrical work began to take truly epic and legendary dimensions when she began to write for Ariane Mnouchkine's renowned Théâtre du Soleil, creating three major historical plays set in the 20th century: *The Terrible but Unfinished Story of Norodom Sihanouk, King of Cambodia* (1985), *The Indiad or the India of Their Dreams* (1987), and *La Ville parjure ou le réveil des Erinyes* (1994). Cixous has also worked with Daniel Mesguich, a theater director who has an exceptional ear for the poetry of her writing, with *On ne part pas, on ne revient pas* (1991) and *L'Histoire (qu'on ne connaîtra jamais)* (1994).

While the strong voices in her fiction have always been women's voices, Cixous has created important male characters in her theater, much to the surprise of certain American feminists. "I have never dared create a real male character in fictional texts," she explains of her fictional and theatrical writing in "Incarnation":

> Why? Because I write with my body, and I'm a woman and a man is a man and I know nothing of his pleasure. And a man without a body and without pleasure, I can't do that. And men in the theater then?
>
> The theater is not the scene of sexual pleasure. Romeo and Juliet love each other but they don't make love. They sing it. At the theater it's the heart that sings, the chest opens, and we see the heart rend itself. The human heart has no sex. The heart feels the same way in a man's chest as in a woman's chest.

The unique intertextuality of her fiction and theater takes root in the treasures of world literature, ranging from mythological and biblical sources, Germanic and Sumerian epics, to Shakespeare, Clarice Lispector and the numerous authors that figure in her seminar readings. For this reason, some familiarity with the scholarly references that circulate in her texts is no doubt indispensable for the reader. Yet this aspect of Cixous's writing, rather than being an end in itself, is best understood as part of the organic adventure her texts embark upon, and in which the infinite richness of language serves as a privileged means of transport. As Derrida writes in his introduction to *The Hélène Cixous Reader,* "Hélène has a genius for making the language speak, down to the most familiar idiom, the place where it seems to be crawling with secrets which give way to thought. She knows how to make it say what it keeps in reserve, which in the process also makes it come out of its reserve."

While the "great" themes of humanity (love, hope, belief, death and life ...) are always on the horizon, Cixous's writing often involves an intense focus on the smallest phenomenological details of the world and subjective experience. The meticulous and unrelenting attention she pays to language, the body, and the subjective world has at times been interpreted superficially as condoning an egocentric escape from political and social responsibility. However the very experience of subjectivity—the fact that one's life and one's death cannot be shared with or communicated to anyone else—is indeed the fundamental experience shared universally by all human beings. In this way, Cixous's absolute faithfulness to the lived world, her "scientific" investigation of reality as a physical *and* poetic reality, in which the smallest particular can catapult us into a universal plane, not only destabilizes the rigid hierarchies that limit our thinking, but offers exciting and vital new perspectives in a landscape that is as old as the earth.

—Sarah Cornell and Eric Prenowitz

CLAY, Rosamund. *See* **OAKLEY, Ann (Rosamund).**

CLIFF, Michelle

Nationality: American. **Born:** Kingston, Jamaica, 2 November 1946; immigrated to the United States in 1949. **Education:** Wagner College, A.B. 1969; Warburg Institute, London, M.Phil. 1974. **Career:** Journalist and researcher, New York, 1969; production supervisor, then manuscript and production editor, "Library" series, W.W. Norton, New York, 1970-80; copublisher and editor, *Sinister Wisdom,* Amherst, Massachusetts, 1981-83; teacher of creative writing and history, Martin Luther King Jr. Public Library, Oakland, California, beginning 1984; visiting writer, 1990, Allan K. Smith Visiting Writer, 1992, Allan K. Smith Professor of English Language and Literature, beginning 1993, Trinity College, Hartford, Connecticut. Instructor at numerous institutions, including Hampshire College, New School for Social Research, Norwich University, Trinity College, University of California at Santa Cruz, University of Massachusetts at Amherst, and Vista College. Visiting lecturer, Stanford University, 1987. Contributor to periodicals, including *Chrysalis, Conditions, Feminary, Feminist Review, Heresies, Ms., Sojourner,* and *Voice Literary Supplement.* **Awards:** MacDowell Colony fellowship, 1982; National Endowment for the Arts fellowship, 1982, 1989; Massachusetts Artists Foundation fellowship and Yaddo Writers Colony fellowship, both 1984; New Zealand Fulbright fellow, 1988. **Address:** Department of English, Trinity College, 300 Summit Street, Hartford, Connecticut 06106-3100, U.S.A.

Publications

Novels

Abeng. Trumansburg, New York, Crossing Press, 1984.

No Telephone to Heaven. New York, Dutton, 1987; London, Methuen, 1988.

Free Enterprise. New York, Dutton, 1993; London, Viking, 1994.

Short Stories

Bodies of Water. New York, Dutton, and London, Methuen, 1990.

Poetry

Claiming an Identity They Taught Me to Despise. Watertown, Massachusetts, Persephone Press, 1980.

The Land of Look Behind: Prose and Poetry. Ithaca, New York, Firebrand Books, 1985.

Other

Editor, *The Winner Names the Age: A Collection of Writings by Lillian Smith.* New York, Norton, 1978.

*

Critical Studies: "Resisting Cultural Cannibalism: Oppositional Narratives in Michelle Cliff's *No Telephone to Heaven*" by Fiona R. Barnes, in *Journal of the Midwestern Modern Language Association,* 25, spring 1992; "Of Mangoes and Maroons: Language, History, and the Multicultural Subject of Michelle Cliff's *Abeng*" by Françoise Lionnet, and "Unspeakable Differences: The Politics of Gender in Lesbian and Heterosexual Women's Autobiographies" by Julia Watson, both in *De/Colonizing the Subject: The Politics of Gender in Women's Autobiography,* edited by Sidonie Smith, Minneapolis, University of Minnesota Press, 1992; "Race, Privilege, and the Politics of (Re)Writing History: An Analysis of the Novels of Michelle Cliff" by Belinda Edmondson, in *Callaloo,* 16, winter 1993; "The Art of History: An Interview with Michelle Cliff" by Judith Raiskin, in *Kenyon Review,* 15, 1993; "An Interview with Michelle Cliff" by Meryl F. Schwarz, in *Contemporary Literature,* 34, winter 1993; "Journey into Speech—A Writer between Two Worlds: An Interview with Michelle Cliff" by Opal Palmer Adisa, in *African American Review,* 28(2), 1994; "After *The Tempest:* Shakespeare, Postcoloniality, and Michelle Cliff's New, New Miranda" by Thomas Cartelli, in *Contemporary Literature,* 36, spring 1995.

* * *

"I consider myself a feminist in the way I chose to define feminism," says Michelle Cliff. "That is, a world view which focuses on the experiences of women. It doesn't mean excluding men. I have real problems with that idea. Feminism should be inclusive, not exclusive. It should concern itself with the liberation of all people." The possibilities of an inclusive feminism—a feminism that addresses issues of race, class, and sexual preference, as well as gender—is one that Cliff explores in her works. Born in Jamaica and educated in the United States and England, Cliff received her doctorate in Italian Renaissance studies from the Warburg Institute in London. Her three novels all address issues of racism and sexism in different countries at different times, moving among the United States, Jamaica, and England, and back and forth through history. Cliff's own background as a mixed-race, light-skinned, middle-class woman of Jamaican heritage is a starting place for some of her writing. She considers herself a "political novelist," rather than a Caribbean writer, and she finds that she cannot limit her writing to "just one place," but also needs to claim a multicultural identity. She not only writes about women's resistances to oppression and the ways that women have fought to overcome patriarchy, but she also explores the intersections of oppression, the ways in which color, class, and sexuality affect women's experiences of discrimination. Cliff's writing reveals the connections between types of oppressions across national boundaries and foregrounds the complexities of colonization.

Cliff wanted to write from a young age, but it was "almost taboo to be a writer." After reading *The Diary of Anne Frank* when she was 13 years old, she was inspired to keep her own diary, recounting her school experiences, her first menstruation, and a crush she had on another girl. Her parents broke into her bedroom, found her diary and read it. They then read the diary out loud in front of Cliff, her aunt, and her sister. This humiliating experience stopped Cliff's writing until she wrote her dissertation, and kept her from creative writing until she was in her 30s and active in the women's movement. Cliff would rework the memory of losing her diary in the title story from her collection, *Bodies of Water,* centering on a gay boy whose diary is discovered by his parents.

Cliff's writing depicts the contradictions of mixed-race experience; she attributes her style to the many aspects of her identity as a colonized, "not mainstream" writer. In two early works, "Claiming an Identity They Taught Me to Despise" and "If I Could Write This in Fire I Would Write This in Fire," she explores the implications of her identity as a colonized person and a light-skinned Jamaican. These pieces, written in a fragmented form, blur the boundaries between fiction, non-fiction, and poetry. This fragmented form permeates Cliff's novels as well and exemplifies a postmodern style: she finds that her position outside mainstream culture leads her to more experimental forms that don't rely on a linear style and allow her to "really mix the media." In "If I Could Write This In Fire I Would Write This In Fire," Cliff explores the importance of female friendship through her memories of her childhood friend Zoe, who was separated from Cliff by the effects of class and color. In writing about her own experiences, she never downplays complexity or oversimplifies power relations. "Because every little piece of reality exists in relation to another little piece," Cliff writes, "our situation was not that simple." The juxtaposition of fragments works to complicate the reader's notions of good and bad and right and wrong, revealing the interconnected nature of prejudice.

Cliff continues her postmodern style in her three novels and describes her first two novels, *Abeng* and *No Telephone to Heaven,* as "semiautobiographical." The heroine of both books, Clare Savage, is, like Cliff, a light-skinned Jamaican. Both novels chronicle Clare's attempts to reconcile her contradictory identities. According to Cliff, Clare Savage is named both for her color and her position: Clare is almost white; "savage" symbolizes the ideas held by the colonizers about the native peoples, and Cliff uses the word ironically. In both novels Clare searches for Jamaican history in order to understand her relationship to the past; understanding the past helps her to achieve wholeness. A particularly important aspect of *Abeng* is female friendship. Clare has a close relationship with a dark-skinned, poor girl named Zoe, who lives on Clare's grandmother's land. After Clare accidentally shoots her grandmother's bull, she is banished from her grandmother's house and her relationship with Zoe ends.

Clare's story continues in *No Telephone to Heaven,* a novel set in Jamaica during the late 1970s, a period of political and social unrest on the island. In addition to Clare, *No Telephone to Heaven* features Harry/Harriet, a homosexual, cross-dressing character. Cliff describes Harry/Harriet as the most heroic character in the novel, a character she created to address the issue of homophobia in Jamaica. As a political novelist, Cliff creates diverse characters to explore a variety of different social situations. Much of her work has included sexuality as a subtext.

In Cliff's most recent novel, *Free Enterprise,* she retells the life of Mary Ellen Pleasant, the woman who financed John Brown's attempted raid on Harper's Ferry prior to the Civil War. In telling stories about the people who were omitted from the official record, Cliff uses many forms, including letters, poetry, prose, and dialogue, and again stretches the boundaries of what is generally considered a novel. Her imaginative recovery of the past gives voice to the resistances that have been erased from history. Cliff wrote *Free Enterprise* to "correct received versions of history.... It seems to me that if one does not know that one's people have resisted, then it makes resistance difficult." Michelle Cliff continues to write important stories, stories that reveal the multifaceted nature of what any one culture may hold up as "history."

—Ann E. Green

COBBE, Frances Power

Nationality: Anglo-Irish. **Born:** Dublin, 4 December 1822. **Education:** Educated by governesses and at Brighton, 1836-38. **Career:** Italian correspondent for *London Daily News,* early 1860s; journalist for the *Echo,* 1868-75, and the *Standard,* 1875; with Mary Carpenter, aided in founding urban "ragged schools" and in workhouse reform, 1858-59; active in the antivivisection cause; cofounder, Victoria Street Society for the Protection of Animals from Vivisection, 1875; founder, British Union for the Abolition of Vivisection, 1898; campaigned for women's suffrage. Contributor to numerous periodicals, including *Fortnightly Review, Fraser's, Macmillan's,* and *Theological Review.* **Died:** 5 April 1904.

Publications

Political/Social Theory

Friendless Girls and How to Help Them: Being an Account of the Preventive Mission at Bristol. London, E. Faithfull, 1861.
The Sick in Workhouses. London, J. Nisbet, 1861.
Workhouse as an Hospital. London, E. Faithfull, 1861.
The Education of Women, and How It Would Be Affected by University Examinations. London, E. Faithfull, 1862.
The Red Flag in John Bull's Eyes. London, E. Faithfull, 1863.
Essays on the Pursuits of Women. London, E. Faithfull, 1863.
Rejoinder to Mrs Stowe's Reply to the Address of the Women of England (published anonymously). London, E. Faithfull, 1863.
Why Women Desire the Franchise. London, London National Society for Women's Suffrage, 1869.
Criminals, Idiots, Women, and Minors: Is the Classification Sound? A Discussion of the Laws concerning the Property of Married Women. Manchester, A. Ireland, 1869.
"The Final Cause of Women," in *Woman's Work and Woman's Culture,* edited by Josephine Butler. London, Macmillan, 1869.
Darwinism in Morals and Other Essays. London, Williams & Norgate, 1872; Boston, G. H. Ellis, 1883.
The Nine Circles; or, The Torture of the Innocent. Being Records of Vivisection, English and Foreign. London, Society for the Protection of Animals from Vivisection, 1873.
The Hopes of the Human Race, Hereafter and Here. London and Edinburgh, Williams & Norgate, 1874; New York, J. Miller, 1876.
The Moral Aspects of Vivisection. London and Edinburgh, Williams & Norgate, 1875; Philadelphia, n.p., 1876.
"Wife Torture," in *Contemporary Review,* 32, 1878.
The Duties of Women. A Course of Lectures. London and Edinburgh, Williams & Norgate, 1881; Boston, G. H. Ellis, 1882.
The Fallacy of Restriction Applied to Vivisection. London, Victoria Street Society, 1886.
Our Policy. An Address to Women concerning the Suffrage. London, London National Society for Women's Suffrage, 1888.
The Scientific Spirit of the Age and Other Pleas and Discussions. London, Smith Elder, 1888.
The Modern Rack. Papers on Vivisection. London, Swan Sonnenschein, 1889.

Religion/Spirituality

An Essay on Intuitive Morals, Being an Attempt to Popularize Ethical Science (published anonymously). London, Longmans, 1855-57; Boston, Crosby Nichols, 1859; 3rd edition revised as *The Theory of Intuitive Morals,* London, Sonnenschein, 1902.
Religious Duty. London, Trübner, 1864; Boston, G. H. Ellis, 1883.
Broken Lights: An Inquiry into the Present Condition & Future Prospects of Religious Faith. London, Trübner, and Boston, J.E. Tilton, 1864.
Dawning Lights: An Inquiry concerning the Secular Results of the New Reformation. London, E. T. Whitfield, 1868.
Alone to the Alone: Prayers for Theists by Several Contributors, with others. London, Williams & Norgate, 1871.
The Peak in Darien, with Some Other Inquiries Touching Concerns of the Soul and the Body. London, Williams & Norgate, 1882.
Rest in the Lord and Other Small Pieces. London, Pewtress, 1887.

Essays

Italics. Brief Notes on Politics, People, and Places in Italy in 1864. London, Trübner, 1864.
Hours of Work and Play (includes short fiction). London, Trübner, 1867.
False Beasts and True: Essays on Natural and Unnatural History. London, Ward Lock & Tyler, 1876.
Re-Echoes (originally appeared in the *Echo).* London, Williams & Norgate, 1876.

Autobiography

Life of Frances Power Cobbe. By Herself. London, R. Bentley & Son, and Boston and New York, Houghton Mifflin, 1894; revised, London, Sonnenschein, 1904.

Other

The Cities of the Past. London, Trübner, 1864.
Bernard's Martyrs. A Comment on Claude Bernard's 'Leçons de physiologie operatoire.' London, Society for the Protection of Animals from Vivisection, 1879.
A Charity and A Controversy. London, Victoria Street Society, 1889.
The Friend of Man; and His Friends—the Poets. London, G. Bell, 1889.
Somerville Hall, A Misnomer. A Correspondence with Notes. London, Victoria Street Society, 1891.

Editor, *The Collected Works of Theodore Parker.* London, n.p., 1863.

Editor, *Lessons from the World of Matter and the World of Man,* by Theodore Parker. London, n.p., 1865.

*

Manuscript Collections: British Library; British Library of Political and Economic Science; Bodleian Library, Oxford University; Fawcett Library, London Guildhall University; Huntington Library, San Marino, California; Pennsylvania Historical Society.

Critical Studies: *Antivivisection and Medical Science in Victorian England* by Richard French, New Jersey, Princeton University Press, 1975; *Women of Ideas and What Men Have Done to Them* by Dale Spender, London, Ark, 1983; "'A Husband Is a Beating Animal': Frances Power Cobbe Confronts the Wife Abuse Problem" by Lawrence Bauer and Carol Ritt, in *International Journal of Women's Studies,* 6(3), 1983, and their "Wife Abuse, Late-Victorian English Feminists, and the Legacy of Frances Power Cobbe," in *International Journal of Women's Studies,* 6(3), 1983; "Women and Anti-vivisection in Victorian England, 1870-1900" by Mary Ann Elston, in *Vivisection in Historical Perspective,* edited by Nicholaas Rupke, London, Croom Helm, 1987; *Victorian Feminists* by Barbara Caine, Oxford, Oxford University Press, 1992; "Vicegerent of God: The Public Crusades of Frances Power Cobbe, 1822-1904" (dissertation) by Lori Lynn Williamson, University of Toronto, 1994.

* * *

Frances Power Cobbe was one of England's most respected feminist theorists and activists; she was involved in everything from furthering women's education and employment opportunities to demanding female enfranchisement. While she preferred to support the 19th-century English women's movement independently rather than collaboratively, withdrawing from organized suffrage activity soon after the London National Society was founded in 1866, Cobbe produced some of the most witty, original, and powerful feminist treatises of her day. She condemned patriarchal society and supported the rights of women to lead productive, and if they chose, public lives, free from husbands and children.

Cobbe was born in Dublin on 4 December 1822, the fifth child and only daughter of Charles Cobbe and his wife, Frances Conway. Cobbe had a rather lonely but also privileged childhood as part of Ireland's landed Anglo-Irish community. She certainly had no financial wants, and in her autobiography she claimed that neither was she made to feel inferior to her brothers, even though her birth was "by no means welcome.... If I have become in mature years a 'Woman's Rights Woman' it has not been because in my own person I have been made to feel a Woman's Wrongs," she would come to write in her *Life of Frances Power Cobbe.*

Regardless of this claim, however, Cobbe was treated differently than her brothers. She was taught by governesses until she was sent to a boarding school in Brighton in 1836, where she proved, much to her father's dismay, to be a dismal failure in the feminine arts that she was taught. He tried, unsuccessfully, a number of times to propel her into Dublin society so that she could conform to the norm and marry.

Soon after her mother's death in the late 1840s, Cobbe rejected Evangelicalism in favor of Theism. She was banished to her brother's farm at Donegal; after ten months she was summoned home to look after her aging father, a task she accepted as one of her duties as an unmarried daughter.

When Charles Cobbe died in 1857, Frances cut her hair, symbolic perhaps of her liberation from patriarchal control, and travelled throughout Europe and the Middle East. Upon her return ten months later she was confronted with a rather common problem. Like other genteel women, Cobbe was not trained to do anything productive outside the domestic realm and essentially had no purpose in life other than to care for family members. Her father had left her £200 a year so she was not destitute. Nor was she forced to seek remunerative labor, although she would later supplement this allowance with journalistic activity, working as the Italian correspondent for the *Daily News* in the early 1860s and, from 1868 until 1875, writing leaders for the *Echo.* Cobbe also wrote for most of the major journals and published a number of books on a wide range of social and ethical subjects.

In 1858 Cobbe decided to launch a philanthropic career for herself. This began in Bristol with reformatory and Ragged School work which she pursued alongside Mary Carpenter, eventually moving on to workhouse visiting. This activity enabled Cobbe to see clearly the extent to which the state victimized the powerless, especially women, and she began to be drawn into the English women's movement.

She was outraged when, in 1862, a student named Elizabeth Garrett was denied permission to sit for the matriculation exam required to obtain her medical degree. Cobbe drafted a conservative argument defending a woman's right—as long as she was either single or a childless wife without family responsibilities—to an education and a useful and remunerative life. Cobbe argued that education would enhance rather than eradicate the differences between men and women, and it was the difference between the sexes, coupled with an individual's moral autonomy, that formed the basis of her feminism.

Cobbe's feminist consciousness developed further when she moved to South Kensington with her companion, the Welsh sculptor, Mary Lloyd, in 1864. She found herself surrounded by other women's rights activists such as Lydia Becker, Bessie Rayner Parkes, and Barbara Bodichon, and she was encouraged to think not only of educational opportunities, but political ones as well. In 1866 she signed the petition for women's suffrage that was presented to Parliament by John Stuart Mill. Just over two years later one of her best-known women's rights publications, *Criminals, Idiots, Women, and Minors: Is the Classification Sound?,* appeared. In this pamphlet Cobbe attacked the inequitable social and legal systems that reduced women—rational free agents created by God in His image—to the quasi-legal status of "Criminal, Idiot, Minor." She was particularly critical of marriage and the common law that victimized women, destroying their individuality and potential while consolidating male power in the private and public sphere.

Cobbe sat on the committee that formed in 1868 to secure property rights for wives and from the mid-1870s publicized cases of wife abuse; this latter activity was instrumental in passing the 1878 Matrimonial Causes Act. "The notion that a man's wife is his PROPERTY," Cobbe wrote in her essay "Wife Torture" the year the act was passes, "in the sense in which a horse is his property ... is the fatal root of incalculable evil and misery." Women were victimized because they were the legal and economic dependents of their spouses, and it was because of their dependence, Cobbe argued, that abuse would stop only if women were separated from violent men and provided with the economic support that would enable them to live independently. And until women received political power their interest would never be seriously considered in Parliament.

From 1875 until her death in 1904, Cobbe's women's rights activities took a back seat to her antivivisection work, yet she remained active in the woman's cause. A few days before her death in April she was asked to allow her name to be given to the Council of the National Union of Women Workers of Great Britain and Ireland as an honorary vice-president.

Frances Power Cobbe was a "different" feminist. She combined a radical demand for suffrage with a moderate view of woman as being the equivalent rather than the equal of man. Although she emphasized the differences between the sexes, and was convinced that women had particular duties associated with their sex, she was also adamant that they have equal access to the public sphere for it fell within their natures to purify and improve society. And because God had created women as morally autonomous individuals, they were as capable as men of deciding what was best for themselves, of living up to their potential, and of determining the direction their lives would take.

—Lori Williamson

COLETTE, (Sidonie-Gabrielle)

Also wrote as Colette Willy. **Other Pseudonym:** Willy. **Nationality:** French. **Born:** Saint-Sauveur-en-Puisaye, Burgundy, 28 January 1873. **Family:** Married 1) Henri Gauthier-Villars (Willy) in 1893 (separated 1906, divorced 1910); 2) Baron Henri de Jouvenel des Ursins in 1912 (divorced 1924), one daughter; 3) Maurice Goudeket in 1935. **Career:** Music hall dancer and mime, 1906-11; columnist, 1910-19, and literary critic, 1919-24, *Le Matin*, Paris; drama critic, *La Revue de Paris*, 1929, *Le Journal*, 1934-39, *L'Eclair, L'Petit Parisien*, and *Le Film;* operated a beauty clinic, Paris, 1932-33. **Awards:** Légion d'Honneur chevalier, 1920, officer, 1928, commandeur, 1936, grand officer, 1953; Académie Royale de Langue et de Littérature Françaises de Belgique, 1935, Anna de Noailles chair, c. 1936; Médaille d'Or de la Ville de Paris, 1953; elected to Académie Goncourt (first female member; president, 1949), 1945; received state funeral, France's highest posthumous honor. **Died:** Paris, 3 August 1954.

Publications

Novels

Claudine à l'école (as Willy). Paris, Ollendorff, 1900; translated as *Claudine at School*, London, Gollancz, 1930; New York, A. & C. Boni, 1930.

Claudine à Paris (as Willy). Paris, Ollendorff, 1901; translated as *Claudine in Paris*, London, Gollancz, 1931; translated as *Young Lady of Paris*, New York, A. & C. Boni, 1931.

Claudine en ménage (as Willy). Paris, Mercure de France, 1902; as *Claudine amoureuse*, Paris, Ollendorff, 1902; translated as *The Indulgent Husband*, New York, Farrar & Rinehart, 1935.

Claudine s'en va: Journal d'Annie (as Willy). Paris, Ollendorff, 1903; translated as *The Innocent Wife*, New York, Farrar & Rinehart, 1935; translated as *Claudine and Annie*, London, Secker & Warburg, 1962.

Minne; Les Egarements de Minne (as Willy). Paris, Ollendorff, 2 vols., 1904-5; as *L'Ingénue libertine* (as Colette Willy). Paris, Ollendorff, 1909; translated as *The Gentle Libertine*, New York, Farrar & Rinehart, and London, Gollancz, 1931.

Le Retraite sentimentale (as Colette Willy). Paris, Mercure de France, 1907; translated as *Retreat from Love*, London, Owen, and Bloomington, Indiana University Press, 1974.

Les Vrilles de la vigne (as Colette Willy). Paris, Editions de la Vie Parisienne, 1908.

La Vagabonde (as Colette Willy). Paris, Ollendorff, 1910; translated as *Renée la vagabonde*, Garden City, New York, Doubleday, 1931; translated as *The Vagabond*, London, Secker & Warburg, 1954.

L'Entrave. Paris, Librairie des Lettres, 1913; translated as *Recaptured*, London, Gollancz, 1931; Garden City, New York, Doubleday Doran, 1932; translated as *The Shackle*, London, Secker & Warburg, 1964; as *The Captive*, New York, Penguin, 1970.

Les Enfants dans les ruines. Paris, Editions de la Maison du Livre, 1917.

Dans la foule. Paris, Georges Crès, 1918.

La Chambre éclairée. Paris, Edouard Joseph, 1920.

Chéri. Paris, Fayard, 1920; translated, New York, A. & C. Boni, 1929; London, Gollancz, 1930.

Le Blé en herbe. Paris, Flammarion, 1923; translated as *The Ripening*, New York, Farrar & Rinehart, 1932; translated as *Ripening Seed*, London, Secker & Warburg, 1955; New York, Farrar, Straus & Cudahy, 1956.

Quatre saisons. Paris, Philippe Ortiz, 1925; translated as *Journey for Myself: Selfish Memories*, London, P. Owen, 1971.

Le Fin de Chéri. Paris, Flammarion, 1926; translated as *The Last of Chéri*, New York, Putnam, 1932; London, Secker & Warburg, 1951.

La Naissance du jour. Paris, Flammarion, 1928; translated as *A Lesson in Love*, New York, Farrar & Rinehart, 1932; translated as *Morning Glory*, London, Gollancz, 1932; translated as *Break of Day*, New York, Farrar Straus, 1961.

La Seconde. Paris, Ferenczi, 1929; translated as *The Other One*, New York, Cosmopolitan Book, 1931; translated as *Fanny and Jane*, London, Gollancz, 1931; translated as *The Other Woman*, London, P. Owen, 1971, and Indianapolis, Bobbs-Merrill, 1972.

La Chatte. Paris, Grasset, 1933; translated as *Saha the Cat*, New York and London, Farrar & Rinehart/T. W. Laurie, 1936; with *Gigi*, London, Secker & Warburg, 1953; *Gigi, and The Cat*, Harmondsworth, Penguin, 1958.

The Married Lover. N.p., 1935.

- *Duo*. Paris, Ferenczi, 1934; translated, New York, Farrar & Rinehart, 1935.
- *Le Toutounier*. Paris, Ferenczi, 1939; translated as *The Toutounier*, with *Duo*, New York, Dell, 1974.

Julie de Carneilhan. Paris, Fayard, 1941; translated with *Chambre d'hôtel*, London, Secker & Warburg, 1952; with *Chambre d'hôtel* and *Gigi*, New York, Farrar Straus & Young, 1952.

Le Képi. Paris, Fayard, 1943.

Short Stories

L'Envers du music-hall. Paris, Flammarion, 1913; translated as *Music-hall Sidelights*, with *Mes Apprentissages*, London, Secker & Warburg, 1957, and with *Mitsou*, New York, Farrar Straus & Cudahy, 1958.

Mitsou; ou, Comment l'esprit vient aux filles (includes *En camarades, pièce en deux actes).* Paris, Fayard, 1919; translated as *Mitsou; or, How Girls Grow Wise,* New York, A. & C. Boni, 1930.
La Femme cachée. Paris, Flammarion, 1924; translated as *The Other Woman,* London, Owen, 1971.
Bella-Vista. Paris, Ferenczi, 1937.
Chambre d'hôtel. Paris, Fayard, 1940; translated as *Chance Acquaintances,* with *Julie de Carneilhan,* London, Secker & Warburg, and with *Gigi* and *Julie de Carneilhan,* New York, Farrar Straus & Young, 1952.
Trois ... six ... neuf. Paris, Corrêa, 1944.
Gigi et autres nouvelles. Lausanne, La Guilde du Livre, 1944; translated as *Gigi,* with *Julie de Carneilhan* and *Chambre d'hôtel,* New York, Farrar Straus & Young, 1952; with *La Chatte,* London, Secker & Warburg, 1953.
The Stories of Colette. London, Secker & Warburg, 1958; as *The Tender Shoot and Other Stories,* New York, Farrar Straus & Cudahy, 1959.
Collected Stories, edited by Robert Phelps. New York, Farrar Straus & Giroux, 1983.

Plays

En camerades (produced Paris 1909).
Claudine, music by Rodolphe Berger (based on her novel; produced Paris, 1910). Paris, n.p., 1910.
Chéri, with Léopold Marchand (four-act; based on her novel; produced Paris, 1921). Paris, Librairie Théâtrale, 1922; translated as *Cheri,* n.p., 1959.
La Vagabonde, with Léopold Marchand (based on her novel; produced Paris, 1923). Paris, Impr. de l'Illustration, 1923.
L'Enfant et les sortilèges, music by Maurice Ravel (produced Paris, 1925). Paris, Durand, 1925; translated as *The Boy and the Magic,* London, Dobson, 1964; New York, Putnam, 1965.
La Décapitée (ballet), in *Mes Cahiers,* 1941.
Gigi, with Anita Loos (based on her novel). Paris, France-Illustration, 1954; New York, Random House, 1952.
Jenue filles en uniform, Lac aux dames, Divine (screenplays), in *Au Cinéma,* 1975.

Screenplays: *La Vagabonde,* 1917, 1931; *La Femme cachée,* 1919; *Jeunes filles en uniform* (French dialogue for *Mädchen in Uniform* by Christa Winsloe), 1932; *Lac aux dames,* 1934; *Divine,* 1935.

Essays

Les Heures longues, 1914-1917. Paris, Fayard, 1917.
Discours de réception à l'Académie Royale de Langue et de Littérature Françaises de Belgique. Paris, Grasset, 1936.

Autobiography

Le Voyage égoïste. Paris, Editions d'Art Edouard Pelletan, 1922; portions translated as *Journey for Myself: Selfish Memories,* London, Owen, 1971.
La Maison de Claudine. Paris, Ferenczi, 1922; revised, 1930; translated as *The Mother of Claudine,* n.p., 1937; translated as *My Mother's House,* with *Sido,* London, Secker & Warburg, and New York, Farrar Straus & Young, 1953.
Sido; ou, Les Points cardinaux. Paris, Editions Kra, 1929; revised, Paris, Ferenczi, 1930; translated with *My Mother's House,* London, Secker & Warburg, and New York, Farrar Straus & Young, 1953.
Ces plaisirs. Paris, Ferenczi, 1932; as *Le Pur et l'impur,* Paris, Armes de France, 1941; translated as *The Pure and the Impure,* New York, Farrar & Rinehart, 1933; translated as *These Pleasures,* London, White Owl, 1934.
Mes apprentissages: Ce que Claudine n'a pas dit. Paris, Ferenczi, 1936; translated as *My Apprenticeships,* with *Music-Hall Sidelights,* London, Secker & Warburg, 1957.
Journal à rebours. Paris, Fayard, 1941; translation in *Looking Backwards,* 1975.
De ma fenêtre. Paris, Armes de France, 1942; enlarged as *Paris de ma fenêtre,* Geneva, Milieu du Monde, 1944; translation in *Looking Backwards,* 1975.
L'Etoile vesper. Geneva, Milieu du Monde, 1946; translated as *The Evening Star: Recollections,* London, P. Owen, 1973; Indianapolis, Indiana, Bobbs-Merrill, 1974.
Journal intermittent. Paris, Fleuron, 1949; translation in *Places,* 1970.
Le Fanal bleu. Paris, Ferenczi, 1949; translated as *The Blue Lantern,* London, Secker & Warburg, and New York, Farrar Straus, 1963.
Earthly Paradise: An Autobiography Drawn from Her Lifelong Writings, edited by Robert Phelps. London, Secker & Warburg, and New York, Farrar Straus, 1966.
Looking Backwards (includes *De ma fenêtre* and *Journal à rebours).* Bloomington, Indiana University Press, 1975.

Other

Creatures Great and Small: Creature Conversations; Other Creatures; Creature Comforts. New York, Farrar Straus & Cudahy, 1957.
Dialogues de bêtes (as Colette Willy). Paris, Mercure de France, 1904; enlarged as *Douze Dialogues de bêtes,* 1930; translated as *Barks and Purrs,* n.p., 1913.
Prrou, Poucette, et quelques autres (as Colette Willy). Paris, Librairie des Lettres, 1913; as *La Paix chez les bêtes,* Georges Crès, 1916; translated as *Cats, Dogs, and I,* n.p., 1924.
Rêverie du nouvel an. Paris, Stock, 1923.
Aventures quotidiennes. Paris, Flammarion, 1924; in *Journey for Myself,* 1971.
Renée Vivien. Abbéville, France, Edouard Champion, 1928.
Histoires pour Bel-Gazou. Paris, Stock, 1930.
La Treille Muscate. N.p, 1932.
Prisons et paradis. Paris, Ferenczi, 1932; revised edition, 1935; portions translated in *Places,* 1970.
La Jumelle noire (theater criticism). Paris, Ferenczi, 4 vols., 1934-38.
Splendeur des papillons. Paris, n.p., 1936.
Mes Cahiers. Paris, Armes de France, 1941.
De la patte à l'aile. Paris, Corrêa, 1943.
Flore et Pomone. Paris, Galerie Charpentier, 1943; as *Flowers and Fruit,* edited by Robert Phelps, New York, Farrar Straus and Giroux, 1986.
Nudités. Paris, Mappemonde, 1943.
Broderie ancienne. Monaco, Editions du Rocher, 1944.
Une Amitié inattendue: Correspondance de Colette and Francis Jammes, edited by Robert Mallet. Paris, Emile-Paul, 1945.

Belles Saisons. Paris, Galerie Charpentier, 1945; translated as *Belles Saisons: A Colette Scrapbook,* edited by Robert Phelps, New York, Farrar Straus & Giroux, 1978.
Pour un herbier. Lausanne, Mermod, 1948; translated as *For a Flower Album,* New York, McKay, 1959.
Trait pour trait. Paris, Fleuron, 1949.
La Fleur de l'âge. Paris, Fleuron, 1949.
En pays connu. Paris, Manuel Bruker, 1949.
Oeuvres complètes, compiled and with an introduction by Colette and Maurice Goudeket. Paris, Flammarion, 15 vols., 1948-50; enlarged as *Oeuvres complètes de Colette,* Paris, Club de l'Honnête Homme, 16 vols., 1973-76.
Chats de Colette. Paris, A. Michel, 1949.
Paysages et portraits. Paris, Flammarion, 1958; portions translated in *The Other Woman,* London, Virago, 1971.
Notes Marocaines. Lausanne, Mermod, 1958.
Letters from Colette, edited by Robert Phelps. New York, Farrar, 1980.
Lettres à Hélène Picard, edited by Claude Pichois. Paris, Flammarion, 1958.
Lettres à Marguerite Moréno, edited by Claude Pichois. Paris, Flammarion, 1959.
Lettres de la vagabonde, edited by Claude Pichois and Roberte Forbin. Paris, Flammarion, 1961.
Lettres au petit corsaire, edited by Claude Pichois and Roberte Forbin. Paris, Flammarion, 1963.
Lettres à ses pairs, edited by Claude Pichois and Roberte Forbin. Paris, Flammarion, 1973.
Découvertes. Lausanne, Mermod, 1961.
Contes des mille et un matins. Paris, Flammarion, 1970; translated as *The Thousand and One Mornings,* London, Owen, and Indianapolis, Indiana, Bobbs-Merrill, 1973.
Places (includes *Journal intermittent).* London, Owen, 1970; Indianapolis, Indiana, Bobbs-Merrill, 1971.
Au Cinéma, edited by Alain and Odette Virmaux. N.p., 1975; translated as *Colette at the Movies,* New York, Ungar, 1980.
Colette: Oeuvres, edited by Claude Pichois. Paris, Gallimard, 1984-86.
La Jumelle noir: critique dramatiqe. Paris, Fayard, 1991.
Lettres aux petites fermières, edited by Marie-Thérèse Colléaux-Chaurang. Pantin, Castor Astral, 1992.

*

Media Adaptations: *La Seconde* and *Claudine at School* (drama); *Gigi* (film), Metro-Goldwyn-Mayer, 1958.

Bibliography: *Colette: An Annotated Primary and Secondary Bibliography* by Donna M. Norell, New York, Garland, 1993.

Manuscript Collections: Bibliothèque Nationale, Paris.

Critical Studies: *Colette: A Provincial in Paris* by Margaret Crosland, London, Peter Owen, 1953; *Près de Colette* by Maurice Goudeket, Paris, Flammarion, 1956, translated by Enid McLeod as *Near Colette,* New York, Farrar Straus & Cudahy, 1957; *Colette* by Elaine Marks, New Brunswick, Maine, Rutgers University Press, 1960; *Colette* by Margaret Davies, London, Oliver & Boyd, 1961; *L'Homme-Objet chez Colette* by Marcelle Biolley-Godino, Paris, Klincksieck, 1972; *Colette: The Difficulty of Loving* by Crosland, Indianapolis, Bobbs-Merrill, 1973; *Colette libre et entravée* by Michèle Sarde, Paris, Stock, 1978, translated by Richard Miller as *Colette, Free and Fettered,* New York, Morrow, 1980; *Colette: The Woman, The Writer* edited by Erica M. Eisinger and Mari McCarthy, University Park and London, University of Pennsylvania Press, 1981; Colette issue of *Europe,* November/December 1981; "Possessing Female Space: *The Tender Shoot*" by Mari McCarty, in *Women's Studies,* 8(3), 1981; *Colette* by Joanna Richardson, London, Methuen, 1983; *Colette* by Joan Hinde Stewart, Boston, Twayne, 1983; "Shadow in the Garden: The Double Aspect of Motherhood in Colette" by Susan D. Fraiman, in *Perspectives on Contemporary Literature,* 11, 1985; *Colette* by Nicole Ward Jouve, Bloomington, Indiana University Press, 1987; *Colette* by Diana Holmes, New York, St. Martin's Press, 1991; *Colette and the Fantom Subject of Autobiography* by Jerry Aline Flieger, Ithaca, Cornell University Press, 1992; *Another Colette: The Question of Gendered Writing* by Lynne Huffer, Ann Arbor, University of Michigan Press, 1992; *Colette: A Study of the Short Fiction* by Dana Strand, New York, Twayne, 1995; *The Mother Mirror: Self-representation and the Mother-Daughter Relation in Colette, Simone de Beauvoir, and Marguérite Duras* by Laurie Corbin, New York, Peter Lang, 1996.

* * *

When Sidonie-Gabrielle Colette died in Paris in 1954, she was buried in Père Lachaise cemetery following an elaborate state funeral; yet, it is interesting to note that she was denied a Catholic ceremony. Her end thus appears to sum up her life: She gained a great deal of fame during her lifetime, but made many enemies because she questioned accepted traditions and values. Today we remember her primarily for her many, mostly autobiographical, novels and other works of fiction and nonfiction, memoirs, essays, and reminiscences. As a matter of fact, part of Colette's attraction results from our inability to classify her or her writing as any distinct category or genre. Notorious—for many reasons—throughout her life, Colette has finally gained critical acceptance; during the last 30 years her contributions to women's writing have been explored and fully appreciated.

Most of what we know about her childhood and adolescence originates from Colette's own writing. In both *My Mother's House* and *Sido,* she describes the almost "edenic" happiness she experienced growing up in her mother's garden. This strong maternal attachment continued to influence her well into adulthood and old age. Some of her biographers even claim that it stunted Colette's emotional growth and was a contributing factor in her failed marriages, her lesbianism, and her tepid relations with her own daughter.

Colette undoubtedly assimilated, during these formative years, a sense of freedom and self-worth that contrasted starkly with the image of woman embraced by late 19th-century French society. During the so-called Belle Epoque, the public schools of the Third Republic imparted to their female pupils a staunch patriotism and a firm desire to remain in the domestic sphere. Colette witnessed first-hand the oppressive nature of a middle-class marriage. She knew that her mother's first marriage had failed. She also saw her half-sister Juliette's unhappy submission to a well-to-do doctor. In her marginally bourgeois family, Colette became, however, also acquainted with non-traditional and unconventional social practices. In her mother's second marriage to Captain Jules Colette, she was able to observe a couple truly dedicated to each other. The Captain, furthermore, liked to lead the good life and let his wife Sidonie control the family's affairs.

After the family fortunes failed, 17-year-old Chéri-Minet—or Gabri as her mother called her—accepted an offer of marriage from Henri "Willy" Gauthier-Villars, 24 years her elder. She followed her husband to Paris despite rumors of his dissolute lifestyle. Life in his bachelor's quarters among his Bohemian friends offered a new training ground for the young woman. Miserly and stingy, Willy did not let her have any money of her own, but did introduce her to many of his literary friends and associates. Colette thus became acquainted with many important hetero- and homosexual figures of the demi-monde, broadening her tastes and horizons.

After she recovered from a serious illness, Willy decided to engage Colette as one of his many ghostwriters for spicy novels and reviews. At first he dismissed, but two years later recognized, the potential value of a school girl's diary Colette had written for him. *Claudine at School* had tremendous popular success and was quickly followed by three more Claudine novels. Naturally, Willy encouraged his wife's literary activities, but inadvertently also contributed to her maturation into an independent woman and writer who eventually would risk social disapprobation to divorce him. Her exposure to Parisian bohemia had sufficiently prepared Colette for the next phase of her career, that of actress and dancer. She had also been able to hone her writing in *Creature Conversations* (1904) and another school girl series, this time published under the name Colette Willy. With the help of her friend George Wague, she had taken dance and ballet lessons and was ready to embark on a new life.

Beginning in 1906, the milieu of music-halls and theaters introduced her still to another important layer of society that would eventually shape her fictions. She met many women who made a living, often precariously, but independently and fervently. As Willy's influence on her writing waned, Colette's own interests became more apparent: She consistently created heroines who were strong, earthy, assertive, and robust. In *The Evening Star* (1946), she would arrive at the conclusion that "the will to survive is so alive in us women, and the lust for physical victory is so female." Her life among the dancers and actresses continued Colette's apprenticeship of life. With her friend Missy, the Marquise de Belbeuf, Colette moved among the lesbian crowd of Paris. Their passionate kiss in *Rêve d'Egypte,* a mimodrama in which they starred together at the Moulin Rouge, caused a huge scandal. Despite this fiasco and frequent attacks on her acting ability, Colette's stage career continued until 1913, when she gave birth to her daughter, Bel-Gazou.

Her works of the music-hall years—*The Vagabond, The Shackle, Music-hall Sidelights,* and later reminiscences in *The Pure and the Impure*—are credited with developing believable women characters who experience sexual desires and sexual fulfillment, an element quite uncommon in other works of that time period. In her study of male characters in Colette's works, *L'Homme-Objet chez Colette,* Marcelle Biolley-Godino also points out that the most attractive men in her novels tend to look weak and effeminate, whereas the women often bear masculine traits. Colette experiments with notions of the androgynous and questions gender roles and behaviors.

Colette's marriage to Henri de Jouvenel ushered in another stage of her life. Due to her husband's position and wealth, she left the theater and wrote reviews and columns for *Le Matin,* even served as a war correspondent during World War I. When the marriage failed, Colette did not maintain strong ties to her daughter. As Diana Holmes explains, motherhood in Colette's works is often described as a beautiful physical event, but mothers (with the exception of Sido) wean their children quickly and send them off into the world to become independent individuals.

The 1920s saw Colette's greatest literary successes with *Chéri* and *The Last of Chéri,* two works in which she masterfully describes the relationship between Léa, an older woman, and her young lover Chéri. When Chéri realizes that she is no longer attractive, he returns to his wealthy wife, but, unlike in other sentimental novels, it is not Léa who is crushed by the event, but Chéri. In 1925 Colette herself met a man 16 years her junior, Maurice Goudeket, to whom she lovingly referred as "her best friend"; she and Goudeket would marry ten years later. Colette spent most of the Occupation years in her apartment at the Palais-Royal in Paris, nursed by her husband through a bout with arthritis after a fracture of her fibula in 1931. Disabled by the degenerative disease in the 1950s, she no longer left her apartment but continued to receive many visitors up until her death.

Colette was not wont to make general or abstract comments on political or social events. It is in her detailed and beautifully crafted writing that we must look for her ideas. Much like her life, her writing transcends categories. Her blending of novel, autobiography, essay, memoirs, and reminiscences precedes contemporary genre criticism. Her characters defy easy classification into male or female, but tend to bear traits of both genders. In a time when women were supposed to serve their husbands as faithful domestic ornaments, Colette's fiction anticipated themes of contemporary women writers. She depicts female characters who are fully alive, sexual beings aspiring to their own physical happiness. Her personal quest for a fulfilled life permeates all her works, which, taken together, weave the legend called Colette.

—Susanna Hoeness-Krupsaw

COLLINS, Patricia Hill

Nationality: American. **Born:** Philadelphia, Pennsylvania, 1 May 1948. **Education:** Brandeis University, A.B. 1969, Ph.D. 1984; Harvard University, M.A.T. 1970. **Family:** Married Roger L. Collins; one daughter. **Career:** Teacher, Harvard UTTT program, 1970-73; curriculum specialist, St. Joseph Community School, 1973-76; director of African American Center, Tufts University, 1976-80; assistant, then associate, 1987-93, then professor of African American Studies, beginning 1993, Charles Phelps Taft Professor of Sociology, 1996, University of Cincinnati. Chair, Minority Fellowship Program Committee, beginning 1992. **Awards:** C.Wright Mills award, 1990, for *Black Feminist Thought.* **Member:** American Sociological Association. **Address:** Department of African American Studies, University of Cincinnati, ML 370, Cincinnati, Ohio 45221, U.S.A.

Publications

Political/Social Theory

Black Feminist Thought: Knowledge, Consciousness, and the Politics of Empowerment. Boston and London, Unwin Hyman, 1990.

Fighting Words: Black Feminist Thought and the Sociology of Oppositional Knowledge. Minneapolis, University of Minnesota Press, forthcoming.

Essays

"Getting Off to a Good Start: The First Class in Black Family Studies," in *Teaching Sociology,* 14(3), 1986.

"The Afro-American Work/Family Nexus: An Exploratory Analysis," in *Western Journal of Black Studies,* 10(6), 1986.

"The Social Construction of Black Feminist Thought," in *Signs,* 14(4), summer 1989.

"Learning from the Outsider Within: The Sociological Significance of Black Feminist Thought," in *(En)Gendering Knowledge: Feminists in Academe,* edited by Joan E. Hartman and Ellen Messer-Davidow. Chicago, University of Chicago Press, 1991.

"Shifting the Center: Race, Class, and Feminist Theorizing about Motherhood," in *Representations of Motherhood,* edited by Donna Bassin, Margaret Honey, and Meryle Mahrer Kaplan. New Haven, Connecticut, Yale University Press, 1994.

"The Sexual Politics of Black Womanhood," and "Modes of Sexual Representation 2—Pornography," with Andrea Dworkin, Gayle Rubin, Gail Dines, Kathy Myers, Annette Kuhn, Alice Mayall, Diane E. H. Russell, and Robert Jensen, in *Gender, Race, and Class in Media: A Text-Reader,* edited by Gail Dines and Jean M. Humez. Thousand Oaks, California, Sage, 1995.

"What's in a Name? Womanism, Black Feminism, and Beyond," in *Black Scholar,* 26(1), 1996.

Other

Editor, with Margaret L. Andersen, *Race, Class, and Gender: An Anthology.* Belmont, California, Wadsworth, 1992; 2nd edition, 1994.

*

Critical Studies: Symposium on *Black Feminist Thought* by Robert G. Newby, Deborah K. King, and Barrie Thorn, in *Gender and Society,* 6(3), September 1992.

* * *

Patricia Hill Collins is perhaps best know for her book *Black Feminist Thought: Knowledge, Consciousness, and the Politics of Empowerment,* which was awarded the 1990 C. Wright Mills Award by the National Society of the Study of Social Problems. In this work, she outlines the historical continuity and major tenets of American Black feminist thought by exploring a broad range of sources: from music, fiction, poetry, and oral history to Afrocentric and feminist philosophy and the sociology of knowledge. Collins describes three major threads of coherence in Black feminist thought: the recognition that oppressions are interconnected; that Black women have created alternative world-views due to the need for self-definition and self-determination; and that Black women have had to deal with narrow and restricting external definitions about who they are, which are often internalized —especially racialized concepts of beauty, skin color, and physique. As Collins writes, "Black women's lives are a series of negotiations that aim to reconcile ... contradictions." However, *Black Feminist Thought* does more than outline, identify, and describe the history of Black feminist consciousness: Collins also points to areas that have, historically, been overlooked or which need further analysis, including racialized gender roles within family and work, politics, violence—in the home, on the job, and in the street—and homophobia.

Collins not only identifies the major concepts of Afrocentric feminist philosophy by drawing from a wide range of Black women's experiences and voices; she also discusses the ways in which these concepts have been obscured: institutionally, via education, the law, and government; philosophically, through who has been deemed the knower and who the known, who the subject and who the object; ideologically, whereby Black women have stereotypically been portrayed through the lens of "controlling images" as mammies, Jezebels, and matriarchs in the media, arts, and through government programs; and materially, through who has and has not, historically, had access to a living wage, union membership, or a variety of career options. Collins's interdisciplinary methodology reflects two of her most important concepts: the idea of a matrix of domination and her call for a "both/and" analytical approach to domination and subordination, both on a general level and as it relates to Black women's lived experiences. Collins rejects oppositional thought because "Either/or dichotomous thinking categorizes people, things, and ideas in terms of their differences from one another" in a manner that requires objectification and subordinating "one half of the dichotomy to the other."

Thinking about domination as matric means that apparently different or separate forms of domination, discrimination, and oppression work together, not individually. Tightly interwoven, it is often difficult to distinguish the different "strands" that make up the matrix. Because racism, sexism, classism, and homophobia are therefore interrelated, it is not effective to simply address one form of oppression or another. However, identifying a "political economy of domination" does not mean that oppressions are interchangeable or analogous. Rather, different forms of domination overlap, have what Collins calls "points of convergence" as well as areas of difference or divergence from one another. In addition, Collins rejects the common presupposition that one is either an oppressor or an oppressed person. To reject this binary opposition between oppressor and oppressed entails rejecting the idea that a person can become completely subjugated or colonized. Moreover, because different forms of domination are interconnected, an individual can, on the one hand, be oppressed (because of race, gender, and/or sexuality, for example). On the other hand, that very same individual may also have access to privileges because of her/his rage, gender, and/or sexuality. For example, in our culture a Black woman who is heterosexual faces various forms of domination, but, as a heterosexual, she also has access to privileges. From Collins's perspective, there is no one who simply occupies the position of being purely the oppressor or purely oppressed. She prefers to emphasize the complex ways in which simultaneity operates, that either/or oppositional thinking obscures and elides. Collins therefore advocates a both/and approach to thinking about domination, identity, and epistemology.

In describing Black feminist thought, Collins rejects traditional theories of knowing. She sees positivism as inadequate in that it relies too heavily on oppositional categorization in the name of scientific reasoning. "Positivist approaches aim to create scientific descriptions of reality by producing objective generalizations,..." she writes. "[However the] result of this entire process is often the separation of information from meaning." Meaning and information can become separated because the researcher (knower) is supposed to separate emotion and reason, wisdom and knowledge: s/he must objectify and decontextualize her/him self. Relativism is also an unsatisfactory approach to evaluating and developing truth claims and knowledge because although it does recognize that all groups can be knowers and the subjects of knowledge, no one group's ideas are any more valid than another's. Collins rejects relativism and positivism because both approaches "minimized the importance of specific location in influencing a group's knowledge claims, the power inequities among groups that produce subjugated knowleges, and the strengths and limitations of partial perspective."

Because Collins wants to take into consideration the social, material, and political *positions* of the knower, standpoint epistemology would seem to be the answer. However, she identifies several problems with standpoint theory. Many standpoint theorists have argued that the oppressed's outsider or marginal status *necessarily* provides them with fewer obstructions to finding the truth. Not only does this approach advocate the idea that there is one version of the truth, like positivism, but it also implies a "biological prerequisite" to have access to that subjugated knowledge. Collins argues that because race (and now, to a certain extent, gender) are questionable biological categories (they are certainly not as fixed, distinct, or immutable as once thought), to solidify them as such is implicitly neither feminist nor Afrocentric. She states that we need a "definition of Black feminist thought ... that avoids that materialist position that being Black and/or female generates certain experiences that automatically" lead one to have an Afrocentric feminist consciousness.

Collins's both/and epistemological approach is not only evident in her rejection of traditional forms of positivism, relativism, and standpoint theories, but also in the way that she discusses who can develop and create Black feminist thought. On the one hand she describes Afrocentric feminist thought as rooted in a Black women's standpoint, an "outsider-within" point of view that stems from Black women's particular and distinct economic and material work experiences (such as in domestic service, wherein the employee both does and does not have access to any contact with the employer's world). Collins writes, "being treated as an invisible Other gives Black women a peculiar angle of vision, the outsider-within stance."

On the other hand, because she rejects biological prerequisites as a basis for certain kinds of knowledge, Collins uses both "Black feminist thought" and Afrocentric feminist epistemology" interchangeable throughout her book to suggest that it is not only Black women who can further Black feminist thought. In other words, she simultaneously advocates both standpoint and non-standpoint approaches by discussing bell hooks's idea that to *advocate* an Afrocentric feminism does not require one to *be* black and female. Such an approach still necessitates that Black women's experiences be "at the center of any serious efforts to develop Black feminist thought yet not have that thought become separatist and exclusionary" and not as broadly based in coalitions as it otherwise would be.

In other words, because domination functions within a matrix, we should develop transformational thought and analysis in an interconnected both/and manner in order to be most effective and far-reaching. Some critics have argued that Collins's approach here is contradictory or, at the least, not adequately fleshed out. However, Collins does not necessarily view apparent contradiction as a flaw but, rather, as a source of strength, creativity, and possibility. She is not necessarily aiming to solve our troubles: instead, she wants to trouble or problematize the ways in which Afrocentrism and feminism have traditionally been practiced and conceived.

Though the characteristics of Black feminist thought are similar to both Afrocentrism and feminism, they are not the same as simply adding both approaches together. According to Collins, there are several key concepts to be found in Black feminist thought, all of which embrace a both/and approach to a matrix of domination: a wisdom-knowledge and a thought-activism continuum; a self-community connection; an ethic of care that requires a "dialogue of reason and emotion"; and an ethic of personal responsibility and accountability.

The concept of dialogue, or call and response, is especially central. In order to evaluate and validate the viability of any truth claim or idea, one must think in relation to a larger community (as a self in context, a relational self). Collins uses the analogy of Black women's quilting aesthetic as a way to illustrate the idea of an ethically bound self-in-context. She describes how African-American women's quilts derive symmetry by using contrast and diversity rather than symmetry in order to emphasize "individual uniqueness in a community setting." Dialogue also requires others to respond and participate. Thus morality and ethics play a key role in Afrocentric feminist experience, the way one lives and acts. Collins applies this belief in her own life. For example, she worked in the community schools movement in Boston, has been very active in the Girl Scouts, and has debated about *Black Feminist Thought* with inmates at an Ohio prison. The concept of dialogue is also apparent in her methodological approach and in her writing style. Not only does she utilize a wide variety of interdisciplinary sources and draw from a broad range of Black women's voices and experience (across time, place, work, economics, and education), but she also avoids unnecessary jargon: She writes for a diverse audience and not just a specialized one.

Collins concludes by claiming that although "Alternative knowledge claims in and of themselves are rarely threatening to conventional knowledge," advocating both/and analysis and an ethics of care could transform the ways in which we think about more traditional knowledge claims, which in turn "opens up the question of whether what has been taken to be true can stand the test of alternative ways of validating truth." Patricia Hill Collins's work has been foundational in pushing the boundaries of both Afrocentric and feminist thought to be more accountable, to have a broader scope, and to advocate a more radical, if less safe or easily identifiable, epistemology. She forces her readers to think differently about how they think about oppression, domination, and subordination, and to reexamine the way in which truth and knowledge are produced, reproduced, and validated—or eradicated and obscured.

—Vivian May

CONGXUAN. *See* **DING LING.**

CONSTANTINE, Murray. *See* **BURDEKIN, Katharine.**

COOPER, Anna Julia Haywood

Nationality: American. **Born:** Raleigh, North Carolina, 10 August 1856. **Education:** St. Augustine's Normal and Collegiate Institute, 1868-77; Oberlin College, Oberlin, Ohio, B.A. 1884, M.A. 1887; Sorbonne, University of Paris, Ph.D. 1925; studied at Le Guilde Internationale, Paris, 1911-13, and Columbia University, New York, 1914-17. **Family:** Married the reverend George A.C. Cooper in 1877 (died 1879); raised five foster children. **Career:** Teacher, Oberlin Academy; head of modern languages department, Wilberforce University, c. 1884; instructor in Latin, German, and mathematics, St. Augustine's Normal and Collegiate Institute, Raleigh, North Carolina, 1885-86; teacher, beginning 1887, principal, 1902-06, the teacher of Latin, 1910-30, "M" Street (later Paul Laurence Dunbar) High School, Washington, D.C.; chair, department of languages, Lincoln University, Missouri, 1906-10; cofounder, 1907, then president, 1930-41, Frelinghuysen University (later Frelinghuysen Group of Schools for Colored Working People), Washington, D.C. Founder, Colored Young Women's Christian Association; trustee and director of summer programs, Colored Settlement House, Washington, D.C. Lecturer at schools and conferences throughout the United States; presented paper "The Negro Problem in America" at first Pan-African Conference, London, 1900. Editor, *The Southland* (North Carolina). **Member:** American Negro Academy, **Died:** Washington, D.C., 27 February 1964.

PUBLICATIONS

Essays

A Voice from the South by a Black Woman of the South. Xenia, Ohio, Aldine, 1892; New York and Oxford, Oxford University Press, 1988.

The Social Settlement: What It Is, and What It Does. Washington, D.C., Murray Bros. Press, 1913.

Legislative Measures concerning Slavery in the United States. Privately printed, 1942.

Equality of Races and the Democratic Movement. Privately printed, 1945.

Uncollected Essays

"Angry Saxons and Negro Education," in *Crisis,* November 1913.

History

Le Pèlerinage de Charlemagne: Voyage à Jérusalem et à Constantinople (secondary thesis). Paris, A. Lahure, Imprimeiur-Editeur, 1925.

L'Attitude de la France à l'égard de l'esclavage pendant la Révolution (thesis). Paris, Imprimeire de la Cour d'Appel, 1925; translated as *Slavery and the French Revolutionists (1788-1805),* Lewiston, New York, E. Mellen Press, 1988.

Personal Collections of the Grimké Family and the Life and Writings of Charlotte Forten Grimké. Privately printed, 2 vols., 1951.

Autobiography

The Third Step: An Autobiography. Privately printed, 1950?

*

Manuscript Collections: Moorland-Spingarn Research Center, Howard University, Washington, D.C.

Critical Studies: "Anna Julia Cooper: A Voice for Black Women" by Sharon Harley, in *The Afro-American Woman: Struggles and Images,* edited by Harley and Rosalyn Terborg-Penn, Port Washington, New York, Kennikat Press, 1968; *Black Women in White America: A Documentary History* edited by Gerda Lerner, New York, Pantheon, 1972; *Anna J. Cooper, a Voice from the South* by Louise Daniel Hutchinson, Washington, D.C., Smithsonian Institution Press, 1981; *From Slavery to the Sorbonne and Beyond: The Life and Writings of Anna J. Cooper* by Leona C. Gabel, Northampton, Massachusetts, Smith College, 1982; *Black Women in 19th-Century American Life: Their Words, Their Thoughts, Their Feelings* edited by Ruth Bogin and Bert Loewenberg, University Park, Pennsylvania State University Press, 1985; "Anna Julia Cooper: The Black Feminist Voice of the 1890s" by Mary Helen Washington, in *Legacy,* 4(2), 1987; *A Singing Something: Womanist Reflections on Anna Julia Cooper* by Karen Baker-Fletcher, New York, Crossroad, 1994.

* * *

Anna Julia Cooper was born into slavery in Raleigh, North Carolina, as the daughter of a slave, Hannah Stanley Haywood, and her master, George Washington Haywood, whose family owned 271 slaves at the time. Living to the age of 105, Cooper would lead an exemplary life of activism as an educator, community activist, pan-Africanist, and women's rights advocate. Cooper is most well-known for her 1892 collection of speeches and essays, *A Voice from the South by a Black Women of the South.* Although she did not publish extensively after 1892, aside from some pamphlets and her doctoral dissertation, a forthright analysis of the politics of domination is evident throughout her life's work.

In *A Voice from the South,* Cooper underscores how sexual, racial, class, and colonial oppressions are interconnected forms of domination. Her analysis is therefore quite radical in that she speaks against notions of absolute dualism and oppositional and distinct categories of identity; she reveals how "opposites" such as man/woman or black/white are relational, as well as how systems of oppression are mutually reinforcing. It is in this context that Cooper expresses her frustrations with the narrowness of the women's movement:

> The cause of freedom is not the cause of a race or a sect, a party or a class,—it is the cause of human kind, the very birthright of humanity. Now unless we are greatly mistaken the Reform of our day, known as the Women's Movement, is essentially such an embodiment, if its pioneers could only realize it, of the universal good.... It is not the intelligent woman vs. the ignorant woman; nor the whole woman vs. the black, the brown, and the red,—

> it is not even the cause of woman vs. man.... [Woman's] cause is linked with that of every agony that has been dumb—every wrong that needs a voice.

Aside from elucidating blind spots within the late 19th-century American women's movement, Cooper also points to a key paradox of oppression: that one can simultaneously dominate and be dominated. She outlines that whiteness is a factor mitigating white women's oppression and gender black men's. Cooper sarcastically describes the women's group "Wimodaughsis (which, being interpreted for the uninitiated, is a woman's culture club whose name is made up of the first few letters of the four words: wives, mothers, daughters, and sisters)." Upon one occasion, "Pandora's box is opened on the ideal harmony of this modern Eden without an Adam when a colored lady ... applies for admission" because many of the white women had "not calculated that there were any wives, mothers, daughters, and sisters, except white ones." She ironically suggests that perhaps "*Whimodaughsis* would sound just as well, and then it need mean just *white mothers, daughters and sisters.*"

Cooper similarly criticizes male leaders of racial uplift by emphasizing that it is impossible to elevate the race without also elevating black women: African Americans "might as well expect to grow trees from leaves as hope to build up a civilization or a manhood without taking into consideration our women." Just as she points to the futility of a "women's" movement that only includes some women, Cooper draws attention to the paradox underlying racial uplift that only "lifts" half of a people, for women are "at once both the lever and the fulcrum for uplifting the race."

Cooper not only critiques racism within the women's movement and sexism within the racial uplift movement; she also delineates a black feminist viewpoint based on black women's distinct experiences in American society. Her words foreshadow what Frances Beale would describe as a black feminist standpoint when she writes, "The colored woman of to-day occupies, one may say, a unique position in this country.... She is confronted by both a woman question and a race problem, and is as yet an unknown or unacknowledged factor in both."

According to Cooper, black women's position on the margin of society can be seen to be part of a distinctive intellectual tradition squarely positioned in racial and gendered oppression. Clearly placing herself in a black female tradition of activism and uplift, Cooper recognizes other black women of her time, including Frances Watkins Harper, Sojourner Truth, Amanda Smith, Charlotte Fortin Grimké, Hallie Quinn Brown, and Fannie Jackson Coppin. Cooper argues that black women's voices should be heard and their experiences considered. Moreover, their position on the political and social margins can be advantageous: "The colored woman, then, should not be ignored because her bark is resting in the silent waters of the sheltered cove. She is watching the movements of the contestants none the less and is all the better qualified, perhaps, to weigh and judge and advise because [she is] not herself in the excitement of the race."

Aside from analyzing racial and gendered oppression, Cooper also points to class or "caste" as an important consideration for women activists. In *A Voice from the South,* she asks her readers, "Is not woman's cause broader, and deeper, and grander, than a bluestocking debate or an aristocratic pink tea? Why should woman become plaintiff in a suit versus the Indian, or the Negro or any other race or class who have been crushed under the iron heel of Anglo-Saxon power and selfishness?" She writes of the inadequate tenements in which the urban poor are forced to life, the profitless and short life of rural tenant farmers, and black women's limited access to adequate means of employment. "How many have ever given a thought to the pinched and down-trodden colored women bending over washtubs and ironing boards," she queries, "with children to feed and house rent to pay, wood to buy, soap and starch to furnish—lugging home weekly great baskets of clothes for families who pay them for a month's laundry barely enough to purchase a substantial pair of shoes!" Cooper also clearly outlines race, gender, and (implicitly) class to be social constructs and not biological essences. She declares that "there is nothing irretrievably wrong in the shape of the black man's skull" and that "race, color, sex, [and] condition" should be "realized to be the accidents, not the substance of life."

In some rather provocative passages in *A Voice from the South,* Cooper suggests that social Darwinism, sexism, classism, racism, violence, and imperialism all intersect within the arena of male dominance, or the predominance of masculine "spheres" of thought. She asks:

> Whence came this apotheosis of greed and cruelty? Whence this sneaking admiration we all have for bullies and prize-fighters? Whence the self-congratulation of 'dominant' races...? Whence the scorn of so-called weak or unwarlike races and individuals, and the very comfortable assurance that it is their manifest destiny to be wiped out as vermin before this advancing civilization?... The world of thought under the predominant man-influence, unmollified and unrestrained by its complementary force, would become like Daniel's fourth beast.

She delineates that a balance of complementary masculine and feminine forces of power are necessary for a "progressive peace": "There are two kinds of peace in this world.... A nation or an individual may be at peace because all opponents may have found the secret of true harmony in the determination to live and let live."

Her conceptualization of peace does not rest on a belief in absolute and biologically determined spheres of woman and man. Instead, Cooper promotes the idea that there are different but intermeshing masculine and feminine spheres of action, thought, and influence—not male and female spheres: she emphasizes nurture over nature. Thought, for Cooper, is not determined or constrained by one's "natural" body; therefore, men can think "feminine" thoughts and women "masculine" ones. She writes, "All I can claim is that there is a feminine as well as a masculine side to truth ... [which are] complements in one necessary and symmetric whole." In the vein of what some later feminist would identify as a need for more androgynous childrearing in the recognition of a gender continuum rather than a biological binary, Cooper advocates the need for young women to be raised to be self-reliant and independent, whereas young men need also to be tender and sensitive.

Although some critics argue that Cooper's class analysis is inadequate, one can also view *A Voice for the South* it as embryonic, for her community activism during the decades following that book's publication clearly demonstrated her commitment to working-class men and women. It is true that Cooper saw herself as among the intellectual leaders of her time, lifting as she climbed. Her position is not only evidenced by her membership in the elite formerly all-male American Negro Academy and her education at

Oberlin, Columbia, and the Sorbonne, but also by her participation in the 1890 American Conference of Educators, the 1893 Congress of Representative Women, the Second Hampton Negro Conference in 1894, a conference of the National Federation of Colored Women in 1896, and in the Pan African Conference held in London in 1900.

However, Cooper clearly saw her intellectual position as connected to her membership in a broad and diverse black community. Not only was she a founder of the first Colored YWCA—the Phillis Wheatley "Y"—and division of Camp Fire Girls, but she also helped found and run a Colored Settlement House in Washington, D.C., which was an entirely volunteer-run organization for its first three decades. The settlement house offered childcare for working mothers, milk for babies, boys' and girls' activity clubs, training for kindergarten teachers, and evening classes for adults in literacy, music, and art. The house also trained young black women in domestic service with the ideal that improved training would increase their ability to demand higher wages. In addition, as a principal and teacher at Washington's "M" Street High School (later the Paul Laurence Dunbar High School, razed in 1976), Cooper firmly advocated that the African American students of D.C. be offered college preparatory courses as well as vocational education. Like W.E.B. DuBois, Cooper disagreed strongly with Booker T. Washington's call for vocational training as the only or best means of educating African Americans. Instead, she believed in the necessity of offer a range of educational opportunities that would promote skill and dignity in all spheres of life. This does not mean that Cooper disdained educations that did not lead to Ivy League degrees, which many Dunbar students went on to gain. Her advocacy of the tenant that people of all class backgrounds have access to basic reading, writing, and mathematics led to her assistance in founding Frelinhuysen University, for which she later acted as president, even allowing her home to be used for classroom space. The school had "satellite" locations around Washington, D.C., for easy access and offered courses at night when working people could attend. Aside from the basics, Frelinhuysen also offered business, typing, and legal courses in its earlier years.

Anna Julia Cooper was a woman who acted upon her insightful observations about interlocking forms of domination throughout her lifetime. Implicit and explicit in her writing and activism are many ideas that are central to contemporary feminist thought: the distinctions between nature and nurture, sex and gender; the delineation of a standpoint epistemology; the fluidity and interconnectedness of categories of identity; the call for a kind of coalitional peace and politics; and the simultaneity of oppression and discrimination with access to privilege.

—Vivian M. May

COTT, Nancy F(alik)

Nationality: American. **Born:** Philadelphia, 8 November 1945. **Education:** Cornell University, B.A. (magna cum laude) 1967; Brandeis University, Ph.D. 1974. **Family:** Married the architect Leland Cott in 1969; one son, one daughter. **Career:** Instructor in history, Wheaton College, Norton, Massachusetts, 1971, Clark University, Worcester, Massachusetts, 1972, and Wellesley College, Wellesley, Massachusetts, 1973-74; assistant professor, associate professor, then professor of history and American studies, beginning 1975, Stanley Woodward Professor, beginning 1990, chair of women's studies program, 1980-87, 1992-93, and chair of American studies program, beginning 1994, Yale University, New Haven, Connecticut. **Awards:** Rockefeller Foundation humanities fellow, 1978-79; Harvard Law School fellowship, 1978-79, 1993-94; Radcliffe Research scholarship, 1982; Yale Whitney Humanities fellowship, 1983-84, 1987; Guggenheim fellowship, 1985; Harvard University Charles Warren fellowship, 1985; American Council of Learned Societies grant, 1988; Yale A. Whitney Griswold grant, 1984, 1987, 1988, 1991, 1993; Radcliffe visiting research scholar, 1991; National Endowment of the Humanities fellowship, 1993-94. **Member:** American Antiquarian Society, American Historical Association, Society of American Historians, American Studies Association, Coordinating Committee of Women in the Historical Profession, Massachusetts Historical Society, Organization of American Historians, Phi Beta Kappa, Phi Kappa Phi. Journal boards include *American Quarterly*, 1977-80; *Feminist Studies*, beginning 1977; *Journal of Social History*, beginning 1978; *Yale Review*, 1980-88, 1991—; *Reviews in American History*, 1981-85; *Women's Studies Quarterly*, beginning 1981; *Orim: A Jewish Journal at Yale,* 1984-88; *Gender and History*, beginning 1987; *Journal of Women's History,* beginning 1987; *Yale Journal of Law and the Humanities,* beginning 1988; *Readers' Encyclopedia of American History*, 1989-91; and *American National Biography,* beginning 1989. **Address:** American Studies Program, P.O. Box 208236, New Haven, Connecticut 06520, U.S.A. **Online Address:** Nancy.Cott@yale.edu

Publications

History

The Bonds of Womanhood: "Woman's Sphere" in New England, 1780-1835. New Haven, Connecticut, Yale University Press, 1977.

The Grounding of Modern Feminism. New Haven, Connecticut, and London, Yale University Press, 1987.

Uncollected Essays

"Young Women in the Second Great Awakening in New England," in *Feminist Studies,* 3, fall 1975.

"Divorce and the Changing Status of Women in 18th-Century Massachusetts," in *William and Mary Quarterly,* 3(33), October 1976.

"18th-century Family and Social Life Revealed in Massachusetts Divorce Records," in *Journal of Social History,"* 10, fall 1976.

"Passionlessness: An Interpretation of Anglo-American Sexual Ideology, 1790-1840," in *Signs: A Journal of Women in Culture and Society,* 4, 1978.

"Feminist Politics in the 1920s: The National Woman's Party," in *Journal of American History,* 71, June 1984.

"Feminist Theory and Feminist Movements: The Past before Us," in *What Is Feminism? A Re-Examination by Nancy Cott, Linda Gordon, Judith Stacey, Juliet Mitchell, Ann Oakley, and Six Other Major Feminist Thinkers,* edited by Juliet Mitchell and Ann Oakley. Oxford, Basil Blackwell, and New York, Pantheon, 1986.

"What's in a Name? The Limits of Social Feminism or, Expanding the Vocabulary of Women's History," in *Journal of American History,* 73(3), December 1989.

"Historical Perspectives: The Equal Rights Amendment in the 1920s," in *Conflicts in Feminism,* edited by Marianne Hirsch and Evelyn Fox Keller. New York, Routledge, 1990.

"'Giving Character to Our Whole Civil Polity': Marriage and State Authority in the Late 19th Century," in *U.S. History as Women's History,* edited by Linda Kerber and others. Chapel Hill, University of North Carolina Press, 1995.

"Justice for All? Marriage and Deprivation of Citizenship in the United States," in *Justice and Injustice* (Amherst Series in Law, Jurisprudence and Social Thought), edited by Austin Sarat. Ann Arbor, University of Michigan Press, 1996.

Other

Editor, *Root of Bitterness: Documents of the Social History of American Women.* New York, Dutton, 1972; completely revised edition, with Jeanne Boydston, Ann Brande, Lori D. Ginsberg and Molly Ladd-Taylor, Boston, Northeastern University Press, 1996.

Editor, with Elizabeth H. Pleck, *A Heritage of Her Own: Families, Work and Feminism in America.* New York, Simon & Schuster, 1979.

Editor, *A Woman Making History: Mary Ritter Beard through Her Letters.* New Haven, Connecticut, and London, Yale University Press, 1991.

Editor, *History of Women in the United States: Historical Articles on Women's Lives and Activities.* New Haven, Connecticut, and Munich, K. G. Saur, 20 vols., 1992-94.

The Young Oxford History of Women in the United States. New York, Oxford University Press, 11 vols., 1995.

* * *

Nancy F. Cott is widely recognized as one of the foremost voices in the field of women's history. For more than two decades, Cott has made frequent and influential contributions to the field as an author, educator and administrator.

Like many of her contemporaries, Cott's initial interest in feminist approaches to history was fueled by the women's liberation movement of the 1960s. At Brandeis University in the early 1970s, she studied under John Demos, a noted authority on family history. There, Cott conducted the research that would inform her 1977 work, *The Bonds of Womanhood.* As a newly minted instructor, she was also able to help meet a growing demand for classes in women's history, teaching at several colleges including Wheaton College and Clark University. After receiving her Ph.D. from Brandeis in 1974, she was hired by the American studies department at Yale University in 1975, where she has remained. Cott is currently the Stanley Woodward Professor of History and American Studies at Yale.

Cott's first published book, *Root of Bitterness,* was a response to the author's own need to provide a wide range of primary documents for her college undergraduates. The collection includes essays, poems and letters from a wide range of women, famous and relatively anonymous, on topics ranging from housewifery to slavery. The collection continues to function as a useful vantage point from which to explore the world of women, accessed through "women's own words and the words addressed to them." Cott provides a brief introduction to each selection that provides the context for the primary document. The book was revised in 1996; four of Cott's former graduate students served as coeditors.

Her 1977 work, *The Bonds of Womanhood: "Woman's Sphere" in New England, 1780-1835,* is a path-breaking study of women's community. Cott examines the letters and diaries of middle-class New England women, as well as the "domestic literature" that became so popular in this era. Cott argues that "womanhood bound women together even as it bound them down." While much about the private female world of women was affirming—providing fellowship and support—it was restrictive and limited women to a narrow sphere of influence. Cott argues that the women's sphere "became ... more clearly articulated" in the era she studies, and formed the basis for the moral reform activities and feminist activism of later generations. This work, along with that of fellow historians Barbara Welter and Carroll Smith-Rosenberg, offers a vivid and intimate portrait of the day-to-day lives of white women in ante-bellum New England. *The Bonds of Womanhood* continues to be a core work assigned in many women's history courses.

Cott's 1987 work, *The Grounding of Modern Feminism,* serves to historicize feminism and place it within an appropriate social context. Cott reveals that feminism as an ideology emerged in the 1910s, and differed in important ways from the suffrage movement. "[I]t was both broader and narrower: broader in intent, proclaiming revolution in all the relations of the sexes," Cott explains, "and narrower in the range of its willing adherents." Perhaps most interesting is Cott's discussion of voluntarist politics in the 1920s. She complicates our vision of women's activities, laying the foundation for current-day rifts. Clearly, women did not act as a monolithic bloc prior to or following passage of the 19th Amendment; conservative and more radical elements continue to be at cross purposes to this day.

As the editor of the 1987 *A Heritage of Her Own,* Cott brought together articles by many pioneers in women's history. Her more recent publication—with a long biographical introduction—of the letters of Mary Ritter Beard allows scholars and students access to the private ruminations of one of the earliest women's historians. Cott identifies Beard as "the only historian [of the pre-World War II era] who paid serious attention to women's lives ... and examined women as actors and agents." For Cott, the task of assembling *A Woman Making History: Mary Ritter Beard through Her Letters* was "a labor of love," as well as a challenge; Beard and her husband, the historian Charles Beard, burned their personal papers during World War II when criticized for their anti-intervention stance. Thus, Cott was faced with the time-consuming task of searching the papers of other individuals who received letters from Mary Ritter Beard to gain insight into the thinking of this remarkable woman.

Cott is the author of dozens of articles published in scholarly journals. Among her most influential essays is "Passionlessness: An Interpretation of Anglo-American Sexual Ideology, 1790-1840," published in *Signs* in 1978. Here Cott examines the view of Victorian women as sexually passive and lacking in sexual appetite, and identifies the cultural reasons for this construction. Another early essay, "18th-century Family and Social Life Revealed in Massachusetts Divorce Records," identifies the extent to which neighbors involved themselves in ostensibly private marital disputes. The work is telling, also, in reminding its readers that infidelity and divorce are not solely late-20th-century aberrations.

Cott is currently at work on her next book, an examination of the history of marriage as a public institution. This study will illuminate the ways that public policy, especially since the latter half of the 19th century, has constructed the gender order by expecting and enforcing a particular model of marriage.

When not writing and teaching, Cott has continued to facilitate the growth of women's history. She was instrumental in efforts to develop a women's studies program at Yale, and served as the chair of that program from 1980-87. She is currently the chair of Yale's American studies program, where she teaches a survey course on the history of American women and mentors the next generation of feminist historians.

—Sara N. Romeyn

CROSS, Amanda. *See* **HEILBRUN, Carolyn G(old).**

CROWE, F. J. *See* **JOHNSTON, Jill.**

CUTRUFELLI, Maria Rosa

Nationality: Italian. **Born:** Messina, Sicily, Italy, 26 January 1946. **Education:** University of Bologna, *Laurea* in literature, 1970. **Family:** Married (separated). **Career:** Writer. Founder, Lotta Feminnista (feminist group), Bologna, Italy, and Gela, Sicily, c. 1970s. Founder and editor, *Tuttestorie* (literary magazine); contributor to periodicals and magazines, including *L'unità, L'indice, Noidonne, Terzo mondo, Marie Claire,* and *Gioia.* **Awards:** Premio Donna Città di Roma, for *La briganta.* **Member:** Coop "Firmato Donna" (president), Circolo "della Rosa," Società delle Letterate. **Address:** Via A. Rendano 41, 00199 Rome, Italy.

Publications

Novels

La briganta [The Female Brigand]. Palermo, La Luna, 1990.
Complice il dubbio [Complicitous Doubt]. Milan, Interno Giallo, 1992
Canto al deserto. Storia di Tina, soldato di mafia [Song to the Desert: Story of Tina, Mafia Soldier]. Milan, Longanesi, 1994.

Short Stories

"Le colline del Nord" [Northern Hills], in *Il pozzo segreto: 50 scrittrici italiane,* edited by Cutrufelli, Rosaria Guacci, and Marisa Rusconi. Florence, Giunti, 1993.
"Madonna Gasparina," in *Sedici racconti italiani* [Sixteen Italian Tales]. Brescia, Libreria Rinascita, 1994.
"Balsamo di tigre" [Tiger Balm], in *Horror Erotico.* Rome, Stampa Alternative, 1995.

Political/Social Theory

L'invenzione della donna: Miti e tecniche di uno sfruttamento [The Invention of Woman: Myths and Techniques of Exploitation]. Milan, Mazzotta, 1974.
Disoccupata con onore: lavoro e condizione della donna [Honorably Unemployed: Labor and Women's Condition]. Milan, Mazzotta, 1975.
Donna perché piangi? Imperialismo e condizione femminile nell'Africa nera. Milan, Mazzotta, 1976; translated as *Women of Africa: Roots of Oppression,* London, Zed, 1983.
Operaie senza fabbrica: inchiesta sul lavoro a domicilio [Women Workers without a Factory: Investigation into Work at Home]. Rome, Editori Riuniti, 1977.
Economia e politica dei sentimenti: la "produzione" femminile [Economics and Politics of Feelings: The "Feminine" Production]. Rome, Editori Riuniti, 1980.
Il cliente: Inchiesta sulla domanda di prostituzione [The Client: An Investigation of Demand in the Prostitution Market]. Rome, Editori Riuniti, 1981.
Il denaro in corpo: Inchiesta sulla domanda di sesso commerciale [Money Embodied: An Investigation of the Demand for Commercial Sex]. Milan, Tropea, 1996.

Literary Criticism

"Alla conquista delle scrittrici: Un nuovo mercato per l'industria editoriale" [The Conquest of Women Writers: A New Market for the Publishing World], in *Scrittura, scrittrici,* edited by Cutrufelli. Rome, Longanesi, 1988.
"Scritture, scrittrici. L'esperienza italiana" [Writings, Women Writers: The Italian Experience], in *Donne e scrittura* [Women and Writing], edited by Daniela Corona. Palermo, La Luna, 1990.
"Un mondo di parole che parte dal corpo" [A World of Words that Starts from the Body], in *Noidonne: Legendaria,* June/August 1990.
"On the Difficulty of Writing about Oneself," in *The Flawed Diamond: Essays on Olive Schreiner,* edited by Itala Vivan. Sydney, Dangaroo Press, 1991.
"La spietatezza di una scrittrice moderna" [The Mercilessness of a Modern Woman Writer], in *Ciao bella: Percorsi di critica letteraria femminile* [Hello Beautiful: Paths of Female Literary Criticism]. Milan, Lupetti, 1996.

History

L'unità d'Italia: Guerra contadina e nascita del sottosviluppo del sud [The Unity of Italy: Peasant War and the Origins of Underdevelopment in the South]. Verona, Bertani, 1974.

Essays

"Sordità tra noi donne: ecco che cosa può renderci più deboli" [Deafness among Women: This Is What Can Weaken Us], in *L'unità,* 30 October 1990.
"Quei calci presi dalla mia ragazza di mafia" [Those Kicks from My Mafia Girl], in *L'unità,* 15 November 1994.

"In Persephone's Kingdom," translated by Edvige Giunta in *VIA: Voices in Italian Americana,* 7(2), 1996.

Plays

Radio Plays: *Lontano da casa* [Far From Home]. Radio-RAI-Fiction, 1996.

Autobiography

Mama Africa: Storia di donne ed utopie [Mama Africa: Story of Women and Utopia]. Milan, Sipiel, 1989.

Other

Editor, *Le Donne protagoniste nel movimento cooperativo: la questione femminile in un'organizzazione produttiva democratica* [Women as Protagonists in the Cooperative Movement: The Feminine Question in a Democratic Organization]. Milan, Feltrinelli, 1978.

Editor, *Scritture, scrittrici.* Rome, Longanesi, 1988.

Editor, with Rosaria Guacci and Marisa Rusconi, *Il pozzo segreto: 50 scrittrici italiane* [The Secret Well: 50 Italian Women Writers]. Florence, Giunti, 1993.

Editor, with Elena Doni and Elena Gianini Belotti, *Piccole italiane: un raggiro durato 20'anni* [Little Italians: A Deception That Lasted 20 Years]. Milan, Anabasi, 1994.

*

Critical Studies: "Under Western Eyes: Feminist Scholarship and Colonial Discourses" by Chandra Talpade Mohanty, in *Third World Women and the Politics of Feminism,* edited by Mohanty, Ann Russo, and Lourdes Torres, Bloomington, Indiana University Press, 1991; "Re-Thinking History: Women's Transgression in Maria Rosa Cutrufelli's *La briganta*" by Monica Rossi, in *Italian Herstory: Re-Reading History through Women's Fiction,* edited by Gabriella Brooke and Maria Ornella Marotti, n.d., n.p; "Briganta contro borghese" (interview) by Sandra Rizza, in *L'isola delle donne: mensile di donne siciliane,* November 1993; *From Margin to Mainstream: Feminism and Fictional Modes in Italian Women's Writing, 1968-1990* by Carol Lazzaro-Weis, Philadelphia, University of Pennsylvania Press, 1993, and her "History, Fiction, and the Female Autobiographical Voice," in *Romance Languages Annual* 7, 1995; "Come salvare Tina, la 'masculedda' della mafia?" (interview) by Adele Cambria, in *Il Giorno,* 13 February 1995.

* * *

Maria Rosa Cutrufelli is one of the most influential figures in Italian feminism. She was born in 1946 in Messina, Sicily, where she lived until age nine, when her family moved to Florence. She studied literature at the University of Bologna and wrote a dissertation on Russian formalism. In 1972 she went back to Sicily and lived in Gela, on the western coast of the island, while teaching high school in the nearby town of Riesi. During this formative period, Cutrufelli developed her ideas about women and class that would lead to the writing of a handful of groundbreaking texts in the history of Italian feminism. Cutrufelli, who had founded Lotta Femminista (Feminist Struggle), the first feminist group in Bologna, acted as the catalyst for a group of young feminists in Gela and started the first feminist group in Sicily, also called Lotta Femminista. This group tried to integrate the feminist practice of consciousness-raising with political activism. From Gela, the feminist movement spread to other Sicilian towns, although this chapter of Italian feminist history has yet to be adequately recorded or documented. Three years later, intolerant of the political corruption that paralyzed the island and of a cultural milieu hostile to assertive female voices, Cutrufelli moved back North.

A self-described "Sicilian in exile," Cutrufelli has produced an extensive body of work that explores, in various genres, problematics of women's exploitation and cultural marginalization. In her first feminist study, *L'invenzione della donna: Miti e tecniche di uno sfruttamento* (The Invention of Woman: Myths and Techniques of Exploitation) (1974), she examines the connections between the division of labor and the construction of mythologies of femininity in capitalist societies, differentiating between European and American forms of capitalism. Cutrufelli's concern with rooting her cultural analyses in historical and economic contexts is evident in *Disoccupata con onore* (Honorably Unemployed), a study of women's labor in Sicily published in 1975, and in *Donna perché piangi? Imperialismo e condizione femminile nell'Africa nera/Women in Africa: Roots of Oppression* (1976, translated 1983), which examines the ways in which imperialist policies have shaped women's condition in Africa. Cutrufelli sees the subjection of women as inextricably linked to the dynamics of neo-colonialism, a position that has been criticized by Chandra Talpade Mohanty, who argues that, like other texts of Western feminism, *Women in Africa* offers a reductive and essentialist view of African women. However, relying solely on the translation's title, Mohanty does not take into account that Cutrufelli wrote *Donna perché piangi?* (which literally translates as "Woman, Why Do You Cry? Imperialism and Women's Condition in Black Africa") in the early 1970s, before the publication of the large body of more recent work on Third World feminism and post-colonial criticism.

Cutrufelli's career demonstrates a continued commitment to political and social transformation pursued through careful analyses of the circumstances of oppression of particular groups. *Operaie senza fabbrica* (1977) (Women Workers without a Factory) furthers her exploration of the history of the working class, also the topic of the earlier *L'unità d'Italia: Guerra contadina e sottosviluppo del sud* (1974) (The Unity of Italy: Peasant War and The Origins of Underdevelopment in the South). *Mama Africa* (1989) blends historical and personal analyses in a powerful autobiographical narrative rooted in the years of the war for the independence of Angola. Based on a journal Cutrufelli kept in 1975-76 while in Angola and Zaire, this book, the title of which is taken from a poem by the Angolan guerrilla Deolinda Rodriguez, has received much critical attention in Italy and was reprinted in 1993.

In 1990 Cutrufelli published her first novel, *La briganta* (The Female Brigand), set in late 19th-century Southern Italy, the protagonist of which is an aristocratic woman who joins a band of brigands. In her *From Margin to Mainstream: Feminism and Fictional Modes in Italian Women's Writing, 1968-1990,* Carol Lazzaro-Weis argues that *La briganta* recounts "not only the story of forgotten female bandits, but also ... a version of the history of Italian feminism in recent years." Cutrufelli's second novel, *Complice il dubbio* (Complicitous Doubt), focuses on the development of the relationship between two women who meet accidentally in the shadow of a man's murder. *Canto al deserto. Storia di Tina, soldato di mafia* (Song to the Desert: Story of Tina, Mafia Soldier), possibly the first feminist novel on women and mafia, combines autobiography and history and is loosely based on the real-life events of Emanuela Azzarelli, a Sicilian girl who became the leader of a mafia gang of adolescent boys in Gela. Through this book Cutrufelli, who returned to Sicily after 20 years of self-imposed exile to do research for her novel, finds a way to come to terms with her conflicted relationship with Sicily. While traveling to Gela for a presentation of her book, Cutrufelli was assaulted by Azzarelli, who resented the author's fictional portrayal of her life. In the essay "In the Kingdom of Persephone," Cutrufelli explores her response to this peculiar and frightening meeting between an author and her character. In "History, Fiction, and the Female Autobiographical Voice," Lazzaro-Weis discusses Tina's story as being "another part of the intellectual autobiography of a writer struggling with *il problema del sud,* its relationship to the feminine and to the practice of her own arts."

In her novels, Cutrufelli both relies on and subverts the genre of historical fiction in order to question the parameters through which history has been written at the expense and exclusion of women. Both Margherita, the protagonist of *La briganta,* and Tina, the protagonist of *Canto al deserto,* articulate the author's attempt to reclaim the silenced voices of women. Cutrufelli's concern with supporting the voices of women is evident in her fictional and theoretical work as well as in her work as the founding editor of *Tuttestorie,* a magazine that continues to provide an important forum for Italian women's fiction. In 1993 she co-edited *Il pozzo segreto: 50 scrittrici italiane,* a collection of short stories published in *Tuttestorie* in 1990-93. She has also been instrumental in organizing readings of women's literature, such as those of the Circolo "della Rosa" in Rome.

Cutrufelli's most recent critical studies examine prostitution (in *Il cliente: Inchiesta sulla domanda di prostituzione* (The Client: An Investigation of Demand in the Prostitution Market) and the sex industry and its customers (in *Il denaro in corpo: Inchiesta sulla domanda di sesso commerciale* [Money Embodied: An Investigation of the Demand for Commercial Sex]). Aligning herself with Teresa De Lauretis, Cutrufelli warns against the division that has occurred within U.S. feminism around the issue of pornography. She argues for the necessity of separating a discussion of the pornography market from a discussion of the legitimacy of sexual fantasies and behaviors, which should not be subjected to scrutiny and censorship.

Cutrufelli's work has been translated in German, French and Portuguese. She is well-known among American scholars of Italian literature and feminist scholars, but her work, though available in American libraries, remains untranslated in English with the exception of *Women in Africa.*

—Edvige Giunta

D

DALL, Caroline Wells Healey

Nationality: American. **Born:** Boston, Massachusetts, 22 June 1822. **Education:** Educated privately; two years of classical studies with Joseph Hale. **Family:** Married the Rev. Charles Henry Appleton Dall in 1844 (died 1886); one son and one daughter. **Career:** Attended Margaret Fuller's "conversations," Boston, c. 1841; vice-principal, Miss English's school for Young Women, Georgetown, D.C., 1842-44; coeditor, with Paula Wright Davis, *Una* magazine, 1854; co-organizer, with Davis, women's rights convention, Boston, 1855; organizer and speaker, New England Woman's Rights Convention, Boston, 1859; cofounder, director, and librarian, American Social Science Association, 1865-1905; moved to Washington, D.C., 1879. **Awards:** LL.D., Alfred University, 1877. **Member:** American Social Science Association (vice-president, beginning 1880). **Died:** Washington, D.C., 17 December 1912.

Publications

Political/Social Theory

Woman's Right to Labor; or, Low Wages and Hard Work (lectures). Boston, Walker Wise, 1860; in *Low Wages and Great Sins: Two Antebellum American Views on Prostitution and the Working Girl,* edited by David J. Rothman and Sheila M. Rothman, New York and London, Garland, 1987.
Woman's Rights under the Law (lectures). Boston, Walker Wise, 1861.
The College, the Market, and the Court; or, Woman's Relations to Education, Labor, and Law. Boston, Lee & Shepherd, 1867.

Literary Criticism

Romance of the Association: or, One Last Glimpse of Charlotte Temple and Eliza Wharton. Cambridge, Massachusetts, J. Wilson, 1875.
What We Really Know about Shakespeare. Boston, Roberts Bros., 1885.
Sordello: A History and a Poem. Boston, Roberts Bros., 1886.

History

Historical Pictures Retouched: A Volume of Miscellanies. Boston, Walker Wise, 1860.
The Life of Dr. Marie Zakrzewska. Boston, n.p., 1860.
Egypt's Place in History. Boston, Lee & Shepherd, 1868.
The Life of Dr. Anadabai Joshee, a Kinswoman of the Pundita Ramabai. Boston, Roberts Bros., 1888.
Barbara Fritchie: A Study. Boston, Roberts Bros., 1892.

Essays

The Liberty Bell. N.p., 1847.
Essays and Sketches. N.p., 1849.

Autobiography

"Alongside"; Being Notes Suggested by "A New England Boyhood" of Dr. Edward Everett Hale. Boston, privately printed, 1900; New York, Arno, 1980.

For Children

The Bible Story Told for Children. N.p., 1866.
Patty Gray's Journey to the Cotton Islands: From Boston to Baltimore [From Baltimore to Washington] [From Washington to the Cotton Islands]. Boston, Lee & Shepherd, 3 vols., 1869-70.

Other

Sunshine: A New Name for a Popular Lecture on Health. Boston, Walker Wise, 1864.
Genealogical Notes and Errata to Savage's Genealogical Dictionary, Etc. Lowell, Massachusetts, Elliott, 1881.
My First Holiday; or, Letters Home from Colorado, Utah, and California. Boston, Roberts Bros., 1881.
Margaret Fuller and Her Friends; or, Ten Conversations with Margaret Fuller upon the Mythology of the Greeks and Its Expression in Art. Boston, n.p., 1895; New York, Arno Press, 1972.
Memorial to Charles Henry Appleton Dall. N.p., 1902.

Editor, *A Practical Illustration of "Woman's Right to Labor"; or, A Letter from Marie E. Zakrzewska.* N.p., 1860.

*

Manuscript Collections: Schlesinger Library, Radcliffe College; Massachusetts Historical Society, Boston.

Critical Studies: *American Feminists* by Robert E. Riegel, Lawrence, University Press of Kansas, 1963; "The Merchant's Daughter: A Tale from Life" by Barbara Welter, in *New England Quarterly,* March 1969; *Perish the Thought: Intellectual Women in Romantic America, 1830-1860* by Susan Phinney Conrad, n.p., 1976; *True Love and Perfect Union: The Feminist Reform of Sex and Society* by William Leach, n.p., 1980.

* * *

The first of eight children born into a well-to-do Boston family, Caroline Wells Healey Dall was educated in private schools, learned to speak five foreign languages, and developed an independent nature early in life. Her father, who wished that his daughter had been a boy, was responsible for bestowing upon Caroline Healey a dedication to hard work, autonomous thinking, and assertiveness. When he was faced with a financial crisis during the Panic of 1837, forcing his family into bankruptcy, the elder Healey's influence prompted his daughter to go to work as a vice-principal in a school for young ladies in the District of Columbia. Dall never felt attractive enough to be called feminine and was not willing to be dubbed masculine, so she referred to herself as neuter. Opinionated and individualistic, she had trouble relating to anyone other than her father. These characteristics created conflict when she became part of the feminist movement in the 1860s and as a consequence of her unpopularity she was kept from assuming leadership roles. Dall's strong ideas and convictions spilled over into her writing, which she considered to be of the utmost consequence: she copied and saved all of the over 85,000 letters she wrote.

Although she claimed she was not an abolitionist, Dall attempted to start a school for blacks while living in Washington, D.C. After the mid-1840s, she wrote articles for the *Liberty Bell*, an anti-slavery annual, and became a part of the underground network helping slaves escape to Canada. She also had exposure to the Transcendentalist movement and was present at several of Margaret Fuller's "conversations" in Boston during the same period. In 1895 Dall would published a book based on her noted and recollections of these "conversations," entitled *Margaret and Her Friends.*

Dall's independent nature also clashed with her father's ideas that she pursue a literary career. Instead, she became more intensely devoted to religion; she married the Reverend Charles Henry Appleton Dall in 1844 and had two children, a boy and a girl, from the union. Caroline Dall shared ministerial duties with her new husband, taught classes, and sometimes took to the pulpit. Her strong tendency to voice her opinions coupled with a strident belief that women were superior to men to lead to an unhappy conclusion of the marriage: by 1855 Reverend Dall had left his wife and children to escape to a missionary post in India. Until his death in 1886 he would only return to Boston to visit with his wife and children on rare occasions.

The absence of a husband and the necessity to support her family fueled Dall's writing career. While many of her early works, such as *Essays and Sketches* (1849) dealt mainly with religious issues, Dall's development as a feminist became more pronounced after her husband's departure for Calcutta. In 1855 and 1859 she helped to organize a woman's rights convention in Boston with Pauline Wright Davis and was the corresponding editor of *Una*, a woman's journal. Unlike many fellow suffragists, Dall's primary concern for women was not that they had the right to vote, but that they had the right to obtain a decent education, could work in competitive jobs, and draw equal pay with men.

Receiving virtually no money from her husband, Dall never relied solely on her father's support, but took in boarders and lectured to supplement her income. While the New York *Evening Post* considered the content of her lectures "eloquent and forceful" as they related to the Woman Question, her lackluster appearance and poor speaking voice prevented her talks from attaining the impact that her writing did. From a collection of her lectures Dall assembled her most notable work, *The College, the Market, and the Court: or, Woman's Relation to Education, Politics, and Law*. This well-written book, published in 1867, was the first of its kind and marked an important epoch in women's feminist history. In it Dall stated that "the educational rights of women" were "those of all human beings." Women had been excluded from most jobs, she contended, and she asked that women be allowed "free, untrammelled access to all fields of labor." Many women, she felt, found it necessary to turn to prostitution because they could not earn enough in any employment, and she criticized middle-class women for sitting idly as their working sisters became impoverished.

Dall encouraged women not to rely on charity but to work hard to attain self-reliance and to enter into fields of medicine, pharmacy, and business because they had as much ability to do so as men. She cited many accomplished women in her published works, as in *The Life of Dr. Marie Zakrzewska* (1860), the story of the female physician who founded the New England Hospital for Women and Children, and *The Life of Dr. Anadabai Joshee*, the first East Indian woman to become a physician. And in *Historical Pictures Retouched* Dall offered the reader a revisionist approach to historical women. In other speeches and writings, she also forcefully disputed the contention of Dr. Edward H. Clarke that women's health would deteriorate through the exertion of education. In *Woman's Rights under the Law*, published in 1861, Dall thoroughly examined the laws of Britain and France and showed what effect they had on women in regard to marriage, divorce, and elective franchise. While she thought that women should have the vote, women's employment opportunities continued to be of much greater significance to her. As Dall's writings increasingly promoted women's energies, her activism in feminist ideals led her to cofound the American Social Science Association (ASSA), an organization that would serve as a starting point for many social reform movements of the Progressive Era.

During her long lifetime Caroline Wells Healey Dall experienced episodes of chronic illness, sometimes believing that she was at death's door. However, she was a forceful and idiosyncratic personality, and never let that deter her in her quest to enlighten the world with what she knew was the right opinion. Until her death in 1912 at the age of 90, she remained resolute in her belief in the superiority of women and in pursuit of the goal of attaining equality of educational and vocational opportunity for women.

—Marilyn Elizabeth Perry

DALY, Mary

Nationality: American. **Born:** Schenectady, New York, 16 October 1928. **Education:** College of St. Rose, Albany, New York, B.A. in English 1950; Catholic University of America, M.A. in English 1952; School of Sacred Theology, St. Mary's College, Notre Dame, Indiana, Ph.D. in religion 1954; University of Fribourg, Switzerland, S.T.B. (basic degree in sacred theology) 1960, S.T.L. (licentiate in sacred theology) 1961, S.T.D. (doctorate in sacred theology) 1963, Ph.D. in philosophy 1965. **Career:** Visiting lecturer, St. Mary's College, Notre Dame, Indiana, 1952-54; teacher of philosophy and theology, Cardinal Cushing College, Brookline, Massachusetts, 1954-59; teacher of theology and philosophy, US Junior Year Abroad programs, University of Fribourg, Switzerland, 1959-66; assistant professor of theology, Boston College, Chestnut Hill, Massachusetts, 1966-69; associate professor of theology, Boston College, Chestnut Hill, Massachusetts, beginning 1969. **Member:** American Catholic Philosophical Association, American Academy of Religion, American Academy of Political and Social Science, American Association of University Professors, National Organization for Women, Society for the Scientific Study of Religion. **Agent:** Charlotte Raymond, 23 Waldron Court, Marblehead, Massachusetts 01945, U.S.A. **Address:** Department of Theology, Carney Hall, Boston College, Chestnut Hill, Massachusetts 02167, U.S.A.

PUBLICATIONS

Political/Social Theory

The Church and the Second Sex. New York, Harper, 1968; revised edition, with a new feminist postchristian introduction by the author, 1975; revised edition, with new archaic afterwords by the author, Boston, Beacon Press, 1985.
Beyond God the Father: Toward a Philosophy of Women's Liberation. Boston, Beacon Press, 1973; revised edition, 1985.
Gyn/Ecology: The Metaethics of Radical Feminism. Boston, Beacon Press, and London, Women's Press, 1978; revised edition, with a new intergalactic introduction by the author, 1990.
Pure Lust: Elemental Feminist Philosophy. Boston, Beacon Press, 1984.
Websters' First New Intergalactic WICKEDARY of the English Language, with Jane Caputi. Boston, Beacon Press, 1987.

Religion/Spirituality

Natural Knowledge of God in the Philosophy of Jacques Maritrain. Rome, Catholic Book Agency, 1966.

Autobiography

Outercourse: The Be-dazzling Voyage: Containing Recollections from My Logbook of a Radical Feminist Philosopher (Be-ing an Account of my Time/Space Travels and Ideas—Then, Again, Now, and How). San Francisco, HarperSanFrancisco, 1992.

Play

Screenplay: *Rape Culture,* with Emily Culpepper, 1975.

*

Critical Studies: "Taking Off on a Daly Journey" by Erica Smith, in *Herizons,* June 1984; "Embracing Motherhood: New Feminist Theory" by Heather Jon Maroney, in *Canadian Journal,* winter 1985; "Surviving to Speak New Language: Mary Daly and Adrienne Rich" by Jane Hedley, in *Hypatia,* 7(2), spring 1992; "What's So Good about the Goddess? (Christianity and Goddess Worship; Theologian Mary Daly)" by Dale Youngs, in *Christianity Today*, 37(9), 16 August 1993; "Rejected, Reclaimed, Renamed: Mary Daly on Psychology and Religion" by Susan E. Henking, in *Journal of Psychology and Theology,* 21(3), fall 1993; "Outercourse, by Mary Daly" by Barbara Krasner, in *Teaching Philosophy,* 16(4), December 1993; *Anglo-Feminist Challenges to the Rhetorical Traditions: Virginia Woolf, Mary Daly, and Adrienne Rich* by Krista Ratcliffe, Carbondale, Southern Illinois University Press, 1995.

* * *

Although she had dreamed from her youth of one day becoming a writer, Mary Daly recalls this desire as existing long before she had any idea about what to write. Indications are, however, that she was drawn to philosophy early; though her bachelor's and master's degrees are in English, she explains this as the result of her undergraduate institution's failure to offer a philosophy major, forcing her to make do with literary theory as a surrogate for philosophy. When she earned her Ph.D. in religion in 1954, at the age of 26, there was no university in the United States which would allow a woman to study for the Ph.D. in Catholic theology she so wanted to pursue. However, the Swiss University of Fribourg could not exclude her because of her gender: its theology faculty was under state control and consequently legally prohibited from barring women. In 1954, after five years of college teaching, Daly set off for Fribourg to satisfy her passion to study the highest levels of philosophy and theology. By the conclusion of her studies at age 37, she possessed a grand total of seven degrees, three of them doctorates.

It was only two years after her return to the United States in 1966—to assume an appointment as assistant professor of theology at Jesuit-run Boston College—that Daly leapt into public prominence with the publication of her second book, *The Church and the Second Sex,* an uncompromising criticism of the Catholic church's subjugation of women. This book, and the round of talk-show appearances that rapidly followed, may well have contributed to Boston College's decision to deny her tenure and promotion the following year. A storm of protest from faculty and students—in which Daly was defended as one of the most popular and best-credentialed members of the faculty by a supporting petition of 2,500 names—ensued, attracting national media coverage and ultimately convincing Boston College to change its position on her promotion and tenure. The granting of tenure did not mean that the college endorsed Daly's philosophical positions: despite her numerous publications, her many degrees, her high public profile, and her 30 years on the faculty, Daly is still an associate professor, having twice been denied promotion to full professor (once in 1974, after the publication of *Beyond God the Father,* and a second time in 1989). Although she sees her experiences at Boston College—by serving "as a laboratory and microcosm, enabling [her] to understand even more deeply not only the banal mechanisms of phallocentric evil but also possibilities of transcendence"—as having contributed to the radicalization of her philosophy, she has, nonetheless, personally suffered as a result of her colleagues' rejection of the radical brand of feminism that permeates her work. In her intellectual autobiography, *Outercourse*—itself centrally concerned with the development of her feminist philosophy—Daly recounts numerous examples of the struggles she has faced during her years at that institution. Were she a philosophical radical of any other stripe, it is arguable that she would, as a matter of course, have received more collegial protection and support than the administration and faculty of Boston College has seen fit to grant her.

Though she is clearly one of the most important of the second-wave radical-feminist thinkers, Daly's feminism is of a somewhat different sort than that of most other radical feminists. Where these others have their primary roots in the secular activist traditions of Marxism and the Left, Daly's intellectual influences are, instead, derived from Catholicism, from the academy, and from the existentialist tradition in theology. In particular, the legacies of Paul Tillich and Martin Buber (who was himself a follower of Heidegger) are seen in her first major work of feminist theory, *Beyond God the Father* (1973). She abandoned her primary identification as a radical Catholic and a practicing Christian—an identification that had been prominent during the writing of 1968's *The Church and the Second Sex.* In *Beyond God the Father,* Daly's new primary identification is as a radical feminist, outside the Christian church and its conventional theology.

Beyond God the Father seeks to provide a radical analysis of patriarchy, arguing that the women's movement can become a "spiritual revolution" in which women have the potential to transform human consciousness" through their "search for ultimate meaning and reality, which some would call God," and thereby to "generate human becoming." To make her argument, she draws on the existentialist theologians' idea that existence proceeds on two levels: the fixed, reified, "profane" level, exemplified by "I-It" (i.e., subject-object, or self-other) relationships, which are most characteristically embodied in the image of a scientist dissecting dead nature; and the intense, charged, "sacred" level, exemplified by "I-Thou" relationships, which involve mutual recognition of personhood. In Daly's view, the conventional notion of the power relationship between fallen humanity, and God-the-Father as patriarchal Supreme Being, is the paradigm example of an "I-It" relationship.

In this image, God is seen as a fixed and reified Self—in other words, as a Noun—instead, of as a "Verb—the Verb of Verbs," a description that conceives of God as an experience of Being in which we all participate in the web of existence, rather than as a person. It is the patriarchal, Christian, reified God who upholds the "Most Unholy Trinity" of patriarchy—Rape, Genocide, and War—combining in one patriarchal person the origins of sexism, racism, and classism, and thereby also becoming an idol which impedes humans' discovery of Becoming, of transcendence, of their own participation in the experience of being alive and of knowing the aliveness of all other organic Being. This God is the father of all patriarchs, possessed of ultimate power-over and, therefore, also characterized by absolute separation-from. Such a transcendent God is wholly unlike the natural world He created out of nothingness, and also consequently wholly removed from woman, whose reproductive powers inextricably implicate her in that world. Instead, she is "It" or Other not only to God's heavenly subject self—His "I"—but also to the "I" of His image and likeness on earth, man, whose superiority to woman has been reinforced by Christian, and especially Catholic, theology's particularization of the maleness of Jesus as a vehicle to the diminution and subordination of women.

In *Gyn/Ecology* Daly moves further to press her claims against patriarchy, arguing that its Unholy Trinity is indeed three-in-one, with but one driving ethos, "necrophilia," the "obsession with and usually erotic attraction toward and stimulation by corpses, typically evidenced by overt acts (as copulation with a corpse)." In patriarchy's death-loving culture, women are meant not only to be mentally oppressed, but also to be physically and spiritually mutilated by means of a "Sado-Ritual Syndrome" which manifests itself in such practices as Hindu suttee, Chinese foot binding, African genital mutilation, European witch burning, and Western gynecology. All of these aim to destroy women's wholeness and integrity, to tame and domesticate her wild, natural being, to shape her into a given culture's image of "femininity"—"a man-made construct, having essentially nothing to do with femaleness." Also important in this shaping is the power of patriarchal language, which smuggles into consciousness the values of patriarchy.

It is in *Gyn/Ecology* that Daly begins to develop the critique of language, as symbolic action and as the creator and the reifier of what we perceive to be reality, which is integral to her subsequent work, and *Gyn/Ecology*'s last section offers a preliminary dictionary of a new language. Daly's linguistic intentions are twofold: both to uncover or elicit new meanings for words with which the reader may think she is familiar (as when therapist becomes the/rapist), and to re-value, reclaim, or reinvent terms for women which in patriarchy have pejorative connotations, giving them a new positive and even celebratory valence (as when she redefines "hag" from the standard meaning of "an ugly, repulsive, perhaps evil old woman" to mean a woman whom patriarchy sees as old and ugly because of its phallic and ageist standards, as well as because she is clever and strong enough to reject its demands for female submission, obedience, and service). In *Gyn/Ecology* Daly also offers a new meaning for the concept of Being, transposing it into Be-ing, which is "the Final Cause, the Good who is Self-communicating, who is the Verb for whom, in whom, and with whom all true movements move."

Pure Lust: Elemental Feminist Philosophy builds on *Gyn/Ecology*'s project of language critique and of feminist theory and language building. Daly's primary concern here is with the two possible meanings for the title of the book: phallic (male) lust—which she describes as "genital fixation and fetishism" that oppresses "women and all living things within its reach" by raping, dismembering, and killing them—and the pure lust of the "high humor, hope, and cosmic accord/harmony of those women who choose to escape, to follow our hearts' deepest desire...out of the State of Bondage." She writes the book in three "Realms" (parts)—entitled "Archespheres," whose theme is origins and female power; "Pyrospheres," which deals with passion and emotion; and "Metamorphospheres," exploring women's relatedness—each of which begins with a "foreground" describing the patriarchal obstacles a woman must understand before she can enter the Realm. Ultimately, *Pure Lust* is an exploration of the possibilities of pure female friendship, freed from the baggage of patriarchy by female Be-ing.

In *Websters' First New Intergalactic WICKEDARY of the English Language*, Daly (in collaboration with Jane Caputi) collects the work she has done on language in her two previous books into a dictionary of her feminist philosophy as well as of her words. The book is written in three "Webs," the second of which is a long section devoted to word entries, some with illustrations. As a whole the work is creative, challenging, and even sometimes funny, full of puns and redefinitions that by turns amuse and startle, frustrate and exasperate, leaving the reader reeling under the impact of the revolution in language and meaning it aims to effect. As such, it is pure Daly—at once inventive and trite, engaging and maddening, subtle and painfully obvious—but always dense, and rich, and full of energy and passion. Finally, one is left not knowing whether we should feel more sympathy for Daly, over her shabby treatment by Boston College, or for Boston College itself, for having survived so long with such an electric, alien, and unsettling presence in its conservative midst.

—Eileen Bresnahan

DART, Helga. *See* **H.D.**

DAS, Kamala

Pseudonym: Madhavi Kutty. **Nationality:** Indian. **Born:** Malabar (now Kerala), 31 March 1934; daughter of poet Balamani Amma. **Education:** Educated at a Catholic convent school, Calcutta. **Family:** Married the banker K. Madhava Das in 1949; three sons. **Career:** Writer and activist; director, Book Point, Bombay; poetry editor, *Illustrated Weekly of India,* 1971-72, 1978-79; founder and president, Bahutantrika Group (artist's collective), Bombay; vice-president, State Council for Child Welfare, Trivandrum; chairman, Forestry Board, Kerla; president, Jyotsna Art and Education Academy, Goregaon, Bombay, and Kerala Children's Film Society; former member, State Planning Board subcommittee on art, literature, and mass communications; independent candidate for Parliament, 1984; member, governing council, Indian National Trust for Cultural Heritage, New Delhi. Conducts seminars on protection of the environment. Artist; exhibits work in Cochin, India. **Awards:** PEN Asian Poetry Prize, 1963; Kerala Sahitya Academy Awards, 1986, and 1970, for *Thanuppu;* Chimanlal Award for journalism, 1971; Asan World Prize for literature, 1985; D.Litt., World Academy of Arts and Culture, Taiwan, 1984; Kamala Das Research Center, St. Berkmans College, Changasasseery, Kerala, has been named in her honor. **Address:** c/o *Times* of India, Chittoor Road, Cochin, India.

Publications

Poetry

Summer in Calcutta. Delhi, Everest Press, 1965; Chicago, Intercultural, 1975.
The Descendants. Calcutta, Writers Workshop, 1967; East Glastonbury, Connecticut, Ind-US, 1975.
The Old Playhouse and Other Poems. Madras, India, Orient Longman, 1973.
Tonight, This Savage Rite: The Love Poetry of Kamala Das and Pritish Nandy. New Delhi, Arnold/Heinemann, 1979.
Collected Poems. Privately printed, 1984.
Selections from Kamala Das. Kottayam, India, D.C. Books, n.d.
Best of Kamala Das. Calicut, Bodhi Books, n.d.
Kamala Das: A Selection with Essays on her Work, edited by S. C. Harrex and Vincent O'Sullivan. Adelaid, Centre for Research in the New Literatures in English, 1986.

Novels

The Alphabet of Lust. New Delhi, Orient Paperback, 1976.
Madhavikkuttiyute munnu novalukal (collection; as Madhavi Kutty). Trivandum, India, Navadhara, 1977.
Asrita (as Madhavi Kutty). Kataka, Odisa Buk Shrora, 1980.
Tvamasi mama (as Madhavi Kutty). Calcutta, Natha Pabalisim, 1983.
Amrtam Bibbhati. Calcutta, Niu Bengala, 1984.
Anoraniyan (as Madhavi Kutty). Calcutta, Paribesaka Natha Bradarsa, 1985.
Manomi (as Madhavi Kutty). Trissur, India, Current, 1988.

Short Stories

Tharisunilam [Fallow Fields] (as Madhavi Kutty). Trissur, India, Current, 1962.
Tanuppa (as Madhavi Kutty). Trissur, India, Current, 1967.
Pathu kathakal (as Madhavi Kutty). Trissur, India, Current, 1968.
Thanuppu [Cold] (as Madhavi Kutty). Trissur, India, Current, 1970.
Premathinté vilapa kavyam [Requiem for a Love] (as Madhavi Kutty). Trissur, India, Current, 1971.
A Doll for the Child Prostitute. New Delhi, India Paperbacks, 1977.
Kisah secebis hati (as Madhavi Kutty). Singapore, Choice, 1978.
Amrtam bibhati (as Madhavi Kutty). Calcutta, Niu Bengala, 1984.
Enté cherukathakal (as Madhavi Kutty). Calcutta, Matrbhumi, 1985.
Bhayam ente nisavasthram (as Madhavi Kutty). Calcutta, Matrbhumi, 1986.
Swatantrasenaniyude makal (as Madhavi Kutty). Calcutta, Purna, 1991.
Padmavati, the Harlot and Other Stories. New Delhi, Sterling, 1992.
Neermatalam poothakalam (as Madhavi Kutty). Kottayam, D.C. Books, 1993.
Narachirukal parakkumbol [When the Bats Fly] (as Madhavi Kutty). Trissur, India, Current, n.d.
Enté snehita Aruna [My Friend Aruna] (as Madhavi Kutty). Trissur, India, Current, n.d.
Chuvanna pavada [The Red Skirt] (as Madhavi Kutty). Trissur, India, Current, n.d.
Rajavinte premabajanam [The King's Beloved] (as Madhavi Kutty). Trissur, India, Current, n.d.
Mathilukal [Walls] (as Madhavi Kutty). Trissur, India, Current, n.d.
Collected Stories. N.p., n.d.

Uncollected Short Stories

"Summer Vacation," in *The Inner Courtyard.* N.p., n.d.

Essays

The Heart of Britain. Calcutta, Firma KLM, 1983.

Plays

Kamala Das: A Collage (collection of one-act plays), compiled by Arum Kuckreja. New Delhi, Vidfa Prakashan Mandir, 1984.

Autobiography

My Story. Jullundur, India, Sterling, 1976; East Glastonbury, Connecticut, Ind-US, 1977.

For Children

Draksakshi Panna [Eyewitness] (as Madhavi Kutty). London, Longman, 1973.

*

Critical Studies: *Contemporary Indian Poetry in English* by Lakshmi Raghunandan, n.p., n.d.; *Kamala Das* by Devindra Kohli, New Delhi, Arnold/Heinemann, 1975; "Mary and Mira: A Study of Kamala Das" by I.K. Sharma, in *Commonwealth Quarterly,* 3(10), 1979; *Contemporary Indian English Verse* by Chirantan

Kulshrestha, New Delhi, Arnold Heinemann, 1980; *Kamala Das and Her Poetry* by A.N. Dwivendi, New Delhi, Doaba, 1983; *Expressive Form in the Poetry of Kamala Das* by A. Rahman, New Delhi, Abhinav, 1981; *Family Quarrels: Towards a Criticism of Indian Writing in English* by Feroza F. Jussawalla, London, P. Lang, 1985; "The Short Stories of Kamala Das" by Mohamed Elias, in *World Literature Written in English,* 25(2), 1985; *Kamala Das: A Selection with Essays on her Work,* edited by S.C. Harrex and Vincent O'Sullivan, Adelaid, Centre for Research in the New Literatures in English, 1986; *Living Indian English Poets* by Madhusudan Prasad, New Delhi, Sterling, 1989; "Watching Herself/Watching Her Self: Kamala Das's Split Texts" by Marilla North, in *New Literatures Review,* 21, summer 1991; "Terms of Empowerment in Kamala Das's *My Story*" by Shirley Geok Lin Lim, in *De/Colonizing the Subject: The Politics of Gender in Women's Autobiography,* Minneapolis, University of Minnesota Press, 1992; *The Endless Female Hungers: A Study of Kamala Das* by Vrinda Nabar, New Delhi, Sterling, 1993; "Text as History, History as Text: A Reading of Kamala Das's 'Anamalai Poems'" by P.P. Raveendran, in *Journal of Commonwealth Literature,* 29(1), spring 1994.

* * *

Kamala Das, with her poem, "Introductions," written in 1965, confidently introduces herself:

> "I am Indian, very brown, born in Malabar/... speak three languages, write in two, dream in one/... the language I speak becomes mine/... it is half English, half Indian/... it is as human as I am human."

Das, schooled at home and in a Catholic convent school in post-colonial India, was literate in English at an early age. She had a culturally rich childhood surrounded by artists, writers, and thinkers, including her poet-mother and her granduncle, a poet-philosopher. At the age of 15 she was taken out of this intellectual milieu and married, in proper Indian fashion, to a banker.

Her wedding night brought bruises and forced intercourse but no love. She constantly searched for this love in extra-marital affairs but found it elusive. These personal experiences and feelings about relationships, as well as about her three sons and their births, her childhood with a beloved grandmother in the 300-year-old matriarchal family house in Malabar, and her mental and physical illnesses frame the dynamic poetry that Das began to write in her early 1920s. Probably her most well-known, albeit controversial, writing, particularly for the 1950s and 1960s, was about sex. She wrote frankly and often explicitly about this taboo subject and to do that, according to critic Dorothy Jones in *Kamala Das: A Selection with Essays on Her Work,* "in a society which expects women to be modest, submissive and unobtrusive is in itself an act of rebellion which imparts energy and vigour" to Das's writing.

In 1974, while in the hospital after suffering a heart attack, Das started writing her autobiography, *My Story,* which would be serialized in *The Current Weekly,* Bombay. As this memoir was even more explicitly about her life, her marriage, and her affairs than her poetry had been, and reached a much broader audience, her personal life was in full view to India. As Das rather graphically explains in her poem, "Loud Posters" from *Summer in Calcutta:* "I've stretched my two-dimensional/Nudity on sheets of weeklies, monthlies,/Quarterlies, a sad sacrifice."

My Story "is rather more figurative and poetic than it is orthodox autobiographical prose," according to critic Marilla North in *New Literature Review,* but has abiding importance as the story of an independent Indian woman, brave and strong in her writing but also submissive and drowning in her love affairs with men. Das is always aware of the role of women and has always understood that marriage meant a show of wealth and social status to the family: only the beauty of the bride is important, not her happiness. In her writings she tenderly relates her childhood: free from cares, swimming nude in the pond, but as an adolescent she had to put away these childish pleasures and be a girl, then a wife. The lines "I was taught to break saccharine into your tea/... to offer at the right moment the vitamins/... I lost my will and reason," reflect the sentiments that echo throughout "The Old Playhouse." The brief poem "Herons" begins and ends with this refrain: "On sedatives I am more lovable says my husband/... my ragdoll limbs adjust better to his versatile lust."

Das has written 30 stories in Malayalam, her birth language, using the name Madhavi Kutty, in addition to her three books of poetry, her autobiography, *My Story,* several short stories and novellas, and journalism articles written in English. Excerpts from *My Story,* plus four short plays that deal with a variety of male-female relationships featuring a woman protagonist, were performed as *The Collage* in New Delhi in 1984 by the Ruchika Theatre Group.

Although Das's writing reflects her life as an independent and courageous woman, continually questioning her identity, she would not call herself a feminist—Vrinda Nabar in *The Endless Female Hungers* writes of a newspaper column of Das's denigrating the Women's Movement; she wants to join the movement to "have the fun of walking around with no bra." However Das has a heightened awareness of the role of women, whether it is as a poor prostitute, a young, raped girl, or an ill wife. Such women figure prominently in her stories, which are told in a sometimes poignant, sometimes ironic style. Her *Doll for a Child Prostitute* is a deceptively simple tale of a 12-year-old girl named Rukmani who is sold to a house of prostitution after being raped by her stepfather and therefore presumably unmarriageable. Once there she is given to a man her grandfather's age who becomes infatuated with her and buys her a doll. The juxtaposition of Rukmani playing at a marriage ceremony of her dolls with her friend, Sita, and then being called to have sex with this old man is shocking. Even more distressing, perhaps, is her fondness for him—he is the only one who cares at all for her.

It is not surprising that these prostitutes have Hindu goddesses' names, such as Sita and Rukmani; mythology and religion permeate Das's poetry and presumably her life as a Hindu. She often uses the images of Radha's love for Krishna as "an image of the transcendent bliss and union with the divine which a woman may experience through sexual love," according to Dorothy Jones.

Important critical studies on Das, such as *The Endless Female Hungers,* which contains interviews with the writer, as well as numerous essays, are beginning to proclaim her importance as a writer outside of her native India. Not only is her work being studied in the English-speaking world, but Das has also introduced herself to U.S., Canadian, and British audiences through lectures on such topics as the "Writer as Emotional Revolutionary" that she gives on college campuses. Kamala Das is following in the footsteps of a long line of Indian female writers with powerful voices, from the 12th-century poet Saint Mahadevi to her own mother, Balamani Amma.

—Jacquelyn Marie

DAVIS, Angela (Yvonne)

Nationality: American. **Born:** Birmingham, Alabama, 26 January 1944. **Education:** Brandeis University, B.A. (honors) in philosophy, c. 1965; studied at Institut für Sozialforschung, Frankfurt; University of California, San Diego, M.A. 1968. **Family:** Married Hilton Braithwaite. **Career:** Lecturer in philosophy, University of California, Los Angeles; joined Communist Party, 1968; travelled to Cuba, 1969; active in Soledad Brothers Defense Committee; acquitted of charges of murder, kidnapping, and conspiracy, 1972; ran for vice-president on the Communist Party ticket, 1980, 1984; lecturer at colleges and universities, including Berkeley, Cal-Santa Cruz, and San Francisco University. Contributor of articles to periodicals, including *Ebony.* **Awards:** Honorary Ph.D., Lenin University. **Member:** National Committee of the Communist Party, National Alliance against Racist and Political Repression, National Black Women's Health Project.

Publications

Political/Social Theory

Women, Race, and Class. New York, Random House, 1981.
Women, Culture, and Politics. New York, Random House, 1989.

Uncollected Essays

"Reflections on the Black Woman's Role in the Community of Slaves," in *Black Scholar,* 3(4), December 1971.

Autobiography

Angela Davis: An Autobiography. New York, Random House, 1974.

Other

Editor, with others, *If They Come in the Morning.* N.p., Third Press, 1971.

Recording: *Angela Davis Speaks,* Folkways, 1971.

*

Critical Studies: *The People vs. Angela Davis* by Charles R. Ashman, Pinnacle, 1972; *From Where I Sat* by Nelda J. Smith, New York, Vantage, 1973; *Black Macho and the Myth of the Superwoman* by Michele Wallace, New York, Dial Press, 1978.

* * *

In a decade of activism, Angela Davis stands out as a radical activist and as an author of tremendous influence. She is certainly one of the best-known black women in America—a charismatic, brilliant educator who continues to infuriate the academic and political establishment and has been a consistent critic of America's racism, sexism, and imperialism for over 30 years. A writer of uncommon power, Davis has been one of the best chroniclers of the anti-war and Black Power movements as well as one of the first scholars to write extensively on the history of black women. Her seminal essay, "Reflections on the Black Woman's Role in the Community of Slaves," written while Davis was in jail charged with murder, kidnapping, and conspiracy to commit both, has been cited as an early call—which few heeded—to consider the unique role of slave women. Davis wrote: "We, the black women of today, must accept the full weight of a legacy wrought in blood by our mothers in chains.... as heirs to a tradition of supreme perseverance and heroic resistance, we must hasten to take our place wherever our people are forging on towards freedom."

Born 26 January 1944, in Birmingham, Alabama, Davis is the daughter of middle-class professionals who fostered their talented child's ambition to learn. Her mother, Sallye E., and her father, B. Frank Davis were schoolteachers, although Davis's father later started his own gas station to better support his family. Her mother and grandmother instructed Angela in African American history, and the child's keen awareness of the social inequities of her surroundings grew as she participated in civil rights actions with her mother. Her education molded the radical woman she became, from the Elizabeth Irwin High School she attended in New York on scholarship (where Davis became a Marxist-Leninist) to Brandeis University, where she studied French literature. She spent a watershed year at the Sorbonne in Paris, deepening her commitment to helping the oppressed as she learned of the struggle in Algeria against the French. When the infamous church bombing in Birmingham in 1963 killed four little girls Davis knew, she was ready to advance politically, and found the mentor she sought in the philosopher Herbert Marcuse. As Marcuse's student, Davis became a philosopher and studied in Germany with Theodore Adorno and Oskar Negt. She earned her Masters in philosophy in 1969 from the University of California at San Diego and moved swiftly to complete her Ph.D. requirements other than her dissertation. During these years, her campus activism led her to the Student Non-violent Coordinating Committee and Franklin and Kendra Alexander, who became her close friends and advisors. Franklin was active in the Black Panthers and the Communist Party, and Davis herself joined the Party in 1968.

This action would have tremendous repercussions on Davis's academic life, as she lost her faculty position in philosophy at the University of California at Los Angeles at the behest of the then-governor, Ronald Reagan, in 1969. She was reinstated, but not rehired the next year on the pretext of her radical activity and citing her lack of a doctorate. At this time she became involved with the effort to free the "Soledad Brothers," three Black inmates charged with the murder of a white prison guard. Davis threw herself into giving speeches on their behalf and, through a correspondence with George Jackson, one of the Soledad Brothers, she became personally involved. Despite the fact that the charges against him had been dropped, Jackson remained in prison and was killed by guards in an alleged escape attempt; his brother Jonathan attempted a rescue of another inmate from San Quentin and was killed along with two prisoners and the judge. Angela's guns had been used in the hostage-taking, and even though she had obtained them legally and had purchased them for her protection, she was forced into hiding when the FBI placed her on its

"Ten Most Wanted" list in 1970. She was found in New York and placed in jail in California without bail.

Davis's celebrity peaked with the "Free Angela" movement of the early 1970s, which made her the focus of a groundswell of popular opinion demanding her release, and in 1972, she was acquired of all charges. Despite Ronald Reagan's and the Board of Regents' mandate that she would never again teach in a California university, Davis has taught at San Francisco State and the University of California at Santa Cruz and remains politically active as a speaker and a writer. She travels extensively and lectures throughout the world. Her work on black women is provocative and challenges easy assumptions—increasingly her focus has been on health issues, and she has been on the board of the National Black Women's Health Project since 1986.

Her best-known books are her 1988 autobiography, and *If They Come in the Morning* (1971). She is as direct and fearless as ever: in an essay entitled "Rape, Race and the Myth of the Black Racist," her aim is not only to eviscerate this persistent myth but to take to task two respected feminist writers, Susan Brownmiller and Shulamith Firestone (among others) for their being deceived by it. Two essay collections, *Women, Race and Class* (1983) and *Women, Culture and Politics* (1989), best represent the maturation of Angela Davis as an activist and an intellectual. She has said she is surprised and gratified that young people continue to be interested in her and her ideas. With characteristic modesty, Davis wrote, "My own work over the last two decades will have been wonderfully worthwhile if it has indeed assisted in some small measure to awaken and encourage this new activism."

—Mary A. Hess

DAVIS, Rebecca (Blaine) Harding

Nationality: American. **Born:** Washington, Pennsylvania, 24 June 1831. **Education:** Washington Female Seminary, 1844-48, graduated (valedictorian), 1848. **Family:** Married L(emuel) Clarke Davis in 1863; three children. **Career:** Regular contributing editor, *New York Tribune*, 1869-89; regular contributor of editorials and fiction to *New York Independent*, 1875-1910, and *Saturday Evening Post*, 1902-06. Contributor of essays and short fiction to other periodicals, including *Atlantic Monthly, Galaxy, Harper's, Hearth and Home, Lippincott's, Peterson's Magazine, St. Nicholas,* and *Youth's Companion.* **Died:** 29 September 1910.

PUBLICATIONS

Novels

Margret Howth: A Story of To-Day (originally published in *Atlantic Monthly,* 1861-62). Boston, Ticknor & Fields, 1862.
Waiting for the Verdict. New York, Sheldon, 1867.
Dallas Galbraith. Philadelphia, Lippincott, 1868.
John Andross. New York, Orange Judd, 1874.
A Law unto Herself. Philadelphia, Lippincott, 1878.
Natasqua. New York, Cassell-Rainbow, 1886.
Kent Hampden. New York, Scribners, 1892.
Doctor Warrick's Daughters. New York, Harper, 1896.
Frances Waldeaux. New York, Harper, 1897.
Bits of Gossip. Boston, Houghton Mifflin, 1904.

Short Stories

"Life in the Iron Mills" (originally published in *Atlantic Monthly,* April 1861), in *Atlantic Tales.* Boston, Ticknor & Fields, 1866; as *Life in the Iron Mills and Other Stories,* introduction by Tillie Olsen, Old Westbury, New York, Feminist Press, 1972.
Kitty's Choice, or Berrytown and Other Stories. Philadelphia, Lippincott, 1873.
Silhouettes of American Life. New York, Scribners, 1892.
A Rebecca Harding Davis Reader: Life in the Iron Mills, Selected Fiction, and Essays, edited by Jean Pfaelzer. Pittsburgh, University of Pittsburgh Press, 1995.

Uncollected Short Stories

"The Murder of the Glenn Ross," in *Peterson's Magazine,* November-December 1861.
"The Second Life," in *Peterson's Magazine,* January-June 1863.
"The Promise of the Dawn," in *Atlantic Monthly,* January 1863.
"Paul Blecker," in *Atlantic Monthly,* May-June 1863.
"Ellen," in *Peterson's Magazine,* July 1863.
"The Wife's Story," in *Atlantic Monthly,* July 1864.
"In the Market," in *Peterson's Magazine,* January 1868.
"A Pearl of Great Price," in *Lippincott's Magazine,* December 1868.
"Captain Jean," in *Peterson's Magazine,* November 1869.
"Put Out of the Way," in *Peterson's Magazine,* May-June 1870.
"Earthen Pitchers," in *Scribner's Monthly,* November 1873-April 1874.
"Pepper-Pot Woman," in *Scribner's Monthly,* September 1874.
"The Middle-Aged Woman," in *Scribner's Monthly,* July 1875.
"Across the Gulf," in *Lippincott's Magazine,* July 1881.
"Here and There in the South," in *Harper's New Monthly,* July-November 1887.
"Elizabeth's Thanksgiving," in *Good Housekeeping,* November 1893.
"An Old-Time Love Story," in *Century,* December 1908.
"The Coming of Night," in *Scribner's Monthly,* January 1909.

Uncollected Essays

"Leebsmall," in *New York Independent,* 4 August 1887.
"Low Wages for Women," in *New York Independent,* 8 November 1888.
"Women in Literature," in *New York Independent,* 7 May 1891.
"On Trial," in *New York Independent,* 24 November 1892.
"The Newly Discovered Woman," in *New York Independent,* 30 November 1893.
"On the Jersey Coast," in *New York Independent,* 15 November 1900.
"The Disease of Money-Getting," in *New York Independent,* 19 July 1902.
"The Trained Nurse," in *New York Independent,* 3 October 1907.
"One or Two Plain Questions," in *New York Independent,* 22 October 1908.

For Children

"A Hundred Years Ago," in *Riverside,* June-July 1870.

"The Paw Paw Hunt" in *Youth's Companion*, 9 November 1871.
"Naylor o' the Bowl" in *St. Nicholas,* 1 December 1873.
"The Shipwreck" in *Youth's Companion,* 17 February 1876.
"Two Brave Boys" in *St. Nicholas,* July 1910.

*

Bibliography: "A Bibliography of Fiction and Non-Fiction by Rebecca Harding Davis" by Jane Atteridge Rose, in *American Literary Realism*, 22(3), spring 1990.

Manuscript Collections: Clifton Waller Barrett Library, University of Virginia; The Huntingdon Library, San Marino, California.

Critical Studies: *The Richard Harding Davis Years: A Biography of a Mother and Son* by Gerald Langford, New York, Holt Rinehart, 1961; "Success and Failure of Rebecca Harding Davis" by James C. Austin, in *Midcontinent American Studies Journal,* 3, 1962; "Literary Contexts of 'Life in the Iron Mills'" by Walter Hesford, in *American Literature,* 49, 1977-78; "Assailant Landscapes and the Man of Feeling: Rebecca Harding Davis's *Life in the Iron Mills"* by John Conron, in *Journal of American Culture*, 3, 1980; "Rebecca Harding Davis: Domesticity, Social Order, and the Industrial Novel" by Jean Pfaelzer, in *International Journal of Women's Studies,* 4, 1981; "Rebecca Harding Davis: From Romanticism to Realism" by Sharon M. Harris, in *American Literary Realism*, 21(2), 1989; "Sculpture in the Iron Mills: Rebecca Harding Davis's Korl Woman" by Maribel W. Molyneux, in *Women's Studies*, 17, 1990; "The 'Feminization' of Rebecca Harding Davis" by Jean Fagan Yellin, in *American Literary History*, 2(2), 1990; "Redefining the Feminine: Women and Work in Rebecca Harding Davis's 'In the Market'" by Sharon M. Harris, in *LEGACY*, 8, 1991, and her *Rebecca Harding Davis and American Realism,* Philadelphia, University of Pennsylvania Press, 1991; *Rebecca Harding Davis* by Jane Atteridge Rose, New York, Twayne, 1993.

* * *

Rebecca Harding Davis was a prolific author of novels, short stories, and essays during the late 19th century. Such eminent contemporaries as Ralph Waldo Emerson and Nathaniel Hawthorne admired her work; she is now recognized for her pioneering short fiction, in which she combines psychologically complex characters with astute social critique. Davis was at the forefront of the literary realism movement and produced over 500 fiction and nonfiction prose pieces in almost 50 years as a writer. Her work is especially remarkable for its consistent focus on social and female concerns, a reflection of the author's own position as a working woman of the 19th century.

Davis was raised, for the most part, in Wheeling, West Virginia. Her hometown was situated at the border of military activity during the Civil War, a fact that would influence her work. Davis consistently refused to glorify war; rather, in her writing she sympathetically explored the universal misery occasioned by battle and highlighted its effect upon women. In her 1867 novel, *Waiting for the Verdict,* she illustrates the need for regional and racial reconciliation during and following the Civil War, and suggests that familial love and interracial friendships are essential to the realization of America's ideals.

In her prose Davis would also combine the urgent social concerns she had developed during a childhood spent witnessing men and women struggling to make ends meet in industrial Wheeling with an exploration of such an environment's effect upon one's psyche. In 1861, the same year that the northwest portion of Virginia seceded from the Confederacy, Davis's first—and most critically acclaimed—short story, "Life in the Iron Mills," appeared in the *Atlantic Monthly.* The story is remarkable for its psychological insight into the conflict, repression, and hopelessness of factory workers struggling to maintain their humanity in the face of an increasingly mechanistic and materialistic society. Throughout her career Davis would demonstrate a consistent concern for individuals alienated within a changing society and sensitively explore the psychological interiority of those on the fringes—particularly women and slaves.

"Life in the Iron Mills" also introduces several of Davis's characteristically unusual female protagonists. Neither Deb nor the korl woman conform to 19th-century standards of womanhood: Deb is stronger than her markedly feminized cousin Hugh "Molly" Wolfe and balances her domestic duties with her work at the mill while evincing strong spiritual beliefs. Many of Davis's female protagonists lack the conventional beauty expected of fictional women, but the framing narrator's voice compels her readers to reconsider established stereotypes and to reevaluate the positioning of women and the societal constraints placed upon them. Emblematic of Davis's concerns is the naked, muscular korl woman, "coarse with labor, the powerful limbs instinct with some one poignant longing," which Hugh explains as a hunger for "'Summat to make her live.'" In her fiction, Davis explores her female characters' desires for a vocation that can satiate their souls, as well as the actual possibilities open to them. "Life in the Iron Mills" also exhibits another of Davis's prominent concerns: the connection between the spiritual and material worlds. She urges social reform through the rediscovery of real Christian values; she juxtaposes seemingly disparate beliefs in an impulse to reconcile and to reform, a reflection of her own ambivalence about her role as a woman artist. Davis would also explore the compromise she perceived as a woman's price for love, viewing marriage and motherhood as inhibiting creativity in her story "Earthen Pitchers," first published in 1873.

Davis challenged the accepted belief of the privileging of social work over domestic work and demonstrated that women are capable of, and even expected to fulfill, both roles. The realism of her work is also critical: her stories also demonstrate the need for reform and for education. Davis's vision was ultimately informed by her personal experience with—and her need to further explore—the conflict of the woman artist. She contended with a male publisher who wanted her to alleviate her serious vision, and with her husband, L. Clarke Davis, whom she married in 1863 and who influenced her toward a more overt didacticism. As early as 1864's "The Wife's Story" Davis would denounce the egotism of the artist as she struggled to reconcile her aesthetic goals with her new domestic role. The responsibilities of marriage and children can be clearly discerned through her continuing development as a writer, since, for financial reasons, Davis was compelled to modify her own artistic and aesthetic goals to realize the expectations of her readership. Jane Atteridge Rose's comprehensive 1993 *Rebecca Harding Davis,* a study of Davis's life and works, reveals many of the conflicts Davis experienced along these lines.

During the 1860s, Davis produced many gothic, supernatural pieces that were carefully orchestrated to appeal to a broad readership. She also began publishing tales for children in the 1870s. But female characters consistently remained the emotional centers of her stories, and the tension between the several roles that Davis fulfilled in real life can be found in much of her work. She came to accept her primary role as wife and mother, but wrote frequently of the need for vocational employment for women. In stories such as 1868's "In the Market," her delineation of the uselessness of women's expected passivity in waiting for marriage is a dominant concern. Davis opposed the accepted belief of the separateness of "male" and "female" spheres and, through her fiction, explored the difficulties of women caught within that belief system.

Davis was able to fulfill the socially accepted 19th-century role of wife and mother while maintaining her writing through a career as an editorial journalist. Her later works focus on the individual and demonstrate an increasing social optimism—as well as an increasing element of moralizing—as their author found domestic contentment. Many of her editorials were based on historical events; her journalism was well researched and highly respected. Nevertheless, Davis's fascination with interior female psychology remained dominant: in 1907's "The Trained Nurse" she insists that women need vocational training for their duties in the domestic sphere. Rebecca Harding Davis's work as a critical realist concerned with psychological interiority and regional realism continues to lend readers valuable insights into the tension and conflicts of a 19th-century woman attempting to fulfill both the expectations of society and her desire for personal expression.

—Lucy Morrison

---

de ASBAJE y RAMÍREZ de SANTILLANA, Juan Inéz. *See* **JUANA INÉS de la CRUZ, Sor.**

---

de BEAUVOIR, Simone (Lucie Ernestine Marie Bertrande)

Nationality: French. **Born:** Paris, France, 9 January 1908. **Education:** Cours Désir, Paris, 1913-25; Institut Sainte Marie, Neuilly; Ecole Normal Supérieure, Paris, agrégation de philosphie 1929. **Family:** Companion of the philosopher Jean-Paul Sartre beginning 1929; adopted one daughter. **Career:** Taught at the Lycée Victor Duruy, Paris, 1929-31, Lycée in Marseilles, 1931, Lycée Jeanne d'Arc in Rouen, 1932, Lycée Molière, Paris, 1936-39, and Lycée Camille-Sée and Lycée Henri VI, Paris, 1939-43; editor, with Jean-Paul Sartre, *Les Temps Modernes,* Paris, beginning 1945; signed *Manifeste des 343* in *Le nouvel observateur,* 1971; cofounder, with Monique Wittig and Christine Delphy, *Questions feministes* (journal), 1979. Member, Consultative Committee, Bibliothèque Nationale, 1969. **Member:** Choisir (president, 1972), League for the Rights of Women (president, beginning 1974). **Awards:** Prix Goncourt, 1954, for *Les Mandarins;* Jerusalem Prize, 1975; State Prize, Austria, 1978; Sonning Prize for European Culture (Denmark). Honorary doctorate, Cambridge University. **Died:** Paris, 14 April 1986.

Publications

Novels

L'Invitée. Paris, Gallimard, 1943; translated as *She Came to Stay,* London, Secker & Warburg, 1949; Cleveland, Ohio, World, 1954.

Le Sang des autres. Paris, Gallimard, 1945; translated as *The Blood of Others,* London, Secker & Warburg, and New York, Knopf, 1948.

Tous les hommes sont mortels. Paris, Gallimard, 1946; translated as *All Men Are Mortal,* Cleveland, Ohio, World, 1956.

Les Mandarins. Paris, Gallimard, 1954; translated as *The Mandarins,* London, Collins, 1957; Cleveland, Ohio, World, 1960.

Les Belles Images. Paris, Gallimard, 1966; translated, New York, Putnam, 1968; London, Fontana, 1969.

La Femme rompue, with *Monologue* and *L'Age de discrétion.* Paris, Gallimard, 1968; translated as *The Woman Destroyed, with The Monologue and The Age of Discretion,* London, Collins, 1969.

Short Stories

Quand prime le spirituel. Paris, Gallimard, 1979; translated as *When Things of the Spirit Come First: Five Early Tales,* New York, Pantheon, 1982.

Philosophy

Pyrrhus et Cinéas. Paris, Gallimard, 1944.

Pour une morale de l'ambiguité. Paris, Gallimard, 1947; translated as *The Ethics of Ambiguity,* New York, Philosophical Library, 1948.

L'Existentialisme et la sagesse des nations. Paris, Nagel, 1948.

Que peut la littérature? with others. Paris, Union Générale d'Éditeurs, 1965.

Play

Les Bouches inutiles. Paris, Gallimard, 1945; translated as *Who Shall Die?* Florissant, Missouri, River Press, 1983.

Essays

Le Deuxième Sexe: I. Les Faits et Les Mythes [II. L'Expérience Vécue]. Paris, Gallimard, 2 vols., 1949; translated as *The Second Sex,* London, Cape, and New York, Knopf, 1953.

Must We Burn Sade? London, Peter Neville, 1953; reprinted in *Privilèges,* 1955.

Privilèges. Paris, Gallimard, 1955.

La Longue Marche: Essai sur la Chine. Paris, Gallimard, 1957; translated as *The Long March,* London, Deutsch, and Cleveland, Ohio, World, 1958.

Brigitte Bardot and the Lolita Syndrome. London, Deutsch, and New York, Reynal & Hitchcock, 1960.

Djamila Boupacha, with Giselle Halimi. N.p., 1962.

La Viellesse. Paris, Gallimard, 1970; translated as *Old Age,* London, Deutsch, and New York, Putnam, 1972.

Autobiography

Mémoires d'une jeune fille rangée. Paris, Gallimard, 1958; translated as *Memories of a Dutiful Daughter,* London, Deutsch, and Cleveland, Ohio, World, 1959.

La Force de l'age. Paris, Gallimard, 1960; translated as *The Prime of Life,* London, Deutsch, and Cleveland, Ohio, World, 1962.

La Force des choses. Paris, Gallimard, 1963; translated as *Force of Circumstance,* New York, Putnam, 1964; London, Deutsch, 1965.

Une Mort très douce. Paris, Gallimard, 1964; translated as *A Very Easy Death,* London, Deutsch, and New York, Putnam, 1972.

Tout compte fait. Paris, Gallimard, 1972; translated as *All Said and Done,* London, Deutsch, and New York, Putnam, 1964.

La Cérémonie des adieux. Paris, Gallimard, 1981; translated as *Adieux: A Farewell to Sartre,* New York, Pantheon, 1984.

Other

L'Amérique au jour le jour (travel). Paris, Morihien, 1948; translated as *America Day by Day,* London, Duckworth, 1948; New York, Grove, 1953.

Lettres au Sartre, edited by Sylvie Le Bon de Beauvoir. Paris, n.d.; translated as *Letters to Sartre,* London, Radius, 1991.

Editor, *Lettres au Castor: et à quelques autres.* Paris, Gallimard, 1983; translated as *Witness to My Life: The Letters of Jean-Paul Sartre to Simone de Beauvoir, 1926-1939,* London, Hamish Hamilton, 1992; translated as *Quiet Moments in a War: The Letters of Jean-Paul Sartre to Simone de Beauvoir, 1940-1963,* New York, Scribners, 1993; London, Hamish Hamilton, 1994.

*

Media Adaptations: *Daughters of de Beauvoir* (film on her work); *Simone de Beauvoir: Un Film de Josée Dayan et Malka Ribowska,* Paris, Gallimard, 1979, New York, Interama Video Classic, 1989.

Bibliography: In *Les Écrits de Simon de Beauvoir* by Claude Francis and Fernande Gontier, Paris, Gallimard, 1979; *French Feminist Criticism: Women, Language, and Literature* edited by Elissa Gelfland and Virginia Hules, New York, Garland, 1985; *Simone de Beauvoir: An Annotated Bibliography* by Joy Bennett and Gabriella Hochmann, New York, Garland, 1988; *Simone de Beauvoir: A Bibliography* by Joan Nordquist, Santa Cruz, References & Research Services, 1991.

Critical Studies: *Simone de Beauvoir: Encounters with Death* by Elaine Marks, New Brunswick, New Jersey, Rutgers University Press, 1973; *Simone de Beauvoir on Woman* by Jean Leighton, Rutherford, New Jersey, Fairleigh Dickinson University Press, 1975; *Simone de Beauvoir* by Robert Cottrell, New York, Ungar, 1975; *Hearts and Minds: The Common Journey of Simone de Beauvoir and Jean-Paul Sartre* by Axel Madsen, New York, Morrow, 1977; "Mothers, Madness, and the Middle Class in *The Bell Jar* and *Les Mots pour le dire*" by Elaine A. Martin, in *French-American Review,* 5, spring 1981; *Simone de Beauvoir and the Limits of Commitment* by Anne Whitmarsh, London, Cambridge University Press, 1981; *Simone de Beauvoir: A Life of Freedom* by Carol Asher, Boston, Beacon, 1981; *Simone de Beauvoir heute* by Alice Schwartzer, Hamburg, Rowohlt, 1983, as *Simone de Beauvoir Today: Conversations, 1972-1982,* London, Hogarth Press, 1984, as *After the Second Sex: Conversations with Simone de Beauvoir,* New York, Pantheon, 1984; *Simone de Beauvoir: A Study of Her Writings* by Terry Keefe, London, Harrap, 1983; *Simone de Beauvoir, a Feminist Mandarin* by Mary Evans, London, Tavistock, 1985; *Simone de Beauvoir* by Judith Okeley, London, Virago, and New York, Pantheon, 1986; *Simone de Beauvoir* by Claude Francis and Fernande Gontier, London, Sidgwick & Jackson, 1987; *Feminist Literary Theory and Simone de Beauvoir* by Toril Moi, Oxford, Blackwell, 1990, and her *Simone de Beauvoir: The Making of an Intellectual Woman,* Oxford, Blackwell, 1994; *Simone de Beauvoir: A Biography* by Deirdre Blair, London, Cape, 1990; *Simone de Beauvoir Revisited* by Catherine Savage Brosman, Boston, Twayne, 1991; *Simone de Beauvoir: The Woman and Her Work* by Margaret Crosland, London, Heinemann, 1992; *Simone de Beauvoir and Jean-Paul Sartre: The Remaking of a 20th-Century Legend* by Kate Fullbrook and Edward Fullbrook, New York and London, Harvester, 1993; *Feminist Interpretations of Simone de Beauvoir* edited by Margaret A. Simons, University Park, Pennsylvania State University Press, 1995; *A Disgraceful Affair: Simone de Beauvoir, Jean-Paul Sartre and Bianca Lamblin* by Bianca Lamblin, Boston, Northeastern University Press, 1996; *The Mother Mirror: Self-Representation and the Mother-Daughter Relation in Colette, Simone de Beauvoir, and Marguérite Duras* by Laurie Corbin, n.p., 1996.

* * *

We best remember Simone de Beauvoir for her 1949 study entitled *The Second Sex,* which quickly turned into a feminist compendium for women all around the world. Over the years, as women have improved their situation, some of Beauvoir's ideas have come under attack while others apply as much today as they did 50 years ago. With less emphasis now being placed on *The Second Sex,* critics have begun to reassess Beauvoir's many other works of fiction and nonfiction.

Many of Beauvoir's works deal with her own experiences, sometimes concealed in fictional terms, sometimes revealed in her autobiography. This is how, in *Memoirs of a Dutiful Daughter,* we learn of her growing up in a bourgeois Parisian family. Her childhood and adolescence seem to have been quite happy although she does not share any intimate details, only that she commanded her younger sister Helène (called Poupette) and her other playmates. Her attachment to Elizabeth Le Coin—called Zaza in her memoirs—set a pattern for the many important friendships with women Beauvoir would maintain throughout her life.

Beauvoir excelled in school, and her father at first supported her intellectual aspirations. Later he resented her success, and Beauvoir eventually began to rebel against the constraints of her bourgeois upbringing. She also rejected her mother's Catholicism. Her parents expected Beauvoir to get married as other girls from her social class did, but she insisted on attending university and becoming a teacher so that she would be able to support herself.

While preparing for her final examinations, she met Jean-Paul Sartre and associated with his friends, a group of young philosophers who appreciated Beauvoir's specialization on Leibniz. As Toril Moi points out, Beauvoir was "a pioneering woman in her own time" when, as only the ninth woman and the youngest student ever, she completed the impressive final examination in philosophy. She passed the exam with flying colors and took second place to Sartre. Her professors admitted that they arrived at this final ranking only with great difficulty. After graduation, Beauvoir began a teaching career at various *lycées*, where she was much admired by her students for her unconventional approach and fascinating lectures. She, thus, established her professional independence by working outside the home. All her life she cherished her individuality and travelled extensively.

While the extent of her impact on contemporary women may be disputed, Beauvoir, nonetheless, managed to model the persona of a successful, professional woman writer. She also believed that such work constituted a valid alternative to motherhood. Beauvoir's writing was first published during the 1940s and elaborated her philosophical ideas in fictional form. Otherwise uninvolved in the political events of the day, in *Letters to Sartre* she describes, in detail, the German Occupation and displays her fears for Sartre's safety during his internment as a prisoner-of-war in Germany. It was only after the war that her thinking became more politicized.

In *The Ethics of Ambiguity,* Beauvoir would clarify various points of Sartre's existentialism for a post-war world. As Kate and Edward Fullbrook argue in *Simone de Beauvoir and Jean-Paul Sartre: The Remaking of a 20th-Century Legend* (1994), Sartre may actually have been influenced by Beauvoir's ideas before he formulated his philosophy. Soon after the war, Beauvoir also went on a long lecture tour of the United States where she met the novelist Nelson Algren, with whom she had a long-distance relationship for nearly 15 years. Both Beauvoir and Sartre, despite their lifelong "essential" relationship, continued to see other people in "contingent" relationships, because they rejected marriage as an outdated and oppressive bourgeois institution.

Her long novel, *The Mandarins*—usually considered a key to understanding the leftist intelligentsia's experience of the postwar years—features characters reminiscent of Beauvoir, Sartre, Algren, and Albert Camus. In great detail, Beauvoir describes how various characters try to reconfigure their lives and relationships after the war. Focusing on two characters, Henri Perron and Anne Dubreuilh, Beauvoir alternates their accounts of the events, letting them overlap at times and, thus, affording the reader two perspectives of the same incident. Despite some stylistic flaws, the novel received the Prix Goncourt because of its philosophical depth and political and historical significance.

Despite her literary success, Beauvoir suddenly became aware of her situation as a woman in a male world and decided to explore this idea in *The Second Sex.* The study employs existentialist philosophy and an historical approach in an effort to explain women's secondary social status. Man sees woman as "a sexual being" and imposes many of his ideas and dreams on his image of woman, making her his other. Beauvoir explains that woman "is defined and differentiated with reference to man and not he with reference to her." Thus, all women, become "the second sex."

She traces this evolution from prehistory and classical antiquity, through the Middle Ages and the Enlightenment into our own time. Particularly interesting are her insights into mythology and her close analysis of images of women in the works of Montherlant, D. H. Lawrence, Claudel, Breton, and Stendhal. The work's greatest significance rests on the premise that woman is <u>not</u> biologically predetermined to become mother and wife but free to determine her own fate. Contemporary critics point to flaws in Beauvoir's argument: hasty generalization resulting from insufficient and dated evidence, for instance. They also deplore her negative attitude toward the female body and motherhood. Furthermore, many have deemed her whole approach Eurocentric and phallocentric.

Although Beauvoir had previously described women in her novels, *The Second Sex* marked a turning point in her writing career: *The Woman Destroyed* and *Les Belles Images* would discuss women's issue even more overtly. Until her death in 1986, Beauvoir continued her political and philosophical pursuits. A lifelong opponent of colonialism, she supported the independence of both French Indochina and Algeria. In *Djamila Boupacha* (1962), she exposed the torture of an Algerian girl by the French military. *The Long March* is a detailed account of Communist China in the late 1950s. Several of her last works discussed the impact of old age and death.

Despite her many other accomplishments, we remember Beauvoir as a pioneering feminist. This reputation originated in *The Second Sex* and continued with her involvement in the French women's struggle for equal rights and greater participation in the politic arena. She also took a firm stand in favor of abortion. Due to the current interest in post-structural and post-modern criticism and dismissal of existentialist ideas, French feminists such as Julia Kristeva and Hélène Cixous have dismissed Beauvoir's ideas as well. Publication of Beauvoir's correspondence and notebooks has, however, opened up new possibilities for the study of the Sartre-Beauvoir relationship and Beauvoir's gender identity. A survey of recent feminist writing reveals that many authors, indeed, owe a great deal to Simone de Beauvoir—even if it is only their efforts in rejecting her ideas.

—Susanna Hoeness-Krupsaw

DEGONWADONTI. *See* **BRANT, Beth (E.).**

---

de GOURNAY, Marie le Jars

Nationality: French. **Born:** 6 October 1566. **Education:** Self-educated. **Career:** Became "adopted daughter" to the philosopher Michel de Montaigne, serving as his secretary; became Montaigne's literary executor, 1592; accused of witchcraft due to jealousy of her intellect and independence. **Died:** 13 July 1645.

Publications

Political/Social Theory

Égalité des hommes et des femmes. Paris, A la Reyne, 1622; translated by Eva M. Sartori as "Of the Equality of Men and Women," in *Allegorica 9,* winter 1987.

Le Grief des dames. Paris, n.p., 1626; translated by Eva M. Sartori as "The Complaint of the Ladies," in *Allegorica 9,* winter 1987.

Essays

De l'education des enfants de France. Paris, n.p., 1600.

La Bienvenue à Monseigneur le duc d'Anjou. Paris, Fleury Bourriquant, 1608.
Adieu de l'Ame du Roy de France. Paris, Fleury Bourriquant, 1610.
Le Prince de Corse. Paris, n.p., 1624.
Les advis ou les présens. Paris, Toussainct Du-Bray, 1634.

Poetry

Remerciement au Roy. Paris, n.p., 1624.

Autobiography

Copie de la vie de la demoiselle de Gournay [Imitation of the Life of the Demoiselle de Gournay]. Paris, n.p., 1616.
Apologie puir celle qui escrit [Apology of She Who Writes]. Paris, n.d.
Peincture de moeurs [Portrait of Manners]. Paris, n.p., 1626.

Other

Le Proumenoiur de Monsieur de Montaigne par sa fille d'alliance [The Promenade of Montaigne]. Paris, Abel L'Agnelier, 1594.
L'ombre de la demoiselle de Gournay [In the Shadow of the Demoiselle de Gournay] (collected works). Paris, Jean Libert, 1626; as *Les Advis ou les presens de la demoiselle de Gournay* [The Opinions or the Presents of the Demoiselle de Gournay], Paris, Toussainct Du-Bray, 1634; revised, Paris, Jean Du-Bray, 1641.

Editor, *Les essais de Michel Seigneur de Montaigne.* Paris, Abel L'Angnelier, 1595; revised, 1598; revised as *Ediction troisieme, plus correcte et plus ample que les précédentes,* Rouen, 1607.

Translator, *Eschantillons de Virgile* [Selections from the Aeneid]. Paris, n.p., 1620.
Translator, *Versions de quelques pièces de Virgile, Tacite et Saluste.* Paris, Fleury Bourriquant, 1619.

*

Critical Studies: *Marie de Gournay* by M. Schiff, Paris, Champion, 1910; *A Daughter of the Renaissance: Marie le Jars de Gournay* by M. Ilsley, The Hague, Mouton, 1963; "Marie le Jars de Gournay: The Self-Portrait of an Androgynous Her" by Tilde Sankovitch, in *French Women Writers and the Book: Myths of Access and Desire,* Syracuse, New York, Syracuse University Press, 1988.

* * *

Marie de Gournay recognized the power of writing and used that medium not only to make known her views on such subjects as women, their education, and the French language, but also to leave a record of her experiences as a woman in early modern France. At a time when women who wrote were rare and those who lived by their pen even rarer, de Gournay's writing earned her both fame and scorn.

As the eldest daughter of an aristocratic, albeit not particularly wealthy family, de Gournay's entry into the world of letters would have been considered unusual. When a young girl, she was an avid reader, despite her mother s repeated disparagement of reading as a useless pastime. Her determination to expand her knowledge led her to teach herself Latin through the comparison of original texts and their translations. Then, at about age 18, de Gournay read the *Essais* of Michel de Montaigne. This work made a lasting impression on her, so much so that five years later, when she discovered that both she and Montaigne were visiting Paris at the same time, she contacted him by letter. The ensuing meeting and close relationship that developed during that year led to Montaigne's naming her his *fille d'alliance* (adopted daughter).

These encounters inspired de Gournay's first work, *Le Proumenoiur de M. de Montaigne,* written in 1588 and published in 1594. After learning of Montaigne's intervening death in 1592, she set to work on a posthumous edition of the *Essais* that would include the changes Montaigne had made since their last publication in 1588. The new edition, published in 1595, gave rise to a great debate over its authenticity, and de Gournay eventually deemed it prudent to retract her introduction since it was judged too self-serving. Did de Gournay insert her own writings into Montaigne's as claimed? Or was it simply that Montaigne was influenced by de Gournay just as she had been by him? The controversy surrounding that edition will probably never be satisfactorily resolved. Nonetheless, Montaigne's family respected her editorial skills and selected her to prepare the next edition of his *Essais* as well.

By 1599 de Gournay had settled in Paris, determined to earn her living as a writer. Her treatise, *De l'education des enfants de France,* occasioned by the birth of a son to Marie de' Medici and Henri IV, brought her praise and facilitated her admission to the intellectual circles of the French capital. There de Gournay would spend the rest of her life, alternately extolled and reviled for her works and the ideas they espoused. Even when she was not being criticized for her opinions, de Gournay suffered too from prejudice against her lifestyle: an unmarried women, supporting herself through writing, whose interest in alchemy did not go unremarked. She often found herself mocked as a spinster and pedant, and even accused of witchcraft. Yet none of these circumstances dissuaded her from following her own mind.

Although it might not appear obvious, de Gournay's commentary on the French language that appeared in the treatise on poetry she published along with her translations of Virgil and other Latin writers in 1622 can be seen as forming a consistent whole with her feminist thought. What she objected to in the nascent neo-classical style in literature as elaborated by Malherbe was its emphasis on order and conformity and its "purification" of the language through the elimination of older words. De Gournay remained a partisan of the view of poet as inspired individual, with the creative liberty of the rich language of the Renaissance. This position, which allowed more readily for a construction of a unique self than a self constructed according to a set of pre-existing rules, led to another controversy, this time over the role of the poet and poetic language in the 17th century. Following her own principles of language, de Gournay created another stir a few years later through her edition of a restored version of a poem by Ronsard, designed to show the superiority of the 16th-century poet.

De Gournay's *Égalité des hommes et des femmes* ("On the Equality of Men and Women"), published in 1622, provides a striking example of her feminist writings. The premise of the *Égalité,* evident in its title, depicts men and women as equally endowed. De Gournay maintains education acts as a determining force in one's life: if women appear to be inferior to men, it is precisely because they have not be allowed the same educational opportunities. The *Grief des dames* ("The Complaint of the Ladies") of 1626 offers a less attenuated version of women's mistreatment. She begins with the conclusion: "Happy are you, reader, if you do not belong to that sex to which all good is forbidden." De Gournay clearly recognized the inequality with which women were treated in her society and spoke out against it. Thus by the mid-1620s, we find her known as an advocate for women's rights and as a maverick critic and editor.

Finally, among de Gournay's most original works are her autobiographical writings: the *Copie de la vie de Mademoiselle de Gournay,* written in 1616 as the result of a practical joke played on her; the *Peincture de moeurs* dating from 1626, and the *Apologie pour celle qui escrit* that appeared in her collected works in 1634. Not only are these texts remarkable as historical documents that chronicle the life of a women of letters in the period of transition from the Renaissance to Classicism, but they are equally remarkable as experiments in style, form, vocabulary, and theme in the genre of women's autobiography. The *Copie* presents a "conventional" account of her life through her work on the 1590's editions of Montaigne; the *Peincture,* a moral self-portrait, and the *Apologie,* a self-defense against her detractors and examination of her development.

Marie de Gournay, whose advocacy of women's issues inspired Theodore Joran to call her the "mother of modern feminism," remains an intriguing though enigmatic figure for, despite her importance in feminist and literary theory, the majority of her works has not been reprinted since 1641. Thus, a complete evaluation of her significance must wait until her complete works become more readily available.

—Edith J. Benkov

DEMING, Barbara

Nationality: American. **Born:** New York, New York, 23 July 1917. **Education:** Bennington College, Bennington, Vermont, B.A. 1938; Western Reserve University (now Case Western Reserve University), M.A. 1941. **Family:** Companion of Jane Gapen. **Career:** Political activist and writer; codirector, Bennington Stock Theatre, Bennington, Vermont, 1938-39; teaching fellow, Bennington School of the Arts, 1940-41; film analyst for Library of Congress film project, 1942-44. Contributor to periodicals, including *The Liberator, Ms.,* and *The Nation.* **Awards:** War Resisters League Peace Award, 1967. **Member:** American Society of Journalists and Authors, Women's Institute for Freedom of the Press, Feminist Writers Guild. **Died:** Sugarloaf Key, Florida, 2 August 1984.

Publications

Short Stories

Wash Us and Comb Us. New York, Grossman, 1972.

Political/Social Theory

Revolution and Equilibrium. New York, Grossman, 1971.
We Cannot Live Without Our Lives. New York, Grossman, 1974.
Remembering Who We Are. Tallahasse, Pagoda/Naiad Press, 1981.

Essays

Prison Notes. New York, Grossman, 1966; in *Prisons That Could Not Hold,* 1985.
We Are All Part of One Another: A Barbara Deming Reader. Philadelphia, New Society, 1984.
A Humming under My Feet: A Book of Travail. London, Women's Press, 1985.
Prisons That Could Not Hold, introduction by Grace Paley. San Francisco, Spinsters Ink, 1985.

Other

Running away from Myself: A Dream Portrait of America Drawn from the Films of the '40s. New York, Grossman, 1969.
Women and Revolution: A Dialogue. National Interim Committee For Mass Party of the People, 1975

*

Critical Studies: Articles in *Ms.,* November 1978 and December 1984.

* * *

If one searches reference books for the name "Barbara Deming," chances are you will come up empty-handed. Deming, who proclaimed and lived her beliefs in a quiet way and shared her wisdom and truths with others in the same gentle, unassuming manner, left little public record of herself. Those who knew her, who marched by her side and who shared jail cells with her, and those lucky enough to be her friends recognized that her gentleness did not mean a weakness of conviction or a lack of strength. They knew just how committed to the causes of civil rights and world peace she was, as she had showed them many times over. However, Deming did not attract the media spotlight; she was not a darling of the airwaves, she did not garner adulation from masses of people in this, or any other country. To learn about Barbara Deming, one must read her books.

Deming began her long years of activism through her belief in and struggle for world peace. On 26 May 1963 a group of men and women began a Peace Walk from Quebec to Quantanamo Bay, Cuba. The walkers were pacifists, schooled in the non-violent resistance ways of Indian leader Mahatma Ghandi. They faced hostile attitudes from local law enforcement agencies and hatred from those who did not understand or agree with the purpose of the march. Deming joined the group in October, planning to walk for three weeks. She found her outlook on achieving world peace shifting slightly as she moved with her fellow marchers through the Southern states. In November the group would be jailed in Macon, Georgia, for passing out leaflets. As she wrote what would become *Prison Notes* from her jail cell in 1964, Deming began to feel the peace movement could not be separated from the civil rights movement.

Ironically, President John Kennedy was assassinated while the group was locked in Macon's jail. Some of the marchers' signs bore the word "Cuba"—the local sheriff, fearing repercussions from the already rampant rumors about Cuba's possible involvement in Kennedy's murder, hustled the group out of jail and out of town. Down the road in nearby Albany the police chief, determined to be in control of "his" town, and the peace group, convinced they could change his political philosophy if he saw how determined they were to support their beliefs, came to a stalemate. The marchers went to jail again, receiving varying sentences. Some, like Deming, would be incarcerated for up to three months. Many of them fasted during the last 27 days before their release. Some men and women were force-fed, some finally quit the fast on their own, or, like Deming, chose a partial fast, taking only a few bites of food each morning. When the marchers were released on 24 February 1964 Deming went home to recover, to write, and to reformulate her thoughts. The walkers continued to Miami, Florida, arriving there on 29 May 1964 after a trip of 2800 miles.

Deming would be a notable presence at another march, for women's rights, two decades later. Before then, however, she would incur the wrath of the United States government by accepting North Vietnam's invitation, through their embassy in what was then the USSR, to visit Hanoi as a "war observer." In December 1966 Deming and three other women made the trip to Hanoi at their own expense. The women's activities were reported by the *New York Times* on an almost daily basis. They visited bombed sites and Hanoi radio reported they were shocked by "evidences of crimes." Some of the women kept a tally of U.S. bombings and what they cited as civilian casualties. Upon return to the United States the women, including Deming, held a news conference in New York City, stating that Ho Chi Minh, in a Hanoi interview, had vowed to fight forever rather than capitulate, that he held the American people blameless for the military intervention in Vietnam, and that he accused the U.S. government of "capitalistic designs." The State Department responded by announcing that the women had obtained no official permission to travel to Hanoi; Deming's passport was immediately revoked.

Much of Deming's writing was done in the 20 years between 1964 and 1984. She used correspondence from friends as jumping-off points to explore the works of such thinkers as Karl Marx, Friedrich Engels, and Sigmund Freud. In her book *Remembering Who We Are,* published in 1981, she is receptive to new ways of thinking, just as she demonstrates a generosity in guiding others to consider political changes, particularly in the feminist movement. Deming, who had once said she realized she was a lesbian at the age of 16, held an abiding interest in figuring out just where women fit into the world and was disturbed to find no real place for women who loved other women. As she grew older, she found herself acknowledging that lesbians were as invisible to the women's movement as blacks were to white society. That discovery cost some people her friendship, for she refused to be invisible.

In 1983 women from around the country joined together in Romulus, New York, to participate in the New York City Women's Pentagon Action Feminist Walk. Deming, whose health was now failing, joined the group on 25 July. The walk took place five days later, beginning in historic Seneca Falls and following a route back to the women's encampment in Romulus. In Waterloo, an angry mob blocked the marchers' path. Choosing not to force their way through the crowd, the women sat in the road; 54 of them, including Deming, would be arrested and held for five days. After her release Deming spent another week at the encampment and then returned home. Despite this experience, she continued to believe that non-violent struggles were the way to effect change within the feminist movement.

In March 1984 Deming was told she had ovarian cancer. She was then living among a community of women on Sugarloaf Key in Florida with her longtime friend Jane Gapen. Aware of the consequences, Deming decided to discontinue chemotherapy treatment. As Grace Paley would later recall in her introduction to *Prisons That Could Not Hold,* Deming told her that she had decided to die: "I'm happy now, I'm serene and I want to die in that serenity". Less than two weeks later, after having the opportunity to say good bye to her many friends and with a mind unclouded by drugs, Deming died in her home. She was 68.

—María Elena Raymond

---

de PISAN, Christine. *See* **CHRISTINE de PISAN.**

DESAI, Anita

Nationality: Indian. **Born:** Mussoorie, India, 24 June 1937. **Education:** Delhi University, B.A. 1957. **Family:** Married Ashvin Desai in 1958; four children. **Career:** Writer. Visiting professor at numerous colleges and universities, including Cambridge University, 1986-87, 1989; Smith College, Northampton, Massachusetts, 1987-88, Mount Holyoke College, South Hadley, Massachusetts, beginning 1988; Barnard College, New York, 1989; American University of Cairo, 1992; and Massachusetts Institute of Technology, beginning 1993. Former member, advisory board for English, Sahitya Akademi, New Delhi. Contributor of short stories to periodicals, including *Envoy, Femina, Harper's Bazaar, Illustrated Weekly of India, Indian Literature, Quest, Thought,* and *Writers Workshop.* **Awards:** Royal Society for Literature Winifred Holtby Prize, 1978, for *Fire on the Mountain;* Sahitya Academy Award, 1978; *Guardian* Award for children's fiction, 1982, for *The Village by the Sea; Hadassah* Prize, 1989, for *Baumgartner's Bombay;* Columbia University Taraknath Das Award, 1989; awarded title of Padma Shri (India), 1990; Scottish Arts Council Neil Gunn Award, 1994. **Member:** Royal Society of Literature (fellow), American Academy of Arts and Letters (honorary member). **Address:** c/o William Heinemann Ltd., 10 Upper Grosvenor St., London W1X 9PA, England.

Publications

Novels

Cry the Peacock. London, P. Owen, 1963.
Voices in the City. London, P. Owen, 1965.
Bye-Bye Blackbird. India, Orient Paperbacks, 1968.
Where Shall We Go This Summer? India, Vikas, 1975.
Fire on the Mountain. New York, Harper, and London, Heinemann, 1977.
Clear Light of Day. London, Heinemann, and New York, Harper, 1980.
In Custody. London, Heinemann, 1984; New York, Harper, 1985.
Baumbartner's Bombay. London, Heinemann, 1988; New York, Knopf, 1989.

Journey to Ithaca. New York, Knopf, and London, Heinemann, 1995.

Short Stories

Games at Twilight and Other Stories. London, Heinemann, 1978; New York, Harper, 1980.

Plays

Screenplay: *In Custody,* 1992.

For Children

The Peacock Garden. London, Orient Longman, n.d.
Cat on a Houseboat. Calcutta, Orient Longmans, 1976.
The Village by the Sea. London, Heinemann, 1982.

*

Media Adaptations: *In Custody* (film; produced by Merchant-Ivory), 1992; *The Village by the Sea* (radio play), 1992.

Manuscript Collections: The University of Texas at Austin.

Critical Studies: *Language and Theme in Anita Desai's Fiction* by Kunja Bala Goel, Jaipur, Classic Publishing House, 1989; *Voice and Vision of Anita Desai* by S. Jena, New Delhi, Ashish Publishing House, 1989; *Perspectives on Anita Desai* by R.K. Srivastava, Ghaziabad, Vimal, 1984; *The Novels of Anita Desai* by Usha Bande, New Delhi, Prestige Books, 1988; *Symbolism in Anita Desai's Novels* by Kajali Sharma, New Delhi, Abhinav Publications, 1991; *Anita Desai's Fiction: Patterns of Survival Strategies*, Delhi, Kanishka Publishing House, 1992; *Anita Desai as an Artist* by Indira Sivanna, New Delhi, Creative Books, 1994.

* * *

The term "feminism" occupies a peculiar position in many nations of the so-called "Third World." Its western origins make it suspect from a nationalist perspective, while its seemingly exclusive focus on women (which, for many, implies an anti-male position) is perceived as a divisive factor that endangers third-world solidarity against the forces of global capitalism and neo-colonialism. Consequently, many third-world women writers resist the "feminist" label and, instead, project a new kind of humanism that gives women a voice as historical agents rather than being subsumed under the generic category of "Man." In doing so, these writers challenge any simplistic notion of "women" as a homogenous category and, implicitly, provide alternatives to certain dominant trends in "western feminism."

Anita Desai is perhaps one of the best known and most highly regarded Indian women writers at both the national and international levels. Hailed as a sensitive and poetic writer whose psychological insights take us deep into the closed interior world of her characters, Desai is mainly known for her portrayal of "feminine sensibility" in novels like *Cry the Peacock* and *Clear Light of Day*. Not all her novels, however, are concerned with an exploration of female consciousness. Her primary focus in all her novels is on the individual's (both male and female) struggle for self-expression in a socially restrictive atmosphere that is often inimical to personal freedom. Her work, therefore, cannot be called "feminist" in the sense of being exclusively concerned with women and their relationship with society. However, each of her novels contains an awareness of gender as a basic structuring principle that has a significant impact on every aspect of both private/domestic as well as public/political life. Consequently, even in novels like *In Custody* and *Baumgartner's Bombay*, where the narrative focuses on a male protagonist, there is an implicit recognition of the patriarchal social and its lack of providing space for women in the public/political sphere.

Four of Desai's novels—*Cry the Peacock, Fire on the Mountain, Where Shall We Go This Summer,* and *Clear Light of Day*—are most easily accessible to a feminist reading. Characterized as domestic novels, these texts place women at the center of the narrative and explore the female psyche. Desai, however, does not use her women characters as feminist spokespersons who embody women's liberation. While characters like Bim in *Clear Light of Day* and Nanda Kaul in *Fire on the Mountain* do emerge as strong independent women, Desai also reveals the sense of isolation and feeling of entrapment that often underlies the apparent bid for personal freedom. By doing so, Desai does not negate the importance of women's power to make their own life-choices; rather, she foregrounds the hidden patriarchal family politics that determine the form of these "choices." In Bim's case, for example, it is the patriarchal notion that women are the chief caretakers of the family that forces Bim to remain unmarried and take care of her younger brother after her other siblings get married and move out of the family home.

Desai also strongly believes in the importance of establishing and maintaining meaningful human connections. The desire for relationships is not, for her, an essential trademark of the "feminine" sensibility. Instead, she views it as a necessary part of being human, and the male characters, such as Gautama in *Cry the Peacock* and Nirod in *Voices in the City*, who refuse such contact are portrayed as leading a dry and lifeless existence. She is, therefore, wary of endorsing a woman's sense of independence that is based upon a negation of human contact as is the case with Nanda Kaul in *Fire on the Mountain.* Real courage and dignity are marked by the ability to relate to others and to retain a faith in the human community—it is evident in Nanda Kaul's reaching out for her great-grandchild and in Bim's decision to re-establish contact with her estranged brother.

A belief in relationality, however, does not led Desai into advocating a universal sisterhood of women. She is acutely aware of differences that separate women ideologically as well as in practical socio-economic terms. In *Cry the Peacock*, for example, Maya's hypersensitivity, which is implicitly related to her upper-middle-class background, is contrasted with her friend Leila's resigned acceptance of life as the hard-working wife of a dying husband. By highlighting such differences within the seemingly homogenous category of "middle-class Indian women," Desai is able to reveal the inadequacy of a single-focus feminist agenda. While the murder of Ila Das in *Fire on the Mountain* and the suicide of Monisha in *Voices in the City* are symptomatic of the violence women face in a patriarchal society, there is no simple solution for such problems. By presenting these problems in all their stark brutality, after carefully tracing the complex network of socio-economic factors that lead up to them, Desai forces us to reconceptualize "feminism" as a multi-faceted form of resistance against interlocking structures of oppression.

Such a re-defined feminism is not merely a "third-world" version of western feminism. At least three of Desai's novels—*Bye*

Bye Blackbird, Baumgartner's Bombay, and *Journey to Ithaca*—are constructed as East-West encounters, but the inclusion of European characters does not result in any significant alteration in her portrayal of women. Sarah in *Bye Bye Blackbird* and Lotte in *Baumgartner's Bombay* are subject to the same kinds of patriarchal constraints as their Indian counterparts. By thus expanding the geographical scope of her fictional universe, Desai is able to make her brand of humanist feminism globally relevant.

—Suchitra Mathur

---

de SANTILLANA, Juana Inés de Asbaje y Ramírez. *See* **JUANA INÉZ de la CRUZ, Sor.**

DEXTER, John. *See* **BRADLEY, Marion Zimmer.**

DINESEN, Isak. *See* **BLIXEN, Karen (Christentze Dinesen).**

DING LING

Name also transliterated as Ting Ling. **Pseudonyms:** Bingzhi; Congxuan. **Nationality:** Chinese. **Born:** Jiang Bingzhi or Ding Bingzhi, in Linli, Hunan Province, 4 September 1904?. **Education:** Attended Communist sponsored-Shanghai University, c. 1922. **Family:** Lived with worker-poet Hu Yepin, c. 1925-31 (executed 1931), one son; lived with translator Feng Da, c. 1931-35, one daughter; married scriptwriter Chen Ming in 1942. **Career:** Moved to Shanghai, 1920; joined the Anarchist Party; editor of *Women's Voice* (paper of the Common Girls' School), 1920-22; moved to Nanjing, Shanghai, then Beijing, 1924; editor, *Honghei Congshu* (literary journal), 1928; joined League of Left-Wing Writers and edited *Beidou* (Communist magazine), 1931; secretly joined Communist Party, 1932; kidnapped and later put under house arrest by Nationalist government of Chiang Kai-shek, Nanjing, 1933; escaped to Red Army base in North China with help of Communist underground, 1936; with husband, organized Northwest Front Service Corps (traveling theatre), 1937; taught at Party universities; literary editor, *Jiefang ribao* (Communist newspaper), until 1942; participated in land reform movement, 1946; gave address to All-China Federation of Literature and Art Circles, 1949; editor, *Wenyi bao,* 1950-52; deputy chief editor, *Renmin wenxue,* 1950-53; condemned by resolution of Writer's Union, 1955, 1956; books banned, 1957-1978; expelled from Party and exiled to Heilongjiang Province, 1958-70; publicly humiliated and held in solitary confinement, Peking, 1970-75; with husband, exiled to Chanzhi, Shaanxi Province, 1975-78; returned to Peking, 1978; officially "rehabilitated," 1979; editor, literary magazine, 1985. Contributor of short stories to periodicals, including *Xiaoshuo yuebao* and *Renijian yuekan.* **Awards:** Stalin Prize in literature (Soviet Union), 1951, for *The Sun Shines over the Sanggan River.* **Member:** Union of Chinese Writers (vice-chair), Chinese People's Political Consultative Conference. **Died:** Peking, 4 March 1986.

Selected Publications

Novels

Yijusanlinhian chun Shanghai zhiyi [Shanghai Spring], in *Xiaoshuo yuebao* (China), 1-2, 1930; translated in *I Myself Am a Woman,* 1989.
Wei Hu, in *Xiaoshuo yuebao,* (21 (1-5), January-May 1930.
Muqin [Mother], in *Dalu xinwen* (China), 1933.
Xin de xinnian [New Faith], in *Wenyi zhanzian* (China), 1939; as *Leiyan mohu zhong zhi xinnian* [Faith through Tear-blurred Eyes]. China, n.p., 1943.
Taiyang zhao zai Sangganhe shang. China, n.p., 1948; translated by Yang Xianyi and Gladys Yang as *The Sun Shines over the Sanggan River,* n.p., 1984.
Zai yiyuan zhong [During the Coldest Days or In the Bitter Winter], in *Renmin wenxue* (China), 1956.
Qingming [Brightness]. China, n.p., 1979.

Short Stories

"Shafei nushi de riji," in *Xiaoshuo yuebao,* 1927; translated in *Miss Sophie's Diary and Other Stories,* China, n.p., 1928; as *Miss Sophie's Diary,* Beijing, Panda Books, 1985; in *I Myself Am a Woman,* 1989.
"Yige muren he yige nanren" [A Woman and a Man], in *Xiaoshuo yuebao,* 1928; translated in *I Myself Am a Woman,* 1989.
"Wo zai Xiacun de shihou [When I Was at Zia Village], in *Zhongguo wenhua,* 1941; in *I Myself Am A Woman,* 1989.

Other

Chongfeng [Reunion] (play), in *Wenji yuekan,* 1936; translated in *Liberation Weekly,* 1938.
"Zanbajie you gan" [Thoughts on March 8], in *Liberation Daily,* 1942.
I Myself Am a Woman: Selected Writings of Ding Ling, edited by Tani E. Barlow, with Gary J. Bjorge. Boston, Beacon Press, 1989.

*

Critical Studies: *Reminiscences of Ding Ling* by Shen Cogwen, n.p., n.d.; *Ding Ling's Fiction: Ideology and Narative in Modern Chinese Literature* by Yi-tsi Mei Fuerwerker, Cambridge, Harvard University Press, Cambridge, 1982.

* * *

Ding Ling, surrounded by the teachings and examples of her progressive mother, took like a duck to water and swam in feminist currents all of her life. She is considered one of the most influential writers in modern Chinese literature, combining startling novels and short stories with essays discussing whichever political revolution was ongoing at the time and thereby sustaining a writing career much longer than many of her contemporaries. How Ding survived the seemingly endless number of purges and revolutions before finally being punished as too "rightist" in 1957 can be found in her willingness to slightly shift her public political stances, while continuing to write stories that bordered on being politically objectionable. It was a narrow path she chose to walk.

Ding clearly had a mind of her own. She was among the first group of girls to integrate a boys-only school in Changsha. When her uncles informed her of their plans to marry her to a man of their choice, she promptly told them that her body belonged only to herself and they would not decide what she should do with it. Coming from a Chinese woman in 1920, this was an astonishing stance. Ding Ling later elected not to marry her early lovers, saying she believed marriage to be legalized prostitution. During the late 1920s, she became well known as a writer, especially after the 1927 publication of *Miss Sophie's Diary,* about women's lot in semi-feudal and restrictive China. Ding wrote explicitly about Sophie's sexuality, her masturbation to relieve sexual tensions, and pictured the two men in Sophie's life as either well-intentioned but whiny or physically beautiful but vacuous; Sophie was portrayed without the will to take charge of her own life.

In her short stories, Ding Ling wrote often of women's sexual passions, their restricted circumstances due to class or political status, or the everyday situations encountered just by being a woman. While many stories depict women as the victims of men and social convention, at the same time Ding broke away from the traditional Chinese portrayal of the hapless woman. She tried to imbue her female characters with a sense of personal strength and purpose. In 1928's "A Woman and A Man," for example, this dichotomy is seen clearly when the female takes the lead in arranging a sexual liaison and feels excited by the "danger and secrecy ... she had aroused." Ding stirred controversy with many of her writings; in fact, the public's perception of her personal "immorality" that resulted from the contents of her many love stories would come back to haunt her during the purge in 1957.

After she became a communist in 1932, Ding Ling gave her then-two-year-old child to her mother to raise, so that she could move forward with her political activities. Ding's second child, born in 1934, was also given to the grandmother. The children would join their mother briefly when she was living along the northern border of China, but little is known of their lives. Ding acknowledged the great influence her mother had on her life in serving as the role model of an independent female; although she trusted her children to her mother, Ding also had deep conflicts about her relationship with her mother. Some of this is addressed in the 1933 novel, *Mother.*

As Ding Ling became more powerful within the Communist Party she was given the task of writing many propaganda essays, which were then published in the party newspapers. If she felt any conflict in performing this duty because of her personal feelings about the party's poor treatment of women, it may be seen in her critical short story "When I Was at Xia Village," about a peasant girl who is raped by Japanese occupying troops and then forced by the Chinese to be a spy for the communists. Her feelings were nowhere more apparent than in her famous article, "Thoughts on March 8" (1941), which describes the discrimination against women in a communist community. Yet in 1948 she then swung back to the party line in her novel about land reform, *The Sun Shines over the Sanggan River.* This novel, widely acclaimed, was quickly translated into many languages, including English. Despite this novel's publication, it was too late for Ding Ling to redeem herself in the eyes of party members; during Mao's Hundred Flowers Campaign she was labeled a "rightist," publicly humiliated, condemned, and sent into exile. She spent most of the next two decades on a farm in northeastern China, tending small animals with her husband. During the Cultural Revolution Ding was taken to Peking and kept in solitary confinement for five years. It was not until she was released in 1979 that she realized her husband had been incarcerated in the cell next to hers for that entire time.

Ding Ling wrote a few stories after her release and spent time giving interviews to the Chinese and foreign press. She visited the United States in 1981 to attend the Ames Writers' Conference in Ames, Iowa, and reportedly stated that she did not understand Western feminism as she saw it. In 1981 Ding wrote the following about Chinese literature: "No matter what we write, we must proceed from life and describe it in depth, warm-heartedly and in a detailed and bold fashion. No matter how much we shock or anger the readers, in the end we must give them strength, leaving them with a picture of the future. Our literature must be thought-provoking and encourage people to march forward." In painting her own vision of the future in over 300 works, Ding Ling dedicated six decades of her life. She died in Peking in 1986, having reached the age of 82.

—Maria Elena Raymond

DOMINI, Rey. *See* **LORDE, Audre (Geraldine).**

DOOLITTLE, Hilda. *See* **H.D.**

DORN, Helga. *See* **H.D.**

---

d'OSSOLI, Marchesa. *See* **FULLER, (Sarah) Margaret.**

DOUGLASS, Frederick

Nationality: American. **Born:** Frederick Augustus Washington Bailey, in Tuckahoe, Maryland, 1818. **Education:** Self-educated.

Family: Married 1) Anna Murray in 1838, three sons, one daughter; 2) Helen Pitts in 1879. **Career:** Born into slavery; started clandestine Bible school for fellow slaves; escaped from a Baltimore shipyard, 1838; settled in New Bedford, Massachusetts; began speaking against slavery as an agent for the Massachusetts Anti-Slavery Society, beginning 1841; lectured against slavery in Great Britain, 1945-47; freedom purchased for $700, 1847; founder and editor, *Frederick Douglass's Paper* (later, *The North Star*), Rochester, New York, 1847-63; speaker at first Seneca Falls Women's Convention, 1848; recruited troops for Massachusetts 54th Regiment (first Northern all-black unit), 1863; U.S. Minister to Haiti, 1889. **Died:** 20 February 1895.

Publications

Autobiography

Narrative of the Life of Frederick Douglass, an American Slave, Written by Himself, preface by William Lloyd Garrison. Boston, Anti-Slavery Office, 1845; Dublin, Webb & Chapman, 1846; edited by Benjamin Quarles, Cambridge, Massachusetts, Belknap Press, 1960; enlarged as *My Bondage and My Freedom,* New York, Miller Orton & Mulligan, 1855; enlarged as *Life and Times of Frederick Douglass, Written by Himself,* Hartford, Connecticut, Park, 1881; as *The Life and Times of Frederick Douglass, from 1817 to 1882, Written by Himself,* London, Christian Age Office, 1882; revised edition, Boston, DeWolfe, 1893; abridged by Barbara Ritchie, New York, Crowell, 1966.

Frederick Douglass: Autobiographies, edited by Henry Louis Gates Jr. Library of America, 1994.

Political/Social Theory

Frederick Douglass on Women's Rights, edited by Philip S. Foner. Westport, Connecticut, and London, Greenwood Press, 1976.

Essays

Abolition Fanaticism in New York. Speech of a Runaway Slave from Baltimore.... Baltimore, Thomas & Evans, 1847.

"Editorial," in *The North Star,* 28 July 1848; in *History of Women Suffrage,* Vol. 1, edited by Elizabeth Cady Stanton, Susan B. Anthony, and Matilda Joslyn Gage. New York, Fowler & Welles, 1881.

Novel

The Heroic Slave, in *The Classic African-American Novels,* edited by William L. Andrews. New York, Mentor, 1990.

Other

Frederick Douglass: Selections from His Writings, edited by Philip Foner. New York, International Publishers, 1945.

The Mind and Heart of Frederick Douglass: Excerpts from Speeches of the Great Negro Orator, adapted by Barbara Richie. New York, Crowell, 1968.

The Frederick Douglass Papers: Speeches, Debates, and Interviews, 1841-46 [1847-54] [1855-63] [1864-80] [1881-95], edited by John W. Blassingame. New Haven, Connecticut, and London, Yale University Press, 5 vols., 1979-92.

Frederick Douglass: New Literary and Historical Essays, edited by Eric J. Sundquist. Cambridge, Cambridge University Press, 1990.

The Oxford Frederick Douglass Reader, edited by William L. Andrews. New York, Oxford University Press, 1996.

*

Media Adaptations: *The Angry Prophet: Frederick Douglass,* 1970; *What, to the American Slave, Is Your Fourth of July?* (sound recording; read by James Earl Jones), 1973; *An Evening with Frederick Douglass* (radio broadcast), 1979; *Fighter for Freedom: The Frederick Douglass Story* (video recording), 1987; *Narrative of the Life of Frederick Douglass* (sound recording; read by Charles Turner), 1991.

Bibliography: *Frederick Douglass: The Colored Orator* by Frederic May Holland, n.p., 1891, revised, New York, Haskell House, 1969.

Critical Studies: *Frederick Douglass, the Orator* by James Monroe Gregory, n.p., 1893 *In Memoriam Frederick Douglass*, Philadelphia, J.C. Yorson, 1897; *Frederick Douglas* by Charles Waddell Chesnutt, Boston, Small Maynard, 1899; *Frederick Douglass* by Booker T. Washington, Philadelphia, G.W. Jacobs, 1907; *The Life and Writings of Frederick Douglas* by Philip S. Foner, New York, International Publishers, 4 vols., 1950-55, and his *Frederick Douglass: A Biography,* New York, Citadel Press, 1964; *Young Frederick Douglass: The Maryland Years* by Dickson J. Preston, Baltimore, Johns Hopkins University Press, 1980; *Slave and Citizen: The Life of Frederick Douglass* by Nathan Irvin Huggins, Boston, Little Brown, 1980; *The Mind of Frederick Douglass* by Waldo E. Martin Jr., Chapel Hill, University of North Carolina Press, 1984; *Critical Essays on Frederick Douglass,* edited by William L. Andrews, Boston, G. K. Hall, 1991; *Frederick Douglass* by William S. McFeely, New York, Norton, 1991; *A Man from Seneca Falls: Elizabeth Cady Stanton, Frederick Douglass, and the Women's Rights Convention of 1848* by Bradford Miller, Hudson, New York, Lindisfarn Press, 1995; *"We Are All Together Now": Frederick Douglass, William Lloyd Garrison, and the Prophetic Tradition* by William B. Rogers, New York, Garland, 1995.

* * *

Abolitionist leader, orator, journalist, and diplomat: the man who would one day be known to the world as Frederick Douglass transcended the oppression of his childhood to become one of the most forward-thinking social reforms of his age. An intellectual and political leader, Douglass harnessed an ever-increasing public profile to promote and defend the causes of full civil rights for all men and women, be they black or white.

Born into slavery in 1818—although the exact year of his birth was not known even to Douglass, who later guessed it to be 1817—the future orator's path in life was influenced by several circumstances unusual for one in his unfortunate position. As a young boy he was taught the rudiments of reading by the kindly wife of an owner; these few, simple words of less than four letters each would be the seeds from which his later intellectual curiosity would spring. Transferred to Baltimore to work at a local shipyard as a young man, Douglass observed the intellectual society of educated white men of his age; the bustling urban environment allowed him the relative freedom to learn from such young men, engage them in conversation and debate, and even purchase a book of his own.

After fleeing Baltimore for the north when he was 20, Douglass settled in New Bedford, Massachusetts, where his skill as a speaker soon brought him to the attention of noted abolitionist William Lloyd Garrison. Garrison quickly recruited the young, charismatic former slave as an agent of his Anti-Slavery Society. Speaking around the country on the ills of slavery, Douglass's platform grew to include a discussion of the hypocrisy of a "Christian" church that would condone such inhumanity and an analysis of the character of the basic freedoms outlined in the U.S. Constitution. Such topics, based as they were on a sophisticated understanding of political and religious theory, were, many began to contend, too sophisticated to be covered so astutely by one of Douglass's self-professed educational dearth; his authority as a former slave began to be questioned.

By 1844 Douglass had decided to put these doubts to rest; he set down on paper *The Narrative of the Life of Frederick Douglass, an American Slave,* which was published the following year; ten years later he would revise and expand his narrative as *My Bondage and My Freedom,* including a greater discussion of his childhood and family members. While eliminating the names of all those who had aided in his escape to freedom, Douglass told the full story of his life, framing it with a full-force abolitionist argument against the institution of slavery.

A speaking tour of Great Britain—undertaken to avoid capture after divulging his true name and status as a runaway slave—found Douglass even more radicalized upon his return to the United States two years later; he began to break with the structured abolitionism advanced by Garrison. *The North Star,* a newspaper that Douglass founded in 1847, would give increasing voice to his own abolitionist theories. It would also publicize and support the cause of equality of women of both races. Bearing the slogan "Right Is of No Sex" upon its masthead, *The North Star* kept the cause of women's rights before the American people even as the cause was voluntarily eclipsed by its key proponents with the issue of slavery, both before and during the Civil War.

"When the true history of the antislavery cause shall be written, women will occupy a large space in its pages," Douglass wrote in his autobiography, "for the cause of the slave has been peculiarly woman's cause." Recognizing the plight of women as similar to that of African Americans in that they lacked most of the same economic and political rights, Douglass added his stature as a public figure to the cause of women's suffrage. Invited to the July 1848 meeting at Seneca Falls by Elizabeth Cady Stanton, he spoke eloquently in favor of supporting women's right to vote and hold public office, a demand that, while included in Stanton's *Declaration of Sentiments,* was still hotly debated by many present at that historic meeting.

Douglass would become a major speaker at most of the Women's Rights conventions held during the next 21 years, partly in gratitude for "woman's agency, devotion, and efficiency in pleading the cause of the slave." When the first National Woman's Rights Convention met in 1850, signs and banners proclaimed a slogan—"Equality before the Law without Distinction of Sex or Color"—that reflected the efforts of many of the women present to aid in the battle to end slavery. More significantly however, Douglass's continued support rested on his belief that the rights of African Americans and women were almost equivalent. However, this qualified difference would become apparent when the moment of victory for his people—"the Negro's hour," as he termed it—finally became immanent. The signing of the Fifteenth Amendment in February 1869 marked a split between Douglas and former allies Stanton and Susan B. Anthony after he refused to continue pressing for the combined voting rights of blacks and women. Speaking at the annual assembly of the Equal Rights Association that year, he stated: "When women, because they are women, are dragged from their homes and hung upon lampposts; when their children are torn from their arms and their brains dashed upon the pavement;... then they will have the urgency to obtain the ballot." White women had the indirect access to the vote—through husbands, fathers, brothers, and sons—that black men lacked, Douglass maintained. Their right to the franchise, then, was less immediate.

The break between Frederick Douglass, Stanton, and Anthony—a break mirrored in the movement for women's suffrage nationwide—would eventually heal; the three would share the podium at the Woman's Suffrage Convention in 1888. "When I ran away from slavery, it was for myself," Douglass would one day write; "when I advocated emancipation, it was for my people; but when I stood up for the rights of women, self was out of the question, and I found a little nobility in the act."

—Pamela Kester-Shelton

DRABBLE, Margaret

Nationality: British. **Born:** Sheffield, Yorkshire, 5 June 1939; sister of writer A.S. Byatt. **Education:** Mount School, York; Newnham College, Cambridge, B.A. (honours) 1960. **Family:** Married 1) Clive Swift in 1960 (divorced 1975), two sons and one daughter; 2) the writer Michael Holroyd in 1982. **Career:** Deputy chair, 1978-80, and chair, 1980-82, National Book League. **Awards:** Rhys Memorial prize, 1966; James Tait Black Memorial prize, 1968; American Academy E.M. Forster award, 1973. D.Litt: University of Sheffield, 1976; University of Keele, Staffordshire, 1988; University of Bradford, Yorkshire, 1988; York University, 1995. C.B.E. (Commander, Order of the British Empire), 1980. **Agent:** Peters Fraser & Dunlop, 503-504 The Chambers, Chelsea Harbour, Lots Road, London SW10 OXF, England.

Publications

Novels

A Summer Bird-Cage. London, Weidenfeld & Nicolson, 1962; New York, Morrow, 1964.

The Garrick Year. London, Weidenfeld & Nicolson, 1964; New York, Morrow, 1965.

The Millstone. London, Weidenfeld & Nicolson, 1965; New York, Morrow, 1966; as *Thank You All Very Much,* New York, New American Library, 1969.

Jerusalem the Golden. London, Weidenfeld & Nicolson, and New York, Morrow, 1967.

The Waterfall. London, Weidenfeld & Nicolson, and New York, Knopf, 1969.

The Needle's Eye. London, Weidenfeld & Nicolson, and New York, Knopf, 1972.

The Realms of Gold. London, Weidenfeld & Nicolson, and New York, Knopf, 1975.
The Ice Age. London, Weidenfeld & Nicolson, and New York, Knopf, 1977.
The Middle Ground. London, Weidenfeld & Nicolson, and New York, Knopf, 1980.
The Radiant Way. London, Weidenfeld & Nicolson, and New York, Knopf, 1987.
A Natural Curiosity. London and New York, Viking, 1989.
The Gates of Ivory. London and New York, Viking, 1991.
The Witch of Exmoor. London and New York, Viking, 1996.

Short Stories

Hassan's Tower. Los Angeles, Sylvester & Orphanos, 1980.

Uncollected Short Stories

"A Voyage to Cythera," in *Mademoiselle* (New York), December 1967.
"The Reunion," in *Winter's Tales 14,* edited by Kevin Crossley-Holland. London, Macmillan, and New York, St. Martin's Press, 1968.
"The Gifts of War," in *Winter's Tales 16,* edited by A.D. Maclean. London, Macmillan, 1970; New York, St. Martin's Press, 1971.
"Crossing the Alps," in *Mademoiselle* (New York), February 1971.
"A Day in the Life of a Smiling Woman," in *In the Looking Glass,* edited by Nancy Dean and Myra Stark. New York, Putnam, 1977.
"A Success Story," in *Fine Lines,* edited by Ruth Sullivan. New York, Scribner, 1981.
"The Dying Year," in *Harper's* (New York), July 1987.
"The Dower House at Kellynch—A Somerset Romance," in *Persuasions: The Jane Austen Society of North America* (Tucson, Arizona), 15, December 1993.

Plays

Bird of Paradise (produced London, 1969).

Screenplays: *Isadora,* with Melvyn Bragg and Clive Exton, 1969; *A Touch of Love (Thank You All Very Much),* 1969.

Television Play: *Laura,* 1964.

Other

Wordsworth. London, Evans, 1966; New York, Arco, 1969.
Virginia Woolf: A Personal Debt. New York, Aloe, 1973.
Arnold Bennett: A Biography. London, Weidenfeld & Nicolson, and New York, Knopf, 1974.
For Queen and Country: Britain in the Victorian Age (for children). London, Deutsch, 1978; New York, Seabury Press, 1979.
A Writer's Britain: Landscape in Literature. London, Thames & Hudson, and New York, Knopf, 1979.
Wordsworth's Butter Knife: An Essay. Northampton, Massachusetts, Catawba Press, 1980.
The Tradition of Women's Fiction: Lectures in Japan, edited by Yukako Suga. Tokyo, Oxford University Press, 1985.
Case for Equality. London, Fabian Society, 1988.
Stratford Revisited: A Legacy of the Sixties. Shipston-on-Stour, Warwickshire, Celandine Press, 1989.
Safe as Houses: An Examination of Home Ownership and Mortgage Tax Relief. London, Chatto & Windus, 1990.
Angus Wilson: A Biography. London, Secker & Warburg, 1995.

Editor, with B. S. Johnson, *London Consequences* (a group novel). London, Greater London Arts Association, 1972.
Editor, *Lady Susan, The Watsons, Sanditon,* by Jane Austen. London, Penguin, 1974.
Editor, *The Genius of Thomas Hardy.* London, Weidenfeld & Nicolson, and New York, Knopf, 1976.
Editor, with Charles Osborne, *New Stories 1.* London, Arts Council, 1976.
Editor, *The Oxford Companion to English Literature.* Oxford and New York, Oxford University Press, 1985; concise edition, edited with Jenny Stringer, 1987.
Editor, *Twentieth-Century Classics.* London, Book Trust, 1986.

*

Bibliography: *Margaret Drabble: An Annotated Bibliography* by Joan Garrett Packer, New York, Garland, 1988.

Manuscript Collections: Boston University; University of Tulsa, Oklahoma.

Critical Studies: *Margaret Drabble: Puritanism and Permissiveness* by Valerie Grosvenor Myer, London, Vision Press, 1974; *Boulder-Pushers: Women in the Fiction of Margaret Drabble, Doris Lessing, and Iris Murdoch* by Carol Seiler-Franklin, Bern, Switzerland, Lang, 1979; *The Novels of Margaret Drabble: Equivocal Figures* by Ellen Cronan Rose, London, Macmillan, 1980, and *Critical Essays on Margaret Drabble* (includes bibliography by J.S. Korenman) edited by Rose, Boston, G. K. Hall, 1985; *Margaret Drabble: Golden Realms* edited by Dorey Schmidt and Jan Seale, Edinburg, University of Texas-Pan American Press, 1982; *Margaret Drabble: Existing within Structures* by Mary Hurley Moran, Carbondale, Southern Illinois University Press, 1983; *Guilt and Glory: Studies in Margaret Drabble's Novels 1963-1980* by Susanna Roxman, Stockholm, Almquist & Wiksell, 1984; *Margaret Drabble* by Joanne V. Creighton, London, Methuen, 1985; *The Intertextuality of Fate: A Study of Margaret Drabble* by John Hannay, n.p., 1986; *Margaret Drabble* by Lynn Veach Sadler, Boston, Twayne, 1986; *Women Novelists Talk* by Olga Kenyon (interview), New York, Carroll & Graf, 1989; *Margaret Drabble: Symbolic Moralist* by Nora Foster Stovel, San Bernardino, California, Borgo Press, 1989; *Womanist and Feminist Aesthetics: A Comparative Review* by Tuzyline Jita Allan, Athens, Ohio University Press, 1995.

* * *

Margaret Drabble was one of the first of a new generation of women novelists responding to the feminist movement of the 1960s. Soon after the germinal feminist texts that launched the women's liberation movement in the early part of the decade—Doris Lessing's blockbuster novel *The Golden Notebook* in 1962 and Betty Friedan's study *The Feminine Mystique* in 1963—Drabble published the first of a dozen novels that portray that recent phenomenon, the graduate wife and mother.

Born in the large industrial Midlands city of Sheffield, England in 1939, the first year of World War II, the second child in a family consisting of three girls and a younger boy, Drabble identified with the Brontës, about whom she would later write. Her mother, Marie Bloor, a Cambridge graduate and English teacher, was depressive. Her father, John Frederick Drabble, a Queen's Counsel and District Court Judge, who published detective novels after his retirement, was away at war when Maggie, as she is known to her family, was a young child. Drabble's siblings include the writer A.S. Byatt, author of several novels and critical studies and winner of the Booker Prize for *Possession* (1990). The third sister is an art historian and the brother a barrister, like his father.

Educated, like her mother and elder sister, at the Mount School in York, with its Quaker leanings, Drabble also followed her sister up to Newnham College, Cambridge, as a scholar. There she came under the influence of F.R. Leavis and the Great Tradition of English Literature. Upon graduation in 1960 she married fellow student and actor Clive Swift and together with him joined the Royal Shakespeare Company, where she understudied Vanessa Redgrave and Dame Judy Dench at Stratford-on-Avon. Swift has gone on to a successful career on stage and screen, especially British television, but Drabble's theatrical career was cut short when, pregnant with her first child, she was relegated to the wings. Not in a condition to carry, let alone shake, spears, she was obliged to write novels, fortunately for her readers, although all her fiction is very dramatic.

After three children, the marriage ended in divorce in 1975. Drabble married Michael Holroyd, biographer of Lytton Strachey, Augustus Johns, and George Bernard Shaw, in 1982. For over a decade the pair maintained their separate houses, spending weekends and holidays together. Drabble only recently gave up her home near Keats's house in Hampstead to join Holroyd. They purchased a country home by the sea in Porlock, Somerset.

Drabble's novels of the sixties reflect the contemporary dilemma of the graduate wife and professional mother, experiencing conflict between her responsibility to herself and her duty to her children, between the demands of family and the pressures of career. These first-person narratives are semi-autobiographical, with the heroines contemporaneous with the author and the dilemmas reflecting the author's own. Each novel explores the female identity by examining one specific feminine role, as wife, mother, lover, daughter, sister, or professional woman—all roles that Drabble has played. *A Summer Bird-Cage* (1963) portrays two sisters, reflecting Drabble and Byatt perhaps, with Sarah Bennett, the younger, a recent Oxford graduate trying to choose between marriage and a career, observing her glamorous sister Louise's marriage to a successful novelist. *The Garrick Year* (1964) presents Emma Evans, nee Lawrence, who has already made the choice to marry and have children, during a theatrical season with her flamboyant actor husband at the Garrick Festival, where the relationship is tested by adulterous affairs. *The Millstone* (1965), titled *Thank You All Very Much* in the United States and filmed as *A Touch of Love* (1969), portrays Rosamund Stacey, a doctoral candidate preparing a dissertation on the Elizabethan sonnet, who is imprisoned in an ivory tower of scholarship, but finally delivered from her solitary confinement by giving birth as an unmarried mother to Octavia, who initiates her into the real world of humanity and affection through Octavia's surgery to correct a congenital defect of the heart. *Jerusalem the Golden* (1967) dramatizes the fraught relationship between an intelligent young woman who escapes from her home town of Northam and her repressive mother to the metropolis of London by a lucrative university scholarship, only to discover that her own mother cherished similar ambitions that were thwarted by marriage and maternity. In *The Waterfall* (1969), which Drabble has called "the most female of all my books," the protagonist is solipsistic to the point of paralysis, living in her poetry, rather than in reality, until a sexual passion revitalizes her so that the word can be made flesh.

Drabble's novels of the seventies paint a broader canvas of a kaleidoscopic panorama of British society that has earned her the title of Chronicler of Britain. Her heroines develop from claustrophobia to community, reflecting the author's own emancipation from the pressures of childrearing into the public sphere as a media celebrity with a social conscience. Similarly, her technical command of narrative method develops to enable her to progress from subjective first-person accounts to multiple viewpoints that encompass a wide range of society. *The Needle's Eye*, the novel that brought Drabble to the attention of North American readers, marks the beginning of a more mature phase in her fiction, for this Jamesian novel concerns money and morality in the modern world, as its heroine, Rose Vertue Vassiliou, attempts to achieve virtue by voluntarily divesting herself of her fortune inherited from her capitalist father. A bitter custody battle with her husband Christopher Vassiliou, son of an impoverished Greek family, who appreciates the virtues of wealth, enables Drabble to probe the peculiarities of the British legal system at a point when she was considering separation from her own husband. In *The Realms of Gold* (1975) Drabble counters the objections of feminist critics who disliked Rose's decision to return to her husband by creating a powerful female protagonist in the person of Frances Wingate, whose successful career as archaeologist and single mother concludes with the comic closure of marriage, as Drabble employs archaeology, history, and geology to span the evolution of man from the primal slime to the final cinder. Drabble takes the temperature of the times in *The Ice Age* (1977), a study of the real estate market during the oil crisis, as she portrays Britain fighting a cold war with a new ice age. The male protagonist, Anthony Keating, is petrified in a prison behind the Iron Curtain, but Drabble declines to follow the fortunes of his female partner Alison, for "Her life ... will not be imagined." In *The Middle Ground* (1980), Drabble explores the cesspool of contemporary British society through the multiple viewpoints of a lively mixture of characters around feminist journalist Kate Armstrong, representing the political, economic, and scientific aspects of society.

After a hiatus during the eighties imposed by her five-year contract to reedit *The Oxford Companion to English Literature*, Drabble composed a trilogy of novels: *The Radiant Way* (1987), *A Natural Curiosity* (1989) and *The Gates of Ivory* (1991). *The Radiant Way* features three women friends—Liz Headleand, psychiatrist, Alix Bowen, social worker, and Esther Breuer, art historian, as well as Liz's sister, Northam housewife Shirley Harper—tracing their friendship to Cambridge in the fifties and following their careers to London in the eighties, culminating in the capture of serial murderer Paul Whitmore, a specialist in severed heads. As the "Author's Note" states, "*A Natural Curiosity* is a sequel to *The Radiant Way*," because Alix Bowen follows Paul Whitmore to his Yorkshire prison to discover what formative influences led him to a career of decapitations. The "Author's Note" concludes: "At the moment of writing this, I intend to write a third but very different volume, which will follow the adventures of Stephen Cox in Kampuchea." Drabble's state-of-the-nation novel becomes a way-of-the-world saga, as she follows Stephen Cox from England into the heart of the Indonesian darkness where mounds of skulls mounting under the rule of demagogue Pol Pot in Cambodia mock poor Yorick. *The Gates of Ivory,* which opens with Liz Headleand receiving in the mail a package containing fragments of Stephen's journals, plus two finger bones, is Drabble's most postmodernist narrative to date, for the package, known as "The Text," must be decoded in the quest to save Stephen or to discover his cause of death.

Following a 1993 story entitled "The Dower House at Kellynch: A Somerset Romance," inspired by Jane Austen's novel *Persuasion,* Drabble announced that she planned to turn from her panorama of international networks to a more intimate focus on the web of related family and friends in the countryside of Somerset, where her 1966 novel, *The Witch of Exmoor,* is set.

Drabble has sustained so successfully the conflicting demands of personal and professional life that she constitutes a role model for modern women. Much more than a novelist, she is also a critic, editor, and scholar of note, as well as a public literary personality. Graduating from Cambridge with a double, starred first, she had a brilliant career as an academic ahead of her. But deciding, like her first heroine Sarah Bennett, that "One can't be a sexy don," she entered the theatre and matrimony instead of the academy. While becoming a successful novelist, however, she has also become a significant scholar. Moreover, her critical studies parallel her fictional texts. In *Wordsworth* (1966), a monograph on the Romantic poet, Drabble's emphasis on the subjective self escaping from oppressive society into communion with nature and on use of natural imagery to symbolize the life of the psyche parallels the subjective focus of her early domestic novels of the sixties with their imagery of flora and fauna to symbolize the life of the affections. *Arnold Bennett: A Biography* (1974) emphasizes the early modern novelist's commitment to the community, paralleling her mature fiction of the seventies where her protagonists' urge for emancipation is resolved in acknowledgment of the individual's responsibility to the community. Both Bennett and Drabble symbolize their social vision in architectural imagery, especially the traditional emblem of the house to embody the concept of the extended family, the continuity of the present with the communities of both past and future. *Angus Wilson: A Biography* (1995), a study of the life and work of the later-20th-century British novelist, parallels Drabble's recent fiction, particularly her trilogy, in its celebration of Wilson's trenchant and macabre social satire.

Drabble is also an editor of note, having published *London Consequences* (1972), a group novel coedited with B.S. Johnson, *Lady Susan, The Watsons, Sanditon* (1974) by Jane Austen, *The Genius of Thomas Hardy* (1976), *New Stories I* (1976), *Twentieth-Century Classics* (1986), and, most impressively, the fifth edition of *The Oxford Companion to English Literature* (1985). Drabble has also published various literary studies: *For Queen and Country: Britain in the Victorian Age* (1978), *A Writer's Britain: Landscape in Literature* (1979), *The Tradition of Women's Fiction* (1982), and she has introduced the Virago editions of Jane Austen's six novels. Not only a novelist of note, Drabble has published several short stories; *Bird of Paradise,* a play produced in London in 1969; screenplays for *Isadora* (1969), starring Vanessa Redgrave, and *A Touch of Love* (1969), starring Sandy Dennis, as well as *Laura* (1964), a television play.

In addition to her career as a writer, Drabble has been a teacher in adult education at Morley College in London, a lecturer for the Arts Council and British Council, and a broadcaster and journalist with many articles, reviews and interviews to her name. She has received numerous awards for her achievements: the Rhys Memorial prize in 1966, the James Tait Black Memorial prize in 1968 and the American Academy E.M. Forster award in 1973. She was named Commander of the British Empire by Queen Elizabeth in 1980 in recognition of her achievements.

—Nora Foster Stovel

DUFFY, Maureen (Patricia)

Pseudonym: D. M. Cayer. **Nationality:** British. **Born:** Worthing, Sussex, 21 October 1933. **Education:** King's College, London, 1953-56, B.A. in English (with honours) 1956. **Career:** Teacher of creative writing, 1951-53, 1956-60. Co-founder, Writers Action Group, 1972; fiction editor, *Critical Quarterly,* Manchester, 1987; editor, *The Sixties,* London, 1960. **Awards:** City of London Festival Playwrights's prize, 1962, for *The Lay-Off;* Arts Council bursary, 1963, 1966, 1975; Society of Authors travelling scholarship, 1976; Royal Society of Literature fellow, 1985. **Member:** Gay and Lesbian Humanist Association, European Writers Congress (vice-president), Writers Guild of Great Britain (joint chair, 1977-78, president, 1985-89), Greater London Arts Literature Panel (chair, 1979-81, 1989—, vice-chair, 1981-86), Authors Lending and Copyright Society (chair, 1982-94), British Copyright Council, Beauty without Cruelty (vice-president), Copyright Licensing Agency (chair, beginning 1996). **Agent:** Jonathan Clowes Ltd., Ironbridge House, Bridge Approach, London NW1 8BD, England.

Publications

Novels

That's How It Was. London, Hutchinson, 1962; New York, Dial, 1984.
The Single Eye. London, Hutchinson, 1964.
The Microcosm. London, Hutchinson, and New York, Simon & Schuster, 1966.
The Paradox Players. London, Hutchinson, and New York, Simon & Schuster, 1967.
Wounds. London, Hutchinson, and New York, Knopf, 1969.
Love Child. London, Weidenfeld & Nicolson, and New York, Knopf, 1971.
I Want to Go to Moscow: A Lay. London, Hodder & Stoughton, 1973; as *All Heaven in a Rage,* New York, Knopf, 1973.
Capital: A Fiction. London, Cape, 1975; New York, Braziller, 1976.
Housespy. London, Hamish Hamilton, 1978.
Gor Saga. London, Methuen, 1981; New York, Viking, 1982.
Scarborough Fear (as D. M. Cayer). London, Macdonald, 1982.
Londoners: An Elegy. London, Methuen, 1983.
Change. London, Methuen, 1987.
Illuminations. London, Sinclair-Stevenson, 1991.
Occam's Razor. London, Sinclair-Stevenson, 1993.

Short Stories

"The City As Archeological Dig," in *A Female Vision of the City: London in the Novels of Five British Women.* Knoxville, University of Tennessee Press, 1989.

"The Last Priestess," in *God: An Anthology of Fiction.* London and New York, Serpent's Tail, 1992.

Poetry

Lyrics for the Dog Hour. London, Hutchinson, 1968.
The Venus Touch: London, Weidenfeld & Nicolson, 1971.
Actaeon. Rushden, Northamptonshire, Sceptre Press, 1973.
Evesong. London, Sappho, 1975.
Memorials of the Quick and the Dead. London, Hamish Hamilton, 1979.
Collected Poems 1949-1984. London, Hamish Hamilton, 1985.

Plays

The Lay-Off (produced London, 1962).
The Silk Room (produced Watford, Hertfordshire, 1966).
Rites (produced London, 1969), in *New Short Plays 2.* London, Methuen, 1969; in *Plays by Women.* London, Methuen, 1983.
Solo, Olde Tyme (produced Cambridge, England, 1970).
A Nightingale in Bloomsbury Square (produced London, 1973), in *Factions,* edited by Giles Gordon and Alex Hamilton. London, Joseph, 1974.
The Masque of Henry Purcell (produced London, 1995).

Television Plays: *Josie,* 1961.

Radio Plays: *Only Goodnight,* 1981.

Literary Criticism

The Passionate Shepherdess: Aphra Behn 1640-1689. New York, Avon, and London, Cape, 1977.
The Erotic World of Faery. London, Hodder & Stoughton, 1972; New York, Avon, 1980.

History

Inherit the Earth: A Social History. London, Hamish Hamilton, 1980.

Other

Men and Beasts: An Animal Rights Handbook. London, Paladin, 1984.
A Thousand Capricious Chances: A History of the Methuen List 1889-1989. London, Methuen, 1989.
"The Progress of Love," in *Tony Harrison,* edited by Neil Astley. Newcastle upon Tyne, Bloodaxe, 1991.
Henry Purcell. London, Fourth Estate, 1994.

Editor, with Alan Brownjohn, *New Poetry 3.* London, Arts Council, 1977.
Editor, *Oroonoko and Other Stories,* by Aphra Behn. London, Methuen, 1986.
Editor, *Love Letters between an Nobleman and His Sister,* by Aphra Behn. London, Virago, 1987.
Editor, *Five Plays,* by Aphra Behn. London, Methuen, 1990.

Translator, *A Blush of Shame,* by Domenico Rea. London, Barrie & Rockliffe, 1963.

*

Manuscript Collections: King's College, University of London.

Critical Studies: *Lesbian Images* by Jane Rule, London, Peter Davies, 1976; "In a Class by Herself" by Leah Fritz, in *Women's Review of Books,* November 1987, p. 25; "Keepers of History: The Novels of Maureen Duffy" by Susan Crecy in *Lesbian and Gay Writing: An Anthology of Critical Essays,* Philadelphia, Temple University Press, 1990; *Maureen Duffy,* London, Book Trust/British Council, 1989; "Three Recent Versions of the Bacchae" by Elizabeth Hale Winkler, in *Madness in Drama,* edited by James Redmond, Cambridge, Cambridge University Press, 1993; "A Portrait of Virginia Woolf in Maureen Duffy's play, *A Nightingale in Bloomsbury Square*" by Christine W. Sizemore, in *Virginia Woolf: Themes and Variations,* edited by Turk Vara Neverow and Mark Hussey, New York, Pace University Press, 1993; "Fiction As Historical Critique: The Retrospective World War II Novels of Beryl Bainbridge and Maureen Duffy" by Phyllis Lassner, in *Phoebe,* 3(2), fall 1991; "Mary and the Monster: Mary Shelley's *Frankenstein* and Maureen Duffy's *Gor Saga*" by Jenny Newman in *Where No Man Has Gone Before: Women and Science Fiction,* edited by Lucie Armitt, London, Routledge, 1991; "'How Sweet the Kill': Orgiastic Female Violence in Contemporary Re-visions of Euripides' *The Bacchae*" by Allison Hersh, in *Modern Drama,* 35(3), September 1992.

* * *

Maureen Duffy writes as a lesbian and a socialist, her work often focusing on misfit characters searching for happiness in modern society. In several novels, Duffy employs sexually ambiguous protagonists to examine the roles gender and sexual identity play in marginalizing characters from society. While her poetry deals with lesbian subjects, in her nonfiction Duffy has proven to be a forceful advocate for animal rights, a topic that also figures prominently in her novel *All Heaven in a Rage.* Duffy has also written stage plays, reflecting an early interest in Shakespearean drama.

For her first novel, *That's How It Was,* Duffy drew upon her own childhood for the story of a gifted girl growing up in an impoverished family during World War II. The character Paddy, whose father leaves when she is two months old and whose mother struggles to raise her alone, is an autobiographical portrait of Duffy herself, bright and determined to rise above her working-class origins. The strong mother-daughter relationship and Paddy's efforts to overcome poverty and social isolation have ensured a continuing readership for the book. Duffy's next novel, *The Single Eye,* is the story of a photographer, Mike, who has an affair with his sister-in-law. But the novel's larger theme concerns the many varieties of sexual preference and the necessity for acceptance of all emotional relationships as valid. Mike not only has an affair with a woman, but is the focus of a homosexual friend's romantic interest as well. As these events in his life unfold, characters discuss forms of sexual attraction, argue for tolerance, and decry society's push for uniformity of expression.

These arguments set the stage for Duffy's one explicitly lesbian novel, *The Microcosm.* The novel is set in the London lesbian scene of the early 1960s and tells the story of Matt, a butch lesbian with a dead-end job at a gas station who feels that she is alienated from her wife, Rae. Matt spends weekends at the House of Shades, a lesbian bar that serves as the novel's focal point. Bringing in the stories of other club customers, Duffy creates a sometimes disjointed account of lesbian life in 1960s London, following the women as they meet, break up, and search for new lovers at the club. Some reviewers criticized the book's uneasy structure. It is not clear, for example, who is speaking for the first fifty pages, and the many episodic accounts of different characters' lives can seem unrelated to each other. But viewed as a panoramic story of lesbian life, one intended not to recount a particular story but rather to recreate a demi-monde, the novel is more successful. The often disorienting nature of the narrative can be seen as a reflection of the lesbian reaction to the straight world, for example. Indeed, Duffy first planned *The Microcosm* to be a nonfiction study of lesbian life, interviewing a number of subjects for her book, some of whose stories are presented fictionally within the novel. In addition she incorporated the stories of people she actually knew into her fictional world as well.

In other novels Duffy explores the relationships between sex, gender, and the larger society. In *Wounds,* for example, recurring scenes featuring a nameless couple making love are punctuated by longer episodes involving a variety of people in modern England who face painful restrictions on their lifestyle. This contrasting of sex with societal limitations sets up a number of questions about the power of love in the modern world and the relationships between personal and public concerns. In *Love Child* Duffy relates the story of Kit, a child of indeterminate sex who takes a deadly revenge on his/her mother's lover. Combining elements of Freudian psychology and Greek mythology, *Love Child* examines a world where gender is subordinate to wealth, power, and the kind of permissiveness that sanctions even the most destructive behavior. A similarly gender-ambiguous narrator is found in *Londoners,* the story of Al, a struggling writer in a London of predatory inhabitants who dreams of writing a filmscript about the French poet François Villon. Al's essential loneliness and isolation amid the incessant activity of the bustling metropolis, brought on by his/her vocation as a writer as well as by his/her sexual preferences, confronts the issue of private versus public behavior and how sexual identity can serve to marginalize people from the larger society.

—Denise Wiloch

DUNBAR, Alice. *See* **DUNBAR-NELSON, Alice Moore.**

DUNBAR-NELSON, Alice Moore

Also wrote as Alice Ruth Moore and Alice Dunbar. **Nationality:** American. **Born:** New Orleans, Louisiana, 19 July 1875. **Education:** Straight University (now Dillard University), B.A. 1892. **Family:** Married 1) the writer Paul Laurence Dunbar in 1898 (divorced 1902); 2) Arthur Callis in 1910 (divorced); 3) Robert J. Nelson in 1916. **Career:** Teacher, New Orleans Public School System, 1892-96; moved to Harlem, New York, 1897; co-founder and teacher, White Rose Mission, Harlem, 1897-89; moved to Washington, DC, 1898; instructor at Howard High School, Wilmington, Delaware, and Howard University and State College for Colored Students (now Delaware State College). Coeditor and writer for *AME Review,* 1913-14; Mid-Atlantic States' field organizer for woman's suffrage movement, 1915; field representative, Woman's Committee of the Council of Defense, 1918; editor and publisher, *The Dunbar Speaker and Entertainer,* 1920; coeditor, with Robert Nelson, Wilmington, Delaware *Advocate;* contributed columns and articles to numerous publications, including *Crisis, Ebony, Opportunity,* and *Topaz.* **Died:** Philadelphia, 18 September 1935.

Publications

Short Stories

Violets and Other Tales (as Alice Ruth Moore; includes verse). Boston, Monthly Review Press, 1895.
The Goodness of St. Rocque and Other Stories (as Alice Dunbar). New York, Dodd Mead, 1899.

Uncollected Short Stories

"The Little Mother," in *Standard Union* (Brooklyn), 7 March 1900.
"The Ball Dress," in *Leslie's Weekly,* 93, 12 December 1901.
"Science in Frenchtown—A Short Story," in *Saturday Evening Mail,* 7 December 1912.
"Hope Deferred," in *Crisis,* 8, September 1914.

Essays

"Appointed, Some Points of View," in *Daily Crusader,* 2 July, 1894.
"Training of Teachers of English," in *Education,* 29, October 1908.
"Wordsworth's Use of Milton's Description of Pandemonium," in *Modern Language Notes,* 24, April 1909.
"What Has the Church to Offer the Men of Today?" in *A.M.E. Church Review,* 30, July 1913.
"The Poet and His Song," in *Paul Laurence Dunbar: Poet Laureate of the Negro Race* (special issue of *A.M.E. Church Review*), October 1914.
"People of Color in Louisiana," in *Journal of Negro History,* 1, October 1916.
"'Hysteria': The Old-Time Mass Meeting Is Dead," in *Competitor,* 1, February 1920.
"Negro Literature for Negro Pupils," in *Southern Workman,* 51, February 1922.
"These 'Colored' United States," in *Messenger,* 9, March 1927.
"Textbooks in Public Schools: A Job for the Negro Woman," in *Messenger,* 9, May 1927.
"Facing Life Squarely," in *Messenger,* 9, July 1927.
"The Negro Looks at an Outworn Tradition," in *Southern Workman,* 57, May 1928.
"The Big Quarterly in Wilmington," in *Journal Every Evening,* 27 August 1932.

Poetry

"Rainy Day," in *Advertiser* (Almira, New York), 18 September 1898.
"Summit and Vale," in *Lippincott's,* December 1902.

"Violets" and "Sonnet," in *Crisis,* August 1917.
"To Madame Curie," in *Public Ledger,* 21 August 1921.
"I Sit and I Sew," and "Sonnet," in *Negro Poets and Their Poems,* edited by Robert T. Kerlin. Washington, DC, Associated Publishers, 1923.
"Communion," "Music," and "Of Old St. Augustine," in *Opportunity,* 3, July 1925.
"Snow in October," in *Caroling Dusk,* edited by Countee Cullen. New York and London, Harper, 1927.
"Forest Fire," in *Harlem: A Forum of Negro Life,* 1, November 1928.
"Canto—I Sing," in *American Interracial Peace Committee Bulletin,* October 1929.

Play

"The Author's Evening at Home," in *Smart Set,* September 1990.

Other

Give Us Each Day: The Diary of Alice Dunbar-Nelson, edited by Gloria T. Hull. New York, Norton, 1984.
The Works of Alice Dunbar-Nelson, edited by Gloria T. Hull. New York, Norton, 3 vols., 1988.

Editor (as Alice Dunbar), *Masterpieces of Negro Eloquence: The Best Speeches Delivered by the Negro from the Days of Slavery to the Present Time.* Harrisburg, Pennsylvania, Douglass, 1914.
Editor and contributor, *The Dunbar Speaker and Entertainer.* Naperville, Illinois, J. Nichols, 1920.

*

Bibliography: "Works by and about Alice Ruth (Moore) Dunbar-Nelson: A Bibliography" by Ora Williams, in *CLA Journal,* 19, March 1976.

Manuscript Collections: Ohio Historical Society, Columbus; Morris Library, University of Delaware, Newark.

Critical Studies: *Color, Sex, and Poetry: Three Women Writers of the Harlem Renaissance* by Gloria T. Hull, 1987; *Afro-American Women Writers, 1746-1933* edited by Ann Allen Shockley, Boston, G.K. Hall, 1988.

* * *

An energetic woman whose written achievements would help lay the foundation for later efforts to establish an African American literary tradition, Alice Dunbar-Nelson transcended the stereotypical black woman of the turn of the century through her pursuit of education, her refinement of her creative talents, and her untiring sense of responsibility for the social and intellectual betterment of men and women of color. A writer whose work preceded the literary bloom of the Harlem Renaissance, she was nonetheless influential within that movement.

Born in New Orleans in 1875, into a secure middle-class family, Dunbar-Nelson was inspired from a young age by the industrious, creative atmosphere of the city. After graduating from Straight University in 1892, she began a career as an educator, which would remain her primary occupation and commitment for the remainder of her life. Writing became both her creative outlet and an increasing viable avenue through which to affect the social changes that she felt were needed. Dunbar-Nelson is often remembered as the wife of fellow writer Paul Laurence Dunbar; the two were married in a quiet ceremony in 1898. Putting his career ahead of her own, she would move with Dunbar to Washington, DC, but their marriage ended rather tumultuously four years later; although she married for a second time shortly after, she would continue to write under his name, augmenting her surname to Dunbar-Nelson upon marrying Robert J. Nelson in 1916.

Dunbar-Nelson's most widely read works were the poetry and stories collected in *Violets and Other Tales* (1895) and *The Goodness of St. Rocque and Other Stories* (1899). Hailed as among the first collections of short fiction published by an African American woman, the stories in these collections reflect the then-current call for "dialect" stories, rather than fiction that dealt with serious racial issues. Published while Dunbar-Nelson was in her early twenties, the stories, such as "Little Miss Sophie" and "A Carnival Jangle," reflect the writer's familiarity with the Creole culture of her native New Orleans, as well as her relative naivete. Later works, in which she addressed racism and women's oppression, found a more difficult time finding a publisher; most of Dunbar-Nelson's mature fiction and nonfiction would be printed in magazines such as *Crisis, Journal of Negro History, Opportunity,* and *Messenger.* Her poem "I Sit and I Sew," published in 1918, reflects an increasing sophistication. Inspired by the nation's involvement in World War I, the female voice within the poem's 21 lines protests war, racism, and the powerlessness of women:

> The little useless seam, the idle patch;
> Why dream I here beneath my homely thatch,
> When there they lie in sodden mud and rain,
> Pitifully calling me, the quick ones and the slain?
> You need me, Christ! It is no roseate dream
> That beckons me—this pretty futile seam,
> It stifles me—God, must I sit and sew?

In addition to writing stories and articles focusing on woman's oppression in traditionally mandated roles, Dunbar-Nelson was active in the suffrage and social reform movement of the early decades of the 20th century. In 1915 she actively organized the suffragist membership of the Mid-Atlantic states, and 1918 saw her working in an important capacity within the Women's Committee of the Council of Defense. Energetic in her commitment to educating, informing, and improving the quality of life of African Americans, Dunbar-Nelson balanced her job as a teacher with editorship of several publications, including her own *Dunbar Speaker and Entertainer,* which she published in 1920. Her columns "From a Woman's Point of View" (Pittsburgh *Courier,* 1926), "As in a Looking Glass" (Washington, DC, *Eagle,* 1926-30), and "So It Seems to Alice Dunbar-Nelson" (Pittsburgh *Courier,* 1930), as well as her editorship of *Masterpieces of Negro Eloquence: The Best Speeches Delivered by the Negro from the Days of Slavery to the Present Time* (1914) place her as the literary foremother of such writers as Ann Allen Shockley in her efforts to preserve and promote the literary legacy of African American writers.

—Pamela Kester-Shelton

DUPIN, Amandine-Aurore-Lucile. *See* **SAND, George.**

DWORKIN, Andrea

Nationality: American. **Born:** Camden, New Jersey, 26 September 1946. **Education:** Bennington College, B.A. 1968. **Family:** Lives with the writer John Stoltenberg. **Career:** Has worked as a waitress, receptionist, secretary, typist, salesperson, factory worker, paid political organizer, and teacher. Contributor to periodicals, including *America Report, Christopher Street, Feminist Studies, Gay Community News, Los Angeles Times, Mother Jones, Ms., Social Policy,* and *Village Voice.* **Member:** International Women's Media Foundation, Women's Institute for Freedom of the Press, Authors League of America. **Agent:** Elaine Markson, 44 Greenwich Avenue, New York, New York 10011, U.S.A.

Publications

Novels

Notes on Burning Boyfriend. N.p., n.d.
Ice and Fire. London, Secker & Warburg, 1986.
Mercy. London, Secker & Warburg, 1990; Four Walls Eight Windows, 1991.

Short Stories

the new woman's broken heart. Frog in the Well, 1980.

Political/Social Theory

Women Hating. New York, Dutton, 1974.
Pornography: Men Possessing Women. New York, Putnam, 1981.
Right-wing Women. New York, Putnam, 1983.
Intercourse. New York, Free Press, 1987.
Pornography and Civil Rights: A New Day for Women's Equality, with Catharine A. MacKinnon. Minneapolis, Organizing against Pornography, 1988.

Essays

Our Blood: Prophecies and Discourses on Sexual Politics. New York, Harper, 1976.
Letters from a War Zone: 1976-1987. London, Secker & Warburg, 1988; New York, Dutton, 1989.
"Andrea Dworkin," in *Contemporary Authors Autobiographical Series,* Vol. 21. Detroit, Gale, 1994.
Life and Death. New York, Free Press, forthcoming.

Poetry

Child. N.p., 1966.
Morning Hair (includes fiction). Privately published, 1968.
(Vietnam) Variations. N.p., n.d.

*

Critical Studies: "Is One Woman's Sexuality Another Woman's Pornography?" by Mary Kay Blakely, in *Ms.,* 13, April 1985; *Pornography, Feminism and the Individual* by Alison Assiter, n.p., 1989; "Fighting Talk" (interview) with Michael Moorcock, in *New Statesman & Society,* 21 April 1995.

* * *

Andrea Dworkin is one of the best-known and consistently active radical feminists to emerge from the U.S. women's movement of the 1970s and 1980s. Through her prolific writing and her many public speaking engagements, Dworkin is American feminism's most outspoken critic of pornography. Her books, articles, and campus speeches advocate the position that pornography violates women's civil rights, and this controversial stance has earned Dworkin a highly visible but contested place in the feminist community. Applauded by many for her striking analysis of sexual violence against women, she has also been personally attacked in print by both men and women who believe her opposition to pornography equals censorship of free speech. Although her writings encompass a wide range of topics concerning sexual relations, violent social practices affecting women, and contemporary feminist politics, Andrea Dworkin—along with legal scholar Catharine A. MacKinnon—continues to be noted most often in the media as a symbolic leader in the feminist campaign against pornography.

Born in New Jersey in 1946 and educated at the all-women's Bennington College, Dworkin grew up with a strong awareness of Jewish heritage and human suffering, becoming involved in the antiwar movement of the late 1960s while still a teenager. Both her brief incarceration at the Women's House of Detention after being arrested at an antiwar rally and her experiences among male left-wing activists awakened Dworkin to the hostility expressed toward radical women in "Amerika," and she left the United States, first for Crete, where she lived for a year, then (after returning for two years to Bennington) for a five-year stint in the Netherlands to develop her own identity as an emerging writer. Her own emotional and physical pain as a battered wife during an abusive marriage to a Dutch man (which ended when she was 25), added to Dworkin's growing political analysis of male control over women, and her career as a notable feminist author began with the 1974 publication of *Woman Hating.* This text exposed cross-cultural practices, traditions, and myths hostile or hurtful to women throughout history. Included in Dworkin's analysis of cultural misogyny were fairy tales, foot-binding, female genital mutilation, and popular male pornographic writings celebrating the degradation of women during sex.

The response to Dworkin's work in the feminist community launched her career as a public speaker and activist, and led to a decade of travel, campus appearances, articles, speeches at "Take Back the Night" rallies, and public debates—supplemented by part-time jobs, for the controversial nature of Dworkin's writings often limited publishers' interest in promoting reviews or sales of her next works (such as her 1976 book *Our Blood: Prophecies and Discourses on Sexual Politics*). Several times in her writing career she turned to English publishers when American presses drew back from her strong rhetoric. Her 1981 book, *Pornography: Men Possessing Women,* developed her stance against the industry of pornography as well as the imagery, responding to her critics with the argument that modern gender inequity had its roots in historic male dominance. Pornography, Dworkin suggested, was not merely fantasy, but a form of social practice, controlling women by insisting that they serve as objects for male sexual use and abuse.

In 1983 antipornography legislation drafted by Dworkin and MacKinnon passed the Minneapolis City Council as a landmark ordinance, declaring pornography to be a form of sex discrimination. Among other definitions, the ordinance declared that pornography, the sexually explicit subordination of women, violated the civil rights of women, and under the proposed law any woman who had been coerced into pornography, been trafficked in, been forced to watch pornography, or been sexually assaulted or physically hurt because of pornography could sue for damages. The ordinance was vetoed by the Minneapolis mayor, but a similar ordinance passed in Indianapolis in 1984—only to be struck down by a federal court as an unconstitutional infringement upon freedom of speech and a violation of the First Amendment.

During the 1980s many conservative groups, such as the Moral Majority, also denounced pornography and sought bans on its availability. But Dworkin's 1983 text *Right-Wing Women* made clear that she did not seek a political alliance with religious conservatives, most of whom were also staunchly anti-feminist. Instead, her new book examined female participation in the conservative movement of the 1980s and the attraction of many women to right-wing political affiliations. *Right-Wing Women* suggested that some women gladly participated in the backlash against other women to preserve their own reputations, or in order to remain attractive to powerful men.

While some right-wing religious women did share Dworkin's concerns about pornography, some feminists in the 1980s insisted themselves that pornography could excite women as well as men and should remain freely available. Thus the 1980s saw the so-called "sex wars" escalate in the feminist community as writers and activists took sides over whether Dworkin and her supporters were "sex negative" and "the new censors." Feminists uncomfortable with the Minneapolis ordinance expressed concern that women's bookstores might be affected by any new curtailment of sexual images, such as those depicting lesbianism.

Throughout the 1980s, while she was often viciously attacked or jeered at, her sexuality questioned and her personal appearance mocked, Dworkin continued to teach, lecture, and publish. *Intercourse,* published in 1987, examined the historic and cultural meanings behind male sexual possession of women, offering legal and religious narratives on subjects such as virginity and defilement. Dworkin also departed from her standard essay format with a novel, *Ice and Fire,* in 1986, which depicted a woman making the journey from violent sexual abuse and street life to a writer's identity.

Dworkin's collection, *Letters from a War Zone,* published in 1993, gathered many of her early columns and essays, including those most freely responding both to the First Amendment question and to Dworkin's often unkind depiction in the American media. The book's cover deliberately showed a proudly imposing Dworkin in her trademark overalls, an image her critics have often jeered at as unfeminine. The collected essays, framed with new introductory notes and reminiscences, provide personal insight into the tireless career of a radical feminist who once declared that both writing *and* legislation were ways to change society. Dworkin continues to write on issues of women, pornography, and the U.S. Constitution from her home in Brooklyn, New York.

—Bonnie Morris

E

EDGEWORTH, Maria

Nationality: British. **Born:** Black Bourton, Oxfordshire, 1 January 1768. **Education:** Educated in Derby, England, 1775-80, and London, 1780-82. **Career:** Lived at family estate in Edgeworthstown, Ireland, from 1782; visited Scotland and met Sir Walter Scott, 1823. **Died:** 22 May 1849.

Publications

Novels

Castle Rackrent: A Hibernian Tale Taken from the Facts, and from the Manners of the Irish Squires, before the Year 1782 (published anonymously). London, J. Johnson, 1800; Boston, T. B. Wait & Sons, 1814.
Belinda. London, J. Johnson, 3 vols., 1801; Boston, Wells & Lilly, 2 vols, 1814.
The Modern Griselda: A Tale. London, J. Johnson, 1805.
Leonora. London, J. Johnson, 2 vols., 1806.
Patronage. London, J. Johnson, 4 vols., 1814.
Harrington [and] *Ormond.* London, R. Hunter, 3 vols., and New York, Kirk & Mercein, 1817.
Helen. London, R. Bentley, 3 vols., 1834.

Short Stories

Tales of Fashionable Life (includes *The Absentee*). London J. Johnson, 6 vols, 1809-12.
The Most Unfortunate Day of My Life: Being a Hitherto Unpublished Story, Together with the Purple Jar and Other Stories. London, Cobden-Sanderson, 1931.

Political/Social Theory

Practical Education, with Richard Lovell Edgeworth. London, J. Johnson, 2 vols., 1798; New York, G. F. Hopkins, 1801.
Essays on Professional Education, with Richard Lovell Edgeworth. London, J. Johnson, 1809.

Essays

Letters for Literary Ladies, to Which Is Added an Essay on the Noble Science of Self-Justification. London, J. Johnson, 1795.
Essays on Irish Bulls, with Richard Lovell Edgeworth. London, J. Johnson, 1802; New York, J. Sevaine, 1803.

For Children

The Parent's Assistant, or, Stories for Children. London, J. Johnson, 3 vols., 1796.
Moral Tales for Young People. London, J. Johnson, 5 vols., 1801; New York, W. B. Gilley, 1810.
Early Lessons. London, J. Johnson, 5 vols., 1801-02; Philadelphia, J. Maxwell, 4 vols., 1821.
Rosamond. London, R. Hunter, 2 vols., and Philadelphia, J. Maxwell, 1821.
Frank. London, R. Hunter, 3 vols., and New York, W. B. Gilley, 2 vols., 1822.
Harry and Lucy. London, R. Hunter, 4 vols., and Boston, Munroe & Francis, 3 vols., 1825.
Popular Tales. London, J. Mercer, 2 vols., 1804.
Continuation of Early Lessons. London, J. Johnson, 2 vols., 1814; Boston, Bradford & Reed, 1815.

Plays

Comic Dramas in Three Acts. London, R. Hunter, and Philadelphia, T. Dobson & Son, 1817.
Little Plays for Children. London, R. Hunter, 1827; as *Little Plays for Children, Being an Additional Volume of The Parent's Assistant,* Philadelphia, Thomas T. Ash, 1827.

Other

Chosen Letters. London, Cape, 1931.
Memoirs of Richard Lovell Edgeworth, Esq.; Begun by Himself and Concluded by His Daughter, Maria Edgeworth, vol. 2, with Richard Lovell Edgeworth. London, R. Hunter, 2 vols., 1820; Boston, Wells & Lilly, 1821.

*

Manuscript Collections: Henry E. Huntington Library, San Marino, California; Beinecke Library, Yale University, New Haven, Connecticut; William Andrews Clark Memorial Library, University of California at Los Angeles; Bodleian Library, Oxford; National Library of Ireland, Dublin; National Archives, Dublin.

Critical Studies: *Maria Edgeworth: A Literary Biography* by Marilyn Butler, Oxford, Oxford University Press, 1972; "Introduction," by Gina Luria, to *Letters for Literary Ladies*, by Maria Edgeworth, New York, Garland Press, 1974; *Sex and Subterfuge: Women Writers to 1850* by Eva Figes, London, Macmillan, 1982, New York, Persea, 1987; "Maria Edgeworth" by Butler, in *British Women Writers: A Critical Reference Guide*, edited by Janet Todd, New York, Continuum, 1989; "A Novel of Their Own: Romantic Women's Fiction, 1790-1830" by Anne K. Mellor, in *Columbia History of the British Novel*, edited by John Richetti, New York, Columbia University Press, 1994; "Class, Gender, Nation, and Empire: Money and Merit in the Writing of the Edgeworths" by Gary Kelly, in *The Wordsworth Circle,* 25(2), 1994; "De-Romanticizing the Subject: Maria Edgeworth's `The Bracelets's Mythologies of Origin, and the Daughter's Coming to Writing" by Mitzi Myers, in *Romantic Women Writers*, edited by Paula R. Feldman and Theresa M. Kelley, University Press of New England, 1995.

* * *

Her nine novels, several essays, and numerous children's stories made Maria Edgeworth one of the most popular authors of her time and, as Marilyn Butler points out in *Maria Edgeworth: A Literary Biography,* "the most commercially successful," rivalled only by Walter Scott. Edgeworth was not only esteemed by the masses of middle-class readers who thronged the circulating libraries, making "Novels by Miss Edgeworth, and Moral and Religious Novels" a book category label, but contemporary authors and critics also praised her work. Although Edgeworth is known today for creating the regional novel, a form later popularized by Scott, she should also be recognized for a vision that produced strong heroines, influencing such later novelists as Jane Austen, Elizabeth Gaskell, and George Eliot.

Edgeworth, who was already writing by the age of 12 and penned tales for children in the late 1780s, first published in 1795. *Letters for Literary Ladies* is an epistolary treatise that insists on the importance of female education. The book is comprised of two series of letters—"Letter from a Gentleman upon the Birth of a Daughter, with the Answer" and "Letters of Julia and Caroline"—and "An Essay on the Noble Science of Self-Justification." Perhaps Edgeworth's most forthright defense of women's rights, the conclusion of the father's answer, which explains his plans for his new daughter, demonstrates her reformist aims for women's education: ". . . I wish to give her the habit of industry and attention, the love of knowledge and the power of reasoning: these will enable her to attain excellence in any pursuit of science or of literature."

Edgeworth's focus on education came from her father, Richard Lovell Edgeworth, who performed semi-Rousseauistic experiments on his 22 children (by four wives). Maria, his eldest daughter, assisted him in compiling the results of this educational research into *Practical Education,* published in 1798. She was shielded from any negative criticism for exploring the unfeminine social sciences by coauthoring this book with her father. However, she wrote 18 of the 25 chapters and continued examining education, focusing on the proper education for young men in 1809's *Essays on Professional Education,* also a collaborative piece with her father. Because she was so involved with the education of her brothers and sisters, Edgeworth saw a definite need for children's books. To fill this literary void, and to facilitate her duties as a teacher, she created moralistic tales for children and published them in several multi-volume works, such as *The Parent's Assistant* (1796-1802) and *Early Lessons* (1801-02). Thus, Edgeworth is also an important figure in the history of children's literature.

With the exception of her most popular novel, the regional tale published in 1800 as *Castle Rackrent,* Edgeworth's novels and stories feature strong heroines. Edgeworth's first novel, *Belinda,* published in 1801, is a classic example of a nascent female-inspired Romanticism in which women are rational beings. In *Belinda,* the tale of a young woman entering society, Edgeworth highlights the importance of proper education and conduct. Although at this time still an immature writer who borrowed plot devices and stylistic dialogue from such contemporaries as Elizabeth Inchbald and Frances Burney, Edgeworth successfully fictionalized the feminist beliefs of Mary Wollstonecraft. As Gary Kelly explains in "Class, Gender, Nation, and Empire: Money and Merit in the Writing of the Edgeworths," Edgeworth "consistently promoted the Enlightenment discourse of reason, even for women. In this way, she exemplified in both her fictional heroines and her own implied identity as author a figure of woman at once intellectual and domestic." Edgeworth's varied female characters—which are prominently featured in every novel, from *Belinda* to 1834's *Helen,* a highly autobiographical work, as well as in many of her children's stories, including her first piece of juvenalia, "The Bracelets"—reflect her commitment to portraying women non-stereotypically, thereby offering alternatives to the traditional view at a time when society's conception of "woman" was evolving. Edgeworth consistently used these female characters to emphasize her primary theme: women's educational rights.

Maria Edgeworth's fictional presentation of her views did not offend audiences. On the contrary, her novels were in high demand, as her commercial success reveals: Scott received £700 for *Waverly* (1814) and Austen earned £300 for *Emma* (1816), while Edgeworth was paid £2100 for *Patronage* (1814). Such popularity can partially be attributed to her awareness of and avoidance of the later stigma attached to outspoken liberal feminists such as Wollstonecraft. For example, in 1799, when Edgeworth proposed founding a woman's political journal, *The Feminead,* to Anna Letitia Barbauld, she was persuaded to abandon the idea because of a probable association with Wollstonecraft. As Butler points out: "Like other moderate feminists, Maria Edgeworth was clearly embarrassed by Wollstonecraft's unconventional career," yet she assisted in disseminating Wollstonecraft's ideas through fiction. According to Butler, Edgeworth "is the first novelist to apply an insight articulated by Wollstonecraft, that women have their own language."

—Staci L. Stone

EHRENREICH, Barbara

Nationality: American. **Born:** Butte, Montana, 26 August 1941. **Education:** Reed College, B.A. in chemistry and physics 1963; Rockefeller University, Ph.D. in cell biology 1968. **Family**: Married 1) John Ehrenreich in 1966 (divorced 1974); one son, one daughter; 2) Gary Stevenson in 1983 (divorced 1994). **Career:** Program research analyst, Bureau of the Budget, New York, 1968-69, and Health Policy Advisory Center, 1969-71; assistant professor of health sciences, State University of New York, College at Old Westbury, 1971-74; Distinguished Visiting Professor, Sangamon State University, 1980, and University of Missouri at Columbia, 1981; fellow, Institute for Policy Studies, Washington, D.C., 1982-87; Regents' Lecturer, University of California at Santa Barbara, 1989; writer-in-residence, Ohio State University, Athens. Features editor, *Seven Days,* 1978-80; member of editorial board: *Social Policy; Sociology of Health and Illness; Critical Social Policy; Radical America; Ms.,* 1979-89; *Mother Jones,* 1988-90; *Lear's,* 1989-94; *The New Press,* beginning 1990; *Culturefront,* beginning 1992. Columnist, *Guardian, Mother Jones, Ms., Time,* and *New York Woman;* contributor to numerous periodicals, including *Atlantic Monthly, Esquire, Harpers, Lear's, Liberation, New York Times, Mother Jones, Ms., Nation, New Republic, New Statesman, Newsday, New York Woman, Radical America, Socialist Review, Vogue,* and *Wall Street Journal.* **Awards:** National Magazine Award (shared), 1980, for excellence in reporting; Ford Foundation Award, 1981, for humanistic perspectives on contemporary society; New York Institute for the Humanities fellow, 1981-93; Institute for Policy Studies fellow; Guggenheim fellowship, 1987; honorary D.Phil.: Reed College, 1987, College of Old Westbury, SUNY, 1990; Long Island Women on the Job Award; Long Island NOW Women's Equality Award, 1988; National Book Critics' Award nominee, 1989, for *Fear of Falling;* New York University Society of Fellows, 1992; National Magazine Award finalist, 1992; National Women's Political Caucus Exceptional Media Merit Award, 1993; MacArthur Foundation grant, 1994. **Member:** Society for Study of Social Problems (program committee cochair, 1980); Democratic Socialists of America (cochair beginning 1983); NOW's Commission on Responsive Democracy; National Women's Health Network; National Abortion Rights Action League; Women's Health Education Project; National Self-Help Clearinghouse; Nationwide Women's Program of the American Friends Service Committee; Association for Union Democracy; Jan Palach Information and Research Trust; Network of East-West Women; Long Island Workers' Rights Center; Boehm Foundation; Feminists for Free Expression; Women's Committee of 100. **Address:** P.O. Box 87, Sugarloaf Key, Florida 33044, U.S.A.

Publications

Novel

Kipper's Game. New York, Farrar Strauss, 1993; London, Virago, 1994.

Political/Social Theory

Long March, Short Spring: The Student Uprising at Home and Abroad, with John Ehrenreich. New York and London, Monthly Review Press, 1969.
The American Health Empire: Power, Profits, and Politics, with John Ehrenreich. New York, Random House, 1970.
For Her Own Good: 150 Years of the Expert's Advice to Women, with Deirdre English. Garden City, New York, Doubleday, 1978; London, Pluto Press, 1979.
The Hearts of Men: American Dreams and the Flight from Commitment. Garden City, New York, Doubleday and London, Pluto Press, 1983.
Remaking-Love: The Feminization of Sex, with Elizabeth Hess and Gloria Jacobs. Garden City, New York, Doubleday, 1986; London, Fontana, 1987.
The Mean Season, with Fred Block, Richard Cloward, and Frances Fox Piven. New York, Pantheon, 1987.
Fear of Falling: The Inner Life of the Middle Class. New York, Pantheon, 1989.

Essays

The Worst Years of Our Lives: Irreverent Notes from a Decade of Greed. New York, Pantheon, 1990; London, Lime Tree, 1991.
The Snarling Citizen: Essays. New York, Farrar Strauss, 1995.

Uncollected Essays

"The Professional-Managerial Class," in *Between Labor and Capital,* edited by Pat Walker. Boston, South End Press, 1977.

Other

Complaints and Disorders: The Sexual Politics of Sickness, with Deirdre English. New York, The Feminist Press, 1973.
Witches, Midwives, and Nurses: A History of Women Healers, with Deirdre English. New York, The Feminist Press, 1973; London, Compendium, 1974.
Women in the Global Factory, with Annette Fuentes. Boston, South End Press, 1983.
Poverty in the American Dream: Women and Children First, with Karin Stallard. Boston, South End Press, 1983.
Toward Economic Justice for Women, with the Women's Economic Agenda Working Group. Washington, DC, Institute for Policy Studies, 1985.

*

Critical Studies: "Science vs. Women: Settling the Accounts of the Past" by Elizabeth Cagan, in *Social Policy,* May/June 1979; review of *The Hearts of Men* by Arlene Kaplan Daniels in *Signs: Journal of Women in Culture and Society,* spring 1986.

* * *

Barbara Ehrenreich is a social critic, feminist, and political activist. Her work ranges from examinations of the oppression of women by the health care industry to reasoned defenses of feminism against a social backlash, to complex political and social critiques suggesting that modern America has lost its heart. Throughout her numerous books, articles, and essays, Ehrenreich displays her intelligence, wit, and unfailing political agenda.

Ehrenreich's values of caring for society are rooted in her family; her parents—a copper miner father and a mother who combined homemaking with being active in the Democratic party—espoused the same vision of responsibility and support for those in need. While Ehrenreich would receive both her B.A. and Ph.D. in the sciences, her progressive work in the 1960s—helping to expand low-income housing and educational opportunities for the underprivileged, organizing union activists, advocating health-care reform, and launching a student antiwar group—influenced her to become a social activist and writer rather than a scientist.

In 1970 Ehrenreich was further radicalized with the birth of her daughter, Rosa, when she realized that her best interests were secondary to the wishes and schedule of her doctor. "The experience made me a feminist," she would later state. She began to explore the power of the American medical establishment and to document the sexist assumptions of its reigning health care "experts." In *Complaints and Disorders: The Sexual Politics of Sickness,* coauthored with Deirdre English in 1973, Ehrenreich presented a history of medicine that highlights the gender, class, and race differences in patients' treatment. The women extended their analysis of the power that doctors and the primarily male medical establishment holds over women's lives from the late 19th century into the present; as they demonstrate, a woman's rights to birth control, abortion, or even medical care during childbirth is still primarily accessed through male doctors.

As social commentary and critique became more central to her work, Ehrenreich made writing her full-time career. She also became deeply involved in the New American Movement (NAM), which embraced a vision of socialism for American society. Her involvement in NAM, coupled with her position as features editor of the news magazine *Seven Days,* provided her with the impetus to tie her arguments about specific issues like health care to a larger critique of American society. In their 1979 book, *For Her Own Good,* Ehrenreich and English reassess the advice often given women by "experts" of different professional stripes—from physicians to psychologists to home economists—and argue that this advice works ultimately to usurp women's traditional roles by institutionalizing the experts' roles in society. Her work during this time helped establish Ehrenreich as an outstanding feminist social critic.

Having won a number of prestigious awards in the early 1980s, Ehrenreich continued to write throughout the decade, focusing particularly on the backlash to the women's movement that was beginning to emerge. One of the most serious threats that this backlash posed to feminism was its charge that the women's movement had led to a breakdown in the stability of the American family, thus laying at women's feet the responsibility for a climbing divorce rate, an increasing crime rate, single-parent families, and a host of other social ills. In her *The Hearts of Men: American Dreams and the Flight from Commitment,* Ehrenreich counters such allegations by claiming that, in fact, men's freedom from family commitment had been increasingly legitimized since the 1950s by such sources as the hedonistic *Playboy* image of the "swinging" single man. She also contends that men's revolt from the breadwinner role actually preceded the women's movement, provocatively making the case that the erosion of the nuclear family began with men, rather than women. Ehrenreich was also concerned with the way that the "sexual revolution" had been redefined as an embarrassing sidetrack from the "real issues" of the women's movement. In *Remaking-Love: The Feminization of Sex,* she and coauthors Elizabeth Hess and Gloria Jacobs argue that the sexual revolution was an important component of women's increasing freedom. They show how sex relates to larger cultural issues such as equal rights, equal pay, and abortion rights.

In *Fear of Falling: The Inner Life of the Middle Class,* published in 1989, Ehrenreich examines the changing values and motivations of the American middle class since the 1950s. The members of the middle class, she argues, in their attempts to maintain a high standard of living, have drawn exclusive boundaries around themselves by withdrawing their political support and physical presence from the larger community. She contends that only by reaffirming a moral standpoint of caring and inclusivity will American society be revitalized. In *The Worst Years of Our Lives* and *The Snarling Citizen,* two collections of acclaimed essays that first appeared in such periodicals as the *Nation, Mother Jones, Ms., New Republic,* and *Time,* Ehrenreich pens incisive, provocative, and humorous pieces reflective of the same values she set forth in *Fear of Falling.* Her 1994 novel, *Kipper's Game,* an ambitious dystopian fantasy, also reflects her stern social critiques.

In three decades as a writer and journalist, Ehrenreich has clearly demonstrated that, for her, writing is an act inspired by a personal commitment to social justice. Currently an essayist for *Time* magazine and a columnist for the London *Guardian,* she continues to contribute numerous pieces to various newspapers, magazines, and journals, raising her strong, clear, compassionate voice to address the relentless political and social shifts within U.S. society as we move into the next century.

—Ivy Kennelly and Joya Misra

---

el-SADAAWI, Nawal. *See* **al'SADAAWI, Nawal.**

EMECHETA, (Florence Onye) Buchi

Nationality: Nigerian/British. **Born:** Yaba, Lagos, Nigeria, 21 July 1944. **Education:** Methodist Girls' High School, Lagos; University of London, B.Sc. (honors) in sociology 1972. **Family:** Married Sylvester Onwordi in 1960 (separated 1969); two sons and three daughters. **Career:** Librarian, 1960-64; library officer, British Museum, London, 1965-69; Inner London Education Authority, youth worker and sociologist, 1969-76; community worker, Camden, New Jersey, 1976-78; visiting lecturer at 11 universities in the United States, 1979; senior research fellow and visiting professor of English, University of Calabar, Nigeria, 1980-81; lecturer, Yale University, New Haven, Connecticut, 1982. Since 1982, lecturer, University of London. Proprietor, Ogwugwu Afo Publishing Company, London; since 1979, member of the Home Secretary's Advisory Council on Race. **Awards:** *New Statesman* Jock Campbell Award for literature by new or unregarded talent from Africa or the Caribbean, 1978; named Best Black British writer, 1978; selected as one of the Best British Young Writers, 1983. **Address:** 7 Briston Grove, London N8 9EX, England.

Publications

Novels

Second-Class Citizen. London, Allison & Busby, 1974; New York, Braziller, 1975.

The Bride Price. London, Allison & Busby, and New York, Braziller, 1976.

The Slave Girl. London, Allison & Busby, and New York, Braziller, 1977.

The Joys of Motherhood. London, Allison & Busby, and New York, Braziller, 1979.

Destination Biafra. London, Allison & Busby, 1982.

Double Yoke. London, Ogwugwu Afo, 1982; New York, Braziller, 1983.

Adah's Story. London, Allison & Busby, 1983.

The Rape of Shavi. London, Ogwugwu Afo, 1983; New York, Braziller, 1985.

A Kind of Marriage. London, Macmillan, 1987.

Gwendolen. London, Collins, 1989; as *The Family,* New York, Braziller, 1990.

Kehinde. Oxford, Heinemann, 1994.

For Children

Titch the Cat. London, Allison & Busby, 1979.

Nowhere to Play. London, Allison & Busby, 1980.

The Moonlight Bride. Oxford, Oxford University Press, 1981; New York, Braziller, 1983.

The Wrestling Match. Oxford, Oxford University Press, 1981; New York, Braziller, 1983.

Naira Power. London, Macmillan, 1982.

Plays

Television Plays: *A Kind of Marriage,* 1976; *The Ju Ju Landlord,* 1976.

Autobiography

In the Ditch. London, Barrie & Jenkins, 1972.
Head above Water. London, Ogwugwu Afo, 1986.

Other

Our Own Freedom, photographs by Maggie Murray. London, Sheba, 1981.

*

Critical Sources: "The Death of the Slave Girl: African Womanhood in the Novels of Buchi Emecheta" by Katherine Frank, in *World Literature Written in English,* 21(3), autumn 1982; "Womanhood/Motherhood: Variations on a Theme in Selected Novels of Buchi Emecheta" by Ketu H. Katrak, in *Journal of Commonwealth Literature,* 22(1), 1987; "Emecheta's Social Vision: Fantasy or Reality" by Chimalum Nwankwo, in *Ufahamu,* 17(1), 1988; "'Second Class Citizen': The Point of Departure for Understanding Buchi Emecheta's Major Fiction" by Michael Porter Abioseh, in *International Fiction Review,* 15(2), summer 1988; "Feminism in the Literature of African Women" by Nancy Topping Bazin, in *Black Scholar,* summer/fall 1989; "Buchi Emecheta: An African Storyteller" by Daphne Topouzis, in *Africa Report,* May/June 1990; "Engaging Dreams: Alternative Perspectives on Flora Nwapa, Buchi Emecheta, Ama Ata Aidoo, Bessie Head, and Tsitsi Dangarembga's Writing" by Maggi Phillips, in *South Central Review,* 1995.

* * *

Florence Onye Buchi Emecheta is perhaps the most prominent African woman novelist of this century. Her writing in English includes 11 novels, an additional five works of fiction for children and young adults, several plays written for television, and autobiography. Although English is her second language (Ibo is her first), Emecheta believes it is important to write and publish in English so that her work reaches the widest possible audience. Emecheta enjoys a truly international reputation since her fiction is read throughout Africa, Europe, and North America. Her wide appeal may be attributed to the fact that she chooses to write about what she considers to be universal subject matter: the relative insignificance of girls in the patriarchal family, the secondary status of women in African society, male privilege within the institution of marriage, and the impact of Western culture on traditional society.

Emecheta herself experienced some of the same hardships and injustices that are the focus of her fiction. Born in the small village of Yaba near the more urban Lagos, Nigeria, Emecheta knew first-hand the tensions between Western values represented by the city of Lagos and the claims of traditional culture retained in African village life. Emecheta's parents died while she was quite young, and as a result, she was sent to live with foster parents who treated her harshly. Although she was able to attend school until the age of 16, she followed tradition by marrying the man to whom she had been engaged since the age of 11. By the age of 17, she gave birth to her first child, and by the time she was 22, she had given birth to five children. In both her fiction and in interviews, Emecheta speaks forcefully about the constraints of childbearing and childrearing on the artistic capabilities of African women.

After her second child was born, Emecheta departed Nigeria for London to join her husband who had left a year earlier to study there. Supporting her family through menial jobs and public assistance, she balanced the responsibilities of motherhood with her writing. Despite the fact that her husband was abusive to her and even burned one of her early manuscripts in an attempt to thwart her drive for independence, Emecheta managed to publish sequential installments of her diary in the *New Statesman.* Her marriage ended in divorce several years later. This first publication, an autobiographical narrative titled *In the Ditch,* recounts her early experiences of hardship in London and her struggle as a young mother and writer. Her first novel, *Second Class Citizen,* also includes many autobiographical elements told from the viewpoint of the main character, Adah: her early desire for an education, her move to London, and the difficulties of being a working mother, student, and writer in a Western culture often in opposition to the traditions that she had previously known.

In her fiction, Emecheta constantly questions the traditional values of Ibo society, such as the primacy of motherhood, the subservience of women in marriage, and the formation of women's identity only as mothers and wives. Although Emecheta might hesitate to label herself a feminist, one of the primary concerns that her fiction addresses is the status of women in Nigerian and Western Africa, as well as African women who live abroad. Emecheta firmly believes that writing about women's problems and the contradictions of African women's social status will draw attention to the many inequities they face, which, in effect, becomes the first step toward social change. In *The Bride Price,* a young couple in love learns the difficulty of trying to overcome the constraints of tradition. Aku-nna, studying to become a teacher, falls in love with her instructor, Chike, who is a descendant of slaves. Since custom forbids girls from respectable families to marry ancestors of slaves, Aku-nna is caught in a dilemma of rejecting her uncle's chosen suitor, Obiajulu, who will pay the highest bride price for her. Aku-nna is subsequently kidnapped by Obiajulu's family, but in order to prevent Obiajulu from violating her, she tells him that she has already consummated her love with Chike. Chike helps Aku-nna escape and takes her as his wife. Despite her happiness, Aku-nna fears that she will eventually die in childbirth because her uncle refuses to accept the generous bride price offered by Chike's family.

If *The Bride Price* exposes how the onset of puberty for women is linked to their subsequent loss of freedom in the traditional arranged marriage, then Emecheta's next novel, *The Slave Girl,* further depicts the full extent of women's ownership by men in the traditional African society. The story opens in the early 1900s with the celebrated birth of the only girl child to survive infancy in Okwueku's household. Ojebeta, this favored daughter, is treated lavishly by her parents until their deaths, at which time her brother sells her into slavery. Emecheta's story is poignantly told as Ojebeta slowly realizes that her brother's abandonment of her into the hands of strangers marks the end of her illusion of security and autonomy.

In Emecheta's most celebrated novel, *The Joys of Motherhood,* the heroine Nnu Ego, like other women in traditional African society, must develop her identity and self-worth only within her role as a wife and mother. Faced with barrenness in her marriage to Naife, she is rejected by her husband, who further humiliates her by taking a new co-wife. When Nnu Ego eventually bears children, she becomes totally consumed by their needs and finds no fulfillment in her maternal status. This novel, with its ironic title, is perhaps Emecheta's most blistering attack on the traditional status and treatment of African women.

Education always presents conflicts for Emecheta's African women characters, who are seldom liberated through their efforts to achieve learning. In *Double Yoke* Nko, a young undergraduate woman at a large Nigerian university, must face family and societal pressure to marry as she is determined to continue her education. Ete Kamba, who wants to marry Nko, is torn between his insistence that she follow traditional expectations and his obvious pride in her intellectual independence.

Readers may classify Emecheta as a political writer solely on the basis of her questioning of gender stereotypes and the subservient roles this entails for African women. However, Emecheta's political focus extends beyond the family and local society to issues of national and international perspective. In *Destination Biafra* Emecheta weaves the personal narrative of a young woman, Debbie Ogedemgbe, into the larger historical tapestry of Nigeria's devastating Biafran civil conflict. Debbie, against the wishes of her parents, decides to join in her country's struggle to survive the competing claims of Nigeria's political and cultural forces. In *The Rape of Shavi* Emecheta constructs a traditional civilization located in an imaginary African country that becomes "invaded" by Westerners who arrive as a result of a plane crash. This richly ironic novel is Emecheta's most sustained criticism of the disastrous effects of Western colonialism on traditional society.

In her more recent novels such as *The Family* and *Kehinde,* Emecheta returns to her most competent form of storytelling by delineating the plight of the individual female within the constraints of the patriarchal family. *The Family* traces the tragic life of Gwendolen Brillianton from her childhood in Jamaica to her teen years in London. Gwendolen endures sexual molestation, incest, and other forms of violence, but like many of Emecheta's heroines, learns to survive in a hostile world. *Kehinde* is the story of a Nigerian woman living in London with a husband who convinces her to have an abortion, then eventually betrays her by returning to Nigeria and remarrying without her knowledge.

Emecheta was first impressed by the power of storytelling through the compelling oral narratives of her maternal ancestors. Their performances convinced her that storytelling is not just an art but one of the most important activities in life. Her own childhood delight in oral narrative has perhaps inspired her remarkable children's novels such as *Titch the Cat* and *Nowhere to Play* (both based on stories by her own children), *The Moonlight Bride,* and the enchanting story of adolescent competition, *The Wrestling Match.* Buchi Emecheta's stylistic agility and captivating narratives account for her continued popularity and success as a contemporary English novelist.

—Janet J. Montelaro

EMSHWILLER, Carol

Nationality: American. **Born:** Carol Fries, Ann Arbor, Michigan, 12 April 1921. **Education:** University of Michigan, Ann Arbor, B.A. in music and B.Design 1949; Ecole Nationale Supérieure des Beaux-Arts, Paris (Fulbright fellow), 1949-50. **Family:** Married the filmmaker and artist Edmund Emshwiller in 1949 (died 1990); two daughters and one son. **Career:** Since 1978, member of the Continuing Education Faculty, New York University. Conducted workshops for Science Fiction Bookstore, New York, 1975, 1976, and Clarion Science Fiction Workshop, 1978, 1979; guest teacher, Sarah Lawrence College, Bronxville, New York, 1983. Contributor to periodicals, including *Croton Review, Epoch,* and *TriQuarterly.* **Awards:** MacDowell fellowship, 1971; Creative Artists Public Service grant, 1975; National Endowment grant, 1979; New York State grant, 1988; New York University continuing education award for teaching excellence, 1989. **Address:** 210 East 15th Street, Apartment 12E, New York, New York, 10003, U.S.A.; (summer) Rt. 1, Box 36 E, Cherrytree Circle, Bishop, CA, 93514, U.S.A.

Publications

Novels

Carmen Dog. London, Women's Press, 1988; San Francisco, California, Mercury House, 1990.
Ledoyt. San Francisco, Mercury House, 1995.

Short Stories

Joy in Our Cause. New York, Harper, 1974.
Verging on the Pertinent. Minneapolis, Minnesota, Coffee House Press, 1989.
The Start of the End of It All. London, Women's Press, 1990; revised edition, San Francisco, Mercury House, 1991.
Venus Rising. Cambridge, Massachusetts, Edgewood Press, 1992.

Plays

Television Plays: *Pilobolis and Joan,* 1974; *Family Focus,* 1977.

*

Critical Studies: "Carol Emshwiller" by Janet Bogstadt, in *St. James Guide to Science Fiction Writers,* edited by Jay Pederson, Detroit, St. James Press, 1995.

Carol Emshwiller comments:

I've always hoped my stories and books (such as *Carmen Dog*) make fun of women's ways as much as of men's.

With the novel *Ledoyt* my writing changed completely—no longer satire and humor. After my husband's death I felt I'd lost my material for the battle between the sexes. Also writing served a different purpose for me. I needed a family to live with since my children were grown and scattered all over.

I wanted to write a long, relaxed novel. I had to research the style. I read all sorts of things I'd never thought to read before, such as Wallace Stegner's *Angle of Repose* and Wendell Berry's *A Place on Earth.* I don't think I ever really mastered the long line I was after.

And I wanted to write from the omniscient point of view for a change. I did get some omniscient in, but mostly I lapsed back into one person's point of view—sequentially.

And about feminism! Just as Flaubert said, "Mme Bovary, c'est moi," I felt about my male character, "Ledroit, c'est moi." I am Ledoyt and am also madly in love with him. More so all the time as I got to know him better (and as he got uglier and uglier). All my growing up I wanted to be a man. Being Ledoyt was fun.

And all my growing up I was brainwashed into thinking men were better at everything and in every way than women. On my 16th birthday my father told me no woman had ever done anything significant. I think he told me as a kindness. He didn't want me going off and making a big mistake.

Of course I know it's not true, but I'm still brainwashed by my father and brothers, and yet, when I think about it, I prefer the company of women or of men with a lot of "womanish" qualities.

* * *

Since the 1950s, Carol Emshwiller has written feminist science fiction and fantasy stories that are by turns experimental in their use of language and character and whimsical in their flights of fancy. Emshwiller's short stories are often Kafkaesque takes on contemporary relations between the sexes, with both genders receiving their share of satirical examination. Her novel *Carmen Dog* is a fantasy fable in which animals and human women exchange places. In the novel *Ledoyt,* Emshwiller turns from her usual fantasy to a realistic story of a marriage that endures against great odds. In all her fiction, Emshwiller's biting wit and ability to turn a phrase have drawn critical acclaim from both genre and mainstream critics alike.

Emshwiller began her writing career in the mid-1950s by publishing short stories in the science fiction magazines of the time. Her first story, "This Thing Called Love," appeared in *Future* in 1955. (Her late husband, Edmund Emshwiller, illustrated science fiction magazine covers during the 1950s under the name Ed Emsh.) Although Emshwiller's work continued to appear regularly in magazines and anthologies, not until 1974 did a collection of her stories appear. *Joy in Our Cause,* containing 20 of Emshwiller's early stories, brought the author to critical attention for her accurate presentation of female interior monologues and for her experiments with language and character in her stories. The title story, for example, consists of a dialogue between two unnamed people who are trying to repair a troubled relationship. Parenthetical asides present the female character's thoughts and sarcastic commentary on the conversation. Typical of Emshwiller's best work, the story examines the feminine psyche in a fantastical, quirky and individualistic way, granting insights that might have been less obvious in a story following a traditional narrative form.

Emshwiller's later collections continue her explorations of both the female mind and experimental forms of literature. In *Verging on the Pertinent,* for example, she employs fable and allegory to explore the relationships between the sexes. The story "Yukon" concerns an unhappy married woman who leaves her husband to live quietly in the woods with a bear. The use of fable appears again in the collection *The Start of the End of It All,* where the title story tells of Earth's divorced women aligning themselves with aliens seeking to conquer the male-dominated world. Emshwiller's fables capture the alienated essence of her estranged women characters by presenting their everyday frustrations and resentments in strange and otherworldly settings. Like a distorting mirror or magnifying glass, Emshwiller's fiction renders its subject in an outlandishly exaggerated manner that makes clear its often overlooked aspects.

For her novel *Carmen Dog,* Emshwiller returns to allegory and fable. A feminist fable in which human women evolve into animals while animals become human women, *Carmen Dog* comments on the relative power of the sexes in a society where women are often treated as dogs. The story focuses on one family in which the wife is transforming into a snapping turtle and the family dog is growing into a woman. Soon the dog, Pooch, is caring for the baby, washing dishes and cooking dinner, but finds these traditional female activities unsatisfying. Advised by a psychiatrist to try catching a frisbee now and then, to satisfy the animal side of her inner self, she rebels. What she really wants to do, Pooch decides, is sing opera. Taking the baby with her, she travels to New York to fulfill her dream by appearing in *Carmen.* Despite some uneven moments, Emshwiller's allegory succeeds in whimsically scoring points about sexual inequalities and commenting on the destructive behavioral tendencies of both women and men. Women who seek to be pampered and men who try to dominate others are both satirized in Emshwiller's animal tale.

Emshwiller turns to a more realistic setting in her novel *Ledoyt,* an historical novel of the American West of the early 20th century. Revolving around the love relationship between Oriana Cochran and Beal Ledoyt, two seeming opposites who overcome their differences in order to marry, the story moves to the couple's daughter, Lotti, who attempts to destroy her parents' marriage. The novel's realistic approach, its conventional narrative style and its development of rounded characters mark *Ledoyt* as a major shift away from Emshwiller's earlier, more fantastic fiction. Yet, despite its differences in presentation, *Ledoyt* shares the same concern for examining relationships between the sexes, here exemplified by the unlikely pairing of Oriana and Beal. Emshwiller examines their marriage, its shared trials and joys, its conflicts and contentments, in an unflinching, realistic manner not marred by either hard-line feminist ideology or demeaning prejudices. *Ledoyt,* then, although far different from the kind of fiction for which Emshwiller is best known, is perhaps her most successful work in terms of examining the fundamental relationship between the sexes she has always explored in her writing.

—Denise Wiloch

ENCHI, Fumi. *See* **ENCHI, Fumiko.**

ENCHI, Fumiko

Pseudonym for Fumi Enchi. **Nationality:** Japanese. **Born:** Fumi Ueda, in Asakusa Ward, Tokyo, 2 October 1905. **Education:** Attended Higher School of Japan Women's University, Tokyo, 1918-22. **Family:** Married Yoshimatsu Enchi in 1930; one daughter. **Career:** Writer, playwright, translator, and essayist. **Awards:** Women Writers' Award, 1954, for "Himojii tsukihi"; Noma Prize for Literature, 1957, for *Onnazaka;* Women Writers' Award, 1966, for *Namamiko monogatari;* Tanizaki Jun'ichirō Prize, 1969, for trilogy *Ake wo ubau mono, Kizu aru tsubasa,* and *Niji to shura;*

Japanese Literature Grand Prize, 1972, for *Yūkon;* Order of Culture, 1985, for lifetime achievement. **Member:** Association of Women Writers (president 1958-76), Academy of Art. **Died:** 14 November 1986.

Publications

Novels

Ake wo ubau mono [Vermilion Thief]. Tokyo, Kawade shobō, 1956.
Onnazaka. Tokyo, Kadokawa shoten, 1957; translated as *The Waiting Years,* Kodansha International, 1971.
Onnamen. Tokyo, Kōdansha, 1958; translated as *Masks,* New York, Knopf, 1983; London, Tuttle, 1984.
Kizu aru tsubasa [Scarred Wings]. Tokyo, Chūō Kōronsha, 1962.
Namamiko monogatari [Tales of the False Shamaness]. Tokyo, Chūō Kōronsha, 1965.
Komachi hensō [Komachi in Disguise]. Tokyo, Kōdansha, 1965.
Niji to shura [Rainbow and Asura]. Tokyo, Bungei shunjū, 1968.
Yūkon [Playful Spirits]. Tokyo, Shinchōsha, 1971.
Shokutaku no nai ie [House without a Kitchen Table]. Tokyo, Shinchōsha, 1979.

Short Stories

"Himojii tsukihi" [Days of Hunger], in *Chūō Kōron,* December 1953.
"Yō," in *Chūō Kōron,* September 1956; translated as "Enchantress" in *Japan Quarterly,* 5(3), 1958; in *Rice Bowl Women: Writings by and about the Women of China and Japan,* edited by Dorothy Blair Shimer. New York, Mentor, 1982.
"Otoko no hone," in *Bungei shunjū,* July 1956; translated as "Skeletons of Men" in *Japan Quarterly,* 35(4), 1988.
"Nise no en—shūi," in *Bungakkai,* January 1957; translated as "A Bond for Two Lifetimes—Gleanings," in *Rabbits, Crabs, Etc.,* edited by Phyllis Birnbaum. Honolulu, University of Hawaii Press, 1983; translated as "Love in Two Lives: The Remnant" in *Stories by Contemporary Japanese Women Writers,* edited by Noriko Mizuta Lippit and Kyoko Selden. New York, M.E. Sharpe, 1983.
"Hokuro no onna" [Woman with a Mole], in *Bungei asahi,* September 1962.
"Mekura oni," in *Shōsetsu Chūō Kōron,* December 1962; translated as "Blind Man's Bluff" in *The Mother of Dreams and Other Stories,* edited by Makoto Ueda. Tokyo, Kodansha, 1986.
"Miyako no onna" [Women of the Capital], in *Shōsetsu Shinchō,* February 1965.
"Kikuguruma," in *Gunzō,* July 1967; translated as "Boxcar of Chrysanthemums" in *This Kind of Woman: Ten Stories by Japanese Women Writers 1960-1976,* edited by Yukiko Tanaka and Elizabeth Hanson. New York, Putnam, 1982.
"Hana kui uba" [The Old Woman Who Eats Flowers], in *Shinchō,* January 1974.
"Kiku" [Chrysanthemum], in *Gunzō,* January 1980.

Other

Translator, *Genji monogatari* [The Tale of Genji]. Tokyo, Shinchōsha, 10 vols., 1972-73.

*

Bibliography: *Japanese Women Writers in English Translation: An Annotated Bibliography* by Mamola Claire Zebronski, New York, Garland, 1989.

Critical Studies: "Eroticism and the Writings of Enchi Fumiko" by Yoko McClain, in *Journal of the Association of Teachers of Japanese,* 15(1), 1980; *Daughters of the Moon: Wish, Will, and Social Constraint in Fiction by Modern Japanese Women* edited by Victoria V. Vernon, Berkeley, Institute of East Asian Studies, University of California Press, 1988; "Spirit Possession in the Context of Dramatic Expressions of Gender Conflict: The Aoi Episode of the *Genji monogatari*" by Doris G. Bargen, in *Harvard Journal of Asiatic Studies* 48(1), 1988, and her "Twin Blossoms on a Single Branch: The Cycle of Retribution in *Onnamen,*" in *Monumenta Nipponica* 46(2), 1991; "Double Weave: The Fabric of Women's Writing" by Amy V. Heinrich, in *World Literature Today: A Literary Quarterly from the University of Oklahoma,* 1988; "Echoes of Feminine Sensibility in Literature" by Van C. Gessel, in *Japan Quarterly,* 35(4), 1988, her "The `Medium' of Fiction: Fumiko Enchi as Narrator," in *World Literature Today,* 1988, and her "Due Time: Modern Japanese Women Writers," in *Journal of Japanese Studies,* 15(2), 1989; "Enchi Fumiko's Literature in Translation" by Shari L. Thurow, in *International Association of Orientalist Librarians,* 34-35, 1989; "Echoes of Feminine Sensibility in Literature" by Juliet Winters Carpenter, in *Japan Quarterly,* 37(3), 1990; "Enchi Fumiko and the Hidden Energy of the Supernatural" by Wayne Pounds, in *Journal of the Association of Teachers of Japanese,* 24(2), 1990; "Women Writers Past and Present: Murasaki Shikubu and Enchi Fumiko" by Chieko Irie Mulhern, in *Review of National Literatures,* 18, 1993; "Enchi Fumiko" by S. Yumiko Hulvey, in *Japanese Women Writers: A Bio-Critical Sourcebook,* edited by Chieko Mulhern, Westport, Connecticut, Greenwood Press, 1994.

* * *

Enchi Fumiko would hardly have considered herself a "feminist." Indeed, the word itself has been misconstrued in the Japanese language since the 1900s to refer to men who "worship women." Be that as it may, Enchi did not see herself as an advocate of women's rights. If anything, she consistently denied her own ambitions, choosing marriage over social activism and endurance over divorce after that marriage faltered. And yet her many stories and novels tell another story—that of a woman's silent rebellion—thus bequeathing to generations of later readers the subversive nature of submission. Few can read Enchi's better known works—*The Waiting Years, Masks,* "Skeletons of Men"—and not be impressed by the undercurrent of strength and passion that courses just beneath the surface of the subdued feminine.

Enchi was born Fumi Ueda, to a prosperous family. Her father was Kazutoshi Ueda (1867-1937), a highly respected professor at the prestigious Tokyo Imperial University whose theories on Japanese historical phonology are still revered. Because she was a sickly girl, Enchi spent her childhood in her father's library, where she developed a fondness for classical Japanese literature. As a child she also accompanied her grandmother to performances at the Kabuki and Noh theaters, an experience that nurtured her early interests in drama. In fact, Enchi made her debut as a playwright in 1926, and though she dabbled in fiction, it was not until the 1950s that she established herself as a novelist and story writer. By this time she had married Yoshimatsu Enchi, a journalist ten years her senior. Most biographers suggest that she married in order to remove herself from associations with both a left-wing group and an illicit affair. The daughter of a prominent scholar, Enchi was always acutely aware of her reputation.

Throughout her life Enchi was plagued with poor health. She was treated for breast cancer in 1938 and uterine cancer in 1946. In addition to ill health, she also found marriage a profound disappointment. Perhaps as an escape from her pain, Enchi turned to the world of fiction. Not surprisingly, many of her works concern unhappy marriages. Frequently she writes of matronly women who, unfulfilled and desperate, take flight in fantasies and dreams. Here Enchi's childhood reading in the Japanese classics stood her in good stead: Many such works present the world of dreams as a tangible sphere just beyond the realm of waking. Lovers unsatisfied by day can find passion by night—in dreams. Enchi invoked the spirituality and mystery of the classics, thus providing her texts with extra layers of meaning, while at the same time imbuing the classical tales with new readings.

Enchi also began posing questions in her novels and stories about what constituted womanhood. The classics often associated female sexuality with vengefulness and jealousy. Were women monsters, then? Were they indelibly tied to their biology? Or were their sexual identities social constructions? Having undergone both a mastectomy and a hysterectomy, Enchi wondered what, after all, defined women as women. During the 1960s many of her works would deal with the issues of womanliness and Womanhood; many contain the word "woman/women" in the title: "The Woman's Cocoon," " Woman with a Mole," "To Live as a Woman," and "Women of the Capital."

Her novel *The Waiting Years,* from this period in Enchi's life, is considered by many to be her first significant work. The Japanese title, *Onnazaka,* means literally "the woman's hill" and refers to the woman's entrance to a shrine. The man's entrance approaches from the front—up a long line of steep stairs, whereas the woman's path winds gently, slowly through the dark grove behind the shrine. The woman's entrance is not as physically demanding, it would seem, but requires patience and perseverance—attributes associated with Tomo, the central character in the novel. Set in the Meiji era (1868-1912), the story concerns the tension between Tomo, her husband, and the young concubine he has Tomo acquire for him. Tomo, a model wife, does not complain, but it is clear that she seethes within. Enchi very subtly sculpts her heroine's psychology by alluding to the Japanese classics, particularly *The Tale of Genji* (written by the court lady, Murasaki Shikibu, ca. 1000), and the hideous toll jealousy takes on women who are forced into positions of rivalry. Unable to give vent to her frustrations by day, one character in this earlier tale finds her living spirit leaving her body by night to attack the object of her envy. Although Enchi's character, Tomo, struggles to control her passions, in the end her spirit will out.

Enchi began collecting material for this work in the late 1930s, intending to write about her maternal grandmother's generation. Unfortunately, all her notes would be destroyed in a fire during one of the Allied air raids during World War II. Some years later, while Enchi was recuperating from her hysterectomy, her mother entertained her by telling her stories about her grandmother. It was from these stories, as well as from memories of her own, that Enchi culled *The Waiting Years*. The novel maintains a sense of orality—of women's voices. But the story is not limited to an individual history. In a greater sense it is the story of all women. Although set in an age when concubinage was not only allowed but expected, the story nevertheless moves beyond the particulars of one outrage to suggest the oppression of women in general. The suffering of the characters in the novel is painful to behold. But at the same time, the author reveals the strength these women share—strength that allows them to persevere up the "woman's hill."

A woman's hidden strength would be a topic Enchi explored repeatedly. At times this hidden strength could be beautifully sinister, as in her next significant novel, *Masks (Onnamen).* Here again she relies on the classics, weaving the traditional theatrical presentation of woman as spiritual medium into a modern setting. Again she writes of the deadly nature of a woman's suppressed emotions. But whereas in the classics the woman was either pitied or reviled for the aggressiveness of her inner nature, Enchi presents this nature in a positive light. In *Masks* her protagonists are ultimately empowered by their femaleness.

Enchi's exploration of female power is always mediated by her presentation of the exploitation of women in patriarchal systems. The bonds that link women together are also the bonds that keep them in check. In "Skeletons of Men," which some critics contend offers an alternative conclusion to *The Waiting Years*, Enchi unravels a tale of suppressed passion. Purportedly the story of an ancient sash and the mysterious "blood letter" found within its lining, the narrator soon discovers that the loss and loneliness of one woman's life is equal to that of all women, despite their marital status or the age within they lived. Like the sash that binds the narrative together, the women in the story are inextricably bound one to another.

The narrative structure in "Skeletons of Men" is typical of Enchi. She frequently employed story-within-a-story-type devices, lending her works richly layered depths. She was especially adept at impregnating her works with the spirit of the classics. In 1967, at the age of 62, Enchi put her love of *The Tale of Genji* to the test by undertaking a translation of the great classic into modern Japanese, a task that would occupy her for eight years. By the time she had finished she was nearly blind, having suffered a detached retina in 1969. From this point on Enchi pursued completed the translation and continued crafting original fiction, by employing an amanuensis, a scenario she had ironically imagined in her earlier story "A Bond for Two Lifetimes—Gleanings" ("Nise no en—shūi," 1957). In addition to her translation of *The Tales of Genji,* Enchi also wrote frequently on other classical texts. Although Japanese women writers are fortunate to have had female predecessors in the literary past, few others have so effectively engaged their foremothers in the kind of dialogue for which Fumiko Enchi is noted. Her works remain as a testament to the beauty and durability of the female literary tradition in Japan.

—Rebecca L. Copeland

ENGEL, Marian (Passmore)

Nationality: Canadian. **Born:** Toronto, Ontario, 24 May 1933. **Education:** McMaster University, B.A. 1955; McGill University, M.A. 1957. **Family:** Married Howard Engel in 1962 (divorced 1977); one son, one daughter (twins). **Career:** Lecturer, Montana State University, Missoula extension, 1957-58; teacher, St. John's School (Royal Air Force school), Nicosia, Cyprus, 1963;

writer-in-residence, University of Alberta, Edmonton, 1977-78, and University of Toronto, 1980-81; Chairman, Writers' Union of Canada, 1973-74; member, Toronto Book Prize Committee, 1974-77. Author of scripts on literary figures for Canadian Broadcasting Corp.; contributor of short stories and articles to periodicals, including *Globe & Mail, MacLean's, New York Times Book Review, Redbook,* and *Saturday Night.* **Awards:** Canada Council senior arts fellowships, 1968, 1973, 1976; Governor General Award, 1976, for *Bear;* Toronto Book Award, 1982, for *Lunatic Villas;* made officer of Order of Canada, 1982. **Member:** Writers Union of Canada, Association of Canadian TV and Radio Artists. **Died:** 1985.

Publications

Novels

No Clouds of Glory. New York, Harcourt, 1968; as *Sarah Bastard's Notebook,* Toronto, Paperjacks, 1971.
The Honeyman Festival. New York, St. Martin's Press, 1970.
Monodromos. Toronto, House of Anansi Press, 1973; as *One-Way Street,* London, Heinemann, 1975.
Joanne: The Last Days of a Modern Marriage (first broadcast on CBC). Toronto, Paperjacks, 1975.
Bear. New York, Atheneum, 1976.
The Glassy Sea. Toronto, McClelland & Stewart, 1978; New York, St Martin's Press, 1979.
Lunatic Villas. Toronto, McClelland & Stewart, 1981; as *The Year of the Child,* New York, St. Martin's Press, 1981.

Short Stories

Inside the Easter Egg. Toronto, House of Anansi Press, 1975.
The Tattooed Woman. Markham, Ontario, Penguin, 1985.

Play

Radio Play: *Joanne,* 1975.

For Children

Adventurer at Moon Bay Towers. Richmond Hill, Ontario, Irwin Clarke, 1974.
My Name Is Not Odessa Yarker. Toronto, Kids Can Press, 1977.

Other

The Islands of Canada. Edmonton, Alberta, Hurtig, 1982.

*

Manuscript Collections: William Ready Division of Archives and Research Collections, Mills Memorial Library, McMaster University, Hamilton, Ontario.

Critical Studies: Interview in *Eleven Canadian Novelists* edited by Graeme Gibson, House of Anansi Press, 1973; *Room of One's Own* (special Marian Engel issue), 9(2); *Private and Fictional Words* by C. Howells, London and New York, Methuen, 1987; "Affairs with Bears: Some Notes towards Feminist Archetypal Hypotheses for Canadian Literature" by Annis Pratt, in *Gynocritics: Feminist Approaches to Canadian and Quebec Women's Writing,* edited by Barbara Godard, Toronto, ECW Press, 1987; "Articulating the Female Subject: The Example of Marian Engle's *Bear*" by Margery Fee, in *Atlantis,* 14(1), spring 1988; "Explod/ing/ed Fictions: Marian Engel's Writing" by Christie Verduyn, in *Atlantis* 14(1), fall 1988; "Marian Engle's *Bear:* Pastoral, Porn, and Myth" by Coral Ann Howells, in *Ariel,* 14 February 1992.

* * *

One of the most articulate feminist writers of contemporary Canada, Marian Engel insightfully portrayed the ongoing war between the sexes and highlighted the few, often devastatingly poignant, options left for heterosexual women of her generation.

Born in Toronto to parents who were both teachers, and raised in several Ontario towns, where she claimed to have had a happy childhood, Engel attended McMaster University, in Hamilton, Ontario, and McGill University, in Montreal, Quebec. As a university student, she was actively involved in the production of the university newspaper and literary magazine, as well as in the dramatic society and debating society. One of the major influences that informed Engel's concern with the power of words and directed her approach to writing was her continuing friendships with the fellow students from these academic times, many of whom went on to teach at universities, became writers, or engaged in politics.

Her travels and residence outside Ontario, including several years spent in France and Cyprus, also served as a rich source of inspiration. One of Engel's novels, *Monodromos,* is set in Cyprus and depicts the summer adventures of a Canadian woman abroad. Critics have commented on the ways in which her fiction seems to mix the various places she had been; for example, Latin Mediterranean imagery and western Ontario landscape inform her second novel, *The Honeyman Festival,* which depicts the experiences of a pregnant Toronto woman during a single night. In an early 1970s interview, however, Engel herself claimed that, even though she found foreign places fascinating, she was becoming more and more Canadian and that the Great Lakes was her heartland.

In *Bear* (1976), probably her most widely read novel, Engel sheds light on the unendurable positions in which Canadian society has placed its intelligent older women and proposes an option that should appear more than commonly shocking, or even somewhat repugnant, to the average reader. The protagonist, Lou, who is a veteran archival librarian in Toronto, receives a commission to spend a whole summer on a river island in northern Ontario sorting out what has been left in a colonial mansion recently bequeathed to the institute she works for. What she discovers in the colossal house on the mystical island is not so much valuable historical documents as her (authentic) self. She forms a peculiarly erotic friendship with a pet bear that belongs to the house, as a potential alternative to, and a possible compensation for, the humiliating and disappointing relationships she has had with men. The novel's ending has been hailed by some as a victory over the misogyny of mainstream Canadian society, with which Engel constantly takes issue. At other times *Bear* been interpreted as a rather passive gesture of resignation and acceptance of the status quo, not unlike the way some critics have read the closing of fellow Canadian writer Margaret Atwood's *Surfacing.*

In *The Glassy Sea* (1978), Engel again creates a lone, middle-aged female protagonist who may at first seem simply confused about what she wants, yet who in fact embodies—and eventually manages to articulate and condemn—the relational dead-end that the contemporary skirmishes between conventional cultural norms and feminist beliefs have led Western societies to. A one-time Anglican nun and now dispirited divorcee who has barely survived her self-righteous, religiously fanatic, lawyer/politician husband and the battle to save her hydrocephalic, and only, child, Rita Bowen (née Heber) muses over the current status of affairs in heterosexual relationships. Rita suggests the radical solution of having all women die at age 30 or in childbirth as older women are considered useless and at the same time feared for their intelligence and independence. The bulk of the novel consists of Rita's letter to the bishop who has requested that she resume her vows, become sister superior, and reopen the Eglantine house; she provides him with the often desolate details of her past by way of enumerating the reasons why she could not comply. The decision Rita makes at the close of the book indicates that her concern is clearly not religious, but rather constitutes an ardent desire to offer refuge to the many women who have been battered or discarded.

In contrast to the lucid sense of loneliness and loss that pervades *The Glassy Sea, Lunatic Villas* (1981) carries a generally cheerful tone. This Margaret Drabblesque novel offers a great deal of entertainment, even though it may have been deemed of much less literary value than Engel's other fiction. The novel's protagonist, Harriet Ross, is a Toronto freelance writer who signs her weekly magazine column, with a considerable amount of honesty, "Depressed Housewife." Harriet fiercely protects her brood of seven mismatched children as well as a few helpless friends, managing on the side to harbor a married lover. Even though Harriet's battles are endless and her responsibilities dauntingly enormous, Engel's buoyant sense of humor adds a great deal of warmth and hopefulness to this urban narrative.

As Engel herself scoffed at the current trend to label every piece of fiction a *roman á clef,* it would be incorrect to see her women characters as direct reflections and outgrowths of the author. It would be quite proper, on the other hand, to regard them as literary vehicles through which Engel voiced her views of contemporary women's lives, their difficulties and strengths. Even though Engel considered herself experiential—in the sense that she tended to jump into situations—rather than theoretical or analytical, her fiction presents her feminist principles quite unambiguously and cerebrally, in highly charged political language. As a committed, even if somewhat disillusioned—or maybe realistic—feminist, Engel was happy to be called a "women's writer," as long as this "women" meant intelligent women—those whose experiences, thoughts, and beliefs very much paralleled her own.

—Tomoko Kuribayashi

F

FADERMAN, Lillian

Nationality: American. **Born:** Bronx, New York, 18 July 1940. **Education:** University of California, Berkeley, A.B. 1962; University of California, Los Angeles, M.A. 1964; Ph.D. 1967; Harvard Institute of Educational Management, certificate 1974. **Career:** Associate professor, then professor of English, beginning 1967, chair of English department, 1971-77, dean of School of Humanities, 1972-73, and assistant vice-president of academic affairs, 1973-76, California State University, Fresno; visiting professor of English and women's studies, University of California, Los Angeles, 1989-91. Associate editor, *Journal of the History of Sexuality,* Chicago, 1989-93; general co-editor, "Between Men/Women" series, Columbia University Press, beginning 1993; columnist, *Advocate,* beginning 1995. Member of editorial board, *Journal of Homosexuality,* beginning 1982; Gay Caucus of MLA Lesbian and Gay Newsletter, 1986-90; *Signs: Journal of Women in Culture and Society,* 1989-91, 1992-95; June Mazer Lesbian Archives, Los Angeles, beginning 1991; *Women's History Review* (United Kingdom), beginning 1991; *Thamyris* (The Netherlands), beginning 1993; and *Journal of Lesbian Studies,* beginning 1995. Contributor to numerous journals, including *New England Quarterly, Journal of Popular Culture, Journal of the History of Sexuality,* and *Signs.* **Awards:** American Library Association Social Responsibility Task Force awards, 1982, for *Surpassing the Love of Men,* and 1992, for *Odd Girls and Twilight Lovers;* National Gay Academic Union Literature Award, 1982, for *Surpassing the Love of Men;* named California State University outstanding professor, 1982-83; Gay & Lesbian Alliance against Defamation (GLAAD) Visibility Award, and Lambda Editor's Choice Award, both 1992, for *Odd Girls and Twilight Lovers;* Lambda Literary Award for best anthology, 1995, for *Chloe Plus Olivia.* **Address:** Department of English, California State University, 5245 North Baker St., Fresno, California 93740-8001, U.S.A.

PUBLICATIONS

History

Scotch Verdict: Miss Pirie and Miss Woods v. Dame Cumming Gordon. New York, Morrow, 1983; London, Quartet, 1985.
Surpassing the Love of Men: Romantic Friendship and Love between Women from the Renaissance to the Present. New York, Morrow, 1981; London, Women's Press, 1985.
Odd Girls and Twilight Lovers: A History of Lesbian Life in Twentieth-Century America. New York, Columbia University Press, 1991; London, Penguin, 1992.

Essays

"Lesbian Magazine Fiction in the Early 20th Century," in *Journal of Popular Culture,* 11(4), spring 1978; in *History of Women in the United States,* edited by Nancy F. Cott. New Haven, Connecticut, and Munich, K.G. Sauer, 1992.
"Who Hid Lesbian History?" in *Frontiers: A Journal of Women's Studies,* 4(3), fall 1979; in *Lesbian Studies,* edited by Margaret Cruikshank. New York, Feminist Press, 1982.
"A History of Romantic Friendships," in *Gender in Intimate Relationships,* edited by Barbara Risman and Pepper Schwartz. New York, Wadsworth, 1988.
"What Is Lesbian Literature?: Creating a Historical Canon," in *Professions of Desire,* edited by Bonnie Zimmerman and George Haggerty. New York, Modern Language Association, 1995.

Other

Editor, with Barbara Bradshaw, *Speaking for Ourselves: American Ethnic Writing.* Glenview, Illinois, Scot Foresman, 1969.
Editor, with Luis Omar Salinas, *From the Barrio: A Chicano Anthology.* San Francisco, Canfield Press 1973.
Editor, with Brigitte Eriksson, *Lesbian-Feminism in Turn-of-the-Century German.* Tallahassee, Naiad Press, 1980; as *Lesbians in Germany: 1890s to 1920s,* 1990.
Editor, with Larry Gross, *Between Men—Between Women: Lesbian and Gay Studies.* New York and Oxford, Columbia University Press, 1992.
Editor, *Chloe Plus Olivia: An Anthology of Lesbian Literature from the 17th Century to the Present.* New York, Viking, 1994; London, Viking, 1995.

*

Critical Studies: "Women Who Love Women" by Carolyn G. Heilbrun, in *New York Times Book Review,* 5 April 1981; "The Invention of the Lesbian" by Joanna Russ, in *Washington Post Book World,* 3 May 1981; "Women in Love" by Susan Brownmiller, in *Washington Post Book World,* 23 June 1991; "Talking Heads" by Jane Mills, in *New Statesman & Society,* 17 July 1992.

* * *

Lillian Faderman, born in New York in 1940, is the author of many significant works of history, literary criticism, and creative writing. She consistently explores themes of women's lives, ethnic identities and experiences, and lesbian history and literature. Faderman received her B.A. from Berkeley in 1962, her M.A. from the University of California, Los Angeles, in 1964, and her Ph.D. from the University of California, Los Angeles, in 1967. Currently distinguished professor of English at California State University, Fresno, Faderman has also taught at University of California, Los Angeles, as a visiting professor. She has written numerous articles about lesbian life and literature, published in journals including *Signs: Journal of Women in Culture and Society, Journal of the History of Sexuality, Journal of Popular Culture,* and *New England Quarterly.*

In 1969, with Barbara Bradshaw, Faderman edited *Speaking for Ourselves: American Ethnic Writing,* an anthology that includes short stories, poems, plays, essays, and excerpts from novels by such writers as Langston Hughes, Gwendolyn Brooks, Hisaye Yamamoto, N. Scott Momaday, and Muriel Rukeyser. The goal of this collection, as stated in the foreword, was to introduce college students of English literature to American writers of marginalized ethnic backgrounds. To this end, Faderman and

Bradshaw included discussion questions and writing suggestions with each work in the collection. In 1973, with Luis Omar Salinas, Faderman co-edited *From the Barrio: A Chicano Anthology.*

Interestingly enough, though a professor of English, Faderman has also written several historical texts about lesbians and women in same-sex relationships. These include *Lesbian-Feminism in Turn-of-the-Century Germany,* written with Brigitte Eriksson (1980; as *Lesbians in Germany: 1890s to 1920s,* 1990); the award-winning *Surpassing the Love of Men: Romantic Friendship and Love Between Women from the Renaissance to the Present* (1981); and *Odd Girls and Twilight Lovers: A History of Lesbian Life in Twentieth-Century America* (1991).

Odd Girls and Twilight Lovers is an expansive history of lesbian life in the U.S., from the "romantic friendships" between women of turn-of-the-century New England, to 1990's Queer Nation politics. To research such an immense project, Faderman interviewed 186 women—self-identified lesbians—about their lesbian identities, their sexualities, and their various communities. Faderman posits a trajectory of lesbian life and experiences in which she documents and historicizes sexology and notions of sexual inversion in the early part of the 20th century; lesbian "chic" in the Harlem Renaissance; butch/femme communities and lesbian bar culture of the 1950s and 1960s; early political organizing and the roots of the gay and lesbian liberation movement; lesbian feminism in the 1970s; and the lesbian sex wars of the 1980s. Much of Faderman's discussion revolves around the idea that "lesbian" itself was a constructed category, formulated in the late 19th century, and affecting the cultural meanings of same-sex relations between women. This, according to Faderman, allowed for the construction of lesbian identity and the establishment of lesbian subcultures and communities. In her introduction to *Odd Girls and Twilight Lovers,* she writes: "Before women could live as lesbians the society in which they lived had to evolve to accommodate, however grudgingly, the possibility of lesbianism—the conception needed to be formulated.... The possibility of a life as a lesbian had to be socially constructed in order for women to be able to choose such a life."

Faderman's historical writings about lesbianism are significant for a number of reasons. *Surpassing the Love of Men* and *Odd Girls and Twilight Lovers* establish histories of lesbians in a social and cultural environment that often marginalizes and excludes lesbians and gay men. In other words, texts such as these construct and provide us with a much-needed history. They allow us to claim as our predecessors the "passing" women of the 19th century; women in long-term "romantic friendships"; as well as any women in history who loved other women, who asserted her independence, and who espoused feminist ideas and positions. Like many other lesbian feminist scholars and writers, including Bonnie Zimmerman, Adrienne Rich, and Barbara Smith, Faderman posits a strong connection between lesbianism and feminism.

In 1983 Faderman published *Scotch Verdict,* an historical recreation of the trial on which Lillian Hellman's *The Children's Hour* was based. And her most recent book, *Chloe Plus Olivia: An Anthology of Lesbian Literature from the 17th Century to the Present* (1994), is an enormous collection of literature about women loving women, from romantic friendship to contemporary "post-lesbian-feminist" literature. Faderman includes sections such as "Men's Writing on Romantic Friendship," "Carnivorous Flowers: The Literature of Exotic and Evil Lesbians," and "In the Closet: The Literature of Lesbian Encoding." She brings together in one volume the writings of Aphra Behn, Emily Dickinson, Richard von Krafft-Ebing, Radclyffe Hall, Virginia Woolf, Djuna Barnes, Jewelle Gomez, Irena Klepfisz, Kitty Tsui, Pat Califia, Cherrie Moraga, and many more writers, artists, and poets. Here, as elsewhere, Faderman continues to engage questions of history and historiography, lesbian identity, and feminism.

—Patti Duncan

FAITHFULL, Emily

Nationality: British. **Born:** Headley Rectory, Surrey, England, 27 May 1835. **Career:** Presented at court, 1856; journalist for *English Women's Journal,* 1858; founder and owner, Victoria Press, London, beginning 1860; appointed printer and publisher-in-ordinary to Queen Victoria; founder and editor, *Victoria Magazine,* 1863-80; editor, *Women and Work,* 1974-76, and *West London Express,* 1877-78. Contributor to periodicals, including *Lady's Pictorial.* **Died:** 1895.

Publications

Autobiography

Three Visits to America. Edinburgh, D. Douglas, 1884.

Novels

Change upon Change. London, n.p., 1868.
A Reed Shaken with the Wind. London, n.p., 1873.

*

Critical Studies: *Emily Faithfull, Victorian Champion of Women's Rights* by James S. Stone, Toronto, P.D. Meany, 1994.

* * *

Emily Faithfull, born 27 May 1835, was the youngest child of Reverend Ferdinand Faithfull. Her family had been solidly upper-middle class from at least the middle of the 18th century, when her great-grandfather William Faithfull was listed as "Gent.," according to a family genealogy. Emily's own presentation at court in 1856 confirmed her gentlewoman's status.

From early childhood, Faithfull suffered from asthma and bronchitis; indeed, these tandem conditions would cause problems for her during her subsequent travels to America. The troubles (and her triumphs) are documented in a volume she wrote called *Three Visits to America.* Not only was she well received by both the women's community and by women's clubs in the United States, but during one of these trips she was offered the use of Potter Palmer's Colorado Springs home to aid in her recovery from asthma by undergoing a pure-air cure. Faithfull spent her first trip to the United States, during 1872, visiting scenes of co-education and employment; as a pioneer in women's training and employment she was interested in opportunities for employment in America.

According to a Faithfull biographer, many of the details of her life had to be gleaned from a column she wrote for *Lady's Picto-*

rial as she ultimately destroyed her private papers. She was also ignored by some of the early historians of the women's movement in Victorian England, notably Vera Karsland and Bessie Parkes, an early associate and an original editor of the *English Women's Journal,* a vehicle for some of Faithfull's early efforts. Her biographer James Stone asserts that the probable reason for Faithfull's exclusion from many of these volumes is the scandal that surrounded the Codrington divorce. Whether Faithfull had been the lesbian lover or the arranger of a meeting place for Mrs. Codrington and one of her lovers seems to be the central question, as yet unanswered. Whatever Faithfull's role, the notoriety surrounding the divorce and its salacious details resulted in her being dropped by most of the her social peers.

What we do know of Faithfull's life must be pieced from the details of her writings and from her work. She was a member of the Langham Place Circle of feminists led by Bessie Parkes and Barbara Bodichon. In 1858 she began her work as a journalist and worked at the *English Woman's Journal* where Parkes described her as strong minded. Her work was described as spare and unsentimental; according to Stone she was an able synthesizer and forceful writer, "sprightly and effective." Her later travel stories provide an interesting picture of the American woman of the 19 century.

In 1860, having decided that the compositors' trade was eminently suitable to women, Faithfull established the Victoria Press with her own resources and the backing of G.W. Hastings of the National Association for the Promotion of Social Sciences. The goal was to give women training and work in the printing trades. A year later, both the *Illustrated London News* and Queen Victoria reported visiting the press and provided sketches. The success of Victoria Press, however, resulted in problems and sabotage because men closed ranks when it came to females joining their union; as late as 1875 male compositors went on strike because a printer had employed women as compositors. In 1886 the union issued a statement saying that women were not physically capable of performing the duties of a compositor; one woman was admitted to the London Society of Compositors in 1892, but this signaled no major progress; by 1941 women were still excluded from membership in the Society of Compositors.

Despite problems with trade unions, Faithfull kept the press going by hiring male printers and by soliciting help from rich and generous friends. Her being appointed "Printer and Publisher in Ordinary to Her Majesty" and receipt of a medal for good printing from the jurors of the international exposition in 1862 also helped.

In 1863 Faithfull established *Victoria Magazine,* which was printed at Victoria Press and which continued through 1880. *Victoria Magazine* has been described as an attempt to combine serious articles on women's issues with fiction and light reading material that would appeal to a broad readership. Another periodical, *Women and Work,* a weekly newspaper reporting work and arranging emigration to the colonies, was edited by Faithfull from 1874-1876; she edited the *West London Express* between 1877 and 1878. From 1874-1880 no more than three titles were published by Victoria Press; and although Faithfull had not succeeded in getting women accepted as printers' union members, she had proved that her apprentices could do quality work.

Faithfull's continued visits to America helped her raise needed funds by lecturing and in 1882, during her last visit, Jennie June Croly, who had included Faithfull in a select group of women journalists, arranged the journalist a New York welcome; Julia Ward Howe was the arranger of greetings in Boston. This visit even included a lecture in Cincinnati during an Ohio River flood. As Stone noted, some of the audience arrived by skiff. Faithfull's first arrival in the States had coincided with a presidential election campaign and she was able to meet both Ulysses S. Grant and Horace Greeley, the two candidates for high office. "The Grant and Greeley contest was said to be one of the bitterest on record," she would write, adding that Greeley had "committed the unpardonable offense in the eyes of the Woman's Suffrage supporters of opposing their movement." Faithfull went on to add that they had accordingly seemed to forget his earnest advocacy of women's industrial interests and that he was the first (with Margaret Fuller) to open New York journalism to women.

During her extensive travels about the United States Faithfull visited and wrote about the Mormons and plural marriages; about the Boston literary scene; about general progress since Harriet Martineu's visit in 1836; about visits to University of Michigan and Kansas State University; about "hotel despotism" in American hotels; about silk worm culture; about the kindergarten movement; about divorce; about the West Coast, San Francisco, Fresno, and Los Angeles. She showed especial interest in the affairs of the Riverside Press at Harvard, where men and women worked side by side in the composing area. It was only during her final visit that Faithfull would have to take time away from her travelling to find refuge in the Colorado mountains because of her health.

In April 1884 Faithfull returned to England for the last time. She continued her support for women in various trades but her active involvement in editing publications appears to have lessened. Occasional writings from this period are still discovered, providing more pieces to the puzzle of Faithfull's life and work. Much more are still needed to adequately reconstruct Faithfull's career and impact on the British feminist movement, although Stone has made remarkable progress from the sketchy materials currently available. Emily Faithfull would die in England in 1895; because of her objections to typical funeral procedures, she was cremated.

—Ann Mauger Colbert

FALLACI, Oriana

Nationality: Italian. **Born:** Florence, 29 June 1930; daughter of Edoardo Fallaci, a hero of the Italian Resistance. **Education:** Attended Liceum Galileo Galilei, Florence; attended Faculty of Medicine, University of Florence, for two years. **Family:** Companion of poet and patriot Alexandros (Alekos) Panagoulis (died 1976). **Career:** Reporter for *Il mattino dell'Italia centrale* (daily newspaper), beginning 1946, and *Epoca* (Italian magazine), c. 1951, Florence; special correspondent, *Europeo* (Italian magazine), beginning mid-1950s. Lecturer at universities, including University of Chicago, Columbia University, Harvard University, and Yale University. Contributor to periodicals, including *Corriere della Sera, Der Stern, La Nouvelle Observateur, Life, New Republic, New York Times Magazine, Look, Washington Post,* and publications in eastern Europe, India, Japan, China, Thailand, and Korea. **Awards:** St. Vincent prize for journalism (Italy), twice; Bancarella Prize, 1971, for *Niente e cosi sia;* honorary D.Let., Columbia College, Chicago; Viareggio Prize, 1979, for *Un uomo;* Le Prix Antibes (France), 1993, for *Insciallah.* **Address:** c/o Rizzoli Editore Corp.,

31 West 57th St., 4th floor, New York, New York 10019, U.S.A.

Publications

Novels

Penelope alla guerra. Milan, Rizzoli, 1964; translated as *Penelope at War,* London, M. Joseph, 1966.
Lettera a un bambino mai nato. Milan, Rizzoli, 1975; translated as *Letter to a Child Never Born,* London, Arlington, and New York, Simon & Schuster, 1976.
Un uomo. Milan, Rizzoli, 1979; translated as *A Man,* New York, Simon & Schuster, 1980; London, Bodley Head, 1981.
Insciallah. Milan, Rizzoli, 1990; translated as *Inshallah,* London, Chatto & Windus, and New York, Doubleday, 1992.

Nonfiction

I sette pecati di Hollywood. Milan, Longanesi, 1958; translated as *The Seven Sins of Hollywood,* preface by Orson Welles,
Il sesso inutile: Viaggio intorno alla donna. Milan, Rizzoli, 1961; translated as *The Useless Sex, Voyage around the Woman,* London, M. Joseph, and New York, Horizon Press, 1964.
Gli antipatici. Milan, Rizzoli, 1963; translated as *Limelighters,* London, M. Joseph, 1967; as *The Egotists: 16 Surprising Interviews,* Chicago, Regnery, 1968.
Se il sole muore. Milan, Rizzoli, 1965; translated as *If the Sun Dies,* New York, Atheneum, 1966; London, Collins, 1967; third edition, Milan, Rizzoli, 1984.
Niente e cosi sia. Milan, Rizzoli, 1969; translated as *Nothing and So Be It,* Garden City, New York, Doubleday, 1972; as *Nothing and Amen,* London, M. Joseph, 1972.
Quel giorno sulla Luna (textbook). Milan, Rizzoli, 1970.
Intervista con la Storia. Milan, Rizzoli, 1974; translated as *Interview with History,* London, M. Joseph, and New York, Liveright, 1976.

*

Critical Studies: "Lady of the Tapes" by D. Sanford, in *Esquire,* 83, June 1975; "Behind the Fallaci Image" by L. Franks, in *Saturday Review,* 8, January 1981; "War and Terror" by John Bemroth, in *MacLean's,* 8 February 1993; unpublished interview with Maria Elena Raymond, April 1996.

* * *

Oriana Fallaci, world famous as a war correspondent, novelist, and interviewer, is a difficult writer to category. She is perhaps most widely known for conducting blunt, high-profile interviews with such prominent public figures as former U.S. Secretary of State Henry Kissinger, Iran's Ayatollah Khomeini, and Palestinian resistance leader Yasir Arafat. Fallaci's direct, yet intimate, technique, which draws out her subject—sometimes to his or her later regret—in revealing ways, is best illustrated by 1976's *Interview with History.* Yet she has shown open frustration with being hailed as a great interviewer: Fallaci considers herself to be a writer who happens to do interviews, rather than the other way around.

Working part-time as a journalist while attempting to put herself through medical school, Fallaci quickly realized her talent for writing. In 1946 she joined the staff of *Il mattino dell'Italia centrale,* Florence's daily paper. From there Fallaci would join the magazines *Epoca* and *Europeo* during the 1950s. In her travels around the world she interviewed subjects from the glamour and entertainment world—these interviews, which the politically minded Fallaci considered shallow, were published as *The Egoists* in 1963—and documented her evolving world view of women in *The Useless Sex* (1961). It wasn't until 1964 that Fallaci would complete her first novel, *Penelope at War,* a book that would set the tone for its author's future work.

Born in Florence, Italy, in 1930, Fallaci was raised in the shadow of Fascist oppression. Her father, Edoardo, a hero of the Italian resistance movement, was captured and tortured; her lover Alekos Panagoulis would also be tortured and twice condemned to death by the Fascist junta. Carrying messages for the resistance as a teenager, Fallaci was made acutely aware of the value of personal and political freedom. It is no surprise, then, that war and death are often the focus of her writing. What has consistently set her work apart from that of other war correspondents, however, has been Fallaci's subjective, rather than objective, viewpoint. She integrates her personal feelings and experiences into her stories, and while that has made critics comment on her disregard for the rules of "objective" reporting it has made reading her novels a riveting experience. Fallaci's books have been translated into more than 30 languages and published world wide.

Because of the author's personal participation both in her novels and her nonfiction works, reviewers have been quick to classify most of Fallaci's writing as autobiographical. 1969's *Nothing and So Be It* is almost a diary of her 12 trips to Vietnam as a reporter and interviewer. Her worldwide bestselling novel *A Man* is an open tribute to her lover, Alexos Panagoulis, who was murdered in 1976. *If the Sun Dies* is an account of NASA and space exploration, yet Fallaci wrote it in the form of dialogue between herself and her father.

Fallaci's risk-taking has not merely been in the realm of the printed page. As a reporter she has put herself in dangerous positions numerous times, with the possibility of death of injury a constant reality. "I envy those who believe in God," she confessed. "Because it must be such a consolation, such a help. And (for me) knowing that God doesn't exist gives such a solitude. Such a loneliness. Each time I was in combat, or I was shot, each time I had a tremendous grief; for instance, because a beloved person died, I thought: 'What a pity I don't believe in God, that God doesn't exist!'"

Fallaci's controversial 1975 novel *Letter to a Child Never Born,* considered to be one of the finest feminist writings about pregnancy, abortion, and emotional torture, is often perceived as yet another autobiographical account on the part of its author. "No, it is not," Fallaci has stated. "The story I tell is totally invented. I have said it many times and I have always been hurt by those who want to see in it a kind of personal memoir. I have always found that an insult to my writer creativity." The novel does, however, reflect one of its author's profound personal regrets: "It is terrible to die without leaving a son or daughter," she explained. "It is really dying.... I will die leaving only paper-children. Books. But it is not my fault. When I tried to have them [children], I lost them all."

Fallaci's 1990 novel, *Inshallah,* is set in Beiruit, Lebanon, immediately after the tragic 1983 suicide bombings of buildings occupied by French and American peacekeeping troops. While the book is termed a "war novel," it may better be termed an *anti*-war novel. Through the interweaving of the thoughts and actions of over 100 characters, *Inshallah* recreates the tensions faced by a troop of Italian peacekeepers as they try to stop any attempt on their lives while striving to keep the fighting Muslim and Christian factions apart. The novel earned Fallaci the French Prix Antibes in 1993; it was the first time this award has ever been bestowed upon an Italian writer.

In 1993 Fallaci joined the front lines of a more personal battle—a fight against breast cancer. In characteristic style, she has aggressively confronted this challenge to her personal freedom. "I fight," she explained. "I wait for its return because it always returns. To kill. But I fight, mainly working. It seems that cancer gets more scared by this kind of fight than by the stupid pills I take, and the radiotherapy, the chemotherapy, and so on." Fallaci has also channeled her creative energies into a new novel: "a very long novel, a very complex one, a very difficult one. So difficult and complex and long that I never had the guts to start it before I got cancer. In fact, it is a book I have in mind since ... let's say 30 years.... But when the Alien came, (this is the name I give to my cancer), I said: 'Well, the moment to write the damn book has arrived.' I work at it daily, incessantly ... So I live in the nightmare of leaving it uncompleted, unfinished,... If I die after I have written the last word of it, I die the happiest person in the world."

—María Elena Raymond

FALUDI, Susan

Nationality: American. **Born:** New York, New York, 18 April 1959. **Education:** Harvard University, Cambridge, Massachusetts, B.A. (summa cum laude) 1981. **Career:** Copy clerk, *New York Times,* 1981-82; reporter for *Miami Herald,* 1983, and *Atlanta Constitution,* 1984-85; staff writer, *West* magazine, San Jose, California, 1985-89; affiliated scholar, Stanford University Institute for Research on Women and Gender, 1989-91; staff writer, *Wall Street Journal* San Francisco bureau, 1990-92. Contributor of articles to periodicals, including *California Business, Mother Jones* and *Ms.* **Awards:** Robert F. Kennedy Memorial Journalism Award citation, c. 1987; John Hancock Award, 1991; Pulitzer Prize, 1991, for *Wall Street Journal* article "The Reckoning"; National Book Critics Circle Award, 1992, for *Backlash: The Undeclared War against American Women.* **Address:** c/o Crown Publishers, 201 East 50th Street, Author's Mail, New York, New York 10022, U.S.A.

Publications

Political/Social Theory

Backlash: The Undeclared War against American Women. New York, Crown, 1991; London, Chatto & Windus, 1992.

Other

Recordings: *Backlash: The Undeclared War against American Women* (audiocassette; read by Faludi), Publishing Mills, 1992.

* * *

Susan Faludi has been described as more reporter than theorist. Indeed, it is this ability to uncover and report the facts that makes her book *Backlash: The Undeclared War against American Women* so important to people who have dismissed feminism as "finished." As she would later tell interviewers, her reaction to a widely circulated *Newsweek* story about women's diminishing marriage prospects was to question it. Indeed, when she checked the facts behind the story touting this so called "marriage crunch," she discovered that the research itself was flawed. Her criticism, then, indicted the reporting of unsubstantiated facts—particularly those relating to women. She was especially critical of media who have set themselves up as "trend-watchers." This media investment in "trend-watching" and reporting has resulted in what Faludi calls a "backlash" of reports critical of women and of the women's movement. As she continued her examination, she discovered that much information was more than "trendy"; it was inaccurate and myth-building.

Faludi's work provides evidence of a backlash from practically every sector, from the rewriting of the script of the movie *Fatal Attraction* to misreporting women's enthusiasm for breast implants to boost underwear sales. One of the most important of the cultural myths that Faludi unravels and challenges is the "infertility epidemic." Women over the age of 30 who were having trouble getting pregnant were troubled, not by careerism as was widely purported in the media, but by chlamydia, a disease frequently spread by men.

Faludi, born in New York City on 18 April 1959, is the daughter of Steven Faludi, a photographer, and Marilyn Faludi, a writer and editor. The couple was divorced in 1976, and Ms. Faludi has been quoted as saying that her mother's frustrated existence and buried, ignored talents were key to her understanding of women's circumscribed existence. It is to her mother that Faludi would dedicate *Backlash.*

She attended Harvard University on an Elks Club scholarship and wrote about sexual harassment for the *Harvard Crimson.* Despite objections of a dean and the professor accused of the crime, Faludi's story was published. The professor was asked to take a leave of absence.

In 1980 Faludi was named Phi Beta Kappa; she graduated summa cum laude in 1981 after receiving an Oliver Dabney History Award for her senior thesis. She then joined the *New York Times* as a news and copy clerk; when she tried to move up the ranks of the prestigious New York paper her efforts were rebuffed by a male reporter who told her that because women were able to carry a baby for nine months, they were "biologically more patient." Accordingly, Faludi was thus better suited for an assistantship position.

Leaving the *Times* in 1982, Faludi accepted a job with the *Miami Herald* and then a general reporting position at the *Atlanta Journal-Constitution.* In 1985 she won a first prize for news reporting and feature writing from Georgia's Associated Press. After moving to the West Coast in 1985, she worked at *West,* the Sunday magazine supplement of the *San Jose Mercury News.* At the same time, she worked as a freelance writer and contributor to *Mother Jones, Ms.,* and *California Business.* Her work received honors and awards from a number of professional organizations.

In 1990 Faludi became a staff writer for the San Francisco bureau of the *Wall Street Journal.* Two years later an investigative piece on the human costs of the $5.65 billion leveraged buyout of Safeway Stores won her the Pulitzer Prize. Meanwhile, she was growing increasingly concerned about misreported information about women and the "media backlash," as she came to call it. Faludi decided that she was one of the "voiceless" affected by the media's reports on women and that she would begin an investigation of the media's role in perpetuating myths about women. One of the first myths to receive her attention was the "marriage crunch" that had been accepted without question by both the media and the American public. No one had suggested that women's marrying "late" was related to a lack of compelling reasons for marrying at all. Further, Faludi noted, women's deliberation on the issue of marriage is threatening to men; after the *Newsweek* article, she perceived the "same theme of women who asked for equality being punished. It appeared in popular novels, movies."

Backlash was written during an 18-month leave from other work. Faludi's resulting compendium of examples of the backlash against women has been reviewed widely, for the most part, favorably. Excerpts from her book appeared during its first month of publication in both *Mother Jones* and *Glamour,* a measure of her ability to reach a wide range of audiences. While most reviews were positive, reviewers for more conservative magazines like *New Republic* and *Forbes* were critical. All agree that Faludi's style is readable and that her extensive evidence is clearly presented; not all agree that a backlash exists.

—Ann Mauger Colbert

FAUSET, Jessie Redmon

Nationality: American. **Born:** Camden County, New Jersey, 27 April 1882. **Education:** Cornell University, B.A. 1904; University of Pennsylvania, M.A. 1919; attended the Sorbonne, Paris, c. 1925. **Family:** Married Herbert Harris in 1929 (died 1958). **Career:** Teacher in Baltimore, Maryland, 1905; teacher of French, M Street School, Washington, D.C., 1906-19; literary editor, *Crisis* magazine, New York, 1919-26; edited *Brownie's Book* (children's magazine), 1920-21. **Awards:** Phi Beta Kappa. **Died:** Philadelphia, Pennsylvania, 30 April 1961.

Publications

Novels

There Is Confusion. New York, Boni & Liveright, and London, Chapman & Hall, 1924.
Plum Bun. New York, Stokes, and London, Elkin Mathews, 1929.
The Chinaberry Tree: A Novel of American Life. New York, Stokes, 1931; London, Elkin Mathews, 1932.
Comedy: American Style. New York, Stokes, 1933.

Uncollected Short Stories

"The Gift of Laughter," in *The New Negro,* edited by Alain Locke. New York, Boni, 1925.
"Emmy,"in *Crisis,* 5, December 1912-January 1913.
"My House and a Glimpse of My Life Therein," in *Crisis,* 8, July 1914.
"'There Was One Time,' A Story of Spring," in *Crisis,* 13, 14, April-May 1917.
"The Sleeper Wakes," in *Crisis,* 20, September-October 1920.
"When Christmas Comes," in *Crisis,* 25, December 1922.
"Double Trouble," in *Crisis,* 26, August-September 1923.

Uncollected Essays

"New Literature on the Negro," in *Crisis,* 20, June 1920.
"Impressions of the Second Pan-African Congress," in *Crisis,* 22, November 1921.
"What Europe Thought of the Pan-African Congress," in *Crisis,* 22, December 1921.

Uncollected Poetry

"Rondeau," in *Crisis,* 3, April 1912.
"Again It Is September," in *Crisis,* 14, September 1917.
"The Return," in *Crisis,* 27, January 1919.
"Mary Elizabeth," in *Crisis,* 19, December 1919.
"Oriflamme," in *Crisis,* January 1920.
"La Vie C'est La Vie," in *Crisis,* 24, July 1922.
"Dilworth Road Revisited," in *Crisis,* 24, August 1922.
"Song for a Lost Comrade," in *Crisis,* 25, November 1922.
"Recontre," in *Crisis,* 27, January 1924.
"Here's April!," in *Crisis,* 27, April 1924.
"Rain Fugue," in *Crisis,* 28, August 1924.
"Stars in Alabama," in *Crisis,* 35, January 1928.
"'Courage!' He Said," in *Crisis,* 36, November 1929.

*

Bibliography: "An Index of Literary Materials in *The Crisis,* 1910-1934: Articles, Belles-Lettres, and Book Reviews" by Jean Fagan Yellin, in *CLA Journal,* 14, 1971.

Critical Studies: "Jessie Fauset" by Marion Starkey (interview), in *Southern Workman,* May 1932; *The Way of the New World: The Black Novel in America* by Addison Gayle, Garden City, New York, Doubleday, 1976; "Literary Midwife: Jessie Redmon Fauset and the Harlem Renaissance" by Abby Arthur Johnson, in *Phylon,* June 1978; *Jessie Redmon Fauset, Black American Writer* by Carolyn Wedin Sylvander, Troy, New York, Whitston, 1981; "The Neglected Dimension of Jessie Redmon Fauset" by Deborah E. McDowell, in *Conjuring: Black Women, Fiction, and Literary Tradition,* edited by Marjorie Pryse and Hortense Spillers, Bloomington, Indiana University Press, 1985; *The Coupling Convention: Sex, Text, and Tradition in Black Women's Fiction* by Ann duCille, New York, Oxford University Press, 1993; *Women of the Harlem Renaissance* by Cheryl Wall, Bloomington, Indiana University Press, 1994; *The Politics of Color in the Fiction of Jessie Fauset and Nella Larsen* by Jacquelyn Y. McLendon, Charlottesville, University Press of Virginia, 1995.

* * *

As literary editor of *The Crisis* from 1919 to 1926, Jessie Redmon Fauset featured and thereby fostered the talents of numerous young black artists, for which she was dubbed literary "midwife" of the Negro Renaissance. The title "midwife" and its implicit stereotypical association of women, in all matters, with reproductivity eventually overshadowed Fauset's productivity as a writer of poetry, essays, short fiction, and novels. Recollections of Fauset by contemporaries such as Langston Hughes and Claude McKay focus almost entirely on her as a nurturer of fledgling writers or as hostess of "refined" social gatherings, the latter accounting, in part, for criticism both then and later that she was a "prim and proper" writer of "genteel" novels about people too much like herself. For decades after, critics not only misread her novels but also passed along misinformation about her life in a foundationless conflation of the author and her sentiments with her characters and theirs, missing the political and subversive aspects of her work, especially in her treatment of black women.

Although examining the broad range of Fauset's writings—literary and extraliterary—is essential to fully understanding her aesthetics, many of the most interesting aspects of her work may be addressed through examining the novels, which were published over a nine-year period. These novels reveal that, among other aims, Fauset sought to politicize issues of color, class, and gender through the revision of conventional literary forms and themes. Light-skinned, educated blacks, some of whom "pass" for white, are always central characters in her novels because through figurations of the mulatto and passing she explores identity and difference as they concern blacks generally and black women specifically. These characterizations also enable her to express her belief that black middle-class society could be interesting and dramatic, despite the demands of the day.

The content of her first novel, *There Is Confusion,* was inspired by the publication of T.S. Stribling's *Birthright* (1922), a story about a young black man who, even with a Harvard education, finally falls victim to idealistic and unattainable desires aroused by his mixed blood. Fauset, along with Harlem Renaissance writers Nella Larsen and Walter White, believed the mulatto protagonist of Stribling's book to be unrealistic. Thus, she deliberately set about revising these stereotypical representations of black life. While she does indeed address issues of race representation by challenging precursory white writers' conventional mulatto tales, she also focuses on black women's psychological reactions under conditions of sexual and racial socialization, and herein lies the strength of her novels.

In *There Is Confusion,* the black woman protagonist, Joanna Marshall, struggles against the double jeopardy of race and gender in her attempt to become a famous singer and dancer. An interesting subplot involves Maggie Ellersley, whose difficulties are compounded by her lower class status. Through these interwoven plots, Fauset critiques and finds wanting black middle-class attitudes but, more important, she creates women whose careers come first, who call into question normative roles of wife and mother. Critics have suggested that these women capitulate in the end by marrying and, as Joanna does, forcing themselves to find "pleasure" in the "ordinary." However, total independence for women may not have seemed a realistic narrative choice for Fauset. Indeed, the book leaves strong impressions of Fauset's criticisms through descriptions, albeit understated, of marriage as not very "interesting" or "picturesque" and of a protagonist who feels that women who give up everything for love are "poor silly sheep."

In her first novel, Fauset simply reverses the implications of the blood theory, a donnee of conventional mulatto tales; that is, she attributes her mulatto characters' weaknesses and failures to their "white" blood. In subsequent novels, however, she uses the mulatto and passing as metaphor, making many of the same points but avoiding the didacticism of her earlier work. In bringing other literary conventions and rhetorical strategies to bear—ironic inversion, drama analogue, mythology, for example—she shows a stylistic sophistication absent in *There Is Confusion.* Further, ideas about women's roles explored tentatively perhaps in the earlier work reach fruition in the later ones. In *Plum Bun,* Angela Murray does not get married at the end but goes off to pursue an art career in Europe. *The Chinaberry Tree* depicts a woman-centered family in which its members fight the stigma attached to miscegenation, illegitimacy, and black female sexuality. Drawing on the myths of the destructive mother in her last book, *Comedy: American Style,* Fauset presents the most scathing indictment of a black mother written by a black woman up to this time. In all her novels she focuses on the psychology of black women and foregrounds vital women's concerns.

Like other Harlem Renaissance writers, Fauset explored a wide range of social and political issues, but she strove always simply to tell a "good story." In the most comprehensive study of Fauset's life and writings to date—*Jessie Redmon Fauset: Black American Writer* (1981)— Carolyn Wedin Sylvander makes a compelling argument for Fauset's stylistic sophistication and dispels many myths about the author and her work. Sylvander and others have made great strides in reviving and re-evaluating Fauset's work, ensuring that her voice is heard among the chorus of voices that emerge from the Harlem Renaissance.

—Jacquelyn Y. McLendon

FAY, Erica. *See* **STOPES, Marie (Charlotte).**

FIGES, Eva

Nationality: British. **Born:** Eva Unger in Berlin, Germany, 15 April 1932; immigrated to England in 1939. **Education:** Kingsbury Grammar School, 1943-50; Queen Mary College, University of London, 1950-53, B.A. (honours) in English 1953. **Family:** Married John George Figes in 1954 (divorced 1963); one daughter and one son. **Career:** Editor, Longman, 1955-57, Weidenfeld & Nicolson, 1962-63, and Blackie, 1964-67, London. Since 1987 co-editor, Macmillan Women Writers series. **Awards:** *Guardian* fiction prize, 1967; C. Day Lewis fellowship, 1973; Arts Council fellowship, 1977-79; Society of Authors traveling scholarship, 1988. Fellow, Queen Mary and Westfield College, 1990. **Agent:** Rogers Coleridge and White Ltd., 20 Powis Mews, London W11 1JN, England. **Address:** 24 Fitzjohn's Avenue, London NW3, England.

Publications

Novels

Equinox. London, Secker & Warburg, 1966.
Winter Journey. London, Faber, 1967; New York, Hill & Wang, 1968.

Konek Landing. London, Faber, 1969.
B. London, Faber, 1972.
Days. London, Faber, 1974.
Nelly's Version. London, Secker & Warburg, 1977; New York, Pantheon, 1988.
Waking. London, Hamish Hamilton, 1981; New York, Pantheon, 1982.
Light. London, Hamish Hamilton, and New York, Pantheon, 1983.
The Seven Ages. London, Hamish Hamilton, 1986; New York, Pantheon, 1987.
Ghosts. London, Hamish Hamilton, and New York, Pantheon, 1988.
The Tree of Knowledge. London, Sinclair Stevenson, 1990; New York, Pantheon, 1991.
The Tenancy. London, Sinclair Stevenson, 1993.
The Knot. London, Sinclair Stevenson, 1996.

Uncollected Short Stories

"Obbligato, Bedsitter," in *Signature Anthology*. London, Calder & Boyars, 1975.
"On the Edge," in *London Tales*, edited by Julian Evans. London, Hamish Hamilton, 1983.

Plays

Radio Plays: *Time Regained*, 1980; *Dialogue between Friends*, 1982; *Punch-Flame and Pigeon-Breast*, 1983; *The True Tale of Margery Kempe*, 1985.

Television Plays: *Days*, from her own novel, 1981.

For Children

The Banger. London, Deutsch, and New York, Lion Press, 1968.
Scribble Sam. London, Deutsch, and New York, McKay, 1971.

Political/Social Theory

Patriarchal Attitudes: Women in Society. London, Faber, and New York, Stein & Day, 1970.
Tragedy and Social Evolution. London, Calder, 1976; New York, Persea, 1990.

Literary Criticism

Sex and Subterfuge: Women Novelists to 1850. London, Macmillan, 1982; New York, Persea, 1988.

Autobiography

Little Eden: A Child at War. London, Faber, 1978; New York, Persea, 1987.

Other

Editor, *Classic Choice 1*. London, Blackie, 1965.
Editor, *Modern Choice 1* and *2*. London, Blackie, 2 vols., 1965-66.
Editor, with Abigail Mozley and Dinah Livingstone, *Women Their World*. Gisburn, Lancashire, Platform Poets, 1980.
Translator, *The Gadarene Club*, by Martin Walser. London, Longman, 1960.
Translator, *The Musicians of Bremen: Retold* (for children). London, Blackie, 1967.
Translator, *The Old Car*, by Elisabeth Borchers. London, Blackie, 1967.
Translator, *He and I and the Elephants*, by Bernhard Grzimek. London, Deutsch-Thames & Hudson, and New York, Hill & Wang, 1967.
Translator, *Little Fadette*, by George Sand. London, Blackie, 1967.
Translator, *A Family Failure*, by Renate Rasp. London, Calder & Boyars, 1970.
Translator, *The Deathbringer*, by Manfred von Conta. London, Calder & Boyars, 1971.

*

Critical Studies: "Eva Figes" by Peter Conradi, in *Dictionary of Literary Biography*, 14: *British Novelists since 1960*, Detroit, Gale, 1983; *Women Writers Talk: Interviews with 10 Women Writers* (interview) by Olga Kenyon, London, n.p., 1989; New York, Carroll & Graf, 1990.

* * *

Eva Figes is a novelist and nonfiction writer whose work in both genres has been widely praised. In her novels, Figes focuses on presenting her characters' states of mind. Often compared because of this to the novelist Virginia Woolf, whose innovative techniques also inspire her, Figes explores in her fiction female psychology over women's social concerns. As a nonfiction writer, she is best known as the author of *Patriarchal Attitudes*, an historical analysis of male domination in a variety of social, economic, religious, and political contexts throughout history. Published in 1970, the work is now regarded as a forerunner of much of the feminist scholarship that has followed in its wake. The work's emphasis on the patriarchal nature of most of the world's civilizations gave the women's movement's demands for gender equality and justice a larger perspective from which to criticize modern society.

Figes employs experimental techniques and unreliable narrators in her fiction as a means of examining the psychology of isolated characters. In the early novel *Winter Journey*, the primary character is an elderly deaf man, while in *Days*, Figes focuses on a woman confined to a hospital bed. Her more explicitly feminist novels present allegories for the female condition in contemporary society. In *Nelly's Version*, for example, Figes tells the story of an amnesiac searching for her real identity. Containing elements of the mystery thriller, the novel takes the form of a search for self-identity, with Nelly embodying the search of all women to find who they are in a male-dominated culture. Figes's novel *Waking* depicts the seven ages of a female character's life in seven chapters, each of which begins with the woman waking in the morning at a different period in her long life. Through this unique narrative structure, Figes presents the woman's thoughts—there is only one line of dialogue in the novel—as she raises questions about the many roles a woman is obliged to fulfill in the course of her life. A similar structure informs *The Seven Ages*, a novel in which seven midwives from different periods of British history speak of the pain women suffer both by bringing children into the world and by living in a patriarchal society which oppresses them. In the novel *Ghosts*, Figes recalls *Nelly's Version* in her story of a nameless woman who has so identified with the daily monotony of her routine that she no longer has a sense of self. The basic tension between the individual and society is here dressed in feminist garb as a struggle between individual women and the patriarchal society which tries to steal away their individuality. *The Tree of Knowledge* fictionalizes the life of poet John Milton, who married three times and had troubled relationships with his three daughters. Figes paints Milton as a misogynist who was cruel and insensitive to the women in his life, criticizing in this way not only Milton's personal behavior but also his written work. Figes' *The Tenancy* is a prolonged examination of a woman's powerless life. It begins as middle-aged Edith, who has just placed her aging mother in a nursing home, sits desolately in her empty apartment and looks back over her unhappy life. Her recollections of the years spent tending her sickly mother, and the ensuing loneliness this duty entailed, make up the novel's narrative.

Many of the concerns raised by Figes in her fiction are addressed more directly in her nonfiction works. In her first such book, *Patriarchal Attitudes,* Figes examines the nature of patriarchal society throughout history. As Peter Conradi explains in the *Dictionary of Literary Biography,* "The book is a levelheaded, politically undoctrinaire account of the ideology underlying male-female relations." In this study Figes discusses not only the conditions women have endured during human history, but also the various political, religious, and philosophical ideologies which have served to justify and support the domination of women. Figes shows that seemingly disparate societies have nonetheless shared a fundamental basis in patriarchal power. Although criticized by some reviewers for not offering constructive ways to counter or transcend patriarchy, Figes was praised for her detailed historical analysis of the subject. Published at a time when the women's movement had quickly won widespread support for the idea of gender equality in economic and social spheres, Figes' book served to widen the scope of feminist critical activity. *Patriarchal Attitudes* has inspired much later feminist scholarship into gender relations throughout history. The book also gave Figes enough name recognition to ensure a steady income as a contributing journalist with British newspapers and magazines, something that her early novels had not provided.

In 1976's *Tragedy and Social Evolution* Figes argues that literary tragedy involves a central character who breaks a fundamental law of society and suffers the painful consequences. She takes this definition further, however, by arguing that, in societies from the ancient Greeks onward, the laws violated in tragedy are those that support the existing patriarchal social structure. Thus, tragedy often concerns a woman who violates the gender norms of her society or who challenges their validity. Citing examples from Euripides, Shakespeare, Plato, and Ibsen to make her case, Figes compares the role of literary tragedy in Western Civilization to certain rituals found among primitive tribes wishing to preserve their own social orders.

Figes turns to the development of the novel in English literature in her book *Sex and Subterfuge: Women Novelists to 1850.* Focusing on a 70-year period during which the novel was created as a distinctive literary genre, Figes highlights the role of women writers in the genre's evolution. Looking at the careers of such authors as Fanny Burney, Mary Wollstonecraft, Ann Radcliffe, and Elizabeth Gaskell, she illustrates how the novel genre was shaped by women authors—who also composed some of its earliest masterpieces. As she states in the book's introduction, women authors "took over the novel in England, gave it a new shape, structure and unity of intention which was to have a lasting impact to this day."

Speaking to Olga Kenyon in *Women Writers Talk: Interviews with 10 Women Writers,* Figes gave this advice: "I feel that fundamentally all women writers must write about an experience that *all* human beings can identify with, including men.... If it's true, then it's almost always true for men as well as women."

—Denise Wiloch

FIRESTONE, Shulamith

Nationality: Canadian. **Born:** Ottawa, Ontario, 1945. **Education:** Attended Yavneh of Telshe Yeshiva and Washington University, St. Louis; Art Institute, Chicago, B.F.A. in painting. **Family:** Married; children. **Career:** Cofounder: with Pam Allen, New York Radical Women, 1967; with Ellen Willis, Redstockings, 1969; with Anne Koedt, New York Radical Feminists, 1969. **Address:** c/o William Morrow Publishers, 1350 Avenue of the Americas, New York, New York 10019, U.S.A.

Publications

Political/Social Theory

The Dialectic of Sex: The Case for Feminist Revolution. New York, Morrow, 1970; London, Cape, 1971; revised edition, New York, Bantam, 1971; London, Paladin, 1972.

Other

Editor, *Notes from the First Year: Women's Liberation.* New York, NYRW, 1968.

Editor, *Redstocking.* New York, 1969.

Editor, with Anne Koedt, *Notes from the Second Year: Radical Feminism.* New York, 1970.

*

Critical Studies: *Daring to Be Bad: Radical Feminism in America, 1967-1975* by Alice Echols, Minneapolis, University of Minnesota Press, 1989; *Feminist Thought: A Comprehensive Introduction* by Rosmarie Tong, Boulder, Colorado, Westview Press, 1989; *Feminist Theory: The Intellectual Traditions of American Feminism* by Josephine Donovan, New York, Ungar, 1994.

* * *

A founding member of New York Radical Women, the Redstockings, and New York Radical Feminists, Shulamith Firestone was among the most important of early "second-wave" radical feminist thinkers and organizers, and a leading figure in the creation of an autonomous women's liberation movement. The women's movement Firestone helped create saw itself not as an outgrowth, or necessary ally, of liberal feminist groups such as the National Organization for Women (NOW), whose goal was to achieve equal opportunity for women within the extant political system, but, at least initially, as a part of the larger radical movement which, in the 1960s, was working to fundamentally transform the conditions and assumptions that shaped American social and political life.

It was within this larger "Movement"—a term embracing the various left-wing protest movements of the time, including the movement to end the Vietnam War, the black freedom movement, the student movement, and the more theoretically sophisticated New Left—that many of the radical women who in 1967 first began discussing the problem of male supremacy had first experienced militant politics. For most of them, the cause of women's oppression could be most persuasively attributed to capitalism, making the achievement of women's liberation dependent on the creation of a socialist revolution. This analysis lead them to the position than any movement for women's liberation must be permanently subordinated to the goals and strategies of the Movement as a whole.

Firestone and the other women who would one day form the core of an autonomous radical feminist movement soon wearied of the rejection, trivialization, and downright misogynist hostility that even the most moderate demands for a discussion of women's oppression elicited from the vast majority of men on the Left. It was after one such personal experience of the Movement's contempt for women's concerns (this, ironically, at a conference whose stated purpose was to unify and solidify the Movement as a whole) that Firestone decided that the campaign for women's liberation could not be effectively pursued within a Movement that saw economic class as the primary contradiction, and therefore believed that women's attempts to focus on their own oppression were at least misguided, if not divisive and counter-revolutionary. Along with Jo Freeman, she decided to find other women who had come to this conclusion, in order to talk about organizing an independent radical women's movement. The result was the Chicago Westside group, which at its initial meeting in fall 1967 became the United States's first women's liberation group.

Despite her initial influence, however, Firestone's association with the Westside group was brief. By October 1967 she had moved halfway across the country to New York City for the explicit purpose of organizing, along with Pam Allen, a women's liberation group there. It is significant that they named their new group "New York Radical Women" (NYRW)—implying an organization *of* radical women, rather than an organization *for* women's liberation—in reflection of their continuing sensitivity to the Left's distaste for the term "feminist" on the ground that the first-wave feminism it connoted was bourgeois and reformist and for "women's liberation" as too radical. NYRW was the first women's liberation group in New York City.

Writing was not Firestone's first avocation: she had received her bachelor's degree in painting at the Art Institute of Chicago. But the frustration that gave life to the women's liberation movement also had a way of making writers out of women who had never thought of themselves as such. Firestone may have been one such woman: her only previous political involvement appears to have been with a socialist Zionist group, and although she continued to struggle during her years of feminist activism to become a professional artist, it is as a feminist theorist and early architect of radical feminism that she has so far achieved her greatest public recognition.

The beginnings of Firestone's writing career lay in her association with NYRW, which published *Notes from the First Year: Women's Liberation,* a compilation of writings analyzing women's oppression and the relationship of the women's liberation to the Movement, in June 1968. Firestone edited and contributed to this volume, a role she continued to fill, with the addition of assistant editor Anne Koedt, for *Notes from the Second Year: Radical Feminism,* published in April 1970. In both *Notes*, the articles Firestone wrote were concerned primarily with theoretical analysis of movement controversies in which she had been personally embroiled, and with the development of unifying principles and position statements, often called "Manifestos," for the feminist projects with which she was affiliated. This sort of writing was very characteristic of radical feminists, and hers are some prime examples.

By the time *Notes from the Second Year* appeared Firestone had moved on from New York Radical Women to help found two more women's liberation groups. The first of these was Redstockings, which she and Ellen Willis organized in New York in February 1969 to be, in Willis's words, "an action group based on a militantly independent, radical feminist consciousness." Once again the impetus was disgust with the blatant antagonism toward women's liberation shown by leftist men, in this case as directed against a women's protest (during which Firestone gave a speech) scheduled as part of a program of the Counter-Inaugural demonstration organized by the National Mobilization Committee to End the War in Vietnam held in Washington, D.C., in January 1969.

This time, however, it was not only the reaction of the men that was troubling, but also the support their hostility received from many leftist women, some of whom allegedly shared Firestone's concern over the oppression of women. She left the Counter-Inaugural all the more resolved to build a women's movement independent of the Left, a resolve that the experience also engendered in several other NYRW members, who had formerly believed that women's liberation should remain closely tied to the larger Movement. These women formed the core of Redstockings, which was designed to be unequivocally radical feminist (unlike NYRW, which had some radical feminists in it, but also others who did not so identify).

The Redstockings took their name in reference to the 19th-century feminist intellectuals who were insultingly referred to as "Bluestockings" by some of their (male) contemporaries. Redstockings accepted the feminist mantle from these women, but did so within the militant radical political tradition, whose color is the red of revolution. Firestone was, no doubt, instrumental in this choice of name, since in *Notes from the First Year* she had been the first to challenge in print the tendency of the Left to belittle first-wave feminism. Her reclamation of this heritage was a direct challenge to the Movement position that this earlier feminism was thoroughly bourgeois and reformist, often cited as "proof" that any autonomous women's movement was bound to be counterrevolutionary.

Although Firestone and Willis organized the Redstockings with the idea that it would be a militant public-action group, it quickly became apparent to Firestone that this was not the direction it was taking. Besides distributing large quantities of women's movement literature, the group organized a successful disruption of New York state legislative hearings on abortion reform and helped to organize both Congresses to Unite Women, as well as a sit-in at the *Ladies' Home Journal.* Its attention, though, was increasingly directed toward consciousness-raising, a process that Firestone supported, although not as an end in itself. As her *The Dialectic of Sex* was to make clear, Firestone had serious reservation about the "pro-woman line" so integral to the group-definition of the Redstockings.

The pro-woman line argued that women's social submissiveness was due, not to psychological factors or to socialization, but to constant daily pressure to conform to female gender-role expectations that was applied to them by men. It considered any attempt to blame sexism on social institutions a dodge designed to allow men to escape their responsibility for women's subordination, and saw such institutions as tools wielded by the oppressors. This line clashed with Firestone's position that the family was the site of "psychosexual" construction of social domination; in her view neither psychology nor socialization—nor, indeed, biology—could be so easily dismissed as causes of women's subordination.

By fall 1969, Firestone's impatience had grown to such an extent that she decided it was time to form another group. Besides disagreeing with Redstockings' determination to devote most their energies to consciousness-raising—a strategy often criticized within the movement as only leading to *more* consciousness-raising—she was also concerned that Redstockings did not seem willing to actively organize the large numbers of women who were by then anxious to become part of the women's liberation movement. Firestone saw this as a serious mistake. She had wanted Redstockings to be militant, active, and open; since that did not seem to be the majority position, she decided, along with Anne Koedt, to found a group that would be. The result was New York Radical Feminists (NYRF).

Like Redstockings, members of NYRF agreed that the primary social contradiction is not class or race, but gender, arguing that every other form of social domination has its origin in male supremacy. Firestone and Koedt saw the formation of this group as the first step toward building a radical feminist movement on a mass scale. However, by summer 1970, a mere six months after the group's inception, charges by newer members that the group's founders were behaving in an elitist fashion resulted in a confrontation. Such charges were common in the women's movement, which tended to value non-hierarchical forms of organization. In this case, they seem to have been at least in part fueled by the realization among the new women that Firestone was becoming increasingly involved in the writing of *The Dialectic of Sex,* and that she, Koedt, and a few others were becoming somewhat well-known.

Radical feminism attracted more women of poor and working-class origins than did liberal feminism, and many of these women were suspicious that the women's movement's commitment to egalitarianism was more a matter of theory than of practice. They mistrusted those women in the movement who were "more privileged" (of middle-class or upper-class origin) and who might try to "cash in" as individuals on feminism. Rather than a matter of jealousy, the concern was over whose version of feminism would become popularized: the fear was that women with more access to the media would be in a position to become leaders of a movement that officially rejected the idea of leadership. But it also touched on the realization that the supposed "sisterhood" of all feminists often concealed sharp differences in educational backgrounds, access to social resources, and opportunities among them.

Confronted with allegations of elitism, Firestone countered that it was not the founding members but the newer members of NYRF who were the problem. In her view, these new women were guilty of vitiating and adulterating the women's movement because many of them were more concerned with their own narrow self-interests than with radically restructuring society. Firestone's problem with the Left had been that it was not radical *enough* in believing that socialism alone would liberate women; she was not now prepared to accept that feminism could be compatible with capitalism. Because many of the newer women saw feminism as an ideology of self-improvement, NYRF was clearly not the organization she had planned.

Although it seems the breach in NYRF could have been healed, Firestone no longer had the stomach to struggle for it. She, along with the other founding members, withdrew from the organization. By the time *The Dialectic of Sex* was published in October 1970, Firestone's involvement with the organized women's liberation movement was already a thing of the past. *Notes from the Third Year,* published in 1971, listed her as co-editor (along with Anne Koedt), but noted that she was "on leave."

In *The Dialectic of Sex,* Firestone offered a feminist revision of Marxism's materialist theory of history in which sex class and the relations of reproduction, rather than economic class and the relations of production, are seen as the driving force moving history along. She argued that the original class distinction is the one between men and women: women's and men's different roles in the work of reproducing the species are the source of the division of labor that forms the basis for the two sex classes, as well as for patriarchy and its ruling ideology, sexism. This sexual division of labor is also the source of the psychology of domination that ultimately led to economic classes, as well as to racial and cultural relations of subordination.

In Firestone's view, then, the roots of women's oppression are biological, and just as the liberation of the proletariat requires an economic revolution, women's liberation requires a biological revolution. To eliminate the sex class system, women must seize the means of reproduction and ultimately obliterate the distinction between the sexes, creating an androgynous, sex-classless society. Androgynous culture offers the possibility of complete human social integration. But as long as gender roles in biological reproduction exist, no amount of political, social, or educational equality will be sufficient to fundamentally change things for women.

Firestone saw the means of eliminating sex class in the technologizing of reproduction: through artificial devices like test-tube conception and gestation in artificial wombs. Once women and men stopped playing different roles in reproduction, she argued, all sex roles could be eliminated and the "tyranny of the biological family" would disappear, along with the needs to impose heterosexuality as a means to species survival and to maintain an incest taboo. Humanity could then "finally revert to its natural polymorphous sexuality" in which "all forms of sexuality would be allowed and indulged."

With the end of the sexual division of labor would also come the end of the need to confine women in the home and to send men out into public to work. Women would then be free to enter the workplace, depriving capitalism of their unpaid productive work in the home and of the role in consumption women at home with children have traditionally played, finally eliminating the family as an economic unit. This would set the stage to eliminate, by means of technology, the role of man as producer (just as technology has also eliminated the role of woman as reproducer). Once distinctive productive and reproductive roles were overcome, the possibility of eliminating all the structures, relations, and ideologies that have historically divided the human community would, for the first time, exist.

The publication of *The Dialectic of Sex* created a national stir. It was widely reviewed, almost always negatively, and became a topic of general public discussion, much of it critical. Not surprisingly, it became a national best-seller, considered by one *Publisher's Weekly* poll to be one of the 20 most influential books of the next two decades. No survey of feminist theory can be considered complete unless it includes *The Dialectic of Sex* as one of the leading expressions of the radical feminist perspective; no history of second-wave feminism can be written without acknowledging Shulamith Firestone as one of the movement's major architects.

—Eileen Bresnahan

FOX-GENOVESE, Elizabeth

Nationality: American. **Born:** Boston, Massachusetts, 28 May 1941. **Education:** Bryn Mawr College, A.B. (cum laude) 1963; Institut d'Etudes Politiques, Paris, France, 1961-62; Harvard University, Cambridge, Massachusetts, A.M. 1966, Ph.D. 1974; studied at Center for Psychoanalytic Training and Research, Columbia University, 1977-79, and Institute in Qualitative Methods, Newberry Library, 1979. **Family:** Married Eugene Dominick Genovese in 1969. **Career:** Assistant editor in history, Houghton Mifflin Co., Boston, 1966-67; picture researcher, Prentice-Hall, New York, 1971-72; assistant professor of history and liberal arts, 1973-76, associate professor of history, 1976-80, developer and chairperson, Cluster on Interdisciplinary Study of Women in Culture and Society, 1978-80, University of Rochester, Rochester, New York; instructor, Newberry Library, 1980; professor of history, State University of New York at Binghampton, 1980-86; directeur associé d'etudes, École des Hautes Études en Sciences Sociales, Paris, 1982; professor of history, beginning 1986, and women's studies, 1986-91, Eléonore Raoul Professor of Humanities, beginning 1988, Emory University, Atlanta, Georgia. Director, Project on Integrating Materials on Women into Traditional Survey Courses, Office of Education, 1978-83; consultant for women's history, UNESCO, 1980, University of Maine at Orono and Canisius College, both 1982, and William Patterson College and Grinnell College, both 1987. Editor for international affairs, 1977-80, contributing editor since 1982, *Marxist Perspectives;* member of advisory board, *Women and History.* Contributor to periodicals, including *Antioch Review, Journal of American History, Nation, New Left Review, New Republic,* and *Partisan Review.* **Awards:** Eleutherian Mills-Hagley Foundation grant, 1972-73; University of Rochester grant, 1975, fellowship, 1975, 1978; National Endowment for the Humanities fellowship, 1976-77; New York Institute for the Humanities fellowship, 1978-79; Newberry Library fellowship, 1979; Rockefeller Foundation fellowship, 1979-80; American Council of Learned Societies fellowship, 1984; Ford Foundation fellowship, 1984; National Humanities Center fellowship, 1984-85; Fund for the Improvement of Post-Secondary Education grant, 1979-80; Lily Endowment, 1982-83. **Member:** American Historical Association, National Council of History Education, American Academy of Religion, Society of American Historians, American Antiquarian Society, Federalist Society, Society for the History of the Early Republic, American Studies Association, American Political Science Association, Modern Language Association, Southern Association of Women Historians, Southern Historical Association, Georgia Historical Association. **Address:** Department of Women's Studies, 210 Physics, Emory University, Atlanta, Georgia 30322, U.S.A.

Publications

Political/Social Theory

Feminism without Illusions: A Critique of Individualism. Chapel Hill and London, University of North Carolina Press, 1991.

Feminism Is Not the Story of My Life: How Today's Feminist Elite Has Lost Touch with the Real Concerns of Women. New York, Doubleday, 1996.

Essays

"Placing Women's History in History," in *New Left Review,* May/June 1982.

"The Claims of a Common Culture," in *Salmagundi,* fall 1986.

"Feminist Rights, Individual Wrongs," in *Tikkun,* 7(3), May/June 1992.

"From Separate Spheres to Dangerous Streets: Postmodernist Feminism and the Problem of Order," in *Social Research,* spring 1993.

"Class, Race, and an Agenda for the Women's Movement," in *Experiences of Gender: Color, Class and Country,* edited by Gay Young and Bette J. Dickerson. London, Zed Books, 1994.

"Feminism, Children, and the Family," in *Harvard Journal of Law and Public Policy,* 18(2), spring 1995.

History

The Origins of Physiocracy: Economic Revolution and Social Order in 18th-Century France. Ithaca, New York, Cornell University Press, 1976.

Fruits of Merchant Capital: Slavery and Bourgeois Property in the Rise and Expansion of Capitalism, with Eugene D. Genovese. New York, Oxford University Press, 1983.

An American Portrait: A History of the United States, with David Burner, Eugene D. Genovese, and Forrest McDonald. New York, Macmillan, 2nd edition, 1985; revised, with D. Burner and Virginia Bernhard, as *Firsthand America: A History of the United States,* St. James, New York, Brandywine Press, 1991.

Within the Plantation Household: Black and White Women of the Old South. Chapel Hill and London, University of North Carolina Press, 1988.

Other

Editor, with Susan Mosher Stuard and others, and contributor, *Restoring Women to History: Western Civilization I [United States I] [Western Civilization II] [United States II].* Bloomington, Indiana, Organization of American Historians, 4 vols., 1983.

Editor and translator, *The Autobiography of Pierre Samuel Du Pont de Nemours.* Wilmington, Delaware, Scholarly Resources, 1984.

Editor, *Beulah,* by Augusta Jane Evans. Baton Rouge and London, Louisiana State University Press, 1992.

Editor, with others, *Southern Women: Histories and Identities.* Columbia, University of Missouri Press, 1992.

Editor, with others, *Hidden Histories of Women in the South.* Columbia, University of Missouri Press, 1994.

Editor, with Virginia Bernhard, *The Birth of American Feminism.* St. James, New York, Brandywine Press, 1995.

* * *

Elizabeth Fox-Genovese is one of the preeminent scholars of women in world history as well as the history of women in the United States, and particularly in the southern United States. While not widely read by the general public, her work has been praised by many in academic and historical circles. She is credited with adding "women" back into history studies in university and college programs around the United States through her work on the groundbreaking curriculum guide *Restoring Women to History* (1983). With the help of other historians Fox-Genovese gave needed impetus to the ongoing fight to accord women in their rightful places in the panorama of U.S. and European history.

Fox-Genovese seems to have defied the law of physics that states you cannot be in two places at once. For five years she developed and directed a nationwide program to integrate materials on women into traditional studies, as well as developing a program of interdisciplinary study of women in culture and society at the University of Rochester in New York. During that same period she was, at various times and places, an assistant professor and associate professor of history in New York and an associate director of social science studies in Paris. After publication of *Restoring Women to History,* Fox-Genovese wrote the award-winning book *Within the Plantation Household* (1988) before turning her writing focus toward interpreting feminism, all the while attaining increasingly more prestigious teaching positions.

Basing them on her characteristically meticulous research, Fox-Genovese has clearly set forth her interpretations of feminism, interpretations that have the power to change the academic world's perception of the modern feminist movement. 1991's *Feminism without Illusions* is her theoretical look at where feminism has been, who it has benefited, and what it has not accomplished. The book caused controversy among the educational elite, as well as within the upper echelons of the community of white, professional women—perceived by many critics as the *only* members of the present feminist movement. If the controversy remains only within those circles, the debate may shift to what difference, if any, the book will make.

Seeing a great need for a more "readable" book on feminism, Fox-Genovese showcased the impact of feminism on a practical level in her 1996 book, *Feminism Is Not the Story of My Life.* Here she throws out most of the theoretical language and talks with women who have never felt a part of the feminist movement, or felt, at most, only tenuous connections on some issues. The women interviewed spell out what they need (and don't need) in their lives; Fox-Genovese draws on their input to propose that feminism shift to meet those needs, and transform itself into a movement of inclusion instead of exclusion.

Fox-Genovese has often indicated her great love of writing; her ability to write about complex subjects without burying her meaning in theoretical terms and dense academic jargon is a characteristic that even her critics grant her. With the publication of *Feminism Is Not the Story of My Life* she has used that ability to great effect, and has made a successful effort to reach those women—and men—who would otherwise have no access to, or even interest in, the feminist debate that has so frequently engaged academics.

—Maria Elena Raymond

FRANKLIN, (Stella Marian Sarah) Miles

Pseudonym: Brent of Bin Bin. **Nationality:** Australian. **Born:** Talbingo, near Tumut, New South Wales, 14 October 1879. **Education:** Primarily educated at home and at local schools. **Military Service:** Worked with unit of Scottish Woman's Hospital, Ostrovo, Serbia, 1917-18. **Career:** Governess, Sydney, Australia, 1897; worked as a nurse, c. 1902, and as a housemaid; freelance journalist, Sydney *Daily Telegraph* and *Morning Herald,* until 1906; moved to California, 1906; secretary to Alice Henry, Women's Trade Union League; coeditor, *Life and Labor,* 1908-15; moved to London and worked as a cook, 1915; assistant secretary, National Housing and Town Planning Council, London, 1919-25; returned to Australia, 1927-30; lived in England, 1931-32; settled in Sydney from 1933; founded Miles Franklin literary award, 1948; lecturer, Commonwealth Literary Fund, University of Western Australia, Perth, 1950. **Awards:** Prior Memorial prize, 1936, for *All That Swagger,* and 1939, for *Joseph Furphy: The Legend of a Man and His Book.* **Died:** 19 September 1954.

Publications

Novels

Some Everyday Folk—and Dawn. Edinburgh, Blackwood & Sons, 1909; New York, Penguin, 1987.

The Net of Circumstance. N.p., 1915.

Up the Country: A Tale of the Early Australian Squattocracy (as Brent of Bin Bin). Edinburgh, n.p., 1928; London, Angus & Robertson, 1966; as *Up the Country: A Saga of Pioneering Days,* New York, Beaufort Books, 1987.

Ten Creeks Run: A Tale of the Horse and Cattle Stations of the Upper Murrumbidgee (as Brent of Bin Bin). N.p., 1930.

Back to Bool Bool: A Ramiparous Novel (as Brent of Bin Bin). N.p., 1931.

Old Blastus of Bandicoot: Opuscule on a Pioneer Tufted with Ragged Rhymes. London, C. Palmer, 1931.

Bring the Monkey. Sydney, Endeavour Press, 1933.

All That Swagger. Sydney, Angus & Robertson, 1936; London, Allen & Unwin, 1952.

Pioneers on Parade, with Dymphna Cusack. London, Angus & Robertson, 1939; North Ryde, New South Wales, Angus & Robertson, 1988.

Prelude to Waking (as Brent of Bin Bin). Sydney, Angus & Robertson, 1950.

Cockatoos: A Story of Youth and Exodists. N.p., 1954.

Gentlemen at Gyang Gyang: A Tale of the Jumbuck Pads on the Summer Runs (as Brent of Bin Bin). Sydney, Angus & Robertson, 1956.

On Dearborn Street. St. Lucia, Queensland, University of Queensland Press, 1981.

Plays

No Family. In *Best Australian One-Act Plays,* 1937.

Call Up Your Ghosts, with Dymphna Cusack (produced 1945). In *Penguin Anthology of Australian Women's Writing,* edited by Dale Spender, London and New York, Penguin, 1988.

Literary Criticism

Laughter, Not for a Cage: Notes on Australian Writing, with Biographical Emphasis on the Struggles, Function, and Achievements of the Novel in Three Half-Centuries (lectures). London, Angus & Robertson, 1956.

For Children

Sydney Royal. N.p., 1947.

Autobiography

My Brilliant Career (as Brent of Bin Bin). Edinburgh, Blackwood & Sons, 1901; London, Virago, 1954; San Francisco, Tri-Ocean Books, 1965.

My Career Goes Bung, Purporting to Be the Autobiography of Sybylla Penelope Melvyn. Melbourne, Georgian House, 1946; as *The End of My Career,* New York, St. Martin's Press, and London, Virago, 1981.

Childhood at Brindabella: My First Ten Years. London, Angus & Robertson, 1963.

Other

Joseph Furphy: The Legend of a Man and His Book, with Kate Baker. London, Angus & Robertson, 1944.

My Congenials: Miles Franklin and Friends in Letters, edited by Jill Roe. Pymble, New South Wales, State Library of New South Wales/Angus & Robertson, 1993.

*

Media Adaptations: *My Brilliant Career* (film), 1979.

Manuscript Collections: Mitchell Library, Sydney, Australia.

Critical Studies: *Miles Franklin* by Marjorie Barnard, New York, Twayne, 1967; *Miles Franklin in America: Her Unknown (Brilliant) Career* by Verna Coleman, London, Angus & Robertson, 1981; *Miles Franklin: Her Brilliant Career* by Colin Roderick, Adelaide, Rigby, 1982; "Alias Miles Franklin" by Val Kent, in *Gender, Politics, and Fiction,* edited by Carole Ferrier, n.p., 1985.

* * *

Miles Franklin's *My Brilliant Career,* first published in 1901, has proved perennially popular but the book's reception itself caused the author significant dismay. Her first novel was presumed to be an autobiography and while containing many elements of her life in Australia's bush country, she did not anticipate the estrangement from her family that occurred because of her unflattering portrayal of them in the novel. One of Australia's most famous novelists, she lived in self-imposed exile in America and England for much of her adult life and always maintained a conflicted relationship with her homeland. Her heroine Sybylla Melvyn (presumed by critics and readers to be Franklin herself) yearns for a wider world and a life given over to artistic expression, rejecting the tedium and exhausting labor she depicts so vividly in *My Brilliant Career.* She also rejects a suitor, the eminently suitable and archetypical Australian Harold Beecham. Franklin meant her novel to be a parody of the romance novels of the 1890s that were so popular, but it was read (and criticized) as if she had been entirely sincere in her broadly drawn characterizations. Her career as a writer was of productivity and frustration: Franklin was a prolific writer, often employing pseudonyms, but yearned for critical approval as an artist, which largely eluded her after the promise of *My Brilliant Career.*

Stella Miles Franklin, the daughter of a pioneering family of the "Squattocracy" of Australia's bush, inherited her mother's artistic nature and the ambition of her father. Susannah Franklin was a well-educated and gifted woman who married John Franklin and followed him to Brindabella, a fertile valley near Canberra that was primarily ranch country. The first ten years of the author's life were spent there and she recalled them fondly in her autobiography *Childhood at Brindabella.* Eventually her father moved the family to Stillwater, which was to figure so prominently in *My Brilliant Career.* Franklin portrayed Stillwater as desolate and uncouth, and longed for her mother's family's homestead at Old Talbingo. Yet without this bush experience, Franklin would have no subject, since the hard life forced her to seek fulfillment outside its limitations. Her feminism was equally a product of her exposure to strong women (particularly her mother and her beloved grandmother) and her rebellion against a proscribed role as wife and mother. Tied to childcare at an early age (minding her younger siblings), Stella clashed with her mother over her dreams of a musical career. She also kept her faithful suitor, Edwin Brindle, waiting for her to satisfy her ambitions but Franklin never found the opportunity to marry anyone. The young author was elated and stung by the reception of her first novel, and alternately repudiated it and justified it throughout her life: hence the "sequel," *My Career Goes Bung,* in which the somewhat chastened Sybylla is reworked and the happenings of the previous book are rewritten in a more cynical fashion. It was written shortly after her first novel but only published in 1946, having been rejected by publishers as odd or containing too much sexual content. Franklin's audacity and her very persona as a woman writer was her worst impediment as an author. She was a novelty, a little bush girl, but Australia was not prepared for her opinions or for a serious artist.

In 1905 Franklin visited the United States, where she met Alice Henry, an Australian reformer who, with Franklin, founded the Women's Trade Union League. Her life in America was revealed by Verna Coleman in *Her (Unknown) Brilliant Career,* in which she described the young Franklin's various employments as a shopgirl and possibly as a barmaid in a Chicago hotel, as well as the emergence of Franklin as a political activist, fostered by her friendships with Alice Henry and Jane Addams of Hull House. Her experiences during the general strike called by the United Garment Worker's Union in 1910 were seminal to the growth of her feminist consciousness, and in *Life and Labor,* the league magazine, Franklin and Henry wrote that "Whatever the nominal result the tremendous pressure has embodied will have an incalculable educational effect on the strikers themselves, while the general public has been awakened to a far deeper understanding of the industrial problem at its door."

Franklin, unwell and dispirited at her largely unrecognized contribution to the magazine, left America in 1915 for England, declining to become a naturalized citizen. The war years found her in Macedonia as an orderly with the Scottish Women's Hospital Unit. She had published one novel, *Some Everyday Folk—and Dawn,* in 1909, and until *Up the Country,* written under the name

"Brent of Bin-Bin"—the first of three books that would return to the bush country and the Squattocracy—Franklin was largely forgotten. *Up the Country* was the first of her efforts to be successful, despite frequent attempts to change her focus from the Australian material to plays and novels with a drawing-room setting. Her pretense to a male authorship benefited her as there was much guessing as to the book's true author and the series went far in reestablishing Franklin as a author and giving her a living as a writer.

Franklin returned to Australia to live in 1933, and published the Prior Prize-winning *All That Swagger* in 1936. She lived with her mother near Sydney until 1938, when Franklin was greatly saddened by her passing, having learned to co-exist with her at last. Her life was enlivened particularly by her friendships with women, in particular author Pixie O'Harris, who urged her to write *Childhood at Brindabella.* Franklin's final years were difficult; she was ill and preferred her solitude. She was not writing, which caused her great distress. When she died on 19 September 1954, her ashes were scattered at Talbingo. The success of the film version of *My Brilliant Career* in 1979 sparked a revival of critical interest in both Franklin and Australian women writers, yet another irony in the unusual career of her most famous work.

—Mary A. Hess

FREEMAN, Mary E. Wilkins

Also wrote as Mary Wilkins. **Nationality:** American. **Born:** Randolph, Massachusetts, 1852. **Education:** Attended Mount Holyoke Female Seminary, South Hadley, Massachusetts, 1970; studied at Glenwood Seminary, West Brattleboro, Vermont. **Family:** Married Charles Manning Freeman in 1902 (legally separated in 1922). **Career:** Teacher at a girl's school, 1873; lived with childhood friend Mary Wales in Randolph until 1889; contributed short stories to periodicals, including *Boston Daily Budget* and *Harper's Bazaar.* **Awards:** American Academy for Arts and Letters' Howells Medal for fiction, 1926. **Member:** National Institute of Arts and Letters. **Died:** Metuchen, New Jersey, 13 March 1930.

PUBLICATIONS

Novels

Jane Field. London, Osgood McIlvaine, 1892; New York, Harper & Bros., 1893.
Pembroke. New York, Harper & Bros., and London, Osgood McIlvaine, 1894.
Madelon. New York, Harper & Bros., and London, Osgood McIlvaine, 1896.
Jerome, A Poor Man. New York and London, Harper & Bros., 1897.
The Jamesons. New York, Doubleday & McClure, 1899.
The Heart's Highway: A Romance of Virginia in the 17th Century. New York, Doubleday Page, and London, Murray, 1900.
The Portion of Labor. New York and London, Harper & Bros., 1901.
The Debtor. New York and London, Harper & Bros., 1905.
By the Light of the Soul. New York and London, Harper & Bros., 1906.
"Doc" Gordon. New York and London, Authors and Newspapers Association, 1906.
The Shoulders of Atlas. New York and London, Harper & Bros., 1908.
The Whole Family: A Novel by 12 Authors, with William Dean Howells, Henry James, and others. New York and London, Harper & Bros., 1908.
The Butterfly House. New York, Dodd Mead, 1912.
The Yates Pride: A Romance. New York and London, Harper & Bros., 1912.
An Alabaster Box, with Florence Morse Kingsley. New York and London, D. Appleton, 1917.

Short Stories

A Humble Romance, and Other Stories. New York, Harper & Bros., 1887; as *A Far-Away Melody and Other Stories,* Edinburgh, Douglas, 1890.
A New England Nun, and Other Stories. New York, Harper & Bros., and London, Osgood McIlvaine, 1891.
Silence and Other Stories. New York and London, Harper & Bros., 1898.
The People of Our Neighborhood. Philadelphia, Curtis, and New York, Doubleday McClure, 1898; as *Some of Our Neighbors.* London, Dent, 1898.
The Love of Parson Lord and Other Stories. New York and London, Harper & Bros., 1900.
Understudies. New York and London, Harper & Bros., 1901.
Six Trees. New York and London, Harper & Bros., 1903.
The Wind in the Rose Bush and Other Stories of the Supernatural. New York, Doubleday Page, and London, Murray, 1903.
The Givers. New York and London, Harper & Bros., 1904.
The Fair Lavinia and Others. New York and London, Harper & Bros., 1907.
The Winning Lady and Others. New York and London, Harper & Bros., 1909.
The Copy-Cat and Other Stories. New York and London, Harper & Bros., 1914.
Edgewater People. New York and London, Harper & Bros., 1918.

Essays

"Good Wits, Pen and Paper," in *What Women Can Earn,* by G.H. Dodge, et. al. New York, Stokes, 1899.
"Emily Brontë and Wuthering Heights," in *The Booklovers Reading Club Handbook to Accompany the Reading Course Entitled The World's Greatest Women Novelists.* Philadelphia, Booklover's Library, 1901.
"The Girl Who Wants to Write: Things to Do and Avoid," in *Harper's Bazaar,* 47, June 1913.
"An Autobiography," in *Saturday Evening Post,* 190, 8 December 1917.

Plays

Eglantina: A Romantic Parlor Play, in *Ladies' Home Journal,* 27, July 1910.
Giles Corey, Yeoman. New York, Harper & Bros., 1893.
Red Robin, A New England Drama. N.p., 1892.

Screenplay: *The Pilgrim's Progress* (adaptation of the book by John Bunyan), with William Dinwiddie, 1915.

For Children

Decorative Plaques (poems), illustrated by George F. Barnes. Boston, Lothrop, 1883.
Goody Two-Shoes and Other Famous Nursery Tales, with Clara Doty Bates. Boston, Lothrop, 1883.
The Cow with the Golden Horns and Other Stories. Boston, Lothrop, 1884.
The Adventures of Anne: Stories of Colonial Times. Boston, Lothrop, 1886.
The Pot of Gold and Other Stories. Boston, Lothrop, and London, Ward Lock, 1892.
Young Lucretia and Other Stories. New York, Harper & Bros., and London, Osgood McIlvaine, 1892.
Comfort Pease and Her Gold Ring. New York, Chicago, and Toronto, Revell, 1895.
Once upon a Time and Other Child-Verses. Boston, Lothrop, 1897; London, Harper, 1898.
The Green Door. New York, Moffat Yard, 1910; London, Gay & Hancock, 1912.

Other

The Infant Sphinx: The Collected Letters of Mary E. Wilkins Freeman, edited by Brent L. Kendrick. Metuchen, New Jersey, Scarecrow Press, 1985.

*

Media Adaptations: *An Alabaster Box* (film), Vitagraph, 1917; *False Evidence* (film; based on *Madelon*), Metro, 1919.

Manuscript Collections: Library of the American Academy of Arts and Letters, New York Public Library; Columbia University; Princeton University; University of Virginia; University of Southern California.

Critical Studies: "Miss Wilkins: An Idealist in Masquerade" by Charles M. Thompson, in *Atlantic Monthly,* 83, May 1899; *Mary E. Wilkins Freeman* by Edward Foster, New York, Hendricks House, 1956; *The New England Art of Mary Wilkins Freeman* by Abigail Ann Hamblen, 1966; "A Defiant Light: A Positive View of Mary Wilkins Freeman" by Susan A. Toth, in *New England Quarterly,* 46, March 1973; "The Dissolving Vision: Realism in Jewett, Freeman, and Gilman" by Julia Bader, in *American Realism: New Essays,* edited by Eric J. Sundquist, Baltimore, Johns Hopkins University Press, 1982; *New England Local Color Literature: A Women's Tradition* by Josephine Donovan, 1983; *Mary Wilkins Freeman* by Perry D. Westbrook, revised edition, Boston, Twayne, 1988; *Critical Essays on Mary Wilkins Freeman* edited by Shirley Marchalonis, Boston, G.K. Hall, 1991; *A Web of Relationship: Women in the Short Fiction of Mary Wilkins Freeman* by Mary R. Reichardt, Jackson and London, University Press of Mississippi, 1992; *In a Closet Hidden: The Life and Work of Mary E. Wilkins Freeman* by Leah Blatt Glasser, Amherst, University of Massachusetts Pres, 1996.

* * *

Mary E. Wilkins Freeman was a prolific regionalist writer who brought a new realism to the characters that populated her New England landscape. Women's regional writing, in which a careful depiction of simple village life goes beyond mere description to a fuller awareness of the human condition, flourished in the late 19th century. The trend started with Harriet Beecher Stowe's *Oldtown Folks* and continued in the writing of Rose Terry Cooke, Celia Thaxter, Helen Hunt Jackson, Elizabeth Stuart Phelps, Alice Brown, and the contemporary with whom Freeman's work is most frequently compared, Sarah Orne Jewett. Freeman's current reputation rests primarily on her feminist consciousness in well-known short stories such as "The Revolt of 'Mother,'" "A New England Nun," "A Church Mouse," and "The Village Singer." Freeman paints realistic psychological portraits of aging women isolated within their communities, made to stand alone against the forces of nature, societal tensions, and economic hardship; the typical Freeman heroine must rely on her own resources for her physical and emotional survival.

Born in 1852 in Randolph, Massachusetts, Mary Ella Wilkins moved at age 15 to Brattleboro, Vermont, where her father had bought a partnership in a dry goods shop. After attending high school, she left for Mount Holyoke Seminary in 1870, returning home after one year to take classes at a local female seminary. In an effort to supplement the family's dwindling income, she tried teaching at a girl's school; however, the venture failed and she soon turned to writing instead. The deaths of her immediate family members (her sister Anna in 1876, her mother in 1880, and her father in 1883) left Wilkins on her own; she returned to Randolph, where she continued writing and lived in the house of her close childhood friend Mary Wales over the next 20 years.

Freeman's reputation as a successful American writer was established with her first two collections of short fiction for adults, *A Humble Romance and Other Stories* (1887) and *A New England Nun and Other Stories* (1891). In 1892 she met Dr. Charles Manning Freeman, whom she married in 1902 after a three-year, on-and-off-again engagement. Although the relationship apparently began happily, by 1909 her husband entered a sanitorium because of his alcoholism, and in 1920 Freeman committed him to the New Jersey State Hospital for treatment. She obtained a legal separation from him in 1922, and he died the next year, leaving her one dollar in his will; Freeman later successfully contested the settlement.

Their relationship likely had an impact on Freeman's creative output, as did changing American literary tastes. After 1918 Freeman published no more books and only a few essays. Although her greatest literary successes were behind her, she was such a respected national figure that in 1926 she was awarded the William Dean Howells medal for distinction in fiction from the American Academy of Arts and Letters, and she was one of the first four women ever to be elected to the National Institute for Arts and Letters, sharing that honor with Agnes Repplier, Margaret Deland, and Edith Wharton.

Among the foremost female authors of her day, Freeman worked in many genres, including children's literature, poetry, drama, and novels, to which she turned her attention later in her career; her most significant work, however, is her short fiction, which appeared in book form and in women's magazines such as *Women's Home Companion, Ladies' Home Journal,* and *Harper's Bazaar.* In her stories, Freeman challenged the basic assumptions of sentimental and domestic fiction—a devotion to home and family and a loving trust in God—made popular by an earlier generation of women writers such as Susan Warner, E.D.E.N. Southworth, and Maria Susanna Cummins. Advocating instead the literary realism of William Dean Howells, Freeman's fiction looks beyond this conventionally defined women's sphere and points to the places where this ideal collides with the reality many rural women faced.

One assumption Freeman questions is on the advantages of marriage. In "A New England Nun," for instance, we have an example of Freeman's ambivalence toward the institution and the recognition of the threat marriage poses to an independent woman, Louisa Ellis. Engaged to Joe Dagget in her youth, she waited patiently for 15 years as he, like so many men of his generation, left the community to seek his fortune. Joe dutifully returns, but Louisa has, in his absence, developed an orderly, almost monastic existence that marriage will entirely upset. When Louisa unexpectedly learns that Joe is in love with another woman but intends to honor his original promise, she chooses to dissolve their engagement and remain in a lifestyle that, though unimaginative at best, gives this woman her greatest pleasures.

When Freeman's characters are married it is almost never contentedly. In "The Revolt of Mother," for example, a dutiful, God-fearing wife makes the ultimate act of protest against a husband who has ignored her opinions and desires for years. Early in her marriage, "mother" Sarah Penn was promised a new home. She has raised her children to near-adulthood in a rundown cottage, however, while her husband's attentions were focused on his farm. As the story opens, Sarah learns that he has begun to build a new and unnecessary barn for his livestock. When her husband is called away on business, she stages her great rebellion, moving all her possessions and her family into the new barn. After the initial shock, her husband concedes to her long-denied wishes. This story was most closely identified with Freeman throughout her career, and revealingly, it is one she looked back upon with some reservation. In an essay published in the *Saturday Evening Post* (8 December 1917), she wrote that "all fiction ought to be true, and The Revolt of Mother is not in the least true.... There never was in New England a women like Mother. If there had been she most certainly would not have moved into the palatial barn... She simply would have lacked the nerve." Freeman exhibits an awareness of the tension between the fact that her society only conferred a social identity on those who were married (those who did not were "outsiders" in one sense or another all their lives), and the reality that when married, women lost much of their independence and individual voice. The stories that have revived interest in Freeman's career are those in which she urges women to challenge, rather than accept, societal roles.

—Deborah Evans

FRENCH, Marilyn

Pseudonym: Mara Solwoska. **Nationality:** American. **Born:** Marilyn Edwards, New York, New York, 21 November 1929. **Education:** Hofstra College (now University), Hempstead, Long Island, B.A. 1961, M.A. 1964; Harvard University, Cambridge, Massachusetts, Ph.D. 1972. **Family:** Married the lawyer Robert M. French in 1950 (divorced 1967); one daughter and one son. **Career:** Instructor, Hofstra University, 1964-68; assistant professor of English, College of the Holy Cross, Worcester, Massachusetts, 1972-76; artist-in-residence, Aspen Institute for Humanistic Study, 1972; Mellon Fellow in English, Harvard University, 1976-77. Contributor to journals, sometimes under the name Mara Solwoska, including *Free Inquiry, Ohio Review,* and *Soundings.* **Agent:** Sheedy Literary Agency, 65 Bleeker St., New York, New York 10012, U.S.A.

Publications

Novels

The Women's Room. New York, Summit, 1977; London, Deutsch, 1978.

The Bleeding Heart. New York, Summit, and London, Deutsch, 1980.

Her Mother's Daughter. New York, Summit, and London, Heinemann, 1987.

Our Father. Boston, Little Brown, and London, Hamish Hamilton, 1994.

Literary Criticism

The Book as World: James Joyce's Ulysses. Cambridge, Massachusetts, Harvard University Press, 1976; London, Abacus, 1982.

Shakespeare's Division of Experience. New York, Summit, and, London, J. Cape, 1981.

Essays

Beyond Power: On Women, Men, and Morals. New York, Summit, and London, J. Cape, 1985.

The War against Women. New York, Summit, and London, Hamish Hamilton, 1992.

*

Media Adaptations: *The Women's Room* (television movie), 1980.

Critical Studies: In *Virginia Quarterly Review,* 54(2), 1978; "The French Definition" by Linda W. Wagner, in *Arizona Quarterly,* 38(4), winter 1982; "Breaking the Silence: Marilyn French's *Her Mother's Daughter*" by Mary Rose Sullivan, in *Mother Puzzles: Daughters and Mothers in Contemporary American Literature,* edited by Mickey Pearlman, n.p., 1983.

* * *

Marilyn French has added a strong voice to feminist fiction and scholarship since her arrival on the literary scene in the late 1970s. While her first scholarly publication, *The Book as Word: James Joyce's Ulysses,* offers an extensive examination of male suffering, French would leave this theme to explore more thoroughly issues of female suffering in the rest of her canon. Only a year after the publication of *The Book as Word,* French achieved her first commercial, mainstream success with her 1977 novel *The Women's Room.* An explosive best-seller and a classic novel of the women's movement, *The Women's Room* takes a highly provocative look at the plight of modern women through the lens of feminism. The novel is based on French's own experiences and transformations from a sheltered wife and mother in the 1950s to a Harvard graduate student in the 1960s who gradually gains self-confidence as well as social independence. *The Women's Room* tells the story of Mira Ward, a woman whose sense of victimization by men and, more specifically, by the failure of men and women to communicate and trust each other, colors the novel. Mira's progression from naive housewife to divorced and liberated but lonely professional offers readers a poignant portrait of the betrayal that women suffer at the hands of men and society. French couches Mira's story within the stories of other middle-class women who also face the violence and injustice that permeate the female experience in a male-dominated culture; this suggests that, far from being isolated incidents, the experiences of Mira and her friends are rather typical of those in modern life.

French's next two novels, *The Bleeding Heart* and *Her Mother's Daughter,* would not achieve the same level of notoriety as *The Women's Room*, although they tackled similar issues concerning the damage that patriarchy does to women and how (if at all) women can protect their daughters from suffering the same physical and psychological damage. Published in 1980, *The Bleeding Heart* explores the life of Dolores Durer, a tenured professor and writer, who suffers a divorce, her daughter's suicide, and a failed love affair with a married, conventional executive before finally turning to her students and her female friends for personal fulfillment and emotional sustenance. *Her Mother's Daughter* (1987) examines the female experience over the course of four generations by tracing the relationships of the women in a family of Polish immigrants. Anastasia, a famous photographer, struggles to understand the silence of her mother and her grandmother, and to prevent the psychological abuse that results from that silence in her relationship with her own daughter.

French's books of essays, *Beyond Power: On Women, Men, and Morals*, and *The War against Women,* continue her investigation into the continuous and relentless subjugation of women by men. While certain critics have denounced French's polemical style and strong anti-male stance, her enduring popularity and importance to the women's movement suggest that many readers continue to identify with Marilyn French's portrayals of female relationships and embrace her suggestion that women assert their personal independence by distancing themselves from the role of "victim."

—Kathleen Drowne

FRIEDAN, Betty (Naomi)

Nationality: American. **Born:** Peoria, Illinois, 4 February 1921. **Education:** Smith College, A.B. (summa cum laude) 1942; University of California, Berkeley, M.A. in psychology; attended University of Iowa and Esalen Institute. **Family:** Married Carl Friedan in 1947 (divorced 1969); two sons, one daughter. **Career:** Instructor in creative writing and women's studies, New York University, 1965-73; visiting professor, Yale University, 1974, and Queens College of the City University of New York, 1975. Feminist organizer, writer, and lecturer at universities, institutes, and professional associations worldwide, including Harvard Law School, University of Chicago, Vassar College, Smithsonian Institution, New York Bar Association, U.S. Embassy in Bogota, Colombia, and in Sweden, the Netherlands, Brazil, Israel, and Italy, beginning in the 1960s; organizer and director, First Women's Bank & Trust Co., New York, beginning 1974. Organizer, Women's Strike for Equality, 1970, International Feminist Congress, 1973, and Economic Think Tank for Women, 1974; consultant to President's Commission on the Status of Women, 1964-65, and Rockefeller Foundation project on education of women, 1965. Contributor of articles to periodicals, including *Harper's, Ladies' Home Journal, Mademoiselle, Newsday, New York Times Magazine, Redbook, Saturday Review,* and *Working Woman;* contributing editor and columnist, *McCall's,* 1971-74; member of editorial board, *Present Tense.* **Member:** National Organization for Women (NOW; founding president, 1966-70; member of board of directors of legal defense and education fund), National Women's Political Caucus (founder; member of national policy council, 1971-73), National Association to Repeal Abortion Laws (vice-president, 1972-74), National Conference of Public Service Employment (member, board of directors), Girl Scouts of the USA (member of national board), Women's Forum, American Sociological Association, Association for Humanistic Psychology, Gerontological Society of America, American Federation of Television and Radio Artists (AFTRA), American Society of Journalists and Authors, Authors Guild, Authors League of America, Society of Magazine Writers, Phi Beta Kappa, Coffee House. **Awards:** New World Foundation/New York State Education Department grant, 1958-62; Wilhelmina Drucker Prize 1971; Humanist of the Year award, 1975; American Public Health Association citation, 1975; American Society of Journalists and Authors Mort Weisinger Award, 1979; American Society of Journalists and Authors Author of the Year. L.H.D.: Smith College, 1975; State University of New York at Stony Brook, 1985; Cooper Union, 1987.

Publications

Political/Social Theory

The Feminine Mystique. New York, Norton, 1963; revised edition, 1974; twentieth-anniversary edition, 1983.

The Second Stage. New York, Summit, 1981; revised edition, 1986.

The Fountain of Age. New York, Simon & Schuster, and London, Cape, 1993.

Essays

It Changed My Life: Writings on the Women's Movement. New York, Random House, 1976; revised, with a new introduction by the author, New York, Norton, 1985.

Uncollected Essays

"Feminism Takes a New Turn," in *New York Times Magazine,* 18 November 1979.

"Twenty Years after *The Feminine Mystique,*" in *New York Times Magazine,* 27 February 1983.

*

Manuscript Collection: Schlesinger Library, Radcliffe College, New York.

Critical Studies: *Psychoanalysis and Feminism* by Juliet Mitchell, New York, Random House, 1974; "Humanism and Feminism: New Directions" (interview) by Paul Kurtz, in *Humanist,* 34(3), May/June 1974; "The Emancipation of Betty Friedan" by

Marilyn French, in *Esquire,* 100(6), December 1983; "Women's Choices as Seen by H. L. Mencken and Betty Friedan" by Joan Call, in *Menckeniana,* 107, fall 1988; *Breaking Barriers: The Feminist Revolution from Susan B. Anthony to Margaret Sanger to Betty Friedan* by Jules Archer, New York, Viking, 1991.

* * *

It wasn't until the late 1950s that Betty Friedan emerged from American domesticity into the life she was destined for, that of a feminist activist. Before the writing of her well-known non-fiction work *The Feminine Mystique,* she had little interest in women's causes. Energetic in her high school and college studies and activities Friedan was firmly enmeshed in the traditional role of a woman in American society. Her identity—indeed, her destiny—was to be someone's wife, someone's children's mother, a sex object.

Friedan's own mother was like many of the women that Friedan would eventually write about in *The Feminine Mystique:* Miriam Goldstein had left a job as an editor of a local newspaper's women's page after her marriage and become a housewife, as was expected. Although an active, talented, and energetic woman who volunteered in community work and played sports, Miriam vented her frustration on her family by spending money incessantly and creating feuds with her husband. Despite family tensions, both parents doted on Betty and thought her a marvelous writer. Her father saved all she wrote and her mother encouraged her to expand her talents by joining the school paper and writing and editing her own literary magazine.

Friedan sailed through school with high marks, was an excellent organizer and took drama lessons. At Smith College she edited the college paper, interviewed Eleanor Roosevelt, and created the *Smith College Monthly.* Her writing skills were enhanced when she attended a writers' conference in Tennessee and felt a leaning toward Socialism. After graduation from Smith, where she was class valedictorian, Friedan went on to complete her master's degree in psychology at Berkeley. Although she was offered a fellowship to continue on for her Ph.D., she volunteered for service in the American Red Cross during World War II because she wanted to fight against Fascism. However, she was turned down from service because she had severe asthma.

Moving to Greenwich Village, New York, Betty married Carl Friedan in 1947. She also wrote freelance articles and gave speeches for political candidates before retired into housewife domesticity in 1949, a lifestyle advocated by popular women's magazines. Her satisfaction with the quiet life subsided after attending a Smith College fifteen-year reunion where she was invited to survey 200 of her fellow graduates to determine to what benefit they had used their educations. She was shocked to learn the results. Nearly 89 percent of the women had not utilized their years of schooling other than by becoming housewives. While men related to themselves and each other in terms of their careers, women had lost their individuality in marriage and domestic lifestyles. They found that they were unhappy but had no idea why.

Friedan received an assignment to put her research results into an article for *McCalls* and later for *Ladies' Home Journal.* But the magazine's male editors skewed her results into line with their own thinking and edited out Friedan's ideas, stating that such findings could not be true. In addition to dealing with such frustrations, Friedan—who was by now balancing a job as a journalist with being a wife and mother—would find herself subjected to job discrimination in the early 1960s. Expecting her second child, she requested maternity leave, which her union contract allowed for. Her employer, however, felt differently and fired Friedan. The union refused to back up her claims of discrimination, stating that her second pregnancy was a "personal matter." This "personal matter" provided a disgruntled Friedan ample opportunity to strengthen her research and write. In 1963 she completed her book. Its subject, "the problem that has no name" had become *The Feminine Mystique.*

Friedan wondered why women had been portrayed differently in the years prior to World War II. Women's magazines of that era had offered women readers the same extensive subject matter that appeared in men's magazines. Many women of that generation were career women, and some accelerated their positions during the war. However, following the war women fell out of the job market and into the routines of housewives. By scanning the magazine articles of past eras, Friedan realized that media advertising played a large part in the stay-at-home agenda. Her research, analysis, and writing enlightened not only a world of women but raised her own level of thinking as well. Women, she felt, needed education, training, creativity, and courage to break out of the mold that had been prepared for them.

Eventually translated into 13 languages, *The Feminine Mystique* created a furor after it became an instant best-seller. In its pages, Friedan raises issues, not only of women's identity, but of the masculine identity as well. Men, she insists, are far from being the enemy; they are trapped by a masculine role that they have to play in order to be accepted by society, just as women are trapped in the feminine domestic roles. The book sparked discussions between men and women all over America who debated, attacked, and denounced its contents. The Friedans were exiled from suburbia and moved back to the city.

Despite the opposition, many women were relieved that someone had identified the cause of their unhappiness, anxieties, and depressions and gave them reason to hope for new lives. Many of these women became part of the women's movement of the 1960s. Friedan continued getting the message out as she traveled the lecture circuit nationally and internationally. The magazines that had once edited out her words now clamored for book excerpts and new articles.

Friedan soon realized that her activism could not be kept to writing and speaking alone; it took a new form after her organizational talents resurfaced in 1966 and she helped found the National Organization for Women (NOW). Friedan wrote the new organization's statement of purpose and was elected as NOW's first president. With NOW's members behind her, Friedan fought against discriminatory practices by, for example, staging a sit-in at a restaurant catering to an exclusively male clientele. After such extreme measures gained popular attention, laws started to change. Friedan progressed to other avenues, offering criticism on the way women were depicted as sex objects on television programming. As she worked on one issue, others surfaced: employment equality, wage discrimination, racial discrimination.

In 1970, after stepping down as NOW's president, Friedan continued her activism in women's rights. Organizing a 24-hour general Women's Strike for Equality, she and fellow members of NOW were able to show their solidarity by marching in numerous cities across the United States. Founding the first National Abortion Rights Action League (NARAL), Friedan helped in the passage of New York laws allowing women the right of choice. She also encouraged women's participation in the political arena, helped to form the National Women's Political Caucus (NWPC), and sought to ease others into the movement who did not want the label of "libber" or "feminist." She worked on gaining support for the Equal Rights Amendment. Her views did not always mesh with feminists who took radical steps and turned away potential support. At one time she lashed out at lesbians, calling them the "lavender menace," but she eventually changed her position to become a supporter of lesbian rights.

In Friedan's second book, *It Changed My Life: Writings on the Women's Movement,* written in 1976, she documents her work on behalf of women and includes a journal of her personal experiences. The book also contains a number of letters that Friedan received from readers of *The Feminine Mystique*. She reiterates the need for feminists not to exclude men from the movement nor to chastise those women who wish to be attractive by wearing cosmetics. Friedan continues to encourage the women's movement to avoid alienating men and women who are a part of mainstream America but whose experiences might lead them to identify with aspects of the women's movement.

In the 1981 publication, *The Second Stage*, Friedan writes about the emergence of the Superwoman myth. Although able to juggle her career, marriage, and children without a great deal of trouble, the "superwoman" is the antithesis of the women of the "feminine mystique" genre; she could be compared to the 1960s perfect housewife because both are so far removed from reality. In order to gain stronger control of their families, Friedan suggests that women should begin to rely on support networks. Women had made great strides thus far, she felt. Now it was time for men and women to join forces to create true equality. In *The Second Stage,* Friedan also takes to task more militant feminists who, she feels, have turned away many women from the movement by not respecting those who chose to embrace the domestic life and motherhood. Not surprisingly, militant feminists did not agree with Friedan, and countered that she was no longer in touch with the objectives of the women's movement.

Continuing interviewing and researching, Friedan completed an analysis of aging, which was inspired by considering the prospects she personally faced in growing old. *The Fountain of Age,* written in 1993, depicts the aging process as not necessarily the time of decline that the media would paint it. Women, especially, have become attuned to new cycles of life as a result of becoming more focused on redefining themselves. Such a heightened involvement with the process of living—one of the results of the women's movement, she notes—has allowed women to remain vigorous.

A new way of looking at life was revealed to millions of women in the aftermath of Friedan's publication of *The Feminine Mystique*. Generations after the release of this famous book, its author finds herself "still awed by the revolution" that the "book helped spark." A woman whose personal search brought others to frontiers of unrealized possibility, Betty Friedan has helped women join forces, find new careers, explore new, more positive images of themselves, and express their true nature in any lifestyle they chose—with pride.

—Marilyn Elizabeth Perry

FRYE, Marilyn

Nationality: American. **Born:** 1941. **Education:** Stanford University, B.A. 1963; Cornell University, Ph.D. 1969. **Career:** Currently professor of philosophy, Michigan State University, Lansing. Contributor of essays to journals, anthologies, and periodicals. **Address:** Department of Philosophy, Michigan State University, East Lansing, Michigan 48824, U.S.A.

Publications

Philosophy

The Politics of Reality: Essays in Feminist Theory. Trumansburg, New York, Crossing Press, 1983.

Willful Virgin: Essays in Feminism, 1976-1992. Freedom, California, Crossing Press, 1992.

Essays

"The Necessity of Differences: Constructing a Positive Category of Women," in *Signs: Journal of Women in Culture and Society,* summer 1996.

*

Critical Studies: "Philosophy and Passion" by Helene V. Wenzel, in *Women's Review of Books,* November 1983.

* * *

In her now-classic *The Politics of Reality: Essays in Feminist Theory* (1983), feminist philosopher Marilyn Frye defines feminist "separatism"—an overly political act manifested through personal choice—as "separation of various sorts or modes from men and from institutions, relationships, roles and activities which are male-defined, male-dominated, and operating for the benefit of males and the maintenance of male privilege—this separation," Frye adds, "being initiated or maintained, at will, *by women.*" The complete withdrawal or separation from a patriarchal society, which includes lesbianism as part of that separatist ideology, becomes a means, then, of gaining empowerment and redefining oneself outside of the narrow confines of male-centered judgement. Choosing *not to* becomes non-collaboration, an active rather than passive resistance to woman's oppression.

Indeed, separatism was adopted by many radical feminists during the decades of the late 1960s and early-to-mid-1970s (Shulamith Firestone and Kate Millett, to name but two), and Frye carries their politics forward into the present. The nine essays in *The Politics of Reality* express the theories and aims of radical lesbian feminism as it remains: an effort to redefine the political, social, and economic structure of male oppression directly, rather than by working "within the system" as more mainstream feminism attempts to. Frye's style is lucid; her straightforward analysis of all terms she brings to the table—from "sexism" to "male chauvinism" to "oppression"—makes her work accessible to both non-academics and neo-feminists. Her work is groundbreaking: as Helene V. Wenzel notes, "At a time when professional respectability and security again demand that lesbian feminists in academe keep one foot in the closet while women's studies goes about its projects of 'mainstreaming' and 'integration,' based in large part on 'gentlemen's agreements,' Frye's book is a bold and courageous *tour de force.*"

In "Lesbian Feminist in the Academy," the first section of *Willful Virgin: Essays in Feminism* (1992), Frye continues her examination of patriarchy, this time engaging with the "second-hand" patriarchy of heterosexual academics—both male and female—as it continues to unconsciously marginalize lesbians. Reaffirming her belief that no women engaged in the institutions or relationships that constitute a patriarchal system can be free, she challenges all women to liberate themselves and manifest "women-directed sexuality and eroticism as a way of breaking the grip of men on women's minds and women's bodies ... and as a way of promoting women's firm and reliable bonding against oppression." While women may not all choose to become lesbians, they can at least chose to be at choice in their sexual expression, rather than to play the traditional submissive role. In addition to a collection of book reviews, *Willful Virgin* contains the essay "White Women Feminist," a forthright primer on how to break away the blinders of a Caucasian perspective in viewing a multicultural world.

—Lynn MacGregor

FULLER, (Sarah) Margaret

Also know as the Marchesa d'Ossoli. **Nationality:** American. **Born:** Boston, Massachusetts, 1810. **Education:** Educated by her father. **Family:** Married Marchese Giovanni Angelo Ossoli, c. 1847; one son. **Career:** Teacher at Bronson Alcott's School, Boston, then headmistress at private school, Providence, Rhode Island, until 1938; conducted "conversations" for educated women, Boston, 1839-44; co-founder, with Ralph Waldo Emerson, and editor, *Dial* magazine, 1840-42; moved to New York City, 1844; European correspondent and literary critic, *New York Tribune,* beginning 1844; travelled in Europe and met George Sand, 1846; settled in Italy; worked in hospitals during Italian war for liberation. **Died:** In a shipwreck off Fire Island, New York, 19 July 1850.

Publications

Essays

Summer on the Lakes, in 1843 (travel). Boston, Little Brown, 1844.

Woman in the 19th Century. New York, Greeley & McElrath, 1845; expanded as *Woman in the 19th Century, and Kindred Papers Relating to the Sphere, Condition and Duties of Woman,* edited by Arthur B. Fuller, New York, Sheldon Lamport, 1855.

Papers on Literature and Art. London and New York, Wiley & Putnam, 1846; as *Literature and Art,* with an introduction by Horace Greeley, New York, Fowlers & Wells, 1853.

Life Without and Life Within: or, Reviews, Narratives, Essays, and Poems, edited by Arthur B. Fuller. Boston, Taggard & Chase, and New York, Sheldon, 1859.

Autobiography

Memoirs, edited by Ralph Waldo Emerson, W.H. Channing, and J.F. Clarke. Boston, Phillips Sampson, and London, R. Bentley, 1852.

At Home and Abroad; or, Things and Thoughts in America and Europe, edited by Arthur B. Fuller. Boston, Crosby Nichols, 1856; second edition, 1884.

Other

Love-Letters of Margaret Fuller, 1845-1846, introduction by Julia Ward Howe. New York, Appleton, 1903.

The Writings of Margaret Fuller, edited by Mason Wade. New York, Viking, 1941.

Margaret Fuller, American Romantic: A Selection from Her Writings and Correspondence, edited by Perry Miller. Garden City, New York, Doubleday, 1963.

The Letters of Margaret Fuller, edited by Robert N. Hudspeth. Ithaca, New York, Cornell University Press, 5 vols., 1983; London, Cornell University Press, 1985.

"These Sad but Glorious Days": Dispatches from Europe, 1846-1859, edited by Larry J. Reynolds and Susan Belasco Smith. New Haven, Connecticut, and London, Yale University Press, 1991.

Translator, *Conversations with Goethe in the Last Years of His Life,* by Johann Eckermann. Boston, Hilliard Gray, 1839.

Translator, *Correspondence of Fraulein Günerode and Bettina von Arnim.* Boston, Peabody, 1842.

Translator, *Torquato Tasso* by Johann Wolfgang von Goethe, in *Art, Literature and the Drama,* edited by Arthur B. Fuller. Boston, Roberts, 1889.

*

Bibliography: In *The Writings of Margaret Fuller,* edited by Mason Wade, New York, Viking, 1941; *Margaret Fuller: An Annotated Secondary Bibliography* by Joel Myerson, New York, Burt Franklin, 1977, and his *Margaret Fuller: A Descriptive Bibliography,* Pittsburgh, University of Pittsburgh Press, 1978.

Manuscript Collections: Houghton Library, Harvard University, and Boston Public Library.

Critical Studies: *Margaret Fuller Ossoli* by Thomas Wentworth Higginson, Boston, Houghton Mifflin, 1884; *Brook Farm and Margaret Fuller* by Karl Knorz, New York, Druck von Hermann Bartsch, 1886; *Margaret Fuller and Her Friends; or, 10 Conversations with Margaret Fuller upon the Mythology of the Greeks and Its Expression in Art* by Caroline Wells Healey Dall, Boston, n.p., 1895, New York, Arno Press, 1972; *Margaret Fuller: A Psychological Biography* by Katharine Anthony, New York, Harcourt Brace, 1920; *Margaret Fuller* by Margaret Bell, n.p., 1930; *The Life of Margaret Fuller* by Madeleine B. Stern, New York, Dutton, 1942; *The Roman Years of Margaret Fuller* by Joseph Jay Deiss, New York, Crowell, 1969; *The Woman and the Myth: Margaret Fuller's Life and Writings,* edited by Bell Gale Chevigny, Old Westbury, New York, Feminist Press, 1976; *Margaret Fuller: Bluestocking, Romantic, Revolutionary,* New York, Farrar Straus, 1977; *Margaret Fuller: From Transcendentalism to Revolution* by Paula Blanchard, New York, Delacort, 1978; *In Search of Margaret Fuller* by Abby Slater, New York, Delacorte, 1978; *The Achievement of Margaret Fuller* by Margaret Vanderhaar Allen, University Park, Pennsylvania, Pennsylvania State University Press, 1979; *Critical Essays on Margaret Fuller* compiled by Joel Myerson, Boston, G.K. Hall, 1980; *Margaret Fuller's "Woman in the 19th Century": A Literary Study of Form and Content* by Marie Mitchell Olesen Urbanski, Westport, Connecticut, Greenwood Press, 1980; *Delicate Subjects: Romanticism, Gender, and the Ethics of Understanding* by Julie Ellison, Ithaca, New York, Cornell University Press, 1990; *Margaret Fuller: A Life of Passion and Defiance* by Carolyn Feleppa Balducci, New York, Bantam, 1991; *Margaret Fuller: An American Romantic Life* by Charles Capper, Vol. 1: *The Private Years,* New York and London, Oxford University Press, 1992; *Margaret Fuller: Writing A Woman's Life* by Donna Dickenson, New York, St. Martin's Press, and London, Macmillan, 1993; *Minerva and the Muse* by Joan von Mehren, Amherst, University of Massachusetts Press, 1994; *Liberty, Equality, Sorority: The Origins and Interpretation of American Feminist Thought* by Elizabeth Ann Bartlett, Brooklyn, New York, Carlson, 1994; *Periodical Literature in 19th-Century America* edited by Kenneth M. Price and Susan Belasco Smith, Charlottesville, University Press of Virginia, 1995; *Gender Roles, Literary Authority, and Three American Women Writers* by Theresa Freda Nicolay, New York, Lang, 1995.

* * *

A strong advocate of a woman's right and need to fulfill her potential, Margaret Fuller presented radical views to antebellum American society, which was not yet fully prepared to accept them. The author of the landmark feminist work, *Woman in the 19th Century,* Fuller was also an intellectual, a teacher, an editor, a journalist and a revolutionary. Her published writing only begins to reflect the impact her intellectual exploration had on her contemporaries, both male and female, and her contribution to the development of American feminism cannot be overestimated.

Fuller was the eldest of seven children born to Timothy and Margaret Crane Fuller of Cambridgeport, Massachusetts; disappointed that his first born was a daughter, Timothy Fuller, a lawyer and politician, nevertheless educated her in a manner more typically reserved for male children in that era. Fuller began learning English and Latin grammar at the age of six and later read extensively in classical texts. For a brief period she attended the Cambridge Port School, where boys learned Latin and Greek to prepare for college study, and she later enrolled in Dr. Park's Boston Lyceum for Young Ladies, a rather progressive institution with a focus on rigorous academic challenges. Despite these early advances, Fuller's education was not without obstacles; as a young woman, she faced the confines of the woman's sphere that her male counterparts did not. While they would enter the university, she briefly attended Miss Susan Prescott's Young Ladies Seminary in Groton, Massachusetts, where the academic curriculum was balanced by a focus on developing social accomplishments and provided a more standard education for a young woman in Fuller's circumstances. Fuller found little to challenge her intellectually at the school, and after a somewhat difficult year, she rejected this educational model and returned home to take up a program of independent study guided by her father. She developed a strong interest in the works of Goethe and hoped eventually to write his biography.

When Timothy Fuller died, leaving his family with only limited means of support, Fuller became head of the household for all practical purposes. This meant that she was in need of an income and, as a middle-class white woman, teaching was one of the very few respectable avenues open to her. She first worked with Bronson Alcott, educational reformer, Transcendentalist, and father of author Louisa May Alcott, at his experimental Temple School in Boston. The controversial nature of Alcott's religious views and Socratic teaching methods limited the school's financial success, however, and Fuller eventually left for an uncharacteristically high salary of $1,000 a year as an instructor at Hiram Fuller's (no relation) Greene Street School in Providence. This new position met her needs financially and allowed her more free time to pursue her intellectual interests.

From 1839 to 1844 Fuller ran a series of highly successful lectures, known as her "Conversations," which were immediately popular among educated, reform-minded women and grew increasingly so over the five years of their run. The Conversations began in the winter of 1839 in Boston; as Fuller explained in a letter to Sophia Ripley, the purpose of the venture was "to systematize thought and give precision and clearness in which our sex are so deficient, chiefly, I think, because they have so few inducements to test and classify what they receive. To ascertain what pursuits are best suited to us, in our time and state of society, and how we may make the best use of our means for building up the life of thought upon the life of action." Within this description Fuller identifies her key challenge: to encourage women, who were not traditionally challenged intellectually, to develop their thinking and speaking skills and to examine topics such as art, mythology, or history in intellectual, rather than emotional, terms. The educational tools she had learned from Alcott and put into practice in her own classroom were particularly effective in her Conversations. And Fuller's power of expression, her commanding presence, and her ability to draw her audience into intellectual interaction all worked to make the lecture series highly popular. As biographer Charles Capper notes, one significant feature of the lectures is their contribution to the growth of organized American feminism. The series influenced a group of her contemporaries, including Ednah Dow Littlehale Cheney, Caroline Healey Dall, and Julia Ward Howe, who would contribute to the feminist movement. Capper also claims that the series had a lasting impact, noting that "prominent feminist leaders—like Elizabeth Cady Stanton and Pauline Wright Davis of New York and Lucinda Chandler of Chicago—would later look back on these Conversations as the central precedent and model for many of their clubs and organizations through which they would seek to nurture American women's intellectual autonomy and self-emancipation."

As important as Fuller was to these women, she also befriended some of the most significant male intellectuals of her day. Her friendship with Ralph Waldo Emerson began in 1836, as did her involvement with the local Transcendentalist movement, some participants of which, such as James Freeman Clarke and William Henry Channing, she had known for years. Fuller was also a regular visitor at Brook Farm, George Ripley's communal experiment, begun in 1841. Because of her devotion to Emerson, in July 1840 Fuller became editor, at his urging, of *The Dial: A Magazine for Literature, Philosophy, and Religion,* founded as a vehicle for the writings of the Transcendentalists, who were displeased with the publishing alternatives open to them. The task was difficult, as people failed to honor promises to contribute prose and poetry; transcendentalism, a philosophical system that emphasized individualism and self-reliance, was loosely organized and defined, and therefore not conducive to group projects. This left Fuller with an increasing burden of responsibility; in the October 1841 issue, for example, she wrote 85 of 136 pages herself. Despite her growing exhaustion with the work, she held the position until July

1842, when she resigned and Emerson took up the editorship himself.

As well as providing transcendentalism a vehicle for expression, Fuller's work for *The Dial* was important in another way: it established her, along with Edgar Allan Poe, as one of the two most important literary critics in 19th-century America. As a critic both for *The Dial* and later for Horace Greeley's *New York Tribune,* Fuller was demanding and consistent, advocating a "comprehensive" criticism that balanced an emphasis on what she termed "genius," in a move to educate her fellow readers. She also supported the serious efforts of less talented writers and lesser known women writers such as Caroline Kirkland and Lydia Sigourney, in an effort to promote the formation of a new national literature.

After resigning the editorship of *The Dial,* Fuller was able to re-focus her intellectual energies. The Conversations were so financially successful that she was able to join Clarke and his wife Sarah in the spring of 1843 on a tour of the Great Lakes region, at that time still the frontier. When she returned to New England she collected her documents and observations from the journey (on, among other subjects, how ill-equipped a woman's education made her for a rugged life on the prairie) and supplemented them with research materials from the Harvard College library, where she raised a few eyebrows as the sole female scholar in the exclusively male facility. The result was *Summer on the Lakes, in 1843;* this book gained the attention of Horace Greeley, who appreciated her work on the west, and invited her to join the staff at the *New York Tribune.* He also encouraged Fuller to expand her very successful *Dial* essay, "The Great Lawsuit. Man versus Men. Woman vs. Woman" into a full-length volume, *Woman in the 19th Century,* which appeared in 1845.

Woman in the 19th Century was the first major feminist book by an American woman. The book quickly sold out its first printing of 1,500 copies and a pirated edition of the volume soon appeared in England. Fuller's primary argument revolved around the fact that neither men nor women should be confined into stereotyped gender roles, but that "male and female represent the two sides of the great radical dualism," and that each person should instead develop his/her individual strengths. As for women, she would argue, instead of relegating them to the confining roles of wife and mother, "Let them be sea-captains, if you will." Although in the American tradition of this era the women's sphere was a place where the woman was elevated to a state that demanded veneration for its purity and sanctity, Fuller rejected the limits—and the adulation—of this pedestal and championed instead a broader range of choices for women. "What Woman needs is not as a woman to act or rule, but as a nature to grow, as an intellect to discern, as a soul to live freely and unimpeded, to unfold such powers as were given to us when we left our common home." Believing that women possess the same intuitive intellect as men, she denigrates the unequal education that women of her era received and drew on her own experience to develop her argument. Through the character of Miranda, a female intellectual, she explores a balance of masculine and feminine traits portrayed in famous female role models from literature, myth, history, and contemporary society.

In 1846 Fuller fulfilled a long-held wish to tour Europe; after travelling through Britain and France and meeting some of her literary idols, such as Thomas Carlyle, William Wordsworth, and George Sand, she went to Italy. There her interest in social causes peaked; she became directly involved with the Italian Revolution and through her foreign correspondence offered U.S. readers a sympathetic view of the Italian people's plight. She also developed a romantic relationship with a young Italian nobleman, Giovanni Angelo Ossoli, who was a fellow supporter of the cause; they may have married secretly in 1847 (scholars have debated the fact for years; documentation supporting the marriage is inconclusive, but Fuller referred to herself as Margaret Ossoli); the couple had a committed relationship and a son, Angelo, who was born in 1848. At the same time, Fuller was working on what she considered the best writing she had ever done, a manuscript on the history of the Italian Revolution. After Rome fell and their cause was defeated, Fuller and Ossoli, who had been disinherited by his family due to his political leanings and his relationship with Fuller, decided to travel to America in 1851. Sadly, Fuller never returned home. Within sight of Fire Island, New York, her ship ran aground. Although some travelers survived the wreck, Fuller and her family drowned. Emerson asked Henry David Thoreau to search the shore for her body—but neither the body nor her final manuscript was ever recovered.

In an effort to preserve their friend's reputation, Emerson, Clarke, and Channing edited Fuller's *Memoirs* (1852); their cuts were rather extensive, however, de-emphasizing Fuller's writing and social activism, and downplaying the controversial aspects of her personal life. As a result, Fuller was considered as one of the secondary figures of the transcendentalist group, and much of the early criticism tends to be biographical. Recent scholarship has done much to change this, however. Her works have come back into print through the '80s and '90s, and scholars more fully consider Fuller's formidable intellect and her early contributions to redefining gender expectations. She stands therefore as a pivotal figure in the development of American feminism in the 19th century.

—Deborah Evans

G

GAGE, Matilda Joslyn

Nationality: American **Born:** Cicero, New York, 25 March 1826. **Education:** Clinton Liberal Institute, Clinton, New York, 1841-44. **Family:** Married Henry Gage in 1845; five children. **Career:** Speaker, National Woman's Rights Convention, Syracuse, New York, 1852; contributor to *Revolution* (newspaper of National Woman Suffrage Association), beginning 1869; author of numerous pamphlets on the subject of women's rights, c. 1870-80s; editor, *National Citizen and Ballot Box,* 1878-81; founder, Woman's National Liberal Union, 1890; advisor to Elizabeth Cady Stanton's *Women's Bible,* 1895. **Member:** National Woman Suffrage Association (NWSA; founding member), New York Woman Suffrage Association (vice-president and secretary). **Died:** Greenwich, Connecticut, 18 March 1898.

Publications

Political/Social Theory

"Declaration of Rights of the Women of the United States," with Elizabeth Cady Stanton. Philadelphia, n.p., 1876.

History

A History of Woman Suffrage, Volumes 1-3, with Elizabeth Cady Stanton and Susan B. Anthony. New York, Fowler & Welles, 3 vols., 1881-88.

Woman, Church, and State: A Historical Account of the Status of Woman through the Christian Ages. Chicago, C.H. Kerr, 1893.

*

Manuscript Collections: Library of Congress, Washington, DC; Schlesinger Library, Radcliffe College; Fayetteville Public Library, Fayetteville, New York; Onondaga Historical Society, Syracuse, New York.

Critical Studies: *A Woman of the Century; 1400 Biographical Sketches,* edited by Frances E. Willard and Mary Livermore, Buffalo, New York, C. W. Moulton, 1893.

* * *

Speaking before the National Woman's Rights Convention held in Syracuse, New York, in September of 1852, 26-year-old Matilda Joslyn Gage let her strong feelings be known regarding the obsequious acceptance of male authority expected of women. An ardent advocate of reforms to gain women both educational and political equality, Gage would dedicate much of her life to writing, editing, and speaking out on suffrage and other feminist issues. Indeed, her fight extended past her death in 1898; Gage's headstone reads, "There is a word sweeter than Mother, Home, or Heaven; that word is Liberty."

A founding member of the National Woman Suffrage Association (NWSA) in 1869, Gage would contribute numerous articles to the pages of its house organ, the *Revolution.* She joined NWSA's first advisory council and was elected secretary and vice-president, moving to the office of president of that organization in 1875. A year later, on Independence Day, she and Susan B. Anthony would present the "Declaration of Rights of the Women of the United States" to the nation's vice-president; the document, which had been cowritten by Gage and Elizabeth Cady Stanton, was a radical manifesto demanding that "all the civil and political rights that belong to citizens of the United States, be guaranteed to us and our daughters forever." Leaving the NWSA shortly thereafter, Gage continued to remain active in the organization as editor of its newsletter, *National Citizen and Ballot Box,* as well as serving as president of a local branch, the New York State Woman Suffrage Association.

Working with suffragists Stanton and Anthony, Gage produced the first three parts of the four-volume *History of Woman Suffrage,* which was published from 1881-86. The chapters written by Gage include "Preceding Causes," "Woman's Patriotism in the War," and "Woman, Church and State." The latter chapter reflected a concern that would prove central to Gage's later work: the belief that the religious indoctrination received by women via organized Christianity perpetuated the social inferiority of women. She felt, therefore, that the teachings of the Church were a key obstacle to female equality. Her preoccupation with this belief led her to found the Woman's National Liberal Union in 1890, through which Gage promoted the dissolution of the socially accepted interrelationship between church and government. Three years later, in 1893, she would publish an expansion of her work for *History of Woman Suffrage* entitled *Woman, Church and State.*

Sparking a great deal of public controversy, *Woman, Church and State* began by attacking the accepted view that following the tenants of modern Christianity would improve the lot of women. Using evidence gleaned from contemporary anthropological findings and her study of ancient civilizations, Gage contended that pre-Christian societies valued women's contribution to a much greater extent than did modern ones, and that women were formerly accorded "a much greater degree of respect and power than she has at the present age." Examining historic matriarchal social structures, Goddess worship, the history of witchcraft, and the various legal restrictions placed on overt female sexual activity through the centuries, *Woman, Church and State* would prove a paradigmatic work. In casting a new light on one of the weightiest cornerstones of patriarchy, the work of Matilda Joslyn Gage prefigured much of the critical examination of late 20th-century radical feminists, as well as the Goddess studies of such writers as Merlin Stone and Charlene Spretnak.

—Pamela Kester-Shelton

GARDNER, Miriam. *See* **BRADLEY, Marion Zimmer.**

GEARHART, Sally Miller

Nationality: American. **Born:** Pearisburg, Virginia, 15 April 1931. **Education:** Sweet Briar College, B.A. in English 1952; Bowling Green State University, M.A. in public address 1953; University of Illinois, Ph.D. in theatre 1956; post-doctoral study in philosophy, University of Kansas, 1969-70. **Career:** Associate professor of speech, Stephen F. Austin State College, Nacogdoches, Texas, 1956-60; visiting associate professor of theatre, MacMurray College, Jacksonville, Illinois, 1959-60; associate professor of speech and drama, 1960-70, head of department, 1965-70, Texas Lutheran College, Seguin; instructor of speech communication, 1972-74, assistant professor, then professor of speech, 1972-92, chair, Department of Speech Communication, 1981-84, acting associate dean, School of Humanities, 1984-86, acting coordinator of women studies, 1989-1990, Professor Emerita, beginning 1992, San Francisco State University. Member of board of directors, San Francisco Family Service Agency; cochairperson, Council on Religion and the Homosexual; member, San Francisco Women's Centers; lecturer and consultant, National Sex Forum. Writer, speaker, and activist in San Francisco Bay Area. Contributor to periodicals, including *Ms., Quest: A Feminist Quarterly* and *WomanSpirit.* **Member:** Speech Communication Association of America, American Civil Liberties Union, National Center for Lesbian Rights, People for the Ethical Treatment of Animals. **Address:** P.O. Box 1027, Willits, California 95490, U.S.A.

Publications

Short Stories

The Wanderground: Stories of the Hill Women. Boston, Alyson, 1978; London, Woman's Press, 1979.

Uncollected Short Stories

"The Chipko," in *Love, Struggle and Change,* edited by Irene Zahava. Trumansburg, New York, Crossing Press, 1988

"Flossie's Flashes," in *Lesbian Love Stories,* edited by Irene Zahava. Trumansburg, New York, Crossing Press, 1989.

"Roja and Leopold," in *And a Deer's Ear, Eagle's Song, and Bear's Grace: Animals and Women,* edited by Theresa Corrigan and Stephanie Hoppe. Pittsburgh, Cleis Press, 1990.

"The Pit Bull Opportunity," in *Reality Change: The Global Seth Journal,* summer 1994.

"Small Town Girl Makes Dyke," in *Testimonies: Lesbian Coming Out Stories,* edited by Karen Barber and Sarah Holmes. Boston, Alyson, 1994.

"First Love at Sweet Briar," in *The Next Our Right to Love,* edited by Ginny Vida. New York, Simon & Schuster, 1996.

Essays

"The Miracle of Lesbianism," in *Loving Women/Loving Men: Gay Liberation and the Church,* edited by Gearhart and William Johnson. San Francisco, Glide, 1974.

"If the Mortarboard Fits: Radical Feminism in the Academe," in *Learning Our Way,* edited by Charlotte Bunch. Plainfield, Vermont, Daughters Press, 1977.

"The Womanization of Rhetoric," in *Women Studies International Quarterly,* 2, summer 1979.

"Womanpower: Energy Resourcement," in *Politics of Women's Spirituality,* edited by Charlene Spretnak. Garden City, New York, Doubleday, 1982.

"The Future—If There Is One—Is Female," in *Reweaving the Web of Life: Nonviolence and Women,* edited by Pam McAllister. Philadelphia, New Society, 1982.

"An End to Technology: A Modest Proposal," in *Dea ex Machina: Women and Technology,* edited by Joan Rothschild. N.p., Pergamum Press, 1984.

"Notes from a Recovering Activist," in *Sojourner: The Women's Forum,* September 1995.

Other

Loving Women/Loving Men; Gay Liberation and the Church, with William R. Johnson. San Francisco, Glide, 1974.

A Feminist Tarot, with Susan Rennie. Boston, Alyson, 1975; 4th edition, 1981.

*

Manuscript Collections: University of Oregon Library.

Critical Studies: "The Politics of Transliteration: Lesbian Personal Narratives," in *Signs,* 9(4), summer 1984; "Feminist Novel Approaches to Conflict" by Cheris Kramarae and Jana Kramer, in *Women & Language,* 11(1), winter 1987; *Alien to Femininity: Speculative Fiction and Feminist Theory* by Marleen S. Barr, Westport, Connecticut, Greenwood Press, 1987; *Radical Imagination: Feminist Conceptions of the Future in Ursula Le Guin, Marge Piercy, and Sally Miller Gearhart,* New York, P. Lang, 1991; Re-Membering Men Dismembered in Sally Miller Gearhart's Exofeminist Utopia *The Wanderground*" by Mario Klarer, in *Extrapolation,* 32(4), 1991; "The Politics of Separatism and Lesbian Utopian Fiction" by Sonya Andermahr, in *Between Men—Between Women: Lesbian and Gay Studies,* edited by Lillian Faderman and Larry Gross, New York and Oxford, Columbia University Press, 1992; "Sally Miller Gearhart," in *Feminist Rhetorical Criticism,* by Karen A. Foss, Sonja K. Foss, and Cindy L. Griffin, Sage, 1997.

Sally Miller Gearhart comments:

Here. Let me put my hand on this Bible or this stone or this plow or this mortarboard or on anything else you'd like me to swear by. And let it be duly noted that I've struggled very hard to be a materialist, to believe and to act as if this physical plane—the tangible, tasteable, smellable, seeable, hearable world around us—is the source not only of our physical selves but of our ideas and feelings. Let me swear as well that I've always believed in Evil, in enemies, in the necessity to fight those Satanic forces that would deprive us all of peace, freedom, jobs, justice, and self-determination.

But always there have been dreams and hunches and laughter and play and "the arts," things that whispered different messages: "The source of it all is not solid or measurable or reasonable," they would say. Sometimes they whispered, even as I was confronting him in my brightest feminist armor, "This guy is not the enemy. He, too, is love."

So I've always saved time for writing stories, singing songs, playing parts, dreaming dreams, and dancing dances. And for listening to what animal friends tell me of deeds and essences, of how the stars brush our quiet minds. It is in these things that I've found my most enduring joy.

Now I know that indulging in these joy-full things is our best chance of creating a world of peace, freedom, Jobs, justice, and self-determination, a world where there are no enemies and it's clear that "evil" is only a turning away from love. For whatever I create in that joy, whether it's a feminist utopia or a cautionary tale, can gather energy to itself and become a reality.

What? The biggest change in my thinking? It's happening right now, thanks to a seven-year writing block only very slowly dissolving into a novel. Though I have loved individual people, even individual men, I have never had a high regard for *Homo sapiens* as a species.

In my eyes the human race has been an evolutionary blunder, up far past its bedtime. It needs to fold its tents and silently steal away, leaving the Earth to sigh her relief at our departure as she begins her long but ecstatic recuperation from our presence. But the book that should be saying these things is resisting being written. And the Earth suggests to me that the human enterprise may actually be a crucial part of her life. I think I shall find out pretty soon.

* * *

Sally Gearhart has secured a recognized place among the writers of "classic" feminist utopias. Her name is most often invoked—along with Ursula K. Le Guin and Joanna Russ—as one of the premier writers of feminist science-fiction critiques of patriarchy. Gearhart's reputation rests almost entirely on her collection of interlocking narratives, *The Wanderground: Stories of the Hill Women.* However, her commitment to a feminism that incorporates both lesbian feminist politics and an attention to spirituality can be seen not only in *The Wanderground,* but also in her works *Loving Women/Loving Men: Gay Liberation and the Church* and *A Feminist Tarot.* A self-proclaimed practitioner of "philogyny"—"the love of women"—Gearhart states "my love of myself as a woman and my love of other women motivates all my writing (and my creative existence)." This woman-centered focus is manifested throughout all her works, even to its publication by small feminist and gay/lesbian presses.

In her 1981 introduction to the fourth edition of *A Feminist Tarot,* co-authored with Susan Rennie, Gearhart sets the goal of using Tarot and pre-Christian/non-Christian spiritualities to encourage dialogue between "hardcore politicos" and spiritual feminists. She is committed to a consideration of both the "material" and the "psychic" in feminist projects. As she and Rennie write: "we think of ourselves as political activists *and* as spiritually concerned feminists." The goal of *A Feminist Tarot* is the "recovery of Tarot from traditional masculinist bias" so that it may become "an instrument for women's self-discovery and self-exploration."

This same commitment is brought to life in the *Wanderground* stories. The women who occupy the Hills (the place is called Wanderground) base their lives on spiritual and material connections with other women and with nature. This self-sufficient lesbian separatist community is often referred as an "ecofeminist" utopia. Critics Cheris Kramarae and Jana Kramer see the political organization of the community as an embodiment of the "consciousness-raising groups of the '70s" because the community practices "rotating leadership, limited speaking time for any individual, and the necessity of *lots* of talk." The Wanderground community is held together not by either physical or emotional force, but by the practice of consensus in all community decisions, by an "enfolding" rather than a "penetrating" love, and without forced submission to anyone else's will.

The Wanderground not only offers an alternative to hierarchical social organizations, but also to a linear narrative structure. The stories in the collection are discrete, yet interconnected. By reading them together it is possible to construct a history of the creation of the community, but that construction is left to the reader. The women of Wanderground keep no written history; they store their past through collective memory and orally recounted tales that are ritually re-told in "Remember Rooms." It is in these "rooms" that Gearhart makes her most pointed critiques of patriarchy and its violence against women. Through ritual accountings of rape and violence, the memories of why the Hill women have separated themselves from men is re-lived and re-affirmed. Gearhart promotes a well-guarded separatism from men.

One narrative thread tells of a few women's journey to meet with a small group of men who have rejected masculine values and left The City, a place where such values are still at work objectifying and enslaving women. These men, called Gentles, are portrayed, cautiously, as "men who knew that the outlaw women were the only hope for the earth's survival. Men who, knowing that maleness touched women only with the accumulated hatred of centuries, touched no women at all." And yet, as far as they have both physically and emotionally distanced themselves from their abusive City counterparts, the Gentles fail in the ability to "enfold"; they seem irredeemably wedded to linear-thinking and the use of force. This tentative and mistrustful alliance with the Gentles suggests some possibility for political alliances with gay men, but also, according to Sonya Andermahr, shows *The Wanderground* as "deeply skeptical of men's ability to change for the good."

June Howard, who sees Gearhart as influenced by Mary Daly's *Gyn/Ecology*, critiques *The Wanderground* as positing an "innate polarity between men and women"—a doctrine that might serve to uphold stereotypes of women as nurturers who are innately closer to "nature." This portrayal of maleness as essential—able to be suppressed by some gentle men but never completely reformed—has caused some to label Gearhart an "essentialist" for whom sex and gender determine behavior. Howard cautions us against reading Gearhart's utopian fiction "too literally." Rather, it can also be seen as a compensatory fantasy that attempts to value attributes and skills which have not previously been given a value in a male-dominated society. The problem with this utopian project, according to Howard, is that it leaves women "essentially powerless on any terrain which resembles the present." In other words, escape and separatism are the only answers, given essential male violence against the female and essential female non-aggression.

Gearhart's utopia has also been criticized for its race neutrality. While women of different ethnic and racial backgrounds are depicted, all cultural and ethnic differences have been erased. In Wanderground there exists one uniform culture: women loving women existing in harmony with nature. Nevertheless, Gearhart's utopia, with its driving metaphor of sisterhood and natural balance, is a powerful fantasy that has stimulated a great deal of critical discussion. Sally Gearhart herself, if the open, honest debate depicted in her *Wanderground* is any guide, would most certainly welcome further discourse about both political and spiritual feminist goals.

—Nancy Jesser

GEMS, Pam

Nationality: British. **Born:** New Forest, Dorset, 1 August 1925. **Education:** Manchester University, B.A. (honors) in psychology, 1949. **Military Service:** Women's Royal Naval Service, 1941-45. **Career:** Playwright; research assistant for BBC, London 1950-53. **Agent:** ACTAC, 16 Cadogan Lane, London SW1, England.

Publications

Plays

Betty's Wonderful Christmas (produced London, 1972).
My Warren (produced London, 1973).
After Birthday (produced London, 1973).
The Amiable Courtship of Miz Venus and Wild Bill (produced London, 1973).
Go West, Young Woman (produced London, 1974).
Up in Sweden (produced Liecester, 1975).
The Rivers and Forests, adapted from the play by Marguerite Duras (produced London, 1976).
My Name Is Rosa Luxemburg, adapted from the play by Marianne Auricoste (produced London, 1976).
The Project (produced London, 1976).
Dead Fish (produced Edinburgh, 1976; as *Dusa, Fish, Stas, and Vi,* Hampstead, 1977). New York, Dramatists Play Service, 1977; London, French, 1978.
Guinevere (produced Edinburgh, 1976).
Queen Christina (produced London, 1977). London, St. Luke's Press, 1982.
Franz into April (produced London, 1977).
Piaf (produced London, 1978). London, Amber Lane Press, 1979.
Sandra (produced London, 1979).
Ladybird, Ladybird (produced London, 1979).
Uncle Vanya, adapted from the play by Anton Checkov (produced London, 1979). As *Uncle Vanya: A New Version,* London, Eyre Methuen, 1979.
A Doll's House, adapted from the play by Henrik Ibsen (produced London, 1980).
Sketches in *Variety Night* (produced London, 1982).
The Treat (produced London, 1982).
Aunt Mary (produced London, 1982). In *Plays by Women, Volume Three* edited by Michelene Wandor, London, Methuen, 1984.
The Cherry Orchard, adapted from the play by Anton Checkov (produced Leicester, 1984).
Camille, adapted from *La Dame aux Camelias* by Alexander Dumas (produced London, 1984). London, Samuel French, 1987.
Loving Women (produced London, 1984). In *Three Plays,* London, Penguin, 1985.
Passionaria (produced Newcastle, 1985).
The Danton Affair, adapted from a work by Stanislawa Przybyszewska (produced London, 1986).
The Blue Angel (produced London, 1991).
The Seagull: A New Version, adapted from Anton Checkov's play. (produced London, 1994). London, Nick Hern, 1994.
Deborah's Daughter (produced London, 1995). London, Nick Hern, 1995.

Television Plays: *A Builder by Trade,* Associated Television, 1961; *We Never Do What They Want,* Thames Television, 1979.

Novels

Mrs Frampton. London, Bloomsbury, 1989.
Bon Voyage, Mrs Frampton. London, Bloomsbury, 1990.

*

Theatrical Activities: Actress in *1984* (film), 1984.

Critical Studies: "Pam Gems" in *Stages in the Revolution: Political Theatre in Britain since 1968* by Catherine Itzin, London, Eyre Methuen, 1980; "Pam Gems" in *Carry on Understudies: Theatre and Sexual Politics* by Michelene Wandor, London, Routledge, 1986; "Pam Gems" in *Interviews with Contemporary Women Playwrights* by Kathleen Betsko and Rachel Koenig, New York, Beech Tree, 1987; "Pam Gems: Reinterpreting the Stereotype" in *Modern British Drama 1890-1990* by Christopher Innes, Cambridge, Cambridge University Press, 1990; "The Plays of Pam Gems: Personal/Political/Personal" by Katherine H. Burkman, in *British and Irish Drama since 1960* edited by James Acheson, New York, St. Martin's Press, 1993.

* * *

Pam Gems, one of the handful of British feminist dramatists who has been successful in the mainstream theater, once told an interviewer that "women are particularly well adapted to theatrical writing because theatre is subversive." Raised by a widowed single mother and in the presence of two widowed grandmothers, Gems had early role models for strong womanhood. She served in the Women's Royal Naval Service (WRENS) during World War II and after the war studied psychology at Manchester University. In the 1950s and 1960s she devoted herself to raising her four children but still found time to work for the BBC in London and to write three television dramas, including *A Builder by Trade,* which was broadcast in 1961.

In the early 1970s, when she was in her 40s, Gems became increasingly involved in both the theater and the burgeoning women's movement. She wrote a number of plays for the alternative or "fringe" theater scene, including work for the lunchtime series by the feminist collective, Almost Free. In 1976 she exploded onto the theatrical scene with *Dead Fish,* which played at the Edinburgh Festival and later transferred to London for a very successful run under the new title *Dusa, Fish, Stas, and Vi.* The play concerns four young women living together in a small flat who are, in various ways, oppressed or disappointed by their relationships with men. Their troubles range from anorexia and drugs to economic pressures to children kidnapped by an estranged husband. Despite these hardships and the suicide that ends the play,

Dusa, Fish, Stas, and Vi is ultimately about solidarity and the strength women find in their friendships.

Gems's next success was *Queen Christina,* produced by the Royal Shakespeare Company (RSC) in 1977 as an answer to Greta Garbo's classic, romantic film portrayal of the 17th-century Swedish queen. Raised as a boy to prepare her for leadership of her country, the boisterous and frankly sexual Christina grows up to find herself discontented with the limitations of women's roles. The play makes clear Gems's contention that gender and sexuality are not merely biologically but also socially constructed. *Queen Christina,* which involves a huge cast and has a complex and episodic structure, helped earn Gems a reputation for experimentation. It was also the first play by a woman to be produced at the RSC's Other Place in London.

The playwright's greatest commercial success was *Piaf,* which premiered in 1978, though it had been written several years earlier. This play tells the story of singer Edith Piaf's rise from the slums of Paris to international stardom. Though Piaf becomes wealthy and powerful, she will, as one of her many young lovers reminds her, "never be a lady." The star drinks and uses drugs, curses, seduces younger men, and behaves in a variety of shocking and vulgar ways, debunking the myth of the singer as the tragic "Little Sparrow." In *Piaf,* Gems continued her formal experiments, using short, film-like scenes and integrating songs into a non-linear chronology. It is this sort of playmaking which, says Gems, has led many (usually male) critics to accuse women of writing "non-plays."

Gems continued her prolific output, and 1982 brought production of *The Treat,* a play set in a French brothel in the 1920s, which shocked many critics and audiences. It is a cruel and sexually explicit work dealing with men's objectifying, and consequently abusing women, both physically and emotionally. The same year, *Aunt Mary* showed audiences a different side of Gems's talent. A quirky, campy story of two transvestites and their female friend, the play examines the various types of commitment one person can make to another and celebrates the support and love to be found in such commitment. This interest in relationships surfaced again in *Loving Women,* a revised version of 1976's *The Project,* which was produced in 1984. It is a chronicle of the lives of two women and one man: Crystal, a pretty and traditional hairdresser, and Suzannah, a socialist and feminist radical committed to revolutionary change, both love Frank, a somewhat weak man who is politically minded but still longs for the comforts of a traditional marriage and family. In the end, the women decide—without Frank's help—to share him, and even to live together, whether he joins them or not.

In the 1980s Gems also became involved with the Women's Playhouse Project, a group working to bring theatrical works by women to a larger audience. The group commissioned work by women playwrights and sought to have a theater run at all levels by women, involving men but, according to Gems, "practicing positive discrimination." In addition to this and to her continuous work in writing original plays, Gems has adapted classics of the modern theater and other works. These adaptations include new versions of Anton Checkov's *Uncle Vanya* (1979) and *The Cherry Orchard* (1984), Isben's *A Doll's House* (1980), and *Camille* (1984), based on Alexander Dumas's *La Dame aux Camelias.* Each of these considers the original story from a new angle; in *Camille,* for example, Gems deromanticizes the story and shows the heroine forced to give up her one love for economic considerations and a promise of education for her child. In 1990 Gems completed a stage adaptation of *The Blue Angel,* based on the classic Marlene Dietrich film, and turned her pen to fiction with two novels, 1989's *Mrs Frampton* and *Bon Voyage, Mrs Frampton,* published in 1990.

—Janet E. Gardner

A GENTLEMAN. *See* **SOPHIA.**

GILBERT, Sandra M(ortola), and Susan Gubar

Nationality: Americans.

GILBERT, Sandra M(ortola). Born: Brooklyn, New York, 27 December 1936. **Education:** Cornell University, B.A. (honors) 1957; New York University, M.A. in English 1961; Columbia University, Ph.D. 1968. **Family:** Married Elliot Gilbert in 1957 (died 1991); one son, two daughters. **Career:** Assistant professor of English, California State University, Hayward, 1968-71; associate professor, Indiana University, 1973-75; associate professor, 1975-85, then professor, beginning 1989, University of California, Davis; associate professor, Princeton University, 1985-89. **Awards:** AWP Poetry Series Prize, 1979, for *In the Fourth World;* International Poetry Foundation Charity Randall Award; *Poetry* (New York) Eunice Tietjens Memorial Prize; Guggenheim fellowship; Rockefeller Foundation Humanities fellowship; with Susan Gubar, named *Ms.* Woman of the Year, 1986. **Address:** Department of English, University of California, Davis, California 95616-8581, U.S.A.

GUBAR, Susan. Born: 1944. **Education:** University of Iowa, Ph.D. 1972. **Career:** Instructor in English, University of Illinois, Chicago; associate professor of English, University of Indiana, Bloomington, beginning 1973; co-taught course with Sandra M. Gilbert, 1974. **Awards:** With Gilbert, named *Ms.* Woman of the Year, 1986. **Address:** Department of English, Indiana University, Bloomington, Indiana 47405, U.S.A.

Publications

Literary Criticism

The Madwoman in the Attic: The Woman Writer and the 19th-Century Literary Imagination. New Haven and London, Yale University Press, 1980.

No Man's Land: The Place of the Woman Writer in the 20th Century: The War of the Words [Sexchanges] [Letters from the Front]. New Haven, Yale University Press, 3 vols., 1988-94.

Other

Editors, *Shakespeare's Sisters: Feminist Essays on Woman Poets.* Bloomington and London, Indiana University Press, 1979.
Editors, *The Norton Anthology of Literature by Women: The Tradition in English.* New York, Norton, 1985; revised edition, 1996.
Editors, *The Female Imagination and the Modern Aesthetic.* New York, Gordon & Breach, 1987.

Poetry; by Sandra M. Gilbert

In the Fourth World. University, University of Alabama Press, 1979.
The Summer Kitchen. Woodside, California, Heyeck, 1983.
Emily's Bread. New York, Norton, 1984.
Blood Pressure (includes *The Summer Kitchen*). New York, Norton, 1988.
Ghost Volcano. New York, Norton, 1995.

Other; by Sandra M. Gilbert

Acts of Attention: The Poems of D. H. Lawrence. Ithaca, New York, and London, Cornell University Press, 1972; revised, Carbondale, Southern Illinois University Press, 1990.
Wrongful Death. New York, Norton, 1995.

Editor, *Kate Chopin's "The Awakening" and Selected Stories.* New York, Penguin, 1984.

Other; by Susan Gubar

"'The Blank Page' and the Issues of Female Creativity," in *Critical Inquiry,* 8, 1981.
"Sapphistries," in *Signs: Journal of Women in Culture and Society* (Durham, North Carolina), autumn 1984.

Editor, with Joan Hoff, *For Adult Users Only: The Dilemma of Violent Pornography.* N.p., 1989.

*

Critical Studies: "Women of the Year: Sandra Gilbert and Susan Gubar, Editors, *The Norton Anthology of Literature by Women*" in *Ms.,* January 1986; *Making Feminist History: The Literary Scholarship of Sandra M. Gilbert and Susan Gubar* edited by William E. Cain, New York and London, Garland, 1994.

* * *

North American writers Sandra Gilbert and Susan Gubar have collaborated upon several works that have contributed to the growing body of woman-centered criticism published since the 1970s, the aim of which is to construct a tradition of women's writing. Gilbert is a poet, critic, and professor at the University of California, Davis; Gubar is a professor of English at Indiana University. The two writers met in 1973 at Indiana University, where they team-taught a course in women's literature.

The experience they shared in that course led to the writing of *The Madwoman in the Attic* (1979), a landmark study of women writers in the 19th century. This work was the first attempt to write a literary history of women's writing, and it is prefaced by Gilbert and Gubar's theory of feminist poetics. They use the work of Jane Austen, Mary Shelley, Emily and Charlotte Brontë, and George Eliot to develop a narrative of women's writing that cuts against the grain of the New Criticism that had dominated literary study for three decades. Their theory impels the reader's awareness of the biographical circumstances of the woman author, whose own life may not be in accord with the stories that she tells, the narratives she shapes, or the plots she contrives. *The Madwoman in the Attic* challenged traditional literary history by insisting on its partiality, its exclusions, its failure to acknowledge the foundational work of woman writers. However, the book also came under fierce attack from not only the defenders of the New Criticism, but from other feminist writers who saw the book as writing feminist history from a middle-class, heterosexual, white woman's perspective. According to their critics, Gilbert and Gubar had ignored the experience of working-class and lesbian writers as well as women of color. For better or for worse, *Madwoman* set off a proliferation of responses that point to the diversity of the women's experience as readers and authors.

Gilbert and Gubar's classic study of women writers included a portion on women poets that is reprinted from their *Shakespeare's Sisters: Feminist Essays on Women Poets* (1979). This edited collection, the title of which alludes to Virginia Woolf's "Judith Shakespeare," contains essays on a range of women poets, including Anne Bradstreet, Anne Finch, Elizabeth Barrett Browning, Emily Dickinson, and Adrienne Rich, among others.

The controversy over Gilbert and Gubar's work again reemerged with their collaborated editorial work on *The Norton Anthology of Women's Literature* (1985), the first anthology to represent the variety and continuity of literature that English-speaking women have produced between the 14th century and the present. By putting together a history of women's literature for classroom study, Gilbert and Gubar put in place a tradition of women's writing that has been criticized for being biased and inaccurate. While Gilbert and Gubar did include minority, working-class, commonwealth, and lesbian writers, they only included 13 writers before the 18th century (approximately 96 pages of their 2390-page anthology). The lack of representation of earlier writers fired a debate around Gilbert and Gubar's emphasis on the professional female writer and their neglect of the coterie writer. As a result, there has been significant work done to recuperate and establish the work of women writers before the 18th century.

Gilbert and Gubar, however, have never claimed to be experts on women writers of all centuries: *The Madwoman in the Attic* is subtitled, *The Woman Writer and the 19th-Century Literary Imagination.* Their more recent collaborative effort, *No Man's Land,* is a three-volume feminist history of the modern period. *The War of the Words* (1988), volume 1 of *No Man's Land,* literalizes and starkly dramatizes women's attack on and warfare against patriarchy in society, politics, and literature; in it they include a number of major and minor female and male writers. *Sexchanges* (1989), volume 2 of the series, opens by laying out the sociocultural contexts—imperialism and the suffrage movement in particular—of the late Victorian and modern period. Among the issues addressed are the rise of the New Woman, the late Victorian and early modern crises of masculinity, the femme fatale, turn-of-the century feminist fantasies and utopias, and lesbian writers and relationships. The third volume, *Letters from the Front* (1994), examines primarily works by representative women writers from three periods: those of the modernist period (Millay, H.D., Hurston, and Woolf); those after the World War II (Bishop,

McCullers, Brooks, Lessing, Spark, Rhys); and those of the second wave of the women's movement (Plath, Rich, Atwood, Wakoski, Carter, Morrison, Kingston). These writers are discussed in terms of their access to the cultural unconscious of the modern period, and their desire to examine the historical representation of the traditional middle-class family plot.

Gilbert and Gubar have also written works individually. Gilbert is an accomplished poet with several collections of poetry that are a personal record of her political development as a feminist. She has also published a study of D. H. Lawrence's poetry, *Acts of Attention* (1990). Gubar has published the uncollected essays "Sapphistries" and "'The Blank Page' and the Issues of Female Creativity," as well as edited, with Joan Hoff, *For Adult Users Only: The Dilemma of Violent Pornography* (1989).

However, Sandra M. Gilbert and Susan Gubar continue to be most recognized for their collaborative efforts. Their most significant contributions to scholarship have been the product of working together; as a successful writing team they have demonstrated the importance of collaboration as a feminist enterprise and discourse. In addition to the discussion of literary history that their work has provoked, they have inspired a body of scholarship on feminist collaboration.

—Beth Carole Rosenberg

GILLIGAN, Carol

Nationality: American. **Born:** New York, New York, 28 November 1936. **Education:** Swarthmore College, B.A. (with highest honors) 1958; Radcliffe College, M.A. (with distinction); Harvard University, Ph.D. 1964. **Family:** Married psychiatrist James Frederick Gilligan; three sons. **Career:** Established practice in psychology, beginning 1964; lecturer, beginning 1968, assistant professor, 1971-78, asociate professor, 1978-86, then professor, since 1986, Harvard University, Cambridge, Massachusetts. Laurie Chair in Women's Studies, Rutgers University, 1986-87; Pitt Professor, University of Cambridge, 1986-87; faculty fellow, Bunting Institute, 1982-83; senior research fellow, Spencer Foundation, 1989-93. Co-director, The Company of Women (theatre group), Cambridge, Massachusetts. **Awards:** *Ms.* Woman of the Year award, 1984; Grawemayer Award in Education, 1992; honorary degrees: Swarthmore College, Haverford College, Wesleyan University, Regis College, and Framingham State Teachers College. **Address:** Larsen Hall 503, Harvard University, Cambridge, Massachusetts 02138, U.S.A.

Publications

Political/Social Theory

In a Different Voice: Psychological Theory and Women's Development. Cambridge, Harvard University Press, 1982; with new preface by the author, 1993.

Making Connections: The Relational Worlds of Adolescent Girls at Emma Willard School, with Nona P. Lyons and Trudy J. Hanmer. Cambridge, Harvard University Press, 1991.

Women, Girls, and Psychotherapy: Reframin Resistance. Cambridge, Harvard University Press, 1991.

Meeting at the Crossroads: Women's Psychology and Girls' Development, with Lyn Mikel Brown. Cambridge, Harvard University Press, 1992.

Between Voice and Silence, with Jill McLean Taylor and Amy M. Sullivan. Cambridge, Harvard University Press, 1996.

Other

Editor, with Janie Victoria Ward, Jill McLean Taylor, and Betty Bardige, *Mapping the Moral Domain: A Contribution of Women's Thinking to Psychological Theory and Education.* Cambridge, Harvard University Press, 1989.

*

Critical Studies: *Backlash: The Undeclared War against American Women* by Susan Faludi, New York, Crown, 1991; *Moral Voices, Moral Selves: Carol Gilligan and Feminist Moral Theory* by Susan J. Hekman, University Park, Pennsylvania State Press, 1995.

* * *

The name Carol Gilligan has become almost synonymous with the title of her often-quoted and best-selling 1982 book, *In a Different Voice: Psychological Theory and Women's Development.* Certainly it was Gilligan, a feminist writer, psychologist, and teacher, who, by listening to the diverse ways men and women talk about moral issues, first called attention to an alternate and previously unheard note in psychological theories of human development: the different voice of her title. Countering the "massive cultural blindness" she perceived in regard to the research on women's psychological development, Gilligan began to fill in the blanks: where previously there had been silence or scorn on the subject—women's more relational sense of self is considered a developmental "failure" according to male-defined norms—Gilligan found instead different paradigms that stressed the importance of maintaining relationships in the lives of girls and women.

Listening to women talk about moral issues, Gilligan found a recurrent theme: women made choices based on an "ethics of care" for the people involved rather than on principles of abstract justice, which caused them to do poorly on a hierarchical scale (developed by Gilligan's teacher, Lawrence Kohlberg) measuring moral maturity in terms of rights rather than relationships. The disparity between Gilligan's findings and those of the psychological theorists who used predominantly male models was great, but rather than listen to the theorists, Gilligan chose, "to listen to the women." She has been doing so ever since.

Like the contextual nature of her findings, Gilligan credits "the convergence of my life, the historical moment, and where I happened to be at that particular time," with being able to perceive these other voices. Trained as a clinical psychologist at Harvard, from which she received her Ph.D. in 1964, Gilligan left the field for a time—where the voices she heard about human lives were very "flat"—to become active in politics and the arts. The historical moment that gave rise to her research refers to the civil rights and feminist movements, and the Supreme Court Decision in *Roe v. Wade* to legalize abortion. For Gilligan based part of her moral development study on the difficult relational choices women face when confronting the possibility of abortion. It was also as a mother raising three young children that helped, as Gilligan notes, to make women's "issues very real."

Listening to the women has meant that Gilligan had to develop a new methodology as well. Drawing on her lifelong interest in music and literature—she did her undergraduate work in literature and history at Swarthmore—Gilligan helped develop what she terms a "Listener's Guide," a process that involves listening at least four times for different themes to the stories that women and girls tell about themselves. This process, as Gilligan and Lyn Mikel Brown describe in *Meeting at the Crossroads: Women's Psychology and Girl's Development* (1992), in which they interview adolescent girls from the Laurel School in Cleveland, Ohio, is much more open-ended and narrative-driven: it allows the researchers to both hear a "polyphony" of girl's voices, and to enter into real relationships with the girls they interview.

This emphasis on collaboration and dialogue, particularly between girls and women, is a theme that runs through all of Gilligan's research and writing. A professor at Harvard in the Human Development and Psychology Program, Graduate School of Education, Gilligan was instrumental in founding the Harvard Project on Women's Psychology and Girls' Development. Like the titles of the numerous books she has co-edited and co-authored, many with members of the Harvard group, *Mapping the Moral Domain: A Contribution of Women's Thinking to Psychological Theory and Education* (1988), *Making Connections: The Relational Worlds of Adolescent Girls at the Emma Willard School* (1990), *Women, Girls & Psychotherapy: Reframing Resistance* (1991), and most recently, *Between Voice and Silence: Women and Girls, Race and Relationship* (1996), Gilligan's work strongly advocates, as she states in *Meeting at the Crossroads,* that "resonant relationships between girls and women are crucial for girls' development, for women's psychological health, and also for bringing women's voices fully into the world."

What Gilligan and her colleagues discovered, or uncovered, through listening to the voices of young women on the "crossroads" of adolescence, was that this stage is "a watershed in female development, a time when girls are in danger of drowning or disappearing." While pre-adolescent girls often speak with surety and confidence about themselves and their relationships, these same girls, once crossing the juncture between childhood and adolescence, tend to lose their voices, repeatedly peppering their statements with phrases like "I don't know." In *Meeting at the Crossroads,* Gilligan and Brown discuss the cultural forces at work—such as the pressure to conform to images of the "nice" "perfect" and "selfless" girl—which help cause girls to separate from their feelings, thus trading "real" relationships with themselves and others for false and idealized ones. Adolescence, they found, was a time of great psychological risk.

Gilligan continued to explore the self-silencing of adolescent girls in *Between Voice and Silence,* this time examining the numerous ways ethnicity, race, class, and gender shape both the girls' stories and the interviewers' responses. Furthermore, Gilligan makes clear that listening and responding to these different voices is both crucial for the psychological health of girls and women as well as an overtly political act that could potentially lead to changing racism and sexism in the society at large. Though Gilligan's work has been criticized by feminists and non-feminists—some feminists, like Susan Faludi, see the potential for harmful misapplication in the psychologist's attention to women's difference (which could be construed as an echo of the separate and unequal separate spheres of the Victorians)—there is no doubt that Gilligan's message has been popularly and widely heard. *In a Different Voice* has sold over 600,000 copies and has been translated into nine languages. Gilligan herself continues to work on "freeing women's voices," both in her research/writing life and as the director, with Kristin Linklater, of an all-woman theater company called The Company of Women.

—Cynthia Boufis

GILMAN, Charlotte (Anna) Perkins (Stetson)

Nationality: American. **Born:** Hartford, Connecticut, 3 July 1860. **Family:** Married 1) Walter Stetson in 1884 (divorced), one daughter; 2) George Houghton Gilman in 1900. **Career:** Writer and lecturer. Editor, writer, and publisher, *The Forerunner* (magazine), 1909-16; co-founder, with George Gilman, Charlton Press, New York. Contributor to periodicals, including *Century, Cosmopolitan, Forum, Harper's Bazaar, Nationalist, New England, Times,* and *Worthington's Illustrated.* **Died:** Ended her own life after diagnosis of breast cancer, Pasadena, California, 17 August 1935.

Publications

Novels

The Yellow Wall Paper. Boston, Small Maynard, 1899.
What Diantha Did (first serialized in *The Forerunner,* 1, 1909-10). New York, Charlton, 1910; London, Unwin, 1912.
The Crux (first serialized in *The Forerunner,* 2, 1911). New York, Charlton, 1911.
Moving the Mountain (first serialized in *The Forerunner,* 2, 1911). New York, Charlton, 1911.
Herland (first serialized in *The Forerunner,* 6, 1915). New York, Pantheon, and London, Women's Press, 1979.
Benigna Machiavelli (first serialized in *The Forerunner*). Santa Barbara, California, Bandanna Books, 1994.

Short Stories

The Charlotte Perkins Gilman Reader: The Yellow Wallpaper and Other Fiction, edited by Ann J. Lane. New York, Pantheon, 1980; London, Women's Press, 1981.
The Yellow Wallpaper and Other Writings, edited by Lynne Sharon Schwartz. New York, Bantam, 1989.
Herland and Selected Stories, edited by Barbara H. Solomon. New York, Signet, 1992.
"The Yellow Wall-Paper" and Selected Stories of Charlotte Perkins Gilman, edited by Denise D. Knight. Newark, Delaware, University of Delaware Press, 1994.
The Yellow Wall-Paper and Other Stories, edited by Robert Schulman. Oxford, Oxford University Press, 1995.

Poetry

In This Our World: Poems and Sonnets. Oakland, California, McCombs & Vaughan, 1893; London, Unwin, 1895; enlarged edition, Boston, Small Maynard, 1898.
Suffrage Songs and Verses. New York, Charlton, 1911.

Play

Three Women (one-act), in *Success,* 11, August 1908; in *Images of Women in Literature,* edited by Mary Anne Ferguson. Boston, Houghton Mifflin, 1986.

Political/Social Theory

A Clarion Call to Redeem the Race! Mt. Lebanon, New York, The Shaker Press, 1890.
The Labor Movement. Oakland, California, Alameda County Federation of Trades, 1893.
Women and Economics: A Study of the Economic Relation between Men and Women as a Factor in Social Evolution. Boston, Small Maynard, 1898; London, Putnam, 1899; 3rd edition, Boston, Small Maynard, 1900.
Concerning Children. Boston, Small Maynard, 1900; London, Putnam, 1901.
The Home: Its Work and Influence. New York and London, McClure Phillips, 1903.
Human Work. New York, McClure Phillips, 1904.
The Punishment that Educates. Cooperstown, New York, Crist Scott, 1907.
Women and Social Service. Warren, Ohio, National American Woman Suffrage Association, 1907.
The Man-Made World; or, Our Androcentric Culture (originally published in *The Forerunner,* 1, 1909). New York, Charlton, and London, T.F. Unwin, 1911; 3rd edition, 1914.
Does A Man Support His Wife? with Emmeline Pethick Lawrence. New York, National Woman Suffrage Association, 1915.
His Religion and Hers: A Study of the Faith of Our Fathers and the Work of Our Mothers. New York and London, Century, 1923.

Essays

"Social Darwinism," in *American Journal of Sociology,* 12, March 1907.
"The Waste of Private Housekeeping," in *Annals of the American Academy of Political and Social Science,* 48, July 1913.
"Toward Monogamy," in *Nation,* 118, 11 June 1924.
"Feminism and Social Progress," in *Problems of Civilization,* edited by Baker Brownell. New York, Van Nostrand, 1929.
"Parasitism and Civilized Vice," in *Woman's Coming of Age,* edited by S.D. Schmalhausen and V.F. Calverton. New York, Boni & Liveright, 1931.
Charlotte Perkins Gilman: A Nonfiction Reader, edited by Larry Ceplair. New York, Columbia University Press, 1991.

Autobiography

The Living of Charlotte Perkins Gilman, forward by Zona Gale. New York and London, Appleton-Century, 1935.
The Diaries of Charlotte Perkins Gilman, edited by Denise D. Knight. Charlottesville, Virginia, University Press of Virginia, 2 vols., 1994.

Other

A Journey from Within: The Love Letters of Charlotte Perkins Gilman, 1897-1900, edited by Mary A. Hill. Lewisburg, Pennsylvania, Bucknell University, 1995.
The Forerunner, Volumes 1-7. New York, Charlton, 1909-1916; with an introduction by Madeleine B. Stern, New York, Greenwood Press, 1968.

*

Media Adaptations: *The Yellow Wallpaper* (film), 1978.

Bibliography: *Charlotte Perkins Gilman: A Bibliography* by Gary Scharnhorst, Metuchen, New Jersey, Scarecrow Press, 1985.

Manuscript Collections: Schlesinger Library on the History of Women in America, Radcliffe College.

Critical Studies: "'The Yellow Wallpaper': A Rediscovered 'Realistic' Story" by Beate Schöpp-Schilling, in *American Literary Realism 1870-1910,* 8(3), summer 1975; *Charlotte Perkins Gilman: The Making of a Radical Feminist, 1860-1896* by Mary A. Hill, Philadelphia, Temple University Press, 1980; "The Dissolving Vision: Realism in Jewett, Freeman, and Gilman" by Julia Bader, in *American Realism: New Essays,* edited by Eric J. Sundquist, Baltimore, Johns Hopkins University Press, 1982; *Building Domestic Liberty: Charlotte Perkins Gilman's Architectural Feminism* by Polly Wynn Allen, Amherst, University of Massachusetts Press, 1988; *Feminist Utopias* by Frances Bartkowski, Lincoln, University of Nebraska Press, 1989; *Charlotte Perkins Gilman: The Woman and Her Work* by Sheryl L. Meyering, Ann Arbor, Michigan, UMI Research Press, 1989; *To Herland and Beyond: The Life and Work of Charlotte Perkins Gilman* by Ann J. Lane, New York, Pantheon, 1990; *The Captive Imagination: A Casebook on The Yellow Wallpaper,* edited by Catherine Golden, Old Westbury, New York, Feminist Press, 1992; *Critical Essays on Charlotte Perkins Gillman,* edited by Joanne B. Karpinski, New York, G. K. Hall, 1992.

* * *

Charlotte Perkins Gilman was recognized as one of the foremost intellectuals in the United States womens' rights movement during the late 19th and early 20th centuries. Her key work *Women and Economics* was considered her highest achievement; however, her current reputation rests more on her fiction, including the often-anthologized short story, "The Yellow Wallpaper." Although none of Gilman's works were in print by 1930, a resurgence of interest in her work began in the mid-1960s and continues to this day.

Through her father, Frederick Beecher Perkins, Gilman was related to the prominent Beecher family, which included her aunts Catherine Beecher and Harriet Beecher Stowe, the author of *Uncle Tom's Cabin* (1852), both models for women's social service. After her father left his wife and family when Gilman was very young, she saw little of this intellectual man throughout her life; he provided only sporadic financial support for the family, and his contact with his daughter was limited to infrequent correspondence and suggested reading lists. Her mother, Mary Westcott, struggled with the emotional and financial demands of raising two children alone and starved her children emotionally.

Gilman's early education was irregular, having moved 19 times in 18 years, but she was ambitious to develop an identity that combined a career and public service with a private life. She attended the Rhode Island School of Design, worked as an artist and briefly as a governess to earn her way, and was determined to remain unmarried. At age 24, however, Gilman married young artist Charles Walter Stetson after a long courtship; their only daughter, Katherine, was born ten months later. Friction began between the pair almost immediately over the inequality of the roles of husband and wife, and following their daughter's birth, Gilman suffered from a severe depression. She consulted famed neurologist S. Weir Mitchell and undertook his well-known "rest cure," which included relaxation and seclusion for the patient, overfeeding and massage, all of which helped to bring an adult women to a coddled, childlike state. After a month Gilman left his treatment, with the admonition never to paint or write again, and to have, as she would later recall in *The Living of Charlotte Perkins Gilman,* "but two hours' intellectual life a day." This regimen only exacerbated Gilman's condition; she soon stopped the treatment and formally separated from her husband. She then moved to California, where she shared a home with her lifetime friend Grace Ellery Channing and became involved in the Nationalist movement. Channing would later marry Stetson—with Gilman's blessing—and play an active role in raising Gilman's daughter.

During this period Gilman gave attention to her writing. She had always been a prolific correspondent and kept a series of diaries and journals, but her first national recognition as writer came with the publication of her early satirical poetry. "Similar Cases" appeared in the *Nationalist* in April 1890. Gilman credits this as the starting point of her literary reputation and her popularity as a lecturer.

Gilman's early work is important because most recent criticism has tended toward reexamining her literary output. Without question, her best known story, which is atypical of her canon, is "The Yellow Wall-Paper," also written in 1890. William Dean Howells, who had noticed Gilman's poetry, brought the story to *Atlantic Monthly* editor Horace E. Scuddler's attention. Scudder refused to print the story, writing to Gilman that "I could not forgive myself if I had made others as miserable as I have made myself"; she could not find a publisher until two years later, when it was printed in *New England* magazine. Gilman claimed "the real purpose of the story was to reach Dr. S. Weir Mitchell and convince him of the error of his ways." She sent him a copy and later, learning through friends that he had modified his treatments since its publication, remarked that "If that is a fact, I have not lived in vain." "The Yellow Wall-Paper" is indeed grim, tracing the first-person narrator's descent into madness under a regimen of treatment much like Dr. Mitchell's; Gilman emphasizes her heroine's obsession with the yellow wallpaper in her room and the figures she sees trapped inside it. Early critics regarded the heroine with a horror more typically associated with Poe's protagonists. The story is significant as a criticism of the oppression women faced in their restrictive late-19th-century society; however, not until the Feminist Press reprinted the text in 1973 with Elaine Hedges's explication did critics begin to examine the story as a feminist commentary on sexual politics. Subsequent readings of the story range from autobiographical analysis to consideration of the literary craft to psychoanalytic interpretations.

In 1893 Gilman published a small volume of poetry, *In This Our World;* as contemporary critic Henry Austin noted, the cover of this work, which Gilman designed, is based on British feminist Olive Schreiner's *Three Dreams in a Desert* (*The Bookman,* June 1895). The poems outline Gilman's economic and social views, admonishing women to reconsider their situations. In one poem, "Young Wife," she writes:

Are you content with work? To toil alone,
To clean things dirty and to soil things clean,
To be a kitchen maid—be called a Queen—
Queen of a cook-stove throne?

Reviews of this volume were positive, but public opinion of Gilman, who had left her daughter for long periods to pursue a career, was hostile; she was referred to in the press as an "Unnatural Mother," a phrase she would take later as the title of one of her short stories.

Despite the negative press, Gilman continued her work and achieved the height of her fame with the publication of *Woman and Economics* (1898), a social treatise based on the arguments of Darwinian and the work of American sociologist Lester Frank Ward. Gilman's work follows the tradition of Mary Wollstonecraft's *A Vindication of the Rights of Women* (1792) and Margaret Fuller's *Woman in the 19th Century* (1845) in its consideration of women's roles and responsibilities. Although associated with feminists of her day, Gilman preferred to refer to herself as a "sociologist" and distanced herself from the women's suffrage movement, claiming in *The Living* that "the political equality demanded by the suffragists was not enough to give real freedom." As she outlines in *Woman and Economics,* this real freedom, and any genuine improvement in society, could come only through recognizing and reforming the social structure in which women, because of their economic dependence on men, do not make a full contribution to social progress. The work firmly established her reputation as a social theorist in England and in the United States, where it was used as a textbook in the 1920s.

During this time Gilman consulted her cousin George Houghton Gilman on a legal matter; they began an intimate correspondence and were married on 11 June, 1900. She continued producing nonfiction works, including *Concerning Children, The Home,* and *Human Work,* all of which expand on themes identified in *Woman and Economics:* day care, the weaknesses of the single-family home, and the necessity of work.

After years of writing for other editors, Gilman decided to publish a periodical of her own that would afford her some independence and a chance to speak her mind free of restrictions. *The Forerunner* (1909-1916) was indeed a remarkable achievement. During the seven years of its run, Gilman wrote, edited, and published the magazine virtually on her own; her essays, commentary, short fiction, poetry, and several serialized novels appeared in its pages before Gilman stopped production because of lack of readership. Gilman published some of the serialized works, *The Man-Made World, What Diantha Did, The Crux,* and *Moving the Mountain* with the Charlton Press, which she formed with her husband; other novels, such as *Herland* and *Benigna Machiavelli,* a female coming-of-age tale, have only recently been reprinted.

Unlike "The Yellow Wall-Paper," much of the fiction in *The Forerunner* is optimistic in tone and best characterized as more concerned with a reformist agenda than with literary craft. Of primary interest is the feminist utopian novel, *Herland* (1915). In *Herland* Gilman fictionalizes her social program and demonstrates that the utopian novel suits her literary agenda. As Ann Lane notes in her introduction to the novel, the form allows Gilman to appeal to a broad audience "and at the same time make socialism a legitimate, appealing and reasonable idea."

In the text, three male explorers discover a society composed entirely of females that has become so self-sufficient that it reproduces parthogenically—effectively recreating the "virgin birth."

The tale is told by one of the male travelers, whose views of women fall between his companions'—one of whom idealizes women, the other who objectifies them. The men see a world in which communal living, standardized practical fashions, and labor for each member according to her skills contribute to the maintenance of a non-violent, progressive order. Expecting that any "civilized" society could not function without a male presence, the travelers find their attitudes about gender, as well as most social institutions, challenged when they learn that the inhabitants construct their identity as "people," not around preconceived qualities of femininity or masculinity—and they view their visitors in the same light. According to Gilman, reform can come only when people are willing to be open-minded and reject established definitions.

After the demise of *The Forerunner,* Gilman continued a productive public and personal life, publishing several works and appearing frequently on the lecture circuit. Her most significant later work is the autobiography titled *The Living of Charlotte Perkins Gilman.* At the age of 75 Gilman was diagnosed with inoperable breast cancer; in a characteristic act, she approached death on her own terms and died of a self-administered overdose of chloroform on 17 August 1935. In a letter explaining this final decision, Gilman wrote: "When one is assured of unavoidable and imminent death, it is the simplest of human rights to choose a quick and easy death in place of a slow and horrible one."

Continuing interest in Gilman's works stems form its unquestionable relevance to issues facing women today. Her vision of the need for social reform remains pertinent, and much of what she said resonates within the attitudes and actions of the Women's Movement in the later 20th century.

—Deborah Evans

GODWIN, Wollstonecraft Mary. *See* **WOLLSTONECRAFT, Mary.**

GOLDMAN, Emma

Also known as Red Emma. **Nationality:** Russian. **Born:** Kovno, Lithuania, 27 June 1869; immigrated to United States 1886. **Education:** Attended *Realschule,* Königsberg, Prussia; studied midwifery, Allgemeines Krankenhause, Vienna, Austria, 1885-96. **Family:** Married 1) Jacob Kershner in 1887 (divorced, remarried, then divorced); 2) James Colton in 1925. **Career:** Worked at garment factories in St. Petersburg, Russia, 1881-85, and Rochester, New York, 1886; moved to New York City and became involved in anarchist movement led by Johann Most and Alexander Berkman, 1889; aided her lover, Berkman, in the attempted assassination of industrialist Henry Clay Frick, 1892; convicted of inciting a riot and served 12 months in Blackwell's Island prison, 1893-84; toured Europe, 1885-89; worked as a nurse, 1900; lectured widely on birth control and free speech; founder and coeditor, with Berkman, *Mother Earth* 1903-17; convicted of obstructing draft and served two years in Missouri State Prison, 1917-19; deported to Russia, 1919; became disenchanted with new Soviet regime and moved to Riga, Latvia, 1921, England, 1924-26, and St. Tropez, France, c. 1931; visited United States, 1934; served as advocate of anti-Franco movement during Spanish Civil War; made lecture tour of Canada, 1940. **Died:** Toronto, Canada, 14 May 1940.

PUBLICATIONS

Political/Social Theory

Patriotism: A Menace to Liberty. New York, Mother Earth, 1908.
The White Slave Traffic. New York, Mother Earth, 1909.
Anarchism and Other Essays. New York, Mother Earth, 1910; London, A. C. Fifeld, 1911; revised, 1917.
My Disillusionment with Russia. Garden City, New York, Doubleday, and London, Heinemann, 1923.
My Further Disillusionment with Russia. Garden City, New York, Doubleday, 1924.
The Traffic in Women, and Other Essays of Feminism, with a biography by Alix Kates Shulman. New York, Times Change Press, 1970.
Red Emma Speaks: Selected Writings and Speeches, introduction by Alix Kates Shulman. London, Wildwood House, 1979.
Vision on Fire: Emma Goldman on the Spanish Revolution, edited by David Porter. New Paltz, New York, Commonground Press, 1983.

Literary Criticism

The Social Significance of the Modern Drama (lectures). Boston, R. G. Badger, 1914.

Autobiography

Living My Life. New York, Knopf, 1931; London, Duckworth, 1932; with introduction by Sheila Rowbotham, London, Pluto, 1987.

Other

Nowhere at Home: Letters from Exile of Emma Goldman and Alexander Berkman, edited by Richard and Anna Maria Drinnon, New York, Schocken, 1975.

*

Media Adaptations: *Emma Goldman* (film), Toronto, Avco Embassy, 1975.

Bibliography: In *Rebel in Paradise: A Biography of Emma Goldman* by Richard Drinnon, Chicago, University of Chicago Press, 1961.

Manuscript Collections: Labadie Collection, University of Michigan Library; New York Public Library; Yale University Library; University of Illinois Library, Chicago Circle; Schlesinger Library, Radcliffe College; International Institute for Social History,

Amsterdam; Emma Goldman Web site at http://sunsite.berkeley.edu/Goldman/.

Critical Studies: "What Is There in Anarchy for Woman?" (interview), in *St. Louis Post Dispatch Sunday Magazine,* 24 October 1897; *Emma Goldman: A Challenging Rebel* by Joseph Ishill, Berkeley Heights, New Jersey, Oriole Press, 1957; *Rebel in Paradise: A Biography of Emma Goldman* by Richard Drinnon, Chicago, University of Chicago Press, 1961; *To the Barricades: The Anarchist Life of Emma Goldman* by Alix Kates Shulman, New York, Crowell, 1971; *Love, Anarchy, and Emma Goldman* by Candace Falk, New York, Holt, 1984, revised, New Brunswick, New Jersey, Rutgers University Press, 1990; *Emma Goldman: An Intimate Life* by Alice Wexler, New York, Pantheon, 1984, as *Emma Goldman in America,* Boston, Beacon Press, 1984; *Emma Goldman* by Martha Solomon, Boston, Twayne, n.d.; *Emma Goldman: American Individualist* by John Chalberg, New York, HarperCollins, 1991; *Emma Goldman and the American Left: Nowhere at Home* by Marian J. Morton, New York, Toronto, and London, Twayne, 1992; *Emma Goldman: Sexuality and the Impurity of the State* by Bonnie Haaland, Montreal, Black Rose Books, 1993.

* * *

Called "Red Emma" and a "most dangerous woman," spirited and rebellious Emma Goldman stood for freedom and the individual. Impacted by the events of the Haymarket bombing in Chicago and the martyrdom of immigrant radicals shortly after her arrival in America from Russia in 1886, Goldman became a vocal anarchist. Throughout her thirty-year residency in the United States, she crossed the country, energetically addressing issues of concern—especially those addressing women's rights. Despite police interference and occasional arrest, Goldman attracted large audiences as she advocated birth control, elevated the position of the "working girl," and criticized the deplorable economic situation that, she believed, forced many young women into prostitution.

Goldman's birth in Russia was neither welcomed nor happy. Her mother, trapped in an arranged marriage shortly after being widowed, feared pregnancy; with two daughters from her first marriage, she did not want the additional strain of more children. Goldman's father, disappointed by the birth of a girl, would physically and verbally abuse Emma throughout her growing years. A sad and isolated child, Goldman sought the individual within herself; she would emerge from her tragic beginnings to fight repression and encourage women to stop being victims of their own female circumstances.

During her childhood, Goldman secretly read many novels and radical political books. She idolized revolutionary women and Russian nihilists and believed that she, too, could stop the injustices in her native country. Unable to attend medical school and facing an arranged marriage herself, Goldman fled Russia for the United States, where her radical ideology would crystallize.

Her years spent in her adopted country would be newsworthy ones: arrested for agitation in 1893, accused of involvement in President McKinley's assassination, forced underground and deported, Goldman became almost notorious. Goldman would express her anarchist viewpoints in *Mother Earth,* a journal she founded in 1903 and edited with her lover, the anarchist Alexander Berkman. The journal featured established authors such as Ibsen and Whitman and introduced new artists and literary talents as well. Publication would cease in 1917 when its editorial board—Goldman and Berkman—was arrested for opposing the conscription of young men during World War I. After serving her two-year sentence Goldman would be exiled; although she longed to return to the United States she would only be permitted a three-month stay in 1934 for a lecture tour. Goldman's anarchist stance was misunderstood by many; in *My Disillusionment with Russia* she claimed that her vision of anarchy was constructive rather than destructive, as she was so perceived.

Anarchy without violence and the drive to achieve individual rights for women were related ideologies, according to Goldman, who pursued both vigorously. Within her writings she maintained that women needed to loosen the bonds which held them psychologically. Four feminist essays in *Anarchism and Other Essays*—"Marriage and Love," "Woman Suffrage," "The Traffic in Women," and "The Tragedy of Woman's Emancipation"—stressed this theme, describing the constant victimization that women endured. Goldman wrote in a direct style, confrontational rather than mollifying, and she ended each essay with a brief but emotionally focused finale.

Although twice married, Goldman denounced the institution of marriage as destructive to woman's identity. In an interview for the *St. Louis Post Dispatch* she stated that when married women lost their names they became the "servant, the mistress, and the slave of both husband and children." Instead of a married state, Goldman promoted free love. To her, free love referred not to indiscriminate sex but to mutuality in a relationship. Her essay "Marriage and Love" related that women should not look to marriage as an ultimate goal but should seek free love in liberating themselves and finding their individuality. Because she felt that love was "the strongest and deepest element in all life," Goldman believed that a relationship should not be one of dependency, but rather of separate and equal existence.

Goldman realized that free love required that women have access to birth control to prevent pregnancy, thus avoid the dangers of abortion. Skilled as both a nurse and midwife, she had seen first-hand how women's health was endangered by frequent pregnancies. Goldman vehemently crusaded on behalf of women's right to dictate what happened to their own bodies, writing the pamphlet, *Why and How the Poor Should Not Have So Many Children.* She was jailed for two weeks after distributing contraception information alongside birth-control advocate Margaret Sanger in 1915. The uncompromising efforts of both Goldman and Sanger would pave the way for the free access by women to information on contraception methods, as well as the nationwide formation of birth control clinics.

In her *The Traffic in Women and Other Essays on Feminism,* Goldman took on the issue of prostitution, stating that a correlation existed between a woman's substandard wages and her need to exchange her sexual favors for money. In fact, argued Goldman, economic necessity was not only the motive behind prostitution; it was the basis of marriage. Contending that women had not yet fully realized their oppressed condition, she noted that they erroneously imagined that full rights would be gained by winning the vote.

The essay "Woman Suffrage" exemplified Goldman's belief that even with the power to vote, women would still be still bound to oppression and the home, where the "life-energy of woman" was sapped. Concerned with the plight of women workers, Goldman did not dispute that women should be eligible to vote but she did not agree that it gave women true emancipation. "The Tragedy of Woman's Emancipation" portrayed women's right to vote as superficial because, while it gave women equal opportunity to compete professionally with men, they were ill-equipped for the task because they had not been trained to be competitive. Goldman also disagreed with several of her prominent feminist contemporaries who had a puritanical view of sex, encouraged chastity, and banished men from their existence. Goldman dismissed this "New Woman" and although she agreed that a woman should not be treated as a sex commodity she believed that women should not repress their healthy sexual instincts, which had too few outlets in civilized society.

Emma Goldman was a woman of restless ambition who attempted to meld the forces of the free individual with a cooperative spirit. A compelling orator, she delivered her powerful message to audiences around the world. Yet, unhappily, no recordings of Goldman's spirited speeches have survived. Her legacy remains in essays, in her autobiography *Living My Life,* in memoirs, and in letters that provide modern readers with a clear picture of the woman who sought justice in a unified world and demanded personal liberty for men and women equally.

—Marilyn Elizabeth Perry

GOMEZ, Jewelle

Nationality: American. **Born:** Boston, Massachusetts, 11 September 1948. **Education:** Northeastern University, B.A. 1971; Columbia University School of Journalism, M.S. 1973. **Family:** Companion of Diane Sabin, beginning 1992. **Career:** Worked in production, WGBH-TV, Boston, for *Say Brother,* 1968-71; WNET-NY, New York, New York, 1971-73; and for the Children's Television Workshop, New York, 1970s; worked in various capacities, including stage manager, at Off-Broadway theatres, 1975-80; lecturer in women's studies and English, Hunter College, 1989-90; director of Literature Program, New York State Council on the Arts, 1989-93. Founding board member, Gay and Lesbian Alliance against Defamation (GLAAD); member of Feminist Anti-Censorship Taskforce (FACT); member of board of advisors, Cornell University Human Sexuality Archives, National Center for Lesbian Rights, and *Multi-Cultural Review* magazine. Contributor to periodicals, including *Black Scholar, Conditions, Outlook,* and *Ms.* **Awards:** Ford Foundation fellowship, 1973; Beards Fund award for fiction, 1985; Barbara Deming/Money for Women Award for fiction, 1990; Lambda Literary awards for fiction and science fiction, 1991, for *The Gilda Stories.* **Agent:** Frances Goldin, 305 East 11th Street, New York, New York 10003, U.S.A.

Publications

Poetry

The Lipstick Papers. Jersey City, New Jersey, Grace Publications, 1980.

Flamingoes and Bears. Jersey City, New Jersey, Grace Publications, 1986.

Novel

The Gilda Stories. Ithaca, New York, Firebrand Books, 1991.

Essays

"A Celebration of Butch-Femme Identities in the Lesbian Community," in *The Persistent Desire: A Butch-Femme Reader,* edited by Joan Nestle. Boston, Alyson Publications, 1992.

Forty-three Septembers. Ithaca, New York, Firebrand Books, 1993.

Over the Rainbow: Lesbian and Gay Politics in America since Stonewall, with others, edited by David Deitcher. N.p., Boxtree, 1995.

*

Critical Studies: "Bold Types" by Barbara Findlen, in *Ms.,* July/August 1991; "No Either/Or" by Victoria Brownworth, in *Outweek,* 22 May 1991; "Jewelle Gomez and Minnie Bruce Pratt" by Jane Troxell, in *Washington Blade,* 8 November 1991; interview in *Out/Look,* spring 1992; "A Novelist's Sense of Family" by Esther Ivrem, in *New York Newsday,* 28 July 1992.

* * *

The work of Jewelle Gomez is a mixture of politics and fancy. Noted for her popular novel *The Gilda Papers,* she is also known for her lesbian-feminist activism, as well as for her work in support of multiculturalism, due to her own roots in both the African American and Native American communities.

Born in Boston in 1948, Gomez obtained her M.A. from the Columbia School of Journalism in 1973. She worked for the Boston-based series *Say Brother,* one of the first weekly African American television programs in the United States, from 1968 to 1971. By the mid-1970s she was assisting the production of New York's award-winning Children's Television Workshop. An instructor in both creative writing and Women's Studies, Gomez also served as director of the Literature Program of the New York State Council on the Arts from 1989 to 1993. Her social activism has also been a prominent part of her life: Gomez is a member of the Feminist Anti-Censorship Taskforce, which works to provide a feminist, sex-positive analysis of anti-pornography campaigns, as well as being a founding board member of GLAAD (Gay and Lesbian Alliance against Defamation). While her poetry, which includes *The Lipstick Papers* (1980) and *Flamingoes and Bears* (1986), celebrates a lesbian lifestyle, the essays included in *Forty-three Septembers* (1993), as well as her contribution to *Over the Rainbow* (1995), attempt to come to terms with how lesbians and feminists, as well as gay men, can articulate and understand erotic and political difference.

Though seductive as a work of popular fiction, Gomez's 1991 novel *The Gilda Stories* is yet another expression of her activism. Taking place from 1850 to 2050, the novel features a female vampire who travels through time and across cultures in an effort to understand her purpose in being. Revamping both the horror story and the picaresque novel tradition to suit herself, Gomez frames her lesbian-feminist politics within literary genres that have been traditionally male. *The Gilda Stories* is not only an entertaining and imaginative novel, is fun to read. Through Gilda's many incarnations within the novel—beginning as a runaway slave in the antebellum south, she is transformed variously into a Native American, a lesbian, and a feminist; her travels taking her from California, Missouri, New England, and the Big Apple to a futuristic New England—Gomez makes an implicit statement about traditional writing; that, by excluding women, gays, and people of color, it itself becomes confined, trapped by its own exclusivity.

—Lynn MacGregor

GORDON, (Irene) Linda

Nationality: American. **Born:** Chicago, Illinois, 19 January 1940. **Education:** Swarthmore College, B.A. (magna cum laude) 1961; Yale University, M.A. in Russian studies 1962, M.A. in history 1963, Ph.D. (with distinction) in history 1970. **Family:** Married Allen Hunter; one daughter. **Career:** Instructor, 1968-69, assistant professor, 1970-75, associate professor 1975-80, then professor of history, 1981-84, University of Massachusetts, Boston; professor of history, 1984-90, Florence Kelly Professor of History, beginning 1990, and Vilas Distinguished Research Professor, beginning 1993, University of Wisconsin, Madison. Scholar-in-residence, Stanford University, 1979, and Dickinson College, 1987; visiting professor, University of Amsterdam, 1984; Bird Memorial lecturer, University of Maine, 1986; invited residency, Bellagio Center, Italy, 1992, and Stanford Center for Advanced Study. Member: advisory board, Margaret Sanger Papers Project, New York University and Smith College; Scholarly Advisory Council, Indiana University Center on Philanthropy; review panel, National Endowment of Humanities Research Grants, 1982; advisory committee, Project on Reproductive Laws for the 1990s, American Civil Liberties Union and Rutgers University School of Law, 1985-87; Advisory Council on Violence against Women, U.S. Department of Justice, beginning 1995. Consultant, Curriculum Development Project for Working Women, 1979-84, Schlesinger Library Project for Collection and Preservation of Women's Organizational Records, beginning 1979, Canadian Broadcasting Corporation (CBC), 1983, Wisconsin Coalition on Sexual Assault, 1987; consultant and historian on numerous films, television series, and documentaries, International Reference Group on Development of Western Welfare States. Member of editorial board, *Journal of American History,* 1994-97, *Journal of Policy History,* 1994-97, *Contemporary Sociology,* 1994-97, *American Historical Review,* 1990-93, *Signs, Feminist Studies, Journal of Women's History, Contention,* and *Gender and History.* Contributor of articles to periodicals, including *Clarion, Dissent, Harper's, Ms., Nation,* and *Radical America.* **Awards:** National Endowment for Humanities fellow, 1979; National Institute of Mental Health Research grant, 1979-82; American Council of Learned Societies travel grant, 1980; Antonovych Prize, 1983, for *Cossack Rebellions;* Guggenheim fellowship, 1983-84; Radcliffe College Bunting Institute fellow, 1983-84; Ford Foundation fellowship, 1985; Guggenheim fellow, 1987; American Historical Association Joan Kelly Award and Wisconsin Librarian's Association Award, both 1988, both for *Heroes of Their Own Lives,* 1988; American Philosophical Society research award, 1988-89; elected honorary member of Simon Fraser University Feminist Institute for Studies on Law and Society, 1991; Berkshire Prize, Gustavus Myers Award, and Wisconsin Library Association outstanding book designation, all 1995, all for *Pitied but Not Entitled.* **Member:** Berkshire Conference on Women in History (program committee, 1974, 1976), Social Science History Association, American Historical Association (member of program committee, 1981), Organization of American Historians (member of nominating committee, 1988-90, executive board, 1991-94, lecturer, beginning 1991, minority historians committee, 1992-94, Turner Prize committee, 1994-95), Institute for Research on Poverty (executive committee, beginning 1990), Society of American Historians, (beginning 1995). **Address:** Department of History, 3211 Humanities Building, University of Wisconsin—Madison, 455 North Park St., Madison, Wisconsin 53706-1483, U.S.A.

Publications

History

Woman's Body, Woman's Right: A Social History of Birth Control in America. New York, Viking, 1976; Penguin, 1977; revised edition, 1990.
Cossack Rebellions: Social Turmoil in the 16th-Century Ukraine. New York, State University of New York Press, 1983.
Heroes of their Own Lives: The Politics and History of Family Violence, Boston 1880-1960. New York, Viking, 1988; London, Virago, 1989.
Pitied but Not Entitled: Single Mothers and the History of Welfare 1890-1935. New York, Free Press, 1994.

Uncollected Essays

"Voluntary Motherhood," in *Feminist Studies,* 1(3-4), winter/spring 1973-74.
"The Struggle for Reproductive Freedom: Three Stages of Feminism," in *Capitalist Patriarchy and the Case for Socialist Feminism,* edited by Zillah R. Eisenstein. New York, Monthly Review Press, 1978.
"What Should Women's Historians Do: Politics, Social Theory, and Women's History," in *Marxist Perspectives,* 3, fall 1978.
"Birth Control and Social Revolution," in *A Heritage of Her Own,* edited by Nancy Cott and Elizabeth Pleck. New York, Simon & Schuster, 1979.
What Is Women's History?" in *History Today,* 35, June 1985.
"Feminism and Social Control: The Case of Child Abuse and Neglect," in *What Is Feminism?* edited by Juliet Mitchell and Ann Oakley. London, Basil Blackwell, and New York, Pantheon, 1987.
"Single Parenthood in 1900," in *Journal of Family History,* 16(2), 1991.
"On Difference," in *Genders,* spring 1991.
"A Right Not to Be Beaten: The Agency of Battered Women," in *Gendered Domains: Rethinking Public and Private in Women's History,* edited by Dorothy O. Helly and Susan M. Reverby. Ithaca, New York, Cornell University Press, 1992.
"A Genealogy of 'Dependency': Tracing a Key Word of the U.S. Welfare State," in *Signs: A Journal of Women in Culture and Society,* winter 1993.

Other

Editor, with Rosalyn Baxandall and Susan Reverby, *America's Working Women: A Documentary History.* New York, Random House, 1976.

Editor, *Maternity: Letters from Working Women.* New York, Norton, 1979.

Editor, *Women and the State: Historical and Theoretical Essays.* Madison, University of Wisconsin Press, 1991.

*

Critical Studies: Review of *Woman's Body, Woman's Right* by Edward Shorter, in *Journal of Social History,* 2, 1977-78; interview with Carol Lasser, in *Visions of History: Conversations with Radical Historians,* edited by Henry Abelove, Betsy Blackmar, Dimock, and others, New York, Pantheon, 1984.

* * *

Historian Linda Gordon has been a leading feminist scholar since the early 1970s. Gordon's work has been pathbreaking, not only in its inclusion of women's history or the ways in which gender centrally impacts society, but also due to its author's painstaking, detailed research, which captures the voices of those she studies in their roles as both subordinates and resistors. One of Gordon's main achievements as a Marxist historian has been to accord "gender" a status within historical discussion equivalent to that which it has achieved through the centuries in everyday life.

Gordon's world view has been largely shaped by her leftist Jewish immigrant parents, although for a time she struggled to assert her identity in opposition to their standpoint. She began her career studying Russia at Yale University, became disillusioned with the extreme politicization of the field of Russian history after the onset of the Cold War, and left academia for a short time, returning to complete her dissertation on rebellions in 16th-century Ukraine in 1983. She took a position at the University of Massachusetts, Boston, in the late 1960s, and was almost immediately drawn into the women's liberation movement. "It was an instant transformation," she later told Carol Lasser in an interview. "The moment I heard a feminist, I knew everything she was saying was true. I had no resistance. It made my whole previous life more explicable and understandable to me. It was as if I had previously been seeing everything through a distorted glass."

Gordon became deeply involved with a women's liberation collective that would eventually found the feminist/socialist collective "Bread and Roses," and changed her intellectual focus to studying U.S. women's history. She explored every book she could find in the Harvard and Radcliffe libraries that focused on women's history, and was stunned to discover a rich vein of women's history from the 1910s and 1920s that had been buried during the intervening years. At this time, Gordon began writing essays and articles that uncovered forgotten women's concerns and protests. In addition, she edited two collections of primary documents, *America's Working Women,* with Rosalyn Baxandall and Susan Reverby in 1976, and *Maternity: Letters from Working Women* in 1979, both of which illustrate the changing nature of women's dual roles as workers and mothers over time.

Gordon's 1976 book, *Women's Body, Women's Right,* was immediately recognized as a significant work for its novel approach to thinking about women's history, the history of sexuality, and the changing social relations of men and women. *Women's Body, Women's Right* showed that control over women's bodies has always been politicized, that birth control and sexual activity cannot be viewed in terms of medical/technological advances or individual choices, but must be seen as part of the overall power relations in society. Gordon identified three distinct stages of the birth control movement and showed how these stages were connected to feminist movements and the class and gender struggles of the last century. She showed that the birth control movement both benefitted and delayed complete freedom for women, and explained the current movement for birth control and abortion rights. Her work would be attacked for its feminist standpoint; in *Journal of Social History,* Edward Shorter wrote "The name of the game becomes getting the goods on chauvinists, rather than tracing changes in social reality."

Gordon's *Heroes of Their Own Lives,* published in 1988, was lauded by Kenneth Keniston in the *New York Times* as "an example of feminist scholarship at its best." In this book, Gordon examined the ways that families, and family violence, have been historically, politically, and socially constructed over time. In case studies of three Boston welfare agencies from 1880-1960, she showed that although the incidence of family violence—spousal abuse, incest, and child abuse—which occurred over time has been relatively constant, the social agencies approached and defined family violence in different ways at different times, due to changing ideologies of the family as well as norms of acceptable violence. For example, during the Depression, welfare agencies deemphasized intra-family violence in order to shore up male authority, which had been impacted by high levels of unemployment. Gordon's complex interweaving of class, gender, and social history again helped explain the current visibility of family violence in the media, while also noting and deploring the actual lack of change in family violence. As Gordon told Lasser, "I think I have a strong tendency to optimism, and to trying to find the good endings if there are any. Sometimes they just don't exist."

In her edited volume *Women, the State, and Welfare,* Gordon would help define the scholarship on women and the welfare state for researchers in history, political science, social work, and sociology. She traced the intellectual development of feminist scholarship on the state in her introductory essay and then included articles that exemplified the best of the research being done. This volume shows that women were critical actors in the struggle for an American welfare state, although they limited their gains by appealing to women's "special" qualities—for example, women often pushed for legislation "protecting" women from the harmful conditions of the workplace, protection which benefitted women while simultaneously limiting their opportunities. Gordon also included articles by Gwendolyn Mink and Barbara Nelson, who were among the first to argue systematically that the U.S. welfare state was shaped not only by gender but also by race, and that welfare programs reinforced racial inequality.

Gordon's more recent work, *Pitied but Not Entitled* (1995), traces the evolution of economic aid for poor women and children from the late 19th century through the passage of the Social Security Act of 1935 to current debates about welfare policy. Gordon's analyses are again very complex, stressing the interaction of politics, class, gender, and race in determining the resulting welfare policies. In explaining why the welfare programs that primarily serve women are so stigmatized—for example, Aid to Families with Dependent Children (AFDC)—as compared to those programs that serve men—for example, Social Security—she demonstrates that the weaknesses of the policy have mainly been due to the gendered and racialized structures of political power, but also in part due to the nature of feminism at the time: the women's rights activists who fought for the policy were unable to move past assumptions of women's economic dependence on men. She argues that for a better policy to emerge, poor women must be involved in policymaking, and prevailing assumptions about female dependency must be challenged.

Gordon is presently Florence Kelly Professor of History and Vilas Research Professor at the University of Wisconsin—Madison. Her latest research has focused on orphans, motherhood, and race in Arizona. Linda Gordon's work continues to shape scholarship and contribute to larger societal debates about women's roles in society.

—Frances Akins and Joya Misra

GORDON, Mary (Catherine)

Nationality: American. **Born:** Far Rockaway, Long Island, New York, 8 December 1949. **Education:** Holy Name of Mary School, Valley Stream, New York; Mary Louis Academy; Barnard College, New York, B.A. 1971; Syracuse University, New York, M.A. 1973. **Family:** Married 1) James Brain in 1974 (divorced); 2) Arthur Cash in 1979, one daughter and one son. **Career:** English teacher, Dutchess Community College, Poughkeepsie, New York, 1974-78; lecturer, Amherst College, Massachusetts, 1979; currently MacIntosh Professor of English, Barnard College. Contributor to periodicals, including *Ladies' Home Journal, Mademoiselle, Ms., Southern Review,* and *Virginia Quarterly.* **Awards:** Janet Kafka prize, 1979, 1982. **Address:** c/o Viking Penguin, 375 Hudson Street, New York, New York 10014, U.S.A.

Publications

Novels

Final Payments. New York, Random House, and London, Hamish Hamilton, 1978.

The Company of Women. New York, Random House, and London, Cape, 1981.

Men and Angels. New York, Random House, and London, Cape, 1985.

The Other Side. New York, Viking, 1989; London, Bloomsbury, 1990.

Short Stories

Temporary Shelter. London, Bloomsbury, and New York, Random House, 1987.

The Rest of Life: Three Novellas. New York, Viking, 1993; London, Bloomsbury, 1994.

Uncollected Short Stories

"Vision," in *Antaeus* (New York), spring 1989.

"Separation," in *Antaeus* (New York), spring-autumn, 1990.

"At the Kirks'," in *Grand Street* (New York), winter 1990.

Essays

"The Parable of the Cave or: In Praise of Watercolors," in *The Writer on Her Work,* edited by Janet Sternburg. New York, Norton, 1980.

Good Boys and Dead Girls and Other Essays. New York, Viking, and London, Bloomsbury, 1991.

Autobiography

The Shadow Man. New York, Viking, and London, Bloomsbury, 1996.

*

Critical Studies: "On Maternal Splitting: A Propos of Mary Gordon's *Men and Angels*" by Susan Rubin Suleiman, in *Signs: Journal of Women in Culture and Society,* 14(1), 1988.

* * *

Mary Gordon's arrival on the American literary scene with her best-selling novel *Final Payments* in 1978 met with immediate acclaim and her career has been remarkably successful ever since. Critics praise Gordon's craftsmanship and her thoughtful probing of the thorny relationship of women to the Catholic church. Gordon's own conservative upbringing in the American church of the 1950s and 1960s certainly shapes her fiction, but she explicitly rejected the identity of a "Catholic writer," though she is frequently labelled as such. In an early interview with the Catholic weekly *Commonweal,* the author explained the schism between the Church and American literature: as a church of immigrants, "The Catholic Church in America has been phenomenally anti-intellectual ... it's also a profoundly anti-sexual tradition." Her contention was that to be Irish Catholic in America was outside of the literary establishment and that scholarship and sexual exploration isolated a Catholic from the faith, and that this was particularly true of women. As a young writer, she described the novel's "function" as "Pleasure. If it's accidentally instructive, then that's all to the good. But its main function is to be beautiful and, in some sense, true in a very large way I can't even begin to explain."

Her novels, beginning with *Final Payments,* involve journeys of spirit and the flesh; with her belief that the Irish Catholic Church rejects the educated and sexual adventurous, Gordon's heroines suffer for their independence and any rebellion against patriarchal authority costs them dearly. Working through guilt, they come to a personal awareness of the cost and the gain, a realistic feminist message by an author who rarely flinches from a painful but emotionally honest rendering of her characters. *The Company of Women,* her second novel, goes beyond the emotional bondage of a daughter to a father to a second loyalty, of the traditional Catholic woman to the priest. This emotional attachment to a sexually unavailable man provides tension to the plot of escape and return, and the young heroine Felicitas's child (conceived out of wedlock) will take her place among the priest's women. In *Men and Angels* an academic woman, Anne, temporarily alone, finds her work eroding her previous beliefs about family and her profession. The au pair hired to help her with her children is a sinister figure who intends to "save" Anne. *The Other Side* finds Gordon dealing with a familiar (and challenging) plot device—the events of a single day but with a male protagonist, an sympathetically drawn Irish-American patriarch. It is to Gordon's credit that critics acclaimed her efforts—she had previously stated she felt she had difficulty with male characters.

In 1988's essay "Getting Here from There: A Writer's Reflections on a Religious Past," Gordon examines her own growth as a writer. She describes the regular attendance at Mass as "an excellent training ground for an aspiring novelist," as a dramatic event composed of rituals and evocative language that she "absorbed ... unconsciously." In that same essay she recalled the parent who most shaped her as a Catholic and as a novelist. Gordon's father, who was a convert to Catholicism, was a figure the novelist began to examine in this essay. Her quest for the true history of her father, "who had a very wild life ... [and] he also lied a lot," culminated in 1996's *The Shadow Man,* in which Gordon's father was revealed to have been not only a pathological liar but a anti-Semite while being a self-hating Jew, a publisher of a girlie tabloid called *Hot Dog,* and a McCarthyite. He claimed to have attended Harvard and styled himself as a Midwestern Protestant, neither of which was true. With her characteristic honesty, Gordon took stock of how his life of fabrications created her as an artist, and what her altered portrait of her family and herself meant to her.

Gordon was born 8 December 1949 to David and Anna (Gagliano) Gordon in Long Island, New York, into an intensely Catholic environment. Her father was involved in publishing right-wing Catholic magazines and encouraged religiosity in his daughter. Her mother, a legal secretary of Irish and Italian heritage, was the parent who raised her after her father's death when Mary was eight. Mary's mother, also a devout Catholic, figures in her essay "More Catholic than the Pope." Gordon's mother has a sense of humor her daughter has inherited—often Gordon is very funny. She began a dissertation on Virginia Woolf, but never finished it, though she counts Woolf and Jane Austen as having helped her learn to shape fiction, and she is an admirer of Ford Maddox Ford. As a writer who is also a teacher, Gordon has taught at Amherst College and is presently the McIntosh Professor of English at Barnard College. She has been married twice; in 1979 she married Arthur Cash, an English professor and is the mother of two children. Her personal life as a daughter, wife, and mother is occasionally a source of inspiration, but she never exploits the emotions but rather finds connections to philosophy or literature. She is intensely personal yet reserved.

Gordon rebelled against the Catholic Church as a teenager, but has since reconciled herself with reservations: her criticisms of the Pope, of dogma, of the Church's sexism are blistering and uncompromising. Some of the best writing Gordon has produced are in her 1991 collection of essays *Good Boys and Dead Girls.* Gordon the critic emerges: her essays on authors she admires, such as Flannery O'Connor and Edith Wharton, are finely constructed and learned. In her essay "The Parable of the Cave" Gordon responds to the left-handed compliment of being called a "woman writer" and deftly exposes the sexism implied in that term while embracing the legacy of her mother and acknowledging she became a writer to please her father: "But now I see I am the kind of writer I am because I am my mother's daughter." Gordon's feminist consciousness and her iconoclastic temperament have produced a remarkable and exemplary body of work.

—Mary A. Hess

GRAFTON, Sue

Nationality: American. **Born:** Louisville, Kentucky, 24 April 1940. **Education:** University of Louisville, Louisville, Kentucky, B.A. 1961. **Family:** Married 1) (divorced), one son; 2) (divorced), one son, one daughter; 3) Steven F. Humphrey in 1978. **Career:** Novelist and screenwriter, beginning 1966. **Awards:** Christopher Award, 1979, for teleplay *Walking through the Fire;* Cloak and Clue Society Mysterious Stranger Award, 1982-83, for *"A" Is for Alibi;* Private Eye Writers of America Shamus Award, 1985; Mystery Readers of America Anthony Award, 1985, for *"B" Is for Burglar;* Macavity Award and Anthony Award, both 1986, both for short story "The Parker Shotgun"; Edgar Award nomination, 1986, for teleplay *Love on the Run;* Anthony Award, 1987, for *"C" Is for Corpse;* Doubleday Mystery Award, 1989, 1990, 1991, 1992; Anthony Award, 1991. **Agent:** Molly Friedrich, Aaron Priest Agency, 122 East 42nd Street, New York, New York 10168, U.S.A.

Publications

Novels

Keziah Dane. New York, Macmillan, 1967; London, P. Owen, 1968.
The Lolly-Madonna War. London, P. Owen, 1969.
"A" Is for Alibi. New York, Holt, 1982; London, Macmillan, 1986.
"B" Is for Burglar. New York, Holt, 1985; London, Macmillan, 1986.
"C" Is for Corpse. New York, Holt, 1986; London, Macmillan, 1987.
"D" Is for Deadbeat. New York, Holt, and London, Macmillan, 1987.
"E" Is for Evidence. New York, Holt, and London, Macmillan, 1988.
"F" Is for Fugitive. New York, Holt, and London, Macmillan, 1989.
"G" Is for Gumshoe. New York, Holt, and London, Macmillan, 1990.
"H" Is for Homicide. New York, Holt, and London, Macmillan, 1991.
"I" Is for Innocent. New York, Holt, and London, Macmillan, 1992.
"J" Is for Judgement. New York, Holt, and London, Macmillan, 1993.
"K" Is for Killer. New York, Holt, and London, Macmillan, 1994.
"L" Is for Lawless. New York, Holt, and London, Macmillan, 1995.

Uncollected Short Stories

"The Parker Shotgun," in *Mean Streets,* edited by Robert J. Randisi. New York, Mysterious Press, 1986.
"She Didn't Come Home," in *Redbook* (New York), April 1986.
"Murder between the Sheets," in *Redbook* (New York), October 1986.
"Falling Off the Roof," in *Sisters in Crime,* edited by Marilyn Wallace. New York, Berkeley, 1989; London, Robinson, 1990.
"A Poison That Leaves No Trace," in *Sisters in Crime II,* edited by Marilyn Wallace. New York, Berkeley, 1990.

Plays

Screenplays: *Lolly-Madonna XXX,* adaptation of her own novel, with Rodney Carr-Smith, 1973.

Television Plays: *With Friends Like These* ("Rhoda" series), 1975; *Walking through the Fire,* 1979; *Sex and the Single Parent,* 1979; *Nurse,* 1980; *Mark, I Love You,* 1980; *Seven Brides for Seven Brothers* (series pilot), with Steven F. Humphrey, 1982; *I Love You, Molly McGraw* and *A House Divided* ("Seven Brides for Seven Brothers" series), with Humphrey, 1983; *A Caribbean Mystery,* with Humphrey, 1983; *A Killer in the Family,* with Humphrey and Robert Aller, 1983; *Sparkling Cyananide,* with Humphrey and Robert Malcolm Young, 1983; *Love on the Run,* 1985; *Tonight's the Night,* with Humphrey, 1987.

* * *

One of several women writers who came to prominence in the mystery field during the 1980s, Sue Grafton is best known for creating the female private detective character Kinsey Millhone. Millhone plies her trade in Southern California, where she walks the mean streets in the manner defined by such writers of the hard-boiled detective genre as Raymond Chandler and Dashiell Hammett. While she successfully updates the familiar formulas of the detective genre for a contemporary audience, Grafton also makes changes to the genre from a feminist perspective by downplaying the macho violence and posturing commonly found in detective novels and emphasizing the suspense instead. Her creation of Millhone—part hard-boiled detective and part feminist icon—has proven popular with a mass audience. Millhone's cases focus on women in trouble, with the detective often called upon to prove a woman's innocence of a crime or locate a missing relative.

Grafton first began writing as a teenager, took a college course in fiction writing, and wrote in the evening and on weekends while raising a family. She published her first novel in 1967. The story of a female matriarch who struggles against great odds to hold her family together, *Keziah Dane* met with moderate critical praise. Her second novel, *The Lolly-Madonna War,* concerns a feud between rival mountain families. During the 1970s Grafton turned from novels to television script writing, authoring a number of made-for-television movies, an episode of the "Rhoda" series, and adaptations of other writers' works. In the 1980s she adapted two Agatha Christie novels for television.

Grafton published her first Kinsey Millhone mystery novel—*"A" Is for Alibi*—in 1982. She was drawn to the genre partly because of her father's enthusiasm for mysteries. He had published two mystery novels under the name C.W. Grafton, writing the books in the evenings after work. In addition to the affection for mysteries inspired by her father, Grafton was intrigued too by her father's book titles, which used lines from an old children's nursery rhyme. The idea of interconnecting the book titles in an ongoing series appealed to her. When she read a book written by cartoonist Edward Gorey—an alphabet book of gruesome deaths—Grafton found her final inspiration. The Kinsey Millhone novels have titles taken from the alphabet: *"A" Is for Alibi, "B" Is for Burglar,* and so on.

In the first book of the series, *"A" Is for Alibi,* Millhone is hired to clear a woman who has just spent eight years in prison for poisoning her husband. In *"B" Is for Burglar,* the feisty detective must track down a missing sister whose signature is required on family papers, uncovering a murder plot along the way. Grafton's mystery novels contain gripping suspense and suitable plot twists that insure their popularity with a large audience of mystery readers who consistently push series titles onto the bestseller lists. For more serious genre fans, the books are often reminiscent of or play off of the works of earlier mystery writers like Ross Macdonald, whose books feature similar plots in which long-concealed family secrets are uncovered, and Raymond Chandler, whose detective Philip Marlowe is an obvious model for Millhone.

But perhaps the strongest appeal of Grafton's mysteries lies in the character of Millhone herself. Grafton has told interviewers that the fictional Millhone is a version of herself, what she would have been if she had not married young and had children. A twice-divorced, 32-year-old when she is first introduced in the series, Millhone is a believable character, both as a private investigator working in a male-dominated profession and as a strong and independent woman. She cuts her own hair, refuses to wear make-up, and has no interest in fashion. She lives alone and owns a total of one dress. When she is forced to kill someone in the line of duty, she is emotionally bothered by the act. Millhone's unsentimental approach to family and emotional relationships gives her wise-cracking attitude—common to private eyes in dozens of other mystery series—an edge that few other fictional detectives possess. This wise-cracking, combined with her brains and fortitude, make Millhone a character whose exploits would be of interest to readers even if she were not a detective. More than that, they make Millhone one of the few strong and believable woman characters in popular fiction today.

—Denise Wiloch

GRAVES, Valerie. *See* **BRADLEY, Marion Zimmer.**

GRAY, Edith. *See* **H.D.**

GREEN, Judith. *See* **RODRIGUEZ, Judith.**

GREER, Germaine

Pseudonym: Rose Blight. **Nationality:** Australian. **Born:** Melbourne, 29 January 1939. **Education:** Star of the Sea Convent, Gardendale, Victoria; University of Melbourne, B.A. in English and French languages and literature (with honors) 1959; University of Sydney, M.A. in English (with honors) 1962; Newnham College, Cambridge, Ph.D. with thesis on Shakespeare's Early Comedies, 1968. **Family:** Married Australian journalist Paul de Feu in 1968 (divorced 1973). **Career:** Taught at girls' schools in Australia; senior tutor in English, Sydney University, 1963-64; assistant lecturer, then lecturer in English, University of Warwick, Coventry, England, 1967-72; broadcast journalist, 1972-present; lecturer with American Program Bureau, 1973-1978; visiting professor, graduate faculty of modern letters, University of Tulsa, Oklahoma, 1979; professor of modern letters, University of Tulsa, 1980-83; founder and editor, Tulsa Center for the Study of Women's Literature, 1980-83, founder and editor, Tulsa Studies in Women's Literature, 1981; director, Stump Cross Books, beginning 1988; special lecturer and unofficial fellow, Newnham College, Cambridge, beginning 1989. Columnist, *Sunday Times,* London, 1971-73. Contributor to periodicals, including *Oz, Esquire, Harper's Magazine, Listener, Playboy, Spare Rib, Private Eye* (as Rose Blight), *Rolling Stone,* and *Spectator.* Co-founder of *Suck* (pornographic newspaper), Amsterdam. Actress on television comedy show in Manchester, England. Frequent appearances on BBC programs from 1972 until present. **Awards:** Australian Junior Government scholarship, 1952; Diocesan scholarship, 1956; Senior Government scholarship, 1956; Teacher's College studentship, 1956; Newnham College Commonwealth Scholar, 1964; J.R. Ackerly Prize and Premio Internazionale Mondello, both 1989, for *Daddy We Hardly Knew You.* **Agent:** Aitken & Stone, 29 Fernshaw Road, London SW10 0TG, England.

PUBLICATIONS

Political/Social Theory

The Female Eunuch. London, MacGibbon & Kee, 1969; New York, McGraw Hill, 1971; with new author's forward, London, Paladin, 1991.

The Obstacle Race: The Fortunes of Women Painters and Their Work. New York, Farrar Straus, 1979.

Sex and Destiny: The Politics of Human Fertility. New York, Harper, 1984.

The Change: Women, Ageing, and the Menopause. London, Hamish Hamilton, 1991; New York, Knopf, 1992.

Literary Criticism

Shakespeare. Oxford, Oxford University Press Past Masters Series, 1986.

Slip-Shod Sibyls: Recognition, Rejection and the Woman Poet. London, Viking, 1995.

Essays

"Women and Power in Cuba," in *Women: A World Report.* N.p., United Nations, 1985.

The Madwoman's Underclothes: Essays and Occasional Writings. London, Picador, 1986; Boston, Atlantic Monthly Press, 1987.

Other

The Revolting Garden (as Rose Blight). London, Andre Deutsch, 1979.

Daddy, We Hardly Knew You. London, Hamish Hamilton, 1989; New York, Knopf, 1990.

Editor, with Jeslyn Medoff, Melinda Sansone, and Susan Hastings, *Kissing the Rod: An Anthology of 17th-Century Women's Verse.* New York, Farrar, Straus, 1989.

Editor, *The Uncollected Verse of Aphra Behn.* Stump Cross, Essex, Stump Cross Books, 1989.

Editor, with R. Little, *The Collected Works of Katherine Philips, the Matchless Orinda.* Stump Cross, Essex, Stump Cross Books, 1993.

*

Critical Studies: Interview in *Women Writers Talking* edited by Janet Todd, New York, Holmes & Meier, 1983.

* * *

Germaine Greer's first book, *The Female Eunuch,* caused the feminist consciousness of women and men in the United States to sky-rocket; in the process, she became the most popular figure then associated with the so-called "women's movement." Greer, with a rather bawdy, brutally honest writing style, proclaimed women were symbolically castrated by American society, forced to be passive by their designated roles, and that men were also made victims by the passivity of women. She advocated not a rebellion of women, but a change in spirit, allowing women to embrace their own sexuality, whether actively or even promiscuously. Until Greer emerged on the U.S. literary scene, most "women's libbers" were perceived by the general public—many women, in addition to most men—as masculine in nature, man-hating, hostile, and lesbian by sexual orientation. Ironically, it took a self-proclaimed heterosexual with an attractive Australian accent, long legs, a pretty face, and fly-away brown hair to make the U.S. public more comfortable with the idea of a feminist movement. Greer clearly enjoyed the media attention, yet she proved to be no one's fool, certainly no overnight "media darling."

The *Female Eunuch,* which would eventually be published in 12 languages, launched its author on a year-long North American book tour. She then spent more than ten years between Tuscany, London and the United States, as both a professor and an in-demand lecturer. However it may have seemed at the time, Greer didn't just suddenly pop up from "Down Under" with a hat-full of feminist theories. While women's rights may not have been a top concern at the start of her academic career—in a 1971 interview in the *New York Post* she admitted that she was a late starter as far as feminism was concerned—Greer was a frequent contributor to so-called "underground" newspapers and magazines throughout Great Britain. She led an idiosyncratic lifestyle. She loved jazz and was well-known to the local rock musicians and other personalities; she lectured in English literature at the University of Warwick; she even appearing on a local television comedy show. By the time she was ready to write a book on the failures of the women's movement, Greer was already known to British talk show audiences. A mirror of this versatility, *The Madwoman's Underclothes: Essays and Occasional Writings* (1986) is a compilation of Greer's newspaper and magazine essays, including some that were previously rejected by publishers as too racy or not "helpful." It is here that readers will find Greer's explanation for her participation in the founding of *Suck,* a short-lived pornographic newspaper based in Amsterdam; her description of her debate with Norman Mailer in 1971; some of the first writing done on the rape of women in refugee camps; her opinions on the abortion debate; her well-crafted essay on women in power in Cuba; and a stunning portrait of the pathos of Ethiopia as well as her blistering report on the Ethiopian resettlement effort.

Greer has continued to be a prolific, controversial author. In 1984 she drew fire from several feminists over her *Sex and Destiny: The Politics of Human Fertility.* Perceived by many as a reversal of the hard line taken in her *The Female Eunuch, Sex and Destiny* advocated increasing importance for motherhood and criticized the West's emphasis on family planning as a matter of policy in underdeveloped nations. In 1989 Greer published the story of her search in Australia for her father's true identity. In the pages of *Daddy We Hardly Knew You* readers can catch a glimpse of the unusual environment in which Greer was raised. Her father, ashamed of being abandoned as a child and made a ward of the state, changed his name and made up an entire childhood history. His emotional distance from his daughter is understood by her as his fear of the many questions she was always asking about family. Greer's mother did not seem to be overly interested in the truth about the man who had become her husband; indeed, she seemed disinterested in most of what went on around her during her marriage. Greer writes candidly, with caring, and *Daddy We Hardly Knew You* is seen as one of her best works.

1991 found Greer back on the attack, this time on the subject of menopause or "climacteric," as she alternately refers to it. In *The Change: Women, Ageing, and the Menopause,* Greer takes a fairly balanced look at menopause: how she feels women should deal with the death of their womb (with appropriate grieving and a moving on), what life looks like coming out the other side of the climacteric, and what options women have for dealing with the pre-menopausal, menopausal, and post-menopausal parts of their lives. Characteristically, Greer has again taken fire from critics who contend that *The Change* discourages women from receiving hormone replacement treatment (HRT). In actuality, Greer's motive is to educate the reader about what s/he should know in order to make informed choices; the advertising dollars spent by large pharmaceutical companies in pushing their products to uninformed women is one of many topics she feels compelled to bring to light.

Beneath the prime-time persona of Greer-the-combative-journalist is Greer-the-educator, a perceptive scholar of literature who is often buried under the fallout from her feminist writings. An acknowledged expert on Shakespeare, she has also worked hard to resurrect the works of forgotten women poets, coediting *Kissing the Rod: An Anthology of 17th-Century Women's Verse* and *The Collected Works of Katherine Philips,* in addition to editing *The Uncollected Verse of Aphra Behn.* With *Slip-Shod Sibyls: Recognition, Rejection and the Woman Poet* (1995), the combative journalist and the educator seemed to join forces; Greer threw down the gauntlet to other literary scholars in her conclusions regarding the worth of the early female poets, as well of such 20th-century "confessional" poets as Sylvia Plath and Anne Sexton. In this book Greer maintains that these poets were forced to walk a tight-rope by male counterparts and often fell into oblivion while trying to reach the heights of their endeavors. While *Slip-Shod Sybils* may not be the definitive work on the woman poet, it is certain to spark animated discussion in many classrooms. Perhaps that is exactly what Greer intended.

Germaine Greer lives outside of London where, through the power of her words, she continues to stretch the parameters of "acceptable" and "comfortable" feminism. Considering herself to be an atheist and anarchist she remains in self-exile from her native Australia in protest of that country's treatment of its aboriginal peoples.

—Maria Elena Raymond

GRIFFIN, Susan

Nationality: American. **Born:** Los Angeles, California, 26 January 1943. **Education:** University of California, Berkeley, 1960-63; San Francisco State College (now University), B.A. (cum laude) 1965; California State University, San Francisco (now San Francisco State University), M.A. 1973. **Family:** Married John Levy in 1966 (divorced 1970); one daughter. **Career:** Assistant editor, *Ramparts* magazine, San Francisco, 1966-68; San Francisco State College (now University), instructor in English, 1970-71; high school poetry instructor, Poetry in the Schools program, Oakland, California, 1972-73; instructor in creative writing and women's studies, University of California, Berkeley, extension school, 1973-75; instructor, San Francisco State University, 1974-75. Visiting writer, Delta College of San Joaquin and Cazenovia College. Contributor to numerous periodicals, including *Aphra, Los Angeles Times, Ms., Ramparts, Shocks, Sundance,* and *Whole Earth Review.* **Awards:** Ina Coolbrith Prize for Poetry, 1963; Emmy Award, 1975, for *Voices;* National Endowment for the Arts grant, 1976; Malvina Reynolds Award for cultural achievement, 1982; Schumacher fellow, 1983; honorary Ph.D., Graduate Theological Union, 1985; Kentucky Foundation for Women grant, 1987; Commonwealth Medal, 1987, for *Unremembered Country;* Women's Foundation Award for Women in the Arts, 1988; MacArthur Foundation grant, 1990. **Address:** 904 Keeler Ave., Berkeley, California 94708, U.S.A.

Publications

Poetry

Dear Sky. Berkeley, Shameless Hussy Press, 1971.
Like the Iris of an Eye. New York, Harper, 1976.
Unremembered Country: Poems. Port Townsend, Washington, Copper Canyon Press, 1987.

Short Stories

The Sink. Berkeley, Shameless Hussy Press, 1973.

Plays

Voices (produced San Francisco, 1974). Old Westbury, New York, Feminist Press, 1975.
Thicket (produced San Francisco, 1992), in *Kenyon Review,* spring 1994.

Radio Plays: *Enter the Circle,* National Public Radio, 1984.

Political/Social Theory

Woman and Nature: The Roaring inside Her. New York, Harper, 1978; London, Harper Collins, 1985.
Rape: The Power of Consciousness. San Francisco, Harper, 1979.
Pornography and Silence: Culture's Revolt against Nature. New York, Harper, 1981.
A Chorus of Stones: The Private Life of War. Garden City, New York, Doubleday, 1992.

Essays

"Thoughts on Writing a Diary," in *The Writer on Her Work,* edited by Janet Sternburg. New York, Norton, 1980.
"Red Shoes," in *Politics of the Essay: Feminist Perspectives,* edited by Ruth-Ellen Boetcher Joeres and Elizabeth Mittman. Bloomington, Indiana University Press, 1993.
The Eros of Everyday Live: Essays on Ecology, Gender and Society. New York, Doubleday, 1995.

Other

Le Viol. Montreal, L'Etincelle, 1972.
Let Them Be Said. Berkeley, Ma Ma Press, 1973.
Letters. Berkeley, Effie's Press, 1973.
Made from This Earth: Selections from Her Writing, 1967-82. London, Women's Press, 1982, published as *Made from This Earth: An Anthology of Writings,* New York, Harper, 1983.

*

Media Adaptations: *Voices* (television film), 1974.

Critical Studies: Interview with Nannerl Koehane, in *Women Writers of the West Coast: Speaking of Their Lives and Careers,* edited by Marilyn Yalom, Santa Barbara, Capra Press, 1983; "Romance Fiction: Porn for Women?" by Alison Assiter, in *Perspectives on Pornography: Sexuality in Film in Literature,* edited by Gary Day and Clive Bloom, New York, St. Martin's Press, 1988; "In Defense of Separatism" by Susan Hawthorne, in *A Reader in Feminist Knowledge,* edited by Sneja Gunew, New York, Routledge, 1991; "Poetry and the Pity of War" by K.K. Roeder, in *Women's Review of Books,* 17(3), winter 1992; "Marginality and Epistemic Privilege" by Bat-Ami Bar On, in *Feminist Epistemologies,* edited by Linda Alcoff and Elizabeth Potter, New York, Routledge, 1993; *Skirting the Issue: Pursuing Language in the Works of Adrienne Rich, Susan Griffin, and Beverly Dahlen* by Alan Shima, Uppsala, Uppsala University Press, 1993; *Feminist Theory: The Intellectual Traditions of American Feminism* by Josephine Donovan, New York, Continuum, 1993.

* * *

Susan Griffin is a prolific writer who works in many different forms. When asked by Nannerl Koehane how she decided which form to use and when to use it, Griffin replied: "I do decide, but it's not in the way that we usually think of decision-making. You don't sit there and say, 'Now I'm going to decide.' I have to go through a whole process and sometimes it is very painful. It's not just trial and error, it's having to do battle with my own preconceptions." Griffin's forms include poetry, short fiction, drama, theory, essays, and memoir. Her subject matter ranges from mysticism to war, and her slant, evident throughout her writing, is feminist.

Born and educated in California, Griffin has participated in many variations of the literary career. She has been an editor, a university English teacher, a high school poetry instructor, a visiting writer at a variety of universities. She has also won numerous awards for her writing: the Ina Coolbrith Prize in poetry (1963), Emmy Award for *Voices* (1975), NEA Grant (1976), Malvina Reynolds Award for cultural achievement (1982), Kentucky Foundation for Women Grant (1987), and more. Griffin, who has one daughter, currently resides in Berkeley, California.

Although most of Griffin's awards have been for her overall achievements, her individual texts offer profound cultural insights into an evolving feminist mind. The books that provide the most powerful insight into Griffin's feminism include *Woman and Nature: The Roaring inside Her* (1978), *Rape: The Power of Consciousness* (1979), *Pornography and Silence* (1981), and *The Eros of Everyday Life: Essays on Ecology, Gender and Society* (1995). Most frequently, scholars refer to Griffin as a radical feminist in search of a new moral vision; a separatist looking for the "freedom to think thoughts that leap beyond the bounds of patriarchy," in the words of Susan Hawthorne; and a "cultural feminist" who appeals to "prepatriarchal practices and symbols more than other feminists," according to Bat-Ami Bar On. In her later works, she writes like postmodern feminists by experimenting with borders of forms and interruptions in language.

In one such postmodern text, *A Chorus of Stones: The Private Life of War,* Griffin deftly interrupts the language of traditional war memoirs. She inserts both the subjective thoughts of a family involved in the war and scientific discussions of war devices. She purposefully writes in this interruptive style to design an accumulation of thought and emotions regarding war and its importance to history: "I do not see my life as separate from history. In my mind my family secrets mingle with the secrets of statesmen and bombers." Griffin's feminism evolves in this text beyond subject matter into style. She evidences none of her famed separatism in this text. Instead she calls attention to a convoluted, yet uncanny and holistic, inclusiveness.

Likewise, in her 1993 essay "Red Shoes," Griffin employs the same method of inclusiveness and accumulation of data. She writes alternating paragraphs of italicized private moments and non-italicized theoretical issues. The subject matter in this instance is the imprisonment of the female mind: "The imprisonment which was at one and the same time understood as the imprisonment of the female mind has a larger boundary, and that is the shape of thought itself within Western civilization. *It is an early memory. Red shoes. Leather straps criss-crossing. The kind any child covets. That color I wanted with the hot desire of a child.*"

Griffin questions whether writing can ever aptly capture the multitudes of discourse needed to bring a fuller understanding of existence to a text. When she walks away from her writing table, she feels as though she enters a different discourse world. She questions how to make the world of writing and the world of living interact with one another: "And when I return to write, will I be able to reshape the form so that more of this world falls on the page?" In an interview with Griffin, K. K. Roeder discusses the author's "interview" pose as one similar to these postmodern texts in that "she discusses a number of subjects almost simultaneously." But Griffin is after neither chaos nor theory; she ends the interview with Roeder by claiming that "those people who have been abused and go through those feelings and out the other side: they're the pioneers for the rest of us. I think the unveiling of secrets will be the thing of our time."

Griffin is one such pioneer. One of the secrets that she has discussed with great clarity, as well as with the aim of "coming out the other side" is her 1981 book, *Pornography and Silence: Culture's Revenge against Nature.* The thesis of this text is clear: "These pages will argue that pornography is an expression not of human erotic feeling and desire, and not of a love of the life of the body, but of a fear of bodily knowledge, and a desire to silence eros." In this text, Griffin traces the relationship between pornography, silence, and soullessness. She discusses pornography as the cultural choice to forget eros, as humiliating another into denying her sexuality, as robbing the body of its power, as asserting that women's beauty means nothing, as steeping us in an unfeeling nature, as taking its revenge on feeling, as ultimately about the loss of the soul. "The pornographer steals the soul of the other, and among those who believe his myths, no one remembers soulfulness," she writes. *Pornography and Silence* is groundbreaking in its revelation of cultural secrets. Although the roots of pornography may threaten us, Griffin asserts that we must become aware of our own soullessness to design a new civilization. In fact, as critic Alison Assiter maintains, "Griffin goes a lot further than producing a definition of porn; in fact she is less interested in that than in producing an account of the formation of the 'pornographic mind.'"

Susan Griffin continues to bring to feminist scholarship a fearlessness in the face of cultural secrets about gender, aggression, and our souls. Call it radical, cultural, or postmodern feminism; Griffin always keeps the bodies and souls of women near the heart of her texts.

—Renee R. Curry

GRIMKÉ, Sarah Moore, and Angelina (Emily) Grimké Weld

Nationality: Americans.

GRIMKÉ, Sarah Moore. Born: Charleston, South Carolina, 29 November 1752. **Education:** Educated at home. **Career:** Converted to Quakerism on a trip to Philadelphia, 1819; moved to Philadelphia, 1820; lectured on abolition of slavery throughout New England, 1836-37; taught at Theodore Weld's interracial school, Perth Amboy, New Jersey, 1848-62; moved to West Newton, Massachusetts, and then to Boston. **Died:** 23 December 1873.

WELD, Angelina (Emily) Grimké. Also wrote as Angelina Grimké. **Born:** Charleston, South Carolina, 20 February 1805. **Education:** Educated at home. **Family:** Married the abolitionist Theodore Weld in 1838; three children. **Career:** Moved to Philadelphia, 1820; lectured on abolition of slavery throughout New England, 1836-37; taught at Theodore Weld's interracial school, Perth Amboy, New Jersey, 1848-62; moved to West Newton, Massachusetts, and then to Boston. **Died:** 26 October 1879.

PUBLICATIONS

Essays; by Sarah Grimké

An Epistle to the Clergy of the Southern States. New York, n.p., 1836.

Letters on the Equality of the Sexes and the Condition of Women (originally published in *New England Spectator*). Boston, I. Knapp, 1838.

Essays; by Angelina Grimké Weld

Appeal to the Christian Women of the South. New York, American Anti-Slavery Society, 1836.

Appeal to the Women of the Nominally Free States. New York, n.p., 1837; as *Slavery in America,* Edinburgh, n.p., 1837.

Letter to Catherine Beecher, in Reply to An Essay on Slavery and Abolitionism. Boston, I. Knapp, 1838.

Other

Slavery as It Is: Testimony of a Thousand Witnesses, with Theodore Dwight Weld. 1839.

The Letters of Theodore Dwight Weld, Angelina Grimké, and Sarah Grimké, 1822-1844, edited by Gilbert H. Barnes and Dwight L. Dumond. Gloucester, Massachusetts, 2 vols., 1934.

The Public Years of Sarah and Angelina Grimké: Selected Writings, 1835-1839, edited by Larry Ceplair. New York and Oxford, Columbia University Press, 1989.

*

Critical Studies: *The Grimké Sisters from South Carolina: Rebels against Slavery* by Gerda Lerner, Boston, Houghton Mifflin, 1967; *Liberty, Equality, Sorority: The Origins and Interpretation of American Feminist Thought* by Elizabeth Ann Bartlett, Brooklyn, New York, Carlson, 1994.

* * *

Sarah and Angelina Grimké, born into a prominent slaveholding family, rebelled against their heritage and became America's first female abolition agents. They gained national notoriety in the 1830s not only by speaking out against slavery but by addressing "mixed" audiences, that is, audiences composed of men as well as women. As would be the case with other female abolitionists, the hostility they met in publicly agitating against slavery awakened their feminist consciousness and they became part of the first generation of woman's rights advocates in the United States.

While Sarah, the sixth of John and Mary Grimké's 14 children, and Angelina, the last, both disliked slavery from an early age, it was Sarah's trip to the North in 1819 that proved pivotal to the development of the sisters' involvement in abolition. Travelling with her father to find a cure for his ill health, Sarah became acquainted with the Quakers and their antislavery views. Her father died during the trip but she remained in Philadelphia and returned to Charleston for only a brief time before moving permanently to the North in 1821. Under Sarah's influence, Angelina also became a Quaker and an abolitionist, but she decided to remain in Charleston, attempting to fight against slavery from within the South. By 1829, however, Angelina's antislavery convictions had so eroded her relationships with her family that she, too, moved to Philadelphia and joined her sister.

Between 1835, when Angelina Grimké joined the Philadelphia Female Anti-Slavery Society, and 1838 when she married Theodore Dwight Weld, the Grimké sisters became figures of national prominence, stirring controversy by speaking and writing about the oppression of slaves and women. Angelina first gained notoriety unwittingly in 1835 when William Lloyd Garrison, editor of *The Liberator,* a journal that promoted the immediate emancipation of both African Americans and women, published a letter she had written. As a member of a prominent southern family, Angelina's public endorsement of Garrison's position drew national attention.

Although she had not asked for her letter to be printed, Angelina chose to remain a public opponent of slavery by publishing in 1836 *An Appeal to the Christian Women of the South,* an abolitionist pamphlet that condemned slavery as a violation of Christianity, human law, and the Declaration of Independence. Speaking directly to her former southern sisters, Angelina urged them to free their slaves and to pay them wages. She followed with another abolitionist pamphlet, her *Appeal to the Women of the Nominally Free States,* in 1837.

Recognizing the attraction of first-hand witnesses to slavery speaking out against the institution, abolitionist leaders invited the sisters to New York to speak to groups of women. Initially conceived as "parlor talks," so many women flocked to these meetings that they were moved to larger locations. More reluctant than her sister in becoming involved in large-scale antislavery agitation, Sarah Grimké also eventually made her hatred of slavery public. In her 1836 *Epistle to the Clergy of the Southern States,* Sarah challenged southern clergymen's support for slavery and countered their biblical defense of slavery by arguing that the enslavement of Africans violated Christian principles.

The success of their talks in New York and their rising reputation as articulate and compelling critics of slavery led New England-based abolitionists to urge the sisters to speak in their region, beginning in the spring of 1837. Although the Grimké sisters had planned to continue to address only all-female gatherings, by June of 1837 men began to attend these meetings, adding further controversy to their endeavor. The tour culminated in February of 1837 when Angelina became the first woman to address the Massachusetts legislature.

The Grimkés's trip spurred not only antislavery activism—most importantly, the circulation of antislavery petitions by New England women—but it also generated further criticism of the sisters for disregarding the accepted norms of womanly behavior. Even their fellow abolitionists questioned the wisdom of the Grimké's activities, concerned that the furor raised by the women addressing mixed audiences would distract attention from the antislavery cause and further discredit the movement. Yet, as Angelina stated in a letter written in the fall of 1837 to Theodore Dwight Weld (the man she would marry), she and her sister had come to see the oppression of slaves and the oppression of women as linked: "We are activated by the full conviction that if we are to do any good in the Anti Slavery cause, our *right* to labor in it *must* be firmly established."

Those outside the abolitionist ranks levelled much more serious charges against the sisters for the antislavery activism. A *Pastoral Letter* issued by the Congregational Churches condemned women, clearly the Grimkés, "Who so far forget themselves as to itinerate in the character of public lecturers and teachers." Their behavior, according to this letter, violated "the appropriate duties and influence as clearly stated in the New Testament." Sarah Grimké replied to this attack in 1838 in her *Letters on the Equality of the Sexes,* one of the first feminist manifestos published in the United States. She refuted the claim that the Bible supported the inferiority of women by arguing that the Bible simply expressed the patriarchal views of its authors and that God had created men and women equal. Outlining the central arguments of the 19-century woman's rights movement, she demanded that women be offered equal educational opportunities, condemned the laws that excluded women from the rights of citizenship, and insisted that women receive equal pay for equal work. Noting the similarities between the status of slaves and the status of women, Sarah called on women to reject all forms of dependency and to accept the same responsibilities and duties that men shouldered.

Although Angelina delivered a public speech in Philadelphia only two days after her marriage to Theodore Dwight Weld in May of 1838, the sisters's careers as abolitionist activists were largely over. Exhausted by a year of lecturing, the Welds and Sarah (they agreed that Sarah would always live with them) retreated from the forefront of the abolitionist battle. The sisters aided Weld in compiling *American Slavery As It Is: Testimony of a Thousand Witnesses,* the book that Harriet Beecher Stowe would consult in writing *Uncle Tom's Cabin,* and they circulated antislavery petitions, but they never again took to the podium to oppose slavery. Beginning in the late 1840s they devoted themselves to various teaching endeavors. Yet despite the brevity of their tenure as abolition agents, the Grimké sisters's riveting testimony against slavery and incisive analysis of the systematic oppression of women and slaves helped lay the foundation for the further development of both the antislavery and woman's rights movements.

—Anne Lewis Osler

GUILLAUMIN, Colette

Nationality: French. **Born:** 1934. **Education:** University of Paris, Sorbonne, doctorate in sociology 1969. **Career:** Researcher, "Migrations et Sociétés" unit, Centre National de la Recherche Scientifique, University of Paris VII; lecturer on feminist social theory. Member of editorial board, *Questions Féministes* until 1980, and *Le Genre Humain.* **Member:** International Association for the Study of Racism (The Netherlands), Association Nationale des Etudes Féministes (ANEF). **Address:** Unité de Recherche Migrations et Sociétés, Centre National de la Recherche Scientifique, Université de Paris VII Denis Diderot, 2, place Jussieu, Tour Centrale, 75251 Paris Cedex 05, France.

Publications

Political/Social Theory

L'idéologie raciste. Genèse et langage actuel. Paris and The Hague, Mouton, 1972.

Sexe, race et pratique du pouvior. L'idee de nature. Paris, côté-femmes, 1992; translated as *Racism, Sexism, Power, and Ideology,* London, Routledge, 1995.

Uncollected Essays

"Changes in Interethnic 'Attitudes' and the Influence of the Mass Media as Shown by Research in French-Speaking Countries," in *Race as News.* Paris, UNESCO Press, 1974.

"Race et race ... La mode 'naturel' en sciences humaines," with Marion Glean O'Callaghan, in *L'Homme et la Société,* 31-32, 1974.

"Sciences sociales et définitions du terme 'race,'" in *L'idée de race dans la pensée politique contemporaine,* edited by P. Guiral and E. Temime. Paris, CNRS, 1977.

"'Race' and Discourse," in *Race, Discourse and Power in France,* edited by M. Silverman. Aldershot, Surrey, Avebury, 1991.

"La 'différence culturelle,'" in *Racisme et modernité,* edited by M. Wieviorka. Paris, La Découverte, 1993.

"The Constructed Body," in *Reading the Social Body,* edited by Catharine Burroughs and Jeffrey Ehrenreich. Iowa City, University of Iowa Press, 1993.

"Quelques considérations sur le terme 'culture,'" in *Ethnicisation des rapports sociaux, Racismes, nationalismes, ethnicismes, et culturalismes,* edited by M. Fourier and G. Vermès. Paris, L'Harmattan, 1994.

"Le naturalisme, les orientations politiques et les femmes," in *L'extréme-droite et les femmes.* Brussels, Université des femmes, 1996.

*

Critical Studies: *Sex in Question: French Materialist Feminism,* edited by Lisa Adkins and Diana Leonard, Philadelphia, Taylor & Francis, 1996.

* * *

Colette Guillaumin is one of the most important writer in France on the construction of sexual and racial "difference." She has until relatively recently been little known in the English-speaking world; fortunately, the recent publication of a collection of her essays, *Racism, Sexism, Power and Ideology,* is helping to counter this anonymity.

Guillaumin is a sociological researcher for the Centre National de la Recherche Scientifique, France's national research institute. She has contributed to a number of books, in French and in English, and her work has also been published in other European languages. She participates in colloquia in France and has been invited to give seminars at a number of Canadian universities as well as in Belgium, Switzerland, and Germany.

Guillaumin's work on racism is considered by many in her field to be groundbreaking. Central to this work is the critique of the ideologies of "difference" and of "Nature." Her book *L'Idéologie raciste. Genèse et langage actuel,* which traces the history of contemporary racism back to its ideological roots in the 19th century, stresses that the active construction and maintaining of the idea of difference as "natural" is the foundation of racist ideology. She discusses "specificity" (as opposed to "generality") as the defining characteristic of racialised "minorities" and emphasizes that the relationship between such "minorities" and "the majority" is not founded in difference in value systems; on the contrary, the very existence of "majority-vs-minority" relies on a shared value system, on a "common symbolic universe." Guillaumin also examines the (often tautological) language used, within this value system, to categorize people according to sex, race, and class.

One of Guillaumin's more recent essays on racism is "Usages théoriques et usages banals du terme 'race,'" a contribution to a colloquium organized to debate whether or not the term "race" in the French Constitution should be changed to "culture" or some other term. (Article 2 of the Constitution states that all citizens are equal before the law, "without distinction of background, race or religion." An attempt during the 1980s to amend this article to include the word "sex" was not successful.) In this essay, Guillaumin argues that terms such as "culture" or "difference," used as euphemisms for "race," have taken on the same connotations; removing the term "race" from the Constitution will not remove the problem it describes.

Guillaumin has been involved in an editorial capacity in two journals, *Le Genre Humain* and *Questions Féministes.* The latter journal, which contained some of her best-known essays, was regrettably short-lived, for a split developed between radical lesbians and radical feminists in the collective over the political analysis of heterosexuality and how this analysis informed the content of the journal. According to radical lesbians Guillaumin, Monique Plaza, Monique Wittig, and Nicole-Claude Mathieu, heterosexuality and lesbianism were "not a matter of lifestyle," as Guillaumin puts it, but political choices. Radical feminists Christine Delphy and Emmanuelle Lesseps, on the other hand, considered that, although heterosexuality was imposed as a social norm rather than necessarily chosen freely, heterosexuality and lesbianism per se were not political choices but questions of sexual orientation. Although there had been an agreement to cease publication of the journal, the split was not amicable and Delphy subsequently started a new journal under the title *Nouvelles Questions Féministes,* which is still in publication.

It was in *Questions Féministes* that three of Guillaumin's best-known essays on male domination of women appeared, namely: "Pratique du pouvoir et idée de Nature" (published in two parts), "Le discours de la Nature," and "Question de différence." All three essays were subsequently translated in the American journal *Feminist Issues.* Once again, the themes of "Nature" and "difference" are central. Guillaumin also makes an important distinction in the first two essays between the appropriation of a worker's or a slave's labor, which is also a form of physical appropriation, and the *sexual* appropriation of women. In the third essay, "Question de différence," Guillaumin argues that the celebration of women's "difference" leads us into a number of traps, not the least of which is the fact that the assertion of difference implies a "norm," a yardstick against which this "difference" is measured. Other traps are those of reinforcing sociobiologizing ideas of women's intrinsic "nature," and of mystifying and "celebrating" what is in fact a state of social, cultural, and political powerlessness, or disempowerment. The issue is rather, not that women "are different from men," but that women are "different from what men assume us to be."

In two later essays, "Folie et norme sociale" (on the Montréal massacre of 1989, when a man shot and killed 14 female engineering students, simply because they were women), and "Le Corps construit," Guillaumin develops her analysis of "difference" through an examination of the ways in which women and men are socialized. In "Folie et norme sociale" she argues that the behavior of the Montréal killer is not "an act of madness" (*folie* = madness), nor an aberration or deviation from a social norm, but on the contrary, a particular manifestation of the "normal" woman-hatred that forms the basis of relationships between the sexes. In "Le Corps construit," Guillaumin discusses how men and women learn to appropriate physical space (or fail to do so, or let others do so), and to relate (or not) to their own bodies and the bodies of others in their sex. She argues that men learn "cooperation among peers" in a free space, whereas women, whose space is constrained, learn asymmetrical ways of relating to others and are not allowed the experience of meeting other women as peers. Guillaumin maintains that women are experts in solidarity, but that they have yet to experience "parity."

Guillaumin regularly gives postgraduate seminars at the Université de Paris VII (Jussieu) and is currently working on the theme of the role of the appropriation of women in the construction of national, cultural, and religious identity.

—Bronwyn Winter

H

HACKER, Marilyn

Nationality: American. **Born:** New York, New York, 27 November 1942. **Education:** New York University, B.A. in romance languages 1964. **Family:** Married the writer Samuel R. Delany in 1961 (separated 1974), one daughter; companion of Karyn J. London since 1986. **Career:** Poet and editor. Antiquarian bookseller in London, England, 1971-76; editor, *City,* 1967-70, and *Quark* (speculative fiction quarterly), 1969-71; editor, *Woman Poet: The East,* 1982, *13th Moon,* 1982-86, *Ploughshares,* 1990, 1996, and *Kenyon Review,* Gambier, Ohio, 1990-94. Writer-in-residence, American Studies Institute, Columbia University, New York, 1988; George Elliston Poet-in-Residence, University of Cincinnati, 1988; distinguished writer-in-residence, American University, 1989; visiting professor of creative writing at S.U.N.Y., Binghamton, University of Utah, Barnard College, and Brandeis University. **Awards:** Academy of American Poets Lamont Poetry selection and New York YWHA Poetry Center discovery award, both 1973, both for *Presentation Piece;* National Book Award in Poetry, 1975, for *Presentation Piece;* Guggenheim fellowship, 1980; Lambda Literary Award, 1991, for *Going Back to the River;* Academy of American Poets Lenore Marshall Award, and Lambda Literary award, both 1995, both for *Winter Numbers;* Poets' Prize, 1995, for *Selected Poems.* **Member:** American Civil Liberties Union, National Organization for Women, N.A.R.A.L., Poetry Society of America. **Agent:** Frances Collins, 210 Conestoga Road, Wayne, Pennsylvania 19087-9403, U.S.A. **Address:** c/o W.W. Norton, 500 Fifth Ave., New York, New York 10110, U.S.A.

Publications

Poetry

The Terrible Children. New York, privately printed, 1967.
Highway Sandwiches, with Thomas M. Disch and Charles Platt. New York, privately printed, 1970.
Presentation Piece. New York, Viking, 1974.
Separations. New York, Knopf, 1976.
Taking Notice. New York, Knopf, 1980.
Assumptions. New York, Knopf, 1985.
Love, Death, and the Changing of the Seasons. New York, Arbor House, 1986; London, Onlywomen Press, 1986.
Going Back to the River. New York, Random House, 1990.
The Hang-Glider's Daughter: Selected and New Poems. London, Onlywomen Press, 1990.
Selected Poems, 1965-1990. New York, Norton, 1994.
Winter Numbers. New York, Norton, 1994.

Other

Editor, *Woman Poet, The East.* Reno, Nevada, Women in Literature, 1982.

Translator, *Edge,* by Clair Malvoux. Winston-Salem, North Carolina, Wake Forest University Press, 1996.

Recordings: *The Poetry and Voice of Marilyn Hacker,* Caedmon, 1976; *Treasury of American Jewish Poets Reading Their Poems,* Spoken Arts, 1979; *Marilyn Hacker,* University of Missouri, New Letters, 1979.

*

Media Adaptation: *Five Poems of Marilyn Hacker: Soprano and Chamber Ensemble* (musical score), by Dennis Riley, 1989; *Hub of Ambiguity: For Soprano and Eight Players* (musical score for poem "Prism and Lens") by Enrique Raxach, 1992.

Critical Studies: "An Interview with Marilyn Hacker" by Karla Hammond, in *Frontiers,* 5(3), 1981; "Marilyn Hacker" by Felicia Mitchell, in *Dictionary of Literary Biography,* Vol. 120, Detroit, Gale Research, 1992; interview by Suzanne Gardinier in *AWP Chronicle,* March/April 1996; "An Interview on Form" by Annie Finch, in *American Poetry Review,* 25(3), May/June 1996.

*   *   *

Since the private publication of *The Terrible Children* (1967), Marilyn Hacker has written ten books of poetry. All of them concentrate on two relationships: 1) women's relationships with other women and their worlds, and 2) women poets' relationships to literary forms. Hacker was born on 27 November 1942, to Jewish immigrants Albert Abraham Hacker and Hilda Rosengarten Hacker. She grew up in the Bronx and attained most of her formal education in New York, earning a B.A. degree from New York University. In 1961 Hacker married the African American novelist Samuel R. Delany. They had a child, Iva Alyxander Hacker-Delany, about whom Hacker has written continuously throughout their lives together. Hacker, a lesbian, and Delany, a gay man, remained married for 13 years; since their divorce, Hacker's poetry has focused with a range of emotion on her love relationships with women. She entered into a life partnership with her lover, Karyn London, in 1986.

Hacker tells interviewer Karla Hammond that her earliest education about women writers and feminism occurred through adolescent reading that she did on her own. Similar to many successful writers, she views her education about poetry and writing as synonymous with the reading she did from an early age. Along with her formal education, Hacker considers the reading of poetry, especially women's poetry, as a great influence on the formation of herself as a writer. "Adrienne Rich is the one who first comes to mind," she explained to Hammond. "I've been reading her with great interest since about 1972.... Another writer with whom I've felt a strong affinity is Judy Grahn. I was lucky enough to know about her work since 1968 or 1969 when we were both in San Francisco. Audre Lorde is awfully good: both on the page and to hear aloud." Although Hacker has both voiced and acted on her commitments to women throughout her life, she never confuses this commitment with deference to their politics. She strives to establish and maintain her voice among the many women writers she cherishes, rather than to echo their concerns.

In 1974 Hacker became a National Book Award winner. *Presentation Piece* immediately established her as one of the most significant feminist writers of the times. In "She Bitches about Boys" the female persona gazes at the male's inadequacies:

> Girls love a sick child or a healthy animal.
> A man who's both itches them like an incubus,
> but I, for one, have had a bellyful
> of giving reassurances and obvious
> advice with scrambled eggs and cereal

This gaze constitutes a flash of the feminist knowledge and resistance to prescribed gender roles that compels Hacker's poetry.

In her poem "Sestina," Hacker first displays the graphic language of sexuality that will become part and parcel of her expressive system of feminist poetics throughout her career, portraying male genitalia: "Your cock whispers/inside my thigh that there is language/without memory." She includes as well a number of fixed forms, including the sonnet sequence, "A Christmas Crown," as well as villanelles and sestinas.

All of Hacker's poetic skills are apparent and honestly delivered in *Presentation Piece.* What comes thereafter will be further enhancement of these skills. As Felicia Mitchell reminds us, "The images of the body, the harsh and honest sounds and words of common language, which are held by the form, and the sense of humor ensuring that disappointment never seems like despair constitute Hacker's mark." The book continues to demand attention, for all the reasons that Hacker has proved worthwhile reading throughout her career.

Another book that still demands attention is *Love, Death, and the Changing of the Seasons* (1986). This collection chronicles in sonnets the cycle of love between two lesbians. The cycle begins simply, with mere hugs: "Hug; hug; this time I brushed my lips/just across yours, and fire down below/in February flared," and ends one year—212 pages—later: "I drank our one year out in brine instead/of honey from the seasons of your tongue." Throughout the sequence Hacker captures emotions in the slowest, most minute details: mundane intimacies, out-of-control moments, heartwrenching rejections, warnings unheeded, ensuing neediness and suffocating clinginess, cooling off, loneliness, loss, absence, anger, and ultimate acceptance of a love ended. *Love, Death, and the Changing of the Seasons* is a book that you cannot put down; it reads like a narrative about those for whom you care deeply. Hacker creates people with stunning emotional capacities, capacities that we see in ourselves, capacities from which we want to protect ourselves, and capacities we want to enjoy again. At times you want to call out to the "I," "hold back," "be careful," and at other times, you want to say: "call her," "take a risk." It is an incredibly interactive piece of writing, an engaging, humble, loving text, a text about human beings at their most vulnerable: Human beings in love.

Hacker writes about her relationships with women, and she writes in fixed forms because it brings her pleasure. "I write the way I do because it's the way that gives me most pleasure, and which finds me my way into the poem." When Hacker uses phrases such as "my way," she means more than just the simple "my" of a singular individual. She believes that "as a woman becomes more and more politicized, as a feminist, she realizes that her concerns are concrete, that while they apply to the world at large, her perceptions of them begin as perceptions of her own life. The political concerns express something that permeates her whole life, permeates *my* whole life." Through her verse Hacker continues to chronicle the process of women making changes and making connections, both in their own worlds and the world at large.

She also knows firsthand that sometimes women are unable to connect with one another. Hacker is especially compassionate about this inability, and she is not afraid to use her own experience as grounds for poetic musing: In the last poem, "August Silence," she includes in *Selected Poems, 1965-1990,* Hacker painfully and courageously resurrects the relationship she had with her dying mother-in-law, Iva's grandmother:

> Because you are
> my only daughter's only grandmother,
> because your only grandchild is my child
> I would have wished you to be reconciled
> to how and what
> I live. No name frames our connection, not
> "in-laws." I hoped, more than "your son's ex-wife."
> I've known you now for two-thirds of my life.

Much of Hacker's life work has been to frame the nameless inside the names, to work on providing forms for the formless. She has already succeeded, and she has not yet run out of stamina for the future. Marilyn Hacker's importance to contemporary poetry is synonymous with her persistent and heroic contribution of her own life experiences and her own life's wisdom to the feminist lesbian canon.

—Renee R. Curry

HAMILTON, Cicely Mary

Nationality: British. **Born:** Cicely Mary Hamill, in London, 15 June 1872. **Education:** Attended private schools in Malvern, England, and Homburg, Germany. **Military Service:** Clerk at the military hospital at Abbeye de Royaumont, France; Women's Auxiliary Corps; Concerts at the Front. **Career:** Worked as a pupil-teacher, translator, actor, and writer (journalist, novelist, dramatist, and social historian). **Awards:** Femina Vie Heureuse 1919; Civil List pension, 1938, for services to literature. **Member:** Women Writers' Suffrage League, Actresses' Franchise League, Women's Freedom League, Women's Tax Resistance League, British League for European Freedom, Society of Authors, League of Nations Union, Open Door Council, New Generation League, Six Point Group, Pioneer Players, Chelsea Fire Service, Soroptomists. **Died:** London, 6 December 1952.

Publications

Plays

The Sixth Commandment (produced London, 1906).
The Serjeant of Hussars (produced London, 1907).
Mrs. Vance (produced London, 1907).
Diana of Dobson's (produced London, 1908). London, Chapman & Hall, 1908.
A Pageant of Great Women (produced London, 1909, as *A Pageant of Famous Women*).
How the Vote Was Won, with Christopher St. John (produced London, 1909).

The Pot and the Kettle with Christopher St. John (produced London, 1909).
Just to Get Married (produced London, 1910).
The Home Coming (produced London, 1910; produced as *After 20 Years,* 1914).
The Cutting of the Knot (produced Glasgow, 1911; produced as *A Matter of Money,* London, 1913).
Jack and Jill and a Friend (produced London, 1911; produced as *Jack and Jill,* 1912).
The Constant Husband (produced London, 1912).
Lady Noggs (adaptation of story by Edgar Jepson; produced London, 1913).
Phyl (produced Brighton, 1913).
The Lady Killer (produced London, 1914).
The Child in Flanders (produced Abbeville, France, 1917; produced London, 1919).
Mrs. Armstrong's Admirer (produced London, 1920).
The Fair and the Brave (produced London, 1920).
The Human Factor (produced Birmingham, 1924; produced as *The Old Adam,* London, 1925).
The Beggar Prince (as *The Fairy Prince*, produced London, 1929).
Caravan (adaptation of *Katherina Knie,* by Carl Zuckmayer; produced London, 1932).
Mr Pompous and the Pussy-cat.

Novels

Just to Get Married. London, Chapman & Hall, 1911.
A Matter of Money. London, Chapman & Hall, 1916.
William an Englishman. London, Skeffington, 1919.
Theodore Savage. London, Leonard Parsons, 1922; revised as *Lest Ye Die,* London, Cape, 1928.
Full Stop. London, Dent, 1931.

Essays

"Triumphant Women," in *Edy: Recollections of Edith Craig,* edited by Eleanor Adlard. London, Frederick Muller, 1949.

Autobiography

Life Errant. London, Dent, 1935.

Political/Social Theory

Marriage as a Trade. London, Chapman & Hall, and New York, Moffat Yard, 1909.
Lament for Democracy. London, Dent, 1940.

Other

Senlis. London, Collins, 1917.
The Old Vic, with Lilian Baylis. London, Cape, and New York, Doran, 1926.
Modern Germanies as Seen by an Englishwoman. London, Dent, 1931.
Modern Italy as Seen by an Englishwoman. London, Dent, 1932.
Modern France as Seen by an Englishwoman. London, Dent, 1933.
Little Arthur's History of the 20th Century. London, Dent, 1933.
Modern Russia as Seen by an Englishwoman. London, Dent, 1934.
Modern Austria as Seen by an Englishwoman. London, Dent, 1935.
Modern Ireland as Seen by an Englishwoman. London, Dent, 1936.
Modern Scotland as Seen by an Englishwoman. London, Dent, 1937.
Modern Sweden as Seen by an Englishwoman. London, Dent, 1939.
Modern England as Seen by an Englishwoman. London, Dent, 1938.
The Englishwoman. London, British Council/Longman's Green, 1940.
Holland Today. London, Dent, 1950.

*

Bibliography: "Cicely Hamilton on Theatre: A Preliminary Bibliography" by Sue Thomas, in *Theatre Notebook,* 19(2), 1995.

Manuscript Collections: Edith Craig Archive, Ellen Terry Memorial Museum, Tenterden, Kent; Lord Chamberlain's Play Collection, British Library, London; Bodleian Library, Oxford; Harry Ransom Humanities Research Center, University of Austin, Texas.

Theatrical Activities:
Actor: **Plays**—several of her own plays, and Hannele's Dead Mother in *Hannele* by Gerhart Hauptmann, London, 1908; Sister Regina in *Sister Beatrice* by Maurice Maeterlinck, London, 1909; Mary Swayne in *Before Sunrise* by Bessie Hatton, 1911; Lady Simms in *The Twelve-Pound Look* by James M. Barrie, London, 1911; Mrs Knox in *Fanny's First Play* by George Bernard Shaw, London, 1911; Wilhelmina in *In the Workhouse* by Margaret Wynne Nevinson, London, 1911; Virginia in *The Sentimentalists* by George Meredith, 1911; role in *Pains and Penalties* by Laurence Housman, 1911; Mrs Barfield in *Esther Waters* by George Moore, 1911; Lady Macbeth in *Shakespeare's Dream* by Guyton Heath, 1912; Mrs Bretherton in *The Tide* by Basil Macdonald Hastings, 1912; Madame in *The Great Gamble* by Jerome K. Jerome, London, 1914; role in *The Golden Moth* by Fred Thompson and P.G. Wodehouse, London, 1921; role in *Coloman* by Edward Percy and Wallace B. Nichols, London, 1923.
Director: **Plays**—several of her own plays.

Critical Studies: *Barry Jackson and the London Theatre* by George W. Bishop, London, A. Baker, 1933; *Myself a Player* by Lena Ashwell, London, M. Joseph, 1936; *Women of Ideas and What Men Have Done to Them* by Dale Spender, London, Routledge & Kegan Paul, 1982, and her *Time and Tide Wait for No Man,* London, Pandora Press, 1984; *The Life and Rebellious Times of Cicely Hamilton* by Lis Whitelaw, London, Women's Press, 1990; "Cicely Hamilton, Independent Feminist" by Harriet Blodgett, in *Frontiers,* 11(1-2), 1990; "Re[pre]senting Eroticism: The Tyranny of Fashion in Feminist Plays of the Edwardian Age" by Sheila Stowell, in *Theatre History Studies,* 11, 1991; *A Stage of Their Own: Feminist Playwrights of the Suffrage* Era, by Sheila Stowell, Manchester, Manchester University Press, 1992; .

* * *

Cicely Hamilton's writing ranged from drama and the novel to socio-political theory and journalism, but her career as a writer was securely established in 1908 with the success of her play *Diana of Dobson's.* Formerly a teacher and actor, she had been exposed to both financially precarious and exploitative working conditions, which would in turn shape her writing. Raised in a military family, the future author's formative experiences included the early death of her mother and the frequent absence of her father; the unhappy experiences in various surrogate families that followed led to Hamilton's childhood suicide attempt. All of these events helped to prompt an independence of spirit and self-reliance that inspired her writings.

Hamilton's critique of the commodification of women and the celebration of women's autonomy in *Marriage as a Trade* (1909) is compatible with more recent lesbian feminist critiques of the institution of marriage. In her own life and throughout her writings Hamilton rejected marriage and defended women's right to do so, even going so far as to devote an entire chapter to "The Unmarried Woman" in her social history for the British Council, *The Englishwoman* (1940). Hamilton's single life was not solitary (until 1929 she lived with her sister, Evelyn Hamill) and her primary relationships were with women such as Elizabeth Abbott and Elizabeth Montizambert.

The women's suffrage movement found Hamilton politically active at branch level, as well as known nationally for her public speaking and writings. She was a member of various organizations, including the Pioneer Players, and was a founder member of the Women Writers' Suffrage League, the Actresses' Franchise League, and the editorial board of *The Englishwoman.* The success of plays such as *A Pageant of Great Women* (1910), *Jack and Jill and a Friend* (1911) and those co-written with Christopher St. John (Christabel Marshall)—*The Pot and the Kettle* and *How the Vote was Won*—was ensured by Hamilton's ability to engage with controversial issues in a humorous and original manner. She appropriated popular forms, subverting them through parody or mimicry, taking a familiar aphorism, stereotype, or cultural form and inexorably exposing the values inscribed within it. The role of the exceptional, individual woman in resisting oppressive systems is emphasized in Hamilton's feminist writings. This is exemplified by *A Pageant of Great Women,* devised by Cicely Hamilton and Edith Craig, in which Hamilton and Christopher St. John played cross-dressing women warriors. In *How the Vote Was Won* it is the collective action of comparatively undistinguished women that forces change, a positive outcome which, in Hamilton's later writings, seems remote.

Aware of the petty antagonisms and competition that impede a political movement, Hamilton dwelled at length on the dynamics of change. She identified the diverse attitudes of women, including the support some women provide to patriarchy in perpetuating notions of women's passivity. The development of Hamilton's feminist thinking reflects the difficulty of resisting social norms and bringing about social change. Her insistence on individualism and criticism of the psychological effects of collective action to some extent posed problems for her feminist position.

Hamilton's critique of patriarchy extended beyond marriage to explore war and international relationships. The years 1914-17 were spent in France, working as a clerk in the Abbeye de Royaumont while it was transformed into a military hospital. Hamilton performed plays for troops in France and Britain, joining Lena Ashwell's Concerts at the Front and forming a repertory company with Gertrude Jennings. Her response to World War I was, like that of many women involved in woman suffrage, one of conflicting emotions. The battle for women's enfranchisement was overshadowed by war. The war was a manifestation of women's disempowerment on an international scale, rendering visible the exclusion of women from the so-called public spheres of employment. While the prize-winning novel, *William an Englishman* seems to mark Hamilton's disillusionment with the women's suffrage movement, it embodies the profound displacement of gender by national identities that the war brought about. Hamilton's post-war writings constitute more than a series of nation-centered travelogues; they sustain her interest in the political dimension of all manner of relationships and national cultures.

An active member of many organizations, Hamilton developed a critique of the way organizations conventionally operate. In her later works, *Lament for Democracy* (1940) and *Life Errant,* she criticized the "herd mind" that developed in organizations, hindering any effective change and reinforcing dominant ideologies. Thus the changes women brought about after enfranchisement appeared to be less dramatic than anticipated, leaving institutions and their manner of operating relatively unaltered. What appears to be Hamilton's disillusionment is based on a developing understanding that social change depends not on individuals but on widespread institutional and organizational change, that the inclusion of hitherto marginalized groups can be used to reproduce rather than transform social norms.

Such insights were gained from a lifetime of activism. Hamilton remained vigilant, retaining a commitment to social change; she campaigned in support of women's rights to abortion and contraception. She sustained her commitment to theatre, writing for *Time & Tide* and *Woman's Leader.* Although *Lament for Democracy* is concerned with the "reason for the widespread failure of government by and for the people," in the same year *The Englishwoman* presented its author's relatively optimistic survey of both the progress achieved by women and the challenges still facing women who challenge patriarchy.

—Katharine Cockin

HANSBERRY, Lorraine

Nationality: American. **Born:** Chicago, Illinois, 19 May 1935. **Education:** Attended University of Wisconsin, 1948-50, Roosevelt College, Chicago School of Art Institute, and New School for Social Research, New York. **Family:** Married Robert Nemiroff in 1953 (divorced 1964). **Career:** Worked as a department store clerk, tag girl in a fur shop, and aide to a theatrical producer; waitress, hostess, and cashier in Greenwich Village restaurant, New York; associate editor, *Freedom* magazine, New York, c. 1952. Contributor to periodicals, including *Negro Digest, Theatre Arts,* and *Village Voice.* **Awards:** New York Drama Critics Circle Award, 1959, for *A Raisin in the Sun;* Cannes Film Festival special award, 1961, for *A Raisin in the Sun* (screenplay). **Member:** Dramatists Guild, Ira Aldrich Society, Institute for Advanced Study in the Theatre Arts. **Died:** New York, New York, 12 January 1965.

Publications

Plays

A Raisin in the Sun (three-act; produced New York, 1959). New York, Random House, 1959.

The Sign in Sidney Brustein's Window (three-act; produced New York, 1964). New York, Random House, 1965.

Les Blancs (two-act; produced New York, 1970). New York, Hart Stenographic Bureau, 1966; adapted by Robert Nemiroff as *Lorraine Hansberry's "Les Blancs,"* New York, S. French, 1972.
The Drinking Gourd. In *Les Blancs: The Collected Last Plays of Lorraine Hansberry,* 1972.
Les Blancs: The Collected Last Plays of Lorraine Hansberry, edited by Robert Nemiroff. New York, Random House, 1972.
What Use Are Flowers? (one-act). In *Les Blancs: The Collected Last Plays of Lorraine Hansberry,* 1972.

Screenplays: *A Raisin in the Sun,* 1960.

Essays

"Simone de Beauvoir and *The Second Sex:* An American Commentary." 1957.
"In Defense of the Equality of Men," in *The Norton Anthology of Literature by Women,* edited by Sandra M. Gilbert and Susan Gubar. New York, Norton, 1985.

Other

The Movement: Documentary of a Struggle for Equality, with others. New York, Simon & Schuster, 1964; as *A Matter of Colour: Documentary of the Struggle for Racial Equality in the U.S.A.,* London, Penguin, 1965.

Recordings: *A Raisin in the Sun* (cassette), Caedmon, 1972; *Lorraine Hansberry Speaks Out: Art and the Black Revolution,* Caedmon, 1972.

*

Media Adaptations: *To Be Young, Gifted, and Black: Lorraine Hansberry in Her Own Words* (play; adaptation of Hansberry's works by Robert Nemiroff), 1969; *Raisin* (musical stage adaptation of *A Raisin in the Sun*), 1974.

Bibliography: In *Hansberry's Drama: Commitment amid Complexity* by Steven R. Carter, Champaign, University of Illinois Press, 1991.

Critical Studies: "The Significance of Lorraine Hansberry" by Ossie Davis, in *Freedomways,* 5(3), summer 1965; *Confrontation and Commitment: A Study of Contemporary Drama* by C. W. E. Bigsby, Columbia, University of Missouri Press, 1968; "Lorraine Hansberry's Last Dramas" by E. Edward Farrison, in *CLA Journal,* 16(2), December 1972; "The Black Experience in Margaret Walker's *Jubilee* and Lorraine Hansberry's *The Drinking Gourd* by Bertie J. Powell, in *CLA Journal,* 21(2), December 1977; special Lorraine Hansberry edition of *Freedomways,* 19, 1979; *Lorraine Hansberry* by Anne Cheney, Boston, G. K. Hall, 1984; *Their Place on the Stage: Black Women Playwrights in America* by Elizabeth Brown-Guillory, n.p., 1988; "Colonialism and Culture in Lorraine Hansberry's *Les Blancs"* by Stephen R. Carter, in *MELUS,* 15(1), 1988, and his *Hansberry's Drama: Commitment amid Complexity,* Champaign, University of Illinois Press, 1991.

* * *

Lorraine Hansberry, the first black women to have a play produced on Broadway (*A Raisin in the Sun,* 1959), was concerned with the fight for civil, human, and women's rights. Her works reflect the race and women's movements of the late 1950s and early 1960s but are not militant. Ultimately life- and love-affirming, they focus on the bonds and conflicts of family and romantic relationships, the pursuit of individual fulfillment, and the clashes between traditions and modern life. All of the plays portray very strong women who stand up for their beliefs, an ideal that Hansberry herself exemplified in her focus on artistic, intellectual, and political pursuits. Tragically, such pursuits would be cut short by her early death as a result of cancer at the age of 34.

A Raisin in the Sun (also adapted for film and musical theater) is about a black family's struggle to leave a Chicago ghetto. The family members have different ideas about spending an inheritance: The mother, Lena, wants a house; her son, Walter Lee (whose wife, Ruth, is accidentally pregnant with their second child), to invest in a liquor store; his sister, Beneatha, to go to medical school. Lena finds the best house for the money in a pleasant, white neighborhood, but Walter Lee feels that the store was his last chance for success. Seeing his broken spirit, Lena bravely decides to settle for a small deposit on the house and allow him to invest in his dream, as long as enough money remains for Beneatha's education. Unfortunately, he is conned. Ruth considers an abortion, and the family argues over selling the house to a realtor who wants to keep the neighborhood segregated.

Lena and Beneatha represent traditional and modern types of female strength, and Hansberry respects what each has to offer. Lena is in tune with nature and acts as the moral head of the household. Beneatha is an atheist who feels that a career is more important than marriage and pursues self-expression through various hobbies. Ruth falls in the middle. Inevitably all three women clash and ultimately influence each other: Lena protests Ruth's planned abortion and admonishes Beneatha not to judge her brother. All the women must contend with Walter Lee's sexist attitudes: "Be a nurse, or get married, and shut up"; "If there's anyone you can't persuade to take a larger view of life, it's a woman." Beneatha's suitors are also representative—the rich, traditional man she doesn't love, and the less chauvinistic but more challenging African suitor, who asks her to come home with him and be a doctor in Africa. He points out her mother's courage: "Your mother still believes she can change things, still acts ... [she] represents more of the future that you... can you understand what a great thing she did?"

The only other play Hansberry would complete during her lifetime is *The Sign in Sidney Brustein's Window* (1964). Brustein, a liberal Jewish ex-activist in Greenwich Village, is reluctantly persuaded to reenter politics by actively supporting a candidate for public office. His wife Iris, a struggling actress, is in psychoanalysis and only now learning to think for herself: "... the first couple of years I just wanted to do what you wanted to do ... now something is ... changing me," she tells her husband. Brustein does not take Iris too seriously: "She always has opinions. If I paid them any attention I'd never accomplish anything." He wishes she would be more like his fantasy, more like her old self. Iris, in turn, takes out her career frustrations on him, expecting his help. As the relationship falters, Iris undergoes a dramatic transformation, actively trying to improve her career even though her husband thinks it silly.

Iris's sisters are also central to Hansberry's plot. Gloria, a call girl, plans to marry a friend of the Brustein's, and Mavis seems the paragon of stability but has silently suffered her own marital problems. Both of these women are shown to be victims of their efforts to fit into traditional roles—"There's a different style of 'man trap' in every kind of women." But despite their disillusionment, each woman ultimately takes some action to try to improve things: Iris with her job, Gloria with her marriage plans, and Mavis by backing Sidney politically. The play culminates when Sidney too, after a political setback, becomes truly motivate to stand up for his belief: "It takes too much energy not to care." Though there are tragedies, all hope is not lost for the characters struggling to come to terms with their beliefs and each other.

The play *Les Blancs* (1970), incomplete at the time of Hansberry's death, was adapted and completed by her ex-husband Robert Nemiroff. The story centers in black liberation in Africa, and its female characters include a white missionary doctor, who tells a curious male visitor that "Something went 'wrong' in my life ... it has been unutterably satisfying!... I've lived without a confidant for years; it isn't the strain it's painted to be." Other works include *The Drinking Gourd,* a TV movie script about slavery that was commissioned and then rejected for being too powerful. The story depicts heinous events that cause a submissive women to act aggressively. *What Use Are Flowers?* is an anti-war play that takes place after a nuclear holocaust wherein a dying hermit must impart all of his knowledge to the only other known human survivors, six boys and girls. Nemiroff also compiled Hansberry's writings, speeches, and letters into the patchwork play *To Be Young, Gifted, and Black* (1969).

Hansberry's unpublished writings directly reveal her feminist sentiments. She encouraged women to think socially instead of personally and to see their connection with other oppressed groups. In a letter submitted anonymously to *The Ladder* in 1957, she speaks of how female homosexuals are less likely to stand up for their rights than gay men because women "are not considered definitively human." And while in the yet-unpublished essay "Simone de Beauvoir and *The Second Sex:* An American Commentary" she argues that "if by some miracle women should not ever utter a single protest against their condition there would still exist among men those who could not endure in peace until her liberation had been achieved," Hansberry also acknowledges that "The station of women is hardly one that she would assume by choice." The secondary status of women in relation to men, not of women's choosing "is necessarily one of oppression, and the oppressed are by their nature ... forever in ferment and agitation against their condition and what they understand to be their oppressors. If not by overt rebellion or revolution," Hansberry prophetically states, "then in the thousand and one ways they will devise with and without consciousness to alter their condition."

—Leslie-Anne Skolnik

HARDING, Sandra G.

Nationality: American **Born:** San Francisco, California, 29 March 1935. **Education:** Douglass College, Rutgers University, B.A. 1956; New York University, M.A. and Ph.D. 1973. **Family:** Married (divorced); two children. **Career:** Assistant professor of philosophy, State University of New York at Albany, 1973-76; assistant professor, 1976-79, professor of philosophy since 1986, and director, women's studies program, 1985-92, University of Delaware, Newark; adjunct professor of philosophy and women's studies, University of California, Los Angeles, beginning 1994. Visiting professor of philosophy and women's studies, University of Amsterdam, 1987, University of Costa Rica, 1990, University of California, Los Angeles, 1992, and Swiss Federal Institute of Technology, 1993. **Awards:** Fund for the Improvement of Postsecondary Education fellowship, 1982-83; National Science Foundation fellowship, 1983; Mellon fellowship, 1984-85; named Woman Philosopher of the Year, 1990. **Member:** American Philosophical Association, Society for Values in Higher Education, Society for Women in Philosophy. **Address:** Department of Philosophy, University of Delaware, Newark, Delaware 19716; Department of Philosophy, University of California, Los Angeles, Los Angeles, California 90024, U.S.A.

Publications

Nonfiction

The Science Question in Feminism. Ithaca, New York, Cornell University Press, 1986.

Whose Science? Whose Knowledge? Thinking from Women's Lives. Ithaca, New York, Cornell University Press, 1991.

Essays

"Rethinking Standpoint Epistemology: 'What Is Strong Objectivity'?" in *Feminist Epistemologies,* edited by Linda Alcoff and Elizabeth Potter. New York and London, Routledge, 1994.

Other

Editor, *Can Theories Be Refuted?* Dordrecht, D. Reidel, 1976.

Editor, with Merrill Hintikka, *Discovering Reality: Feminist Perspectives on Epistemology, Metaphysics, Methodology, and Philosophy of Science.* Dordrecht, D. Reidel, 1983.

Editor, *Feminism and Methodology.* Bloomington, Indiana University Press, 1987.

Editor, with Jean O'Barr, *Sex and Scientific Inquiry.* Chicago, University of Chicago Press, 1987.

Editor, *The "Racial" Economy of Science: Toward a Democratic Future.* Bloomington, Indiana University Press, 1993.

* * *

Sandra Harding has written and edited several books that examine the relationship between feminist theory and science. In *The Science Question in Feminism* (1986) and *Whose Science? Whose Knowledge: Thinking from Women's Lives* (1991), she focuses on the realms of scientific epistemology and methodology, bringing to the table a long-overdue discussion of how such bodies of knowledge might be transformed or revisioned within a feminist context.

An antiessentialist philosopher—Harding views the continuation of racism and sexism to be the result of the erroneous assumption that observable trends in history are *ipso facto* "natural" or universal laws—she believes women capable of challenging the status quo of oppression and subordination by social constructs through their intuitive analysis of these same constructs as oppressive and subordinative. *The Science Question in Feminism* reveals the gender biases of Western science by attempting an answer to the question "Is it possible to use for emancipatory ends sciences that are apparently so intimately involved in Western, bourgeois, and masculine projects?" Beyond this, what would a "feminist" science be like?

Whose Science? Whose Knowledge? is an overview of feminist theories on these very same issues. Drawing on writers from Francis Bacon to Evelyn Fox Keller, she outlines the prevailing feminist position: that Western science is *not* an objective, disinterested, culture-neutral search for "knowledge." Rather, it is sexist, culturally biased, financially motivated, and invasive of the subject of study by its very methodology. Because of their intuitive nature and their position outside the dominant masculine ideology, woman can provide the missing ingredient that can transform science into its creative, objective ideal. Able to see beyond the surface they can discern the subtle, even hidden, biases that color hypothetical reasoning; as outsiders to the social and political scientific network, their vision is more complete. "We cannot 'strip nature bare' to 'reveal her secrets' as conventional views have held," notes Harding using a rape metaphor typical of science-speak, "for no matter how long the striptease continues or how rigorous its choreography, we will always find under each 'veil' only nature-as-conceptualized-within-cultural projects; we will always (but not only) find more veils."

In addition to her own work on the subject, Harding has edited several important collections on the relationship between women and science. *Discovering Reality: Feminist Perspectives* (1983), which she edited with Merrill B. Hintikka, contains 16 essays that respond to the question "Are there—can there be—distinctive feminist perspectives on epistemology, metaphysics, methodology, and philosophy of science?" In *The "Racial" Economy of Science: Towards a Democratic Future* (1993) she broadens her appraisal of science by collecting and introducing a number of essays that question the supposed universality of Western scientific study, reevaluate the scientific optimism remaining as a legacy of the Enlightenment, and raise a variety of other social, multicultural, and ethical concerns.

—Lynn MacGregor

H.D.

Pseudonym for Hilda Doolittle. **Other Pseudonyms:** Delia Alton; J. Beran; Helga Dart; Helga Dorn; Edith Gray; John Helforth; D. A. Hill; Sylvania Penn; Rhoda Peter. **Nationality:** American. **Born:** Bethlehem, Pennsylvania, 10 September 1886. **Education:** Bryn Mawr College, 1904-06. **Family:** Married Richard Aldington in 1913 (divorced 1938); one daughter. **Career:** Literary editor of the *Egoist*, 1916-17; contributing editor of the cinema journal *Close-Up*, 1927-31; contributor of poetry to newspapers and periodicals, sometimes under various pseudonyms. **Awards:** *Poetry* Guarantors Prize, 1915, for "The Wind Sweepers," "Storm," "Pool," "The Garden," and "Moonrise"; *Little Review* Vers Libre Prize, 1917, for "Sea Poppies"; *Poetry* Helen Haire Levinson Prize, 1938, for "Sigel XV"; Harriet Monroe Memorial Prize, 1958, for "In Time of Gold," "Nails for Petals," and "Sometimes and After"; Brandeis University Creative Arts Award for Poetry, 1959; Bryn Mawr College Citation for Distinguished Service, 1960; American Academy of Arts and Letters Award of Merit Medal, 1960. **Died:** Zurich, 27 September 1961.

Publications

Poetry

Sea Garden. London, Constable, and Boston and New York, Houghton Mifflin, 1916.
The Tribute and Circe: Two Poems. Cleveland, Clerk's Private Press, 1917.
Hymen. London, Egoist Press, and New York, Holt, 1921.
Heliodora and Other Poems. London, Cape, and Boston, Houghton Mifflin, 1924.
Collected Poems of H.D. New York, Boni & Liveright, 1925.
H.D., edited by Hugh Mearns. New York, Simon & Schuster, 1926.
Red Roses for Bronze. London, Chatto & Windus, Boston and New York, Houghton Mifflin, 1931.
The Usual Star. Dijon, France, Darantière, 1934.
Trilogy. New York, New Direction, 1973.
- *The Walls Do Not Fall.* London and New York, Oxford University Press, 1944.
- *Tribute to the Angels.* London and New York, Oxford University Press, 1945.
- *The Flowering of the Rod.* London and New York, Oxford University Press, 1946.

By Avon River (includes prose). New York, London, and Toronto, Macmillan, 1949; revised, Redding Ridge, Connecticut, Black Swan, 1986.
What Do I Love? London, Brendin, 1950.
Selected Poems of H.D. New York, Grove, 1957.
Helen in Egypt. New York, Grove, 1961.
Two Poems (originally published in *Life and Letters Today,* 1937). Berkeley, ARIF, 1971.
Hermetic Definition. New York, New Directions Press, and Oxford, Carcanet, 1972.
Temple of the Sun. Berkeley, ARIF, 1972.
The Poet and the Dancer (originally published in *Life and Letters Today,* December 1935). San Francisco, Five Trees Press, 1975.
Priest and A Dead Priestess Speaks. Port Townsend, Washington, Copper Canyon Press, 1983.
Collected Poems 1912-1944, edited by Louis L. Martz. New York, New Directions Press, 1983.
Selected Poems, edited by Louis L. Martz. New York, New Directions Press, 1988.

Novels

Palimpsest. Dijon, France, Darantière, and Boston, Houghton Mifflin, 1926; revised, Carbondale, Southern Illinois University Press, 1968.
Hedylus. Boston, Houghton Mifflin, and Oxford, Blackwell, 1928; revised, Redding Ridge, Connecticut, Black Swan, and Cheadle, Carcanet, 1980.
Kora and Ka. Dijon, France, Darantière, 1934; Berkeley, Bios, 1978.
Nights (as John Helforth). Dijon, France, Darantière, 1935; New York, New Directions Press, 1986.

Bid Me to Live (A Madrigal). New York, Grove, 1960; enlarged edition, Redding Ridge, Connecticut, Black Swan, 1983.
HERmione. New York, New Directions, 1981; as *Her,* London, Virago, 1984.
Asphodel, edited by Robert Spoo. Durham and London, Duke University Press, 1992.
Paint It Today. New York, New York University Press, 1992.

Plays

Hippolytus Temporizes: A Play in Three Acts. Boston, Houghton Mifflin, 1927; revised, Redding Ridge, Connecticut, Black Swan, 1986.
Borderline—A Pool Film with Paul Robeson. London, Mercury Press, 1930.

For Children

The Hedgehog. London, Brendin, 1936; New York, New Directions Press, 1988.

Autobiography

The Gift. New York, New Directions Press, 1982.

Other

Tribute to Freud, with Unpublished Letters by Freud to the Author. New York, Pantheon, 1956; 2nd edition as *Tribute to Freud: Writing on the Wall,* Boston, Godine, 1974.
End to Torment: A Memoir of Ezra Pound, edited by Norman Holmes Pearson and Michael King. New York, New Directions Press, 1979.
Notes on Thought and Vision and The Wise Sappho. San Francisco, City Lights, 1982.

Translator, *Choruses from the Iphigenia in Aulis,* by Euripides. London, Ballantyne Press, and Cleveland, Ohio, Clerk's Private Press, 1916.
Translator, *Ion,* by Euripides. London, Chatto & Windus, and Boston and New York, Houghton Mifflin, 1937; revised, Redding Ridge, Connecticut, Black Swan, 1986.

*

Manuscript Collection: Beinecke Library, Yale University, New Haven, Connecticut.

Bibliography: "H.D.: A Preliminary Checklist" by Jackson R. Bryer and Pamela Roblyer, in *Contemporary Literature,* 10, autumn 1969; *H.D.: A Bibliography 1905-1990* by Michael Boughn, London and Charlottesville, University of Virginia Press, 1993.

Critical Studies: "The Art of H.D." by Kathryn Gibbs Gibbons, in *Mississippi Quarterly,* 15, fall 1962; *Hilda Doolittle* by Vincent Quinn, New York, Twayne, 1967; "Who Buried H.D.? A Poet, Her Critics, and Her Place in 'The Literary Tradition'" by Susan Stanford Friedman, in *College English,* 36, March 1975, and her "Creating a Woman's Mythology: H.D.'s *Helen in Egypt,"* in *Women's Studies,* 5, 1977; *Images of H.D.* by Eric Walter White, London, Enitharmon Press, 1976; "The Echoing Spell of H.D.'s *Trilogy"* by Susan Gubar, in *Contemporary Literature,* 19, spring 1978; "Family, Sexes, Psyche: An Essay on H.D. and the Muse of the Woman Writer" by Rachel Blau duPlessis, in *Montemora,* 6, 1979; *Psyche Reborn: The Emergence of H.D.* by S. Friedman, Bloomington, Indiana University Press, 1981; "Hilda in Egypt" by Albert Gelpi, in *Southern Review,* 18, spring 1982; *H.D.: The Life and Work of an American Poet* by Janice S. Robinson, Boston, Houghton, 1982; *Herself Defined: The Poet H.D. and Her World* by Barbara Guest, New York, Doubleday, 1984; *Women of the Left Bank, Paris, 1900-1940* by Shari Benstock, Austin, University of Texas Press, 1986; *H.D.: The Career of That Struggle* by R. duPlessis, Bloomington and Indianapolis, Indiana University Press, 1986; "Recovering the Human Equation: H.D.'s *Hermetic Definition*" by Burton Hatlen, in *Sagetrieb,* 6, fall 1987; *Thought and Vision: A Critical Reading of H.D.'s Poetry* by Angela DiPlace Fritz, Washington D.C., Catholic University of America Press, 1988; *H.D.: Modern Critical Views* edited by Harold Bloom, New York and Philadelphia, Chelsea House, 1989; *H.D. between Image and Epic: The Mysteries of Her Poetics* by Gary Burnett, Ann Arbor, University of Michigan Research Press, 1989; *Penelope's Web: Gender, Modernity, H.D.'s Fiction* by Friedman, Cambridge, Cambridge University Press, 1990; *H.D.: The Poetics of Childbirth and Creativity* by Donna Krolik Hollenberg, Boston, Northeastern University Press, 1991; "Lesbian Romanticism: H.D.'s Fictional Representations of Frances Gregg and Bryher" by Cassandra Laity, in *Paint It Today,* New York, New York University Press, 1992; *Out of Line: History, Psychoanalysis, and Montage in H.D.,'s Long Poems* by Susan Edmunds, Stanford, California, Stanford University Press, 1995.

* * *

Hilda Doolittle is better known as H.D. and her use of initials as a mark of authorship indicates much about her as a literary figure. H.D. was a leading figure in the Imagist movement at the start of her career, but developed to become a leading poet intimately concerned with the identity of woman both as woman and as author. She departed from literary and cultural conventions throughout her life in an attempt to reconcile her personal inner conflicts about her own identity. H.D. is now recognized as a vital figure in the development of American poetry; more recently, her novels have also been rediscovered as worthy of further consideration.

Born in 1886 and raised by an artistic mother and scientific father in a Moravian community in Pennsylvania, H.D. determined to devote herself to literature after meeting Ezra Pound in Bryn Mawr in 1901. Pound adopted what would become a familiar role of teacher to his friend; the couple became engaged in 1907, but H.D. already had doubts about the constrictions and possibilities of conventional marriage. She simultaneously developed a close friendship with fellow student Frances Gregg and was confused over her newly recognized bisexuality. In perhaps her best novel, *HERmione,* the love triangle of the characters Hermione Gart, George Lowndes, and Fayne Rabb is an autobiographical fictionalization of the relationship between H.D., Ezra Pound, and Frances Gregg, respectively. The novel reveals H.D.'s exploration of her own retrospective interiority, as she struggles to find her own identity by attempting to define and to order her experiences.

In 1911 H.D. followed Pound to Europe and became a member of his literary circle, which included such eminent personalities as William Butler Yeats, Ford Madox Ford, and F.S. Flint. While Pound became engaged to Dorothy Shakespear and Gregg returned to America to marry Louis Wilkinson, H.D. achieved her first poetic success: Her first three published poems appeared in the influential *Poetry* magazine in January 1913. Pound promoted and approved of their Imagist mode, and he affixed "H.D. Imagiste" to the bottom of the manuscript. H.D. maintained these initials as her signature throughout her career as the shield against any gendered authorial identity. The Imagist movement proclaimed a determination for a new poetry favoring precise language, a focus on musical rhythm, and an image that concerned itself directly with the "thing" under consideration. "Priapus: Keeper-of-Orchards," retitled "Orchard" for inclusion in her 1925 *Collected Poems,* is an exemplary Imagist text. The androgynous narrator pleas with a "god of the orchard" to be spared from loneliness and from the simultaneous death and promise of rebirth implicit in the Fall. The language of the poem is exact and direct with sharply defined feminine imagery of satiation. The poem can also be interpreted as an encoded plea for release from the constrictions of conventional society, and especially as the plea of a woman desirous of freedom from the societal definition of "woman."

H.D.'s first volume of poetry, 1916's *Sea Garden,* confirmed her place as a renowned author at the forefront of the Imagist movement and furthered her popularity as a poet. Many of H.D.'s characteristic themes are evident within these pages. Her frequent revisions of the usual portrayals of Greek mythological figures are an aspect of H.D.'s consistent re-visioning of the male-dominated formation of history, culture, and tradition. She thus recreates traditional mythology in an attempt to redetermine the masculine conceptions of women that dominate culture.

As Louis L. Martz points out in his introduction to her *Collected Poems 1912-1944,* H.D. was to "inhabit constantly the borderline" as a bisexual woman poet. Her poetry is also steeped in the dualities that she finds necessary of investigation as part of her movement toward synthesis. The human passion of the speaker of the poems is a mask for the impersonalized identity of the poet, and as a bisexual American woman living in Europe, H.D. herself transgressed established cultural, traditional, and gender boundaries. H.D.'s work maintained a focus upon the problems of identity, and a poem such as "Sea Rose" explores her difficulties as a woman author while at the same time defying society's definitions of feminine beauty and celebrating her own unique difference. Her imagery is also distinctively feminine; for example, she frequently presents flowers as symbols invested with an almost sacred eroticism celebrating the female body.

H.D. never stopped questioning masculine definitions of women, and, in challenging established gender roles, she evoked androgynous personas and imagery in her early career. She married Richard Aldington in 1913, but his participation in World War I and subsequent affair with another woman drove them apart, and their divorce was finalized in 1938 (her only child, Perdita, was born in 1919). H.D. began a lifelong relationship with Winifred Ellerman (known as Bryher) in 1918, but the personal traumas of 1919 were succeeded by her first breakdown. She recovered for a trip to Greece in 1920 and also visited Egypt in 1923 (the recollection of which was to become a fertile source in her poetry), but the years between the world wars were principally ones of self-definition for H.D. She experimented in prose and attempted to find a definition of self through exploration of masculine-defined traditions. Many of her novels have not been reprinted, but those available reveal that H.D.'s experimentation between the world wars centered upon an introspective reconsideration of her own life, as in *Bid Me to Live (A Madrigal).* As Robert Spoo points out in his introduction to the novel, "part of *Asphodel* overlaps with the period covered by *Madrigal,*" but *Asphodel*—an early version of the same novel—focuses on the characterization of D.H. Lawrence, who was a close friend of H.D. toward the end of World War I. H.D.'s novels are concerned principally with the interiority of the central female protagonist, and many of her techniques, such as repetition and fragmented syntax, belong to the central concerns of the Modernist literary movement and simultaneously reflect her interest in the cinema.

In "Eurydice," H.D. re-visions mythology by retelling the familiar myth of Orpheus and Eurydice from Eurydice's perspective. Preoccupied with the injustice of the voicelessness of women in a male-dominated culture, she frequently revised myths or other literature by providing the woman's perspective. In *By Avon River* she gives voice to the offstage character of Claribel from William Shakespeare's *The Tempest.* Many of H.D.'s poems demand that readers reconsider the masculine domination of literature and culture. In "Helen," the poem's speaker suggests that "All Greece hates / the still eyes in the white face" only because hatred of and desire for traditional feminine beauty are conflicted in the traditional masculine construction of women. In a later, longer poem, *Helen in Egypt,* H.D. revises the masculine epic tradition. Helen is the central consciousness in an exploration of the Trojan Wars as seen from her own retrospective viewpoint, and Helen's inner journey—representative of women's search for identity—is one central theme of the poem. H.D. simultaneously integrates the mythical and personal into a predominantly female perspective. Her own conflicts over her identity as a bisexual are inextricably intertwined with her conflicts about the links between love, identity, and creativity.

In the early 1930s, H.D.'s previously established interest in psychoanalysis culminated in her becoming both student and patient of Dr. Sigmund Freud. Through these sessions, she became more reconciled to her divisive identity as a bisexual. She began to see her personal experiences in terms of the universal and developed her own psychic experiences through a continuing interest in and practice of the occult. This increased self-knowledge enabled H.D. to conquer the writing block of the 1930s, and culminated in an emotional and powerful series of three poems which she wrote around 1935. "The Dancer" celebrates the speaker's love for a woman and the relationship with a "sister" who has "only leisure; / infinite leisure / to proclaim / harmony." "The Master" is a tribute to Freud, and the speaker affirms that the psychological difficulty necessitating their sessions was the need of reconciliation for the "I" who "had two loves separate." But H.D. also demonstrates that she had problems with Freud's male-oriented psychoanalytical theories. She challenges his phallocentrism with the proclamation that "*woman is perfect*" (emphasized by her italics), but the phrase can also be interpreted as a protest against conventional male expectations and positioning of women. Culminating in "The Poet," this sequence demonstrates H.D.'s acceptance of herself as a bisexual as she attempts to mediate between reason and imagination and demonstrates a renewed confidence in her ability and role as poet.

In *Trilogy,* published in three separate parts as *The Walls Do Not Fall, Tribute to Angels,* and *The Flowering of the Rod* during World War II, H.D. revises male religion and posits a matriarchal goddess as the force of love that dominates the universe. The woman figure thus incorporates the promise of rebirth and new creation in response to the destruction of the war. Susan Stanford Friedman points out in her *Psyche Reborn* that "mother-symbols appear in H.D.'s epics to inspire the daughter's search for autonomous identity and the principle of love in a hate-filled world dominated by the forces of death." Again heavily dominated by polarities in need of unity, H.D.'s poems celebrate the powers of survival. The three-part epic also exhibits the palimpsestic nature of the poet's later perceptions of humanity and time as she insists upon a universality of experience. Following her immersion in psychoanalysis, her later work reveals her belief that history is a many layered text but her views remain affirmative in her embrace of a matriarchal figure and the omnipresence of the possibility for renewal.

In the 1950s, H.D. renewed her ties with both Pound and Aldington, and her long poem, *Hermetic Definition,* draws together many of her dominant themes once again. For H.D., autonomy as a woman author could only be achieved through her creative attempts to redefine literary traditions with a woman's voice. Creating a palimpsest of her life and works reveals a woman poet striving not only to enter a man's world, but also to reinvest it with a woman's perspective and insights. Recent criticism has rightfully removed the constrictive label of "Imagist" from H.D. The achievements of her career as an influential and developing woman poet, as well as the wealth of her texts and unique female perspective, are finally being recognized.

—Lucy Morrison

HEAD, Bessie

Nationality: South African; granted Botswanan citizenship, 1979. **Born:** Bessie Amelia Emery, Pietermaritzburg, South Africa, 6 July 1937; immigrated to Botswana, 1964. **Education:** Studied at Umbilo Road High School; trained to be a primary teacher in South African schools. **Family:** Married journalist Harold Head in 1962 (divorced); one son. **Career:** Teacher in primary schools, South Africa and Botswana, 1956-59; journalist with Drum Publications, Johannesburg, c. 1960-62; writer, beginning 1963; voluntary unpaid farm work in Botswana; representative of Botswana at the University of Iowa international writers conference, 1977-78, and in Denmark, 1980. Contributor to periodicals, including *Presence Africane, New African,* London *Times,* and *Transition.* **Awards:** *New Statesman* Jock Campbell award nomination, 1978, for *The Collector of Treasures and Other Botswana Village Tales.* **Died:** Botswana, of hepatitis, 17 April 1986.

PUBLICATIONS

Novels

When Rain Clouds Gather. New York, Simon & Schuster, 1968; London, Gollancz, 1969.
Maru. London, Gollancz, and New York, McCall, 1971.
A Question of Power. London, Davis Poynter, and New York, Pantheon, 1973.

Short Stories

The Collector of Treasures and Other Botswana Village Tales. London, Heinemann, and Cape Town, Philip, 1977.
Tales of Tenderness and Power, edited by Gillian Stead Eilersen. Johannesburg, Donker, 1989; London, Heinemann, 1990.

Poetry

"Things I Don't Like," in *The New African* (London), 1(7), 1962.

History

Serowe: Village of the Rain Wind. Cape Town, Philip, and London, Heinemann, 1981.
A Bewitched Crossroad: An African Saga. Johannesburg, Donker, 1984.

Autobiography

A Woman Alone: Autobiographical Writings, selected and edited by Craig MacKenzie. Oxford, Heinemann, and Portsmouth, New Hampshire, Heinemann, 1990.

Other

"Letter from Botswana," in *New York Times,* 1971.
"Dear Tim, Will You Please Come to My Birthday Party...," in *One Parent Families,* edited by Dulan Barber. London, Davis-Poynter, 1975.
"Notes from a Quiet Backwater...," in *Drum* (Johannesburg), 1982.
Foreword to *Native Life in South Africa,* by Sol Plaatje. Johannesburg, Ravan, 1982.
"A Search for Historical Continuity and Roots," in *Momentum: On Recent South African Writing,* edited by M. J. Daymond, J. U. Jacobs, and Margaret Lenta. Pietermaritzburg, University of Natal Press, 1984.
Foreword to *Call Me Woman,* by Ellen Kuzwayo. Johannesburg, Ravan, and London, Women's Press, 1985.
"Some Happy Memories of Iowa," in *The World Comes to Iowa: Iowa International Anthology,* edited by P. Engle, R. Torrevillas, and H.N. Engle. Ames, Iowa State University Press, 1987.
A Gesture of Belonging: Letters from Bessie Head, 1965-1979, edited by Randolph Vigne. London, SA Writers, and Portsmouth, New Hampshire, Heinemann, 1991.

*

Bibliography: *Bessie Head: A Bibliography* by Susan Gardner and Patricia E. Scott, Grahamstown, National English Literary Museum, 1986; *Bessie Head: A Bibliography* by Cathy Giffuni, Gaborone, Botswana, 1987.

Manuscript Collection: Khama III Memorial Museum, Serowe; Mugar Memorial Library, Boston University.

Critical Studies: "Women in Literature" by Lewis Nkosi, in *Africa Woman* (London), 6, 1976; *The Novel in the Third World* by Charles R. Larson, Washington, D.C., Inscape, 1976; "Bessie Head's Alienated Heroine: Victim or Villain?" by Femi Ojo-Ade, in *Ba Shiru* (Madison, Wisconsin), 8(2), 1977; "Bessie Head's *A Question of Power:* The Journey through Disintegration into Wholeness" by Linda Susan Beard, in *Colby Literary Quarterly* (Waterville, ME), 15, 1979; *Women Writers in Black Africa* by Lloyd W. Brown, Westport, Connecticut, Greenwood Press, 1981;

"Bessie Head: Restless in a Distant Land" by Charlotte H. Bruner, in *When the Drumbeat Changes,* edited by Carolyn Parker and Stephen Arnold, Washington, D.C., Three Continents, 1981; *Conversations with African Writers: Interviews with 26 African Writers,* edited by Lee Nichols, Washington, D.C., Voice of America, 1981; "Womanism: The Dynamics of the Contemporary Black Female Novel in English" by Chikwenye Okonyo Ogunyemi, in *Signs: Journal of Women in Culture and Society* (Chicago), 11(1), 1985; "Feminist Perspectives in African Fiction: Bessie Head and Buchi Emecheta" by Nancy Topping Bazin, in *Black Scholar* (Oakland, California), 17(2), March/April 1986; "Women's Role in Bessie Head's Ideal World" by Virginia U. Ola, in *Ariel* (Calgary, Alberta), 17(4), October 1986; "'A Nice-Time Girl' Strikes Back: An Essay on Bessie Head's *A Question of Power*" by Margaret E. Tucker, in *Research in African Literatures* (Bloomington, Indiana), 19(2), summer 1988; "Myth, Exile, and the Female Condition: Bessie Head's *The Collector of Treasures*" by Sara Chetin, in *Journal of Commonwealth Literature* (Oxford), 24(1), 1989; *Bessie Head: An Introduction* by Craig MacKenzie, Grahamstown, National English Literary Museum, 1989; *The Tragic Life: Bessie Head and Literature in Southern Africa,* edited by Cecil Abrahams, Trenton, New Jersey, Africa World, 1990; "'We Bear the World and We Make It': Bessie Head and Olive Schreiner" by Robin Visel, in *Research in African Literature,* 21, fall 1990; "Mother/lands: Self and Separation in the Work of Buchi Emecheta, Bessie Head, and Jean Rhys" by Elaine Savory Fido, in *Motherlands: Black Women's Writing from Africa, the Caribbean, and South Asia,* London, Women's Press, 1991.

* * *

Bessie Head is one of Southern Africa's most powerful voices of the 1970s and 1980s. She matches the vigor and passion of other women authors in that region writing in English—Nadine Gordimer, Ellen Kuzwayo, and Doris Lessing. Born to a white mother and a black father, in a colonialist and severely apartheid society especially hostile to people of racially mixed heritage, Head suffered the anguish of being an alien to both races. Yet out of the torture of political and spiritual displacement grew a body of work that is an unique blend of unflinching depiction of oppressive forces and lyrical beauty. Head's writing creates new worlds out of harsh realities in which despair is redeemed by hope, often through the figure of the woman-outsider.

Head's own state as an outcast influenced the path her life and work would take. After an early marriage, a brief teaching career, and a stint as journalist for Drum Publications in Johannesburg, she found herself unable to live in South Africa. Facing unrelenting racial strife and a growing sense of alienation from the community of "coloreds" (as people of mixed heritage were called), Head emigrated, with her son, to Botswana in 1963. She considered Botswana unique because, in remaining unconquered by foreigners, it retained some of the unassuming majesty and the non-exploitative communities of ancient Africa.

Head's longing for the beauty of pre-colonial southern Africa, her experience of exile, and the attempt to understand the causes and injustices of racism, created a compelling set of forces in her writing. The struggle was to recover a sense of one's own history and the dignity of a self stamped down by colonialist exploitation, especially that of women who were usually subject to state as well as patriarchal ideologies. The answer lay not in abstract concepts, but in human relationships that revealed the good and evil hidden in the recesses of their souls.

Head's first novel, *When Rain Clouds Gather* (1969), depicts these issues with scathing political commentary and inspiring idealism. This work, which the author herself described as authentic to a South African black point of view, drew upon her experience in living with a refugee community in Northern Botswana. Corruption (on the part of both black and white) and interracial wariness plague Makhaya, a Zulu, who is the author's symbol of the refugee-exile. It is the help of the strong, calm Paulina Sebeso that enables the achievement of harmony and new faith in black leadership which Head presents as alternatives to war and abusive power.

In *Maru* (1971), Head exposes this unjust exercise of power in black-against-black racism. Masarwa (or Bush people) are oppressed by Botswanans in a country to which Head had fled in the hope of escaping atrocities. The conflict of good and evil becomes morally ambiguous because the antagonists, Maru and Moleka, both reflect and contrast each other. In this narrative of the resilient goodness of Margaret Cadmore, a San (Bushman) outsider, who fascinates both of them, Head presents a more contemplative tale of the equivocal triumph of love and peace over arrogance and ferocity.

This co-existence of good and evil, not their mere opposition, informs the most well-known and widely acclaimed of Head's writing—her third novel, the semi-autobiographical *A Question of Power* (1974). Not many have explored with such depth the force of evil that grips people and leads them with irresistible momentum towards destruction. The protagonist, Elizabeth, born to a white mother and a black stable boy, illegitimate and illegal (the Immorality Act of 1957 prohibited inter-racial union), carries the stigma of madness attached to anyone of mixed origins. Despite the trauma of experiencing unrelenting savagery from the men in her dreams, Elizabeth gains a faith in goodness and love. Even her madness becomes a potentially subversive act, because it breaks the prescribed pattern of linear development. This process of liberation from an internalized oppression is the means by which Elizabeth attains self-reliance. Her victory symbolizes an inversion of traditional narratives written about women's powerlessness, and the end result is serenity, with an almost mystic quality in the insistence on the sacredness of life.

Elizabeth's story depicts the gender politics of male brutality and female resistance. In this setting, the rebellion by the marginalized woman provides the potential for revolution against oppressive forces. Head's short stories are crystallizations of similar issues. *The Collector of Treasures* (1977) creates a tapestry that complements her other work in describing her philosophy of humanism and communality, especially of love as a magical force strong enough to bring hope in a sordid world. The narrative technique of both the longer and shorter works reveal the origins of her material in oral traditions, with Head frequently weaving her commentary into the stories.

In a different genre, *Serowe: Village of the Rain Wind* (1981) is a factual account of ancient migrations and recent crises, linking the political with the spiritual, as do her other works; but here, Head offers a new perspective on issues such as the conflict between Christianity and indigenous religions, the debilitating impact of belief in witchcraft, and the erosion of communal values resulting from this. In this, Head attempts a revisioning of Africans in this region against the accounts written by foreign historians, interpreting their migrations as efforts more to prevent war than to indulge in savage blood-baths.

Head's novels, plays, and diaries, as well as her stories for children, are characterized by a tenacity of conviction that power and hierarchy are key sources of imbalance and injustice, and that the struggle for freedom and equality is the answer towards transformation. Thus, Head's vocabulary is not one of nihilism, but of an invincible belief in women's strength and wisdom that emerge from brutal experiences to become sources of inspiration to other women. In combining grotesque evil with profound beauty, Bessie Head herself fulfills what she describes as the main function of a writer—infusing life with magic and conveying its wonder.

—Sonita Sarker

HEILBRUN, Carolyn G(old)

Pseudonym: Amanda Cross. **Nationality:** American. **Born:** East Orange, New Jersey, 13 January 1926. **Education:** Wellesley College, Wellesley, Massachusetts, B.A. 1947; Columbia University, New York, M.A. 1951, Ph.D. in English literature 1959. **Family:** Married James Heilbrun in 1945; two daughters and one son. **Career:** Instructor in English, Brooklyn College of the City University of New York, 1959-60; instructor, 1960-62, assistant professor, 1962-67, associate professor, 1967-72, professor of English, beginning 1972, Avalon Foundation professor in the humanities, 1986-93, Columbia University, New York. Visiting lecturer at Union Theological Seminary, 1968-70, Swarthmore College, 1970, and Yale University, 1974; visiting professor at University of California, Santa Cruz, 1979, and Princeton University, 1981. Member of policy advisory council, Danforth Foundation, beginning 1978. Editor, with Nancy K. Miller, of New Gender and Culture series, Columbia University Press. Contributor to periodicals, including *New York Times Book Review, Saturday Review,* and *Texas Quarterly.* Member of editorial boards of *Virginia Woolf Newsletter,* 1971-72, *Virginia Woolf Quarterly,* 1971-73, *Twentieth-Century Literature,* beginning 1973, and *Signs,* beginning 1975. **Awards:** Mystery Writers of America Scroll, 1964, for *In the Last Analysis;* Guggenheim fellow, 1965-66; Rockefeller fellow, 1976; Radcliffe Institute fellow, 1976; Nero Wolfe Award, 1981, for *Death in a Tenured Position;* National Endowment for the Humanities fellow, 1983; Wellesley College Alumnae Achievement Award, 1984; honorary degrees from University of Pennsylvania, 1984, Bucknell University, 1985, Rivier College, 1986, and Russell Sage College, 1987. **Member:** Modern Language Association of America (member of executive council, 1976-79, 1982-84; president, 1984), Mystery Writers of America (member of executive board, 1982-84), Authors Guild. **Agent:** Ellen Levine Literary Agency, 15 East 26th St., Suite 1801, New York, New York 10010, U.S.A.

Publications

Novels

In the Last Analysis (as Amanda Cross). New York, Macmillan, 1964; London, Virago, 1992.

The James Joyce Murder (as Amanda Cross). New York, Macmillan, 1967; London, Virago, 1989.

Poetic Justice (as Amanda Cross). New York, Knopf, 1970; London, Virago, 1990.

The Theban Mysteries (as Amanda Cross). New York, Knopf, 1972; London, Virago, 1989.

The Question of Max (as Amanda Cross). New York, Knopf, 1976; London, Virago, 1989.

Death in a Tenured Position (as Amanda Cross). New York, Dutton, 1981; as *A Death in the Faculty,* London, Gollancz, 1981.

Sweet Death, Kind Death (as Amanda Cross). New York, Dutton, 1984.

No Word from Winifred (as Amanda Cross). New York, Dutton, 1986; London, Virago, 1987.

A Trap for Fools (as Amanda Cross). New York, Dutton, 1989; London, Virago, 1990.

The Players Come Again (as Amanda Cross). New York, Dutton, and London, Virago, 1990.

An Imperfect Spy (as Amanda Cross). New York, Dutton; London, Virago, 1995.

Literary Criticism

The Garnett Family. New York, Macmillan, 1961.

Christopher Isherwood. New York, Columbia University Press, 1970.

Toward a Recognition of Androgyny: Aspects of Male and Female in Literature. New York, Knopf, 1973; as *Toward Androgyny,* London, Gollancz, 1973.

Reinventing Womanhood. New York, Norton, 1979.

Hamlet's Mother and Other Women: Feminist Essays on Literature. New York, Columbia University Press, 1990; London, Women's Press, 1991.

Essays

Writing a Woman's Life. New York, Norton, 1988; London, Women's Press, 1989.

Other

The Education of a Woman: The Life of Gloria Steinem. New York, Dial Press, 1995.

Editor, *Lady Ottoline's Album.* New York, Knopf, 1976.

Editor, with Margaret R. Higgonet, *The Representation of Women in Fiction.* Johns Hopkins University Press, 1983.

*

Critical Studies: *Ten Women of Mystery* edited by Earl F. Bargannier, Bowling Green University, 1981; *Designs of Darkness: Interviews with Detective Novelists* by Diana Cooper-Clark, Bowling Green University, 1983.

* * *

In 1957, in her first published essay, "Hamlet's Mother," author and educator Carolyn Heilbrun signaled the themes she would refine and amplify through the next four decades, both in her literary criticism and in the Amanda Cross mysteries, featuring detective-cum-English professor Kate Fansler. Primary is the generosity toward other women, real or fictional, which underlies her defense of Gertrude, whom she portrays as the much-maligned mother of Hamlet and queen of Denmark.

"Hamlet's Mother" presents the idea—revolutionary in 1957 and even today in some circles—that a woman of middle age or beyond might not only still be interested in sex, but might even have full use of her mind. Heilbrun believes that the failure to understand the strength of Gertrude's lust, which the queen herself sees as her critical flaw, has been the basis for misunderstanding about her character, allowing critics to see her as "well-meaning but shallow ... superficial and flighty." Heilbrun, who was 31 when she wrote the essay, sees Gertrude as "strong-minded, intelligent, succinct, and, apart from the passion, sensible." In her analysis of Gertrude (who, being fictional, has no opportunity to rewrite her own life) Heilbrun rewrites our view of the queen.

Writing is the metaphor for another of Heilbrun's continuing themes: taking control of one's own life and expanding its possibilities. It is a theme most richly developed in the title essay from *Writing a Woman's Life.* Here we find the genesis of mystery writer Amanda Cross, the adventurous alter ego of a discreet Columbia professor; a warm discussion of women's friendships; an agreeably acidic comment on Margaret Thatcher; an incisive look at the egalitarian marriage of Virginia Woof, with glances at Colette, George Eliot, Elizabeth Barrett Browning, Gertrude Stein and Ivy Compton-Burnett; and some delicious glimpses of what makes Carolyn tick. "I believe now that I must have wanted, with extraordinary fervor, to create a space for myself," she writes of her entry into mystery writing in 1963, when she had a demanding job, three children, a large dog, and a husband newly working on his Ph.D. Or perhaps she was writing herself an unencumbered alternate life, in giving Kate Fansler the same job but no children, no husband (as yet), no parents, independent wealth.

Aging, and the liberating and often surprising courage of middle age and beyond, is another favorite theme, first addressed in "Hamlet's Mother" and expressed with great compassion and humor in *An Imperfect Spy,* an Amanda Cross novel published in 1995. In this adventure, "Harriet Furst" does the ultimate life rewrite, disappearing from her life as (what else?) a college professor, and resurfacing in a totally different persona to nudge Kate towards helping a battered wife imprisoned for killing her husband. In the brilliant *Towards a Recognition of Androgyny,* Heilbrun would write: "I am confident that great androgynous works will soon be written." And indeed they have been, in particular in the oft-dismissed field of detective fiction, with Heilbrun helping to define the now-common feminist detective novel. She takes some pride in the fact that the detective story, particularly in the United States, has been in the forefront of the difficult move towards androgynous, or non-gender-stereotyped, heroes and heroines. Heilbrun/Cross gives Fansler women colleagues, students, and relations for friendship and reality checks, and an admiring, supportive, male friend, and later, husband, who is comfortable in his own success as a lawyer and never threatened by her intellectual brilliance. Nor is the marriage of Kate and Reed Amhearst threatened by Kate's extra-marital affairs, admitted in *An Imperfect Spy.* The thing that worries both of them is the possibility of going stale in one's work.

Escaping "the prison of gender" is a constant theme. "I felt that, unlike so many of the women I had read of and known personally, I had been born a feminist and never wavered from that position," she writes in the preface to *Reinventing Womanhood.* This deeply moving chapter explores what Heilbrun perceives as the "outsider" position, which she believes permitted and encouraged her career. For years, she perceived herself as outside the mainstream of academe because of her feminism. Finally, she realized that her nearly-ignored Jewishness also contributed to that position. Here she also explores on a very intimate level that favorite theme of middle-age. Fifty when she started writing the book, she declares her whole life had been leading up to it, and rejoices in the freedom conferred by having grown children, a solid and constantly evolving marriage, the strength to do one's work, and for the first time, to be part of a supportive community of women.

No stranger to biography, Heilbrun published in 1995 what must have been a deeply satisfying work, a biography of feminist pathfinder Gloria Steinem. All the familiar themes converge here in the story of a beautiful and brilliant revolutionary woman who successfully wrote herself out of the prison of gender and, with the support of a loyal community of women friends and colleagues, changed the face of women's magazines by founding *Ms.*

—Sophie Annan Jensen

HELFORTH, John. *See* **H.D.**

HELLMAN, Lillian

Nationality: American. **Born:** New Orleans, Louisiana, 20 June 1906. **Education:** Attended New York University, 1922-24, and Columbia University, New York, 1925. **Family:** Married press agent Arthur Kober in 1925 (divorced 1932); companion of author Dashiell Hammett (died 1961). **Career:** Manuscript reader for Horace Liveright, New York; play reader and book reviewer, *New York Herald Tribune;* scenario reader, Metro-Goldwyn-Mayer, Hollywood, California; as a journalist, covered the Spanish Civil War; co-producer, with Ernest Hemingway and others, *The Spanish Earth* (film), 1937; blacklisted as Communist sympathizer by Hollywood producers, from 1948; testified before House Committee on Un-American Activities, 1952; co-founder, Committee for Public Justice, 1970; brought libel suit against Mary McCarthy, 1980. Contributor to numerous newspapers and periodicals, including *American Spectator, Collier's, New Republic,* and *Ladies' Home Journal.* **Awards:** New York Drama Critics Circle Award, 1941, for *Watch on the Rhine,* and 1960, for *Toys in the Attic;* elected to American Academy of Arts and Sciences, 1960, and American Academy of Arts and Letter, 1963; Brandeis University Creative Artist Medal, 1960-61; Albert Einstein College of Medicine, Yeshiva University, Achievement Award, 1961; National Institute of Arts and Letters Gold Medal, 1964; National Book Award, 1970, for *An Unfinished Woman;* elected to Theatre Hall of Fame, 1973; Edward MacDowell Medal, 1976. Litt.D.:

Wheaton College, 1961; Douglass College of Rutgers University, 1963; Brandeis University, 1965; Yale University, 1974; Smith College, 1974; New York University, 1974; Franklin and Marshall College, 1975; Columbia University, 1976. **Member:** National Institute of Arts and Letters (vice-president, 1962). **Died:** 30 June 1984.

PUBLICATIONS

Plays

The Children's Hour (three-act; produced New York, 1934). New York, Knopf, 1934; London, Hamilton, 1937.
Days to Come (three-act; produced New York, 1936). New York and London, Knopf, 1934.
The Little Foxes (three-act; produced New York, 1939). New York, Random House, and London, Hamilton, 1939.
Watch on the Rhine (three-act; produced New York, 1941). New York, Random House, 1941; London, English Theatre Guild, 1946.
Four Plays. New York, Random House, 1942.
The Searching Wind (two-act; produced New York, 1944). New York, Viking, 1944.
Another Part of the Forest (three-act; produced New York, 1946). New York, Viking, 1947.
Montserrat, adapted from the play by Emmanuel Roblès (two-act; produced New York, 1949). New York, Dramatists Play Service, 1950.
The Autumn Garden (three-act; produced New York, 1951). Boston, Little Brown, 1951.
The Lark, adapted from *L'Alouette* by Jean Anouilh (produced New York, 1955). New York, Random House, 1956.
Candide: A Comic Operetta, adapted from the novel by Voltaire, score by Leonard Bernstein, lyrics by Richard Wilbur, John Latouche, and Dorothy Parker (produced New York, 1956). New York, Random House, 1957.
Toys in the Attic (three-act; produced New York, 1960). New York, Random House, 1960.
tit *Six Plays*. New York, Random House, 1960.
My Mother, My Father and Me, adapted from *How Much?* by Burt Blechman (produced New York, 1963). New York, Random House, 1963.
Lillian Hellman: The Collected Plays. Boston and Toronto, Little Brown, 1972.

Screenplays: *The Dark Angel,* with Mordaunt Shairp, 1935; *These Three* (based on her play *The Children's Hour*), 1936; *Dead End,* 1937; *The Little Foxes* (based on her own play), 1941; *The North Star,* 1943; *The Searching Wind* (based on her own play), 1946; *The Chase,* 1966.

Autobiography

Three. Boston and Toronto, Little Brown 1979.
An Unfinished Woman: A Memoir. Boston and Toronto, Little Brown, and London, Macmillan, 1969.
Pentimiento: A Book of Portraits. Boston and Toronto, Little Brown, 1973; London, Macmillan, 1974.
Scoundrel Time. Boston and Toronto, Little Brown, 1976; London, Macmillan, 1977.
Maybe: A Story. Boston, Little Brown, 1980.

Other

Editor, *The Selected Letters of Anton Chekhov.* New York, Farrar Straus, and London, Hamilton, 1955.
Editor, *The Big Knockover,* by Dashiell Hammett. New York, Random House, and London, Cassell, 1966.

*

Media Adaptations: *Julia* (film adaptation of *Pentimiento*), 1977; *Lillian* by William Luce (play; based on Hellman's memoirs), 1986.

Bibliography: *Lillian Hellman, An Annotated Bibliography* by Steven Bills, New York, Garland, 1979; *The Lillian Hellman Collection at the University of Texas* by Manfred Triesch, Austin, University of Texas Press, 1979; *Lillian Hellman, A Bibliography: 1928-1978* by Mary Marguerite Riordan, Metuchen, Scarecrow, 1980; *Lillian Hellman, Plays, Films, Memoirs: A Reference Guide* by Mark W. Estrin, Boston, G.K. Hall, 1980.

Manuscript Collections: Humanities Research Center, University of Texas at Austin.

Theatrical Activities: Director, *Another Part of the Forest, Montserrat,* 1952 revival of *The Children's Hour.*

Critical Studies: *Lillian Hellman, Playwright* by Richard Moody, New York, Pegasus, 1972; " A Still Unfinished Woman: A Conversation with Lillian Hellman" by Christine Doudna, in *Rolling Stone,* 24 February 1977; Lillian Hellman by Katherine Lederer, Boston, Twayne, 1979; "On Apocryphism" by Martha Gellhorn, in *Paris Review,* 79, spring 1981; *Hellman in Hollywood* by Bernard F. Dick, n.p., 1982; *Conversations with Lillian Hellman,* edited by Jackson R. Bryer, n.p., 1986; *Lillian Hellman: The Image, the Woman* by William Wright, New York, Simon & Schuster, 1986; *Lillian Hellman, Her Legend and Her Legacy* by Carl Rollyson, n.p., 1988; *Critical Essays on Lillian Hellman,* edited by Mark W. Estrin, n.p., 1989.

* * *

Lillian Hellman, though undeniably ambivalent about feminism, emerges nonetheless as a writer whose work in various genres and life itself resonate with themes integral to feminism. From the 1934 Broadway production of the first of her eight plays, through the publication of three memoirs, to her death in 1984, Hellman generated controversy to the point of becoming a legend in the course of an amazing half-century-long literary career. As a consequence, her personal life and political positions came to be so inextricably merged with her writings that scholarship has yet to accord to Hellman's work, especially the drama, the recognition it deserves as formally innovative and prophetically feminist.

Born in New Orleans in 1906 (this date itself the subject of controversy for years), Hellman, an only child, moved at aged five to New York City following her father's bankruptcy; however, regular visits to her maiden aunts' boarding house in New Orleans fed the Southern roots that ground so many of her plays. Having dropped out of New York University and worked in publishing, she moved to Paris with her husband in 1926 and published what she later disparaged as "lady-writer stories." Witnessing mounting anti-Semiticism in Germany dissuaded Hellman, who was Jewish, from plans to study in Bonn and resulted in a move to Hollywood in 1930. There she met Dashiell Hammett, with whom she returned to New York and lived until his death 31 years later. Though divorced in 1932, Hellman never married Hammett, a controversial personal decision that marked her as an extraordinarily independent woman and signaled the professional and political controversy to follow.

The opening of *The Children's Hour* confirmed this life-pattern; the play caused an immediate sensation, bringing the playwright overnight fame and financial success. Centering on accusations of lesbianism against two headmistresses of a girls' school, the play, which had deterred name actors and precluded pre-opening-night tryouts, was banned in Boston, Chicago, and London and was refused a viewing by the Pulitzer committee despite the favorable reviews of New York critics. Not only the homoerotic element—deleted from Hellman's film adaptation entitled *These Three*—but the theme of female oppression in the play provide evidence of the feminist perspective that would underlie Hellman's future works. Occluded for years by critical debate over the drama's genre as realism or melodrama and the playwright's politics as pro-American or pro-Communist, Hellman's feminist impulse is currently producing some of the most insightful re-examination of her writing. Feminist critics, however, should take heed of the ambiguity of the conclusion of *The Children's Hour* as the focus shifts from accuser to accused, one of whom confesses lesbian desires and thus renders her victimization and suicide more tragic complexity than melodramatic convention.

This ambiguity pervades subsequent plays like *Days to Come*, Hellman's one failure, which incurred charges ranging from Marxian propaganda to middle-class morality in portraying a factory owner calling in strikebreakers. A 1937 tour of the Spanish Civil War zone cemented a life-long determination on the part of the playwright to fight totalitarianism despite criticism, a determination soon evidenced in Hellman's refusal to allow a benefit performance of her next play, *The Little Foxes,* for relief of the "pro-Nazi little republic" of Finland. Consequently attacked by the play's star, Tallulah Bankhead, Hellman nevertheless earned praise for an integrity "rare among her native playwriting sex" and the title of "American Woman Playwright Number One." The feminist impulse inherent in Hellman's repeatedly expressed objection to this categorization emerges powerfully in *The Little Foxes,* her most acclaimed play. Based on her mother's Southern family, the characterization shifts from the culturally inscribed female passivity in *The Children's Hour* to an active female villainy regarded by many feminist critics as the product of a patriarchal system. The greedy triumph of Regina over her brothers counterpointed by her daughter's moral awakening ends the play on an ambiguous note, which reflects Hellman's deliberate but often overlooked irony and comic subversion of realism.

Ambiguity and controversy characterize Hellman's wartime plays as well, though both are avowedly anti-fascist. *Watch on the Rhine,* depicting a wealthy Southern family shaken by Nazism, immediately brought praise for patriotism and a request from President Roosevelt for a benefit performance. Some critics, however, descried Communist overtones in this play and in the subsequent *The Searching Wind,* an indictment of the apathy of the well bred as breeding ground for the war. Detesting political message-drama, Hellman scorned *Wind* for too closely approaching one, but her anti-polemical stance was ignored in reviews of the postwar *Another Part of the Forest* as an anti-capitalist protest. Such political message-mongering overshadows Hellman's deepest insight, that the personal is political, which confirms a feminist perspective, if not politics, in the plays. Set in 1880 and directed by Hellman herself, *Forest* traces the inception of the familial power struggle of *Foxes,* suggesting that both Regina and her mother are victims of gender constraints who nevertheless become catalysts of action.

This fusion of the personal and political was brought home to Hellman in 1948, when, having written film adaptations and an original screenplay, she discovered that her name was on Hollywood's blacklist, where it was to remain until the 1960s. Returning to the theatre, she adapted *Montserrat* and wrote her own favorite play, *The Autumn Garden,* a study of moral paralysis set in the South which again portrays female characters determinedly attaining self-awareness in the face of inscribed passivity. Evidence of the playwright's own resistance to passivity soon surfaced in her now-famous reply to a 1952 subpoena from the House UnAmerican Activities Committee; refusing to testify about any but her own activities, Hellman wrote:

> I do not like subversion or disloyalty in any form and if I had ever seen any I would have considered it my duty to have reported it to the proper authorities. But to hurt innocent people whom I knew many years ago in order to save myself is, to me, inhuman and indecent and dishonorable. I cannot and will not cut my conscience to fit this year's fashions, even though I long ago came to the conclusion that I was not a political person and could have no comfortable place in any political group.

Recently cited evidence of Hellman's Communist Party membership should in no way detract from the courage of this stance. With Hammett already in prison for contempt of court, Hellman only reluctantly took the Fifth Amendment at the hearing; though excused, she had suffered drastic emotional and financial setbacks.

Thus vividly reminded of the consequences of allegations, Hellman directed that same year a revival of *The Children's Hour,* which was well received except for one critic's later recanted accusation of pro-Communist liberalism. Subsequent unsuccessful adaptations of two French texts were followed by *Toys in the Attic,* which was to be Hellman's last original script; it centers, like her first, on two repressed female characters, New Orleans spinsters who are obviously based on her aunts. *Toys*' selection by the Pulitzer Jury having been overruled by the Advisory Board and the adaptation *My Mother, My Father, and Me* having failed in 1963, Hellman bitterly exited the theater, commenting that "[Y]ou can make a very good case for pictures being a lot better than the theater these days, and I ain't crazy about pictures." This statement proved prophetic as Hellman quit screenwriting only a few years later when, only recently removed from the blacklist, she again acted upon her convictions in protesting drastic revisions of her screenplay for *The Chase.*

The feminist consciousness implicit in Hellman's drama and explicit in her life found voice in a second career writing memoirs. The title of the first of three, 1969's *An Unfinished Woman,* bespeaks Hellman's awareness of the defining quality of biologically determined sex and of culturally determined gender. Though acknowledging the "self-made foolishness" that left her unfinished, Hellman also examines in each memoir familial, societal, and national power structures and the evils thereof which constitute the subject matter of her drama. The commitment to anti-totalitarianism and personal responsibility that led her to declare a moral imperative in the plays pervades her autobiographical reflections as well and reflects a feminist resistance to hierarchies rooted in money or power. *Pentimiento*'s portraits underscore this ethic, especially the one of "Julia," a childhood friend and anti-fascist activist who convinced Hellman to smuggle money into Berlin in 1937. The film adaptation *Julia*, which starred Jane Fonda as Hellman, catapulted the author to legendary status as a liberated woman, although Hellman equivocated on her link to feminism. Detesting the label of "Ms." and dismissing some of the causes of the Women's Movement as "small battles," she nevertheless insisted that "Women *have* been put down" and that "The big battle is equal rights, whether one likes to face it or not."

Allegations of fabrications in her autobiographical accounts, including *Julia,* and the publication of *Scoundrel Time,* her reminiscences of the McCarthy era, served to fuel further the controversy that had surrounded Hellman for over three decades; having charged certain liberals and intellectuals, including her friends the Trillings, with complicity and betrayal, Hellman was publicly implicated when her publisher canceled publication of Diana Trilling's book, which included a rebuttal of the charges. In *Three,* Hellman defends the morality of her stand, and, when Mary McCarthy accused Hellman on national television of being a chronic liar, Hellman sued. Though the suit did not come to trial before Hellman's death, it is emblematic of the diametrically opposed views of Hellman as courageous or corrupt. Vastly contradictory perspectives continue to be reflected not only by her biographers, whose tones range from adulation to malice, but also by her critics, whose assessments of the work, particularly the drama, range from praise to disparagement. To categorize Hellman is to ignore the complexity of both the work and the woman who resisted all labels but whose moral vision of personal responsibility as political action marks her legacy as intrinsically, if not avowedly, feminist.

—Janet V. Haedicke

HENLEY, Beth

Nationality: American. **Born:** Jackson, Mississippi, 1952. **Education:** Southern Methodist University, B.F.A. 1974; University of Illinois, 1975-76. **Family:** One son. **Career:** Playwright and actress. **Awards:** Pulitzer Prize for Drama, 1981, New York Drama Critics Circle Best Play award, 1981, *Newsday* Guggenheim Award, 1981, Tony Award nomination for best play, 1981, and Academy Award nomination for best adapted screenplay, 1986, all for *Crimes of the Heart.* **Agent:** c/o Gilbert Parker, William Morris Agency, 1350 Avenue of the Americas, New York, New York 10019, USA. **Address:** Los Angeles, California, USA.

Publications

Plays

Am I Blue? (one-act; produced Dallas, 1973). New York, Dramatists Play Service, 1982.

Crimes of the Heart (three-act; produced Louisville, Kentucky, 1979; produced on Broadway, 1981). New York, Dramatists Play Service, 1981.

The Miss Firecracker Contest (two-act, produced Los Angeles, 1980; produced Off-Broadway, 1980). New York, Dramatists Play Service, 1985.

The Wake of Jamey Foster (two-act; produced Hartford, Connecticut, then Broadway, 1982). New York, Dramatists Play Service, 1985.

The Debutante Ball (produced Costa Mesa, California, 1985).

The Lucky Spot (produced Williamstown, Massachusetts, 1986; produced on Broadway, 1987). New York, Dramatists Play Service, 1987.

Abundance (produced Costa Mesa, California, 1989; produced Off-Broadway, 1990).

Beth Henley: Four Plays. Portsmouth, New Hampshire, Heinemann, 1992.

Control Freaks (produced Los Angeles, 1992).

Revelers (produced New York; produced Chicago, 1993).

Screenplays: *Nobody's Fool* (original title, "The Moonwatcher," 1977), 1986; *True Stories,* with Stephen Tobolowsky and David Byrne, 1986; *Crimes of the Heart,* 1986; *Miss Firecracker,* 1988; *Paying Up,* with Nora Ephron, Terrence McNally, and others; *The Lucky Spot,* forthcoming; *A Long and Happy Life* (based on book by Reynolds Price), forthcoming.

*

Critical Studies: "The Tragicomic Vision of Beth Henley's Drama" by Nancy D. Hargrove, in *Southern Quarterly,* 22(4), summer 1984; "Criminality, Desire, and Community: A Feminist Approach to Beth Henley's *Crimes of the Heart*" by Karen L. Laughlin, in *Women and Performance,* 3(1), 1986; "Diverse Similitude: Beth Henley and Marsha Norman" by Lisa J. McDonnell, in *Southern Quarterly,* 25(3), spring 1987; "Familial Bonds in the Plays of Beth Henley" by Billy J. Harbin, in *Southern Quarterly,* 25(3), spring 1987; "Beth Henley: Female Quest and the Family-Play Tradition" by Jonnie Guerra, in *Making a Spectacle: Feminist Essays in Contemporary Women's Theatre,* edited by Lynda Hart, Ann Arbor, University of Michigan Press, 1989; "The Ghosts of Chekhov's *Three Sisters* Haunt Beth Henley's *Crimes of the Heart*" by Joanne B. Karpinski, in *Modern American Drama: The Female Canon,* edited by June Schlueter, Rutherford, Fairleigh Dickinson University Press, 1990; "Feeding the Hungry Heart: Food in Beth Henley's *Crimes of the Heart*" by Lou Thompson, in *Southern Quarterly,* 30(2-3), winter/spring 1992; "Aborted Rage in Beth Henley's Women" by Alan Clarke Shepard, in *Modern Drama* 36(1), March 1993; "'A Population [and Theater] at Risk': Battered Women in Henley's *Crimes of the Heart* and Shepard's *A Lie of the Mind*" by Janet V. Haedicke, in *Modern Drama* 36(1), March 1993.

* * *

Raised in Jackson, Mississippi, the second of four daughters born to parents who loved the stage, Beth Henley grew up watching her mother, an actor, rehearse various roles with the Jackson Community Theater. Captivated by the sights and sounds of the theater, young Beth not only attended rehearsals regularly with her mother, Elizabeth Josephine Henley, but also pursued her actor parent about the house, prompting her to learn her lines. Thus, Henley's affinity for drama developed early, especially her interest in regional theater. Henley's father, a Mississippi state senator and a lawyer, equally displayed a flair for the dramatic, most notably evidenced when he stood before the podium at political rallies. When her father campaigned, Beth often joined him and the rest of the family center stage, quickly learning about the importance of both appearance and presentation. Attuning her ears to the sounds and rhythms of the stage, Henley already had decided by the time that she graduated from high school to embark upon an acting career.

Enrolling at Southern Methodist University in Dallas, Texas, the future Pulitzer Prize-winner pursued the acting craft with vigor, reading the world's great playwrights and writing plays herself. In its embryonic form, *Crimes of the Heart* began as a playwriting class assignment. In 1976 Henley's first play, *Am I Blue* was produced on the Southern Methodist University campus.

After working summer stock at New Salem State Park and completing a year of graduate school, Henley moved to Los Angeles to live with actor-director Stephen Tobolowsky. Finding acting roles in Los Angeles proved a disheartening process, so Henley turned to writing screenplays, which, at first, seemed a fruitless endeavor, given the fact that the writer had no agent to facilitate getting her scripts read, much less produced. As a matter of fact, Henley's first screenplay, *Nobody's Fool,* though written in the 1970s, did not get produced until 1986.

Receiving the Pulitzer Prize in 1981, Henley's first full-length play, *Crimes of the Heart,* focused on the lives of women, the McGrath sisters. Thanks to Henley's close friend, screenwriter Frederick Bailey, the play was submitted to the Actors Theatre of Louisville, enjoying its world premiere in 1979. Feminists prize the play especially because of its resilient heroines; even in the midst of despair, they find humor. The play revolves around the reunion of the McGraths, who return to their hometown of Hazelhurst, Mississippi, in an effort to aid their sister, Babe, who stands accused of attempting to murder her husband, State Senator Zackery Botrelle. As the plot unfolds, however, the audience becomes increasingly aware of other "crimes," ones equally serious, which have been perpetuated not just against Babe, but against her sisters as well. These "crimes" implicate important males who have figured prominently in the lives of the women, including their father, and the eldest of the patriarchs, Old Granddaddy, who attempts to control the futures of his granddaughters, forcing upon them his will and expectations. Subtly, he even attempts to control Lenny's fertility. This household patriarch requires sacrifice of all women—a sacrifice, Henley intimates, that is cyclical in nature. At one point Babe complains that Lenny, pictured wearing her deceased grandmother's gardening gloves and working in the garden, seems to be "turning into Old Grandmama." Despite Old Granddaddy's best efforts to manipulate and to control the sisters, the playwright suggests that the McGrath women will prevail. Even though they sometimes misdirect their anger against themselves, they simultaneously sustain and heal one another with their strength and unconditional love. During the course of the play, Old Granddaddy's physical condition worsens, but the unexpected reaction of the McGrath sisters—a surprise even to them—intermingles, paradoxically, remorse with glee, with more of the latter apparent than of the former.

Eventually, Babe's lawyer, Barnette, exposes medical records that reveal that Botrelle has beaten his wife for years, his "crimes" going unpunished, and unacknowledged, in a South that expects its women to remain passive, silently silhouetted on verandas sipping lemonade. *Crimes of the Heart,* with its predominant themes of wife-beating, female sacrifice, hidden secrets and hidden anger, confused identity, female rebellion, and sisterhood, fares well with most women because it unmasks important feminist issues beneath the glossy veneer of its comical plot. The ostensible mixing of Southern grotesque humor with rebellious female antics won Henley an Oscar nomination when she adapted *Crimes* for the screen. Following its extraordinary success with an equally uproarious, yet thought-provoking, drama posed a challenge for the talented playwright. Indeed, *Crimes of the Heart* had only whetted the appetites of the critics for more Pulitzer Prize winners.

Henley received further critical acclaim by introducing *The Miss Firecracker Contest,* again a play about a troubled, disintegrating Southern family. Carnelle Scott, Henley's protagonist, wishes to fulfill her greatest dream, to win the coveted crown of "Miss Firecracker," a title awarded to the most beautiful and talented female in the small town of Brookhaven, Mississippi. In the past, Carnelle's first cousin, Elain Rutledge, a famous local beauty, donned her flowing dress and led the parade through town, seated atop her pedestal on the "Miss Firecracker" float. To the chagrin of many feminists, Henley's apparent focus on Carnelle's attempt to qualify for the beauty contest, to don the appropriate dress, to color her hair, and to "out-perform" other dancing, singing, and twisting females on the stage—who entertain a taunting, primarily male audience—seems, at first, antithetical to feminist ideals. These critics, however, misinterpret Henley, assuming that she approves, tacitly, of Carnelle's obsession with "beauty" and with the "Miss Firecracker" title. Recognizing the dangers of woman's attempt to transform herself into patriarchy's "ideal," a "role" created and manufactured by men for women, these critics, perhaps, fail to see beyond the parade of women's bodies. Thus, they may miss Henley's point: Carnelle, the loser of the beauty contest, ultimately wins in the greater contest, life itself! Her undaunted courage, perseverance, and the depth of her humanity, far exceed her cousin Elain's surface attributes. While undermining Carnelle, Elain unwittingly divulges the restrictions inherent for females who "win" the coveted title of "Miss Firecracker": "Poor Carnation. She wants to be beautiful without understanding the limitations it brings," sighs Elain.

Indeed, during the course of the drama, Elain never fully recognizes her own limitations, nor does she break from patriarchy's bonds, those tying her to servitude, either to husband, to town, or to beauty. For Carnelle's brother Delmount, however, Henley prophesies hope—even a cure! Before being influenced by the restorative powers of Popeye, Carnelle's seamstress—a strong, female figure—Delmount's imagination can envision women only from a limited, warped, or distorted perspective. Even Elain appears frightened by the "truth" of her brother's vision of femininity. Delmount's vision appears prescriptive, "either/or"; woman either adheres to patriarchal "prescriptions" and looks "beautiful," or she becomes violently fragmented, disembodied, a portrait of beauty aborted:

> DELMOUNT. I don't understand you. I know you're probably a kind person. You gave Popeye your earrings; you have a need to be excited by life. So why do you go back to being what Mama wanted? You know she was mean!

ELAIN. (Turning to him angrily.) Yes, I know she was mean and you know it too. So why do you straighten your wild hair? Why do you have horrible, sickening dreams about pieces of women's bodies? Some all beautiful; some all mutilated and bloody! I hate those dreams. I wish you didn't tell me about them. They scare me.

Ultimately, Henley's protagonist doesn't need a gown, a title, or a parade to recognize who she is. Refusing to be defined—or confined—by others, Carnelle learns to feel good about herself.

Though the critics became somewhat satiated with *The Miss Firecracker Contest,* Henley's autobiographical play, *The Wake of Jamey Foster,* proved not to their tastes. Failing miserably at the New York box office, *The Wake of Jamey Foster* disappointed critics, for they felt that Henley's female characters amounted to little more than McGrath sister "make-overs." Despite criticism levied against the play, the playwright blotted out past defeats, affixing her pen to the "coming out" of her next play, *The Debutante Ball,* in the spring of 1985, which was followed hard upon by *The Lucky Spot,* a tragicomedy, in the summer of 1986.

In *Abundance,* an 1880s tale of the Western Frontier, Henley intrigues audiences with her typical biting humor, uncovering the psychological cruelties of the marriage bed—a structure that exacts more pain than any torture wild Indians could inflict upon settlers. The playwright's more recent work includes a dark comedy, *Control Freaks,* which opened at Los Angeles' Met Theatre in 1993. Here, Henley made her directorial debut as well as co-produced the play, along with her favorite leading actor, star Holly Hunter.

Beth Henley creates rebellious females who challenge patriarchal authority and win. Her portraits, though sometimes shadowed by the past or by seeming imperfections, continue to inspire women, for they show us not just what we were, but what we can be.

—Linda Rohrer Paige

HEWETT, Dorothy

Nationality: Australian. **Born:** Perth, Western Australia, 21 May 1923. **Education:** University of Western Australia, B.A. 1961, M.A. 1963. **Family:** Married 1) Lloyd Davies in 1944 (divorced 1949); 2)Les Flood in 1950 (divorced 1959); three sons; 3) the writer Merv Lilley in 1960; two daughters. **Career:** Joined communist party, c. 1942; worked as a millworker, 1950-52; advertising copywriter in Sydney, 1956-58; senior tutor in English, University of Western Australia, Perth, 1964-73; writer-in-residence, Monash University, 1975. Head of Australian Playwrights Conference; Member of editorial committee, *Overland,* beginning 1970; poetry editor, *Westerly,* 1972-73; review editor, *New Poetry,* 1979. **Awards:** Australian Broadcast Corp. poetry prize, 1945 and 1965; Literature Board Historical Council grants, 1973-76, 1976-79, and 1980-81; Australian Writers Guild awards, 1974 and 1981; Australian Poetry Prize, 1986; Grace Leven Award, 1989; awarded the Order of Australia, 1986. **Member:** Australian Writers Guild. **Address:** 49 Jersey Rd., Woollahra, New South Wales 2025, Australia.

Publications

Novels

Bobbin Up. Melbourne, Australasian Book Society, 1959; London, Virago, 1985.
The Toucher. Ringwood, Victoria, McPhee Gribble/Penguin, 1993.

Short Stories

"Joey," in *The Tracks We Travel,* edited by Jack Bensley. Sydney, Australasian Book Society, 1961.
"The Wire Fences of Jarrabin," " The Strawberry Pickers," "Joe Anchor's Rock," in *The Australians Have a Word for It: Short Stories from Down Under,* edited by G. Gelbin. Berlin, Seven Seas, 1964.
"On the Terrace," in *Summer's Tales 3,* edited by John Iggulden. Melbourne, Macmillan, 1966.
"The Galle Face," in *Coast to Coast: Australian Short Stories,* edited by Frank Moorhouse. Sydney, Angus & Robertson, 1973.
"Homeland," in *Homeland,* edited by George Papaellinas. Sydney, Allen & Unwin, 1991.
"The Darkling Sisters," in *Sisters,* edited by Drusilla Modjeska. Sydney, Harper Collins, 1993.

Poetry

What about the People!, with Merv Lilley. Sydney, Realist Writers, 1962.
Windmill Country. Melbourne, Overland, 1968.
The Hidden Journey. Launceston, Wattles Grove Press, 1968.
Late Night Bulletin. Launceston, Wattles Grove Press, 1968.
Rapunzel in Suburbia. Sydney, New Poetry, 1975.
Greenhouse. Sydney, Big-Smoke Books, 1979.
Alice in Wormland. Paddington, New South Wales, Paperback Press, 1987; as *Alice in Wormland: Selected Poems,* edited by Edna Longley, Newcastle upon Tyne, Bloodaxe, 1991.
A Tremendous World in Her Head: Selected Poems. Sydney, Kangaroo Press, 1989.
Selected Poems: Dorothy Hewett. South Fremantle, Western Australia, Fremantle Arts Centre Press, 1991.
Peninsula. South Freemantle, Western Australia, Fremantle Arts Centre Press, 1994.
Collected Poems, edited by Bill Grono, South Freemantle, Western Australia, Fremantle Arts Centre Press, 1995.

Plays

This Old Man Comes Rolling Home (produced Perth, 1968). Sydney, Currency Press, 1976.
Mrs Porter and the Angel (produced Sydney, 1970).
The Chapel Perilous; or, The Perilous Adventures of Sally Banner (produced Perth, 1971). Sydney, Currency Press, 1972; London, Eyre Methuen, 1974; revised edition, Currency Press, 1977.
Bon-Bons and Roses for Dolly [and] *The Tatty Hollow Story* (produced, respectively, Perth, 1972, and Sydney, 1976). Sydney, Currency Methuen, 1976.
Catspaw (produced Perth, 1974).
Miss Hewitt's Shenanigans (produced Canberra, 1975).
The Beautiful Mrs Portland (two-act), in *Theatre Australia,* 1(4) and 3(5), 1976.

Joan (produced Canberra, 1975). Yackadandah Playscripts, 1984.
Pandora's Cross (produced 1978), in *Theatre Australia,* 3(2-3), 1978.
The Man from Mukinupin (two-act). South Freemantle, Western Australia, Fremantle Arts Centre Press, 1979.
Susannah's Dreaming [and] *The Golden Oldies.* Sydney, Currency Press, 1981.
The Fields of Heaven (produced 1982).
Joan. Montmorency, Victoria, Yackadandah Playscripts, 1984.
Golden Valley: Song of the Seals. Sydney, Currency Press, 1985.
Beyondie (two-act; n.d.).
Dorothy Hewett: Collected Plays. Paddington, New South Wales, Currency Press, 1992-.

Screenplays: *Five Acts of Violence,* 1976; *For the First Time,* 1976.

Autobiography

Wild Card: An Autobiography, 1923-1958. Ringwood, Victoria, McPhee Gribble/Penguin, 1990.

Other

Editor, *Sandgropers: A Western Australia Anthology.* Nedlands, University of Western Australia Press, 1973.

*

Media Adaptations: *Rapunzel in Suburbia* (play), adapted by Kim Carpenter, 1984.

Critical Studies: *The Making of Australian Drama* by Leslie Rees, London, Angus & Robertson, 1978; "Dorothy Hewett: Playwright of Splendid Moments" by Alrene Sykes, in *World Literature Written in English,* 17(1), 1978; "Time Passed/Time Past: The Empowerment of Women and Blacks in Australian Feminist and Aboriginal Drama" by Joanne Tompkins, in *Australasian Drama Studies,* October 1991; "Representations of Female Identity in the Poetry of Dorothy Hewett" by Jenny Digby, in *Southerly,* 52(2), 1992; *Dorothy Hewett: The Feminine as Subversion* by Margaret Williams, Paddington, New South Wales, Currency Press, 1992; *Dorothy Hewett: Selected Critical Essays* edited by Bruce Bennett, South Fremantle, Fremantle Arts Centre Press, 1995.

* * *

Dorothy Hewett's writing often rouses extreme and contradictory responses from readers and audiences, both feminists and fellow Australians. Crossing all literary genres, it has won plaudits from scholars, who admire her avant garde vision and styles and her dedicated social commentary. It also offends the thin-skinned with its rowdy sexually explicit language and social critiques. Although she is Australia's leading female dramatist of the 1970s and 1980s, possibly of the 20th century, Hewett has yet to be discovered outside of Australia.

Hewett's autobiography *Wild Card* (1990), which covers her life from 1923 to 1958 (up to the publication of her first novel), received more media attention that any of her fiction, drama, or poetry. The rich sensual details of her early life as a leftist politico and scandals about much-publicized love affairs titillated journalists more than her art. In her life and her art, as a controversial free-spirit, Hewett embraces contradictions with passionate political convictions, raucous and bittersweet satire, typically Australian raunchiness, and the colorful patois of working class neighborhoods in Sydney.

Her earliest and most famous novel *Bobbin Up* (1959), based on her own experiences as a mill worker and Communist Party organizer, exposes the cynical hypocrisy of the ruling capitalist class exploiting factory workers in the textile mills. Typical of Hewett's early writing, the novel contrasts the squalid living conditions with the resilient hopes of 1950s workers in Sydney, who believed that collective struggle would achieve a social and economic revolution, although her naturalistic portrayal of wild, undisciplined early organizers offended Party leaders who preferred to exhibit sober, respectable workers. Hewett immerses readers in the popular culture of the 1950s through frequent echoes of popular songs and styles. She uses the Russian satellite Sputnik circling the globe as a symbol of hope for the global class struggle. Rather than focusing the novel on a single hero, Hewett creates a collective female protagonist drawn from women of different ages, in different economic crises, whose lives are loosely connected. The radical form departs from most modern novels to construct a collective outcry appropriate for both feminist and working class fiction.

From the 1945 ABC poetry prize received in her early 20s through her *Collected Poems* (1995), published in her early 70s, Hewett has echoed the ideas, images, rhythms, forms, and whole phrases of her favorite British mentors from Blake, Coleridge, Keats, Brontë, and Tennyson to Yeats and Eliot. *Rapunzel in Suburbia* (1975) established her reputation as a neo-Romantic poet craftily recasting mythic archetypes in contemporary urban settings. In "Grave Fairytale" Rapunzel takes responsibility for her erotic desire, her shadow/mirror dual identity, and her fate to free/isolate herself from male lust and the world. Shadows of the Lady of Shallot flicker across both her poetry and drama of this period as dark and desirable undertow. Influenced by the notion of a split subject and Lacanian mirroring, she writes "Me is not a stable reality" in "Creeley in Sydney" (*Greenhouse*). The title, *Alice in Wormland* (1987), and the cover photograph of a black caped poet reclining in a garden and holding a falcon aloft, suggests parodic mythic contrasts between innocence and experience, ego and id, birth and death, madness and rationality.

The archetypal contrast between the garden (represented by her birthplace in Western Australia) and the city (usually Sydney) recurs in both poetry and drama. The setting for Hewett's earliest major play first produced in 1967, *This Old Man Comes Rolling Home* (1976) is the working class inner city of *Bobbin Up* but with much less optimism. Urban lives of quiet desperation peter out with a whimper of alcoholism, denial, death, and departure for the fringes—the Northern Territory or Tasmania. *The Man from Mukinupin*, commissioned for Western Australia's sesquicentennial celebration in 1979, may seem superficially to foster optimism corn-fed on bucolic bliss. But the spritely musical balances the banality of the surface romance through double casting to reveal the dark side of each character and situation.

Hewett attracted major feminist attention with several major plays performed and published from the mid-'70s to mid-'80s featuring a female protagonist as object/victim/hero. Sally, Dolly, Tatty, Joan, and others in *Bon Bons and Roses for Dolly*, *The Tatty Hollow Story*, *The Chapel Perilous*, *Susannah's Dreaming*, *The Golden Oldies*, *Joan*, and other plays recognize and flaunt themselves as objects of the male gaze constructed by Hollywood cinematic expectations of flawless beauty that never changes or ages—a celluloid version of Grecian urn figures. Critics have identified Sally Banner in *The Chapel Perilous* as a thinly veiled self-portrait of the artist struggling to be the subject of her own erotic desire and political commitment amidst a sea of shark-like censors, sexual predators, and authority figures who seek to shred and consume her. Neither Alice, Rapunzel, Lady of Shallot, nor Joan, Sally seeks a simple vision of self unclouded by the smoke of orthodoxy. Tatty Hollow, the most transparent construction of male lust, appears only through the narrative fantasies of the various men who have desired and destroyed her. With echoes of Shaw's *Saint Joan*, Hewett presents Joan the Peasant, Joan the Soldier, Joan the Witch, and Joan the Saint as four perspectives of one historic person reconstructed through history to question and triumph over authoritarian detractors in a manner inaccessible to Sally Banner.

Hewett's unconventional and controversial writing spans the latter half of the 20th century. Especially in her drama and poetry, an alienated, decentered subject challenges the center of power with uniquely feminist wit and subversive power. Her Brechtian anti-heroes ridicule spectators who would form sentimental attachments to the oppressed, asserting that collective organizing always outweighs alleviating individual suffering. Dorothy Hewett's characteristically feminist representation of women's status through the device of a collective protagonist foregrounds women's liberation as a class struggle.

—Rosemary Keefe Curb

HILL, D. A. *See* **H.D.**

HOLTBY, Winifred

Nationality: British. **Born:** Rudstone, Yorkshire, 1898. **Education:** Somerville College, Oxford, B.A. 1920. **Military Service:** Signals Unit, Women's Auxiliary Army Corps, Huchenneville. **Career:** Lived with Vera Brittain in London, beginning 1921; director, *Time and Tide* (magazine), London, from 1926; lectured throughout Europe for League of Nations Union. **Award:** James Tait Memorial prize, 1936, for *South Riding: An English Landscape.* **Died:** In London, of kidney disease, 25 September 1935.

Publications

Novels

Anderby Wold. London, J. Lane, 1923.
The Crowded Street. London, J. Lane, 1924.
The Land of Green Ginger. London, J. Cape, 1927; New York, R. M. McBride, 1928.
Poor Caroline. London and Toronto, J. Cape, and New York, R. M. McBride, 1931.
Mandoa! Mandoa! London, Collins, and New York, Macmillan, 1933.
South Riding: An English Landscape. London, Collins, and New York, Macmillan, 1936.

Short Stories

Truth Is Not Sober and Other Stories. London, Collins, and New York, Macmillan, 1934.
Pavements at Anderby: Tales of 'South Riding' and Other Regions, edited by Vera Brittain. London, Collins, 1937; New York, Macmillan, 1938.

Poetry

The Frozen Earth and Other Poems. London, Collins, 1935.

Play

Take Back Your Freedom, with Norman Ginsbury. London, J. Cape, 1939.

Political/Social Theory

Women and a Changing Civilisation. London, J. Lane, 1934; New York, Longmans Green, 1935.
A New Voter's Guide to Party Programs. London, Kegan Paul, 1929.

Literary Criticism

Virginia Woolf, A Critical Study. London, Wishart, 1932.

Essays

Eutychus: or, The Future of the Pulpit. London, Kegan Paul, and New York, Dutton, 1928.

Other

The Astonishing Island. London, Lovat Dickson, 1933.
Letters to a Friend, edited by Alice Holtby and Jean McWilliam. London, Collins, 1937; New York, Macmillan, 1938.
Selected Letters of Winifred Holtby and Vera Brittain. London, A. Brown, 1960.
Testament of a Generation: The Journalism of Vera Brittain and Winifred Holtby, edited by Paul Berry and Alan Bishop. London, Virago, 1985.

*

Media Adaptations: *South Riding* (film), 1938.

Bibliography: *Winifred Holtby: A Concise and Selected Bibliography, Together with Some Letters* by Geoffrey H. Taylor, London, 1955.

Critical Studies: *Testament of Friendship: The Story of Winifred Holtby* by Vera Brittain, London, Macmillan, 1940, with introduction by Carolyn Heilbrun, New York, Wideview Books, 1981; "Feminism and Fiction between the Wars: Winifred Holtby and Virginia Woolf" by Marion Shaw, in *Women's Writing: A Challenge to Theory,* edited by Moira Monteith, Brighton, Harvester Wheatsheaf, 1986; *Vera Brittain and Winifred Holtby: A Working Partnership* by Jean E. Kennard, Hanover, New Hampshire, University Press of New England, 1989; "Love and Marriage in the Works of Winifred Holtby" by Sally Brown, in *It's My Party: Reading Twentieth Century Women's Writing,* edited by Gina Wisker, London, Pluto Press, 1994.

* * *

Novelist Winifred Holtby was born in Rudstone, six miles from Bridlington, in the East Riding of Yorkshire. In the fall of 1917 she went up to Somerville College in Oxford to read modern history, but interrupted her studies the following summer to join Queen Alexandra's Women's Army Auxiliary Corps (WAAC). Holtby spent the last months of World War I working in a WAAC camp in France. When she returned to Oxford, she met the woman who was probably the most significant figure in her life, the writer Vera Brittain. The fact that both women had actively served in the war—Brittain had been a VAD nurse—created an early bond between them. They had also chosen to study history for the same reason, which stemmed directly from their experience of the war: a desire to study the mistakes of the past in the hope of prevented such a conflict from happening again.

The two women were closely associated for the rest of Holtby's life, in spite of Brittain's marriage in 1925, and Brittain was at Holtby's bedside when she died. Her biography of Holtby, *Testament of Friendship,* records the strength of their mutual attachment, and it remains impossible to discuss the life or career of one without mentioning the other. Their obvious and enduring intimacy led to inevitable rumors of a lesbian relationship, rumors which both women refuted. Whatever the nature of their partnership, however, it is certain that Holtby and Brittain were a great influence on each other's work and political activity. Both were regular contributors to various newspapers and journals, including the feminist publication *Time and Tide,* of which Holtby would eventually become a director, and were active members of the Six Point Group, which campaigned for equal opportunities for women.

Together with Brittain, Holtby was a significant figure in the interwar feminist debate between so-called "old" feminism, which maintained that complete equality between men and women was achievable through political legislation, and "new" feminism, which focused on the biological differences between the sexes in order to argue that women had distinct social needs. Brittain and Holtby were passionate "old" feminists and their views were summed up by Holtby in an article printed in *Time and Tide* in 1926, where she defended her vision of "a society in which there is no respect of persons, either male or female, but a supreme regard for the importance of the human being." It was an argument on which she would elaborate further in her 1934 publication *Women and a Changing Civilisation.*

Of the two women, it was Holtby who would be the most successful novelist; her first book, *Anderby Wold,* was published in 1923, while Brittain was still trying to find a publisher for her manuscript *The Dark Tide.* Although *Anderby Wold* was not outstandingly successful, Brittain noted in *Testament of Friendship* that it did establish Holtby "as a young writer to be watched with expectation." Viewed now in retrospect, the book is also significant for introducing many of the themes and settings that would become central to much of Holtby's more mature fiction. With the exception of *Mandoa Mandoa!,* a political satire set in Africa, Holtby drew heavily on the landscapes of her childhood in the writing of her fiction. *Anderby Wold* can be seen as the beginning of a process, continued in subsequent novels such as *The Crowded Street, The Land of Green Ginger,* and *South Riding,* where she constructed an entire fictional geography in which names and places remain constant from book to book. She called this imaginary area the "South Riding," although it corresponds to the East Riding where she was brought up, and to which she constantly returned throughout her career.

Holtby's views regarding "equal opportunities" feminism are clearly exhibited in her fiction, in which her major female characters are often denied the easy resolutions offered by conventional romantic narratives. Instead she vigorously asserts women's right to personal and professional fulfillment, which she portrays as usually—although not always—incompatible with marriage. Muriel Hammond's response to a proposal at the end of *The Crowded Street* is typical: "'I can't be a good wife until I've learnt to be a person ... and perhaps in the end I'll never be a wife at all. That's very possible. But it doesn't matter.'"

Tragically, Holtby did not live to witness the reception of *South Riding,* the book that is now widely regarded as her greatest work. The novel was published six months after her death in 1935 to widespread and immediate acclaim, winning the James Tait Memorial Prize for the best novel of 1936. In 1938, it was also made into a highly successful feature film. *South Riding* has been compared with George Eliot's *Middlemarch,* in that both are books that employ an epic scope in order to explore the impact of national social and political change on the lives of individuals. Within a huge cast of characters, Holtby's heroine is Sarah Burton, tempestuous headmistress of a girls' school, who falls in love with the local landowner, Robert Carne. Their abortive romance embodies the major theme around which the book as a whole is based; the clash between the old, prewar, feudal order represented by Carne and the emergent postwar socialism so passionately espoused by Sarah.

Brittain observes in *Testament of Friendship* that *South Riding* was the most autobiographical of Holtby's novels. The debt her artistic imagination owed to her personal origins is acknowledged through Holtby's dedication of the novel to her mother, whose own career in local government as county alderman is echoed in the character of Alderman Mrs. Beddowes. In addition, the book also demonstrates a growing preoccupation with illness and death, reflecting Holtby's own knowledge that she might not live to complete it. Nevertheless, *South Riding* is not a morbid novel, but a masterpiece of feminist fiction in which Holtby's political and artistic preoccupations, in Brittain's words, "met and mingled in final co-operation."

—Sarah Gamble

hooks, bell

Pseudonym for Gloria Watkins. **Nationality:** American. **Born:** 1955. **Education:** Attended Stanford University. **Career:** Assistant professor of Afro-American studies and English, Yale University, New Haven, Connecticut, beginning c. 1985. **Address:** c/o Department of Afro-American Studies, Yale University, New Haven, Connecticut 06520, U.S.A.

Publications

Political/Social Theory

Ain't I a Woman: Black Women and Feminism. Boston, South End Press, 1981.
Feminist Theory: From Margin to Center. Boston, South End Press, 1984.
Yearning: Race, Gender, and Cultural Politics. N.p., Between-the-Lines, 1990.
Breaking Bread: Insurgent Black Intellectual Life, with Cornell West. Boston, South End Press, 1991.
Black Looks: Race and Representation. Boston, South End Press, 1992.
Sisters of the Yam: Black Women and Self-Recovery. Boston, South End Press, 1993.

Essays

Talking Back: Thinking Feminist, Thinking Black. N.p., Between-the-Lines, 1988.
Outlaw Culture: Resisting Representations. New York, Routledge, 1994.

Other

A Woman's Mourning Song. Writers and Readers, 1992.

*

Critical Studies: "A Name for Herself" (interview) by Courtney Leatherman, in *The Chronicle of Higher Education,* 19 May 1995.

* * *

Perhaps best known for her controversial work *Ain't I a Woman: Black Women and Feminism,* bell hooks has consistently written works that investigate the role of black women in society and within feminist criticism. Despite the critical attacks launched at this work for historical inaccuracies, *Ain't I a Woman* remains an important part of any study of feminist criticism.

Born Gloria Watkins, she writes under the pseudonym of bell hooks, which was her great-grandmother's name. The use of her great-grandmother's name is symbolic of hooks's concern with the past especially when it relates to the status of African American women. Fascinated by the roles that race and sex play within U.S. culture, hooks has produced a number of works that address these complexities in an attempt to define a place for all women and, in particular, women of color. As hooks would write in the introduction to *Ain't I a Woman,* her book "attempts to further the dialogue about the nature of black woman's experience that began in 19th-century America so as to move beyond racist and sexist assumptions about the nature of black womanhood to arrive at the truth of our experience." In addition to her focus on the experience of black women, hooks also argues that *Ain't I a Woman* doesn't just focus on the black woman; she states "our struggle for liberation has significance only if it takes place within a feminist movement that has as its fundamental goal the liberation of all people." These goals permeate the majority of hooks's many writings.

Following the great attention received by *Ain't I a Woman,* hooks published *Feminist Theory: From Margin to Center.* Again this work focuses on the role of black women in society and more specifically their role in the feminist movement. By criticizing the initial racism of the feminist movement, the importance of including black women's experience into feminist criticism is explored. Feminist criticism, according to hooks "actually referred to the plight of a select group of college-educated, middle and upper class, married white women." While acknowledging that the women's movement had to begin somewhere, hooks argues that the real concern of feminism extended far beyond this initial narrow scope. *Feminist Theory* further supports hooks's idea that if women are going to be liberated then all women should be included in the feminist movement. hooks states, "it is essential that black women recognize the special vantage point our marginality gives us and make use of this perspective to criticize the dominant racist, classist, sexist hegemony as well as to envision and create a counter-hegemony." While this work seems at times an open assault on the beginnings of the feminist movement, an issue that hooks is often criticized for, *Feminist Theory* develops further questions about the role of feminism in today's society.

Talking Back, a collection of essays, continues hooks's examination of the role of black women within the feminist movement. Here hooks expands her scope to include issues such as the teaching of women's literature, black homophobia, physical violence, racist feminists, black pornography, and academic politics.

hooks's fourth work, *Yearning: Race, Gender, and Cultural Politics,* while continuing the cultural dissection typical of her work, also includes much introspection on hooks's part. In this work, she attempts to redefine her purpose, an effort that is centered on the struggle to find a place for herself and to understand the place of black womanhood in a society that defines itself in relation what is different or marginalized.

Breaking Bread: Insurgent Black Intellectual Life includes hooks's dialogue with Cornell West, an African American social critic. West and hooks discuss various issues that affect black Americans today including the depiction of black Americans in the media and the struggles faced by African Americans in society. Many of these themes have been explored by hooks in earlier works as well. This work is useful for its dual perspective on the issues.

Outlaw Culture: Resisting Representations continues the investigation of the depiction of African Americans in modern culture that hooks explored in *Breaking Bread. Outlaw Culture* specifically focuses on cinematic, artistic, and musical representations of race, and is particularly interesting due to hooks's commentary on figures such as Madonna and gangster rap. Aside from cultural commentary, hooks also offers her commentary, critical as it is, on the "new feminism" of figures such as Camille Paglia.

The work of bell hooks is notable for the important issues she raises concerning the goals of feminism and the place of black women within the feminist movement. Her criticisms of the feminist movement, although controversial, served as a reminder that the goal of feminism should be the inclusion of all women, not just white women. She began to lend a voice to a formally silent group of women; black women who were, and continues to be, in a struggle to define their role within the women's movement. hooks is worthy of respect in feminist circles if for no other reason than that she continued to question the socially defined order of things rather than accepting it.

—Melissa L. Evans

HORNEY, Karen

Nationality: German. **Born:** Karen Clementine Theodore Danielssen, Hamburg, 16 September 1885; immigrated to the United States, 1932; naturalized, 1938. **Education:** Studied at University of Freiburg and University of Göttingen; University of Berlin, M.D. 1915. **Family:** Married Dr. Heinrich Horney in 1909; three daughters. **Career:** Worked at the Berlin-Lankwitz Sanatorium, 1915-18; training analyst and lecturer, Berlin Psychoanalytical Institute and Society, beginning 1920; after immigrating to United States, associate director, Chicago Institute for Psychoanalysis, 1932-34; in private practice beginning 1934. Lecturer and training analysis, Washington-Baltimore Institute of Psychoanalysis, New York Institute for Psychoanalysis, and the New School for Social Research, New York. Co-founder, Association for the Advancement of Psychoanalysis, 1941. **Member:** New York Psychoanalytic Association. **Died:** New York, 4 December 1952.

Publications

Nonfiction

The Neurotic Personality of Our Time. New York, Norton, and London, Routledge, 1937.

New Ways in Psychoanalysis. New York, Norton, and London, Routledge, 1939.

Self-Analysis. New York, Norton, and London, Routledge, 1942.

Our Inner Conflicts: A Constructive Theory of Neurosis. New York, Norton, 1945; London, Routledge, 1946.

Neurosis and Human Growth: The Struggle toward Self-Realization. New York, Norton, 1950; London, Routledge, 1951.

Feminine Papers, edited by Harold Kelman. New York, Norton, and London, Routledge, 1967.

Autobiography

The Adolescent Diaries of Karen Horney. New York, Basic Books, 1980.

Other

Editor, *Are You Considering Psychoanalysis?* New York, Norton, 1946.

*

Bibliography: In *Helping People: Karen Horney's Psychoanalytic Approach* by Harold Kelman, New York, Science House, 1971.

Critical Studies: *Helping People: Karen Horney's Psychoanalytic Approach* by Harold Kelman, New York, Science House, 1971; *Karen Horney: Gentle Rebel of Psychoanalysis* by Jack L. Rubins, New York, Dial Press, 1978; *The Feminist Legacy of Karen Horney* by Marcia Westcott, New Haven, Connecticut and London, Yale University Press, 1986.

* * *

Therapist, teacher, lecturer, writer—Karen Horney was a pioneer who laid the groundwork for the development of a "feminine psychology," and also made great contributions to the concepts of anxiety and neurosis. In 1922, in her very first public presentation, Dr. Horney would shock the world by challenging Sigmund Freud's theory of penis envy. It was not so much the penis itself that females envied, she asserted, but the benefits of having one!

Horney had experienced this inequality first-hand. Growing up in a strict, middle-class, German family at the turn of the century, her parents made no apologies about preferring her older brother. Germany at that time abided by the adage "*Kinder, Kirsche, Kuche*"—"children, church, and kitchen"—in defining the scope of women's allotted sphere. To add to this restrictive cultural milieu, Horney's father, a stern and harsh sea captain, often belittled both her physical appearance and her intellectual prowess. This disparagement culminated in his attempt to block her entry into medical school. Finally, however, her mother intervened, and in 1913 Horney became one of the first women to graduate from medical school in Berlin.

Her relationship with Freud continued to mimic her relationship with her father. As part of Freud's exclusive inner circle, and one of only a handful of women in the entire world to practice psychoanalysis at that time, Horney persisted in bucking Freud's hierarchy, in which women were continually cast in the subservient role. "Our whole civilization is a masculine civilization...," she would write. "If we are clear about the extent to which all our being, thinking, and doing conform to these masculine standards, we can see how difficult it is ... to really shake off this mode of thought." Cultural norms are predominantly created by men, she posited, and therefore reflect their values. Horney often referred to the traditional psychology of women as a "deposit of the desires and disappointments of men."

This constant devaluation, said Horney, made women conflicted between wanting to comply (gain approval from big daddy) and wanting to rage and triumph over them (hostility towards men). It is this inner conflict between an internalized self-hatred and the idealized self-image of cultural stereotypes that creates an underlying basic anxiety; this anxiety, in turn, often produces neurotic ways of coping in both women and men. In her book, *The Neurotic Personality of Our Time* (1937), she organized these coping mechanisms into three basic types: compliance, or seeking love and approval; aggression, or seeking power and dominance; and detachment, or seeking self-sufficiency through withdrawal.

Although everyone employs coping mechanisms at times—from escapist TV shows to a drink after work to unwind—Horney defined a neurotic need as a fixed, compulsive response that permits no spontaneity, often resulting in inappropriate responses to the ups and downs of daily life. These rigid behavior patterns create further problems because they often become entrenched as part of the personality, and are often felt to be in conflict with each other. (For instance, the need for affection and the need for dominance.)

As a whole, women, she felt, primarily clung to the first type of neurosis: approval-seeking. This was exemplified by their desperate need for love. In a paper entitled "Overvaluation of Love" (1934), Horney reveals that it is not love per se that is overvalued, but men, and men's approval.

Conversely, "The Dread of Woman" (1932) postulated that every man suffers to some extent from an anxiety of inadequacy; to allay their fears, men often fall victim to a compulsion to power to "prove" their worth. Others withdraw, too afraid to even risk intimacy.

Horney had true empathy for the damaged of both sexes, alternatively chasing the phantoms of "love" and "power." She also foresaw—and experienced in her own life—the modern woman's dilemma. By fusing both stereotypical strategies, the modern woman has become, as psychologist and author of *The Feminist Legacy of Karen Horney* Marcia Westcott so aptly penned, "torn between love and work and consequently dissatisfied in both."

After a rocky marriage, Horney divorced her husband in 1927. She continued to come under increasing pressure from orthodox psychoanalytic circles in Berlin largely because of her feminist ideas. Still, ever true to her beliefs, she continued to develop psychological theories that diverged from the Freudian doctrine of the day. She pointed to the influences of family and culture rather than biology or instincts as the determining factors of one's personality and psychological health. People develop *in relationship* to others close to them, and within the context of a specific social milieu.

Immigrating to the United States in 1932, Horney became associate director of the Chicago Institute for Psychoanalysis before founding the American Institute of Psychoanalysis, all the while continuing private practice. There, in the New World, Horney found her ideas further validated. Many psychological problems manifested themselves differently in 1930s America—therefore, the dominant culture must indeed play a significant part. How could universal biological factors explain the wide variations in problems suffered in differing places? The enthusiastic response to her work from respected anthropologists such as Ruth Benedict and Margaret Mead further encouraged Horney that she was on course.

As a therapist and now mother of three, Horney also had great faith in the individual's innate urge and potential to grow, as well as the constructive tendency to heal, again in contrast to Freud's pessimistic theory of a static biological determinism. She exhibited a respect for people, both in her personal relationships and in her work, and an uncommon modesty towards her own profession. "We must not forget, however, that life may be the best therapist," she admitted in her paper "Personality Changes in Female Adolescence" (1934).

In many ways and across many fields, Horney's work has had considerable impact. For example, her view of feminine psychology is akin to the philosophical concept of woman as "the other" as expressed in Simone de Beauvoir's groundbreaking *The Second Sex* (1949)—only Horney's hypothesis predated de Beauvoir by more than 25 years! Clearly, Horney took a bold turn away from the patriarchal goose-step of her time so that future feminists might also cut a wider path. Her other notable achievements include the establishment of the Karen Horney Clinic and the Karen Horney Psychoanalytic Institute (a training center for therapists) in New York City, both still active today.

What, finally, constitutes a woman's worth? Karen Horney dedicated her life to attempting to answer that question. At age 18, on New Year's Day 1904, she wrote in her diary that her goal in life was "to learn how to listen to the delicate vibrations of my soul, to be incorruptibly true to myself and fair to others, and to find in this way the right measure of my own worth." It is an admirable measure of any human being, and certainly one that she achieved.

—Victoria Larimore

HOWE, Julia Ward

Nationality: American **Born:** New York, New York, 27 May 1819. **Education:** Privately educated. **Family:** Married the philanthropist Samuel Gridley Howe in 1843 (died 1876); four daughters and one son. **Career:** Visited Boston and met Margaret Fuller, 1839; co-editor, with Samuel Howe, *The Commonwealth* (abolitionist newspaper), prior to 1865; travelled to Greece, 1867; made first speech on behalf of woman suffrage, Boston, 1868; delegate to World's Prison Reform Congress, London, 1872; promoted international peace association after 1870. Unitarian preacher and lecturer in the United States, Rome, and Santo Domingo. Founder and editor, *Northern Lights* (literary journal), 1867; founder and associate editor, *Woman's Journal,* beginning 1870; contributor to numerous periodicals. Co-founder, Association of Advancement of Women, and General Federation of Women's Clubs. **Awards:** Inducted into American Academy of Arts and Letters, 1908; L.L.D., Tufts College, 1904; Litt.D., Brown University, 1910. **Member:** American Woman Suffrage Association, American Authors' Guild (president, 1898), New England Woman Suffrage Association (president, 1868-77, 1893-1910), New England Club (president), Massachusetts Woman Suffrage Association (president, 1870-78, 1891-93). **Died:** Newport, Rhode Island, 17 October 1910.

Publications

Essays

Is Polite Society Polite? Boston and New York, Lamson Wolfe, 1885.

Julia Ward Howe and the Woman Suffrage Movement: A Selection from Her Speeches and Essays, edited by Florence Howe Hall. Boston, D. Estes, 1913.

Plays

Leonora, or The World's Own (produced New York, 1855). Boston, Ticknor & Fields, 1857.

Hippolytus. N.p., 1941.

Poetry

Passion Flowers (published anonymously). Boston, Ticknor Reed & Fields, 1854; 3rd edition, 1854.

Words for the Hour. Boston, Ticknor & Fields, 1857.

"Battle Hymn of the Republic," in *Atlantic Monthly,* February 1862.

Later Lyrics. Boston, J.E. Tilton, 1866.

From Sunset Ridge: Poems Old and New. Boston and New York, Houghton Mifflin, 1899.

Other

A Trip to Cuba. Boston, Ticknor & Fields, 1860.
From the Oak to the Olive. Boston, n.p., 1868.
The Massachusetts Philanthropist: Memoir of Dr. Samuel Gridley Howe. Boston, A.J. Wright, 1876.
Modern Society. Boston, Roberts Bros., 1881.
Margaret Fuller (Marchesa Ossoli). Boston, Roberts Bros., 1883.
The Julia Ward Howe Birthday Book: Selections from her works, edited by Laura E. Richards. Boston, Lee Shepard, 1889.
Reminiscences, 1819-1899. Boston and New York, Houghton Mifflin, 1899.
The Walk with God (diary entries and poetry), edited by Laura E. Richards. New York, E.P. Dutton, 1919.

Editor, *Sex and Education: A Reply to Dr. E.H. Clarke's "Sex in Education."* Boston, Roberts Bros., 1874.
Editor and contributor, *Sketches of Representative Women of New England.* Boston, New England Historical Publishing Co., 1905.

*

Media Adaptations: *Robert E. Lee* (musical adaptation of "Battle Hymn of the Republic") by Linda Betts Frazier, 1992.

Critical Studies: *Two Noble Lives: Samuel Gridley Howe, Julia Ward Howe* by Laura Elizabeth Howe Richards, Boston, D. Estes, 1911; *Julia Ward Howe, 1819-1910* by Florence Howe Hall, Maude Howe Elliot, and Laura Elizabeth Howe Richards, Boston, Houghton, 1915; *The Story of the Battle Hymn of the Republic* by Florence Howe Hall, New York and London, Harper, 1916; *Three Saints and a Sinner: Julia Ward Howe, Louisa, Annie, Sam Ward* by Louise Hall Tharp, Boston, Little Brown, 1956. *Mine Eyes Have Seen the Glory: A Biography of Julia Ward Howe* by Deborah Pickman Clifford, Boston, Little Brown, 1979; *Private Woman, Public Person: An Account of the Life of Julia Ward Howe from 1819-1868* by Mary Hetherington Grant, Brooklyn, New York, Carlson, 1994.

* * *

The first woman to be inducted into the prestigious American Academy of Arts and Letters, Julia Ward Howe was esteemed in her day not only as the author of the "Battle Hymn of the Republic" but as an ardent suffragist and abolitionist. The wife of prominent Boston philanthropist Dr. Samuel Gridley Howe, Julia devoted her life to social activism, which she married to her quick intellect, broad educational background, and her skill as a writer.

Howe was born in New York City in 1819. The daughter of a successful banker, Howe received the benefit of a liberal education that included both classical and Romance languages, geometry, history, and European literature. After her father's death when she was 20 the independent Howe travelled to Boston, where she visited the noted intellectual Margaret Fuller, about whom she would later write a biography after Fuller's tragic death in 1850. Four years later she was married; she and her husband would live in Italy for a year, during which her first child was born. Returning to New York, the Howes jointly edited and published the abolitionist newspaper *The Commonwealth,* which remained in circulation up until the outbreak of the Civil War. Despite her husband's adamant protests, Julia also began to write fiction; from 1854, when she anonymously published her first volume of poetry, entitled *Passion Flowers,* Howe's writing was primarily entertaining and included plays, verse, and travel essays. The "Battle Hymn of the Republic," which Howe later claimed was written on a single sheet of paper in the middle of the night and was based on the traditional tune "John Brown's Body," was published in the *Atlantic Monthly* in 1862 and earned its author nation-wide acclaim.

In 1869 Howe transferred her activist zeal from the cause of abolition to that of woman suffrage. As one of her first public pronouncements of her support of women's right to the vote she spoke before a legislative committee in the Boston State House. Active in organized suffrage activities on both the state and regional level, and involved in the formation of the American Woman Suffrage Association, Howe used the opportunity provided as a delegate to the 1872 World's Prison Reform Congress held in London to further women's solidarity overseas. A pacifist lecturer and preacher within the Unitarian church, Howe also strongly supported the foundation of a woman's association in support of international peace, a cause on which she wrote an appeal at the end of the Franco-Prussian War in 1870. Her social activism reached its zenith in a lecture tour on the West Coast in 1888; Howe died in 1919, at the age of 91.

—Lynn MacGregor

HOWE, Susan

Nationality: American. **Born:** Boston, Massachusetts, 10 June 1937. **Education:** Boston Museum School of Fine Arts, B.A. 1961. **Family:** Married 2) the sculptor David von Shlegell (deceased); two children. **Career:** Worked as a painter, actress, stage set designer, and radio producer until 1971; professor of English, State University of New York at Buffalo, beginning 1991; numerous traveling appointments. **Awards:** Before Columbus Foundation American Book Award, 1980, 1987. **Address:** 115 New Quarry Road, Guilford, Connecticut 06437, U.S.A.

Publications

Literary Criticism

My Emily Dickinson. Berkeley, California, North Atlantic, 1985.

Essays

The Birth-Mark: Unsettling the Wilderness in American Literary History. Middletown, Connecticut, Wesleyan University Press, 1993.

Poetry

Hinge Picture. Cherry Valley, New York, Cherry Valley/Telephone Books, 1974.

Chanting at the Crystal Sea. Boston, Fire Exit/Corbett, 1975.
The Western Borders. Willits, California, Tuumba, 1976.
A Secret History of the Dividing Line. New York, Telephone Books, 1978.
Deep in a Forest of Herods. New Haven, Connecticut, Pharos, 1979.
Cabbage Gardens. Chicago, Fathom, 1979.
The Liberties. Guilford, Connecticut, Loon, 1980.
Pythagorean Silence. New York, Montemora Foundation, 1982.
Defenestration of Prague. New York, Kulchur Foundation, 1983.
Articulation of Sound Forms in Time. Windsor, Vermont, Awede, 1987.
A Bibliography of the King's Book, or, Eikon Basilike. Providence, Rhode Island, Paradigm, 1989.
Singularities. Middletown, Connecticut, Wesleyan University Press, 1990.
The Europe of Trusts: Selected Poems. Los Angeles, Sun & Moon, 1990.
Silence Wager Stories. Providence, Rhode Island, Paradigm, 1992.
The Nonconformist's Memorial. New York, New Directions Press, 1993.

*

Critical Studies: "Canon and Loaded Gun: Feminist Poetics and the Avant-Garde" by Marjorie Perloff, in *Stanford Literature Review,* 4, spring 1987, and her "'Collision or Collusion with History': The Narrative Lyric of Susan Howe," in *Contemporary Literature,* 30, winter 1989; "'Whowe': On Susan Howe" by Rachel Blau DuPlessis, in her *The Pink Guitar: Writing as Feminist Practice,* New York, Routledge, 1990; *Talisman: A Journal of Contemporary Poetry and Poetics* (special Howe issue), 4, spring 1990; "And The Without: An Interpretive Essay on Susan Howe" by Peter Quartermann, in his *Disjunctive Poetics: From Gertrude Stein and Louis Zukofsky to Susan Howe,* New York, Cambridge University Press, 1992; "Susan Howe" by Linda Reinfeld, in her *Language Poetry: Writing as Rescue,* Baton Rouge, Louisiana State University Press, 1992; "My Susan Howe" by Eric Murphy Selinger, in *Parnassus: Poetry in Review,* 20, 1995; "Articulating the Inarticulate: Singularities and the Counter-Method in Susan Howe," in *Contemporary Literature* 36, 1995; "An Interview with Susan Howe" by Lynn Keller, in *Contemporary Literature* 36, 1995.

* * *

Susan Howe belongs to the experimental, avant-garde tradition in American women's poetry. She falls specifically in the line of both Emily Dickinson (about whom she has written at length in *My Emily Dickinson*) and of Gertrude Stein. She also has affinities with a recent development in American poetry—a school known as "Language Poetry." In general, Language Poets deliberately disrupt both syntax and the typographical appearance of a poem on a page. Howe uses these techniques, and others, to call particular attention to the voices of women who, throughout history, have been silenced by the ideologically dominant languages.

Throughout, Howe's writing demonstrates an acute awareness of the manner in which women have been excluded from both literacy and literary history. For example, early in *The Europe of Trusts,* Howe writes: "I wish I could tenderly lift from the dark side of history, voices that are anonymous, slighted—inarticulate." Howe grew up in Cambridge, Massachusetts, and notes, in *The Birth-Mark: Expressions and the Wilderness,* that her father, a Harvard professor, would have to go into the stacks for her to retrieve books so that, as a woman, she would not be trespassing. The often unusual appearance of a Howe poem on the page—she will on occasion roll a page into the typewriter at a diagonal or even print words upside down on a page—dates in part to her early training as a painter. She was trained at the Boston Museum of Fine Arts, and switched gradually to the production of poetry after she discovered that she was doing more and more with words on canvas.

After the publication by mainstream presses of *The Europe of Trusts* and *Singularities* in 1990, Howe's work began to be more widely recognized. The latter contains a previously published sequence entitled *The Liberties,* which centers on the story of Hester Johnson (whom Jonathan Swift refers to as Stella and who was probably the daughter of Sir William Temple). At Swift's encouragement, both Stella and her companion, Rebecca Dingley, moved to Ireland to settle on land inherited from William Temple and to become lifelong companions of Swift. Because Stella, and any words she may have written, now survive only in Swift's writing, Howe must (through imagination) recreate what Stella's life may have been like.

Singularities reprints *Articulation of Sound Forms in Time,* which contains an imaginative historical account based loosely on the journal of a Puritan minister named Hope Atherton, who wandered on the fringes of a battle between American settlers and Native Americans. Howe's work throughout the volume assigns a special weight to the voices of both Native Americans and women, noting that those voices were not, until very recently, in the received accounts of American history. The remainder of *Singularities* stands as a larger meditation on what seems to have gone wrong with the American voice and point of view from almost the first step on the shores. The long poems "Thorow" and "Scattering as a Behavior toward Risk" also appear in *Singularities.* "Thorow" comprises an extended meditation on what Howe terms the "Elegiac Western Imagination" and which she filters through a particularly American landscape.

In *The Birth-Mark,* Howe explains: "It's the stutter in American literature that interests me.... I hear the stutter as a sounding of uncertainty. What is silenced or not quite silenced. All the broken dreams.... A return is necessary, a way for women to go. Because we are in the stutter. We were expelled from the Garden of the Mythology of the American Frontier. The drama's done. We are the wilderness. We have come on to the stage stammering." That women have historically been silenced, prevented from writing, not listened to, is not a new point. What is new, however, is the seriousness with which Howe asks the question of whether we have learned all that we need to know about how to read that silencing. "Is a poetics of intervening absence an oxymoron?" she asks. "Do we go anywhere?" and then answers "I will twine feathers, prickings, rulings, wampum beads, chance echoes, sprays of lace in the place of your name."

The poetry collection *The Nonconformists's Memorial* was published simultaneously with *The Birth-Mark,* and it is clear that the works are intended to gloss one another. Especially in the opening section of *Nonconformist's Memorial,* Howe focuses on women's stories that need to be re-thought, including most noticeably the stories of Mary and of the early American dissenter Anne Hutchinson. Near the end of the opening poem, we read a representative example that captures Howe's stress on recovering both silences and the inner lives of women: "Dense in parameter space/the obscure negative way.... Moving away into depth/of the sea/Her love once said in her mind/Enlightenedly to do." This passage, and many others, demonstrate Howe's consistent focus on women in her work.

Because Howe's work may seem inaccessible to readers who encounter her for the first time, it may be helpful to conclude with a brief statement of who Howe considers her influences to be. In a 1995 interview with Lynn Keller, she listed among her influences for poetry H.D. (Hilda Doolittle) and Virginia Woolf. Among those who have influenced her prose, she refers to Hélène Cixous and Julia Kristeva, and also to the early American critic Patricia Caldwell. Susan Howe's work is demanding, but then, perhaps appropriately so: the task of recovering women's voices in history and in literary history is, in fact, an intellectually demanding—and rewarding—one.

—Jane Hoogestraat

HULME, Keri

Nationality: New Zealander **Born:** Christchurch, 9 March 1947. **Education:** University of Canterbury, 1967-68. **Career:** Worked as a fisher, television director, cook, and postwoman; writer-in-residence, Otago University, Dunedin, 1978, and University of Canterbury, Christchurch, 1985. Painter. **Awards:** New Zealand Book Award, and Pegasus Award for Maori literature, both 1984, and Booker McConnell Prize, 1985, all for *the bone people.* **Member:** New Zealand Literary Fund (member advisory committee), New Zealand Indecent Publications Tribunal. **Address:** Okarito Private Bag, Westland, New Zealand.

Publications

Novels

the bone people. Auckland, Spiral, 1983; Baton Rouge, Louisiana University Press, and London, Hodder & Stoughton, 1985.

Short Stories

Te Kaihau/The Windeater. Wellington, Victoria University Press, 1986; New York, Braziller, and London, Hodder & Stoughton, 1987.

Poetry

The Silence Between: Moeraki Conversations. Wellington, Victoria University Press, and Oxford, Oxford University Press, 1982.
Strands. Auckland, Auckland University Press, 1992.

Uncollected Poetry

"He Hoha," in *Into the World of Light: An Anthology of Maori Writing,* edited by Witi Ihimaera and D.S. Long. Auckland, Heinemann, 1982.

Uncollected Essays

"Okarito and Moeraki," in *Te whenua, te iwi: The Land and the People,* edited by Jock Phillips. Wellington, New Zealand, Allen & Unwin, 1987.

Other

Lost Possessions. Wellington, Victoria University Press, 1985.
Homeplaces: Three Coasts of the South Island of New Zealand, photographs by Robin Morrison. Auckland and London, Hodder & Stoughton, 1989.

Recordings: *Keri Hulme and Les.A. Murray Reading from Their Work,* 1985.

*

Media Adaptations: *Hooks and Feelers* (film; adaptation of her short story), 1983; *Hinekaro Goes on a Picnic and Blows up an Obelisk* (film; adaptation of her short story), 1995.

Critical Studies: "Keri Hulme: Breaking Ground" by Shona Smith, in *Untold,* 2, spring 1984; "Sandi Hall and Keri Hulme Talk about 'the bone people' in *Broadsheet,* 121, July/August 1984; "Rewriting Their Stories: Postcolonialism and Feminism in the fictions of Keri Hulme and Audrey Thomas" by C. Prentice, in *Span,* 23, September 1986; interview with Harry Ricketts, in his *Talking about Ourselves: 12 New Zealand Poets in Conversation,* Wellington, Mallison Rendel, 1986; "Violence as lingua franca: Keri Hulme's *The Bone People*" by M. Dever, in *World Literature Written in English,* 29(2), autumn 1989; interview with Elizabeth Alley in *In the Same Room: Conversations with New Zealand Writers,* edited by Alley and Mark Williams, Auckland, Auckland University Press, 1992.

Keri Hulme comments:

My mother comes from a line of covert matriarchs, women who run their households surely, but—and most importantly—also let their families run.—

She has had six very different children. One way or another, we have all made our mark. I have, for example, two sisters who are midwives, inventive women-centered tautoko domiciliary midwives. They are partners in a business: they have different emphases in their individual practices: they are family-oriented people.

I am, by nature, a loner. I have been, since I was very young indeed. I was always trailing off up a beach, bemazed by the buzzing wondrous everything around, sand insects surf birdcries wind stink yearn—

I am also, in my depths/heights, family-oriented.

Our family comes from diverse people: Kai Tahu, Kati Mamoe (South Island Maori iwi); Orkney islanders; Lancashire folk; Faroese and/or Norwegian migrants. I have a mother—my father died when I, eldest of my siblings, was 11—and two maternal uncles; I have two paternal aunts; I have three sisters and two brothers, and a helluva lot of small fry (some of them now in their 20's) engendered thereby. I won't start on the cousin rings...

I have always been pro-female, not least because I come from a line of matriarchs. Being female is a position of strength, like being Maori. Yes, it can be eroded. Yes, it is eroded by economic factors and historical factors and societal factors. But together, all of us, we survive. We not only survive, we laugh. We eat fatly, we drink well, and we weep when it is time to weep, and we laugh—

from this base I live and move and have my being. From this base, I write—

* * *

Keri Hulme is primarily known for her novel *the bone people,* which in 1984 won the New Zealand National Book Award, the prize for Maori literature, and in 1985 went on to win the prestigious British Booker Prize, the first New Zealand book to do so. Of Maori, Scots (Orkney) and English ancestry, Hulme identifies strongly as Maori:

> I am lucky to have got two extremely rich and potent mythological traditions, one is Kai Tahu or Maori in general and the other is Celtic—I can't section me up, but I think of myself as Maori rather than Pakeha [white] and where this may seem ridiculous to someone who goes through the whakapapa, the family tree, and says, oh but you're only an eighth Maori, how can you feel like that? Well—that's where I draw my strength from, that's where I learnt about works first and that's the side I learnt to tell stories from.

During the 1970s her short stories appeared in a New Zealand magazines and a collection, *Te Kaihau,* appeared in 1986, but her first published book, *The Silences Between* (1982), was poetry. In an impressive long poem, "He Hoha," about being a woman in a woman's body she writes:

> Bones tuned, the body sings-
> See me,
> I am wide with swimmer's muscle, and a bulk and luggage I carry curdled on hips;
> I am fat rich as a titi-chick, ready for the far ocean flight.
> See me,
> I have skilled fingers with minimal scars, broad feet that caress beaches,
> ears that catch the music of ghosts, eyes that see the landlight, a pristine womb
> untouched except by years of bleeding, a tame unsteady heart

and continues:

> It is cliché that once a month, the moon stalks through my body
> rendering me frail and still more susceptible to brain spin;
> it is truth that cramp and clot and tender breast beset—but then
> it is the tide of potency, another chance to walk the crack between worlds

The bone people, refused by three mainstream publishers as too long, too different, and too unwieldy, was published by a feminist collective, Spiral, whose small initial edition sold out in weeks. Unusual in New Zealand literature, the novel is a mixture of realism, fantasy and myth. It fuses Pakeha and Maori mythology and suggests that biculturalism is fundamental to the future of New Zealand. It uses the local landscape, Maori names, Maori spiritual beliefs, the rhythms of colloquial speech, and to many readers seemed the first literary work to capture the distinctive qualities of post-colonial bicultural New Zealand. Hulme creates a protagonist, Kerewin Holmes, who in many ways resembles herself: a strong eccentric artist, witty, bitter, self-deprecating and wise, skilled at fishing and aikido, who can defeat a man in a fight or at chess, and drink any man under the table. She lives in a wish-fulfillment tower by the sea, and struggles to find ways of relating to a deaf pakeha child and his Maori foster father who, when drunk, violently batters his child. Kerewin, a fluent and complex wordspinner with a wide and eclectic knowledge dominates the novel. She rejects conventional women's roles, and refuses to enter into a couple relationship. The novel ends in a vision of a new way of relating for male and female, adult and child, pakeha and Maori, moving beyond gender and racism—"something perilous and new, something strange and growing and great." Hulme sees Maori spirituality as central to her novel. In an interview with Sandi Hall she says:

> it's taken a very long time, nearly two centuries, for Maori spiritual attitudes to regain their former standing, to regain their mana. Because of that—we all know the deplorable statistics—the gross disproportion of Maori in jail, other institution-type places. Pakeha people are taking more notice of things that indicate people are in considerable pain. The amount of rape, wife and child assault, drinking, committal for various mental read spiritual diseases, among Maori people.

Although Kerewin appealed to many female readers as an independent and "self-caretaking" woman, and although Hulme agreed that "to me she was an option that maybe other women would be interested in" she added that "when I was writing it feminism wasn't really a driving force, certainly wasn't in my life anyway." But speaking of her family she says "I have always been pro-female, not least because I come from a line of matriarchs. Being female is a position of strength, like being Maori." In interviews she has spoken of herself as "gender neuter": "A neuter to me is not so much standing on the fence as being on both sides of the track at once," she told Shona Smith. "You are then free to adopt whatever blend of qualities society deems to be specifically male or specifically female without being put on the line as to where your loyalties lie—sexual loyalties lie—you don't have them."

With the success of *the bone people* the New Zealand media publicized Hulme as a loner and raconteur, living in a remote tiny coastal settlement famous for its white herons, smoking a pipe, drinking whisky, a skilful whitebaiter (fisherwoman). She and her novel have become part of the New Zealand mythos.

—Aorewa Pohutukawa McLeod

HURST, Fannie

Nationality: American. **Born:** Hamilton, Ohio, 18 October 1887. **Education:** Washington University, St Louis, B.A. 1909; attended

Columbia University, New York, 1910. **Family:** Married the pianist Jacques S. Danielson in 1915 (died 1952). **Career:** Teacher, 1909-10; moved to New York and worked as an actress before becoming full-time writer. Chair, Woman's National Housing Commission, 1936-37; member of the National Advisory Committee of the WPA, 1940-41; U.S. delegate to the UN World Health Assembly, Geneva. Trustee, Heckscher Foundation, 1940-60. **Awards:** D.Litt.: Washington University, 1953; Fairleigh Dickinson University, Rutherford, New Jersey. **Member:** Authors League (president, 1936-37; vice-president, 1944-46, 1947). **Died:** 23 February 1968.

Publications

Novels

Star-Dust: The Story of an American Girl. New York and London, Harper, 1921.
Lummox. New York, Harper, 1923; London, Cape, 1924.
Appassionata. New York, Knopf, and London, Cape, 1926.
Mannequin. New York, Knopf, 1926.
A President Is Born. New York, Harper, and London, Cape, 1928.
Five and Ten. New York, Harper, and London, Cape, 1929.
Back Street. New York, Cosmopolitan, and London, Cape, 1931.
Imitation of Life. New York and London, Harper, 1933.
Anitra's Dance. New York, Harper, and London, Cape, 1934.
Great Laughter. New York, Harper, 1936; London, Cape, 1937.
Sister Act. New York, Longmans, 1941.
Lonely Parade. New York, Harper, and London, Cape, 1942.
White Christmas. New York, Doubleday, 1942.
Hallelujah. New York and London, Harper, 1944.
The Hands of Veronica. New York, Harper, and London, Lane, 1947.
Anywoman. New York, Harper, and London, Cape, 1950.
The Name Is Mary. New York, Dell, 1951.
The Man with One Hand. London, Cape, 1953.
Family! New York, Doubleday, 1960.
God Must Be Sad. New York, Doubleday, 1961.
Fool—Be Still. New York, Doubleday, 1964; London, Hale, 1966.

Short Stories

Just around the Corner: Romance en Casserole. New York and London, Harper, 1914.
Every Soul Hath Its Song. New York and London, Harper, 1916.
Gaslight Sonatas. New York, Harper, and London, Hodder and Stoughton, 1918.
Humoresque: A Laugh on Life with a Tear behind It. New York and London, Harper, 1919.
The Vertical City. New York and London, Harper, 1922.
Song of Life. New York, Knopf, and London, Cape, 1927.
Procession. New York, Harper, and London, Cape, 1929.
We Are Ten. New York and London, Harper, 1937.

Plays

The Land of the Free, with Harriet Ford (produced New York, 1917).
Back Pay (produced New York, 1921).
Humoresque (produced New York, 1923).
It Is to Laugh (produced New York, 1927).

Screenplays: *The Younger Generation,* with Sonya Levien and Howard J. Green, 1929; *Lummox,* with Elizabeth Meehan, 1930.

Other

No Food with My Meals. New York, Harper, 1935.
Today Is Ladies' Day. New York, Home Institute, 1939.
Anatomy of Me: A Wonderer in Search of Herself. New York, Doubleday, 1958; London, Cape, 1959.

*

Media Adaptations: *Five and Ten,* 1931; *Symphony of Six Million (Melody of Life),* 1932; *Back Street,* 1932, 1941, 1961; *Anatomy of Me,* 1934, 1959; *Four Daughters* (adapted from the novel *Sister Act*), 1938; *Humoresque,* 1946; *Young at Heart,* 1956.

Manuscript Collections: Olin Library, Washington University, St Louis; Goldfarb Library, Brandeis University, Waltham, Massachusetts; University of Texas, Austin.

Critical Studies: "Fannie Hurst: By Her Ex-Amanuensis" by Zora Neale Hurston, in *Saturday Review of Literature,* 16, 9 October 1937; *Myths about Love and Women: The Fiction of Fannie Hurst* by Mary Rose Shaughnessy, New York, Gordon Press, 1980; "White Patron and Black Artist: The Correspondence of Fannie Hurst and Zora Neale Hurston" by Gay Wilentz, in *Library Chronicle of the University of Texas,* 35, 1986; "Fanny Hurst" by Susan Currier, in *Dictionary of Literary Biography,* Vol. 86: *American Short Story Writers, 1910-1945,* Detroit, Gale, 1989.

* * *

Often dismissed by contemporary and later critics as the "Queen of the Sob Sisters," the fiction of Fanny Hurst can be seen as relevant within the cannon of feminist writers due to her prolific dramatization of the multitude of oppressions endured by turn-of-the-century women. The right of a woman to retain her birth name after marriage, equal pay for equal work, spouse abuse, sexual harassment, the availability of birth control, the need for sex education, age discrimination, the plight of poor women attempting to raise children on their own; Hurst addressed each of these issues and more in her many novels, short stories, and plays.

Born on a farm in Hamilton, Ohio, Hurst graduated from Washington University in 1909 and then did what educated women usually did: became a school teacher. However, she believed her talents could be put to greater use as a writer and a year later she moved to New York City to begin what would be a long and lucrative literary career. Short fiction was the first form she tried her hand at. The short story collections *Just around the Corner, Every Soul Hath Its Song, Gaslight Sonatas,* and *Humoresque* were published between 1914 and 1919. *Humoresque* is notable for its focus on Jewish Americans and the problems they faced in trying to assimilate into U.S. culture; *Just around the Corner* for championing the efforts of the young, working woman.

An established writer by her mid-twenties, Hurst's most popular works were the novels *Back Street* (1931) and *Imitation of Life* (1933). While her heroines were often trapped by their emotional necessity for men—indeed for some of her woman protagonists the energy they invest into a career is merely a replacement for the love they would otherwise expend upon a man—the vivid, sentimental manner she used to address and win her audience endeared her to thousands of female readers. Especially during the Depression era, Hurst's escapist tales of confinement, futile existences, and controlling relationships with egotistical males provided readers with the sense that their emotional experiences were somehow shared, albeit with much less pathos, by others.

—Pamela Kester-Shelton

HURSTON, Zora Neale

Nationality: American. **Born:** Eatonville, Florida, 7 January 1901 (some sources say 1891). **Education:** Attended Morgan Academy, Baltimore, Maryland, 1917; Howard University, Washington, DC, 1918; Barnard College, New York, B.A. 1928; Columbia University, 1935. **Family:** Married 1) Herbert Sheen in 1927 (divorced 1931); 2) Albert Price in 1939 (divorced). **Career:** Moved to Harlem, New York, 1925; secretary to novelist Fanny Hurst c. 1926; director and producer of plays and storytelling events for Federal Theatre Project, Harold Golden Theatre, New York, and around the U.S.; script writer, Paramount Pictures and Warner Brothers, Hollywood, California; head of drama department, North Carolina College for Negroes, Durham; false charge of child abuse brought against her, 1948; returned to Florida and worked as a librarian and a maid. **Awards:** *Opportunity Magazine* award, 1925, for "Spunk"; first African American woman to receive a Guggenheim fellowship; Honorary Doctor of Letters degree from Morgan State College, 1939; Anisfield-Wolf Award, 1943, for *Dust Tracks on a Road;* Howard University's Distinguished Alumni Award, 1943. **Died:** 28 January 1960.

Publications

Novels

Jonah's Gourd Vine. Philadelphia and London, Lippincott, 1934.
Their Eyes Were Watching God. Philadelphia and London, Lippincott, 1937.
Moses, Man of the Mountain. Philadelphia, New York, London, and Toronto, Lippincott, 1939; as *The Man of the Mountain,* London, Dent, 1941.
Seraph on the Suwanee. New York, Scribner's 1948.

Short Stories

Mules and Men. Philadelphia and London, Lippincott, 1935.
Tell My Horse. Philalelphia, New York, London, and Toronto, Lippincott, 1938; as *Voodoo Gods: An Inquiry into Native Myths and Magic in Jamaica and Haiti,* London, Dent, 1939.
The Sanctified Church: The Folklore Writings of Zora Neale Hurston, edited by Toni Cade Bambara. Berkeley, Turtle Island Press, 1981.
Spunk. The Selected Short Stories of Zora Neale Hurston. Berkeley, California, Turtle Island Foundation, 1985.

Essays

I Love Myself when I Am Laughing. . . and Then Again When I Am Looking Mean and Impressive: A Zora Neale Hurston Reader, edited by Alice Walker. New York, Feminist Press, 1979.

Plays

Color Struck, in *Fire!!,* 1 November 1926.
"The First One," in *Ebony and Topaz,* edited by Charles S. Johnson. New York, National Urban League, 1927.
The Great Day (revue). N.p., 1932.
Singing Steel. N.p., 1934.
Mule Bone: A Comedy of Negro Life, with Langston Hughes, in *Drama Critique,* spring 1964.

Autobiography

Dust Tracks on the Road. Philadelphia and London, Lippincott, 1942.

*

Manuscript Collections: Yale University, New Haven, Connecticut; Moorland-Spingarn Research Center, Howard University, Washington, DC; Fisk University Library.

Critical Studies: *Zora Neale Hurston: A Literary Biography* by Robert E. Hemenway, Urbana, University of Illinois Press, 1977; "Zora Neale Hurston: Changing Her Own Words" by Cheryl A. Wall, in *American Novelists Revisited: Essays in Feminist Criticism* edited by Fritz Fleischmann, Boston, G.K. Hall, 1982; *The Character of the Word: The Texts of Zora Neale Hurston* by Karla F.C. Holloway, Westport, Connecticut, Greenwood Press, 1987; *Sorrow's Kitchen: The Life and Folklore of Zora Neale Hurston* by Mary E. Lyons, New York, Scribner's, 1990; *New Essays on Their Eyes Were Watching God* by Michael Awkward, Cambridge, Cambridge University Press, 1990; *Zora in Florida* edited by Steve Glassman and Kathryn Lee Seidel, Orlando, University of Central Florida Press, 1991; *Alice Walker and Zora Neale Hurston: The Common Bond* edited by Lillie P. Howard, Westport, Connecticut, Greenwood Press, 1993; *Jump at the Sun: Zora Neale Hurston's Cosmic Comedy* by John Lowe, Urbana & Chicago, University of Illinois Press, 1994; *Every Tub Must Sit on Its Own Bottom: The Philosophy and Politics of Zora Neale Hurston* by Deborah G. Plant, Champaign, University of Illinois Press, 1995; *Women of the Harlem Renaissance* by Cheryl A. Wall, Bloomington, Indiana University Press, 1995: *The Voices of African American Women: The Use of Narrative and Authorial Voice in the Works of Harriet Jacobs, Zora Neale Hurston, and Alice Walker* by Yvonne Johnson, New York, P. Lang, 1995.

* * *

Zora Neale Hurston expressed her creative genius and zest for life through her work as a writer, anthropologist, and folklorist. A visionary, Hurston realized many of her dreams during her lifetime and wrote prolifically, publishing short stories, essays, plays, historical narratives, ethnographies, an autobiography, and several novels. Although she was a well-known figure of the Harlem Renaissance, Hurston's writing was often unread or misunderstood by her contemporaries and virtually ignored by the time of her death in 1960. Since the 1970s, contemporary black women writers, led by Alice Walker, have revived Hurston's work. Her most powerful novel, *Their Eyes Were Watching God,* has become a model of "womanist" writing. New readers continue to discover and appreciate Hurston's contributions to American literature.

Growing up in Eatonville, Florida (the first all-black town in the United States), Hurston was fascinated by stories swapped among townsfolk gathered at local store porches. Rural black folk characters, both real and imagined, shaped Hurston's world as a child and inspired much of her writing, both fiction and non-fiction, in later years. Hurston's secure childhood ended abruptly with her mother's death. "Mama died at sundown and changed a world," she would later write in her autobiography, *Dust Tracks on a Road.* Hurston and her seven siblings were separated, and Hurston's father, a Baptist preacher and community leader, remarried soon after. The loss marked the beginning of Hurston's "wanderings"—living with relatives, traveling, and working odd jobs—before attending Morgan Academy (now Morgan State University) in Baltimore, Maryland.

After graduating from Morgan Academy, Hurston relocated to Washington, D.C., and attended Howard University. An avid storyteller since childhood (her mother had been her first audience), Hurston began writing seriously at this time. The publication of "John Redding Goes to Sea" in *Stylus* (Howard University's literary society magazine) launched her career as a writer. Arriving in Harlem, New York, in 1925, Hurston joined other black artists active in the Harlem Renaissance movement. She continued writing essays and short fiction, introducing readers to the characters who would remain central to Hurston's work throughout her career.

At Barnard College in New York, Hurston began her studies in cultural anthropology. Encouraged by anthropologist Franz Boas, she journeyed south to collect Negro folk-lore, conducting field research in Florida, Alabama, Louisiana, and the Bahamas from about 1927 to 1932. A collection of folklore, *Mules and Men,* remains a unique ethnographic account of Southern black culture during the Great Depression. During this time Hurston also began her study of voodoo, a focus she maintained throughout her anthropological career. In the late 1930s Hurston traveled to Jamaica and Haiti, recording her findings in *Tell My Horse.* Hurston's ethnographic contributions (largely ignored within the discipline of anthropology) offer innovative models of both fieldwork practice and ethnographic writing. She was a keen listener and active participant in the field, and she refused to ignore her presence or the voices of her informants in her textual accounts.

The "spy-glass of Anthropology" (as she described it in the opening pages of *Mules and Men*) gave Hurston a tool for seeing the world. Her attempts to incorporate folk traditions and black dialect in her stories were strengthened by her field experiences. Rooted in the rhythms and struggles of Southern rural life, Hurston's novels—*Jonah's Gourd Vine; Moses, Man of the Mountain;* and *Their Eyes Were Watching God*—bring humor, wisdom, and dignity to the lives of African American women and men. A witness to the diversity of black experiences (in her autobiography she proclaimed "There is no *The Negro* here"), Hurston gave voice to a variety of ways to live, laugh, love, and learn.

Experiences of black women—both her sisters' and her own—were of particular concern to Hurston. They are survivors struggling to renew and redefine themselves and their communities in spite of the uncertainties and inequalities of their worlds. As the "mule of the world," black women bear enormous burdens with strength and endurance. Despite these burdens, women—like Missie May (the new bride of "The Gilded Six Bits") and Delia Jones (the washwoman of "Sweat")—find humor in the everyday while dreaming of better tomorrows. In *Their Eyes Were Watching God,* Nanny, Janie Crawford's grandmother, faithfully seeks (by word and deed) to imagine and create a better world for her granddaughter. As the elder woman tells Janie, "Ah was born back due in slavery so it wasn't for me to fulfill my dreams of whut a woman oughta be and to do. Dat's one of de hold-backs of slavery. But nothing can't stop you from wishin'. You can't beat nobody down so low till you can rob'em of they will." Like many of Hurston's female characters, Janie Crawford seeks to create an identity for herself in a way that is both faithful to the inner yearnings of her spirit and mindful of her relations to others.

Women find strength from the land and from each other as they travel alone, and at times, together. Like young Isis Watts (who first appeared in "Drenched in Light"), women in Hurston's stories often stop and look down the road, wondering what possibilities might lie ahead. In her own journey, Hurston navigated previously untraveled roads as a black woman writing during the first half of the 20th century. Despite meeting "roadblocks" along the way and changing course whenever she saw fit, Zora Neale Hurston never stopped writing. Readers who have followed Hurston's tracks might guess who Alice Walker had in mind when she defined "womanist " as one who "Loves music. Loves dance. Loves the moon. *Loves* the Spirit. Loves love and food and roundness. Loves struggle. *Loves* the Folk. Loves herself. *Regardless.*" As her stories continue to be shared, the spirit of Zora Neale Hurston lives.

—Laura McLeod

I-J

IRIGARAY, Luce

Nationality: French. **Born:** Belgium, 1930; immigrated to France c. 1962. **Education:** University of Louvain, M.A. in philosophy and literature 1955; University of Paris, M.A. in psychology 1961; Institut de Psychologie de Paris, diploma in psychopathology 1962; University of Paris X at Naterre, Ph.D. in linguistics 1968; University of Paris VIII, Ph.D. in philosophy 1974; École Freudienne, Ph.D. (honors). **Family:** Married once; children. **Career:** High school teacher in Brussels, 1956-59; assistant researcher, Fondation Nationale de la Recherce Scientifique, Belgium 1962-1964; assistant researcher, then director of research beginning 1986, Centre National de la Recherche Scientifique, Paris. Taught at University of Paris VIII, Vincennes, 1970-74; named to Chaire International de Philosophie, Erasmus University, Rotterdam, 1982; teacher at Ecole des Hautes Etudes en Sciences Sociales, 1985-86, Collège International de Philosophie, Paris, 1988-90, and Centre Américain d'Etudes Critiques, 1989-90; Speaker at women's groups and conferences throughout Europe and North America. **Address:** Paris, France.

PUBLICATIONS

Political/Social Theory

Le Langage des déments (thesis). The Hague, Mouton, 1973.

Speculum de l'autre femme (thesis). Paris, Minuit, 1974; translated by Gillian C. Gill as *Speculum of the Other Woman,* Ithaca, Cornell University Press, 1985.

Ce Sexe qui n'en est pas un (includes "Quand nos lèvres se parlent"). Paris, Minuit 1975; translated by Catharine Porter as *This Sex Which Is Not One,* Ithaca, Cornell University Press, 1985.

Et l'une ne bouge pas sans l'autre. Paris, Minuit, 1979; translated by Hélène V. Wenzel as "And the One Doesn't Stir without the Other," in *Signs: Journal of Women in Culture and Society,* 7(1), 1981.

Amante marine. De Fredrich Neitzsche. Paris, Minuit, 1983; portions translated by Sara Speidel as "Veiled Lips," in *Mississippi Review,* 11(3), 1983; translated as *Marine Lover of Friedrich Nietzsche,* New York, Columbia University Press, 1991.

Le Corps-à-corps avec le mère. Ottawa, La Pleine Lune, 1981.

Passions élémentaires. Paris, Minuit, 1982; translated by Joanne Collie and Judith Still as *Elemental Passions,* London, Athlone Press, and New York, Routledge, 1992.

La Croyance même. Paris, Galilée, 1983.

L'Oubli de l'air: Chez Martin Heidegger. Paris, Minuit, 1983.

Ethique de la différence sexuelle. Paris, Minuit, 1984; translated by Gillian C. Gill and Carolyn Burke as *An Ethics of Sexual Difference,* London, Athlone Press, and Ithaca, New York, Cornell University Press, 1993.

Parler n'est jamais neutre. Paris, Minuit, 1985.

Sexes et parentés. Paris, Minuit, 1987; translated by Gillian C. Gill as *Sexes and Genealogies,* New York and Chichester, Columbia University Press, 1993.

Le Temps de la différence: pour une révolution pacifique. Paris, Livre de Poche, 1989; translated by Karin Montin as *Thinking the Difference: For a Peaceful Revolution,* London, Athlone, 1994.

Sexes et genres à travers les langues. Paris, Grasset, 1990.

J'aime à tois: esquisse d'une félicité dans l'histoire. Paris, Grasset, 1992; translated by Alison Martin as *I Love to You: Sketch for a Happiness within History,* New York, Routledge; as *I Love to You: Sketch of a Possible Felicity in History* London, Routledge, 1995.

Je, tu, nous: pour une culture de la différence. Paris, Grasset, 1990; translated by Alison Martin as *Je Tu, Nous: Toward a Culture of Difference,* New York and London, Routledge, 1993.

Uncollected Essays

"L'Ordre sexuel du discours," in *Langages,* 85, March 1987.

"Corps, sexes et genres linguistiques," in *Bulletin du Centre de Recherches sur les Arts et le Langage* 4(3), 1988.

"Sujet de la science, sujet sexué?" in *Sens et place des connaissances dans la sociéte.* Paris, Editions du CNRS, 1988.

"Egalies à qui?" in *Critique,* May 1987; translated as "Equal to Whom?, in *differences,* 1, 1989.

Other

The Irigaray Reader, edited by Margaret Whitford. Oxford and Cambridge, Massachusetts, Blackwell, 1991.

*

Bibliography: In *French Feminist Criticism: Women, Language, and Literature: An Annotated Bibliography* by Elissa D. Gelfand and Virginia Thorndike Hules, New York, Garland, 1985; *French Feminist Theory: Luce Irigaray and Hélène Cixous: A Bibliography* by Joan Nordquist, Santa Cruz, Reference & Research Services, 1990.

Critical Studies: *Sexual/Textual Politics: Feminist Literary Theory* by Toril Moi, New York, Methuen, 1985; "Difference on Trial: A Critique of the Maternal Metaphor in Cixous, Irigaray, and Kristeva" by Domna C. Stanton, in *The Poetics of Gender,* edited by Nancy K. Miller and Carolyn G. Heilbrun, New York, Columbia University Press, 1986; "The Absent Text: Luce Irigaray's Foray into the Dark Continent of Femininity" by Mary E. Papke, in *Literature and Psychology,* 32(1), 1986; *Sexual Subversions: Three French Feminists* by Elizabeth Grosz, Sydney, Allen & Unwin, 1989; *Luce Irigaray: Philosophy in the Feminine* by Margaret Whiford, London and New York, Routledge, 1991; *Transfigurations: Theology and the French Feminists* by C.W. Maggie Kim, Susan M. St. Ville, and Susan M. Simonaitis, Minneapolis, Fortress Press, 1993; *Ethics of Eros: Irigaray's Re-Writing of the Philosophers* by Tina Chanter, New York, Routledge, 1994; *Engaging with Irigaray: Feminist Philosophy and Modern European Thought* by Carolyn L. Burke, Margaret Whitford, and Naomi Schor, New York, Columbia University Press, 1994; *God between Their Lips: Desire between Women in Irigaray, Brontë, and Eliot* by Kathryn Bond Stockton, Stanford, California, Stanford University Press, 1994; *Plenishment in the Earth: An Ethic of Inclusion* by Stephen David Ross, Saratoga Springs, State University of New York Press, 1995.

* * *

One of the most widely know and referenced feminist theorists of this century, Luce Irigaray's influence extends far beyond academic circles. Currently director of research in philosophy at the Centre National de la Recherche Scientifique in Paris, her works, which include *This Sex Which Is Not One* (1975), "And the One Doesn't Stir without the Other" (1979), and *Thinking the Difference: For a Peaceful Revolution* (1989), have firmly established her as a philosopher of international repute.

Born in Belgium in 1930, Irigaray moved to France in the early 1960s, from whence she has continued to study and write. Aside from her academic activities, she was active in the French women's movement of the 1970s, rallying on behalf of both pro-choice platforms and the legalization of contraception.

The recipient of advanced numerous degrees and an active teacher and researcher, Irigaray also became the subject of considerable controversy after presenting her doctorate dissertation *Speculum de l'autre femme* to philosopher Jacques Lacan's prestigious École Freudienne in 1974. A critique of Freud's theories as patriarchal and phallocentric, *Speculum* indirectly criticized the work of the school's founder; its subsequent publication caused Irigaray not only to be deemed *persona non grata* in many Parisian intellectual circles but also eliminated any aspirations she held to teach in that city's universities. Nonetheless, her talents have since been increasingly recognized within French academic circles.

Beginning with *Le Langage des déments* (1973), a study of pathological linguistic collapse in patients suffering from senile dementia, Irigaray's work has continued to be groundbreaking in her examination of the psycho-linguistic relationship, particularly that between language and gender. It is also what some would term "difficult"—she assumes from her readers a basic understanding of her theories, as well as a solid grounding in the classics of Western philosophy. Her style is a stringing together of wordplay, allusion, metaphor, neologisms, and analogy, broken here and there by direct interjections framed by brackets, quotes, ellipses, dashes, underlines, and the like, words often pulled apart to reveal their hidden components. While this style has often rattled the uninitiated and resulted in confusion and misunderstanding, it is an essential part of her message: the necessity to deconstruct, break apart patriarchal language to allow for the interjection of female subjectivity within its cracks.

Irigaray's ultimate goal is both to accept and reaffirm sexual differences in order to create a more equitable society. While many have criticized her solution to this problem as overly theoretical, she maintains that only by a multilevel restructuring of society's theoretical and intellectual foundations can the patriarchal forces that threaten to destroy modern society, and indeed our planet, be abated. Such a foundation is built upon language, upon thought, upon discourse; systems that re-present, translate, lived experiences and ultimately reaffirm the forces of patriarchy. She looks to more natural principals to serve as systems within a more equitable society, and contends that those based on a respect for sexual difference rather than a hierarchical view of sexual difference would serve as such. More than legislation or other forced methods of eliminating domination of one sex by another, the representation of the relationship between males and females becomes central to any consideration of eliminating oppression.

Throughout her body of work Irigaray reevaluates Freudian psychoanalytic theories in the light of Jacques Derrida's concept of binaries: combining two terms, such as man/woman, in an implicit hierarchical arrangement. She also challenges Lacanian theorists by criticizing their view of feminine sexuality as rooted in a female's "lack" (as of a phallus, there by making her incomplete, less than whole, and therefore inferior). Accepting, indeed celebrating, sexual differences, Irigaray views women's "otherness" in a positive light: she credits them with being not only more versatile—in "Quand nos lèvres se parlent" she identifies women's genital and oral lips as representing a multiple sexuality, in opposition to male's single sex organ—but also possessing a distinct feminine psycho-linguistic capability that she terms "*parler-femme*—"speaking [as a] woman."

Irigaray's ideas on feminine sexuality and writing can be more easily encountered in *This Sex Which Is Not One,* a relatively accessible book within her oeuvre, and certainly more so than *Speculum.* Evaluations and interpretations of her works have been undertaken by numerous feminist philosophers and theoreticians, including Toril Moi, Gayatri Chakravorty Spivak, and Judith Butler. In addition to her numerous theoretical works, Irigaray's writing has also found its way into the arena of politics; she is a regular contributor to the newspaper of the Italian Communist Party.

—Lynn MacGregor

IRON, Ralph. *See* **SCHREINER, Olive (Emilie Albertina).**

IVES, Morgan. *See* **BRADLEY, Marion Zimmer.**

JACOBS, Harriet Ann

Pseudonym: Linda Brent. **Nationality:** American. **Born:** Edenton, North Carolina, 1813. **Family:** One son, one daughter. **Career:** Abolitionist; Civil War relief volunteer, 1862-65; continued to report on conditions in the South until 1868; supported herself as a domestic worker. **Died:** 1897.

Publications

Autobiography

Incidents in the Life of a Slave Girl: Written by Herself (as Linda Brent), edited by Lydia Maria Child. Boston, privately printed, 1861; revised edition, edited by Jean Fagan Yellin, Cambridge, Massachusetts, and London, Harvard University Press, 1987.

*

Critical Studies: *Self-Discovery and Authority in Afro-American Narrative* by Valerie Smith, Cambridge, Harvard University Press, 1987; *Black Women Writing Autobiography: A Tradition within a Tradition* by Joanne Braxton, Philadelphia, Temple University Press, 1989; *Touching Liberty: Abolition, Feminism, and the Politics of the Body* by Karen Sanchez-Eppler, Berkeley, University of California Press, 1993; *The Voices of African American Women: The Use of Narrative and Authorial Voice in the Works of Harriet Jacobs, Zora Neale Hurston, And Alice Walker* by Yvonne Johnson, New York, P. Lang, 1995.

* * *

Harriet Jacobs's slave narrative survives as an important example of the genre. One of the last such narratives published, and one of the few in book-length form, Jacobs offers an early black feminist perspective on slavery, an institution that was most commonly critiqued by black male writers. Born the daughter of a South Carolina planter, Jacobs's fair skin and good looks attracted the unwanted attention of her owner. She recounts her experiences of what we would now call sexual harassment, though the morality of the day may have left her silent about more serious forms of sexual abuse or rape. In any case, she acknowledges that black women bear the burden of both race and gender under slavery, writing "Slavery is terrible for men; but it is far more terrible for women." Indeed, her autobiography includes five chapters that discuss the sexual oppression slave women faced.

Though Jacobs escaped to the North in 1842, she did not publish *Incidents in the Life of a Slave Girl* until almost two decades later. Active in the abolitionist movement and busy caring for a white family's children, Jacobs squeezed work on her manuscript into the evening hours. Written in the style of sentimental fiction that was popular in 19th century America, Jacobs's narrative espouses the virtues of modesty, chastity, and domesticity that would have been familiar to her mostly white female readers. At the same time, her text offers important black feminist challenges to that sentimental script. For example, she writes about sexuality at a time when the topic would have been largely off-limits in both conversation and writing, particularly for women. Further, though most sentimental fiction would have presented marriage as the ultimate goal for its heroines, Jacobs deviates from that aspect of the genre. Instead, her autobiography ends with the themes of freedom and family connection and emphasizes the crucial role both the black community and family members play in aiding her escape. Finally, Jacobs' text clearly critiques the ways that patriarchy and chattel slavery work in tandem.

Incidents in the Life of a Slave Girl bears witness to its author's ingenuity and determination to gain her freedom. At the same time, Harriet Jacobs's text is far more than one woman's personal tale; it remains as a lasting critique of slavery and insures that future generations will remember the institution's power not only to oppress those who labored under it, but also to foster an enduring spirit of resistance.

—Allison Kimmich

JACOBUS, Mary

Nationality: British. **Born:** Cheltenham, Gloucestershire, 4 May 1944. **Education:** Oxford University, B.A. (first class honors) 1965, M.A. and Ph.D 1970. **Family:** Married Reeve Parker in 1981; two children. **Career:** Randall McIver research fellow, Oxford University, Oxford, 1968-70; lecturer in English, Victoria University of Manchester, 1970-71; fellow and tutor, Lady Margaret Hall, 1971-80, lecturer in English, 1972-80, Oxford University; associate professor of English, 1980-82, professor of English and women's studies, 1982-89, John Wendell Anderson Professor of English beginning 1989, Cornell University, Ithaca, New York. Visiting professor, Georgetown University, 1976; visiting fellow, Humanities Research Centre, Canberra, 1985; guest professor, CEKVINA, University of Aarhus, Denmark, 1992, visiting overseas scholar, St. John's College, University of Cambridge, 1993. **Awards:** Cornell University Society for the Humanities Faculty fellowship, 1986-87; Guggenheim fellowship, 1988-89; National Endowment for the Humanities grant, 1995. **Member:** Modern Language Association. **Address:** Department of English, Cornell University, 252 Goldwin Smith Hall, Ithaca, New York 14853-3201, USA. **Online Address:** mlj2@cornell.edu.

Publications

Literary Criticism

"William Huntington's 'Spiritual Sea-Voyage': Another Source for "The Ancient Mariner," in *Notes and Queries* (Oxford), 16(11), November 1969.

"The Idiot Boy," in *Bicentenary Wordsworth Studies,* edited by Jonathan Wordsworth. Ithaca, New York, and London, Cornell University Press, 1970.

"Southey's Debt to *Lyrical Ballads* (1798)," in *The Review of English Studies* (Oxford), 22(20-36), February 1971.

"'Tintern Abbey' and Topographical Prose," in *Notes and Queries* (Oxford), 18(10), October 1971.

"*Peter Bell* the First," in *Essays in Criticism* (Oxford), 24(3), July 1974.

"Sue the Obscure," in *Essays in Criticism* (Oxford), 25(3), July 1975.

"Tess's Purity," in *Essays in Criticism* (Oxford), 26(4), October 1976.

Tradition and Experiment in Wordsworth's Lyrical Ballads (1798). Oxford, Clarendon Press, 1976.

"*Villette*'s Buried Letter," in *Essays in Criticism* (Oxford), 28(3), July 1978.

"Tess: The Making of a Pure Woman," in *Tearing the Veil: Essays on Femininity,* edited by Susan Lipshitz. London, Routledge, and Boston, Kegan Paul, 1978.

"Women's Writing: *Jane Eyre, Shirley, Villette, Aurora Leigh*" with Cheris Kramer, Cora Kaplan, Helen Taylor, Jean Radford, Jennifer Joseph, Margaret Williamson, and Maud Ellman, in *Ideology and Consciousness* (Oxford), 3, spring 1978.

"Wordsworth and the Language of the Dream," in *English Literary History* (Baltimore, Maryland), 46(4), 1979.

"Tree and Machine: *The Woodlanders,*" in *Critical Approaches to the Fiction of Thomas Hardy,* edited by Dale Kramer. London, Macmillan, 1979.

"The Question of Language: Men of Maxims and *The Mill on the Floss,*" in *Critical Inquiry* (Chicago), 8(2), winter 1981.

"Hardy's Magian Retrospect," in *Essays in Criticism* (Oxford), 32(3), July 1982.

"Is There a Woman in This Text?" in *New Literary History* (Baltimore, Maryland), 14(1), autumn 1982.

"'That Great Stage Where Senators Perform': *Macbeth* and the Politics of Romantic Theatre," in *Studies in Romanticism* (Boston), 22(3), fall 1983.

"The Law of/and Gender: Genre Theory and *The Prelude*," in *Diacritics* (Baltimore, Maryland), 14(4), winter 1984.

"The Art of Managing Books: Romantic Prose and the Writing of the Past," in *Romanticism and Language*, edited by Arden Reed. Ithaca, New York, Cornell University Press, 1984.

"Apostrophe and Lyric Voice in *The Prelude*, in *Lyric Poetry: Beyond New Criticism*, edited by Chaviva Hosek and Patricia Parker. Ithaca and London, Cornell University Press, 1985.

Reading Woman: Essays in Feminist Criticism. New York, Columbia University Press, 1986.

"Madonna: Like a Virgin; or, Freud, Kristeva, and the Case of the Missing Mother," in *Oxford Literary Review* (Stirling, Scotland), 8(1-2), 1986.

"Freud's Mnemonic: Women, Screen Memory, and Feminist Nostalgia," in *Michigan Quarterly Review* (Ann Arbor), 26, winter 1987.

"'The Third Stroke': Reading Woolf with Freud," in *Grafts: Feminist Cultural Criticism*, edited by Susan Sheridan. London and New York, Verso, 1988.

Romanticism, Writing and Sexual Difference: Essays on the Prelude. Oxford, Clarendon Press, and New York, Oxford University Press, 1989.

"'Tea Daddy': Poor Mrs. Klein and the Pencil Shavings," in *Women: A Cultural Review* (Oxford), 1, summer 1990.

"'Incorruptible Milk': Breast Feeding and the French Revolution," in *Rebel Daughters: Women and the French Revolution*, edited by Sarah Melzer and Leslie Rabine. New York, Oxford University Press, 1991.

"The Woman who Mistook Her Art for a Hat," in *Art History: Special Issue on Representation and the Politics of Difference* (London and Boston), 16(3), 1993.

First Things: Reading the Maternal Imaginary, New York, Routledge, 1995.

"Berthe Morisot: Inventing the Psyche" in *Women: A Cultural Review* (Oxford), 6, autumn 1995.

Other

Editor, *Women Writing and Writing about Women* (includes "The Difference of View" and "The Buried Letter: Feminism and Romanticism in *Villette*"). London, Croom Helm, 1979.

Editor, *Diacritics* (special issue: "Cherchez la Femme: Feminist Critique/Feminine Text"; Baltimore, Maryland), 12(2), summer 1982.

Editor, *Body/Politics: Women and the Discourses of Science*, with Evelyn Fox Keller and Sally Shuttleworth (includes "In Parenthesis: Immaculate Conceptions and Feminine Desire"). New York and London, Routledge, 1990.

*

Mary Jacobus comments:

My feminist work came out of the feminist movement in England in the '70s, which had a strongly psychoanalytic (and often, Marxist) flavor, with its roots in the New Left movement of the '60s. Although I began by writing about canonical texts such as the Victorian novel, a move to the U.S. in 1980 made it possible to do psychoanalytic feminist work with a more theoretical focus and a broader range, in a context where a large and energetic feminist community existed within the universities.

I continue to want to work closely with literary texts and try to bring my feminist, psychoanalytic, and theoretical concerns to bear in the reading of literature itself. Alongside a commitment to psychoanalytic work, I've returned to the Romantic period as a reader and teacher of texts by women written during and in the wake of the French Revolution; the period of Wollstonecraft and her circle remains a reference-point for me.

As a feminist, I've chosen to work within the academy where feminism has created the space for lively intellectual debate as well as allowing new and energizing concerns with gender to emerge. My current interests are moving in two main directions: British (and French) post-Kleinian object relations psychoanalysis and the generational feminisms of the women of the Romantic period. What has enabled me most as a feminist literary critic is the context that the universities have provided in the past decade or so for women to work on women's writing and feminist literary theory. But as a writer, I write mostly from a submerged set of personal concerns that are my own and sometimes (I hope) those of other women too; I think this is where the best writing comes from in the end.

* * *

Mary Jacobus is a prolific writer whose contributions to literary theory have helped define some of the most compelling issues at stake in contemporary feminist criticism. Jacobus would first articulate the direction of her own work in the still influential essay "The Difference of View," published in 1979's *Women Writing and Writing about Women*. Here, she questions untheorized assumptions about language and gender and brings psychoanalytic, poststructuralist, and French feminist thought to bear on the question of sexual difference and the appropriate reach of feminist literary criticism.

The difference of view that Jacobus calls for in women's writing and feminist criticism is a rethinking of the notion of difference itself: just as women cannot gain access to "male-dominated culture" by employing masculinist modes of literary criticism, neither can they do so by embodying notions of "woman" as man's opposite. According to Jacobus, feminist critics should instead think of difference as "a traversal of ... boundaries" and question "the terms of language itself, as well as the terms of psychoanalysis and of literary criticism."

In her work Jacobus vigorously questions the terms of theory, taking nothing for granted and refusing to settle for easy answers when she finds it more productive to keep questions open. As she explains in *Reading Woman: Essays in Feminist Criticism*, her intention is neither to usher underrepresented women writers into the literary canon, nor to apply particular feminist methods to interpret the texts she reads. Rather, Jacobus takes as her object theory itself, which she reads through the lens of various literary, psychoanalytic, and historical works by both men and women in order to "raise theoretical questions" and attempt the "investigation of 'theory' by way of 'reading'."

The central theoretical question underlying much of Jacobus's work is that of the relation between reading (and writing) and sexual difference. She distrusts gender theories that depend upon biological and experiential differences between men and women, being more sympathetic to French feminism, which takes a psychoanalytic/poststructuralist approach to language and gender. In her introductory essay to *Reading Woman,* Jacobus suggests that sexual difference is textually, rather than biologically, formed. She investigates how the category "woman" is constituted in the act of reading, and how readers are constituted as gendered. Taking her cue from Derridian deconstruction, according to which the meaning of a text is never stable or fixed, she finds gender to be equally ambiguous. She insists that "It is in language—in reading and in writing woman—that femininity at once discloses and discomposes itself, endlessly displacing the fixity of gender identity by the play of difference and division which simultaneously creates and uncreates gender, identity, and meaning."

Jacobus's analyses of gender, identity, and meaning have evolved as her own interests have developed and shifted. In the final three chapters of *Romanticism Writing and Sexual Difference,* she offers readings of Wordsworth's *The Prelude,* as well as works by De Quincey and Rousseau, to argue that Romantic notions of the individual depend upon the excision of "woman" and the suppression of sexual difference in Romantic writing. In *Reading Woman,* Jacobus further explores what she calls "the deflection of gender harassment ... onto the 'body' of the text" or "textual harassment," which results in "the specular appropriation of woman, or even her elimination altogether."

Jacobus devotes equal attention in *Reading Woman* to literary texts by women, to psychoanalytic writings such as Freud's case studies and writings on female sexuality, and to French feminist discourses on the feminine by Julia Kristeva and Luce Irigaray. She frequently reads two or more texts through or against one another. For example, in "*Dora* and the Pregnant Madonna" she contrasts Freud's dismissal of the possible significance of feminine and maternal presences in his most famous patient's life to Kristeva's emphasis on the maternal as a highly relevant component of women's relation to language. In the three essays that comprise the fourth section of the collection, Jacobus reads a Freudian case history with short stories by Charlotte Perkins Gilman and George Eliot in order to test her speculation that hysteria in women's writing is "the shadow of male hysteria about women."

"In Parenthesis: Immaculate Conceptions and Feminine Desire," her contribution to *Body/Politics: Women and the Discourses of Science* (a volume she also co-edited), furthers Jacobus's analysis of the suppression of the feminine in masculine discourse. Here she demonstrates how in three very different texts—a short story by Heinrich von Kleist, Freud's *Three Essays on the Theory of Sexuality,* and theological arguments about reproduction and surrogate motherhood—female sexuality is "subsumed under the sign of maternity," suggesting that feminine desire poses a serious threat to the patriarchal thought systems that these various texts represent.

With her 1995 collection of essays, *First Things: The Maternal Imaginary in Literature, Art, and Psychoanalysis,* Jacobus completes a shift in focus begun five years earlier, with *Body/Politics,* toward discourses of the body, the various cultural images and narratives that have shaped Western conceptions of the feminine body and which also have material effects on real women. Jacobus loosely defines the term "maternal imaginary" as "the fantasmatic mother ... who exists chiefly in the realm of images and imagos." Her analyses of this encompassing figure includes a critique of feminist attempts to replace Freud's Oedipal narrative with mother-centered myths; a reading of de Sade along with Thomas Malthus's writings on population to show that both contain matriphobic undertones; a reassessment of the value of Melanie Klein's work on mother-child relations to psychoanalytic feminism; and essays on breast-feeding, mastectomy, and Berthe Morisot's paintings of her daughter, in which Jacobus considers the cultural, historical, and psychological significance of the image of the breast.

As a feminist working within academia, Jacobus naturally assumes a certain familiarity with current theory on the part of her readers. Therefore, her writing may strike some readers as difficult. But this difficulty is the inevitable result of the complex thinking and penetrating analysis that is Mary Jacobus's trademark.

—Megan Simpson

JAYAWARDENA, Kumari. *See* **JAYAWARDENA, Visakha Kumari.**

JAYAWARDENA, Visakha Kumari

Also writes as Kumari Jayawardena. **Nationality:** Sri Lankan. **Born:** 16 June 1931. **Education:** London School of Economics and Political Science, University of London, B.Sc. 1955, Ph.D. 1964. **Family:** Married Lal Jayawardena; one son. **Career:** Associate professor in political science, Colombo University, 1969-85; member of faculty of Women's Studies Programme, Institute of Social Studies, the Hague, 1981-82; director, Workers Education Programme; currently professor of Women's Studies, Colombo University. Author of numerous publications in Sinhalese. **Address:** Department of Women's Studies, Colombo University, Sri Lanka.

PUBLICATIONS

Political/Social Theory

Ethnic and Class Struggles in Sri Lanka. Colombo, Colombo University Press, 1985.
Feminism and Nationalism in the Third World. London, Zed, 1982; revised edition, London, Zed, 1986.
The White Woman's Other Burden: Western Women and South Asia during British Colonial Rule. New York and London, Routledge, 1995.

History

The Rise of the Labour Movement in Ceylon. Durham, North Carolina, Duke University Press, 1972.
Feminism in Europe: Liberal and Socialist Strategies, 1789-1919, with Maria Mies. The Hague, Institute of Social Studies, 1981.

* * *

In the late 19th and early 20th centuries, colonized countries challenged Western imperialism. Thinking about such nationalist movements evokes thoughts of notable male leaders such as Ghandi, or bloody military confrontations. Feminism or women's movements rarely, if ever, come to mind. But Kumari Jayawardena challenges readers to confront this way of thinking. Her goal is to "re-place" women into accounts of national liberation movements. Like histories of other areas at other times, the history of de-colonization usually overlooks the contributions of women, and Jayawardena wants to acknowledge a tradition of feminism in the Third World. She also wants to encourage Western and non-Western feminists to recognize their differences and similarities, so that they can build a cross-national sense of sisterhood without ignoring distinctions among women.

Although she addressed social movements and inequality in her earliest work, Jayawardena did not always write from a feminist standpoint. Her first book, part of her thesis at the London School of Economics, was *The Rise of the Labor Movement in Ceylon.* Already interested in the ways class, religion, and national identity affect people's lives, Jayawardena argued that Sri Lankans were divided along many lines. For example, while factory workers organized into labor groups at the turn of the century, plantation workers were isolated from them and did not join labor movements until much later. On the other hand, sometimes people from different groups could work for common goals, and nationalist movements in Ceylon provided the training ground for middle-class leaders who would eventually organize lower-class workers. In *The Rise of the Labor Movement in Ceylon,* published in 1972, Jayawardena paid significant attention to ethnicity and class, but did not extensively discuss the contributions of either women or feminism in Sri Lanka.

Women's studies and feminism would soon became crucial to Jayawardena's work. After receiving her Ph.D. she worked in the Political Science Department at Colombo University in Sri Lanka. In 1981-82 she was affiliated with the Women's Studies Programme at the Institute of Social Studies (I.S.S.) in the Hague. There she worked with Maria Mies, and the two feminists wrote *Feminism in Europe.* In the preface to *Feminism and Nationalism in the Third World,* first published in 1982, Jayawardena thanks Mies, "who pioneered the women's studies programme in the ISS and inspired many Third World feminists." In her native Sri Lanka, Jayawardena is an active supporter of both civil rights and the women's movement; she currently teaches in the Department of Women's Studies at Colombo.

Jayawardena's most recent work reflects her current interests in feminism and gender. In *Feminism and Nationalism in the Third World,* she argues that women's movements significantly impacted nationalist and democratic movements in the Third World. During the economic development that imperialism brought, middle-class women gained education and a certain amount of freedom. They united around "women's issues," such as polygamy, female education, ownership rights, the vote, and *sati* (the tradition of a woman throwing herself on her husband's funeral pyre). At the same time, they tried to strengthen their native cultures against Western imperialism by fighting restrictions on local suffrage and the imposition of Christianity.

Consequently, for Jayawardena feminism is not just a Western phenomenon, but one which also took seed in the context of the Third World and has relevance to women there. Of course, Third World women may be oppressed in different ways than Western women are, and non-Western women may differ tremendously from one another. Their ethnic or national ties may mean that they are treated differently and expected to do different things. Jayawardena argues that women are not the same everywhere, and differences such as class, race, and ethnicity matter.

However, Jayawardena does not claim that Third World feminism emerged in a vacuum. In *The White Women's Other Burden* she argues that Western women—missionaries, reformists, Socialists, and others who lived in colonized areas—influenced the development of women's movements in colonized countries. Some of these women, who often opposed nationalist movements, tried to reform local practices they saw as barbaric and make them more Western. Others supported nationalist movements and saw local practices as more emancipatory for women. Both types of women influenced local versions of both feminism and nationalism.

Jayawardena's works lead her to an important conclusion. The development of Third World feminist movements, the influence of Western women, and the interaction of feminism with nationalism show the tension between two approaches to women's oppression. The first argues that all women are universally oppressed, and that feminism should address similar issues all over the world. The second says that women are *so* different they cannot possibly unite as one movement or speak about each others' oppression. Seeking to reconcile the two outlooks, Jayawardena states in *The White Women's Other Burden:*

> I advocate a perspective that combines universalist discourse with the recognition of difference.... This approach does not lose sight of the universal condition of subordination that women are subject to, and claims the right of every woman to speak out against women's oppression and exploitation everywhere. But it also recognizes the distortion that can arise from a universalism that only takes gender into account, as well as the pitfalls of focusing exclusively on ethnic or racial collectivities, disregarding internal class and gender divisions.

To Kumari Jayawardena, gender, nationality, and class influence each other in differing degrees from society to society, but still manifest characteristics that are common to all cultures around the world. While crucial differences most certainly exist among them, women worldwide each experience some form of oppression around which they can build their own unique form of feminism.

—Amy Caiazza

JELINEK, Elfriede

Nationality: Austrian. **Born:** Mürzzuschlag, Steiermark, 20 November 1946. **Education:** Studied art, art history, and theatre at University of Vienna; attended Vienna Conservatory of Music. **Family:** Married to Gottfried Hüngsberg. **Career:** Freelance writer. **Awards:** Austrian Youth Culture award, 1969; Austrian State Scholarship for Literature, 1972; City of Bad Gandersheim's Roswitha Memorial award, 1978; Interior Ministry of West Germany award for best screenplay, 1979; honored by Austrian Minister for Education and Art, 1983; Heinrich-Böll award, 1986; Honorary Award for Literature of Vienna, 1989. **Member:** Graz Writers Union. **Address:** Vienna, Austria, and Munich, Germany.

Publications

Novels

Lisas Schatten. München, Relief Verlag Eilers, 1967.
wir sind lockvögel baby! Reinbek bei Hamburg, Rowohlt, 1970.
Michael. Ein Jugendbuch für de Infantilgesellschaft. Reinbek bei Hamburg, Rowohlt, 1972.
Die Liebhaberinnen. Reinbek bei Hamburg, Rowohlt, 1975; translated by Martin Chambers as *Women as Lovers,* London, Serpent's Tail, 1994.
bukolit. hörroman. Wien, Rhombus, 1979.
Die Ausgesperrten. Reinbek bei Hamburg, Rowohlt, 1980.
Die Klavierspielerin. Reinbek bei Hamburg, Rowohlt, 1983; translated by Joachim Neugroschel as *The Piano Player,* New York, Weidenfeld & Nicholson, 1988.
Oh Wildnis, oh Schutz vor ihr. Reinbek bei Hamburg, Rowohlt, 1985.
Lust. Reinbek bei Hamburg, Rowohlt, 1989; translated by Michael Hulse, London, Serpent's Tale, 1992.
Isabelle Huppert in Malina (film novelization), adapted from *Malina* by Ingeborg Bachmann. Frankfurt am Main, Suhrkamp, 1991.
Totenauberg. Reinbek bei Hamburg, Rowohlt, 1991.
Die Kinder der Toten. Reinbek bei Hamburg, Rowohlt, 1995.
Sturm und Zwang. Schreiben als Geschlechterkamp, with Jutta Heinrich and Adolf-Ernst Meyer. Hamburg, Klein, 1995.

Plays

Was geschah, nachdem Nora ihren Mann verlassen hat. München, dtv, 1980.
Theaterstücke. Clara S. Was geschah, nachdem Nora ihren Mann verlassen hat. Burgtheater, edited by Ute Nyssen. Köln, Prometh, 1984.
Krankheit oder moderne Frauen, edited by Regine Friedrich. Köln, n.p., 1987.
Präsident Abendwind, in *Anthropophagen im Abendwind* (Berlin), 1988.
Wolken. Heim. Göttingen, Steidl, 1993.
Raststätte. N.p., 1995.
Stecken, Stab und Stangle—Eine Handarbeit. N.p., 1996.

Screenplays: *Die Ausgesperrten,* 1982; *Was die Nacht verspricht,* 1987; *Malina,* 1990.

*

Critical Studies: *Political Ideology and Aesthetics in Neo-Feminist Fiction: Verena Stefan, Elfriede Jelinek, Margot Schroeder* by Tobe Levin, Ithaca, New York, Cornell University, 1979; "Access Routes into Postmodernism: Interviews with Innerhoffer, Jelinek, Rosei, and Wolfgrubber" by Donna Hoffmeister, in *Modern Austrian Literature,* 20, 1987; *Against the Horizon: Feminism and Postwar Austrian Women Writers* by Jacqueline Vansant, New York, Greenwood Press, 1988; "Elfriede Jelinek's Political Feminism: *Die Ausgesperrten*" by Dagmar C.G. Lorenz, in *Modern Austrian Literature,* 23, 1990; *Elfriede Jelinek* edited by Kurt Bartsche and Gunther A. Hofler, Graz, Droschl, 1991; *Elfriede Jelinek: Framed by Language* edited by Jorun B. Johns and Katherine Adams, Riverside, California, Ariadne Press, 1994; *Rewriting Reality: An Introduction to Elfriede Jelinek* by Allyson Fiddler, Oxford, Berg, 1994; *Critical Plays, Feminist Pleasures: 20th-Century Women's Theatre in German* by Katrin Sieg, Ann Arbor, University of Michigan Press, forthcoming.

* * *

One of Austria's most prolific and talented writers, Elfriede Jelinek has become very well known for her outspoken feminism and her sharp criticism of capitalist patriarchy. Born in 1948, she made her literary debut in 1969, and has published novels, plays, audio plays, film scripts, essays, literary translations, and much more ever since. But sparked by the topics she chooses to write about—such as domestic violence, sexual exploitation, and human alienation—she has been accused by male critics of possessing the "evil eye," or writing "cold, analytical" prose not becoming to a woman writer, while her female critics have charged her with being a traitor to the feminist cause because of her depiction of female sexuality, masochism, and self-mutilations. All this has turned Jelinek into Austria's "best-hated author," a title to which the media immediately took. Jelinek herself has appeared to revel in the controversy sparked by her writings and in her role as trouble-maker, which she furthers by granting numerous interviews in which she perpetuates the mystique of literary *enfant terrible.*

Although openly admitting to a feminist agenda, as a "Marxist feminist" Jelinek's primary concern is with the material conditions of the working class in a capitalist society, with special attention paid to its effects on the position of women. Therefore, an analysis of the conditions of oppression to her must always look at capitalist structures, while at the same time including a feminist perspective. In her writings Jelinek intentionally shifts the gaze from the male spectator to the position of women as objects, and turns it back on the position of power and domination. Through the lens of her analytical gaze, she looks at the ways in which patriarchy defines and objectifies women as commodities. Therefore, instead of searching for the notion of "authentic female subjectivity" or "true womanhood," Jelinek refuses to represent "authentic" female identity, even as a utopian possibility, and concentrates instead on the effacing effects of capitalist patriarchy on women.

Besides Marxism, Jelinek is heavily influenced by the critical theory of the Frankfurt School, Bertholt Brecht's epic theater, as well as by poststructural and postmodern theories and contemporary pop culture. She combines these different strands in a very innovative and linguistically challenging approach to literature in which she uses graphic descriptions and crude and deliberately shocking language. In a cascade of verbal images borrowed from the world of media, TV, cartoons, comic strips, Beatles' songs, and science fiction, the author ruptures cultural assumptions, conventions, and taboos. She calls herself a "satirist" and a "language artist" with the aim to exaggerate and stretch reality to the point of caricature in order to make visible its governing structures of power and manipulation.

Although most of her novels are set in a fictitious rural Austrian village, her writings are by no means restricted by geographical boundaries. Because she is not interested in describing individual fates and characters but rather in illuminating patterns of oppression and exploitation, her works transcend national and geographical limitations and instead rigorously deconstruct myths of family, love, self-determination, and free will. In *Women as Lovers* the author portrays two women, Brigitte and Paula, and their struggle for personal and financial independence. While both aspire to find true love, Brigitte settles for the financially stable marriage with an electrician. Paula, however, who demands more from life, ends up married to a drunkard who beats her and her children, and she is outcast by her own society for wanting a better life. In *The Piano Teacher* a 30-year-old woman struggles to free herself from her oppressive and dominating mother, whose controlling behavior has caused the daughter profound self-alienation to the point of emotional and physical numbness. In *Lust* Jelinek portrays the impossibility of female desire through the wife of a factory owner who is treated by her husband as his property.

In all her works Jelinek challenges a society centered around a capitalist-patriarchal value system that victimizes its members. With the arrival of *Lust* in 1989—which caused a great controversy over allegations of supposedly having written a "female pornography"—she has finally secured the attention of literary scholars and critics that alluded her for so long in favor of her male colleagues Thomas Bernhard, Peter Handke, and Werner Schwab.

—Karin U. Herrmann

JELLICOE, (Patricia) Ann

Nationality: British. **Born:** Middlesbrough, Yorkshire, 15 July 1927. **Education:** Attended Central School of Speech and Drama, London, 1944-47. **Family:** Married 1) C.E. Knight-Clarke in 1950 (divorced 1961) 2) Roger Mayne; two children. **Career:** Actress, stage manager, and director in repertory, beginning 1947; founder, Cockpit Theatre Club, London, 1951-53; acting teacher, Central School of Speech and Drama, London, 1953-55; literary manager, Royal Court Theatre, 1973-74; writer and director, Colway Theatre Trust, Lyme Regis, beginning 1979. **Awards:** Elsie Fogerty Prize, 1947; London *Observer* prize, 1956, for *The Sport of My Mad Mother.*

Publications

Plays

Romersholm, adapted from the play by Henrik Ibsen (produced London, 1952; revised version produced London, 1959).
The Sport of My Mad Mother (produced London, 1958; revised 1964). London, Faber & Faber, 1964.
The Lady from the Sea, adapted from the play by Henrik Ibsen (produced London, 1961).
The Knack (produced Cambridge, 1961; produced New York, 1964). London, Encore, and New York, French, 1962.
Der Freischütz, translation of libretto by Kriedrich Kind; music by Karl Maria von Weber (produced London, 1963).
The Seagull, adapted from the play by Anton Chekhov (produced London, 1964). New York, Avon, 1975.
Shelley; or The Idealist (produced London, 1965). London, Faber & Faber, and New York, Grove Press, 1966.
The Rising Generation (produced London, 1967), in *Playbill 2,* edited by Alan Durband. London, Hutchinson Education, 1970.
The Giveaway (produced Edinburgh, 1968). London, Faber & Faber, 1970.
The Reckoning (produced Lyme Regis, 1978).
The Tide (produced 1980).

For Children

You'll Never Guess (produced London, 1973), in *Three Jelliplays.* 1975.
Clever Elsie, Smiling John, and Silent Peter, and *A Good Thing or a Bad Thing* (produced London, 1974), in *Three Jelliplays.* 1975.
Three Jelliplays (includes *You'll Never Guess, Clever Elsie, Smiling John, Silent Peter,* and *A Good Thing or a Bad Thing).* London, Faber & Faber, 1975.

Other

Some Unconscious Influences in the Theatre. London and New York, Cambridge University Press, 1967.
Devon, with Roger Mayne. London, Faber & Faber, 1975.

*

Media Adaptations: *The Knack* (film), 1965.

Bibliography: *Twenty Modern British Playwrights: A Bibliography* by Kimball King, New York and London, Garland, 1977.

Theatrical Activities: Director, all her own plays.

Critical Studies: Review of *The Sport of My Mad Mother* in the *Times* (London), 26 February 1958; "Presented at Court: Ann Jellicoe" by John Russell Taylor, in his *Anger and After: A Guide to the New British Drama,* London, Methuen, 1962; interview with Robert Rubens in *Transatlantic Review,* 12, spring 1963; "Autumn 1864; 'The Knack'" by John Simon, in his *Uneasy Stages: A Chronicle of the New York Theatre, 1963-1973,* New York, Random House, 1975; *At the Royal Court: 25 Years of the English Stage Company* edited by Richard Findlater, New York, Grove, 1982.

* * *

Ann Jellicoe's plays range from the extremely experimental to the more conventional, with women's roles and effects on their surroundings among the primary driving forces. The more abstract works include such diverse female characters as Greta, the pregnant street gang leader in *The Sport of My Mad Mother;* Mother, the head of an anti-male army of women in *The Rising Generation;* and Nancy, the confused ingenue in *The Knack. Shelley; or, The Idealist,* a more traditional play, highlights the constraints upon women in the 19th century. It powerfully depicts the poet Shelley's opposition to patriarchy and marriage and the result of his philosophies in his personal life.

The Sport of My Mad Mother (1958) was the work that first gained Jellicoe notoriety. Centering on a band of violent teenagers, it is a visceral kind of play—an "anti-intellect play," in Jellicoe's words—with much dialogue reduced to rhythmic chants, and actions taking precedence over words. Jellicoe preferred the audience to experience the action rather than to be intellectually processing during the performance. Some critics were unable to decipher the play's themes, but the general feeling was that it explores "the predicament of a generation ruled by fear," an "aimlessness

... not easy to dramatize" in the words of a *London Times* critic. The story involves the pregnancy of Greta, the charismatic, red-headed gang leader, with the opposing gang leader's child. With her fertility in the midst of violence, she is symbolically paralleled with the Hindu goddess Kali, who both gives and destroys life. Jellicoe quotes an Indian hymn: "All creation is the sport of my mad mother Kali."

Because of *Sport*'s interest in teens, the Girl Guides Association then commissioned Jellicoe to write a play. Their choice was considered hardly appropriate because Jellicoe's work was more risque than wholesome. The result was the radical play *The Rising Generation*—which the Girl Guides not surprisingly rejected. However, it was published and eventually produced. It is a parable-like work about a totalitarian regiment of women, ruled by the awesome Mother, that aims to exterminate men. The girls recite in school, "Shakespeare was a woman," and "Men will tear you, beat you, eat you." But male-female attraction threatens to disrupt the regime. As in most of Jellicoe's plays, people are more influenced by feelings than ideologies, and idealistic views of relations between the sexes conflict with messy, uncontrollable forces.

The Knack (1961, filmed 1965), though still free-form, abstract, and anti-intellect, was written in a more accessible comedy-of-manners style, intended as it was for commercial success. It is a somewhat lighthearted portrayal of the game-playing and insecurities between young men and women. A lost 17-year-old, Nancy, accidentally enters the lives of three male roommates: Tolen, a macho ladies' man, Colin, a nerd, and Tom, who is in between. Tensions and conflicts arise as the men try to connect with Nancy and demonstrate their womanizing skills to each other in a sometimes insensitive, immature way. Tolen tries to teach Colin his secret to success: "Women are not individuals, but types ... not even types, just women. They want to surrender but they don't want the responsibility of surrendering.... If you feel it necessary in order to get the woman you must even be prepared to humiliate yourself.... Once you've got her it's the woman that grovels... Very few men ... are real masters. Almost all women are servants." Nancy vacillates between defending herself and acquiescing, as when Tom asks her to get him tea: "What do you think I am? ... Oh, all right." It is eventually she who immaturely outmanipulates them by threatening to cry "rape."

Jellicoe's biographical play, *Shelley; or, The Idealist* (1965) was fairly successful, and its Victorian melodrama style surprised her followers. Percy Bysshe Shelley held many views extreme for his time, such as atheism, belief in women's liberation, and preference for cohabitation over marriage: "Oh, you couldn't think of a situation more studiously hostile to human happiness than marriage.... Women and men must live together in friendship: free, equal and pure." His sister Hellen, ostracized in school for defending him, sends Shelley messages through her friend Harriet, with whom Shelley forms a relationship. He exhorts his sister and Harriet to fight against the oppression of women("It degrades me as a man") at school and at home. Harriet is soon in a compromised position, her father expecting a proposal, her sister urging her to use deceit if necessary, and Shelley marries her. But when he later meets Mary, daughter of his intellectual idols William Godwin and Mary Wollstonecraft, who shares his opinions and proffers her affection, he recognizes her as his soul mate. Not wishing to abandon Harriet, he asks her to live platonically with him and Mary, with whom his relationship eventually sours after many tragedies. Jellicoe shows here, as well as in her fictional plots, that while equality between the sexes is a legitimate ideal, going to extremes to implement it without regard for feelings can backfire.

Other plays by Jellicoe include *The Giveaway,* a farce about a family who wins a 10-years' supply of corn flakes, and *The Reckoning,* a regional theatre piece about an episode in the history of Lyme Regis. She has also written a number of children's plays and a widely used book about producing community theatre, and is active in directing community productions.

—Leslie-Anne Skolnik

JEWETT, Sarah Orne

Nationality: American. **Born:** South Berwick, Maine, 3 September 1849. **Education:** Studied at home and at Miss Raynes School; graduated from Berwick Academy, 1866. **Career:** Contributed short stories, sketches, and essays to periodicals, including *Atlantic Monthly, Century, Cosmopolitan, Flag of Our Union, Harper's Bazaar, Harper's Magazine, Independent, Our Folks, St. Nicholas, Scribner's* and *Youth's Compendium;* lost the ability to write after suffering a spinal injury in a carriage accident, 1902. **Awards:** Litt.D, Bowdoin College, 1901. **Died:** 24 June 1909.

Publications

Novels

A Country Doctor. Boston and New York, Houghton Mifflin, 1884.
A Marsh Island. Boston and New York, Houghton Mifflin, 1885.
The Tory Lover. Boston, Houghton Mifflin, and London, Smith Elder, 1901.

Short Stories

Deephaven (originally appeared in *Atlantic Monthly,* 1873-76). Boston, Osgood, 1877; London, Osgood McIlvaine, 1893.
Old Friends and New. Boston, Houghton Osgood, 1879.
Country By-Ways. Boston, Houghton Mifflin, 1881; London, Trübner, 1882.
The Mate of the Daylight, and Friends Ashore. Boston, Houghton Mifflin, 1884.
Strangers and Wayfarers. Boston and New York, Houghton Mifflin, 1890; London, Osgood, McIlvaine, 1891.
A White Heron and Other Stories. Boston and New York, Houghton Mifflin, 1886.
The King of Folly Island and Other People. Boston and New York, Houghton Mifflin, 1888; London, Duckworth, 1903.
Tales of New England. Boston, Houghton Mifflin, 1890; London, Osgood McIlvaine, 1893.
A Native of Winby and Other Tales. Boston, Houghton Mifflin, 1893.
The Life of Nancy. Boston and New York, Houghton Mifflin, and London, Longman's, 1895.
The Country of the Pointed Firs (originally appeared in *Atlantic Monthly*). Boston and New York, Houghton Mifflin, and London, Unwin, 1896.

The Queen's Twin and Other Stories. Boston and New York, Houghton Mifflin, 1899; London, Smith Elder, 1900.
Stories and Tales. Boston and New York, Houghton Mifflin, 7 vols., 1910; London, Constable, 1911.
An Empty Purse: A Christmas Story. Boston, privately printed, 1905.
The Best Stories of Sarah Orne Jewett, edited by Willa Cather. Boston, Houghton Mifflin, 2 vols., 1925.
The Only Rose and Other Tales, London, Cape, 1937.
The Uncollected Short Stories of Sarah Orne Jewett, edited by Richard Cary. Waterville, Maine, Colby College Press, 1971.
The Country of the Pointed Firs and Other Stories, selected and introduced by Mary Ellen Chase, New York, Norton, 1982.
Novels and Stories, New York, Library of America, 1994.

Poetry

Verses, edited by M. A. DeWolfe Howe. Boston, privately printed, 1916.

For Children

Play Days: A Book of Stories for Children. Boston, Houghton Osgood, 1878.
The Story of the Normans, Told Chiefly in Relation to Their Conquest of England. New York, Putnam's, 1887; London, Unwin, 1898.
Betty Leicester, A Story for Girls. Boston and New York, Houghton Mifflin, 1890.
Betty Leicester's English Xmas, A New Chapter of an Old Story. Baltimore, privately printed, 1894; as *Betty Leicester's Christmas,* Boston and New York, Houghton Mifflin, 1899.

Other

Letters of Sarah Orne Jewett, edited by Annie Fields. Boston and New York, Houghton Mifflin, 1911.
Letters of Sarah Orne Jewett Now in the Colby College Library. Waterville, Maine, Colby College Press, 1947.
Sarah Orne Jewett Letters, edited by Richard Cary. Waterville, Maine, Colby College Press, 1956; enlarged edition, 1967.
The World of Dunnet Landing: A Sarah Orne Jewett Collection, edited by David Bonnell Green. Lincoln, University of Nebraska Press, 1962.

*

Bibliography: *A Bibliography of the Published Writings of Sarah Orne Jewett* by Clara C. Weber and Carl J. Weber, Waterville, Maine, Colby College Press, 1949; "Sarah Orne Jewett: A Critical Bibliography of Secondary Comment" by Clayton L. Eichelberger, in *American Literary Realism,* 2, fall 1969; *Sarah Orne Jewett: A Reference Guide* by Gwen L. Nagel and James Nagel, Boston, G. K. Hall, 1978.

Manuscript Collections: Houghton Library, Harvard University; Society for the Preservation of New England Antiquities; Boston Public Library; Colby College, Waterville, Maine; Folger Shakespeare Library; Library of Congress.

Critical Studies: *Sarah Orne Jewett* by Richard Cary, New York, Twayne, 1962; *Appreciation of Sarah Orne Jewett: Twenty-nine Interpretive Essays* edited by Cary, Waterville, Maine, Colby College Press, 1973; "The New Woman Revisited" by Carolyn Forrey, in *Women's Studies,* 2, 1974; *Sarah Orne Jewett* by Josephine Donovan, New York, Ungar, 1980; "Sarah Orne Jewett and the World of the Mothers" by Donovan, in her *New England Local Color Literature,* New York, Ungar, 1983; *Critical Essays on Sarah Orne Jewett* edited by Gwen L. Nagel, Boston, G. K. Hall, 1984; *Sarah Orne Jewett: An American Persephone* by Sarah Way Sherman, Hanover, University Press of New England, 1989; *Folk Roots and Mythic Wings in Sarah Orne Jewett and Toni Morrison: The Cultural Function of Narrative* by Marilyn Sanders Mobley, Baton Rouge, Louisiana State University Press, 1991; "Sarah Orne Jewett" by Helen Fiddyment Levy, in her *Fiction of the Home Place* Jackson, University Press of Mississippi, 1992; *New Essays on The Country of the Pointed Firs* edited by June Howard, New York and Cambridge, Cambridge University Press, 1994; *Sarah Orne Jewett: Her World and Her Work* by Paula Blanchard, New York, Addison-Wesley, 1994.

* * *

Foremost among American women writers of the late 19th century, Sarah Orne Jewett once observed that, "a dull little village is just the place to find the real drama of life." Equally comfortable in both urban and rural New England, Jewett chose its rural villages and farms, especially those of the Maine seacoast, as the wellspring of most of her fiction. Yet for more than 30 years, Jewett was at the heart of a vibrant, urban community of women writers, artists, and scholars in Boston; creating her fiction in a unique period when 19th-century middle-class feminism was firmly embedded in the mainstream culture of New England.

Jewett's work has been traditionally classified as "regional" or, more specifically, as "local color" literature in which detailed, authentic portrayals of a geographic region's scenery, people, dialect, and customs are depicted. In recent decades, the rise of feminist scholarship has led to a groundswell of interest in Jewett and subsequently, to many new interpretations of her work. Feminist or not, today most scholars and critics agree that much of Jewett's work transcends the narrow boundaries of both regional and local color literature.

Born Theodora Sarah Orne Jewett on 3 September 1849 into a prosperous middle-class family in the village of South Berwick, Maine, Jewett was plagued by frequent illnesses as a child. Her father, a country doctor and intellectual, encouraged her to be out of doors as much as possible, hoping it would improve her health. She was an average student, and much preferred curling up with a book or exploring the woods, fields, and river near her home to scholarly pursuits. As a young teenager, Jewett frequently accompanied her father throughout the countryside as he called on his patients. During this period, her father taught her the skill of close, sympathetic observation of people and nature. This training motivated her to consider medicine as a career. Although her ill health ultimately made this option impossible (Jewett suffered from severe arthritis from her teen years on), she redirected her longing for a vocation and her powers of observation toward writing.

As an older child Jewett was fond of writing occasional stories and verse. She was 18 when "Jenny Garrow's Lovers," her first story to be published in a mainstream publication appeared in *The Flag of Our Union,* a Boston weekly, in 1868. The next few years were a period of extensive experimentation as she struggled to find a niche, submitting works in many genres for adults and children. Later in life, in a letter to a friend, Jewett reflected on the early discovery of what came to be the focus of her writing. "I determined to teach the world that country people were not the awkward, ignorant set those people seemed to think. I wanted the world to know their grand, simple lives; and, so far as I had a mission, when I first began to write, I think that was it."

With the publication of the first of four *Deephaven* sketches, each published successively in the *Atlantic Monthly* between 1873-1876 and then collectively as a book in 1878, Jewett captured the praise and attention of the magazine's editor, the writer William Dean Howells, who introduced her to Boston literary society. She soon met James T. Fields, the celebrated Boston publisher, and his wife Annie Adams Fields, writer and social reformer. Jewett became a close friend of the Fieldses and, after James's death in 1881, her friendship with Annie deepened. The two women became intimate companions, Jewett living approximately half the year with Annie Fields in Boston and the rest of the year in South Berwick with her family. Although many Jewett scholars have suggested that Jewett and Fields may have had a lesbian relationship, the exact nature of their attachment is not known, though their correspondence is a testament to the deeply loving, intimate, and mutually supportive nature of their relationship.

It is in *Deephaven* that Jewett first explores the themes, form, and style that characterize much of her later work. In this series of loosely woven character and nature sketches, two young women from Boston spend a summer in a Maine coastal village. There the two city sophisticates are drawn into a world far beyond their experience, a universe of old sea captains, a fisherman, and a strong woman of wisdom, all of whom have tales to tell and a philosophy to impart. Although *Deephaven* lacks the polished lyrical style that was to become Jewett's signature, it does artfully convey her profound reverence for the past and her affection and respect for her rural subjects. And, in the character of Mrs. Bonny, Jewett presents one of the first of many strong female characters she was to create. Mrs. Bonny lives in a cabin deep in the woods, wears men's clothes, smokes, and possesses the emotional steadiness that comes with age, wisdom, and a spiritual affinity with the natural world.

Literary scholars have criticized Jewett for what has been described as deficiencies in plot structure. While it is true that her plots do not follow traditional structure and form, feminist critics have long argued that Jewett's apparent plotlessness does not derive from a weakness or absence of plot but rather from the deliberate creation and elaboration of other structures, such as the sketch and vignette, which are better suited to conveying feminine experience.

The Country Doctor is considered Jewett's most feminist novel and also her most autobiographical. In this work, Nan, a young orphan, is fascinated by nature and outdoor activity but disdains all things domestic. With her foster parent Dr. Leslie as her guide and mentor (modelled on Jewett's own father), Nan realizes as she matures that she has an undeniable vocation to pursue a career in medicine. When she falls in love and is asked to marry, Nan discovers that marriage is completely incompatible with her more urgent goals. She refuses her suitor and courageously embraces her future "in an ecstasy of life and strength, and gladness."

According to Jewett's vision as portrayed in *The Country Doctor,* marriage cannot exist alongside a woman's devotion to a career. Through the voice of Dr. Leslie, Jewett states her belief that "some [women] are set apart by nature for other uses and conditions than marriage." Jewett, then, was most concerned with declaring a woman's right and duty to refuse marriage if she is not suited for it, a stance that may have derived from her need to defend her own choice to devote her life to her writing career and to relationships aside from marriage.

With the publication of the short story "A White Heron" in 1886, Jewett entered her full maturity as a writer, perfecting her control of symbols, themes, and the sketch-like structure of her fiction. Young Sylvia, a tomboy and lover of nature, decides to help a hunter and rare bird enthusiast who seeks to add a white heron to his collection of stuffed birds. At first Sylvia is happy that she is to be instrumental to the man's goals. But the experience of sighting the bird changes her and she chooses not to reveal its whereabouts. Some feminist scholars have viewed "A White Heron" as an antiromance, in which the prince seduces the heroine but is ultimately rejected by her. More important than the rejection, however, is the transformation that takes place within Sylvia when she discovers the heron. This pivotal alteration allows her to remain in harmony with the natural world as its protector, a distinctly feminine role.

From the moment *The Country of the Pointed Firs* first appeared, critics and readers agreed that its quality far surpassed Jewett's previous work. Since that time it has often been identified as her masterpiece. Like *Deephaven, The Country of the Pointed Firs* was first published as four separate sketches in the *Atlantic Monthly,* then published in book form in 1896. Of all Jewett's works, *The Country of the Pointed Firs* best exemplifies her recurring theme of the power of female relationships. Indeed, Jewett lavishes the most attention on portrayals of women's relationships in all her fiction, particularly friendships that are interdependent, mutually nourishing, and life-supporting connections.

Jewett invented the term "imaginative realism" to explain to a fellow writer how the realism in her fiction differed from conventional concepts of literary realism. She often noted that her work involved much more than the mere observation and recording of reality. In *Deephaven,* and in the bulk of her later work, the reality of everyday life—people, events, the natural world—is transformed through the individual and shared spiritual experiences of her characters.

In *The Country of Pointed Firs,* the middle-aged, nameless narrator is a writer who journeys to a Maine fishing village named Dunnet Landing. She rents a room from Mrs. Todd, herbalist, healer, and quintessential Jewett wise-woman. As the narrator is drawn into the lives and relationships of the villagers, there is the sense that the rural world is disappearing with the accompanying necessity to savor and celebrate its final moments. The narrator not only listens to the villagers' stories, rituals, and customs, she and the rest of the community internalize them and are transformed, thereby enriching their individual and collective experiences with new meanings and understandings.

In 1901 Bowdoin College awarded Jewett an honorary doctorate in literature, the first time the college bestowed this honor upon a woman. The following year, on her 53rd birthday, she would seriously injure her head and spine in a carriage accident. Jewett never completely recovered from her injuries and, tragically, lost the ability to write more than a few lines at time. She spent her remaining years in Boston and in South Berwick, and died of a cerebral hemorrhage on 24 June 1909.

With the recent resurgence of interest in Sarah Orne Jewett, more and more of her previously out-of-print works have been reprinted. Modern readers now have the opportunity to discover her infectious optimism about the multi-dimensional potential of women's relationships and the richness of middle-aged and older women's experience. Portraits of vigorous, independent, rock-solid, mature women have been especially lacking in American literature, and Jewett's oeuvre can be celebrated for broadening narrow, conventional literary conceptions of the female experience.

—Judith E. Harper

JOHNSTON, Jill

Pseudonym: F.J. Crowe. **Nationality:** British-American. **Born:** London, 17 May 1929. **Family:** Married Richard John Lanham in 1958 (divorced 1964); one son, one daughter. **Career:** Author of column, "Dance Journal," *Village Voice,* New York, 1959-75; critic, *Art in America,* New York, 1983-87. Contributor to periodicals, including *Art News.*

Publications

Political/Social Theory

Lesbian Nation: The Feminist Solution. New York, Simon & Schuster, 1973.

Essays

Marmalade Me (originally published in *Village Voice*). New York, Dutton, 1971.
Gullibles Travels. New York, Links Books, 1974.
Secret Lives in Art. Chicago, A Capella, 1994.

Autobiography

Autobiography in Search of a Father: Mother Bound [Paper Daughter]. New York, Knopf, 2 vols., 1983-85.

Other

Editor, with Bertha Harris, Esther Newton, and Jane O'Wyatt, *Amazon Expedition: A Lesbian-Feminist Anthology.* San Rafael, California, Times Change Press, 1973.

*

Critical Sources: "Johnston Preserved" by Rosalind Constable, in *New York,* 1(24), 24 May 1971; *Between Marriage and Divorce* by Susan Braudy, New York, Morrow, 1975; "Consciousness as Style; Style as Aesthetic" by Julia Penelope and Susan J. Wolfe, in *Language, Gender, and Society,* edited by Barrie Thorne, Cheris Kramarae, and Nancy Henley, n.p., 1983.

* * *

Jill Johnston remains best known for her 1973 work *Lesbian Nation: The Feminist Solution,* which fused her eclectic style as a critic for the *Village Voice* with her strident political analysis of lesbian identity. The book's intentionally daring title typified Johnston's personal and intellectual impatience with the mainstream feminist leadership of the early 1970s, an era when feminist leaders chose to alienate or disclaim lesbians in the growing women's movement.

Born in 1929 in London, Johnston was the illegitimate daughter of a high-ranking British father and an American mother, who had met aboard a ship bound for Europe. Johnston's mother, Olive, elected to have the baby Jill in England and, in order to avoid scandal, claimed widowhood upon returning to the United States. Raised by her mother, aunt, and grandmother and spending the first five years of her life traveling with her mother between Europe and New York, Johnston grew up with a unique perspective for writing about both woman-identified relationship ties and patriarchal codes of law that judged women according to marital status. Of her own childhood and adolescence, Johnston has said "Having grown up in a kind of fugitive matriarchy, knowing only my mother and various maternal relatives and finally only women in prep schools and colleges, I was given the most unusual illusion of freedom." While her mother worked to support her, Johnston attended the Episcopal boarding school St. Mary's, where she achieved distinction as both an athlete and, in her words, a "delinquent."

After attending college in Minnesota and in Greensboro, North Carolina, Johnston moved to New York and studied at Columbia University while involving herself in the dance and art worlds of the 1950s. Here she established numerous contacts in the gay male and beatnik-intellectual-artist communities, socializing with experimental artists like John Lennon and Yoko Ono, yet finding little validation for her lesbian relationships. As she later wrote in *Lesbian Nation,* "The conspiracy of silence prevailed.... There was no lesbian identity. There was lesbian activity." This primarily male world of avant-garde arts and letters that Johnston explored as both a student and review writer would later fuel her criticism of sexism in the male counterculture.

Despite her early orientation toward women, Johnston attempted a marriage to Richard Lantham in 1958, and had two children with him while establishing her own career as dance critic for the *Village Voice.* Their 1964 divorce re-introduced Johnston to the common plight of women separated from a legally recognized husband: a reduced standard of living. Writing about her subsequent loss of child custody in the 1972 essay "The Return of the Amazon Mother," Johnston said "I didn't give up my children as a lark. I was living in desperate circumstances alone with the children in a tenement either on welfare or on $25 a week from the father whenever it was forthcoming and trying to establish myself as a writer."

Johnston's first book, *Marmalade Me,* featured her collected art and dance reviews from the *Village Voice* column she had written since 1959, and established her as a respected critic with a stream-of-consciousness style hailed as "important, radical, innovative ... fractured, anecdotal ... iconoclastic ... the theatre of total concern." Her subsequent writings for the *Voice* in the early 1970s shifted toward coverage of the women's movement, its treatment by the male press, and feminists' own discomfort with the question of lesbian identity. *Lesbian Nation* challenged both the sexism of male counterculture—which Johnston found as conservative in its views of women as the "establishment" culture it defied artistically—and the homophobia of mainstream feminism. Calling herself a lesbian chauvinist at a time when lesbianism was still labeled deviant and treated as criminal behavior, Johnston shocked some readers and intrigued the lesbian community by dedicating the book "To my mother, who should've been a lesbian, and for my daughter, in hopes she will be."

Johnston often drew on the language of her own illegitimate birth to define larger moments in political consciousness, defining gay liberation as counterculture's "most important bastard," for instance, or lamenting of her difficult circumstances "After all, who was I but an impoverished American female posing as an important British bastard." Although she continued to write and speak on lesbian issues after the publication of *Lesbian Nation* and, with Bertha Harris and others, *Amazon Expedition,* such later works as *Gullibles Travels* and *Mother Bound* returned to the question of her own paternity and her relationship to her mother's struggle of childrearing out of wedlock. This theme has continued in Johnston's more recent writing for the feminist journal *On the Issues:* a 1996 piece, "Family Values," described the author's journey back to London shortly after her 66th birthday to establish herself as heir to her deceased father. The title of her 1994 work *Secret Lives in Art* similarly reflects the unique tension of Johnston's writing: that society more readily accepts the avant-garde in art than in its socially sanctioned family arrangements. Still living in New York and writing, Jill Johnston has contributed a body of work that suggests the possibility of lesbian freedom against the restraints of propriety so many women, including her own mother, struggled with in work and family life.

—Bonnie Morris

JONES, LeRoi. *See* **BARAKA, Amiri.**

JONG, Erica

Nationality: American. **Born:** Erica Mann, New York, New York, 26 March 1942. **Education:** High School of Music and Art, New York; Barnard College, New York (George Weldwood Murray fellow, 1963), 1959-63, B.A. 1963 (Phi Beta Kappa); Columbia University, New York (Woodrow Wilson fellow, 1964), M.A. 1965; Columbia School of Fine Arts, 1969-70. **Family:** Married 1) Michael Werthman in 1963 (divorced 1965); 2) Allan Jong in 1966 (divorced 1975); 3) the writer Jonathan Fast in 1977 (divorced 1983), one daughter; 4) Kenneth David Burrows in 1989. **Career:** Lecturer in English, City College, New York, 1964-66, 1969-70, and University of Maryland European Division, Heidelberg, Germany, 1967-68; instructor in English, Manhattan Community College, New York, 1969-70. Since 1971 instructor in poetry, YM-YWHA Poetry Center, New York. Member of literary panel, New York State Council on the Arts, 1972-74. **Awards:** Academy of American Poets award, 1963; Bess Hokin prize (*Poetry,* Chicago), 1971; New York State Council on the Arts grant, 1971; Madeline Sadin award (*New York Quarterly*), 1972; Alice Fay di Castagnola award, 1972; National Endowment for the Arts grant, 1973; Creative Artists Public Service grant, 1973; Premio Internationale Sigmund Freud (Italy), 1979; United Nations Award of Excellence. **Member:** Authors Guild (president, 1991-93). **Address:** c/o Erica Jong Productions, 205 East 68th Street, New York, New York 10021, U.S.A.

Publications

Novels

Fear of Flying. New York, Holt Rinehart, 1973; London, Secker & Warburg, 1974.
How to Save Your Own Life. New York, Holt Rinehart, and London, Secker & Warburg, 1977.
Fanny, Being the True History of the Adventures of Fanny Hackabout-Jones. New York, New American Library, and London, Granada, 1980.
Parachutes and Kisses. New York, New American Library, and London, Granada, 1984.
Serenissima: A Novel of Venice. Boston, Houghton Mifflin, and London, Bantam, 1987.
Any Woman's Blues. New York, Harper, and London, Chatto & Windus, 1990.

Uncollected Short Stories

"From the Country of Regrets," in *Paris Review,* spring 1973.
"Take a Lover," in *Vogue,* April 1977.

Poetry

Fruits & Vegetables. New York, Holt Rinehart, 1971; London, Secker & Warburg, 1973.
Half-Lives. New York, Holt Rinehart, 1973; London, Secker & Warburg, 1974.
Here Comes and Other Poems. New York, New American Library, 1975.
Loveroot. New York, Holt Rinehart, 1975; London, Secker & Warburg, 1977.
The Poetry of Erica Jong. New York, Holt Rinehart, 1976.
Selected Poems 1-2. London, Panther, 2 vols., 1977-80.
At the Edge of the Body. New York, Holt Rinehart, 1979; London, Granada, 1981.
Ordinary Miracles: New Poems. New York, New American Library, 1983; London, Granada, 1984.
Becoming Light: Poems: New and Selected. New York, HarperCollins, 1991.

Other

Four Visions of America, with others. Santa Barbara, California, Capra Press, 1977.
Witches (miscellany). New York, Abrams, 1981; London, Granada, 1982.
Megan's Book of Divorce: A Kid's Book for Adults. New York, New American Library, 1984; London, Granada, 1985.
The Devil at Large: Erica Jong on Henry Miller. New York, Turtle Bay, and London, Chatto & Windus, 1993.
Fear of Fifty: A Midlife Memoir. New York, HarperCollins, and London, Chatto & Windus, 1994.

Recordings: *Fear of Flying,* 1990; *Becoming Light,* 1992; *Serenissima,* 1986; *Fear of Fifty,* 1995.

*

Critical Studies: Interviews in *New York Quarterly,* 16, 1974, *Playboy* (Chicago), September 1975, and *Viva* (New York), September 1977; "Dorothy Parker, Erica Jong, and New Feminist Humor" by Emily Toth, in *Regionalism and the Female Imagination,* 3, fall/winter 1977; "Isadora and Fanny, Jessica and Erica: The Feminist Discourse of Erica Jong" by Julie Anne Ruth, in *Australian Women's Book Review* (Melbourne), September 1990; "Nothing to Fear but Fear Itself?" by Isabelle de Courtivron, in *Womens Review of Books,* November 1994; *Feminism and the Politics of Literary Reputation: The Example of Erica Jong* by Charlotte Templin, Lawrence, University Press of Kansas, 1995.

* * *

"A writer is a person of his or her own age," Erica Jong has written, an expression that rings particularly true when contemplating her own work. Jong is best known for employing a bawdy, ribald writing style traditionally reserved for male writers, a style that became associated with the burgeoning tide of women's sexual liberation that coincided with the women's movement in the 1970s.

When Jong went to college, as she herself notes, there were "no women's studies courses, no anthologies that stressed a female heritage, no public women's movement." Although her education included degrees from prestigious institutions, it was not until the women's movement that she was able to construct her trademark intersection of female creativity and female sexuality in poems and prose.

Jong has never been a writer to shy away from a blatantly female physicality in her work. In fact, in her landmark first novel, *Fear of Flying* (1973), one of the subplots occurs within the time frame of a woman's menstrual cycle. The title refers to the thinly disguised autobiographical antagonist's voyage toward self-esteem and independence, and her persistent uncertainty about her ability to thrive as a mature woman. Isadora Wing's coming-of-age journey involves liberation through marriage, affairs, travel, and analysis, which lead her finally to confront her fears and find the ultimate freedom of self-acceptance, an acceptance that is especially predicated on claiming her womanly sexual self.

Fear of Flying generated widespread critical and popular attention for its energetic style, its humor, and its ability to capture the contradictions of the contemporary woman's search for love and liberation. The novel contributed a slang expression to the popular lexicon, the "zipless fuck," referring to a woman's fantasy of sex without physical or emotional consequences, a condition most men of the time could take for granted. Although considered by some to be a trivial work, the novel was also praised by such literary heavyweights as Henry Miller as a "Female Tropic of Cancer."

In *Fanny: Being the True History of the Adventures of Fanny Hackabout-Jones,* Jong creates a novel in the picaresque mode—a fictional genre dealing with the episodic adventures of a roguish protagonist. Traditionally, that rogue has been a male. Jong skillfully uses the language of the 18th century as her eponymous heroine retells her life story in order to revise the false, "sugar'd Tale of cloying Fanny Hill" composed by John Cleland in *Fanny Hill: Memoirs of a Woman of Pleasure.* The novel details Fanny's difficulties in achieving respect and acclaim as a writer upon revealing her female identity, and questions the assignment of rigid gender roles. The protagonist's difficulties stem from her insistence on stepping outside of the role deemed proper for a woman writer. Jong uses this tale as a metaphor for women reclaiming their stories from male presentations of female subjects.

In her poetry, as well, Jong insists on writing as a woman, and acknowledges her debt to other female writers such as Sylvia Plath and Anne Sexton, who wrote from an acute awareness of the female body, its bleeding cycles and fertility, its passage through menopause. Jong follows their example by incorporating explicitly female images in her work, from the oral sensuality in *Fruits & Vegetables,* to her search to comprehend the possibilities and perils of a woman's life in *Half-Lives* and *Bloodroot.*

Jong's poems frequently challenge the prevailing cultural ideals of beauty for women, using comedy to help the reader see that the concept really is somewhat absurd. For example, her poem "Aging" moves from the speaker's search for wrinkle creams to fight advancing age, to an acceptance and appreciation of the body's increasing wisdom.

Jong's most recent work includes *Fear of Fifty: A Midlife Memoir,* a volume which proves that in midlife she has lost none of her younger raunchy style. In a passage about the royal family's boring sex lives, for example, she claims, "If I were queen, I would have as many beautiful men as I wanted. Kill or castrate them later—or even marry them off."

In an early essay, "The Artist as Housewife/The Housewife as Artist," Jong wrote that a woman has more difficulty becoming a writer than a man because "she has greater problems becoming a self. She can't believe in her existence past thirty. She can't believe her own voice." As a prizewinning writer translated into 15 languages whose work is accepted by a wide popular audience, Erica Jong should no longer have any problem believing her own voice.

—Kate Lynn Hibbard

JOYAUX, Julia. *See* **KRISTEVA, Julia.**

JUANA INÉS de la CRUZ, Sor

Pseudonym of Juana Inés de Asbaje y Ramírez de Santillana. **Nationality:** Mexican. **Born:** San Miguel Napantle, Amecameca, 1648. **Education:** Self-educated. **Career:** Invited to become a lady of honor in the court of the Marquise of Mancera, 1665; joined the convent of St. Jeronimo, Mexico City, 1669; entered the Convent of the Unshod Carmelites, 1677; reprimanded by Bishop of Puebla de los Angeles, and ceased writing and academic studies, after signing her *Prótesta que Rubricada con su sangre, hizo de su fe y amor a dios,* 1691. **Died:** Mexico City, 1695.

Publications

Poetry

Villancicos, que se cantaron ... a la Purísima Concepción. Mexico City, n.p., 1676.
Villancinos, que se cantaron ... a S. Pedro Nolasco. Mexico City, n.p., 1677.
Villancinos, que se cantaron ... al Señor San Pedro. Mexico City, n.p., 1677.
Villancinos, que se cantaron ... en honor de María Santísima ... en su Asunción triunfante. Mexico City, n.p., 1685-86.
Villancicos, con que se solemnizaron ... los maitines del gloriosísimo patriarca Señor S. Joseph. Puebla de los Angeles, Mexico, n.p., 1690.
Villancicos, que se cantaron ... al Señor San Pedro. Mexico City, n.p., 1691.
Explicación succinta del arco triunfal .... Mexico City, n.d.; as *Loa con la descripción poética,* Mexico City, n.p., 1952.
Neptuno alegórica. Mexico City, n.p., 1690.
Auto sacramental del Divino Marciso. Mexico City, n.p., 1690.
Primero sueño. Madrid, c. 1680; edited by Ermilo Abreu Gómez, in *Contemporáneos,* 1(3), 1928; edited by Geraldo Moldenhauer and Juan Carlos Merlo, Buenos Aires, n.p., 1953; translated as *Sor Juana's Dream,* New York, Lumen, 1986.
Selected Sonnets. Saskatoon, Saskatchewan, Peregrina, 1987.

Essays

Crisis en un sermón: Carta athenagórica (with "Carta de Sor Philotea"). Puebla de los Angeles, Mexico, n.p., 1690.
La Repuesta de la poetisa a la muy ilustre Sor Philotea de la Cruz. N.p., 1691; edited by Emilio Abreu Gómez, 1929; translated as *A Woman of Genius: The Intellectual Autobiography of Sor Juana Inés de la Cruz,* Salisbury, Connecticut, Lime Rock Press, 1982; translated as *The Answer/Repuesta,* edited and translated by Electa Arenal and Amanda Powell, New York Feminist Press, 1994.

Plays

Los empeños de una casa. Seville, Joseph Padrino, 1683; as *The Obligations of a House,* n.p., n.d.
Amor es más labyrinto, with Juan de Guevara. Seville, Diego López de Haro, 1689.
El mártir del Sacramento, San Hermenegildo. In *Poesia y teatro,* 1946.
El cetro de José. In *Poesia y teatro,* 1946.
El divino Narciso. In *Poesia y teatro,* 1946.
Poesia y teatro, edited by Matilde Muñoz. Madrid, n.p., 1946.

Other

Inundación castálida de la única poetisa, musa dézima, sor Juana Inés de la Cruz.... Vol. 1, Madrid, 1689, vol. 2, Seville, 1692; vol. 3, Madrid, 1700.
Obras completas, edited by Alfonso Méndez Plancarte and Alberto G. Salceda. Mexico City and Buenos Aires, F.C.E., 4 vols., 1951-57.
A Sor Juana Anthology. Cambridge, Harvard University Press, 1988.

*

Bibliography: *Sor Juana Inés de la Cruz: Bibliografía y biblioteca* by Ermilo Abreau Gómez, Mexico City, n.p., 1934.

Critical Studies: "Tenth Muse" by Royer Fanchón, in *The Américas,* 8(2), 1951; "Sor Juana Inés de la Cruz: Speaking the Mother Tongue" by Electa Arenal, in *University of Dayton Review,* 16(2), 1983; *Sor Juana, or, the Traps of Faith* by Octavio Paz, Cambridge, Harvard University Press, 1988; "Sor Juana" by Georgina Sabat Rivers, in *Latin American Writers,* New York, Scribners, 1989; *Feminist Perspectives on Sor Juana Inés de la Cruz,* edited by Stephanie Merrim, n.p., 1991.

* * *

Sor Juana Inés de la Cruz, the "10th Muse," was a nun who dared to write amorous poetry during the time of the Inquisiton in 17th-century Mexico. She has also been called the first feminist of the Americas because of her defense of women's right to learn in response to the strict patriarchal doctrines of the Church. Sor Juana heralded not only the Age of Enlightenment but the modern era as well. Three hundred years after her death, she is still a compelling presence.

She was born Juana Inés Ramirez de Asbaje, a poor illegitimate *criolla,* a child prodigy largely educated in her grandfather's library. By age 15, as one of the most learned women in Mexico, she was presented at court in Mexico City to the Viceroy Marquis de Mancera and his wife, Doña Leonor Carreto. The couple, who were fond of literature, were captivated by Juana Inés. As a lady-in-waiting to the Marquise, Juana Inés would become known at court for her wit and beauty, as well as for her erudite intelligence. To ascertain the extent of her learning, the Marquis gathered together some of the most astute minds of the day—poets, historians, theologians, philosophers, and mathematicians. Juana Inés deftly answered the questions and arguments directed at her, impressing them all with her mental prowess.

At age 20, having captured the admiration of the court society, she entered the Convent of San Geranium. Why did one so beautiful, though not especially devout, choose to be a nun? Many women at that time sought shelter in a cloister. At that time there was really no other option for a women with such an independent spirit and a passion for learning.

As a nun Sor Juana's life was not a rigorously ascetic one. She lived in a two-storey cell where she read insatiably and amassed an impressive library while pursuing her writing and intellectual pursuits. She brought the elegance of the court with her by transforming the convent locutory into an intellectual salon. The next Viceroy, the Marquis de La Laguna and the Marquise María Luisa, the Countess de Pareda, were among the court society and literary devotees who came to talk and debate with Sor Juana.

María Luisa and Sor Juana were nearly the same age and a close relationship developed. Sor Juana wrote exquisitely beautiful poems to her friend, using the courtly love conventions of the time; in turn, Sor Juana wore a ring given to her by the Countess de la Pareda. The women were a community of two, surrounded by a patriarchal world during a period of total subjugation of women. They had only each other as true reflections for their souls.

Sor Juana also wrote sacred poems and erotic love poems, vocal music, villancicos performed in the cathedral, plays, secular comedies, and some of the most significant documents in the history of feminism and philosophical literature. Her use of language, though characterized by the Baroque style, has a modern essence.

Her public face reveals the impiousness of an undaunted spirit who appears, not as a nun, but as an independent woman. As she wrote in "Romance 48":

> As I will never be a woman
> who as wife nay serve a man.
> I know only that my body,
> not to either state inclined,
> is neuter, abstract, guardian
> of only what my soul consigns.

Her later *La Repuesta* would reveal a private, melancholy side, one that experienced an essential aloneness; she was truly unique in the world:

> ... I and only I must be
> my family and lineage
> Can anything compare with knowing
> I depend on no one,
> that I choose death, then birth myself
> whenever I take the notion?...
> That all my species is only I
> and I need incline toward none,
> since any creature is only obliged
> to love one of its own?
> That my inkwell is the simple pyre
> where I set myself aflame....

Sor Juana was a pivotal figure who lived at a unique point in history bound by two opposing world views: one the closed universe of Ptolemy and of the Inquisition, which still held sway in Mexico/New Spain; the other characterized by the new science of Copernicus, Newton, and Galileo. Of her monumental philosophical poem *Primero sueño/First Dream,* Nobel Prize-winner Octaio Paz notes that something in the world ended and something else began: the beginning of the modern impulse in poetry. A soul goes on a journey in search of divine revelation and finds none. In *First Dream,* the soul is pictured as intellect, not a religious pilgrim. At the height of the journey, at the fullest understanding reason can attain, there was no vision. Instead, the soul drew back at the immensity of the universe and foundered in confusion.

Sor Juana's genius gained recognition on two continents. She was commissioned to write poems, her plays were performed. Suddenly her world turned upside down, precipitated by the departure of the Marquis de La Laguna and María Luisa, who returned to Spain, leaving Sor Juana without the protection of the Viceregal palace, which had shielded her from the misogynist church. Fortunately, María Luisa brought Sor Juana's writings to Spain, where they were published for the first time.

In 1690, at the request of the Bishop, she wrote her only theological criticism, the *Carta Athenagórica,* a "letter worthy of Athena," which she insisted was not for public view. However, the Bishop published it with an accompanying letter from an imaginary nun—"Sor Philotea"—to censure Sor Juana publicly for her devotion to secular letters. In defiant response, Soe Juana wrote *La Repuesta de la poetisa a la muy ilustre Sor Philotea de la Cruz,* a feminist manifesto defending women's right to be educated and pursue learning, citing over 40 women who had made significant contributions throughout history. *La Respuesta* ignited the church's wrath.

External events also conspired against her. Endless rain resulted in a shortage of food, which caused riots. Widespread terror and superstition reigned. In a climate of intimidation and fear, her confidence sapped, Sor Juana signed *Prótesta que Rubricada con su sangre, hizo de su fe y amor a dios,* a statement of self-condemnation in blood. She renewed her vows and surrendered her musical and scientific instruments, as well as her library of 4,000 volumes, considered at that time to be the largest in Mexico. Two years of silence and penance followed. Then in 1695, while ministering to nuns struck by an epidemic, she herself succumbed and died.

—Sandia Belgrade

JULIA. *See* **ROBINSON, Mary (Darby).**

JUVENAL, Horace. *See* **ROBINSON, Mary (Darby).**

K

KENNEDY, Adrienne

Nationality: American. **Born:** Pittsburgh, Pennsylvania, 1931. **Education:** Ohio State University, B.A. in education 1953. **Family:** Married Joseph Kennedy in 1954 (divorced 1966); two sons. **Career:** Lecturer in playwriting, Yale University, New Haven, Connecticut, 1972-73, and Princeton University, 1977; visiting associate professor, Brown University, Providence, Rhode Island, 1979-80; chancellor and distinguished lecturer, University of California, Berkeley, 1986; visiting lecturer, Harvard University, Cambridge, Massachusetts, 1990-91. Co-founder, Women's Theatre Council, New York, 1971. **Awards:** Obie award, 1965, for *Funnyhouse of a Negro;* Guggenheim fellowship, 1967; Rockefeller grant, 1967-1969, 1973; New England Theatre Conference grant; National Endowment for the Arts grant, 1972; CBS-Yale University fellowship, 1973; Creative Artists Public Service Grant, 1974. **Address:** 325 West 89th Street, Apt. 5, New York, New York 10024, U.S.A.

Publications

Novel

Deadly Triplets: A Theatre Mystery and Journal. Minneapolis, University of Minnesota Press, 1990.

Uncollected Essays

"Letter to My Students," in *Kenyon Review,* 1993.

Plays

Funnyhouse of a Negro (produced New York, 1964; London, 1968). New York, S. French, 1969.

The Owl Answers (produced Westport, Connecticut, and New York, 1965). In *Cities of Bezique,* 1969.

A Beast's Story (produced New York, 1965). In *Cities in Bezique,* 1969.

A Rat's Mass (produced Rome, 1966; New York and London, 1970), in *New Black Playwrights,* edited by William Couch Jr. Baton Rouge, Louisiana State University Press, 1968.

The Lennon Play: In His Own Write, with John Lennon and Victor Spinetti (produced London, 1967; revised version produced London, 1968; Albany, New York, 1969). London, Cape, 1968; New York, Simon & Schuster, 1969.

A Lesson in Dead Language (produced New York and London 1968). In *Collision Course.* New York, Random House, 1968.

Boats (produced Los Angeles, 1969).

Sun: A Poem for Malcolm X Inspired by His Murder (produced London, 1969), in *Scripts 1* (New York), November 1971.

Cities in Bezique (includes *The Owl Answers* and *A Beast's Story).* New York, S. French, 1969.

An Evening with Dead Essex (produced New York, 1973).

A Movie Star Has to Star in Black and White (produced New York, 1976), in *Wordplays 3.* New York, Performing Arts Journal Publications, 1984.

Orestes [and] *Electra* (produced New York, 1980).

Black Children's Day (produced Providence, Rhode Island, 1980).

A Lancashire Lad (for children; produced Albany, New York, 1980).

Adrienne Kennedy in One Act (contains *Funnyhouse of a Negro, The Owl Answers, A Lesson in Dead Language, A Rat's Mass, Sun, A Movie Star Has to Star in Black and White, Electra,* and *Orestes).* Minneapolis, University of Minnesota Press, 1988.

She Talks [and] *Beethoven: 2 One-Act Plays,* in *Antaeus* (New York), 66, spring 1991.

The Alexander Plays (includes *She Talks to Beethoven, The Ohio State Murders, The Film Club,* and *The Dramatic Circle).* Minneapolis, University of Minnesota Press, 1992.

Autobiography

People Who Led to My Plays. New York, Knopf, 1987.

*

Bibliography: *American Women Dramatists of the 20th Century* by Brenda Coven, Metuchen, New Jersey, Scarecrow Press, 1982.

Critical Studies: "Theatre of Identity: Adrienne Kennedy's Portrait of the Black Woman" by Robert L. Tener, in *Studies in Black Literature,* 6, summer 1975; "*Cities in Bezique:* Adrienne Kennedy's Expressionistic Vision" by Kimberly W. Benston, in *CLA Journal,* 20, December 1976; *Interviews with Contemporary Women Playwrights* by Kathleen Betsko and Rachel Koenig, Beech Tree Books, 1987; *Intersecting Boundaries: The Theatre of Adrienne Kennedy* edited by Paul K. Bryant-Jackson and Lois More Overbeck, Minneapolis, University of Minnesota Press, 1992; *The Subject's Tragedy: Political Poetics, Feminist Theory, and Drama* by Linda Kintz, Ann Arbor, University of Michigan Press, 1992.

* * *

Playwright Adrienne Kennedy employs fantasy and dream-like images to portray the multi-faceted identities of her African American women characters as they struggle against an oppressive society. Heavily symbolic, hallucinatory, and filled with violence, Kennedy's plays operate in a fantastic milieu where troubled characters use psychodramatic means to confront racial and gender questions.

Kennedy's first play, *Funnyhouse of a Negro,* winner of the 1965 Obie Award, presents a young woman named Sarah as she unravels the complexities of her own identity as the daughter of a black man and a white woman. Her inner selves, characterized on stage by such varied figures as Queen Victoria, Jesus Christ, Patrice Lumumba, and the Duchess of Habsburg, dramatize the conflicting parts of Sarah's personality. These inner conflicts center on questions of gender and race as Sarah discusses her feelings with the various personas contained within her. Images of masks and skulls recur throughout the play, as Sarah rekindles buried memories of violence and rape that eventually lead her to commit suicide.

In *The Owl Answers,* Kennedy again presents a female character with multiple personalities. Clara Passmore contains within her the Virgin Mary, the Bastard, and the Owl—characters who appear to her while she rides on a New York subway car. The subway doors open to reveal such historical personages as Chaucer, Shakespeare, and Anne Boleyn, some of these visitors transforming in turn into her father and mother. Like Sarah in *Funnyhouse of a Negro,* Clara is of mixed heritage—her mother is a black cook in Georgia and her father is a wealthy white man. Her conversations with the characters inside and outside of herself become an exploration of her own past and a means of discovering who she truly is. Finally imprisoned within the Tower of London, Clara becomes an owl, a symbol of her mother. Filled with Christian and surrealistic imagery, *The Owl Answers* is an examination of one woman's attempt to find herself amid a confusing racial heritage.

In *A Beast's Story,* a young bride named Beast Girl is married to Dead Human by her father. Later she is raped by Dead Human when she refuses his advances. She then kills her baby to please her parents and, overcome by despair, murders her husband as well. More hallucinatory than Kennedy's earlier plays, *A Beast's Story* has a dreamlike quality and, like a dream, seems to circle around itself repetitively as obsessive images recur and the protagonist's confusion mounts. Also hallucinatory in approach, *A Rat's Mass* parodies the Catholic mass as it tells the story of Brother and Sister Rat, two siblings who find that their incestuous love for each other has replaced the love they once had for Rosemary, a descendant of the Pope, Julius Caesar, and the Virgin Mary. Blood plays a prominent role as symbol of both guilt and religious sacrament. The play, Kennedy has explained, was inspired by a dream she had while riding a train in Europe. A religious dimension reappears in the play *A Lesson in Dead Language,* set in a classroom where a teacher dressed as a White Dog joins with Joseph, Mary, and two Wise Men to confront seven young girls with religious guilt.

In more recent plays Kennedy has often drawn on actual biography for inspiration. She was inspired by the death of black leader Malcolm X to write the short play *Sun: A Poem for Malcolm X,* in which a single actor stands before such changing symbols as a moon, a severed head, and various colored suns as he reads the text of a poem of homage. In *The Lennon Play: In His Own Write,* Kennedy adapted stories written by John Lennon as a stage play featuring a young British boy growing up in an absurdist small town. *A Lancashire Lad* is a fictionalized account of the boyhood of famed silent-film star Charlie Chaplin.

In addition to the plays she has written, Kennedy joined with five other women playwrights in 1971 to found a theatre cooperative, the Women's Theatre Council. The group was founded to counter what the women believed was a neglect of female playwrights by the established New York theatrical community.

—Denise Wiloch

KINCAID, Jamaica

Nationality: Antiguan/American. **Born:** Elaine Potter Richardson, St. John's, Antigua, West Indies, 25 May 1949; immigrated to United States 1965; changed her name to Jamaica Kincaid 1973; naturalized U.S. citizen. **Education:** Attended government schools in Antigua; studied photography at New School for Social Research, New York; attended Franconia College. **Family:** Married the composer Allen Shawn; two children. **Career:** Worked as an au pair, secretary, and freelance journalist upon arrival in New York, c. 1966; staff writer, *New Yorker,* New York, 1976-95. Teacher in creative writing, Harvard University, beginning 1995. Contributor to periodicals, including *Ingenue.* **Awards:** American Academy's Morton Dauwen Zabel Award, 1983, for *At the Bottom of the River.* **Address:** Bennington, Vermont, U.S.A.

Publications

Novels

Annie John. New York, Farrar Straus, 1985.
Lucy. New York, Farrar Straus, 1991.
Autobiography of My Mother. New York, Farrar Straus, 1996.

Short Stories

At the Bottom of the River. New York, Farrar Straus, 1983.

Other

A Small Place. New York, Farrar Straus, 1988.
Annie, Gwen, Lilly, Pam, and Tulip, illustrated by Eric Fischl. New York, Whitney Museum of Modern Art, 1989.

*

Critical Studies: *Fifty Caribbean Writers,* edited by Daryl Cumberdance, 1986; "Jamaica Kincaid and the Modernist Project" (interview) by Selwyn R. Dudjoe, in *Callalo,* 12(2), spring 1989; "Merge and Separate: Jamaica Kincaid's Fiction" by Wendy Dutton, in *World Literature Today,* 63(3), summer 1989; interview with Donna Perry in *Reading Black, Reading Feminist* edited by Henry Louis Gates Jr., New York, Meridian, 1990; *Where the Land Meets the Body: Jamaica Kincaid* by Moira Ferguson, Charlottesville, University Press of Virginia, 1994, and her "A Lot of Memory: An Interview with Jamaica Kincaid," in *Kenyon Review,* 16(1), winter 1994; *Jamaica Kincaid* by Diane Simmons, New York, Twayne, 1994.

* * *

Jamaica Kincaid left Antigua for the United States at the age of 16, but continues to return to the island of her childhood and adolescence in her fiction. Much of her work is autobiographical, naming the relations of power as they are perceived, suffered, or resisted in the intensely private world of her female protagonists. The first three works of fiction, *At the Bottom of the River, Annie John,* and *Lucy,* explore the subjectivity of a young girl/woman whose experiences of growing up in colonial Antigua and migrating to the U.S. are similar to the author's. Her nonfictional work, *A Small Place,* written in the first person, was inspired by Kincaid's visit to Antigua, after 19 years.

Two intertwined themes recur in most of her work: the adolescent daughter's traumatic separation from the mother is articulated alongside the impact of colonial education and the attendant displacement of the narrator from her homeland. Migration to England (or North America) is a difficult rite of passage that has been told in many ways by male Caribbean writers, notably George Lamming, Aime Cesaire, Edward Brathwaite, and V.S. Naipaul. Kincaid's is a distinctly female version of that rite of passage, where exile from the subordinated homeland is first experienced as a state of exile from the mother. Feeling betrayed by both mother and motherland, Kincaid's protagonists respond to these divisions with bitter anguish.

Both *At the Bottom of the River* (1978) and *Annie John* (1983) may be read as variations on the same theme; in both works the first-person narrator takes us to the difficult place where she is "no longer a child but not yet a woman." In both works, the perspective is that of a dissenting daughter. The mother's unfortunate role of disciplining the daughter in accordance with the civilizing mission of a colonial, patriarchal society earns her the daughter's profound resentment.

The intermeshing of patriarchal and colonial ideology is evident in the first chapter of *Bottom,* "Girl," with its inventory of maternal directives impressed upon the narrator's consciousness. Along with practical injunctions on performing domestic chores come bourgeois codes of respectability with their policing of female sexuality. Blending Victorian codes of conduct with Creole recipes for making salt fish and pepper pot, the maternal voice attempts to shape her daughter into the desired mould of conformity.

In *Annie John* we begin to understand the severity of the mother-daughter split narrated elliptically in Kincaid's first book. By relentlessly policing the daughter's libido, as it were, putting an end to all undesirable friendships and conduct inappropriate to middle-class, feminine modes of behavior, the mother earns the daughter's heart-felt hatred. The mother herself appears secure in her black Caribbean female identity, mixing the colonial culture with older Afro-Caribbean forms of healing and ritual. The schooled daughter seems to feel no such assurance. She is caught between her education—the word-worlds of Enid Blyton, Charles Kingsley, the Brontës, Milton, and Wordsworth—where what she learns is inimical to her black Caribbean identity, and her mother's expectations of domesticity and virtue, where what she learns is inimical to an unfettered female identity. Set adrift from the anchoring matrix of mother and motherland, the narrator goes to sea. As we follow Annie John on her last walk to the jetty—"the road ... to school, to church, to Sunday school, to choir practice, to Brownie meetings, to Girl Guide meetings..."— we realize that the entire educational and cultural apparatus had done just what she had accused her mother of doing: "proposing separation after separation" from the world in which she lived, making England the obvious destination.

In *A Small Place,* her only work of nonfiction, Kincaid is able to go beyond the self to write the nation of which the self is a part. An exposé of colonial power and neo-colonial corruption in Antigua (independent since 1981), it is in her own words, "a prolonged visit to the bile duct." The scorn and irony directed at the first-world complacency of the white tourist, who makes a spectacle of Antiguan poverty and necessity, is surpassed only by the scathing criticism of the elite in power, who sell the interests and sovereignty of the people for their own profit. Kincaid insists on showing her reader that this corruption is in itself a legacy of colonial rule, that the national industry of tourism is located in a nexus of power relations between first and third worlds that preclude the term "independence" for Antiguan people.

Lucy continues where *Annie John* left off; Annie John ends with Annie's last day in Antigua, while *Lucy* opens with the 19-year-old narrator's first day in the U.S. working as an au pair for a white family. From her subordinate position, the narrator purveys her employer's subject position (one of complacent mastery vis-a-vis her) with bristling irony. In her luciferous discontent, both sick of home and home-sick, the narrator finds that exile provides no escape from the bonds that tie her to her Mother/land. The novel continues the saga of the mother's "betrayal" of her daughter.

Autobiography of My Mother, Kincaid's latest novel, set in the land of Dominica, voices the daughter Xuela Richardson's longing for her Carib mother, a figure from whom she is natally alienated, the mother having died upon giving birth. It turns out this mother too was unmothered, abandoned at birth. This lovelessness haunts Xuela's life, upon whom the "spell of history" is irrevocable; through her, the novel gestures towards the loss of Carib origins, and of the rupture of ancestral lineage that founds Caribbean nationhood. The 70-year-old Xuela has remained childless for she does not have "the courage to bear" what she calls "the crime of these identities."

In all of Jamaica Kincaid's work the personal register of rage, loss, and disappointment of her female narrators becomes a way of critiquing the violent processes of history. Writing turns ammunition: a way of repossessing the female self in language.

—Gurleen Grewal

KINGSTON, Maxine Hong

Nationality: American. **Born:** Maxine Ting Ting Hong, Stockton, California, 27 October 1940. **Education:** University of California, Berkeley, B.A. 1962, teaching certificate, 1965. **Family:** Married Earll Kingston in 1962; one son. **Career:** Teacher of English and mathematics, Sunset High School, Hayward, California, 1965-67; teacher of English, Kahuku High School, Hawaii, 1967; teacher, Kahaluu Drop-In School, 1968; teacher of English as a second language, Honolulu Business College, Hawaii, 1969; teacher of language arts, Kailua High School, Hawaii, 1969, and Mid-Pacific Institute, Honolulu, 1970-77; visiting professor of English, University of Hawaii, Honolulu, 1977-78; workshop conductor, Asian-Pacific Women's Conference, University of Southern California, 1980; Thelma McCandless Distinguished Professor in the Humanities, Eastern Michigan University, 1986; Chancellor's Distinguished Professor, University of California at Berkeley, beginning 1990. Contributor to periodicals, including *American Heritage, Caliban, Hungry Mind Review, Los Angeles Times, Mother Jones, Ms., New Yorker,* and *Redbook.* **Awards:** National Book Critics Circle award, 1976, for *The Woman Warrior: Memoirs of a Girlhood among Ghosts; Mademoiselle* award, 1977; Anisfield-Wolf Race Relations award, 1978; National Endowment for the Artd writing fellowship, 1980; American Book award, 1981, for *China Man;* Stockton Arts Commission award, 1981; named Asian/Pacific Women's Network Woman of the Year, 1981; Guggenheim fellowship, 1981; Hawai'i Writers award, 1982; Governor's award for the arts, 1989; PEN Award, 1989; Brandeis University National Women's Committee award, 1990; American Academy award, 1990; Lila Wallace *Reader's Digest* award, 1992. Honorary degrees: Eastern Michigan University, 1988; Colby College, 1990; Brandeis University, 1991; University of Massachusetts, 1991; Starr King School for the Ministry, 1992. **Member:** American Academy of Arts and Sciences. **Address:** c/o Alfred A. Knopf Inc., 201 East 50th Street, New York, New York 10022, U.S.A.

Publications

Novel

Tripmaster Monkey, His Fake Book. New York, Knopf, and London, Pan, 1989.

Essays

"The Coming Book" in *The Writer and Her Work,* edited by Janet Sternburg. New York, Norton, 1980.

The Making of More Americans. Honolulu, Hawaii, InterArts, 1980.

Hawai'i One Summer (originally appeared in the *New York Times*). Port Jefferson, New York, Meadow Press, 1987.

Through the Black Curtain. Berkeley, University of California Press, 1987.

Autobiography

The Woman Warrior: Memoirs of a Girlhood among Ghosts. New York, Knopf, 1976; London, Allen Lane, 1977.

China Men. New York, Knopf, 1980; London, Pan, 1981.

*

Critical Studies: Interview with Timothy Pfaff in *New York Times Book Review,* 15 June 1980; *Approaches to Teaching Kingston's "The Woman Warrior"* edited by Shirley Geok-Lim, New York, Modern Language Association of America, 1991; *Articulate Silences: Hisaye Yamamoto, Maxine Hong Kingston, Joy Kogawa,* by King-Kok Chueng, Ithaca, Cornell University Press, 1993.

* * *

Maxine Hong Kingston, American novelist and nonfiction writer, was born of Chinese immigrant parents on 27 October 1940. She was the oldest daughter of Tom and Ying Lan Chew Hong, who operated a laundry in the Chinatown of Stockton, California. Kingston's parents had two children in China prior to Tom Hong's emigration to the United States in 1924. He worked as a laundryman in New York for the next 15 years, while supporting his wife's medical training at the To Keung School of Midwifery in Canton, China. During the couple's separation, their two children died. Tom Hong was finally able to bring his wife to the United States in 1939; soon after she arrived, the couple moved to Stockton to open a laundry of their own.

Because Cantonese was spoken at home, young Maxine did not learn English until she went to kindergarten. Her inability to speak fluent English, coupled with her ethnic background, made her a reserved and self-conscious child. In fact, Kingston kept silent during her first few years of schooling: "My silence was thickest—total—during the three years that I covered my school paintings with black paint," she would later recall in *The Woman Warrior: Memories of a Girlhood among Ghosts.* By age nine, however, her English improved enough to allow the youngster to write poetry in her second language. She enjoyed reading and writing and was, like her mother, good at storytelling. With impressive academic records in high school, Kingston went to the University of California at Berkeley, first studying engineering but soon changing her major to English literature. She received both a B.A. degree and a teaching certificate from Berkeley, in 1962 and 1965, respectively.

While in college, Kingston met acting student Earll Kingston and, after graduation, married him. The couple taught from 1966 to 1967 at the Sunset High School in Hayward, California, before they moved to Hawaii. There Kingston would teach English as various institutions—at Kahuku High School in 1967, Kahaluu Drop-In School in 1968, both Honolulu Business College and Kailua High School in 1969, and Mid-Pacific Institute in Honolulu beginning in 1970. It was in 1976, during her last year as a teacher at Mid-Pacific Institute, that she published her first biographical nonfiction work, *The Woman Warrior: Memories of a Girlhood among Ghosts.*

The immediate financial success of *The Woman Warrior* allowed Kingston to concentrate solely in writing, but she also chose to teach at universities across the country. She was a visiting associate professor of English at the University of Hawaii in Honolulu from 1977 to 1978, a workshop conductor at the University of Southern California's Asian-Pacific Women's Conference in 1980, and Thelma McCandless Distinguished Professor in the Humanities at Eastern Michigan University in 1986. Since 1990 Kingston has been teaching at the University of California at Berkeley as a senior lecturer.

During the 1980s Kingston published three significant works: a sequel to *The Woman Warrior* called *China Men* and published in 1980; 1987's *Hawai'i One Summer,* a collection of 12 prose sketches originally published in the *New York Times;* and *Tripmaster Monkey: His Fake Book,* her first work of fiction, released in 1989.

Kingston's works clearly reflect her dual cultural background: Chinese and American. The "talk-stories" she heard from her mother and from Chinese immigrants while she was a child deeply affected her literary imagination. These oral stories—myths, legends, ghost stories, and familial anecdotes from China—would eventually find their way into her written work. Kingston assumes the role of an Asian-American feminist when she resents male chauvinism, reflects on the strength of women, and empowers herself through the act of writing. Meanwhile, she plays the role of spokesperson for Chinese immigrants when she dwells on the racism and sexism they have been subjected to in American society.

The Woman Warrior, which won the National Book Critics Circle Award for the best nonfiction book of 1976, recounts Kingston's childhood, haunted as it was by two "ghosts": the Chinese ghost created by numerous "talk-stories," and the Caucasian ghost manifested in the form of bewildering American language and culture. In the first episode of the book, "No Name Woman," the narrator, who has reached womanhood, hears from her mother a story about her Chinese aunt. The aunt, who brings shame on her family by being impregnated through adultery, is condemned by both the community and her own family. As a spiteful response to their cruelty, she kills herself and her newborn baby. With an understanding heart, the narrator identifies with the forgotten aunt and feels obligated to pay tribute to her. In another episode, "White Tigers," the legendary Chinese swordswoman Fa Mu Lan shows how powerful a woman can be in a male-dominated society. In the story, the heroine masters a martial art and avenges her village. Fa Mu Lan is the type of a woman that Kingston wants to emulate. Like Fa Mu Lan, she believes in the self-empowerment of women. She resists the Chinese patriarchy symbolized by Chinese sayings like "There's no profit in raising girls. Better to raise geese than girls." As a writer, however, she realizes that in 20th-century America revenge can be done not through violence, but through the power of the pen. While the mythic Fa Mu Lan beheads and guts her oppressors, says Kingston, the modern writer will take her revenge through her pen. She remarks confidently, "And I have so many words—'chink' and 'gook' words too—that they do not fit on my skin." *The Woman Warrior* has been applauded as a feminist text by female and male critics alike.

In her next book, *China Men,* which won the American Book Award in 1981, Kingston explores the life stories of her father, brothers, and male ancestors and relatives who emigrated from their native country to the "Gold Mountain," America. As in her previous work, she blends historical facts, legends, myths, and autobiography in an effort to illuminate the strength and the struggle of the story's male characters. These Chinese men came to America in search of better lives but were troubled by discriminatory immigration laws, by racial and sexual prejudices, and by concerns about the family members they had left behind in China. As Kingston said in an interview with Timothy Pfaff in the *New York Times Book Review,* she wanted to proclaim through this work these Chinese immigrants' right to belong to American society: "What I am doing in this new book is claiming America." The author shows how the Chinese men contributed to the United States as laundrymen, railroad workers, sugar plantation laborers, farmers, miners, cooks, and members of the U.S. armed forces.

In *Tripmaster Monkey: His Fake Book,* a novel set in San Francisco during the 1960s, Kingston explores the life of a young man named Wittman Ah Sing. A recent graduate of the University of California at Berkeley, Wittman is a fifth-generation Chinese American, hippie, draft-dodger, playwright-director, poet, and tireless talker. Wittman, who was named by his father after the American poet Walt Whitman, wants to sing a song of himself as a Chinese American, a legitimate American. "Where's our jazz? Where's our blues?" he deplores. "Where's our ain't-taking-no-shit-from-nobody street-strutting-language? I want so bad to be the first bad-jazz China Man bluesman of America." In one such effort, he adapts the old Chinese romance novel *Romance of the Three Kingdoms* but adds the elements of legends, operas, vaudeville, and "talk-stories." The book ends with Wittman's lengthy monologue, in which he rants about racial stereotypes against Asian Americans and other social issues of the day.

Maxine Hong Kingston's literary achievements have been widely recognized. In 1980 a Honolulu Buddhist sect named her as a Living Treasure of Hawaii. She is the recipient of numerous awards, including the 1978 Anisfield-Wolf Race Relations Award, the Stockton Arts Commission Award and Asian/Pacific Women's Network Woman of the Year Award, both in 1981, and the 1983 Hawai'i Writers Award. She has also received a National Education Association writing fellowship and a Guggenheim fellowship. But perhaps her greatest achievement has been in giving voice to the past—to forbearers divided by the gulfs of culture, gender, economics, and tradition—and transforming her Asian American legacy into a bridge for future generations.

—Jae Nam Han

K.M. *See* **MANSFIELD, Katherine.**

KOGAWA, Joy

Nationality: Canadian. **Born:** Vancouver, British Columbia, 6 June 1935. **Family:** One son and one daughter. **Awards:** Books in Canada First Novel award, 1981, Canadian Authors Association Book of the Year award, Before Columbus Foundation American Book award, and American Library Association Notable Book designation, all 1982, all for *Obasan;* Periodical Distributors' Best Paperback Fiction award, 1983. D.L.: University of Lethbridge, 1991; Simon Frazer University, 1993. D. Litt.: University of Guelph, 1992. **Member:** Order of Canada, 1986. **Address:** 845 Semlin Dr., Vancouver, British Columbia V5L 4J6, Canada.

Publications

Novels

Obasan. Toronto, Lester & Orphen Dennys, 1981; New York, Anchor, 1994.

Itsuka. Toronto, Viking Canada, 1992; revised edition, New York, Anchor, 1993.

Poetry

The Splintered Moon. St. John, University of New Brunswick, 1967.

A Choice of Dreams. Toronto, McClelland & Stewart, 1977.

Jericho Road. Toronto, McClelland & Stewart, 1977.

Woman in the Woods. Oakville, Ontario, Mosaic Press, 1985.

For Children

Naomi's Road. Toronto, Oxford University Press, 1986.

*

Critical Studies: "Witnessing the Japanese Canadian Experience in World War II: Processual Structure, Symbolism, and Irony in Joy Kogawa's *Obasan*" by Cheng Lok Chua in *Reading the Literatures of Asian America,* edited by Amy Ling, and others, Philadelphia, Temple University Press, 1992; *Articulate Silences: Hisaye Yamamoto, Maxine Hong Kingston, Joy Kogawa* by King-Kok Cheung, Ithaca, Cornell University Press, 1993; interview with Janice Williamson in *Sounding Differences: Conversations with 17 Canadian Women Writers,* Toronto, University of Toronto Press, 1993; "Canadian Women of Color in the New World Order: Marlene Nourbese Philip, Joy Kogawa, and Beatrice Culleton Fight Their Way Home" by Heather Zwicker, in *Canadian Women Writing Fiction,* edited by Mickey Pearlman, Jackson, University Press of Mississippi, 1993; interview with Jeanne Delbaere in

Kunapipi, 16(1), 1994; "Memory and the Matrix of History: Joy Kogawa's *Obasan* and Toni Morrison's *Beloved*" by Gurleen Grewal, in *Memory and Cultural Politics: New Essays in American Ethnic Literatures,* edited by Robert Hogan and others, Boston, North Eastern University Press, 1996.

* * *

Joy Kogawa was born in Vancouver, Canada, in 1935 and, like her fictional character Naomi Nakane, suffered the uprooting of her well-to-do parents during World War II, when all those of Japanese ancestry were evacuated from the West Coast. Kogawa's own mother, a musician, did not recover from the shock of displacement. With her justly celebrated first novel *Obasan,* about the Japanese Canadian community's experience of dispersal and dispossession during World War II, Kogawa proved herself to be among the finest of feminist-humanist writers. Living in both Toronto and Vancouver, Kogawa has, for many years now, been involved with political work concerning the rights of Japanese Canadians.

It is not surprising to learn that Kogawa is a seasoned poet who has turned to fiction. Her best-selling *Obasan* was preceded by three collections of poetry published between 1967 and 1977: *The Splintered Moon, A Choice of Dreams,* and *Jericho Road.* Many of her poems have taken root in recollected dreams. For Kogawa (as she explained to interviewer Janice Williamson), "the practice of poetry ... is the sweeping out of the debris between the conscious and the unconscious." In fiction too, her endeavor is the same.

Through protagonist Naomi Nakane's recollection of her painful childhood, *Obasan* lays bare the inter-generational pain of Japanese Canadians affected by the Canadian government's relocation and internment of its citizens during World War II. A tribute to the integrity of the broken and the enduring Nisei—particularly those of the second generation, such as her old aunt and uncle—*Obasan* is a protest against the government's racially prejudiced policies, and a refusal to be thus marginalized by the nation. Incorporating letters and documents, this beautifully crafted novel with its moving resonances has done invaluable service to its varied readers. It has opened necessary dialogue; it has healed. Its language has wrought a gently forceful transformation of tragic and discordant forces.

Through the poetic and quiet ruminations of the intense first person narrator, Naomi, both novels, *Obasan* (1981) and *Itsuka* (1992), chart the long process of recovering from a traumatic past. *Obasan* begins in 1972, three decades after the fateful war year of 1942 (the year the collective crisis began), with Naomi Nakane, the 36-year-old survivor acknowledging life's imperative to heal. In her effort to emerge from the numbing world of grief and silence, she grapples with speech: Naomi struggles with fear, rage, and the despondent sense of futility. Urged by her maternal Aunt Emily's activist voice against injustice, Naomi's haltingly persistent and poignant reliving of the past enables her to release the deep, dark secrets held in silence: the memory of the shame-instilling and speech-robbing act of her childhood molestation by a neighbor; the suppressed truth about her mother's death in the other holocaust, the nuclear bombing of Nagasaki. Devastating as it is, truth frees; difficult though it may be, the coming to speech liberates the victimized from their isolation.

Itsuka picks up where *Obasan* ends, allowing the reader to witness Naomi's personal growth and fulfillment. If *Obasan* successfully releases the long-repressed memories of the past, *Itsuka* brings about the reconciliation between past and present. The process of healing, initiated so powerfully in *Obasan,* comes full circle when, Naomi, now 40, finds a comrade in Father Cedric, a French Canadian priest in whose presence she learns to replace old fears with trust. *Itsuka* openly bears the message of hope and trust implicit in *Obasan;* we recall the old Uncle's sigh of "itsuka...," meaning "someday." Befittingly, the final page of *Itsuka* carries a retrospective apology by the Government of Canada; it admits of policies "influenced by discriminatory attitudes" against Japanese Canadians, listing acts that were "unjust...,"[d]espite perceived military necessities at the time."

A writer whose concern is both the world of politics and the spiritual world of the psyche that bears the scars of history, Kogawa's fiction emphasizes compassion and the arduous work of healing. She is a feminist who feels the necessity of identifying with oppressed humanity, regardless of gender; as she puts it in her interview with Williamson, she is wary of the "uglification of the soul that happens with one-dimensionality, and [which] is one of the dangers of political endeavor," including that of feminism.

—Gurleen Grewal

KOLLONTAI, Aleksandra M(ikhailovna Domantovich)

Nationality: Russian. **Born:** St. Petersburg, 1 April 1872; daughter of Czarist general. **Education:** Studied in Switzerland until 1917. **Family:** Married Vladimir Kollontai in 1893 (separated); one son. **Career:** Social revolutionary, lecturing throughout Russia and abroad, beginning 1896; participated in "Bloody Sunday" demonstration, St. Petersburg, Russia, 1905; went into voluntary exile to avoid arrest, 1908; toured United States to agitate against World War I, 1915; joined Bolshevik party, 1915; elected to Central Committee as Commissar for Public Welfare, 1917; joined Worker's Opposition party, 1920-21; appointed, by Stalin, as Soviet Minister to Norway, 1923-35 and 1927-30, Mexico, 1925-57, and Sweden, 1930-35; negotiated peace agreement between Moscow and Helsinki, 1944; advisor to Ministry of Foreign Affairs until 1952. Contributor to periodicals, including *Pravda.* **Awards:** Order of Lenin, 1933; Order of the Red Banner, 1942. **Died:** 9 March 1952.

Publications

Political/Social Theory

The Life of the Finnish Workers. [Russia], n.p., 1903.
On the Question of the Class Struggle. [Russia], n.p., 1905.
Sotsīal'nyīā osnovy zhenskago voprosa [The Social Basis of the Woman Question]. St. Petersburg, Izd. t-va Znanīe, 1909.
Society and Maternity. [Russia], n.p., 1916.
The New Morality and the Working Class (includes "Sexual Relations and the Class Struggle," "Love and the New Morality," and "The New Woman"). [U.S.S.R.], 1918.

Sem'īā i kommunisticheskoe gosudarstvo. Moscow, Kn-vo Kommunist, 1918; translated as *Communism and the Family,* London, Worker's Socialist Federation, 1918.
Rabotnitsa i krest'īānka v Sovetskoi Rossii. Petrograd, Mezhdunarodnyi sekritariat po rabote sredi, c. 1922.
Women Workers Struggle for Their Rights. 3rd edition, Bristol, Falling Water Press, 1973.
Selected Writings of Alexandra Kollontai. Westport, L. Hill, and London, Allen & Busby, 1977.
Selected Articles and Speeches. New York, International Publishers, 1984.

Novel

Free Love. [U.S.S.R.], 1932.

Short Stories

Love of Worker Bees (includes "Sisters"). N.p., 1923; translated by Cathy Porter, London, Virago, 1977.
A Great Love. N.p., 1923; second edition, 1927; translation by Lily Lore, New York, Vanguard Press, 1929; translation by Cathy Porter, London, Virago, 1981.
Red Love. New York, Seven Arts, 1927.

Autobiography

The Autobiography of a Sexually Emancipated Communist Woman, translated by Salvator Attanasio. N.p., 1926; New York, Herder & Herder, 1971; London, Orbach & Chambers, 1972.

*

Critical Studies: *Bolshevik Feminist: The Life of Alexandra Kollontai* by Barbara Evans Clements, Bloomington, Indiana University Press, 1979; *Aleksandra Kollontai: Socialism, Feminism, and the Bolshevik Revolution* by Beatrice Farnsworth, Stanford, California, Stanford University Press, 1980; *Alexandra Kollontai: The Lonely Struggle of the Woman Who Defied Lenin* by Cathy Porter, London, Virago, 1980.

* * *

The daughter of wealth and privilege, young Aleksandra Kollontai read extensively from the shelves of her grandfather's sizable library collection and learned of the revolutionary changes taking place in her Russian homeland. Nicknamed Shura, Kollontai dreamed of not only being involved in aiding the cause of the Russian peasants, but also of becoming a writer. However, when she finally made her first attempt at writing a short story it was rejected as propaganda. The year was 1894; the czarist government of Russia was carrying the seeds of its later destruction, and the would-be writer had attacked the stabilizing conventions of marriage, allowing her heroine to leave her husband for her lover. The story may well have been a scene from Kollontai's own life; her mother, one of the "New Women" of the period, had deserted her husband to live with Aleksandra's father before the girl was born.

Exposed to the crushing poverty of Russian workers through the work of her husband, an engineer, Kollontai pursued her interest in revolutionary philosophy in 1896 when she studied the works of Karl Marx and published an article in a Marxist journal. Wishing to continue her study of Marxism but under pressure from the government, Kollontai was forced to leave her husband and young son behind in St. Petersburg in order to study economics at the University of Zurich. Upon her return to Russia a year later she shed both her traditional domestic role and her husband, committed to political activism.

Regarding the rights of women, Kollontai differed with the bourgeois feminist views so prevalent in the 1890s. Her perspective on the women's rights issue stemmed from her involvement with socialism, an ideology that expanded the meaning of "feminism" for late 19th-century Russian women with its promotion of a collective atmosphere. Once free from domesticity and family responsibilities, a socialist woman was obligated to move toward a collective atmosphere and work to better the human condition. Such was the attitude of Kollontai on her return from Zurich, as she began to concentrate on women's liberation. By 1905 she had become totally immersed in the woman question.

Voluntarily exiling herself in 1908 due to political pressures, Kollontai fled to Germany. Following her departure, her *Social Basis of the Woman Question* was published in Russia but received little recognition. The work sought to clarify the meaning of the term "free love" and separate it from the common perception of promiscuity and situations where men were able to take sexual advantage of supposedly willing women. Because of the furor then existing in Russia over the large amount of explicit sexual material in circulation—much of which associated free love with depravity—her work was relegated to the status of a fourth-rate novel.

During Kollontai's period of exile she wrote a number of articles in which she broke from the feminist dogma of Lenin and the Russian revolutionary movement and began to shape a more defined, individualistic view. In an essay written in 1913 on the "New Woman" she stressed that women needed to discover a sense of autonomy from within themselves. Woman had lost "her identity," she would eventually write in her *Autobiography of a Sexually Emancipated Communist Woman,* and had renounced "her own 'ego' for the sake of the beloved, for the protection of love's happiness." A new conception of being a "woman" would help women everywhere become productive citizens, not tied solely to the needs of the family.

After 1917 the aftermath of revolution in Russia provided a new forum for Kollontai. The overthrow of the czarist regime, with its ties to tradition, was now gone; women would now have the opportunity to pursue their lives independent of male support. Traveling throughout Russia, she spoke out against the continued oppression that she found, imploring women to be open to the new ideas of the Soviet revolution and see the possibilities. Kollontai soon realized, however, that the revolutionary movement would not bring women's liberation to complete fruition. Through her international travels she had lost touch with the conservativism that would become a traditional Soviet attitude. As Kollontai became increasingly outspoken in her attempt to gain women more than basic civil rights, encouraging them to break from the conventional male attitudes that kept them hard at work both in and outside of the home, she became increasingly unpopular with the Soviet government.

Kollontai's efforts to liberate women workers would not materialize while she lived within Soviet boundaries. Although, as Commissar for Public Welfare, she would be the only woman appointed to a post in the first Bolshevik government, officials disapproved of her strong opinions on free love and considered her proposed changes in family life to be disruptive. Commissioned to the low-visibility post of trade delegate to Norway, Mexico and Sweden beginning in 1922, she was effectively kept out of the public eye, although she kept the debates about women's role alive through her writings.

In Oslo, Norway, Kollontai immediately began her work of fiction, *The Love of Worker Bees*, a collection of two novellas and a short story that would be published in 1923. The stories candidly dealt with subjects she had touched on previously in articles regarding the New Woman: sexuality, dilemmas regarding family life, and economic worth. Believing that writing should resemble a woman's own reality, Kollontai structured her second novel, *A Great Love*, to resemble incidents that had occurred in her own life during the period 1908-17, while she was exiled from Russia in Europe. The protagonist in *A Great Love* has an affair with a married Russian revolutionary and economist, parallels to the author's life that classify the work as a *roman à clef.* Characters appear who closely mimic figures such as Lenin and others in the Soviet government. But the romance dies when the woman's lover fails to realize how important her work is to her; a good socialist, she departs to work for the betterment of her comrades.

Unlike several of her lovers and many of her political associates, Kollontai would survive the purges of the Communist party. She lived to the age of eighty, dying one year before Stalin, in 1952. After the Communist government relaxed the Iron Curtain, a great deal of archival material concerning of Kollontai emerged; many of her works were translated into English in the 1970s and she became the subject of several biographies. Through her essays, novels, and especially through her autobiography, Aleksandra Kollontai made manifest the paradox of communism and feminism, and clearly illustrated the struggle faced by the Russian women of her generation.

—Marilyn Elizabeth Perry

KRISTEVA, Julia

Pseudonym: Julia Joyaux. **Nationality:** French. **Born:** Silven, Bulgaria, 24 June 1941. **Education:** Attended French schools in Bulgaria; Université de Sofia, Bulgaria, diplômée de philologie romane, 1963; studied at Académie des Sciences en Littérature comparée, Sofia, and l'École practique des Hautes-Études, France; University of Paris 7, Ph.D. in linguistics 1973. **Family:** Married Phillippe Sollers (divorced); one son. **Career:** Worked as a journalist in Bulgaria; travelled to France in 1966; research assistant, Claude Lévi-Strauss's Laboratoire d'anthropologie sociale, 1967-73; instructor, 1972, then professor of linguistics, beginning 1973, University of Paris 7—Denis Diderot; visiting professor, Columbia University, New York, 1974; visiting professor in comparative literature, University of Toronto, 1992. Member of editorial board, *Tel quel,* beginning 1971; research trip to China with husband, Phillippe Sollers, and Roland Barthes, 1974; established psychoanalytic practice in Paris, 1978. Contributor to periodicals, including *Critique, Langages, Langues françaises, L'Infiniti, Partisan Review,* and *Revue français de psychanalyse.* **Awards:** Chevalier des Arts et des Lettres; Chevalier de l'Ordre du Mérite. **Member:** Société psychanalytique de Paris. **Address:** Université de Paris 7—Denis Diderot, UFR de Sciences des Textes et Documents, 34-44, 2e étage, 2, place Jussieu, 75006 Paris, France.

Publications

Philosophy

Sémèiôtikè, Recherce pour une sémanalyse. Paris, Le Seuil, 1969; abridged and translated in *Desire in Language: A Semiotic Approach to Literature and Art,* New York, Columbia University Press, and Oxford, Basil Blackwell, 1980.

Le Langage, cet inconnu, Une initiation à la linguistique (as Julia Joyaux). Paris, Le Seuil, 1969; as Julia Kristeva, 1981; translated as *Language: The Unknown: An Initiation into Linguistics,* New York, Columbia University Press, and London, Harvester Wheatsheaf, 1989.

Le Texte du roman: approache semiologique d'une stucture discursive transformationnelle. The Hague, Mouton, 1970.

La Révolution du langage poétique, L'avant-garde à la fin du XIXe siècle, Lautréamont et Mallarmé. Paris, Le Seuil, 1974; translation abridged as *Revolution in Poetic Language,* New York and Guilford, Columbia University Press, 1984.

Des Chinoises. Paris, Editions Des Femmes, 1974; as *About Chinese Women,* London, Marion Boyars, and New York, Urizen, 1977.

La Traversée des signes, with others. Paris, Le Seuil, 1975.

Polylogue. Paris, le Seuil, 1977; translated in *Desire in Language: A Semiotic Approach to Literature and Art,* New York, Columbia University Press, and Oxford, Basil Blackwell, 1980.

Folle Vérité, vérité et vraisemblance du texte psychotique, with Jean Michel Ribettes. Paris, Le Seuil, 1980.

Histoires d'amour. Paris, Denoël, 1983; translated as *Tales of Love,* New York and Guilford, Columbia University Press, 1987.

Au commencement était l'amour, Psychanalyse et foi. Paris, Hachette, 1985; translated as *In the Beginning Was Love: Psychoanalysis and Faith,* New York, Columbia University Press, 1987.

A Kristeva Reader, edited by Toril Moi. New York, Columbia University Press, 1986.

Soleil noir: depression et mélancolie. Paris, Gallimard, 1987; translated as *Black Sun: Depression and Melancholia,* New York, Columbia University Press, 1989.

Étrangers à nous-mêmes. Paris, Fayard, 1988; translated as *Strangers to Ourselves,* New York, Columbia University Press, and London, Harvester Wheatsheaf, 1991.

Les Nouvelles Maladies de l'âme. Paris, Fayard, 1993; translated as *New Maladies of the Soul,* New York, Columbia University Press, 1995.

Le Temps sensible, Proust et l'Expérience littéraire. Paris, Gallimard, 1994; as *Time and Sense: Proust and the Experience of Literature,* New York, Columbia University Press, and London, Faber & Faber, 1993.

Sens et no-sens de la revolte (Volume 1). Paris, Fayard, 1996.

Possession. Paris, Fayard, 1996.

Essays

"Le temps des femmes," in *34/44 Cahiers de recherche de sciences de textes et documents,* 5, 1979; translated as "Women's Time," in *Signs: A Journal of Women in Culture and Society,* 7(1), 1981.

Pouvoirs de l'horreur, Essai sur l'abjection. Paris, Le Seuil, 1980; translated as *Powers of Horror: An Essay on Abjection,* New York and Guilford, Columbia University Press, 1982.

Lettre ouverte à Harlem Désir. Paris, Rivages, 1990; as *Nations without Nationalism,* New York and Chichester, Columbia University Press, 1993.

Novels

Les Samouraïs. Paris, Fayard, 1990; as *The Samurai,* New York, Columbia University Press, 1992.

Le Vieil Homme et les loups. Paris, Fayard, 1991; as *The Old Man and the Wolves,* New York, Columbia University Press, 1994.

Other

Editor, with Thomas Sebeok, *Approaches to Semiotics, Vol. 1.* The Hague, Mouton, 1969.

Editor, *Epistémologie de la linguistique. Hommage à Émile Benveniste.* Paris, Didier, 1971.

Editor, with Josette Rey Debove and Donna Jean Umiker, *Essays in Semiotics: Essais de Sémiotique.* The Hague, Mouton, 1971.

Editor, with Jean-Claude Milner and Nicolas Ruwet, *Langue, discours, société: pour Emile Benveniste.* Paris, Le Seuil, 1975.

*

Bibliography: "Julia Kristeva" by Joan Nordquist, in *Social Theory: A Bibliographic Series* (Santa Cruz, California), 16, 1989; "Julia Kristeva: A Selected Bibliography" by Hélène Volat, in *Review of Existential Psychology and Psychiatry,* 22(1-3), 1990-91; "Julia Kristeva" by Lynne Huffer, in *French Women Writers: A Bio-Bibliographic Sourcebook,* edited by Eva Martin Sartori and Dorothy Wynne Zimmerman, New York, Greenwood Press, 1991; *Julia Kristeva* by Kathleen O'Grady, Bowling Green, Ohio, Philosophical Documentation Center, 1997.

Critical Studies: *New French Feminisms: An Anthology,* edited by Elaine Marks and Isabelle de Courtivron, Amherst, University of Massachusetts Press, 1980 (interview); "French Feminism in an International Frame" by Gayatri Chakravorty Spivak, in *Yale-French Studies,* 62, 1981; "Criticism of Julia Kristeva: A New Mode of Critical Thought" by Evelyn H. Zepp, in *Romantic Review* (New York), 73(1), January 1982; "The Phallic Mother: Freudian Analysis" by Jane Gallop, in *Feminism and Psychoanalysis: The Daughter's Seduction,* London, Macmillan, 1982; "Difference on Trial: A Critique of the Maternal Metaphor in Cixous, Irigaray, and Kristeva" by Domna C. Stanton, in *The Poetics of Gender,* edited by Nancy K. Miller and Carolyn G. Heilbrun, New York, Columbia University Press, 1986; *Sexual Subversions: Three French Feminists* by Elizabeth Grosz, Sydney, Allen & Unwin, 1989; "The Body Politics of Julia Kristeva" by Judith Butler, in *Hypatia,* 3(3), 1989; *Abjection, Melancholia, and Love: The Works of Julie Kristeva* edited by Andrew E. Benjamin and John Fletcher, London and New York, Routledge, 1990; *Julie Kristeva* by John Lechte, New York and London, Routledge, 1990; *Body/Text in Julia Kristeva: Religion, Women, and Psychoanalysis* by David Drownfield, Albany, State University of New York Press, 1992; *From Klein to Kristeva: Psychoanalytic Feminism and the Search for the "Good Enough" Mother* by Janice L. Doane and Devon L. Hodges, Ann Arbor, University of Michigan Press, 1992; *Transfigurations: Theology and the French Feminists* by C. W. Maggie Kim, Susan M. St. Ville, and Susan M. Simonaitis, Minneapolis, Fortress Press, 1993; *Ethics, Politics, and Difference in Julia Kristeva's Writings* by Kelly Oliver, New York, Routledge, 1993, and her *Reading Kristeva: Unraveling the Double-Bind,* Bloomington, Indiana University Press, 1993; *Reading Theory: An Introduction to Lacan, Derrida, and Kristeva* by Michael Payne, Oxford, Blackwell, 1993; *Womanizing Nietzsche: Philosophy's Relation to the "Feminine"* by Oliver, London, Routledge, 1995.

* * *

Julia Kristeva is one of the most influential and prolific of the contemporary French intellectual writers. Her writings span the disciplines and are studied by scholars from departments of philosophy and psychology to linguistics, theology and women's studies. Her impact on current feminist theory is significant, yet Kristeva's relationship to feminism has always been marked by ambivalence. She has never taken the title of "feminist" herself, and her critics have continuously labelled her work as everything from anti-feminist propaganda to radical feminist theory. Her latest work continues to obscure rather than clarify her position to feminism.

Kristeva was born and raised in communist Bulgaria, where she was educated by nuns in a Catholic school. She began her early career as a journalist, but in 1966, at age 25, she left her home to pursue a doctoral fellowship in linguistics at the University of Paris. Almost immediately she surprised French intellectuals of the time by publishing several ground-breaking articles in linguistic philosophy. Her work brought her into contact with many of the major thinkers of the time: she was supervised by Roland Barthes and Émile Benveniste, while attending lectures given by Jacques Lacan and working as a laboratory assistant for Claude Lévi-Strauss. And her involvement with the *Tel quel* journal, a marxist and avant-garde publication, introduced her to many of the central French thinkers of the latter half of this century: Jacques Derrida, Philippe Sollers (who later became her husband) and Michel Foucault, among many others.

Though Kristeva's writings reflect much of the spirit of 1960s Paris (the May 1968 revolution, flirtations with communism and the emergence of poststructuralism), her texts have always maintained a distinctly individual quality. Kristeva herself has attributed this to her position as the *étranger* (stranger/foreigner)—as a Bulgarian and a woman—of her peer group. This position has marked much of her theoretical work and contributes to her ability to understand the place of that which is other, marginalized, and outcast.

While excelling in the field of linguistics and semiotics for many years, Kristeva's increasing interest in Freudian and Lacanian theory propelled her toward psychoanalysis. She became a qualified and practicing analyst in 1979, and today continues her work as an analyst in addition to her post as professor of linguistics at the University of Paris 7. Her publications weave together these two fields of interest. In addition to her early linguistic works and later psychoanalytic texts, Kristeva has also completed two novels that augment her theoretical work. A woman of many genres, Kristeva has never abandoned the field of linguistics, but has found a variety of ways to communicate her interest.

Kristeva is most widely known for her contribution to literary studies, particularly her theory of *poetic language,* which emerged from such works on modernist poetry and prose as 1974's *Revolution in Poetic Language* and her *Desire in Language: A Semiotic Approach to Literature and Art. Poetic language*, Kristeva insists, is that aspect of language that cannot be accounted for in standard grammatical theories. She identifies two components that together constitute all linguistic operation: the *semiotic* and the *symbolic*. She names the *symbolic* (masculine) that part of language which expresses univocal meaning. It is the referential and communicative facet of language, its denotative property. The *semiotic* (feminine) on the other hand, is the rhythmic part of any language use, its playful, illogical element. It is that aspect of language that denies the linear and logical sequence of the *symbolic*. The *chora,* a term Kristeva borrows from Plato, is a maternal and nourishing space, the place from which the *semiotic* receives its motivation to rupture the sequential logic of the *symbolic*. The chora provides the *semiotic* aspect of language with its rhythm and lyrical movement. The chora is biological (undeniably maternal and dictated by bodily drives), but always already shaped by social forces.

Poetic language is the operation of the *semiotic* aspect of language in dialogue with the *symbolic* component. Any language use is an expression of these two forces intermingling, transforming and renewing one another, while providing multiple and varied meanings to any given utterance. Both the reader and the writer are implicated in the *semiotic-symbolic* dialogue as a *subject-in-process*. There is no judging, unified subject that exists outside of language, Kristeva insists, but a split-subject that results from the confrontation between the two forces. The subject of language is created and destroyed and constructed again (forever in process) by and through the rhythms of the *semiotic* in dialogue with the *symbolic*. The subject is not stagnant, but dynamic, open to the process within language itself.

Kristeva's theory of poetic language is not openly feminist, but provides a structure for a feminist critique of texts by theorizing the hitherto unspoken aspect of linguistic practice (the feminine, though not necessarily *female*). She accounts for the way in which linear language is disrupted by *semiotic* libidinal forces, and replaces a dangerously normative (masculine) subject with a dissolved and decentered subject of language. In addition she provides a means for understanding the speech of marginalized and oppressed groups (through their use of the *semiotic*). Kristeva's *About Chinese Women* is her first notably "feminist" work—feminist, in that it applies her theory of the *semiotic* to her understanding of the place of women in Chinese society. She has, however, been highly criticized, primarily by Gayatri Chakravorty Spivak, for perpetuating an inaccurate and imperialistic view of Chinese culture. Though most critics will agree that her contribution of the *semiotic* component of language provides a useful tool for feminist critique, many have also criticized Kristeva's tendency to highlight the artistic practices of male writers while ignoring the poetic and prose productions of women.

The most widely cited of Kristeva's texts is undoubtably "Women's Time," a small essay that outlines most definitively her position on the women's movement. Kristeva delineates three stages of feminism that have emerged from disparate applications of *time*. Borrowing terms from Nietzsche, she declares that *linear* or *cursive* time refers to an historical, temporal dimension. This is the arena where suffragists and liberal-socialist feminists fight to achieve equality and strive for a place within traditional institutional power. A second type of feminism has also emerged, Kristeva contends, but this position is based on a *monumental* and *cyclical* conception of time. This is the dimension which expresses the eternal and the universal. It rejects political activity and instead rests on an artistic and psychoanalytic practice that is outside of *linear* time. As a creative expression, this type of feminism, radical in its aims, locates its struggle within the realm of signs. It embodies in its linguistic productions the repetitive and cyclical realm of the feminine, the place of biological rhythms, and drives. Both types of feminism are universal and global in their approach, ignoring different social and cultural heritages. They forcibly catalogue a variety of women under a single unified identity: Woman.

Kristeva rejects both the liberal feminist agenda and radical feminist aesthetics in favor of a combination of the two conceptions of time employed by each. A successful feminism cannot be merely a shift in legal or political legislation (according to *linear* time) nor a refusal to acknowledge anything but the feminine (in *monumental* time) but must be achieved by restructuring each individual's connection with *power itself,* particularly as it is embodied in language. A comprehensive feminism would also understand that the opposition between man and woman is a *metaphysical* distinction and that this very conception of identity must be challenged. Kristeva agrees with Lacan that there is no such thing as "Woman", but her aim is to emphasize *individual identity,* structured on the difference found at the base of the self. This challenge constitutes Kristeva's proposed "third" generation of feminism.

It is no coincidence that Kristeva spurns the group identification necessary in both *linear* and *monumental* feminism. Her own disillusionment with communism and subsequently with Maoism has left her with a distrust of any political theory that places the unity of the group above the diversity of its individuals. It is psychoanalysis that provides Kristeva with the means to focus on the singularity of the individual as the site of difference, multiplicity, and otherness.

Kristeva's more recent psychoanalytic works, particularly *Powers of Horror, Tales of Love,* and *Black Sun,* have again brought her theory close to feminist concerns, but Kristeva has still refrained from adopting the title "feminist" and again centers her attention on individual (male or female) psychic identity. Much of her psychoanalytic project has been marked by her attempt to expand and amplify the Freudian and Lacanian views of early childhood development. Kristeva has chosen to construct an earlier, pre-Oedipal stage of development that grants *the mother* a larger role in the process of language acquisition. Texts like "Stabat Mater" (in *Tales of Love)* describe, both through content and stylistically, the relationship between the mother and child (and the mother's mother) during pregnancy and childbirth and consequently, the impact this relationship has on the language contract. It is also in this text that Kristeva outlines something called *herethics* (implying both "*her*-ethics" and "heretics"). Kristeva outlines a theory of ethics that includes the feminine and is modelled on the pregnant woman who is both a double and a split subject.

Again, many of Kristeva's critics have deemed this maternally based ethics regressive and anti-feminist, while others, like Kelly Oliver, have understood it as a radical feminist move to refuse the effacement of the physical female body in the political realm. And texts like *Black Sun,* which examines closely the melancholic woman, and *Powers of Horror,* which details the abjection of the maternal body, do not detract, but add to the debate. *Is Julia*

Kristeva a feminist? Perhaps this question is not the appropriate one. Perhaps, as Kristeva advocates, we should refrain from rigid categorization and ask instead, *Is feminism itself based on a metaphysical understanding of identity?* and look to ourselves for the answer.

—Kathleen A. O'Grady

KUTTY, Madhavi. *See* **DAS, Kamala.**

L

A LADY OF QUALITY. *See* BAGNOLD, Enid.

LARSEN, Nella

Also wrote as Nella Larsen Imes. **Pseudonym:** Allen Semi. **Nationality:** American. **Born:** Chicago, Illinois, 13 April 1891. **Education:** Attended Fisk University as a Normal Preparatory student, Nashville, Tennessee, 1907-08; studied nursing at Lincoln Hospital, New York, New York, 1912-15. **Family:** Married the physicist Elmer S. Imes in 1919 (divorced 1933). **Career:** Assistant superintendent of nurses, Tuskegee Institute, Tuskegee, Alabama, 1915-16; nurse, Lincoln Hospital, New York, 1916-18, and New York City Department of Health, 1918-21; assistant librarian, 1922-23, assistant children's librarian, 1924-26, New York Public Library, Harlem branch; returned to nursing, Gouverneur Hospital, New York, 1941-61; Metropolitan Hospital, New York, 1961-64. Contributor of short fiction to periodicals, including *Brownie's Book* and *Young's Magazine,* sometimes under the name Nella Larsen Imes. **Awards:** Harmon Foundation Bronze Medal, 1928, for *Quicksand;* Guggenheim fellowship (first African American female recipient), 1930. **Died:** 30 March 1964.

PUBLICATIONS

Novels

Quicksand. New York, Knopf, 1928.
Passing. New York, Knopf, 1929.

Uncollected Short Stories

"The Wrong Man" (as Allen Semi), *Young's Magazine,* January 1926.
"Freedom" (as Allen Semi), *Young's Magazine,* April 1926.
"Sanctuary," n.p., 1931.

For Children

"Three Scandinavian Games," in *Brownie's Book,* June 1920.
"Danish Fun," in *Brownie's Book,* July 1920.

Other

An Intimation of Things Distant: The Collected Fiction of Nella Larsen, edited by Charles R. Larson. New York: Anchor Books, 1992.

*

Critical Studies: *The Negro Novel in America* by Robert Bone, New Haven, Yale University Press, 1965; *The Harlem Renaissance Remembered* edited by Arna Bontemps, New York, Dodd Mead, 1972; *Silence to the Drums: A Survey of the Literature of the Harlem Renaissance* by Margaret Perry, New York, Greenwood Press, 1976; "Nella Larsen: Mystery Woman of the Harlem Renaissance" by Mary Helen Washington, in *Ms.,* December 1980; *The Coupling Convention: Sex, Text, and Tradition in Black Women's Fiction* by Ann duCille, New York, Oxford University Press, 1993; *Invisible Darkness: Jean Toomer and Nella Larsen* by Charles R. Larson, Iowa City, University of Iowa Press, 1993; *Nella Larsen, Novelist of the Harlem Renaissance* by Thadious M. Davis, Baton Rouge, Louisiana State University Press, 1994; *The Politics of Color in the Fiction of Jessie Fauset and Nella Larsen* by Jacquelyn Y. McLendon, Charlottesville, University Press of Virginia, 1995.

* * *

Nella Larsen Imes herself laid claim to the "awful truth" of her first novel, *Quicksand,* in a letter to her friend Carl Van Vechten, white writer, critic, and patron of the arts. To the extent that the facts of Larsen's life are known, she did indeed share some similarities with her protagonist Helga Crane, and some of the book's events were obviously drawn from her own experiences. Like Helga, Larsen was born of mixed parentage—a Danish mother and a black father. She seems to have grown up in predominantly white surroundings and, later in life, to have become estranged from her mother and sister, the latter of whom at Larsen's death denied knowledge of her. Larsen also suffered from feelings of alienation, writing explicitly in her letters that she identified with Helga's racial ambivalence.

To some extent, because of this background, Larsen felt she was more qualified to write about mulattoes than white writers were. Having been negatively "affected," according to contemporary Jessie Fauset, by portraits of mulattoes in precursory American fiction such as T. S. Stribling's *Birthright* (1922), Larsen set out, along with Fauset and Walter White, to challenge the prevailing conventions and thereby inscribe black difference. Through a fusion of autobiography and fiction, Larsen explores the psychological effects of racial dualism and marginality on a black bourgeois class, especially on its women. Both *Quicksand* and *Passing* contrast the black and white worlds within which her women protagonists search for individuality and freedom from racial and gender oppression in the face of a fragmented and often hostile environment. Thus, seen against the backdrop of respectable society, are the horrors of hatred, disloyalty, jealousy, greed, sexual promiscuity, and murder, a far cry from the preoccupation with "refined" upper middle class values that many critics have read into her novels and also from the traditional mulatto narratives that treat such horrors as the effects of an admixture of "black" and "white" blood.

In her novels, Larsen, like Fauset, satirizes the middle class and finds in it a correlation with the concept of passing, for characteristic of the members of such a class is their propensity for behaving in ways designed to disguise the truth. Also like Fauset, she uses the tragic mulatto and passing as metaphor. That is to say, appearance vs. reality, marginality, and entrapment, all intrinsic to the figure of the mulatto, are consonant with the strategies she employs in structuring her novels and with their content. Larsen and Fauset are worth comparing because of the similarities in the strategies they use to politicize issues of color, class, and gender and because of the shared subversive aspects of their work.

In *Quicksand* Larsen daringly raises questions about marriage and motherhood; these become central themes in *Passing*. In the former, the strain of having too many babies and bringing them into a world hostile to blacks causes Helga to sigh with relief over the death of her newborn infant; in the latter, Clare and Irene declare openly that being a mother is cruel and that children aren't everything. Further, both novels make central the complexities of female desire. Helga's feelings of lust, which are normally the exclusive privilege of men, prompt her to marry a man she does not love and to continue during her marriage to ignore "her first disgust at the odor of sweat and stale garments" and wait eagerly for "night ... at the end of every day. Emotional, palpitating, amorous, all that was living in her sprang like rank weeds at the tingling thought of night, with a vitality so strong that it devoured all shoots of reason."

In *Passing* Larsen concerns herself with exploring the causes of women's sexual reticence, which adds another dimension to psychological passing. Irene Redfield's references to "ideas about sex" as "queer ideas about things" and "dreadful jokes" indicate her discomfort in broaching the subject of sexuality. An attempted conversation about sex with her husband, Brian, makes clear that while it is "necessary education" for males, it is a taboo subject for females. Irene, therefore "passes" as a lady by keeping silent about topics deemed unladylike. The consequences of her repression, however, prove deadly: "She wanted ... to shock people, to hurt them, to make them notice her, to be aware of her suffering," and at the end of the novel there is strong evidence of her pushing Clare to her death. Considered by many critics to be melodramatic, this ending nevertheless is grounded in the reality that violence to the self or others is a consequence of fear and repression. Moreover, Irene shows no signs of remorse for her hand in Clare's death; in fact, a "sob of thankfulness . . . rose in her throat" at the news that Clare had died "instantly." That her female character is able to punish with impunity is not only a bold stroke for Larsen but also a clear revision of stereotypical mulatto tales and portraits of women.

Nella Larsen showed promise of becoming one of the major figures of the Harlem Renaissance but she never completed a third book. Scholars have long speculated about why she stopped writing and eventually dropped out of sight. Some say that an accusation of plagiarism was partially responsible, even though she was exonerated. Others say it was the failure of her marriage to Imes. Whatever the reason, Larsen returned to the occupation of nursing and worked at several New York City hospitals until her death in 1964. Although she wrote only two novels, her legacy is not slight, for her writings helped to shape the literature of the Harlem Renaissance and, more important, a tradition of black women writers as well.

—Jacquelyn Y. McLendon

LAURA. *See* **ROBINSON, Mary (Darby).**

LAURA MARIA. *See* **ROBINSON, Mary (Darby).**

LAURENCE, (Jean) Margaret (Wemyss)

Nationality: Canadian. **Born:** Neepawa, Manitoba, 18 July 1926. **Education:** University of Manitoba, B.A. 1947. **Family:** Married John Fergus Laurence in 1947 (divorced 1969); one son, one daughter. **Career:** Reporter with *Winnipeg Citizen;* writer-in-residence, University of Toronto, 1969-79, and University of Western Ontario, 1973; writer-in-residence, 1974, then chancellor, 1981-83, Trent University, Peterboro, Ontario. **Member:** Royal Society of Canada. **Awards:** Beta Sigma Phi First Novel award, 1961; University of Western Ontario President's Medal, 1961, 1962, 1964; Governor General's Literary Award in fiction, 1967, for *A Jest of God;* Companion of Order of Canada, 1971; Moulson Prize, 1975; B'nai Brith award, 1976; Periodical Distributors award, 1977; City of Toronto award, 1978; Canadian Booksellers Association Writer of the Year award, 1981; Banff Centre award, 1983; honorary degrees from numerous universities. **Died:** Lakefield, Ontario, 5 January 1987.

Publications

Novels

This Side Jordan. New York, St. Martin's Press, 1960.
The Stone Angel. New York, Knopf, 1964.
A Jest of God. New York, Knopf, 1966; as *Rachel, Rachel,* Popular Library, 1968; as *Now I Lay Me Down,* Panther, 1968.
The Fire-Dwellers. New York, Knopf, 1969.
The Diviners. New York, Knopf, 1974.

Short Stories

The Tomorrow-Tamer and Other Stories. New York, Knopf, 1964.
A Bird in the House. New York, Knopf, 1970.
Heart of a Stranger. Toronto, McClelland & Stewart, 1976; New York, Lippincott, 1977.

For Children

Jason's Quest. New York, Knopf, 1970.
Six Darn Cows. Lorimer, 1979.
The Olden Days Coat. Toronto, McClelland & Stewart, 1979.
The Christmas Birthday Story. New York, Knopf, 1980.

Autobiography

The Prophet's Camel Bell. London, Macmillan, 1963; as *New Wind in a Dry Land,* New York, Knopf, 1964.
Dance on the Earth: A Memoir. Toronto, McClelland & Stewart, 1989.

Other

Long Drums and Cannons: Nigerian Dramatists and Novelists 1952-1966. New York, Macmillan, 1968.

Editor, *A Tree for Poverty.* Nairobi, Eagle Press, 1954.

*

Media Adaptations: *Rachel, Rachel* (film adaptation of *The Jest of God*), 1968.

Bibliography: "Margaret Laurence: An Annotated Bibliography" by Susan J. Warwick, in *the Annotated Bibliography of Canada's Major Authors,* edited by Robert Lecker and Jack David, Downsview, Ontario, ECW, 1979.

Critical Studies: *Margaret Laurence* by Clara Thomas, Toronto, McClelland & Stewart, 1969, and her *The Manawaka World of Margaret Laurence,* Toronto, McClellan & Stewart, 1975; *Three Voices: The Lives of Margaret Laurence, Gabrielle Rosy, and Frederick Philip* by Joan Hind-Smith, Irwin, 1975; "The Wild Garden and the Manawaka World" by Clara Thomas, in *Modern Fiction Studies* (Purdue, Indiana), autumn 1976; *Margaret Laurence: The Writer and Her Critics* edited by William H. New, Toronto, McGraw-Hill Ryerson, 1977; *A Place to Stand On: Essays by and about Margaret Laurence* edited by George Woodcock, Edmonton, NeWest, 1983; "Margaret Laurence: Prairie, Ancestors, Woman" by Anne Burke, in *Cross-Canada Writers' Quarterly,* 9(2), 1987; *Critical Approaches to the Fiction of Margaret Laurence* edited by Colin Nicholson, London, Macmillan, 1990; *Margaret Laurence: The Long Journey Home* by Patricia Morley, Kingston, McGill-Queens, 1991.

* * *

Margaret Laurence is perhaps best known for her five books set in "Manawaka," a fictional town based on her childhood home of Neepawa, Manitoba. However, as critic Patricia Morley cogently argues in *Margaret Laurence: The Long Journey Home,* Laurence's Manawaka fiction is a continuation of ideas and beliefs first explored in her writings set in Africa. After writing poetry and short stories for her university's literary magazine *Vox,* Laurence launched her literary career by writing about her experiences in Africa, where her awareness of the dynamics of imperialism and colonialism deepened her beliefs about the need for social justice held since childhood. After leaving Africa and starting her Manawaka fiction, Laurence began to see women's liberation, anticolonialism, and Canada' search for national identity as interrelated political, cultural, and historical moments. Within her Manawaka fiction, feminism, nationalism, and pacifism intersect with her anti-imperial and anti-colonial beliefs, suggesting not only that fiction and history are intertwined, but also that literature can provide readers with the means to discover or create their own identities.

Laurence applies this belief not only to her fiction written for adult audiences, but also to her children's books. For example, in *The Christmas Birthday Story,* Laurence rewrites or subverts dominate biblical interpretation by suggesting that Mary and Joseph would be happy to have either a girl or a boy, that Christ could just as easily have been female as male. Many critics underscore how Laurence subverts dominant biblical stories as well as literary plot conventions, such as the quest, by inserting female protagonists as central to such stories. Moreover, Laurence writes against the grain of social stereotypes, such as the belief that (white) women are less sensually and sexually inclined than are men. Many of her female characters overtly enjoy their sexuality, and heterosexuality is not the only arena for women's sexual self-expression, as suggested by the lesbian character Calla in *A Jest of God.* Laurence's Manawaka novels encompass female representatives of different generations, classes, and races in order to explore women's various material and psychological realities across the last century.

Thus stories, be they historical, fictional, or anthropological, serve as models by which we live and plan our futures but also as the lenses through which we (re)interpert the past. Fiction functions for Laurence much like the river that flows two ways in *The Diviners:* our understandings of our private personal histories and broader social histories continuously ebb and flow. In other words, our comprehension of the past and our visions of the future are in a continuous state of flux in that private and public histories are always being reinterpreted, rerepresented. Thus, although Laurence's female protagonists find themselves caught in different but related webs of stifling social conventions because they are women and because they are white, they all also come to modify or subvert those conventions to suit their own needs and desires.

Laurence's approach not only allows for subverting and rewriting dominant beliefs and conventions, but also hints at the ways in which writing and communication are political acts. Literature, for Laurence, is not only social or cultural, but also political and historical. Laurence's female protagonists' individual quests for a sense of self and for spiritual, psychic, and political freedom have larger political and social implications. Laurence's fiction connects family politics and socially constructed gender roles to Canada's national politics, both as a former British colony and as a nation built on racial distinctions and hierarchies. Central to the individual heroines' quests and to the implied broader cultural quest is the need for communication and for language(s) that can allow the many different facets of human potential to blossom.

Language and form are therefore central to Laurence's writing. Her novels experiment with dialects that delineate class, education, racial, and ethnic differences. In addition, some of Laurence's overtly sexual language has been controversial, leading some to call for books such as *The Diviners* to be banned from high school libraries due to explicit sexual language or content. Laurence creates linguistic nuances between young and old, anglophone and allophone, lower class and upper class, Native and those of European descent. Moreover, Laurence mixes genres (e.g. autobiography, short story, novel), and time and place (e.g., though memory and movie-like sequences). By creating, in her Manawaka fiction, an arena for multiple and conflicting voices, Laurence implicitly calls for a more pluralistic understanding of spirituality, politics, history, and individual and collective identities. By subverting linear time, genre boundaries, and plot conventions, Laurence points to the need for creating new and different forms of communication as simultaneous to the need for new identities and ways of categorizing the self. Her fiction suggests that categories of identity such as femininity are socially constructed, but never stable, static, or completely determined.

Thus several themes emerge from Margaret Laurence's exploration of female or feminine subjectivity in her Manawaka fiction:

that it is necessary to pursue the search for spiritual and psychological freedom in the face of alienation; how the quest for one's identity is connected to finding or creating an adequate language; that we need to recognize and accept differences, both in terms of an individual's many selves and in terms of accepting Otherness or outsiders; and, finally, a call to understand our collective and individual pasts, recognizing that this understanding can never be complete as it is always in the process of becoming.

—Vivian May

LAVIN, Mary

Nationality: British. **Born:** East Walpole, Massachusetts, 11 June 1912; immigrated to Ireland. **Education:** Attended Loreto Convent, Dublin; University College, Dublin, B.A. (with honors) 1934; National University of Ireland, M.A. (first-class honors), 1938. **Family:** Married 1) the lawyer William Walsh in 1942 (died 1954), three daughters; 2) Michael MacDonald Scott in 1969. **Career:** Writer. Worked as a farmer; teacher of French, Loreto Convent school, Dublin. **Awards:** James Tait Black Prize, 1944, for *Tales from Bective Bridge;* Guggenheim fellowships, 1959, 1961, 1962; Katherine Mansfield-Melton Prize, 1962, for *The Great Wave and Other Stories;* Ella Lyman Cabot fellowship, 1969; Boston Eire Society Gold Medal, 1974; Gregory Medal, 1974; American Irish Foundation award, 1979; Allied Irish Bank award, 1981. D.Litt: National University of Ireland, 1968. **Member:** Irish Academy of Letters (president 1971-73). **Died:** In Dublin, 26 March 1996.

Publications

Novels

The House in Clewe Street (first published as "Gabriel Galloway" in *Atlantic Monthly,* 1944-45). Boston, Little Brown, 1945.
Mary O'Grady. Boston, Little Brown, 1950.

Short Stories

Tales from Bective Bridge. Boston, Little Brown, 1942; revised edition, Poolbeg, 1978.
The Long Ago and Other Stories. London, M. Joseph, 1944.
The Becker Wives and Other Stories. London, M. Joseph, 1946; as *At Sallygap and Other Stories,* Boston, Little Brown, 1947.
A Single Lady and Other Stories. London, M. Joseph, 1951.
The Patriot Sun and Other Stories. London, M. Joseph, 1956.
Selected Stories. New York and London, Macmillan, 1959.
The Great Wave and Other Stories (first published in *New Yorker*). New York and London, Macmillan, 1961.
The Stories of Mary Lavin. London, Constable, 3 vols., 1964-85.
In the Middle of the Field and Other Stories. London, Constable, 1967; New York, Macmillan, 1969.
Happiness and Other Stories. London, Constable, 1969; Boston, Houghton, 1970.
Collected Stories. Boston, Houghton, 1971.
A Memory and Other Stories. London, Constable, 1972; Boston, Houghton, 1973.
The Shrine and Other Stories. Boston, Houghton, 1977.
Mary Lavin: Selected Stories. London and New York, Penguin, 1981.
A Family Likeness. London, Constable, 1985.
In a Cafe, edited by E. Peavy Lavin Walsh. Dublin, Townhouse, 1995.

For Children

A Likely Story. New York and London, Macmillan, 1957.
The Second-Best Children in the World. Boston, Houghton, 1972.

*

Critical Studies: *Mary Lavin* by Zack Bowen, Lewisburg, Pennsylvania, Bucknell University Press, 1975; *Mary Lavin* by Richard F. Peterson, New York, Twayne, 1978; *Mary Lavin, Quiet Rebel: A Study of Her Short Stories* by Angeline A. Kelly, New York, Barnes & Noble, 1980; "Mary Lavin, Elizabeth Bowen, and a New Generation: The Irish Short Story at Midcentury" by Janet Egleson Dunleavy, in *The Irish Short Story: A Critical History,* edited by James F. Kilroy, Boston, Twayne, 1984; interview in *Irish Women Writers: An Uncharted Tradition* by Ann Owens Weekes, Lexington, University Press of Kentucky, 1990; "Sacrificial Women in Short Stories by Mary Lavin and Edna O'Brien" by Jeanette Roberts Shumaker, in *Studies in Short Fiction,* 32, spring 1995.

* * *

Mary Lavin is often placed in the company of the great Irish short story writers known as "the three O's": Liam O'Flaherty, Frank O'Connor, and Sean O'Faolain. Unlike them, however, Lavin didn't write about political issues; rather, her fiction focuses on women's lives, domestic tragedy, affairs of the heart. Although born in Massachusetts in 1912, Lavin and her Irish-born parents returned to Ireland when she was nine, and her fiction details the silently desperate lives of the Irish middle class; perhaps it is this dual sensibility that makes her stories both specifically grounded in Ireland, yet universal.

At the National University of Ireland Lavin wrote her Master's thesis on Jane Austen's novels, and like Austen, her stories are replete with irony so subtle that, as A.A. Kelly has noted, she is one of the "few leading Irish writers whose work was never banned by the Censorship Board." Lavin wrote her first short story on the back of a draft of her Ph.D. thesis on Virginia Woolf, a thesis she never completed. *Tales from Bective Bridge,* her first short story collection, was published in 1942, the same year she married William Walsh, a classmate at the University College in Dublin. Two daughters, born in 1943 and 1945, could have taken her away from writing. Yet her oldest daughter claims that Lavin always wrote in the company of her daughters rather than in a private study. And she was prolific, writing two novels, *Mary O'Grady* and *The House on Clewe Street,* and publishing four short fiction collections between 1944 and 1951. Her third daughter was born in 1953 and her husband died a year later. In 1969 she married an old school friend, Michael Scott, who had been a priest since 1940. He left the church to marry Lavin.

Although some critics denounce her characters as "shopkeepers, schoolgirls and widows," most recognize Lavin's style: small details that slowly peel away reality's shell to reveal a character's denials, pains, and failures. Her early stories often examine how misunderstanding and miscommunication, as well as the rules and traps of family, religion, and society, can come between two people.

However, Lavin refuses to place all the blame on social or outside forces; rather she recognizes the individual's complicity in her own tragic existences. In "A Nun's Mother," a woman's fears unconsciously push her daughter, Angela, into the convent. Angela's mother secretly meditates on the honor she will have as a nun's mother, and expresses relief at not having to be a grandmother, while the daughter, unable to communicate with her mother, nevertheless absorbs her fears and enters the convent without a true vocation.

In "Sarah," the sexually free woman is ostensibly punished because she refuses to follow convention, but, like everyone else in the story, she is punished because she is unable to love. After Sarah becomes pregnant yet another time with a married man's baby, the priest coerces her brothers into kicking her out of the house; meanwhile her lover's wife, Mrs. Kedrigan, humiliates the adulterers, maintaining her respectability in the community by viciously seeking revenge. The tragedy of the story is that no one—Sarah, the married couple, Sarah's brothers, or the priest—has felt love. It is this story that most represents Lavin's early fiction: she is a moralist speaking out against denial, conformity and hypocrisy, and against using the institutions of the church or marriage as a crutch. For Lavin, in an ideal world, spirituality, love, and communion would triumph over conformity, hypocrisy and revenge.

The stories written in the 1950s and '60s are known collectively as the "widow stories" because of a common heroine, the autobiographical Vera. Although Vera begins as an emotionally isolated, grieving widow, she gradually gains the strong sense of self often denied Lavin's younger heroines. In many of the widow stories death is ultimately a positive force. Perhaps it is Lavin's own experiences as a widow that allows her fictional widow a release from unhappiness, a release denied many of her earlier characters. "In a Cafe" and "Happiness" frame a widow's life from the start of her widowhood till her death. In the first story, the widow, this time named Mary, has lunch with a younger widow, a woman who recognizes that she is still desirable, while Mary, being older and past childbearing age, is not. Mary gets angry at this and wallows in her bitterness. Ironically, the reader sees that her widowhood frees her, permitting her to approach men, and to try new restaurants, like the cafe. Almost humiliating herself by begging a stranger to help ease her loneliness, she suddenly realizes that it is Richard himself, her husband, that she misses, not simply the stability of marriage. The epiphany frees her, and she is no longer trapped by an internalization of society's definition of a widow. This realization that her love for Richard did not die with him allows her to assert her identity outside the roles of wife and mother and hence begin a new life.

"Happiness" brings us to the death of the widow figure. As she lies dying, the widow tries to define happiness for her daughters and Father Hugh, a family friend. She realizes that happiness is that which cannot be altered by the tragedies of life. Like her love for her husband, happiness is inviolate. As in "In a Cafe," love survives death and tragedy. In both stories, love is both indestructible and transformative.

Up until her death in 1996, like the subject of her unfinished Ph.D. thesis Lavin's fictional motto was: "Examine for a moment an ordinary mind on an ordinary day." In a 1980 interview, she, like many feminist-thinking women of her generation, denied that she was a "feminist." However, her works of short fiction from the 1940s to her last published short story, which appeared in the *New Yorker* in 1976, concern the lives of ordinary women: their relationships to each other, to men, to society, and to themselves. Through these themes, Mary Lavin directly addresses several central feminist concerns.

—Stacey Donohue

Le GUIN, Ursula K(roeber)

Nationality: American. **Born:** Berkeley, California, 21 October 1929; daughter of anthropologist Alfred L. Kroeber and writer Theodora Kroeber. **Education:** Radcliffe College, Cambridge, Massachusetts, B.A. 1951 (Phi Beta Kappa); Columbia University, New York (Faculty fellow, 1952; Fulbright fellow, 1953), M.A. 1952. **Family:** Married the historian Charles A. Le Guin in 1953; two daughters and one son. **Career:** Instructor in French, Mercer University, Macon, Georgia, 1954, and University of Idaho, Moscow, 1956; department secretary, Emory University, Atlanta, 1955; has taught writing workshops at Pacific University, Forest Grove, Oregon, 1971, University of Washington, Seattle, 1971-73, Portland State University, Oregon, 1974, 1977, 1979, in Melbourne, Australia, 1975, at the University of Reading, England, 1976, Indiana Writers Conference, Bloomington, 1978, 1983, and University of California, San Diego, 1979. **Awards:** *Boston Globe/Horn Book* award 1968, for *A Wizard of Earthsea;* Nebula awards, 1969, 1975 (twice), 1990; Hugo awards, 1969, 1973, for *The Word for World Is Forest,* 1974, for "The Ones Who Walked away from Omelas," 1975, for *The Dispossessed,* 1988, for "Bufallo Gals"; National Book award 1972, for *The Farthest Shore:* Jupiter award, 1974 (twice), 1976; World Science Fiction Convention guest of honor, Melbourne, Australia, 1975; Gandalf award, 1979; University of Oregon Distinguished Service award, 1981; *Locus* award, 1973 for *The Lathe of Heaven,* 1984, for *The Compass Rose,* 1995, for "Forgiveness Day"; Janet Heidinger Kafka award, 1986; Pushcart Prize, 1986, for *Always Coming Home;* American Academy and Institute of Arts and Letters Harold D. Vursell award, 1991; James Tiptree Jr. award, 1995, for "The Matter of Seggri"; Theodore Sturgeon award, 1995, for "Forgiveness Day." Honorary degrees: Bucknell University, 1978; Lawrence University; University of Oregon; Western Oregon State; Lewis & Clark College, 1983; Occidental College, 1985; Emory University; Kenyon College; Portland State University. **Agent:** Virginia Kidd, P.O. Box 278, Milford, Pennsylvania 18337, U.S.A.

Publications

Novels

Rocannon's World. New York, Ace, 1966; London, Tandem, 1972.
Planet of Exile. New York, Ace, 1966; London, Tandem, 1972.
City of Illusion. New York, Ace, 1967; London, Gollancz, 1971.
The Left Hand of Darkness. New York, Walker, and London, Macdonald, 1969.
The Lathe of Heaven. New York, Scribner, 1971; London, Gollancz, 1972.

The Word for World Is Forest, in *Again, Dangerous Visions,* edited by Harlan Ellison. New York, Doubleday, 1972; London, Millington, 1976; published separately, New York, Berkley, 1972; London, Gollancz, 1977.
The Dispossessed: An Ambiguous Utopia. New York, Harper & Row, and London, Gollancz, 1974.
Very Far Away from Anywhere Else. New York, Atheneum, 1976; as *A Very Long Way from Anywhere Else,* London, Gollancz, 1976.
The Eye of the Heron, in *Millennial Women,* edited by Virginia Kidd. New York, Delacorte, 1978; published separately, London, Gollancz, 1982; New York, Harper & Row, 1983.
Malafrena. New York, Berkeley, 1979; London, Gollancz, 1980.
Always Coming Home (includes audio tape, music by Tod Barton). New York, Harper & Row, 1985; London, Gollancz, 1986.
The Earthsea Quartet. London, Penguin, 1993.
A Wizard of Earthsea. Berkeley, California, Parnassus Press, 1968; London, Gollancz, 1971.
The Tombs of Atuan. New York, Atheneum, 1971, London, Gollancz, 1972.
The Farthest Shore. New York, Atheneum, 1972; London, Gollancz, 1973.
Tehanu: The Last Book of Earthsea. New York, Atheneum, and London, Gollancz, 1990.

Short Stories

The Wind's Twelve Quarters. New York, Harper & Row, 1975; London, Gollancz, 1976.
Orsinian Tales. New York, Harper & Row, 1976; London, Gollancz, 1977.
The Water Is Wide. Portland, Oregon, Pendragon Press, 1976.
Gwilan's Harp. Northridge, California, Lord John Press, 1981.
The Compass Rose. Portland, Oregon, Pendragon Press, 1982; London, Gollancz, 1983.
The Adventure of Cobbler's Rune. New Castle, Virginia, Cheap Street, 1982.
The Visionary: The Life Story of Flicker of the Serpentine of Telina-Na, bound with *Wonders Hidden,* by Scott Russell Sanders. Santa Barbara, California, Capra Press, 1984.
Buffalo Gals and Other Animal Presences. Santa Barbara, California, Capra Press, 1987; London, Gollancz, 1990.
The New Atlantis, bound with *The Return from Rainbow Bridge,* by Kim Stanley Robinson. New York, Tor, 1989.
Searoad: Chronicles of Klatsand. New York, HarperCollins, 1991; London, Gollancz, 1992.
Nine Lives. Eugene, Oregon, Pulphouse, 1992.
The Ones Who Walk away from Omelas. Mankato, Minnesota, Creative Education, 1993.
A Fisherman of the Inland Sea. Norwalk, Connecticut, Easton Press, 1994.
Buffalo Gals, Won't You Come out Tonight. San Francisco, Pomegranate, 1994.
Four Ways to Forgiveness. New York, HarperPrism, 1995.
Unlocking the Air and Other Stories. New York, HarperCollins, 1996.

Plays

No Use to Talk to Me, in *The Altered Eye,* edited by Lee Harding. Melbourne, Norstrilia Press, 1976; New York, Berkeley, 1978.
King Dog, with *Dostoevsky,* by Raymond Carver and Tess Gallagher. Santa Barbara, California, Capra Press, 1985.

Screenplays: *King Dog,* 1985.

Poetry

Wild Angels. Santa Barbara, California, Capra Press, 1975.
Tillai and Tylissos, with Theodora K. Kroeber. N.p., Red Bull Press, 1979.
Torrey Pines Reserve. Northridge, California, Lord John Press, 1980.
Hard Words and Other Poems. New York, Harper & Row, 1981.
In the Red Zone, illustrations by Henk Pander. Northridge, California, Lord John Press, 1983.
Wild Oats and Fireweed. New York, Harper & Row, 1988.
Blue Moon over Thurman Street, photographs by Roger Dorband. Portland, Oregon, NewSage Press, 1993.
Going out with Peacocks and Other Poems. New York, HarperPerennial, 1994.

Literary Criticism

The Language of the Night: Essays on Fantasy and Science Fiction, edited by Susan Wood. New York, Putnam, 1979; revised edition, edited by Le Guin, London, Women's Press, 1989; New York, HarperCollins, 1992.
Myth and Archetype in Science Fiction. Eugene, Oregon, Pulphouse, 1991.

Essays

From Elfland to Poughkeepsie (lecture). Portland, Oregon, Pendragon Press, 1973.
Dreams Must Explain Themselves. New York, Algol Press, 1975.
Dancing at the Edge of the World: Thoughts on Words, Women, Places. New York, Grove Press, and London, Gollancz, 1989.

For Children

Leese Webster. New York, Atheneum, 1979; London, Gollancz, 1981.
Cobbler's Rune. New Castle, Virginia, Cheap Street, 1983.
Solomon Leviathan's 931st Trip around the World. New Castle, Virginia, Cheap Street, 1983.
The Beginning Place. New York, Harper & Row, 1980; as *Threshold,* London, Gollancz, 1980.
Catwings. New York, Orchard, 1988.
A Visit from Dr. Katz. New York, Atheneum, 1988; as *Dr. Katz,* London, Collins, 1988.
Catwings Return. New York, Orchard, 1989.
Fire and Stone. New York, Atheneum, 1989.
A Ride on the Red Mare's Back. New York, Orchard, 1992.
Fish Soup. New York and London, Atheneum, 1992.
Wonderful Alexander and the Catwings. New York, Orchard, 1994.

Other

The Way of the Water's Going, photographs by Ernest Waugh and Alan Nicholson. New York, Harper & Row, 1989.
Talk about Writing. Eugene, Oregon, Pulphouse, 1991.

Findings. Browerville, Minnesota, Oxhead Press, 1992.
Earthsea Revisioned (lecture). Cambridge, Children's Literature New England/Green Bay, 1993.

Editor, *Nebula Award Stories 11.* London, Gollancz, 1976; New York, Harper & Row, 1977.
Editor, with Virginia Kidd, *Interfaces.* New York, Ace, 1980.
Editor, with Virginia Kidd, *Edges: 13 New Tales from the Borderlands of the Imagination.* New York, Pocket Books, 1980.
Editor, with Brian Atteberg, *The Norton Book of Science Fiction: North American Science Fiction, 1960-1990.* New York and London, Norton, 1993.

Recording: *The Ones Who Walk away from Omelas,* Alternate World Recording, 1976.

*

Media Adaptations: *The Word for World Is Forest* (sound recording), 1968; *The Lathe of Heaven* (teleplay), 1979; *The Tombs of Atuan* (filmstrip), 1980; *The Earthsea Trilogy* (abridged sound recording), 1981; *The Ones Who Walk away from Omelas* (musical drama with dance; produced Portland, 1981).

Bibliography: *Ursula K. Le Guin: A Primary and Secondary Bibliography* by Elizabeth Cummins Cogell, Boston, G.K. Hall, 1983; *Ursula K. Le Guin: A Primary Bibliography* by David S. Bratman, n.p., 1995.

Manuscript Collection: University of Oregon Library, Eugene.

Critical Studies: *The Farthest Shores of Ursula K. Le Guin* by George Edgar Slusser, San Bernardino, California, Borgo Press, 1976; "Ursula Le Guin Issue" of *Science-Fiction Studies* (Terre Haute, Indiana), March 1976; *Ursula Le Guin* by Joseph D. Olander and Martin H. Greenberg, New York, Taplinger, and Edinburgh, Harris, 1979; *Ursula K. Le Guin: Voyager to Inner Lands and to Outer Space* edited by Joseph W. De Bolt, Port Washington, New York, Kennikat Press, 1979; *Ursula K. Le Guin* by Barbara J. Bucknall, New York, Ungar, 1981; *Approaches to the Fiction of Ursula K. Le Guin* by James Bittner, Ann Arbor, Michigan, UMI Research Press, and Epping, Essex, Bowker, 1984; *Ursula Le Guin* by Charlotte Spivack, Boston, Twayne, 1984; *Ursula K. Le Guin* edited by Harold Bloom, New York, Chelsea, 1986; "Ursula K. Le Guin" (interview) in *Contemporary Authors New Revisions,* 32, Detroit, Gale, 1989; *Understanding Ursula K. Le Guin* by Elizabeth Cummins Cogell, Columbia, University of South Carolina Press, 1990; *Radical Imagination: Feminist Conceptions of the Future in Ursula Le Guin, Marge Piercy, and Sally Miller Gearhart,* New York, P. Lang, 1991; "Places Where a Woman Could Talk: Ursula K. Le Guin and the Feminist Linguistic Utopia" by Kristine J. Anderson, in *Women and Language,* spring 1992; "Feminist Sci-Fi: a Brave New World" by Julie Phillips, in *Ms.,* 1994.

* * *

Ursula K. Le Guin's work challenges critics and readers to examine society; as she has stated, "one of the essential functions of science fiction ...[is] question-asking." Her books are "thought-experiments" meant to engage readers in "reversals of a habitual way of thinking" by investigating the role of gender, sexuality, and economic structures in our society through imagined worlds. Le Guin is an important cross-over writer because she is both a popular success and a critical success. She consistently downplays the distinctions between literary and popular fiction. As she says in her introduction to *Dancing at the Edge of the World: Thoughts on Words, Women, Places,* she is not able "to make distinctions between High art and low (*sic*) stuff, between being a woman and being a feminist, and so on"; her goal, rather, is "to subvert as much as possible without hurting anybody's feelings."

Both of Le Guin's parents' own work as writers influenced her. Her father, Alfred L. Kroeber, was a noted anthropologist known for his influential studies of California's Native American cultures. Her mother, Theodora Kroeber Quinn, was educated as a psychologist and began her writing career in her 50s. Le Guin addresses her mother's role in the development of both her own writing and her feminist outlook in several essays in *Dancing on the Edge of the World.* Quinn's best-known book was *Ishi in Two Worlds* (1961), the biography of a yahi Indian who entered white California society in 1911 as the last of his people. Like Le Guin's later fictional heroes, Ishi negotiated between two radically different worlds, two sets of values, and two ways of living. Le Guin credits her mother with being a powerful storyteller and with, telling her "to write about women, not men, years before I (the 'women's libber') was able to do so."

From Le Guin's earliest novels—five "Hainish" novels and *The Lathe of Heaven*—her exposure to both anthropology and varied cultures informs her fiction. She has created an anthropology of the future, imagining whole cultural systems and conflicts. In the "Hainish" novels—*Rocannon's World, Planet of Exile, City of Illusions, The Left Hand of Darkness,* and *The Word for World Is Forest*—Le Guin writes about actual and emotional journeys her protagonists make when they venture into cultures and communities strikingly different from their own. The Hainish are a people from the planet Hain who planted themselves across all the livable planets of our part of the Universe. Through adaptation, chance, and planetary environment, they develop into distinct and diverse cultures. According to critic Charlotte Spivack, "most of Le Guin's protagonists assume the role of anthropologist if not by profession then by circumstance." These "anthropologist" heroes journey from planet to planet, from society to society, exposing each culture's assumptions and habits of thought.

By the mid-1970s, *The Left Hand of Darkness* and *The Dispossessed* had secured Le Guin's reputation among readers and academic literary critics; as Spivack states, Le Guin "escaped the science-fiction ghetto and entered the realm of serious academic consideration." With these two novels Le Guin intensifies her investigation of gender roles and cultural attitudes toward sexuality, focusing on the consequences of sexist gender roles, male dominance, and economic and political oppression. She imagines contrasting worlds: one familiar and fraught with violence and inequality; one unfamiliar, a place of relative peace and equality. This juxtaposition of two possible worlds—usually one violent, hierarchical, and greed-centered and the other self-sufficient, economically small-scale, and build on interdependence—occurs frequently in her works. Some critics resolve the dualities and oppositions present in Le Guin's work into a unity defined by the balance of those tensions—ideas derived from the Taoist philosophy of balanced opposites, the *yin-yang*. These critics see the exploration of androgyny in *The Left Hand of Darkness* as an extension of this larger theme. However, feminist critics such as Pamela Annas have seen androgyny as the center of the novel because it shows how crucial cultural constructions of male/female are to a sexist world. Readers learn, as the male Genly learns from the androgynous Estraven, to ask if they "fit" into culturally defined gender roles. According to Annas, *The Left Hand of Darkness* is the "story of Genly's gradual coming to consciousness, his own conceptual transcendence of dualism and sexual polarization."

Like *The Left Hand of Darkness, The Dispossessed* (1974) also explores the social consequences of gender roles. On the planet Urras gender roles are rigid: women are excluded from property ownership and education, and are confined to the home and child-rearing. This world is on the brink of war and its governments constantly use violent methods of repression. On Anarres, women have equal access to education, there is no private property, and parental roles are shared equally and communally. In this way *The Dispossessed* answers *The Left Hand of Darkness,* in which androgyny only exists in a people biologically different from humans. In her later novel, Le Guin imagines the potentially more radical possibility of gender equality given our biology. Another consequence of the biological androgyny of the Gethenians in *The Left Hand of Darkness* is the obliteration of same-sex relationships. This issue, too, is revisited in *The Dispossessed.* On the planet Anarres bisexuality, homosexuality, and heterosexuality are presented as alternatives without one being compulsory. Still, Le Guin's treatment of same-sex relationships is cursory, limited to the protagonist Shevek's brief affair with his gay friend Bedap; she spends greater effort developing the heterosexual partnership between Shevek and Takver. Whatever their degree, however, Le Guin's treatment of androgyny, gender roles, and sexuality in these two books would pave the way for an explosion of science fiction/fantasy books treating similar topics.

After the Hainish novels, Le Guin continued to be innovative in her world creation—from the "historical" 1979 novel *Malafrena,* which takes place in a mythical, early 19th-century European country, to *Always Coming Home.* This second novel, published in 1985, combines poetry, music (a cassette was included with the book), anthropologist's notes, legends, and stories of the Kesh, a group of people that inhabits a future California, after ecological disasters have fundamentally changed North America. Though in *Malafrena* and similar novels events and characters may exist in other time periods and in imaginary landscapes, they reflect the author's commitment to the present-day world. For instance, the plot of *The Word for World Is Forest* presents readers with a stark and explicit analogy to the Vietnam War, as well as commenting on attacks on rain forests and indigenous peoples in South America and Indonesia. In the novel, the colonizing Terrans violently react to the forest-dwelling Athsheans by a deforestation process rooted in economic greed and fear of an alien culture.

In addition to boundaries in time and space, Le Guin also crosses literary boundaries between juvenile and adult fiction by writing books that attract readers of many ages. Her *Earthsea Quartet,* often described as young-adult fiction, is considered by some to be among her greatest artistic achievements. The series, in which the protagonist is a young male wizard—magic is a male province—began in 1968 with the publication of *A Wizard of Earthsea,* followed in 1970 by *The Tombs of Atuan.* According to Spivack, "Earthsea is a convincingly authenticated world, drawn with a sure hand for fine detail. A mature narrative of growing up, a moral tale without a moral, a realistic depiction of a fantasy world." While the series temporarily ended in 1972 with *The Farthest Shore,* by 1990 Le Guin would return to Earthsea with a sequel entitled *Tehanu: The Last Book of Earthsea,* a novel inspired by some negative criticism by feminists and her own changes as a feminist writer. According to Julie Phillips in "Feminist Sci-Fi: a Brave New World," Le Guin changes her focus from wizards and male protagonists to "acknowledging motherhood and home as realms of heroines' powers and desires." The main characters of this last Earthsea novel are a young girl and an old woman, neither of whom are traditionally represented as heroes in works for either children or adults. Le Guin has continued to write works for children, providing much-needed alternatives to traditional, sexist fairy tales. Works like *Catwings* and *Catwings Return* evoke imaginary worlds: worlds at once fantastic—flying cats—and ethically compelling—the flying kittens are adopted by a girl and a boy who learn about love and care-taking.

In addition to her novels Le Guin has published numerous collections of short stories, poetry, and essays. While she has been continually praised for breaking ground for women in the male-dominated genre of science fiction, some have criticize her for being wedded to a liberal humanism, or rather, a masculinism masquerading as humanism by universalizing western, male, heterosexual experience as human experience. This kind of humanism has, according to some feminists, obscured the different presences and contributions of women, as well as the experiences of members of other cultures, lesbians, and gay men. Le Guin is most criticized by feminist critics for her reliance, especially in her early works, on male protagonists, male-centered civilizations, and the use of the pronoun "he" to describe the ostensibly androgynous inhabitants of the planet Gethen in *The Left Hand of Darkness.* Lesbian and gay critics have also noted that she has downplayed same-sex relationships and idealizing heterosexual partnerships. In answer to some of these criticisms, Le Guin has revised her former position that the pronoun "he" is neutral and that alternatives would "mangle English," as she once noted. She has also made increasing efforts to place women at the center of her imagined worlds and novels.

Le Guin continues to offer her readers new visions of the future and of society. Her writings in *Dancing at the Edge of the World* address such varied subjects as menopause "On Becoming a Crone," women and writing, and reproductive rights. Her growing body of writing consistently reflects what she called, in a 1989 interview in *Contemporary Authors New Revisions,* the "process" of how she "learned to be a better feminist." Le Guin's development both as a writer and a feminist follows the changes and adjustments undergone by the North American feminist movement itself since the mid-1960s. Rather than seeking to edit or revise her earlier writings, she has chosen to see her previous work as manifestations of change in her own feminism. In the essay "Is Gender Necessary? Redux," Le Guin explains why she simply did not revise the essay—originally published in *Aurora,* a groundbreaking 1976 anthology of women's science fiction—to remove what would be seen in hindsight as embarrassing. In the "Redux" she does not rewrite the essay, but adds to it by interspersing her more recent thoughts and ideas: "It is rather in the feminist mode to let one's changes of mind, and the processes of change, stand as evidence—and perhaps remind people that minds that don't change are like clams that don't open." This commitment to change and constant reexamination may be Ursula K. Le Guin's greatest contribution to feminist writing.

—Nancy Jesser

LERNER, Gerda

Nationality: Austrian and American. **Born:** Vienna, 30 April 1920; immigrated to the United States 1939; naturalized 1943. **Education:** New School for Social Research, New York, B.A. 1963; Columbia University, New York, M.A. 1965, Ph.D. 1966. **Family:** Married the filmmaker Carl Lerner in 1941 (died 1973); one son and one daughter. **Career:** Professional writer and translator since 1941; lecturer and instructor, New School for Social Research, New York, 1963-65; assistant professor, 1965-67, associate professor of American history, 1967-68, Long Island University, Brooklyn; member of history faculty, 1968-80, director of graduate program in women's history, 1972-76, educational director, summer institutes in women's history, 1976, 1979, Sarah Lawrence College, Bronxville, New York; Robinson-Edwards professor of history, beginning 1980, director and codirector, graduate program in women's history, 1981-90, Alumni Research Foundation Senior Distinguished Research Professor, 1984-90, University of Wisconsin—Madison. Member, Columbia University seminars on American Civilization and Women and Society, both 1972; codirector, Fund for the Improvement of Secondary Education Grant for Promoting Black Women's History, 1980-83; project director, "Documenting the Midwest Origins of 20th-Century Feminism," 1990-93. Contributor of short stories, articles, and reviews to periodicals. **Awards:** Social Science Research Council research fellow, 1970-71; Emmanuel College Robert H. Lord Award, 1974; National Endowment for the Humanities fellow, 1976; Ford Foundation fellow, 1978-79; Lilly Foundation fellow, 1979; Berkshire Conference of Women Historians Special Book Award, 1980, for *The Majority Finds Its Past: Placing Women in History;* Guggenheim fellow, 1980-81; Organization of American Historians grant, 1980-83; American Association of University Women (AAUW) Educational Foundation Achievement Award, 1986; American Historical Association Joan Kelly Award, 1986, for *Woman and History;* Lucretia Mott Award, 1988; American Historical Association award, 1992; Kathë Leichter-Preis, Austrian State Prize for Women's History and the History of the Labor Movement, both 1995; Austrian Cross for Science and Art, 1996; recipient of ten honorary degrees from colleges and universities. **Member:** Organization of American Historians (president, 1981-82), American Historical Association, AAUW, American Studies Association, Authors League of America. **Address:** Department of History, University of Wisconsin, 3211 Humanities Building, 455 North Park Street, Madison, Wisconsin 53706, U.S.A. **Online Address:** glerner@facstaff.wisc.edu.

Publications

Novel

No Farewell. New York, Associated Authors, 1955.

History

The Grimké Sisters from South Carolina: Rebels against Slavery. Boston, Houghton Mifflin, 1967.

The Woman in American History (textbook). Reading, Massachusetts, Addison-Wesley, 1971.

Women Are History: A Bibliography in the History of American Women. New York, Sarah Lawrence College, 1975; 4th edition, with Marie Laberge, Madison, University of Wisconsin Press, 1986.

The Majority Finds Its Past: Placing Women in History. New York and London, Oxford University Press, 1979.

Teaching Women's History. Washington, D.C., American Historical Association, 1981.

Women and History, Volume 1: The Creation of Patriarchy [Volume 2: The Creation of Feminist Consciousness, from the Middle Ages to 1870]. New York and London, Oxford University Press, 2 vols., 1986-93.

Plays

Stage Plays: *Singing of Women* (musical), with Eve Merriam, 1956.

Screenplays: *Black like Me,* with Carl Lerner, based on book by John Howard Griffin. Walter Reade, 1964.

Autobiography

A Death of One's Own. New York, Simon & Schuster, 1978.

Other

Editor, *Black Women in White America: A Documentary History.* New York, Pantheon, 1972.

Editor, *The Female Experience: An American Documentary.* Indianapolis, Indiana, Bobbs-Merrill, 1976.

Recordings: *Dorthea Dix* (sound recording), Pacifica Tape Library, n.d.; *Elizabeth Cady Stanton and Susan B. Anthony* (sound recording), Pacifica Tape Library, n.d.

* * *

Gerda Lerner has been hailed as one of the pioneers in the growing field of women's history. Beginning in the mid-1960s, Lerner's research, combined with her commitment to organize programs designed to train future generations of feminist scholars, helped establish women's history as an essential component of contemporary history curriculums in colleges and universities both in the United States and abroad.

A native of Austria, Lerner fled Vienna in 1939 at the age of 18 to escape persecution by the Nazis. Settling in New York, she married, raised a family, and after teaching herself English, began writing. She published *No Farewell,* a novel, in 1955. The following year she would collaborate with Eve Merriam on a musical, *Singing of Women,* and in 1964 she completed the screenplay *Black like Me.* In 1959, when she was 39, Lerner resumed the formal education that had been cut short by the Nazis and entered New York's New School for Social Research as an undergraduate. Her love of history awakened, she received her B.A. in 1963 and entered the graduate program in history at Columbia University.

Lerner's battle to establish women's history as a legitimate field of study began during her student years at Columbia. Despite the skepticism of her advisors, she insisted on writing a women's history dissertation. Her dissertation, completed in 1966 and published a year later as *The Grimké Sisters from South Carolina,* demonstrated that Sarah and Angelina Grimké played a critical role in the early stages of the abolition movement and that the woman's rights movement had its roots in the fight against slavery.

As a professor at Sarah Lawrence College beginning in 1968, Lerner not only began and directed the first program to offer a graduate degree in women's history, but the books and articles she published during the 1960s and 1970s lay the foundation for the development of women's history as a recognized field of study. Committed to writing women's history in a way that recognized both the complexity of women's lives as well as the role that gender has played in important historical developments, Lerner made race and class analysis central to her scholarship. "The Lady and the Mill Girl," first published in 1969, underlined the importance of class differences in understanding the history of American women in the early nineteenth century. In 1972 Lerner published *Black Women in White America: A Documentary History,* a volume important to the growth of African American women's history. Lerner's success in collecting documents that many assumed had been lost proved that with persistence and ingenuity the long-suppressed history of African American women could be told. 1975's *The Majority Finds Its Past: Placing Women in History* outlined directions for research on women, while her *The Female Experience: An American Documentary,* published the following year, proposed new ways of periodizing history to better explain the contours of women's lives.

In 1980 Lerner moved to the University of Wisconsin—Madison, where she became the Robinson-Edwards Professor of history and started a graduate program in women's history. Her achievements in the field were recognized by her peers in 1981 when she was elected president of the Organization of American Historians. Lerner retired from the University of Wisconsin in 1990.

It was during the 1980s, while she was at Madison, that Lerner would embark on her most ambitious scholarly project. Moving away from the study of American women's history, she examined ancient history to ascertain the roots of women's oppression. As she argued in 1986's *The Creation of Patriarchy,* patriarchy was the oldest form of social domination; she illustrated this by tracing its development in Western Civilization over two millennia, an effort that earned her the American Historical Association's Joan Kelly Prize for the best book in women's history in 1986. The companion volume, *The Creation of Feminist Consciousness,* published in 1993, traced European and American women's attempts to know and tell their history from the middle ages to 1870.

Lerner has also worked to make women's history accessible to those outside academic circles. As the educational director for two summer institutes at Sarah Lawrence College in 1976 and 1979, she offered high school teachers and leaders of women's organizations training in women's history. The idea for a "Women's History Week," which has grown into "Women's History Month," originated at the institute for women leaders that met in the summer of 1979. Between 1990 and 1993 Lerner directed "Documenting the Midwest Origins of Twentieth-Century Feminism," a project that resulted in a comprehensive record of the beginnings of the most recent women's movement and culminated in a reunion of the participants.

In the mid-1990s Lerner returned as an honored scholar to the land she once fled. In 1995 she would receive the Kathë Leichter Preis, the Austrian state prize for women's history and the history of the labor movement. And in March 1996 the Austrian government awarded Lerner with the Austrian Cross for Science and Art.

—Anne Lewis Osler

LESBIA. *See* **ROBINSON, Mary (Darby).**

LESSING, Doris

Pseudonym: Jane Somers. **Nationality:** British. **Born:** Kermansha, Persia, 22 October 1919; moved with her family to England, then to Banket, Southern Rhodesia, 1924. **Education:** Dominican Convent School, Salisbury, Southern Rhodesia, 1926-34. **Family:** Married 1) Frank Charles Wisdom in 1939 (divorced 1943), one son and one daughter; 2) Gottfried Lessing in 1945 (divorced 1949), one son. **Career:** Au pair, Salisbury, England, 1934-35; telephone operator and clerk, 1937-39, then typist, 1946-48, Salisbury; journalist, *Cape Town Guardian,* 1949; moved to London and worked as a secretary, 1950; writer. Member of editorial board, *New Reasoner* (later *New Left Review*), 1956. **Awards:** Somerset Maugham award, 1954; Modern Language Association honorary fellow, 1974; Médicis prize (France), 1976; Austrian State prize, 1981; Shakespeare prize (Hamburg), 1982; W.H. Smith literary award, 1986; Grizane Cavour award (Italy), 1989; University of East Anglia Distinguished Fellow in Literature, 1991; *Los Angeles Times* Book Prize and James Tait Memorial Prize, both 1995, both for *Under My Skin.* D.Lit., Princeton University, 1989, Durham University, 1990, Warwick University, 1994; D.Let., Bard College, 1994, Harvard University, 1995, Oxford University, 1996. **Member:** National Institute of Arts and Letters, American Academy (associate member), Institute for Cultural Research. **Agent:** Jonathan Clowes Ltd., Iron Bridge House, Bridge Approach, London NW1 8BD, England.

Publications

Novels

The Grass Is Singing. London, Joseph, and New York, Crowell, 1950.

Children of Violence:

Martha Quest. London, Joseph, 1952.

A Proper Marriage. London, Joseph, 1954, with *Martha Quest,* New York, Simon & Schuster, 1964.

A Ripple from the Storm. London, Joseph, 1958.

Landlocked. London, MacGibbon & Kee, 1965; with *A Ripple from the Storm,* New York, Simon & Schuster, 1966.

The Four-Gated City. London, MacGibbon & Kee, and New York, Knopf, 1969.

Retreat to Innocence. London, Joseph, 1956; New York, Simon & Schuster, 1959.

The Golden Notebook. London, Joseph, and New York, Simon & Schuster, 1962.
Briefing for a Descent into Hell. London, Cape, and New York, Knopf, 1971.
The Summer before the Dark. London, Cape, and New York, Knopf, 1973.
The Memoirs of a Survivor. London, Octagon Press, 1974; New York, Knopf, 1975.
The Diaries of Jane Somers. New York, Random House, 1984; London, Joseph, 1985.
The Diary of A Good Neighbour (as Jane Somers). London, Joseph, and New York, Knopf, 1983.
If the Old Could (as Jane Somers). London, Joseph, and New York, Knopf, 1984.
The Good Terrorist. London, Cape, and New York, Knopf, 1985.
The Fifth Child. London, Cape, and New York, Knopf, 1988.
Canopus in Argos: Archives. New York, Vintage, 1992.
Re: Colonized Planet 5, Shikasta. London, Cape, and New York, Knopf, 1979.
The Marriages between Zones Three, Four, and Five. London, Cape, and New York, Knopf, 1980.
The Sirian Experiments: The Report by Ambien II, of the Five. London, Cape, and New York, Knopf, 1981.
The Making of the Representative for Planet 8. London, Cape, and New York, Knopf, 1982.
Documents Relating to the Sentimental Agents in the Volyen Empire. London, Cape, and New York, Knopf, 1983.
Love Again. New York, HarperCollins, 1996.

Short Stories

Collected African Stories:
This Was the Old Chief's Country. London, Joseph, 1951; New York, Crowell, 1952.
The Sun between Their Feet. London, Joseph, 1973; New York, n.p., 1981.
Five: Short Novels. London, Joseph, 1953.
The Habit of Loving. London, MacGibbon & Kee, and New York, Crowell, 1957.
A Man and Two Women. London, MacGibbon & Kee, and New York, Simon & Schuster, 1963.
African Stories. London, Joseph, 1964; New York, Simon & Schuster, 1965.
Winter in July. London, Grafton, 1966.
The Black Madonna. London, Grafton, 1966.
The Story of a Non-Marrying Man and Other Stories. London, Cape, 1972; as *The Temptation of Jack Orkney and Other Stories,* New York, Knopf, 1972.
A Sunrise on the Veld, London, Joseph, 1975.
(Stories), edited by Alan Cattell. London, Harrap, 1976.
A Mild Attack of Locusts, London, Cape, 1977.
Collected Stories. London, Cape, and New York, Knopf, 2 vols., 1978.
London Observed: Stories and Sketches. London, HarperCollins, 1992; as *The Real Thing,* New York, HarperCollins, 1992.
Spies I Have Known and Other Stories. Glasgow, Collins Educational, 1995.

Plays

Before the Deluge (produced London, 1953).
Mr. Dollinger (produced Oxford, 1958).
Each His Own Wilderness (produced London, 1958), in *New English Dramatists.* London, Penguin, 1959.
The Truth about Billy Newton (produced Salisbury, Wiltshire, 1960).
Play with a Tiger (produced London, 1962; New York, 1964). London, Joseph, 1962.
The Storm, adaptation of a play by Alexander Ostrovsky (produced London, 1966).
The Singing Door, in *Second Playbill 2,* edited by Alan Durband. London, Hutchinson, 1973.

Television Plays: *The Grass Is Singing* (from her own novel), 1962; *Please Do Not Disturb,* 1966; *Care and Protection,* 1966; *Between Men,* 1967.

Libretto: *The Making of the Representative for Planet 8* (from her own novel), with music by Philip Glass, 1988.

Poetry

Fourteen Poems. Northwood, Middlesex, Scorpion Press, 1959.

Essays

A Small Personal Voice: Essays, Reviews, Interviews, edited by Paul Schlueter. New York, Knopf, 1974.
African Laughter: Four Visits to Zimbabwe. London and New York, HarperCollins, 1992.
Autobiography
Under My Skin: Volume 1 of My Autobiography, to 1949. New York, HarperCollins, 1994.

Other

Going Home. London, Joseph, 1957.
In Pursuit of the English: A Documentary. London, MacGibbon & Kee, 1960; New York, Simon & Schuster, 1961.
Particularly Cats. London, Joseph, and New York, Simon & Schuster, 1967; expanded as *Particularly Cats and Rufus the Survivor,* New York, Knopf, 1981.
Prisons We Choose to Live Inside. Montreal, CBC Enterprises, 1986; London, Cape, and New York, Harper & Row, 1987.
The Winds Blow away Our Words: And Other Documents Relating to the Afghan Resistance. London, Panther, and New York, Vintage, 1987.
The Doris Lessing Reader. New York, Knopf, 1988; London, Cape, 1989.
Doris Lessing: Conversations, with Earl G. Ingersoll. Princeton, New Jersey, and New York, Ontario Review Press/Braziller, 1994.

*

Bibliography: *Doris Lessing: A Bibliography* by Catharina Ipp, Johannesburg, University of the Witwatersrand Department of Bibliography, 1967; *Doris Lessing: A Checklist of Primary and Secondary Sources* by Selma R. Burkom and Margaret Williams, Troy, New York, Whitston, 1973; *Doris Lessing: An Annotated Bibliography of Criticism* by Dee Seligman, Westport, Connecticut, Greenwood Press, 1981; *Doris Lessing: A Descriptive Bibli-*

ography of Her First Editions by Eric T. Brueck, London, Metropolis, 1984; *Doris Lessing* by Elizabeth Maslen, Plymouth, British Council, 1994.

Critical Studies: *Doris Lessing* by Dorothy Brewster, New York, Twayne, 1965; *The Novels of Doris Lessing* by Paul Schlueter, Carbondale, Southern Illinois University Press, 1973; *Doris Lessing* by Michael Thorpe, London, Longman, 1973; *Doris Lessing: Critical Studies* edited by Annis Pratt and L.S. Dembo, Madison, University of Wisconsin Press, 1974; *The City and the Veld: The Fiction of Doris Lessing* by Mary Ann Singleton, Lewisburg, Pennsylvania, Bucknell University Press, 1976; *Boulder-Pushers: Women in the Fiction of Margaret Drabble, Doris Lessing, and Iris Murdoch* by Carol Seiler-Franklin, Bern, Switzerland, Lang, 1979; "The Feminist Apologues of Lessing, Piercy, and Russ" by Rachel Blau DuPlessis, in *Frontiers,* 4, 1979; *The Novelistic Vision of Doris Lessing: Breaking the Forms of Consciousness* by Roberta Rubenstein, Urbana, University of Illinois Press, 1979; *Notebooks/Memoirs/Archives: Reading and Re-reading Doris Lessing* edited by Jenny Taylor, London, and Boston, Routledge, 1982; *Substance under Pressure: Artistic Coherence and Evolving Form in the Novels of Doris Lessing* by Betsy Draine, Madison, University of Wisconsin Press, 1983; *Doris Lessing* by Lorna Sage, London, Methuen, 1983; *Doris Lessing* by Mona Knapp, New York, Ungar, 1984; *Doris Lessing and Women's Appropriation of Science Fiction* by Mariette Clare, Birmingham, Centre for Contemporary Cultural Studies, 1984; *Fiction; or, The Language of Our Discontent: A Study of the Built-In Novelist in the Novels of Angus Wilson, Lawrence Durrell, and Doris Lessing* by Guido Kums, New York, P. Lang, 1985; *The Unexpected Universe of Doris Lessing: A Study in Narrative Technique* by Katherine Fishburn, Westport, Connecticut, Greenwood, 1985; *Doris Lessing* edited by Eve Bertelesen, New York, McGraw Hill, 1985; *Critical Essays on Doris Lessing* edited by Claire Sprague and Virginia Tiger, Boston, Hall, 1986; *Rereading Lessing: Narrative Patterns of Doubling and Repetition* by Claire Sprague, Chapel Hill and London, University of North Carolina Press, 1987, and *In Pursuit of Doris Lessing: Nine Nations Reading* edited by Sprague, New York, St. Martin's Press, and London, Macmillan, 1990; *The Theme of Enclosure in Selected Works of Doris Lessing* by Shirley Budhos, Troy, New York, Whitston, 1987; *Doris Lessing: The Alchemy of Survival* edited by Carey Kaplan and Ellen Cronan Rose, Athens, Ohio University Press, 1988; *Doris Lessing* by Ruth Whitaker, New York, St. Martin's Press, and London, Macmillan, 1988; *Doris Lessing* by Jeannette King, London, E. Arnold, 1989; *The Other Side of the Story: Structures and Strategies of Contemporary Feminist Narrative* by Molly Hite, Ithaca, New York, Cornell University Press, 1989; *Understanding Doris Lessing* by Jean Pickering, Columbia, University of South Carolina Press, 1990; *Engendering the Subject: Gender and Self-Representation in Contemporary Women's Fiction* by Sally Robinson, Albany, State University of New York Press, 1991; *Nayantara Sahgal and Doris Lessing: A Feminist Comparison* by Neena Arora, New Delhi, India Study for Commonwealth Studies, 1991; *Doris Lessing: Sufi Equilibrium and the Form of the Novel* by Shadia S. Fahim, New York, St. Martin's Press, 1993; *Woolf and Lessing: Breaking the Mold* edited by Ruth Saxton and Jean Tobin, New York, St. Martin's Press, 1994; *Doris Lessing* by Margaret Moan Rowe, New York, St. Martin's Press, 1994.

* * *

Doris Lessing is considered one of the finest novelists of the 20th century. There is no lack of study of her work to support that conclusion—the acclaim of both the academic and psychological communities is complimentary—but proof of her accomplishments is seen in the many dedicated readers that Lessing continues to attract.

While Lessing left school at age 14, she holds honorary degrees from some of the finest universities in the world. She seemed born with a talent for writing, but she worked to attain a realistic approach to character development through her keen sense of observation and her devotion to the many small details that make up the daily lives of her characters. Lessing is indeed a graduate of the university of life. From the publication of her first novel, *The Grass Is Singing,* in 1950, she has stirred controversy, touched chords of emotions that people had long forgot were present in their lives, and opened the eyes and minds of countless readers.

The Grass Is Singing was hailed as a breakthrough look at the horrors of South African apartheid. However, upon a second reading, the novel may seem focused on the desperate situation of a lively woman who is beat down by the grayness of her married life and the bleakness of anything the future might hold. Yet another reading of the novel brings out the harshness of the African landscape, the overwhelming power of nature, and the impending defeat of any human who tries to challenge those obstacles. Therein lies the strength of Lessing's talent, the layering of story within story, detail upon detail, emotion piled on top of emotion, until something or someone cracks. Lessing uses her personal interest in psychology and Persian mysticism to dig endlessly into the minds and souls of her characters, compelling the reader to face often unpleasant, uncomfortable, or ugly results, found not only found in the story's characters, but oft-times also recognized within themselves.

When the first volume of Lessing's "Children of Violence" series—five self-contained novels—appeared it became clear that she was also an outstanding observer of the world political scene. Beginning with *Martha Quest,* the novels's subjects run the gamut: war and race, the Cold War as an outgrowth of World War II, the struggle against capitalism, the attendant problems of violence. In her idealistic youth, Lessing had been a member of the Communist Party in Southern Rhodesia, believing in the original intent of communism to provide an equal forum for all people. She left the Party within a couple of years, remaining a critic and analyst of global politics, as well becoming a socialist in her personal politics.

Lessing's complex and perhaps most famous novel, 1962's *The Golden Notebook,* was seized upon by the feminist movement as proof of its author's support, as well as her understanding of the oppression of women. At the time Lessing indicated more than a little irritation at the book being pigeon-holed as a feminist tract. She felt no one paid any attention to the structure or ideas of the book, which she was then quoted as describing as "certain political and sexual attitudes that have force now; [the book] is an attempt to explain them, to objectivize them, to set them in relation with each other. So in a way it is a social novel." While she acknowledged the continued oppression of women and women's right to be free, she was dismayed that people would miss what she felt were the "truths" of the novel, including the idea of the rights of the individual. In her 1993 introduction to a newly released edition of *The Golden Notebook,* Lessing expressed surprise that the novel was still in demand, and that it was being read by second and third generations of women and men: "I am indeed flattered," she wrote.

In the 1970s, just when critics thought they had Lessing figured out, she took a side-trip into the world of writing science fiction. Several novels written early in that decade, such as 1971's *Briefing for a Descent into Hell* and 1974's *The Memoirs of a Survivor,* hinted at science-fiction themes, including suggestions of the use of spiritual insights in an attempt to save a city on the edge of collapse. But her five-volume series, "Canopus in Argos: Archives," left no doubt about Lessing's total immersion in the genre. *Shikasta,* the first volume of the series, has the planet (Shikasta/Earth) headed toward self-destruction due to the influence of another deadly planet. The following volumes all feature worlds on the brink of extinction. One volume, *The Marriages between Zones Three, Four, and Five* deals with integrating female qualities in a male-warrior world, a theme that wouldn't be adopted again until the mid-1990s. While Lessing was roundly criticized by many in the science-fiction community as being out of her league, the continued popularity of these novels belies those critics.

Doris Lessing continues to write her probing novels and short stories. One increasing focus is on women and how they deal with solitude, whether they live alone, are single by choice or widowed, or whether they are married and still alone. Such concerns are especially prevalent in her fiction, as in the short stories in 1978's *Collected Stories.* "To Room Nineteen" is a short story on a par with the works of Poe, and reminiscent of Charlotte Perkins Gilman's *The Yellow Wallpaper.* 1983's *The Diary of a Good Neighbour* and the following year's *If the Old Could...* are written in Lessing's familiar style: detailed descriptions, the influence of nature, and spare, no-nonsense language. The fact that these two works were published under the pseudonym of Jane Somers and not recognized by most Lessing fans as her work is astonishing. Lessing says she was trying to prove the point that writers without an established name cannot get published, and if they do, don't sell many books. Lessing's latest work is the first volume of her autobiography, *Under My Skin.* It does not disappoint. Written bluntly and with the detail for which she is now famous, Lessing clearly records the making of her youth and offers no apologies for her choices in a life in Southern Rhodesia. No apologies are needed.

—Maria Elena Raymond

LEVERTOV, Denise

Nationality: American. **Born:** Ilford, Essex, England, 24 October 1923; immigrated to the United States 1948, naturalized 1955. **Education:** Privately educated; also studied ballet. **Military Service:** Nurse for Britain, 1943-45. **Family:** Married writer Mitchell Goodman in 1947 (divorced 1972); one son. **Career:** Worked in an antique store and a bookstore in London, 1946; briefly taught English in Holland; teacher of poetry, YM-YWHA Poetry Center, New York, 1964; visiting lecturer, Drew University, Madison, New Jersey, 1965; writer-in-residence, City College of the City University of New York, 1965-66; visiting lecturer, Vassar College, Poughkeepsie, New York, 1966-67; visiting professor, University of California, Berkeley, 1969; visiting professor and poet-in-residence, Massachusetts Institute of Technology, Cambridge, 1969-70; visiting professor, Kirkland College, Clinton, New York, 1970-71; Elliston Lecturer, University of Cincinnati, 1973; professor, Tufts University, Medford, Massachusetts, 1973-79; Fannie Hurst Professor, Brandeis University, Waltham, Massachusetts, 1981-83; professor of English, Stanford University, beginning 1981. Poetry editor, *Nation,* 1961-62, and *Mother Jones,* 1976-78. Co-initiator of Writers and Artists Protest against the War in Vietnam, 1965; active in the anti-nuclear movement. **Member:** American Academy and Institute of Arts and Letters, Academie Mallarmé. **Awards:** Bess Hokin Prize (*Poetry*, Chicago), 1959, for "With Eyes at the Back of Our Heads"; Longview Award, 1961; Guggenheim fellowship, 1962; Harriet Monroe Memorial Prize, 1964; Inez Boulton Prize, 1964; American Academy grant, 1965; Morton Dauwen Zabel Memorial Prize (*Poetry*), 1965; Lenore Marshall Poetry Prize, 1976; Elmer Holmes Bobst Award, 1983; Poetry Society of America Shelley Memorial Award, 1984, 1989; Robert Frost Medal, 1990; National Education Association senior fellowship, 1990. D.Litt.: Colby College, 1970, University of Cincinnati, 1973, Bates College, 1984, Saint Lawrence University, 1984; **Address:** c/o New Directions Press, 80 Eighth Avenue, New York, New York 10011-5126, U.S.A.

Publications

Poetry

The Double Image. London, Cresset, 1946; Waldron Island, Washington, Brooding Heron Press, 1991.
Here and Now. City Lights, 1957.
Overland to the Islands. Jargon, 1958.
Five Poems. White Rabbit, 1958.
With Eyes at the Back of Our Heads. New York, New Directions Press, 1959.
The Jacob's Ladder. New York, New Directions Press, 1961.
O Taste and See: New Poems. New York, New Directions Press, 1964.
City Psalm. Oyez, 1964.
Psalm concerning the Castle. Perishable Press, 1966.
The Sorrow Dance. New York, New Directions Press, 1967.
Penguin Modern Poets 9, with Kenneth Rexroth and William Carlos Williams. London, Penguin, 1967.
A Tree Telling of Orpheus. Black Sparrow Press, 1968.
A Marigold from North Vietnam. Albondocani Press-Ampersand, 1968.
Three Poems. Perishable Press, 1968.
The Cold Spring and Other Poems. New York, New Directions Press, 1969.
Embroideries. Black Sparrow Press, 1969.
Relearning the Alphabet. New York, New Directions Press, 1970.
Summer Poems 1969. Oyez, 1970.
A New Year's Garland for My Students, MIT 1969-1970. Perishable Press, 1970.
To Stay Alive. New York, New Directions Press, 1971.
Footprints. New York, New Directions Press, 1972.
The Freeing of the Dust. New York, New Directions Press, 1975.
Chekhov on the West Heath. Woolmer/Brotherston, 1977.
Modulations for Solo Voice. Five Trees Press, 1977.
Life in the Forest. New York, New Directions Press, 1978.
Collected Earlier Poems, 1940-1960. New York, New Directions Press, 1979.
Pig Dreams: Scenes from the Life of Sylvia. Countryman Press, 1981.

Wanderer's Daysong. Copper Canyon Press, 1981.
Candles in Babylon. New York, New Directions Press, 1982.
Poems, 1960-1967. New York, New Directions Press, 1983.
Oblique Prayers: New Poems with 14 Translations from Jean Joubert. New York, New Directions Press, 1984.
El Salvador: Requiem and Invocation. William B. Ewert, 1984.
The Menaced World. William B. Ewert, 1984.
Selected Poems. Newcastle upon Tyne, Bloodaxe, 1986.
Breathing the Water. New York, New Directions Press, 1987.
Poems, 1968-1972, New York, New Directions Press, 1987.
A Door in the Hive. New York, New Directions Press, 1989.
Evening Train. New York, New Directions Press, 1993; as *A Door in the Hive; Evening Train,* Newcastle upon Tyne, Bloodaxe, 1993.
Sands of the Well. New York, New Directions Press, 1996.

Essays

The Poet in the World. New York, New Directions Press, 1973.
Light Up the Cave. New York, New Directions Press, 1981.
New and Selected Essays. New York, New Directions Press, 1992.

Other

In the Night: A Story. Albondocani Press, 1968.

Recordings: *Today's Poets 3,* Folkways; *The Acolyte,* Watershed, 1985.

Editor, *Out of the War Shadow: An Anthology of Current Poetry.* War Resisters League, 1967.

Translator and editor, with Edward C. Dimock Jr., *In Praise of Krishna: Songs from the Bengali.* Garden City, New York, Doubleday, 1967.
Translator, with others, *Selected Writings,* by Jules Spervielle. New York, New Directions Press, 1968.
Translator, *Selected Poems,* by Eugene Guillevic. New York, New Directions Press, 1969.
Translator, with others, *Poets of Bulgaria,* edited by William Meredith. Unicorn Press, 1985.
Translator, *Black Iris,* by Jean Joubert. Copper Canyon Press, 1988.

*

Bibliography: *Denise Levertov: An Annotated Primary and Secondary Bibliography* by Liana Sakelliou-Schultz, n.p., 1988.

Manuscript Collections: Humanities Research Center, University of Texas at Austin; Washington University, St. Louis, Missouri; Indiana University, Bloomington; Fales Library, New York University; Beinecke Library, Yale University, New Haven, Connecticut; Brown University, Providence, Rhode Island; University of Connecticut, Storrs; Columbia University, New York City; State University of New York at Stony Brook.

Critical Studies: *Assays* by Kenneth Rexroth, New York, New Directions Press, 1961; *Poets in Progress* edited by Edward Hungerford, Northwestern University Press, 2nd edition, 1967; *Denise Levertov* by Linda W. Wagner, Boston, Twayne, 1967; *With Eye and Ear* by Rexroth, Herder & Herder, 1970; *Out of the Vietnam Vortex: A Study of Poets and Poetry against the War* by James Mersmann, University Press of Kansas, 1974; *Denise Levertov: In Her Own Province* edited by Wagner, New York, New Directions Press, 1979; "Levertov and Rich: The Later Poems" by Wagner, in her *American Modern: Essays in Fiction and Poetry,* Port Washington, New York, Kennikat, 1980; *The Imagination's Tongue: Denise Levertov's Poetic* by William Slaughter, Aquila, 1981; *From Modern to Contemporary American Poetry, 1945-1965* by James E. B. Breslin, University of Chicago Press, 1984; *Modern American Women Poets* by Jean Gould, New York, Dodd, 1985; *Critical Essays on Denise Levertov* edited by Linda Wagner-Martin, Boston, G. K. Hall, 1990; *The Poet's Gift: Towards the Renewal of Pastoral Care* by Donald Capps, Louisville, Westminister, 1993; *Denise Levertov: Selected Criticism* edited by Albert Gelpi, Ann Arbor, University of Michigan Press, 1993; *Denise Levertov: The Poetry of Engagement* by Audrey T. Rodgers, London and Cranbury, New Jersey, Associated University Presses, 1993; *Poetics of the Feminine: Authority and Literary Traditions* by Linda A. Kinnahan, Cambridge and New York, Cambridge University Press, 1994.

* * *

Late in the Vietnam War, Denise Levertov came to Chicago to do a poetry reading. I climbed to the top balcony of Orchestra Hall and sat, waiting among a sprinkle of young beatniks dotted here and there with old activists (of whom I was one), until a rather small, hesitant figure came on stage holding a sheaf of papers. We were respectfully silent, perhaps less interested in the poems, per se, than in finding how the poet integrated her much-criticized social action with her primary work.

We were not to find out. Orchestra Hall is a cavernous and echoing place, Miss Levertov was obviously chilled through and in the grip of stage fright, and while she read all that she had planned to, I think, the listeners missed a great deal of it. She finally left the immense stage with an air of escape. For at least one listener, too, it was a relief to get home and go back to the books, which never falter.

Not that public appearances held any terrors for Levertov. Already an established poet, wife of a poet—some people thought her husband, Mitchell Goodman a better writer than his famous brother Paul—she was the author of several books, with more to come. Never formally educated, Levertov had made a place for herself in the literary world. Born in London in 1923, she had served as a nurse in World War II, worked at various jobs and worked quietly to find her own voice. Her first work was published when she was 16, and thereafter her life was blended of poetry and social concern, a blend that seemed to work well.

When the American Mitchell Goodman came to England to study on the G.I. Bill, he and Levertov met and married, lived in France and Italy and then in Mexico, fetching up in New York City where they produced a son, Nik, and became a part of the exciting post-war days. They were separated in the late 1970s.

In what might have been called the Allen Ginsberg era, when the voice of the poet was often a raucous one, Levertov spoke quietly but with authority. Whether she was writing about the Holocaust or about a cat eating roses, she spoke her feelings. She was involved in civil rights, the Huac trials—Goodman would be a codefendant in the 1968 trial of Dr. Benjamin Spock—in the noisy tumult of the Eichmann trials, and the general social unrest of the civil rights movement. Writing and direct action seemed to her parts of one engrossing whole. Degrees, lectureships, and grants came her way—even a Guggenheim—but one suspects that the story is not over. What a pleasure a new Levertov poem would be!

—Valerie Taylor

LISPECTOR, Clarice

Nationality: Brazilian. **Born:** Tchetchelnik, Ukraine, 10 December 1925; immigrated to Brazil, 1926. **Education:** Studied law, 1944. **Family:** Married diplomat Mauri Gurgel Valente in 1943; two sons. **Career:** Worked as a journalist, Rio de Janeiro; lived in Europe, 1945-49, and in United States, 1952-59. **Died:** Of cancer, 9 December 1977.

Publications

Novels

Perto do coração selvagem. Rio de Janeiro, Noite, 1944; as *Near to the Wild Heart,* New York, New Directions Press, and Manchester, England, Carcanet, 1990.
O lustre. Rio de Janeiro, AGIR, 1946.
A cidade sitiada. Rio de Janeiro, Noite, 1949; revised, Rio de Janeiro, Alvaro, 1964.
Alguns contos. Rio de Janeiro, Ministério de Educação e Saúde, 1952.
A maçã no escuro. Rio de Janeiro, Alves, 1961; as *The Apple in the Dark,* New York, Knopf, 1967; London, Virago, 1985.
A paixão segundo G.H. Rio de Janeiro, Autor, 1964; as *The Passion according to G.H.,* Minneapolis, University of Minnesota Press, 1988.
Uma aprendizagem; ou, O livro dos prazeres. Rio de Janiero, Sabiá, 1969; as *An Apprenticeship; or, The Book of Delights,* Austin, University of Texas Press, 1986.
Agua viva. Rio de Janeiro, Artenova, 1973; as *The Stream of Life,* Minneapolis, University of Minnesota Press, 1989.
A vida íntima de Laura. Rio de Janeiro, Olympio, 1974.
A hora de estrela. Rio de Janeiro, Olympio, 1977; as *The Hour of the Star,* Manchester, England, Carcanet, 1986.

Short Stories

Laços de família. Sãu Paulo, Alves, 1960; as *Family Ties,* Austin, University of Texas Press, 1972; Manchester, England, Carcanet, 1985.
Felicidade clandestina. Rio de Janeiro, Sabiá, 1971.
Onde estivestes de Noite. Rio de Janeiro, Artenova, 1974; in *Soulstorm,* New York, New Directions Press, 1989.
A via crucis do corpo. Rio de Janeiro, Artenova, 1974; in *Soulstorm,* New York, New Directions Press, 1989.

For Children

O mistério do coelho pensante. Rio de Janeiro, Alvaro, 1967.
A mulher que matou os peixes. Rio de Janeiro, Sabiá, 1968; as *The Woman Who Killed the Fish,* in *Latin American Literary Review,* 11, fall/winter 1982.

Essays

Visão do esplendor: Impressões leves. Rio de Janeiro, Alves, 1975.
De corpo inteiro. Rio de Janeiro, Artenova, 1975.
A descoberta do mundo. Rio de Janeiro, Nova Fronteira, 1984; translated as *Discovering the World,* Manchester, Carcanet, 1992.

Other

A legião estrangeira. Rio de Janeiro, Autor, 1964; as *The Foreign Legion,* New York, Center for Inter-American Relations, 1979; Manchester, England, Carcanet, 1986.
A imitação da rosa. Rio de Janeiro, Artenova, 1973.
Seleta, edited by Renato Cordeiro Gomes. Rio de Janeiro, Olympio, 1975.
Um sopro de vida: Pulsações. Rio de Janeiro, Nova Fronteira, 1978.
Quase de verdade. Rio de Janeiro, Rocco, 1978.
Para não esquecer. São Paulo, Atica, 1978.
A bela e a fera. Rio de Janeiro, Nova Fronteira, 1979.

Translator, *O retrato de Dorian Grey,* by Oscar Wilde. Rio de Janeiro, Ouro, 1974.

*

Media Adaptations: *A hora de estrela* (film).

Bibliography: "Clarice Lispector: A Complete English Bibliography" by Cathy Giffuni, in *Lyra,* 1(3), 1988.

Critical Studies: "The Passion according to C.L." (interview) by Elizabeth Lowe, in *Review,* 24, June 1979; *Clarice Lispector* by Olga Borelli, Rio de Janeiro, Nova Fronteira, 1981; *Clarice Lispector* by Earl E. Fitz, Boston, Twayne, 1985; "Introduction" to *Family Ties* by Giovanni Pontiero, Austin, University of Texas Press, 1991; *Passionate Fictions: Gender, Narrative and Violence in Clarice Lispector* by Marta Peixoto, Minneapolis, Minnesota University Press, 1994.

* * *

As an emigré from the Ukraine to Brazil, as a young woman in Brazilian intellectual society, and as a diplomatic wife living abroad for many years, Clarice Lispector acquired a unique sense of being on the outside, and her writing helped her to find a way back in—a way just for her. Even before her long absence from Brazil helped her to develop a global perspective, Lispector was a notable author. Her unconventional storytelling style earned her praise immediately upon the publication of her first novel in 1944, just after her graduation from law school. *Perto do coração selvagem* (*Near to the Wild Heart*) takes its title from an epigram contained in James Joyce's *Portrait of the Artist as a Young Man,* and indeed, reminds the reader of Joyce's detailed narration of the mind's interior, in the story of the artistic development of Joana, the novel's protagonist.

In *Near to the Wild Heart* the author established not only an unconventional form of expression, but also she openly declared her desire for independence and her need to eliminate traditional roles for women who expected to develop artistically. As Giovanni Pontiero explains, the protagonist of *Near to the Wild Heart* bears a close resemblance to the author who created her. Lispector also rebelled against the constraints of marriage, which in Brazil followed a prescription of women who had to be subservient and dependent on men, who deferred to the men's careers, and relied on child-bearing as validation of personal value. Instead, Joana reveals a spirit that wishes to unburden itself from such a destiny, because it will result in the suffocation of any artistic capabilities that she has. The themes in this first novel are revolutionary enough. The language and its introspection defy conventional development of plot, preferring instead to delve into the realm of discovery through language. Joana, a reflection of Lispector, explores words and gleans from them new meanings when she examines the very words she uses to describe her world and her state of mind.

As with later novels, the plot of *Wild Heart* is minimal, with much greater importance being devoted to the development of characters, as these reflect subtle evolutions of the author's emotional states. Lispector's literary characters seek to discover who they really are by searching among splintered pieces of the subconscious mind. A person's transcendence and spirituality can be uncovered amidst seemingly trivial details that all the senses perceive. Lispector welcomed the moments of solitude that allowed her to reflect on these details and transform them into a portrayal of the human soul,

In addition to her literary debt to Joyce, Lispector nods to Franz Kafka for his depiction of a world full of confusing signs that people must struggle to decipher. When Lispector turned to the creation of her own world in literature, it became a process of discovery as well. She relies on sensations from the outside world, and the way in which these lead her to the bottom of her own feelings, through the discovery zone of words. Words acquire an organic quality, growing as though they were leaves on a tree, with free associations, and sensuous reiterations, from which she expects, ultimately, to make some sense of the world around her.

Laços de família (*Family Ties*), her collection of short stories from 1967, is perhaps one of the best examples of this attempt to glean meaning from absurd and seemingly insignificant gestures. As with so many of Lispector's works of fiction, characters move through a world in which very little happens. What does take place is the sweeping of the eye over a scene, the awakening of a memory, the exploration of a disturbing thought. Lispector's narrative style is admired by many younger authors throughout Latin America, including Marta Traba of Argentina and Colombia. The younger generation especially prizes Lispector's work for her psychological introspection, but also because she was one of the first women writers in Latin America to receive wider recognition through her novels, which reject traditional, restrictive roles for women in the continent. As *Wild Heart* and *Family Ties* both amply demonstrate, women who expect more from themselves than the domestic role assigned to them by men in their society have to openly reject these assignments. They must take a stand, as Joana does in Lispector's first novel, and accept solitude, boredom, or rejection, because these are ultimately the paths to independence.

Clarice Lispector did ultimately separate from her husband and, with her children, returned to Brazil from Washington, D.C., in 1959. She continued to work as a journalist, as well as a novelist, and she translated Oscar Wilde's *Portrait of Dorian Gray.* Her work, as a discoverer within the Portuguese language, brought her much deserved attention before her death from cancer in 1977. With her unique introspective narrative style, Lispector introduced contemporary readers in both her native Brazil and throughout Latin America a little-trodden path—one that led towards female independence and discovery.

—Helena Antolin Cochrane

LIVESAY, Dorothy

Nationality: Canadian. **Born:** Winnipeg, Manitoba, 12 October 1909. **Education:** Trinity College, University of Toronto, 1927-31, B.A. 1931; Sorbonne, Paris, Diplôme d'études supérieures 1932; University of Toronto, Diploma in social work 1934; attended Institute of Education, University of London, 1959; University of British Columbia, M.A. in education 1966. **Family:** Married Duncan Macnair in 1937 (died 1959); two children. **Career:** Worked as a social worker in Montréal and New Jersey during the Depression; a high school teacher; a journalist in postwar London for the *Toronto Daily Star;* an English teacher, Zambia, 1960-63. Lecturer and writer-in-residence at numerous colleges and universities. Regional editor, *New Frontier* (journal); founder and editor, *CV II* (journal); contributor of articles, short stories, and verse to periodicals, including *Canadian Forum, Canadian Literature, Educational Record, Fiddlehead, Impulse, Journal of Canadian Fiction, Poetry, Quarry,* and *Saturday Night.* **Awards:** Jardine Memorial Prize for English Verse, 1929; Governor General Award for Poetry, 1944, 1947; Royal Society of Canada Lorne Pierce Medal, 1947; University of Western Ontario President's Medal, 1954; Canadian Council fellowship, 1958-59; St. John's College, University of Manitoba fellowship, 1976; Canada Council Senior Arts grant, 1977; Governor General Persons Award, 1984; Order of Canada, 1987; Trinity College, University of Toronto fellowship, 1987; D.Litt.: University of Waterloo, 1972; Althabaska University, 1983; McGill University, 1985; Simon Fraser University, 1987. **Member:** Amnesty International, World Federalists, Federation of Canadian University Teachers of English. **Address:** Galiano Island, British Columbia, Canada.

Publications

Poetry

Green Pitcher. Toronto, Macmillan, 1928.
Signpost. Toronto, Macmillan, 1932.
Day and Night. Boston, Humphries, and Toronto, Ryerson, 1944.
Poems for People. Toronto, Ryerson, 1947.
Call My People Home (radio documentary). Toronto, Ryerson, 1950.
New Poems, edited by Jay Macpherson. Toronto, Emblem, 1955.
Selected Poems: 1926-1956. Toronto, Ryerson, 1957.
The Colour of God's Face. Vancouver, Unitarian Service Committee, 1964; revised as "Zambia" in *The Unquiet Bed,* 1967.
The Unquiet Bed. Toronto, Ryerson, 1967.
The Documentaries: Selected Longer Poems. Toronto, Ryerson, 1968.

Plainsongs. Fredericton, Fiddlehead, 1969; revised edition, 1971.
Disasters of the Sun. Burnaby, British Columbia, Blackfish Broadsides, 1971.
Collected Poems: The Two Seasons. Toronto, McGraw Hill Ryerson, 1972.
Nine Poems of Farewell, 1972-1973. Windsor, Ontario, Black Moss, 1973.
Ice Age. Erin, Ontario, Porcépic, 1975.
The Woman I Am: Best Loved Poems from One of Canada's Best Loved Poets. Erin, Ontario, Porcépic, 1977.
The Phases of Love: Adolescence, 1925-1928. Toronto, League of Canadian Poets, 1980.
The Raw Edges: Voices from Our Time. Winnipeg, Turnstone, 1981.
Feeling the Worlds: New Poems. Fredericton, Fiddlehead & Goose Lane, 1984.
Beyond War: The Poetry. Vancouver, privately printed, 1985.
The Self Completing Tree: Selected Poems. Victoria and Toronto, Porcépic, 1986.

Novel

The Husband. Charlottetown, Prince Edward Island, Ragweed, 1990.

Short Stories

A Winnipeg Childhood. Winnipeg, Peguis, 1973; revised as *Beginnings: A Winnipeg Childhood,* Toronto, New Press, 1975.

Plays

Joe Derry: A Pantomime in Seven Scenes, in *Masses* (Toronto), 10, September 1933; in *Eight Men Speak and Other Plays from the Canadian Workers' Theatre,* edited by Richard Wright and Robin Endres. Toronto, New Hogtown Press, 1976.

Uncollected Essays

"The Native People in Our Canadian Literature," in *English Quarterly* (Winnipeg), 4(1), spring 1971.
"Tennyson's Daughter of Wilderness Child" The Factual and Literary Background of Isabella Valancy Crawford," in *Journal of Canadian Fiction,* 2(3), 1973.
"A Putting Down of Roots," in *CV II* (Winnipeg), 1(1), 1975.
"Carr and Livesay," in *Canadian Literature* (Vancouver), 84, spring 1980.
"The Woman Writer and the Idea of Progress," in *Canadian Forum* (Toronto), 62, November 1982.
"On Being in Love: A Reminiscence by Dorothy Livesay." in *NeWest Review* (Edmonton), 15(2), December 1989/January 1990.

Autobiography

Right Hand Left Hand: A True Life of the '30s, edited by David Arnason and Kim Todd. Erin, Ontario, Porcépic, 1977.
Journey with My Selves: A Memoir, 1909-1963. Vancouver, Douglas & McIntyre, 1991.

Other

Editor, *Collected Poems of Raymond Knister.* Toronto, Ryerson, 1949.
Editor, with Seymour Mayne, *Forty Women Poets of Canada.* Montreal, Ingluvin, 1971.
Editor, *Woman's Eye: 12 B.C. Poets.* Vancouver, Air, 1978.
Editor, with Louisa Loeb, *Down Singing Centuries: Folk Literature of the Ukraine,* translated by Florence Randal Livesay. Winnipeg, Hyperion, 1981.

Recordings: *Canadian Poets on Tape,* 1971; *Dorothy Livesay Reading from Her Work: Poetry 1920-1973,* 1973; *A Poetry Reading by Dorothy Livesay,* 1982.

*

Media Adaptations: *The Woman I Am* (documentary film), National Film Board of Canada, 1982; *Women Writing around the World* (video recording), University of Toronto Media Centre, 1990.

Bibliography: "Dorothy Livesay: An Annotated Bibliography" by Alan Ricketts, in *The Annotated Bibliography of Canada's Major Authors,* edited by Robert Lecker and Jack David, vol. 4, Downsview, Ontario, ECW, 1983; *The Papers of Dorothy Livesay: A Research Tool,* University of Manitoba Libraries, Department of Archives & Special Collections, 1986.

Manuscript Collections: Elizabeth Dafoe Library, University of Manitoba, Winnipeg; Cameron Library, University of Alberta, Edmonton; Douglas Library Archives, Queen's University, Kingston, Ontario.

Critical Studies: "My New Found Land" by W. E. Collin, in his *White Savannahs,* Toronto, Macmillan, 1936; *On Canadian Poetry* by E. K. Brown, Toronto, Ryerson, 1943; "The Poetry of Dorothy Livesay" by Robert Weaver, in *Contemporary Verse,* 26, fall 1948; "Dorothy Livesay and the Transcendentalist Tradition" by Jean Gibbs, in *Humanities Association Bulletin* (Fredericton, New Brunswick), 21, spring 1970; "Dorothy Livesay, Poet of Nature" by D. Leland, in *Dalhousie Review* (Halifax, Nova Scotia), 51, autumn 1971; "Dorothy Livesay: The Love Poet" by Peter Stevens, in *Canadian Literature* (Vancouver), 47, winter 1971; "Livesay's Coming of Age" by Lorraine Vernon, in *Lakehead University Review,* 6, fall/winter 1973; Livesay issue of *Room of One's Own* (Vancouver), 5(1-2), 1979; "The Poet as Radical: Dorothy Livesay in the '30s" by Henry Kreisel, in *CV II* (Winnipeg), 4(1), 1979; "Dorothy Livesay at 73—The Unquiet Thoughts of a Romantic Feminist" by Heather Robertson, in *Quill & Quire* (Toronto), 49, March 1983; "'A Thankful Music': Dorothy Livesay's Experiments with Feeling and Poetic Form" by Lorraine M. York, in *Canadian Poetry,* 12, 1983; *A Public and a Private Voice: Essays on the Life and Work of Dorothy Livesay* edited by Lindsay Dorney and others, Waterloo, University of Waterloo Press, 1986; *Dorothy Livesay* by Lee Briscoe Thompson, Boston, G.K. Hall, 1987; *Dorothy Livesay and Her Works* by Paul Denham, Toronto, ECW Press, 1987; "Daddy's Little Girl: Dorothy Livesay's Correspondence with her Father" by Pamela Banting, in *Canadian Poetry,* 22, 1988; *Dorothy Livesay: Patterns in a Poetic Life* by Peter Stevens, Toronto, ECW Press, 1992; *Dorothy Livesay's Poetics of Desire* by Nadine McInnis, Winnipeg, Turnstone Press, 1994.

* * *

Dorothy Livesay is one of the most important Canadian poets of the 20th century. The central feature of her six-decade-long writing career is a ceaseless renewal of poetic form to accommodate new influences and experiences. As she wrote in 1937, the poet's individual mark is to be found in her way of giving form: "[p]oets are not independent philosophers, they are gleaners. The experience is common; the way it is transmitted is personal." Livesay's poetic expression has found diverse forms and rhythms ranging from the compression of imagist lyrics to longer, dramatic poems based on historical events, which she calls "documentaries."

There are, however, several constant interests in Livesay's writing. She has been consistently committed to the ideal of poetry as a popular form of communicative, "living speech," rather than a rarefied aesthetic object. The particular struggle of the woman writer, as the inheritor of a patriarchal literary tradition as well as maternal and sexual roles that threaten her with isolation and silence, has been an important theme in her writing. In the foreword to her *Collected Poems: The Two Seasons,* she underlines the prominence in her work of natural and domestic symbols such as the seasons, day and night, sun, wind, snow, the garden, the house, the door, and the bed. Livesay has also been preoccupied, from her earliest writing days, with the relationship between the life of the senses and the life of work and struggle in the social, political world. This relationship has conventionally been read as an opposition between private and public voices, each of which are seen to have been prominent at different times in her writing career. However, Livesay's "private," lyrical voice is very often concerned with sexual politics and her adoption of a recognizably "public" voice is at least partly determined by a hierarchy of speech genres established by the authority of her father.

Livesay's parents, Florence Randal Livesay, a poet and translator of Slavic folk songs and verse, and John Frederick Bligh Livesay, manager of The Canadian Press, Were among her earliest literary influences. Her father was an avid reader who introduced his teenaged daughter to the writing of women novelists and Engels's *Origin of the Family,* and took her to a lecture by the anarchist Emma Goldman. Livesay was also reading the poetry of Emily Dickinson and H.D. at this time. She saw her impulse to work with lyricism and rhythm, rather than the prose which her father so admired, as the choice of an insubordinate form of speech that carried the risks of inaudiblilty and insignificance.

Livesay was only 19 when her first book of poetry, *Green Pitcher* (1928), was published during her first year of studies in French and Italian at the University of Toronto. These finely crafted free verse poems were quite new in a literary context that was still largely steeped in romantic and patriotic poetry. It was not, however, just the compressed style of *Green Pitcher* and *Signpost* (1932), Livesay's second book, that was bold. Many of these poems address rhetorical questions to an implicitly male audience in a tone that wavers between mocking defiance and a sense of defeat. They also stage a contest between the female poet, ecstatically identified with nature in spring, and an alluring but dangerous masculine force which threatens her autonomy. These poems often end without firm conclusions but the presence of sun or wind as dark counterpoints to the poet's joyful isolation is striking.

By the time *Signpost* was published, Livesay had returned from her year at the Sorbonne, during which time she had seen political unrest first-hand and become aware of the rise of Fascism. Renouncing the "Decadence in Modern Bourgeois Poetry" (a CBC radio talk she gave in the 1930s), she enrolled in the School of Social Work at the University of Toronto and became active in the Young Communist League, the Canadian League against War and Fascism, and the Progressive Arts Club of Toronto. The latter group's commitment to the direct involvement of art with the class struggle stimulated her to write the agitprop play *Joe Derry,* as well as revolutionary poetry and mass chants for the Toronto communist paper, *Masses.* Livesay also contributed radical journalism, poetry on the Spanish Civil War, and (under the pseudonym Katherine Bligh) short fiction based on her work as a social worker in Montreal and New Jersey during the Depression to the left-wing journal *New Frontier.* The writings from her life as a communist cultural worker during this period are collected in *Right Hand, Left Hand,* an autobiographical collage of poems, photographs, letters, plays, and addresses written for CBC radio.

Livesay was inspired by her reading of the left-wing English poets W. H. Auden and C. Day Lewis in the mid- to late 1930s with a new hope of poetry. Her attempt to marry politics with lyricism was enormously successful and in 1944, *Day and Night* won the Governor General's Award for Poetry. The joyful season of spring was now identified with the coming revolution, and it was poetry that would help us to imagine that revolution. The book represents Livesay's first sustained work with the long poem form and the techniques of discontinuous narrative, and collage of language styles and rhythms. The title poem, about alienated factory labor, racist industrial practices, and imposition of mechanical upon natural rhythms, weaves allusion to Cole Porter, the spiritual, the comic book, and the biblical fiery furnace. The theme of racial discrimination is also central in *Call My People Home* (1950), Livesay's documentary radio play about the internment of Japanese-Canadians in British Columbia during World War II.

After her marriage to the Glaswegian, Duncan Macnair, in Vancouver in 1937, Livesay was force by law to relinquish her job as a social worker to make way for the employment of married men. She continued to write poetry during her years of marriage and motherhood in the 1940s, in "time snatched in the basement supervising an old washing machine with hand wringer, or waiting until everyone was asleep," as she recalls in her memoir *Journey with My Selves* (1991). Images of silence and invisibility return in the poems of these years, published as *New Poems* in 1955 and in the 1957 *Selected Poems.* In these poems, the only solution to the precarious integrity of the female subject, dependent on the external support of "sun's round" and threatened by an invasive masculine force, is a form of androgyny that obliterates female difference.

Livesay's husband died suddenly whilst she was studying the teaching of English in London in 1959. She then went to work for UNESCO as a teacher in training colleges in Zambia, during the years in which that country emerged as an independent nation. She returned to Canada in 1963 and enrolled as a graduate student in Education at the University of British Columbia. Here she came into contact with a vital new poetry movement influenced by the American Black Mountain School and its interest in integrating natural breath rhythms into the forms and rhythms of poetry. This reassertion of the immediacy of the body was something to which Livesay was already headed with *The Colour of God's Face* (1964), a series of poems inspired by the rhythms of African drumming and tribal chants.

Livesay brought the focus of her Masters' thesis on the contemporary poem as "the event itself" to what is arguable her most original and revolutionary poetic achievement, *The Unquiet Bed* (1967). In this book, poems that celebrate the victory of the spontaneous over the orderly and controlled take a serial form, with irregular lines and spacing. Explicitly sexual poems in this book, as well as in *Plainsongs* (1971) and *Disasters of the Sun* (1971) are written from a specifically female perspective. Often addressed to a male lover, they reveal an ambivalence about an erotic enjoyment in which the speaker is implicated as muse, not poet. Livesay inscribes the female lover's visceral presence through graphic anatomical detail to differentiate her from the beloved who is the projection of male fantasy in traditional love poetry.

An explicitly feminist world view emerges in Livesay's late poetry. In *Ice Age* (1975) and *Feeling the Worlds* (1984), the poetry is increasingly addressed to a female "we" in the process of evolving an alternative moral order and ecological consciousness. She explores themes of aging, and begins to write lesbian love poetry, returning to a highly economical style but self-consciously altering some of the images in her earlier poetry to highlight her evolving vision.

As a critic and editor, Livesay has wrestled with some of the central questions confronting modern Canadian literature. Her 1932 thesis for a Diplôme d'Etudes Supérieures from the Sorbonne was on the influence of metaphysical and symbolist poetry on modern English poetry. She thus brought to her reading of fellow Canadian poets what critic Northrop Frye called and "unusually cosmopolitan knowledge of modern poetry."

Livesay founded the Winnipeg-based journal *CV II* with the goal of providing serious criticism of Canadian poetry. (The title of the journal was a tribute to *Contemporary Verse,* one of the few outlets for the work of new poets in Canada in the 1940s, and a journal which Livesay also helped to found.) Livesay's knowledge of international developments in poetry has not prevented her from strongly siding with those who call for poetry that expresses the way people live and struggle in Canada. In an important 1969 address, she defined the documentary as a distinctly Canadian genre and launched a debate about the boundaries between historical and literary writing in the national literature. Another important contribution to Canadian literary criticism was her recover of a neglected 19th-century Canadian woman poet from obscurity. Livesay saw in Isabella Valancy Crawford a literary foremother "intoxicated with language and metaphor" and identified with her struggles against silence and inauthenicity in the absence of a community to which she could address her work. In a 1975 editorial for *CV II,* Livesay declared a commitment to the creation of a readership for women writers. She included in the journal's mandate exploration of "the true feelings of women," not a straight-forward task since, as she put it, "[m]any women poet today are either looking into mirrors or speaking from behind masks." Livesay continued this engagement with the writing of other women in her editing of the anthologies *Forty Women Poets of Canada* (1971) and *Woman's Eye: 12 B.C. Poets* (1978).

—Jennifer Henderson

LORDE, Audre (Geraldine)

Pseudonym: Rey Domini. **Nationality:** American. **Born:** New York City, 18 February 1934. **Education:** National University of Mexico, 1954; Hunter College (now Hunter College of the City University of New York), B.A. 1960; Columbia University, New York, M.L.S. 1962. **Family:** Married Edwin Ashley Rollins in 1962 (divorced 1972); one son, one daughter. **Career:** Librarian, Mount Vernon Public Library, Mount Vernon, New York, 1961-63; head librarian, Town School Library, New York City, 1966-68; lecturer in creative writing, City College, New York City, 1968; lecturer in education department, Herbert H. Lehman College, Bronx, New York, 1969-70; associate professor of English, John Jay College of Criminal Justice, New York City, beginning 1970; professor of English, Hunter College, New York City, 1981-87, Thomas Hunter professor, 1987-92. Visiting professor, Tougaloo University, Tougaloo, Mississippi, and Atlanta University, Atlanta, Georgia, both 1968. Visiting lecturer throughout the United States, Europe, Africa, and Australia. Founder, Kitchen Table—Women of Color Press and Sisterhood in Support of Sisters in South Africa. Poetry editor, *Chrysalis* and *Amazon Quarterly.* Contributor of short stories to *Venture* magazine as Rey Domini. **Awards:** National Endowment for the Arts grants, 1968, 1981; Creative Artists Public Service grant, 1972, 1976; National Book Award nominee, 1974; American Library Association Gay Caucus Book Award, 1981, for *The Cancer Journals;* Borough of Manhattan President's Award, 1987, for literary excellence; Before Columbus Foundation American Book Award, 1989; Bill Whitehead Award for lifetime contribution to literature, 1990; Sappho Award for contribution to literature on multicultural lesbian identity, 1990; Fund for Free Expression Award, 1991; named New York State Poet Laureate, 1992. Honorary doctorates: Oberlin College, Haverford College, State University of New York at Binghampton. **Died:** In St. Croix, Virgin Islands, 20 November 1992.

Publications

Poetry

The First Cities. New York, Poets Press, 1968.
Cables to Rage. London, Breman Press, and Detroit, Broadside Press, 1970.
From a Land Where Other People Live. Detroit, Broadside Press, 1973.
The New York Head Shop and Museum. Detroit, Broadside Press, 1974.
Coal. New York, Norton, 1976.
Between Our Selves. Point Reyes, California, Eidolon Editions, 1976.
The Black Unicorn. New York, Norton, 1978.
Chosen Poems, Old and New. New York, Norton, 1982; revised as *Undersong: Chosen Poems Old and New,* 1992.
Our Dead behind Us. New York, Norton, 1986.

Essays

Sister Outsider: Essays and Speeches. Trumansburg, New York, Crossing Press, 1984.
A Burst of Light. Ithaca, New York, Firebrand Books, 1988.

Uncollected Essays

"Poems Are Not Luxuries," in *Chrysalis,* 3, 1977.
"Scratching the Surface: Some Notes on Barriers to Women and Loving," in *Black Scholar,* April 1978.

"Man Child: A Black Lesbian-Feminist's Response," in *Conditions: Four,* winter 1979.

"An Open Letter to Mary Daly," in *Top Ranking: A Collection of Articles on Racism and Classism in the Lesbian Community,* edited by Joan Gibbs and Sara Bennett. Brooklyn, February 3rd Press, 1980.

Autobiography

The Cancer Journals. Argyle, New York, Spinsters Ink, 1980.

Zami: A New Spelling of My Name (biomythography). Freedom, California, Crossings Press, 1982.

Other

Uses of the Erotic: The Erotic as Power. Brooklyn, New York, Out and Out Books, 1978.

*

Bibliography: *Modern American Woman Poets* by Jean Gould, New York, Dodd Mead.

Critical Studies: "Nothing Safe: The Poetry of Audre Lorde" by Joan Larkin, in *Margins,* August 1975; "On the Edge of the Estate" by Sandra M. Gilbert, in *Poetry* (Chicago), 104(24), 1977; The Phenomenal Woman and the Severed Daughter" by R. B. Stepto, in *Parnassus,* 8(1), 1979; "The Re-Vision of the Muse: Adrienne Rich, Audre Lorde, Judy Grahn, Olga Broumas" by Mary J. Carruthers, in *Hudson Review,* summer 1983; "The Re-Vision of the Muse: Unnaming and Renaming in the Poetry of Audre Lorde, Pat Parker, Sylvia Plath, and Adrienne Rich" by Pamela Annas, in *Hudson Review* (New York), summer 1983; *Black Women Writers at Work* by Claudia Tate (interview), New York Continuum, 1983; "No More Buried Lives: The Theme of Lesbianism in Lorde, Naylor, Shange, Walker" by Barbara Christian, in *Feminist Issues,* spring 1985; "Audre Lorde" by Irma McClaurin-Allen, in *Dictionary of Literary Biography,* Vol. 41: *Afro-American Poets since 1955,* Detroit, Gale, 1985; "The Black Woman as Artist and Critic: Four Versions" by Margaret B. MacDowell, in *Kentucky Review* (Lexington), spring 1987; "'Which Me Will Survive?': Audre Lorde and the Development of a Black Feminist Ideology" by Sharon Patricia Holland in *Critical Matrix* (Princeton), 1, 1988; "*Zami*: A Portrait of the Artist as a Black Lesbian" by Barbara DiBernard, in *Kenyon Review* (Gambier, Ohio) 13(4), 1991; "*Zami* and the Politics of Plural Identity" by Erin Carlston, in *Sexual Practice, Textual Theory* edited by Susan Wolfe and Julan Penelope, Cambridge, Massachusetts, Blackwell, 1993.

* * *

"In the cause of silence," Audre Lorde writes in *The Cancer Journals*, "each one of us draws the face of her own fear—fear of contempt, of censure, or some judgment, or recognition, of challenge, of annihilation." Yet her written work as a black lesbian feminist poet activist—a list like the ones that Lorde herself was fond of using to emphasize each aspect of her identity—constantly campaigns against the cause of silence. Indeed, for two decades Lorde raised her voice through essays, autobiography, and poetry in order to speak out about everything from motherhood to lesbianism to breast cancer.

Lorde's art and her activist voice are never separated, and she is consequently known for her feminist essays as well as her poetry. Sometimes—in the essay "Poems Are Not Luxuries," for example—the two concerns meet as Lorde discusses the important role that intimacy between women plays in the creative process. In "Poems Are Not Luxuries" she explains that, for women, poetry "is a vital necessity of our existence. It forms the quality of the light within which we predicate our hopes and dreams toward survival and change, first made into language, then into an idea, then into more tangible action." Here Lorde underscores what she regards as the essential links among creativity, language, and activism.

Lorde's longer nonfiction pieces sound similar themes, perhaps because writing serves as the lens through which she views her world. *The Cancer Journals*, for example, reflect both the courage and the fear that Lorde feels as she faces breast cancer. She uses the disease as the impetus to reflect on the importance of her life as a writer and to find renewed energy to create. Lorde seems to translate that energy into telling her life's story with *Zami: A New Spelling of My Name*, published in 1982. The narrative traces what she calls "an unfolding of my life and loves," and she terms the text a biomythography rather than autobiography as if to emphasize the importance of women's communities in contrast with one individual's life. *Sister Outsider* and *A Burst of Light*, published in 1984 and 1988 respectively, contain a series of essays and speeches on topics like the generative power of anger and Lorde's view of her role as a lesbian mother.

Even in her prose, however, the poet's voice sings through; perhaps Lorde sprinkles much of her prose with snatches of poetry because that has long seemed the surest way to communicate. Born to West Indian immigrant parents, Lorde grew up in New York a quiet and inarticulate child. Poetry, she explains, served as her most powerful connection with the world: "I didn't speak until I was five, in fact, not really until I started reading and writing poetry." Ignoring the criticism of the Hunter High School English teachers who described an early love poem as being "too romantic," Lorde sent it to *Seventeen* magazine where it was published. After graduating from high school, Lorde attended Hunter College in New York City from 1951 to 1960, where she earned her degree in library science. Spending a year at the University of Mexico in 1954 played an important role in affirming Lorde's identity as a black woman. Recalling the experience in *Zami*, she writes: "Wherever I went there were brown faces of every hue meeting mine, and seeing my own color reflected upon the streets in such great numbers was an affirmation for me that was brand-new and very exciting."

Lorde received her master's degree in library science from Columbia University in 1962, the same year that she married lawyer Edwin Ashley Rollins. The two divorced a decade later, and the marriage left her with two children, Elizabeth and Jonathan. In 1968 Lorde published her first book of poetry, *The First Cities.* Critics regarded Lorde's poetic voice as a refreshing contrast to much of the more confrontational black poetry of the time. Her second volume, *Cables to Rage*, contains the first poem in which she explicitly writes about erotic love between two women. In "Martha" the narrator shares thoughts of hope and anxiety as she waits for her lover to recover from an accident: "yes Martha we have loved each other and yes I hope we still can/ no Martha/ I do not know if we shall ever sleep in each other's arms again."

Lorde's next two publications mark an increasingly political poetic voice. Her 1973 collection, *From a Land Where Other People*

Live, turns its attention on global political issues even as it continues to explore more personal concerns. *New York City Head Shop and Museum* provides the reader with the poet's sometimes admiring, sometimes angry view of the city where she spent her life. In "A Birthday Memorial to Seventh Street," for example, Lorde thinks with some nostalgia of the place where "I became a woman" even as the place calls to mind friends who lost their lives to drugs and violence.

When W. W. Norton published *Coal* in 1976, Lorde's work had its first encounter with the wider audience a major publisher could offer. The volume compiles poems from *The First Cities* and *Cables to Rage*. It is *The Black Unicorn*, however, that critics regard as her finest work. Drawing on the African landscape and its people, Lorde emphasizes her identity as a black woman and as a lesbian. Critic R. B. Stepto called *The Black Unicorn* "a personal triumph for Lorde" and "an event in contemporary letters." In *Our Dead behind Us*, as its title suggests, the poet scans the global map and writes about how violence interrupts people's lives in South Africa, Central America, and here at home. *Chosen Poems, Old and New* along with the revised collection, *Undersong: Chosen Poems Old and New* contain poems from Lorde's earlier volumes.

Throughout all of Audre Lorde's writing, both nonfiction and fiction, a single theme surfaces repeatedly. The black lesbian feminist poet activist reminds her readers that they ignore differences among people at their peril, a point that black feminists have long made. Instead, Lorde suggests, differences in race or class must serve as a "reason for celebration and growth." Though liver cancer claimed her life in 1992, Lorde's words will continue to ring out against silence.

—Allison Kimmich

LOVELACE, Maud Hart

Nationality: American. **Born:** Mankato, Minnesota, 25 April 1892. **Education:** University of Minnesota, 1911-12. **Family:** Married Delos Wheeler Lovelace in 1917 (died 1967); one daughter. **Career:** Professional writer, beginning 1911. Contributor of short fiction to periodicals, including *Jack and Jill.* **Awards:** Spring Book Festival Award, 1950, for *The Tune in the Tree.* **Died:** 11 March 1980.

Publications

Novels

The Black Angels. Day, 1926.
Early Candlelight. Day, 1929.
Petticoat Court. Day, 1930.
The Charming Sally. Day, 1932.
One Stayed at Welcome, with Delos Wheeler Lovelace. Day, 1934.
Gentlemen from England, with Delos Wheeler Lovelace. New York, Macmillan, 1937.

For Children

"Betsy-Tacy" series:
- *Betsy-Tacy,* illustrated by Lois Lenski. New York, Crowell, 1940; revised edition, 1979.
- *Betsy-Tacy and Tib,* illustrated by Lois Lenski. New York, Crowell, 1941; revised edition, 1979.
- *Over the Big Hill,* illustrated by Lois Lenski. New York, Crowell, 1942; as *Betsy and Tacy Go over the Big Hill,* 1942; revised edition, 1979.
- *Down Town,* illustrated by Lois Lenski. New York, Crowell, 1943; as *Betsy and Tacy Go Downtown,* 1943; revised edition, 1979.
- *Heaven to Betsy,* illustrated by Vera Neville. New York, Crowell, 1945.
- *Betsy in Spite of Herself,* illustrated by Vera Neville. New York, Crowell, 1947.
- *Betsy Was a Junior,* illustrated by Vera Neville. New York, Crowell, 1947.
- *Betsy and Joe,* illustrated by Vera Neville. New York, Crowell, 1948.
- *Betsy and the Great World,* illustrated by Vera Neville. New York, Crowell, 1952.
- *Betsy's Wedding,* illustrated by Vera Neville. New York, Crowell, 1955.

The Golden Wedge: Indian Legends of South America, with Delos Wheeler Lovelace, illustrated by Charlotte Chase. New York, Crowell, 1942.
Carney's House Party, illustrated by Vera Neville. New York, Crowell, 1949.
The Tune Is in the Tree, illustrated by Eloise Wilken. New York, Crowell, 1950.
Emily of Deep Valley, illustrated by Vera Neville. New York, Crowell, 1950.
The Trees Kneel at Christmas, illustrated by Gertrude Howe. New York, Crowell, 1951.
Winona's Pony Cart, illustrated by Vera Neville. New York, Crowell, 1953.
What Cabrillo Found, illustrated by Paul Galdone. New York, Crowell, 1958.
The Valentine Box, illustrated by Ingrid Fetz. New York, Crowell, 1966.

*

Bibliography: In *Between Deep Valley and the Great World: Maud Hart Lovelace in Minneapolis* by Amy Dolnick, Minneapolis, Betsy-Tacy Society, 1993.

Manuscript Collections: University of Oregon Library, Eugene.

Critical Studies: "Maud Hart Lovelace and Mankato" by Jo Anne Ray, in *Women of Minnesota,* edited by Barbara Stuhler and Gretchen Kreuter, St. Paul, Minnesota Historical Society Press, 1977; *The Betsy-Tacy Companion: A Biography of Maud Hart Lovelace* by Sharla Scannell Whalen, Whitehall, Pennsylvania, Portalington Press, 1995.

* * *

Maud Hart Lovelace can perhaps best be described as an unconscious feminist for most of her life. Growing up in the era of the suffrage movement, she supported the feminism of the suffragists through the words of her alter ego, Betsy Ray, in *Betsy and the Great World.* Lovelace's books for children and young adults are a scarcely masked autobiographical account of her own life and that of her friends. As Sharla Whalen has meticulously detailed, virtually every character and incident has a real life counterpart. Occasionally, Lovelace changes the time, place, and characters in order to create a clearer story line, but the real-life parallels are omnipresent. The leading character of Betsy Ray, whom she tracks from kindergarten through her early married life, is Maud herself. Of all Lovelace's characters, Betsy is perhaps the natural feminist; her close friend Tacy, whose real-life counterpart was Maud's lifelong friend, Bic, is by contrast a more traditional woman. But even Tacy has bursts of independence.

Lovelace's many books for children and young adults are based on the lives of both she and her friends, the major exception being the development of her relationship with her husband, Delos Lovelace. While in real life Maud met Delos when they were both adults—the couple were married not long afterward—Betsy meets Joe, the fictional Delos, when both are entering their freshman year of high school. Their friendly rivalry as budding writers and their growing rapport is a theme throughout Lovelace's young adult books.

In her children's books, it would be hard to discover a overt feminist philosophy, but little Betsy and her friends have a sense of adventure that develops at an early age and increases through their elementary years. The early childhood adventures give way to more mature escapades in the high school series, which begins with *Heaven to Betsy* and ends with *Betsy and Joe.* After a brief break, the activities of Betsy and her friends are recaptured in *Betsy and the Great World* and *Betsy's Wedding.* In these books written for teenagers, one starts to glimpse a subtle, implicit feminism. As one becomes immersed in the characters and their lives, one realizes that Betsy and her sister Julia have aspirations far exceeding the typical women of their day. Lovelace, like Louisa May Alcott, created characters whose dreams and ideals inspired women to greater heights. Like Alcott's Jo March, Lovelace's Betsy Ray is a woman who inspires young women to greater heights. This is a reason why many adult women have returned to the stories of Betsy and her friends and are keeping the legend alive. The national Betsy-Tacy Society and the regional Maud Hart Lovelace Society both enroll Lovelace devotees.

Not surprising, Lovelace originally wrote the "Betsy" stories for her own daughter Merian, perhaps to inspire the young girl to dream dreams and aspire to higher achievement than even her mother. An independent-minded woman, Lovelace had begun her writing career as a young child and continued to write until she was quite elderly. Continuing her career after marriage to writer-journalist Delos, she and her husband lived a quiet, intellectual life in New York and in California. Although Lovelace's Minnesota roots—especially Mankato, the fictional Deep Valley—and Minneapolis were special to her, she actually spent relatively little of her adult life in Minnesota, coming back periodically only to visit. In 1961 she was honored by her beloved hometown with a special Betsy-Tacy Day, which was marked by a reunion of many of Lovelace's childhood friends. During her peak writing years for the Betsy series, she had maintained active correspondence with these friends, frequently tapping their recollections of times and places. For example, when she wrote *Carney's House Party,* which features one of Betsy's closest friends, Lovelace corresponded with Carney's real-life counterpart, Marion Willard Everett, in an attempt to recapture details of her friend's college years and romance with her husband-to-be.

In addition to her books for younger readers, Lovelace wrote historical novels during the 1920s and 1930s, but, although well researched, they never achieved the popularity or success of her children's works. The adult fiction is rooted primarily in the history of Minnesota and is also characterized by strong heroines. Because of the strong resurgence of interest in Lovelace, these too have been re-issued in recent years by the Minnesota Historical Society.

Fans of Lovelace include those who grew up in the 1940s, 1950s, and 1960s when her books were first published, as well as their daughters and grand-daughters. The Betsy-Tacy Society boasts about 1,000 members throughout the United States; a local Maud Hart Lovelace Society is based in the Twin Cities of Minneapolis and St. Paul.

—Norma C. Noonan

LUCAS, Victoria. *See* **PLATH, Sylvia.**

LYNX. *See* **WEST, Rebecca.**

M

MacKINNON, Catharine A.

Nationality: American. **Born:** 7 October 1946. **Education:** Smith College, Northampton, Massachusetts, B.A. in government (magna cum laude with distinction) 1969; Yale University, New Haven, Connecticut, J.D. 1977, Ph.D. in political science 1987. **Career:** Admitted to bar of Connecticut, 1978, and U.S. Supreme Court, 1986. Visiting professor of law, Yale University, Harvard University, Stanford University, University of California Los Angeles, and University of Chicago, 1980-82 and 1984-88; assistant professor of law, University of Minnesota, 1982-84; professor of law, Osgoode Hall, York University, Toronto, Ontario, 1988-90; professor of law, University of Michigan Law School, Ann Arbor, beginning 1990. Designed legal claim for sexual harassment, 1975, and, with Andrea Dworkin, conceived and drafted antipornography ordinances for Minneapolis, Minnesota, 1983, and Indianapolis, Indiana, 1984; represented Bosnian and Croatian women survivors of genocidal rape, beginning 1991. Contributor to periodicals. **Address:** University of Michigan School of Law, 625 South State St., Ann Arbor, Michigan 48109-1210, U.S.A.

PUBLICATIONS

Political/Social Theory

Sexual Harassment of Working Women: A Case of Sex Discrimination. New Haven, Yale University Press, 1979.

Feminism Unmodified: Discourses on Life and Law (speeches). Cambridge, Harvard University Press, 1987.

Pornography and Civil Rights: A New Day for Women's Equality, with Andrea Dworkin. Minneapolis, Organizing against Pornography, 1988.

Toward a Feminist Theory of the State. Cambridge, Massachusetts, and London, Harvard University Press, 1989.

Only Words (lectures). Cambridge, Harvard University Press, 1993.

*

Critical Studies: *Feminist Thought: A Comprehensive Introduction* by Rosemarie Tong, Boulder and San Francisco, Westview Press, 1989; "Eccentric Subjects: Feminist Theory and Historical Consciousness" by Teresa De Laurentis, in *Feminist Studies* 16(1), spring 1990; "Feminism and Pragmatism" by Richard Rorty, in *Michigan Quarterly Review* 30(2), spring 1991; "Catharine MacKinnon, May I Speak?" by Suzanne Rhodenbaugh, in *Michigan Quarterly Review* 30(3), summer 1991; "Catharine MacKinnon and Feminist Jurisprudence: A Critical Appraisal" by Emily Jackson, in *Journal of Law and Society* 19(2); "The Logic of the Development of Feminism; or, Is MacKinnon to Feminism as Parmenides Is to Greek Philosophy?" by Susan E. Bernick, in *Hypatia,* 7(1), winter 1992; "The New Legal Puritanism of Catharine MacKinnon" by Dan Greenberg and Thomas H. Tobiason, in *Ohio State University Law Journal* 54(5), 1993; "Sex and the Feminists" by Carol Iannone, in *Commentary* 96(3), September 1993; *States of Injury: Power and Freedom in Late Modernity* by Wendy Brown, Princeton, Princeton University Press, 1995; "Pornography: The Theory" by Frances Ferguson, in *Critical Inquiry* 21(3), spring 1995.

* * *

Considered by many to be the central figure in modern feminist legal theory, law professor, lawyer, political theorist, and political activist Catharine MacKinnon's writing is singularly focused on changing minds and changing laws. Her project, most consistently, is to convince her readers that they live in and contribute to a social climate that has almost uniformly failed to take seriously the harm certain widely tolerated social practices inflict on women—and often, as well, on children. In particular, the areas of pornography and sexual harassment have received her attention, and in both these areas—whose "convergence," she has commented, the law is increasingly willing to see—MacKinnon has had startling impact, her thought and argument transforming law and jurisprudence by fundamentally redefining the basic understandings from which thinking on these matters proceeds.

The daughter of Federal appellate judge George E. MacKinnon and Elizabeth Davis MacKinnon, Catharine Alice MacKinnon attended Smith College, as had her mother and grandmother, graduating magna cum laude with a B.A. in government in 1969. In some sense, she was bred to politics, though clearly not activism of the change-seeking sort in pursuit of which she has made her name: her father was a Republican Party true-believer, an adviser to the Presidential campaigns of both Eisenhower and Nixon, and himself a one-term congressman and Republican nominee for governor of Minnesota. But MacKinnon attributes her political and intellectual perspectives to her tenure in New Haven, Connecticut, where she spent much of the 1970s involved in radical projects. First working in opposition to the war in Vietnam and in support of the Black Panther Party, MacKinnon became part of the women's movement, as did many women during that decade. It is from this movement, she says, that she "learned everything" she knows.

While still at Yale, from which she would earn a J.D. in 1977 and a Ph.D. in political science in 1987, MacKinnon worked at designing a legal argument to address sexual harassment on the job. Her pioneering work on sex equality generally resulted in the "dominance" approach that has become so pivotal to feminist legal theory. MacKinnon's work on developing this approach began when she became aware that the law regarding sexual discrimination, as it then stood, made it virtually impossible to address the real situations women faced, including those resulting from sexual advances or pressure at work. This awareness fed her growing conviction that much of the law had "nothing whatever to do with the problem of sexual inequality as it's experienced by women." She therefore set out to create a legal approach capable of dealing with the practical realities of women's experiences of sex discrimination.

Traditionally, the law sees discrimination to exist only where two *equivalent* or comparable groups are treated differently. In this view, because women could be seen as *sexually different,* their different sexual treatment would become a private matter, the natural and understandable outcome of males' personal or biologically driven pursuit of women. As a result, when women left their jobs to escape abusive sexual behaviors, pressures, or propositions, this could also be seen as a personal decision for which no legal remedy could be sought. Under the dominance approach, however, discrimination exists whenever a social practice is part of the systematic deprivation of one sex *because* of sex, making sexual harassment an instance of sex discrimination under federal law.

Her successful argument that sexual harassment is sex discrimination formed the basis for MacKinnon's first book, *The Sexual Harassment of Working Women*, published in 1979 and still considered the definitive work on the subject. In this book MacKinnon argued that there exist two forms of sexual harassment, both of which are sexual discrimination. The first of these is the "quid pro quo" or tit-for-tat form of sexual harassment, in which a supervisor ties specific rewards or punishments to an employee's acceptance or rejection of certain sexual conditions (as in, "if you sleep with me, I won't fire you"). This form of harassment was recognized by the lower courts beginning in 1976. MacKinnon first made a visible contribution to U.S. law in 1986, when, as co-counsel in *Meritor Savings Bank v. Vinson,* she wrote the brief that argued to the Court that Mechelle Vinson had been a victim of sex discrimination when she left her bank job to escape the second kind of harassment, a "hostile environment" created by her male supervisor's alleged two-and-a-half years of rape and sexual molestation. Although the man had never stated that he would fire Vinson, MacKinnon argued that he had still discriminated against her under Title VII of the Civil Rights Act of 1964 because she had to endure his sexual attacks or leave her job, to which she had a right, free of sex discrimination.

In MacKinnon's argument, the two seemingly distinct forms of sexual harassment were revealed actually to be just two different points in time. A woman working in a hostile environment suffered that environment as a condition of employment. Were she to reject such treatment or leave, that would clearly transform her into a victim of quid pro quo harassment. But why should she be forced to bring such "intensified injury" upon herself in order to prove any injury at all? Wouldn't this requirement amount to sanctioning the clever harasser who, as long as he left the woman's job "formally undisturbed," could otherwise, without consequence, make her worklife a constant punishment because of her sex? The Court agreed that it would, finding unanimously that hostile environment sexual harassment, as much as quid pro quo, was illegal sex discrimination under the laws of the United States. Ensuing decisions have further strengthened this ruling.

If MacKinnon's position on sexual harassment has been accepted by the legal establishment, the same cannot be said about her efforts to eliminate pornography, at least in the United States. On this issue, her work has been deeply entwined with that of activist Andrea Dworkin. Since the early 1970s, Dworkin had been building a body of work that argues that the roots of women's subordination lie in the construction of sexuality, and that pornography is central to that construction. In the early 1980s, she and MacKinnon joined forces to design a course on pornography at the University of Minnesota Law School, where MacKinnon was then teaching; they were consequently asked by a group of Minneapolis residents to aid in a battle those residents were waging against the zoning of pornography *into* their neighborhood (a poor and largely African American one, as are most of the neighborhoods in to which municipalities zone regulated sex businesses).

In response, MacKinnon and Dworkin developed a new legal basis on which to attack pornography, which was requested by the Minneapolis City Council in the form of a proposed anti-pornography ordinance that recognized the harm of pornography to women's equality. This new approach argued that the problem with pornography is not that it is "obscene" or that it appeals to "prurient interests," but that it *harms* women in a whole range of ways, concretely from coercion into pornography, forcing pornography on a person, to assault due to pornography, defamation, and finally, all the harms of second-class citizenship due to its trafficking. MacKinnon and Dworkin presented evidence in testimony and from scholarly experts that pornography is dangerous and injurious to women. Among its harms are that, as the evidence shows, as men see increasing amounts of pornography they begin to enjoy it more and become desensitized to the violence against women that such pornographic materials depict. They also act it out, their evidence showed.

MacKinnon and Dworkin's strategy was to take pornography out of the criminal courts (where the obscenity laws had located it) and to attack it in civil court, where money damages are the remedy and the burden of proof is lower. But it was not tort law that MacKinnon and Dworkin were invoking, but sex equality law, anti-discrimination law; theirs was a civil rights approach that allowed women—or anyone who is used in pornography in place of women—to sue anyone who coerced them to appear in pornography, who forced pornography on them, or who produced a particular piece of pornography that caused them to be assaulted. Further, under the proposed ordinance, any woman could bring suit against pornography traffickers on behalf of all women, provided they could prove women are subordinated by its traffic.

The Minneapolis City Council held two extensive hearings to investigate the evidence on the harm of pornography and to determine if women had been damaged by it. Then, satisfied that this was the case, they enacted it, twice. The Mayor vetoed it. MacKinnon and Dworkin were then successful in getting a similar ordinance—limited to violent acts or materials—passed by the city of Indianapolis, but in that case the courts invalidated it in actions that were summarily affirmed without comment by the Supreme Court in 1986 (the same year the Court handed MacKinnon her precedent-setting victory on hostile-environment sexual harassment).

It is significant that, in the legal battles over the proposed ordinances, some of the most prominent opposition came from prominent feminists as well as from liberal organizations, among them the Feminist Anti-Censorship Task Force (FACT), the American Civil Liberties Union, and the American Booksellers Association. FACT weighed in with a legal brief, signed by more than 50 prominent feminists including Betty Friedan and Adrienne Rich, which argued that MacKinnon and Dworkin's ordinance is vague, amounts to censorship, and tends to reinforce the society's "central sexist stereotypes." In response, MacKinnon accused the members of FACT of being the women's movement's equivalents to "Uncle Toms," asking pointedly why they were betraying sexually abused women and stating that FACT's opposition to the ordinances amounted to "fronting for male supremacists."

MacKinnon early argued the now common feminist view that gender is not an expression of nature but is instead a *construction* created by society. Where she and Dworkin part company with some other feminists is in the analysis that pornography is part of constructing "the social reality of gender." It "*does*" this, MacKinnon says in *Feminism Unmodified,* by defining "in pornographic terms" "what a woman is," thereby creating a harm that is difficult to address by law as harm because it is embodied in the make-up of gender, seeming to be "just the way things are." Pornography is not an example of free speech protected by the First Amendment, she contends, but rather a practice of the subordination of women, an *act* of sex discrimination. If society insists on defining men's freedom as including the freedom "to make or consume pornography," she argues, it does so at the expense of women's equality, purchasing "men's freedom to use [women] in this way" at the cost of women's "second-class civil status."

Pornography "sexualizes inequality," making "dominance and submission into sex." In pornography, we can find "in one place, all of the abuses" women suffer. Pornography "sexualizes" these abuses, "eroticiz[ing] the dominance and submission that is the dynamic common to them all," thereby "legitimiz[ing] them" and making "hierarchy sexy." By means of "this process pornography constructs what a woman is as what men want from sex," so that in pornography's "harmonious" world, acts of sexual violence "become acts of sexual equality." In this pornographic world, the most "liberated" woman is the one who most wants to acquiesce to what men want from her sexually. But although in pornography the "victim must look free," this ostensible freedom always coexists with a communication of "forcing," making pornography itself "a form of forced sex, a practice of sexual politics, and an institution of gender inequality" that "institutionalizes the sexuality of male supremacy, fusing the erotization of dominance and submission with the social construction of male and female." In society, "men treat women as who they see woman as being" and it is pornography that "constructs who that is."

Rather than retreating in the aftermath of her ordinances' defeat, MacKinnon has stepped up her campaign against pornography, frequently lecturing on its harms. Some leading constitutional theorists predict that she may succeed in convincing the U.S. courts that pornography is no more protected by the First Amendment than is sexual harassment. In the meantime, the civil rights approach to pornography has found some vindication in Canada, whose Supreme Court in 1992 redefined obscenity to include materials that degrade, dehumanize, or subordinate women, ruling that it is permissible for the government to prohibit materials that harm women or sex equality. In the Canadian Court's reasoning, such materials pose a threat to women's equality, because they portray women "as a class as objects for sexual exploitation and abuse," resulting in damage to "the individual's sense of self-worth and acceptance," and to their personal security.

MacKinnon's most recent work is directed toward recognizing women's rights as human rights internationally. She is currently representing Bosnian women survivors of Serbian genocidal sexual atrocities, attempting to secure international justice. Her U.S. lawsuit on their behalf under the Alien Tort Statute for genocidal rape and murder, torture, and war crimes has established new human rights for aliens to assert in U.S. courts under international law. The case, *Kad c v. Karadz c,* marks the first time rape and forced pregnancy have been legally recognized as acts of genocide.

As is typical of significant works that challenge the status quo, although her books are widely read and reviewed, critical reaction to MacKinnon's writing (excepting, to some extent, her writing on sexual harassment) has been mixed. While widely cited by both courts and experts in a variety of fields, MacKinnon has also been termed rigid, elitist, and even accused of alienating people from feminism. Such comments have had little effect on her career; in 1990 she was appointed, with tenure, to the University of Michigan Law School. Although the controversy that has surrounded her work on behalf of women may have compromised her career, that same controversial scholarship has also earned MacKinnon numerous ardent disciples, who concur in the opinion of University of Michigan Law School's Dean, Lee Bollinger, that "the force of her scholarship and the quality of her mind" make her an important scholar and a "major social theorist." It has become apparent that, whether or not one agrees with her, Catharine MacKinnon remains a legal force to be reckoned with: a woman who has achieved the rare distinction of having, in her own lifetime, through her determination and the power of her intellect, changed social presumptions that were all too recently almost beyond questioning.

—Eileen Bresnahan

MAITLAND, Sara (Louise)

Nationality: English. **Born:** London, 27 February 1950. **Education:** Oxford University, B.A. (with honours) 1971. **Family:** Married the priest Donald Hugh Thomson Lee in 1972; one daughter and one son. **Career:** Freelance researcher, Oxford, England, 1972-73; freelance writer, journalist, and lecturer, beginning 1973. Cofounder, with Zoë Fairbairns, Michèle Roberts, Valerie Miner, and Michelene Wandor, Feminist Writers Group. Contributor to periodicals, including *Bananas, City Limits, Guardian, Listener, New Society, New Statesman, Spare Rib,* and *Time Out.* **Awards:** Somerset Maugham Award, 1979, for *Daughter of Jerusalem.* **Member:** National Union of Journalists. **Agent:** Anne McDernird, Curtis Brown Ltd., 162-168 Regent St., London W1R 5TA, England. **Address:** St. Chad's Vicarage, Dunloe St., London E 2 England.

PUBLICATIONS

Novels

Daughter of Jerusalem. London, Blond & Briggs, 1978; as *Languages of Love,* Garden City, New York, Doubleday, 1980.
Virgin Territory. London, M. Joseph, and New York, Beaufort Books, 1984.
Arky Types, with Michelene Wandor. London, Methuen, 1987.
Ancestral Truths. New York, Holt, 1994.
Home Truths. London, Chatto & Windus, 1993.

Short Stories

Tales I Tell My Mother, with Zoë Fairbairns, Michèle Roberts, Michelene Wandor, and Valerie Miner. London, Journeyman Press, 1978; Boston, South End Press, 1980.
More Tales I Tell My Mother, with Zoë Fairbairns, Michèle Roberts, Michelene Wandor, and Valerie Miner. London, Journeyman Press, 1987.
Telling Tales. London, Journeyman Press, 1983.
Weddings and Funerals, with Aileen La Tourette. London, Brilliance, 1984.
A Book of Spells. London, M. Joseph, 1987.

Women Fly When Men Aren't Watching. London, Virago Press, 1993.
Angel and Me: Short Stories for Holy Week. London, Mowbray, 1995.
Angel Maker: The Collected Short Stories of Sara Maitland. New York, Holt, 1996.

Uncollected Short Stories

"Let Us Now Praise Unknown Women and Our Mothers Who Begat Us," in *Stepping Out: Short Stories on Friendships between Women.* London and New York, Pandora Press, 1986.
"Fag-hags: A Field Guide," in *Critical Quarterly,* 33(2), summer 1991.
"Lullabye for My Dyke and Her Cat," in *The Penguin Book of Lesbian Short Stories.* London and New York, Viking, 1993.
"Siren song," in *By the Light of the Silvery Moon.* London, Virago Press, 1994.

Essays

"Abortion and the Sanctity of Life," in *Catholicism and Conflict: The Jubilee Lectures.* London, Jubilee Group, 1982.
"Futures in Feminist Fiction," in *From My Guy to Sci-Fi: Genre and Women's Writing in the Postmodern World.* London, Pandora, 1989.
"Biblicism, a Radical Rhetoric," in *Refusing Holy Orders: Women and Fundamentalism in Britain.* London, Virago, 1992.

Other

A Map of the New Country: Women and Christianity. London, Routledge, 1983.
Vesta Tilley (biography). London, Virago, 1986.
Very Heaven: Looking Back at the 60s. London, Virago, 1988.
Three Times Table. London, Chatto & Windus, 1990.
A Big-enough God: A Feminist's Search for a Joyful Theology. New York, Holt, 1995.

Editor, with Jo Garcia, *Walking on the Water: Women Talk about Spirituality.* London, Virago, 1983.
Editor, with Lisa Appignanesi, *The Rushdie File.* London, ICA, Fourth Estate, 1989; Syracuse, New York, Syracuse University Press, 1990.

*

Media Adaptations: "Lullabye for My Dyke and Her Cat" (audio recording) 1995; "The Wicked Stepmother's Lament" (audio recording) in *Woman's Hour: Short Stories,* 1990; *Pandora's Box: A 3-Dimensional Celebration of Greek Mythology,* with Christos Kondeatis (video), 1995.

Critical Studies: "Traditional Myth and the Feminine" by Richard Martin, in *American Book Review,* 7(5), July/August 1985; *Writers Revealed* by Rosemary Hartill, London, BBC Books, 1989; "Three Women and a Dragon" by Anita Brookner, in *Spectator,* 14 April 1990; "Iris Murdoch—a Revisionist Theology?: A Comparative Study of Iris Murdoch's *Nuns and Soldiers* and Sara Maitland's *Virgin Territory*" by Caroline Guerin, in *Literature and Theology: An International Journal of Theory, Criticism and Culture,* 6(2), June 1992; "Bewitched: Sara Maitland Stirs It Up," by Laurie Muchnick in *Village Voice Literary Supplement,* 123, March 1994.

* * *

In her novels and short fiction, Sara Maitland draws on both her Christian beliefs and her feminist politics in an attempt to come to terms with the treatment of women within a patriarchal society. Praised for her use of language and for the broad knowledge she brings to bear on her subject, her novels and short fiction present the reader with real characters whose resolution of conflict within their fictional worlds becomes relevant and real to our own.

During her education at Oxford University, Maitland became heavily involved in both English Catholicism and socialist-inspired English feminism. These two doctrines have, in turn, greatly influenced her work as a writer; a characteristic concern of her fiction is an exploration of the historic relationship, as well as the continued relevancy, between orthodox Christianity and female empowerment, most particularly as a result of 20th-century feminist enlightenment.

Maitland's first novel, 1978's *Daughter of Jerusalem* (published in the United States as *The Languages of Love*) would set the pace of her later works in its use of Old Testament narratives as a means of addressing the concerns of 20th-century women. Liz, while a self-proclaimed feminist, still wishes to incorporate some of womanhood's traditional aspects into her life. Alas, she is unable to bear children; in the course of the novel she endures invasive medical exams and the suggestion that her barrenness is psychosomatic by insensitive physicians, is pressured by ultra-feminist friends to add her voice to their pro-choice campaign, and deals with marital stresses caused by her husband's need for progeny.

Virgin Territory (1984) deals with the conflict between religious devotion and lesbianism. A member of a South American convent, Sister Anna is devastated after learning that fellow nun Sister Kitty has been raped; her quest for understanding is pulled by the divergent forces of an unforgiving, patriarchal Yahweh and a growing sense of her alternate possibilities as a radical lesbian. Maitland's 1990 novel, *Three Times Table,* introduces three generations of women: a paleontologist; her daughter, a former flower child who now works in a community garden; and *her* daughter, who lives in a world of imagination. Within Maitland's mix of evolutionary theory, the confrontation of mortality brought on by a diagnosis of cancer, and an adolescent's coming of age, *Three Times Table* was described by Anita Brookner as "a superior version of the [three-generations-of-women] formula."

A co-founder of the Feminist Writers group with Zoë Fairbairns, Michèle Roberts, and Michelene Wandor, Maitland has collaborated in *Tales I Tell My Mother* (1978) and the 1987 sequel, *More Tales I Tell My Mother.* Maitland and Wandor have also co-authored the novel *Arky Types* (1987). In addition to publishing several essays and works of nonfiction, including a feminist-focused, historic survey called *A Map of the New Country: Women and Christianity* (1983), she has edited *Walking on the Water: Women Talk about Spirituality* (1983), with Jo Garcia. Maitland's biography of a brassy British socialite, *Vesta Tilley* was published in 1986.

—Pamela Kester-Shelton

MALPEDE, Karen

Also writes as Karen Taylor. **Nationality:** American. **Born:** Wichita Falls, Texas, 29 June 1945. **Education:** University of Wisconsin—Madison, B.S. (with honors) 1967; Columbia University, M.F.A. 1971. **Family:** One daughter. **Career:** Cofounder and resident playwright, New Cycle Theatre, Brooklyn, New York, 1976-85; member of field faculty, Smith College, Northampton, Massachusetts, 1982-86; member of adjunct faculty, 1987-90, assistant professor of theatre, beginning 1991, New York University. Conductor of playwriting workshops and lecturer; has given readings at universities, festivals, and conventions throughout the United States. Contributor of articles and reviews to professional journals. **Awards:** Windward Foundation production grants, 1976, 1977; PEN Writers grant, 1981; Creative Artists Public Service grant, 1982-83; Smith College travel grant, 1984, Harnish Fund for Visiting Artists, 1985; Ludwig Vogelstein Foundation writer's grant, 1987. **Member:** Dramatists Guild. **Address:** New York, New York U.S.A.

Publications

Plays

A Lament for Three Women (produced Cummington, Massachusetts, 1974), in *A Century of Plays by American Women,* edited by Rachel France. New York, Richards Rosen Press, 1979.
Rebecca (produced 1974).
The End of War (produced Dallas, 1976). Privately printed, 1977; in *A Monster Has Stolen the Sun and Other Plays,* 1987.
Making Peace: A Fantasy (produced Brooklyn, New York, 1979).
A Monster Has Stolen the Sun (produced Brooklyn, 1981). In *A Monster Has Stolen the Sun and Other Plays,* 1987.
Sappho and Aphrodite (produced Northampton, Massachusetts, then New York 1984; produced London, 1987). In *A Monster Has Stolen the Sun and Other Plays,* 1987.
Us (produced New York, 1987). In *Us. Women on the Verge,* 1992.
A Monster Has Stolen the Sun and Other Plays. Marlboro, Vermont, Marlboro Press, 1987.
Better People (produced 1990). In *Better People. Angles of Power,* 1991.
Better People. Angles of Power, edited by Susan Hawthorne and Renata Klein. Melbourne, Spinifex, 1991.
Us. Women on the Verge, edited by Rosette C. Lamont. New York, Applause, 1992.
Blue Heaven (produced New York, 1992).

Other

People's Theater in Amerika (as Karen Taylor). New York, Drama Books, 1972.

Editor, with Joseph Chaikin, *Three Works by the Open Theater.* New York, Drama Book Specialists, 1974.
Editor, *Women in Theater: Compassion and Hope.* New York, Limelight, 1983.

*

Critical Studies: "Rebeccah Rehearsal Notes" by Helen Krich Chinoy and Linda Walsh Jenkins, in *Women in American Theatre,* New York, Theatre Communications Group, 1981; Interview with Rachel Koenig in *Interviews with Contemporary Women Playwrights,* edited by Koenig and Kathleen Betsko, New York, Morrow, 1987; "Karen Malpede" by Cindy Rosenthal, in *Jewish American Woman Writers,* edited by Ann R. Shapiro, Westport, Connecticut, Greenwood Press, 1994.

* * *

Karen Malpede has a reputation. Committed: to her pacifism, her Jewish roots, and her feminist politics. Radical: She has made a courageous, unique contribution to feminist-inspired, avant garde theatre in works that include *Sappho and Aphrodite, Us,* and *The End of War.* And controversial: criticism of her works has run the gamut, from high praise for her lyrical prose to dismay over her use of graphic violence to drive home a political point. Indeed, driving home a political point is the sole function of Malpede's performance art. "Feminism released me to write plays," she explained to Cindy Rosenthal. "If one was to pursue non-violence, the next logical place to pursue it was in gender issues. The feminist movement was a totally transformative experience ... the sense that my story mattered, that I had a story that could be read in a universal way." In addition to her plays, Malpede is also the author of *Women in Theatre: Compassion and Hope* (1983), an anthology of works by feminist playwrights.

Born in Texas in 1945, Malpede was raised in a Chicago suburb and grew up knowing she would one day be a writer. As an undergraduate student in English at the University of Wisconsin—Madison during the mid-1960s she wrote for the college paper and got caught up in the antiwar movement of the time. When she began to study the work of Ireland's Abbey Theatre playwrights she sensed an affinity, a sense of the Abbey Theatre as "a social/political/poetic force" able to "create a community, create poetry and ... have an effect on the culture of [one's] time."

Her notions of theatre as a political avenue became more pronounced when Malpede entered the graduate program at Columbia University in 1969. For her Master's thesis she chose to study New York's Theatre Union, a radical, left-wing theater in operation during the 1930s. The thesis would metamorphosize into *People's Theatre in Amerika,* published in 1972. The years following graduation from Columbia found her at Brooklyn's New Cycle Theatre, "a very positive space" that encouraged Malpede to complete her first full-length play, *A Lament for Three Women.* An effort to resolve the tangle of mixed emotions that remained following the death of her father while she was a sophomore at Madison, *A Lament* features three women in a hospital waiting room awaiting the moment of death: of a man, a society, a race. Their voices are sometimes raised in ritualistic incantatory lamentation, bringing to mind another trio of sisters: the three witches in Shakespeare's *Macbeth.* Their names recall even older sisters: Naomi, Ruth, and Rachel, with roots leading back to the Jewish mythos of the Old Testament.

Darker and more experimental works would follow. *The End of War* (1976) contains a shocking monologue describing the rape of a young girl, while *Us* (1987) explores the more violent manifestations of sexuality, childbearing, and family life: incest and child abuse. A marked contrast to much of her oeuvre, *Sappho and Aphrodite* (1983) must be considered one of Malpede's most popular plays—it has performed for audiences both in New York and

London. Here again are women, a community of women, who by engaging in lyrical rituals of song and dance and creativity embrace the joy of life rather than death and the violence that often precedes it.

Karen Malpede has continued her dedication to theatre, both on and off the stage. In addition to her continued production of plays, which include *A Monster Has Stolen the Sun* (1981) and *Blue Heaven* (1992) she is an assistant professor of theatre at New York University, where she inspires new generations of playwrights with her confrontative feminist vision.

—Lynn MacGregor

MANNING, Olivia

Also wrote as O. M. Manning. **Pseudonym:** Jacob Morrow. **Nationality:** British. **Born:** Portsmouth, England, 1908. **Education:** **Family:** Married Reginald Donald Smith in 1939. **Career:** Writer; spent most of her childhood in Ireland; moved to Bucharest, 1939; press officer to U.S. Embassy, Cairo, Egypt, and press assistant to Public Information Office, Jerusalem, during World War II; returned to London, 1946. Contributor to periodicals, sometimes as O. M. Manning or under the pseudonym Jacob Morrow, including *Horizon, Observer, New Statesman, Spectator,* and *Sunday Times* (London). **Awards:** Named Commander of the Order of the British Empire, 1976; *Yorkshire Post* Book of the Year, 1977, for *The Danger Tree.* **Died:** Isle of Wight, 23 July 1980.

PUBLICATIONS

Novels

The Wind Changes. London, J. Cape, and New York, Knopf, 1937.
School for Love. London, Heinemann, 1951.
A Different Face. London, Heinemann, 1953; New York, Abelard-Schulman, 1957.
The Doves of Venus. London, Heinemann, 1955; New York, Abelard-Schulman, 1956.
The Balkan Trilogy. London, Penguin, 1981.
 The Great Fortune. London, Heinemann, 1960; Garden City, New York, Doubleday, 1961.
 The Spoilt City. London, Heinemann, and Garden City, New York, Doubleday, 1962.
 Friends and Heroes. London, Heinemann, and Garden City, New York, Doubleday, 1965.
The Crimson Dawn. N.p., Merlin Press, 1963.
The Camperlea Girls. New York, Coward-McCann, 1969.
The Play Room. London, Heinemann, 1969.
The Rain Forest. London, Heinemann, 1974.
The Levant Trilogy. London, Penguin, 1984.
 The Danger Tree. London, Weidenfeld & Nicolson, and New York, Atheneum, 1977.
 The Battle Lost and Won. London, Weidenfeld & Nicolson, 1978; New York, Atheneum, 1980.
 The Sum of Things. London, Weidenfeld & Nicolson, 1980; New York, Atheneum, 1981.

Short Stories

Growing Up: A Collection of Short Stories. London, Heinemann, 1948.
A Romantic Hero and Other Stories. London, Heinemann, 1967.

Play

Screenplay: *The Playroom* (adapted from her novel), with Ken Annakin, 1970.

Other

The Remarkable Expedition: The Story of Stanley's Rescue of Emin Pasha from Equatorial Africa. London, Heinemann, 1947; as *The Reluctant Recluse: The Story of Stanley's Rescue of Emin Pasha from Equatorial Africa,* New York, Doubleday, 1947.
The Dreaming Shore (Irish travelogue). London, Evans Bros., 1950.
Summer Companions. N.p., Leisure Books, 1982.
Extraordinary Cats. London, M. Joseph, 1967.

Editor, *Romanian Short Stories.* Oxford, Oxford University Press, 1971.

*

Media Adaptations: *The Balkan Trilogy* (radio play), BBC-Radio; *The Fortunes of War* (television adaptation of *The Balkan Trilogy* and *The Levant Trilogy*), *Masterpiece Theatre,* BBC-TV.

Critical Studies: *Tradition and Dream: The English and American Novel from the '20s to Our Time* by Walter Allen, London, J.M. Dent, 1964; *The Novel Now* by Anthony Burgess, New York, Norton, 1967; *Continuance and Change: The Contemporary British Novel Sequence* by Robert K. Morris, Carbondale, Southern Illinois University Press, 1972; "Introduction" to Manning's *The Wind Changes* by Isobel English, London, Virago, 1988.

* * *

In Olivia Manning's short story "The Romantic Hero," the heroine says: "Everyone's unhappy ... even if they don't parade their sorrows, they have them. People are full of anxiety; they don't know what hangs over them.... No one believes in anything, yet they want to believe"; to which the eponymous hero replies, "Whatever you say, individual relationships are the most important thing in life." Manning's novels concentrate on individuals, and, through their stories, evoke the world-shattering nature of the events taking place around them. Her protagonists' search for personal definition and belonging in a rapidly changing world is a recurrent theme in Manning's work, as well as in her own life.

Manning was born in 1908 in Portsmouth, England, where her father served in the Royal Navy. He had been brought up through Navy ranks at a time when it quite literally ruled the seas, and the British Empire was the largest and most powerful the world had ever known. It was from her father that Manning, despite her stated sympathy with Fabian socialism and radicalism, inherited her admiration for British imperialism, and her firm belief that Britain had been a benevolent colonial power (though she felt this did not apply to Ireland). The Empire has long been an important source of national identity for the British, a fact that readers do well to remember when encountering her novels, which chronicle the Empire's close during World War II.

Manning's childhood was divided between Portsmouth and her mother's native Ireland, giving her, as she would later describe it, "the usual Anglo-Irish sense of belonging nowhere." The family had very little money and during Commander Manning's periods of active duty at sea—which would sometimes last more than a year—would stay with Irish relations. The differences in class and language between the two places led to the young and sensitive Manning being teased by other children, and meant, she said, that she and her brother "suffered an identity crisis at a young age." As with much of her personal history, a heroine in Manning's fiction will later have similar feelings; in the short story "Portrait of a Hungarian Doctor" the narrator describes herself as "a sort of mongrel" who does "not seem to belong anywhere." Such loneliness can be traced to the early part of Manning's upbringing.

Manning attended art school in both Portsmouth and Dublin and exhibited in the former, but she eventually gave up painting in favor of writing. Her family's chronic lack of money was certainly a factor—painter's materials are expensive—but, as a harsh self-critic, she perhaps also felt that her painting lacked discipline and effort; as Manning once told an interviewer, she thought a "novel should not be written too easily." However, the powers of observation and description developed through this training would become a defining quality of her fiction.

She began writing while living in Portsmouth with her parents, supporting herself as a typist, but feeling, as she later described it, as if she "existed in a limbo of loneliness." She published three mystery serials under the name Jacob Morrow, and articles and short stories under the name O. M. Manning, later explaining that she did so "because of a prejudice against women writers at the time." Manning disliked the term "woman novelist," regarding herself as a novelist who was also a woman. In 1935 she began an affair with Hamish Miles, a publisher and editor; they met after he rejected one of her manuscripts but invited the young author to London. Miles would become her teacher as well as her lover, carefully working on with her on her writing while allowing her to feel part, if only by proxy, of the Bloomsbury movement. Their affair lasted three years, until his untimely death in 1938.

Manning's first novel, *The Wind Changes,* was published in 1937. In many ways, it introduces the themes characteristic of the rest of her work. Set in Ireland, it is her only novel about the "troubles," but focuses on individuals and their experience of historical events, rather than on history itself. It is written, as Isobel English argues in her Virago introduction, "with a noticeable masculine impersonality, which was to become the hallmark of her work." The critic points out that in the last chapter of the novel, the heroine Elizabeth Dearborn sees "as though she were Adam and this the first morning of creation." Manning's novels tend to have more male characters than female, though the major women characters tend to be semi-autobiographical: Dearborn in *The Wind Changes,* or Harriet Pringle in *The Balkan Trilogy* and *The Levant Trilogy.*

In 1939 Manning married R. D. Smith and travelled with him, first to Romania and then to Greece. As the Germans advanced across Europe the couple were evacuated to Egypt and then to Jerusalem, where Smith was in charge of a radio station. Manning served as press officer to the U.S. Embassy in Egypt and as press assistant to the Public Information Officer in Jerusalem. These experiences gave Manning the material for her best-known works, the two trilogies that would be know as "The Fortunes of War": *The Balkan Trilogy* (*The Great Fortune,* 1960; *The Spoilt City,* 1962; *Friends and Heroes,* 1965) and *The Levant Trilogy* (*The Danger Tree,* 1977; *The Battle Lost and Won,* 1978; and *The Sum of Things,* 1980). Describing the adventures of the newly married Guy and Harriet Pringle, they are, according to novelist and critic Anthony Burgess, "the finest fictional record of the war produced by a British writer," because "her gallery of personages is huge, her scene painting superb, her pathos controlled, her humour quiet and civilized." Though she based her novels on her own experiences, Olivia Manning was not hasty in completing them. She believed that time should pass between the event and its fictionalization; otherwise the work would be mere journalism. As she pointed out, Tolstoy, an obvious model for her own work, waited 30 years after the Napoleonic wars to begin *War and Peace.*

—Meredith E. Hyde

MANNING, O. M. *See* **MANNING, Olivia.**

MANSFIELD, Katherine

Pseudonym for Kathleen Mansfield Beauchamp; also wrote as K.M. **Other Pseudonyms:** Boris Petrovsky, Elizabeth Stanley. **Nationality:** New Zealand. **Born:** Wellington, New Zealand, 14 October 1888. **Education:** Attended Karori primary school, Wellington Girls' High School, and Miss Swainson's, Wellington; Queen's College, London, 1903-06. **Family:** Married 1) George Bowden in 1909 (separated 1909; divorced 1918); 2) John Middleton Murry in 1918. **Career:** Writer. Co-editor of periodicals, including *Rhythm, The Blue Review,* and *Signature,* c. 1912-15; translator, with S.S. Koteliansky, of diaries and letters of Anton Chekhov; author of verse for children. Contributor to periodicals, including *New Age, English Review, Open Window,* and *Athenaeum.* **Died:** Fontainebleau, France, 9 January 1923.

Publications

Short Stories

In a German Pension. London, Swift, 1911; with introduction by John Middleton Murry, New York, Knopf, and London, Constable, 1926.

Prelude. London, Hogarth Press, 1918.

Je ne parle pas français. Hampstead, Heron Press, 1920.

Bliss and Other Stories. London, Constable, 1920; New York, Knopf, 1921.

The Garden Party and Other Stories. London, Constable, and New York, Knopf, 1922.

The Doves' Nest and Other Stories, edited by John Middleton Murry. New York, Knopf, 1923.

Something Childish, and Other Stories, edited by John Middleton Murry. London, Constable, 1924; as *The Little Girl and Other Stories,* New York, Knopf, 1924.
The Aloe. London, Constable, and New York, Knopf, 1930; as *The Aloe, with Prelude,* Wellington, Port Nicholson Press,1982.
The Short Stories of Katherine Mansfield. New York, Knopf, 1937; with illustrations by John D. Dawson, Franklin Center, Pennsylvania, Franklin Library, 1982.
Collected Stories of Katherine Mansfield. London, Constable, 1946; as *The Complete Short Stories of Katherine Mansfield,* Auckland, New Zealand, Golden Press/Whitcombe & Tombs, 1974; edited by Antony Alpers, Auckland, Oxford University Press, 1984.
Thirty-four Short Stories, edited by Elizabeth Bowen. London, Collins, 1957.
Undiscovered Country: The New Zealand Stories of Katherine Mansfield, edited by Ian A. Gordon. London, Longmans, 1974.

Poetry

Poems. London, Constable, 1923; New York, Knopf, 1924.
To Stanislaw Wyspianski. London, Favil Press, 1938.
Four Poems, edited by Jeffrey Meyers. London, E. & J. Stevens, 1980.

Autobiography

Journal of Katherine Mansfield, edited by John Middleton Murry. London, Constable, 1927.
The Urewera Notebook, edited by Ian A. Gordon. Oxford, Oxford University Press, 1978.

Literary Criticism

Novels and Novelists (originally published in *Athenaeum,* April 1919-December 1920), edited by John Middleton Murry. London, Constable, and New York, Knopf, 1930.
The Critical Writings of Katherine Mansfield, edited by Clare Hanson. Houndsmill, Basingstoke, Hampshire, and New York, St. Martin's Press, 1987.

Other

Letters of Katherine Mansfield, edited by John Middleton Murry. London, Constable, 2 vols., 1928; special edition, New York, Knopf, 1932.
The Scrapbook of Katherine Mansfield, edited by John Middleton Murry. London, Constable, and New York, Knopf, 1939.
Letters to John Middleton Murry, 1913-1922, edited by Murry. London, Constable, 1951.
Passionate Pilgrimage: A Love Affair in Letters; Katherine Mansfield's Letters to John Middleton Murry from the South of France, 1915-1920, edited by Helen McNeish. London, M. Joseph, 1976.
The Letters and Journals of Katherine Mansfield: A Selection, edited by C.W. Stead. London, Allen Lane, 1977.
The Collected Letters of Katherine Mansfield: Vol. 1: *1913-1917* [Vol. 2: *1918-1919*] [Vol. 3: *1919-1920*], edited by Vincent O'Sullivan and Margaret Scott. Oxford, Clarendon Press, 3 vols., 1984-93.
Letters Between Katherine Mansfield and John Middleton Murry, edited by Cherry Hankin. London, Virago, 1988.
Dramatic Sketches. Palmerston North, New Zealand, Nagare Press, 1989.

Translator, with S.S. Koteliansky, *Reminiscences of Leonid Andreyev,* by Maxim Gorky. London, Heinemann, 1922.

*

Media Adaptations: *The Two Tigers: A Play on Katherine Mansfield and John Middleton Murry,* 1977; *A Picture of Katherine Mansfield* (television film), 1973; *The Garden Party* (film), 1973, 1985; *The Woman at the Store* (television film), 1975; *Bliss* (ballet), 1986.

Bibliography: *The Critical Bibliography of Katherine Mansfield* edited by Ruth Elvish Mantz, London, Constable, 1931; *Katherine Mansfield: Publications in Australia, 1907-1909* by Jean E. Stone, n.p., 1977; "Katherine Mansfield: A Bibliography of International Criticism, 1921-1977" by Jeffrey Meyers, *Bulletin of Bibliography,* 34(2), April/June 1977; *Mansfieldiana: A Brief Katherine Mansfield Bibliography* by G.N. Morris, Folcroft, Pennsylvania, Folcroft Library, 1979; "A Bibliography of Katherine Mansfield References, 1970-1984" by Nelson Wattie, in *Journal of New Zealand Literature,* 3, 1985; *A Bibliography of Katherine Mansfield* by B.J. Kirkpatrick, Oxford, Clarendon Press, 1989.

Manuscript Collection: Alexander Turnbull Library, National Library of New Zealand, Wellington.

Critical Studies: *The Life of Katherine Mansfield* by Ruth Elvish Mantz, London, Constable, 1933; *Katherine Mansfield: A Biography* by Isabel C. Clarke, Wellington, Beltane Book Bureau, 1944; *Katherine Mansfield: A Critical Study* by Sylvia Berkman, New Haven, Yale University Press, 1951; *Katherine Mansfield: A Biography* by Antony Alpers, London, J. Cape, and New York, Knopf, 1953, revised as *The Life of Katherine Mansfield,* London, J. Cape, and New York: Knopf, 1980; *Katherine Mansfield* by Ian A. Gordon, London and New York, Longman2 Greens, 1954, revised 1963; *Katherine Mansfield* by Saralyn R. Daly, New York, Twayne, 1965, revised edition, New York and Toronto, Twayne/Macmillan, 1994; *Katherine Mansfield: An Appraisal* by Nariman Hormasji, London, Collins, 1967; *The Edwardianism of Katherine Mansfield* by Frederick J. Foot, Wellington, Brentwoods Press, 1969; *The Fiction of Katherine Mansfield* by Marvin Magalaner, Carbondale, Southern Illinois University Press, 1971; *Katherine Mansfield: The Memories of L.M.* by Ida Baker, London, M. Joseph, 1971, with an introduction by A.L. Barker, London, Virago, 1985; *Katherine Mansfield: A Biography* by Jeffrey Meyers, London, Hamish Hamilton, 1978; *Katherine Mansfield* by Clare Hanson and Andrew Gurr, London, Macmillan, and New York, St. Martin's Press, 1981; *Katherine Mansfield And Her Confessional Stories* by Cherry A. Hankin, London, Macmillan, 1983; *Katherine Mansfield* by Kate Fullbrook, Brighton, Harvester Press, and Bloomington, Indiana University Press, 1986; *Dear Miss Mansfield: A Tribute to Kathleen Mansfield Beauchamp* by Witi Ihimaera, New York, Viking, 1989; *Katherine Mansfield: A Secret Life* by Claire Tomalin, London, Viking, and New York, St. Martin's Press, 1987; *Katherine Mansfield: The Woman and the Writer* by Gillian Boddy, New York, Penguin, 1988; *Katherine Mansfield* by Rhoda B. Nathan, New York, Continuum, 1988; *Katherine Mansfield: A Study of the Short Fiction* by J.F. Kobler, London and Boston, Twayne, 1990; *Critical Essays on Katherine Mansfield,* edited by Nathan, New York, G.K. Hall, and Toronto, Macmillan, 1993; *Katherine Mansfield's Fiction* by Patrick D. Morrow, Bowling Green, Bowling Green State University Popular Press, 1993; *Illness, Gender, and Writing: The Case of Katherine Mansfield* by Mary Burgan, Baltimore, Johns Hopkins University Press, 1994; *Katherine Mansfield: In from the Margin,* edited by Roger Robinson, Baton Rouge, Louisiana State University Press, 1994.

* * *

In her 34 years, Katherine Mansfield led a life that was quintessentially modern in both its social and literary content. Born in Wellington, New Zealand, Mansfield experienced early sexual attractions to Maata Mahupuku, a Maori princess and classmate at Miss Swainson's school, and Edith Kathleen Bendall, a friend, 1906-08. She also had an emotional and probable sexual involvement with Ida Constance Baker—also known as L.M. (or Leslie Moore)—a classmate of Mansfield's at Queen's College; the two women would remain close until Mansfield's death. Mansfield immigrated to England in the summer of 1908 and became romantically involved with Garnet Trowell, originally an acquaintance from New Zealand; she became pregnant, probably in December of 1908. It is unknown if Trowell was ever told of the pregnancy. Instead, Mansfield made a hasty marriage to George Bowden, a singing teacher whom she barely knew, on 2 March 1909. The marriage was never consummated and they separated on their wedding day, though they did not legally divorce until April 1918. Mansfield left England for Bavaria in May of 1909, where she suffered a miscarriage in June or July.

Mansfield remained for a time in Bavaria and, as she recovered her health, took up with Polish intellectual Floryan Sobienowski. Sobienowski probably introduced Mansfield to the work of Anton Chekhov. Mansfield's story "The Child-Who-Was-Tired" is essentially a translation of Chekhov's "Spat khochetsia," though Mansfield was later considered to have plagiarized the story because of her failure to acknowledge the Russian writer's story as a source for her own. It is likely that, late in 1909, Mansfield was infected with gonorrhea, probably by Sobienowski. Her illness was ineffectually treated and thus began the assault on her health by an accumulation of illnesses that eventually led to the tuberculosis which took her life.

Mansfield returned to London in December 1909. She contacted Bowden, and he introduced her to A.R. Orage, editor of the literary magazine *New Age,* one of a series of British literary, artistic, and political journals that the writer would be associated with. Mansfield met the writer John Middleton Murry in December of 1911 and, in the spring of 1912, they became lovers; they vacillated over the years between living together and apart. They survived on a combination of Mansfield's allowance from her family and what income they could generate from writing fiction and criticism for and editing periodicals. Only three volumes of Mansfield's stories were ever published prior to her death.

People of note whom Mansfield came to know include Henri Gaudier-Brzeska, Lady Ottoline Morrell, D.H. Lawrence, Frieda von Richthofen Weekley Lawrence, Bertrand Russell, Dora Carrington, Lytton Strachey, and Virginia Woolf (they met in 1916). Lawrence's *Bildungsroman* titled *Sons and Lovers* probably provided Mansfield with the inspiration for the autobiographical coming-of-age novel she never finished, *Maata* (the name was borrowed from her childhood friend). It is commonly believed that the character Gudrun in Lawrence's *Women in Love* (1916) is based on both Mansfield and Murry. Just after the start of World War I, Lawrence introduced Mansfield and Murry to S.S. Koteliansky, a Jewish Ukrainian law student who would grow to be an important friend with whom she collaborated on some translation projects. The war claimed the lives of several people of importance to Mansfield, but none more so than her brother, Leslie Beauchamp. His death in France at the front in 1915 was one of the great crises of Mansfield's life.

Mansfield was diagnosed in late 1917 or early 1918 with tuberculosis. She spent the first few months of 1918 in the south of France trying to recuperate and returned to England in April 1918. At this time she finally secured a divorce from Bowden, and Mansfield and Murry married on 3 May 1918. The last years of Mansfield's life were marked by her declining health and the search for a cure (involving much travel), and the drive to write. She had long since had only a very distant relationship with her family. Mansfield's mother died in 1918, and Mansfield went years without seeing her father or sisters, though they did see each other prior to her death. After enduring a variety of useless or even harmful medical treatments, Mansfield looked into the possibility of regaining her health through spiritual means. She encountered the teachings of George Gurdjieff, and on 16 October 1922, accompanied by her friend Ida Baker, Mansfield arrived at Gurdjieff's Institute for the Harmonious Development of Man in Fontainebleau, France. At first instructing Murry not to visit her until the spring, on 31 December 1922 she wrote to her husband, urging him to come to her. He arrived on the afternoon of 9 January 1923. That night, as Murry helped her to her room, she suffered a lung hemorrhage; within moments, she was dead.

Mansfield was the premier short story writer of the modern period. While she wrote some poetry and began what was intended to be a novel-length piece, she concentrated on the short story form. In her stories, she was instrumental in defining many of the literary hallmarks of modernism, including an emphasis on the internal musings of her characters and an emphasis on the significance of epiphanic moments in the lives of her protagonists. Mansfield wished to write stories that were "plotless"; hence, in many of her stories dilemmas are presented or realizations are achieved by her characters while situations remain essentially unresolved. In "Bliss," for example, Bertha Young, a wife and mother, throws a dinner party. One of her guests, Pearl Fulton, holds a special fascination for Bertha; "Bertha had fallen in love with her, as she always did fall in love with beautiful women who had something strange about them." At the party Bertha experiences both a desire for her husband Harry and an intense moment with Pearl Fulton, as the two women look out over the pear tree in the garden. As the evening ends, however, she catches sight of Harry and Pearl in the hall, as Harry "put his hands on [Pearl's] shoulder and turned her violently to him. His lips said: 'I adore you.'" Bertha is left with the realization of Harry and Pearl's betrayal and, as the story ends, cries, "Oh, what is going to happen now?" No other resolution is provided.

Mansfield's literary ability interested Virginia Woolf, and the two became friends. Woolf and her husband, Leonard Woolf, published Mansfield's story "Prelude" at their Hogarth Press. Woolf and Mansfield were generally fond of each other's writing, though Woolf disliked "Bliss," for instance, and Mansfield wrote a critical review of Woolf's *Night and Day.* Still, they talked about writing for hours, and Mansfield wrote in a letter to Woolf, "You are the only woman with whom I long to talk work. There will never be another." Throughout Woolf's life, she occasionally recalled Mansfield in her journal entries, though she outlived Mansfield by nearly two decades.

Mansfield's stories generally center around a female protagonist or protagonists, though many deal in detail with relations between women and men. She often explored relations within families, and she wrote a great number of stories that have female children or adolescents as primary characters. She wrote several stories, known as her New Zealand stories, which were set in her native country and rely to some degree on autobiographical details. Because many of her stories are about the perceptions of children and because Mansfield sometimes mined her personal experiences for her stories, some critics have downplayed the significance of her writing by arguing that it is confessional and concerned with her private past and therefore not sufficiently directed to a wider audience. However, such claims have often been made to devalue writing by women, and it is unlikely that similar accusations would be made against James Joyce's *Dubliners,* a collection that also relies to some degree on autobiographical content and contains many stories centered around child characters.

Mansfield does not write of childhood and the relationships between mothers and children or husbands and wives simply as an autobiographical gesture or an attempt at nostalgia for the past. Rather, many of her stories are somber and even dark in tone. In "The Woman at The Store," for example, a young girl and her mother live alone at a remote location, where the mother runs a store. The mother has murdered her husband in front of the daughter. A group of travelling men stop at the store and the mother becomes sexually involved with one of them. The girl draws a picture of the murder of her father by her mother and shows the picture to the men as a retaliatory gesture against her mother. While the majority of Mansfield's stories are less shocking, there is at the very least in these tales a challenge to the notion of childhood as a time of innocence.

Themes that Mansfield explores in her stories include class attitudes, class and gender indoctrination as they are expressed through the socialization of children, and the relationship between femaleness and creativity. She is concerned with oppression, specifically gender oppression and the falseness of personality it forces upon both women and men. Elaine Showalter has argued that Mansfield is pessimistic and draws her women characters too brutally. Kate Fullbrook, however, calls this pessimism a strength of Mansfield's:

> Katherine Mansfield sees the failure of many human relationships as grounded in a collaboration of victim and victimizer who are caught in a cycle of self-falsification.... Through her exposure of the base of psychological oppression, Katherine Mansfield ... both truly portrays the nature of objectification and reveals the secret mechanisms that support it. To refuse such writing on the grounds that it is "brutal", or to dismiss it as "miniaturist", or to bracket it off as "mere" confessional, is to fail to understand the pressures against which anything that might legitimately be called freedom might be won, and to miss one of the main reasons for Katherine Mansfield's impact as a modern writer.

Early in her life as a writer, Mansfield was enamored of the writings of Oscar Wilde and his dictum that one could develop oneself into a self-chosen image. Mansfield often visited this possibility, weighing the ability to sculpt a self against the forces of socialization. In her exploration of this theme, and in the literary techniques she employed, her impact as a modernist writer is great indeed.

—Martha Henn

MARIE de FRANCE

Nationality: French. **Born:** Possibly Normandy, fl. c. 1160. **Died:** c. 1190.

Publications

Poetry

Lais. N.p., c.1167; edited by B. Roquefort as *Poésies de Marie de France, poéte anglo-normand de XIIIe siécle,* Paris, Chasseriau, 2 vols., 1819-20; translated by Glyn S. Burgess and Keith Busby as *Lais of Marie de France,* Harmondsworth, Penguin, 1986.

L'Ysopet (adaptation of Aesop's fables). N.p., c. 1170; edited by Leopold Hervieux as *Les Fabulistes latins, depuis le siécle d'Auguste jusqu'à la fin du moyen âge;* edited by Harriet Spiegel as *Fables,* Toronto, University of Toronto Press, 1987.

Other

Translator, *Espurgatoire Saint Patriz* [St. Patrick's Purgatory] (translation of *Tractatus de Purgatorio Sancti Patricii*). N.p., c.1190; edited by T.A. Jenkins, Chicago, University of Chicago Press, 1903.

*

Critical Studies: *Marie de France* by Emanuel J. Mickel Jr., New York, Twayne, 1974.

* * *

While the poetry of Marie de France represents the work of one of the earliest identifiably female voices to emerge from the Middle Ages, we know almost nothing about her. The century in which she lived, her country of residence, and the precise extent of her body of work, have all been the subject of intense scholarly debate. Still unresolved, and likely to remain a contentious question, is the degree to which she can be considered, in any modern sense of the term, a "feminist writer."

Although there may well have been more, three works are generally attributed to Marie de France: the *Lais* (*The Lays*), a collection of 12 short stories on the power of love, presented in poetic form; *L'Ysopet* (*The Fables*), a grouping of 103 fables, supposedly translated from some now lost source; and *Espurgatoire Saint Patriz* (*St. Patrick's Purgatory*), a faithful translation of a popular legend. In all three texts, ignoring the medieval tradition of anonymity, the author proudly gives her name, most explicitly in the epilogue to the *Fables:*

> Me numerai pur remembrance:
> Marie ai num, si sui de France.
> [I shall name myself for remembrance,
> Marie is my name, I am of France.]

In the *Lais,* the author appears in the prologue to the first poem, the tale of Guigemar: "Oez, seignurs, ke dit Marie" ["Hear, lords, the words of Marie"], and in *Espurgatoire* she reveals herself at the close:

> Jo, Marie, ai mis, en memoire,
> Le livre de l'Espurgatoire.
> [I, Marie, have set down for posterity
> The book of Purgatory.]

Marie was once thought to have lived during the 13th century, but scholars are now generally agreed that she produced her works during the second half of the 12th century, and that while she wrote in French, she lived in England. The dedication, in the prologue of the *Lais,* to a "noble king" has led scholars to conclude that Marie was attached in some way to the court of Henry II (1154-1189), although there is no agreement on the identity of the "Count William" whom she identifies as her patron in the epilogue to the *Fables.*

A tantalizingly small amount of external evidence gives some weight to the chronology, tentatively proposed by the most recent editor of the *Fables,* which places the composition of the *Lais* around 1155-1160, the *Fables* somewhere between 1160 and 1190 and the *Espurgatoire* no earlier than 1190. As Harriet Spiegel plausibly suggests, such a sequence would have Marie starting her career "with youthful questions of love and romance, of fidelity and conflicting loyalties" in the *Lais,* moving, in her middle years "to skillfully rendered entertainment directed toward contemporary social and political concerns" with the *Fables* and turning, in her last years, "to sober and religious matters" in the *Espurgatoire.*

Marie claimed that all three of her works were either translations or transmissions; she says, in the preface to the *Lais,* that she is setting down stories that she has heard and that she has made poems out of them, later identifying them as Breton lays. She claims to be using King Alfred's English translation of Aesop for her *Fables,* but only in the case of the *Espurgatoire* has an immediate source been identified. Most critics are agreed that, whatever her sources, Marie's own creative contribution to both the *Lais* and the *Fables* was significant and considerable.

Any attempt to discuss Marie de France within the context of feminist writing is fraught with potential pitfalls. Since we know nothing of her life except what we can tease out from her works—she was well-educated, she knew Latin and probably English, as well as her native French, she was connected with the court and wrote for a courtly audience, she had a well-developed sense of the value of her work—we cannot view her work within a framework of other activity. Looking at the two works which appear to contain her most original writing—and we can never be sure how original it is—the reader is not immediately made aware of a writer dealing with issues related directly to women.

The *Lais,* Marie's courtly adventures on the theme of love, concern themselves with situations so diverse as to admit no overall theme or moral and, within the brief compass of each story, the characters are skillfully portrayed as individuals; there are evil and deceitful women, such as the wife of the seneschal in *Equitan* and the queen in *Lanval,* as well as evil men. Within the courtly love convention, it was the quality of the love that was all-important, and Marie's tales reflect the prevailing literary practices in a way that reveals neither more nor less understanding of or sympathy for the female character.

Spiegel has argued that in the *Fables* Marie shows a special concern for her female characters; details concerning the devastation wrought by unruly pups in *The Pregnant Hound* or the misery of a bear raped by a wily fox in *The Fox and the Bear* are not contained in the Latin originals of these stories. However, it is difficult to disentangle the standard medieval habit of ornamenting and improving upon a source from any possible sense of solidarity Marie may have felt towards the female figures in her tales.

Certainly some of Marie's fables appear to share the misogyny so prevalent in the literature of the Middle Ages; tales such as *The Peasant Who Saw Another with His Wife* and *The Peasant Who Saw His Wife with Her Lover* conform to the traditional fabliaux mode of the simpleton husband, cuckolded by his scheming wife and the closing couplets of latter (Speigel's translation) faithfully reflect the sardonic anti-feminist irony of the genre:

> And so, forewarned all men should be
> That women know good strategy.
> They've more art in their craft and lies
> Than all the devil can devise.

In a similar vein Marie concludes her fable of *The Peasant and the Snake* with the observation that:

> Of many women this is so;
> Their men they counsel in such ways
> That turn on them and bring disgrace.

While it may be noteworthy that Marie transforms all the gods who appear in the animal fables into goddesses, it is difficult to view her as a feminist writer by even the widest modern definition. However, given the patriarchal nature of the medieval period, Marie's ample literary talents, and her professional pride in her work make her an exceptional figure and an example for women who were to follow her; ample reason for her achievements to be remembered.

—Kathleen E. Garay

MARLATT, Daphne (Buckle)

Nationality: Canadian. **Born:** Melbourne, Australia, 11 July 1942; immigrated to Canada 1951. **Education:** University of British Columbia, B.A. in English 1964; University of Indiana, M.A. in comparative literature 1968. **Family:** Married Gordon Alan Marlatt (divorced 1970); one son. **Career:** Instructor in English, Capilano Community College, North Vancouver, British Columbia, 1968, 1973-76; writer-in-residence, University of Manitoba, 1982, University of Alberta, 1985-86; and University of Western Ontario, 1993; Ruth Wynn Woodward Professor of Women's Studies, Simon

Fraser University, Burnaby, British Columbia, 1988-89; instructor in poetry, University of British Columbia, Vancouver, 1989-90. Poetry editor, *Capilano Review,* 1973-76; co-editor, *periodics,* 1977-80; associate editor, *Island,* 1980-83; member of editorial collective, *Tessera,* 1983-91. Contributor of verse to periodicals, including *TISH* , *Canadian Forum, Capilano Review, Ellipse, Origin, Tessera,* and *West Coast Line.* **Awards:** Canada Council arts grants, 1969-70, 1973-74, 1985, 1987-88; L.L.D., University of Western Ontario, 1996. **Member:** Writers Union of Canada, West Coast Women and Words. **Address:** c/o Writers Union of Canada, 24 Ryerson Ave., Toronto M5T 2P3, Canada.

Publications

Novels

Zocalo. Toronto, Coach House Press, 1977.
Ana Historic. Toronto, Coach House Press, 1988.
Taken. Toronto, Coach House Press, 1996.

Poetry

leaf leaf/s. Santa Rosa, California, Black Sparrow Press, 1968.
Rings. Vancouver, Vancouver Community Press, 1971; included in *What Matters,* 1980.
Vancouver Poems. Toronto, Coach House Press, 1972.
Steveston. Vancouver, Talonbooks, 1974; revised, Edmonton, Alberta, Longspoon Press, 1984.
Our Lives. Carrboro, Truck Press, 1975; revised, Lantzville, B.C., Oolichan, 1979.
Here and There. Island Writing Series. Lantzville, B.C., 1981.
Mauve, with Nicole Brossard. Vancouver, Kootenay School of Writing, 1985.
Character/Jeu de lettres, with Nicole Brossard. Vancouver, Kootenay School of Writing, 1986.

Plays

Radio Play: *Steveston,* 1976.

Uncollected Essays

"In the Mouth of Hungry Ghosts," in *Capilano Review,* 16/17, 1979.
"Entering In: The Immigrant Imagination," in *Canadian Writers in 1984,* edited by W.H. New. Vancouver, University of British Columbia Press, 1984.
"Musing with Mothertongue," in *Gynocritics: Feminist Approaches to Canadian and Quebec Women's Writing,* edited by Barbara Godard. Toronto, ECW Press, 1987.

Other

Frames of a Story. Toronto, Ryerson Press, 1968.
The Story, She Said. Vancouver, Monthly Press, 1977.
Selected Writings: Net Work, edited by Fred Wah. Vancouver, Talonbooks, 1980.
What Matters: Writing 1968-70. Toronto, Coach House Press, 1980.
How Hug a Stone. Winnipeg, Turnstone Press, 1983.
Touch to My Tongue. Edmonton, Longspoon Press, 1984.
Double Negative, with Betsy Warland. Charlottetown, P.E.I., Gynergy Books, 1988.
Salvage. Red Deer, Alberta, Red Deer College Press, 1991.
Ghost Works. Edmonton, NeWest Press, 1993.
Two Women in a Birth, with Betsy Worland. Guernica Editions, 1994.

Editor, *Steveston Recollected: A Japanese-Canadian History.* Victoria, B.C., Provincial Archives of British Columbia, 1975.
Editor, with others, *Opening Doors: Vancouver's East End.* Victoria, B.C., Provincial Archives of British Columbia, 1979.
Editor, *Lost Language,* by Maxine Gadd. Toronto, Coach House Press, 1982.
Editor, with others, *In the Feminine: Proceedings of the Women and Words/Les Femmes et les mots Conference, 1983.* Edmonton, Longspoon Press, 1985.
Editor, with others, *Telling It: Women and Language across Cultures.* Vancouver, B.C., Press Gang, 1990.

*

Manuscript Collections: Literary Manuscripts Collection, National Library of Ottawa.

Critical Studies: Interview by George Bowering in *Open Letter,* 4(3), 1979; "'Body I': Daphne Marlatt's Feminist Poetics" by Barbara Godard in *American Review of Canadian Studies,* 15(4), 1985; essay by Laurie Ricou in *A Mazing Space: Writing Canadian Women Writing,* edited by Shirley Neuman and Smaro Kamboureli, Edmonton, Longspoon Press, 1986; *Line* (special Marlatt issue), 13, 1989; *The Bees of the Invisible: Essays in Contemporary English Canadian Writing* by Stan Drugland, n.p., 1991; "Each Move Made Here (me) Moves There (you)" by Sarah Harasym, in *boundary 2* (Durham, North Carolina), 18(1), 1991; *Beyond TISH,* edited by Douglas Barbour, Edmondton, NeWest Press, 1991.

Daphne Marlatt comments:

Reading, writing, editing, all three of these activities have, for me, involved a "collaboration in the feminine" (to use Barbara Godard's phrase). This collaboration in the feminine is not only a pleasure, one I am grateful for, but an experience of continual growth and enlargement of my/our notions of literature, reality, and women's lives.

Impossible to list here all the reading paths which led me to the hidden and astonishingly varied tradition of women's writing—the other side of that man-in-the-moon face polished and presented to us as the shining side of "Contemporary Literature" (predominantly male) when I was a student. The dark side, a wonderful colloquy of women's voices writing about the "trivial," taboo, and tacit: solitude verging on madness, women's social roles and loss of self, excessive passion, a whole female erotic, daily doubts that give the lie to philosophic certainties, companionship with animals and trees, women's companionship with each other despite double standards in (and within) sex and race, double standards everywhere with one another's difficult balance there. And that has been the excitement, the lifting of a horizon, that here is an ongoing dialogue where women are central, not marginal, where women are delighting in writing the complex i (fem.) and listening to other women's words/realities in a delicate balance between recognition of difference and recognition of shared ground.

* * *

An important contemporary Canadian literary leader, poet, writer, teacher, and editor, Daphne Marlatt has shared the innovative literary concerns of such poetic flagbearers as Frank Davey, George Bowering, and Fred Wah since the 1960s and is a strong voice among West Coast Canadian poets. She is also a self-proclaimed feminist whose ideas evoke those of French Canadian women writers like Nicole Brossard and Barbara Godard, and the theoretical writings of French academics such as Hélèn Cixous and Luce Irigaray.

Born in Melbourne, Australia, in 1942 to British parents and raised in post-World War II Penang, Malaysia, Marlatt immigrated to Western Canada via England with her family in 1951. She attended the University of British Columbia, where she received her B.A. in English and then obtained an M.A. in comparative literature at the University of Indiana. She now lives in Vancouver.

From the beginning of her life in Canada, Marlatt developed a strong sense of belonging to the geographical location of Vancouver, its surrounding areas, and the province of British Columbia in general, especially the forest that was near her childhood home in North Vancouver. At the same time, she was keenly aware of the different English spoken by the people of the region, and even though she was an Anglophone by birth, she sensed her position as a cultural outsider rather keenly; she remembers making a special effort to belong linguistically as well as culturally.

This early experience no doubt had a role in sharpening Marlatt's sense of sounds and syntax, which later led to her preoccupation with experimenting with poetic as well as prose language—actually many readers find it impossible to distinguish between the two in her writing. In addition, her strong interest in French—as is evident in her choice for her master's thesis, which was a translation of French poet Francis Ponge's *Le parti pris des choses*—challenged her to "explore the limits of English syntax," to push at a linguistic edge. Indeed, pushing at a linguistic edge is exactly what Marlatt has been doing most of her writing career, as attested by the carefully arranged lines, purposefully fragmented words, and lack of adherence to conventional sentence structures in her poetry and prose.

Marlatt's preoccupation with language has much to do with her belief that language possesses the power to form and transform, that language is closely tied up with our consciousness, and that consciousness can change through linguistic changes. This political belief led Marlatt to engage in works that concern the internment of Japanese Canadians during World War II: *Steveston,* a 1974 collection of poems; *Steveston Recollected: A Japanese-Canadian History,* a documentation published by the Provincial Archives of British Columbia in 1975; and *Steveston,* a C.B.C. radio playscript Marlatt herself adapted from the first two. Marlatt gives poetic voice to the unjustly underpublicized internment experiences of the ethnic minority group who was forcibly moved from the coast of British Columbia to the interior region west of the Rockies. These mixed-genre projects well exemplify her commitment to justice and to uncovering of hidden sides of history, a commitment that parallels her concern with the poor and the female.

The Steveston projects also testify to Marlatt's belief in the power of words to allow both the writer and the reader to relive the moment that the poems recreate. Marlatt has long been a disciple of the concept of "proprioception," a writing that accurately reflects the condition of the writer—especially the bodily and sensory condition—at the moment of the writing, and that also requires that the reader go through the same sort of experiences during the perusal. Her adherence to "proprioception" stems from her belief that writing is, or should be, an organic outgrowth of the body, which echoes the theoretical beliefs of many French and French Canadian feminists.

All these creative principles that Marlatt embraces and applies to her writing—the importance of the sense of location, the concern with history, especially with the history of the oppressed, and the belief in the transformative power of language, as a potential political as well as aesthetic tool—have combined to make her second novel, *Ana Historic,* a powerful and highly complex book. Of primary importance as Marlatt's coming-out novel, *Ana Historic* traces the intellectual, emotional, and sexual reawakening of a contemporary Canadian woman, Ana Richards. Initially a bored and depressed British Columbia housewife and mother, Ana discovers her new erotic potential in the company of her friend Zoë, as her interest in the hitherto unexplored aspects of local history, her frustration with women's roles in Canadian society, and her desire to recover her childhood interests in female camaraderie converge to give birth to her new identity and perspective.

Marlatt is widely admired for what she has accomplished in terms of poetic experimentation as well as for representing, in the last decade or so, the sensitivity and sensuality of many lesbian writers and readers. As more than one critic have noted, in Marlatt's poetry and fiction, what is said is often far less important than how it is said. Her value as writer resides in the persistence with which she explores and refines her language and the way in which she draws her reader into her writing, to experience, as if firsthand, the writer's bodily, emotional, spiritual, and cerebral sensations at the moment of literary creation.

—Tomoko Kuribayashi

MARTIN, Del

Nationality: American. **Born:** San Francisco, California, 5 May 1921. **Education:** Attended University of California, Berkeley, 1938-39, and San Francisco State College (now University), 1939-1941. **Family:** Married James Martin (divorced), one daughter, two grandchildren; companion of Phyllis Lyon since 1953. **Career:** Reporter, *Pacific Builder,* San Francisco, 1948-49; editor, *Daily Construction Reports,* Seattle, Washington, 1949-51; cofounder, 1955, founding president of San Francisco chapter, 1955-56, and national president, 1957-60, Daughters of Bilitis; editor, *Ladder,* 1960-62. Cofounder: Council on Religion and the Homosexual, 1964; Citizens Alert, 1965; San Francisco Women's Centers, 1970; Lesbian Mothers Union, 1971; Alice B. Toklas Memorial Democratic Club, 1972; Community Advisory Board of the Center for Special Problems, 1973; Bay Area Women's Coalition, 1974; Coalition for Justice for Battered Women, 1975; La Casa de las Madres, 1976; California Coalition against Domestic Violence, 1977; Lesbian Lobby, 1978; San Francisco Feminist Democrats, 1978. Member of Bishop Pike's Diocesan Commission on Homosexuality, 1965-66; Task Force on Homosexuality,

San Francisco Mental Health Association, 1971-72; Bishop Myers's Diocesan Commission on Human Sexuality, 1972-73; National Organization for Women (NOW) National Task Force on Battered Women and Household Violence (cochair), 1976-77; San Francisco Commission on the Status of Women (chair, 1976-77), 1976-79. Member of advisory board, Senior Action in a Gay Environment, 1980-83; California Commission on Crime Control and Violence Prevention, 1980-83; Gay/Lesbian Outreach to Elders, beginning 1984; San Francisco Board of Supervisors Senior Services Plan Task Force, 1994-95; San Francisco Family Violence Council, beginning 1995; appointed by Senator Dianne Feinstein as delegate, White House Conference on Aging, 1995. Contributor to periodicals, including *Challenge: A Theological Arts Journal, Entre Nous, New York Times, Motive, Ms., On Our Backs, Open Hands, Osteopathic Physician, San Francisco Bay Guardian, Sinister Wisdom,* and *Trends.* Consultant to television documentaries, including *Last Call at Maud's,* 1994, *Pride Divide,* and wife-battery episodes of *Mary Hartman, Mary Hartman.* **Awards:** American Library Association Gay Book Award, 1972, for *Lesbian/Woman;* Prosperos Award of Merit, 1972; Humanist Community of San Jose certificate of recognition, 1973; San Antonio Gay Community Lavender Alcade Service Award, 1978; San Francisco Board of Supervisors merit awards, 1978, 1980, 1991; named honorary citizen of Austin, Texas, 1978; Southern California Women for Understanding First Lesbian Rights Award, 1979; Family Violence Project Gold Star Award, 1981; California State Assembly commendation, 1983; David Award, 1983, City and County of San Francisco Award of Merit, 1985; NOW certificate of Appreciation, 1986; honorary D.A., Institute for Advanced Study of Human Sexuality, San Francisco, 1987; Cable Car Award of Merit, 1988; Franklin E. Cook Memorial Award, 1989; American Civil Liberties Union Earl Warren Civil Liberties Award, 1990; George Washington High School Alumni Hall of Merit, 1991. **Member:** Women's Institute for Freedom of the Press, National Gay Task Force, National Women's Political Caucus, Feminists for Free Expression, Feminists Anti-Censorship Task Force, Working Group on Women, Censorship, and Pornography for National Coalition against Censorship, National Lesbian Feminist Organization, Lesbian Caucus, Religious Coalition for Abortion Rights, Mobilization against AIDS, Lesbian Agenda for Action, American Association of Retired Persons, Old Lesbians Organized for Change. **Address:** 651 Duncan Street, San Francisco, California 94131, U.S.A.

Publications

Political/Social Theory

Lesbian/Woman, with Phyllis Lyon. San Francisco, Glide Publications, 1972; updated edition, New York, Bantam, 1983; revised and updated, Volcano, California, Volcano Press, 1991.

Lesbian Love and Liberation, with Phyllis Lyon. San Francisco, Multi Media Resource Center, 1973.

Battered Wives. San Francisco, Glide Publications, 1976; revised, Volcano, California, Volcano Press, 1981.

The Male Batterer: A Treatment Approach, with Daniel Jay Sonkin and Lenore E.A. Walker. New York, Springer, 1985.

Domestic Violence on Trial, edited by Daniel Jay Sonkin. New York, Springer, 1987.

Uncollected Essays

"If That's All There Is," in *Vector,* November 1970.

"Afterthought: Lesbians as Gays and as Women," with Sally Gearhart, in *We'll Do It Ourselves: Combating Sexism in Education,* edited by David Rosen, Steve Werner, and Barbara Yates. Lincoln, University of Nebraska Press, 1974.

"Society's Vindication of the Wife Batterer," in *Bulletin of the American Academy of Psychiatry and the Law,* 5(4), 1977.

"Reminiscences of Two Female Homophiles," with Phyllis Lyon, in *Our Right to Love,* edited by Ginny Vida. Englewood Cliffs, New Jersey, Prentice-Hall, 1978; revised edition, New York, Simon & Schuster, 1996.

"The Older Lesbian," with Phyllis Lyon, in *Positively Gay,* edited by Betty Berzon and Robert Leighton. Millbrae, California, Celestial Arts, 1979; revised, 1992.

"What Keeps a Woman Captive in a Violent Relationship? The Social Context of Battering," in *Battered Women,* edited by Donna M. Moore. Beverly Hills, Sage, 1979.

"Anniversary," with Phyllis Lyon, in *The Lesbian Path,* edited by Margaret Cruikshank. Monterey, California, Angel Press, 1980; revised and enlarged, San Francisco, Grey Fox Press, 1985.

"Wife Beating: A Product of Sociosexual Development," in *Women's Sexual Experience: Explorations of the Dark Continent,* edited by Martha Kirkpatrick. New York, Plenum Press, 1981.

"Lesbian Women and Mental Health Policy," with Phyllis Lyon, in *Women and Mental Health Policy,* edited by Lenore E. Walker. Beverly Hills, Sage, 1984.

"The Historical Roots of Domestic Violence," in *Domestic Violence on Trial,* edited by Daniel Jay Sonkin. New York, Springer, 1987.

"A New Political Twist," with Phyllis Lyon, in *Dyke Life,* edited by Karla Jay. New York, Basic Books, 1995.

*

Critical Studies: In *Christian Century,* 23 December 1964; *Lesbian Images* by Jane Rule, New York Pocket Books, 1976; "A History of the Lesbian Periodical—*The Ladder*" (master's thesis) by Sarah Elizabeth Boslaugh, University of Chicago, 1984.

Del Martin comments:

My domestic/business/life partner of 43 years, Phyllis Lyon, and I are erroneously credited as the founders of the Daughters of Bilitis (pronounced Bil *ee* tis). In 1955 we were invited by a lesbian we had met to join her and her friends to form a secret lesbian club. We had felt isolated and jumped at the chance to meet others like ourselves. Little did we know how that would change our lives.

Both of us were journalists and political activists before we met. We both had wanted to write the great American novel. Instead we lived it. Our writing turned from poetry and fiction to nonfiction. We have chronicled four decades of lesbian/gay/feminist/bisexual/transgender political activism.

We are often referred to as the inseparable duo, but our careers diverged in the '70s. Phyllis was a founder of the National Sex Forum at Glide Urban Center and became a sexologist/professor at the Institute for Advanced Study of Human Sexuality. I became involved in the domestic violence issue through our publisher, Ruth Gottstein.

Writing *Battered Wives* put the feminist movement as a whole in perspective for me. Every issue that feminists had addressed in the late '60s and early '70s, either directly or indirectly, related to the plight of battered women. Phyllis in her work and writing advanced our theory that women will not be liberated until they are free sexually—free from sex role stereotyping, free to make informed choices, free to find and attain their potential as equal human beings.

Obviously we are for drastic social change. We have seen changes we could never have dreamed of back in the '50s. We are proud to have played a part in that. We liked the challenge. We had fun. Feminism has become global. There is no turning back.

* * *

Indefatigable in her advocacy of women for almost half a century, activist and writer Del Martin has been at the forefront of many of the social movements that have advanced the causes of both lesbians and feminists. In 1955 she and life partner and fellow-activist Phyllis Lyon helped to organize the first national association to advance the cause of lesbians. The Daughters of Bilitis, or DOB, through its publication, *The Ladder,* reached out to the heterosexual community with an eye toward mutual acceptance and toleration rather than confrontation and exclusion; in her role as editor of *The Ladder* from 1960-62, Martin was responsible for promoting this positive relationship.

Chief among the many causes that Martin has dedicated not only her time, but her vast energy and enthusiasm to, has been that of battered women. Believing spousal abuse to be an outward manifestation of women's entrapment in a patriarchal system that affords them no real power, she has devoted her time to serving on advisory boards such as the Coalition for Justice for Battered Women, the California Coalition against Domestic Violence, NOW's National Task Force on Battered Women and Household Violence (of which she was cochair), and the California Commission on Crime Control and Violence Prevention. In addition, Martin has also helped to found San Francisco's La Casa del las Madres, a shelter for battered women and their children. Her *Battered Wives,* first published in 1976, has aided in raising women's consciousness about the abuse that many once accepted in silence; Martin's book has helped this issue emerge from behind locked doors and be addressed openly, on a national level. In several articles she has helped to both define and address wife battering as an actual crime of assault; in "What Keeps a Woman Captive in a Violent Relationship? The Social Context of Battering," she examines the reasons why, for a woman undergoing systematic abuse, such legal definitions can be psychologically invalidated. In *The Male Batterer: A Treatment Approach* (1987), written with Daniel Jay Sonkin and Lenore E.A. Walker, Martin suggests ways to combat such violence towards women.

With Lyon, Martin had also written several groundbreaking books on lesbianism. *Lesbian/Woman* (1972) and *Lesbian Love and Liberation* (1973) have been important in educating women as to the realities of lesbian life, providing information that, most certainly at the time of their initial publication, was not openly available. In more recent years, Martin has also become personally involved in problems confronted by the aged in America, and has volunteered her time and expertise as an advocate with her characteristic energy and enthusiasm. In 1995 she was invited by U.S. Senator Dianne Feinstein to serve as California's delegate to the White House Conference on Aging, held in Washington, D.C. Feinstein could not have made a better choice.

—Pamela Kester-Shelton

MARTINEAU, Harriet

Nationality: British. **Born:** Norwich, England, 12 June 1802. **Career:** Visited United States, 1834-36; was an invalid at Tynemouth, 1839-44. Frequent contributor to the *Athenaeum, Chambers' Journal, Cornhill Magazine, Edinburgh Review, Household Words, The Leader, London Daily News, Macmillan's Magazine, Monthly Repository, National Anti-Slavery Standard, New Monthly Magazine, Once a Week, Penny Magazine, People's Journal, Quarterly Review, Spectator, Tait's Edinburgh Magazine, London & Westminster Review,* and *Westminster Review.* **Died:** 27 June 1876.

Publications

Novels

Deerbrook. London, Moxon, 3 vols., and New York, Harper, 1839.

Political/Social Theory

The Rioters; or, A Tale of Bad Times. London, Houlston, 1827.
The Turn Out; or, Patience the Best Policy. London, Houlston, 1829.
Illustrations of Political Economy. London, Fox, 25 vols., 1832-34; Boston, Bowles, 8 vols., 1833.
Poor Laws and Paupers. London, Fox, 4 vols., 1833-34; Boston, Bowles, 1833.
Illustrations of Taxation. London, Fox, 5 vols., 1834.
Society in America. Boston, Hilliard Gray, 3 vols., 1836.
The Hamlets. Boston, Munroe, 1836.
Retrospect of Western Travel. London, Saunders & Otley, 3 vols., and New York, Lohman, 2 vols., 1838.
Dawn Island. Manchester, England, Gadsby, 1845.
Forest and Game-Law Tales. London, Moxon, 3 vols., 1845-46.
Household Education. London, Moxon, and Philadelphia, Lea & Blanchard, 1849.
Two Letters on Cow-Keeping, Addressed to the Governor of the Guiltcross Union Workhouse. London, Charles Gilpin, Edinburgh, Black, and Dublin, J.B. Gilpin, 1850.
The Factory Controversy: A Warning against Meddling Legislation. Manchester, England, National Association of Factory Occupiers, 1855.
Corporate Tradition and National Rights: Local Dues on Shipping. London, Routledge, 1857.
Suggestions towards the Future Government of India. London, Smith Elder, 1858.

Religion/Spirituality

Devotional Exercises for the Use of Young Persons. London, Hunter, 1823; Boston, Bowles, 1833.
Addresses with Prayers and Original Hymns for the Use of Families and Schools. London, Hunter, 1826.

The Essential Faith of the Universal Church Deduced from the Sacred Records. London, Unitarian Association, 1831; Boston, Bowles, 1833.
The Faith as Unfolded by Many Prophets: An Essay Addressed to the Disciples of Mohammed. London, Unitarian Association, 1832; Boston, Bowles, 1833.
Providence as Manifested through Israel. London, Unitarian Association, 1832; Boston, Bowles, 1833.
Letters on the Laws of Man's Nature and Development, with Henry George Atkinson. London, Chapman, and Boston, Mendum, 1851.

History

The Hour and the Man. London, Moxon, 3 vols., and New York, Harper, 2 vols., 1841.
The Billow and the Rock. London, Knight, 1846.
History of England during the 30 Years' Peace 1816-46. London, Knight, 2 vols., 1849; Philadelphia, Porter & Coates, 2 vols., 1864.
Introduction to the History of the Peace from 1800 to 1815. London, Knight, 1850.
British Rule in India: A Historical Sketch. London, Smith Elder, 1857.
The Hampdens: A Historiette. London, Routledge, 1880.

Essays

Life in the Sick-Room. London, Moxon, and Boston, Bowles & Crosby, 1844.
Letters on Mesmerism. London, Moxon, and New York, Harper, 1845.

For Children

Principle and Practice; or, The Orphan Family. Wellington, England, Houlston, 1827; New York, Printed for W. B. Gilley, 1828.
Five Years of Youth; or, Sense and Sentiment. London, Harvey & Darton, 1831; Boston, Bowles & Green, 1832.
Sequel to Principle and Practice. London, Houlston, 1831.
Christmas-Day; or, The Friends. London, Houlston, 1834.
The Playfellow. London, Knight, 4 vols., 1841-43; London and New York, Routledge, 1883.

Autobiography

Harriet Martineau's Autobiography, with Memorials by Maria Weston Chapman. London, Smith Elder, 3 vols., and Boston, Osgood, 2 vols, 1877.

Other

Mary Campbell; or, The Affectionate Granddaughter. Wellington, England, Houlston, 1828.
My Servant Rachel. London, Houlston, 1838.
The Children Who Lived by the Jordan. Salem, Massachusetts, Landmark, 1835; London, Green, 1842.
Miscellanies. Boston, Hilliard Gray, 2 vols., 1836.
How to Observe Morals and Manners. London, Knight, and New York, Harper, 1838.
The Martyr Age of the United States of America. Boston, Weeks Jordan & Otis Broaders, 1839; Newcastle upon Tyne, Emancipation & Aborigines Protection Society, 1840.
The Land We Live In, with Charles Knight. London, Knight, 4 vols., 1847.
Eastern Life, Present and Past. London, Moxon, 3 vols., and Philadelphia, Lea & Blanchard, 1848.
Letters from Ireland. London, Chapman, 1852.
Guide to Windermere, with Tours to the Neighbouring Lakes and Other Interesting Places. London, Whittaker, 1854.
A Complete Guide to the English Lakes. London, Whittaker, 1855.
A History of the American Compromises. London, Chapman, 1856.
Sketches from Life. London, Whittaker, 1856.
Guide to Keswick and Its Environs. London, Whittaker, 1857.
The "Manifest Destiny" of the American Union. New York, American Anti-Slavery Society, 1857.
Endowed Schools of Ireland. London, Smith Elder, 1859.
England and Her Soldiers. London, Smith Elder, 1859.
Health, Husbandry, and Handicraft. London, Bradbury & Evans, 1861; portion published as *Our Farm of Two Acres,* New York, Bunce & Huntingdon, 1865.
Biographical Sketches. London, Macmillan, and New York, Leopoldt & Holt, 1869.
Harriet Martineau's Letters to Fanny Wedgwood, edited by Elisabeth Sanders Arbuckle. Stanford, California, Stanford University Press, 1983.
Harriet Martineau: Selected Letters, edited by Valerie Sanders. Oxford, Clarendon University Press, 1990.

Editor, *Traditions of Palestine.* London, Longman Rees, 1830; as *The Times of the Saviour,* Boston, Bowles, 1831.
Editor and translator, *The Positive Philosophy of Auguste Comte.* London, Chapman, 2 vols., 1853; New York, 1854.

*

Bibliography: *Harriet Martineau: A Bibliography of Her Separately Printed Books* by Joseph B. Rivlin, New York, New York Public Library, 1947.

Critical Studies: *Harriet Martineau* by John Cranstoun Nevill, London, Muller, 1943; *The Life and Work of Harriet Martineau* by Vera Wheatley, London, Secker & Warburg, 1957; *Harriet Martineau: A Radical Victorian* by R. K. Webb, London, Heinemann, 1960; "An Abominable Submission: Harriet Martineau's Views on the Role and Place of Women" by Valerie Kossew Pichanick, in *Women's Studies,* 5(1), 1977; *Harriet Martineau: The Woman and Her Work* by Pichanick, Ann Arbor, University of Michigan Press, 1980; "*Harriet Martineau's Autobiography:* The Making of a Female Philosopher" by Mitzi Myers, in *Women's Autobiography: Essays in Criticism,* edited by Estelle C. Jelinek, Bloomington, Indiana University Press, 1980; *Sex and Subterfuge: Women Writers to 1850* by Eva Figes, London, Macmillan, 1982, and New York, Persea, 1987; *Harriet Martineau* by Gillian Thomas, Boston, G. K. Hall, 1985; *Reason over Passion: Harriet Martineau and the Victorian Novel* by Valerie Sanders, Sussex, Harvester, 1986.

* * *

"I admire her and wonder at her more than I can say" wrote Charlotte Brontë of Harriet Martineau in 1850. "Her powers of labour, of exercise, and social cheerfulness are beyond my comprehension." This estimation of Martineau, whom Brontë considered a "colossal intellect," was one shared by most of the intelligentsia of 19th-century England, as Martineau was unquestionably one of the most productive and influential members of the Victorian literati. As the author of hundreds of political, economic, and historical tracts and stories, fictional works and travel pieces, as well as children's books and religious essays, Martineau is perhaps unsurpassed in the sheer volume of her contributions to the literature of the period. As friend, confidant, and sometimes adversary to figures of such renown as William and Dorothy Wordsworth, Samuel Taylor Coleridge, Charles Dickens, William Makepeace Thackeray, Elizabeth Gaskell, Thomas and Jane Carlyle, John Stuart Mill and Harriet Taylor, Elizabeth Barrett Browning, Florence Nightingale, George Eliot, as well as Charlotte Brontë, she was clearly a force to be reckoned with in English literary circles. Yet what elevated Martineau to such a position of prominence was her identification as a powerful example of the fact that women could write intelligently about political, religious, and economic matters in what had primarily been a males-only milieu. This, if nothing else, serves to identify Martineau as one of the earliest and most influential of all British feminist writers.

As the sixth of eight children born into a relatively affluent Norwich manufacturing family, Martineau's early life was characterized by illnesses, the effects of which would plague her throughout her life. Born with neither the sense of smell nor taste, at age twelve she would also begin to go deaf, though her repeated entreaties to her parents for help were dismissed as the hypochondrial ravings of a child. Unfortunately, by the time that her parents realized that she was in fact losing her hearing, she was fifteen-years-old and almost totally deaf. Yet despite her handicaps, Martineau continued to apply herself to her the study of languages and the classics that she had undertaken both at home and during a two-year stint at school; as a result, the girl who had read Milton at the age of seven, who began to study political economy at fourteen, and who claimed to even think in Latin, was by the age of 18 an intellectual prodigy.

It was at about this time that she wrote "Female Writers of Practical Divinity," which was published in the Unitarian journal *Monthly Repository* in 1820. Her younger brother James, a prominent theologian, was so impressed with his sister's literary acumen that he told her to "leave it to other women to make shirts and darn stockings," and encouraged her to devote herself to writing. "That evening," Martineau recalled in her *Autobiography*, "made me an authoress."

With her first book, *Devotional Exercises for the Use of Young Persons* (1823), Martineau embarked on a career that would position her as one of the 19th century's most productive writers, and after the publication of *Illustrations of Political Economy* (1832-1834), she became one of England's most celebrated authors as well. *Illustrations* was the prototype for almost all of Martineau's later works, in that she illustrated her political and economic beliefs by writing a short story that conveyed her message in a highly didactic fashion. *Illustrations* was not only financially successful—it sold more than 10,000 copies by subscription—but it, like many of her later works, was socially influential as well. The polemic *Poor Laws and Paupers Illustrated,* written in 1833-34, was similarly significant: in it Martineau described destitute families abusing the system of welfare for the poor, having found that a life of dependency in the poorhouses was highly preferable to an existence of hard work and honest labor. For many British citizens, Martineau's tales only confirmed what they had believed all along, that many of the poor were good-for-nothing idlers. A few years later, Dickens would sarcastically rebut this type of dogma in *Oliver Twist,* but despite his contentions, Martineau was clearly writing literature that echoed the beliefs of many English citizens.

Although Martineau wrote politically and economically centric literature, she also branched out into other fields of interest. She not only continued to write the religious essays that had fueled her early career, but she also wrote a number of morally didactic stories for children, the most included in 1841's *The Playfellow.* In 1839 she wrote a novel, *Deerbrook,* and although a popular success, some critics, like Thomas Carlyle, found little to admire in this novel that was "very trivial-didactic, in fact very absurd for the most part." Nevertheless, Martineau continued to be a popular and productive author, despite the fact that in 1839 she became bed-ridden and remained so until cured by mesmerism in 1844.

In the late 1840s she became what would later be termed an agnostic, much to the chagrin of her highly religious siblings. In 1855, after recurring health problems, Martineau began what may well be her most well-known work, her *Autobiography.* Although she would regain her health and live until 1876, for a brief period in 1855 she labored furiously to finish her life story, which would remain unaltered and locked away until her death 21 years later. In this work Martineau criticized and passed judgement on most of her contemporaries, many of whom would have been shocked to hear her opinions of them and their work. Among the criticisms leveled at her contemporaries were the charges that Sir Walter Scott was unoriginal and that he had "only one perfect plot," that Thomas Macaulay was a plagiarist, and that Dickens should refrain from writing novels like *Oliver Twist* and *Hard Times* because he knew nothing about political economy. As George Eliot said of the *Autobiography*, "The account of her childhood and early youth is most pathetic and interesting; but ... one regrets that she continually felt it necessary not only to tell of her intercourse with many more or less distinguished persons—which would have been quite pleasant to everybody—but especially to pronounce upon their entire merits and demerits, especially when, if she had died as soon as she expected, these persons would nearly all have been living to read her gratuitous rudeness." Indeed, the vituperative Martineau often let her proclivity for criticizing others destroy friendships, including those she had with both Eliot and Charlotte Brontë.

Although Martineau produced only two book-length works during the last sixteen years of her life, she remained politically active, especially in the forum of women's rights. She worked with Florence Nightingale during the 1860s to force Parliament to repeal the Contagious Diseases Acts, which allowed the forcible physical examination of any woman suspected of being a prostitute in a military town, on no more evidence than hearsay. Although the acts were not repealed until after her death, Martineau was undeniably influential in organizing their early opposition. Still mentally alert, the aging Martineau, who had outlived almost all of her friends and contemporaries, finally joined them when she died in 1876.

While Martineau's name is now primarily familiar to students of the 19th century, she was one of history's most significant literati—male or female. Because she was an opinionated intellectual, Charlotte Brontë noted that "some of the gentry dislike her, but the lower orders have great regard for her." Yet in spite of this—or perhaps because of it—Harriet Martineau was one of the most influential and important writers that England ever produced.

—James R. Simmons Jr.

MARTINES, Julia. *See* **O'FAOLAIN, Julia.**

McCARTHY, Mary (Therese)

Nationality: American. **Born:** Seattle, Washington, 21 June 1912; sister of actor Kevin McCarthy. **Education:** Vassar College, New York, A.B. 1933. **Family:** Married 1) actor/playwright Harold Johnsrud in 1933 (divorced 1936); 2) writer Edmund Wilson in February 1938 (divorced 1946), one son; 3) Bowden Broadwater in 1946 (divorced 1961); 4) U.S. State Department official James Raymond West in 1961. **Career:** Founder, with Elizabeth Bishop, Muriel Rukeyser, and Eleanor Clark, of a literary magazine to protest the policies of the *Vassar Review* (the two magazines later merged), c. 1932; book reviewer for the *Nation* and *New Republic,* typist and editor for Benjamin Stolberg, and brochure writer for Manhattan art gallery proprietor, New York, 1933-36; editor, Covici Friede (publishers), New York, 1936-37; ghostwriter for H.V. Kaltenborn, 1937; editor, 1937-38, and drama critic, 1937-62, *Partisan Review,* New York; instructor in literature, Bard College, Annandale-on-Hudson, New York, 1945-46; instructor in English, Sarah Lawrence College, Bronxville, New York, 1948; Northcliffe Lecturer, University College, University of London, 1980. Contributor of essays to periodicals, including *New York Review of Books, New York Times Book Review, Observer, Partisan Review,* and *Sunday Times.* **Awards:** Horizon prize, 1949, for *The Oasis;* Guggenheim fellowships, 1949-50 and 1959-60; National Institute of Arts and Letters grant in literature, 1957; named Officier de L'Ordre des Arts et Lettres (France), 1983; Edward MacDowell Medal, 1984; Harold K. Guinzburg Foundation National Medal for Literature, 1984; D.Litt.: Syracuse University, 1973; University of Hull, 1974; Bard College, 1976; Bowdoin College, 1981; University of Maine at Orono, 1982; LL.D.: University of Aberdeen, 1979. **Member:** National Institute of Arts and Letters, Authors League of America, Phi Beta Kappa. **Died:** Of cancer, in New York, New York, 25 October 1989.

Publications

Novels

The Company She Keeps. New York, Simon & Schuster, 1942; London, Weidenfeld & Nicolson, 1957.
The Oasis (first published in *Horizon*). New York, Random House, 1949; as *A Source of Embarrassment,* London, Heinemann, 1950.
The Groves of Academe. New York, Harcourt, 1952.
A Charmed Life. New York, Harcourt, 1955.
The Group. New York, Harcourt, and London, Weidenfeld & Nicolson, 1963.
Winter Visitors. New York, Harcourt, 1970; expanded as *Birds of America,* 1971.
Cannibals and Missionaries. New York, Harcourt, 1979.

Short Stories

Cast a Cold Eye. New York, Harcourt, 1950; enlarged as *The Hounds of Summer and Other Stories: Mary McCarthy's Short Fiction,* New York, Avon, 1981.

Literary Criticism

Ideas and the Novel. New York, Harcourt, 1980.
The Writing on the Wall and Other Literary Essays. New York, Harcourt, 1970.

Essays

On the Contrary. New York, Farrar Straus, 1961; London, Weidenfeld & Nicolson, 1980.
The Humanist in the Bathtub. New York, New American Library, 1964.
Occasional Prose. New York, Harcourt, 1985.
Intellectual Memoirs: New York, 1936-1938. New York, Harcourt, 1992.

Nonfiction

Vietnam. New York, Harcourt, 1967.
Hanoi. New York, Harcourt, 1968.
Medina. New York, Harcourt, 1972.
The Mask of State: Watergate Portraits. New York, Harcourt, 1974.
The Seventeenth Degree (includes *Vietnam, Hanoi,* and *Medina*). New York, Harcourt, 1974.

Autobiography

Memories of a Catholic Girlhood. New York, Harcourt, 1957; London, Penguin, 1975.
How I Grew. San Diego, Harcourt, 1987; London, Penguin, 1989.

Other

Sights and Spectacles, 1937-1956 (theater criticism). New York, Farrar Straus, 1956; enlarged as *Sights and Spectacles, 1937-1958,* London, Heinemann, 1959; enlarged as *Mary McCarthy's Theatre Chronicles, 1937-1962,* Farrar Straus, 1963.
Venice Observed. New York, Reynal, 1956; 2nd edition, 1957; with *The Stones of Florence,* London, Penguin, 1972.
The Stones of Florence. New York, Harcourt, 1959; with *Venice Observed,* London, Penguin, 1972.
Between Friends: The Correspondence of Hannah Arendt and Mary McCarthy, 1949-1975, edited by Carol Brightman. New York, Harcourt, 1994; London, Secker & Warburg, 1995.

Translator, *The Iliad; or, The Poem of Force,* by Simone Weil. Politics Pamphlets, 1947.

Translator, *On the Iliad,* by Rachel Bespaloff. New York, Pantheon, 1948.

*

Bibliography: *Mary McCarthy: An Annotated Bibliography* by Joy Bennett and Gabriella Hochmann, New York, Garland, 1992.

Critical Studies: *Mary McCarthy* by Barbara McKenzie, Boston, Twayne, 1966; *Critical Occasions* by Julian Symons, London, Hamish Hamilton, 1966; *Mary McCarthy* by Irvin Stock, Minneapolis, University of Minnesota Press, 1968; *The Company She Kept: A Revealing Portrait of Mary McCarthy* by Doris Grumbach, New York, Coward, 1976; *The New York Intellectuals: The Rise and Decline of the Anti-Stalinist Left, from the 1930s to the 1980s* by Alan M. Wald, University of North Carolina Press, 1987; *Mary McCarthy: A Life* by Carol W. Gelderman, New York, St. Martin's Press, 1988; *Conversations with Mary McCarthy* edited by Gelderman, Jackson, University Press of Mississippi, 1991; *Writing Dangerously: Mary McCarthy and Her World* by Carole Brightman, San Diego, Harcourt, 1994.

* * *

During her professional career Mary McCarthy was a prolific writer, producing novels, short stories, essays, literary criticism, and social, political, and cultural commentary. She also worked as an editor and a translator and maintained a 26-year correspondence with the political theorist Hannah Arendt. Best known perhaps for her 1963 block-buster novel *The Group* and the autobiographical *Memories of a Catholic Girlhood,* McCarthy associated with left-wing intellectuals during the 1930s and '40s and in her works from the '50s to the '70s offered critiques of 20th-century liberalism. Disparaging the feminist movement of the '60s and '70s, which she characterized as full of "self-pity, shrillness and greed," McCarthy, nevertheless, explores in her works issues involving women's search for identity, relationships with men and other women, and intellectual development.

The first child of Therese Preston McCarthy and Roy Winfield McCarthy, McCarthy was orphaned in 1918 when her parents died in an influenza epidemic. While her paternal grandparents provided monetarily for her and her three brothers, the children lived for five years with an aunt and her husband, a man whom McCarthy characterizes in her autobiography as brutally Dickensian. In 1923 McCarthy's maternal grandfather, Harold Preston, took her to live in Seattle and sent her to Catholic school. She returned east to attend Vassar, from which she graduated in 1933; after graduation, she began her professional career, writing book reviews occasionally for the *New Republic* and *Nation.* By 1937 she was on the editorial board of *Partisan Review,* an anti-Stalinist magazine; however, because the male editors did not value her political beliefs, they gave her a permanent assignment as drama critic. It was her second husband, the literary critic and writer Edmund Wilson, who encouraged McCarthy to write fiction; in 1941, four years after their marriage, she published *The Company She Keeps.*

Intended originally simply as a series of stories, *The Company She Keeps* eventually became for McCarthy a novel centered on the protagonist, Margaret ("Meg") Sargent. Focusing on individuals whom Meg meets, part of the work recounts their relationships to her; in "Portrait of the Intellectual as a Yale Man," McCarthy analyzes a married man with whom Meg has a brief affair. An average young man who becomes a Marxist, Jim eventually abandons his political convictions for success, while Meg retains her integrity. The episodes dealing directly with Meg portray her effort to maintain her intellectual honesty and her search for selfhood. "The Man in the Brooks-Brothers Suit" relates not only Meg's affair with a businessman, but also her assessment of her former marriage and her critical scrutiny of her role in the affair.

Through the next decade McCarthy produced social satire about intellectualism in *The Oasis, The Groves of Academe,* and *A Charmed Life.* In the first novel, published in 1949, New York intellectuals establish a colony called Utopia and soon fall into two factions. It is a teacher named Katy Norell who has the intellectual honesty to understand why the community will not succeed for either of the groups. *The Groves of Academe* depicts another kind of idealistic community, a women's liberal college, in which a faculty member about to be dismissed pretends to have been a communist to gain faculty support. *A Charmed Life,* set in an artists' colony, again deals with a woman's moral struggle. The protagonist, Martha Sinnott, unlike the other characters in the colony, is an individual who cannot live falsely. Therefore, as McCarthy develops the narrative, Martha makes a moral decision when she resolves to have an abortion. In the last chapter, just when she has learned not to be afraid of her past, she dies in a car accident. In these works, while McCarthy ridicules the follies of the intellectual elite, she also portrays the moral integrity of female characters.

In *The Group,* which draws upon its author's Vassar experiences, McCarthy details the attitudes and constricted worlds of middle-class, college-educated women of the 1930s. The novel opens as the women are leaving school, confident in their abilities and in the notion of progress; one of them, Kay Strong, is about to get married. The novel ends when the group reunites seven years later for Kay's funeral. During the course of the work, McCarthy offers accounts of the women's lives and careers, their miserable sexual relationships with husbands and lovers, and their loss of moral boldness.

While McCarthy produced well-received political and social commentary during the late 1960s and early 1970s, her current literary reputation rests on her first autobiographical account, *Memories of a Catholic Girlhood.* Published in 1954, this volume has received the most critical praise of all of her work. Like her novels, *Memories,* with its characteristic ironic style, also deals with questions of moral integrity and passivity and a woman's developing awareness—central themes in all of Mary McCarthy's work.

—Phyllis Surrency Dallas

McCLUNG, Nellie

Nationality: Canadian. **Born:** Nellie Letitia Mooney, in Chatsworth, Ontario, 20 October 1873. **Education:** Graduated from Winnipeg Normal School, Manitoba, 1889. **Family:** Married Robert Wesley McClung in 1896; five children. **Career:** Homesteaded with family in Manitoba, beginning 1880; teacher in rural Manitoba, 1889-96; moved to Winnipeg; co-founder, Political Equality League, Winnipeg; moved to Alberta, 1914; elected to provincial assembly, 1921-25; moved to Victoria, British Columbia, 1935; appointed to board of governors, Canadian Broadcasting Corporation, 1936; delegate to League of Nations, 1938; retired due to illness, 1943. **Died:** 1 September 1951.

PUBLICATIONS

Novels

Sowing Seeds in Danny. Toronto, Briggs, and New York and London, Doubleday Page, 1908; as *Danny and the Pink Lady,* Hodder & Stoughton, 1908.
The Second Chance. Toronto, Briggs, and New York, Doubleday, 1910; London, Hodder & Stoughton, 1922.
Purple Springs. Toronto, Allen, 1921; Boston and New York, Houghton, and London, Huchinson, 1922.
The Beauty of Martha. London, Hutchinson, 1923.
Painted Fires. Toronto, Allen, and New York, Dodd Mead, 1925; London, Fisher, 1926.

Short Stories

The Black Creek Stopping-House and Other Stories. Toronto, Briggs, 1912.
The Next of Kin: Stories of Those Who Wait and Wonder. Toronto, Allen, and Boston and New York, Houghton Mifflin, 1917.
When Christmas Crossed "The Peace." Toronto, Allen, 1923.
All We like Sheep and Other Stories. Toronto, Allen, 1926.
Be Good to Yourself: A Book of Short Stories. Toronto, Allen, 1930.
Flowers for the Living: A Book of Short Stories. Toronto, Allen, 1931.

Essays

In Times like These. Toronto, McLeod & Allen, and New York, Appleton, 1915.
Leaves from Lantern Lane. Toronto, Allen, 1936.
More Leaves from Lantern Lane. Toronto, Allen, 1937.

Autobiography

Clearing in the West: My Own Story. Toronto, Allen, 1935; New York, Revell, 1936.
The Stream Runs Fast: My Own Story. Toronto, Allen, 1945.

Other

Three Times and Out: Told by Private Simmons, with Mervin C. Simmons. Toronto, Allen, and New York and Boston, Houghton Mifflin, 1918.

*

Manuscript Collections: Provincial Archives of British Columbia, Victoria.

Theatrical Activities: Actor: The premier, in *Women's Parliament,* produced Winnipeg, 1914.

Critical Studies: "Introduction to Nellie L. McClung" by Veronica Strong-Boag, in *In Times like These,* Toronto, University of Toronto Press, 1972; "Nellie McClung: 'Not a Nice Woman'" by Given Matheson and V. E. Lang, in Matheson's *Women in the Canadian Mosaic,* Toronto, Martin, 1976; *Our Nell: A Scrapbook Biography of Nellie L. McClung* by Candace Savage, Saskatoon, Western Producer, 1979; "Ever a Crusader: Nellie McClung, First-Wave Feminist," in *Rethinking Canada: The Promise of Women's History,* Toronto, Copp Clark, 1986; "Canadian Women's Autobiography: A Problem of Criticism" by Susan Jackel, in *Gynocritics,* Toronto, ECW, 1987; "Introduction" to *Purple Springs* by Randi R. Warne, Toronto, University of Toronto Press, 1992; *Firing the Heather: The Life and Times of Nellie McClung* by Mary Hallett and Marilyn Davis, Saskatoon, Fifth House, 1993; *Literature as Pulpit: The Christian Social Activism of Nellie L. McClung* by Randi R. Warne, Wilfred Laurier University Press, 1993; article in *The Literary Review of Canada* by Arun P. Mukherjee, July/August 1995.

* * *

In discussions of reclaiming women's writing, Canadian women are all too often overlooked or forgotten. The result of this is that fascinating women of significant actions and great rhetorical abilities do not receive the attention they deserve. Listening to Canadian women like Nellie McClung opens up important new perspectives on feminism, the women's suffrage movement, women's rhetoric, and, ultimately, women's history.

In 1880 Nellie Letitia Mooney and her family moved from Ontario to Manitoba to homestead. McClung graduated from a Winnipeg normal school in 1990 and received her first teaching assignment in Manitou, Manitoba. Manitou offered her many opportunities that provided a training ground for her later political work. Her awareness of the plight of everyday rural people inspired McClung to an impressive range of actions and roles. In *Clearing in the West* she writes of being inspired by Dickens' social critiques to become a writer and "to do for the people around me what Dickens had done for his people."

In addition to publishing 16 volumes of essays, speeches, novels, and autobiography, McClung was also an influential activist for workers' rights, women's suffrage, temperance, and married women's property rights. In 1921 she was elected to Alberta's legislature, where she fought for women's rights and prohibition. When, in 1928, the Supreme Court of Canada unanimously decided against women holding public office on the grounds that they were not "persons," McClung and four other women (known as The Famous Five) fought " The Persons Case" all the way to the Privy Council in Britain. In 1929 the Privy Council reversed this decision and called women's exclusion from public office "a relic of days more barbarous than ours." McClung was also active in the Winnipeg Political Equality League, the Canadian Women's Press Club, and well as suffrage and temperance organizations in Alberta. She was the first woman member of the Canadian Broadcasting Corporation from 1936-1942 and was a Canadian delegate to the League of Nations in 1938.

While McClung has a reputation as an important Canadian woman, her writings hover on the brink of obscurity. While it is important to acknowledge her profound influence on Canadian cultural and political life, what is perhaps most urgent to current McClung scholarship is reclaiming and restoring her voice by attempting to reconstruct and acknowledge the cultural and political milieu in which she wrote and spoke. As Randi R. Warne notes in *Literature as Pulpit: The Christian Social Activism of Nellie L.*

McClung, McClung's feminism eventually came to be seen as "old-fashioned and irrelevant." McClung, Warne writes, "had lost her voice. Her language—religious, feminist, activist—was no longer the language of common parlance." All too often scholarship on McClung either overly romanticizes her as a person and overlooks her writing or dismisses her writing for being too out of date, too sentimental, or not "feminist enough" by late-20th-century standards.

Because both of these critical stances lead to an impasse, it is important to find alternative ways of looking at McClung's writings in order to rescue them from obscurity. Agreeing with Warne that through "investigating the whole context of McClung's life and work, it is possible to learn to hear McClung's voice clearly once again," one can see McClung as a skilled rhetorician and her work as well-crafted rhetoric. Looking at her through the context of her world, her cultural and political locations, we can attempt to see why it was that she achieved so much and was so influential.

In reading McClung's writings, it is important to remember that in her world women had very few legal rights and that women's suffrage was characterized as bringing the downfall of civilization. Her work was constantly shaped by the goals she wanted to achieve, the audience she was addressing, and her insight into the rhetorical strategies that would transform people's imaginations. Numerous newspaper accounts report how McClung captivated audiences and changed even the most stubborn minds. Her most effective rhetorical stance was her ability to make people laugh; an oft-cited example of McClung's use of humor is "Woman's Parliament," a play she and other suffrage activists staged in 1914 in Winnipeg. In the play, gender roles are reversed; women hold all the political power and men come to them to plead for voting rights. A contemporary *Montreal Herald* report describes McClung's skillful rhetoric:

> Last Thursday Sir Rodmond [premier of Manitoba] spoke here and on Monday his feminine tormentor made him look ridiculous. She has introduce into this campaign the most telling weapon with which the bombastic Premier of Manitoba could be attacked and one which no person has ever wielded against him before so poignantly and effectively. All Manitoba has been made to laugh at Sir Rodmond Robling by Mrs. McClung.

At present, scholarship concerning McClung has not adequately addressed the complexities and contradictions that she negotiates within her writing. Reviewing current critical works on McClung, Arun P. Mukherjee writes: "A complete assessment of Nellie McClung cannot be made unless racism, social Darwinism, and imperialism, the three major forces of McClung's era, are considered. When all evidence is taken into account, McClung looks a lot better than her contemporaries.... However, not responding to certain aspects of her texts and her life and focusing only on her championing of women's rights presents an incomplete picture."

Returning to Warne's argument that we need to investigate the whole context of McClung's life and work in order that "the full significance of this vital, courageous and fascinating Canadian be articulated," much work remains to be done. Indeed, the "full significance" of McClung's work needs to be investigated in order to restore her voice and writings to the place they deserve.

—Heidi L. M. Jacobs

McCULLERS, (Lula) Carson

Nationality: American. **Born:** Lula Carson Smith, in Columbus, Georgia, 19 February 1917. **Education:** Attended Columbia University, New York, and New York University, 1934-36. **Family:** Married Reeves McCullers in 1937 (divorced 1941, remarried 1945, divorced 1948; committed suicide 1953). **Career:** Held a variety of jobs; suffered throughout life with rheumatic fever; moved to New York City, 1934; resident artist, Breadloaf Writers Conference, 1940, and Yaddo Writers Conference, 1941, 1943, 1944, 1945, 1954. **Awards:** Houghton Mifflin fellowship, 1939; Guggenheim fellowships, 1942, 1966; National Institute of Arts and Letters grant, 1943; Donaldson Awards, 1950, Theatre Club Gold Medal, 1950, and New York Drama Critics' Circle Award, 1951, all for *The Member of the Wedding; Die Welt* prize (Germany), 1965, for *The Heart Is a Lonely Hunter.* **Member:** American Academy of Arts and Letters (fellow). **Died:** From a brain hemorrhage, 29 September 1967.

Publications

Novels

The Heart Is a Lonely Hunter. Boston, Houghton Mifflin, 1940.
Reflections in a Golden Eye. Boston, Houghton Mifflin, 1941.
The Member of the Wedding. Boston, Houghton Mifflin, 1946.
The Ballad of the Sad Cafe: The Novels and Stories of Carson McCullers (collection; "The Ballad of the Sad Cafe" first published in *Harper's Bazaar,* 1943). Boston, Houghton Mifflin, 1951; as *The Shorter Novels and Stories of Carson McCullers,* London, Barrie & Jenkins, 1972.
Clock without Hands. Boston, Houghton Mifflin, 1961.

Short Stories

Collected Short Stories and the Novel, The Ballad of the Sad Cafe. Boston, Houghton Mifflin, 1955.

Plays

The Member of the Wedding (adapted from her novel; produced New York, 1950). New York, New Directions Press, 1951.
The Square Root of Wonderful (produced New York, 1957). Boston, Houghton Mifflin, 1958.

Television Plays: *The Sojourner* (adapted from her short story), 1951.

For Children

Sweet as a Pickle, Clean as a Pig (verse). Boston, Houghton Mifflin, 1964.

Other

The Mortgaged Heart: The Previously Uncollected Writings of Carson McCullers, edited by Margarita G. Smith. Boston, Houghton Mifflin, 1971.

*

Media Adaptations: *The Ballad of the Sad Cafe* (play; adapted by Edward Albee), produced New York, 1963; *The Member of the Wedding* (film), Columbia, 1952; *Reflections of a Golden Eye* (film), Seven Arts, 1967; *The Heart Is a Lonely Hunter* (film), Warners/Seven Arts, 1968.

Bibliography: *Carson McCullers: A Descriptive Listing and Annotated Bibliography of Criticism* by Adrian M. Shapiro and others, New York, Garland, 1980.

Critical Studies: *Lies like Truth* by Harold Clurman, New York, Macmillan, 1958; *The Lonely Hunter: A Biography of Carson McCullers* by Virginia Spencer Carr, New York, Doubleday, 1975; *Carson McCullers* by Margaret B. McDowell, New York, Twayne, 1980; *Carson McCullers* edited by Harold Bloom, New York, Twayne, 1986; *Sacred Groves and Ravaged Gardens: The Fiction of Eudora Welty, Carson McCullers and Flannery O'Connor* by Louise Westling, Athens, University of Georgia Press, 1985.

* * *

The haunting photographs of Carson McCullers with her round, child-like face and her intense gaze may provide a visual link to her writing. Androgynous misfits, freak shows, and one-eyed cooks dominate the fiction of McCullers, who often felt herself to be an outcast and misfit.

A youthful success, McCullers moved to New York City from Georgia when she was 17 years old. When she first arrived in the city, she would often go to Macy's Department Store and sit in a phone booth and read, secured by the surrounding glass. This action is, perhaps, a metaphor for McCullers's life—isolated yet often only too visible.

McCullers published her first short story, "Wunderkind" at age 19. Often anthologized,"Wunderkind" is a story of frustrated female creativity. A young girl, Frances, becomes separated from the music she knows so well and is silenced. By the end of the story, she runs from her music teacher's apartment, her place as the "wunderkind" usurped by a more talented young man. Frances has outgrown her creativity.

This fear of growing up is a recurrent theme in much of McCullers's fiction. Mick Kelly, the main character in *The Heart Is a Lonely Hunter,* is a young girl caught between youth and adulthood, between female and male. Like Frances in "Wunderkind," Mick has music caught in her head, music that goes unfulfilled. In this first novel by McCullers, we also encounter Singer, the deaf man who plays records for Mick, and Biff, the cafe owner who likes women's perfume and is the watcher of the town. We are also introduced to Doctor Copeland, the African American doctor, who is trapped by his race in this small southern town. Like Copeland, many of McCullers's characters are encased by the expectations of a traditional, patriarchal society.

McCullers again offers an analysis of maturation, race, and gender in *The Member of the Wedding,* perhaps her most perfect novel. The main character, Frankie Addams, is caught in that blurry world between child and woman, and for McCullers maturation into womanhood is not freedom. The three characters of this novel—Frankie; Berenice, the African American cook with one blue eye; and John Henry, the young boy-cousin from next door who likes to dress like a girl—spend an intense summer in one of the most remarkable kitchens in American literature. In *The Member of the Wedding,* McCullers brings to the forefront a world too often seen as unimportant—a black woman, a clumsy, masculine girl, and a young, feminine boy. The lines of color and gender and age are blurred; in fact, this odd trio often play word games in which they create a more perfect world than God has done.

After a life-long battle with illness and alcoholism, McCullers died while in a coma in 1967 at the age of 50. Trapped by a society determined to place limitations on both gender and identity, McCullers transcended these limitations by falling in love with both men and women, by retaining her child-like obsessions and imagination, and by writing fiction filled with crossed boundaries.

—Jennifer Brantley

MEAD, Margaret

Nationality: American. **Born:** Philadelphia, Pennsylvania, 16 December 1901. **Education:** Attended DePauw University, 1919-20; Barnard College, B.A. 1923; Columbia University, M.A. 1924, Ph.D. 1929. **Family:** Married 1) Luther Cressman in 1923 (divorced); 2) the anthropologist Reo Fortune in 1928 (divorced); 3) the anthropologist and biologist Gregory Bateson in 1936 (divorced 1945), one daughter. **Career:** American Museum of Natural History, New York, assistant curator, 1926-42, associate curator, 1942-64, curator of ethnology, 1964-69, then curator emeritus, 1969-78; adjunct professor of anthropology, Columbia University, New York, 1954-78; professor of anthropology and chairman of Division of Social Sciences, Fordham University, Lincoln Center, New York, 1968-70. Did field work in Samoa, 1925-26, New Guinea, 1928-29, 1931-33, 1938, 1953, 1964, 1965, 1967, 1971, 1973, 1975, Nebraska, 1930, and Bali, 1936-38, 1957-58. Jacob Gimbel Lecturer, Stanford University and University of California, 1946; Mason Lecturer, University of Birmingham, 1949; Inglis Lecturer, Harvard University, 1950; Jubilee Lecturer for New Education Fellowship, Australia, 1951; Philips Visitor, Haverford College, 1955; Terry Lecturer, Yale University, 1957; Sloan Professor, Menninger School of Psychiatry, 1959; Reynolds Lecturer, University of Colorado, 1960; Alumni Distinguished Lecturer, University of Rhode Island, 1970-71; Fogarty Scholar-in-Residence, National Institutes of Health, 1973. Visiting lecturer, Vassar College, 1939-41; visiting professor, University of Cincinnati, beginning 1957, Emory University, 1964, New York University, 1965-67, and Yale University, 1966; taught Harvard seminars on American civilization, Salzburg, Austria, 1947, and at the UNESCO Workshop on International Understanding, Sevres, France, 1947; conducted courses for American Museum's audio-visual program on culture and communication in collaboration with Columbia University's Teacher's College, 1947-51. Directed Wellesley School of Community Affairs, 1943, and Columbia University "Research in Contemporary Cultures" project for the Office of Naval Research, 1948-50. Secretary of committee on food habits, National Research Council, 1942-45; former member of World Health Organization study group on the psychological development of the child, Hampton Institute board of trustees, Josiah H. Macy Conference on Group Processes, and Macy Conference on Problems of Consciousness; member and co-editor of Macy Conference on Cybernetics. Editor of a manual on cultural patterns and technical change for UNESCO, World Federation for Mental Health, 1950; prepared case materials for the International Seminar on Mental

Health and Infant Development, Chichester, England, 1950. Contributor to scholarly and popular periodicals; contributing editor, *Redbook,* 1961-78. **Awards:** Chi Omega National achievement award, 1940; Society of Women Geographers gold medal award, 1942; Viking Medal in anthropology, 1958; Rice University medal of honor, 1962; Nationwide Woman Editors Women's Hall of Fame award, 1965; Scientific Research Society of America's William Proctor Prize for Scientific Achievement, 1969; Pacific Science Center Arches of Science Award, 1971; UNESCO/government of India's Kalinga Prize, 1971; Vanier Institute of the Family's Wilder Penfield Award, 1972; New York Academy of Sciences Lehmann Award, 1973; Omega Achievers Award for Education, 1977; Presidential Medal of Freedom, 1979. Honorary degrees from Columbia University, Rutgers University, University of Leeds, and numerous other colleges and universities. **Member:** American Academy of Arts and Sciences, American Anthropological Association (fellow; past president), American Association for the Advancement of Science (past president; past chairman of board), Institute for Intercultural Studies (secretary), American Association of University Women, Society of Applied Anthropology (past president), American Ethnological Society, Society of Woman Geographers (fellow), American Orthopsychiatric Association (fellow), World Society of Ekistics (past president), Scientists Institute for Public Information (past president), Society for General Systems Research (past president), Institute for Intercultural Studies, World Federation of Mental Health (past president), American Council of Learned Societies (past vice-president), New York Academy of Science (fellow), Phi Beta Kappa, Delta Kappa Gamma, Sigma Xi. **Died:** New York, New York, 15 November 1978.

Publications

Nonfiction

An Inquiry into the Question of Cultural Stability in Polynesia (Ph.D. thesis). New York, Columbia University Press, 1928.
Coming of Age in Samoa: A Psychological Study of Primitive Youth for Western Civilization. New York, Morrow, 1928.
Social Organization of Manua. Bernice P. Bishop Museum, 1930, 2nd edition, 1969.
Growing Up in New Guinea. New York, Morrow, 1930.
The Changing Culture of an Indian Tribe. New York, Columbia University Press, 1932.
Sex and Temperament in Three Primitive Societies. New York, Morrow, 1935.
Cooperation and Competition among Primitive Societies, with others. Boston, McGraw, 1937.
From the South Seas (includes *Coming of Age in Samoa, Growing Up in New Guinea,* and *Sex and Temperament in Three Primitive Societies*), New York, Morrow, 1939.
And Keep Your Powder Dry: An Anthropologist Looks at America. New York, Morrow, 1942; expanded edition, Books for Libraries, 1971.
Balinese Character: A Photographic Analysis, with Gregory Bateson. New York, New York Academy of Sciences, 1942.
Male and Female. New York, Morrow, and London, Gollancz, 1949.
Soviet Attitudes toward Authority. New York, McGraw-Hill, 1951.
The School in American Culture. Boston, Harvard University Press, and Oxford, Oxford University Press, 1951.
Growth and Culture: A Photographic Study of Balinese Childhood, with Frances Cooke MacGregor. New York, Putnam, 1951.
Themes in French Culture: A Preface to a Study of French Community, with Rhoda Metraux. Stanford, California, Stanford University Press, 1954.
New Lives for Old. New York, Morrow, and London, Gollancz, 1956.
Technique and Personality, with Junius B. Bird and Hans Himmelheber. New York, Museum of Primitive Art, 1963.
Anthropology, A Human Science: Selected Papers, 1939-1960. New York, Van Nostrand, 1964.
Continuities in Cultural Evolution. New Haven, Connecticut, Yale University Press, 1964.
Family, with Ken Heyman. New York and London, Macmillan, 1965.
The Wagon and the Star: A Study of American Community Initiative, with Muriel Brown. Curriculum Resources, 1966.
The Small Conference: An Innovation in Communication, with Paul Byers. Paris, Ecole Pratique des Hautes Etudes, 1966.
The Changing Cultural Patterns of Work and Leisure (booklet). Washington, D.C., U.S. Department of Labor, 1967.
The Mountain Arapesh. Natural History Press, 3 vols., 1968-71.
Culture and Commitment: A Study of the Generation Gap. Natural History Press, and London, Bodley Head, 1970; as *Culture and Commitment: The New Relationships between the Generations in the 1970s,* Garden City, New York, Doubleday, 1978.
A Way of Seeing, with Rhoda Metraux. McCall, 1970.
A Rap on Race, with James Baldwin. Philadelphia, Lippincott, and London, Joseph, 1971.
Twentieth-Century Faith: Hope and Survival. New York and London, Harper & Row, 1972.
World Enough: Rethinking the Future, with Ken Heyman. Boston, Little Brown, 1975.
Aspects of the Present, with Rhoda Metraux. New York, Morrow, 1980.

Essays

Some Personal Views, edited by Rhoda Metraux. London, Angus & Robertson, 1979.

Poetry

Time & Measure. Northampton, Massachusetts, Hypatia Press, 1986.

Plays

Screenplays: *Films in Character Formation in Different Cultures,* 1952.

Television Play: *Margaret Mead's New Guinea Journal,* 1968.

For Children

People and Places. World Publishing, 1959; Edinburgh, Blackie, 1964.
Anthropologists and What They Do. New York, F. Watts, 1965.
An Interview with Santa Claus, with Rhoda Metraux. New York, Walker, 1978.

Autobiography

Blackberry Winter: My Earlier Years. New York, Morrow, 1972; London, Angus & Robertson, 1973.

Letters from the Field, 1925-1975. New York and London, Harper, 1977.

Other

A Creative Life for Your Children (booklet). Washington, D.C., U.S. Department of Health, Education, and Welfare, 1962.

Food Habits Research: Problems of the 1960s (booklet), Washington, D.C., National Academy of Sciences-National Research Council, 1964.

Ruth Benedict (biography). New York and London, Columbia University Press, 1974.

Editor, *Cultural Patterns and Technical Change: A Manual.* Paris, UNESCO, 1953; Westport, Connecticut, Greenwood Press, 1985.

Editor, with Rhoda Metraux, *The Study of Culture at a Distance.* Chicago, University of Chicago Press, and Cambridge, Cambridge University Press, 1953.

Editor, with Nicolas Calas, *Primitive Heritage: An Anthropological Anthology.* New York, Random House, 1953.

Editor, with Martha Wolfenstein, *Childhood in Contemporary Cultures.* Chicago, University of Chicago Press, 1955.

Editor, *An Anthropologist at Work: Writings of Ruth Benedict.* Boston, Houghton, 1959.

Editor, with Ruth L. Bunzel, *The Golden Age of American Anthropology.* New York, Braziller, 1960.

Editor, with others, *Science and the Concept of Race.* New York, Columbia University Press, 1968.

*

Media Adaptations: *Margaret Mead: Taking Notes* (video recording), 1981.

Critical Studies: *Margaret Mead: A Voice for the Century* by Robert Cassidy, New York, Universe Books, 1982; *Margaret Mead and Samoa: The Making and Unmasking of a Myth* by Derek Freeman, Cambridge, Massachusetts, Harvard University Press, 1983; *Mead's Coming of Age in Samoa: A Dissenting View* by Richard A. Goodman, Oakland, California, Pipperine Press, 1983; *Margaret Mead: A Life* by Jane Howard, New York, Simon & Schuster, 1984; *With a Daughter's Eye: A Memoir of Margaret Mead and Gregory Bateson* by Mary Catherine Bateson, New York, Morrow, 1985; *Quest for the Real Samoa: The Mead/Freeman Controversy and Beyond* by Lowell D. Holmes, South Hadley, Massachusetts, Bergin & Garvey, 1987; *Margaret Mead* by Phyllis Grosskurth, London, Penguin, 1988; *Confronting the Margaret Mead Legacy: Scholarship, Empire, and the South Pacific* edited by Lenora Foerstel and Angela Gilliam, Philadelphia, Temple University Press, 1992; *Adolescent Storm and Stress: An Evaluation of the Mead-Freeman Controversy* by James E. Côté, Hillsdale, New Jersey, Erlbaum, 1994.

* * *

Although Margaret Mead's prominence in the field of anthropology remains virtually unmatched, many would not recognize her solely by such foreign endeavors. The author of over forty books—a number written on domestic social activism and human relations—Mead committed her life to building a sense of community. In active pursuit of both scholarly and social contributions, she invested her enormous energy and intellect wherever and whenever she believed a situation called for attention. While inciting controversy over her idiosyncratic stance against certain aspects of the blossoming women's movement during the 1960s, Mead can be credited with helping to disarm age-old perceptions about a woman's proper "role" in society. Through both her work and her life, she illustrated that, although they might be bound by culture, gender alone presented no obstacle, and set no limit, to what women could accomplish.

Born on December 16, 1901, in Philadelphia, Pennsylvania, Mead learned early on the influence of both knowledge and independence. Her father, Sherwood Mead, taught economics at the Wharton School of Business; her mother, Emily Fogg Mead, was a graduate of Wellesley College and an avid feminist. In fact, Mead's mother was one of few women to pursue higher education at a time when a woman's place was deemed to be "in the home." In addition to the influence of her parents, her grandmother, Martha Mead, encouraged her young granddaughter to observe and record the activities of her younger siblings.

Even within her relatively forward-thinking family, Mead clearly understood the social limitations placed on women. Although her father accepted that his daughter's success in life would be hampered because of her gender, Mead refused to accept this unfair destiny. Seeking to continue her education through college, she set her sights on preeminent women's schools such as her mother's alma mater. Unfortunately, the family could not afford the fees. Again, in an attempt to curtail her ambitions, Mead's father asked their doctor to try to dissuade the young scholar. The doctor's comments to his young patient to the effect that she was helpless and weak because she was a woman, only motivated Mead more.

Eventually, her father agreed to send her to his own alma mater, Indiana's De Pauw University. While Mead expected to find college life intellectually provoking, at De Pauw, students seemed more interested in fraternities and sororities. Her homemade dresses and East-Coast accent made her a social outsider within the campus world. Mead pleaded with her family for assistance and was grateful when, after one miserable year at De Pauw, she transferred to Barnard College's all-female campus in New York City.

At Barnard, not only did Mead gain excellent academic training, but she was also able to create a friendship circle true to her interests and beliefs. Mead and the Ash Can Cats, as the group of friends called themselves, enjoyed many cultural and intellectual activities together. In one especially memorable event, the "cats" arrived at the door of Greenwich Village-resident Edna St. Vincent Millay at midnight on May 1, to present the noted poet with a May basket.

Mead had entered Barnard still undecided as to her eventual course of study. While contemplating politics because she felt well prepared as a public speaker, she recognized the insecurity of this arena. Instead, she opted to pursue her love of literature and writing as an English major, also selecting classes in psychology because of her interest in the human mind. It was not until her senior year, when Mead sought to fill a gap in her schedule, that she noticed a course in anthropology, taught by professor Franz Boas. A new science, anthropology and its study of "people" piqued Mead's interest, so she registered.

Boas taught his students that through anthropology a real human community could be understood. Contrary to the race sentiment of the era, he contended that all people are basically the same; that differences could be attributable to culture or lifestyle rather than biology. Receiving inspiration from both Boas and his teaching assistant and fellow anthropologist, Ruth Benedict, Mead eventually changed her academic path. After completing her Bachelor's degree and also a Master's thesis in psychology, Mead then dedicated her life to the study of anthropology. Accompanying this shift in career was a shift in her personal life: Mead married longtime sweetheart Luther Cressman in 1923, causing quite an uproar by keeping her own last name.

Both Boas and Benedict believed that the study of primitive cultures—those still untouched by any forced adaption or assimilation to modernization—was essential. Although Boas suggested that Mead remain in the United States due to the danger of travel, the young anthropologist insisted upon overseas research. She set off for Samoa, an island in the South Pacific. Here, her task would be to study adolescent transition among young women and cross-culturally compare this period of growth. "[T]he originality of her project was that no one had concentrated exclusively on women and children before," Phyllis Grosskurth noted in her *Margaret Mead: A Life of Controversy.* During her nine-month stay, Mead's eyes were opened to many new and intriguing concepts. In her best-selling book, *Coming of Age in Samoa,* written after her return to the United States in 1928, she submits that, even more so than the biologically induced changes in human adolescence, social environments enhance the many difficulties faced by teenagers. In response to this finding, she suggested methods for easing teenage stress within American society.

In other famous books, including 1935's *Sex and Temperament in Three Primitive Societies* and *Male and Female,* published in 1949, Mead used her research from such places as New Guinea and Bali to counter the influential findings of the renown psychologist Sigmund Freud. Mead asserted that Freud "was so bound up in his own 19th-century European interpretation of culture that he failed to consider how sexuality could be viewed under different conditions," as Robert Cassidy explained in *Margaret Mead: A Voice for the Century.* Freud maintained that biology dictated one's place in society, and that women who went against their natural instinct suffered from "penis envy." Conversely, Mead argued that, both historically and culturally, women's status changed depending on their societal condition. She demonstrated that ample evidence existed from many cultures to indicate the existence of a corresponding "womb envy" among men. Overall, she contended, by constantly adapting as time and culture demanded, women were doing nothing less than furthering an age-old need for flexibility.

Mead wrote more than forty books—eighteen with other people—and over a thousand monographs and articles. Within these works she made the mysteries of science comprehensible to the common person. Her writing was easily understood; it allowed readers to interpret her findings in relation to their own situation. She also lectured throughout the world, not only speaking about her experiences in the field, but frequently making commentary on contemporary political issues.

In addition to holding positions in the American Museum of Natural History, she also taught at colleges and universities throughout the country. Mead served on numerous committees and received over twenty-five honorary degrees. She was also inaugurated into the National Women's Hall of Fame. While such fame was important to Mead, even more important was her desire to have a family. Having been married and divorced again since her first marriage to Cressman, Mead married Gregory Bateson in 1936, a partnership that resulted in a daughter, Mary Catherine, before the couple divorced a decade later.

Interestingly enough, the achievements made by Mead led to public controversy in a surprising arena. Although her success, especially as a pioneer woman in the field, established her as a feminist role model, Mead would voice disagreement with many of her contemporaries. "[W]hen it was very clear that a feminist revolution was under way, Mead poured scorn on the middle-aged women who complained that they had been victimized by a male-dominated society," commented Grosskurth, "because, so far as she could see, they had passively allowed themselves to be the objects of discrimination."

Betty Friedan, in her groundbreaking book *The Feminine Mystique,* criticized Mead for this typification of women. Friedan claimed that Mead divided women into two groups: either "childbearing" or, like herself, uncommon individualists who dared to transcend social boundaries. In fact, Grosskurth submitted, Mead "never hesitated to take advantage of being a woman.... She took no part in a whole range of activities such as sport. She concentrated only on those things in which she felt confident that she could excel."

Despite the challenge from activists such as Friedan, the average woman in the United States could identify with Mead, as Robert Cassidy stated in his *Mead: A Voice for the Century,* "the average woman could sense that Mead had a personal stake in their more mundane problems: Even with all her degrees and honors, they felt, she knew how to change a diaper." These commonalities were not only extended in Mead's speeches and academic articles. She also wrote a monthly column for the popular *Redbook* magazine, in which she often discussed the women's movement and her opinion of its principles and progressions. Mead agreed that the country offered contradictory opportunity for men and women, putting forth the view that, although in school girls are taught to work towards the same values as boys, after they reach adulthood—the childbearing years—their sole option becomes marriage and motherhood.

Although Mead had been a vocal proponent of greater rights for women, she believed that some of the more radical feminist agendas of the 1960s failed to address what she considered to be the real needs either of women or of society. She felt that the movement was too anti-male, pointing to a heightening social tension between men and women as one result. She continued to stress that, without a bipartisan coalition, the movement would only create more inequity for both men and women. Mead also believed that some feminist platforms either disregarded or shamed many of the feminine attributes which she considered to be positive.

Mead knew, moreover, that this middle-class-generated movement did not speak to the needs of the majority of women, particularly those in traditionally underprivileged segments of society. In 1963, as a Presidential commission headed by the late John F. Kennedy sought to open up the job market to women, Mead criticized its members for their shortsightedness. While the commission's report advocated access, it developed to plan to assist the average housewife and mother in gaining such access. Until her death in 1978, Mead consistently raised her voice against such similarly negligent attitudes, attitudes that would continue to bar women from making choices.

As a whole, however, Mead worked toward building a society wherein the gender roles of men and women would blur; where society would become "reshaped, by both sexes, to suit the needs of both sexes." "If we are to achieve a richer culture," she wrote in *Sex and Temperament,* "rich in contrasting values, we must recognize the whole gamut of human potentialities, and so weave a less arbitrary social fabric, one in which each diverse human gift will find a fitting place." As she wrote, spoke, and lived for that goal, Margaret Mead exemplified the role of humanitarian. Her named will continue to stand for much more than that of a mere "anthropologist," as we as a society struggle to achieve her dreams.

—Naomi M. Barry

MERNISSI, Fatima

Nationality: Moroccan. **Born:** Fez, 1940. **Education:** Studied at the Sorbone, Paris; Brandeis University, Ph.D. in sociology. **Career:** Currently professor of sociology, University Mohammed V, Rabat, Morocco. Contributor to numerous women's conferences worldwide; member of editorial board of several publications.

Publications

Political/Social Theory

Beyond the Veil: Male-Female Dynamics in a Modern Muslim Society. Cambridge, Massachusetts, Schenkman, 1975; revised, London, Al Saqi, 1985; Bloomington, Indiana University Press, 1987.

Sexe Idéologie Islam. N.p., 1983; revised edition, Rabat, Éditions Maghrebines, 2 vols., 1985.

Al-Hubb fi hadaratina al-Islamiyah. Beirut, Lebanon, al-Dar al-Alamiyah lil-Tibaah wa-al-Nashr wa-al-Tawzi, 1984.

Le Maroc raconté par ses femmes. Rabat, Société marocaine des éditeurs réunis, 1984; translated as *Doing Daily Battle: Interviews with Moroccan Women,* London, Women's Press, 1988; New Brunswick, New Jersey, Rutgers University Press, 1989; revised as *Le monde n'est pas un harem: paroles de femmes du Maroc,* Paris, A. Michel, 1991.

Women in Moslem Paradise. New Delhi, Kali for Women, 1986.

L'Amour dans les Pays Musulmans. Casablanca, Éditions Maghrebines, 1986.

Le harem politique: le prophète et les femmes. Paris, A. Michel, 1987; translated as *The Veil and the Male Elite: A Feminist Interpretation of Women's Right in Islam,* Reading, Massachusetts, Addison-Wesley, 1991.

Chahrazad n'est pas marocaine: autrement, elle serait salariée! [Shaharazad Is Not Moroccan]. Casablanca, Morocco, Éditions Le Fennec, 1988.

Sultanes oubliées: femmes chefs d'État en Islam. Casablanca, Éditions Le Fennec, 1990; translated as *The Forgotten Queens of Islam,* Cambridge, Polity Press, 1993.

Women and Islam: An Historical and Theological Inquiry. London, Basil Blackwell, 1991.

La peur-modernité: conflit Islam démocratie. Paris, A. Michel, 1992; translated as *Islam and Democracy: Fear of the Modern World.* Reading, Massachusetts, and Wokingham, Addison-Wesley, 1992.

Women's Rebellion and Islamic Memory. Atlantic Highlands, New Jersey, Zed Books, 1996.

Essays

"Effects of Modernization on the Male-Female Dynamics in a Muslim Society," (Ph.D. thesis), in *Sexe Idéologie Islam,* vol. 2.

Can We Women Head a Muslim State? Lahore, Pakistan, Simorgh Women's Resource and Publications Centre, 1991.

Other

Country Reports on Women in North Africa, Libya, Morocco, Tunisia. Addis Ababa, African Training and Reserach Center for Women, U.N. Economic Commission for Africa, 1978.

Al-Suluk al-jinsi fi mujtama' Islāmi ra'smāli taba'i. Beirut, Lebanon, 1982.

Kayd al-nisa'? Kayd al-rijal? hikayah sha'biyah Maghribiyah / rawiyat al-hikayah, Lallah La'azizah al-Tazi; i'dad Fatimah al-Marnisi; rusum Saladi; khutut 'Abd al-Rahman Ra'd; hay'at al-ishraf al-thaqafi wa-al-fanni, Muhammad Sha'bah ...et al. Al-Dar al-Bayda', Mu'assasat Bansharah, 1983.

al-Mar'ah wa-al-sulat / silsilah bi-ishr-af F-atimah al-Mern-iss-i. Al-Dar al-Bayda', Nashr al-Fannak, 1990.

The Harem Within: Tales of a Moroccan Girlhood, photographs by Ruth V. Ward. London, Doubleday, 1994; as *Dreams of Trespass: Tales of a Harem Girlhood,* Reading, Massachusetts, Addison-Wesley, 1994.

*

Critical Studies: *al-Khitab al-nisa'i fi al-Maghrib: namudhaj Fatimah al-Marnisi* by Ahmad Sharrak, al-Dar al-Bayda', Afriqiya al-Sharq, 1990.

* * *

Fatima Mernissi is a Moroccan woman sociologist who has made her mark in the second half of the twentieth century as a Moslem feminist. Her reputation is largely due to her numerous works, which have been translated into several languages, and to her unmovable stance, in these works, as a champion of women's rights in the Moslem Arab world. It is not possible to place Mernissi's work solely in sociology, women's studies, or religion, for it crosscuts all three, gaining importance precisely from this multidimensionality. All contemporary woman scholars writing on the relationship between Islam and woman tread on the path she first opened.

Mernissi made her name heard for the first time in the 1970s with *Beyond the Veil: Male-Female Dynamics in a Modern Muslim Society* (1975). She has since published a number of other essays or reminiscences, which includes the critically acclaimed *Dreams of Trespass: Tales of a Harem Girlhood* (1994) and which center around women, Islam, and Moslem Arab society. She is a frequent participant in international conferences and seminars, during which she does not refrain from pronouncing her feminism. A professor of sociology at Muhammed V University in Rabat for several years, Mernissi has also been visiting professor at the University of California at Berkeley and Harvard University.

Mernissi studied at the Sorbonne in Paris and later received her Ph.D. from Brandeis University. Thus familiar with both French and American cultures, Mernissi writes in French as well as in English. Her Western academic discourse and perspective, coupled with her access to Arab sources, put her in a unique position. She is heard in the West because she provides scholarship about and insight into an unknown area using Western tools, while the methodology she has acquired and her seriousness of intent enable her to study Islam, its history, and catechism in a new light. Her writings call into question some of the basic premises of traditional Islam as it has been lived; what Mernissi envisages for the Moslem Arab woman is nothing less than a total conceptual revolution.

Her main message is that Islam should not be written off as merely an unenlightened system of belief that imprisons women behind the veil and fixates societies in a backward state. Rather, it is the men's attitude that is responsible for women's position in Islam, a position that is ineluctably being altered with the forceful modernity of our time.

In *Beyond the Veil* Mernissi points to the difference between the Judeo-Christian tradition of Western societies and the Moslem Arab tradition concerning women. While Westerners consider women as inferior and refuse to see in them anything but passive sexual partners, Islam acknowledges the powerful sexuality of women and as such is afraid of it; that is why women are barred, made to remain within boundaries, outside of the male "space," or hidden, covered by the veil. The goal is to protect men. In the introduction to the 1987 revised edition of the book, she discusses the issue of present-day Islamic fundamentalism and asserts that if there is such a cry today in Moslem societies for women to be veiled, it must be because women are *not,* because they must have been shedding it. She believes that a return *en masse* to the veil is unlikely and doomed to remain a dream of Moslem men. But she indicates that the call to the veil has an unspoken dimension that should not be neglected, since "far from being a regressive trend," it is, "on the contrary a defense mechanism against profound changes in ... sex roles." She explains that what is at stake are male concerns about power. Knowledge, for one, leads to power, and women, at least in her native Morocco, are fast getting it and all that it provides, disrupting and disturbing the traditional Arab society, in a manner in which there is no going back.

An unquestioning believer in God, and very much admirative of the Prophet Muhammed, Mernissi decides in *The Veil and the Male Elite: A Feminist Interpretation of Women's Rights in Islam* (1987, English translation 1991) to go to the roots of Moslem ideology to see why it is misogynist. Analyzing the first years of Islam, as it was in the making, she finds a situation that is not at all unfavorable to women. She encounters a democratic Muhammmed, who envisions an egalitarian society, with women enjoying equal status with men. As Mernissi points out, his wives had "extraordinary freedom in the public sphere," and were "directly involved in the affairs of the Muslim state."

It is only later, while in Medina, as he was aging and had suffered military defeats, which made him vulnerable, that the Prophet had to bow in to his conservative Companions, such as Umar (later the second Caliph), who wished to see pre-Islamic tribal male prerogatives retained. He thus instituted the *hijab* (literally "curtain" in Arabic) that segregated the sexes and forced women to conceal themselves from the public gaze, thus forbidding them public life and aspirations. Mernissi considers that this was a compromise the Prophet felt he had to make if he did not want to see everything he had achieved so far founder in the hands of his opponents.

Nothing prevents the Moslem Arab woman from reverting to the Prophet's initial dream and fulfilling it, of course, except 15 centuries of social conventions, which, Mernissi believes, are no longer insurmountable.

—Gönül Pultar

MILL, Harriet Taylor, and John Stuart Mill

Nationality: British.

MILL, Harriet (Hardy) Taylor. Born: 1807. **Family:** Married 1) the merchant John Taylor (died 1849), three children; 2) John Stuart Mill in 1851. **Career:** Member of London intellectual community; since 1838, aided Mill in drafting several of his works, including *On Liberty,* 1859. **Died:** Avignon, 3 November 1858.

MILL, John Stuart. Born: 20 May 1806; son of the economist James Mill. **Education:** Educated at home; studied in France c. 1820. **Family:** Married Harriet Taylor in 1851 (died 1858). **Career:** Clerk in examiner's office, India House, 1823-56; founded the Utilitarians, 1823; co-owner and editor, *London Review,* 1835-40; elected to Parliament, 1865-68; rector of St. Andrew University, 1866. **Died:** 8 May 1873.

Publications

By Harriet Taylor Mill

The Enfranchisement of Women (originally published in *Westminster Review,* July 1851, and *New York Tribune for Europe,* 4 October 1850). Rochester, New York, n.p., 1851.

By John Stuart Mill

A System of Logic. London, J. W. Parker, 1843; New York, Harper Bros., 1848; 8th edition, London and New York, Harper Bros., 1900.

Essays on Some Unsettled Questions of Political Economy. London, J. W. Parker, 1844.

Principles of Political Economy. London, J. W. Parker, and Boston, Little Brown, 1848.

On Liberty. London, J. W. Parker, 1859; Boston, Ticknor & Fields, 1863.

Dissertations and Discussions (originally published in *Edinburgh Review* and *Westminster Review*). London, n.p., 1859; Boston, Spencer, 4 vols., 1865-68.

Considerations on Representative Government. London, Parker, 1861; New York, Harper Bros., 1867.

Utilitarianism. London, J. W. Parker, 1863; revised edition, 1871; revised edition, Boston, W. Small, 1887.

An Examination of Sir William Hamilton's Philosophy. London, Longmans Green, 1865; Boston, Spencer, 1866.

Auguste Comte and Positivism. London, Trübner, 1865.

Suffrage for Women (speech given in British Parliament). London, Ticknor & Fields, and New York, American Equal Rights Association, 1867.

The Subjection of Women. London, Longmans Green, and Philadelphia, Lippincott, 1869; 3rd edition, London, Longmans Green, 1879; with a forward by Carrie Chapman Catt, New York, Stokes, 1911.

Speech ... in favor of Woman's Suffrage. Edinburgh, Blackie, 1871.

Autobiography. London, Longmans Green, 1873; New York, Holt, 1874; as *The Early Draft of John Stuart Mill's Autobiography,* edited by Jack Stillinger, Urbana, University of Illinois Press, 1961.

Three Essays on Religion: Nature, The Utility of Religion, and Theism. New York, Holt, 1874.

Essays on Literature and Society, edited by J. B. Schneewind. London, Collier-Macmillan, 1965.

On Politics and Society, edited by Geraint L. Williams. London, Fontana, and New York, International Publication, 1976.

Collected Works of John Stuart Mill. Toronto, University of Toronto Press, 1963-92.

By Harriet Taylor Mill and John Stuart Mill

Essays on Sex Equality, edited by Alice S. Rossi. Chicago and London, University of Chicago Press, 1970.

Sexual Equality: Writings by John Stuart Mill, Harriet Mill, and Helen Taylor, edited by Ann P. Robson and John M. Robson. Toronto, Buffalo, and London, University of Toronto Press, 1994.

John Stuart Mill and Harriet Taylor: Their Correspondence and Subsequent Marriage, edited by Friedrich von Hayek, Chicago, University of Chicago Press, and London, Routledge & Kegan Paul, 1951.

*

Bibliography: *Bibliography of the Published Writings of John Stuart Mill* by J. R. Hainds and James McNab McCrimmon, Evanston, Illinois, Northwestern University, 1945; *John Stuart Mill, a Bibliography* by Robert Goehlert, Monticello, Illinois, Vance Bibliographies, 1982; *John Stuart Mill: The Economic, Political, and Feminist Papers,* Woodbridge, Connecticut, Research Publications, 1988.

Manuscript Collections: Columbia University, New York.

Critical Studies: *John Stuart Mill and Harriet Taylor: Their Correspondence and Subsequent Marriage* by Friedrich von Hayek, Chicago, University of Chicago Press, and London, Routledge & Kegan Paul, 1951; *Mill and the Harriet Taylor Myth* by H. O. Pappe, n.p., 1960; *The Improvement of Mankind: The Social and Political Thought of Mill* by John M. Robson, Toronto, University of Toronto Press, 1968; "Sentiment and Intellect: The Story of John Stuart Mill and Harriet Taylor Mill" by Alice S. Rossi, in *Essays on Sex Equality,* edited by Rossi, Chicago and London, University of Chicago Press, 1970; *John Stuart Mill in Love* by Josephine Kamm, London, Gordon & Cremonesi, 1977; "Harriet Taylor and John Stuart Mill" by Phyllis Rose, in *Parallel Lives: Five Victorian Marriages,* New York, Knopf, 1983; "Mill and Ruskin on the Woman Question Revisited" by Deborah Epstein Nord, in *Teaching Literature: What Is Needed Now,* edited by James Engell and David Perkins, Cambridge, Harvard University Press, 1988; *Mill and Sexual Equality* by Gail Tulloch, Hertfordshire, Harvester Wheatsheaf, 1989; "The Feminization of John Stuart Mill" by Susan Gorag Bell, in *Revealing Lives: Autobiography, Biography, and Gender,* edited by Gorag Bell and Marilyn Yalom, Albany, State University of New York Press, 1990; "John Stuart Mill's *The Subjection of Women:* The Foundations of Liberal Feminism" by Susan Hekman, in *History of European Ideas* (Tarrytown, N.Y.), 15(4-6), August 1992; *Mill and Liberalism* by Maurice Cowling, Cambridge, Cambridge University Press, 1990; *Signifying Woman: Culture and Choas in Rousseau, Burke, and Mill* by Linda M. G. Zerilli, Ithaca, New York, Cornell University Press, 1994; "'The Lot of Gifted Ladies Is Hard': A Study of Harriet Taylor Mill Criticism" by Jo Ellen Jacobs, in *Hypatia: A Journal of Feminist Philosophy* 9(3), summer 1994.

* * *

In 1830 John Stuart Mill met Harriet Taylor, marking the beginning of an ardent relationship and a fruitful collaborative partnership in feminist writing. For the next 21 years, though Taylor was married to successful London merchant John Taylor and had begun a family with him, they wrote to one another, traveled together, discussed issues with one another, and, most importantly, wrote, edited, and rewrote articles, pamphlets, and books together.

It is perhaps difficult for the modern reader to understand the circumstances of their relationship. Although they were much in love with each other, until John Taylor died, marriage was out of the question, due both to the near impossibility of obtaining a divorce in Victorian England and to the sense of duty which they both felt toward Taylor's husband. The couple were finally able to marry in 1851, a proper two years after John Taylor's death; Mill marked the event with a feminist declaration of his objection against the existing laws of marriage, which made a wife absolutely dependent on her husband:

> I declare it to be my will and intention ... that she retains in all respects whatever the same absolute freedom of action, and freedom of disposal of herself and of all that does or may at any time belong to her, as if no such marriage had taken place; and I absolutely disclaim and repudiate all pretension to have acquired any *rights* whatever by virtue of such marriage.

The statement, unromantic though it may seem, illustrates the seriousness with which both Taylor and Mill held their feminist beliefs and introduces some of the basic principles behind their feminism: belief in women's personal liberty, in women's right to hold property, and in the injustice of declaring that a woman becomes the property of the man who marries her, to do with as he wishes.

The details of their feminist philosophy are discussed in *The Enfranchisement of Women*, published by Taylor Mill in 1851, and in *The Subjection of Women*, published by John Stuart Mill in 1869. The documents have much in common. Both condemn unequal treatment of women because it infringes upon personal liberty, the dearest-held tenet of democracy. They each condemn the inequality of women as the last remaining throwback to an earlier, less enlightened time when force was law. Both argue for the innate equality of men and women and deny essentialist Victorian claims that women are the "weaker sex." It is only the unequal treatment of them by society that makes them appear unequal. Both documents propose an empirical experiment to replace legislation that treats women differently: Give women the opportunity to compete on an equal playing field; let them vote, own property, hold office, and compete for jobs. If they are truly unable, biologically, to participate as equal citizens, they will be eliminated by fair competition. And both works also optimistically proclaim that women will play equal roles in private life, business, and politics once the obstacles to their personal liberty are removed.

Taylor Mill and her husband both pinpoint differences in the education of men and women as the primary cause of inequality. But they go farther than classic liberal feminist thought. Modern readers will be able to trace the beginnings of socialist feminism and radical feminism in some of their ideas. For example, they argue that women, in essence, are trained to be slaves because they are taught that their primary function is to serve men. Here, they borrow from rising Socialist thought that describes inequality in terms of power and property. Their argument sets up an important comparison of women's roles to the roles of slaves or lower class workers: women are trapped by their dependence on a more powerful upper class, in this case, men. They point out that women's dependence on men is a behavior cultivated by society for the benefit of men and perpetuated by cultural ideals of femininity. First, women are taught that it is unfeminine and even immoral to assert their own desires or ideas; second, women are told they should depend on men for intellectual guidance and physical sustenance; and, last, they are taught that they can best secure the support upon which their lives depend by attracting a man, which means by playing the required obedient, submissive, "feminine" role. *The Enfranchisement of Women* makes this point in the strongest terms, describing women's training in terms of brainwashing that benefits the powerful by convincing the weak that their weakness is, in fact, their primary virtue: "[N]o other inferior caste that we have heard of, have been taught to regard their degradation as their honour," writes Taylor Mill.

Knowing their personal circumstances, it is not surprising that the earliest feminist writings of John Stuart Mill and Taylor Mill discuss the problem of marriage and divorce—for example, John Stuart Mill's "On Marriage" and Taylor's "On Marriage." In 1832, a year or two after meeting for the first time, they exchanged statements on the topic that concerned them so personally. Both documents argue that marriage is no better than prostitution as long as one of the partners—the woman—participates through intimidation or coercion rather than consent through free choice. In Victorian England, they contend, a woman's consent is neither freely given nor informed. Rather, it is effectively coerced since a woman is educated, not to earn her own living herself, but to earn it by marrying. She cannot make a free choice because she has no other way of surviving. Further, they argue, a woman's consent is not informed. Taylor, especially, concentrates on the inequity of expecting a young girl to enter into a binding contract for life when she is entirely ignorant of its terms, having had no prior relationship with a man. Yet, she argues, society determines a woman's fitness for marriage entirely by this purity—read: virginity. For both thinkers, legal and easily obtainable divorce offers one answer, so that women and men would not spend their whole lives burdened with the result of one bad mistake. Taylor goes a step further in suggesting that all laws regarding marriage should eventually be erased. Once women are given equality with men, she argues, there would be no need for the institution of marriage as we know it, since it functions mainly to limit the rights of women.

In later writings, both before and after their marriage, John Stuart Mill and Taylor address the issue of domestic abuse. To them its prevalence, especially in the lower classes, demonstrates the horrifying results of, first, giving a husband utter control over his wife as his property and, second, refusing the wife any relief through divorce or legal prosecution. Written during the 1840s and 1950s, their newspaper articles—mostly from the *Morning Chronicle* and the pamphlet, *Remarks on Mr. Fitzroy's Bill*—also demonstrate their growing awareness that the powerlessness of women was both exploited in private and approved in public. They cite case after case in which women were repeatedly battered, only to be victimized again in court when they were blamed for provoking their husbands' anger. In these writings, Taylor and Mill attack inequities inherent in a patriarchal legal system in order to expose the injustice of court decisions and laws. Since the law defines a wife as her husband's property, they point out, both husbands' actions and legal decisions are motivated by this value of a wife as something less than human. Moreover, they argue, a woman cannot hope for anything like justice if she presses charges because the system does not recognize her right to participate in it through serving on a jury or acting as a judge. They point out that the injustice is rooted in the very terms of 19th-century British law: this male-dominated system defines domestic violence as less serious than assault between strangers. Together, these unjust conditions amount to legal sanctioning of wife abuse, and both husbands and wives understand it this way. In these writings, Taylor and Mill call for judges to strengthen their judgments against convicted wife-abusers, for juries to exercise equity in determining guilt, and for Parliament to reform laws concerning domestic abuse.

After Taylor Mill died in 1858, her husband continued to voice his opinions on women's rights and to work toward their collective vision of sexual equality. Elected to Parliament in 1865, he worked tirelessly for women's suffrage, along with other Radical causes. In 1866 he brought before Parliament a petition containing 1521 signatures of women who desired to vote; a year later he moved for an amendment to allow unmarried women who held property to vote. Mill's speech in support of the amendment is a model of rational argument, drawing many of its ideas from earlier writings to demonstrate that women both desire and deserve to vote; that, in fact, justice will not be served if they are denied the basic right of exercising a voice in political representation. Although the amendment was rejected by a vote of 196 to 73, Mill wrote later that he was pleased with its relative success: no one had expected it to do so well. He obviously felt that this debate had paved the way for eventual success and wrote in his *Autobiography* that this was the most important event of his Parliamentary career. It certainly did encourage women to continue working for suffrage. Soon afterward, Helen Taylor, Harriet's daughter, formed the National Society for Women's Suffrage, and Mill supported her effort whole-heartedly, speaking at several of their meetings between 1869 and 1871.

"It is doubtful if I shall ever be fit for anything, public or private, again," Mill wrote in a letter to W. T. Thornton after the death of his wife. "The spring of my life is broken." Although history proves that he went on to do much great work after her death, Mill's comment is a touching demonstration of the degree to which he believed he and his wife truly collaborated in everything they did. He had relied on Harriet as his emotional support, his intellectual springboard, and perhaps more. Mill writes in his *Autobiography* that very few of the works which bear his name were written by him alone. *On Liberty* and *The Subjection of Women*, especially, he says, were "joint productions," in which "What was abstract and purely scientific was generally mine; the properly human element came from her: in all that concerned the application of philosophy to the exigencies of human society and progress, I was her pupil." Mill's seeming self-denigration and overly lavish praise of his partner have led many readers to doubt his believability. But if he is truthful in attributing to her an equal share in some of the most influential philosophical and feminist writing of the 19th century, then John Stuart Mill and Harriet Taylor Mill confirm the possibility of a relationship all-too-rarely seen: a husband and wife team collaborating on equal terms, working together toward a common social vision of sexual equality.

—Ellen Arnold

MILLER, Jean Baker

Nationality: American. **Born:** New York, New York, 29 September 1927. **Education:** Sarah Lawrence College, Bronxville, New York, B.A. 1948; Columbia University, New York, M.D. 1952; Montefiore Hospital, New York, internship 1952-53, residency in medicine 1953-54; residency in psychiatry at Bellevue Medical Center, 1955-56, Albert Einstein College of Medicine, 1955-56, and Upstate Medical Center, Syracuse, 1962-63; New York Medical College, psychoanalytic training 1955-60. **Family:** Married; two children. **Career:** Instructor in psychiatry, Upstate Medical Center, University of the State of New York, Syracuse, 1961-66; interdisciplinary research fellow, 1965-67, instructor, 1967-73, Albert Einstein College of Medicine, New York; visiting lecturer, London School of Economics, 1972-73; visiting associate, 1972-73 and 1976-77, co-teacher, 1977, Tavistock Institute and Clinic, London; associate clinical professor, 1974-82, then clinical professor of psychiatry, beginning 1982, Boston University School of Medicine; assistant clinical professor, 1974-81, lecturer in psychiatry, beginning 1981, Harvard Medical School; professor of psychology, Wellesley College, Wellesley, Massachusetts, 1981-84; director, 1981-84, scholar-in-residence, 1984-86, director of education, beginning 1986, Stone Center for Developmental Services and Studies, Wellesley College. Psychiatrist, in private practice, beginning 1956. **Awards:** Association for Women in Psychology Distinguished Career award, 1980; Rockefeller Foundation fellowship, 1981; Massachusetts Psychological Association Allied Professional Award, 1982; National Organization for Women (Massachusetts Chapter) Woman of the Year Award, 1982; D.H.L., Brandeis University, 1987; Unitarian-Universalist Association National Women's Federation Ministry to Women Award, 1987; American Orthopsychiatric Association Blanche F. Ittelson Memorial Award, 1995; D.H.C., Regis College, 1995. **Member:** American Psychiatric Association, American Academy of Psychoanalysis, American College of Psychiatrists, American Orthopsychiatric Association, Massachusetts Psychiatric Society, Society of Medical Psychoanalysts. **Address:** c/o Stone Center, Wellesley College, Wellesley, Massachusetts 02181-8268, U.S.A.

Publications

Political/Social Theory

Towards a New Psychology of Women. Boston, Beacon Press, 1976; London, Allen Lane, 1978; second edition, Boston, Beacon Press, 1986; Harmondsworth, Penguin, 1988.

Women's Growth in Connection: Writings from the Stone Center, with Judith V. Jordan, Alexandra G. Kaplan, Irene P. Stiver, and Janet L. Surrey. New York, Guilford Press, 1991.

Connections, Disconnections, and Violations, with others. New York, Basic Books, forthcoming.

Other

Editor, *Psychoanalysis and Women: Contributions to New Theory and Therapy.* New York, Brunner/Mazel, 1973.

Editor, *Psychoanalysis and Women.* Harmondsworth and Baltimore, Penguin, 1974.

*

Manuscript Collections: Stone Center, Wellesley College, Wellesley, Massachusetts.

* * *

Jean Baker Miller has helped to revolutionize psychology's understanding of women by challenging the traditional, male-centered perspective by which the mental health community has traditionally assessed and treated women. In her book *Toward a New Psychology of Women,* first published in 1978, Miller argued that this perspective looked at men as the model for mental health, thereby pathologizing women.

The traditional view on women was based on the formulations by Sigmund Freud, who is considered the founder of psychoanalytic thinking. Freud defined mental health as related to one's ability to emotionally separate from one's family and to become one's own individual, thus equating maturity with autonomy. Women, with their emphasis on remaining connected to significant others in their lives, were derogatorily assessed by Freud and later clinicians as "dependent" and less mature that men.

Miller suggested that this understanding of the human experience was limited and distorted because it was based on only half of the human population. She pointed out that our society socially mandates gender roles in a way that is restrictive to both genders, expecting women to be the caretakers and men to deny their need for emotional connectedness. However, women's caretaking work is devalued; women are pathologized by society and, relatedly, by the mental health community for the same behaviors that are socially mandated for them. Miller suggested that women's inner sense of connection to others is central to their development and is a strength, not a weakness.

Miller was born in the Bronx to a working-class family in the late 1920s. Contracting polio when she was 11 months old, she wore leg braces until she was seven and had two operations by the time she was 12. However, she was an excellent swimmer and refused to accept that her illness would keep her from doing the things that she wanted to do. During the Great Depression she noted the particularly terrible predicament of the women who were widows or whose husbands had lost a job. Never wishing to find herself in a similar position, Miller decided that she would prepare herself for work.

Two women who would have a great impact on Miller were nurses—twin sisters—whom she met while in treatment for her polio. The "Miss Stones" offered the young Jeanne alternative female role-models to the long-suffering, working-class women of her neighborhood. Eventually they convinced Miller's mother to let her make the hour-long subway trek to Manhattan to attend Hunter College High School, an all-girls school with an emphasis on intellectual achievement and, according to Miller, "marvelous teachers." The teachers at Hunter helped Miller gain a scholarship to Sarah Lawrence College, an all-women's school where she was again encouraged to excel. Graduating with her Bachelor's degree from Sarah Lawrence in 1948, she saw many of her peers move on to menial jobs such as secretarial work. Miller decided to apply to medical school, overlooking others' skepticism in her ability to succeed. Accepted to Columbia University, she eventually pursued a specialization in psychiatry.

Miller did not actually become interested in feminism until she reviewed Betty Friedan's *The Feminine Mystique* in the early 1960s. When she wrote *Toward a New Psychology of Women* a decade later, she had 20 years of clinical experience from which to develop her observations on women's development. In the early 1980s Miller helped found Wellesley College's Stone Center for Developmental Services and Studies, an organization that attempts to make the connection between the psychological theory of women and clinical practice. Miller and other researchers at the Stone Center continually publish their findings in a *Work in Progress* series. In 1991, along with Judith V. Jordan, Alexandra G. Kaplan, Irene P. Stiver, and Janet L. Surrey, Miller published a selection of these manuscripts in *Women's Growth in Connection: Writings from the Stone Center.* This and other writings by feminist theorists, including such scholars as Nancy Chodorow, Carol Gilligan, Susie Ohrbach, and Luise Eichenbaum, present a new perspective on women that has been called the self-in-relation theory.

The self-in-relation theory extends the perspective that women's psychological development is not based on separation and individuation, as Freud formulated through his observations of male development. The traditional view holds that boys need to separate from their mother, usually the primary caretaker, in order to identify with their father. However, the self-in-relation theory points out that girls have no need to break this primary connection. Instead, the theory suggests, girls and women develop autonomy and self-direction while in relationship with their mothers. Rather than separate from significant others, women redefine their relationships as they evolve and continue to add others, extending their relational way of being to the larger community.

Miller's distinguished career has included the multiple and usually overlapping roles of theorist, writer, teacher, and psychotherapist. Her contributions to feminist scholarship have been instrumental in helping to remove the derogatory labels that have positioned women as psychologically deficient in relation to men, thereby reframing women's way of being in the world in more positive terms and encouraging society to consider the possibilities in living a life in which affiliation is viewed "as highly as, or more highly than, self-enhancement."

—Yiota Papadopoulos

MILLETT, Kate

Nationality: American. **Born:** Katherine Murray Millett, St. Paul, Minnesota, 14 September 1934. **Education:** University of Minnesota, Minneapolis, B.A. (Phi Beta Kappa) 1956; St. Hilda's College, Oxford University, M.A. (first-class honors) 1958; Columbia University, New York, Ph.D. 1970. **Family:** Married Fumio Yoshimura in 1965 (divorced 1985). **Career:** Professor of English, University of North Carolina at Greensboro, 1958; kindergarten teacher, Harlem, New York, 1960-61; English teacher, Waseda University, Tokyo, 1961-62; professor of English and philosophy, Barnard College, New York, 1964-69; professor of sociology, Bryn Mawr College, Bryn Mawr, Pennsylvania, 1971; distinguished visiting professor, State College of Sacramento, California, beginning 1973. Artist, exhibiting sculpture and drawings at galleries, including Minami Gallery, Tokyo, Japan, 1963, Judson Gallery, Greenwich Village, New York, 1967, Los Angeles Woman's Building, Los Angeles, California, 1977, NoHo Gallery, New York, beginning 1976, and Chuck Levitan Gallery, New York. Contributor of numerous essays to newspapers and periodicals including *Ms., New York Times, Nation,* and *Semiotext(e).* **Member:** National Organization for Women (chairman, education committee, 1966), Congress of Racial Equality (CORE). **Agent:** Georges Borchardt, 136 East 57th Street, New York, New York, U.S.A. **Address:** 295 Bowery, New York, New York 10003, U.S.A.

Publications

Political/Social Theory

Token Learning. New York, NOW, 1967.
Prostitution Papers. New York, Banc Books, 1971.
The Basement: Meditations on Human Sacrifice. New York, Simon & Schuster, 1980; with a new introduction by Millet, 1991.
Going to Iran. New York, Coward McCann, 1981.
The Politics of Cruelty: An Essay on the Literature of Political Imprisonment. London, Viking, 1994.

Literary Criticism

Sexual Politics (Ph.D. thesis, Columbia University). Garden City, New York, Doubleday, 1970.

Autobiography

Flying. New York, Knopf, 1974.
Sita. New York, Farrar Straus, 1977; with a new introduction by Millett, New York, Simon & Schuster, 1992.
The Loony-Bin Trip. New York, Simon & Schuster, 1990.
A.D.: A Memoir. New York, Norton, 1995.

Plays

Screenplay: *Three Lives,* Impact Films, New York, n.d.

*

Critical Studies: "Lib and Lit" by Germaine Greer, in *Listener* (London), 85(2191), 25 March 1971; *Psychoanalysis and Feminism* by Juliet Mitchell, New York, Pantheon Books, 1974; "The Lady's Not for Spurning" by Annette Kolodny, in *Contemporary Literature,* 17(4), autumn 1976; *Lesbiana: Book Reviews from the Ladder* by Barbara Grier, Tallahassee, Naiad Press, 1976; *The Body in Pain: The Making and Unmaking of the World* by Elaine Scarry, London, Oxford University Press, 1985; "Beyond Ideology: Kate Millett and the Case for Henry Miller" by Michael Woolf, in *Perspectives on Pornography,* edited by Gary Day and Clive Bloom, London, MacMillian, 1988; "To Hell and Back" by Karen Malpede, in *Women's Review of Books,* 8(1), October 1990; *The Safe Sea of Women: Lesbian Fiction, 1969-1989* by Bonnie Zimmerman, Boston, Beacon Press, 1990; "To Speak the Unspeakable" by Elissa Gelfand, in *Women's Review of Books,* 11(9), June 1994; *Writing Selves: Contemporary Femininst Autography* by Jeanne Perreault, Minneapolis and London, University of Minnesota Press, 1995.

* * *

Most of Kate Millett's writings are *temoignage,* literature of the witness. Millett describes just such writing in the introduction to her *Politics of Cruelty: An Essay on the Literature of Political Imprisonment* (1994):

> Temoignage, the literature of the witness; the one who has been there, seen it, knows. It crosses genres, can be autobiography, reportage, even narrative fiction. But its basis is factual, fact passionately lived and put into writing by a moral imperative rooted like a flower amid carnage with an imperishable optimism, a hope that those who hear will care, will even take action.

Whether Millett writes about her lesbian lovers, sexual politics, mental health, political imprisonment, or the murder of women by women, she always writes with the passion of the witness calling for an ethical change in our culture.

Born in St. Paul, Minnesota, Millett attained her education in Minnesota, England and in New York City, finally taking her Ph.D. at Columbia University. She has taught at the University of North Carolina, Greensboro; Waseda University, Tokyo; Bryn Mawr College; and, State College of Sacramento, California. An artist as well as a writer, Millet exhibits her drawings and sculptures at galleries in New York, Japan, and Los Angeles. Her published works include five texts of social theory, one literary criticism text, two novels, a screenplay, an autobiography, and numerous essays. Millett currently lives in New York City. She married Fumio Yoshimura in 1965; they divorced in 1985. She has been an ardent feminist ethicist throughout her life.

Millett came into her fame as a feminist writer in 1970 with the publication of *Sexual Politics.* In this text she argues that sex is political. In particular, she outlines and defines patriarchy and its system of birthright priority: "What goes largely unexamined, often even unacknowledged (yet is institutionalized nonetheless) in our social order, is the birthright priority whereby males rule females. Through this system a most ingenious form of 'interior colonization' has been achieved."

Sexual Politics not only defines sex as political, it offers historical background on the sexual revolution and provides feminist reflections on books by D. H. Lawrence, Henry Miller, Norman Mailer, and Jean Genet. Many women's studies and feminist criticism courses now require *Sexual Politics* as core reading. Therefore, many people associate Millett with this text alone, but 1970 was but the start of Millett's career as a writer.

One thing has remained certain throughout Millett's career: she has always been sure to cast the most discerning eye upon herself and her life as a particular woman. We learn the most about Millett's feminist ethics through these texts. In her book, *Sita* (1977), she writes of a lesbian love affair that occurs between her and Sita over a 3,000 mile distance (New York—Los Angeles). The book opens with loving, internal monologues that comment upon aspects of the relationship, and it ends with the realization that the relationship is not going to work. In detail, she writes about the power of love affairs: "The conduct of a love affair, I say to myself, seeing the parking lot finally through the car window—arrived, safe—the conduct of a love affair requires the right moves, adroitness." It is with writing like this that Millett seduces her readers. Simultaneously, the language reads like a how-to manual, a philosophic piece, an autobiography, as well as a romance. Millett knows how to capture the moment in ethical terms; we must be conscious of our conduct in every thing, even, or especially, in our love affairs. Jeanne Perreault says that Millett writes "autography," which she defines as writing that celebrates the feminist "I": "'I' and 'we' are the most important words in the writing(s) of contemporary feminism, continuously transformed and reenacted as feminists claim the rights of self-definition. This process of transformation, these texts, works actively and explicitly in the context of feminist communities, communities that are ... inextricable from discourses of selfhood." *Sita* is a discourse on Millett as the lesbian self trying to capture the self of the lover.

The Basement: Meditations on a Human Sacrifice (1980) is a different discourse of the self. The text is a meditation on the "real life" torture and death of 16-year-old Sylvia Likens in 1965. On the opening page of the meditation, Millett addresses Sylvia: "I will use the first person and I will speak to you directly—it was for this that I waited, all the years waiting to write, my 14-year obsession with you." Millett says that Sylvia's story stayed with her because it was a tale of growing up female in this society, a society that forces young women to feel so ashamed about anything sexual that they feel ashamed even when tortured in sexual ways. The text is riveting. Millett captures as many voices as possible to try to render the last weeks that led to the death of Sylvia Likens. She captures the voices involved in the court proceedings, the voice of the torturer, the voice of the torturer's children, the voices of the neighbors, and even, at the end of the book, the voice of Sylvia herself. Perreault claims that "These languages make an autography that incorporates victim and tormentor, reader and writer, self and other in an interrogation of feminist ethics." Millett wants to dignify the dying girl with an "I" that can proclaim her value, her fear, and her courage. The book ends with Sylvia's internal reflections: "So it's finally here. Then it's like all the insides of me screams. This kinda scream is inside your head. Not even inside the guts, inside the head. And my lips bleedin. I'm scared.... the hurt's so big I can't feel it. Cause where all the terrible trouble is, is in my eyes. Lookin through them basement windows seein the light a minute ago and now I don't see nothin. I'm facin 'em but they ain't there no more. Yeah, it's finally here." What Millett achieves in this work is an incredible homage to the tortured victim as well as an homage to Amnesty International's attempt to keep the tortured voice from silence.

In her subsequent texts, Millett furthers the witnessing and autographic aspects of writing. In *The Loony-Bin Trip* (1990) she writes of her own struggle with lithium treatments as a manic-depressive; in *The Politics of Cruelty* (1994) she addresses in detail the particularities of torturers and victims inside the worlds of political imprisonment; and, in *A.D.* (1995), she writes of her aunt, Aunt Dorothy, who both encouraged her in her love of art and made her witness to an implacable snobbery. Millett is a feminist writer who ventures into torturous worlds and vulnerable worlds herself and then to encourage us to witness with conscience how other people live through her writings. She does not leave her projects at the witnessing stage, however. She concludes by asking us, forcing us, her readers, to "do something about it."

—Renee R. Curry

MILLETT, Katherine Murray. *See* **MILLETT, Kate.**

MINER, Valerie

Nationality: American. **Born:** New York, New York, 28 August 1947. **Education:** University of California, Berkeley, B.A. 1969, M.J. 1970, M.A. 1970; attended University of Edinburgh, 1968, and University of London, 1974-75. **Career:** Reporter, *Daily Review,* Hayward, California, and *Castro Valley Vista,* Castro Valley, California, 1964-65; instructor, Centennial College, Toronto, and University of Toronto, 1972-74, York University, 1973, and California State University, Hayward, and San Francisco State University, both 1977; lecturer, University of California, Berkeley, beginning 1977. Guest lecturer, City Literary Institute, London, 1975, University of Alberta, 1976, Mills College and Contra Costa Press Institute, 1977, and Stanford University, 1979. Broadcaster, Toronto, 1973; freelance writer, London, 1974-76. Former member of editorial staff of *Listener, Time Out,* and Writers and Readers Publishing Cooperative; contributor to periodicals, including *Economist, Feminist Review, Maclean's, Mademoiselle, New Society, New Statesman,* and *Saturday Night.* **Member:** National Feminist Writers Guild (founding member), National Union of Journalists, Women against Violence and Pornography (member, board of directors), Theta Sigma Phi. **Address:** Field Studies Program, University of California, Berkeley, California 94706, U.S.A.

PUBLICATIONS

Novels

Blood Sisters: An Examination of Conscience. New York, St. Martin's Press, 1982.
Murder in the English Department. New York, St. Martin's Press, 1982.
Movement: A Novel in Stories. Trumansburg, New York, Crossing Press, 1982.
Winter's Edge. London, Methuen, 1984; Trumansburg, New York, Crossing Press, 1987.
All Good Women. Freedom, California, Crossing Press, 1987.
A Walking Fire. Albany, State University of New York Press, 1994.

Short Stories

Tales I Tell My Mother, with Zoë Fairbairns, Sara Maitland, Michèle Roberts, and Michelene Wandor. London, Journeyman Press, 1978; Boston, South End Press, 1980.
More Tales I Tell My Mother, with Zoë Fairbairns, Sara Maitland, Michèle Roberts, and Michelene Wandor. London, Journeyman Press, 1987.
Trespassing and Other Stories. London, Methuen, and Freedom, California, Crossing Press, 1989.
"Dropping Anchor," in *Dreamers and Desperadoes: Contemporary Short Fiction of the American West.* New York, Laurel, 1993.
"A Spare Umbrella," in *Ploughshares,* 20(2-3), fall 1994.
"On Earth," in *Virginia Quarterly Review,* 70(2), spring 1994.

Essays

Her Own Woman, with M. Kostash, M. McCracken, E. Paris, and H. Robertson. London, Macmillan, 1975.
"Writing Feminist Fiction: Solitary Genesis or Collective Criticism?" in *Frontiers: A Journal of Women Studies,* 6(1-2), spring/summer 1981.
Competition: A Feminist Taboo? with Helen E. Longino. New York, Feminist Press, 1987.
"An Imaginative Collectivity of Writers and Readers," in *Lesbian Texts and Contexts: Radical Revisions,* edited by Karla Jay, Joanne Glasgow, and Catherine Stimpson. New York, New York University Press, 1990.
"Spinning Friends: May Sarton's Literary Spinsters," in *Old Maids to Radical Spinsters: Unmarried Women in the 20th-Century Novel.* Urbana, University of Illinois Press, 1991.
Rumors from the Cauldron: Selected Essays, Reviews, and Reportage. Ann Arbor, University of Michigan Press, 1992.
"A Walking Fire: Finding Cordelia's Voice as Working-Class Hero," in *Hayden's Ferry Review,* 11, fall/winter 1992.
"Writing and Teaching with Class," in *Working-Class Women in the Academy: Laborers in the Knowledge Factory.* Amherst, University of Massachusetts Press, 1993.

*

Critical Studies: "Lessing's Influence on Valerie Miner" by Ellen Cronan Rose, in *Doris Lessing Newsletter* (Baltimore), 6(2), winter 1982; "Historical Fiction and Fictional History: An Interview with Valerie Miner" by Carole Ferrier in *Meanjin* (Victoria, Australia), 46(4), December 1987; interview in *Backtalk: Women Writers Speak Out,* New Brunswick, New Jersey, Rutgers University Press, 1993.

* * *

A journalist, novelist, and author of short fiction, Valerie Miner uses writing as a means to explore the status of women in society. In works like *Blood Sisters: An Examination of Conscience*

(1981), *Movement* (1982), and *A Walking Fire* (1994), she examines such issues as feminism, abortion, divorce, sexual harassment, political militancy, and lesbianism as they weave in and out of the lives of her politically and socially active, intelligent female protagonists. Later novels have continued to look to the recent past for guidance in traversing what Miner less-than-optimistically perceives as a "post-feminist era." Her 1992 book *Rumors from the Cauldron: Selected Essays, Reviews, and Reportage,* provides a succinct overview of her nonfictional work, compiled, as Miner notes in her introduction, as "my own small resistance to cultural amnesia. We can continue to imagine as feminists only if we can remember."

Miner's first novel, *Blood Sisters* is the story of two Irish-born cousins. In the tradition of their heroic grandmother, Elizabeth O'Brien, herself a dedicated Irish patriot, each is committed to a political cause. London-bred schoolteacher Beth agitates, sometimes violently, for the freedom of Northern Ireland, while Liz, a free-spirited Californian, manifests her pacifist lesbian-feminist ideology through her "new age" religious beliefs. Not surprisingly, philosophical disagreements arise between the two after Liz and her brother, Larry, relocate to London in response to a job offer. While criticized for historical inaccuracy in her use of actual incidents from Irish history, Miner's first novel was praised for its telling comparison of the religious rift in Northern Ireland and the rift between the sexes that sparked the women's movement.

Blood Sisters signals many of Miner's overall concerns, which she would refine and develop in later novels. In *Movement,* for example, the residual social and political upheaval of the late 1960s and early 1970s becomes a backdrop for protagonist Susan Campbell's journey from housewife to feminist author and activist. By weaving short, seemingly unrelated vignettes about women's lives into the central narrative, Miner attempts to emphasize the interconnectedness of human experience. *Murder in the English Department* is more feminist polemic than murder mystery, as English professor Nan Weaver finds herself falsely accused of the murder of a chauvinistic male colleague after she keeps hidden the knowledge that a young student killed the man in self-defense to avoid being raped. *Winter's Edge* tells of the troubled relationship between Chrissie and Margaret, two elderly women who choose to continue vicariously living in their San Francisco home rather than give up their independence and sense of purpose within their community by retiring into the sterile existence offered by Social Security.

In addition to novels, Miner has contributed several volumes of short fiction to the feminist library, including 1978's *Tales I Tell My Mother,* written with Zoë Fairbairns, Sara Maitland, Michèle Roberts, and Michelene Wandor, and *Trespassing and Other Stories,* published in 1989. Her essays on feminist literature have appeared in numerous anthologies.

—Pamela Kester-Shelton

MITCHELL, Juliet (Constance Wyatt)

Nationality: British. **Born:** Christchurch, New Zealand, 4 October 1940; immigrated to England, 1944. **Education:** St. Anne's College, Oxford, B.A. (honors) 1961; graduate study, Oxford University, 1962. **Family:** Married Perry Anderson in 1962 (separated, 1965); one daughter. **Career:** Assistant lecturer in English, University of Leeds, 1962-63; lecturer, University of Reading, 1965-71; freelance writer, broadcaster, and lecturer since 1971; auxiliary nurse, psychiatric unit, University College Hospital, 1974-75; psychotherapist, Paddington Centre for Psychotherapy, 1975-76, and in private practice, 1976-77; psychoanalyst in private practice, beginning 1978. Lecturer at educational institutions in Australia, Canada, Europe, New Zealand, and the United States. A.D. White Professor-at-Large, Cornell University, 1993. Member of editorial board, *New Left Review,* c. early 1960s; contributor to journals, including *Shrew.* **Member:** Institute of Psychoanalysis (associate member). **Agent:** Deborah Rogers, 20 Powis Mews, London W11 1JN, England.

Publications

Political/Social Theory

Women's Estate. Harmondsworth, Penguin, 1971; New York, Pantheon, 1972.

Psychoanalysis and Feminism. New York, Pantheon, 1972; Harmondsworth, Penguin, 1974.

Women: The Longest Revolution: Essays in Feminism, Literature, and Psychoanalysis (title essay originally published in *New Left Review,* 1966). London, Virago, and New York and Toronto, Random House, 1984.

Other

Editor, with Ann Oakley, *The Rights and Wrongs of Women.* Harmondsworth, Penguin, and New York, Pantheon, 1976.

Editor, *The Fortunes and Misfortunes of the Famous Moll Flanders,* by Daniel Defoe. London, Penguin 1978.

Editor, with Jacqueline Rose, *Feminine Sexuality: Jacques Lacan and L'Ecole Freudienne.* London, Macmillan, 1982; New York, Norton, 1983.

Editor, with Ann Oakley, *What Is Feminism?* New York, Pantheon, and Oxford, Basil Blackwell, 1986.

Editor, *The Selected Melanie Klein: The Essential Writings.* Harmondsworth, Penguin, 1986; New York, Free Press, 1987.

Editor, with Michael Parsons, *Before I Was: Psychoanalysis and the Imagination,* by Enid Balint. London and New York, n.p., 1993.

*

Critical Studies: Review of *Women's Estate* by Elizabeth Janeway, in *Book World,* 30 January 1972; "A Fresh Take on Feminists" by David Gelman, in *Newsweek,* 116(84), 29 October 1990; "Psychoanalysis, Feminism, and Politics: A Conversation with Juliet Mitchell" by Toril Moi, in *South Atlantic Quarterly* (Durham, North Carolina), 93(4), fall 1994.

* * *

Marxist socialism and feminism combine in the provocative works of British psychoanalyst and social theorist Juliet Mitchell. Beginning with her groundbreaking essay "Women: The Longest Revolution," originally published in the *New Left Review* in 1966—prior, even, to the beginning of a formalized "women's movement" in Great Britain—and continuing to parallel the intellectual developments generated by feminist theory since the mid-1960s, Mitchell has attempted, through her writing and lecturing, to promote understanding and discussion of the complex evolution of female oppression.

"Whenever I feel confronted by something that interests but baffles me, I decide to write about it," Mitchell states in her introduction to the 1983 retrospective anthology *Women: The Longest Revolution.* The book's title essay—one of several included that clearly reflect the evolution of Mitchell's intellectual development over a crucial 15-year period—remains perhaps her most significant work. Frequently anthologized and reprinted in pamphlets for distribution in both England and the United States, it was also widely translated as the women's movement spread across cultures and nationalities during the late '60s and '70s. Beginning with an overview of socialist theory that encompasses such thinkers as Marx, Lenin, Bebel, and even De Beauvoir, Mitchell goes on to identify the four societal structures that differentiate women's condition from that of her male counterpart: Production (female anatomy as it relates to a woman's physical capability for labor, as well as her capacity for violence and coercive behavior), Reproduction (a seeming biological constraint that signals a causal chain inscribed as "Maternity, Family, Absence from Production and Public Life, Sexual Inequality), Sexuality (women's physical appropriation as a form of sexual "private property"), and Socialization of Children ("an attempt to focus women's existence exclusively on bringing up children"). The lack of socially acceptable alternatives to the institutions of "marriage" and "family" lie at the core of female oppression, concludes Mitchell, calling the present system "a denial of life. For all human experience shows that intersexual and intergenerational relationships are infinitely various ... while the institutionalized expression of them in our capitalist society is utterly simple and rigid." Socialism, she concludes, should not be equated with the abolishment of "family," but rather with "the diversification of the socially acknowledged relationships which are today forcibly and rigidly compressed into it."

Women's Estate, which Mitchell published in 1971, explores the everyday condition of modern women, both at home and on the job, through the writer's characteristic Marxist perspective. Praising the work as a significant contribution to the growing body of feminist literature, fellow feminist Elizabeth Janeway noted of the work that "Mitchell reveals herself ... as a humane, wide-ranging, and toughminded critic and guide [whose] Marxist background has not turned her into a stereotypical thinker."

1974's *Psychoanalysis and Socialism* began as an outgrowth of "Women: The Longest Revolution" but quickly took on a life of its own. Mitchell developed a growing interest in the work of Freudian psychoanalysis as, contrary to anti-Freud feminist orthodoxy, providing a revealing perspective on the causes of female oppression. What she had originally conceived of as "a book on the family, which I thought was going to have a lot of social history in it," as Mitchell would tell Toril Moi, became *Psychoanalysis and Feminism,* "and the publisher didn't mind." While her work would be widely read in feminist circles, Mitchell maintains that much of the book was interpreted out of context. It was intended as an "initiating book.... an open project. It was asking if we could use psychoanalysis to bring feminism into the socialist project." Recall Mitchell's use of writing as a problem-solving device: "When I finish something.... I know the solution is incomplete, fragmentary, will be found wrong, awaits revision, continuation," she explains in her introduction to *Women: The Longest Revolution.* However, ignoring the author's attempt to posit psychoanalysis as a possible agent for the transformation of society toward socialism, *Psychoanalysis and Feminism* was depoliticized by critics into a work of purely psychoanalytic theory. Rather than viewing the book as an attempt to engage in polemic, to foster debate, many readers perceived it as an attack, an act of overt hostility towards other women. "The question of women and aggression comes up so strongly in the whole intellectual enterprise," Mitchell explained to Moi in discussing the criticism she would consequently receive in feminist circles. The reason? The fear of rivalry, of being perceived through open confrontation as identifying with men. "It is as though envy and rivalry between women will be unleashed if one lets any argument or competitiveness of thinking show at all, that it will unleash something too powerful, too deeply hostile—the sibling rivalry of sisters, or of mother-daughter relationships.... In a way, there is not a sufficient trust in women's solidarity for people to realize that they can argue against a woman and still remain feminists."

A trained psychotherapist, Mitchell has supplemented her staunch socialism with the theories of noted French psychoanalyst Jacques Lacan, who departed from acceptance of Freud's "single sex" model by maintaining that sexual difference is in fact due to the existence of a basic femininity rather than a gender identity derived from woman's lack of a male sex organ. Speaking of this symbolic castration, Mitchell notes in her essay "Psychoanalysis: Child Development and Femininity" that "The two famous concepts of the castration complex (in men) and penis-envy (in women) are correlatives; they express an identical fear of (and necessity for) the feminine position.... Freud's psychoanalytic theories are about sexism; that he himself propagated certain sexist views and that his work has been a bulwark of the ideological oppression of women is doubtless of great importance." She concludes *Psychoanalysis and Feminism* by positing the question of whether the human unconscious may, in fact, be a repository of social ideology. What, then is the causal relationship between cultural revolutions such as socialism and the human psyche? Does psychoanalysis, then, become a political tool with the potential to transform society and end the oppression of women? Or is the relationship a converse one? "In what way do we transform social relations by aiming for equality, when that aim in itself does not transform social relationships?," Mitchell has continued to wonder.

In addition to her original contributions to feminist theory, Mitchell has edited several important volumes of theory by other feminist thinkers. Together with noted sociologist Ann Oakley, Mitchell has edited *The Rights and Wrongs of Women,* as well as *What Is Feminism?,* a 1986 anthology bringing together the works of such notable feminist thinkers as Nancy Cott and Linda Gordon. In addition, she has edited a collection of studies in child psychology by controversial British psychoanalyst Melanie Klein as *The Selected Melanie Klein,* published in 1986.

In her continued writing and lecturing in the areas of socialist politics and feminist theory, Juliet Mitchell stresses the interrelation between the two. Feminism should "be about" everything: "It is unbelievable that feminists should think that women shouldn't be a part of the consciousness of, and the struggle against [international political conflicts]," she told Moi. "That is precisely to treat feminism as though it were only about femininity, as though women have no other place in other politics.... There must be women acting as women in the general political struggle as much as acting in the women's struggle.... If we are not there, it is tantamount to saying that fascism, war, etc., don't affect women; that there are no women in the Balkans, in the former Soviet Union."

—Lynn MacGregor

MOERS, Ellen

Nationality: American. **Born:** New York, New York, 9 December 1928. **Education:** Vassar College, B.A. 1948; Radcliffe College, M.A. 1949; Columbia University, Ph.D. 1954. **Family:** Married Martin Mayer in 1949; two sons. **Career:** Lecturer in English, 1956-57, senior research associate, 1957-58, Hunter College (now Hunter College of the City of New York); associate professor of English, Barnard College, New York, beginning 1968. Contributor to periodicals, including *American Scholar, Columbia Forum, Commentary, Harper's, New York Review of Books,* and *Victorian Studies.* **Awards:** Guggenheim fellowship, 1962-63; National Endowment for the Humanities senior fellowship, 1972-73. **Member:** American Studies Association, Phi Beta Kappa. **Died:** New York, New York, 25 August 1979.

PUBLICATIONS

Literary Criticism

Two Dreisers. New York, Viking, 1969; London, Thames & Hudson, 1970.

Literary Women: The Great Writers. Garden City, New York, Doubleday, 1976; London, W.H. Allen, 1977.

Harriet Beecher Stowe and American Literature. Hartford, Connecticut, Stowe-Day Foundation, 1978.

History

The Dandy: Brummell to Beerbohm. New York, Viking, and London, Secker & Warburg, 1960.

*

Critical Studies: *American Scholar,* autumn 1976.

* * *

Ellen Moers's death from cancer at age 51 ended her life, but not her profound influence on the field of women's literature, just flowering in the late 1970s. As long-neglected women authors were restored to print and to the canon, Moers's seminal work *Literary Women: The Great Writers* (1976) inspired numerous students to write on women's fiction and to be literary detectives. Far from Hawthorne's dismissive comments about "scribblers," there proved to be a rich tradition of women writers to explore: as Moers puts it, "Literature is the only intellectual field to which women, over a long stretch of time, have made an indispensable contribution." Moers herself referred to the 1970s as a time when long-silent women writers returned to print to tell their own stories of the writing life: a "golden harvest of memoirs to thicken the air with women's voices, to bring the old and young together in testimony to a woman's life." A prime example of this was Tillie Olsen, who became a friend of Moers during her research for the book.

Moers's first task was to identify women writers of significance and to examine their life experience as writers. A meticulous researcher, she had been preparing her study since the early 1960s, and devoted two years away from teaching in 1972-74 to completing her research (supported by a NEH grant). When the book appeared in 1976, it was hailed by Renee Winegarten in *American Scholar:* "Her book is a witty, provocative, stimulating, and entertaining 'celebration of the great women who have spoken for us all' (men included?)." *Literary Women* quickly became a key resource for women's studies programs and was widely discussed and read by literary scholars in the academy and elsewhere, thanks to Moers's accessible prose. The predictable reaction of more conservative reviewers was to pick at Moers's prose style, which they had done with regularity since the publication of her first book. The book has endured, and on nearly every page one can see where some concept of Moers's has borne fruit; literary researchers followed her lead and countless studies can be traced back to her insights. Her concept of "heroinism" (her term for "literary feminism") was a powerful one: she dealt with the actual impediments (sexism, poverty, ridicule, etc.) that writing women faced and over which they prevailed. She insisted that the writing was just as important to women as it was to men, if not more so because of the repression of women in the Western tradition. Her prime examples were the Brontës, George Eliot, Sylvia Plath, and Virginia Woolf, whose *Room of One's Own* perfectly captures the wishes and anxieties of a brilliant woman who would write—had to write—and yet faced the obstacles of the world solidly set against her. *Literary Women* was also a practical study in that it pointed the reader to further exploration—the last section is a bibliography of women writers and their work that is impressive in itself.

Moers's own story was one of a life dedicated to literature. The daughter of Robert Moers, a lawyer, and Celia Lewis (Kauffmann) Moers, a teacher, she grew up in New York City, where she lived most of her life. Born 9 December 1928, she received an excellent education, first at Vassar College, then at Radcliffe, and finally at Columbia, where she studied with Susanne Howe Nobbe, who taught the history of the novel and Victorian literature. Her dissertation on dandyism in England and France was a remarkable success, later published in an expanded version as "It's a Dandy" in 1960, and was translated into several languages. A specialist in the 19th-century novel, Moers was an intelligent and articulate reviewer. She was a frequent contributor to the *New York Review of Books* among others, as well as academic journals. She married the writer Martin Mayer in 1949 and was the mother of two sons, Thomas and James. Moers's teaching career was distinguished: notably she taught at Barnard and Hunter College and received numerous grants and awards.

As an author, Moers made a significant contribution to the field of the 19th-century novels with her 1969 study *The Two Dreisers.* While some critics were somewhat dismissive of her study of the writer Theodore Dreiser, they also acknowledged that her work illuminated the personal qualities of her subject. Moers received mixed reviews throughout her career, always acknowledging her skills while being somewhat hostile to her methods. Her book on Harriet Beecher Stowe was an influential study, and brought new critical attention to that neglected phenomenon of American literature, the much-maligned author of *Uncle Tom's Cabin,* exactly the sort of woman writer Moers was championing in *Literary Women.* At the time of her death, Moers was writing on the subject of the interrelationship of British and American writers of the 19th century. Ellen Moers died 25 August, 1979 in New York City. Her influence on the field is an enviable one, as her pioneering efforts are considered classics.

—Mary A. Hess

MOI, Toril

Nationality: Norwegian. **Born:** 1953. **Education:** University of Bergen, D. Art, 1985. **Career:** Lecturer, Oxford University, 1983-85; director, Centre for Feminist Research in the Humanities, University of Bergen, Norway; adjunct professor of comparative literature, University of Bergen; currently professor of literature, Duke University. Contributor as a translator and reviewer to journals, including *Vinduet, Edda, Kontrast,* and *French Studies.* **Address:** Literature Program, Duke University, Durham, North Carolina, 27706-8001, U.S.A. **Online Address:** toril@acpub.duke.edu.

Publications

Literary Theory

Sexual/Textual Politics: Feminist Literary Theory. London, Methuen, 1986.
Feminist Literary Theory and Simone de Beauvoir. Oxford, Basil Blackwell, 1990.

Essays

"Representation of Patriarchy: Sexuality and Epistemology in Freud's *Dora,*" in *Feminist Review,* 9, 1981; in *In Dora's Case: Feminism—Psychoanalysis—Hysteria,* edited by Charles Bernheimer and Claire Kahane. New York, Columbia University Press, and London, Virago, 1985.
"Who's Afraid of Virginia Woolf? Feminist Readings of Woolf," in *Canadian Journal of Political and Social Theory,* 9(1-2), winter/spring 1985.
"She Came to Stay," in *Paragraph: A Journal of Modern Critical Theory* (Edinburgh), 8, 1986.
"Men against Patriarchy," in *Gender and Theory: Dialogues on Feminist Criticism,* edited by Linda Kauffman. Oxford, Basil Blackwell, 1989.
"Patriarchal Thought and the Drive for Knowledge," in *Between Feminism and Psychoanalysis,* edited by Tresa Brennan. London and New York, Routledge, 1989.
"Feminism, Postmodernism, and Style: Recent Feminist Criticisms in the United States," in *Criticism in the Twilight Zone: Postmodern Perspectives on Literature,* edited by Zadworna-Fjellestad-danuta and Bjork-Lennart. Stockholm, Almqvist & Wiksell, 1990.
"Simone de Beauvoir's *L'Invité:* An Existentialist Melodrama," in *Paragraph: A Journal of Modern Critical Theory* (Edinburgh), 14(2), July 1991.
"Appropriating Bourdieu: Feminist Theory and Pierre Bourdieu's Sociology of Culture," in *New Literary History: A Journal of Theory and Interpretation* (Baltimore), 22(4), autumn 1991.
"Ambiguity and Alienation in *The Second Sex,*" in *Boundary 2: An International Journal of Literature and Culture* (Durham, North Carolina), 19(2), summer 1992.
"Beauvoir's Utopia: The Politics of *The Second Sex,*" in *South Atlantic Quarterly* (Durham, North Carolina), 92(2), spring 1993.

Other

Simone de Beauvoir: The Making of an Intellectual Woman. Oxford, Basil Blackwell, 1994.

Editor, *The Kristeva Reader.* Oxford, Basil Blackwell, and New York, Columbia University Press, 1986.
Editor, *French Feminist Thought: A Reader.* Oxford, Basil Blackwell, 1987.
Editor, with Janice A. Radway, *Materialist Feminism.* Durham, North Carolina, Duke University Press, 1994.

*

Critical Studies: "Introducing Feminism" by Naomi Schor, in *Paragraph* (Edinburgh), 8, October 1986; "Questions of Feminist Criticism" by Linda Anderson, in *Prose Studies,* 10(2), September 1987; "A Vicious and Corrupt Word: Feminism and Virginia Woolf" by Bev Jackson, in *Dutch Quarterly Review of Anglo American Letters* (Amsterdam), 17(4), 1987; "Escaping the Cave: Luce Irigaray and Her Feminist Critics," by Maggie Berg, in *Literature and Ethics,* Kingston, Ontario, McGill-Queen, 1988; "Two into Three Won't Go: Mimetic Desire and the Dream of Androgyny in *Dancing in the Dark*" by D.S. Neff, in *Modern Fiction Studies,* Baltimore, 34(3), 1988; "Getting into History" by Diana Fuss, in *Arizona Quarterly* (Tucson, Arizona), 45(4), winter 1989.

Toril Moi comments:
I am currently working on a collection of essays tentatively entitled *What Is a Woman? and Other Essays,* to be published by Oxford University Press.

* * *

With the 1985 publication of her first academic book, *Sexual/ Textual Politics: Feminist Literary Theory,* Norwegian-born feminist theorist Toril Moi has introduced the two main approaches to feminist literary theory, the Anglo-American and the French, in a way that is both interesting and negotiable for the novice. Moi's discussions—incisive, critical—uncover the theoretical assumptions at work in both Anglo-American feminist criticism and French theory and attempt to reveal how those assumptions are often in conflict with the political goals of feminism.

Sexual/Textual Politics opens with a chapter on Virginia Woolf. As Moi states, our goal as feminists must be a critical theory that does "both justice and homage to its great mother and sister." She begins with a discussion of the criticism of Elaine Showalter, who accuses Woolf of moving away from her gendered identity "into androgyny" and ends with a critique of noted French theorist Julia Kristeva.

Sexual/Textual Politics received mixed reactions within the academic community—some praising, some critical—and Moi feels that the critical reaction is partly an effect of the "upfront way in which it is written," adding that "one of my points in the book is that a passive, submissive response to a text is not a response that I think feminists should encourage. So to that extent, if people are taking issue with the book or feeling that they want to have their own say after it, I can only say that, after all, I wrote it to stimulate debate, and I can't start to complain if it does so."

Often taken to task for excluding black and lesbian contributions to American feminist criticism—because "so far, lesbian and/or black feminist criticism have presented exactly the same methodological and theoretical problems as the rest of Anglo-American feminist criticism," according to Moi—nevertheless, she has managed to do two difficult things at once: introduce the field of feminist literary theory so as to make it interesting, and produce a text that will spark productive theoretical debate for years to come.

A noted scholar of French intellectual feminist Simone de Beauvoir, Moi has published two books, 1990's *Feminist Theory and Simone de Beauvoir* and *Simone de Beauvoir: The Making of an Intellectual Woman,* released in 1994. Together they cover the life and work of this woman whom Moi refers to as "the most important feminist intellectual of the twentieth century." The later book is not an biography in the traditional sense, for it doesn't seek to cover the subject's whole life in a balanced manner. Nor is it a critical analysis of de Beauvoir's writings, since it is concerned only with three texts: *L'Invité, Le Deuxième sexe,* and *Mémoires d'une jeune fille rangée*. Thus, Moi describes the book as being a "personal genealogy." Although the difference between a biography and a "personal genealogy" may not always be clear to the reader, Moi's subtitle, *The Making of an Intellectual Woman,* gives a clear indication of the substance of her work. For example, de Beauvoir's own biographies are all of her own life, making her both the subject and the object of study, the sympathetic observer of her psychological development, always split yet never distanced from herself. However, Moi examines what de Beauvoir made of what had been made of her, and how de Beauvoir made history on the basis of what history had made her. In other words, Moi examines the *making* of Simone de Beauvoir as an intellectual woman, and does so in more ways than one.

Written using an historical, even dialectical, method, this intellectual biography, of sorts, looks at de Beauvoir—who permitted posterity access to her personal letters in the interests of scholarship and with an explicit distaste for intimate secrets—with both acumen and empathy. Furthermore, this highly readable book is marked in particular by its explicit acknowledgement of its own situated nature, its subjectivity—not as opposed to some impossible objective perspective, but rather recognizing itself as the work of a feminist thinker in the 1900s, half a century after de Beauvoir. And, it is this same "subjectivity" that runs throughout all of Moi's work.

Moi's written work does not dull our senses with jargonized phrases. *Simone de Beauvoir: The Making of an Intellectual Woman* is written in a pleasant and engaging style that can be read with ease and profit by the noninitiated. Its honesty about the private lives, political compromises, and literary achievements of both de Beauvoir and Jean-Paul Sartre (de Beauvoir's lover, intellectual partner, and author of *The Age of Reason* and *What Is Literature?*) is, in fact, quite refreshing. In an interview in 1990 with Laura Payne in *Feminist Theory and Simone de Beauvoir,* Moi states: "it is the problem of the intellectual woman—her speaking position, her concerns, her conflicts, her intellectual styles—which fascinates me ... and obviously I'm interested in the conceptualization of knowledge in Beauvoir." And, it is Moi's interest in the "conceptualization of knowledge" that makes this insightful book well worth reading for the novice or scholar interested in the work and life of Simone de Beauvoir.

—Stacie J. Koochek

MONTAGU, Elizabeth (Robinson)

Nationality: British. **Born:** York, 2 October 1720; sister of novelist Sarah Scott. **Education:** Educated at home. **Family:** Married Edward Montagu in 1742; one son. **Career:** Essayist, scholar, letter writer; known as "Queen of the Bluestockings" for hosting an intellectual salon whose members included Hannah Moore, Fanny Burney, Hester Chapone, Sarah Scott, Horace Walpole, and Samuel Johnson. **Died:** 25 August 1800.

Publications

Essays

Essay on the Writings and Genius of Shakespeare, Compared with the Greek and French Dramatic Poets. London, J. Dodsley, 1769.

Other

"Dialogues XXVI, XXVII, and XXVIII" in *Dialogues of the Dead,* by Lord George Lytton. London, W. Sandby, 1760-65.

Letters of Mrs. Elizabeth Montagu, with Some of the Letters of Her Correspondents, edited by Matthew Montagu. London, T. Cadell, 4 vols., 1809-13; 3rd edition, 1810-13.

Letters from Mrs. Elizabeth Carter to Mrs. Montagu between the Years 1755 and 1800, edited by Montagu Pennington. London, R. & R. Gilbert, 1817.

Elizabeth Montagu, the Queen of the Bluestockings: Her Correspondence from 1720 to 1761, edited by Emily J. Climenson. London, John Murray, and New York, E. P. Dutton, 2 vols., 1906.

Mrs Montagu "Queen of the Blues": Her Letters and Friendships from 1762 to 1800, edited by Reginald Blunt. London, Constable, 2 vols., 1923.

*

Bibliography: "The Eighteenth-Century Englishwoman" by Barbara B. Schnorrenberg with Jean E. Hunter, in *The Women of England from Anglo-Saxon Times to the Present,* edited by Barbara Kanner, Hamden, Archon, 1979.

Manuscript Collections: Montagu Collection, Huntington Library.

Critical Studies: *The Queens of Society* by A. T. Thomson, New York, Harper, 1860; *A Lady of the Last Century: Illustrated in her*

Unpublished Letters; Collected and Arranged, with a Biographical Sketch, and a Chapter on Bluestockings by Dr. John Doran, London, R. Bentley, 1873; *Mrs. Montagu and Her Friends, 1720-1800, a Sketch* by Rene Louis Huckon, London, Murray, 1907; "New Light on Mrs. Montagu" by Katherine Gee Hornbreak, in *The Age of Johnson: Essays Presented to Chauncey Brewster Tinker*, edited by F.W. Hilles, New Haven, Yale University Press, 1949; "The Romantic Bluestocking, Elizabeth Montagu" by W. Powell Jones, in *Huntington Library Quarterly*, 12, 1948-49; "Mrs. Elizabeth Montagu (1720-1800)" by James T. Boulton, in *Burke Newsletter*, 3, 1961-62; "Learning, Virtue, and the Term 'Bluestocking'" by Sylvia H. Myers, in *Studies in 18th-century Culture*, 15, Madison, University of Wisconsin Press, 1986; "A Measure of Power: The Personal Charity of Elizabeth Montagu" by Edith Sedgwick Larson, in *Studies in 18th-century Culture*, 16, Madison, University of Wisconsin Press, 1986; *The 18th-century Feminist Mind* by Alice Browne, Detroit, Wayne State University Press, 1987; *The Bluestocking Circle: Women, Friendship, and the Life of the Mind in 18th-century England* by Sylvia Harcstark Myers, Oxford, Clarendon, 1990; "The Bluestocking Circle: The Negotiation of 'Reasonable' Women" by Susan M. Yadlon, in *Communication and Women's Friendships: Parallels and Intersections in Literature and Life*, edited by Janet Doubler Ward and JoAnna Stephens Mink, Bowling Green, Bowling Green State University Popular Press, 1993.

*   *   *

When Samuel Johnson dubbed Elizabeth Montagu "Queen of the Bluestockings," he intended to praise her as the intellectual leader of one of the most important literary circles of the 18th century. Shortly thereafter, however, the term "bluestocking" took on its current pejorative connotation, identifying an affectedly intellectual woman. But the term itself appears to have derived from a playful inside joke at the expense of scholar, botanist, and poet Benjamin Stillingfleet, who wore blue worsted stockings to the group's night gatherings when polite society dictated that white stockings were more appropriate. In Montagu's early correspondence, she associates "bluestocking" with learned philosophical men of the circle; but to her it later also came to represent the steadfast pursuit of an intellectual life for women.

Members of the Bluestocking circle, which included both women and men, considered themselves part of an elite but informal society founded on learning, friendship, and the free expression and exchange of ideas. At their receptions, the Bluestockings discouraged frivolous entertainments such as drinking, gambling, and dancing, as well as gossip and political discussion. Montagu was the principal host for these gatherings and for nearly a quarter of a century served as the center of the Bluestocking circle, which also included such notables as Johnson, Hester Thrale (later Piozzi), Hannah More, Elizabeth Carter, Catherine Talbot, Hester Mulso Chapone, Fanny Burney, David Garrick, Horace Walpole, Sir Joshua Reynolds, Samuel Richardson, Sir George Lyttleton, and many others.

Montagu herself was a scholar, critic, prodigious correspondent, and a charismatic society lady. Her marriage to the grandson of the earl of Sandwich, 28 years her senior, in 1742 facilitated her social aspirations and gratified her expensive tastes; but their relationship, while amicable, appears to have been distant, particularly after the death of their infant son in 1744. Friendship and scholarship became Montagu's top priority, though she cared for her husband until his death in 1775, when she took over management of the family business. Her friendship with Lyttleton, who encouraged her literary studies, led to her anonymous contribution of three dialogues to his *Dialogues of the Dead,* of which "Dialogue XXVII" is the most delightful in its sharp satire of frivolous modern ladies. Montagu's greatest literary achievement, however, was her celebrated but anonymous *Essay on the Writings and Genius of Shakespeare,* which defended the English dramatist from Voltaire's denigration with much nationalistic fervor and critical insight. Since her death, Montagu perhaps has been best known for her letters, a selection of which was first published by her nephew in 1809; her correspondence, most of which remains unpublished and uncatalogued, reveals much about the celebrated literary figures of the day, as well as about Montagu's own literary and political opinions, her tastes, and her generosity—her patronage would help support writers such as James Beattie, Hannah More, and Anna Laetitia Barbauld. Though she never approached the feminist consciousness of Mary Wollstonecraft, Montagu is noteworthy for her faith in the female intellect and for her belief in the importance of women's friendships, such as those she shared with Elizabeth Carter, Elizabeth Vesey, and her sister, the novelist Sarah Scott.

—Daniel Robinson

MOORE, Alice Ruth. *See* **DUNBAR-NELSON, Alice Moore.**

MORAGA, Cherríe

Nationality: American. **Born:** Whittier, California, 25 September 1952. **Education:** Attended private school, Hollywood, California; B.A. 1974; San Francisco State University, M.A. 1980. **Career:** High school English teacher, Los Angeles, during the mid-1970s; cofounder and administrator, Kitchen Table: Women of Color Press, New York, beginning 1981; playwright-in-residence, INTAR (Hispanic-American arts center), 1984; part-time writing instructor, University of California, Berkeley, beginning 1986. **Awards:** Before Columbus Foundation American Book Award, 1986, for *This Bridge Called My Back: Writings by Radical Women of Color;* National Education Association Theatre Playwrights Fellowship Fund for New American Plays award. **Address:** c/o Chicano Studies Department, University of California, 3404 Dwinelle Hall, Berkeley, California 94720, USA.

Publications

Plays

Giving Up the Ghost: Teatro in Two Acts (produced as stage reading Minneapolis, Minnesota, 1984; produced Seattle, 1987; revised version produced San Francisco, 1987). Minneapolis, Minnesota, West End Press, 1986.

La extranjera (produced 1985).
The Shadow of a Man (produced 1988). N.p., 1991.
Heroes and Saints and Other Plays. N.p., 1994.

Poetry

Loving in the War Years: Lo que nunca pasó por sus labios ["What Never Passed Her Lips"], (includes essays). Boston, South End Press, 1983.
The Last Generation (includes prose). Boston, South End Press, 1993.

Other

Editor, with Alma Gómez and Mariana Romo-Carmona, and contributor, *Cuentos: Stories by Latinas*. New York, Kitchen Table: Women of Color Press, 1983.
Editor, with Gloria Anzaldúa, *This Bridge Called My Back: Writings by Radical Women of Color.* Watertown, Massachusetts, Persephone Press, 1981; revised bilingual edition published as *Esta puente, mi espalda: Voces de mujeres tercermundistas en los Estados Unidos,* edited by Ana Castillo, with Spanish translation by Castillo and Norma Alarcón, San Francisco, Ism Press, 1988.
Editor, with Norma Alarcón, *Third Woman,* Volume 4: *The Sexuality of Latinas.* Berkeley, California, Third Woman Press, 1989.
Editor, with Ana Castillo and Norma Alarcón, *The Sexuality of Latinas.* Berkeley, California, Third Woman Press, 1993.

*

Critical Studies: *New England Review,* summer 1983; "All of Our Art for Our Sake" by SDiane Bogus, in *Sinister Wisdom,* fall 1984; interview with Mirtha N. Quintanales, in *Off Our Backs,* January 1985; "Cherríe Moraga's Giving Up the Ghost: The Representation of Female Desire" by Yvonne Yarbro-Bejarano, in *Third Woman,* 3(1-2), 1986; interview with Norma Alarcón, in *Third Woman,* 3(1-2), 1986; interview with Luz María Umpierre, in *Americas Review,* 14, 1986; *Rocky Mountain Review of Language and Literature,* 41(1-2), 1987; "Cherríe Moraga" by Yvonne Yarbro-Bejarano, in *Dictionary of Literary Biography,* Volume 82: *Chicano Writers,* Detroit, Gale, 1989; "'A Deep Racial Memory of Love': The Chicana Feminism of Cherríe Moraga" by Nancy Saporta Sternback, in *Breaking Boundaries: Latina Writing and Critical Readings,* edited by Asunción Horno-Delgado and others, Amherst, University of Massachusetts Press, 1989; *Mother Jones,* January/February 1991, 15; article in *Ms.,* March 1992.

* * *

In an interview with Norma Alarcón, Chicana author Cherríe Moraga articulates her vision of feminism. "I feel that feminism which takes seriously the specific kinds of oppression suffered by women can also within that context take into consideration how class and racism complicate and increase the kinds of oppression suffered by women," Moraga expains. "The kind of movement that incorporates all those things is feminism to me." With that in mind, it is fair to say that Moraga, a biracial lesbian activist and writer, fully embodies a feminist perspective. Moreover, she not only personifies action but directly opens avenues for women of color internationally.

Born in 1952 in Whittier, California, Moraga came into the world, a product of an interracial marriage, already straddling the cultural borders that would define her later work. The ability to "pass" for white in multicultural California allowed her easy access to an education; she obtained an undergraduate degree in English from a small college in Hollywood, an accomplishment that established Moraga as a forerunner within her own family. Although while in school she attempted to write creatively, her work proved to be personally disillusioning and of poor quality. Despite a personal urge to improve her writing, Moraga accepted a position as a instructor in a Los Angeles high school. She probably would have continued working in this profession had it not been for a writer's seminar offered through the Los Angeles Women's Building. Not only was she motivated by the women around her and the craft, but she also was beginning to confront her own homosexuality. As a result, her expressive abilities became enhanced and unclouded. In an interview with Puerto Rican scholar and poet Luz María Umpierre, Moraga explains that "one of the reasons why they [her early attempts at writing] were so terrible is because I felt very much that I was writing with secrets." Accepting her lesbianism unlocked many doors of confusion and thus freed Moraga to express herself more openly and honestly.

Although she experienced an overwhelming sense of relief, Moraga also faced many new hurdles as a result of "coming out." While her writing flourished she encountered a system of heterosexism that curtailed and at times barred her emotional presentation. The encouragement and support she had once found within her writing group changed as the women found her new material unsettling. Moraga knew, thereafter, that she had to write—readers would just have to alter their expectations. She committed herself to the task, making teaching no longer feasible. She also moved to San Francisco, where she could better concentrate on her work and spiritual transformation. Her decision to remain a writer by profession would hing on the acceptance and success resulting from this first year's travails.

During this trial year not only did Moraga write, but she also read. After building her understanding and technique, she performed her poetry at numerous local readings. Her verse was well received, but most importantly, Moraga herself felt able and accomplished as a novice. She entered a graduate program in feminist writing at San Francisco State University, where she met Gloria Anzaldúa, another influential Chicana lesbian author. The two writers collaborated on a project so that Moraga could successfully complete her thesis: the project was the anthology of minority women's writings called *This Bridge Called My Back: Writings by Radical Women of Color.*

Groundbreaking in scope, *This Bridge Called My Back* went through several printings, won a Before Columbus Foundation American Book Award and, in 1988, was translated into Spanish. The book's success thrilled Moraga who, in addition to long hours, had put a lot of trust and hope into the project, which gave a long-needed voice to multiracial women of color and minority lesbians.

"The original impetus behind [*This Bridge Called My Back*]," Moraga told Alarcón, "was to write this book that was gonna get the White girls right. We were gonna write a book that was gonna say you are racist in 'x' amount of ways, and we've had it. But basically that became only one chapter of the book. As we began to generate interest in the book, we found that we were less interested in White women's racism and more interested in Third World women's feminism." As the first text of its kind, the book illuminated a path long ignored but essential to the understanding of racial and sexual politics.

Frustrated by how difficult the publishing process had been and how difficult in general it was for radical women of color to get published, Moraga and a few other women created Kitchen Table: Women of Color Press, which would republished *This Bridge Called My Back* in 1986 and go on to market many other works by minority women. Among these other texts is Moraga's own coedited book *Cuentos: Stories by Latinas.* Bearing a title reminiscent of the oral storytelling tradition of Latino culture, the collection provides space for women whose lives "have never fully been told, except by word of mouth." Specifically, Moraga's own pieces in the book deal with sexuality and racism and the coping mechanisms needed to live with these struggles.

Though both her previous works were collaborations, Moraga had, by this time, composed a substantive and creative body of her own work. She went to work on her own book, which was published as *Loving in the War Years: Lo que nunca pasó por sus labios.* Included are her famous "For the Color of My Mother" and "A Long Line of Vendidas." The title of the book, as noted by critic Nancy Saporta Sternbach, "connects Moraga to a mestiza Chicana past but also questions, reevaluates, and finally takes issue with it." Like many Chicana authors before her, Moraga invokes the Mexican/Mexican American myth of la Malinche to place herself in the culture. Malinche, or Doña Marina, was the Indian consort to Hernán Cortés (conquistador of Mexico) who subsequently gave birth to the first mestizo or mixed-blood. Malinche thus illustrates the downfall of the Aztec people and shoulders the role of traitor. Moraga reconfigures the myth in an effort to place herself, a half-breed, lesbian, within the culture. "The painful journey she embarks upon in order to discover this truth allows her return to her mother, to her people, to 'la mujer meztiza,' to a new awareness of what it means to be Malinche's daughter," notes Sternbach. Putting women first, respecting their long-neglected contributions, and creating space and tolerance for human experience, Moraga's book secures understanding and voice for those previously silenced.

Most recently, after having written numerous plays, Moraga has presented Chicano and feminist literary canons in *The Last Generation.* Understanding herself as one of the last of her species to remember and record, Moraga comments on the assimilation strategies that pressured people of color during the conservative 1980s. "[W]e're all supposed to quietly accept this passing, this slow and painless death of a cultura, this invisible disappearance of a people. But I do not accept it. I write. I write as I always have, but now I write for a much larger familia." Called to action by the tremulous occurrences of that decade, Moraga presents essays making us, as a society, consider the destructive path we are on. Evoking myth in the essay "La Fuerza Femenina," she recalls the daughter, "la hija Rebelde" of the Goddess Coatlicue. Aligning herself with this persona who "attempts to pick up the fragments of our dismembered womanhood and reconstitute ourselves," Moraga reasserts her connection and commitment to women as a whole and to the Chicana specifically.

When she is not writing, Moraga lectures throughout the country. Always available and interested in the student, the younger generation, she is an inspiring teacher. As a feminist, although she has been dissuaded by popular (i.e., white women's) feminism throughout the years, Cherríe Moraga continues to dedicate herself to creating a society inclusive of all women, to making the "invisible oppression" visible, and to finding inner peace.

—Naomi Barry

MORGAN, Robin

Nationality: American. **Born:** Lake Worth, Florida, 29 January 1941. **Education:** Wetter School, Mount Vernon, New York, graduated 1956 (with honors); Columbia University, New York, 1956-59; attended poetry workshops with Louise Bogan, Babette Deutsch, and Mark Van Doren. **Family:** Married Kenneth Pitchford in 1962 (divorced 1983); one son. **Career:** Freelance book editor, 1961-69; editor, Grove Press, New York, 1967-70; editor and columnist, 1974-87, editor-in-chief, 1989-93, international consulting editor, beginning 1993, *Ms.* magazine, New York. Visiting chair and guest professor of women's studies, New College, Sarasota, Florida, 1973; distinguished visiting scholar and lecturer, Center for Critical Analysis of Contemporary Culture, Rutgers University, 1987; consultant, U.N. Conference to End All Forms of Discrimination against Women, Sao Paulo and Brasilia, Brazil, 1987; member of advisory board, ISIS (international women's network). Cofounder, Women's International Terrorist Conspiracy from Hell (WITCH) and New York Radical Women, 1960s; organizer, first feminist demonstration against Miss America Pageant, Atlantic City, New Jersey, 1968; founder, New York Women's Center, 1969; founder and president, The Sisterhood Fund, 1970, New York Women's Law Center, 1970; cofounder and member of board of directors, Feminist Women's Health Network, National Battered Women's Refuge Network, National Network Rape Crisis Centers; cofounder, Sisterhood Is Global Institute (think-tank), 1984; member of advisory board, Global Fund for Women, Women's Studies International; member, board of directors, Feminist Press. Contributor to numerous periodicals, including *American Voice, Antioch Review, Atlantic, American Poetry Review, Calyx, Chrysalis, Feminist Review, Sojourner, Woman's Vioce,* and *Yale Review.* **Awards:** National Endowment for the Arts grant in poetry, 1979; Yaddo writer-in-residence grant, 1980; Ford Foundation grants, 1982, 1983, 1984; Front Page Award, 1982, for *Ms.* article "The First Feminist Exiles from the USSR"; Wonder Woman award, 1982; Kentucky Foundation for Women Literature grant, 1986; Feminist Majority Foundation Woman of the Year award, 1990; *Utne Reader* award and National Women's Political Caucus award for journalism, both 1991; Asian American Women's Organization Warrior Woman Award, 1992; D.H.L., University of Connecticut, 1992; Association for Education in Journalism and Communications special achievement award, 1993. **Member:** Feminist Writers Guild, Media Women, North American Feminist Coalition, Pan Arab Feminist Solidarity Association (honorary member), Women's Foreign Policy Council, Feminists for Animal Rights, Lesbian Books Association. **Address:** c/o *Ms.* Magazine, 230 Park Avenue, New York, New York 10169-0005, U.S.A.

Publications

Poetry

Monster: Poems. New York, Random House, 1972.
Lady of the Beasts: Poems. New York, Random House, 1976.
Death Benefits: Poems. Port Townsend, Washington, Copper Canyon Press, 1981.
Depth Perception: New Poems and a Masque. New York, Anchor/Doubleday, 1982.

Upstairs in the Garden: Poems Selected and New: 1968-1988. New York, Norton, 1990.

Novel

Dry Your Smile. Garden City, New York, Doubleday, 1987; London, Women's Press, 1988.

Plays

In Another Country, 1960.
The Duel, 1979.

Essays

The Anatomy of Freedom: Feminism, Physics, and Global Politics. Garden City, New York, Doubleday, 1982; London, 1984; revised edition, 1994.
The Demon Lover: On the Sexuality of Terrorism. New York, Norton, and London, Methuen, 1989.
The Word of a Woman: Feminist Dispatches 1968-1992. New York, Norton, 1992; as *The Word of a Woman: Selected Prose, 1968-1992,* London, Virago, 1993; revised edition, 1994.

For Children

The Mer-Child: A Legend for Children and Other Adults, illustrated by Jesse Spicer Zerner. New York, Feminist Press, 1991.

Autobiography

Going Too Far: The Personal Chronicle of a Feminist. New York, Random House, 1977.

Other

Manpower: Photographs, photographs by Sally Soames. London, Deutsch, 1987.

Editor, with Charlotte Bunch-Weeks and Joanne Cooke, *The New Women: A Motive Anthology on Women's Liberation* (originally published in *Motive* magazine). New York, Bobbs-Merrill, 1969.
Editor, *Sisterhood Is Powerful: An Anthology of Writings from the Women's Liberation Movement.* New York, Random House, 1970.
Editor, *Sisterhood Is Global: The International Women's Movement Anthology.* Garden City, New York, Doubleday, 1984; Harmondsworth, Penguin, 1985.

Recordings: *Our Creations Are in the First Place Ourselves* (audiocassettes), Iowa State University of Science and Technology, 1974; *Anatomy of Freedom,* Los Angeles, Pacifica Radio Archive, 1983.

*

Critical Studies: "Robin Morgan" by Blanche Wiesen Cook, in *Contemporary Lesbian Writers of the United States: A Bio-Bibliographical Critical Sourcebook,* edited by Sandra Pollack and Denise D. Knight, Westport, Connecticut, Greenwood Press, 1993.

* * *

Robin Morgan has made important contributions to the international feminist movement through her active involvement in feminist organizations, as well as through her poetry, non-fiction, and fiction. Morgan's involvement with political and economic issues pertaining to women and worldwide patriarchal systems of power has led to her confrontations with such difficult and pervasive problems as illiteracy, refugee populations, pornography, genital mutilation, the welfare and rights of children, education, and the abuse and oppression that women have suffered and are still suffering around the globe. Her politics merge with her art in her several books of poetry, collections of essays, novels, and numerous articles in literary and political journals, all devoted to the empowerment of women.

Born in Florida and raised in Mount Vernon, New York, Morgan tasted fame for the first time at a very early age. Her divorced mother's ambitions for her young and talented daughter resulted in Morgan's own radio program in the 1940s, "The Little Robin Morgan Show," and her later role as Dagmar in the popular 1950s television series *I Remember Mama.* In 1956 Morgan graduated with honors from the Wetter School in Mount Vernon, and from 1956-1959 was taught by private tutors in the United States and Europe. She studied literature and classics at Columbia University (although she did not take a degree) and worked on developing her gift for poetry.

The 1960s found Morgan protesting the Vietnam War, participating in civil rights and anti-segregation movements, involving herself with such organizations as CORE (Congress for Racial Equality), SNCC (Student Nonviolent Coordinating Committee), SDS (Students for a Democratic Society), the Revolutionary Youth Movement, and the New York Radical Women, and helping to establish the Women's International Terrorist Conspiracy from Hell (WITCH). She worked as a freelance editor from 1961-1969, focused seriously on her own writing, and married the poet, novelist, and playwright Kenneth Pitchford in 1962. These various and pressing demands for her time and energy—which would soon include raising the couple's son—taught Morgan firsthand the difficulties of balancing an active political and literary life with the pressures of marriage.

In 1968 Morgan "came out" publicly as a lesbian in the *New York Times.* However, she and her husband—a gay man who was a cofounder of the Gay Liberation Front—remained married until 1983. In 1969 Morgan became part of a female collective that seized and transformed—at least temporarily—the male-dominated underground newspaper *Rat*; in January of 1970, the first entirely female-produced issue included her famous essay "Goodbye to All That," which bade farewell to her working with men in the promotion of Leftist causes. The year 1970 also saw the publication of *Sisterhood Is Powerful*, Morgan's first anthology of writings on the women's liberation movement. A bestseller that is now considered a feminist classic, *Sisterhood Is Powerful* continues to be read as an important chronicle for students of the women's movement.

Morgan's seemingly tireless dedication to the cause of advancing women's rights clearly surfaces in the poetry she has published during the past several decades. While not every one of Morgan's poems deal with overly feminist issues, her deep concerns for women around the world unmistakably color her work. Morgan's first book of poems, 1972's *Monster,* combines her radical politics with powerful images of the female experience. This early collection demonstrates both Morgan's profound love for women as well as her vision of men as the enemy not just of women but of culture as a whole. Her next volume of poetry, *Lady of the Beasts,* published in 1976, continues these themes of feminine love and feminist anger, and also incorporates visions of women assuming their rightful and powerful archetypal roles in each stage of their lives. Although *Lady of the Beasts* was received with somewhat more critical enthusiasm than her first book had been, Morgan has been regarded by many critics as an accomplished and compelling poet from the first. Her subsequent three collections of poetry, 1981's *Death Benefits,* 1982's *Depth Perception: New Poems and a Masque,* and *Upstairs in the Garden: Selected and New Poems,* published in 1990, all present the poet's conceptions of the lives and passions of women living in a patriarchal world, and demonstrate her ability to expose their pain and beauty through her art.

Morgan's contributions to radical feminist thought extend far beyond her poetry; as a writer and editor for *Ms.* magazine from 1984-1987 and a frequent contributor to many journals, much of her influence has been generated through her non-fiction writing. 1977's *Going Too Far: The Personal Chronicle of a Feminist* features some of Morgan's more autobiographical non-fiction collected from 1962 to 1977, and reveals her opinions on diverse feminist issues ranging from marriage to lesbianism to the Miss America Pageant. In her introduction, Morgan celebrates the notion that in confronting the problems, obstacles, and threats that face all women, there really is no such thing as "going too far." Interestingly, she opted to include in this collection some of her earlier writings that she considered to be weaker, dated, or flawed in some way, because she believes that they contribute to a more accurate and honest representation of her long-term development as a writer and an activist. *The Anatomy of Freedom: Feminism, Physics, and Global Politics,* which Morgan published in 1982, also examines the implications of striving toward a future defined by feminism and non-violent politics.

In 1989 Morgan brought out another non-fiction work: *The Demon Lover: On the Sexuality of Terrorism.* Fueled in part by a visit she took in 1986 to the Palestine refugee camps in the Gaza Strip, Morgan explores the worldwide ramifications of male violence and terrorism. In this powerful and painful book, she asserts that the violence perpetrated against women around the globe and over the course of centuries has led, frighteningly, to the normalization of female subjugation. An ardent pacifist, she calls for an end to this terrorism and for women to work toward a transformation of the politics of power.

Morgan's fiction writing has also served her radical feminist politics; in her first novel, 1987's *Dry Your Smile,* she investigates her own personal connections to other women in her life. Highly autobiographical, *Dry Your Smile* tackles issues of female love in the contexts of friendships, marriage, family, and lesbian relationships. *The Mer-Child: A Legend for Children and Other Adults,* written four years later, tells of the loneliness wrought by intolerance and prejudice, and the love that can be generated when one moves beyond one's sense of alienation and difference.

Morgan's devotion to causes that transcend racism, sexism, and all other forms of injustice has led her to found or co-found several organizations that promote feminist change. These include the Sisterhood Is Global Institute, the National Network of Rape Crisis Centers, the New York Women's Center, the Feminist Women's Health Network, and the Battered Women's Refuge Network. She also directs or participates in several other feminist organizations, such as the Women's Law Center and the Women's Institute Freedom Press. Her feminist activism has led her to brief stints in academia; in 1972 she taught in the Women's Studies department at New College in Sarasota, Florida, and in 1987 at Rutgers University's Center for Critical Analysis of Contemporary Culture. Also in 1987 she attended the United Nations Convention in Brazil to End All Forms of Discrimination against Women. Morgan returned to the position of editor of the new, no-advertising *Ms.* magazine in 1990, reinventing it as an independent journal for women, free from the influences of advertising sponsors, before becoming the magazine's international consulting editor in 1993. Describing herself as an apostate Jew and a Wiccean atheist, Robin Morgan's life and work testify to a religion of female love, pacifist activism, personal liberation, and revolutionary feminist politics.

—Kathleen Drowne

MORRISON, Toni

Nationality: American. **Born:** Chloë Anthony Wofford, Lorain, Ohio, 18 February 1931. **Education:** Howard University, Washington, DC, B.A. 1953; Cornell University, Ithaca, New York, M.A. 1955. **Family:** Married Harold Morrison in 1958 (divorced 1964); two sons. **Career:** Instructor in English, Texas Southern University, Houston, 1955-57, and Howard University, 1957-64; senior editor, Random House, New York, 1965-84; associate professor, State University of New York at Purchase, 1971-72; visiting lecturer, Yale University, New Haven, Connecticut, 1976-77, Rutgers University, New Brunswick, New Jersey, 1983-84, and Bard College, Annandale-on-Hudson, New York, 1986-88; Schweitzer Professor of Humanities, State University of New York at Albany, 1984-89; Regents' lecturer, University of California, Berkeley, 1987; Santagata lecturer, Bowdoin College, Brunswick, Maine, 1987; professor of humanities, Princeton University, New Jersey, beginning 1989. **Awards:** American Academy award, 1977; National Book Critics Circle Award, 1977; New York State Governor's award, 1985; Book-of-the-Month Club award, 1986; Before Columbus Foundation award, 1988; Robert F. Kennedy award, 1988; Melcher award, 1988; Pulitzer Prize, 1988; Nobel Prize for literature, 1993. Honorary degree: College of Saint Rose, Albany, 1987. **Agent:** International Creative Management, 40 West 57th Street, New York, New York 10019. **Address:** Department of Creative Writing, Princeton University, Princeton, New Jersey 08544, U.S.A.

Publications

Novels

The Bluest Eye. New York, Holt Rinehart, 1970; London, Chatto & Windus, 1979.
Sula. New York, Knopf, 1973; London, Allen Lane, 1974.
Song of Solomon. New York, Knopf, 1977; London, Chatto & Windus, 1978.
Tar Baby. New York, Knopf, and London, Chatto & Windus, 1981.
Beloved. New York, Knopf, and London, Chatto & Windus, 1987.
Jazz. New York, Knopf, and London, Chatto & Windus, 1992.

Short Story

"Recitatif," in *Confirmation: An Anthology of African American Women,* edited by Amiri Baraka and Amina Baraka. New York, Quill, 1983.

Play

Dreaming Emmett (produced Albany, New York, 1986).

Essays

Playing in the Dark: Whiteness and the Literary Imagination. Cambridge, Massachusetts, Harvard University Press, 1992.

Uncollected Essays

"What the Black Woman Thinks about Women's Lib," in *New York Times Magazine*, 22 August 1971.
"A Slow Walk of Trees (as Grandmother Would Say) Hopeless (as Grandfather Would Say)," in *New York Times Magazine,* 4 July 1976.
"Memory, Creation, and Writing," in *Thought,* 59, December 1984.
"Blacks vs. Browns," in *Arguing Immigration: The Debate over the Changing Face of America,* edited by Nicolaus Mills. New York, Simon & Schuster, 1994.

Other

Editor, *The Black Book.* New York, Random House, 1974.
Editor, *Race-ing Justice, En-gendering Power: Essays on Anita Hill, Clarence Thomas, and the Construction of Social Reality.* New York, Pantheon, 1992; London, Chatto & Windus, 1993.

*

Bibliography: *Toni Morrison: An Annotated Bibliography* by David L. Middleton, New York, Garland, 1987.

Critical Studies: *New Dimensions of Spirituality: A Biracial and Bicultural Reading of the Novels of Toni Morrison* by Karla F.C. Holloway, New York, Greenwood Press, 1987; *Critical Essays on Toni Morrison* by Nellie Y. McKay, Boston, G.K. Hall, 1988; *The Crime of Innocence in the Fiction of Toni Morrison* by Terry Otten, Columbia, University of Missouri Press, 1989; *Race, Gender, and Desire: Narrative Strategies in the Fiction of Toni Cade Bambara, Toni Morrison, and Alice Walker* by Elliott Butler-Evans, Philadelphia, Temple University Press, 1989; *Modern Critical Views: Toni Morrison* by Harold Bloom, New York, Chelsea House, 1990; *Toni Morrison* by Wilfred D. Samuels and Clenora Hudson-Weems, Boston, Twayne, 1990; *Down from the Mountaintop: Black Women's Novels in the Wake of the Civil Rights Movement, 1966-1989* by Melissa Walker, New Haven, Connecticut, Yale University Press, 1991; *The Dilemma of "Double-Consciousness": Toni Morrison's Novels* by Denise Heinz, Athens, University of Georgia Press, 1993.

* * *

Toni Morrison's novels reveal the feminist issues concerning black women, issues often forgotten in many feminist discussions; Alice Walker would coin this expanded definition of feminism that includes issues related to women of color "womanism." In her six novels, Morrison interrogates and deconstructs the long-held stereotypical images of black women as oversexed or desexed, all powerful or powerless, idealized or otherized. Her portraits of black women dismantle these myths by revealing a more complex characterization than these stereotypes suggest. She also resists the pressure to portray only positive or idealistic characters. Instead, Morrison's representation of black women is realistic and varied, ranging from the heroic to the pathetic, from the average to the pariah, from the murdered to the murderer. Her method of characterization is based on empathy, unveiling the humanity in and motives behind silenced voices of the misrepresented and the misunderstood.

Morrison also explores the victimization of black women that goes beyond a simple patriarchy. Whether it is the black men they love, the white men who enslave and violate them, the impossible standards of beauty, or the black community's tendency to label what it does not understand as "evil," the forces that oppress black women have the potential to crush them, body and mind. However, some women survive these odds and point to the possibility of flight.

Morrison's first novel, *The Bluest Eye,* explores the destructive consequences of the standard of white beauty when adopted by a poor, black community. This ideal is symbolized by a young black girl's desire for blue eyes and the way the world must look through them, illustrated by the related image of the perfect middle-class whites found in the Dick-and-Jane primer quoted throughout the novel. Eleven-year-old Pecola Breedlove has been consistently told that she is ugly, so she believes that the only way she can be loved is by having "the bluest eyes," a quest for the impossible which ultimately leads her into madness. The narrator of the novel, Claudia MacTeer, looks back regretfully at these events, partially comprehending the harm of the cultural standards embodied by actress Shirley Temple and little white dolls.

The destruction of the young black girl, however, is not so simple. Pecola reflects the self-hatred of the entire community. Morrison illustrates how the community that is oppressed by white ideals of beauty unknowingly becomes its own oppressor: Pecola's family, her peers, and the community contribute to her gradual demise. Her mother, a maid, values the physical beauty that she sees in her employer's perfect house, with its clean linens and beautiful white children. She thus neglects and abuses her own small house, secondhand clothes, and black children. Pecola's father expresses his love by raping and impregnating his own daughter. The community blames her for the incestuous pregnancy, so they ostracize her. Ultimately, the standard that equates whiteness with beauty evolves into an ideal of light-skinned blacks. Maureen Peal is the community's counterpart to Shirley Temple: despite having six fingers and a dog tooth, she is a "high-yellow dream child" who knows that she is "cute," whereas the other girls are "black" and therefore ugly. The standard of blue eyes that extends beauty only to white girls and the fairy-tale family of the grade-school primer eventually destroys the community, where now marigolds will not grow, black girls will go insane, and adults will only be able to ask how this came to be.

Sula, Morrison's second novel, delves into the lives and sexuality of two best friends, Sula Peace and Nel Wright. While Nel is a repressed woman who tries to live a quiet, average life, Sula is her foil: the amoral free spirit who leaves the town for ten years and returns a pariah for her self-fulfilling sexuality and for accepting no boundaries. Nel is a representative of the community that ultimately brands Sula a witch because they cannot understand or, more importantly, control her behavior. As children, Nel and Sula are inseparable; they are two half-selves, whole only when they are together. When they grow up, however, their friendship is interrupted by Nel's initiation to the standards of morality and possession. When Sula has sex with Nel's husband and fails to understand the consequences on their friendship, Nel cites the code of possession that dictates that Jude belonged to her and therefore not to Sula. The granddaughter of Eva Peace—a one-legged matriarch who fiercely nurtured her family and took pride in her sexuality by wearing one fancy shoe—and the daughter of Hannah Peace—whose promiscuity taught Sula the pleasures of sex—Sula has crossed a boundary she does not understand. In fact, Sula confronts the borders between right and wrong, good and evil. After Nel has heaped all of her anger upon Sula for years, Sula asks Nel "'About who was good. How you know it was you?'" Twenty-five years after Sula's death, Nel finally considers this question and mourns her loyalty to the town's mores over her beloved best friend. She cries, "'We was girls together ... O Lord, Sula ... girl, girl, girlgirlgirl.'"

Her third novel, *Song of Solomon,* explores the perspective of a black man as what Morrison calls "a delight in dominion—a definite need to exercise dominion over place and people." Milkman, the protagonist, gradually learns to fly—a symbol for his surrender to love, family, and history—in the search for his own identity with the necessary guidance of his aunt, Pilate. Like Sula, Pilate is a pariah for her unconventional life; however, Pilate is a survivor, creating a healthy, nurturing environment for her family and eventually finding her own way through the collective consciousness and history of her family. Lacking a navel and following the advice of her father's ghost, she is a supernatural presence who serves as the spiritual mother and guide for Milkman—and herself—through the ancestral songs and stories. However she is very real in her earthy womanhood: She wears men's clothes, cares nothing for material wealth or proper appearances, and supports her family by bootlegging, thus defining her own role as a woman beyond the constraints under which Milkman's mother, Ruth Dead, and her own granddaughter, Hagar, suffer. Ruth is passive and silent, starved for the love of the men in her life. Her only solace is found in nursing Milkman far beyond the appropriate age. Hagar, Milkman's lover, cannot survive his rejection of her smothering love and ultimately fails even at her attempts to kill him. These women are Pilate's foils: if they are the products of the cultural expectations for black women, then Pilate is Morrison's answer.

Tar Baby, Morrison's fourth novel, is unique in that explores the world beyond an insular black community. Morrison unveils the myth of the idealized white woman in the characterization of Margaret Street, the wife of a rich and powerful landowner in the West Indies. Street is a former beauty queen who is pedestalled on Valerian's lush estate, yet she is revealed to be unloved, unstable, and even abusive to her own infant son. In a misguided rebellion against the patriarchal power that has imprisoned her, she strikes back at its weakest point: an innocent child who ultimately grows up to reject that same patriarchy. At the heart of the book, however, is the inner conflict of Jadine, a Sorbonne-educated black woman determined to define her own life. Jadine is torn between the white patriarchy that gave her the education and opportunity to become a wealthy, successful model, the ancestral black women who accuse her of forfeiting her heritage, and the black man who beckons her to sexuality and domesticity. Unable to resolve this conflict, Jadine is Morrison's ambivalent portrait of the successful, self-determined black woman whose status alienates from her cultural heritage.

In her next book, Morrison redefines the conventional genre of the realistic novel by confusing the linear, chronological sequence and by writing magical realism—disruptions that resemble some of her heroines' attempts to negotiate the constraining boundaries of tradition. In *Beloved,* which won the Pulitzer Prize in 1988, Morrison's world is alive with the supernatural: the title character is the adult ghost of a murdered baby. Through this incarnation, Morrison explores why a mother could commit the unthinkable: kill her own child. Based on a historical incident, the novel gives voice to a woman whose actions were condemned by some for murder and hailed by others for asserting the humanity of her race. After Sethe—a pregnant slave valued for her breeding ability—heard the overseer teaching her children that slaves are animals, a different species from human beings, she determined to escape North to shield her family from such dehumanization and to prevent her separation and estrangement from her children, the typical fate of slave families. Before she could escape, however, Sethe survived a symbolic rape by this overseer who stole her milk and then left his mark on her back with a scar resembling a chokecherry tree. After escaping, she sliced her baby girl's throat to prevent her from suffering the same violence that Sethe experienced as a female slave. Eighteen years later, her beloved baby returns as a young woman who craves both affection and answers from her mother. Ultimately, Beloved—the ghostly manifestation of the guilt and blame for the murder—drains Sethe's life force until she is rescued by her now teenage daughter Denver and the women in the community, who exorcise the ghost and the guilt of the past. Thus, *Beloved* is Morrison's powerhouse of womanist writing in its reinscription of literary conventions and traditional portraits of a benevolent slave system and its kindly masters.

Morrison's recent novel, *Jazz,* like *Song of Solomon,* revolves around the significance of personal and collective history. However, the characterizations reveal her continuing interest in interrogating the destructiveness of idealized womanhood, as in her first novel. Bearing the name of a flower—the conventional symbol of beautiful, youthful womanhood—middle-aged Violet Trace knows she falls short of this ideal, for her beauty has faded, as has the love of her husband. Joe has taken a teenage lover and eventually murders her to stop time, thereby holding on to his idealistic love by preventing her from leaving him and from aging. Violet lashes out at the impossible standard of youthful beauty embodied by the dead girl by mutilating her face, the representation of what she should be. In this way, she riffs on the expectations of her name by earning the name "Violent" instead. *Jazz* comes full circle in Toni Morrison's attempt to unveil the debilitating consequences of unattainable ideals of beauty and behavior on black women. She has also subverted the similarly reductionist and confining negative stereotypes: the asexual matriarchs have become sexualized, the black mammy has asserted her humanity by killing her own child, and the pariahs have defied boundaries, interpreted their own histories, and taught us to fly.

—Nancy L. Chick

MORROW, Jacob. *See* **MANNING, Olivia.**

MORTLAKE, G. N. *See* **STOPES, Marie (Charlotte).**

MOTT, Lucretia (Coffin)

Nationality: American. **Born:** Nantucket, Massachusetts, 3 January 1793. **Education:** Educated at Nine Partners Quaker school, Poughkeepsie, New York. **Family:** Married James Mott in 1811 (died 1868); six children. **Career:** Teacher at Nine Partners Quaker boarding school, Poughkeepsie, New York; moved to Philadelphia and became a Quaker minister, c. 1818; charter member, Female Anti-Slavery Society, Philadelphia, Pennsylvania, 1833; delegate to World's Anti-Slavery Convention, London, 1840; founder, Association for the Relief and Employment of Poor Women, Philadelphia; leader, with Elizabeth Cady Stanton, Women's Rights Convention, Seneca Falls, New York, 1848; sheltered fugitive slaves, beginning 1850; appointed president, American Equal Rights Association, 1866-69; chairman, Equal Rights Convention, 1866. **Died:** 11 November 1880.

Publications

Essays

Discourse on Woman (speech delivered December 17, 1849). Philadelphia, T. B. Peterson, 1850.

Lucretia Mott: Her Complete Speeches and Sermons, edited by Dana Greene. New York, E. Mellen Press, 1980.

Other

James and Lucretia Mott: Life and Letters, edited by Anna Davis Hallowell. N.p., 1884.

Slavery and "The Woman Question": Lucretia Mott's Diary of Her Visit to Great Britain to Attend the World's Anti-Slavery Convention of 1840, edited by Frederick B. Tolles. London and Haverford, Pennsylvania, Friends' Historical Association, 1952.

*

Critical Studies: *Lucretia Mott* by Otelia Cromwell, Cambridge, Massachusetts, Harvard University Press, 1958; *Lucretia Mott, Early Leader of the Women's Liberation Movement* by Gerald Kurland, Charlottesville, New York, SamHar Press, 1972; *Valiant Friend: The Life of Lucretia Mott* by Margaret Hope Beacon, New York, Walker, 1980.

* * *

Lucretia Mott, one of the leading figures in the history of 19th-century U.S. reform, fought to extend the promises embedded in the Declaration of Independence to all, but to slaves and to women in particular. Like other prominent female reformers of the era, Mott's experience with gender discrimination within antislavery organizations awakened her to the need to agitate for women's rights. Together with Elizabeth Cady Stanton, she organized the first women's rights convention in Seneca Falls, New York in 1848 and became a revered and unifying force in the movement until well after the Civil War.

The second of seven children born to Anna and Thomas Coffin, Mott received early training in women's rights in the Quaker household on Nantucket Island where she was raised. Mott not only observed the self-sufficiency of Nantucket women who lived independently during their husbands' long absences at sea, but as Quakers, her family believed in the spiritual equality of the sexes. As Mott later recalled, "I grew up so thoroughly imbued with women's rights that it was the most important question of my life from a very early day." She attended schools in Boston from 1804 to 1806 after her family moved to that city. She received further education at Nine Partners, a Quaker boarding school near Poughkeepsie, New York, and became an assistant teacher there at age 15. In 1809 she followed her family to Philadelphia and two years later she married James Mott, a fellow teacher at Nine Partners and an employee in her father's hardware business.

Although busy with domestic responsibilities (she bore six children between 1812 and 1828), in 1821 Mott became a Quaker minister, a position that recognized her spiritual leadership and fluency as a public speaker. By 1827, however, she broke with orthodox Quakers and allied herself with Elias Hicks, leader of the "Hicksite" faction, a group that rejected the tendency toward hierarchical control present within many Quaker meetings. Under the influence of Hicks, Mott began her sustained attack on slavery and from 1825 on, she never knowingly used any products grown or manufactured by slaves.

Mott's opposition to slavery coincided with the development of the organized antislavery movement in America. She attended the convention called by noted abolitionist William Lloyd Garrison in Philadelphia in 1833 that formed the American Anti-Slavery Society; since despite Garrison's support of women's rights this national organization refused to admit women, she helped organize the Philadelphia Female Anti-Slavery Society. Committed to acknowledging and encouraging women's activism in the antislavery movement, Mott was one of the leading figures in the Anti-Slavery Convention of American Women that met in 1837. When the American Anti-Slavery Society changed its policy and began admitting women, Mott assumed a number of leadership roles within that organization.

The World's Anti-Slavery Convention held in London in 1840 proved critical not only to Mott's development as a women's rights activist, but to the history of the women's rights movement in America. Unlike the American Anti-Slavery Society, the antislavery organizations controlling this convention refused to admit female delegates. Seated off the convention floor, "behind the bar," Mott and Elizabeth Cady Stanton, the new wife of antislavery delegate Henry Stanton, resolved to take action against the injustices done to women, injustices evident even within organizations presumably committed to establishing human equality. Eight years later in Seneca Falls, New York, Mott and Stanton, along with Mott's younger sister, Martha Coffin Wright, fulfilled the pledge they had made to each other in London and held the first women's rights convention in America. Presenting a Declaration of Sentiments modeled on the Declaration of Independence, they protested against men's long tyranny over women and made a series of demands, including a call for the right to vote.

Mott became one of the women's rights movement's leading activists, attending and presiding over conventions and using her talent for oratory for the movement's benefit. One of her most persuasive speeches, *Discourse on Woman,* was published in 1850. Prepared as a response to Richard Henry Dana's "Address on Woman," Mott countered his claim that women were in every respect weaker than men and thus best suited to remain at home, outside public life. She offered examples of women's natural ability dating back to biblical times and insisted that Dana's work simply illustrated the effects of the oppression and unequal opportunities that had been women's experience for centuries.

Although she was in her 70s by the time the Civil War ended, Mott remained involved in antislavery and women's rights activism as these movements met with postwar challenges. After emancipation, leading abolitionists, including William Lloyd Garrison, argued that antislavery organizations should disband, their work accomplished. Mott believed otherwise and worked to bring education to the recently emancipated southern blacks. At Elizabeth Cady Stanton's insistence, Mott became the first president of the American Equal Rights Association in 1866, a group committed to agitating for the rights of both blacks and women. This organization splintered three years later, however, when it became clear that the Republican party would support suffrage for black men, but not for women, white or black. Albeit unsuccessfully, it was Mott who tried to effect an early reconciliation between those women willing to postpone their fight for the vote until black men had won the battle for full citizenship and those who believed that the fight for woman suffrage must not be subordinated to any other cause. It would be this issue that would dominate and divide members of the U.S. suffrage movement for decades to come.

—Anne Lewis Osler

MUKHERJEE, Bharati

Nationality: American. **Born:** Calcutta, India, 27 July 1940; became Canadian citizen, 1972; naturalized U.S. citizen. **Education:** Loreto Convent School, Calcutta; University of Calcutta, B.A. (honors) in English 1959; University of Baroda, Gujarat, M.A. in English and ancient Indian culture 1961; University of Iowa, Iowa City, M.F.A. in creative writing 1963, Ph.D. in English and comparative literature 1969. **Family:** Married Clark Blaise in 1963; two sons. **Career:** Instructor in English, Marquette University, Milwaukee, Wisconsin, 1964-65, and University of Wisconsin—Madison, 1965; lecturer, 1966-69, assistant professor, 1969-73, associate professor, 1973-78, and professor, 1978, McGill University, Montreal; professor, Skidmore College, Saratoga Springs, New York; associate professor, Montclair State College, New Jersey, 1984-87, and Queen's College, City University of New York, Flushing, 1987-89; professor, University of California, Berkeley, beginning 1990. **Awards:** Canada Arts Council grant, 1973, 1977; Guggenheim fellowship, 1977; National Book Critics Circle award, 1989, for *The Middleman.* **Agent:** Lynn Nesbit, Yanklow & Nesbit Associates, 598 Madison Ave., New York, New York 10022, U.S.A. **Address:** Department of English, University of California, Berkeley, 322 Wheeler Hall, Berkeley, California 94720-0001, U.S.A.

Publications

Novels

The Tiger's Daughter. Boston, Houghton Mifflin, 1972; London, Chatto & Windus, 1973.
Wife. Boston, Houghton Mifflin, 1975; London, Penguin, 1987.
Jasmine. New York, Grove Weidenfeld, 1989; London, Virago Press, 1990.
The Holder of the World. New York, Knopf, and London, Chatto & Windus, 1993.

Short Stories

Darkness. Toronto, Penguin, 1985; New York, Fawcett, 1990.
The Middleman and Other Stories. New York, Grove Press, 1988; London, Virago Press, 1989.

Play

Screenplay: *Days and Nights in Calcutta,* with Clark Blaise, 1991.

Other

Days and Nights in Calcutta, with Clark Blaise. New York, Doubleday, 1977; London, Penguin, 1986.
The Sorrow and the Terror: The Haunting Legacy of the Air India Tragedy, with Clark Blaise. Toronto, Viking, 1987.

*

Critical Studies: *Bharati Mukherjee: Critical Perspectives* edited by Emmanuel S. Nelson, New York, Garland Press, 1993; "*Jasmine* or the Americanization of an Asian" by Gönül Pultar, in *Journal of American Studies in Turkey,* 2, fall 1995; *Bharati Mukherjee* by Fakrul Alam, New York, Twayne, 1995.

Bharati Mukherjee comments:
I write to discover ideal worlds; I live to repair ruined ones.

* * *

Bharati Mukherjee is perhaps one of the most well-known writers from the Indian diaspora in the United States. Her writing, both fictional and non-fictional, belongs to the growing category of immigrant literature that explores the complex cross-cultural forces which structure the diasporic experience. Mukherjee is specially interested in the cultural dynamics of immigration in relation to women's sense of self-identity. Focusing on the multiple, and at times conflicting, life-scripts that inscribe the lives of women as they move from India to the New World, Mukherjee traces the process of immigrant women's subject-formation. It is her concern with female immigrant subjectivity, and her emphasis on women's agency in the construction of this subject-position as a form of personal liberation, which clearly marks Mukherjee as a feminist writer.

Born in Calcutta, India, in an upper-caste/upper-class Bengali family, Mukherjee first came to the United States as a graduate student at the age of 21. Unlike her sister, who was overcome by homesickness and quickly returned to India, Mukherjee successfully adapted to her life in America. In 1963 she married an American fellow student, Clark Blaise, in a civil ceremony that marked a self-conscious disassociation from her Indian past. Mukherjee thus moved from being a nostalgic expatriate to an exuberant immigrant who forged a new identity for herself through adaptation and assimilation. These personal experiences are reflected clearly in her fictional writing, which celebrates the liberatory potential of the immigrant experience for women. However, despite this celebration, Mukherjee is unable to break away completely from her past; India remains a constant presence in her writing, forcing her female protagonists to live a dual existence that complicates their freedom to create a new sense of identity for themselves.

This sense of being caught between two worlds is most evident in Mukherjee's first two novels, *The Tiger's Daughter* and *Wife*. Both Tara and Dimple are eager to escape from the constricting atmosphere in India and embrace the freedom offered by life in the United States. Tara's decision to marry an American and Dimple's decision to live at a distance from the mini-India created by the insular group of Indian families in Queens, New York, are symbolic acts of autonomous agency that indicate a rejection of the past by the two women. Mukherjee appears to be making a clear distinction between the oppressive socio-cultural traditions of India and the individual freedom characteristic of American society. By rejecting the former and embracing the latter, these two women are able to develop an independent sense of selfhood. But this sense of freedom is complicated by a sense of isolation and guilt. Tara is unable to communicate her feelings during her Indian vacation either to her American husband or her Indian friends, while Dimple experiences psychological problems as she faces the conflicting demands of Indian tradition and American liberation.

Mukherjee's awareness of the psychic trauma that accompanies the construction of an autonomous immigrant identity for Indian women is reflected in the strong undercurrent of violence that runs through her novels. The rapes, riots, and murders that proliferate in these texts have frequently been seen by critics as symbolic of the violence that is endemic to the condition of postcoloniality. More specifically, given Mukherjee's feminist agenda, this violence may be seen as a literal metaphor for the cultural displacement that characterizes the immigrant experience especially for women as they attempt to create a new identity for themselves. While westernization, whether in terms of dress or individualist thinking, is seen as a mark of success in a man, it is viewed as a moral failing in Indian women. Therefore when women like Tara and Dimple consciously adopt certain "western" ways of thinking, this is done at the cost of a violent disruption of their moral sensibilities. This inner conflict is externalized by Mukherjee in the violence that surrounds her female characters. At the same time, this violence is also symptomatic of the actual physical violence that threatens women in both India and America. Mukherjee is careful to emphasize that adapting to an American way of life does not automatically ensure complete liberation for Indian immigrant women.

To adapt and survive, according to Mukherjee, the women have to constantly resist any easy acceptance of a single, monolithic identity, Indian or American. The liberatory aspect of immigrant identity for women lies in its multiplicity and hybridity. This is seen in Mukherjee's later novels, *Jasmine* and *The Holder of the World*. Jyoti/Jase/Jasmine/Jane and "Salem bibi," the female protagonists of these two novels respectively, simultaneously inhabit different cultural spaces as is reflected in their names. The protagonist of *Jasmine* refuses to remain either the submissive Jyoti as demanded by Indian feudal traditions or become the dutiful Midwestern wife Jane; instead she embraces her identity as Jasmine and rebels against traditional expectations in both India and America. Similarly, Hannah, the "Salem bibi," negotiates new identities for herself as she moves between America, England, and India, constantly assimilating the liberating potential offered by each cultural milieu without conforming to the demands of any single tradition.

Mukherjee's two collections of short stories, *Darkness* and *The Middleman and Other Stories,* also concentrate on the immigrant experience, but do not focus exclusively of the woman's perspective. In several of her short stories, like "The Imaginary Assassin" and "Danny's Girls," Mukherjee adopts a male persona. These stories, especially those in *The Middleman* also move beyond an exclusive focus on Indian immigrants to a consideration of various other immigrant experiences. This expanded focus facilitates Mukherjee's questioning of the American Dream and the accessibility of its promise of individual freedom for marginalized immigrants in the United States. Bharati Mukherjee's work, therefore, shows ideological development, moving from an assimilationist celebration of America as the land of freedom and a clear rejection of repressive Indian traditions, to an awareness of the complex multiplicity of immigrant experiences. At the same time, in feminist terms, she moves from an emphasis on the liberating potential of American individualism to an exploration of the possibilities of cross-national/cross-cultural alliances that deconstruct rigid East/West oppositions and foster the construction of a self-affirming hybrid identity for women.

—Suchitra Mathur

MYRDAL, Alva

Nationality: Swedish. **Born:** Uppsala, 31 January 1902. **Education:** University of Stockholm, B.A. 1924; Uppsala University M.A. 1934; studied in London, Leipzig, Geneva, and New York. **Family:** Married the economist (Karl) Gunnar Myrdal in 1924; two daughters, one son. **Career:** Teacher for Workers' Education Association, Stockholm, 1924-32; psychological assistant, Central Prison, Stockholm, 1932-34; founder and director, Training College for Preschool Teachers (Social Pedagogical Institute), Stockholm, 1936-48; principal director, United Nations Department of Social Affairs, New York, 1949-50; director, Department of Social Sciences of UNESCO, Paris, 1951-55; Swedish minister to Burma, 1955-58, ambassador to India and minister to Ceylon, 1955-61, ambassador to Nepal, 1960-61, and ambassador-at-large, 1961-66; elected to Senate as Social Democratic candidate, Swedish Parliament, 1962-70; leader of Swedish delegation, Geneva Disarmament Conference, 1962-70; member of Swedish delegation to UN General Assembly, New York, 1962-73; chairman, expert group on South Africa, 1964; deputy leader, 1967-73, then chairman, committee on disarmament and development; cabinet minister for disarmament, 1966-73; cabinet member for church affairs,

1969-73. Visiting fellow, Center for the Study of Democratic Institutions, Santa Barbara, California, 1973-74; visiting professor of sociology, Massachusetts Institute of Technology, 1974-75; Visiting Distinguished Slater Professor of Sociology, Wellesley College, Massachusetts, 1976; research fellow, Institute for Research on Poverty, Madison, Wisconsin, 1977. Member, government committee on social housing, 1935-38; Royal Population Commission, 1935-38; committee on postwar planning, Social Democratic Party and Trade Union Federation, 1943; Scientific Council for a Swedish Gallup Institute, 1943-44; government committee on the handicapped 1943-47; British Royal Population Commission, 1945; Social Democratic Party's Program Commission, 1944-48; government committee on organization and social information services, 1946-48; Royal Commission on Educational Reform 1946-48; Commission on Disestablishment of the Swedish State Church, 1968-72. Chair, Swedish Civic Organization for Cultural Relief in Europe, 1943-48; Stockholm International Peace Research Institute, 1965-66; Commission on Studies of the Future, 1971-72; Delegation for expanding international laws against brutality in war, 1972-73. Adviser, Education for Peace, 1982-86. Coeditor, *Morgonbris*, 1936-38; editor, *Via Suecia*, 1945-46, and *Round Table on Social Problems*, 1946-48. Contributor to periodicals, including *Bulletin of Atomic Sciences, Foreign Policy, Independent Woman, Parents' Magazine,* and *Scientific American.* **Awards:** Rockefeller Foundation fellowship, 1929-30; Doctor of Law, Mount Holyoke College, 1950, and University of Edinburgh, 1964; Doctor of Humane Letters, Columbia University, 1965, and Temple University, 1968; West German Peace Prize (with Gunnar Myrdal), 1970; Doctor of Divinity, Gustavus Adolphus University, 1971; Hague Academy of International Peace Wateler Prize, 1973; Royal Swedish Institute of Technology prize, 1975; Women's International League for Peace and Freedom Award, 1975; Monismanien Prize for protection of civil liberties, 1976; Royal Swedish Academy of Sciences Gold Medal, 1977; Albert Einstein Peace Award, 1980; Nehru Prize for International Understanding, 1981; People's Peace Prize, 1982; Nobel Peace Prize (with Alfonso García Robles), 1982. Honorary degrees: University of Leeds, 1962; Brandeis University, 1974; University of Gothenburg, 1975; University of East Anglia, 1976; Helsinki, 1981. **Member:** State Commission on Women's Work (chief secretary, 1935-38), Stockholm Organization of Business and Professional Women (vice-chair, 1932-35), Swedish Federation of Business and Professional Women (chair, 1936-38, 1940-42), International Federation of Business and Professional Women (vice-chair, 1938-47), World Council on Preschool Education (chair, 1946-48), Stockholm School of Social Work (member, board of directors, 1944-47), World Federation of United Nations (executive member, 1948-50). **Died:** Stockholm, 1 February 1986.

Publications

Political/Social Theory

Kris i befolkinsfrågen [Crisis in the Population Question], with Gunnar Myrdal. Stockholm, S. Bonnier, 1934; adapted and translated as *Nation and Family: The Swedish Experiment in Democratic Family and Population Policy,* New York and London, Harper Bros., 1941; revised edition, 1965.
Stadsbarn: en bok om deras fostran i storbarnkammare [City Children]. Stockholm, Kooperativa forbundet, 1935.
Women in the Community. Copenhagen, TARP, 1943.
America's Role in International Social Welfare, with Arthur J. Altermeyer and Dean Rusk. New York, Columbia University Press, 1955.
Women's Two Roles: Home and Work, with Viola Klein. New York, Humanities Press, and London, Routledge and Kegan Paul, 1956; revised edition, 1968.
Vårt ansvar für de fattiga folken: Utvecklingsproblem i social närbild [Our Responsibility for the Poor Peoples: Development Problems at Close View]. Copenhagen, Raben & Sjoegren, 1961.
"Disarmament and the United Nations," in *The Quest for Peace,* edited by Andrew W. Cordier and Wilder Foote. N.p., 1962; published separately, New York, Columbia University Press, 1965.
Disarmament: Reality or Illusion? N.p., 1965.
Ökad jämlikhet. N.p., 1969; abridged edition translated as *Towards Equality,* n.p., 1971.
The Right to Conduct Nuclear Explosions: Political Aspects and Policy Proposals. Stockholm, Stockholm International Peace Research Institute, 1975.
The Game of Disarmament: How the United States and Russia Run the Arms Race. New York, Pantheon, and Manchester, Manchester University Press, 1977; revised edition, New York, Pantheon, 1982.
Wars, Weapons, and Everyday Violence. N.p. 1977.
Dynamics of European Nuclear Disarmament, with others. London, Spokesman, 1981.

Other

Right Playthings. Stockholm, Kooperativa forbundet, 1936.
Kontakt med Amerika [Contact with America], with Gunnar Myrdal. Stockholm, Bonnier, 1941.
"Statement by Alva Myrdal upon Receiving the International Award from the Albert Einstein Peace Prize Foundation, 29 May 1980," in *Disarmament: A Periodic Review of the United Nations,* 3, November 1980.
"Nobel Lecture," in *Scandinavian Review,* 71, 1983.

*

Bibliography: *Alva Myrdal: Kommenterad Bibliografi, 1932-1961* (with English translation) by Barbro Terling, Stockholm, Alva och Gunnar Myrdals stiftelse, 1987.

Manuscript Collections: Arbetarrorelsen Arkiv och bibliotek, Stockholm.

Critical Studies: Review of *Women's Two Roles* by Mirra Komarovsky, in *American Journal of Sociology,* 63, November 1957; *The Swedish Experiment in Family Politics: The Myrdals and the Interwar Population Crisis* by Allan Carlson, New Brunswick, New Jersey, Transaction, 1990; *Alva Myrdal: A Daughter's Memoir* by Sissela Bok, Reading, Massachusetts, Addison-Wesley, 1991.

* * *

Alva Myrdal was one of the most influential social reformers of the 20th century. The trajectory of her life's work covered an ever-expanding scope of social concerns. Beginning in the 1930s with a number of books and articles on social issues that influenced the development of the European welfare state, Myrdal's research would eventually encompass nuclear disarmament, winning her the 1982 Nobel Peace Prize. Throughout her life she worked to ameliorate inequality at all levels, between men and women, members of different classes, and nation-states. When Myrdal heard her life's work described as the striving for equality, she commented, "'Equality' is the shape that the dream takes, but the emotional side has to do with 'justice.'"

Myrdal was strongly influenced by her father, Albert Reimer, a building contractor and active councilperson, her mother, Lova Larsson Reimer, mother of five, and an early teacher, Per Sundberg, the leader of the Swedish Quakers. Her Social Democratic parents instilled in her a desire to work to change society for the better. Despite the limited educational prospects for women during the 1920s, Myrdal received a B.A. from the University of Stockholm, even holding the prestigious Sokestraus scholarship, and continued her formal education at several universities in the fields of philosophy, psychology, and sociology. She later earning her M.A. in social psychology.

Right after receiving her B.A., she married Gunnar Myrdal, who became a prominent economist and sociologist. Together they had three children—Jan, Sissela, and Kaj—during the course of their strong marriage; as Alva once admitted, "We have never found anybody else so interesting to talk to." Their relationship also flourished because it allowed both Gunnar and Alva to immerse themselves in separate careers.

Inspired by her early career as a teacher of young children, Myrdal's first books and articles addressed the problems of housing, poverty, access to education, working conditions for parents, and institutionalized support for child rearing. *Kris i befolkinsfrågen* (Crisis in the Population Question), which Myrdal co-authored with her husband, aroused concern over the shrinking birth rate and helped implement national welfare programs in Sweden, Denmark, and Norway after its publication in 1934. The Myrdals' ideas would strongly influence European and American welfare policy as well after Alva adapted and translated their work as *Nation and Family.* She provided an in-depth analysis of the family-oriented policies developed in Sweden, and reiterated her earlier call for policies that would provide benefits and services to help subsidize the costs of raising children, thereby maintaining the birth rate.

The Social Pedagogical Institute, which Myrdal founded and directed from 1936-1948, promoted progressive educational theories in child care. Her work during this period placed her in positions of nation-wide policy formation, heading a government commission on women's work, chairing the Swedish Federation of Business and Professional Women, and vice-chairing the International Federation of Business and Professional Women. Myrdal continued to emphasize issues of equality for women, women's right to work, and the difficulties of single motherhood. Her home in Sweden became an center for European intellectuals intent on planning a postwar vision of Europe. She herself focused on the "refugee question" and served as a member of the labor movement's postwar commission.

Soon Myrdal's policy platform became international as well. When appointed director of the United Nations Department of Social Affairs in 1949, she became the first woman to hold a high-ranking position in the UN. Two years later she was appointed director of the UNESCO Department of Social Sciences in Paris. At the UN she became a well-known and lauded force for humane national and international policy-making. In New York and Paris, Myrdal's work on welfare for children and the poor led her to address the dilemma faced by working women. In her book *Women's Two Roles,* written with psychologist Viola Klein, Myrdal discussed critical issues for women, including their increasing career opportunities, and the difficulty of balancing their roles at work and in the home. Myrdal believed and argued that women should devote themselves to full-time work for the majority of their lives. Although some reviewers suggested that the work/home dilemma was only an issue for very few, usually highly educated, women, others applauded the book's careful, historically contextualized analyses; noted feminist sociologist, Mirra Komarovsky argued in *American Journal of Sociology* that the book "makes an important contribution by its well-argued case for reconciliation of women's two roles." At Myrdal's memorial service, her daughter Sissela spoke about how Myrdal herself had no role models to guide her in her ambition to combine a career with a full family life; and as a mother she was determined to provide such a model for her daughters. Myrdal viewed women's issues as key in ameliorating living conditions for all.

Beginning in 1955 Myrdal accepted appointments as Swedish ambassador to India and Nepal and minister to Ceylon and Burma. In 1961 she returned to Sweden to serve as ambassador-at-large, and was also elected to the Swedish Senate as a Social Democratic candidate. In these positions disarmament and peace became central to Myrdal's concerns. After spending a number of years acting as Swedish Cabinet Minister for Disarmament, she began publishing work in the area of disarmament, drawing upon her experience to examine the strategic interplay between the United States and the Soviet Union. In 1977's *The Game of Disarmament: How the United States and Russia Run the Arms Race,* Myrdal became the first to accuse these superpowers of maintaining the arms race to guarantee their own interests and predominance, arguing that détente helped institutionalize rather than reverse the arms race.

Her single-minded work in pursuing the goal of disarmament won Myrdal the Nobel Peace Prize in 1982, one of a number of impressive prizes she would receive during her career, including the West German Peace Prize (1970), the Wateler Peace Prize (1973), the Albert Einstein Peace Award (1980), and the People's Peace Prize (1982). During the late 1970s and early 1980s, Myrdal extended her work to address more general issues of societal violence, citing connections between wars, weapons, and violence. She critiqued violence from an ethical standpoint, and called for a greater commitment to the pursuit of peace. Myrdal argued vehemently that resources should be directed to social scientific research rather than militaristic technological advances, since social research has the potential of helping the world reach a meaningful state of peace. For a peaceful society to emerge, Myrdal believed, violence must be addressed in all aspects of society and culture. With this goal in mind, she supported the "Education for Peace" program, administered by the Myrdal Foundation.

"The ruin of the planet is there for all to contemplate," Myrdal would write in her 1982 preface to the second edition of *The Game of Disarmament.* "But so, too, is its potential richness if we learn to cooperate. We still have a choice. But we must act now as never before." Through her life of action, during which she expended her vast energy and enthusiasm in an effort toward improving the lot of, not only women and children, but all people, Alva Myrdal proved that one person, every person, could indeed make a difference in creating a richer quality of life.

—P. A. Duffy and Joya Misra

N

NAMJOSHI, Suniti

Nationality: Indian. **Born:** Bombay, 20 April 1941. **Education:** University of Poona, B.A. 1961, M.A. 1963; University of Missouri, M.S. in business administration 1969; McGill University, Ph.D. in English literature 1972. **Family:** Companion of poet Gillian Hanscombe since 1984. **Career:** Lecturer in English literature, University of Poona, Fergusson College, Poona, India, 1963-64; officer, Government of India Administrative Service, New Delhi, 1964-69; lecturer, 1972-73, assistant professor, 1973-78, associate professor of English literature, 1978-89, Scarborough College, University of Toronto, Scarborough, Ontario. **Awards:** Ontario Arts Council award, 1976, 1977; Canada Council award, 1981. **Member:** League of Canadian Poets. **Address:** East Devon, England.

Publications

Short Stories

Feminist Fables. London, Sheba Feminist Press, 1981.
The Conversations of Cow. New Delhi, Rupa, 1985.
The Blue Donkey Fables. London, Women's Press, 1988.
The Mothers of Maya Diip. London, Women's Press, 1989.
"Dusty Distance," in *The Inner Courtyard: Stories by Indian Women.* Calcutta, Rupa, 1991.
Hey Diddle Diddle," with Gillian Hanscombe, in *By the Light of the Silvery Moon: Short Stories to Celebrate the 10th Birthday of Silver Moon Women's Bookshop.* London, Virago, 1994.
Saint Suniti and the Dragon and Other Fables. London, Virago, 1994.

Poetry

Poems. Calcutta, Writers Workshop, 1967.
More Poems. Calcutta, Writers Workshop, 1967.
Cyclone in Pakistan. Calcutta, Writers Workshop, 1971.
The Jackass and the Lady. Calcutta, Writers Workshop, 1980.
The Authentic Lie. Fredericton, New Brunswick, Fiddlehead Poetry Books, 1982.
From the Bedside Book of Nightmares. Fredericton, New Brunswick, Fiddlehead Poetry Books, 1984.
Flesh and Paper, with Gilian Hanscombe. Seaton, Devon, Jezebel Tapes & Books, 1986.
Because of India: Selected Poems and Fables. London, Only Woman Press, 1989.

Play

Circles of Paradise, with Gillian Hanscombe (produced London, 1994).

For Children

Adita and the One-Eyed Monkey. Boston, Beacon Press, 1986; London, Sheba Feminist Press, 1986.

Other

Ezra Pound and Reality: A Study of the Metaphysics of the Cantos (thesis). Toronto, McGill University, 1972.

Translator, with mother, Sarojini Namjoshi, *Poems of Govindagraj,* by Ram Ganesh Gadkari. Calcutta, Writers Workshop, 1968.

Recordings: In *Dykeproud, A Lesbian Poetry Reading from the Third International Feminist Bookfair* (recording), 1988; *Flesh and Blood* (video), with Gillian Hanscombe, 1990.

*

Critical Studies: Articles in *Canadian Woman Studies,* winter 1982, fall 1983; article by Mary Meigs in *Room of One's Own,* February 1984; "Sister Letters: Miranda's Tempest in Canada" by Diana Brydon, in *Cross-Cutural Performances: Differences in Women's Re-Visions of Shakespeare,* edited by Marianne Novy, Urbana, University of Illinois Press, 1993; "'Cracking India': Minority Women Writers and the Contentious Margins of Indian Nationalist Discourse" by Harveen Sachdeva Mann, in *Journal of Commonwealth Literature,* 29(2), summer 1994; *Configurations of Exile: South Asian Writers and Their World* by Chelva Kanaganayakam, Toronto, TSAR, 1995.

* * *

In an epigraph for her poem *The Jackass and the Lady,* Indian poet and fabulist Suniti Namjoshi described herself thus: "Neither snake, nor prince, nor charmer, but the baffled fool for my lady in green in the well-known forest." Her feminist-lesbian self questioned the gender stereotyping of "lady," her femaleness denied her the role of "prince," her Hinduism the role of "snake," therefore, only "fool" was left. This fool, according to Namjoshi, was a "beast" but with a soul; not separated from humans but, in the Hindu tradition, a part of all creation. In *Because of India,* a 1989 compilation of her writings that includes personal introductory essays, Namjoshi elaborates on this same concept with the question, "All right, I was a beast, a creature. But what sort of beast was I?" In her many fables and poems written in English over 23 years and in four different countries, Namjoshi attempts an answer by giving voice to various creatures, including a blue donkey, a jackass, a cow, and a one-eyed monkey. These and others from Hindu and Greek myths, fairy tales, and stories from favorite English authors Lewis Carroll, Jonathan Swift, and even Shakespeare, inhabit the wry imagination of Namjoshi and help her work out her lesbian/feminist Indian diasporic identity through the medium of writing.

Namjoshi was born in Bombay in 1941, and spent her early years at a Protestant boarding school where she learned English and studied the Bible. However, she never lost her Hindu heritage; though not raised as a devout Hindu, this culture has influenced much of her writing. For example, she juxtaposes the idea of reincarnation—that our identity is composed of experiences from past lives—with the Western idea of self-identity. In *Be-*

cause of India Namjoshi recognizes that "identity is arbitrary"; however in this lifetime "as a lesbian creature" she still must "deal with all the other creatures who have their own identities." Today's "core" identities "seem to be based on gender, skin colour, sexual choice, as well as nationality and religion," she observes. "Any threat to the sense of self causes a violent reaction. But then how are we all to live?" She questions these ideas of identity in *Conversations with a Cow,* written in 1985. The cow, Bhadravati, is a lesbian Indian cow, but can change her persona from man to woman to animal. Society's reactions to differences are a main focus of *The Blue Donkey Fables,* written in 1988, which begins "Once upon a time a blue donkey lived by a red bridge. 'Inartistic,' said the councilors who governed that town. 'A donkey who lives by our bright red bridge must be of the purest and silkiest white or we must request that the said donkey be required to move on.' The matter soon turned into a political issue."

In 1964, after graduating from and teaching at the University of Poona, Namjoshi started working for the Indian administrative Service, in part to gain some independence, but was stationed in Poona, the home of her mother's family. At that time she was also fortunate to have several of her poems published by the Writers Workshop, a publisher for Indian poets writing in English. Namjoshi also learned to read and write in Marathi, her mother tongue, and did translations of Marathi poetry with her mother and grandmother.

Namjoshi spent a short time in the United States, earning an M.S. in business administration at the University of Missouri before immigrating to Canada to earn a Ph.D. in English literature at McGill University. In 1972 she was hired as a professor of English literature at the University of Toronto, from where she continued to write poetry. *The Jackass and the Lady* was used as part of her tenure, though it was published in India rather than in Canada. It was on a sabbatical from Toronto spent in London and Cambridge from 1978-79 that Namjoshi underwent a political transformation, meeting lesbian feminists and discovering feminist authors such as Adrienne Rich, to whom she would later dedicate a poem.

Returning to Toronto, Namjoshi's newly formed political consciousness permeated her next book, feminist in both title and publisher: *Feminist Fables* was released by London's Sheba Feminist Press in 1981. In these retellings of fairy tales such as "Blue Beard" and "Red Riding Hood," as well as of various Sanskrit and Greek myths, Namjoshi brings both imagination and comprehension of sexual politics to bear in writing her fables. In one telling and slyly humorous piece, "The Wicked Witch," a "handsome young dyke" asks a witch to tell her what the "real thing" is, as she has been told that lesbian love is not the real thing. The witch says "forget other people, find out for yourself."

The Authentic Lie, written in 1982, would be a slight departure from such feminist retellings. Namjoshi's poems for this collection were written as a means of dealing with her childhood grief at her test-pilot father's death in 1953, when she was only 12. She also wrote a children's story for her niece entitled *Aditi and the One-Eyed Monkey.*

In 1984's *From the Bedside Book of Nightmares* Namjoshi takes on the bard himself, retelling Shakespeare's stories of Prospero, Miranda, and Caliban. Caliban is tranformed into a female and eventually becomes a "sister" to Miranda, a concept that troubles Prospero, the egotist. Other poems view families and social institutions in all their power struggles, though they avoid didacticism through her use of innuendo, humor, and realism.

Viewing Namjoshi's work from an Indian perspective, critic Harveen Sachdeva Mann believes that Namjoshi takes on the difficult task of "construction a'nation' that has hitherto been totally ignored in modern Indian nationalist discourse, one underwritten by egalitarian lesbian sexual politics." In *Mothers of Maya Diip,* 1989, for example, she creates a lesbian who is the lover of the Hindu Goddess Saraswathi—not an typical Indian theme. However the visionary matriarchal world of mothers portrayed in this fable is not all sweetness and light; there are hierarchies and power plays and cruelty even in feminist paradises.

Namjoshi met her lover and intellectual partner, English poet Gillian Hanscombe, in 1984, and the two have collaborated on poems and plays since that time. In *Flesh and Blood,* a video with Pratibha Parmar as interviewer, they both describe falling in love, first on paper, then in person. The interview is interspersed with readings, photos, music, and impressionistic visuals.

Namjoshi retired from academia in 1989 in order to devote more time to her writing, and now lives with Hanscombe in Devon, England. Her short story collection *Saint Suniti and the Dragon,* published in 1994, continues to explore and overturn the mythic and literary images of male warrior-saints (they turn into females), literary monsters such as Grendel's mother dragging her son around, and life-destroying dragons, all in her witty, complex, and imaginative style.

—Jacquelyn Marie

NAYLOR, Gloria

Nationality: American. **Born:** New York, New York, 25 January 1950. **Education:** Brooklyn College of the City University of New York, B.A. in English (summa cum laude) 1981; Yale University, New Haven, Connecticut, M.A. in Afro-American Studies 1983. **Career:** Missionary for Jehovah's Witnesses in New York, North Carolina, and Florida, 1968-75; worked as telephone operator for various hotels in New York, including Sheraton City Squire, 1975-81; contributing editor, *Callaloo,* since 1984; author of column, "Hers," for *New York Times,* 1986. Writer-in-residence, Cummington Community of the Arts, 1983; visiting lecturer, George Washington University, 1983-84, and Princeton University, 1986-87; cultural exchange lecturer, United States Information Agency, India, 1985; scholar-in-residence, University of Pennsylvania, 1986; visiting professor, New York University, 1986, Boston University, 1987, and University of Kent, Canterbury, 1992; Fannie Hurst Visiting Professor, Brandeis University, 1988; senior fellow, Society for the Humanities, Cornell University, 1988. Founder and president, One Way Productions (independent film company), Brooklyn, New York, beginning 1990. Contributor to periodicals, including *Essence, Life, Ms., Ontario Review, People,* and *Southern Review.* **Awards:** American Book Award for best first novel, 1983, for *The Women of Brewster Place;* Mid-Atlantic Writers Association Distinguished Writer Award, 1983; National Endowment for the Arts fellowship, 1985; National Coalition of 100 Black Women Candace Award, 1986; Guggenheim fellowship, 1988; Southern Regional Council Lillian Smith Award, 1989; New York Foundation for the Arts fellowship, 1991; Brooklyn College President's Medal, 1993; D.H.L., Sacred Heart University, 1994. **Agent:** Sterling Lord, One Madison Ave., New York,

New York 10010, U.S.A. **Address:** One Way Productions, 638 2nd St., Brooklyn, New York 11215, U.S.A.

Publications

Novels

The Women of Brewster Place. New York, Viking, 1982.
Linden Hills. New York, Ticknor & Fields, 1985.
Mama Day. New York, Ticknor & Fields, 1988.
Bailey's Cafe. New York, Harcourt, 1992.

Plays

Bailey's Cafe (adaptation of her own novel; produced Hartford, Connecticut, 1994).
Candy (for children; production scheduled, 1997).

Screenplays: *Our 13,* 1985; *Women of Brewster Place* (adaptation of her novel), 1984.

Other

Editor, *Children of the Night: The Best Short Stories by Black Writers, 1967 to the Present.* Boston, Little Brown, 1996.

*

Media Adaptations: *The Women of Brewster Place* (miniseries), 1989, (television series), 1990.

Critical Studies: "No More Buried Lives: The Theme of Lesbianism in Lorde, Naylor, Shange, Walker" by Barbara Christian, in *Feminist Issues,* spring 1985; "The Whole Picture in Gloria Naylor's *Mama Day*" by Susan Meisenhelder, in *African American Review,* 27(3), fall 1993; *Gloria Naylor: Critical Perspectives Past and Present* edited by Henry Louis Gates Jr. and K.A. Appiah, New York, Amistad, 1993; "Recovering the Conjure Woman: Texts and Contexts in Gloria Naylor's *Mama Day*" by Lindsey Tucker, in *African American Review,* 28(2), summer 1994; *Gloria Naylor: In Search of Sanctuary* by Virginia C. Fowler, New York, Twayne, 1996.

* * *

Gloria Naylor achieved national eminence and critical praise when her first novel, *The Women of Brewster Place,* appeared in 1982. In this novel as in her later works, Naylor explores the association between sexism and racism and suggests that through communal bonds individuals can survive these forces. Naylor, like many African American feminists, uses multiple voices to depict the strength of the represented communities.

Born in New York City to Roosevelt and Alberta Naylor, a transit worker and a telephone operator respectively, Naylor worked for seven years as a Jehovah's Witnesses missionary after graduating from high school in 1968. While attending Brooklyn College of the City University of New York, she worked as a telephone operator in various city hotels. While at Brooklyn, she first read Toni Morrison's *The Bluest Eye,* which confirmed her desire to write. As a student at both Brooklyn and, later, at Yale, Naylor studied African American literature; for her Yale thesis, she wrote *Linden Hills.* Since earning her B.A. in English in 1981, Naylor has written professionally and has had teaching appointments at George Washington, Princeton, Pennsylvania, Brandeis, and Cornell universities, among others.

In *The Women of Brewster Place,* winner of the American Book Award for best first novel, Naylor depicts the dynamics of racism and sexism in an disadvantaged urban-housing project. Written in the form of stories, the work portrays six women who have endured violence from men and for whom Brewster Place is a last resort. Only Kiswana Browne, a young, idealistic, middle-class woman, has chosen to live in Brewster Place. Although economic conditions, race, and sexism have brought most of the women to this walled-off street, a sense of community exists. Mattie Michael, a matriarchal figure, consoles several of the women, and Kiswana tries to help a young welfare mother. In the final story, "The Block Party," Mattie envisions the women united in their anger after the gang rape and death of a young lesbian. Mattie imagines that the women destroy the wall separating the street from the rest of the city.

Based on Dante's *Inferno, Linden Hills* again examines racism and sexism, but this time the narrative involves an affluent middle-class black community (Kiswana's former home). The Linden Hills development is the vision of six generations of men, all named Luther Nedeed, who have seen it as "a beautiful, black wad of spit right in the white eye of America." As the wandering poets, Willie and Lester, descend the rings in Linden Hills, they find assimilated blacks who have rejected their racial heritage; eventually the poets reach the bottom, where Luther resides. Besides depicting the torment of the Linden Hills inhabitants, Naylor also portrays the misery of the current Mrs. Luther Nedeed, Willa Prescott Nedeed. Imprisoned with her young son in the basement by her husband, who suspects her of adultery because the baby is light-skinned, she learns through recipes, letters, and photographs the histories of earlier Nedeed wives. These women had been used by their husbands to produce clones of themselves. After escaping from the basement, Willa confronts Luther; the ensuing fight ends with the house catching fire and their deaths. While the novel suggests the patriarchy's destructive effects on black men and women, it also depicts the powerful friendship between Willie and Lester, who have witnessed pain, self-denial, even suicide. They have survived their journey through Linden Hills.

Mama Day, set on a fictional island off the Georgia-South Carolina coast, alludes to Shakespeare's *The Tempest.* Rewriting the story of Prospero's patriarchy, Naylor depicts a matriarchal community led by a powerful conjurer, the descendant of the island's first mother, the slave Sapphira Wade. Named Miranda, she is called Mama Day. Besides presenting Mama Day's voice, the novel offers the first-person accounts of the love story of Ophelia ("Cocoa"), Miranda's great-niece, who lives in New York and George Andrews, an orphan from the city, raised according to individualistic ideals. While the novel portrays Cocoa as estranged from her island heritage, it depicts George as wounded by the loss of his mother and as alienated from his racial heritage. When Cocoa is dying and George realizes that because of a hurricane he cannot get to the mainland for help, he is forced to reject his belief in individualism and to accept the power of communal action. His rationality prevents him, however, from accepting the strength of Mama Day's conjuring powers. He dies, unable through his own action to save his wife; because of Mama Day, Cocoa does survive. The novel suggests that she will eventually learn her family history and accept her heritage, and it depicts matriarchy's power and the human cost of radical individualism.

Bailey's Cafe, which ends with George Andrews' birth, utilizes the method of magical realism to rewrite Biblical accounts of women—Jesse Bell (Jezebel), Eve, Esther, and two Marys—and offers the first-person narrative of Miss Maple, a black man who chooses to wear women's clothes. Through the women's stories, Naylor continues her exploration of the blighting effect of sexism, especially the whore/virgin dichotomy, and uses Miss Maple's history to underscore white capitalist America's efforts to emasculate black men. Although the diner, Bailey's Cafe, exists at "the edge of the world," it does offer these characters a refuge and suggests, through the birth of a baby, the possibility of renewal despite overwhelming odds. As in her other novels, Gloria Naylor implies that community can allay the effects of racism and sexism.

—Phyllis Surrency Dallas

NEAL, John

Pseudonym: Jehu O'Cataract. **Nationality:** American. **Born:** Falmouth (now Portland), Maine, 25 August 1793. **Education:** Attended local schools; studied law, Baltimore, Maryland, c. 1816; Bowdoin College, Brunswick, Maine, M.A. 1836. **Family:** Married Eleanor Hall in 1828, five children. **Career:** Worked as a store clerk in shops in Portland, Maine, then teacher of penmanship and drawing in towns along Kennebec River; moved to Baltimore and opened a dry-goods store, 1814-16; editor of Baltimore *Telegraphy;* admitted to bar, 1819; resided in England as contributor to magazines and secretary to social reformer Jeremy Bentham, 1823-27; returned to Portland to practice law, 1827; editor, *Yankee,* 1828-29, *New England Galaxy,* Boston, a local Portland newspaper, and *Brother Jonathan* (comic), New York, 1843. Contributor to periodicals, including *Atlantic Monthly, Blackwood's, Harper's,* and *North American Review.* **Died:** 20 June 1876.

Publications

Novels

Keep Cool: A Novel, Written in Hot Weather. Baltimore, J. Cushing, 2 vols., 1817.
Logan: A Family History (published anonymously). Philadelphia, H.C. Carey, 1822; London, A. K. Newman, 1823.
Errata; or, The Works of Will Adams. New York, Published for the Proprietors, 2 vols., 1823.
Randolph. Baltimore, n.p., 1823.
Seventy-Six; or, Love and Battle. Baltimore, J. Robinson, and London, G. & W. B. Whittaker, 1823.
Brother Jonathan; or The New Englanders. Edinburgh, Blackwood, and London, Strand, 1825.
Rachel Dyer: A North American Story. Portland, Maine, Shirley & Hyde, 1828.
Authorship: A Tale. Boston, Gray & Bowen, 1830.
The Down-Easters. New York, Harper & Bros., 2 vols., 1833.
True Womanhood: A Tale. Boston, Ticknor & Fields, 1859.
The White-Faced Pacer; or, Before and After the Battle. New York, Beadle, 1863.
The Moose-Hunter; or, Life in the Maine Woods. New York, Beadle, 1864.
Little Mocassin; or, Along the Madawaska: A Story of Life and Love in the Lumber Region. New York, Beadle, and London, n.p., 1866.

Religion/Spirituality

One Word More: Intended for the Reasoning and Thoughtful among Unbelievers. N.p., 1854.

History

A History of the American Revolution, with Paul Allen and Tobias Watkins. Baltimore, printed for F. Betts by W. Wooddy, 1822.
An Account of the Great Conflagration in Portland, July 4th & 5th, 1866. Portland, Maine, Starbird & Twitchell, 1866.

Essays

American Writers: A Series of Papers Contributed to Blackwood's Magazine, edited by Fred Lewis Pattee. Durham, North Carolina, Duke University Press, 1937.

Poetry

The Battle of Niagara (as Jehu O'Cataract). Baltimore, N. G. Maxwell, 1818; enlarged, as Neal, 1819.

Play

Otho: A Tragedy in Five Acts. Boston, West, Richardson & Lord, 1819.

Autobiography

Wandering Recollections of a Somewhat Busy Life. Boston, Roberts Bros., 1869.

Other

Principles of Legislation. Boston, Wells & Lilly, 1830.
Great Mysteries and Little Plagues. Boston, Roberts Bros., 1870.
Portland Illustrated. Portland, Maine, W. S. Jones, 1874.
John Neal to Edgar A. Poe (letters). Ysleta, Texas, E. B. Hill, 1942; enlarged as *Letters to Edgar A. Poe,* Norwood, Pennsylvania, Norwood Editions, 1975.
Observations on American Art: Selections from the Writings of John Neal, edited by Harold Edward Dickson. State College, Pennsylvania, Pennsylvania State College, 1943.
The Genius of Neal: Selections from His Writings, edited by Benjamin Lease and Hans-Joachim Lang. Frankfurt am Main, Lang, 1978.

*

Bibliography: In *Bibliography of American Literature* by Jacob Blanck, n.p., 1973.

Critical Studies: *A Down-East Yankee from the District of Maine* by Windsor Pratt Daggett, n.p., 1920; *That Wild Fellow John Neal and the American Literary Revolution* by Benjamin Lease, Chicago, University of Chicago Press, 1972; *John Neal* by Donald A. Sears, Boston, Twayne, 1978; *A Right View of the Subject: Feminism in the Works of Charles Brockden Brown and John Neal* by Fritz Fleishmann, Erlangen, Palm & Enke, 1983.

* * *

A popular novelist and magazine editor of the mid-19th century, John Neal was credited with being an early American advocate of women's rights, a subject he was first introduced to by reading the works of William Godwin. In a debate on the subject of slavery held in 1823, Neal first publicly argued on behalf of women's rights when he stated that women were no better off than were the black slaves of the time. When the scheduled speaker was unable to attend a Fourth of July celebration in Portland, Maine, in 1833, Neal gave an impromptu lecture on freedom, again tying together the issues of slavery and women's rights. He specifically decried the limited rights of women under English common law, pointing out in particular how women were forced to pay taxes but were not allowed to vote, a clear violation of the principles the nation had been founded upon. The event led him to become a forceful speaker on the subject, often speaking for up to two hours eloquently and without notes. Bostonite Margaret Fuller was much impressed by his ability to argue women's rights from the podium, as was the poet Elizabeth Oakes Smith.

But it was in his work as editor and writer that Neal was able to widely publicize the women's rights movement. In the journal *Brother Jonathan* he printed the texts of his many speeches and held an ongoing debate over women's rights with Mrs. Eliza W. Farnham. Neal's novels often included female characters who are outspoken in their support of women's rights and who live their lives independent of the expected norms of the time. In *Rachel Dyer,* for example, a story of the Salem witchcraft trials, Neal created a female character who, although shunned as a hunchback, possesses great virtue and strength of principle. The novel *Authorship* focuses on Mary, a woman who lives in a menage-a-trois and who argues forcefully that women have the right to pursue their own careers. In *True Womanhood,* Neal presents Julia, a strong and independent woman whose vibrant religious convictions are a role model for the other characters. Julia also argues against marriage: "I do not believe that marriage is a condition absolutely indispensable for the happiness of women, or for the development of true womanhood." In 1852, Elizabeth Oakes Smith would read a letter from Neal to the Woman's Rights Convention in Syracuse, New York.

In addition to his support for women's rights, John Neal was also a social activist associated with a number of other causes. He argued against the custom of dueling, advocated an end to capital punishment and, as a proponent of physical exercise, was credited with popularizing athletic gymnasiums in the United States. Neal was also an early promoter of Edgar Allan Poe, Nathaniel Hawthorne, and Henry Wadsworth Longfellow.

—Denise Wiloch

NORMAN, Marsha

Nationality: American. **Born:** Louisville, Kentucky, 21 September 1947. **Family:** Married 1) Michael Norman (divorced 1974); 2) the theatrical producer Dann C. Byck Jr. in 1978 (divorced); 3) the painter Timothy Dykman; one son and one daughter. **Education:** Agnes Scott College, B.A. 1969; University of Louisville, M.A.T. 1971. **Career:** Worked with disturbed children, Kentucky Central State Hospital, 1969-71; teacher, Brown School, Louisville, Kentucky, 1970-72, and Kentucky Arts Commission, 1972-76; book reviewer and editor, Louisville *Times,* 1974-79; writer-in-residence, Actors Theatre, Louisville, 1977-80. **Awards:** American Theater Critics Association citation, 1977-78, for *Getting Out;* National Endowment for the Arts grant, 1978-79; Outer Critics Circle's John Gassner New Playwrights Medallion and George Oppenheimer-*Newsday* Award, both 1979, both for *Getting Out;* Rockefeller playwright-in-residence grant at the Mark Taper Forum, Los Angeles, 1979-80, Susan Smith Blackburn prize, 1982, Tony award nomination, 1983, and Pulitzer Prize, 1983, all for *'Night, Mother;* Tony Award for Best Book of a Musical, 1991, for *The Secret Garden.* **Address:** c/o The Tantleff Office, 375 Greenwich St., No. 700, New York, New York 10013, U.S.A.

Publications

Plays

Getting Out (two-act; produced Louisville, Kentucky, 1977; produced Off-Broadway, 1978). New York, Avon, 1977.
Third and Oak: The Laundromat [and] *The Pool Hall* (one-acts; produced Louisville, Kentucky, 1978). New York, Dramatists Play Service, 2 vols., 1980-85.
Circus Valentine (two-act; produced Louisville, 1979).
The Holdup (two-act; produced Louisville, 1980). New York, Dramatists Play Service, 1988.
'Night, Mother. New York, Hill & Wang, 1983.
The Shakers (produced Louisville, 1983).
Traveler in the Dark (produced Los Angeles, 1984). New York, Dramatists Play Service, 1988.
Four Plays by Marsha Norman (collection). San Francisco, Theatre Communications, 1988.
Sarah and Abraham (produced Louisville, Kentucky, 1988). N.p., 1992.
The Secret Garden (musical book and lyrics adapted from the book by Frances Hodgson Burnett; produced on Broadway, 1991). San Francisco, Theatre Communications Group, 1992.
Loving Daniel Boone (produced Louisville, 1992). Portsmouth, New Hampshire, Heinemann, 1995.
The Red Shoes (musical book and lyrics). N.p., 1993.
Trudy Blue (produced Humana Festival, 1995; revised version produced Fayettevile, North Carolina, 1996). Lyme, New Hampshire, Smith & Kraus, 1995.

Screenplays: *'Night, Mother,* Universal, 1986; *The Children with Emerald Eyes,* Columbia, n.d.; *The Bridge,* n.d.; *Thy Neighbor's Wife,* United Artists, n.d.; *My Shadow,* 1989.

Television Plays: *It's the Willingness,* Public Broadcasting Service, 1978; *In Trouble at 15* (on television program *Skag*), Lorimar Productions, 1980.

Novel

The Fortune Teller. New York, Random House, 1987.

*

Bibliography: "Marsha Norman: A Classified Bibliography" by Irmgard H. Wolfe, in *Studies in American Drama,* 3, 1988.

Critical Studies: "Norman's *'Night, Mother:* Psychodrama of Female Identity" by Jenny S. Spencer, in *Modern Drama,* 30(3), September 1987; "Doing Time: Hunger for Power in Marsha Norman's Plays" by Lynda Hart, in *Southern Quarterly,* 25(3), spring 1987; *Interviews with Contemporary Women Playwrights* by Kathleen Betsko and Rachel Koenig, New York, Beech Tree, 1987; "Locked behind the Proscenium: Feminist Strategies in *Getting Out* and *My Sister in This House*" by Patricia R. Schroeder, in *Modern Drama,* 32(1), March 1989; *A Casebook on Marsha Norman,* edited by Linda Ginter-Brown, Hamden, Connecticut, Garland Press, 1996.

* * *

Born to religious fundamentalist parents, Marsha Norman always has felt somewhat at odds with her upbringing, though, undeniably, her parents and her Southern roots have furnished many an inspiration for dramatic characterizations. When asked at the 1996 Southern Writers' Symposium, which honored the playwright's work, what her mother thought of her plays, Norman responded somberly, "My mother is dead ... but I think that she would think them ... 'vulgar.'"

Norman's predilection for writing appeared early in her youth. At Louisville's Deride High School, the future Pulitzer Prize winner worked on both the school newspaper and on the yearbook staff. Her high school essay on Job's suffering, later published in the *Kentucky English Bulletin,* took first place at a local writing contest. Awarded a scholarship to attend Agnes Scott College in Decatur, Georgia, a small liberal arts college, Norman majored in philosophy and continued her interest in creative writing. Volunteering part-time in a pediatric burn unit at General Hospital in Atlanta, Georgia, she furthered her understanding of human suffering and of human courage, viewing first hand the anguish of the innocent.

Graduating college in 1969, Norman returned to Louisville, where she married her former English teacher, Michael Norman, a marriage not destined to last. Back in her hometown, she entered graduate school, taking courses at the University of Louisville, from where she later received her Master's Degree in 1971. One of the author's most memorable experiences around this time was working with gifted children at the Brown School in Louisville, where she was hired to teach adolescents filmmaking. Norman soon became engaged in drawing up a humanities curriculum for children in the middle school, focusing her talent upon writing materials appropriate for various grade levels. Feeling this work particularly rewarding, she maintained that this writing experience forced upon her a new level of awareness of language, greatly contributing to her development as a writer. In gearing sentences towards specific levels of difficulty, she argued, one meticulously had to count syllables, one by one.

By 1976 a few of Norman's book reviews and other pieces had appeared in the *Louisville Times*, and the newspaper added a children's weekend supplement, a feature Norman created, named "The Jelly Bean Journal." While attempting to find an audience for her newspaper writing, the future playwright met the artistic director of the Actors Theatre of Louisville, Jon Jory. He suggested that she write a play. Though Jory's initial topic did not spark Norman's interest, she did have an idea worth exploring. Norman had once met a disturbed, young woman with a penchant for violence at the Kentucky Mental State Hospital and, intrigued by her, had kept up with her movements. This young woman's story would materialized into the hit *Getting Out,* a play about a prison parolee, Arlene/Arlie, who struggles with her identity and attempts to survive in a modern, unjust world. Despite emotional and physical abuse, Norman's protagonist chooses to proceed with her struggle, to embrace life. Receiving critical accolades for her innovative presentation of the "divided-self" by placing two characters on stage simultaneously—Arlie and Arlene, one in the same, are played by two different actors)—Norman developed even more intricate combinations of characters and staging, often merging pasts and presents, the real and the fictive.

Having enjoyed a spectacular reception at the Louisville Actor's Theatre for 1977s *Getting Out,* Norman soon became playwright-in-residence there, where she wrote *Third and Oak* (1978), consisting of two one act plays, *The Laundromat* and *The Pool Hall.* Both plays explore loneliness, troubled marriages, death, and hidden secrets. In *The Laundromat,* Norman creates two very dissimilar female characters who chance to meet at a local laundromat to wash their clothes at 3 a.m. Carrying heavier "baggage" than their bundles of clothes, the women have become emotionally weighted, the younger one married to an abusive and philandering husband, and the elder one immersed in grief as a result of her husband's recent death. By listening and by empathizing with one another, each appreciating the other's struggles, the two women bond. The metaphor of "washing clothes," traditionally associated with "women's work," becomes in Norman's hands, a vehicle for communication, for each woman has been going through an emotional "wringer." This night of communion "cleanses," heals, and encourages both females to move forward with their lives and to understand that they do have options. Likewise, in *The Pool Hall,* Norman taps another troubled pair, two black men: a disc jockey dubbed Shooter (his father's nickname) and the pool hall owner, Willie. Both characters, confronting past and current misunderstandings and feelings of despair, unite by the play's end to confirm their friendship, love, and hope for the future.

Norman's fifth play, the 1983 Pulitzer Prize winning *'Night, Mother,* proved a success at both the regional theater and on Broadway. Again, Norman did what she does best: concoct an assortment of hidden pains and secrets and bring them to a boiling point. Delighting in the stirring process, the playwright thickens her plots and delights her audiences with the "overflow of powerful emotions." Norman's best-known play, *'Night, Mother* revolves around Jessie Cates (played on Broadway by actress Kathy Bates), who divulges to her mother, Thelma, her intention of committing suicide this night. Critical to the plot remains the issue of female autonomy, implicitly woman's prerogative to control her own destiny. Inherent in this notion of control lies woman's right to her own body—and the right to determine what she does with it—even if her choice includes suicide. To Jessie, choice remains vital, and despite Mama's threats of patriarchal intervention—calling Jessie's brother, Dawson, or the doctor, who has "prescribed" for Jessie an unexcited, tranquil life, Norman's protagonist refuses to deviate from her plan. By killing herself, Cates chooses an active (traditionally, associated with male suicide) rather than a passive (associated with female suicide) means of self-destruction.

Not content with failure or with letting go of characters she wishes to develop further, Norman sometimes rewrites her dramas, referring to them as plays "in-progress." Having already resurrected the not-so-well-received *Circus Valentine,* Norman reintroduced in March of 1996 another play, *Trudy Blue,* the story of a female writer, Ginger, who appears estranged from her husband, children, and friends. Trudy Blue, the heroine of Ginger's work, serves as a kind of alter-ego for the protagonist herself; sometimes she materializes on the stage and competes with Ginger for love. Intent upon pursuing happiness, despite various obstacles in her path, Ginger gets diagnosed with cancer—or rather, "rediagnosed" with it, the result of original misinformation by a bungling medical establishment. Struggling with her identity, the protagonist attempts to reconcile the real and the imaginary, the past and the present, most notably depicted in flashbacks of a haunting mother, whose criticism—though not humorless—continues to wound her adult child. Unlike the 1995 version of *Trudy Blue,* Norman continues to be innovative, using the same actor to play both Ginger's imaginary lover and her husband.

Marsha Norman continues to explore the female psyche in her plays, capturing moments of women in crises. Her characters confront life—whether they choose to continue it or to destroy it, and they bring to the surface heretofore invisible forces affecting woman's sense of self and self-esteem. Always, autonomy remains central to the plots involving a female protagonist, no matter the character's status or background. Invariably, Norman's protagonist has as her object the desire to communicate, to "touch" another life. Despite repeated themes of patriarchal privilege and subjugation of women, of physical or emotional abuse, of parental rejection and confused identity, Norman's plays speak especially—and poignantly—to women, capturing moments of understanding, of shared sisterhood, and of love. These moments both delight and haunt audiences.

—Linda Rohrer Paige

NOVIS, Émile. *See* **WEIL, Simone (Adolphine).**

O

OAKLEY, Ann (Rosamund)

Pseudonym: Rosamund Clay. **Nationality:** British. **Born:** London, 17 January 1944. **Education:** Chiswick Polytechnic (now West London Institute of Higher Education); Somerville College, Oxford, M.A. (honors), 1965; Bedford College, London University, Ph.D. 1974. **Family:** Married, two daughters, one son. **Career:** Research officer, Social Research Unit, Bedford College, University of London, 1974-79; Wellcome Research fellow, Radcliffe Infirmary, National Perinatal Epidemiology Unit, Oxford, 1980-83; deputy director, Thomas Coram Research Unit, 1985-90, director, Social Science Research Unit, 1990, and professor of sociology and social policy, beginning 1991, Institute of Education, University of London. **Agent:** Rachel Calder, Tessa Sayle Agency, 11 Jubilee Place, London SW3, England.

Publications

Political/Social Theory

Sex, Gender, and Society. London, Temple Smith, 1972; New York, Harper, 1973.
Housewife. London, Allan Lane, 1974; as *Woman's Work: A History of the Housewife,* New York, Pantheon, 1975.
The Sociology of Housework. London, Martin Robinson, 1974; New York, Pantheon, 1975; with new introduction, Oxford, Basil Blackwell, 1985.
Becoming a Mother. London, Martin Robinson, 1979; New York, Schocken, 1980; as *From Here to Maternity,* Harmondsworth, Penguin, 1981; with new introduction, New York, Schocken, 1986.
Women Confined: Towards a Sociology of Childbirth. Oxford, Martin Robinson, and New York, Schocken, 1980.
Subject Women. Oxford, Martin Robinson, and New York, Pantheon, 1981.

Essays

"Interviewing Women: A Contradiction in Terms," in *Doing Feminist Research,* edited by Helen Roberts. New York, Routledge, 1981.
Telling the Truth about Jerusalem: Selected Essays. Oxford, Basil Blackwell, 1986.
Essays on Women, Medicine and Health. Edinburgh, Edinburgh University Press, 1993.

Novels

The Men's Room. London, Virago, 1988; New York, Atheneum, 1989.
Only Angels Forget (as Rosamund Clay). London, Virago, 1990.
Matilda's Mistake. London, Virago, 1990.
The Secret Lives of Eleanor Jenkinson. London. HarperCollins, 1992.
Scenes Originating in the Garden of Eden. London and New York, HarperCollins, 1993.

Autobiography

Taking It like a Woman. London, Cape, and New York, Random House, 1984.

Other

Miscarriage, with M. McPherson and H. Roberts. London, Fontana, 1984; revised edition, Harmondsworth, Penguin, 1990.
The Captured Womb: A History of the Medical Care of Pregnant Women. Oxford, Basil Blackwell, 1984; New York, Oxford University Press, 1985.
Helpers in Childbirth: Midwifery Today, with S. Houd. Washington, DC, World Health Organization, 1990.
Social Support and Motherhood: The Natural History of a Research Project. Oxford and New York, Basil Blackwell, 1992.

Editor, with Juliet Mitchell, *The Rights and Wrongs of Women.* London, Penguin, and New York, Pantheon, 1976.
Editor, with Juliet Mitchell, *What Is Feminism?* New York, Pantheon, and Oxford, Basil Blackwell, 1986.
Editor, with A.S. Williams, *The Politics of the Welfare State.* London, UCL Press, 1994.

*

Media Adaptation: *The Men's Room* (television film), 1990.

Critical Studies: Review of *Social Support and Motherhood* by Dulcie Groves, in *Sociology,* 28, November 1994.

* * *

Ann Oakley is a distinguished academic and one of England's most prominent feminists. Much of her work focuses on the domestic domain, exploring such subjects as the sociology of housework, the discrimination—both socially and medically—faced by pregnant women, and the methodological considerations women face in researching women as a group.

In 1984, after writing a series of sociological books praised for their thorough documentation and well-constructed premises, Oakley published the autobiographical *Taking It like a Woman.* While interesting as a source of information on Oakley's personal history, the book is perhaps, more important as a vehicle to track the development of her feminist ideals and trace the foundations of interest in the topics she chooses to research. Oakley begins the book by asking, What makes someone a feminist? What sort of person is a feminist? How can a feminist be part of society organized in terms of sexual difference and "the family?" She spends much of the book tracing her personal experiences and attempting to answer these questions. While Oakley ends the book without answers, she goes a long way in describing her own feminist ideals and roots.

Oakley describes a lonely and isolated childhood, during which she gave the outward appearance of excelling, but inwardly was falling apart, resulting in a minor breakdown. She recovered to follow the path set for her—complete university, marry, and have children. Yet, she veered from this path, by returning to school for a Ph.D. in which she studied the sociological history of housework in Great Britain. In 1969 neither the topic nor a mother of two as Ph.D. candidate were taken seriously. However, she completed her dissertation and from the project, and those it begot, went on to publish the now classic *Sex, Gender and Society* (1972), as well as *The Sociology of Housework* (1974) and *Housewife* (1974). *Housewife,* and particularly the more academic *Sociology of Housework,* broke new theoretical ground in the analysis of the importance of women's work in the home.

Oakley has gone on to write about motherhood and pregnancy in *Becoming a Mother* (1979), *Women Confined* (1980), and *The Captured Womb* (1984). Her works on pregnancy have focused on uncovering the discrimination women face when pregnant, particularly in regards to the medical care they receive. In *The Captured Womb* Oakley argues that the health care that women received during pregnancy is planned and carried out under the administration of men. She asserts that the function of such care is to exert control over women.

Throughout her career, Oakley has explored the contradictions between feminist and traditional social science research methods. In 1981 she published her ground-breaking, and now often-cited essay "Interviewing Women." The essay aided in opening up debates surrounding the ethics of feminist research and, more specifically, the tensions between feminist research and traditional social sciences methods. In her essay Oakley argues that interviewing women using methods requiring "objectivity" and a hierarchial methodological structure objectifies and further exploits women. She calls for a new model of interviewing that encourages a more open format marked by a give and take between researcher and subject, thereby reducing the one-way, researcher-over-researched position. In light of these concerns, she reissued *The Sociology of Housework* with a new preface criticizing the study's traditional methodology.

In her 1992 book, *Social Support and Motherhood: The Natural History of a Research Project,* Oakley continues to combine her interests in methodological considerations with academic issues. This work joins a sociology of research, i.e., exposing and analyzing the processes by which research is performed, with a study of how social support during pregnancy improves the health of mothers and infants. In a review of the book in *Sociology* Dulcie Groves praises it as an "impressive treatment of the actual history of birthweight," which has "much to offer those who wish to learn about the design, execution and funding of research projects as well as the important substantive concerns of research."

While Oakley's contribution to feminist research and sociology are undeniable, her attempt to universalize the lives of some women as representative of all women diminishes the importance of cultural, (dis)ability status, class, and sexuality in women's experiences. In fact in *Taking It like a Woman* she states that, to her, feminism means:

> that I believe that women are an oppressed social group, a group of people sharing a common exclusion from full participation from certain key social institutions.... Feminism means being more involved on a political level with the situation of women than with that of any other minority or majority group. To be a feminist means putting women first.

In defining feminism as such, Oakley is demanding that in order to be "feminist," women of color, working class women and lesbian/bisexual women must do the impossible; that is, separate out, for example, the issues and experiences of race from gender.
The multi-talented Oakley not only writes works with a scholarly bent; she is also the author of a number of novels and essay collections. One of her fiction works, *The Men's Room* (1988), was well received and was eventually adapted by the BBC into a successful movie.

—Lisa Loutzenheiser

OATES, Joyce Carol

Pseudonym: Rosamond Smith. **Nationality:** American. **Born:** Millersport, New York, 16 June 1938. **Education:** Syracuse University, New York, 1956-60, B.A. in English 1960 (Phi Beta Kappa); University of Wisconsin, Madison, M.A. in English 1961; Rice University, Houston, 1961. **Family:** Married Raymond J. Smith in 1961. **Career:** Instructor, 1961-65, and assistant professor of English, 1965-67, University of Detroit; member of the Department of English, University of Windsor, Ontario, 1967-78. Since 1978 writer-in-residence, and currently Roger S. Berlind Distinguished Professor, Princeton University, New Jersey. Since 1974 publisher, with Raymond J. Smith, *Ontario Review,* Windsor, later Princeton. **Awards:** National Endowment for the Arts grant, 1966, 1968; Guggenheim fellowship, 1967; O. Henry award, 1967, 1973, and Special Award for Continuing Achievement, 1970, 1986; Rosenthal award, 1968; National Book award, 1970; Rea award, for short story, 1990; Bobst Lifetime Achievement award, 1990; Heideman award, 1990, for one-act play; Walt Whitman award, 1995. **Member:** American Academy, 1978. **Agent:** John Hawkins and Associates, 71 West 23rd Street, Suite 1600, New York, New York 10010. **Address:** 185 Nassau Street, Princeton, New Jersey 08540, U.S.A.

Publications

Novels

With Shuddering Fall. New York, Vanguard Press, 1964; London, Cape, 1965.
A Garden of Earthly Delights. New York, Vanguard Press, 1967; London, Gollancz, 1970.
Expensive People. New York, Vanguard Press, 1968; London, Gollancz, 1969.
Them. New York, Vanguard Press, 1969; London, Gollancz, 1971.
Wonderland. New York, Vanguard Press, 1971; London, Gollancz, 1972.
Do with Me What You Will. New York, Vanguard Press, 1973; London, Gollancz, 1974.
The Assassins: A Book of Hours. New York, Vanguard Press, 1975.
Childwold. New York, Vanguard Press, 1976; London, Gollancz, 1977.
Son of the Morning. New York, Vanguard Press, 1978; London, Gollancz, 1979.
Cybele. Santa Barbara, California, Black Sparrow Press, 1979.
Unholy Loves. New York, Vanguard Press, 1979; London, Gollancz, 1980.

Bellefleur. New York, Dutton, 1980; London, Cape, 1981.
Angel of Light. New York, Dutton, and London, Cape, 1981.
A Bloodsmoor Romance. New York, Dutton, 1982; London, Cape, 1983.
Mysteries of Winterthurn. New York, Dutton, and London, Cape, 1984.
Solstice. New York, Dutton, and London, Cape, 1985.
Marya: A Life. New York, Dutton, 1986; London, Cape, 1987.
Lives of the Twins (as Rosamond Smith). New York, Simon & Schuster, 1987.
You Must Remember This. New York, Dutton, 1987; London, Macmillan, 1988.
American Appetites. New York, Dutton, and London, Macmillan, 1989.
Soul-Mate (as Rosamond Smith). New York, Dutton, 1989.
In the Desert. New York, Dutton, 1990
Because It Is Bitter, and Because It Is My Heart. New York, Dutton, 1990; London, Macmillan, 1991.
Nemesis (as Rosamond Smith). New York, Dutton, 1990.
I Lock My Door upon Myself. New York, Ecco Press, 1990.
The Rise of Life on Earth. New York, New Directions, 1991.
Black Water. New York, Dutton, 1992; London, Picador, 1994.
Snake Eyes (as Rosamond Smith). New York, Dutton, 1992.
Foxfire: Confessions of a Girl Gang. New York, Dutton, 1993; London, Picador, 1994.
What I Lived For. New York, Dutton, 1994; London, Macmillan, 1995.
You Can't Catch Me (as Rosamond Smith). New York, Dutton, 1995.
Zombie. New York, Dutton, 1995.

Short Stories

By the North Gate. New York, Vanguard Press, 1963.
Upon the Sweeping Flood and Other Stories. New York, Vanguard Press, 1966; London, Gollancz, 1973.
The Wheel of Love and Other Stories. New York, Vanguard Press, 1970; London, Gollancz, 1971.
Cupid and Psyche. New York, Albondocani Press, 1970.
Marriages and Infidelities. New York, Vanguard Press, 1972; London, Gollancz, 1974.
A Posthumous Sketch. Los Angeles, Black Sparrow Press, 1973.
The Girl. Cambridge, Massachusetts, Pomegranate Press, 1974.
Plagiarized Material (as Fernandes/Oates). Los Angeles, Black Sparrow Press, 1974.
The Goddess and Other Women. New York, Vanguard Press, 1974; London, Gollancz, 1975.
Where Are You Going, Where Have You Been? Stories of Young America. Greenwich, Connecticut, Fawcett, 1974; edited by Elaine Showalter, New Brunswick, New Jersey, Rutgers University Press, 1994.
The Hungry Ghosts: Seven Allusive Comedies. Los Angeles, Black Sparrow Press, 1974; Solihull, Warwickshire, Aquila, 1975.
The Seduction and Other Stories. Los Angeles, Black Sparrow Press, 1975.
The Poisoned Kiss and Other Stories from the Portuguese (as Fernandes/Oates). New York, Vanguard Press, 1975; London, Gollancz, 1976.
The Triumph of the Spider Monkey. Santa Barbara, California, Black Sparrow Press, 1976.
The Blessing. Santa Barbara, California, Black Sparrow Press, 1976.
Crossing the Border. New York, Vanguard Press, 1976; London, Gollancz, 1978.
Daisy. Santa Barbara, California, Black Sparrow Press, 1977.
Night-Side. New York, Vanguard Press, 1977; London, Gollancz, 1979.
A Sentimental Education. Los Angeles, Sylvester & Orphanos, 1978.
The Step-Father. Northridge, California, Lord John Press, 1978.
All the Good People I've Left Behind. Santa Barbara, California, Black Sparrow Press, 1979.
The Lamb of Abyssalia. Cambridge, Massachusetts, Pomegranate Press, 1979.
A Middle-Class Education. New York, Albondocani Press, 1980.
A Sentimental Education (collection). New York, Dutton, 1980; London, Cape, 1981.
Funland. Concord, New Hampshire, Ewert, 1983.
Last Days. New York, Dutton, 1984; London, Cape, 1985.
Wild Saturday and Other Stories. London, Dent, 1984.
Wild Nights. Athens, Ohio, Croissant, 1985.
Raven's Wing. New York, Dutton, 1986; London, Cape, 1987.
The Assignation. New York, Ecco Press, 1988.
Heat and Other Stories. New York, Dutton, 1991.
Where Is Here? Hopewell, New Jersey, Ecco, 1992.
Haunted: Tales of the Grotesque. New York, Dutton, 1994.
Will You Always Love Me? and Other Stories. New York, Dutton, 1995.

Plays

The Sweet Enemy (produced New York, 1965).
Sunday Dinner (produced New York, 1970).
Ontological Proof of My Existence, music by George Prideaux (produced New York, 1972). Included in *Three Plays,* 1980.
Miracle Play (produced New York, 1973). Los Angeles, Black Sparrow Press, 1974.
Daisy (produced New York, 1980).
Three Plays (includes *Ontological Proof of My Existence, Miracle Play, The Triumph of the Spider Monkey*). Windsor, Ontario Review Press, 1980.
The Triumph of the Spider Monkey, from her own story (produced Los Angeles, 1985). Included in *Three Plays,* 1980.
Presque Isle, music by Paul Shapiro (produced New York, 1982).
Lechery, in *Faustus in Hell* (produced Princeton, New Jersey, 1985).
In Darkest America (*Tone Clusters* and *The Eclipse*) (produced Louisville, Kentucky, 1990; *The Eclipse* produced New York, 1990).
American Holiday (produced Los Angeles, 1990).
I Stand Before You Naked (produced New York, 1991).
How Do You Like Your Meat? (produced New Haven, Connecticut, 1991).
Twelve Plays. New York, Dutton, 1991.
Black (produced Williamstown, 1992).
The Secret Mirror (produced Philadelphia, 1992).
The Perfectionist (produced Princeton, New Jersey, 1993). In *The Perfectionist and Other Plays,* 1995.
The Truth-Teller (produced New York, 1995).
Here She Is! (produced Philadelphia, 1995).
The Perfectionist and Other Plays. Hopewell, New Jersey, Ecco, 1995.

Poetry

Women in Love and Other Poems. New York, Albondocani Press, 1968.
Anonymous Sins and Other Poems. Baton Rouge, Louisiana State University Press, 1969.
Love and Its Derangements. Baton Rouge, Louisiana State University Press, 1970.
Woman Is the Death of the Soul. Toronto, Coach House Press, 1970.
In Case of Accidental Death. Cambridge, Massachusetts, Pomegranate Press, 1972.
Wooded Forms. New York, Albondocani Press, 1972.
Angel Fire. Baton Rouge, Louisiana State University Press, 1973.
Dreaming America and Other Poems. New York, Aloe Editions, 1973.
The Fabulous Beasts. Baton Rouge, Louisiana State University Press, 1975.
Public Outcry. Pittsburgh, Slow Loris Press, 1976.
Season of Peril. Santa Barbara, California, Black Sparrow Press, 1977.
Abandoned Airfield 1977. Northridge, California, Lord John Press, 1977.
Snowfall. Northridge, California, Lord John Press, 1978.
Women Whose Lives Are Food, Men Whose Lives Are Money. Baton Rouge, Louisiana State University Press, 1978.
The Stone Orchard. Northridge, California, Lord John Press, 1980.
Celestial Timepiece. Dallas, Pressworks, 1980.
Nightless Nights: 9 Poems. Concord, New Hampshire, Ewert, 1981.
Invisible Woman: New and Selected Poems 1970-1982. Princeton, New Jersey, Ontario Review Press, 1982.
Luxury of Sin. Northridge, California, Lord John Press, 1984.
The Time Traveller: Poems 1983-1989. New York, Dutton, 1989.

Essays

Contraries: Essays. New York, Oxford University Press, 1981.
The Profane Art: Essays and Reviews. New York, Dutton, 1983.
On Boxing, photographs by John Ranard. New York, Doubleday, and London, Bloomsbury, 1987; expanded edition, Hopewell, New Jersey, Ecco, 1994.
(Woman) Writer: Occasions and Opportunities. New York, Dutton, 1988.

Other

The Edge of Impossibility: Tragic Forms in Literature. New York, Vanguard Press, 1972; London, Gollancz, 1976.
The Hostile Sun: The Poetry of D.H. Lawrence. Los Angeles, Black Sparrow Press, 1973; Solihull, Warwickshire, Aquila, 1975.
New Heaven, New Earth: The Visionary Experience in Literature. New York, Vanguard Press, 1974; London, Gollancz, 1976.
The Stone Orchard. Northridge, California, Lord John Press, 1980.
Funland. Concord, New Hampshire, Ewert, 1983.
Conversations with Joyce Carol Oates, edited by Lee Milazzo. Jackson, University Press of Mississippi, 1989.
George Bellows: American Artist. Hopewell, New Jersey, Ecco Press, 1995.

Editor, *Scenes from American Life: Contemporary Short Fiction.* New York, Vanguard Press, 1973.
Editor, with Shannon Ravenel, *The Best American Short Stories 1979.* Boston, Houghton Mifflin, 1979.
Editor, *Night Walks: A Bedside Companion.* Princeton, New Jersey, Ontario Review Press, 1982.
Editor *First Person Singular: Writers on Their Craft.* Princeton, New Jersey, Ontario Review Press, 1983.
Editor, with Boyd Litzinger, *Story: Fictions Past and Present.* Lexington, Massachusetts, Heath, 1985.
Editor, with Daniel Halpern, *Reading the Fights* (on boxing). New York, Holt, 1988.
Editor, with Daniel Halpern, *The Sophisticated Cat: A Gathering of Stories, Poems, and Miscellaneous Writings about Cats.* New York, Dutton, 1992; London, Pan, 1994.

*

Bibliography: *Joyce Carol Oates: An Annotated Bibliography* by Francine Lercangée, New York, Garland, 1986.

Manuscript Collection: Syracuse University, New York.

Critical Studies: *The Tragic Vision of Joyce Carol Oates* by Mary Kathryn Grant, Durham, North Carolina, Duke University Press, 1978; *Joyce Carol Oates* by Joanne V. Creighton, Boston, Twayne, 1979; *Critical Essays on Joyce Carol Oates* edited by Linda W. Wagner, Boston, Hall, 1979; *Dreaming America: Obsession and Transcendence in the Fiction of Joyce Carol Oates* by G.F. Waller, Baton Rouge, Louisiana State University Press, 1979; *Joyce Carol Oates* by Ellen G. Friedman, New York, Ungar, 1980; *Joyce Carol Oates's Short Stories: Between Tradition and Innovation* by Katherine Bastian, Bern, Switzerland, Lang, 1983; *Isolation and Contact: A Study of Character Relationships in Joyce Carol Oates's Short Stories 1963-1980* by Torborg Norman, Gothenburg, Studies in English, 1984; *The Image of the Intellectual in the Short Stories of Joyce Carol Oates* by Hermann Severin, New York, Lang, 1986; *Joyce Carol Oates: Artist in Residence* by Eileen Teper Bender, Bloomington, Indiana University Press, 1987; *Understanding Joyce Carol Oates* by Greg Johnson, Columbia, University of South Carolina Press, 1987; *Joyce Carol Oates: A Study of the Short Fiction* by Greg Johnson, New York, Twayne, 1993.

* * *

One of the most prolific North American writers of this century, Joyce Carol Oates has been both praised and criticized for her tremendous literary output. She has written 32 novels (five under the pseudonym Rosamond Smith), 35 volumes of short stories, over 30 plays (most of which have been produced), 20 collections of poetry, and a number of essays and other works of non-fiction. A precocious child, Oates occupied many of her girlhood hours writing short stories and books. Oates was born in 1938 in rural Millersport, New York, where she received her early education in a one-room schoolhouse. She recreates her early memories of Erie County, New York, in some of her novels, often named as the fictional Eden County. The first in her family to receive a high school diploma, Oates focused her undergraduate studies on English at Syracuse University and was valedictorian of her graduating class in 1960. Throughout her undergraduate career, she continued writing fiction and was awarded first place for her story "In the Old World" in a 1959 college fiction contest sponsored by *Mademoiselle* magazine.

Oates completed her M.A. in English in 1961 at the University of Wisconsin—Madison, where she met Raymond J. Smith whom she later married. In 1961 Oates and Smith moved to Beaumont, Texas, where she planned to study for her Ph.D. in English and where he had accepted a faculty position. Noticing the increasing recognition that her fiction began to receive, Oates put aside her plans for graduate study and devoted herself completely to her writing. She has taught at the University of Detroit, the University of Windsor in Ontario, Canada, and most recently at Princeton University in New Jersey.

Many of Oates's characters find themselves in conflict with forces they cannot control. Oates often constructs situations that seem fatalistic for her characters, and their helplessness in a hostile world often results in their outrage and subsequent acts of violence. Most readers of Oates's fiction have felt compelled either to criticize or to explain the use of violence in her writing. While some complain that violence for Oates is merely gratuitous or sensational, other readers have argued that it is part of Oates's American landscape and that her depiction of violence is a complex one, ranging from subtle social and political commentary to irony as well as parody. *A Garden of Earthly Delights, Expensive People,* and *Them*—comprising Oates's first trilogy—feature individuals whose lives are shaped by tragic circumstances and who face violent resolutions to their conflicts.

Oates considers herself a feminist and many of her literary works, both fiction and nonfiction, attest to this point of view. She resents the designation "woman" writer since she feels strongly that no writer should be limited in her choice of subject matter (as her acclaimed book *On Boxing* demonstrates), literary style, or genre because of her gender. In her collection of essays *(Woman) Writer: Occasions and Opportunities,* she comments on the often ironic, marginalized, and subjugated position of women who also happen to be writers. In her fiction, Oates's female characters represent a wide cross-section of society. While some of her female characters are certainly passive victims of various forms of social violence (such as Elena in *Do With Me What You Will*), others are fully realized agents who directly confront misogyny, patriarchal privilege, and traditional constraining views of women (for example, Maddy and Legs of *Foxfire: Confessions of a Girl Gang*). For Oates's women characters, heterosexual love, marriage, and motherhood are seldom fulfilling events in their lives. In one of Oates's early novels, *Wonderland,* Mrs. Pedersen and Helene Vogel, both married to wealthy physicians, are psychologically despairing and tragic figures. Similarly, Oates's latest collection of short stories *Will You Always Love Me?* features a number of unhappy heterosexual couples, many of whom are in abusive relationships. Rape, incest, physical and psychological abuse are frequent in the lives of Oates's girl and women characters, but their victimization is often a commentary on her male characters' propensity for violence and society's condoning of it.

Oates not only reexamines traditional women's roles in her second trilogy (*Bellefleur, Bloodsmoor Romance, The Mysteries of Winterthurn*) but also employs the conventions of 19th-century novels—the gothic, the romance, and the detective genres, respectively—to create moments of feminist critique and point of view. *Bellefleur,* an allegorical saga about a wealthy American family, examines the unrestrained desire for accumulating vast wealth and power. The heroine and matriarch of the novel, Leah Bellefleur, is determined at all costs to restore the Bellefleur estate, founded by her ancestor Jean Pierre Bellefleur, to its past glory. The novel parodies the myth of the American dream, and Oates's use of a female character to dramatize the Bellefleur family's obsession with wealth and power creates an ironic effect. The many gothic conventions in *Bellefleur* lends an otherworldly atmosphere to the novel that produces an allegorical quality to the text: the haunted Bellefleur castle, mysterious animals with supernatural powers, humans who become transformed into animals, and a variety of deformed or grotesque persons. The second novel, *A Bloodsmoor Romance,* details the history of the Zinn family and their five daughters: Constance, Malvinia, Octavia, Samantha, and Deirdre. Like *Bellefleur,* the story takes place in 19th-century America and focuses on the exploits of female characters to explore a variety of traditional attitudes toward women and sexuality. Constance, the oldest Zinn daughter, spends her life preparing for marriage but flees west before her wedding, returning years later as a male, Philippe Fox. Other Zinn daughters follow similarly unconventional paths: Malvinia runs away from home to become an actress; Deirdre, after her mysterious kidnapping, falls under the influence of a medium and becomes obsessed with the occult; Samantha assists in the laboratory of her father who is an inventor. Octavia, the one daughter who becomes a conventional wife and mother, is subjected to bizarre sexual rituals by her husband. When he and her children die later in the novel, Octavia devotes herself to a life of prayer and contemplation. *The Bloodsmoor Romance* is one of Oates's most successful parodies of the 19th-century romance genre. The final novel, *The Mysteries of Winterthurn,* follows the detective Xavier Kilgarvan through three gruesome murder cases which occur at 12-year intervals. Through the use of antifeminist sentiments voiced throughout the novel, Oates manages to place feminist issues at the forefront of the novel's action. Although these three novels are unrelated in terms of character or plot, they all playfully recast and subvert 19th-century literary conventions while successfully incorporating feminist subtexts.

Many of Oates's subsequent novels return to contemporary American settings and are decidedly feminist in content. *Solstice* tells the story of a relationship between two women, Monica Jensen, who is teaching at a Pennsylvania boarding school for boys after her 8-year marriage has failed, and Sheila Trask, a painter who is older than Monica and recently widowed. Although the two women have quite different personalities and interests, they are nevertheless attracted to each other. Monica, who is the less self-assured of the two is, to an extent, psychologically dependent on Sheila. Midway through the course of their relationship, Sheila experiences a crisis and loss of confidence as a painter and begins insidiously manipulating Monica. Oates's story concerns not only the demands and limits of friendship but is a psychologically compelling account of women's relationships that are defined on their own terms. In *Marya,* Oates focuses on the life of a young girl from a lower middle-class background who suffers multiple abuses from her single-parent mother and her male cousin Lee. Marya's story begins with her precarious childhood of deprivation and neglect, but culminates in her intellectual and material independence through a sequence of brilliant academic successes. Marya's path to academic accomplishment has often been compared to Iris Courtney's similar success in Oates's later novel *Because It Is Bitter, and Because It Is My Heart.* Some of the settings in *Marya* (as in *Because It Is Bitter*) are based on Oates's childhood home in upstate New York, while later scenes are taken from the campus at Syracuse University which Oates attended. Although Marya's deprivation is not a reflection of Oates's own childhood, Marya's love of learning and academic accomplishment are certainly drawn from Oates's personal experience. As this novel concludes, Marya must honestly come to terms with her past, as most of Oates's characters must, in particular, her relationship with her mother.

Two more recent works, *Black Water* and *Foxfire: Confessions of a Girl Gang,* continue Oates's interest in feminist issues. *Black Water* is a fictional recreation of the 1969 Chappaquiddick incident, in which an automobile driven by Senator Edward Kennedy veered off a bridge into eight feet of water killing passenger Mary Jo Kopechne. Kopechne, who becomes the fictional Elizabeth Anne (Kelly) Kelleher of Oates's novel, is represented as a wholesome and intelligent researcher and writer for a Washington political journal. She becomes infatuated with the unnamed Senator of the novel when they meet at a Fourth of July party off the Maine coast and decide to leave together. The narrative is clearly sympathetic to Kelly Kelleher as the incidents leading up to her death gradually unfold and are retold from her points of view. The fact that Oates creates a tortured consciousness and narrative voice for Kelly Kelleher, which displaces and undermines the Senator's authority, lends a greater sense of irony as well as tragedy to this historical event in which political power has, until now, dominated the official script. In *Foxfire: Confessions of a Girl Gang,* Oates creates another female narrator and protagonist, Maddy, who recounts her adolescent experience as a member of a girl gang whose members realize their status as victims of social injustice due to men's abusive authority as well as their impoverished economic status. Their indignation leads them to commit a variety of vengeful acts and test the limits of their newly found power. *Foxfire: Confessions of a Girl Gang* is just one of many coming-of-age stories about the lives of adolescent girls in Oates's fiction. Other notable girl characters in this genre include Enid in *You Must Remember This* and Calla in *I Lock the Door Upon Myself.*

The feminist voice of Joyce Carol Oates is not limited to her novels, short stories, and essays, but it emerges in her poetry as well. Especially in a volume such as *Invisible Woman,* Oates is struggling with the concept of invisibility as it applies to women. She comments in her "Afterword" to this volume that the theme of invisibility in regard to women is so prominent because society places such emphasis on women's physical attributes while a woman's unseen or interior self is largely ignored. For Oates, invisibility is a dynamic concept as it thematizes a movement in women's social evolution from selflessness to an emerging identity (or visibility) accompanied by greater individual autonomy. This movement of her women characters is reflected in Oates's poetry as well as in her fiction.

Oates has also written a series of novels under the pseudonym Rosamond Smith, a feminine variant of her husband's name, Raymond Smith. This doubling effect of authorship reflects the series' thematic focus on relationships between twins, their pairing and doubling. Like her previous works with a feminist perspective, this series finds occasions to scrutinize patriarchal institutions and to address feminist social issues.

Joyce Carol Oates would probably object if readers limited her scope to a feminist perspective. She has been compared to scores of writers, both male and female, ranging from Renaissance to contemporary authors. Her popularity among readers continues to flourish along with her impressive literary production. She has already established her reputation as one of the most significant women of American literature and culture.

—Janet J. Montelaro

OBERON. *See* **ROBINSON, Mary (Darby).**

O'BRIEN, Edna

Nationality: Irish. **Born:** Tuamgraney, County Clare, 15 December 1936. **Education:** Attended Pharmaceutical College of Ireland, Dublin. **Family:** Married the author Ernest Gébler in 1952 (divorced 1964); two sons. **Career:** Full-time writer; teacher of creative writing, City College, New York, New York, beginning 1986. Contributor to periodicals, including *Cosmopolitan, Ladies' Home Journal,* and *New Yorker.* **Awards:** Kingsley Amis Award, 1962, for *The Country Girls; Yorkshire Post* Book of the Year award, 1970, for *A Pagan Place; Los Angeles Times* Book Prize, 1990, for *Lantern Slides.* **Agent:** Sarah Chalfant, Wylie Aitken & Stone, 250 West 57th St., Suite 2114, New York, New York 10107, U.S.A. **Address:** London, England.

Publications

Novels

The Country Girls Trilogy and Epilogue. New York, Farrar Straus, 1986.
- *The Country Girls.* New York, Knopf, 1960.
- *The Lonely Girl.* New York, Random House, 1962; as *Girl with Green Eyes,* London, Penguin, 1964.
- *Girls in Their Married Bliss.* London, J. Cape, 1964.

August Is a Wicked Month. New York, Simon & Schuster, 1965.
Casualties of Peace. London, J. Cape, 1966.
A Pagan Place. London, Weidenfeld & Nicholson, 1970.
Zee and Co. London, Weidenfeld & Nicholson, 1971.
Night. New York, Knopf, 1972.
Johnny I Hardly Knew You. London, Weidenfeld & Nicholson, 1977; as *I Hardly Knew You,* New York, Doubleday, 1978.
The High Road. New York, Farrar Straus, 1988.
Time and Tide. New York, Farrar Straus, 1992.
House of Splendid Isolation. New York, Farrar Straus, 1994.
Down by the River. N.p., forthcoming.

Short Stories

The Love Object. London, J. Cape, 1968.
A Scandalous Woman and Other Stories. New York, Harcourt, 1974.
Seven Novels and Other Short Stories. London, Collins, 1978.
Mrs Reinhardt and Other Stories. London, Weidenfeld & Nicholson, 1978; as *A Rose in the Heart,* Garden City, New York, Doubleday, 1979.
Returning: Tales. London, Weidenfeld & Nicholson, 1982.
A Fanatic Heart: Selected Stories. New York, Farrar Straus, 1984.
Lantern Slides. New York, Farrar Straus, 1990.

Poetry

On the Bone. London, Greville Press, 1989.

Plays

A Cheap Bunch of Nice Flowers (produced London, 1962), in *Plays of the Year,* Vol. 26, edited by J. C. Trewin. New York, Ungar, 1963.
Oh! Calcutta! An Entertainment (produced New York, 1969), with Kenneth Tynan, Sam Shepard, Samuel Beckett, and others. New York, Grove, 1969.
A Pagan Place (produced London, 1972). New York, Knopf, 1970.
The Gathering (produced Dublin, Ireland, 1974; produced New York, 1977).
Virginia (produced London, 1981; produced Stratford, Ontario, 1985; produced New York, 1985). New York, Harcourt, 1981; revised, 1985.
Madame Bovary (adapted from the novel by Gustave Flaubert; produced Watford, England, 1987).
Far from the Land (produced 1989).

Screenplays: *The Girl with the Green Eyes,* 1963; *Time Lost and Time Remembered* (adapted from O'Brien's short story "A Women at the Seaside"), with Desmond Morris, 1966; *I Was Happy Here,* 1965; *Three into Two Won't Go* (adapted from the novel by Andrea Newman), 1969; *X, Y and Zee,* 1972; *The Country Girls,* 1982.

Television Plays: *The Wedding Dress,* 1963; *The Keys of the Cafe,* 1965; *Give My Love to the Pilchards,* 1965; *Which of These Two Ladies Is He Married To?* 1967; *Nothing's Ever Over,* 1968; *The Hard Way,* 1980.

For Children

The Dazzle, illustrated by Peter Stevenson. London, Hodder & Stoughton, 1981.
A Christmas Treat, illustrated by Peter Stevenson. London, Hodder & Stoughton, 1982.
The Expedition. London, Hodder & Stoughton, 1982.
The Rescue, illustrated by Peter Stevenson. London, Hodder & Stoughton, 1983.
Tales for the Telling: Irish Folk and Fairy Stories, illustrated by Michael Foreman. New York, Atheneum, 1986.

Other

The Lotte Berk Book of Exercises, with Lotte Berk. London, MacDonald, 1969.
Mother Ireland, photographs by Fergus Bourke. New York, Harcourt, 1976.
Arabian Days, photographs by Gerard Klijn. New York, Quartet, 1977.
James and Nora: A Portrait of Joyce's Marriage. London, Lord John, 1981.
Vanishing Ireland, photographs by Richard Fitzgerald. New York, C. N. Potter, 1987.
An Edna O'Brien Reader. New York, Warner, 1994.

Editor, *Some Irish Loving: A Selection.* New York, Harper, 1979.

*

Critical Studies: "A Sex By Themselves: An Interim Report on the Novels of Edna O'Brien" by Sean McMahon, *Eire-Ireland,* 2(1), spring 1966; *Edna O'Brien* by Grace Eckley, Lewisburg, Pennsylvania, Bucknell University Press, 1974; "Edna O'Brien's Paradise Lost" by Raymonde Popot, in *Cahiers Irlandais,* 4-5, 1976; "'That Trenchant Childhood Route'?: Quest in Edna O'Brien's Novels" by Lotus Snow, *Eire,* 14(1), spring 1979; "Edna O'Brien: A Kind of Irish Childhood" by Darcy O'Brien, *Twentieth-Century Women Novelists,* edited by Thomas F. Staley, Totowa, New Jersey, Barnes & Noble, 1982; "Tragedies of Remembrance, Comedies of Endurance: The Novels of Edna O'Brien" by Lynette Carpenter, in *Essays on the Contemporary British Novel,* edited by Hedwig Bock and Albert Wertheim, Munich, Max Hueber, 1986; "The Silly and the Serious: An Assessment of Edna O'Brien" by Peggy O'Brien, in *Massachusetts Review,* 28(3), autumn 1987; "Tough Luck: The Unfortunate Birth of Edna O'Brien" by James Haule, *Colby Library Quarterly,* 23(4), December 1987; "Women's Consciousness and Identity in Four Irish Women Novelists" by Tasmin Hargreaves, in *Cultural Contexts and Literary Idioms in Contemporary Irish Literature,* edited by Michael Kenneally, Totowa, New Jersey, Barnes & Noble, 1988; "Edna O'Brien's 'The Doll': A Narrative of Abjection" by Kitti Carriker, in *Notes on Modern Irish Literature,* 1, 1989; "Edna O'Brien's 'Stage-Irish' Persona: An 'Act' of Resistance" by Rebecca Pelan, *Canadian Journal of Irish Studies,* 19(1), July 1993; "Love Objects: Love and Obsession in the Short Stories of Edna O'Brien" by Kiera O'Hara, in *Studies in Short Fiction,* 30(3), summer 1993; "Sacrificial Women in Short Stories by Mary Lavin and Edna O'Brien" by Jeanette Roberts Schumaker, in *Studies in Short Fiction,* 32, spring 1995.

* * *

Edna O'Brien is an important Irish woman writer because she is one of the first to explicitly write about women's emotional and sexual lives. Her female protagonists struggle with love, the failure of love, relationships with men, their mothers and fathers, their pasts, their memories, and the limited roles that Irish Catholic society furnishes for its women. Most of her characters are daughters, mothers, wives, and nuns and they invariably find themselves estranged from their husbands and fathers. They search for love and security in extramarital relationships and even in the arms of other women.

Critics frequently point out the similarities between O'Brien's life and the plots of her novels and short stories. She was born in rural County Clare to a long suffering mother and an alcoholic father. After finishing convent school, she attended pharmacology college in Dublin where she also began to write. In 1952 she married Ernest Gébler and they moved to London in 1959. *The Country Girls* was written immediately after her arrival in England. Her subsequent literary success caused the breakup of her marriage and the beginning of strained relations with her family and her country. O'Brien's first seven novels were banned in Ireland for their portrayals of female sexuality. Her first novel was labeled "a smear on Irish womanhood" and was burned on church grounds by the residents of her childhood home and the local priest. Her mother erased all objectionable passages from her personal copy of the novel.

O'Brien critiques the rigid morality of the west of Ireland and women's place in this rural culture. Her work was not considered feminist until her third, and more explicitly political novel, *Girls*

In Their Married Bliss, where Baba satirically announces that marriage is a facade of propriety. Baba, like most of O'Brien's characters, is not involved with the women's movement; instead, her outrage derives from her limited personal freedom and the impossibility of maintaining her independence from men. O'Brien's examination of what Raymond Popot describes as "women's desperate struggles towards physical, mental, and emotional freedom" from men, Ireland, and Catholicism clearly demonstrate her feminist agenda.

The Country Girls trilogy follows the lives of Kate Brady and Baba Brennan. While Kate is passive and demure, Baba is brash and irreligious. They attend convent school together and, after being expelled for writing lewd comments in a prayer book, they move to Dublin and finally London. By the end of the trilogy, both Kate and Baba find themselves in unsatisfactory marriages and have extramarital affairs. Even the role of motherhood provides little solace. Kate loses custody of her son and Baba's accidental pregnancy results in a daughter with whom she cannot communicate. Kate's "Cinderella" fantasy of being rescued by a handsome man and of being romantically transformed by love leaves her ill-equipped to cope with the reality of a brutal and demanding husband. Furthermore, while the two women try to escape the examples of their mothers, they ultimately end up replicating the drudgery of these same lives.

The theme of women's yearning for a love that never materializes is echoed in much of O'Brien's fiction but with variations. In her collection, *The Love Object,* she creates characters whose desires are left unfulfilled and who, paradoxically, crave this lack. Kiera O'Hara explains that this "cycle of unattainability" gives their lives purpose and it repels the possibility of a dismal and meaningless future. For example, in the title story, Martha describes the progress of a love affair with a married man. After he terminates the affair, she clings to his memory and even considers suicide because she does not know how to live without love and she fears loneliness. Sometimes love produces guilt. In *August Is a Wicked Month,* Ellen consummates a relationship while she is on vacation but, at the same time, her son dies in an accident while camping in Wales. Her guilt over the death of her son and her love affair on the French Riviera manifests itself in a sexually transmitted disease she contracts at the end of her holiday. Similarly, in *Time and Tide* Nell expresses guilt over the failure of her marriage and her subsequent Bohemian lifestyle in light of her son's drowning.

Love comes in many guises in O'Brien's work. Indeed, she demonstrates that "religious and sexual romance" are not only similar but also, in some cases, indistinguishable. For example, in "Sister Imelda," a short story in *Returning,* the unnamed narrator falls in love with her teacher and also wants to become a nun like her. In this case, vocation and desire are fused and exacerbated by the sacrificial model of the Catholic Madonna. O'Brien further explores lesbian desire in *The High Road.* Anna and Catalina fall in love with each other after realizing their disillusionment with domesticity. Both women have unsuccessful relationships with men, yet even their love for each other cannot escape the punishment of the Spanish and staunchly Catholic village where they meet.

O'Brien's most emancipated character is Mary Hooligan in *Night.* She spends a sleepless night remembering her past as a daughter, mother, wife, and lover in order to exorcise her memories. Mary Hooligan demonstrates that O'Brien's women characters are survivors because they wish to learn from their mistakes, to be independent, and to be happy. Mary is middle-aged, no longer married, her son is grown, and she is living in a house that is not her own. Yet, she exhibits strength and resilience in emancipating herself from persistent and sometimes painful memories in order to live more independently.

In her 1994 novel, *House of Splendid Isolation,* O'Brien examines the multiple viewpoints of the Irish "troubles," particularly those of a young IRA terrorist and an old woman whose house he commandeers. She also explores Irish women's political involvement in the terrorist movement. Her forthcoming novel, *Down by the River,* which she has described as "a story of incest and abortion in Ireland," suggests that O'Brien is committed to exposing the grim realities of women's lives in Ireland.

—Helen Thompson

O'BRIEN, Kate

Nationality: British. **Born:** County Limerick, Ireland, 3 December 1897. **Education:** University College, Dublin, B.A. 1919. **Family:** Married the historian Gustaaf Johannes Renier (divorced). **Career:** Worked as a governess, Bilbao, Spain, 1922-23; journalist, *Manchester Guardian,* Manchester, England, c. 1920. **Awards:** James Tait Black Prize, 1932, and Hawthornden Prize, 1931, both for *Without My Cloak.* **Member:** Royal Society of Literature (fellow), Irish Academy of Letters. **Died:** 13 August 1974.

Publications

Novels

Without My Cloak. London, Heinemann, and Garden City, New York, Doubleday Doran, 1931.
The Ante-Room. London, Heinemann, and Garden City, New York, Doubleday Doran, 1934.
Mary Lavelle. London, Heinemann, and Garden City, New York, Doubleday Doran, 1936.
Pray for the Wanderer. London, Heinemann, and Garden City, New York, Doubleday Doran, 1938.
The Land of Spices. London, Heinemann, and Garden City, New York, Doubleday Doran, 1941.
The Last of Summer. London, Heinemann, and Garden City, New York, Doubleday Doran, 1943.
That Lady. London, Heinemann, 1946; as *For One Sweet Grape,* Garden City, Doubleday Doran, 1946.
The Flower of May. London, Heinemann, and New York, Harper, 1953.
As Music and Splendour. London, Heinemann, and New York, Harper, 1958.

Plays

Distinguished Villa (three-act; produced London, 1926). London, Benn, 1926.
The Bridge (produced London, 1927).
The Anteroom (produced London, 1936).
The Schoolroom Window (produced London, 1937).
The Last of Summer (produced London, 1944).

That Lady (produced New York, 1949). New York, Harper, 1949.

Uncollected Essays

"Return in Winter," in *Contemporary Essays,* edited by Sylva Norman. London, Mathews & Marrot, 1933.
"George Eliot: A Moralizing Fabulist," in *Essays by Divers Hands,* vol. 27, edited by Sir George Rostrevor Hamilton. London, Oxford University Press, 1935.
"Writers of Letters," in *Essays and Studies,* 9, 1956.

Autobiography

English Diaries and Journals. London, Collins, 1943.
Presentation Parlour. London, Heinemann, 1963.

Other

Farewell, Spain. London, Heinemann, and Garden City, New York, Doubleday Doran, 1937.
Teresa of Avila. London, Parish, and New York, Sheed & Ward, 1951.
My Ireland. London, Batsford, and New York, Hastings House, 1962.

*

Critical Studies: "Matriarchs" by Margaret Lawrence, in her *The School of Femininity,* New York, Stokes, 1936; "Class and Creed in Kate O'Brien" by Joan Ryan in *The Irish Writer and the City,* edited by Maurice Harmon, Gerrards Cross, Colin Smythe, and Totowa, New Jersey, Barnes & Noble, 1984; "A Not So Simple Saga: Kate O'Brien's *Without My Cloak*" by Adele Dalsimer, in *Eire-Ireland,* 21(3), 1986; *Kate O'Brien: A Literary Portrait* by Lorna Reynolds, Gerrards Cross, Colin Smythe, and Totowa, New Jersey, Barnes & Noble, 1987; *Kate O'Brien: A Critical Study* by Adele Dalsimer, Dublin, Gill & Macmillan, and Boston, Twayne, 1990; *Ordinary People Dancing: Essays on Kate O'Brien* edited by Eibhear Walshe, Cork, Cork University Press, 1993; "Kate O'Brien" by Eavan Boland, in *The Stony Thursday Book* 7 (Limerick), n.d.

* * *

The most outstanding Irish woman writer of early to mid-century, Kate O'Brien wrote about issues that occupied her feminist predecessors and still preoccupy her successors: how is a woman to realize her life, her individualism, her intellectual aspirations, and her sexuality in a culture that inhibits women's pursuit of these very things? For O'Brien, the "personal was political" long before that phrase became a rallying cry for the feminist movement.

Born in 1897, the youngest of Thomas O'Brien and Katherine "Katty" Thornhill O'Brien's nine children, Kate grew up in an atmosphere of privilege near Limerick. She was soon left an orphan, though: her mother died in 1903, followed by her father in 1916. O'Brien was schooled first at the Laurel Hill Convent and then at University College, Dublin, where she received a bachelor of arts degree in 1919. Asserting her independence by breaking free of the sheltered life she had led in Ireland, O'Brien travelled to Spain in the winter of 1922-1923, taking a position as a governess in Bilbao and writing plays. She then moved to England and began writing for the *Manchester Guardian,* but returned to Spain often, in both her life and her writings. Spain and Ireland formed opposite poles in her work, the former representing freedom, passion, and the opportunity for inner growth; the latter the source of identity but also the source of societal constraints.

Influenced by George Eliot, James Joyce, and Virginia Woolf in themes, if not in styles, O'Brien produced some of Ireland's best writing from the 1930s until her death. Her work is preoccupied with women's struggles to create art in the face of family demands for adherence to societal conventions, concerns rooted in O'Brien's artistic struggles in her own life. Unable to remain in Ireland if she wished to be free to cultivate her art, she exiled herself to England for the rest of her adult life. Both her love for Ireland and her keen perception of its shortcomings emerge in her novels, in which there are no easy solutions. Rather, in most of her works, upper-class Irish Catholics fight with themselves and others as they weigh their desires for love or career against religious convictions and familial demands.

O'Brien's first novel, *Without My Cloak* (1931), was a great success, winning the 1931 James Tait Black Memorial Prize and the Hawthornden Prize in 1932. O'Brien set her novel in 19th-century Mellick—a fictionalized version of Limerick—and wrote about her own class, the gentry who lived in beautiful houses and were conscious of societal standards and obligations. In the novel, members of the Considine family suffer various fates as they choose from the roles their world offers them. Teresa, the plainest of the Considine sisters, marries unsuitably, solely to avoid spinsterhood; Caroline, the most beautiful, enters a socially desirable match but is miserable. When she creates a scandal by running away, her brother is dispatched to London to fetch her back to Ireland and the Catholicism that demands that a wife remain in her marriage, no matter what the conditions.

Just as her characters suffer for their art and desires, so too did O'Brien. An author who unblinkingly questioned the mores of Catholic Ireland, she saw two of her novels banned in her own country. The Irish Censorship of Publications Board ruled against *Mary Lavelle* (1936) because of its depiction of an Irish governess's affair with her Spanish employer's married son; they did the same to *The Land of Spices* (1941). Overlooking the beauty of this feminine counterpart to James Joyce's *Portrait of the Artist as a Young Man*, the Censorship Board banned the book on the basis of a single line, in which the protagonist is shocked to find her father "in the embrace of love" with his male student.

Even after these setbacks, O'Brien did not flinch from confronting what were difficult issues honestly and with sympathy. *That Lady*, both a historical novel and a Broadway play, depicts the consequences of the widow Ana de Mendoza's ethical decisions when she takes Antonio Perez as her lover and refuses to allow either King or Church to judge her actions. Sent to prison because she will not renounce her love, Ana dies 15 years later, never yielding to those who would dictate to her.

O'Brien's last two novels go even further in their exploration of women's hearts and the tension between duty and desire, but in these novels of the 20th century, women face society more confidently than in the past. In *The Flower of May*, Fanny Morrow's solitary truth seeking contrasts with the actions of her best friend and sister. Her friend, Lucie, depends on men to feel alive; her married sister, Lilian, has the indelicacy to indulge in an affair even as her mother, Julia Delahunt, is dying. Just when Fanny needs a weapon to help her defend her family and ensure her own independence, she receives from her Aunt Eleanor a gift akin to Virginia Woolf's "£500 and a room of one's own": the Delahunt family home. Financial independence gives Fanny the confidence and the means to stop her sister's affair and to educate herself. In this novel the author concentrates on the more positive aspects of familial strength and represents the power of love between women.

O'Brien's last novel, *As Music and Splendour* (1958), goes even further and depicts the love between women as a lesbian relationship. In this novel set in the Paris opera world of the late 1880s, O'Brien presents the lesbian relationship as being as normal as a heterosexual relationship, with which it is juxtaposed. Both kinds of love produce both pleasure and pain, and when they are over, art remains, and gives hope.

Unlike that of her male contemporaries, Kate O'Brien's works fell out out of print until recently; her books are now, finally, being read again, and she is influencing a new generation of feminists in Ireland and elsewhere.

—Maria M. Davidis

O'CATARACT, Jehu. *See* **NEAL, John.**

O'FAOLAIN, Julia

Also writes as Julia Martines. **Nationality:** Irish. **Born:** Dublin, Ireland, 6 June 1932; daughter of novelist Sean O'Faolain. **Education:** University College, Dublin, B.A. and M.A.; graduate study at Università di Roma and Sorbonne, Paris. **Family:** Married Lauro Martines, one son. **Career:** Writer, translator and language teacher. Contributor of short fiction to periodicals, including *Irish Press, Kenyon Review, New Yorker, New York Times, Saturday Evening Post,* London *Times,* and *Washington Post.* **Awards:** Booker Prize short list, 1980, for *No Country for Young Men.* **Agent:** Deborah Rogers, Ltd., 49 Blenheim Crescent, London W11, England.

Publications

Novels

Godded and Codded. London, Faber, 1970; as *Three Lovers,* New York, Coward, 1971.
Women in the Wall. London, Faber, and New York, Viking, 1975.
No Country for Young Men. London, Allen Lane, and New York, Carroll & Graf, 1980.
The Obedient Wife. London, Allen Lane, and New York, Carroll & Graf, 1982.
The Irish Signorina. London, Allen Lane, and New York, Carroll & Graf, 1984.

Short Stories

We Might See Sights! and Other Stories. London, Faber, 1968.
Man in the Cellar. London, Faber, 1974.
Melancholy Baby and Other Stories. Dublin, Poolbeg Press, 1978.
Daughters of Passion. London, Allen Lane, 1982.
The Judas Cloth. London, Sinclair Stevenson, 1992.

Other

Editor, with Lauro Martines, *Not in God's Image: Women in History from the Greeks to the Victorians.* London, Temple Smith, and New York, Harper, 1973.

Translator (as Julia Martines), *Two Memoirs of Renaissance Florence: The Diaries of Buonaccorso Piti and Gregorio Dati,* edited by Gene Bruckner. New York, Harper, 1967.
Translator (as Julia Martines), *A Man of Parts,* by Piero Chiara. Boston, Little Brown, 1968.

*

Critical Studies: *Two Decades of Irish Writers: A Critical Survey* edited by Douglas Dunn, Dufor, 1975; *Six Irish Writers* by Ann Weeks, Tucson, University of Arizona Press, n.d.

* * *

Julia O'Faolain is one of the best-known novelists in contemporary Anglo-Irish literature. Like most Irish writers of the post-World War II generation, O'Faolain writes about the social changes Ireland has gone through since its independence from England; unlike most of her Irish contemporaries, she has not restricted herself to writing about Ireland. Her wider concerns with the institutional powers of church and family, as well as her concerns with the identity politics of feminism, have led her to expand her field of vision to America, Italy, and even 6th-century Gaul.

Born in 1932 in London and raised in Ireland, O'Faolain is the daughter of Séan O'Faolain, perhaps the most influential Irish literary and social critic of the 20th century—and also a novelist. Julia O'Faolain received her bachelor's and master's degrees from University College, Dublin, then traveled to Europe where she pursued her graduate degree at the Sorbonne in Paris and the Università di Roma. She married Lauro Martines and worked in Italy as an author, translator, and language teacher; the distance from Ireland helped O'Faolain to forge a separate identity, out from under her famous father's shadow. This pressure may explain why her first fiction publication, 1968's *We Might See Sights!,* was a collection of Irish short stories written in Italy; in stories like "Melancholy Baby," "A Pot of Soothing Herbs," and "Turkish Delight," she sketches Irish characters and reveals the limitations of a people too overwhelmed by outdated religious dogma or the heroes of their national past to build a new future. This forthright political agenda singles O'Faolain out from most of the Irish women writers of her time who tend to deal with politics indirectly—often by setting their Irish novels in the past and focusing on nostalgia. O'Faolain, however, represents the oppression of women by both the Church and the Irish State as being too important and pervasive—affecting everything from divorce law to the chances of unification with Northern Ireland—to approach by any but the most direct means.

O'Faolain's work traces the roots of sexism to the door of the Catholic church and to the institution of the family. She characterizes both as repressive, concerned with preserving traditional morality at the expense of personal freedom and happiness. She also sees both placing women in weak positions, subordinate to strong male authority figures these institutions insist must guide them. In this way, O'Faolain examines the manner in which sexism is sanctified by church and state, as well as the manner in which the deadweight of the past—conservative religion and politics—hamper contemporary women from making their own life decisions. This is the message of *No Country for Young Men,* O'Faolain's best-known novel. The story concerns a married woman, Grainne O'Malley, who tries to leave her husband—a man who is also her first cousin—but is thwarted by her uncle, who represents the Irish political machine, the heroic past (the O'Malleys are descendants of a famous patriot), and the Church, and who forbids Grainne to disgrace the family name. Short-listed for the Booker Prize, *No Country for Young Men* holds out little or no hope for the individual locked in struggle against societal mores—no matter how determined or strong that individual may be.

In *The Irish Signorina,* the ancient Cavalcanti family is in danger of dying out with its elderly matriarch Niccolosa, the Marchesa Cavalcanti. Still the Marchesa does all she can, with the help of the local priest, to prevent Anne, a young Irishwoman whose mother was once governess to the family, from marrying Guido Cavalcanti. The Marchesa finally reveals to Anne that Guido is actually her father—although even Guido does not know this. After the Marchesa's death, however, Anne chooses to marry Guido anyway, because she sees the relationship—despite its incestuousness—as her free choice and best chance for happiness. Anne's story is metaphoric in that she must throw off her mother's version of life with the Cavalcantis and the Marchesa's manipulations to create her own story. In *The Obedient Wife,* Carla, an Italian woman living in California, passes over the chance to leave her bullying husband Marco for Leo, a priest who has left orders for her sake, because the combined pressures of Marco's family and her own sense that Leo is still more devoted to the Church than to herself seem to leave her no other choice. In the short story "The Man in the Cellar," Una, a battered wife, manages to get revenge on her abusive husband, but her triumph is an exception rather than the rule.

In *Women in the Wall,* O'Faolain goes back in time to find the roots of the powerless woman, tracing them to the historical moment when family and Church are waging war for control of Europe, in 6th-century Gaul, where the family is represented by pagan Frankish clans. The family is represented as merely a site of power struggle and murder and the Church demands forsaking oneself for the greater good of the institution. Neither of these institutions offers a safe space for personal happiness or freedom—particularly for women, who are on the one hand considered spoils of war by the secular powers that be and opportunities for sin by the Church fathers.

Julia O'Faolain has continued to publish in the decades following her debut. Her steady output through the ensuing decades has included both short story collections (*Man in the Cellar, Daughters of Passion, The Judas Cloth*), and critical articles and reviews in numerous journals and magazines, including the *New York Times Book Review, Times Literary Supplement, New Yorker, Washington Post,* and the *Irish Press.* She has also edited, with Lauro Martines, *Not in God's Image: Women in History from the Greeks to the Victorians,* in which the same social institutions that have been the focus of O'Faolain's literary works are traced through a multitude of historical, legal and literary texts. O'Faolain currently lives and works in Los Angeles and London.

—Lori Rogers

OGUNDIPE-LESLIE, 'Molara

Nationality: Nigerian. **Born:** Lagos, Nigeria. **Education:** University of Ibadan, Nigeria, graduated (first class honors). **Family:** Two daughters. **Career:** Formerly member of faculty, University of Ibadan, and chairman, Department of English, Ogun State University, Nigeria. Lecturer in English and African literature at universities in Africa, Canada, and the United States, including Columbia University, Harvard University, University of California—Berkeley, and Northwestern University. Contributing essayist and member of editorial board, *The Guardian* (newspaper), Nigeria. National director of Social Mobilization, Federal Government of Nigeria, 1987-89. **Member:** Women in Nigeria (founding member), Association of African Women for Research and Development (founding member).

Publications

Essays

Re-Creating Ourselves: African Women and Critical Transformations. Trenton, New Jersey, Africa World Press, 1994.

Uncollected Essays

"The Female Writer and Her Commitment," in *The Guardian* (Lagos), 21 December 1983.

"Not Spinning on the Axis of Maleness," in *Sisterhood Is Global: The International Women's Movement Anthology,* edited by Robin Morgan. Garden City, New York, Doubleday, 1984; Harmondsworth, Penguin, 1985.

"African Women, Culture and Another Development," in *Theorizing Black Feminisms,* edited by Stanlie James and Abena Busia. London and New York, Routledge, 1993.

"Women in Africa and Her Diaspora: From Marginality to Empowerment," in *Moving Beyond Boundaries,* Vol. 1: *International Dimensions of Women's Writing,* edited by Ogundipe-Leslie and Carole Boyce Davies. New York, New York University Press, 1995.

"'Re-creating Ourselves All over the World.' A Conversation with Paule Marshall," and "The Bilingual to Quintulingual Poet in Africa," in *Moving beyond Boundaries,* Vol. 2: *Black Women's Diasporas,* edited by Carole Boyce Davies. New York, New York University Press, 1995.

Poetry

Sew the Old Days and Other Poems. Nigeria, Evans Bros., 1985.

Other

Editor, with Carole Boyce Davies, *Moving beyond Boundaries*, Vol. 1: *International Dimensions of Women's Writing*. New York, New York University Press, 1995.

*

Critical Studies: *Nigerian Female Writers: A Critical Perspective* edited by Henrietta Otukunefor and Obiagele Nwodo, Lagos, Nigeria, Malthouse, 1989; *In Their Own Voices: African Women Writers Talk* (interview) by Adeola James, London, James Currey, 1990.

* * *

The analysis of socioeconomic class, in its provision of a solid global mode for connecting women, is central to the feminist work of Nigerian educator and critic 'Molara Ogundipe-Leslie.

In her essay "The Female Writer and Her Commitment" Ogundipe-Leslie asserts that, for her, "female writers cannot usefully claim to be concerned with various social predicaments in their countries or in Africa without situating their awareness and solutions within the larger global context of imperialism and neocolonialism." Questions of class have been a particularly visible aspect of the colonial and neo-colonial situations in the author's homeland of Nigeria, where many women lost certain measures of economic autonomy they had enjoyed before the onset of British rule and in its aftermath. Similar insights are shared by materialist, socialist, and Marxist feminists in different parts of the globe, both in the "first" and "third" worlds, who believe that women's liberation requires a dismantling of not only oppressive patriarchal rule, but also exploitative capitalist relations.

An activist, poet, scholar, and mother, Ogundipe-Leslie's dynamic participation in global feminism in general, and African feminism in particular, has taken many forms. Born in Lagos, Nigeria, of Yoruba descent, Ogundipe-Leslie, a graduate (with first class honors) of the University of Ibadan, has taught English and African literature, and held numerous posts in various universities in Nigeria and around the world, including Columbia, Berkeley, Harvard, and Northwestern in the United States. A weekly contributing essayist for *The Guardian*, she also served on the editorial board of that Nigerian newspaper. As National Director of Social Mobilization in the Federal Government of Nigeria from 1987-89, her position focused on the political and cultural education of women. She is a founding member of WIN (Women in Nigeria), a women's research and activist group, and AAWORD (Association of African Women for Research and Development), an African women's research organization based in Senegal.

The 1994 publication of *Re-Creating Ourselves: African Women and Critical Transformations*, brings together a number of previously published and unpublished essays in which Ogundipe-Leslie addresses everything from marginalized literary works to masculinist tendencies in revolutionary discourse and liberation movements. In addition, she discusses the grave implications of inequitable contemporary capitalist practices, such as those represented by the power of the International Monetary Fund, on the lives of African men and women.

The diversity of issues analyzed in *Re-Creating Ourselves* reflects the broad range of commitments that constitute 'Molara Ogundipe-Leslie's feminism. This diversity is a testament to her basic premise—stated in her 1984 essay "Not Spinning on the Axis of Maleness" included in Robin Morgan's groundbreaking anthology *Sisterhood Is Global*—that "men are not the enemy. The enemy is the total societal system.... As women's liberation is but an aspect of the need to liberate the total society from dehumanization, it is the social system which must be changed. But," Ogundipe-Leslie adds, "men do become enemies when they seek to retard or even block these necessary historical changes."

—Mahnaz Ghaznavi

OLSEN, Tillie

Also wrote as Tillie Lerner. **Nationality:** American. **Born:** Tillie Lerner, Omaha, Nebraska, 14 January 1913. **Education:** Attended high school. **Family:** 1) Daughter, born 1932; 2) Married Jack Olsen in 1943 (died), three daughters. **Career:** Worked in the service, warehouse, and food processing industries, and as an office typist. Writer-in-residence, Amherst College, Amherst, Massachusetts, 1969-70, Massachusetts Institute of Technology, Cambridge, 1973, and Kenyon College, Gambier, Ohio, beginning 1987; visiting professor, Stanford University, Stanford, California, 1971, and University of Massachusetts, Boston, 1974; visiting lecturer, University of California, San Diego, 1978; International Visiting Scholar, Norway, 1980; Hill Professor, University of Minnesota, Minneapolis, 1986; Regents' professor, University of California, Los Angeles, 1988. Creative writing fellow, Stanford University, 1956-57; fellow, Radcliffe Institute for Independent Study, Cambridge, Massachusetts, 1962-64. **Awards:** Ford grant, 1959; O. Henry Award, 1961, for *Tell Me a Riddle;* National Endowment for the Humanities grant, 1966, 1984; American Academy award, 1975; Guggenheim fellowship, 1975; Unitarian Women's Federation award, 1980; "Tillie Olsen Day" observed in San Francisco, 1981; Bunting Institute fellowship, 1986; Nebraska Library Association Mari Sandoz award, 1991; Rea award, 1994. Doctor of Arts and Letters: University of Nebraska, Lincoln, 1979; D.Litt.: Knox College, 1982; Albright College, Reading, 1986, Mills College, 1995; L.H.D.: Hobart & William Smith Colleges, 1984; Clark University, 1985; Wooster College, 1991. **Address:** 1435 Laguna, No. 6, San Francisco, California 94115, USA.

Publications

Novel

Yonnondio: From the '30s. New York, Delacorte Press, 1974; London, Faber, 1975.

Short Stories

"The Iron Throat" (as Tillie Lerner), in *Partisan Review*, 1, April/May 1934.

Tell Me a Riddle (includes "I Stand Here Ironing," "Hey Sailor, What Ship?," and "O Yes"). Philadelphia, Lippincott, 1962; London, Faber, 1964.

"Requa," in *Iowa Review,* 1(3), summer 1970; as "Requa-I" in *The Best American Short Stories 1971,* edited by Martha Foley and David Burnett. Boston, Houghton Mifflin, 1971.

Poetry

"I Want You Women Up North to Know" (as Tillie Lerner), in *Partisan,* 1, March 1934.
"There Is a Lesson" (as Tillie Lerner), in *Partisan,* 1, April 1934.

Other

"Thousand-Dollar Vagrant" (as Tillie Lerner), in *New Republic,* 29 August 1934.
"The Strike" (as Tillie Lerner), in *Partisan Review,* 1, September/October 1934.
"A Biographical Interpretation" (Afterword), in *Life in the Iron Mills* by Rebecca Harding Davis. Old Westbury, New York, Feminist Press, 1972.
"Women Who Are Writers in Our Century: One out of Twelve," in *College English,* 34, October 1972.
Silences. New York, Delacorte Press, 1978; London: Virago Press, 1980.
"The Word Made Flesh," in *Critical Thinking/Critical Writing: Prize-Winning High School and College Essays.* Cedar Falls, Iowa, University of Northern Iowa, 1984.

Editor, *Mother to Daughter and Daughter to Mother: A Feminist Press Daybook and Reader.* Old Westbury, New York, Feminist Press, 1984; London, Virago Press, 1985.
Editor, with Julie Olsen-Edwards and Estelle Jussim, *Mothers and Daughters: That Special Quality: An Exploration in Photograph.* New York, Aperture, 1987.

*

Media Adaptations: *Tell Me a Riddle* (film), Filmways, 1980.

Manuscript Collection: Berg Collection of English and American Literature, New York Public Library; American Literature Archives, Stanford University Library, Stanford, California.

Critical Studies: "Tillie Olsen: The Weight of Things Unsaid" by Sandy Boucher, in *Ms.*, September 1974; "De-Riddling Tillie Olsen's Writing" by Selma Burkom and Margaret Williams, in *San Jose Studies* 2, February 1976; "Tillie Olsen: Wings of Life" by Barbara Adams, in *Ithaca Times*, April 1980; "Tillie Olsen: Storyteller of Working America" by Sally Cuneen, in *Christian Century,* 21, May 1980; "'I Stand Here Ironing': Motherhood as Experience and Metaphor" by Joanne S. Frye, in *Studies in Short Fiction,* 18, summer 1981; "From the '30s: Tillie Olsen and the Radical Tradition" by Deborah Rosenfelt, in *Feminist Studies,* 7, fall 1981; "Coming of Age in the '30s: A Portrait of Tillie Olsen" by Erika Duncan, in *Book Forum: An International Transdisciplinary Quarterly,* 4, 1982; "Grace Paley and Tillie Olsen: Radical Jewish Humanists" by John Clayton, in *Contemporary Jewish Review,* 46, 1984; "After Long Silence: Tillie Olsen's 'Requa'" by Blanche H. Gelfant, in *Studies in American Fiction,* 12, spring 1984; *Tillie Olsen* by Abigail Martin, Boise, Idaho, Boise State University, 1984; "Literary Foremothers and Writers' Silences: Tillie Olsen's Autobiographical Fiction" by Rose Kamel, in *MELUS,* 12(3), fall 1985; "Sisters in Protest" by Frances M. Malpezzi, in *Artes Liberales,* 12, spring 1986; "Earth, Air, Fire, and Water in *Tell Me a Riddle*" by Naomi M. Jacobs, in *Studies in Short Fiction,* 23, fall 1986; "Tillie Olsen: The Writer as Jewish Woman" by Bonnie Lyons, in *Studies in American Jewish Literature,* 5, 1986; *Tillie Olsen and a Feminist Spiritual Vision* by Elaine Neil Orr, Jackson, University Press of Mississippi, 1987; "'A Child of Anxious, Not Proud, Love': Mother and Daughter in Tillie Olsen's 'I Stand Here Ironing' by Helen Pike Bauer, in *Mother Puzzles: Daughters and Mothers in Contemporary American Literature,* edited by Mickey Pearlman, Westport, Connecticut, Greenwood Press, 1989; "The Unnatural Silences of Tillie Olsen" by Anne Trensky, in *Studies in Short Fiction,* 27(4), fall 1990; *Tillie Olsen* by Abby Werlock and Pearlman, Boston, Twayne, 1991; "On the Side of the Mother: *Yonnondio* and *Call It Sleep*" by Elaine Orr, in *Studies in American Fiction,* 21(2), autumn 1993; *Protest and Possibility in the Writing of Tillie Olsen* by Mara Faulkner, Charlottesville and London, University Press of Virginia, 1993; *The Critical Response to Tillie Olsen* edited by Kay Hoyle Nelson and Nancy Huse, Westport, Connecticut, and London, Greenwood Press, 1994; *Listening to Silences* edited by Elaine Hedges and Shelley Fisher Fishkin, New York and Oxford, Oxford University Press, 1994; *Better Red* by Constance Coiner, New York, Oxford University Press, 1995; *Tillie Olsen: A Study of the Short Fiction* by Joanne Frye, Boston, Twayne, 1995; *Tell Me A Riddle* by Deborah Rosenfelt, Rutgers, Rutgers University Press, 1995; "'People Who Might Have Been You': Agency and the Damaged Self in Tillie Olsen's *Yonnondio*" by Lisa Orr, in *Women's Studies Quarterly,* 1-2, 1995.

* * *

Tillie Olsen's life and art reflect her commitment to providing a voice for working-class men, women, and children silenced in a world divided by gender, class, and race. As a feminist writer, Olsen's vision is filtered through women's traditional roles and often mundane experiences. Her protagonists are not larger than life; if they appear so, it is because Olsen has succeeded in revealing the heroism of individuals engaged in the daily struggle to survive.

Olsen's oeuvre embodies the combination of Jewish humanism and American idealism that characterized her youth. She was born Tillie Lerner in 1913 to Samuel and Ida Lerner, a couple who had fled Russia in 1905 in the wake of the failed revolution, settled in Nebraska, and embraced American socialism. Olsen credits her "Jewish socialist" background with providing the central insights that inform her fiction, including a "knowledge and experience of injustice" and "an absolute belief in the potentiality of human beings." In 1929 Olsen left high school in order to work. However, she furthered her education at the Omaha Public Library, gleaning much from such radical publications as *Modern Quarterly, The Liberator,* and *The Masses*. In 1931 she joined the Young Communist League.

During the decade of the 1930s Olsen became a politically active writer and mother. Recovering from illness in 1932, she began to write *Yonnondio,* a work that would not appear in print until 1974 and then in unfinished form. That same year she gave birth to Karla, the first of four daughters. (Olsen has remained silent on the identification of Karla's father.) In 1933 Olsen settled with her daughter in California. There, as political activist, writer, and mother, Olsen began her first prolific period of writing. During

1934 she published the fictional "The Iron Throat," two poems, and two articles. Although she remained active throughout 1935, participating in the American Writers Conference along with such prominent authors as Michael Gold, Richard Wright, Theodore Dreiser, and Nathaniel West, Olsen did not publish for several years. In 1937 she gave birth to her second child, her first by husband Jack Olsen, whom she had met in 1933. During the nearly two decades between the birth of her second daughter and the publication of "I Stand Here Ironing" in 1957, Olsen's literary voice was silent.

Olsen's goal of using art for political and social purposes reflected the trend of contemporary radical fiction, a genre that grew in popularity during the 1930s. She vowed to write the lives of "despised" or marginalized peoples. The works published during the fruitful year 1934 reflect her ideology: "The Iron Throat" is a polemic against capitalism; "The Strike" is an impressionistic account of Bloody Thursday, a violent clash between striking longshoremen and police; and the related piece, "Thousand Dollar Vagrant," recounts Olsen's arrest during the clash. Her poem "I Want You Women up North to Know" expresses her outrage at the exploitation of sweatshop labor.

These pieces, taken along with *Yonnondio,* are indicative of what separates the writing of women from that of men during the 1930s; namely, a concern with issues of class *and* gender. *Yonnondio* is important both for what it is—a novel left unfinished as a result of the multiple challenges faced by Olsen as artist, mother, activist, and worker—and for what it is not—a work that reflects the conventions dictated by the masculinist tradition of proletariat fiction. The novel examines a brutal period in the life of the Holbrook family as they move from a mining town to a farming community, and from there to the city. Olsen intended to develop the story of father Jim's political awakening and to conclude with two of the Holbrook children, Will and Mazie, as they travel to California to become organizers. Mazie, who was to become an artist and tell her mother's story, would serve as a model of personal achievement, political awareness, and artistic success. Mazie never achieves her success; conflicting responsibilities compelled Olsen to put aside *Yonnondio.* However, it is shadowed in her later work, *Silences,* as Olsen examines the nature and variety of the impediments that confront and silence artists like herself, among them family responsibilities, poverty, and, most importantly, gender.

Yonnondio is not a conventional proletariat novel. The early chapters contain the authorial intrusions offering political commentary and revolutionary prophecy conventions in proletariat fiction—conventions established by the male-dominated preserve of the Communist Party elite. However, as Mazie's struggle becomes a central theme, gender emerges as an issue as important as that of class. Because the Party decried attempts to privilege feminist concerns above those of the proletariat, author Olsen was confronted with the tensions between what she sought to achieve in her novel and what was conventional for leftist writers.

Olsen's work is indicative of the trend among many proletariat women writers of the 1930s, including Josephine Herbst, Tess Slesinger, and Agnes Smedley: to expand the definition and range of radical fiction. Women writers addressed issues of gender and the female experience, particularly maternity and motherhood. These issues inform three of the stories collected in *Tell Me A Riddle*: the title story, "I Stand Here Ironing," and "O Yes." Although the fourth story in the collection, "Hey Sailor, What Ship?," and the later "Requa," feature male protagonists, both examine themes evident throughout Olsen's work: the potential for human creativity and growth, the salvific power of compassion, and the instinct of the members of the working class towards survival.

Contemporary feminists continue to embrace Olsen. Her fiction and essays, including the provocative "Afterword" to Rebecca Harding Davis's *Life in the Iron Mills*, address the challenges faced by women as they seek personal fulfillment in the face of their duties as mothers, artists, and workers. Although Olsen's subjects are rooted in the political activism of the '30s, she recognizes that the shaping influences of gender and race are as significant as those of class. In her work, class consciousness and feminist consciousness intertwine.

—Jeraldine R. Kraver

OSCEOLA. *See* **BLIXEN, Karen (Christentze Dinesen).**

P

PAGELS, Elaine (Hiesey)

Nationality: American. **Born:** Palo Alto, California, 13 February 1943. **Family:** Married the physicist Heinz R. Pagels in 1969 (died 1988); one daughter, two sons (one of them deceased). **Education:** Stanford University, B.A. 1964, M.A., 1965; Harvard University, Ph.D. 1970. **Career:** Assistant professor, 1970-74, professor of history of religion, then head of department, 1974-82, Barnard College, New York; Harrington Spear Paine Professor of Religion, Princeton University, Princeton, New Jersey, beginning 1982. Member of editorial and translation board, *The Nag Hammadi Library in English,* Harper, 1978. Contributor to journals, including *Harvard Theological Review.* **Awards:** National Endowment for the Humanities grant, 1972-73; Aspen Institute of Humanistic Studies Mellon fellow, 1974; Hazen fellow, 1975; Rockefeller fellow, 1978-79; National Book Critics Circle award, 1979, for *The Gnostic Gospels;* Guggenheim fellow, 1979-80; American Book Award, 1980, for *The Gnostic Gospels;* MacArthur Prize fellow, 1981-87. **Member:** Society of Biblical Literature, American Academy of Religion. **Address:** Department of Religion, Princeton University, Princeton, New Jersey 08544, U.S.A.

PUBLICATIONS

Religion/Spirituality

The Johannine Gospel in Gnostic Exegesis: Heracleon's Commentary on John. Nashville, Tennessee, Abingdon, 1973.

The Gnostic Paul: Gnostic Exegesis of the Pauline Letters. Philadelphia, Fortress Press, 1975.

The Gnostic Gospels. New York, Random House, 1979.

The Gnostic Jesus and Early Christian Politics. Tempe, Arizona State University, 1981.

Adam, Eve and the Serpent. New York, Random House, and London, Weidenfeld & Nicholson, 1988.

The Origins of Satan. New York, Random House, 1995.

*

Critical Studies: "Women and the Bible" by Cullen Murphy, in *Atlantic Monthly,* August 1993; "Le Diable au Coer" by Norman Cohn, in *New York Review of Books,* 21 September 1995.

Elaine Pagels comments:

Reflection on feminist issues, during the mid 1970s, initiated a kind of intellectual conversion experience. In graduate school at Harvard, intellectual history was regarded as distinct from social, political, and institutional history; but as I worked on the material to Chapter 3 of *The Gnostic Gospels* ("God the Father/God the Mother"), I experienced the collapse of these categories. From that time on I was, in effect, writing what is called "social history," which *includes* history of culture and what formerly was called "history of ideas"—as if ideas existed in a cloudy stratosphere independent of the human world.

* * *

The feminist aspect of the studies of early Christian history that make up the work of Elaine Pagels can best be understood within the context of the larger feminist enterprise of biblical and historical scholarship. This enterprise, which seeks to undo some of the patriarchal legacy of traditional biblical interpretation and provide a foundation for some of the demands of many women to be allowed a more active role in church and synagogue, proceeds largely by looking for archeological and textual evidence that women living in biblical times participated more fully in the religious institutions of their day than biblical and historical scholars have traditionally acknowledged. By presenting such alternative interpretations, feminist scholars work to reevaluate texts that have historically been read as supporting women's exclusion and oppression.

In spite of the rapid growth of the field of feminist biblical studies in recent years, Pagels remains one of the few scholars of early Christian history who can lay claim to a wide readership outside the halls of academia. Her reputation stems largely from the publication, in 1979, of *The Gnostic Gospels,* a study of a group of texts know generally as the Nag Hammadi Library: writings believed by many scholars to date to the infancy of Christianity that, because of their differences from the more familiar four Gospels of the Christian New Testament, often seem shocking and controversial to modern Christian readers.

Prior to the publication of *The Gnostic Gospels,* Pagels's work was relatively unknown except to other biblical scholars. Her early work, which consisted of scholarly studies of Gnostic interpretations of biblical texts (*The Johannine Gospel in Gnostic Exegesis* and *The Gnostic Paul*), nevertheless laid the groundwork for her later, more popular writings by exploring some common beliefs that linked the early Christian factions that were called "Gnostic" by their enemies in the emerging church.

The Gnostic Gospels, in which Pagels considers the social and historical contexts for the differences between Gnostic and orthodox Christianity, met with both wild enthusiasm and harsh criticism at the time of its publication and continues to find a large, though not always persuaded, audience. A major reason for the book's popularity, as well as its notoriety, is its implicitly feminist claim that in Gnostic Christianity women found greater theological and ecclesiastical freedom and influence than in orthodoxy. Pagels focusses her study on the theological debates that marked the 1st and 2nd centuries following the life of Jesus, a period during which the leaders of the increasingly institutionalized Christian movement were deciding which texts would be included in the New Testament, and which would be judged heretical and thus excluded. One of her major claims with respect to the texts that were labelled heresy is that, while not representing a unified system of beliefs, they contain many common elements, one of the most significant being a recognition of the importance of women and of the feminine aspect of spirituality that was missing from or repressed by orthodox Christianity. She further argues that this recognition of the importance of the feminine had striking implications for both the theologies and the social organizations of various Gnostic groups, often allowing women to assume significant leadership within those groups.

In *Adam, Eve, and the Serpent,* published nine years after *The Gnostic Gospels,* Pagels continues to examine the writings of the

Nag Hammadi Library in order to demonstrate the existence of an alternate tradition of Christian stories about the creation of the universe, a tradition that does not support more conventional understandings of the nature of sin and of woman's place in the cosmic order. Here Eve is not the mother of original sin, men are not the ordained masters of women, and sexuality is not inherently sinful. This alternate interpretive heritage, which until quite recently was largely ignored by most biblical scholars, supports the work of contemporary feminists who attempt to construct ways of reading Jewish and Christian scriptures that do not contribute to the oppression of women. In calling this tradition to the attention of a popular audience Pagels arguably continues to make a significant contribution to the field of feminist biblical criticism.

More recently, however, with the 1995 publication of *The Origins of Satan,* explicitly feminist themes have essentially disappeared from Pagels's work. In this book she explores the development of the idea of Satan within the history of Christian theology, focussing in particular on the process by which the enemies of Christian orthodoxy—from Jews to heretical Christians—are identified as agents of Satan intent on sabotaging Christ's salvation of humanity from sin. Of particular interest to Pagels is the seeming tendency, within Christianity, to demonize those elements of society that are different from, yet closely identified with, Christians themselves. *The Origins of Satan* is not, however, without its value to feminists interested in the history of Christianity. Scholars wishing to draw useful insights from *The Origins of Satan* might well note how Pagels lays the groundwork for the observation that it is women themselves who are most often demonized in this way within the Christian heritage—although this is a claim that Pagels herself stops short of, preferring to point instead to the treatment of Jews and unorthodox Christians at the hands of the early Christian church.

Elaine Pagels has had an important impact within the field of feminist biblical criticism and early Christian history. In fact, many readers outside of the academy have been introduced to feminist themes within these related fields by means of her work. Because of the continued popularity of her work, it is probable that Pagels will continue to influence young feminist scholars, regardless of whether she returns to explicitly feminist issues in her own work.

—Judith Poxon

PAGLIA, Camille (Anna)

Nationality: American. **Born:** Endicott, New York, 2 April 1947. **Education:** State University of New York, Binghamton, B.A. in English (summa cum laude) 1968; Yale University, M.Phil. 1971, Ph.D. 1974. **Career:** Faculty member in literature and languages division, Bennington College, Bennington, Vermont, 1972-80; visiting lecturer in English, Wesleyan University, Middletown, Connecticut, 1980; fellow, Ezra Stiles College, 1981, visiting lecturer in comparative literature, 1981 and 1984, visiting lecturer in English, 1981-83, fellow, Silliman College, 1984, Yale University, New Haven, Connecticut; assistant professor, 1984-86, associate professor, 1987-91; professor of humanities, beginning 1991, Philadelphia College of Performing Arts (now University of the Arts), Philadelphia, Pennsylvania. **Awards:** National Book Critics Circle Award nomination for criticism, 1991, for *Sexual Personae: Art and Decadence from Nefertiti to Emily Dickinson.* **Agent:** Lynn Nesbit, Janklow & Nesbit, 598 Madison Ave., New York, New York 10022, U.S.A. **Address:** Department of Humanities, University of the Arts, 320 South Broad St., Philadelphia, Pennsylvania 19102, U.S.A.

Publications

Political/Social Theory

Sexual Personae: Art and Decadence from Nefertiti to Emily Dickinson. New Haven, Connecticut, Yale University Press, 1990.

Essays

Sex, Art, and American Culture: Essays. New York, Vintage, 1992; London, Viking, 1993.

Vamps and Tramps: New Essays. New York, Vintage, 1994; London, Viking, 1995.

*

Critical Studies: "The Perverse *Kulturgeschichte* of Camille Paglia" by William Kerrigan, in *Raritan,* 10(3), December 1990; "The Politics of the Outrageous" by Teresa L. Ebert, in *Women's Review of Books,* 9(1), October 1991; "Freaked Out: Camille Paglia's *Sexual Personae*" by Sandra M. Gilbert, 1991; "I'm Not a Feminist But I Play One on TV" by Susan Faludi, in *Ms.,* March/April 1995.

* * *

Camille Paglia has transformed herself into a cipher for feminists and commentators in the past several years. Feminist critic Sandra Gilbert, in a review of *Sexual Personae,* describes her as an "idiot savant," and Susan Faludi characterizes her as the precursor to the "pod feminists" who might have as their slogan "I'm not a feminist but I play one on TV." Elsewhere, accusations have been made that Paglia's works are self-advertisement.

Part of Paglia's vicious attraction, even for otherwise dismissive readers, is that she flaunts the stodgy, cautious conventions of academic writing. In a literary frenzy *Sexual Personae* weaves intellectual insights with witty personal reaction and analogies to contemporary culture.

Her reintroduction of the erotic, popular imagination to the intellectual one, however, yields strange fruit. Paglia ambitiously peddles her work as a history of sexual personae, such as the "femme fatale" or the "pretty boy," from Nefertiti to Emily Dickinson. Revitalizing "biology is destiny" arguments she argues for "the truth in sexual stereotypes." "Sex is natural in man," she claims, and "nature has a master agenda we can only dimly know." She rejects feminist claims that society causes women's problems. "Society," she notes, "is the force which keeps crime in check." Without it, our innate cruelty—"the great neglected or suppressed item of the modern, humanist agenda"—would burst forth. Paglia finds evidence for the Hobbesian idea that we would live "short, nasty, and brutish" lives without society's restraints in art and aesthetics, which illustrate the thriving continuity of pagan traditions against Judeo-Christianity and the waxing of the liberal state.

The stronger "civilization"gets, the more decadent sexual personae become.

Art's "parade of sex personae"—"our message from beyond"—are "vehicles of ... assault against nature," male attempts to wrest control from "chthonian," primal female thorough culture, a drama re-staged throughout history with the same ambiguous results. The pretty boy or the homosexual fascinate Paglia as the most cogent, if doomed, defense men stage against aesthetically "grotesque" female bodies. The heroic Marquis de Sade's "sadomasochistic inventions are modes of distancing by which male imagination tries to free itself from female origins," she argues. "Scratch a fabulist and you'll find fear of women and fear of nature. Fable is marshmallow myth—it is myth stripped of chthonian realities."

The book ultimately leaves us with the conversation-stopper that "you can't argue with Mother Nature."

If art enacts male struggles against the awesome (female) power of nature, how can we account for *female* artists? Paglia handles Emily Dickinson through a version of soul cross-dressing, by which the poet is rebaptized as the "Madame de Sade," a "*male genius* and visionary sadist" in her "hidden inner life."

Sexual Personae delights in this sort of bizarre juxtaposition. The Beach Boys' falsetto choir in the otherwise heterosexual anthem "California Girls" reminds Paglia of Lord Byron's sexual ambiguities. The band epitomizes an "annoying self-congratulatory modern youth culture that Byron began." She anoints Tina Turner as "Shakespeare's 'tawny' Cleopatra in all her moods." Her comparisons are consistently thought-provoking and wonderfully jarring. Yet for others they make *Sexual Personae* the intellectual equivalent of a highway accident—parts scattered randomly, the Beach Boys strewn together with Lord Byron, Tina Turner colliding with Cleopatra—its wildness is so horrifying that you can't *help* but look.

This is Paglia's intent—she does not want us to judge her writing by conventional academic rules or disciplinary protocols, which she consistently violates. Yet, there is something disingenuous—and anti-intellectual—in Paglia's ascent to celebrity through caricaturing and annoying feminists but refusing to discuss the wealth of feminist, including Luce Irigaray, Judith Butler, and Gayle Rubin, to name a handful, who have wrestled with the topics she explores in complex ways. "Feminism, like all liberal movements," she states in her introduction, as if all feminism belonged to the liberal tradition, despite a variety—Marxist, poststructuralist, cultural—that move beyond the rhetoric of "rights" Paglia rants against. (Interestingly, her own work reads "natural" superiority to men's destructive cultural impulses). Similarly, her wise confession that "sex is a more powerful force than feminism has admitted" takes a *part* of feminism (antipornography crusaders) as the *whole.* Consequently, she overlooks numerous feminist writers who have done the kind of courageous soul searching about sex's bewildering power that Paglia undertakes in *Sexual Personae.*

She is, as Gilbert notes, a profoundly *self*-conscious author. The space left vacant by Paglia's refusal to engage with conventional standards of accountability or the feminist intellectual tradition is filled by the author's capacious ego. In the absence of any protocol such as the historian's attention to cause and effect or the art historian's sensitivity to cultural context, why should we *believe* Paglia's claims? Evidently, because she *tells* us they are true. Paglia characterizes this "method" of shocking assertion as "a form of sensationalism." Others have described it less charitably as "a pornography of ideas."

In any case, Paglia's technique of recycling conservative clichés about biological determinism, dressing them in stylish costume to give them an innovative, *non* conservative look, and *proclaiming* them true has silenced any ideological criticism of her work before the fact. As Faludi elaborates, Paglia "is more of an attention-seeking generator of outrageous one liner than an conservative in feminist costume. She dons and discards so many masks—from drag queen celebrator to bondage n' leather poster girl—that it's hard to say whether under her veils a person with a coherent set of political beliefs really exists at all." This is unfortunate because Paglia's project is an important one for academic feminists; she is trying to find a way to speak meaningfully about culture outside of arcane academic discourses. Yet there must be something other than the *self*—the author's own quirkiness—which replaces those discourses in order for the work to have *political* value for feminists.

Paglia has continued her odd self-canonization in *Vamps and Tramps,* which serves up a muscled, flamboyant "drag queen feminism" as an antidote to anti-pornography wimps. Here, she reminisces that she was destined to "look in the latrine of culture." She remains unfazed by charges that she has done more than look in it.

—Pamela Haag

PALEY, Grace

Nationality: American. **Born:** Grace Goodside, New York, New York, 11 December 1922. **Education:** Attended Hunter College (now of the City University of New York), 1938-39, and New York University. **Family:** Married 1) Jess Paley in 1942, one daughter and one son; 2) the playwright Robert Nichols in 1972. **Career:** Taught at Columbia University, New York, and Syracuse University during the early 1960s; member of literature faculty, Sarah Lawrence College, Bronxville, New York, beginning 1966, and City College, New York, beginning 1983. Secretary, New York Greenwich Village Peace Center. Contributor to periodicals, including *Accent, Atlantic Monthly, Esquire, Genesis West,* and *Ikon.* **Awards:** Guggenheim fellowship, 1961; National Endowment for the Arts grant, 1966; National Institute of Arts and Letters award, 1970, for short stories; New York State Writers Institute Edith Wharton Citation of Merit, 1986, 1988-89, naming Paley the first "state author" of New York; National Endowment for the Arts senior fellowship, 1987; National Council on the Arts grant. **Member:** American Academy and Institute of Arts and Letters, 1980. **Address:** Box 620, Thetford Hill, Vermont 05074, U.S.A.

Publications

Short Stories

The Little Disturbances of Man: Stories of Men and Women in Love. New York, Doubleday, 1959; London, Weidenfeld & Nicolson, 1960.

Enormous Changes at the Last Minute. New York, Farrar Straus, 1974; London, Deutsch, 1975.

Later the Same Day. New York, Farrar Straus, and London, Virago Press, 1985.

The Collected Stories. New York, Farrar, Straus, 1994.

Uncollected Short Story

"Two Ways of Telling," in *Ms.* (New York), November-December 1990.

Poetry

Leaning Forward. Penobscot, Maine, Granite Press, 1985.
New and Collected Poems. Maine, Tilbury Press, 1991.
Long Walks and Intimate Talks (includes short stories), paintings by Vera B. Williams. Old Westbury, New York, Feminist Press, 1991.

Other

365 Reasons Not to Have Another War: 1989 Peace Calendar. Philadelphia and New York, New Society Publications/War Resisters' League, 1989.

*

Media Adaptations: *Enormous Changes at the Last Minute* (film), 1985.

Bibliography: "Grace Paley: A Bibliography" by Ulrich Halfmann and Philipp Gerlack, in *Tulsa Studies in Women's Literature,* 8(2), fall 1989.

Critical Studies: *Reaching Out: Sensitivity and Order in Recent American Fiction by Women* by Anne Z. Mickelson, Metuchen, New Jersey Scarecrow Press, 1979; *Grace Paley* by Sara Poli, n.p., 1983; "Grace Paley: Chaste Compactness" by Ronald Schleifer, in *Contemporary American Women Writers: Narrative Strategies,* edited by Catherine Rainwater and William J. Scheick, Lexington, University Press of Kentucky, 1985; "Grace Paley's Community: Gradual Epiphanies in the Meantime" by Barbara Eckstein, in *Politics and the Muse,* n.p., 1989; *Grace Paley: Illuminating the Dark Lives* by Jacqueline Taylor, Austin, University of Texas Press, 1990; *Grace Paley: A Study of the Short Fiction* by Neil Isaacs, Boston, Twayne, 1990; "Talking Lives: Storytelling and Renewal in Grace Paley's Short Fiction" by Victoria Aarons, in *Studies in American Jewish Literature,* 9(1), spring 1990.

* * *

In her short stories, Grace Paley uses postmodernist fictional techniques to address feminist concerns. Often focusing on female or Jewish characters, Paley's stories portray women struggling to raise their families alone or trying to regain their balance after a failed love relationship. Contemporary political issues are also present in her stories, as her characters work for world peace or protest against nuclear energy. A hallmark of all Paley's work is her talent for rendering the voices of her characters in a realistic manner, truthfully recreating their varied educational backgrounds, ethnic heritage, and regional accents. As Paley's fiction has developed, she has shown an increasing interest in the nature of fiction itself and its relationship to the life of the reader. In exploring this question, her work has sought to fuse the personal and political in a way that is typical of feminist theoretics.

The Little Disturbances of Man, Paley's first collection of stories, introduces the New York City setting of so many of her later works. It also utilizes the idiomatic speech of native New Yorkers to create realistic characters who accurately reflect their ethnic and racial backgrounds. The critically praised story "An Interest in Life," an account of a man abandoning his wife and four children, is especially noted for its combination of humor and sadness, and for the determination of the main character to overcome what she calls "the little disturbances of man." The story "Goodbye and Good Luck" contrasts the lives of two sisters, one who has married and the other who has had a long-standing relationship with a married man. The relative disappointments and regrets of both lives are examined in a sympathetic way. In "The Pale Pink Roast," Paley tells of Anna, a woman who is remarried but still sleeping with her former husband as well. Many of the stories in *The Little Disturbances of Man* reflect the actual events in Paley's own life at the time. Divorced and left with a family to raise on her own, she was also active in anti-Vietnam War rallies of the 1960s and in the early feminist movement.

The political concerns first introduced in *The Little Disturbances of Man* become more central to the stories of Paley's *Enormous Changes at the Last Minute,* which also explores more experimental fictional techniques and presents a darker vision of life. The collection contains open-ended stories that do not resolve in traditional ways, partly because Paley believes that traditional narrative structures cannot adequately present contemporary political and social realities. Nonlinear narratives, surrealistic plots, and the use of vignettes and metafictional devices mark the stories in *Enormous Changes at the Last Minute.* In "The Long-Distance Runner," a middle-aged Jewish woman jogs into her old neighborhood and spends three weeks living with the black family who now reside at her family's old apartment. In the collection's longest story, "Faith in a Tree," Paley's fictional self, Faith, finds her whole life changing once she sees an anti-war parade chased from the local park. The story "At That Time; or, The History of a Joke" is a satiric parody on the Biblical story of virgin birth, this time set in contemporary America. Paley's reputation was enhanced by these stories of women protesting against government actions or affirming their independence from the men in their lives.

In *Later the Same Day,* Paley reintroduces characters who first appeared in her earlier collections. The characters have aged but are still recognizable in their fierce determination and political commitments. Faith reappears in "Dreamer in a Dead Language," in which she visits her parents in a nursing home only to find that they are considering a divorce. In "Zagrowsky Tells," Faith listens as an elderly Jewish man recounts how his mentally impaired daughter gave birth to a black baby. "Somewhere Else" follows a group of American liberals on their enthusiastic tour of Communist China, where they inadvertently offend the authorities by taking too many photographs of working people. Upon their return to America, one of the tourists offends a group of men in a South Bronx neighborhood by taking their picture as well. In all of these stories, Paley is concerned with the process of storytelling, with the construction of history through memory and image, and with the interaction between reader and writer in creating the meaning of a text. Also injected as a major theme into *Later the Same Day,* although not in a didactic manner, are Paley's leftist political sensibilities. Her characters are seen participating in political activities even as they struggle to advise their children or care for their aging parents.

—Denise Wiloch

PANKHURST, Christabel (Harriette)

Nationality: British.

PANKHURST, Christabel (Harriette). Born: Manchester, 22 September 1880. **Education:** Educated privately; attended Manchester University; obtained a law degree. **Career:** Cofounder, with mother, Emmeline Pankhurst, Women's Social and Political Union, 1903; arrested for militancy at Liberal Party meeting, Manchester, 1905; fled to France in face of conspiracy charge, 1912; founder and editor, *The Suffragette* (newspaper); became Second Adventist and from 1921 lectured on the Second Coming in Great Britain and the United States; moved to United States, 1939. **Awards:** Created Dame of the British Empire, 1936. **Died:** Los Angeles, 13 February 1958.

PANKHURST, Emmeline. Born: Manchester, 4 July 1858. **Education:** Educated in Manchester; attended finishing school, Paris, France. **Family:** Married the lawyer Richard Marsden Pankhurst in 1879 (died 1898); three daughters, two sons. **Career:** Campaigned for Manchester Women's Suffrage Committee; joined Fabian Society; founder, Women's Franchise League, 1889; elected to Chorlton Board of Guardians, 1894; joined Independent Labour Party until 1903, when she cofounded, with daughter, Christabel Pankhurst, Women's Social and Political Union (WSPU); arrested for first time, 1908; supported war effort; went to Canada, 1918, and became involved in activities of National Council for Combating Venereal Disease; returned to England, 1926; joined the Conservative Party and put herself forward as a candidate for election, 1929. **Died:** London, 14 June 1928.

PANKHURST, (Estelle) Sylvia. Born: Manchester, 5 May 1882. **Education:** At home and at Manchester High School; on scholarship, attended art school in Vienna and Royal College of Art, London. **Family:** Common law relationship with Italian anti-fascist Silvio Ersmus Corio; one son. **Career:** Organized Women's Social and Political Union branches; imprisoned several times; founder, East London Federation; founder, *Women's Dreadnought* (socialist journal; renamed *Worker's Dreadnought,* 1917); pacifist during World War I; cofounder, with Charlotte Despard, Women's Peace Army; welcomed Bolshevik Revolution and visited Russia; joined British Communist Party; protested Italian involvement in Ethiopia; founded *New Times and Ethiopian News;* moved to Ethiopia, 1956; editor, *Ethopian Observer.* **Awards:** Decoration of the Queen of Sheba. **Died:** Addis Ababa, Ethiopia, 27 September 1960.

Publications

Political/Social Theory; by Christabel Pankhurst

The Parliamentary Vote for Women. Manchester, A. Heywood, 1896(?).
The Commons Debate on Women Suffrage with a Reply. London, Women's Press, 1908.
The Militant Methods of the NWSPU. London, Women's Press, 1908?
The Great Scourge and How to End It. London, Women's Press, 1913.
Plain Facts about a Great Evil. London, D. Nutt, 1913.
America and the War (speech). London, Women's Social and Political Union, 1914?
The War (speech). London, Women's Social and Political Union, and New York, National Woman Suffrage, 1914.
International Militancy (speech). London, Women's Social and Political Union, 1915.
Pressing Problems of the Closing Age. London, Morgan & Scott, 1924.
Some Modern Problems in the Light of Bible Prophecy. New York and Chicago, F. H. Revell, 1924.
The World's Unrest: Visions of the Dawn. London, Morgan & Scott, 1926.
Seeing the Future. New York and London, Harper & Bros., 1929.
The Uncurtained Future. London, Hodder & Stoughton, 1940.

Autobiography; by Christabel Pankhurst

Unshackled. The Story of How We Won the Vote, edited by Lord Pethick-Lawrence. London, Hutchinson, 1959.

Political/Social Theory; by Emmeline Pankhurst

The Importance of the Vote. London, The Woman's Press, 1908.
Suffrage Speeches Made from the Dock by Mrs Pankhurst, Mrs Pethick Lawrence, Pethick Lawrence and Tim Healy, Counsel for the Defense Made at the Conspiracy Trial, Old Bailey, 15-22 May 1912. London, The Woman's Press, 1912.
Verbatim Report of Mrs. Pankhurst's Speech Delivered 13 November 1913 at Parson's Theatre, Hartford, Connecticut. Hartford, Connecticut Woman Suffrage Association, 1913.

Autobiography; by Emmeline Pankhurst

My Own Story. London, E. Nash, and New York, Hearst's International Library, 1914.

Political/Social Theory; by Sylvia Pankhurst

The Suffragette; The History of the Women's Militant Suffrage Movement, 1905-10. London, Gay & Hancock, and New York, Sturgis & Walton, 1911.
Housing and the Worker's Revolution: Housing in Capitalist Britain and Bolshevik Russia. London, Workers' Socialist Federation, 1917.
Lloyd George Takes the Mask Off. London, Workers' Socialist Federation, 1920.
Rebel Ireland; Thoughts on Easter Week, 1916. London, Workers' Socialist Federation, 1920?
Soviet Russia as I Saw It. London, Workers' Dreadnought, 1921.
Writ on Cold Slate. London, The Dreadnought, 1922.
Education of the Masses. London, The Dreadnought, 1924.
The Truth about the Oil War. London, Dreadnought, n.d.
India and the Earthly Paradise. Bombay, Sunshine Publishing House, 1926.
Delphos; the Future of International Language. London, K. Paul Trench Trubner & Co., and New York, E. P. Dutton, 1927.
Save the Mothers; a Plea for Measures to Prevent the Annual Loss of about 3,000 Child-bearing Mothers and 20,000 Infant Lives in England and Wales, and a Similar Grievous Wastage in Other Countries. London, A. A. Knopf, 1930.

The Home Front; a Mirror to Life in England during the World War. London, Hutchinson, 1932.
The Life of Emmeline Pankhurst; the Suffragette Struggle for Women's Citizenship. London, T. W. Laurie, 1935; Boston and New York, Houghton Mifflin, 1936.
British Policy in Eastern Ethiopia, the Ogaden and the Reserved Area. Woodford Green, Essex, privately printed, 1946.
British Policy in Eritrea and Northern Ethiopia. Woodford Green, Essex, privately printed, 1946.
The Ethiopian People: Their Rights and Progress. Woodford Green, Essex, New Times and Ethiopian News Book Department, 1946.
Eritrea on the Eve; the Past and Future of Italy's "First-Born" Colony, Ethiopia's Ancient Sea Province. Woodford Green, Essex, New Times and Ethiopian News Book Department, 1952.
Ethiopia and Eritrea; the Last Phase of the Reunion Struggle, 1941-52, with Richard Pankhurst. Woodford Green, Essex, Lalibela House, 1953.
Ethiopia, a Cultural History. Woodford Green, Essex, Lalibela House, 1955.
A Sylvia Pankhurst Reader, edited by Kathryn Dodd. Manchester, Manchester University Press, n.d.

Autobiography; by Sylvia Pankhurst

The Suffragette Movement: An Intimate Account of Persons and Ideals. London and New York, Longmans, 1931.

*

Media Adaptation: *Shoulder to Shoulder* (television play), 1974.

Manuscript Collections: Christabel Pankhurst: National Library of Wales; Trinity College Library, Cambridge University; Manchester University. **Emmeline Pankhurst:** Internationaal Instituut voor Sociale Geschiedenis, Amsterdam; Library of Congress, Washington, D.C.; John Rylands Library, Manchester University. **Sylvia Pankhurst:** Instituut voor Sociale Geschiedenis, Amsterdam; National Museum of Labour History, Manchester, England; Wisconsin State Historical Society; John Rylands Library, Manchester University; Trinity College Library, Cambridge University; British Library, London.

Critical Studies: *The Fighting Pankhursts: A Study in Tenacity* by David Mitchell, London, Cape, 1967; *Rise up Women! The Militant Campaign of the Women's Social and Political Union, 1903-1914,* London, Routledge & Kegan Paul, 1974; *Shoulder to Shoulder: A Documentary* by Midge MacKenzie, London, Penguin, and New York, Knopf, 1975; *Queen Christabel: A Biography of Christabel Pankhurst* by D. Mitchell, London, Macdonald & Jane, 1977; *Sylvia Pankhurst, Artist and Crusader: An Intimate Portrait* by Richard Pankhurst, New York and London, Paddington Press, 1979; "Mrs Pankhurst" by Piers Bredon in *Eminent Edwardians,* Harmonsworth, Penguin, 1979; "Sylvia Pankhurst: Suffragist, Feminist, or Socialist?" by Linda Edmondson, in *European Women on the Left: Socialism, Feminism and the Problems Faced by Political Women, 1880 to the Present,* edited by Jane Slaughter and Robert Kern, Westport, Connecticut, Greenwood Press, 1981; "Christabel Pankhurst: Reclaiming the Power" by Elizabeth Sara in *Feminist Theorists,* edited by Dale Spender, London, The Women's Press, 1983; *Sylvia and Christabel Pankhurst* by Barbara Castle, Harmonsworth, Penguin, 1987; *E. Sylvia Pankhurst: Portrait of a Radical* by Patricia Romero, New Haven, Connecticut, Yale University Press, 1987; "Sylvia Pankhurst (1905-1924): Suffragette and Communist" (dissertation) by Barbara Winslow, University of Washington, n.d.

* * *

The Pankhursts are synonymous with the militant wing of the women's suffrage movement in early 20th-century England, and Christabel in particular is often portrayed in histories of the movement as a domineering, aggressive virago. Feminist historians have criticized the negative portrayals of the Pankhursts that have been put forth in recent years; for example, David Mitchell's studies of Christabel have been subject to intense criticism. While Christabel certainly dominated the Women's Social and Political Union (WSPU) that she co-founded with her mother, Emmeline, in 1903, there was much more to the Pankhursts—mother and daughters—than the aggressive stance they took on female enfranchisement.

Emmeline Pankhurst was born in Manchester on 4 July 1858, the eldest daughter and third child of Robert Goulden, a cotton manufacturer. She grew up in a household surrounded by the liberal ideas of mid-century Manchester, and from the age of 14 her mother took her to suffrage meetings. Her upbringing may have been liberal, yet she was reminded early on of her subordinate female status. As Midge MacKenzie notes in her *Shoulder to Shoulder,* one night, as her father bent over her in bed she heard him say, "What a pity she wasn't born a lad."

In 1878 Emmeline met the lawyer, reformer, and advocate of women's suffrage Richard Pankhurst, and they married in 1879. Christabel was born the following year and Sylvia in 1882. Three more children followed; Frank in 1884, Adela in 1885, and Harry in 1889. During their early years in Manchester the Pankhursts drifted to the left in politics; they joined the Fabian Society when women's suffrage was excluded from the 1884 Reform Bill. The family moved to London in 1885, where their home became a social center for an assortment of Fabians, anarchists, and free-thinkers, in whose discussions Christabel and Sylvia were encouraged to take part. In 1893 the Pankhursts returned to Manchester, where Richard and Emmeline joined the Independent Labour Party (ILP) founded by Keir Hardie. In 1894 Emmeline was elected to the Chorlton Board of Guardians.

Workhouse conditions appalled Emmeline, and she was particularly outraged at the treatment endured by women who had borne illegitimate children. It was at these times that she began to consider that only if women possessed political power—namely the vote—would conditions improve. "Though I had been a suffragist before, I now began to think about the vote in women's hands not only as a right, but as a desperate necessity" she would later remark.

In 1898 Richard Pankhurst died from a perforated ulcer. Like many 19th-century women who were not trained for work, Emmeline was thrown upon her resources in order to support herself and her four children (Frank had died from diphtheria in 1889). She decided to open a shop; this was not a successful venture and it was fortunate that as this time a registrarship of births and deaths became vacant. She combined this position with her shop work, and dragged a recalcitrant Christabel into the shop with her.

The death of Richard Pankhurst affected Sylvia more than Christabel. For all of her life Christabel was much closer to her mother, whereas Sylvia was drawn to her father; his socialist views and belief that women's suffrage was just one part of a much larger struggle for social and political equality would profoundly influence the direction that Sylvia's feminist leanings would take.

Soon after her father's death, Sylvia, who was a gifted artist, was awarded a scholarship to art school, followed by study in Venice and later a scholarship to the Royal College of Art. Christabel, who disliked working in her mother's shop, decided to take some courses as Manchester University, where she met two women's rights advocates, Eva Gore Booth (sister of the first woman elected to Parliament) and Esther Roper, who were working to revive the women's movement. Christabel was quickly drawn into the meetings and activities of the Manchester branch of the National Union of Women's Suffrage Societies, and began what she later referred to as her "political apprenticeship" amongst the working women of the north. "Here, then, was an aim in life for me—the liberation of politically fettered womanhood," she would write in *Unshackled: The Story of How We Won the Vote,* which was first published in 1959.

It was Sylvia, however, who set in motion the train of events that would encourage the Pankhurst women to agitate for women's suffrage independently from the Independent Labour Party. On returning home from Venice, she was asked to decorate an ILP hall in memory of her father. When the newly decorated hall opened, Sylvia's mother was shocked to discover that neither she nor her Sylvia—nor indeed, any women—would be allowed admission. This was proof to Emmeline that the ILP was as disinclined as any other political party to treat women equally with men. She came to the conclusion that men would do nothing for women and that the only people upon whom women could rely to effectively change their subordinate status were themselves. In 1903 Emmeline and daughter Christabel founded the Women's Social and Political Union (WSPU).

Christabel agreed with her mother that men would never do anything positive for women. Her anti-male tendencies have been interpreted by some historians as an indication of lesbianism, although in her *Sylvia and Christabel Pankhurst,* Barbara Castle prefers to view them as part of Christabel's suffrage strategy, which evolved into an open sex war endorsing "Votes for Women, Chastity for Men." Men, Christabel argued, were responsible for women's sexual and economic subordination; by their insistance on denying women's suffrage, which women would undoubtedly use to purify both the male race and society, she was also able to hold men responsible for all kinds of social evils, including venereal disease and prostitution.

In May 1905 a private member's bill supporting women's suffrage had been "talked out" in parliament; this suggested to Christabel and Emmeline that the tactics of the constitutional suffragists—which consisted of repeated petitions and deputations—were not getting anywhere. More direct action was needed. Christabel, along with friend and fellow working-class suffragette Annie Kenney, decided to disrupt a speech that Winston Churchill was giving at Manchester's Free Trade Hall during the build-up to a general election. During the assembly, they asked whether the Liberal Party, if it came to power, would support women's suffrage. When no answer was given, Christabel unfurled a banner on which "Votes for Women" was emblazoned. The two women were ejected from the meeting and were promptly arrested outside the Free Trade Hall when Christabel attempted to make a pro-suffrage speech.

Such militant tactics intensified from 1908 onwards. When they escalated to attacks on property and arson the government decided, in 1912, to arrest the leaders of the WSPU on charges of conspiracy. Christabel escaped arrest by fleeing to Paris, where she continued to direct the WSPU campaign and edited *The Suffrage* for the next two years.

Although the first act of militancy was Christabel's, Emmeline Pankhurst was soon to be found beside her daughter; she closed her shop in 1907 and resigned her registrarship. Emmeline went to prison for the first time in 1908, and until the outbreak of World War I she was regularly in and out of jail. Once war did break out she threw herself with patriotic fervor behind her country; women's suffrage took a back seat. With the cessation of hostilities in 1918, she went to Canada where she became involved in Dr. Gordon Bates's National Council for Combatting Venereal Diseases, and by 1922 she was the Council's chief lecturer. Emmeline returned to England in 1926 and joined the Conservative Party.

Sylvia, too, was imprisoned for her pro-suffrage activities; she went to jail for the first time in 1906, and, according to one source, "was hardly less heroic than her mother Emmeline in determining to endure with courage whatever suffering her frequent imprisonments forced upon her." Yet she was never as committed to militancy as were her mother and sister. Unlike them she had not given up membership in the ILP, and she made a concerted effort to bring working-class women into the women's suffrage movement. Emmeline and Christabel, on the other hand, saw suffrage as falling within the middle and upper classes, and believed that female enfranchisement would be thrown off course if it was demanded alongside wider claims of social and political equality. In 1914 Sylvia broke with the WSPU and concentrated her energies on the working-class East London Federation. She established a newspaper, the *Women's Dreadnought,* which was renamed the *Worker's Dreadnought* in 1917; this reflected her decreased support for feminism and her increased socialist sympathies.

With the outbreak of war in 1914 the WSPU ceased its militancy and directed all of its energies towards supporting the war cause. The Union's open support of the war widened the gulf between Sylvia and her sister and mother. Christabel's *The Suffragette* became the pro-war *Britannia;* Sylvia, on the other hand, cofounded the Women's Peace Army with Charlotte Despard and attended the International Congress of Women for Peace at the Hague. In 1917 she welcomed the Bolshevik revolution and at the end of the war she visited Russia. She also joined the British Communist Party; her demands for freedom of expression resulted in her expulsion.

At the end of the war Sylvia became involved with a left-wing exile, Silvio Erasmus Corio, with whom she had a child in 1927. She never married Corio, nor did her son take Corio's name. The birth of this child out of wedlock further strained the relationship between mother and daughter, as did Emmeline's decision to become a Conservative candidate in the general election of 1929. Emmeline died in 1928; the last time that Christabel and Sylvia would meet was at their mother's grave.

Sylvia became even more left-wing over time. She opposed fascism and, in protest over Italy's invasion of Ethiopia, she founded the *New Times and Ethiopia News,* which she edited for 20 years. She also wrote a number of books on Ethiopia and moved there in 1956, where she helped to establish a Social Service Society and edited the *Ethiopia Observer.* She received the decoration of the Queen of Sheba and died in Addis Ababa on 27 September 1960.

Whereas Sylvia became a committed socialist and anti-fascist, Christabel became a committed Second Adventist. She traveled to the United States in 1921 where she lectured on the Second Coming; she moved permanently to the States in 1939 and altered her view that women could purify society; only a spiritual reawakening could effect the social and moral changes that Christabel demanded.

Each of the Pankhurst women brought to the women's suffrage movement their unique understanding of feminism, enfranchisement, and political progress. Although their views divided as much as unified, the name "Pankhurst" will forever be linked in popular imagination with militancy, determination, and women's rights.

—Lori Williamson

PARDO BAZÁN, Emilia, Condesa de

Nationality: Spanish. **Born:** La Coruna, Galicia, 15 September 1851. **Education:** Self-taught. **Family:** Married Don Jose Quiroga in 1867 (separated 1887); three children. **Career:** Writer, beginning 1867; founder, *Nuevo Teatro Crítico* (feminist journal), 1891; professor of Romance languages, Atheneum of Madrid, beginning 1916. **Died:** 1921.

Publications

Novels

Pascual López. Madrid, F. Fé, 1879.
Un viaje de novios. N.p., 1881; translated as *A Wedding Trip,* New York, Cassell, 1891.
La Tribuna [The Female Orator]. N.p., 1883.
La dama joven [The Young Woman]. N.p., 1883.
El cisne de Vilamorta. N.p., 1885; translated as *The Swan of Vilamorta,* New York, Cassell, 1891.
Los pazos de Ulloa. Barcelona, n.p., 1886; translated as *The Son of the Bondswoman,* New York and London, J. Lane, 1908; as *The House of Ulloa,* London, Penguin, 1990; New York, 1991.
La madre naturaleza. N.p., 1887.
Insolación. Barcelona, n.p., 1889; translated as *Midsummer Madness,* Boston, C. M. Clark, 1907.
Morriña. Barcelona, n.p., 1889; translated as *Homesickness,* New York, Cassell, 1891.
La piedra angular. N.p., 1891.
Doña Milagros [Lady Miracles]. N.p., 1894.
Memorias de un solterón [Diary of a Bachelor]. N.p., 1896.
La salud del las brujas. N.p., 1897.
El tesoro de Gascón [Gascon's Treasure]. N.p., 1897.
El niño de Guzmán. In *Obras completas,* 1899.
La quimera [The Chimera]. N.p., 1905.
Misterio. Madrid, n.p., 1903; translated as *The Mystery of the Lost Dauphin,* New York, Funk & Wagnalls, 1906.
La sirena negra [The Dark Siren]. Madrid, n.p., 1908.
Dulce dueño [Sweet Lord]. In *Obras completas,* 1911.

Short Stories

Un destripador de antaño. In *Obras completas,* 1900.
Una cristiana—La prueba. Madrid, La España editorial, 2 vols., 1890-91; translated as *A Christian Woman,* New York, Cassell, 1891.
Cuentos de Marineda. In *Obras completas,* 1892.
Cuentos de Navidad y Año Nuevo. N.p., 1894.
Arco iris. Barcelona, n.p., 1895.
Novelas ejemplares. N.p., 1895.
Cuentos de amor. In *Obras completas,* 1898.
Cuentos sacro-profanos. In *Obras completas,* 1899.
En tranvía, cuentos dramáticos. In *Obras completas,* 1901.
Cuentos de Navidad y Reyes; cuentos de la patria; cuentos antiguos. In *Obras completas,* 1902.
El Fondo de alma. In *Obras completas,* 1907.
Sud-exprés, cuentos actuales. In *Obras completas,* 1909.
Belcebú, cuentos breves. In *Obras completas,* 1912.
Cuentos de la tiera. N.p., 1923.
Cuentos religiosis. Madrid, n.p., 1925.
Short Stories, edited by Albert Shapiro and F. J. Hurley. London, Harrap's, 1935.

Poetry

Los Poetas Épicos Cristianos. In *Obras completas,* 1895.

Essays

La cuestión palpitante [The Burning Question]. Madrid, n.p., 1883.
Polémicos y Estudios literarios. In *Obras completas,* 1892.

Other

Obras completas. Madrid, Aguilar, 43 vols., 1891-1926.

*

Bibliography: *Bibliografía descriptiva de estudios críticos sobre la obra de Emilia Pardo Bazán* by Robert M. Scari, Valencia, Albatros, 1982.

Critical Studies: "Pardo Bazán and Literary Polemics about Feminism" by Ronald Hilton, in *Romanic Review,* 44, 1953; *Emilia Pardo Bazán* by Walter T. Patterson, New York, Twayne, 1971; "A Woman's Place in the Sun: Feminism in *Insolación*" by Ruth A. Schmidt, in *Revista de Estudios Hispánicos,* 8, 1974; "Feminism and the Feminine in Emilia Pardo Bazán's Novels" by Mary Giles, in *Hispania,* 63, 1980; *Emilia Pardo Bazán como novelista (de la teoria a la practica)* by Nelly Clemessy, translated by Irene Gambra, 2 vols., Madrid, Fundación Universitaría, 1981; *Emilia Pardo Bazán: The Making of a Novelist* by Maurice Hemingway, London, Cambridge University Press, 1983; *The 19th-Century Spanish Story: Textual Strategies of a Genre in Transition* by Lou Charnon-Deutsch, London, Tamesis, 1985; "A Privileged View of Pardo Bazán's Feminist Ethos" by Walter Oliver, in *Romance Notes,* 28, 1987; *The Early Pardo Bazán: Theme and Narrative Technique in the Novels of 1879-89* by David Henn, Liverpool, F. Cairns, 1988; "En-Gendering Strategies of Authority: Emilia Pardo Bazán and the Novel" by Maryellen Beider, in *Cultural and Historical Grounding for Hispanic and Luso-Brazilian Feminist Literary Criticism,* edited by Hernán Vidal, Minneapolis, Institute for the Study of Ideologies and Literature, 1989, and her "Emilia Pardo Bazán and Literary Women: Women Reading Women's Literature in Late 19th-Century Spain," in *Revista Hispanica Moderna,* 46(1), 1993; *Portrait of a Woman as Artist* by Francisca

Gonzalez-Arias, New York, Garland, 1992; "Emilia Pardo Bazán" by Ruth El Saffar, in *Spanish Women Writers,* Westport, Connecticut, Greenwood Press, 1994; *Under Construction: The Body in Spanish Novels* by Elizabeth A. Scarlett, Charlottesville, University Press of Virginia, 1994.

* * *

Even by the standards of the late 20th century, a woman of such vast accomplishment as Emilia Pardo Bazán would be considered prodigious. As a woman of letters in the late 19th century, her accomplishments seem even more remarkable. With over a dozen novels, short stories numbering in the thousands, volumes of poetry, plays, and significant essays, the Countess Pardo Bazán far outshone many of her male contemporaries, and served as an example to her female colleagues that a woman was perfectly capable of thinking about matters beyond the domestic circle, and writing literature of admirable quality.

She was a precocious and unusual child, the only daughter of a wealthy and prominent Galician lawyer and his attentive, traditional wife. Doña Emilia had privileged access to a large and diverse library, and erudite conversation among her father's friends and "contertulianos." Her literary inclinations were manifested early, as she published her first novel in a regional journal that featured the work of young ladies from prominent families at the age of 15. With the encouragement of her parents and, initially, of her husband, Doña Emilia threw herself headlong into a life of writing and debate that earned her prominence in circles not traditionally open to women.

Doña Emilia married at the age of 17 to Jose Quiroga, a well-to-do law student from her native La Coruna. Disguised as a man, she joined him in his law classes, in order to further her own education. Everything she read or learned had to be done on her own initiative, as schooling was prohibited for girls and practicing a profession was not allowed for women of a certain class. While the first years of her marriage seemed to have been satisfactory—indeed, she and her husband had three children—after 20 years they separated and went on to lead totally independent lives. Doña Emilia never assumed her husband's surname when she married, a fact that points to her independence of character and her desire to establish an identity as a writer whose vocation was more serious than the brand offered by "literatas" of her time. Instead of being a woman who writes, Doña Emilia became known as a writer who was also a woman.

She gained renown for several of her publications, but she earned disdain and reproach for her treatise on Naturalism, 1883's *La cuestión palpitante/The Burning Question,* in which she discussed the role of scientific investigation and detail in the realist novel. Her position, which never wavered substantively from her staunch Catholicism, was reviled because it admitted the possibility that people can be overpowered by their circumstances, and end up acting more instinctively than intellectually. Two novels that followed closely on the heals of *The Burning Question—Los pazos de Ulloa/Son of a Bondswoman* (1886) and *La madre naturaleza/Mother Nature* (1887)—reinforced in practice what Pardo Bazán had discussed in her theory. She is best known for these two Naturalist novels, but more recent criticism has directed attention to her subsequent works, which delve into psychological examination of characters and introduce the spiritual vein that would eventually overtake her short stories and, finally, her rather less successful plays.

To understand adequately the stature of Doña Emilia, it is useful to be aware of the company she kept. She maintained correspondence with some of the most important literary figures of her day. In France she became acquainted with Victor Hugo, and the Goncourt brothers. She read extensively in order to comment upon Naturalistic novels by these authors, as well as works by Emile Zola. In Spain she corresponded regularly with luminaries of the day, such as Ramon Menedez y Pelayo and Francisco Giner de los Rios, both extremely influential professors of literature at the end of the 19th century. In addition, she exchanged letters and ideas on the novel with the best-known realist novelist of her time, Benito Perez Galdos. In her travels throughout Europe, Doña Emilia had an audience with Pope Pius IX, and made the acquaintance of the deposed King Carlos of Spain. In none of these meetings, correspondences or friendships was she considered to have an inferior, "feminine" intellect.

Doña Emilia has only recently begun to receive the attention she merits for her vast literary production, and only since the 1980s has the body of critical study taken its attention further than her relationship with the Naturalist movement in Spain and France. Scholars Maurice Hemingway and Francisca Gonzalez-Arias have written books that treat her as a complete and profound artist and a feminist who would not capitulate to the prohibitions imposed on women by a closed and retrogressive Spanish society. Despite the frustrations inherent in pursuing a career at a time when other women were unable or unwilling to exercise that option, Pardo Bazán remained dedicated to the production of literature and literary criticism. She also sustained her dedication to the ideal that womanhood not be considered an excuse to shunt away and marginalize half of society. Throughout her life she advocated education and practicality over frivolity and ignorance, for women both in her native Spain and throughout the world.

—Helena Antolin Cochrane

PARKER, Dorothy

Nationality: American. **Born:** Dorothy Rothschild, in West End, New Jersey, 22 August 1893. **Education:** Attended Blessed Sacrament Academy, New York (dismissed) and Miss Dana's School, Morristown, New Jersey, until 1908. **Family:** Married 1) Parker (divorced); 2) the writer Alan Campbell (divorced). **Career:** Editor, *Vogue* magazine, New York, 1916-17; drama critic, *Vanity Fair,* New York, 1917-20, and *Ainslee's*; cofounder, with Robert Benchley, Robert Sherwood, and others, Algonquin Hotel Round Table luncheon group, New York, c. 1923; book reviewer in column "Constant Reader," *New Yorker,* 1927-33; became involved with Communist party, 1934; blacklisted for support of radical causes, including civil rights, 1949; willed estate to Martin Luther King Jr. Contributor of book reviews, short stories, poems, columns, and articles to numerous periodicals, including *American Mercury, Cosmopolitan, Esquire, Nation, New Republic, New Yorker, Saturday Evening Post,* and *Vogue.* **Awards:** National Institute of Arts and Letters Marjorie Peabody Waite Award for achievement and integrity, 1958; inducted into National Institute of Arts and Letters, 1959. **Died:** New York, New York, 7 June 1967.

PUBLICATIONS

Short Stories

Laments for the Living. New York, Viking, and London, Longmans Green, 1930.
After Such Pleasures. New York, Viking, 1933; London, Longmans Green, 1934.
Here Lies: Collected Short Stories. New York, Viking, and London, Longmans Green, 1939; as *The Collected Stories of Dorothy Parker,* New York, Modern Library, 1942.
The Viking Portable Dorothy Parker. New York, Viking, 1944; as *The Indispensable Dorothy Parker,* New York, Book Society, 1944; as *Selected Short Stories,* New York, Editions for the Armed Services, 1944; revised and enlarged as *The Portable Dorothy Parker,* edited by Brendan Gill, New York, Viking, 1973; as *The Collected Dorothy Parker,* London, Duckworth, 1973.

Literary Criticism

Constant Reader (book reviews; originally published in the *New Yorker*). New York, Viking, 1970; as *A Month of Saturdays,* London, Macmillan, 1971.

Poetry

Enough Rope. New York, Boni & Liveright, 1926.
Sunset Gun. New York, Boni & Liveright, 1928.
Death and Taxes. New York, Viking, 1931.
Not So Deep as a Well. New York, Viking, 1936; London, Hamilton, 1937; as *The Collected Poetry of Dorothy Parker,* New York, Modern Library, 1944.

Plays

No Sirree, with others (revue; produced New York, 1922).
Nero, with Robert Benchley (produced New York, 1922).
Round the Town (revue; produced New York, 1924).
Close Harmony, or The Lady Next Door, with Elmer Rice (three-act; produced New York, 1924). New York and London, S. French, 1929.
Shoot the Works (revue; produced New York, 1931).
The Coast of Illyria, with Ross Evans (produced Dallas, Texas, 1949).
The Ladies of the Corridor, with Arnaud d'Usseau (produced New York, 1953). New York, Viking, 1954.

Screenplays: *Business Is Business,* with George S. Kaufman, Paramount, 1925; *Here Is My Heart,* Paramount, 1934; *One Hour Late,* Paramount, 1935; *Mary Burns, Fugitive,* Paramount, 1935; *Hands across the Table,* Paramount, 1935; *Paris in Spring,* Paramount, 1935; *Big Broadcast of 1936,* Paramount, 1935; *Three Married Men,* with Alan Campbell, Paramount, 1936; *Lady, Be Careful,* with Alan Campbell and Harry Ruskin, Paramount, 1936; *The Moon's Our Home,* with Alan Campbell, Paramount, 1936; *Suzy,* with Alan Campbell, Horace Jackson, and Lenore Coffee, Metro-Goldwyn-Mayer (MGM), 1936; *A Star Is Born,* with Alan Campbell and Robert Carson, United Artists, 1937; *Woman Chases Man,* with Joe Bigelow, United Artists, 1937; *Sweethearts,* with Alan Campbell, MGM, 1938; *Trade Winds,* with Alan Campbell and Frank R. Adams, United Artists, 1938; *Weekend for Three,* with Alan Campbell, RKO, 1941; *Saboteur,* with Peter Viertel and Joan Harrison, Universal, 1942; *Smash Up: The Story of a Woman,* with Frank Cavett, Universal, 1947; *The Fan,* with Walter Reisch and Ross Evans, 20th Century-Fox, 1949; *Queen for a Day,* United Artists, 1950.

Television Plays: *The Lovely Leave, A Telephone Call,* and *Dusk before Fireworks,* WNEW-TV, 1962.

Other

Men I'm Not Married To, with *Women I'm Not Married To* by Franklin P. Adams. Garden City, New York, Doubleday Page, 1922.
Soldiers of the Republic. New York, Alexander Woolcott, 1938.
The Best of Dorothy Parker. London, Methuen, 1952.

Editor, *The Portable F. Scott Fitzgerald.* New York, Viking, 1945.
Editor, with Frederick B. Shroyer, *Short Story: A Thematic Anthology.* New York, Scribners, 1965.
Lyricist, with Richard Wilbur and John Latouche, *Candide: A Comic Operetta,* by Lillian Hellman, adapted from the novel by Voltaire, score by Leonard Bernstein (produced New York, 1956). New York, Random House, 1957.

*

Media Adaptations: *The Infamous Dorothy Parker* (film), New Line, 1994.

Manuscript Collections: Houghton Library, Harvard University (letters).

Critical Studies: *While Rome Burns* by Alexander Woolcott, New York, Grosset & Dunlap, 1934; *An Unfinished Woman* by Lillian Hellman, Boston, Little Brown, 1969; *You Might as Well Live* by John Keats, New York, Simon & Schuster, 1970; "Dorothy Parker, Erica Jong, and New Feminist Humor" by Emily Toth, in *Regionalism and the Female Imagination,* 3, fall/winter 1977; *Dorothy Parker* by Arthur F. Kinney, Boston, G.K. Hall, 1978; "'I Am Outraged Womanhood': Dorothy Parker as Feminist and Social Critic" by Suzanne L. Bunkers, in *Regionalism and the Female Imagination,* 4, fall 1978; *What Fresh Hell Is This? A Biography of Dorothy Parker* by Marion Meade, New York, Penguin, 1987; "Dorothy Parker" by Nancy Walker and Zita Dresner, in *Redressing the Balance: American Women's Literary Humor from Colonial Times to the 1980s,* Jackson, University Press of Mississippi, 1988.

* * *

Known as "the wittiest woman in America," Dorothy Parker became a legend during the 1920s as much for her hilarious one-liners at the Algonquin Round Table as for her best-selling poetry, fiction, and reviews. While Parker's vast popularity stemmed from her ability to make people laugh, simmering beneath the surface of her short stories and verse is a suppressed rage at the pervasive inequalities of American society.

Parker was born Dorothy Rothschild on 22 August 1893 to an affluent New York family. Her relatively privileged and happy beginnings were brutally cut short by the death of her mother when Dorothy was four years old, a tragedy that haunted her the rest of her life. Like the vast majority of women during this period, Parker never attended college. She did, however, receive a rigorous classical education at Miss Dana's, an exclusive private high school; more importantly, she educated herself through voracious independent reading.

After Parker's father died in 1913, Dorothy was economically on her own. She began her career by writing fashion captions for the fashion magazine *Vogue*, inventing lines such as "brevity is the soul of lingerie." She was quickly promoted to drama critic for *Vanity Fair*, a prestigious and influential literary magazine. With this position—a very unusual one for such a young and unknown woman—Parker's reputation as a wit began. She made her mark with devastating but humorous reviews of plays, with lines such as "if you don't knit, bring a book." Although theatrical producers dreaded the sight of her, the public loved her, repeated her quips, and begged for more. Parker's writing style is important from a feminist perspective because she completely rejected the prevailing standards for female writing and thinking, standards that expected women to be delicate, romantic, and timid in offering their opinions. Instead, as Parker's biographer Marion Meade explains in *What Fresh Hell Is This?,* she "had chosen to present herself not so much as a bad girl, but as a bad boy, a firecracker who was aggressively proud of being tough, quirky, feisty ... and she managed to carry it off with style and humor."

Parker's literary career and reputation as a humorist quickly took off after that point. After she was fired from *Vanity Fair* for offending too many clients, she worked for other magazines—first for *Ainslee's*, then for *The New Yorker*—continually delighting and shocking audiences with her devastating wit. She is perhaps most famous for her participation as in the Algonquin Round Table, a group of literary friends (mostly male) who met every day for lunch at the Algonquin Hotel in New York to trade witticisms and make each other laugh. This group became famous for their humor, with newspapers and magazines frequently quoting their lines. When asked to use the word "horticulture" in a sentence, for example, Parker responded, without missing a beat, that "you can lead a horticulture but you can't make her think." Her sharp wit, which often played off of sexual themes, belied the prevailing stereotype of women as humorless and prudish.

During the 1930s and 1940s, Parker lived on and off in Hollywood and collaborated with her second husband Alan Campbell as a screenwriter for numerous films. It was during these very financially successful years, ironically, that Parker became politically radicalized. For the rest of her life she fought vigorously against social inequalities of all forms: not only gender inequalities, but also class injustices, racism, and the growing tide of fascism. Because of her involvement with the Communist party in the 1930s, she later became blacklisted by the Hollywood establishment and her screenwriting career came to an end. Nonetheless, she continued writing reviews, essays, and plays until the end of her life in 1967.

Feminist themes are prevalent in many of Parker's most enduring poetry and short stories. Stories such as "Big Blonde," "Mr. Durant," "The Waltz," and "A Telephone Call" document with both humor and sadness the realities of being a woman in a male-dominated world. Male brutality towards women's emotional vulnerability, along with the devastating effects of feminine socialization, are common themes of Parker's work. The ironic contrast between her characters' polite social behavior and the true feelings lying beneath the surface is the source of both her most successful humor and her most powerful critiques of sexism. As Gloria Steinem has argued in the video *The Infamous Mrs. Parker,* Dorothy is important for feminists because, in a world where men are supposed to be the definers of reality, Parker "dared to define—to fight back with her wit and with her words and say 'No, I am going to define what this is.'" Parker's definition of reality refused to countenance male callousness towards women's professional and emotional needs.

Parker was also famous for her feminist life-style. Not only was she was one of the very few women to make it big in the male-dominated world of humorists, but she also refused to subordinate her own professional interests to those of the men in her life. Her relationship with her second husband, Alan Campbell, was marked by a complete reversal of traditional husband-wife roles. Although they wrote as a team for Hollywood films, Parker was by far the more famous and successful of the two. On the domestic front, she was completely and unapologetically lacking in any domestic skills, while Campbell delighted in caring for her and their home.

Sadly, however, swimming against the tide of ladyhood exacted a price. Despite Parker's professional success, her independence, her many friends, and her egalitarian relationship with Campbell, she also knew much pain. She battled alcoholism for most of her adult life and the emotional fallout from some of her disastrous love affairs led to several suicide attempts. Nevertheless, Parker managed to create art and wit out of even the darkest sides of her life. Her famous poem "Resume" is a good example: after detailing the unpleasantness of various methods of suicide, e.g., "razors pain you" and "rivers are damp," the final line declares "you might as well live." Dorothy Parker's serio-comic depictions of the tensions between the sexes and the agony of love are as relevant for today's readers as they were for those of her own time.

—Debra Beilke

PENN, Sylvania. *See* **H.D.**

PERDITA. *See* **ROBINSON, Mary (Darby).**

PETER, Rhoda. *See* **H.D.**

PETROVSKY, Boris. *See* **MANSFIELD, Katherine.**

PHELPS (WARD), Elizabeth Stuart

Pseudonym: Mary Adams. **Nationality:** American. **Born:** Mary Gray Phelps, in Boston, Massachusetts, 31 August 1844; daughter of novelist Elizabeth Stuart Phelps; renamed herself upon mother's death in 1852. **Education:** Attended Abbot Academy and Mrs. Edwards' School for Young Ladies, Andover, Massachusetts. **Family:** Married the journalist Herbert Dickinson Ward in 1888 (separated). **Career:** Professional writer. Sunday school teacher; active in antivivisection activities after 1890; contributor of short stories and articles to periodicals, including *Atlantic Monthly, Century, Harper's Monthly Magazine, Independent, Ladies' Home Journal,* and *Woman's Journal.* **Died:** Newton, Massachusetts, 28 January 1911.

PUBLICATIONS

Novels

The Gates Ajar. Boston, Fields Osgood, 1868; London, Low & Marston, 1869.
Hedged In. Boston, Fields Osgood, and London, Low & Marston, 1870.
The Silent Partner. Boston, Osgood, and London, Low, 1871.
The Story of Avis. Boston, Osgood, and London, Routledge, 1877.
Friends: A Duet. Boston, Houghton Mifflin, and London, Low, 1881.
Dr. Zay. Boston, Houghton Mifflin, 1882.
Beyond the Gates. Boston and New York, Houghton Mifflin, and London, Chatto & Windus, 1883.
Burglars in Paradise. Boston and New York, Houghton Mifflin, and London, Chatto & Windus, 1886.
The Madonna of the Tubs. Boston and New York, Houghton Mifflin, and London, Low, 1887.
The Gates Between. Boston and New York, Houghton Mifflin, and London, Chatto & Windus, 1887.
A Singular Life. Boston and New York, Houghton Mifflin, and London, Clark, 1895.
Confessions of a Wife (as Mary Adams). New York, Century, 1902.
Trixy. Boston and New York, Houghton Mifflin, 1904; London, Hodder & Stoughton, 1904.
Though Life Us Do Part. Boston and New York, Houghton Mifflin, 1908.
Walled In. New York and London, Harper, 1909.

Short Stories

"Margaret Bronson," in *Harper's New Monthly,* 31, September 1865.
Men, Women, and Ghosts (includes "The Tenth of January," originally published in *Atlantic Monthly,* March 1868). Boston, Fields Osgood, and London, Low & Marston, 1869.
Sealed Orders. Boston, Houghton Osgood, 1879.
An Old Maid's Paradise. Boston, Houghton Osgood, and London, Clarke, 1879.
Fourteen to One. Boston and New York, Houghton Mifflin, and London, Cassell, 1891.
The Oath of Allegiance and Other Stories. Boston and New York, Houghton Mifflin, and London, Constable, 1909.
The Empty House and Other Stories. Boston and New York, Houghton Mifflin, 1910; as *A Deserted House and Other Stories,* London, Constable, 1911.

Essays

"The 'Female Education' of Women," in *Independent,* 25, 13 November 1873.
"George Elliot," in *Independent,* 33, 3 February 1881.

Poetry

Songs of the Silent World and Other Poems. Boston and New York, Houghton Mifflin, 1884.

Play

Within the Gates. Boston and New York, Houghton Mifflin, 1901.

For Children

Ellen's Idol. Boston, Massachusetts Sabbath School Society, and London, Ward Lock, 1864.
Up Hill; or, Life in the Factory. Boston, Hoyt, 1865.
Mercy Gliddon's Work. Boston, Hoyt, 1866; London, Ward Lock, 1873.
Gypsy Breynton. Boston, Graves & Young, 1866; London, Ward Lock, 1872.
Gypsy's Cousin Joy. Boston, Graves & Young, 1866; London, Strahan, 1873.
Gypsy's Sowing and Reaping. Boston, Graves & Young, 1866; London, Strahan, 1873.
Tiny. Boston, Massachusetts Sabbath School Society, 1866; London, Ward Lock, 1875.
Tiny's Sunday Nights. Boston, Massachusetts Sabbath School Society, 1867; London, Ward Lock, 1875.
Gypsy's Year at the Golden Crescent. Boston, Graves & Young, 1868; London, Strahan, 1873.
I Don't Know How. Boston, Massachusetts Sabbath School Society, 1868; London, Ward Lock, 1873.
The Trotty Book. Boston, Fields Osgood, 1870; as *That Dreadful Boy Trotty: What He Did and What He Said,* London, Ward Lock, 1877.
Trotty's Wedding Tour, and Story-Book. Boston, Osgood, and London, Routledge, 1877.
My Cousin and I. Boston, Sunday School Union, 1879.
Jack the Fisherman. Boston and New York, Houghton Mifflin, and London, Low, 1887.

Autobiography

Chapters from a Life. Boston and New York, Houghton Mifflin, 1896; London, Clark, 1897.

Other

What to Wear? Boston, Osgood, and London, Low, 1873.
Poetic Studies. Boston, Osgood, 1875.
A Gracious Life: A Eulogy on Mrs. Charlotte A. Johnson. Boston, printed privately, 1888.
Austin Phelps: A Memoir. New York, Scribner, and London, Nisbet, 1891.

A Plea for the Helpless. New York, American Humane Society, 1901.
Vivisection and Legislation in Massachusetts. Philadelphia, American Anti-vivisection Society, 1902.

*

Manuscript Collections: Andover Historical Society, Andover, Massachusetts; Houghton Library, Harvard University; Beinecke Library, Yale University.

Critical Studies: *Elizabeth Stuart Phelps* by Mary Angela Bennett, Philadelphia, University of Pennsylvania Press, 1939; "Elizabeth Stuart Phelps: A Study in Female Rebellion" by Christine Stansell, *Massachusetts Review,* 13, 1972; *The Feminization of American Culture* by Ann Douglas, New York, Knopf, 1977; *Elizabeth Stuart Phelps* by Carol Farley Kessler, Boston, G. K. Hall, 1982; *The Life and Works of Elizabeth Stuart Phelps, Victorian Feminist Writer* by Lori Duin Kelly, Troy, New York, Whitston, 1983; "The Career Woman Fiction of Elizabeth Stuart Phelps" by Susan Ward, in *19th-Century Women Writers of the English-speaking World,* edited by Rhoda B. Mason, New York, Greenwood Press, 1986; *Doing Literary Business: American Women Writers in the 19th Century* by Susan Coultrap-McQuinn, n.p., 1990.

* * *

Elizabeth Stuart Phelps, professional writer, advocate of workers' rights and of women's right to work, wrote prolifically on a variety of topics and created many strong, progressive female characters. One of the heroines of Phelps's pro-labor novel *The Silent Partner,* published in 1871, rejects her suitor with these words: "The fact is ... that I have no time to think of love and marriage.... That is a business, a trade, by itself to women. I have too much else to do." In her many novels—particularly those written early in her career—Phelps created heroines who brought a new voice to fiction, speaking actively for women as a class and presenting a critique of those social institutions that placed limits on women's development.

The daughter of a popular writer, whose name she took after her mother's death when she was eight years old, Phelps had already begun to publish short fiction in periodicals during her teens; approaching writing as a full-time profession, she would produced 56 volumes of fiction, poetry, and other work before her death in 1911. She also wrote more than 150 short stories, including the compelling "The Tenth of January," a portrayal of a crippled factory girl who is trapped during the collapse of the Pemberton Mill. Praised by such contemporaries as Thomas Wentworth Higginson and John Greenleaf Whittier, "The Tenth of January" reflects its author's concern over the social conditions that render women powerless. The experiences of her own mother would affected Phelps's writing as well; she based her most well-known work, 1877's *The Story of Avis,* on her mother's struggle to write while fulfilling the traditional role of wife and mother. Avis, a promising artist whose career is stifled by marriage and motherhood, portrays the impossibility of artistic fulfillment for married women.

Surprisingly, Phelps married Herbert Dickinson Ward—a man 17 years her junior—when she was 44. The marriage would prove to be an unhappy one, and they spent much of their time apart. Despite the aftereffects of a physical breakdown following *The Story of Avis,* Phelps continued to support herself, and later, her husband, through her writing. She also became increasingly active in the antivivisection movement, using her ability as a writer to advance that cause as she had also advanced the cause of women and the poor. As she would write in her 1896 autobiography, *Chapter from a Life,* Elizabeth Stuart Phelps was "proud ... that I have always been a working woman, and always had to be."

—Ann E. Green

PIERCY, Marge

Nationality: American. **Born:** Detroit, Michigan, 31 March 1936. **Education:** University of Michigan, Ann Arbor (Hopwood award, 1956, 1957), A.B. 1957; Northwestern University, Evanston, Illinois, M.A. 1958. **Family:** Married Ira Wood (third marriage) in 1982. **Career:** Instructor, Indiana University, Gary, 1960-62; poet-in-residence, University of Kansas, Lawrence, 1971; visiting lecturer, Thomas Jefferson College, Grand Valley State Colleges, Allendale, Michigan, 1975; visiting faculty, Women's Writers' Conference, Cazenovia College, New York, 1976, 1978, 1980; staff member, Fine Arts Work Center, Provincetown, Massachusetts, 1976-77; writer-in-residence, College of the Holy Cross, Worcester, Massachusetts, 1976; Butler Professor of Letters, State University of New York, Buffalo, 1977; Elliston Professor of Poetry, University of Cincinnati, 1986. Member of the board of directors, 1982-85, and of the advisory board since 1985, Coordinating Council of Literary Magazines; poetry editor, *Tikkun* magazine, since 1988. **Awards:** Borestone Mountain award, 1968, 1974; National Endowment for the Arts grant, 1978; Rhode Island School of Design Faculty Association medal, 1985; Carolyn Kizer prize, 1986, 1990; Shaeffer Eaton-PEN New England award, 1989; New England Poetry Club Golden Rose, 1990; New England Poetry Club May Sarton Award, 1991; Arthur C. Clarke Award, 1993, for *He She and It.* **Agent:** Lois Wallace, Wallace Literary Agency, 177 East 70th Street, New York, New York 10021, USA. **Address:** Box 1473, Wellfleet, Massachusetts 02667, U.S.A.

Publications

Novels

Going down Fast. New York, Simon & Schuster, 1969.
Dance the Eagle to Sleep. New York, Doubleday, 1970; London, W.H. Allen, 1971.
Small Changes. New York, Doubleday, 1973; London, Penguin, 1987.
Woman on the Edge of Time. New York, Knopf, 1976; London, Women's Press, 1979.
The High Cost of Living. New York, Harper, 1978; London, Women's Press, 1979.
Vida. New York, Summit, and London, Women's Press, 1980.
Braided Lives. New York, Summit, and London, Allen Lane, 1982.
Fly Away Home. New York, Summit, and London, Chatto & Windus, 1984.
Gone to Soldiers. New York, Summit, and London, Joseph, 1987.
Summer People. New York, Summit, and London, Joseph, 1989.

He, She and It. New York, Knopf, 1991; as *Body of Glass,* London, Joseph, 1992.
The Longings of Women. New York, Fawcett, and London, Joseph, 1994.

Uncollected Short Stories

"Crossing over Jordan," in *Transatlantic Review* (London), fall 1966.
"Love Me Tonight, God," in *Paris Review,* summer 1968.
"A Dynastic Encounter," in *Aphra* (New York) spring 1970.
"And I Went into the Garden of Love," in *Off Our Backs* (Washington, DC), Summer 1971.
"Do You Love Me?," in *Second Wave* (Cambridge, Massachusetts), 1(4), 1972.
"The Happiest Day of a Woman's Life," in *Works in Progress 7* (New York), 1972.
"Somebody Who Understands You," in *Moving Out* (Detroit), 2(2), 1972.
"Marriage Is a Matter of Give and Take," in *Boston Phoenix,* 3 July and 10 July 1973.
"Little Sister, Cat and Mouse," in *Second Wave* (Cambridge, Massachusetts), fall 1973.
"God's Blood," in *Anon,* 8, 1974.
"Like a Great Door Closing Suddenly," in *Detroit Discovery,* March/April 1974.
"The Retreat," in *Provincetown Poets* (Provincetown, Massachusetts), 2(2-3), 1976.
"What Can Be Had," in *Chrysalis 4* (San Diego, California), 1977.
"The Cowbird in the Eagles' Nest," in *Maenad,* fall 1980.
"I Will Not Describe What I Did," in *Mother Jones* (San Francisco), February/March 1982.
"Spring in the Arboretum," in *Michigan Quarterly Review* (Ann Arbor), winter 1982.
"Of Chilblains and Rotten Rutabagas," in *Lilith* (New York), winter/spring 1985.

Play

The Last White Class: A Play about Neighborhood Terror, with Ira Wood (produced Northampton, Massachusetts, 1978). Trumansburg, New York, Crossing Press, 1980.

Poetry

Breaking Camp. Middletown, Connecticut, Wesleyan University Press, 1968.
Hard Loving. Middletown, Connecticut, Wesleyan University Press, 1969.
A Work of Artifice. Detroit, Red Hanrahan Press, 1970.
4-Telling, with others. Trumansburg, New York, Crossing Press, 1971.
When the Drought Broke. Santa Barbara, California, Unicorn Press, 1971.
To Be of Use. New York, Doubleday, 1973.
Living in the Open. New York, Knopf, 1976.
The 12-Spoked Wheel Flashing. New York, Knopf, 1978.
The Moon Is Always Female. New York, Knopf, 1980.
Circles on the Water: Selected Poems. New York, Knopf, 1982.
Stone, Paper, Knife. New York, Knopf, and London, Pandora Press, 1983.
My Mother's Body. New York, Knopf, and London, Pandora Press, 1985.
Available Light. New York, Knopf, and London, Pandora Press, 1988.
Mars and Her Children. New York, Knopf, 1992.
Eight Chambers of the Heart. London, Penguin, 1995.

Recordings: *Marge Piercy: Poems,* 1969; *Laying Down the Tower,* Black Box, 1973; *Reclaiming Ourselves,* 1973; *At the Core,* 1976; *Reading and Thoughts,* Everett Edwards, 1976; *At the Core,* Watershed, 1976.

Other

Parti-Colored Blocks for a Quilt. Ann Arbor, University of Michigan Press, 1982.
The Earth Shines Secretly: A Book of Days. Cambridge, Massachusetts, Zoland Press, 1990.

Editor, *Early Ripening: American Women's Poetry Now.* London and New York, Pandora Press, 1987.

*

Bibliography: In *Contemporary American Women Writers: Narrative Strategies* edited by Catherine Rainwater and William J. Scheick, Lexington, University Press of Kentucky, 1985.

Manuscript Collection: Harlan Hatcher Graduate Library, University of Michigan, Ann Arbor.

Critical Studies: "Marge Piercy: A Collage" by Nancy Scholar Zee, in *Oyez Review* (Berkeley, California), 9(1), 1975; "In and Out of Time: The Form of Marge Piercy's Novels" by Susan Kress, and "Recent Feminist Utopias" by Joanna Russ, both in *Future Females: A Critical Anthology,* edited by Marlene Barr, Bowling Green, Bowing Green State University, 1981; *Ways of Knowing: Critical Essays on Marge Piercy* edited by Sue Walker and Eugenie Hamner, Mobile, Alabama, Negative Capability Press, 1986; *Alien to Femininity: Speculative Fiction and Feminist Theory* by Marlene S. Barr, New York, Greenwood Press, 1987; *Radical Imagination: Feminist Conceptions of the Future in Ursula Le Guin, Marge Piercy, and Sally Miller Gearhart,* New York, P. Lang, 1991; *The Repair of the World: The Novels of Marge Piercy* by Kerstin W. Shands, Westport, Connecticut, Greenwood Press, 1994.

* * *

Marge Piercy is one of America's foremost feminist writers; and is certainly one of the most prolific. She has achieved distinction as both a novelist and poet, and has also produced a fairly substantial body of criticism. Although she began writing as a teenager, her work wasn't published until she was in her 30s, beginning with a collection of poems, *Breaking Camp* (1968). Her first novel, *Going down Fast,* was published the following year. To date, she has written over a dozen novels and numerous collections of poetry.

Piercy's fiction and poetry interrelate on many levels. By Piercy's own account, the two often cross-fertilize each other—for instance, the title of her second novel, *Dance the Eagle to Sleep,* is an echo of a line from her poem "Curse of the earth magician on a metal land" (*Hard Loving*, 1969). A sequence of 11 poems collected in *Circles on the Water* was the starting point for *Woman on the Edge of Time*. Piercy has also claimed, however, that her poetry is more personal than her fiction, stating in an interview in the British feminist magazine *Everywoman* in June 1992 that "'[b]ecause I write as much poetry as fiction, I get to use up my autobiographical impulses in poetry.'"

Although she is often regarded in a rather uncomplicated way as a writer of contemporary feminist social realism, Piercy's novelistic output actually spans a range of genres. In addition to the works that can be included in the "social realist" category, she has also written a war novel of monumental length, *Gone to Soldiers*, and three works of speculative fiction: *Dance the Eagle to Sleep*, *Woman on the Edge of Time*, and *He, She and It*. Indeed, *Woman on the Edge of Time*, now regarded as a classic example of feminist science fiction, is arguably the novel that has gained Piercy the most critical attention. *He, She and It*, published in 1991, has also been widely commented on as a timely feminist intervention within the masculinist science fiction subgenre of cyberpunk.

In whatever mode she chooses to write, however, Piercy's politics—feminist and left-wing—are always clearly articulated through her art. Novels such as *Going down Fast*, *Dance the Eagle to Sleep*, *Small Changes*, *Vida*, and *Braided Lives* indicate her involvement in the New Left movement of the 1960s and '70s, as well as her doubts concerning women's involvement in non-feminist radical politics. The characters in her novels are nearly always individuals who live on the margins of mainstream society, be it by virtue of their race, gender, sexuality, occupation, or economic status, and the very act of giving them a narrative voice automatically attaches significance to their lives. In this way the value of the personal is consistently upheld against the political. A common scenario, set up in Piercy's first novel, *Going down Fast*, is that of a small countercultural group bravely battling against a faceless system characterized as patriarchal, capitalist, and uncaring. Although she is no idealist, Piercy ultimately asserts the importance of a flexibly egalitarian community in which the specific circumstances of the individual takes precedence over abstract ideology—the similarities between her two speculative utopias, Mattapoisett (*Woman on the Edge of Time*) and Tikva (*He, She and It*) are not accidental.

From *Summer People* onwards, another element in Piercy's work has grown in importance—her interest in her Jewish heritage. Piercy has attributed this to the research she engaged in while writing *Gone to Soldiers*, which deals with both the Holocaust and the Jewish Resistance movement in France. Piercy vigorously asserts the possibility of being both a Jew and a feminist, and is extremely interested in ways in which Jewish feminists are changing rituals and traditions from within the religion. Increasingly, her major female characters speak from a consciously Jewish sensibility, such as Diana in *Summer People*, whose father, a holocaust survivor, bequeaths her a history of suffering and survival.

While Piercy makes the polemical intention behind her novels clear in such statements as her preface to the Women's Press edition of *Vida*, published in 1980: "I want to change consciousness ... If you don't support alternate ways of imagining things, people aren't going to be able to imagine a better world," she is not, however, committed to an inflexible political, religious or feminist stance. On the contrary, Piercy's preference for multi-voiced narration, sharing out the narrative point of view among several main characters (a technique that reaches its apotheosis in *Gone to Soldiers*, which attempts to relate the experience of the Second World War from the perspective of no less than ten major characters) allows her to weave together a variety of different views in order to allow for intricate, and not always completely compatible, shadings of opinion and experience. Her latest novel, *The Longings of Women*, demonstrates this extremely skillfully. It has three separate narrators: Leila Landsman, a Jewish academic; Mary Burke, a homeless woman; and Becky Souza Burgess, a working-class girl who murders her husband. Although all are connected, none know all the details of each others' lives. Thus, none of the characters possess the controlling opinion within the narrative, allowing Piercy to develop each woman's particular predicament subtly and sympathetically.

The feminist nature of Piercy's artistic methodology is neatly indicated in the title of her 1982 collection of interviews and essays entitled *Parti-Colored Blocks for a Quilt* where, rather like Alice Walker in her well-known essay "Everyday Use," Piercy uses the traditional feminine art of quilting as a metaphor for the activity of attributing value to women's lives and histories. In all her writing, Piercy consistently speaks for the downtrodden and the marginalized, seeking to make connections, forge a sense of community, and work towards a better world. It is a project succinctly summed up in her poem "Let Us Gather at the River" (*Stone, Paper, Knife*, 1983): "I am the woman sitting by the river./ I mend old rebellions and patch them new."

—Sarah Gamble

PLASKOW, Judith

Nationality: American. **Born:** Brooklyn, New York, 14 March 1947. **Education:** Clark University, A.A. 1968; Yale University, M.Phil. 1971, Ph.D. 1975. **Family:** Married in 1969; one son. **Career:** Adjunct assistant professor of religion, New York University, 1974-75; lecturer at Hebrew Union College School of Education, Drew Theological School, and Douglas College, 1975-76; assistant professor of religion, 1976-79, Wichita State University, Wichita, Kansas; assistant professor, 1979-84, associate professor, 1984-90, then professor of religious studies, beginning 1990, Manhattan College, Riverdale, New York. Member of advisory board, Women's Studies in Religion program, Harvard Divinity School, 1980-84 and 1985-89; cofounder, *B'not Eh* (feminist collective), 1981; cofounder and coeditors, *Journal of Feminist Studies in Religion*, 1983-94; member of editorial board and columnist, *Tachyon*. **Member:** American Academy of Religion (associate director, 1992-94; vice-president, 1995-96), American Theological Society, Society for Values in Higher Education, Women's Caucus for Religious Studies, New York Feminist Scholars in Religion. **Address:** Department of Religious Studies, Manhattan College, 4513 Manhattan College, Bronx, New York, 10471-4097, U.S.A.

Publications

Religion/Spirituality

Sex, Sin, and Grace: Women's Experience and the Theologies of Reinhold Niebuhr and Paul Tillich. Washington, University Press of America, 1980.

Standing Again at Sinai: Judaism from a Feminist Perspective. San Francisco, Harper & Row, 1990.

Essays

"The Coming of Lilith," in *Religion and Sexism: Images of Women in the Jewish and Christian Traditions,* edited by Rosemary Radford Ruether. New York, Simon & Schuster, 1974.

"Toward a New Theology of Sexuality," in *Twice Blessed,* edited by Christie Balk and Andy Rose. Boston, Beacon Press, 1989.

"Transforming the Nature of Community: Toward a Feminist People of Israel," in *After Patriarchy: Feminist Transformations of the World Religions,* edited by P. Coney, W. Akin, and J. McDaniel. Maryknoll, New York, Obis, 1992.

"We Are Also Your Sisters: The Development of Women's Studies in Religion," in *Women's Studies Quarterly,* 21(1-2), spring/summer 1993.

"Jewish Theology in Feminist Perspective," in *Feminist Perspectives on Jewish Studies,* edited by Lynx Davidman and Shelly Tenenbaum. New Haven, Yale University Press, 1994.

Other

Editor, with Joan Arnold Romeo, *Women and Religion: Papers of the Working Group on Women and Religion, 1972-73.* Chambersburg, Pennsylvania, American Academy of Religion, 1974.

Editor, with Carol P. Christ, *Womanspirit Rising: A Feminist Reader in Religion.* San Francisco, Harper & Row, 1979.

Editor, with Carol P. Christ, *Weaving the Visions: New Patterns in Feminist Spirituality.* San Francisco, Harper & Row, 1989.

* * *

Judith Plaskow, a prominent Jewish feminist theologian, has been a central figure in the transforming of how religion is both studied and practiced in relation to women. In the 1970s, Plaskow, with her colleague Carol Christ among others, began the difficult work of etching out spaces in theology schools where barriers had traditionally stood. Their purpose was to create new theologies and practices more cognizant of the reality of who women are and the complexity of their lives. The stark reality of the restrictions placed on women in theology came to Plaskow during her years as a doctoral student at Yale University, where she struggled to open the academy's eyes to theology's androcentric conception of women.

Plaskow's proposal for her dissertation meant positioning women's experience at the center of her research, an idea initially met with derision by the male faculty. Today, Plaskow credits her friend and colleague Carol Christ, as well as others in the feminist movement, for having given her the strength and knowledge to force her work to completion. She critiques seminaries and university academies on their resistance to feminist theory—a resistance that creates, for many women, insurmountable barriers as they labor to create their own standing in the discipline.

In her dissertation Plaskow broke new ground by examining the notions of sin and grace in the work of two of the 20th century's most prominent theologians, Reinhold Niebuhr and Paul Tillich. Her work was both innovative and provocative, due in part to her perception of the definitions assigned by Niebuhr and Tillich in light of women's lives or experiences. In order to illuminate the complexity of women's lives, Plaskow used literature as a groundwork from which she could then demonstrate the limits of theology. Her conclusion was that, while these men spoke powerfully for their times, too often theologies such as theirs have been applied as if they were universal truths. Such "truths" occlude, or worse still, reject the complexities of many who may be invisible to the dominant theology and yet, in cultural and religious practice, are still subject to their authority.

As a Jewish feminist Plaskow is intimately aware of the differences found among women as a group. Nevertheless, as she says in *Sex, Sin, and Grace: Women's Experience and the Theologies of Reinhold Niebuhr and Paul Tillich,* there are often collective experiences, feelings, thoughts, and ideas between women of diverse cultural, economic, and racial subgroups. While similarities may exist, she stresses that concepts like the *eternal feminine* have functioned to contain women in roles that diminish their humanity and prohibit their full participation in the community.

As a way of turning academic practice on its head, Plaskow has demonstrated her commitment to both feminism and Judaism by living beyond academic corridors. Her publications reflect this commitment by opening venues for other women to illustrate their own commitments to both religious practice and feminism. As early as 1975 she coedited an anthology of articles that dealt not only with women's differing experiences, but critiqued institutional religions and their sacred texts. Later she would coedit two manuscripts with her colleague and friend Carol P. Christ that would become foundational works for women engaged in the study of religion. Their first work, *Womanspirit Rising,* drew together religion and feminism in what is often a precarious relationship. The collection of articles is useful, however, for blending critiques with new alternatives to traditional religious expression. Therefore, while patriarchal institutions and practices are critiqued a new trend is also being created, as women name their own religious experiences by reworking traditional notions of myth, symbol, ritual, and such basic concepts as god and spirituality. Published in 1989, a second book illustrates the changes in feminism and religious practice. Plaskow and Christ note these changes in their introduction to *Weaving the Visions,* changes that reflect the different directions they themselves have taken in their work. Christ has moved to goddess studies; Plaskow works to find a way of drawing her feminism and Judaism together. The force of *Weaving the Visions* is its diversity of resources, including, most significantly, the voices of women of color.

A central component of Plaskow's work and life is the development of community. She credits the women's movement with having raised women's consciousness to the subtle and not so subtle mechanisms of patriarchy. In community, she contends, women have learned to strive beyond cultural expectations. This is why Plaskow says in her 1974 article, "The Coming of Lilith" (reprinted in *Womanspirit Rising*) that process and content are of equal importance; feminist theology is not just talked about or relegated to one avenue of experience, but is integrated into the details of daily living. In community, according to Plaskow, women discover both their worth and their power to say "no" to the pressures in life that constrain them. From community women have discovered affirming friends and energy for continuing the struggle beyond the bounds of the group. In all of Plaskow's work, every aspect of human existence can have religious significance; strong community ties can be seen as an example of grace.

In Judith Plaskow's most recent work, she brings together her feminism and Judaism by reworking the use of sacred texts, images of God, and, certainly, ritual. Her publications—most notably *Standing Again at Sinai: Judaism from a Feminist Perspective*—parallel the work done in her Jewish feminist collective *B'not Eh,* which she helped to found in 1981. Through this group and her academic work, Plaskow exposes the misogynist elements of Judaism. Instead of leaving an empty space, she creates new expressions that allow women's entire realm of body, intellect, and psyche to find full expression.

—Helen-May Eaton

PLATH, Sylvia

Pseudonym: Victoria Lucas. **Nationality:** American. **Born:** Boston, Massachusetts, 27 October 1932. **Education:** Smith College, B.A. (summa cum laude) 1955; attended Harvard University, 1954; Newnham College, Cambridge, 1955-57 (Fulbright scholar), M.A. 1957. **Family:** Married the poet Ted Hughes in 1956 (separated); one son, one daughter. **Career:** Volunteer art teacher, People's Institute, Northampton, Massachusetts, c. 1951-54; guest editor, *Mademoiselle* magazine, New York, summer 1953; instructor in English, Smith College, 1957-58; lived in Boston, 1958-59, and at Yaddo, 1958; moved to London, 1959; moved to Devon, England. Contributor to periodicals, including *Atlantic, Christian Science Monitor, Harper's, London Magazine, Mademoiselle, Nation, Poetry,* and *Seventeen.* Awards: Mount Holyoke College Glascock Poetry Prize, 1955; Bess Hokin Award (*Poetry,* Chicago), 1957; Cheltenham Festival prize, 1961; Eugene F. Saxon fellowship, 1961; Pulitzer Prize, 1982, for *Collected Poems.* **Member:** Phi Beta Kappa. **Died:** In London, 11 February 1963.

Publications

Novel

The Bell Jar (as Victoria Lucas). London, Heinemann, 1963; under real name, London, Faber, 1965; New York, Harper, 1971.

Poetry

The Colossus. London, Heinemann, 1960; revised as *The Colossus and Other Poems,* New York, Knopf, 1962.
Uncollected Poems (booklet). London, Turret Books, 1965.
Ariel, edited by Ted Hughes and Olwyn Hughes. London, Faber, 1965; New York, Harper, 1966.
Wreath for a Bridal. London, Sceptre Press, 1970.
Crossing the Water: Transitional Poems, edited by Ted Hughes. New York, Harper; with different contents, London, Faber, 1971.
Crystal Gazer and Other Poems. London, Rainbow Press, 1971.
Lyonnesse. London, Rainbow Press, 1971.
Million Dollar Month. London, Sceptre Press, 1971.
Winter Trees, edited by Ted Hughes. London, Faber, 1971; New York, Harper, 1972.
Collected Poems, edited by Ted Hughes. New York, Harper, 1981.
Stings (drafts). Northampton, Massachusetts, Smith College, 1983.
Selected Poems, edited by Ted Hughes. London, Faber, 1985.

Play

Three Women: A Monologue for Three Voices (broadcast London, BBC-Radio, 1962). Turret Books, 1968.

For Children

The Bed Book. New York, Harper, 1976.

Other

Letters Home: Correspondence, 1950-1963, edited by Aurelia Schober Plath. New York, Harper, 1975.
Johnny Panic and the Bible of Dreams: Short Stories, Prose, and Diary Excerpts, edited by Ted Hughes. New York, Harper, 1979.
The Journals of Sylvia Plath, edited by Frances McCullough and Ted Hughes. New York, Ballantine, 1983.

Editor, *American Poetry Now.* London, Oxford University Press, 1961.

*

Media Adaptations: *The Bell Jar* (film), Avco-Embassy, 1978; *Letters Home* (stage play; adapted by Rose Leiman Goldemberg), 1979.

Bibliography: *Sylvia Plath: A Bibliography* by Gary Lane and Maria Stevens, Metuchen, New Jersey, Scarecrow Press, 1978; *Sylvia Plath: An Analytical Bibliography* by Stephen Tabor, Westport, Connecticut, Meckler, 1987; *Sylvia Plath: A Reference Guide, 1973-1988* by Sheryl L. Meyering, Boston, G. K. Hall, 1990.

Manuscript Collections: Lilly Library of Indiana University, Bloomington; Smith College Rare Book Room, Northhampton, Massachusetts.

Critical Studies: *The Art of Sylvia Plath: A Symposium* edited by Charles Newman, Bloomington, Indiana University Press, 1970; *Sylvia Plath* by E. M. Aird, New York, Harper, 1973; *A Closer Look at Ariel: A Memory of Sylvia Plath* by N. H. Steiner, New York, *Harper's* Magazine Press, 1973; *Sylvia Plath: A Biography* by Linda Wagner-Martin, New York, Simon & Schuster, 1987; *Bitter Fame: The Undiscovered Life of Sylvia Plath* by Anne Stevenson, Boston, Houghton, 1989; *Rough Magic: A Biography of Sylvia Plath* by Paul Alexander, New York, Viking, 1991; *The Death and Life of Sylvia Plath* by Ronald Hayman, Secaucus, New Jersey, Carol Publishing Group, 1991; *The Haunting of Sylvia Plath* by Jacqueline Rose, London, Virago, 1991; *The Silent Woman: Sylvia Plath & Ted Hughes* by Janet Malcolm, New York, Knopf, 1993; *Revising Life: Sylvia Plath's Ariel Poems* by Susan R. Van Dyne, Chapel Hill, University of North Carolina Press, 1993.

* * *

In the years since her death, Sylvia Plath's life and work has taken on mythic proportions. She has become one of the most well-known poets of the 20th century, in part because of her tragic suicide at age 30. Perhaps as a result, the writings to which most readers and critics refer are those dealing with suicide and death.

This focus is unfortunately narrow, because Plath's writings are much more far-ranging in their ambitions and scope. Larger interests in world politics (especially the Holocaust) and in women's issues can be found throughout Plath's poetry and prose. Determining her relationship to feminism has proven far more difficult, however. Though she is not an anomaly in this regard, Plath's relationship to the second wave of the women's movement has been the subject of a great deal of critical debate.

Born to German immigrants Otto and Aurelia Plath, Sylvia began writing stories and poems at an early age. What might otherwise have been an idyllic childhood came to an end when, at the age of eight, her father died. Otto Plath had taught applied biology at Boston University and had published a well-regarded book on bees. He found out too late that his fatally gangrenous leg resulted from undiagnosed diabetic complications, which would have been treatable if detected earlier. After Otto's death, Aurelia taught secretarial skills and struggled to raise her daughter Sylvia and her younger son Warren.

Sylvia was a model high school student. She won a scholarship to Smith College, where, as Sandra Gilbert and Susan Gubar put it, Plath was a "'superachiever,' accumulating a steady string of honors and prizes along with high grades and accolades from her teachers." One of the honors she received proved formative to her life and work. Plath was chosen as a "guest editor" of *Mademoiselle* magazine in the summer of 1953. After that whirlwind month in New York City and the series of disappointments that followed it, Plath attempted suicide. The details of this period in her life are recounted in her loosely autobiographical novel, *The Bell Jar.*

Plath was hospitalized, received treatment, and rallied from her "nervous breakdown," returning to Smith to graduate summa cum laude in 1955. Shortly thereafter, she left the United States for England, studying on a Fulbright scholarship at Cambridge University. It was there, in 1956, that she met her future husband, the poet Ted Hughes, at a party—a fiery episode she describes in her *Journals.* Hughes and Plath married and had two children, Frieda and Nicholas, who often appear in Plath's poems.

Both Plath's and Hughes's careers as poets prospered during the late 1950s and early 1960s, though Hughes's work was the first to gain wider recognition (partly thanks to Plath's preparation and promotion of her husband's writing). They taught and wrote in England and in the United States, settling eventually in a house in Devon. Their marriage, however, proved a failure. In the summer of 1962 Hughes began an affair with Assia Gutmann, who "had the reputation for having affairs, especially with poets," according to Paul Alexander (tragically, Gutmann, too, later took her own life). Hughes moved to London with Gutmann, and Plath and Hughes officially separated.

Plath, left alone to raise two children as was her mother before her, fought off depression in Devon and then in London during the bitterly cold fall and winter of 1962-63. She produced at the rate of two or three a day what are now regarded as her most brilliant poems, published posthumously in a collection titled *Ariel.* While her earlier poetry had been studied and formally intricate, these last poems had much more of an intense, wry immediacy and a twisted fairy-tale quality to them. On 11 February 1963, she left mugs of milk for her children and stuffed towels in the cracks around the kitchen door so that Frieda and Nicholas would not be harmed. She then turned on the gas in the oven and ended her life.

When reading Plath's writings, it is important to resist the temptation to see her work as in itself a long suicide note—as the central or only focus of her writings. Plath, who (along with the poet Anne Sexton) had studied under poet Robert Lowell, is often labeled a writer of "confessional" poetry. To reduce her output to confessions about her own life would be a mistake, however. Even those famous poems that seemingly describe her personal life also consider broader issues of gender, relationships, and power. Though much of her work is certainly dark, a great deal of it deals with nature, childbearing and childrearing, love, and sexuality.

One of Plath's most renowned poems is "Daddy" (1963), in which the poem's speaker describes a German father who "died before I had time," and whom she "had to kill." This paradoxical sense of longing for his return and longing to destroy him fuels the rest of the poem. The speaker tells her father (and the reader) that she could never talk to him because her "tongue stuck in my jaw" as if in a "barb wire snare." Images of the speaker as imprisoned, like a Jew during the Holocaust, are made even more explicit in the subsequent stanzas. The speaker claims she "may be a bit of a Jew" and says again to "Daddy," "I have always been scared of you," because of his "Luftwaffe," his "gobbledygoo," his "neat mustache," and "Aryan eye." The poem makes the controversial statement that "Every woman adores a Fascist" and says that women like "the boot in the face" and the "Brute heart of a brute like you." Most feminist readers recoil at this line, and it has been discussed often in terms of women's masochism or desire for self-inflicted pain (which feminist psychologist Paula Caplan, for one, has called a "myth"). The remaining stanzas of the poem recount the speaker's "making a model" of "Daddy" in her choice of a husband. The speaker then "kills" both of the men, maintaining that she is "finally through" and comparing "Daddy" and the husband to vampires.

Another famous Plath poem, "Lady Lazarus" (1963), also deals explicitly with death and maintains that "dying is an art." The poem's speaker is a "smiling woman" of 30 who tells about her three suicide attempts, describing them as a "strip tease" and again utilizing Nazi and Jewish imagery. The speaker discusses her suicide attempts as "theatrical" and her eventual comebacks as "A miracle!" She imagines men as her audience with her incantations to "Herr Doktor" and "Herr Enemy," and later "Herr God, Her Lucifer." The poem ends with a warning that the poem's speaker will rise out of the ash with her red hair and "eat men like air." It is easy to understand why readers interested in poetic expressions of women's power and independence would find the last lines of this poem to be compelling, chilling, and important ones. The female speaker's rage and violence here is, however, confusing in a poem that also sees a woman's life as expendable and as primarily a performance for men.

Many other, less famous poems deal with issues such as motherhood, nature, and female relationships. Notable among these are the bee poems, including "The Bee Meeting," "The Arrival of the Bee Box," "Stings," "The Swarm" and "Wintering." The latter sees the female bees as "Maids and the long royal lady," and the male drones as "blunt, clumsy stumblers" and "boors." The poem's speaker describes herself as a midwife of sorts, delivering honey. Perhaps as a result of her father's interest in bees, Plath herself chose to become a beekeeper in her adult years. Many of the bee poems describe women's lives through the lens of the bee community, as in "Stings," where the poem's speaker maintains, "I/ Have a self to recover, a queen."

The Bell Jar, too, has its moment of feminist impulse and insight. Some critics have even seen the novel as illustrating the beginnings of the feminist movement, though this is perhaps an overstatement. The protagonist, Esther Greenwood (whose mental breakdown is chronicled) questions the roles American women are "supposed" to play in the 1950s. Esther finds herself both drawn to and repulsed by many of the women's lives she observes around her—including those of the boring, wholesome, but good-hearted virgins; the fun-loving but sometimes selfish and reckless whores; and the seemingly asexual but successful businesswomen. At a time when women were thought to be either "good" or "bad," Esther tries to find a middle ground on which to tread. One of the best places to see Plath's multi-faceted exploration of femininity is in her radio play for three voices, "Three Women" (1962), which dramatizes the contradictory social messages and desires with which many women struggle.

Carole Ferrier has suggested that Plath "was in many ways a victim of the fifties and its ideology of the family. Women struggling to lead independent lives or pursue the ideal of being writers were under pressure to submerge themselves within monogamous marriage and create households straight out of *Ladies' Home Journal.* Plath died just as the new wave of feminist theory began to surface with the rise of the women's movement." Plath dealt with these contradictions in her life and her work, to be sure. The extent to which she saw either as seeking to improving the lot of women is debatable, though. Many have wanted to claim that Plath was "truly" a feminist, but determining which of the many selves we see in her letters, journals, poems, and prose is the "true" one is an impossible task. Is Plath the woman who adores a fascistic male? Is she the woman who devours men who would seek to control her? Neither? Both?

Calling Plath a feminist, then, presents difficulties. It is unlikely that she herself would have identified with this label. Her struggles, however (in life and in poetry), were clearly understood by her to be gendered and often, as a result, unjust. She struggled to articulate the contradictions that a woman who wanted to be both devoted wife and mother *and* a successful creative writer faced in the late 1950s and 1960s. That her struggles have proved inspirational, fascinating, and tragic to subsequent generations of readers is testimony to the enduring relevance of her insights and to the stunning brilliance of her work.

—Devoney Looser

POLLOCK, Sharon

Nationality: Canadian. **Born:** Mary Sharon Chambers, in Fredericton, New Brunswick, 19 April 1936. **Education:** Attended University of New Brunswick, 1952-54. **Family:** Married Ross Pollock in 1954 (marriage dissolved), five children; one child by Michael Ball. **Career:** Actress, touring with Prairie Players; affiliated with drama department, 1976-77, visiting lecturer, 1976-81, University of Alberta, Edmonton; head of playwright's colony, Banff Centre of Fine Arts, Banff, Alberta, 1977-80; dramaturge and assistant artistic director, 1983-84, artistic director, 1984, Theatre Calgary, Calgary, Alberta. Playwright-in-residence, Alberta Theatre Projects, 1977-79; artist-in-residence, National Arts Centre, Ottawa, 1980-82; Advisory Arts Panel, Canada Council, member, 1978-81, chair, 1979-80; member of advisory committee, National Theatre School, 1979-80; associate artistic director, Manitoba Theatre Centre, 1988; artistic director, Theatre New Brunswick, 1988-90; associate director, Stratford Festival, 1990. **Awards:** Dominion Drama Best Actress Award, 1966; Alberta Playwriting Competition award, 1971, for *A Compulsory Option;* Association of Canadian Television and Radio Artists award, 1981, for *Sweet Land of Liberty;* Canada Council Governor General's Literary Awards, 1981, for *Blood Relations,* and 1986, for *Doc.* **Address:** 319 Manora Drive, NE, Calgary, Alberta T2A 4R2, Canada.

Publications

Plays

A Compulsory Option (produced Vancouver, 1972).

Walsh (produced Calgary, 1973; revised version produced Stratford, Ontario, 1974; aired on CBC Radio 1974; revised version produced Ottawa, 1983). Vancouver, Talonbooks, 1973; revised edition, 1974; revised edition, 1983.

New Canadians (produced Vancouver, 1973).

Superstition throu' the Ages (produced Vancouver, 1973).

Wudjesay? (produced Vancouver, 1974).

The Happy Prince (produced Vancouver, 1974).

The Rose and the Nightingale (produced Vancouver, 1974).

Star-child (produced Vancouver, 1974).

The Great Drag Race, or Smoked, Choked, and Croaked (commissioned by British Columbia Christmas Seal Society; produced in British Columbia secondary schools, 1974).

Lessons in Swizzlery (produced New Westminister, British Columbia, 1974).

And out Goes You (produced Vancouver, 1975).

The Komagata Maru Incident (produced Vancouver, 1976; aired on CBC, Vancouver, 1979). Toronto, Playwrights Co-op, 1978.

My Name Is Lisabeth (produced New Westminister, British Columbia, 1976).

Tracings—The Fraser Story, with others (produced Edmonton, 1977).

The Wreck of the National Line Car (produced Calgary, 1978).

Chautaqua Spelt E-N-E-R-G-Y (produced Alberta, 1979).

Mail vs. Female (produced Calgary 1979).

One Tiger to a Hill (produced Edmonton, 1980; revised version produced Lennoxville, Quebec, 1980; produced New York, 1980; aired on CBC Radio, 1985). In *Blood Relations and Other Plays,* 1981.

Blood Relations (produced Edmonton, 1980). In *Blood Relations and Other Plays,* 1981.

Generations (adaptation of her radio play; produced Calgary, 1980). In *Blood Relations and Other Plays,* 1981.

Blood Relations and Other Plays. Edmonton, NeWest Press, 1981.

Whiskey Six Cadenza (produced Calgary, 1983; aired on CBC Radio, 1983), in *NeWest Plays by Women,* edited by Diane Bessai and Don Kerr. Edmonton, NeWest Press, 1987.

Doc (produced Calgary, 1984; revised version produced Toronto, 1984; revised as *Family Trappings,* produced Fredericton, New Brunswick, 1986; aired on CBC Radio, 1991). Toronto, Playwrights Canada, 1986.

Egg (produced Calgary, 1988).

Getting It Straight (produced Winnipeg, 1989). in *Heroines: Three Plays,* edited by Joyce Doolittle. Red Deer, Red Deer College Press, 1992.

The Making of Warriors, (radio play; aired 1991), in *Airborne: The Morningside Dramas,* edited by Ann Jansen. Winnipeg, Blizzard, 1991.
Saucy Jack (produced Calgary, 1993). Winnipeg, Blizzard, 1994.
Fair Liberty's Call (produced Stratford, Ontario, 1993). Toronto, Coach House Press, 1995.

Television Plays: *Portrait of a Pig,* 1973; *The Larsens,* 1976; "Ransom" (episode of *The Magic Lie* series), 1978; *Country Joy,* with others, 1970-80; *The Person's Case* (originally titled *Free Our Sisters, Free Ourselves*), 1980; *The Komogata Maru Incident,* 1984.

Radio Plays: *A Split Second in the Life Of,* 1971; *31 for 2,* 1971; *We to the Gods,* 1971; *Waiting,* 1973; *The B Triple P Plan,* n.d.; *In Memory Of,* n.d.; *Generation,* 1978; *Sweet Land of Liberty,* 1979; *The Story of the Komogata Maru,* 1979; *Mrs. Yale and Jennifer,* n.d.; *Mary Beth Goes to Calgary,* n.d.; *In the Beginning Was,* n.d.; *Intensive Care,* 1983; *The Making of Warriors,* 1991.

*

Bibliography: *Canadian Playwrights: A Biographical Guide* edited by Don Rubin and Alison Cranmer-Byng, Toronto, CTR, 1980; *Playwriting Women: Female Voices in English Canada* by Cynthia Zimmerman, Toronto, Simon & Pierre, 1994.

Manuscript Collections: University of Calgary, Alberta.

Theatrical Activities: Actor—Role of Lizzie Borden in *My Name Is Lisabeth,* produced New Westminister, British Columbia, 1976; Lizzie Borden in *Blood Relations,* produced Calgary, 1981; Eme in *Getting It Straight,* produced Winnipeg, 1989; Catherine in *Doc,* aired CBC Radio, 1991.

Critical Studies: *The Work: Conversations with English-Canadian Playwrights* (interview) by Robert Wallace and Cynthia Zimmerman, Toronto, Coach House Press, 1982; *A Mazing Space: Writing Canadian Women Writing* edited by Shirley Neuman and Smaro Kamboureli, Edmonton, Longspoon-NeWest, 1987; *Fairplay: 12 Women Speak* (interview) edited by Judith Rudakoff and Rita Much, Toronto, Simon & Pierre, 1990; *Playwrighting Women: Female Voices in English Canada* by Cynthia Zimmerman, Toronto, Simon & Pierre, 1994.

* * *

In the three decades since she was hired to operate the box office at Fredericton's Beaverbrook Playhouse, Sharon Pollock has assumed a leading role in the world of English-Canadian drama. Author of a broad range of dramatic writing, she has also garnered acclaim for her abilities as director, artistic director, and actor. A self-identified feminist playwright, Pollock has increasingly depicted strong women who contest oppressive power relations.

Pollock won a playwriting competition with her first stage play, *A Compulsory Option.* During the 1970s she wrote radio and television scripts and nine children's plays; unfortunately, none of these early works has been published. Pollock came to national attention with her second full-length play, *Walsh.* A depiction of the Sioux' exile in Canada after the defeat of General Custer, the play, like much of Pollock's major early work, interrogates the adequacy of conventional accounts of history. *Walsh* was followed by the naturalistic *The Komagata Maru Incident,* which recreates how almost 400 British subjects of East Indian origin were denied entry to Canada in 1914. *One Tiger to a Hill,* loosely based upon a 1975 penitentiary hostage-taking, solidified Pollock's reputation as a playwright who wielded the theatre as an instrument of social reform. Recently, she has returned to reexamining Canadian history with *Fair Liberty's Call.* The play depicts a Loyalist family gathered in New Brunswick to commemorate the anniversary of the fall of Yorktown. Though born in New Brunswick, Pollock nonetheless identifies herself as a prairie playwright. Southern Alberta is the setting of *Generations* and *Whiskey Six Cadenza.* The former depicts a farming family confronting personal and political change; the latter, two Prohibition-era households headed by domineering parental figures.

That theme of parent-child conflict reappears in *Blood Relations,* the best known of Pollock's plays and the first to feature a female protagonist. Based upon the notorious Lizzie Borden case, the play's primary concern is not with the truth of the murder charges. Rather, Pollock employs the device of a play within a play to reconstruct the circumstances that might have provoked Lizzie to attack her father and stepmother with an axe. Ten years after her acquittal by a court unable to reconcile femininity with murder, Lizzie directs her lover, an actress, in a reenactment of the period just prior to the crimes. The so-called "dream thesis" presents a Lizzie determined to resist the stifling gender scripts imposed upon her by 19th-century society in general and her father in particular. The Actress, in the role of Lizzie, explores and rejects each of the limited choices available to her until ultimately one course of action remains. The play concludes ambiguously, the Actress having discovered what she would do but no more certain about actual events. Still eluding definition by inflexible patriarchal culture, Lizzie implicates that culture in the crime. Her response to the Actress's remark, "Lizzie, you did," is directed towards the audience: "I didn't.... You did."

Like Lizzie Borden, the protagonist of *Doc* is engaged in a conflict with a patriarch who is at once actual and symbolic. The most autobiographical of Pollock's works, Doc dramatizes the playwright's own struggles to reconcile conventional scripts of domestic femininity with contemporary career aspirations. Past and present interact as the adult Catherine, a writer, and Katie, her childhood counterpart, confront painful ancestral legacies. Catherine is haunted by the suicides of the grandmother whose name she bears and a mother whose alcoholism and eventual madness bespoke the strain of maintaining an identity distinct from her husband's. Everett Chalmers (suggestively named after Pollock's own father) is a prominent physician from whom Catherine derives her own uncompromising commitment to her profession. His critique of his daughter's choice of career over family parallels his earlier denunciation of his wife's quest for autonomy, as Catherine is all too well aware. The two characters struggle to reconcile divergent expectations, a possibility tentatively affirmed by the play's conclusion.

Getting It Straight reprises the theme of women and madness introduced in *Doc.* The single character is a schizophrenia patient, Eme, who has escaped her custodian to hide under the bleachers of a now-deserted rodeo arena. Her stream-of-consciousness monologue is a melange of fact and fantasy, memory and conjecture from which repeated motifs gradually resolve themselves. Central among these is a protest against male aggression and power, as manifested in both individual and political violence. Through the ending is no less ambiguous than that of *Blood Relations*, Eme's hauntingly poetic call for solidarity among all women is unmistakable.

Like *Blood Relations, Saucy Jack* revisits one of the most sensationalistic events of the previous century. Set in Victorian England, the play depicts how a scholar and his former pupil, Prince Albert Victor, skirt the truth behind the identity of Jack the Ripper. Duplicity and betrayal reign as friendship becomes a front for murder. Jack's anonymous victims are granted provisional identities, for the actress Kate humanizes the ill-fated prostitutes she has been hired to portray. As *Saucy Jack* progresses, Kate gradually exploits voice and silence to usurp the men's power. In her prefatory remarks, Pollock observes that the actress—the only character alive at the play's conclusion—heralds "the ultimate failure and demise of the supposedly 'Dominant,' be they of class or sex."

Resistance to the "Dominant" is a recurring theme in Pollock's stage plays, as it is too in *The Making of Warriors*, a half-hour radio dramatization of the lives and deaths of activists Sarah Moore Grimké and Anna Mae Pictou Aquash. Pollock's art reflects a conviction she expressed to interviewer Rita Much: "I certainly don't understand how a woman with any sense of justice can not be a feminist."

—Nina van Gessel

PORTIA. *See* **ROBINSON, Mary (Darby).**

POWER, Eileen (Edna Le Poer)

Nationality: British. **Born:** Altrincham, Cheshire, 1889. **Education:** Graduated from Girton College, Cambridge, 1910; studied in Paris and Chartres; London School of Economics, 1911-13. **Family:** Married Michael M. Postan in 1938. **Career:** Director of Historical Studies, Girton College, Cambridge, 1913-21; lecturer and reader, 1921-31, then professor of economic history, beginning 1931, London School of Economics, London. Co-founder and editor, *Economic History Review*, 1927. **Died:** Of heart failure, 1940.

Publications

History

The Paycockes of Coggshall. London, Methuen, 1920.

Medieval English Nunneries c. 1275-1535. Cambridge, Cambridge University Press, 1922.

Medieval People. N.p., 1924; 10th edition, London, Methuen, 1963.

Boys and Girls of History, with Rhoda Power. London, Dobson, 1967; New York, Roy, 1970.

"The Position of Women," in *The Legacy of the Middle Ages*, edited by C.G. Crump and E. F. Jacob. Oxford, Clarendon Press, 1926.

"Peasant Life and Rural Conditions (c. 1100 to c. 1500)," in *Cambridge Medieval History*, Vol. 7, edited by J. R. Tanner and others. [England], n.p., 1932.

The Wool Trade in English Medieval History (Ford lectures given 1939). London and New York, Oxford University Press, 1941.

Medieval Women, edited by Michael Postan. Cambridge, Cambridge University Press, 1975.

Other

Editor, with R. H. Tawney, *Tudor Economic Documents*. London, Longman Green, 1924.

Editor, *Poems from the Irish*, London, Benn, 1927.

Editor, with Michael M. Postan, *Studies in English Trade in the 15th Century*. London, Routledge, 1933.

Editor, with others, *Cambridge Economic History of Europe from the Decline of the Roman Empire*, Vol. 1. Cambridge, Cambridge University Press, 1941.

Translator, *The Goodman of Paris (Le menagier de Paris)*. London, Routledge, 1928.

*

Critical Studies: "History's Two Bodies" by Natalie Zemon Davis, in *American Historical Review*, 93, 1988; *Inventing the Middle Ages* by Norman F. Cantor, New York, Morrow, 1991; "Eileen Power" by Maxine Berg, in *Cambridge Women: 12 Portraits*, edited by Edward Shils and Carmen Blacker, Cambridge, Cambridge University Press, 1996, and her *A Woman in History: Eileen Power 1889-1940*, Cambridge, Cambridge University Press, 1996.

* * *

In the Academy, women have often been active in marginalized fields, but their welcome fades when these areas become mainstream and professionalized. The medievalist Eileen Power was a pioneer scholar in economic history, social history, and women's history. Although not the first woman in these fields, she was the most influential and the best known, because she addressed general readers as well as scholars. Like her friend, H. G. Wells, Power believed that historians should play a meliorating role in society and that familiarity with world history would reduce local and national biases. She contributed to popular journals, gave radio lectures on historical topics, and even wrote books for children. (At her death, she left an unfinished world history for young people.) Unlike many later social historians, Power emphasized the personal factor in history and used individuals to represent types, most memorably in *Medieval People* (1924). Through a lively style backed by solid learning, she shared history with a wide audience that is neglected by most academics.

In her scholarly books and articles, Power demonstrated mastery of interdisciplinary methods, and she advocated organizations and collective publications to win respectability for economic and social history. One of the founders of the Economic History Society, she served as an editor of both *The Economic History Review* and *The Cambridge Economic History of Europe.* In this missionary activity, she was allied with her colleague at the London School of Economics, R. H. Tawney. (Tawney's wife disapproved of his close friendship with Power.) Earlier in her career, while still a student at Girton College, Cambridge, Power had studied with C.G. Coulton, whose anticlerical influence would be reflected in her first major scholarly work, *Medieval English Nunneries* (1922). Important as Coulton and Tawney were to her, Power was gifted with a sensitive historical imagination and could evoke the vitality of the past from the driest and most unpromising evidence. Her humanistic approach to economic and social history included an abiding dislike for economic theory and any reduction of historical variety to rigid theoretical systems such as Marxism.

A vivacious individual, Power rejected the model of prim spinsterhood that academic women had often embraced before World War I. She was an ardent suffragist, a non-Marxist socialist, and an early opponent of fascism. Power was also fond of dancing, nightclubs, and chic clothes. In childhood she had been shamed and impoverished when her father was (more than once) imprisoned for banking frauds, but her mother managed to provide the education Power needed to compete for access to elite circles. With support from scholarships and fellowships, she attended Girton and the London School of Economics and studied briefly in France. A sponsored trip (1920-21) to India, China, and Japan broadened her horizons beyond medieval interests. She disliked Indian religiosity and the harsh modernity of Japan, but China enraptured her as a cultured premodern society. After teaching at Girton since 1913, Power moved to the London School of Economics in 1921, partly because Cambridge refused to grant women degrees, but also because London was livelier both intellectually and socially. On a second trip to China, Power fell in love with Sir Reginald Johnston, but their engagement foundered in the early 1930s. In 1938 she married Michael Postan, a former student, research assistant, and colleague at the London School of Economics, whose academic career she carefully furthered. Postan received a chair in economic history at Cambridge, in part through her efforts. In 1940, at the height of her fame, Power died of a heart attack.

Like many medievalists, Power was attracted to the Middle Ages as a pre-industrial alternative to the modern era, but she did not hide the flaws of the past. The major focus of her research was on the wool trade, which had been conducted by entrepreneurs whose businesses and personalities she skillfully reconstructed. For Power, economic history was not confined to statistics and goods; she was more interested in the actors, their lives, and their roles in society. Her most popular book, *Medieval People,* remains in print because of her skill in presenting history with a human face. The book ignores princes and popes and presents an era through six representative individuals: a Carolingian peasant, a Venetian traveler, a worldly English prioress, a middle-class Parisian housewife, and two Englishmen in the wool trade. In these vivid sketches, Power imparts considerable information and demonstrates great skill in eliciting evidence from documents and artifacts. She also displays her boundless zest for travel ("Cargoes are the most romantic of topics," she notes at one point); and she lauds traders who love and respect their wives and are honest in business matters (unlike her father). Two of the "Medieval people" are women, and one of the wool traders devoted a good deal of correspondence to his betrothed. In her early works, Power dealt with nunneries and with women elsewhere. She contributed a paper on "The Position of Women" to a popular survey (*The Legacy of the Middle Ages,* 1926), but the editors pruned her ideas and she disliked the printed article for its uncritical treatment of the topic. Power was outspoken in her public lectures, and in 1975 Postan edited a few of these talks in a brief, illustrated collection entitled *Medieval Women.* The chapters include ideas on women (clerical and aristocratic stereotypes adopted by middle classes who knew better); the cultural games and managerial duties of aristocratic women; the important roles of women in trade and manufacturing; the rarity of female education even among the upper and middle classes; and life in a nunnery as an alternative to marriage for gentlewomen (Power does not neglect flaws in the religious life). Since the lectures were given mostly in the 1920s, portions of the book are dated, but it is quite readable and still informative.

After World War II rigid professionalism overtook economic and social history and the female presence in the Academy waned both in numbers and influence. In the new social-scientific climate, there was little room for Power's approach to social history, and her fame soon faded. The revival of women's history has restored Eileen Power to the prominence she deserves.

—Sandra J. Peacock

R

RANDALL, Anne Francis. *See* **ROBINSON, Mary (Darby).**

RICH, Adrienne (Cecile)

Nationality: American. **Born:** Baltimore, Maryland, 16 May 1929. **Education:** Radcliffe College, A.B. (cum laude) 1951. **Family:** Married Alfred Haskell Conrad in 1953 (died 1970); three children. **Career:** Conductor of workshops, YM-YWHA Poetry Center, New York, 1966-67; visiting lecturer, Swarthmore College, Swarthmore, Pennsylvania, 1967-69; adjunct professor in writing division, Graduate School of the Arts, Columbia University, New York, 1967-69; lecturer in SEEK English program, 1968-70, instructor in creative writing program, 1970-71, then assistant professor of English, 1971-72 and 1974-75, City College of the City University of New York; Fannie Hurst Visiting Professor of creative literature, Brandeis University, Waltham, Massachusetts, 1972-73; Lucy Martin Donelly Fellow, Bryn Mawr College, Bryn Mawr, Pennsylvania, 1975; professor of English, Douglass College, Rutgers University, New Brunswick, New Jersey, 1976-78; A.D. White Professor-at-Large, Cornell University, 1981-86; Clark Lecturer and distinguished visiting professor, Scripps College, Claremont, California, 1983; Burgess Lecturer, Pacific Oaks College, Pasadena, California, 1986; professor of English and feminist studies, Stanford University, Stanford, California, beginning 1986. Member of advisory boards, Boston Woman's Fund, New Jewish Agenda, and Sisterhood in Support of Sisters in South Africa. **Member:** Modern Language Association (honorary fellow, 1985—). **Awards:** Yale Series of Younger Poets prize, 1951; Guggenheim fellowships, 1952 and 1961; Poetry Society of America Ridgely Torrence Memorial Award, 1955; Chicago Friends of Literature Thayer Bradley Award, 1956; Phi Beta Kappa Poet, College of William and Mary, 1960, Swarthmore College, 1965, and Harvard University, 1966; National Institute of Arts and Letters award for poetry, 1961; Amy Lowell travelling fellowship, 1962; Bollingen Foundation translation grant, 1962; Bess Hokin Prize (*Poetry,* Chicago), 1963; Bautibak Translation Center grant, 1968; Eunice Tietjens Memorial Prize (*Poetry*), 1968; National Endowment for the Arts grant, 1970; Poetry Society of America Shelley Memorial Award, 1971; Ingram Merrill Foundation grant, 1973-74; National Book Award, 1974; National Gay Task Force Fund for Human Dignity Award, 1981; Modern Poetry Association/American Council for the Arts Ruth Lilly Poetry Prize, 1986; Brandeis University Creative Arts medal for poetry, 1987; National Poetry Association award, 1987; New York University Holmes Bobst award for arts and letters, 1989; Lenore Marshall/Nation award, 1992; Lambda Literary Award for lesbian poetry, 1992; Bill Whitehead award for lifetime achievement in lesbian and gay literature, 1992; *Los Angeles Times* Book Award for poetry, 1992; Poets' Prize, 1993; Litt.D.: Wheaton College, 1967; Smith College, 1979; Brandeis University, 1987; and College of Wooster, 1988. **Address:** c/o W.W. Norton Co., 500 Fifth Avenue, New York, New York 10110, U.S.A.

Publications

Poetry

A Change of World, foreword by W.H. Auden. New Haven, Yale University Press, 1951.
Poems. Fantasy Press/Oxford University Poetry Society, 1951.
The Diamond Cutters and Other Poems. New York, Harper, 1955.
The Knight, after Rilke. Privately printed, 1957.
Snapshots of a Daughter-in-Law: Poems, 1954-1962. New York, Harper, 1963, revised edition, New York, Norton, 1967; London, Chatto & Windus, 1970.
Necessities of Life. New York, Norton, 1966.
Focus. Cambridge, Massachusetts, N.p., 1967.
Selected Poems. London, Chatto & Windus, 1967.
Leaflets: Poems, 1965-1968. New York, Norton, 1969; London, Hogarth Press, 1972.
The Will to Change: Poems, 1968-1970. New York, Norton, 1971; London, Chatto & Windus, 1972; excerpts published as *Pieces,* San Francisco, Poythress Press, 1977.
Diving into the Wreck: Poems, 1971-1972. New York and London, Norton, 1973.
Poems: Selected and New, 1950-1974. New York, Norton, 1974.
Adrienne Rich's Poetry: Texts of the Poems, The Poet on Her Work, Reviews and Criticism, edited by Barbara Charlesworth Gelpi and Albert Gelpi. New York, Norton, 1975.
Twenty-one Love Poems. Emeryville, California, Effie's Press, 1977.
The Dream of a Common Language: Poems, 1974-1977. New York and London, Norton, 1978.
A Wild Patience Has Taken Me This Far: Poems, 1978-1981. New York, Norton, 1981.
Sources. Woodside, California, Heyeck Press, 1983.
The Fact of a Doorframe: Poems Selected and New, 1950-1984. New York, Norton, 1984.
Your Native Land, Your Life. New York and London, Norton, 1986.
Time's Power: Poems, 1985-1988. New York and London, Norton, 1989.
Birth of the Age of Woman, with paintings by Susan Morland. Hereford, Wild Caret, 1991.
An Atlas of the Difficult World: Poems, 1988-1991. New York and London, Norton, 1991.
Collected Early Poems, 1950-1970. New York, Norton, 1992.
Dark Fields of the Republic: Poems, 1991-1995. New York, Norton, 1995.

Essays

Of Woman Born: Motherhood as Experience and Institution. New York, Norton, 1976.
Women and Honor: Some Notes on Lying. Pittsburgh, Motheroot Publishing/Pittsburgh Women Writers, 1977.

On Lies, Secrets and Silence: Selected Prose, 1966-1978. New York, Norton, 1979.
Compulsory Heterosexuality and Lesbian Existence. London, Onlywomen Press, 1981.
Blood, Bread and Poetry: Selected Prose, 1979-1986. New York, Norton, 1986; London, Virago, 1987.
What Is Found There: Notebooks on Poetry and Politics. New York and London, Norton, 1994.

Other

Translator, with Aijaz Ahmad and William Stafford, *Poems by Ghalib,* edited by Aijaz Ahmad. New York, *Hudson Review,* 1969.
Translator, *Reflections,* by Mark Insingel. New York, Red Dust, 1973.
Translator, *De amor oscoro/Of Dark Love* by Francisco Alarcon. Santa Cruz, Moving Parts, 1991.

Recordings: *Adrienne Rich Reading at Stanford.* Stanford, 1973; *A Sign I Was Not Alone* (with others), New York, Out & Out, 1978.

*

Critical Studies: "Ghostlier Demarcations, Keener Sounds" by Helen Vendler, in *Parnassus,* fall/winter 1973; "On Adrienne Rich: Intelligence and Will" by Robert Boyers, in *Salmagundi,* spring/summer 1973; "Adrienne Rich: The Poetics of Change" by Albert Gelpi, in *American Poetry since 1960,* edited by Robert B. Shaw, Cheadle, Cheshire, Carcanet Press, 1973; *Adrienne Rich's Poetry: A Norton Critical Edition,* edited by Barbara Charlesworth Gelpi and Albert Gelpi, New York, Norton, 1975; "The Feminist Poet: Alta and Adrienne Rich" by Suzanne Juhasz, in *Naked and Fiery Forms: Modern American Poetry by Women,* 1976; *Five Temperaments* by David Kalstone, New York, Oxford University Press, 1977; "Adrienne Rich and an Organic Feminist Criticism" by Marilyn R. Farwell, in *College English,* October 1977; *Reconstituting the World: The Poetry and Vision of Adrienne Rich* by Judith McDaniel, Argyle, New York, Spinsters Ink, 1979; "Levertov and Rich: The Later Poems" by Linda W. Wagner, in her *American Modern: Essays in Fiction and Poetry,* Port Washington, New York, Kennikat, 1980; "The 'I' in Adrienne Rich: Individuation and the Androgyne Archetype" by Betty S. Flowers, in *Theory and Practice of Feminist Literary Criticism,* edited by Gabriela Mora and Karen S. Van Hooft, Ypsilanti, Michigan, Bilingual Press, 1982; *Women of Ideas and What Men Have Done to Them: From Aphra Benn to Adrienne Rich* by Dale Spender, London, Routledge & Kegen Paul, 1982; "A Poetry of Survival: Unnaming and Renaming in the Poetry of Audre Lorde, Pat Parker, Sylvia Plath, and Adrienne Rich" by Pamela Annas, in *Colby Library Quarterly,* March 1982; "Adrienne Rich: Poet, Mother, Lesbian Feminist, Visionary" by Katherine Arnup, in *Atlantis,* fall/autumn 1982; "Her Cargo: Adrienne Rich and the Common Language" by Alicia Ostriker, in her *Writing like a Woman,* Ann Arbor, University of Michigan Press, 1983; "The Re-Vision of the Muse: Adrienne Rich, Audre Lorde, Judy Grahn, Olga Broumas" by Mary J. Carruthers, in *Hudson Review,* summer 1983; *An American Triptych: Anne Bradstreet, Emily Dickinson, Adrienne Rich* by Wendy Martin, Chapel Hill, University of North Carolina Press, 1984; *Reading Adrienne Rich: Reviews and Re-Visions, 1951-1981* edited by Jane Roberta Cooper, Ann Arbor, University of Michigan Press, 1984; *The Transforming Power of Language: The Poetry of Adrienne Rich* by Myriam Diaz-Diocaretz, Utrecht, Hes Publishers, 1984; *Translating Poetic Discourse: Questions on Feminist Strategies in Adrienne Rich* by Myriam Diaz-Diocaretz, Amsterdam, John Benjamins, 1985; *The Aesthetics of Power: The Poetry of Adrienne Rich* by Claire Keyes, Athens and London, University of Georgia Press, 1986; "Adrienne Rich and Lesbian/Feminist Poetry" by Catharine Stimpson, in *Parnassus,* spring 1986; *My Life, a Loaded Gun: Female Creativity and Feminist Poetics* by Paula Bennett, Boston, Beacon Press, 1986; "Claiming the Bittersweet Matrix: Alice Walker, Sandra Cisneros, Adrienne Rich" by Nancy Corson Carter, *Critique,* 35(4), summer 1994; *Skirting the Subject: Pursuing Language in the Works of Adrienne Rich, Susan Griffin, And Beverly Dahlen* by Alan Shima, Uppsala, Uppsala University, 1993; *The Dream and the Dialogue: Adrienne Rich's Feminist Poetics* by Alice Templeton, Knoxville, University of Tennessee Press, 1994; *Anglo-Feminist Challenges to the Rhetorical Traditions: Virginia Woolf, Mary Daly, and Adrienne Rich* by Krista Ratcliffe, Carbondale, Southern Illinois University Press, 1995.

* * *

In *What Is Found There: Notebooks on Poetry and Politics,* Adrienne Rich speaks of writing herself out of her own divisions. The body of Rich's work reflects her continuous attempts to come to terms with herself as a writer who is "marked by family, gender, caste, landscape, the struggle to make a living." She sees writing as a tool toward achieving change both individually and culturally. Born into a middle-class family of mixed Jewish and gentile heritage, Rich would go on to question the family silences concerning her Jewish ethnicity, claim a lesbian identity, and struggle to bring a clearer consciousness of racism, anti-Semitism, and political oppression to the women's movement and the literary world through her poems and essays.

Her early poems reflect the concern with formal control that quickly won her recognition from the literary establishment. In his preface to *A Change of World,* which he selected for the Yale Younger Poets Prize in 1951 (the same year Rich graduated from Radcliffe), W.H. Auden praises the work for its precision and decorum. He writes that the poems are "neatly and modestly dressed, speak quietly but do not mumble."

Determined to combine the life of a serious writer with that of a wife and mother, Rich married in her 20s and had three children by the time she was 30. Although on the surface she appeared to have it all, her writing of the time reflects much inner turmoil. In her essay "When We Dead Awaken: Writing as Re-Vision," Rich revisits her old journals to trace the birth of her consciousness as a writer and activist. She writes of being "paralyzed by the sense that there exists a mesh of relationships—e.g., between my anger at the children, my sensual relationships, pacifism, sex (I mean sex in its broadest significance, not merely sexual desire)—an interconnectedness which, if I could see it, make it valid, would give me back to myself, make it possible to function lucidly and passionately."

This struggle to make connections between the personal and the political was first reflected in her poetry in *Snapshots of a Daughter-in-Law* (1963), a volume written in a less formal mode than her previous work and which takes as its central concern Rich's cultural experience as a woman. Several books later, in *Leaf-*

lets (1969), Rich grapples with the choices between love and ego, "womanly, maternal love, altruistic love—a love defined and ruled by the weight of an entire culture—and egoism—a force directed by men into creation, achievement, ambition, often at the expense of others."

She later comes to realize that this very dichotomy is a false one, and the concept of love itself is in need of revision. In her 1979 introduction to Judy Grahn's book *The Work of a Common Woman,* Rich scrutinizes our cultural understanding of love, and by extension, how one might responsibly write poetry about love: "The most revealing and life-sustaining love poetry is not 'about' the lover but about the poet's attempt to live with her experience of love, to fathom how she can order its chaos and ride out its storms, to ask what *loving* an individual can mean in the face of death, cruelty, famine, violence, taboo."

Here we also see Rich mapping the unique terrain of the lesbian poet. By virtue of the conditions under which she loves, the lesbian poet must ask questions that would never have occurred to a Donne or a Yeats, questions about our culture's fixation on the female body, about the legacy of violence committed against women by men. For the lesbian poet to be honest about love means rejecting the entire convention of love poetry and creating a new tradition.

Rich has always been insistent on confronting political issues in her work, even at a time when it was not thought to be a proper subject for poetry. Whether it be pacifism, racism, anti-Semitism, or her own burgeoning feminist consciousness, Rich insists that to create separate categories for the personal and the political is to create a false opposition that in essence serves to distract people, particularly women, from claiming the power to effect change.

The Dream of a Common Language (1978) achieved tremendous popularity in the non-literary, non-academic world, and is probably the most important volume for any discussion of lesbian feminist poetry. The title refers to the nature of and reason for writing poetry: "The drive/to connect. The dream of a common language." At that time what many other feminist writers took from Rich's work was permission: to put women at the center of their work; to approach the profound by way of the profane dailiness of a woman's life; to see (and write about) lesbian existence as an inherently political existence.

"Twenty-One Love Poems," a work characteristic of Rich's mid-career poetry, uses the traditional subject of a sequence of love poetry in a form that approximates the sonnet in length. Rich places these lovers firmly in the world; love is not transcendent. There is virtually no safe space for lesbian love to endure without an acknowledgement of the punishing world in which it exists. Rich's lovers exist within the cultural context of patriarchy, yet they attempt to define and create a love that transpires those boundaries.

One way Rich transforms the poetry of love is by challenging the culture's insistence on the separation of mind and body. Since the lovers are two women, the traditional correlations of man with intellect and woman with passion no longer apply. The speaker in "Twenty-One Love Poems" seems to be searching rather for a unification of love and intelligence.

These women's love is grounded in dailiness, in the unremarkable locales of an every day life, serving to both deemphasize the exotic factor of lesbianism and demystify their love's existence: "two people together is a work/heroic in its ordinariness." What ultimately undoes the relationship is silence, the impossibility of creating a relationship without confronting the fear imposed by the culture those lovers must exist within. "I mean to go on living" in that culture, the speaker says, in a place where "there are no miracles." Yet in the final poem she speaks to the creation of a womanly space, not in a specific country or political system, but a place where "solitude,/shared, [can] be chosen without loneliness."

Throughout Rich's poetry we read an affirmation of the value of being a woman, the value of a woman's body, the value of women's sexuality, the value of women's ways of speaking and knowing. In her later volumes, Rich moves beyond the concerns of lesbian identity to occupy a larger poetic canvas, acknowledging the particular historical and social place occupied by many individuals embracing an outsider, minority status. In *Atlas for a Difficult World* (1994) and *The Dark Fields of the Republic* (1996), Rich examines the multiple impacts of political, class, gender, and racial oppression through space and time. This universal sensibility may be in fact her ultimate triumph; she speaks her vision with such authority that the reader can accept it as central rather than as identifiably other.

Rich is an accomplished essayist as well as poet, and her prose work has appeared in many anthologies. *Of Woman Born: Motherhood as Experience and Institution* (1976) was a groundbreaking work in feminist theory, as Rich became one of the first writers to examine motherhood as a cultural construct rather than a "natural" phenomenon. With the publication of *On Lies, Secrets and Silence* (1979), Rich further explores the impact of sexuality and sexual identity on women's cultural position. In "It Is the Lesbian in Us..." she writes: "It is the lesbian in us who drives us to feel imaginatively, render in language, grasp, the full connection between woman and woman. It is the lesbian in us who is creative, for the dutiful daughter of the fathers in us is only a hack."

Indeed, Rich seems to suggest that women's creativity is dependent on the ability to step outside of a paradigm (in this case, the paradigm of heterosexuality) and find new ways of seeing; that sexual orientation, however that is defined, affects consciousness, and therefore, imagination. In her essay "Compulsory Heterosexuality and Lesbian Existence," published in *Blood, Bread, and Poetry* (1986), Rich makes a significant contribution to scholarship in the developing fields of women's history and lesbian studies as she examines in rigorous detail the social construction of women's sexual identities. This volume also includes "Split At The Root: An Essay on Jewish Identity," an important piece that traces Rich's early experiences of assimilation and denial of her Jewish heritage.

Throughout her career, Rich has insisted on facing the violence of racism, classism, and heterosexism that are the legacy of the patriarchy and our complicitousness within it. At the same time she delineates a vision of the transcendence possible via resistance. In her poem "Planetarium," she describes the process of seeing and trying to speak the truth of the human condition as she perceives it:

> I have been standing all my life in the
> direct path of a battery of signals
> the most accurately transmitted most
> untranslatable language in the universe
> I am a galactic cloud so deep
> so involuted that a light wave could take 15
> years to travel through me
> And has taken

I am an instrument in the shape
of a woman trying to translate pulsations
into images
for the relief of the body
and the reconstruction of the mind

—Kate Lynn Hibbard

RICHARDSON, Dorothy M(iller)

Nationality: British. **Born:** Abington, 17 May 1873. **Family:** Married the painter Alan Odle in 1917. **Career:** Governess and teacher in Hanover, 1891; returned to England to teach until 1895; nursed her mother until her death from suicide, 1895; worked as a secretary and journalist; had an affair with H.G. Wells, 1906. Contributor to periodicals, including *Arts & Letters, Close-Up, Life and Letters, Ploughshare,* and *English Story.* **Died:** 17 June 1957.

Publications

Novels

Pilgrimage (includes *Dimple Hill*). London, Dent & Cresset, and New York, Knopf, 4 vols., 1938; revised to include *March Moonlight,* London, Dent, and New York, Knopf, 4 vols., 1967.
- *Pointed Roofs.* London, Duckworth, 1915; New York, Knopf, 1916.
- *Backwater.* London, Duckworth, 1916; New York, Knopf, 1917.
- *Honeycomb.* London, Duckworth, 1917; New York, Knopf, 1919.
- *Interim.* London, Duckworth, 1919; New York, Knopf, 1920.
- *The Tunnel.* London, Duckworth, and New York, Knopf, 1919.
- *Deadlock.* London, Duckworth, and New York, Knopf, 1921.
- *Revolving Lights.* London, Duckworth, and New York, Knopf, 1923.
- *The Trap.* London, Duckworth, and New York, Knopf, 1925.
- *Oberland.* London, Duckworth, 1927; New York, Knopf, 1928.
- *Dawn's Left Hand.* London, Duckworth, 1931.
- *Clear Horizon.* London, Dent & Cresset, 1935.

History

The Quakers Past and Present. London, Constable, 1914; New York, Dodge, 1914.

Essays

"The Reality of Feminism," in *Ploughshare,* 2 September 1917.
"Talent and Genius, n.p., 1923.
"Women and the Future, n.p., 1924.
"About Punctuation," n.p., 1924.
"Women in the Arts: Some Notes on the Eternally Conflicting Demands of Humanity and Art," in *Vanity Fair,* 24 May 1925.
"Continuous Performance: The Film Gone Male, n.p., 1932.
"Adventure For Readers," in *Life and Letters To-Day,* 22 July 1939.
"Novels," in *Life and Letters,* March 1948.

Other

Gleanings from the Works of George Fox. London, Headley, 1914.
John Austen and the Inseparables. London, Jackson, 1930.
Windows On Modernism: Selected Letters of Dorothy Richardson, edited by Gloria Fromm. Chicago, University of Chicago Press, n.d.

Translator, *Consumption Doomed* by Dr. Paul Carton (vol. 7, Healthy Life Booklets). London, Daniel, 1913.
Translator, *Some Popular Foodstuffs Exposed,* by Dr. Paul Carton (vol. 11, Healthy Life Booklets). London, Daniel, 1913.
Translator, *Man's Best Food,* by Dr. Gustav Krüger. London, Daniel, 1914.
Translator, *The Dubarry,* by Karl von Schumacher. London, Harrap, 1932.
Translator, *Mammon,* by Robert Neumann. London, Davies, 1933.
Translator, *André Gide: His Life and His Works,* by Leon Pierre-Quint. London, Cape, 1934.
Translator, *Jews in Germany,* by Josef Kastein. London, Cresset, 1934.
Translator, *Silent Hours,* by Robert de Traz. London, Bell, 1934.

*

Bibliography: *Dorothy Richardson: The Genius They Forgot* by John Rosenberg, London, Duckworth, 1973.

Manuscript Collections: Beinecke Library, Yale University; Henry W. and Albert A. Berg Collection, New York Public Library; University of Texas at Austin; Firestone Library, Princeton University, Rice University; Pennsylvania State University; British Library.

Critical Studies: *Dorothy Richardson: An Adventure in Self-Discovery* by Horace Gregory, New York, Holt Rinehart, 1967; *Dorothy Richardson, The Genius They Forgot: A Critical Biography* by John Rosenberg, London, Duckworth, 1973; *Dorothy Richardson: A Biography* by Gloria G. Fromm, Urbana, Chicago, and London, University of Illinois Press, 1977; *A Literature of Their Own: British Women Novelists from Brontë to Lessing* by Ellen Showalter, Princeton, Princeton University Press, 1977; *Feminine Consciousness in the Modern British Novel* by Sydney Janet Kaplan, Urbana, Chicago, and London, University of Illinois Press, 1975; "Male and Female Consciousness in Dorothy Richardson's *Pilgrimage*" by Suzette Henke, in *Journal of Women's Studies in Literature,* 1, 1979; *The Art of Life: Dorothy Richardson and the Development of Feminist Consciousness* by Gillian E. Hanscombe, London, Owen 1982, Athens, Ohio University Press, 1983; "Dorothy Richardson" by Diane F. Gillespie in *The Gender of Modernism: A Critical Anthology,* edited by Bonnie Kime Scott, Bloomington, Indiana University Press; *Dorothy Richardson* by Jean Radford, Bloomington, Indiana University Press.

* * *

Dorothy Richardson's work, while it remains unfamiliar to a large number of scholars and general readers, is absolutely central to the configuration of a female literary canon and to feminist perceptions of Modernism. Credited as being one of the first to undertake the stream-of-consciousness novel in English, she ranks with contemporaries Virginia Woolf, Marcel Proust, and James

Joyce as one of the most important writers of experimental fiction.

Born in 1873 and raised in a modest English family, Richardson began supporting herself when she was eighteen, first as a governess and later as a teacher. Four years later, in 1895, she left her job in order to nurse her mother, Mary Taylor Richardson, who killed herself a few months later.

Following her mother's tragic death, Richardson took up residence in London where she worked as a secretary and journalist and gradually became involved in the avant-garde art societies so prevalent in the city during the early part of the 20th century. She became acquainted with several renowned intellectuals. Among them was H. G. Wells; an affair between the two would result in a miscarriage in 1906. Wells was essential to Richardson's developing literary career, primarily because his work provided the touchstone against which her own distinctively feminine aesthetic would develop.

Richardson came to writing late in life. She began her 13-volume experimental novel sequence *Pilgrimage* in 1913, at the age of 40. The first "chapter volume," entitled *Pointed Roofs,* was published in 1915, the same year that Virginia Woolf published her own first novel, *The Voyage Out.* Richardson referred to her experimental enterprise as a "cultural autobiography" in which she intended to forge an aesthetic expressive of a specifically female consciousness. She deliberately sought a style which would stand in an antithetical relation to the received masculine Realist tradition of the novel; a tradition best exemplified for Richardson by writers like her paramour Wells.

Richardson's representation of feminine consciousness, as embodied by her heroine Miriam, is one in which plot trajectory, such as it is, depends on the interior world of the mind rather than the external world. Richardson associated the external world with a thoroughly masculine ethos: Her sentences, rather than being anchored by formal grammatical rules or punctuation, are mobile, fragmentary, dissolute, and a form unto themselves in that they refuse to be dictated by linearity and succumb instead to ambiguity and spontaneity. Novelist May Sinclair, in the 1918 issue of *The Egoist,* borrowed William James's term "stream of consciousness" to describe Richardson's work. Richardson herself rejected this summation, preferring instead the metaphor of a fountain as somehow more appropriate to the progression of her project. In essence, she forged a new and distinctive kind of Realism which radically dispensed with traditional novelistic conventions like plot, climax, and conclusion.

Woolf, while she tended to disapprove of Richardson's work as egotistical and, hence, formless, argued in a 1923 review that Richardson had invented a new kind of sentence, "of a more elastic fibre than the old ... the psychological sentence of the feminine gender." Feminine prose, according to Richardson, should "properly be unpunctuated, moving from point to point without formal obstructions." Her goal in the collected works of *Pilgrimage* was to represent Miriam's consciousness with a style that would be indistinguishable from consciousness itself.

In addition to creating a highly original experimental novel, Richardson wrote for the avant-garde film journal *Close-Up* and produced several essays noteworthy for their expression of her own aesthetic, as well as their explorations into and analysis of feminism. One of Richardson's most crucial feminist points—asserted both in her fiction and in her essays—is that if reading and writing shape the lives we live, or at, the very least, the meanings by which we live, then the active and collaborative role of the reader in the process is vital. Richardson perceived her aesthetic as one which necessitated the active role of a participant rather than the passive role of a recipient.

The contribution to literature made by Richardson's extraordinary *Pilgrimage* and her cogent arguments for the necessity of a new novel representative and expressive of a particularly feminine consciousness cannot be overestimated. Her life and her work are fundamental to a complete understanding of literary Modernism.

—Kimberly Engdahl

ROBERTS, Michèle (Brigitte)

Nationality: British. **Born:** Bushey, Hertfordshire, 20 May 1949. **Education:** Oxford University, B.A. (with honors) 1970; University of London Library Associate, 1972. **Career:** Has worked as a librarian, cook, teacher, cleaner, pregnancy counselor, and researcher; writer-in-residence, Lambeth Borough, London, 1981-82, and Bromley Borough, London, 1983-84. Cofounder, with Zoë Fairbairns, Sara Maitland, and Michelene Wandor, Feminist Writers Group. Poetry editor, *Spare Rib,* 1975-77, and *City Limits,* 1981-83. **Awards:** *Gay News* Literary award, 1978, for *A Piece of the Night.* **Agent:** Caroline Dawnay, A.D. Peters, 10 Buckingham St., London WC2, England.

Publications

Novels

A Piece of the Night. London, Women's Press, 1978.
The Visitation. London, Women's Press, 1978.
The Wild Girl. London, Methuen, 1984.
Seven Deadly Sins. London, n.p., 1988.
The Book of Mrs. Noah. London, Methuen, 1987.
In the Red Kitchen. London, Methuen, 1990.
Psyche and the Hurricane. London, Methuen, 1991.
Daughters of the House. London, Virago, and New York, Morrow, 1992.
During Mother's Absence. London, Virago, 1993.
Flesh & Blood. London, Virago, 1994.

Short Stories

Tales I Tell My Mother, with others, edited by Zoë Fairbairns. London, Journeyman Press, 1978.
More Tales I Tell My Mother, with others, edited by Zoë Fairbairns. London, Journeyman Press, 1987.

Poetry

Licking the Bed Clean. London, n.p., 1978.
Smile, Smile, Smile, Smile. London, n.p., 1980.
Touch Papers, with Judith Karantris and Michelene Wandor. London, Allison & Busby, 1982.
The Mirror of the Mother: Selected Poems 1975-1985. London, Methuen, 1985.
All the Selves I Was: New and Selected Poems. London, Virago, 1995.

Other

Editor, with Michelene Wandor, *Cutlasses and Earrings*. London, Playbooks, 1976.

*

Critical Studies: Interview in *Women Writers Talk* by Olga Kenyon, New York, Caroll & Graf, 1990.

* * *

Michèle Roberts—poet, novelist, essayist, and antagonist. During the 1970s, when she published work featuring women's sexuality and lesbianism, such a description might have emanated from the mouths and pens of several critics about *A Piece of the Night* (1978). Indeed, one reviewer wrote that it was full of "shrieking Lesbian banshees"—to which Roberts told Olga Kenyon during an interview, "I thought the reviews wonderful. Reactions were mixed, but it was widely reviewed, which helped." *A Piece of the Night* chronicles the life and times of a woman who evolves from pupil in a convent school to wife and mother to lesbian and feminist.

Reaction to Roberts' third novel, *The Wild Girl* (1984), about Mary Magdalene was explosive. A few people went so far as to seek formal accusation of Roberts for blasphemy. The novel starts out innocently enough: young Mary delights in being able to sleep on the roof so she can watch the stars. However, when she starts menstruating she is no longer allowed this pleasure and must keep her eyes lowered in the fashion of grown women. One day, after Mary Magdalene has grown into a young woman, her brother, Lazarus, introduces her to Jesus—who immediately compliments her on her lovely singing voice. After Lazarus's death, and before his legendary return from the dead, Mary and Jesus share a passionate moment: "He held me against him and I smelt his sweat and his hot skin. His tongue gently exploring my mouth was one of the sweetest and sharpest pleasures I have ever known." They eventually make love, which Mary also describes—though not in so graphic detail—and she announces to her brother and sister the next day that she is going to go away with Jesus. Of course, the story of Jesus and Mary Magdalene is presented in the Bible, though obviously not in such a frank manner.

The Visitation (1983)—as powerful as *The Wild Girl*, but not nearly as controversial—begins with an introduction to Helen, a young girl who is periodically visited by a stranger: an encounter that she obviously must keep secret from her family. Though Helen must run away from the man, she enjoys the exchange because she always eludes him. *The Visitation* follows Helen into her teen years and then into adulthood. All the while, she considers the supernatural while condemning her Catholic faith. Roberts guides her reader through these complex transitions by using lush physical description and enchanting mental imagery. Every once in a while, she also skillfully flashes back to Helen's younger days in order to give her readers a fuller perspective on the adult Helen's attitude toward conventional religion in general, and the Catholic church of her youth, specifically.

Although *Daughters of the House* (1992) is not as immediately provocative as some of Roberts's other works, it is probably the most notable in terms of its literary reception; the novel was shortlisted for England's Booker Prize. *Daughters of the House* begins with the impending arrival of Therese, who has lived in a convent for many years; indeed, her cousin Leonie is so violently moved by the prospect that she has a nightmare that causes her to spring from her bed and rush to the bathroom in time to vomit into the toilet. As it turns out, Therese's arrival is rather anticlimactic; Leonie has no need to fear the stranger who simply wishes to look back at the times the two had shared before Therese entered the convent 20 years before. Both women eventually must face the memories of the horrible, long-ago event that precipitated their separation. As is typical in Roberts's work, the novel is full of spiritual imagery: the convent, imagined concepts of heaven, and a favorite religious statue. Also present are numerous detailed physical descriptions: Therese's feeling too naked in street clothes because she is used to her thick, brown dress, for instance. This combination of highly styled description, heavy symbolism, and riveting plot was very well-received by critics—hence, the Booker Prize nomination.

During Mother's Absence (1993) is a short-story collection featuring works written in the perspectives of both daughters and mothers. Particularly spellbinding is the story "Anger," which illustrates a strange blessing derived from a seemingly devilish incident. A young mother drops her baby daughter into a fire; the child lives and seems to literally become the death of her errant mother. The girl's body is scarred and neighbors speculate on whether she is the devil's spawn. Instead, Roberts presents her as a magical being possessing the human qualities of grace and humility, but to an otherworldly degree. The story "Taking It Easy" is presented from a mother's point of view, though the story is hardly about a mother's relationship with her daughter. Indeed, all of the action takes place between the hours of ten and three, when the little girl is at school. It seems all of the woman's life occurs during these scant five hours; it is during this time that she has written a multitude of short stories for a variety of genres. When she finally gets the chance to take a two-week vacation in France, everything seems to fall into place, both physically and mentally. Roberts suddenly introduces the reader to a full-bodied woman, complete with hunger pangs and a sex drive. Roberts saves her vivid sensory descriptions for this portion of the story, in tune to the mother's experiences of muted existence followed by intense living.

Whatever specific topic Michèle Roberts chooses to address in a given piece of writing, her writing mainly deal with feminism, Catholicism, and women's bodies. Her works, though sometimes highly controversial, are always well-conceived and never skimpy. Roberts's readers often wonder why she places so much stock in representation of women's bodies and simultaneous discussion of the Catholic Church. "The church has never been comfortable with our bodies. It even used to 'church' women after childbirth, to 'cleanse' them," Roberts explained to Kenyon. "You could only hint at what you felt about your body within the Church when I was a girl. That's very disappointing if you're somebody who is interested in words."

—Tracy Clark

ROBINSON, Mary (Darby)

Pseudonyms: Tabitha Bramble; Bridget; Julia; Horace Juvenal; Laura; Laura Maria; Lesbia; Oberon; Perdita; Portia; Anne Francis

Randall; Sappho. **Nationality:** British. **Born:** Bristol, 27 November 1758. **Education:** Taught by Hannah More's sisters at an academy in Bristol, then educated in a Chelsea school run by the learned Maribah Lorington, then attended a finishing school in Marylebone. **Family:** Married Thomas Robinson in 1774; 1 daughter. **Career:** Actress, Drury Lane, London, 1776-83; poet and novelist, often under a variety of pseudonyms; wrote political speeches for lover, Banastre Tarleton, MP for Liverpool. Poetry editor, *Morning Post,* London, 1800. **Died:** 26 December 1800.

Publications

Novels

Vancenza; or, The Dangers of Credulity. London, n.p., 2 vols., 1792.

The Widow; or, A Picture of Modern Times. A Novel, in a Series of Letters. London, Hookham & Carpenter, 1794.

Audley Fortescue. London, William Lane, 1795.

Angelina. London, Hookham & Carpenter, 3 vols., 1796.

Hubert de Sevrac, a Romance of the 18th Century. London, Hookham & Carpenter, 3 vols., 1796.

Walsingham: or, The Pupil of Nature. London, Longman, 1797.

The False Friend, A Domestic Story. London, Longman & Rees, 4 vols., 1799.

The Natural Daughter, with Portraits of the Leadenhead Family. London, Longman & Rees, 1799.

Essays

A Letter to the Women of England, on the Injustice of Mental Subordination (as Anne Francis Randall). London, Longman & Rees, 1799. [attributed]

Thoughs on the Condition of Woman, and on the Injustice of Mental Subordination. London, Longman & Rees, 1799. [attributed]

Poetry

Poems. London, C. Parker, 1775.

Elegiac Verses to a Young Lady on the Death of Her Brother. London, J. Johnson, 1776.

Captivity, a Poem. And Celadon and Lydia, a Tale. London, T. Becket, 1777.

Ainsi va la Monde, a Poem. Inscribed to Robert Merry, Esq. A.M. Member of the Royal Academy of Florence; and, Author of the Laurel of Liberty and the Della Crusca Poems (as Laura Maria). London, J. Bell, 1790.

The Beauties of Mrs. Robinson. London, H. D. Symonds, 1791.

Poems. London, 2 vols., Vol. 1, J. Bell, 1791, Vol. 2, Evans & Becket, 1793.

Monody to the Memory of Sir Joshua Reynolds. London, J. Bell, 1792.

Modern Manners, a Poem. In Two Cantos (as Horace Juvenal). London, J. Evans, 1792.

Monody to the Memory of the Late Queen of France, Marie Antoinette. London, J. Evans, 1793.

An Ode to the Harp of the Late Accomplished and Amiable Louisa Hathaway. London, J. Bell, 1793.

Sight, the Cavern of Woe, and Solitude. London, Evans & Becket, 1793.

Sappho and Phaon, In a Series of Legitimate Sonnets, with Thoughts on Poetical Subjects, and Anecdotes of the Grecian Poetess. London, Hookham & Carpenter, 1796.

The Sicilian Lover. A Tragedy in Five Acts. London, Hookham & Carpenter, 1796.

Lyrical Tales. London, Longman & Rees; Bristol, Briggs & Co., 1800.

The Wild Wreath, edited by Mara Elizabeth Robinson. London, Richard Phillips, 1804.

Poetical Works of the Late Mrs. Mary Robinson. London, Richard Phillips, 3 vols., 1806.

Autobiography

Memoirs of the Late Mrs. Robinson, Written by Herself. With Some Posthumous Pieces, edited by Maria Elizabeth Robinson. London, R. Phillips, 4 vols., 1801.

*

Bibliography: *Romantic Poetry by Women: A Bibliography, 1770-1835* by J. R. de J. Jackson, Oxford, Clarendon, and New York, Oxford University Press, 1993; *British Women Poets of the Romantic Era, 1770-1840* edited by Paula R. Feldman, Baltimore, Johns Hopkins University Press, 1996.

Critical Studies: *Twelve Great Actresses* by Edward Robins, New York and London, G. P. Putnam's, 1900; *The Exquisite Perdita* by L. Adams Beck, New York, Dodd Mead, 1926; *The Lost One: A Biography of Mary—Perdita—Robinson* by Marguerite Steen, London, Methuen, 1937; *Studies in the Literary Backgrounds of English Radicalism, with Special Reference to the French Revolution* by M. Ray Adams, Lancaster, Pennsylvania, Franklin & Marshall College, 1947; *The Green Dragoon: The Lives of Banastre Tarleton and Mary Robinson* by Robert D. Bass, New York, Holt, 1957; "Lost Poem Found: The Cooperative Pursuit and Recapture of an Escaped Coleridge 'Sonnet' of 72 Lines" by David V. Erdman, in *Bulletin of the New York Public Library,* 65, 1961; *Mrs Robinson and her Portraits* by John Ingamells, London, Trustees for the Wallace Collection, 1978; *The 18th-century Feminist Mind* by Alice Browne, Detroit, Wayne University Press, 1987; "Romantic Poetry: The I Altered" by Stuart Curran, in *Romanticism and Feminism,* edited by Anne K. Mellor, Bloomington, Indiana University Press, 1988; Introduction to *Lyrical Tales* by Jonathan Wordsworth, Oxford, Woodstock Books, 1989; "Coleridge, Mary Robinson and *Kubla Khan*" by Martin J. Levy, in *The Charles Lamb Bulletin,* 77, January 1992; "The Spectacular *Flaneuse*: Mary Robinson and the City of London" by Judith Pascoe, in *The Wordsworth Circle,* 23(3), summer 1992; "Selling One's Sorrows: Charlotte Smith, Mary Robinson, and the Marketing of Poetry" by Jacqueline M. Labbe, in *The Wordsworth Circle,* 25(2), spring 1994; "A Stranger Minstrel: Coleridge's Mrs. Robinson" by Susan Luther, in *Studies in Romanticism,* 33(3), fall 1994; "Mary Robinson's *Lyrical Tales* in Context" by Stuart Curran, in *Re-Visioning Romanticism: British Women Writers, 1776-1837,* edited by Carol Shiner Wison and Joel Haefner, Philadelphia, University of Philadelphia Press, 1994; "Becoming an Author: Mary Robinson's *Memoirs* and the Origins of the Woman Artist's Autobiography" by Linda H. Peterson, in *Re-Visioning Romanticism: British Women Writers, 1776-1837,* edited by Carol Shiner Wison and Joel Haefner, Philadelphia, University of Philadelphia Press, 1994; "Mary Robinson and the Literary Marketplace" by Judith Pascoe, in *Romantic Women Writers: Voices and Countervoices,* edited by Paula R. Feldman and Theresa M. Kelley, Hanover and London, University Press of New England, 1995; "From 'Mingled Measure' to 'Ecstatic Meaures': Mary Robinson's Poetic Reading of 'Kubla Khan'" by Daniel Robinson, in *The Wordsworth Circle,* 26(1), winter 1995; "Reviving the Sonnet: Women Romantic Poets and the Sonnet Claim" by Daniel Robinson, in *European Romantic Review,* 6(1), summer 1995; "The Claims of 'real life and manners': Coleridge and Mary Robinson" by Lisa Vargo, in *The Wordsworth Circle,* 26(3), summer 1995.

* * *

Late 20th-century critical commentary on Mary Robinson has focused to a large extent on her relationship with poet Samuel Taylor Coleridge, who called her "a woman of undoubted Genius"—certainly no small praise. Coleridge recognized in Robinson a remarkable ear for poetry and an impressive original talent and even showed her an early version of his poem "Kubla Khan," to which she wrote an enthusiastic poetical reply: her "To the Poet Coleridge" was in circulation 16 years prior to the publication of Colridge's masterwork. Coleridge wrote a reciprocal tribute to Robinson, "A Stranger Minstrel," published in the posthumous collection *The Wild Wreath.* However, by the time she and Coleridge established their mutual admiration, Robinson was nearing the end of a remarkable 25-year literary career, during which time she had been a notorious public figure as well as a respected poet and novelist. Robinson's unusual literary fame during her career was largely due to public interest in her personal life.

Born to respectable parents—a genteel mother and an American sea captain—Robinson exhibited precocious literary talent as a child; however, her father's imprudent commercial investments and eventual abandonment of the family disrupted her formal education, although she was, for brief periods, educated by Hannah More's sisters and by the learned but alcoholic Maribah Lorrington. At age 15, while at a finishing school in Marylebone, she charmed the aging thespian David Garrick, who offered to train her to play Cordelia to his Lear. Instead, she married, upon the insistence of her mother, Thomas Robinson, a law clerk who claimed to be awaiting an inheritance from a wealthy uncle. The "uncle" turned out to be the young man's father, no inheritance was forthcoming, and the couple, who lived beyond their means, soon landed in debtor's prison.

While in prison, Robinson published her first volume of poems, thanks to the patronage of the Duchess of Devonshire, as well as giving birth to the couple's daughter. She soon returned to Garrick, also manager of Drury Lane Theater, and debuted as Juliet on 10 December 1776. Her subsequent success as an actress, lasting for the next four seasons, allowed the Robinsons renewed access to fashionable society, in which her husband renewed his interest in gambling and womanizing. In 1779, during a performance as Perdita in *The Winter's Tale,* Robinson's beauty attracted the attention of the young Prince of Wales, later George IV; shortly thereafter she became his mistress.

The short-lived affair was scandalous and widely publicized, the two lovers appearing in many satirical verses, fake love letters, and cartoons as "Florizel" and "Perdita." But the affair gave Robinson some independence from her wastrel husband. She was both famous and infamous, inciting even the curiosity of Marie Antoinette, who requested an interview during Robinson's visit to Paris where she was feted as *la belle Anglaise*. Robinson later became the mistress of Col. Banastre Tarleton, who, like the Prince, eventually abandoned her. Mounting debt and a debilitating illness encouraged her to pursue what became a successful career as a professional author; she earned much popular and critical praise, as well as the friendship of an impressive circle of literary friends that included Robert Merry, John Wolcot, William Godwin, Mary Wollstonecraft, and Coleridge. In the last year of her life, Robinson succeeded Robert Southey as poetry editor for the *Morning Post,* for which she was also a regular and prolific contributor, and published *Lyrical Tales*, a book which prompted Wordsworth to reconsider the title for the second edition of *Lyrical Ballads*.

Robinson's early poetry is largely in the affected ornamental style associated with the Della Cruscans, led by Merry; however, her verse of the 1790s reveals an innovative and insurgent spirit like that commonly associated with poets of the Romantic period. Composed in highly original meters and forms, poems such as "The Maniac," "The Lascar," and "The Negro Girl" demonstrate Robinson's interest in the marginalized, downtrodden figures of society, while others, such as "The Haunted Beach," "The Lady of the Black Tower," "Stanzas Written after Successive Nights of Melancholy Dreams," and "To the Poet Coleridge," reveal a fascination for the fantastic, the dream-like states of semiconsciousness, and the imagination. In the long blank-verse poem "The Progress of Liberty," Robinson attacks tyrannies, such as slavery and bigotry, that encroach upon the rights of humankind, indicates her democratic and liberal views, and urges reason over the frenzy of revolutionary passions. Certainly no conservative thinker, Robinson nonetheless finds sympathy with Marie Antoinette as a woman and a mother in her poems *Monody to the Memory of the late Queen of France* and "Marie Antoinette's Lamentation in Her Prison of the Temple." Her sonnet sequence, *Sappho and Phaon*, written in 44 strictly Petrarchan sonnets, details the passionate but destructive love of a woman poet for a man who abandons her, clearly bearing the autobiographical resonance of her love affairs with the Prince of Wales and Tarleton. However, the sequence, when combined with its prose preface, also makes a bold claim for the "mental preeminence" of literary women and an important association of its author with the woman's poetic tradition through Sappho. It also boldly subverts the erotic tradition of the sonnet by portraying the woman as the active lover and the man as the passive and unattainable object of desire.

Robinson also wrote eight novels, the first of which—*Vancenza; or the Dangers of Credulity*, a Gothic story of seduction—quickly sold out upon first publication, no doubt due to its author's public notoriety. 1797's *Walsingham, or The Pupil of Nature* bears some influence of Godwin's radical humanitarianism in its exploration of oppression associated with the endemic injustices of political systems and society, and it praises the Enlightenment philosophers Rousseau and Voltaire. Her final novel, *The False Friend, a Domestic Story,* takes aim at the sexism of men who seduce and deceive virtuous women through the portrayal of a villain who bears some likeness to Tarleton. The two proto-feminist tracts long attributed to Robinson, *A Letter to the Women of England, on the Injustice of Mental Subordination* and *Thoughts on the Condition of Woman, and on the Injustice of Mental Subordination*, are fairly radical in their insistence upon the intellectual equality of the sexes, in their critique of marital subordination, societal manners, and decorum, and in their sympathy for laboring women of the lower class. It is also noteworthy that Mary

Robinson served as the subject of several portraits by such renowned British painters as Gainsborough, Reynolds, and Romney.

—Daniel Robinson

RODRIGUEZ, Judith

Also wrote as Judith Green. **Nationality:** Australian. **Born:** Perth, Western Australia, 13 February 1936. **Education:** Brisbane Girls' Grammar School, 1950-53; University of Queensland, St. Lucia, 1954-57, B.A. (honors) 1957; Girton College, Cambridge, 1960-62, M.A. 1965; University of London, Cert. Ed. 1968. **Family:** Married 1) Fabio Rodriguez in 1964 (divorced 1981), three daughters and one son; 2) Thomas W. Shapcott in 1982. **Career:** Resident teacher, Fairholme Presbyterian Girls' College, Toowoomba, 1958; lecturer, University of Queensland Department of External Studies, 1959-60; lecturer in English, Philippa Fawcett College of Education, London, 1962-63, and University of the West Indies, Kingston, Jamaica, 1963-65; lecturer, St. Giles School of English, London, 1965-66, and St. Mary's College of Education, Twickenham, Middlesex, 1966-68; lecturer, 1969-76, and senior lecturer, 1977-85, La Trobe University, Melbourne; writer-in-residence, University of Western Australia, Nedlands, 1978, and Rollins College, Winter Park, Florida, 1986; lecturer on Australian literature, Macquarie University, North Ryde, New South Wales, 1985; visiting fellow, Western Australian Institute of Technology, South Bentley, 1986; lecturer in English, Macarthur Institute of Higher Education, Milperra, Sydney, 1987; lecturer in writing and writer-in-residence, Royal Melbourne Institute of Technology, 1988-89; writer-in-residence, Ormond College University of Melbourne, 1988-89. Since 1989 lecturer in writing, Victoria College; senior lecturer, Deakin University, 1993. Poetry editor, *Meanjin,* Melbourne, 1979-82; poetry columnist, Sydney *Morning Herald,* 1984-86. Since 1989 poetry consultant, Penguin Books Australia. Also artist and illustrator: individual shows in Melbourne, Brisbane, Adelaide, and Paris. **Awards:** Australia Council fellowship, 1974, 1978, 1983; South Australian Government prize, 1978; Artlook Victorian prize, 1979; P.E.N. Stuyvesant prize, 1981; Feminist Fortnight Favourite, 1989, for *New and Selected Poems;* Member of the Order of Australia, 1994; Christopher Brennan award, 1994, for poetry. **Address:** 18 Churchill St., P.O. Box 231, Mount Albert, Victoria 3127, Australia.

Publications

Poetry

Four Poets (as Judith Green), with others. Melbourne, Cheshire, 1962.
Nu-Plastik Fanfare Red and Other Poems. St. Lucia, University of Queensland Press, 1973.
Broadsheet Number 23. Canberra, Open Door Press, 1976.
Water Life. St. Lucia, University of Queensland Press, 1976.
Shadow on Glass. Canberra, Open Door Press, 1978.
Three Poems. Melbourne, Old Metropolitan Meat Market, 1979.
Angels. Melbourne, Old Metropolitan Meat Market, 1979.
Arapede. Melbourne, Old Metropolitan Meat Market, 1979.
Mudcrab at Gambaro's. St. Lucia, University of Queensland Press, 1980.
Witch Heart. Melbourne, Sisters, 1982.
Mrs. Noah and the Minoan Queen, with others, edited by Rodriguez. Melbourne, Sisters, 1983.
Floridian Poems. Winter Park, Florida, Rollins College, 1986.
The House by Water: New and Selected Poems. St. Lucia, University of Queensland Press, 1988.
The Cold. Canberra, National Library of Australia, 1992.

Plays

Poor Johanna (produced Adelaide, 1994), in *Heroines,* edited by Dale Spender. Melbourne, Penguin, 1991.
Lindy (opera libretto), with Robyn Archer, music by Moya Henderson (produced 1992).

Other

Noela Hjorth, with Vicki Pauli. Clarendon, South Australia, Granrott Press, 1984.

Editor, *Mrs. Noah and the Minoan Queen.* Melbourne, Sisters, 1983.
Editor, with Andrew Taylor, *Poems from the Australian's 20th Anniversary Competition.* Sydney, Angus & Robinson, 1985.
Editor, *I sogni cantano l'alba: poesia contemporeana,* translated by G. Englaro. Milan, Lanfranchi, 1988.
Editor, *Jennifer Rankin: Collected Poems.* St. Lucia, University of Queensland Press. 1990.

Translator, *Your Good Colombian Friend,* by Jairo Vanegas. Upper Ferntree Gully, Papyrus Press, 1995.

*

Manuscript Collection: Fryer Research Library, University of Queensland, Brisbane.

Critical Studies: Interviews in the Australian National Archive, 1976; *Women and Writing: Into the Eighties,* Clayton, Victoria, Monash University, 1980; "More Wow than Flutter" by Les A. Murray, in *Quadrant* (Sydney), October 1976; "Bolder Vision than Superintrospection" by P. Neilsen, in *The Age* (Melbourne), 12 March 1977; "Sea Change" by C. Treloar, in *Twenty-Four Hours* (Sydney), August 1977; "The White Witch and the Red Witch: The Poetry of Judith Rodriguez" by Delys Bird, in *Poetry and Gender: Statements and Essays in Australian Women's Poetics,* St. Lucia, University of Queensland Press, 1989; "A Lifetime Devoted to Literature: A Tribute to Judith Rodriguez" by Jennifer Strauss, in *Southerly* (Sydney), 1992; "Judith Rodriguez" by R. P. Rama, in *Dialogues with Australian Poets,* Calcutta, Writers Workshop Press, 1993; "An Interview with Judith Rodriguez" by Peter Haddow, in *Famous Reporter* (Kingston, Tasmania), 1993; "Bathing in a Great Sea of Wonderful Words" (interview) by Jennifer Digby, in her *A Woman's Voice: Conversations with Australian Poets,* Queensland, University of Queensland Press, 1996.

* * *

Australian poet Judith Rodriguez first came to public attention in the 1960s as a member of a group dubbed the "Queensland Octopus," so named for writing a poetry filled with energy and wild imagery. This group, all young and from the Brisbane area of Australia, consisted of David Malouf, Rodney Hall, Don Maynard and Rodriguez. Their poetry focused on a direct expression of emotion, held in check only by adherence to a formal lyrical tradition.

In the mid- to late 1960s Rodriguez lived in Europe and the Caribbean. She taught at the University of the West Indies in Jamaica, at the Philippa Fawcett College of Education and at St. Giles School of English, both in London, and at St. Mary's College of Education in Twickenham, Middlesex, England. Returning to Australia in 1968, she joined the faculty at La Trobe University in Melbourne, where she stayed until 1985. Rodriguez is currently a lecturer in writing at Victoria College.

When Rodriguez returned to Australia in 1968, she began writing a more controlled, condensed, and more openly female poetry. The exuberant energy found in her early poems was still present, but a wider perspective was also evident. This change first appeared in Rodriguez's collection, *Water Life.* These mature poems focus on emotional and intellectual growth and speak not only of personal development but of a larger awareness among all women as well. This larger perspective was inspired, in part, by the women's liberation movement of the time which, Rodriguez has explained, made her aware of the strength she possessed as a woman. She also found that speaking with other women artists stimulated her own creativity. Rodriguez has collaborated with other women artists, writing lyrics for singer Robyn Archer and libretti for composer Mary Mageau. Rodriguez's interest in women's literature culminated in 1983 when she edited the anthology *Mrs. Noah and the Minoan Queen,* a collection of writings by Australian women of her generation. The anthology was published by Sisters Publishing, a feminist press. She also serves as a poetry consultant to Penguin Books Australia, helping the publisher to develop a list of poetry books written by Australians.

—Denise Wiloch

ROWBOTHAM, Sheila

Pseudonym: Sheila Turner. **Nationality:** British. **Born:** Leeds, 27 February 1943. **Education:** Oxford University, B.A. 1966. **Family:** One son. **Career:** Teacher with Workers Educational Association at technical colleges and schools in England, 1964-79; staff writer, *Black Dwarf* (socialist paper), London, 1968-69; writer, *Red Rag* (socialist feminist paper), 1972-73. Visiting professor of Women's Studies, University of Amsterdam, 1981-83; research officer, Economic Policy Unit, Greater London Council, 1983-86; consultant research advisor to the Women's Programme, World Institute for Development Economics Research, United Nations University, 1987-91; currently Simon Senior Research Fellow, department of Sociology, University of Manchester. Freelance writer, researcher, and journalist; involved in women's movement in England since its origins in the late 1960s. **Address:** Department of Sociology, Coupland II Building, University of Manchester, Oxford Road, Manchester M13 9PL, England.

Publications

Political/Social Theory

Women's Liberation and the New Politics. Bertrand Russell Peace Foundation, 1971.
Women's Consciousness, Man's World. London, Penguin, 1973.
Beyond the Fragments: Feminism and the Making of Socialism, with Hilary Wainwright and Lynne Segal. London, 1979; Boston, Alyson, 1981.
The Past Is before Us: Feminism in Action from the Late 1960s. London, Pandora, and Boston, Beacon Press, 1989.
Homeworkers Worldwide. London, Merlin Press, 1993.

History

Women, Resistance, and Revolution: A History of Women and Revolution in the Modern World. New York and London, Pantheon, 1972.
Hidden From History: Rediscovering Women in History From the 17th Century to the Present. New York, Vintage, 1973; as *Hidden From History: 300 Years of Women's Oppression and the Fight against It,* London, Pluto Press, 1973; 3rd edition, 1977.
Socialism and the New Life: The Personal and Sexual Politics of Edward Carpenter and Havelock Ellis, with Jeff Week. London, Pluto Press, 1977.
A New World for Women: Stella Browne, Socialist Feminist. London, Pluto Press, 1978.
Women in Movement: Feminism and Social Action. London and New York, Routledge, 1992.

Other

One Foot on the Mountain. Only Woman Press, 1979.
Dreams and Dilemmas: Collected Writings. London, Virago, 1983.
Friends of Alice Wheeldon. London, Pluto Press, 1986; with introduction by Sandi Cooper and Blanche Wiesen Cook, New York, Monthly Review Press, 1987.
"Retrieval and Renewal," in *Marxism in the Postmodern Age: Confronting the New World Order,* edited by Antonio Callari, Stephen Cullenburg, and Carole Biewener. New York and London, Guilford Press, 1995.

Editor, with Jean McCrindle, *Dutiful Daughters: Women Talk about Their Lives.* Allen Lane, 1977.
Editor, with Swasti Mitter, *Dignity and Daily Bread: New Forms of Economic Organising among Poor Women in the Third World and the First.* London and New York, Routledge, 1994.
Editor, with Swasti Mitter, *Women Encounter Technology: Changing Patterns of Employment in the Third World.* London, Routledge, 1995.

*

Critical Studies: Interview in *Visions of History: Conversations with Radical Historians,* edited by Henry Abelove, Betsy Blackmar, Dimock, and others, New York, Pantheon, 1984; interview in *Once a Feminist: Stories of a Generation,* edited by Michelene Wandor, London, Virago, 1990; *Modern Feminisms, Political, Literary, Cultural,* edited by Maggie Humm, New York, Columbia University

Press, 1992; interview with Bryan D. Palmer in *Left History,* 2(1), spring 1994.

Sheila Rowbotham comments:

My initial research in the 1960s was on the history of the University Extension Movements (1870-1910). I examined the motivation of the middle class lecturers and working class students who contributed not only to the creation of new institutions—including Manchester University—but the shaping of the social sciences as disciplines. This enabled me to engage with the interaction between subordinated intellectual perspectives and shifts in prevailing intellectual attitudes—in this case the emergence of strands of social liberalism and social imperialism.

My research into the case of Alice Wheeldon, about whom I wrote a play, brought out the significance of the First World War in shaping the approach of the Labour Party to the state. It also indicated how the creation of social welfare connects with the structures of surveillance of "subversives." How to relate to the state and to "power" was a theme which was being much discussed in the women's movement in the late 1970s and 1980s. My experience in the Greater London Council (1983-1986) was to give me an insight into the working of administrative structures while the attempt was made to democratize economic policy enabled me to think how demands made in the women's movement about access to resources, the organization of work and daily life, and the forms of politics could link to a wider political project.

While writing about the women's movement in Britain in *The Past Is before Us,* and while writing *Women in Movement* I became interested in women's campaigns for access to social resources in communities. This interest was stimulated by the debates on social movements in Latin America and led to historical research on women and consumption. I am currently writing on women in the 20th century in Britain and America for Penguin Books.

* * *

Associated with second-wave Anglo-European feminism, Sheila Rowbotham was born in Leeds in 1943, attended a Methodist school, and went on to St. Hilda's College, Oxford to study history. She is considered a pioneer of the women's liberation movement that emerged in late 1960s England. An overview of Rowbotham's texts indicates that broader tendencies in this period of feminist thought to interrogate women's subordination not solely in patriarchal hierarchies but rather in multiple and overlapping structures of domination.

While left politics and working-class organizing had been explicit features of social movements in the England of the 1960s, the legacy of McCarthyism and anti-union legislation such as the Taft Hartley Act gave a different shape to prevailing articulations of feminism in the U.S. context. Where feminist consciousness in the United States was deeply impacted by the civil rights movement, other factors shaped its formation in the British context. The analysis of women's relationship to socialist thought and practice, a preoccupation in a number of Rowbotham's early essays, is indicative of the distinct forms feminism adopted during this period.

Rowbotham documents her impressions and experiences of this historical formation in "The beginnings of Women's Liberation in Britain," one of two essays authored by her that appear in the first British women's liberation anthology, *The Body Politic* (1972). She notes in this essay that the first stirrings of the women's movement were to be found in the then-contemporary working-class women's equal work for equal wage campaigns in England. Born amid rumors of movements gathering momentum in other European countries and the United States, the ideas of the women's liberation in England germinated in a context of working class and anti-war consciousness raising. In the late 1960s Ruskin, a trade union college at Oxford, served as a gathering place for politicized students and social activists. Rowbotham's discussions with other participants of the Ruskin History Workshops resulted in the organization of the first conference on women's liberation of its kind in England. Attended by over 500, the Oxford conference is considered a landmark of the British feminist movement.

A prolific writer, Rowbotham has aimed consistently in her work to outline the contours of women's social, political, and economic contributions to history, contours that have been subordinated in predominately male inscriptions of the past. In her early prose she characterizes her perspective on history as Marxist feminist. A focus on working class women and affiliation with socialist political organizations inform the tenor of this phase of her writing. Intended as general surveys, *Hidden from History* (1973) and *Woman's Consciousness, Man's World* (1973) register the challenges posed by the reconstruction of British women's history from a feminist *and* materialist point of view. It is these tensions between gender analysis and class analysis to which Rowbotham returns again and again in her work. Despite the sweeping accounts presented in the studies, Rowbotham cautions readers of her early writings against an understanding of "women" as an abstract ahistorical category in the rewriting of history because, as she acknowledges, race and class dynamics are inextricable dimensions of women's experience.

Attention to the specificity of the historical situation of women becomes more apparent in Rowbotham's work in the latter part of the '70s. In *The Friends of Alice Wheeldon* (1980) she experiments with the genre of drama in order to explore the influence of syndicalism upon feminism and socialism. She reconstructs the activities of Wheeldon, a suffragette in the Women's Social and Political Union, a supporter of the Independent Labour Party, and one of three persons imprisoned by the British state for conspiracy in the closing years of the second decade of the 20th century as a way of highlighting a figure important for radical feminist thought. Amid the rising tide of political conservatism in late 1970s England, Rowbotham, along with Hilary Wainwright and Lynne Segal, coauthored *Beyond the Fragments,* a collection of three essays against the grain of the times that interrogate the scope of power dynamics operating women's participation in socialist politics and a male-dominated left.

With the 1980s came an invisible transformation in the conditions of women worldwide. The emergence of scholarship on and by third world women as a cheap exploited labor force called for a rethinking of some of the former decades' presupposition and assumptions about feminism. These changes are reflected in the focus of Rowbotham's research and writing from the period. *The Past Is before Us* (1989), a collection of essays first presented as lectures at the University of Amsterdam and other prominent universities, assesses the meaning of these changes for feminism in Britain. In a similar vein, *Women in Movement* (1992) explicitly addresses the international dimension of the women's movement.

In "Retrieval and Renewal" (1992) Rowbotham reiterates basic premises and themes fundamental to the direction of her research and analysis over the last three decades. She asserts, on the one hand, the continuing relevance of Marx's ideas on the individual and society for contemporary feminist strategy, particularly over and against a predominant strand of postmodernist thought that squarely rejects his philosophy of social relations. On the other had, Rowbotham notes in this essay the importance of the ways in which women's diverse situations and feminist critiques problematize some of Marx's tenets and, in doing so, call for productive revisions of social theories in light of historical complexities. If at this historic juncture feminism is to maintain any political currency and promise for the future then it must strive to balance self *and* social emancipation, Rowbotham argues. While it is crucial to retrieve insights from the past, it is also imperative that some form of renewal of these insights take place for notions of the individual and the social are historically contingent and constantly in need of redefinition, as are articulations of feminism.

Mother of one son, Rowbotham continues to write and lecture. Until its dissolution by the state in 1986, she served as a member of the Economic Policy Unit of the Greater London Council. Of her numerous accomplishments more recent ones include an appointment as Honorary Fellow in Women's Studies at the University of North London, and residence as a Simon Senior Research Fellow at the Department of sociology, University of Manchester.

—Mahnaz Ghaznavi

RUBIN, Gayle

Nationality: American. **Education:** University of Michigan, Ph.D. in anthropology. **Career:** Anthropologist and writer. Instructor in women's studies, feminist theory, and lesbian history at various schools, including the University of Michigan, University of California at Santa Cruz, and University of California at Berkeley; member of editorial board, *Signs, Journal of Homosexuality,* and *GLQ: A Journal of Lesbian and Gay Studies.* **Address:** San Francisco, California.

Publications

Political/Social Theory

"A Contribution to the Critique of the Political Economy of Sex and Gender," in *Dissemination,* 1(1), 1974.

"The Traffic in Women: Notes on the 'Political Economy' of Sex," in *Towards an Anthropology of Women,* edited by Rayna Rapp Reiter. New York, Monthly Review Press, 1975.

"Thinking Sex: Notes for a Radical Theory of the Politics of Sexuality," in *Pleasure and Danger: Exploring Female Sexuality,* edited by Carole S. Vance. Boston, Routledge, 1984.

"The Leather Menace: Comments on Politics and S/M," in *Coming to Power: Writings and Graphics on Lesbian S/M,* edited by SAMOIS. Boston, Alyson, 1992.

"Of Catamites and Kings: Reflections on Butch, Gender, and Boundaries," in *The Persistent Desire: A Femme-Butch Reader,* edited by Joan Nestle. Boston, Alyson, 1992.

"Misguided, Dangerous, and Wrong: An Analysis of Anti-Pornography Politics," in *Bad Girls and Dirty Pictures: The Challenge to Reclaim Feminism,* edited by Allison Assiter and Avedon Carol. London, Pluto Press, 1993.

Deviations: Essays in Sex, Gender, and Politics. Berkeley, University of California Press, forthcoming.

*

Critical Studies: "'Gender' for a Marxist Dictionary" by Donna Haraway, in her *Simians, Cyborgs, and Women: The Reinvention of Nature,* New York, Routledge, 1991; interview with Judith Butler in *Differences: A Journal of Feminist Cultural Studies,* 6(2-3), 1994.

* * *

Gayle Rubin has been one of the most influential voices in the second wave of the feminist movement. She has worked for many years in the overlapping fields of anthropology, feminist theory, and lesbian/gay history and politics. An activist, feminist, writer, and scholar, she has also been a vocal proponent of sexual minority movements, as well as an ardent critic of the anti-pornography position.

Rubin's groundbreaking work has, in the eyes of many, set the terms and the methodologies for contemporary feminist theory and lesbian and gay studies. Her well-known essay "The Traffic in Women: Notes on the 'Political Economy' of Sex," published in *Toward an Anthropology of Women* and written, incidentally, when she was a graduate student, was one of the most significant works in the history of second wave feminist writing. It continues to be required reading in introductory women's studies and feminist theory courses at universities all around the United States.

Rubin received her Ph.D. in anthropology from the University of Michigan, and has taught women's studies, feminist theory, and lesbian history at several U.S. universities. Among Rubin's other essays and articles are 1984's "Thinking Sex: Notes for a Radical Theory of the Politics of Sexuality," included in *Pleasure and Danger: Exploring Female Sexuality;* "The Leather Menace: Comments on Politics and S/M," in 1992's *Coming to Power: Writings and Graphics on Lesbian S/M;* and 1993's "Misguided, Dangerous, and Wrong: An Analysis of Anti-Pornography Politics," published in *Bad Girls and Dirty Pictures: The Challenge to Reclaim Feminism.* More recently, her work has focused on male homosexuals and the gay male subculture of San Francisco; her Ph.D. dissertation involved ethnographic work on the history and culture of the gay male leather community. A collection of Rubin's writings, *Deviations: Essays in Sex, Gender, and Politics,* is forthcoming.

Rubin introduced the term "sex/gender system" in her 1975 essay "The Traffic in Women: Notes on the 'Political Economy' of Sex." In this essay, she attempted to describe a social "apparatus" that could explain the process by which biological *sex* (woman as raw material) is transformed into social/cultural *gender* (women as products). In other words, the sex/gender system is a means to explain gender as socially constructed, dependent upon social and historical context, as well as political and economic events.

Located near the beginning of an explosion of socialist-feminist writing, "The Traffic in Women" represented a significant intervention in Marxist feminism. It articulated the limitations of Marxist thought with regard to gender oppression. Along with Heidi Hartmann's essay, "The Unhappy Marriage of Marxism and Feminism," and Juliet Mitchell's "Women: The Longest Revolution," Rubin's analysis linked gender oppression to issues of class, demonstrating the interdependence of economics, politics, and sexuality, but argued against the subordination of feminist thought to

Marxist analysis. As Rubin would state in a 1994 interview with Judith Butler in *Differences,* the essay is a sort of "neo-Marxist, proto-pomo exercise.... written on the cusp of a transition between dominant paradigms." She began with a discussion of Marx and Engels and rooted her analysis in Freudian psychoanalytic thought and Levi-Strauss's theory of kinship systems. Rubin, however, went beyond Levi-Strauss's understanding of kinship, arguing that such systems involve much more than the exchange of women between men; also exchanged are names, ancestors, certain rights and kinds of status, and sexual access to women.

As Donna Haraway points out in *Simians, Cyborgs, and Women: The Reinvention of Nature,* all contemporary notions of "gender" in feminism can be traced back to Simone de Beauvoir's claim that "one is not born a woman." Beauvoir's analysis of the social construction of "woman"/women was a major development in feminism, in part because it placed personal and psychologically oriented understandings of womanhood and femininity onto social and political axes. Rooted in the traditional philosophical western distinction between nature and culture, Beauvoir's assertion that one is not born, but rather, *becomes* a woman—as a result of societal pressures and influences—posited an early distinction within the unified notion of "woman." This understanding helped create the possibility for development and analysis of the term sex/gender system.

The political possibilities for feminism enabled by the term were and still are significant. Not only did "sex/gender" provide a means to understand what was then an early phase of the essentialism/social construction debate. It also indicated that feminist *movement* is possible. At such a critical historical juncture, conceptualization of a sex/gender system meant that oppression was not necessarily inevitable, that women's subjugation is not rooted in biology or "nature," and that we can change the lived reality of women by changing the system that oppresses us. This notion of women's position as constructed through culture was what prompted Rubin, in 1975, to call for a feminist revolution in kinship. If gender is socially constructed through specific processes and systems—through social *relations*—then the answer, it seems, is to change those systems and relations; things can be different than they are. The sex/gender system was a way to envision a better future for women.

Nine years later, in "Thinking Sex: Notes for a Radical Theory of the Politics of Sexuality," Rubin extended her analysis of the sex/gender system. In this essay, she offered a powerful critique of the anti-pornography feminist position, as well as an historical overview of "sex panics," periods in which sexual minorities and so-called "deviants," as well as certain sexual practices and identities (e.g., homosexuality, transsexuality, transvestism, sex for money, fetishism, cross-generational sex) become particularly stigmatized due to social and political anxieties. These periods in western culture—identified by Rubin as the 1880s, the 1950s, and the early 1980s—involve renegotiations among social, legal, and medical models, about sexuality. Sexual acts themselves become particularly significant and overvalued with meaning.

During such moral panics, many progressives have turned to feminism as the privileged site for discussion of sexuality. Rubin, however, argued for a more differentiated analytic framework for conceptualizing gender and sexuality. Her reasoning behind this stemmed from the notion that feminist theories, while engaging issues of gender injustice, simply do not and cannot offer adequate explanations for the oppression of sexual minorities. Because the relationship between feminism and sex is so complex, what is needed is a new, autonomous, *radical* theory of sex and the politics of sexuality. Written primarily for a feminist readership, Rubin's argument was never to say that gender and sexuality should be completely separate conceptual domains, though many have understood her to be arguing for such a separation. Rather, gender and sexuality, while related and connected, must be recognized as situational, not universal. Like her critique of Marxism in 1975 that enabled the construction of the sex/gender system, "Thinking Sex" noted the limitations of feminism for discussion about sexuality. Rubin's analysis suggests the overt politicization of sexuality—that sexuality is always political, and is organized into systems of power.

"I am skeptical of any attempt to privilege one set of analytical tools over all other.... I am skeptical of all universal tools," Rubin maintains in her interview with Butler. She also resists the implication that her work has set the terms for feminist and lesbian/gay theories, suggesting instead that her writing represents part of an ongoing process and situating herself within a context of many other scholars and activists thinking and writing about lesbian and gay studies and feminism. Gayle Rubin continues to push the boundaries of contemporary feminist thought, calling for changes in conceptualizations of sex, gender, and sexuality, and challenging us to move beyond familiar paradigms and systems of thought.

—Patricia Duncan

RUETHER, Rosemary Radford

Nationality: American. **Born:** Minneapolis, Minnesota, 2 November 1936. **Education:** Scripps College, B.A. 1958; Claremont Graduate School, M.A. in classics and Roman history 1960, Ph.D. in classics and patrisitics 1964. **Family:** Married Herman J. Ruether in 1958; one son and two daughters. **Career:** Professor of theology, School of Religion, Howard University 1966-76, visiting lecturer, Harvard Divinity School, 1971-72, G.A. Harkness Professor of Theology, Garrett Evangelical Theological Seminary, Evanston, Illinois, beginning 1976; member of graduate faculty, Northwestern University, Evanston. **Awards:** Fulbright scholar in Sweden, 1984; numerous honorary degrees. **Member:** American Academy of Religion. **Address:** Department of Bible Studies, Garrett Evangelical Theological Seminary, 2121 Sheridan Rd., Evanston, Illinois 60201-2926, U.S.A.

Publications

Religion/Spirituality

A Historical and Textual Analysis of the Relationship between Futurism and Eschatology in the Apocalyptic Texts of the Intertestament period. Claremont, California, Claremont University Press, 1958.

A Study of the Political Career of the Domitii Ahenovardi in the Republican Period. Claremont, California, Claremont University Press, 1960.

The Church against Itself: An Inquiry into the Conditions of Historical Existence for the Eschatological Community. New York, Herder & Herder, and London, Sheed & Ward, 1967.

Gregory of Nazianzus, Rhetor and Philosopher. Oxford, Clarendon Press, 1969.
The Radical Kingdom: The Western Experience of Messianic Hope. New York, Harper, 1970.
Liberation Theology: Human Hope Confronts Christian History and American Power. New York, Paulist Press, 1972.
Faith and Fratricide: The Theological Roots of Anti-Semitism. New York, Seabury Press, 1975.
New Woman, New Earth: Sexist Ideologies and Human Liberation. New York, Seabury Press, 1975.
Mary, The Feminine Face of the Church. Philadelphia, Westminster Press, 1977.
To Change The World: Christology and Cultural Criticism. New York, Crossroads, and London, SCM, 1981.
Sexism and God-Talk: Toward a Feminist Theology. Boston, Beacon Press, and London, SCM, 1983.
Womanguides: Readings toward a Feminist Theology. Boston, Beacon Press, 1985.
Women-Church: Theology and Practice of Feminist Liturgical Communities. San Francisco and London, Harper, 1985.
Contemporary Roman Catholicism: Crises and Challenges. Kansas City, Missouri, Sheed & Ward, 1987.
The Wrath of Jonah: The Crisis of Religious Nationalism in the Israeli-Palestinian Conflict, with Herman Reuther. San Francisco, Harper, 1989.
Disputed Questions: On Being a Christian. Nashville, Abingdon, 1982; revised edition, New York, Orbis, 1989.
Gia and God: An Ecofeminist Theology of Earth Healing. 1992; London, SCM, 1993.
God and the Nations, with John Douglas. Minneapolis, Fortress Press, 1995.

Autobiography

"Beginnings: An Intellectual Autobiography," in *Journeys: The Impact of Personal Experience on Religious Thought,* edited by Gregory Baum. New York, Paulist Press, 1975.

Other

At Home in the World: The Letters of Thomas Merton and Rosemary Radford Ruether, edited by Mary Tardiff. Maryknoll, New York, Orbis, 1995.

Editor, *Religion and Sexism: Images of Woman in the Jewish and Christian Traditions.* New York, Simon & Schuster, 1974.
Editor, with Eugene C. Bianchi, *From Machismo to Mutuality: Essays on Sexism and Woman-Man Liberation.* New York, Paulist Press, 1976.
Editor, with Eleanor McLaughlin, *Women of Spirit: Female Leadership in the Jewish and Christian Traditions.* New York, Simon & Schuster, 1979.
Editor, with Rosemary Skinner Keller, *Women and Religion in America: A Documentary History: The 19th Century [The Colonial and Revolutionary Periods] [1900-1968].* San Francisco and London, Harper, 3 vols., 1981-86.
Editor, with Marc H. Ellis, *Beyond Occupation: American Jewish, Christian, and Palestinian Voices for Peace.* Boston, Beacon Press, 1990.
Editor, with Eugene C. Bianchi, *A Democratic Catholic Church: The Reconstruction of Roman Catholicism.* New York, Crossroads, 1992.
Editor, with Naim S. Ateek and Marc H. Ellis, *Faith and the Intifada: Palestinian Christian Voices.* Maryknoll, New York, Orbis, 1992.
Editor, with Rosemary Skinner Keller, *In Our Own Voices: Four Centuries of American Women's Religious Writing.* San Francisco, HarperSanFrancisco, 1995.

*

Critical Studies: *Critical Theory of Religion: A Feminist Analysis* by Marsha Aileen Hewitt, Minneapolis, Fortress Press, n.p.; *Four Modern Prophets: Walter Rasuchenbusch, Martin Luther King Jr., Gustavo Gutiérrez, Rosemary Radford Ruether* by William M. Ramsey, Atlanta, John Knox Press, 1986; *Ruether's Theology of the Church and Its Implications for the Structure of the Local Church* by Kennon L. Callahan, Ann Arbor, Michigan, University Microfilms International, 1986; *The Christology of Rosemary Radford Ruether: A Critical Introduction* by Mary Hembrow Synder, Mystic, Connecticut, 23rd Publications, 1988; "Rereading, Reconceiving and Reconstructing Traditions: Feminist Research in Religion" by June O'Connor, *Women's Studies,* 17(112), 1989; "Crucifixion and Realized Eschatology: A Critique of Some Proposals concerning Feminist Theology" by Frederick Sontag, in *Asian Journals of Theology,* 4(1), April 1990; "The Status of the Anomaly in Feminist God-Talk of Rosemary Ruether" by George Alfred James, in *Zygon,* 25(2), June 1990; *Desperately Seeking Mary: A Feminist Appropriation of a Traditional Religious Symbol* by Els Maeckelberghe, The Netherlands, Pharos, 1991; "Woman, Nature and Power: Emancipatory Themes in Critical Theory and Feminist Theory" by Marsha Aileen Hewitt, in *Studies in Religion,* 20(3), 1991; *Women and the Cross: Atonement in Rosemary Radford Ruether and Dorothy Soelle* by Thelma Megill-Cobbler, Ann Arbor, Michigan, UMI Dissertation Services, 1992; "Enacting the Divine: Feminist Theology and the Being of God" by Richard Grigg, in *Journal of Religion,* 74(4), October 1994; *Escape from Paradise: Evil and Tragedy in Feminist Theology* by Kathleen M. Sands, Minneapolis, Fortress Press, 1994; *On Being the Church in the United States: Contemporary Theological Critiques of Liberalism* by Barry Penn Hollar, New York, Peter Lang, 1994; *"The Woman Will Overcome the Warrior": A Dialogue with the Christian/Feminist Theology of Rosemary Radford Ruether* by Nicholas John Ansell, Lanham, Maryland, University Press of America, 1994; *The Greening of Theology: The Ecological Models of Rosemary Radford Ruether, Joseph Sittler, and Jürgen Moltmann* by Steven Boums-Prediger, Atlanta, Scholars Press, 1995.

* * *

Rosemary Radford Ruether, professor, author, Catholic theologian, and advocate for the oppressed, began her academic career in 1954 at Scripps College in California. She has continued to work in academics and is a professor of theology at Garrett-Evangelical Theological Seminary in Evanston, Illinois. Mother of three, Radford Ruether's political commitments have led her to actively contest oppression in its many guises. Whether as writer or front-line combatant—as in 1965 when she travelled to Mississippi as part of the group of students working with the Delta Ministry in order to support the Civil Rights movement—Radford Ruether believes in active resistance to institutional oppression.

Radford Ruether's notion of family is based on an "exacting sense of history," of having a "consciousness of being rooted in the stories of many generations," as she notes in "Beginnings: an

Intellectual Autobiography." She lived in Greece with her family for two years and during this time she attended a French Ursuline convent. In 1948, while still in Greece and during a period when her mother was absent from home, Radford Ruether's father died. Alone for a brief time until her mother returned, the 12-year-old Rosemary felt a "strange detachment" and was "haunted" by memories of her father being lowered into his grave. This was her first personal experience of death and it left her with "a strong sense of human mortality, the finitude of the individual self." In 1952 she, her mother, and two sisters left Georgetown, Washington, and moved to La Jolla, California, not far from her mother's childhood home of San Diego. Here Radford Ruether spent the rest of her adolescence enveloped in a strong female community that supported her developing sense of self.

Radford Ruether's Catholicism is inherited from her mother, a woman who believed in the benefits of a Christian community. She grew up believing that Catholicism was the cloak of a *mysterium tremendum* but she felt safe in ignoring it when it demonstrated a unrefined or narrowly doctrinaire style. However, with the development of her political consciousness, Radford Ruether went on to critique her own religious tradition and in theological works such as 1967's *The Church against Itself,* 1972's *Liberation Theology: Human Hope Confronts Christian History and American Power,* and 1989's *Disputed Questions: On Being A Christian,* she self-consciously analyzed the Catholic tradition that had enculturated her throughout her childhood.

Radford Ruether came early to a critical awareness of social inequalities. During her high school years, one of her teachers introduced into the class the horrors of American racism. In 1954 she enrolled at Scripps College in Claremont California intending to develop her artistic talent. However, her interest dramatically shifted towards the classics and ancient history. In her junior year of college she married Herman Ruether and went on to major in classics, completing her undergraduate work in 1958. She then went on to do a M.A. in classics and Roman history, and a Ph.D. in classics and patristics. During this formative period, she developed a historical consciousness that was infused with a hermeneutical understanding of religion: an understanding that entailed an awareness of one's own political/theological investments and how they relate to the questions and interpretations brought to one's field of study. Equipped with these tools of analysis, and a critical awareness of social injustices and their historical basis, Radford Ruether began her foray into biblical studies, Christian origins and Catholic theology.

Having developed a sound yet critical knowledge of Christian history, Radford Ruether went on to incorporate liberation theology into her work. She had read Karl Marx during her undergraduate years, and consequently was appreciative of liberation theology, itself grounded in Marxist theory. She focused on the issue of social inequality, framing it within a Catholic paradigm. The writings of liberation theologians Leonardo Boff, Jon Sobrino, and Jose Miranda suggested to her a different starting point for Christology. The theological position of liberation theology situate Jesus within the Jewish prophetic tradition. He is understood to have advocated for the oppressed, the poor, the sick, and social outcasts. According to Radford Ruether, liberation theology "does not start first with a dogma about God becoming "man" or divine epiphany ... [r]ather, liberation theology focuses first on the historical Jesus, specifically on his 'liberating praxis.'"

In her study of Christianity, Radford Ruether built into her method a "fundamental tendency toward dialectical thinking," which meant that she understood thought to proceed from contradiction and the reconciliation of contradiction. She is suspicious of any idea that appears to be one side of a dualism. Using this method she was able to discern a polemic or opposition and develop from it a dialectic. An example of this method is Radford Ruether's writings on Judaism and Christianity, which include *The Radical Kingdom: The Western Experience of Messianic Hope,* 1970, and *Faith and Fratricide: The Theological Roots of Anti-Semitism,* 1974. Christianity's diatribes against Judaism in the Christian gospels are understood by her not to be a justification for anti-Semitism, but rather are the attempts of early Christianity to justify Jesus and itself over and against Judaism as a competitive religion.

Radford Ruether also addresses the problems of the misogynist and patriarchal behavior of the Roman Catholic church. She recognizes and criticizes Catholicism and Christianity for their exclusivity stating in *To Change the World* that "the imaging of God and Christ as white, male ruling class persons ... are not merely intellectual errors, but sins, the sins of idolatry and blasphemy." By squarely situating religion in the realm of historical, social, and political activity the onus for this kind of exclusivity resides with those who practice and perpetuate sexism. According to Radford Ruether, it is not God, God/ess, or Jesus in Christianity who excluded women from the human race, it was the men who attempted to interpret God/ess' actions in history. Although the historical Jesus is male, Radford Ruether maintains that the historical accidents of Jesus's person—maleness, Jewishness, social class—should not be understood as indicative of God's preference for these social particularities. And although this has been evident in the instances of both Jewishness and social class, it has been less clear in the instance of gender.

The historical accident of Jesus's person as male has been used to deify masculinity in the Christian belief systems, especially Catholicism. Radford Ruether maintains that women must continue to argue for their right as human beings to follow a priestly vocation. Jesus's maleness was not a reflection of a male-gendered deity or the deification of the male gender. The theology of the Catholic Church, its organization, and its structures are at best lopsided, reflecting only a male perspective. Within the context of Catholicism and Christianity, Radford Ruether suggests that women create a new midrash, a feminist midrash based on scripture, one that reflects women's interpretations of the Christian gospels, and one that critiques traditional versions for their androcentric perspective. She also suggests that a feminist midrash should "enter into dialogue and controversy with patriarchal religion." Radford Ruether maintains that a Christian feminist midrash must remain open to a feminist exploration of religions in other traditions including alternative forms of goddess religions. Ultimately, she advocates that, as Christian women have been able to identify with the crucified rabbi from Nazareth regardless of his gender, Christian men should be able to identify with the raped woman, understanding her experience as similar to that of the crucified rabbi from Nazareth.

Radford Ruether names a Christian feminist liberation community "Women-church." Women-church needs to establish itself apart from the hierarchal Church in order for it to create a structure that validates those who work toward a Church that is neither patriarchal, hierarchal, nor sexist. As an exodus community, Women-church can provide a space wherein women's experience and knowledge are legitimized: not marginalized or trivialized. Women need a space were they can speak without fear of being humiliated or silenced, where their ideas are honored and taken up as valid contributions to the community. But Women-church, according to Radford Ruether, does not establish itself over and against men, thereby creating a dichotomy between the two. She clearly states that the need for a separate base in order to form critical views should not be confused with ideological separatism. Nor does Women-church deny males the capacity for authentic humanness; but it does deny that patriarchy is the normative of authentic humanity. She believes that until women are recognized as fully human within the Catholic Church, there is no place for women as authentic human beings within the Church. Women-church does not mean a break from the Church in order to form a sectarian group. Instead, Radford Ruether insists that women should participate within the Catholic church on their own terms, not those of the Church. She expands this view in works that include *New Woman, New Earth: Sexist Idealogies and Human Liberation*, 1975; *Mary, The Feminine Face of the Church*, 1977; and *A Democratic Catholic Church: The Reconstruction of Roman Catholicism*, 1992.

When referring to deity, Radford Ruether uses the term God/ess. Humanity's discursive means to actualize deity is metaphorical and analogous. Symbolic images of deity that sanction one gender, color, or class over all others have been used as the means by which to legitimate that gender, class, or color. According to Radford Ruether in "Feminist Theology and Spirituality," images of deity(ies) "must be drawn from the entire range of human experience, from both genders, and all classes and cultures." She draws upon Judaic and Christian traditions that used feminine images, or upon female experiences such as giving birth or breast feeding, in order to develop mythic notions of the Divine and its interactions with humanity. She insists that God/ess is both mother and father, creatrix and creator. Incorporated with Radford Ruether's concern about women's oppression, has been a concern about the destruction of the planet's ecosystems. In this endeavor she points to the underlying impulse beneath all forms of oppression and demonstrates how the will to dominate rather than the will to understand underscores traditional Catholic Christianity.

Radford Ruether's theology arises from traditional Catholicism, but extends beyond it. Although, according to her, deity is God/ess, the symbols developed as analogues for deity have been gendered male. God-talk has neurotically reflected those who have held hegemony in the Western world: white middle class men. But what she most clearly illustrates is how symbols, systems, and theologies are but human discourses about the nature of existence. These symbols and theologies were not parachuted down from on high, but have a context in the social historical reality of human beings. As such, then, they are open to social and historical criticism. Her numerous works have examined the structures and operations of oppression as they function in Western culture. In this, Rosemary Radford Ruether's analyses have furthered the development of critical reflection within Christian Theology.

—Darlene M. Juschka

RUKEYSER, Muriel

Nationality: American. **Born:** New York, New York, 15 December 1913. **Education:** Attended Vassar College and Columbia University, 1930-32; briefly attended Roosevelt Aviation School. **Family:** Married the painter Glynn Collins in 1947 (divorced 1947); one son. **Career:** Co-founder, with Elizabeth Bishop, Mary McCarthy, and Eleanor Clark, *Student Review* (magazine), Vassar College; New York; worked for theatres, theatre magazines, and as a secretary, New York, prior to World War II; instructor, Sarah Lawrence College, New York, 1946, 1956-67; moved to California, 1946; instructor, California Labor School; moved back to New York, 1954; suffered paralysing stroke, 1964; imprisoned for protesting Vietnam war, 1972; with Denise Levertov, protested Vietnam War, Hanoi, 1972; protested death sentence of poet Kim Chi-Ha, Seoul, South Korea, 1975. Vice-president, House of Photography, 1946-60. Contributor to periodicals, including *Nation, New Republic, Poetry,* and *Saturday Review.* **Awards:** Yale Younger Series Poetry award, 1935, for *Theory of Flight;* Oscar Blumenthal Poetry Prize, 1940; Harriet Monroe Poetry award, 1941; National Institute of Arts and Letters grant, 1942; Guggenheim fellowship, 1943; Levinson Prize, 1947; American Council of Learned Societies fellowship, 1963; Swedish Academy translation award, with Leif Sjöberg, 1967, for *Selected Poems of Gunnar Ekelöf;* Copernicus Award, 1977; Shelley Memorial Award, 1977; *New York Quarterly* Poetry Day honors, 1979. D.Litt: Rutgers University, 1961. **Member:** PEN American Center (president, 1975-76), Society of American Historians, American Association of University Professors, National Institute of Arts and Letters, Teachers-Writers Collaborative (member, board of directors, 1967-80). **Died:** 12 February 1980.

Publications

Poetry

Theory of Flight. New Haven, Connecticut, Yale University Press, 1935.
Mediterranean. N.p., Writers & Artists Committee, Medical Bureau to Aid Spanish Democracy, 1938.
U.S. 1. New York, Covici Friede, 1938.
A Turning Wind. New York, Viking, 1939.
The Soul and Body of John Brown. Privately printed, 1940.
Wake Island. Garden City, New York, Doubleday, 1942.
Beast in View. Garden City, New York, Doubleday, 1944.
The Green Wave, with Octavio Paz and Rari. Garden City, New York, Doubleday, 1948.
Elegies. New York, New Directions, 1949.
Orpheus, illustration by Pablo Picasso. N.p., Centaur Press, 1949.
Selected Poems. New York, New Directions, 1951.
Body of Waking, with Octavio Paz. New York, Harper, 1958.
Waterlily Fire: Selected Poems 1935-62. New York, Macmillan, 1962.
The Outer Banks. Unicorn Press, 1967; revised edition, 1980.
The Speed of Darkness. New York, Random House, 1968.
29 Poems. N.p., Rapp & Whiting, 1972.
Breaking Open: New Poems. New York, Random House, 1973.
The Gates. New York, McGraw-Hill, 1976.
The Collected Poems of Muriel Rukeyser. New York, McGraw-Hill, 1978.
Rukeyser Out of Silence: Selected Poems, edited by Kate Daniels. Oak Park, TriQuarterly, 1992.
A Muriel Rukeyser Reader, edited by Jan Heller Levi. New York, Norton, 1994.

Essays

"Under 40: A Symposium of American Literature and the Younger Generation of American Jews," in *Contemporary Jewish Record,* 7(1).
The Life of Poetry. New York, Current, 1949.

Novel

The Orgy. New York, Coward McCann, 1965.

Plays

The Middle of the Air (produced Iowa City, Iowa, 1945).
The Colors of the Day (produced Vassar College, Poughkeepsie, New York, 1961).
Houdini (produced Lenox, Massachusetts, 1973).

Screenplays: *A Place to Live; All the Way Home.*

For Children

Come Back, Paul, with her own illustrations. New York, Harper, 1955.
I Go Out, illustrated by Leonard Kessler. New York, Harper, 1962.
Bubbles, edited by Donald Barr, illustrated by Jeri Quinn. New York, Harcourt, 1967.
Mazes, photographs by Milton Charles. New York, Simon & Schuster, 1970.
More Night, illustrated by Symeon Shimin. New York, Harper, 1981.

Other

Willard Gibbs. Garden City, New York, Doubleday, 1942.
One Life (biography of Wendel Wilkie). New York, Simon & Schuster, 1957.
The Traces of Thomas Hariot. New York, Random House, 1971.
Craft Interview, in *New York Quarterly,* 11, summer 1972.

Translator, with others, *Selected Poems,* by Octavio Paz. Bloomington, Indiana University Press, 1963; revised as *Early Poems, 1935-1955,* New York, New Directions Press, 1973.
Translator, *Sun Stone,* by Octavio Paz. New York, New Directions Press, 1963.
Translator, with Leif Sjöberg, *Selected Poems of Gunnar Ekelöf.* New York, Twayne, 1967.
Translator, *Three Poems,* by Gunnar Ekelöf. N.p., T. Williams, 1967.
Translator, with Leif Sjöberg, *A Molna Elegy: Metamorphoses.* N.p., Unicorn Press, 2 vols., 1984.
Translator, *Uncle Eddie's Moustache,* by Bertolt Brecht. N.p., 1974.

Recording: *The Poetry and Voice of Muriel Rukeyser,* Caedmon, 1977.

*

Critical Studies: *Poetry and the Age* by Randall Jarrell, New York, Knopf, 1953; *Selected Criticism: Prose, Poetry* by Louise Bogan, Noonday Press, 1955; "Muriel Rukeyser: A Retrospective" by Virginia R. Terris, in *American Poetry Review,* 3, May/June 1974; *The Poetic Vision of Muriel Rukeyser* by Louise Kertesz, Louisiana State University Press, 1979; special Rukeyser issue of *Poetry East,* edited by Kate Daniels and Richard Jones, 1985.

* * *

"The great devastating activity in life," Muriel Rukeyser said in an interview in 1972, "is to shred all the unities one knows. It isn't that one brings life together—it's that one will not allow it to be torn apart." Indeed, in the roles she played throughout her life as teacher, war protestor, journalist, pilot, mother, defender of children's rights, and writer, Rukeyser refused to see the distinct aspects of her life, or the events on the world's stage, as disparate or unrelated. In an essay she wrote as a young poet, she affirmed: "To live as poet, woman, American, and Jew—this chalks in my position. If the four come together in one person, each strengthens the others." Her ability to connect one experience to another, one kind of poetry to another, manifests itself in her 1949 treatise, *The Life of Poetry,* which traces the derivations of American poetry to expected sources like the Bible and Walt Whitman, but also to Native American chants, jazz, songs of the railroad workers, modern dance. Rukeyser's poetry shows that the realms of the political, the spiritual, the erotic, and the aesthetic always inform each other. In this way she chartered new territory for women writers who followed her—Adrienne Rich, Sharon Olds, Alice Walker—and who have insisted on making such connections. Erica Jong once called Rukeyser "the mother of us all."

From early on in her career, Rukeyser declared the significance of being a woman to the project of being a poet. The ten-poem sequence "Letter to the Front" (1944), confronting the horrors of the Spanish Civil War and World War II, begins in a visionary voice: "Women and poets see the truth arrive./Then it is acted out .... Women and poets believe and resist forever." Rukeyser made it her life's project to see the "truth" and then to respond to it. Sent as a journalist in the 1930s to report on the tragedies in the West Virginia Gauly Tunnel project, in which an estimated 476 to 2,000 miners died when safety methods for mining silica were ignored, Rukeyser wrote "The Book of the Dead." One of the great American long poems of this century, this work experiments with biography, revisionary myth, and documentary reportage—including the testimony of mothers who lost sons and husbands to silicosis. In this poem, Rukeyser insists on breaking silences: "What three things can never be done?/Forget. Keep silent. Stand alone."

In *The Life of Poetry* Rukeyser wrote that the "universe of poetry is the universe of emotional truth." While she refused to forget or keep silent about emotions, often she did stand alone as a woman poet who could and would write about subjects like war and female sexuality together. From the beginning, Rukeyser turned away from such supposed virtues of women's poetry as sentimentality, coyness, and modesty. Her early poems, such as "Effort at Speech between Two People," explore the personal pain of childhood; in later poems, especially her sequence "Nine Poems for an Unborn Child," she explicitly and unsentimentally establishes pregnancy, lactation, and motherhood as subjects for poetry. Poems like "The Speed of Darkness" and one of her last poems, "The Gates," broke new ground for women poets connecting their own experiences as women and mothers to political conditions ranging from racism in the United States to the imprisonment of the South Korean poet Kim-Chi Ha.

Thus the theme of breaking silences remained consistent throughout her poetry. In "The Poem as Mask," she confessed that when she wrote of the god Orpheus in an earlier poem "it was myself, split open, unable to speak in exile from myself." Recognizing this, she proclaimed the words that became the title of Howe and Bass's anthology of women's poetry: "No more masks! No more mythologies." Similarly, in her poem honoring the German artist Kathe Kollwitz, Rukeyser asked, "What would happen if one woman told the truth about her life?/The world would split open." One of the ways Rukeyser found to tell the truth was through revisionary mythmaking. With poems like "Orpheus," "Icarus," and "Myth"—about Oedipus, Rukeyser initiated a wave of women poets returning to and rewriting classical androcentric myths.

Rukeyser often invoked images of the female body, both because she was determined to give that body a place in poetry and because she trusted her own experience—which included the experience of her physical body in the world—to give her further ways of understanding and bringing together seemingly contradictory elements of life. Thus she is "open like a woman" to the story of the martyrdom of Rabbi Akiba, one of the great figures in the Rabbinic tradition. In her poem about protesting the imprisonment of the South Korean poet Kim-Chi Ha, she writes that the gates of the prison are "also the gates of perception, the gates of the body." Imagining herself as bringing herself "to birth" through writing, Rukeyser knows that the poet's task is not just to dream but to speak and thereby to hold oneself accountable to the present.

Her love poem "Looking at Each Other," shows the transformative power of desire to alter "inner and outer oppression." Though she never identified herself overtly in her writing as a lesbian, this poem and others explore lesbian sexuality and the resistance to it; in the primary relationships in the latter part of her life, women played a significant role. Poems like "Despisals" explicitly identify the "despised" in society, including homosexuals, and expose the fear that perpetuates oppression.

No matter how much Rukeyser spoke out against oppression, she always insisted on building, creating, repairing. Her poem "Wherever" declares, "Wherever/we walk/we will make/Wherever/we protest/we will go planting." Her poems observe and celebrate moments of "meeting" in which individuals are transformed through an encounter with an Other. The last lines of her last book of poem, *The Gates,* reaffirm that as a poet, a woman, a mother, a Jew, her concern ultimately was for the kind of world we create for ourselves and for the next generation: "How shall we speak to the infant beginning to run?/All those beginning to run?" By calling upon her generation to be the one to change, she positions herself as an ally to future generations. She invites us to join in a "we" that dares to break legacies of domination and to stand for freedom.

—Janet E. Kaufman

RULE, Jane (Vance)

Nationality: Canadian. **Born:** Plainfield, New Jersey, 28 March 1931. **Education:** Palo Alto High School, California; Mills College, Oakland, California (Ardella Mills award, 1952), 1948-52, B.A. in English 1952 (Phi Beta Kappa); University College, London, 1952-53; Stanford University, California, 1953. **Career:** Teacher of English and biology, Concord Academy, Massachusetts, 1954-56; assistant director of International House, 1958-59, intermittent lecturer in English, 1959-72, and guest lecturer in creative writing, 1972-73, University of British Columbia, Vancouver. Since 1974; full-time writer. **Awards:** Canada Council award, 1969, 1970; Canadian Authors Association prize, for short story, 1978, for novel, 1978; Gay Academic Union (USA) award, 1978; Fund for Human Dignity (USA) award, 1983; Canadian National Institute for the Blind, 1991, for talking book of the year. D.H.L., University of British Columbia, 1994. **Agent:** Georges Borchardt Inc., 136 East 57th Street, New York, New York 10022, USA. **Address:** The Fork, Route 1 S.19 C17, Galiano, British Columbia V0N 1P0, Canada.

Publications

Novels

Desert of the Heart. Toronto, Macmillan, and London, Secker & Warburg, 1964; Cleveland, World, 1965.
This Is Not for You. New York, McCall, 1970; London, Pandora Press, 1987.
Against the Season. New York, McCall, 1971; London, Davies, 1972.
The Young in One Another's Arms. Garden City, New York, Doubleday, 1977; London, Pandora Press, 1990.
Contract with the World. New York, Harcourt Brace, 1980; London, Pandora Press, 1990.
Memory Board. Tallahassee, Florida, Naiad Press, and London, Pandora Press, 1987.
After the Fire. Tallahassee, Florida, Naiad Press, and London, Pandora Press, 1989.

Short Stories

Theme for Diverse Instruments. Vancouver, Talonbooks, 1975; Tallahassee, Florida, Naiad Press, 1990.
Outlander (includes essays). Tallahassee, Florida, Naiad Press, 1981.
Inland Passage and Other Stories. Tallahassee, Florida, Naiad Press, 1985.

Uncollected Short Stories

"Your Father and I," in *Housewife* (London), 23(8), 1961.
"No More Bargains," in *Redbook* (New York), September 1963.
"Three Letters to a Poet," in *Ladder* (Reno, Nevada), May/June 1968.
"Moving On," in *Redbook* (New York), June 1968.
"Houseguest," in *Ladder* (Reno, Nevada), January 1969.
"The List," in *Chatelaine* (Toronto), April 1969.
"Not an Ordinary Wife," in *Redbook* (New York), August 1969.
"Anyone Will Do," in *Redbook* (New York), October 1969.
"The Secretary Bird," in *Chatelaine* (Toronto), August 1972.
"The Bosom of the Family," in *75: New Canadian Stories,* edited by David Helwig and Joan Harcourt. Ottawa, Oberon Press, 1975.

"This Gathering," in *Canadian Fiction* (Vancouver), autumn 1976.
"Pictures," in *Body Politic* (Toronto), December 1976-January 1977.
"The Sandwich Generation," in *Small Wonders*, edited by Robert Weaver. Toronto, CBC, 1982.
"Ashes, Ashes," in *New:West Coast Fiction*. Vancouver, Pulp Press, 1984.
"Blessed Are the Dead," in *The Vancouver Fiction Book*, edited by David Watmough. Winlaw, British Columbia, Polestar Press, 1985.

Other

Lesbian Images (history and criticism). New York, Doubleday, 1975; London, Davies, 1976.
A Hot-Eyed Moderate. Tallahassee, Florida, Naiad Press, 1985.
Detained at Customs: Jane Rule Testifies at the Little Sister's Trial. Vancouver, Lazara Press, 1995.

*

Media Adaptations: *Fiction and Other Truths: A Film about Jane Rule*, Toronto, Great Jane Productions, 1995.

Manuscript Collection: University of British Columbia, Vancouver.

Critical Studies: "Jane Rule and the Reviewers" by Judith Niemi, in *Margins* (Milwaukee), 8(23), 1975; "Jane Rule Issue" of *Canadian Fiction* (Vancouver), autumn 1976; interview with Michele Kort, in *rara avis* (Los Angeles), summer-fall 1981; "Strategies for Survival: The Subtle Subversion of Jane Rule" by Marilyn R. Schuster, in *Feminist Studies*, 7(3), fall 1981; "The People-Centred Vision of Jane Rule" by Robin Van Heck, in *Dalhousie Review*, fall 1988; "Hell and the Mirror: A Reading of *Desert of the Heart*" by Gillian Spragg, in *New Lesbian Criticism: Literary and Cultural Readings*, edited by Sally Munt, New York, Columbia University Press, 1992; interview with Keith Louise Fulton, in *Herizons* (Canada), winter 1993.

* * *

Jane Rule says she began writing to make a world she could live in. As a lesbian artist, thinker, and teacher in the McCarthy era, there was no found world she could inhabit. In her fiction, she creates characters whose sexualities are part of their being whole human beings. By integrating sexuality (and a range of sexuality) with character, Rule brings it out of the private world. Readers have passed Rule's writing from friend to friend, helping to shape the movement for women's and gay liberation. That her work is widely read by thoughtful people but rarely studied in schools and universities, is a measure of institutionalized homophobia: a reluctance of educators to include knowledge about lesbian lives.

But academic invisibility is changing. In 1994 the University of British Columbia awarded Rule an honorary doctorate; the same university that had nearly fired Rule from her teaching position after she published *Desert of the Heart*, a 1964 novel about two women who find themselves and each other in the desert. She saved her job, Rule says, when someone remembered that authors were not necessarily their characters.

Rule has, of course, long worn "the public label of lesbian" as she puts it in *Lesbian Images*, her 1975 study of how women writers are "influenced by religious and psychological concepts and by their own personal experience in presenting lesbian characters." She writes, "I am so far from objective disinterest that my life, or at least the quality of my life, depends on what people think and feel about what it is to be lesbian."

The worlds of Rule's fiction are recognizable to people who have lived in those times and conditions. She creates characters who feel real and whose sheer variety attest to the difference among women (and men). To do this, she has "subverted," as critic Marilyn Schuster has argued, the conventions of realism and created new strategies. Her second novel, *This Is Not for You*, is written entirely in the second person, dramatizing the narrator's internalized homophobia in the message she sends the woman she loves, "this [loving] is not for you." Far from heroic, her denial drives the other woman finally into a convent and a repudiation of her body.

By her third novel, *Against the Season*, Rule has discovered a way to make a community of people and not a single protagonist the center of the fiction. The world does not revolve around a single person with everyone else a supporting character: "we get birthdays, we get turns at being the centre of attention but they are ceremonies. They aren't really what living is about." Her characters cross national borders as well as sexual and social boundaries. While the community in this novel is from a small coastal town in the United States, the group in *The Young in Each Other's Arms* is a self-defined collective who move from Vancouver to an island.

Rule herself has lived on Galiano Island with her partner since her retirement from teaching, and the island is the setting from her last novel, *After the Fire*. In contrast to the gender balance in Rule's other fictional communities, this group is all women. Though of different ages, sexualities, races, cultures, and classes, their lives have in common their separate experiences of rejection and the support they get from each other, though not always the cozy kind. After the fire destroys the father's house, it is up to them to change the patriarchy in their own lives and actions.

As a citizen and member of a community, Rule take sup responsibilities as diverse and as connected as opening her pool to teach children on the island how to swim and as testifying on behalf of Little Sister's Bookstore in their court case filed against Canadian Customs for stopping lesbian and gay books at the border. *Detained at Customs* contains Rule's testimony: "We are a community speaking with our passion and our humanity in a world that is so homophobic that it sees us as nothing but sexual creatures instead of good Canadian citizens, fine artists, and brave people trying to make Canada a better place for everyone to speak freely and honestly about who they are."

The novel most recently detained, *Contract with the World*, provides a searching exploration of artists, art, and politics. Rule has published two collections of her prose, 1982's *Outlander*—the title suggestive of Virginia Woolf's Society of Outsiders and of Audre Lorde's 1968 title *Sister Outsider*—and *A Hot-Eyed Moderate*, in 1985. Many of these essays first appeared in *The Body Politic*, a now disappeared gay publication in Toronto which Rule pledged herself to write for as long as they were in court fighting an obscenity charge laid by the government: "Whether we like it or not," she would write, "our sexuality isn't a private matter."

Many of Rule's short stories explore themes of autonomy and connection and transform the idea that self and community are opposing realities. A generous number are stories Rule has written for her parents, in which she constructs a fiction from an incident in her own childhood.

Often connecting the struggles of children and adults, Rule's fiction dramatizes the fracturing of community in our society by age segregation, whether in same-age classrooms or in the sequestering of the old. In 1987's *Memory Board,* perhaps Rule's finest novel, a brother seeks reconciliation in their old age with his twin sister and her lover, Constance. Their separation, since he acquiesced to his wife's refusal to acknowledge his lesbian sister, prevented his children from knowing their aunt. In their vacation to the desert, David, Diane, and Constance revisit Dante's burning sands, the circle of hell promised to homosexuals, which Rule had written out of her life in *Desert of the Heart.* Rule realizes in her fiction what W. H. Auden had imagined, "In the deserts of the heart/ let the healing fountain start." The memory board Diane uses to help Constance live with Alzheimers offers a metaphor on writing as an aid to remembering who we are and what we are doing. Writing also provides some protection against falling into memories we cannot get out of, where we can be trapped, by grudge or trauma, short of the present in which we can recognize those we love.

Jane Rule has consistently refused to accept any narrow definition of lesbian; as she writes in *Lesbian Images,* "the reality of lesbian experience transcends all theories about it."

—Keith Louise Fulton

RUSS, Joanna

Nationality: American. **Born:** New York, New York, 22 February 1937. **Education:** Cornell University, Ithaca, New York, B.A. 1957; Yale University School of Drama, New Haven, Connecticut, M.F.A. 1960. **Family:** Married Albert Amateau in 1963 (divorced 1967). **Career:** Lecturer in speech, Queensborough Community College, New York, 1966-67; instructor, 1967-70, and assistant professor of English, 1970-72, Cornell University; assistant professor of English, State University of New York, Binghamton, 1972-73, 1974-75, and University of Colorado, Boulder, 1975-77; associate professor, 1977-84, and professor of English, 1984-94, University of Washington, Seattle. Contributor of book reviews and articles to periodicals, including *Extrapolation, Fantasy & Science Fiction, Feminist Review of Books, Ms., Science-Fiction Studies, Village Voice,* and *Washington Post Book World.* **Awards:** Nebula Award, 1972, 1983; National Endowment for the Humanities fellowship, 1974; O. Henry Award, 1977; Hugo Award, 1983; *Locus* Award, 1983; *Science Fiction Chronicle* Award, 1983. **Agent:** Ellen Levine Literary Agency, 432 Park Avenue South, New York, New York 10016. **Address:** 8961 East Lester St., Tucson, Arizona 85715, U.S.A.

Publications

Novels

Picnic on Paradise. New York, Ace, 1968; London, Macdonald, 1969.

And Chaos Died. New York, Ace, 1970.

The Female Man. New York, Bantam, 1975; London, Star, 1977.

We Who Are About To. . . . New York, Dell, 1977; London, Women's Press, 1987.

The Two of Them. New York, Berkley, 1978; London, Women's Press, 1986.

Kittatinny: A Tale of Magic. New York, Daughters, 1978.

On Strike against God. New York, Out & Out, 1980; London, Women's Press, 1987.

Extra(Ordinary) People. New York, St. Martin's Press, 1984; London, Women's Press, 1985.

Short Stories

Alyx. Boston, Gregg Press, 1976.

The Adventures of Alyx. New York, Pocket Books, 1983; London, Women's Press, 1985.

The Zanzibar Cat. Sauk City, Wisconsin, Arkham House, 1983.

The Hidden Side of the Moon. New York, St. Martin's Press, 1987; London, Women's Press, 1989.

Play

Window Dressing, in *The New Women's Theatre,* edited by Honor Moore. New York, Random House, 1977.

Essays

How to Suppress Women's Writing. Austin, University of Texas Press, and London, Women's Press, 1983.

Magic Mommas, Trembling Sisters, Puritans & Perverts: Feminist Essays. Trumansburg, New York, Crossing Press, 1985.

To Write Like a Woman: Essays in Feminism and Science Fiction. Bloomington, Indiana University Press, 1995.

Putting It All Together. New York, St. Martin's Press, 1996.

*

Manuscript Collection: Popular Culture Library, Jerome Library, Bowling Green State University, Bowling Green, Ohio.

Critical Studies: "Reflections of Science Fiction: An Interview with Joanna Russ" in *Quest, A Feminist Quarterly,* 2, 1975; "Science Fiction and Feminism: The Work of Joanna Russ" by Marilyn Hacker, in *Chrysalis,* 4, 1977; article by Samuel Delany, in *Science-Fiction Studies,* 19, 3 November 1979; "The Feminist Apologues of Lessing, Piercy, and Russ" by Rachel Blau DuPlessis, in *Frontiers,* 4, 1979; "A Female Man? The 'Medusan' Humor of Joanna Russ" by Natalie M. Rosinsky, in *Extrapolation,* 23, 1982; "Profile: Joanna Russ" (interview) by Charles Platt, in *Isaac Asimov's Science Fiction Magazine,* March 1983; "A Dialogue: Samuel Delany and Joanna Russ on Science Fiction" by Charles Johnson, in *Callaloo,* 7, 1984; "Orders of Chaos: The Science Fiction of Joanna Russ," by Samuel R. Delany, in *Women Worldwalkers: New Dimensions of Science Fiction and Fantasy,* edited by Jane B. Weedman, Lubbock, Texas Tech, 1985; *Demand the Impossible: Science Fiction and the Utopian Imagination* by Tom Moylan, New York, Methuen, 1986; *Feminist Utopias* by Frances Bartkowski, Lincoln, University of Nebraska Press, 1989; "An Interview with Joanna Russ" by Larry McCaffery, in *Across the Wounded Galaxies,* Chicago, University of Illinois Press, 1990;

"The Politics of Separatism and Lesbian Utopian Fiction" by Sonya Andermahr, in *New Lesbian Criticism: Literary and Cultural Readings* edited by Sally Munt, New York, Columbia University Press, 1992; "Joanna Russ" (interview) by Donna Perry, in *Backtalk: Women Writers Speak Out,* New Brunswick, New Jersey, Rutgers University Press, 1993.

* * *

In the late 1960s, Joanna Russ integrated her love of science fiction with her commitment to feminism and launched her career as a feminist science fiction and fantasy writer. Through the 1970s and 1980s, her short stories, novels, and essays greatly influenced the rapidly growing field of feminist science fiction and fantasy. Although she is best known as a science fiction writer, Russ has also written a non-science fiction lesbian novel, a children's fantasy story, essays on popular culture, and has contributed significantly to feminist literary criticism.

Born in 1937, Russ grew up in New York City. She recalled in an autobiographical essay in *Magic Mommas, Trembling Sisters, Puritans & Perverts,* that at age 12 she was "a tall, overly bright and overly self-assertive girl, too much so to fit anybody's notions of femininity." In early adolescence, she discovered science fiction and became an immediate fan. Russ graduated from Cornell University in 1957 with a B.A. in English and earned an M.F.A. in playwrighting at Yale Drama School in 1960. Instead of pursuing a career as a playwright, she began to publish science fiction and fantasy short stories, beginning with "Nor Custom Stale" in 1959.

With the "Alyx" stories and the novel *Picnic on Paradise,* published between 1967 and 1970 and collected in *The Adventures of Alyx,* Russ achieved what she called a "breakthrough." She deliberately rejected the gender stereotypes common in fantasy-adventure stories by creating a victorious female protagonist. The character Alyx is smart, tough, a thief and assassin, sensual, intelligent, and *not* beautiful. In an interview with Larry McCaffery, Russ said she "had stumbled upon the chance to create a *new story.*"

In early 1969 Russ attended a feminist colloquium at Cornell University, which she identified as another turning point for her. Feminism and lesbianism became important issues in her life and her fiction. Although science fiction at that time was dominated by male authors, readers, and protagonists, Russ proved that science fiction was entirely compatible with feminism. Because science fiction by definition requires a "different" world—different in one or many ways from the world of the author and reader—Russ could invent worlds from a feminist viewpoint. By presenting such worlds, she suggested to readers that life as we know it could be different.

Like many other feminist writers, Russ turned to the utopian mode to imagine a different and better society. In her 1981 survey "Recent Feminist Utopias," included in *To Write Like a Woman,* she notes that the 1970s had witnessed "a mini-boom of feminist utopias, a phenomenon obviously contemporaneous with the women's movement itself." Russ herself was one of the earliest contributors to this trend. She first presented "Whileaway," an all-female utopia, in the Nebula Award-winning story "When It Changed" (1969) and later developed it in more detail in *The Female Man,* written between 1969 and 1971, although not published until 1975. In the 20-plus years since its publication, *The Female Man* has received a great deal of critical attention—no discussion of feminist utopias is complete without it—and remains Russ's best-known work. Simultaneously angry and funny (characteristics that mark much of Russ's writing), *The Female Man* is based on the premise of alternate worlds. Its four protagonists share the same genotype, but have developed into four very different women according to their environments. Jeannine, the most oppressed and unhappy character, lives in the U.S., but in her "possible universe" World War II was never fought and the Great Depression has lasted into the late 1960s. The only life for a woman in her world is marriage, and she both longs for and dreads that destiny. Joanna (a fictionalized version of Russ) lives in a more historically realistic America, with second-wave feminism on the move in 1969. Joanna has more choices than Jeannine, but she is still expected to orient herself around men and is constantly told "women can't" or "women don't." Jael lives in a near future in which men and women wage a cold war. Her experience of being a woman is much like Joanna's, but Jael's response is violence. Janet represents the ideal, a woman who grew up with no gender stereotypes to shape her life and who thus developed her full human potential. She hails from the utopia Whileaway, a world in which all the men were killed off centuries ago in a plague (or, in a different version of the story, a war). Joanna wistfully calls Janet a woman "whom we don't believe in and whom we deride but who is in secret our savior from utter despair."

No summary can do justice to the complexity and energy of this novel. Whileaway is engagingly detailed in bits and pieces throughout the book; the first-person voice is assumed by various characters with occasional intrusions by the author; and the narrative jumps from genre to genre (in fact, labeling the novel a "utopia" is an over-simplification). *The Female Man* encompasses the themes to which Russ returns in other fiction and non-fiction: the myriad ways in which the sex-class system is maintained, lesbianism as a personal and political response to compulsory heterosexuality, the importance of strong female role models, and the connections between art and life.

Because Russ believes that art can and should influence life, she creates strong female characters to serve as role models for female writers and readers. In the 1972 essay "What Can a Heroine Do? Or, Why Women Can't Write," Russ argues that the actions and roles available to women characters in fiction are absurdly limited. "The lack of workable myths in literature," she writes, affected not only literature but also its readers, because "we interpret our own experience in terms of them." Writing in the early years of the second-wave feminist movement in the United States, Russ called for new "myths," new plots and roles for female characters.

Positive female role models are especially important for the adolescent female. In "Recent Feminist Utopias," Russ notes that puberty "is often not a broadening-out (as it is for boys) but a diminution of life," a time when girls are instructed (even more than in childhood) in the importance of femininity and deference. To resist this socialization, girls need unconventional models. Russ's characters include such non-feminine heroes as Alyx and *The Female Man*'s Janet, as well as the adolescent girls who seek such role models. In *The Female Man,* Joanna describes herself at age "thirteen, desperately watching TV, curling my long legs under me, desperately reading books, callow adolescent that I was, trying (desperately!) to find someone in books, in movies, in life, in history, to tell me it was O.K. to be ambitious, O.K. to be loud.... Being told I was a woman." Similarly, the teenage Laura of *The Female Man* dreams of herself as Genghis Khan and is sent to a therapist who tells her "to look and act more feminine." Zubeydeh of *The Two of Them* and the eponymous protagonist of *Kittatinny* are also adolescent girls who struggle with their cultures' expectations of women.

In exploring the cultural conditioning of girls and women, Russ pays particular attention to the oppression of lesbians. In "Not for Years but for Decades," an essay about her experiences as a lesbian which she includes in *Magic Mommas,* she recalls that as an adolescent, she learned that lesbianism "was bad and it didn't exist. It was bad *because* it didn't exist." The protagonist of her second novel, *And Chaos Died,* is a gay man, but Russ stated in an interview with Donna Perry, "I think he was a stand-in for you-know-who—me—or parts of things of my own that I projected onto him .... What I was trying for was what finally came out in *The Female Man,* and it was a romance between women." Like other writers energized by the feminist movement and the gay liberation movement of the late 1960s and early 1970s, Russ wrote lesbianism into existence. In *The Female Man,* Janet, who is married to a woman in all-female Whileaway, demonstrates to the other characters the possibility and desirability of lesbianism. Joanna, who recognizes and struggles against the cultural pressures to "live for The Man," makes love to another woman and experiences a revelation: "I can't describe to you how reality itself tore wide open at that moment .... If this is possible, anything is possible." In the non-SF *On Strike against God,* Russ details the difficulties and rewards of rejecting heterosexuality for lesbianism.

In her science fiction and fantasy, Russ often rewrote conventional plots from a feminist standpoint. *We Who Are About To ...* begins with a group of tourists stranded on a deserted planet, but Russ rejects the typical Robinson Crusoe story of creating civilization in the wilderness. Instead, the female protagonist refuses the futile survivalism of her companions, especially when she is threatened with forced breeding. *The Two of Them* features another strong female protagonist who rescues an adolescent girl from a male-dominated society. Like many of Russ's short stories—"The Little Dirty Girl," "Bluestocking," "The Autobiography of My Mother"—*The Two of Them* concentrates on a mother-daughter type of relationship. In *Extra(Ordinary) People,* she examines the concepts of gender identity and sexual identity, ranging from hilarious, madcap plotting to poignant depictions of human love. The wide scope of her talent is also evident in two collections of short stories, *The Zanzibar Cat*—which includes "When It Changed"—and *The Hidden Side of the Moon.*

An energetic writer, Joanna Russ has not been as prolific in the past decade because of her struggles with Chronic Fatigue Immune Deficiency Syndrome. Her 1995 book, *To Write like a Woman,* collects new and previously published essays on the two subjects that define her career: feminism and science fiction. *Putting It All Together*, a nonfiction book analyzing sexism, racism and classism, is forthcoming from St. Martin's Press.

—Julie Linden

S

SAND, George

Pseudonym for Amandine-Aurore-Lucile Dupin, Baronne Dudevant; also wrote as G. Sand. **Other Pseudonyms:** Jules Sand (joint pseudonym). **Nationality:** French. **Born:** Paris, 1 July 1804. **Education:** Attended the Convent of the Dames Augustines Anglaises, Paris, 1818-20. **Family:** Married 1) Casimir-François Dudevant in 1822 (separated 1831), two daughters; companion of the poet Alfred de Mussett, until 1835; companion of the composer Frédéric Chopin, 1839-47. **Career:** Moved to Paris, 1831; cofounder, *Revue indépendante,* 1841; retired to the "châtelaine of Nohant," Nohant-sur-Seine, beginning 1848. Contributor to *Le Figaro,* with Jules Sandeau, under joint pseudonym Jules Sand. **Died:** 8 June 1876.

Selected Publications

Novels

Rose et Blanche, with Jules Sandeau (as Jules Sand). Paris, n.p., 1831.

Indiana (as G. Sand). Paris, n.p., 1832; translated as *Indiana: A Love Story,* Philadelphia, T.B. Peterson, 1881.

Valentine. Brussels, J.P. Meline, 1832; translated, Philadelphia, G. Barrie, 1902.

Lélia. Brussels, J.P. Meline, 1833.

Jacques. Brussels, J.P. Meline, 1834; translated, New York, J.S. Redfield, 1847.

Leone-Leoni. Paris, n.p., 1834-36; translated, Philadelphia, G. Barrie, 1900.

Mauprat. Paris, n.p., 1837; translated, London, Churton, 1847; Boston, Roberts Bros., 1870.

L'Uscoque. Paris, n.p., 1837; translated as *The Uscoque: A Venitian Story,* London, G. Slater, 1850; New York, n.p., 1851.

L'Orco. Paris, 1838.

Spiridion. Paris, F. Bonnaire, 1838-39; translated, London, n.p., 1842.

Les sept cordes de la lyre. Paris, n.p., 1839; translated as *A Woman's Version of the Faust Legend: The Seven Strings of the Lyre,* Chapel Hill and London, University of North Carolina Press, 1989.

Le compagnon du tour de France. Paris, n.p., 1840; translated as *The Companion of the Tour of France,* London, Churton, 1847; as *The Journeyman Joiner, or, The Companion of the Tour of France,* Dublin, J. McGlashan, 1849; as *The Compagnon of the Tour of France,* New York, H. Fertig, 1976.

Horace. Paris, n.p., 1841-42; translated, San Francisco, Mercury House, 1993.

Un hiver à Majorque. Paris, 2 vols., 1842; translated as *Winter in Majorca,* London, Cassell, 1956.

Consuelo. Paris, n.p., 1842-43; translated as *Consuelo: A Romance of Venice,* New York, n.p., 1851.

La comtesse de Rudolstadt. Paris, n.p., 1843-44; translated as *The Countess of Rudolstadt,* New York, Dodd Mead, 2 vols., 1891; London, Oxford Library, 1893.

Jeanne. Paris, n.p., 1844.

Le Meunier d'Angibault. Brussels, Meline Cans, 1845; translated as *The Miller of Angibault,* Boston, Roberts Bros., 1871.

La mare au diable. Paris, n.p., 1846; as *The Haunted Pool,* New York, Dodd Mead, 1890.

André. Paris, n.d.; translated, London, Churton, 1847.

François le champi. Brussels, Meline Cans, 1848; translated as *François the Waif,* New York and London, Routledge, 1889.

La petite Fadette. Paris, n.p., 1848-49; translated as *Fanchon the Cricket,* New York, J. Bradburn, 1864; translated as *Fadette,* New York, G.H. Richmond, 1893; translated as *Little Fadette,* London, Scholartis Press, 1928.

Le château des désertes. Brussels, Meline Cans, 1851.

Les maîtres sonneurs. Brussels, Meline Cans, 1853; translated as *The Master Bellringers,* London, n,d; translated as *The Bagpipers,* Boston, Roberts Bros., 1890.

L'homme de neige. Paris, Hachette, 2 vols., 1859; New York, Oxford University Press, 1933.

Elle et lui. Paris, M. Lévy, 1859; translated as *He and She,* Philadelphia, G. Barrie, 1902.

La ville noire. Paris, M. Lévy, 1861.

Le Marquis de Villemer. Paris, M. Lévy, 1861; translated as *The Marquis de Villemer,* Boston, J.R. Osgood, 1871.

Antonia. Paris, M. Lévy, 1863; translated, Boston, Roberts Bros., 1870.

Mademoiselle La Quintinie. Paris, n.p., 1864.

Monsieur Sylvestre. Paris, 1865; translated, Boston, Roberts Bros., 1870.

Les beaux messieurs de Bois Doré. Paris, M. Lévy, 1865; translated as *The Gallant Lords of Bois-Doré,* New York, Dodd Mead, 1890.

Le dernier amour. Paris, n.p., 1866.

Essays

Questions d'art et de littérature (includes "Dialogues familiers sur la poésie de prolétaires"). Paris, n.p., 1842.

Porquoi Les femmes à l'Académie? Paris, M. Lévy, 1863.

Questions politiques et sociales. Paris, Calmann Lévy, 1879.

George Sand: Collected Essays, edited by Janis Glasgow. Troy, New York, Whitston, 1985.

For Children

L'Histoire de Véritable Gribouille. Paris, n.p., 1869; translated as *The Mysterious Tale of Gentle Jack and Lord Bumblebee,* New York, Dial, and London, Methuen, 1988.

Contes d'une grand'mère. Paris, n.p., 1873; selection translated as *Wings of Courage,* London, Blackie, 1884; entire text translated as *Tales of a Grandmother,* Philadelphia and London, J.B. Lippincott, 1930; New York, Feminist Press, 1994.

The Castle of Pictures and Other Stories: A Grandmother's Tales, edited by Holly Erskine Hirko. New York, Feminist Press, n.d.

Autobiography

Lettres d'un voyageur. Paris, n.p., 1834-1836).

Histoire de ma vie. Paris, V. Lecou, 20 vols., 1854-55; translated as *The Story of My Life: The Autobiography of George Sand,* Albany, State University Press of New York, 1991.
Impressions et souvenirs. Paris, M. Lévy, 1873; translated as *Impressions and Reminiscences,* Boston, W.F. Gill, 1877.
Journal intime, edited by Aurore Sand. Paris, Calmann Lévy, 1926; translated as *The Intimate Journal of George Sand,* New York, John Day, 1929.
Oeuvres Autobiographiques, edited by Georges Lubin. Paris, 2 vols., 1970-71.

Other

Oeuvres de George Sand. Paris, Perrotin, 16 vols., 1842-44.
Oeuvres choisies de George Sand. Brussels, 3 vols., 1851.
Oeuvres illustrées de George Sand. Paris, M. Lévy, 9 vols., 1851-56.
Oeuvres complètes de George Sand. Paris, M. Lévy, 115 vols., 1852-1926.
Théâtre compléte de George Sand. Paris, Calmann Lévy, 4 vols., 1866-67.
The Masterpieces of George Sand, translated by G. Burnham Ives and Mary W. Artois. Philadelphia, G. Barrie, 20 vols., 1900-02.
Correspondance de George Sand et d'Alfred Musset, edited by F. Decori. Brussels, E. Deman, 1904.
The George Sand-Gustave Flaubert Letters, edited by Aimée McKenzie. New York, Boni & Liveright, 1921; London, Duckworth, 1922.
George Sand-Marie Dorval: Correspondance inédite, edited by Simone André-Maurois. Paris, n.p., 1953.
Correspondance, edited by Georges Lubin. Paris, Garnier, 16 vols., 1964-81.
Les lettres de George Sand à Sainte-Beauve, edited by Osten Södergard. Geneva, n.p., 1964.
Lettres de George Sand à Alfred de Musset et Gustave Flaubert, edited by Jean-Luc Benoziglio. Paris, n..p., 1970.
Romans. Paris, Presses de la Cité, 1991.
Flaubert-Sand: The Correspondence. London, Harvill, 1993.

*

Bibliography: In *George Sand* by David A. Powell, Boston, Twayne, 1990.

Critical Studies: *Literary Women: The Great Writers* by Ellen Moers, New York, Doubleday, 1973, London, Women's Press, 1977; *George Sand: A Biography of the First Modern Liberated Woman* by Noel B. Gerson, London, Hale, 1973; *George Sand: A Biography* by Curtis Cates, Boston, Houghton Mifflin, and London, Hamilton, 1975; *George Sand: A Biography* by Ruth Jordan, London, Constable, 1976; *Infamous Woman: The Life of George Sand* by Joseph Barry, Garden City, New York, Doubleday, 1977; *The Double Life of George Sand: Woman and Writer* by Renée Winegarten, New York, Basic Books, 1978; "George Sand" by Gita May, in *European Writers: The Romantic Century,* edited by George Stowle, New York, Scribner's, 1985; *Family Romances: George Sand's Early Novels* by Kathryn J. Crecelius, Bloomington, Indiana University Press, 1987; *George Sand: A Brave Man, the Most Womanly Woman* by Donna Dickenson, Oxford, Berg, 1988; *George Sand* by David Powell, Boston, Twayne, 1990; *The Feminization of the Novel* by Michael Danahy, Gainesville, University of Florida Press, 1991; *George Sand: Writing for Her Life* by Isabelle Hoog Naginski, New Brunswick, New Jersey, Rutgers University Press, 1991; *George Sand and Idealism* by Naomi Schor, New York, Columbia University Press, 1993; *George Sand and the 19th-Century Russian Love-Triange Novels* by Dawn D. Eidelman, Lewisburg, Pennsylvania, Buckness University Press, 1994; *Maternal Fictions: Stendhal, Sand, Rachilde, and Bataille* by Maryline Lukacher, Durham, Duke University Press, 1994.

* * *

For those who grew up in France, George Sand evokes such idyllic pastoral novels as *La petite Fadette* (*Little Fadette,* 1848-1849) and *François le champi* (*François the Waif,* 1847-1848). Marcel Proust's case, in this respect, is paradigmatic. His boyhood was brightened and enriched by Sand's rustic novels, gifts to him from his mother and grandmother.

In her own century, Sand gained immense respect and admiration from writers, painters, and composers, despite her controversial reputation. One of the few dissenting voices in this chorus of praise was that of Charles Baudelaire, whose animosity toward her was not without envy of her literary success and abundant creativity. While Proust saw in Sand the very essence of human generosity and moral goodness, Baudelaire regarded her as a dangerous and seductive apologist for romantic utopianism.

Sand's position among French women of letters is crucial by virtue of several factors: her life span embraced an era marked by momentous changes; she welcomed, indeed thrived on, conflict and strife; in both her fiction and nonfictional works she showed a keen awareness of the importance of the historical context in the life of every individual. History, as she saw it, is determined both by events of a cataclysmic nature—such as wars and revolutions—and by the slow, sometimes imperceptible impact of ideas. She recognized that the interrelation between these two sets of events is at once crucial and immensely complex. Events of a portentous nature certainly played a decisive role in shaping Sand's political and social attitudes and beliefs, as her autobiography, *Histoire de ma vie* (*Story of My Life,* 1854-1855), makes clear, and as she proudly acknowledged, in her veins coursed the blood of both patricians and plebeians.

Sand dealt more boldly than any of her predecessors (including Germaine de Stael) with such themes as passion, marriage, and the painful conflicts of love and duty. That she flouted social conventions openly in her own life, and lived her romances fully and intensively, added to her notoriety, but also obscured the seriousness of her commitment as a writer. Her generous, compassionate nature caused her to identify with the poor and oppressed, she maintained strong ideological ties with the ideals of the Enlightenment and French Revolution, and she remained a steadfast admirer and disciple of Jean-Jacques Rousseau.

An uncommonly prolific output, in addition to the gender question, contributed to a basic misunderstanding of Sand's rightful place among the great writers of the 19th century. The general reproach has been that she was too unselfconscious to be ranked with such giants as Stendhal, Balzac, and Flaubert. She could not be a true artist because her easy, flowing style showed no obvious traces of self-torment and self-doubt. Sand, for her part, remained convinced that as a writer she had the right, indeed the duty, to give free rein to her thoughts and feelings without any undue concern for formal niceties. Hence her espousal of a unambiguous, even improvisatory style of writing, which is only now being fully appreciated.

Indiana, which appeared in 1832, was Sand's first major novel. Under the guise of a masculine narrator, *Indiana* tells the story, set during the last years of the Restoration and the 1830 Revolution, of a Spanish Creole, Indiana, unhappily married to an elderly, unfeeling officer, Colonel Delmare. When she eventually escapes the bonds of matrimony in order to rejoin her lover, Raymon de Ramiere, an egotistical nobleman who is also a self-indulgent womanizer and a political conservative, he rejects her in favor of a socially advantageous marriage. In her humiliation and despair, Indiana contemplates suicide, but fortunately finds happiness with her loyal cousin, Sir Ralph Bowen, a noble Englishman. The main impact of the book lies in its eloquent and bold treatment of the "woman question."

Indiana is, in many ways, transposed autobiography, and its heroine, like Sand, finds disappointment in both marriage and passionate love. The happy ending lacks plausibility but hardly detracts from the main thrust of the novel, which powerfully contrasts woman's quest's for fulfillment with man's selfish vanity and sensuality.

Lélia, published in 1833, is Sand's boldest and most confessional novel. It depicts a young poet, Sténio, who is driven to despair and a life of debauchery after being repulsed by the seductive but unmerciful Lélia, in many ways the female counterpart of the romantic conception of Don Juan. The novels bold, erotic scenes of physical passion made a tremendous impact on the contemporary reading public.

Sand's stormy relationship with Alfred de Musset, from 1833 to 1835, had endless repercussions in her writings, notably in her correspondence, in her *Journal intime (Intimate Journal),* in her *Lettres d'un voyageur,* 1834-36, and in her novel *Elle et lui* (*She and He*), published two years after Musset's death in 1857. In this thinly disguised fiction Musset is easily recognizable in the portrayal of the painter Laurent, with his unpredictable moodiness and fits of rage. Thérèse, of the other hand, is given an idealized treatment, and the parallel with Sand is inescapable. In Sand's passionate prose one finds all the major romantic themes: melancholy and restlessness, generosity and suspiciousness, enthusiasm, nihilism, and above all else the pervasive ailment of the soul characterized as *mal du siècle.*

It was while in Venice, partly in order to seek escape from emotional turmoil, that Sand dashed off in a week *Leone-Leoni* (1834), a novel inspired by the abbé Prevost's famous *Manon Lescaut* (1732). She transposed the characters and reversed the situation by endowing the male narrator, Leoni, with Manon's fatal seductiveness and amorality. Like Manon, Leoni is eventually redeemed through love for his adoring, ever-forgiving mistress. Juliette, who like Prevost's Des Grieux, yearns for a quiet existence in some rustic retreat, repeatedly succumbs to passion and adventure. Sand's disastrous Venetian with Musset also found expression in such tales of passion and mystery as *La dernière Aldini* (*The Last Aldini,* 1838), the dramatic story of a patrician Venetian woman enamored of a gondolier; *L'Orco* (1838), a symbolic novella with fantastic overtones; and *L'Uscoque* (1837), a romance with Byronic strains.

In 1835 Sand met Robert Lamennais, the fiery and controversial cleric whose *Paroles d'un croyant (Words of a Believer)* had appeared in 1834. Deeply impressed by his socially minded zeal, which had alienated him from the ecclesiastical hierarchy, she turned to him for guidance and inspiration. But it was Pierre Leroux, whose books and journalistic writings eloquently denounced social inequities, who had the most powerful impact on Sand's political orientation. She did not hesitate to hail him as an authentic spokesperson for the oppressed and to place his political theories alongside Rousseau's.

Some of the novels Sand wrote after her association with Lamennais and Leroux, notably the mystical allegory *Spiridion* (1838-39), the philosophically ambitious *Les sept cordes de la lyre* (*The Seven Strings of the Lyre,* 1839), the religio-socialist *Le compagnon du tour de France* (*The Journeyman-Joiner*, 1840), and the sweeping *Consuleo* (1842-43), with its sequel, *La comtesse de Rudolstadt* (*Countess Rudolstadt,* 1843-44), reflect her spiritual quest and evolution from orthodox Catholicism to Christian socialism. Ernest Renan, the religious historian and author of the famous *Vie de Jésus* (*Life of Jesus,* 1861), was a great admirer of *Spiridion,* and *Consuelo* was the favorite novel by Sand of both Dostoyevsky and Whitman. Henry James considered *Consuelo* her masterpiece and the French philosopher Alain ranked it with Goethe's *Wilhelm Meister.*

Consuelo is a novel of great sweep and scope. The heroine, Consuelo, is a Spanish-born singer and adventurous female Don Juan in quest of perfect love. More significantly, she is the artist in quest of truthful self-expression. Her wanderings take Consuelo from Venice to the courts of Maria Theresa in Vienna and Frederick the Great in Potsdam; they also bring her into contact with the great composers of her day, for music plays an important part in the novel. In *Consuelo* Sand expressed all her personal and artistic aspirations, and with *Countess Rudolstadt,* it constitutes her most ambitious work. Unlike most romantic heroines, Consuelo not only survives misfortunes and persecutions, she even manages to find happiness and serenity. Electing to live among simple, ordinary people, she offers them music in exchange for their hospitality.

Mauprat, published in 1837, despite its initial cool reception is one of Sand's best novels. It is set in the period immediately preceding the French Revolution. In the orphaned, mistreated young hero, Bernard de Mauprat, Sand presents a compelling picture of an illiterate youth, all instinctual impulsiveness, who rises above his stormy, unrestrained nature through suffering and a great love. It is a confessional tale of the old Mauprat, who looks back on his life with unflinching honesty. *Mauprat* is a novel of experience, a *bildungsroman* with a strong didactic component.

Sand's liaison with Chopin, which began in 1838, and their stay in Majorca in the winter of 1838-1839, during which Chopin fell ill, have been amply documented. After the Majorca experience, Sand came to the realization that she was past the age of passionate love affairs. Once she threw her considerable energies into her work, and the result was a cycle of works with rustic settings and characters: *Jeanne* (1844); *Le Meunier d'Angibault* (*The Miller of Angibault,* 1845); *La mare au diable* (*The Devil's Pool,* 1846), a rural story that was to become one of her most popular novels; *François le champi,* which treats the theme of bastardy in provincial France; and *La petite Fadette.*

In these folk tales with a rustic setting, Sand inaugurated a novelistic tradition that continues to thrive to this day. To be sure, to depict French peasantry with authenticity and truthfulness also tempted such 19th-century masters of the novel as Balzac in *Les paysans* (*The Peasant,* 1844), and Zola, in *La terre* (*The Earth,* 1887); vivid glimpses of peasant mentality and mores are also afforded in Flaubert's *Madame Bovary* (1857) and *Un coeur simple* (*A Simple Heart,* 1877). But unlike Balzac, Flaubert, and Zola, who presented their peasant characters in a relentlessly harsh light, Sand endowed her peasant types with considerable nobility and dignity. Her romantic utopianism offers us an idealized and sentimentalized panorama of country manners and mores.

Sand remained steadfast in her beliefs through the double tragedy of the War of 1870 and the Paris Commune. By then she had learned the hard lessons of serenity and detachment, as her novel, *Monsieur Sylvestre* (1865), testifies. Her novel *Le dernier amour* (*The Last Love,* 1866), dedicated to Flaubert and obviously influenced by *Madame Bovary,* is a testimony to their close friendship, as is also their fascinating correspondence. She worked hard and lived fully until her death on 8 June 1876.

From the outset, Sand has had her passionate apologists and vociferous detractors. Feminist criticism has not only rekindled interest in her writing, it has also vigorously fostered a serious and systematic reexamination of her works. Recent critical editions of her novels, autobiography and correspondence, as well as English translations of these works, amply testify to this resurgence of interest. George Sand's place alongside such great French writers of the 19th century as Stendhal, Balzac, Flaubert, and Zola has now been secured.

—Gita May

SAND, Jules. *See* **Sand, George.**

SANGER, Margaret (Higgins)

Nationality: American. **Born:** Corning, New York, 14 September 14 1883. **Education:** Claverack College, Hudson, New York; nursing training at White Plains Hospital; post-graduate studies at School of Manhattan Eye and Ear Hospital; LL.D., Smith College, 1949. **Family:** Married 1) the architect William Sanger in 1902 (divorced 1920), three children; 2) J. Noah Slee in 1922. **Career:** Leader of the birth control movement in the United States. Launched struggle against prohibitions against birth control beginning 1912; maternity nurse, New York; went to Paris and met Malthusian reformers; founded National Birth Control League, 1914; published *Woman Rebel* magazine; indicted for mail fraud after sending pamphlet, *Family Limitation,* through the U.S. mail, 1915; arrested for operating a birth control clinic in Brooklyn, New York, 1916; while in prison, founded and edited *Birth Control Review;* case dismissed, 1916; sentenced to 30 days at a Brooklyn, New York, workhouse after opening birth control clinic in Brownsville, Brooklyn; founded Birth Control Clinical Research Bureau (merged with American Birth Control League to form Birth Control Federation of America, now known as Planned Parenthood Federation of America, 1942), 1921. Organized first World Population Conference, Geneva, 1927. President, International Planned Parenthood Federation, beginning 1953. **Awards:** American Women's Award, 1931; Town Hall award, 1936; Lasker Foundation award, 1950. **Died:** Tucson, Arizona, 6 September 1966.

Publications

Political/Social Theory

What Every Girl Should Know. Reading, Pennsylvania, Sentinel Press, 1913; revised edition, New York, M. N. Maisel, 1916.
What Every Mother Should Know; or, How Six Little Children Were Taught the Truth. New York, Rabelais Press, 1914.
The Case for Birth Control. New York, Modern Art Printing, 1917.
Woman and the New Race, with a preface by Havelock Ellis. New York, Brentano's, 1920; as *The New Motherhood,* London, Jonathan Cape, 1922.
The Pivot of Civilization. N.p., 1922; London, Jonathan Cape, 1923.
Woman, Morality, and Birth Control. New York, New York Women's Publishing Co., 1922.
Happiness in Marriage. New York, Brentano's, 1926.
What Every Boy and Girl Should Know. New York, Brentano's, 1927.
Motherhood in Bondage. N.p., 1928.

Autobiography

My Fight for Birth Control. New York, Farrar & Rinehart, 1931; London, Faber & Faber, 1932.
Margaret Sanger: An Autobiography. New York, Norton, 1938; London, Gollancz, 1939.

*

Bibliography: *Margaret Sanger and the Birth Control Movement: A Bibliography, 1911-1984* by Gloria Moore, Metuchen, New Jersey, Scarecrow Press, 1986.

Critical Studies: *Margaret Sanger: Rebel with a Cause* by Virginia Cigney, Garden City, New York, Doubleday, 1969; *Woman of Valor: Margaret Sanger and the Birth Control Movement in America* by Ellen Chesler, New York, Simon & Schuster, 1992; *The Importance of Margaret Sanger* by Deborah Bachrach, San Diego, California, Lucent Books, 1993.

* * *

Margaret Higgins Sanger was born in 1879 in Corning, New York, the sixth of 11 children. She became her mother's helper and even aided at several of her mother's deliveries. The typical child born to Anne and Michael Higgins was large—14 pounds was not unusual—and in an age when women bore children at home, Peggy, as Sanger was called, assisted at some of the difficult deliveries. She blamed her mother's death in 1896 on frequent and difficult childbearing; indeed the tragic event turned Sanger's attention to women's health and medicine. These interests and personal circumstances no doubt were an impetus toward her future work in birth control (a label she credits herself with originating) and family limitation. She was, she always pointed out, interested in informing and helping women at improving their own health by limiting their pregnancies.

Sanger completed nursing training at White Plains Hospital and also studied at the Manhattan Eye and Ear Clinic in New York City. Six years after her mother's death, she began to see a common pattern more clearly; as a nurse called out on night cases and maternity work, she saw the sickness, poverty, and waste of life for women who had too many children. She felt helpless and was torn by women's pleas for "the secret" that richer women seemed to have that helped them limit family size.

Sanger knew no secrets and when she explained what she did know—that devices or techniques to prohibit pregnancy depended on the husband—she learned that reliance on men to practice any kind of protection was considered foolish by these poor women. They a device or method they themselves could use to protect themselves from pregnancy.

In 1902, as she was finishing her final work at Manhattan Eye and Ear Hospital, Sanger met architect William Sanger. Eight years her senior and already making a good living, he eventually insisted that they marry; in letters to her sisters Sanger herself described the event as unplanned and coercive. About six months later she became pregnant, a development that brought back tubercular symptoms she had been fighting for some time.

In her autobiography Sanger described life downtown during the early years of their marriage as radical and "an interesting phase ... a religion without a name was spreading over the country. The converts were liberals, Socialists, anarchists, revolutionists of all shades," she would write two decades later. The list of the Sanger's friends included Bill Haywood, Will Durant, Emma Goldman, Mabel Dodge, Jack Reed, Elizabeth Gurley Flynn, and Walter Lippman. She wrote that her belief in socialism and activism in the early labor movement was important, but the whole question of strikes for higher wages was based on a man's economic support of his family, and "this was a shallow principle upon which to found a new civilization."

About labor activities, Sanger noted: "I was enough of a Feminist to resent the fact that woman and her requirements were not being taken into account in reconstructing this new world about which all were talking." Life and the quality of life itself were to be the center of her future social activities. Appropriately enough, her biography was dedicated "to all the pioneers of new and better worlds to come."

Sanger's focus was becoming clearer and in 1912, she gave up nursing as a career. She wrote that human growth potentialities must include consideration of women. As her activities had led her into Lower East Side apartments, she had encountered desperate lives: her patients' financial circumstances and the birth of unplanned, unwanted children compounded the problems. She contributed articles on health to a socialist organ, *The Call;* these were later collected into two volumes: *What Every Girl Should Know* (1916) and *What Every Mother Should Know* (1917). What women were seeking was self-protection, because women could not rely on their husbands to assume the burden of protection.

While she worked with the laboring classes, Sanger became increasingly aware of the problems of truly desperate people. No labor union, church or public group reached them; women faced recurrent nightmares of babies born dead, children sick, a situation Sanger called "destitution linked with excessive childbearing."The way of life for these women seemed utterly senseless, she said: these wretched women were destined to be "thrown on the scrap heap" before they were 35. She watched woman after woman die through what she believed to be senseless waste. Those not destroyed by childbearing itself were frequently the victim of unsanitary trial abortions, often self-administered.

In 1913 the Sanger family—by now with three children—traveled to Europe, particularly to countries and communities known for their small families. William's goal was the art colonies of France; Margaret's encounters with helpless women—and her own recurrent illness, no doubt—had finally resulted in a personal crusade to do something, to see what she could learn from countries where family birth limitation was practiced. Their first stop was Scotland, because she had learned that in Glasgow the socialist government supported the need to limit family size. What she discovered, she said, was two Glasgows, one meeting the hopes of those promoting socialism as an answer and one on the fringes where pitiful women overburdened with children lived with unemployed husbands in the worst kind of circumstances.

In 1914 Sanger returned to the United States and started a society called the National Birth Control League. She also began to publish the *Woman Rebel,* an organ that would bring her into direct confrontation with the Anthony Comstock obscenity legislation. She was indicted for sending an obscene publication through the mails and fled to Canada, then to Europe, right before her trial. Her study of birth control continued and in 1915 she returned to face her legal opponents. The indictment was dropped, finally, as a result of widespread sympathy for Sanger and her work.

In 1916 she began a three-month lecture tour focusing on circumstances when birth control should be practiced: when either had a transmissible disease; when wife had heart, lungs, or kidney trouble; when parents had had subnormal children; when prospective parents are adolescent; when earnings of family inadequate; if two or three years since last birth had not passed. Her seventh suggestion was that young couples should wait for at least a year before having children. Sanger's complaint that the rich had benefits of birth control but were unwilling to endorse it for others was another subject for her from behind the rostrum.

The next year she was sent to a workhouse for 30 days. She had been charged with creating a public nuisance: the nation's first birth control clinic in the Brownsville district of Brooklyn. Physically, the trip to the workhouse was devastating, but Sanger's appeal led to a favorable ruling granting doctors the right to give advice about birth control. This was in 1917; it would be 1936 before the medical community could import and prescribe contraceptive devices.

In 1928 Sanger published her fifth book, *Motherhood in Bondage.* An organized compilation of representative letters from women pleading for information about birth control, the volume provided letters from children as well as women and men. Their plea was similar: help us help ourselves by limiting family size and restoring health to mothers. *Motherhood in Bondage* was not just a book about women forced to continue childbearing after their health or economic status made it foolish to have more children, although the letters representing this group are especially poignant. Sanger includes many letters from young women who had been forced to take over the mothering duties when their own mothers died from problems associated with excessive childbearing. Another group of letters came from women whose husbands had been infected with venereal disease and who bore children with birth defects or mental illness. The pleas are sane and eloquent in their simplicity. So are the husbands who write asking for help to make their wives' lives easier.

In a chapter called "The Doctor Warns But Does Not Tell," Sanger concluded that doctors did not know, either, that what passed for lack of seriousness in the face of desperation is really a cover for ignorance. Doctors were blamed by some letter writers for simply saying "Don't do it," without explaining to the husband the critical nature of the problem. Again and again, doctors were blamed for being condescending and instructive without having useful information about prevention of pregnancy; letter writers ask why men are so happy-go-lucky while women are forced to suffer, over and over. The compilations of women's confusions, sicknesses, and worries are almost unbearable, readers have said. Yet Sanger saw the importance of making sure the record was there in a volume.

Several national and international organizations resulted from her work, and Sanger was involved in organizing conventions in both the United States and in Europe. Conferences were held annually in New York City from 1921 to 1925, and in Geneva in 1927. The American Birth Control League was established in 1921; Sanger would serve as its president for eight years. In 1931 she founded a new organization, the National Committee on Federal Legislation for Birth Control. In 1939 the League and the education department of the Birth Control Research Bureau combined and after 1942 would be known as Planned Parenthood Federation. Sanger was honorary chairman of the new Planned Parenthood and was elected president of the International Planned Parenthood Federation in 1953 in Bombay.

In addition to her national and international organizing for women's health and birth control information, Sanger was noted for her clear writing. Many pamphlets and books were written about the need for birth control, including *The Case for Birth Control* (1917), *Women, Morality, and Birth Control* (1922), *Woman and the New Race* (1923), *Happiness in Marriage* (1926), and *Motherhood in Bondage* (1928). Her autobiographical works, which are vague and sometimes contradictory about dates, include *My Fight for Birth Control* (1931) and *Margaret Sanger: An Autobiography* (1938). Birth control pioneer Margaret Sanger died on September 6, 1966, in Tuscon, Arizona.

—Ann Mauger Colbert

SAPPHO

Nationality: Lesbian. **Born:** Eresos, Lesbos, c. 613 B.C. **Family:** Married Cercylas; one daughter. **Career:** Exiled to Sicily as a child; spent adult life in Mytilene; teacher of music and poetry to a following of young girls. **Died:** 508 B.C.

Publications

Poetry

Sapho, translated by Reneé Vivien. Paris, Lemerre, 1909.

Sappho: The Fragments of the Lyrical Poems, edited by Edgar Lobel. Oxford, Clarendon Press, 1925.

"Sappho," in *Lyra Graeca,* translated and edited by J.M. Edmonds. Cambridge, Harvard University Press, 1934.

The Songs of Sappho in English Translation by Many Poets, illustrated by Paul McPharlin. Mount Vernon, New York, Peter Piper Press, 1942.

Sappho, translated by Mary Barnard. Berkeley, University of California Press, 1958.

Sappho, translated by Willis Barnstone. Garden City, New York, Anchor Books, 1965; revised edition, New York, Schocken Books, 1987.

The Art of Loving Women: The Poetry of Sappho, photographs by J. Frederick Smith. New York, Chelsea House, 1975.

Poems and Fragments, translated by Guy Davenport. Ann Arbor, University of Michigan Press, 1965.

Love Songs, translated by Paul Roche. New York, New American Library, 1966.

Poems, translated by Suzy Q. Groden. Indianapolis, Bobbs-Merrill, 1966.

Poems and Fragments, translated by Josephine Balmer. London, Brilliance Books, 1984; revised edition, Newcastle upon Tyne, Bloodaxe, 1992.

Sappho, a Garland, translated by Jim Powell. New York, Farrar Straus, 1993.

*

Bibliography: In *The Poems: Sappho of Lesbos* edited and translated by Terence DuQuesne, Thames, Darengo, 1989.

Critical Studies: *Sappho: 100 Lyrics* by Bliss Carmen, London, Chatto & Windus, 1910; *Sappho and Her Influence* by D.M. Robinson, n.p., 1924; *Sappho of Lesbos, Her Life and Times* by Arthur Weigall, New York, Stokes, 1932; *Sappho and Alcaeus: An Introduction to the Study of Ancient Lesbian Poetry* by Denys Page, Oxford, Clarendon Press, 1955; *Sex Variant Women in Literature* by Jeannette H. Foster, New York, Vantage Press, 1956, revised, Tallahassee, Florida, Naiad Press, 1985; *The Poetic Dialect of Sappho and Alcaeus* by Angus M. Bowie, New York, Arno Press, 1981; *Three Classical Poets: Sappho, Catullus, and Juvenal* by Richard Jenkyns, Cambridge, Harvard University Press, 1982; *Three Archaic Poets: Archilochus, Alcaeus, Sappho* by Anne Pippin Burnett, Cambridge, Harvard University Press, 1982; *The Golden Lyre: The Themes of the Greek Lyric Poets* by David A. Campbell, 1983; *The Highest Apple: Sappho and the Lesbian Poetic Tradition* by Judy Grahn, San Francisco, Spinsters Ink, 1985; *Fictions of Sappho, 1546-1937* by Joan E. DeJean, Chicago, University of Chicago Press, 1989; *Sappho's Immortal Daughters* by Margaret Williamson, Cambridge, Harvard University Press, 1995; *Sappho Is Burning* by Page duBois, Chicago, University of Chicago Press, 1996.

* * *

Born on the island of Lesbos, which lies in the Aegean Sea, over two and a half thousand years ago, it is not surprising that little information remains on the life of the poet Sappho. What is surprising is that so many of her verses have survived the passage of those years and are still read and revered today.

It is known that Sappho was the daughter of Scamandronymus and Cleis; it is believed that she had three brothers but it is not know whether they were older or younger. It is known that she came from an aristocratic background, but not known whether she was given the benefit of learning or whether her poetic vision was a gift of her muse. It is believed that she married young and bore a daughter, whom she named Cleis in honor of her own mother. Her death at her own hand because of unrequited passion for the ferryman Phaon begins to seem more the stuff of legend, as legends did build up around this immensely talented, insightful, and gifted woman.

Sappho instructed a small band of young women in the worship of Aphrodite, the Greek goddess of love and beauty. Her own "Hymn to Aphrodite," the only complete poem that remains, is wishful, asking the aid of this powerful goddess in winning the affections of a young girl whom the poet covets. Fragmented verses remain of other love-torn ruminations: the poet sees a woman she desires at the side of a handsome young man. Sappho is torn by emotion; indeed passion, jealousy, joy, and hatred are the many facets of her brilliant oeuvre. Other verses sing the praises of women with names like Anactoria, and Lydia, names that role off the tongue and resonate: indeed, through Sappho's verse the reader can envision Lydia who, like the vast moon in the night sky, far outshines the stars.

No mere singer of lovesick songs, Sappho's verse contains a level of sophistication that some critics have declared superior to her male contemporary, Alcaeus. Translated into the harsher tones of Latin, her works were used as models by Roman versifiers such as Catullus and Horace; Plato dubbed her "the tenth muse." Of the twelve thousand lines of verse that she is believed to have written, only a few hundred—mere tattered remnants—survive, discovered on fragile sheets of ancient papyrus during archeological digs in Egypt.

Living in an age of political tension, Sappho was exiled from her home several times as a young woman; why can only be conjectured. Her sophistication in the arts was perhaps a result of one of these exiles, to the cosmopolitan city of Sybaris on the island of Sicily. Back again in Mytilene, an ever-changing following of young women, who came to her for instruction in the writing of poetry, in music, and in dance—skills necessary to a Greek woman of fine breeding intent upon marrying well—kept the poet young, alive, inspired by their youth and vigor. Indeed, the issue of the poet's sexuality has been contested for centuries: whether, despite marriage and childrearing, her love for women extended beyond silken words. In *Sex Variant Women in Literature* Jeannette Foster marshals the evidence on both sides, and concludes that conjecture "proves little save the impossibility of objective judgement.... we may leave it that Sappho was ... what modern authorities term bisexual. She experienced marriage and motherhood, and may even have enjoyed other heterosexual relationships, but passion for her own sex inspired most of her poems, to judge from the surviving fragments."

The "sapphic" form, derived from her works, consists of four-line stanza; the first three lines follow the pattern (¯˘/¯¯/¯˘˘/¯˘/¯¯) while the fourth line, shorter in length, finishes each stanza with (¯˘˘/¯˘). Difficult to reproduce in English given the natural stresses of the spoken language, it was nonetheless attempted by adventurous poets during the Victorian era.

—Lynn MacGregor

SAPPHO. *See* **ROBINSON, Mary (Darby).**

SARTON, (Eleanor) May

Nationality: American. **Born:** Wondelgem, Belgium, 3 May 1912; daughter of science historian George Sarton; brought to the United States in 1916; became citizen, 1924. **Education:** The Institut Belge de Culture Française, Brussels, 1924-25; attended Shady Hill School and the High and Latin School, both in Cambridge, Massachusetts. **Career:** Apprentice, then member and director of the Apprentice Group, Eva Le Gallienne's Civic Repertory Theatre, New York, 1930-33; founder and director, Apprentice Theatre, New York, and Associated Actors Inc., Hartford, Connecticut, 1933-36; teacher of creative writing and choral speech, Stuart School, Boston, 1937-40; documentary scriptwriter, Office of War Information, 1944-45; poet-in-residence, Southern Illinois University, Carbondale, 1946; Briggs-Copeland Instructor in English composition, Harvard University, Cambridge, Massachusetts, 1950-53; lecturer, Bread Loaf Writers Conference, Middlebury, Vermont, 1951, 1953, Boulder Writers Conference, Colorado, 1955, 1956, and Radcliffe College, Cambridge, Massachusetts, 1956-58; Phi Beta Kappa Visiting Scholar, 1959-60; Danforth Lecturer, 1960-61; lecturer in creative writing, Wellesley College, Massachusetts, 1960-64; poet-in-residence, Lindenwood College, St. Charles, Missouri, 1964, 1965; visiting lecturer, Agnes Scott College, Decatur, Georgia, 1972. **Awards:** New England Poetry Club Golden Rose, 1945; Bland Memorial prize, 1945 (*Poetry,* Chicago); American Poetry Society Reynolds prize, 1953; Bryn Mawr College Lucy Martin Donnelly fellowship, 1953; Guggenheim fellowship, 1954; Johns Hopkins University Poetry Festival award, 1961; National Endowment for the Arts grant, 1967; Sarah Josepha Hale award, 1972; College of St. Catherine Alexandrine medal, 1975; Before Columbus Foundation award for prose, 1985. Litt.D.: Russell Sage College, Troy, New York, 1959; New England College, Henniker, New Hampshire, 1971; Clark University, Worcester, Massachusetts, 1975; Bates College, Lewiston, Maine, 1976; Colby College, Waterville, Maine, 1976; University of New Hampshire, Durham, 1976; King School of the Ministry, Berkeley, California, 1976; Nasson College, Springvale, Maine, 1980; University of Maine, Orono, 1981; Bowdoin College, Brunswick, Maine, 1983; Union College, Schenectady, New York, 1984; Bucknell University, Lewisburg, Pennsylvania, 1985; Rhode Island College, Providence, 1989; Centenary College, Hackettstown, New Jersey, 1990. **Member:** American Academy of Arts and Sciences (fellow). **Died:** 16 July 1995.

Publications

Novels

The Single Hound. Boston, Houghton Mifflin, and London, Cresset Press, 1938.

The Bridge of Years. New York, Doubleday, 1946.

Shadow of a Man. New York, Rinehart, 1950; London, Cresset Press, 1952.

A Shower of Summer Days. New York, Rinehart, 1952; London, Hutchinson, 1954.

Faithful Are the Wounds. New York, Rinehart, and London, Gollancz, 1955.

The Birth of a Grandfather. New York, Rinehart, 1957; London, Gollancz, 1958.

The Small Room. New York, Norton, 1961; London, Gollancz, 1962.

Joanna and Ulysses. New York, Norton, 1963; London, Murray, 1964.

Mrs. Stevens Hears the Mermaids Singing. New York, Norton, 1965; London, Owen, 1966.

Miss Pickthorn and Mr. Hare: A Fable. New York, Norton, 1966; London, Dent, 1968.
The Poet and the Donkey. New York, Norton, 1969.
Kinds of Love. New York, Norton, 1970; London, Norton, 1980.
As We Are Now. New York, Norton, 1973; London, Gollancz, 1974.
Crucial Conversations. New York, Norton, 1975; London, Gollancz, 1976.
A Reckoning. New York, Norton, 1978; London, Gollancz, 1980.
Anger. New York, Norton, 1982.
The Magnificent Spinster. New York, Norton, 1985; London, Women's Press, 1986.
The Education of Harriet Hatfield. New York, Norton, 1989; London, Women's Press, 1990.

Uncollected Short Stories

"Old-Fashioned Snow," in *Collier's* (Springfield, Ohio), 23 March 1946.
"The Return of Corporal Greene," in *American Mercury* (New York), June 1946.
"The Contest Winner," in *Liberty* (New York), 10 August 1946.
"Mrs. Christiansen's Harvest," in *Ladies Home Journal* (New York), March 1947.
"The Town Will Talk," in *Ladies Home Journal* (New York), June 1947.
"The Miracle in the Museum," in *Church and Home* (London), March 1948.
"The Paris Hat," in *Cosmopolitan* (New York), March 1948.
"Mr. Pomeroy's Battle," in *Better Homes and Gardens* (Des Moines, Iowa), November 1948.
"If This Isn't Love," in *Woman's Home Companion* (Springfield, Ohio), April 1949.
"The Little Purse," in *Redbook* (New York), June 1949.
"Alyosha and His Horse," in *World Review* (London), September 1949-February 1950.
"The Last Gardener," in *Woman's Day* (New York), April 1953.
"The Screen," in *Harper's Bazaar* (New York), October 1953.
"Aunt Emily and Me," in *Woman's Day* (New York), April 1960.

Plays

The Underground River. New York, Play Club, 1947.

Screenplays (documentaries): *Valley of the Tennessee,* 1945; *A Better Tomorrow,* with Irving Jacoby, 1945; *The Hymn of the Nation,* 1946.

Poetry

Encounter in April. Boston, Houghton Mifflin, 1937.
Inner Landscape. Boston, Houghton Mifflin, 1939; with a selection from *Encounter in April,* London, Cresset Press, 1939.
The Lion and the Rose. New York, Rinehart, 1948.
The Leaves of the Tree. Mount Vernon, Iowa, Cornell College, 1950.
Land of Silence and Other Poems. New York, Rinehart, 1953.
In Time like Air. New York, Rinehart, 1957.
Cloud, Stone, Sun, Vine: Poems, Selected and New. New York, Norton, 1961.
A Private Mythology: New Poems. New York, Norton, 1966.
As Does New Hampshire and Other Poems. Peterborough, New Hampshire, Richard R. Smith, 1967.
A Grain of Mustard Seed: New Poems. New York, Norton, 1971.
A Durable Fire: New Poems. New York, Norton, 1972.
Collected Poems 1930-1973. New York, Norton, 1974.
Selected Poems, edited by Serena Sue Hilsinger and Lois Brynes. New York, Norton, 1978.
Halfway to Silence: New Poems. New York, Norton, 1980; London, Women's Press, 1993.
A Winter Garland. Concord, New Hampshire, Ewert, 1982.
Letters from Maine: New Poems. New York, Norton, 1984.
The Phoenix Again: New Poems. Concord, New Hampshire, Ewert, 1987.
The Silence Now: New and Uncollected Earlier Poems. New York, Norton, 1988.
Collected Poems, 1930-1993. New York, Norton, 1993.
Coming into Eighty: New Poems. New York, Norton, 1994; London, Norton, 1995; as *Coming into Eighty: And Earlier Poems.* London, Women's Press, 1995.

Autobiography

In Memoriam. Brussels, Godenne, 1957.
I Knew a Phoenix: Sketches for an Autobiography. New York, Holt Rinehart, 1959; London, Owen, 1963.
Plant Dreaming Deep. New York, Norton, 1968.
Journal of a Solitude. New York, Norton, 1973; London, Women's Press, 1985.
The House by the Sea: A Journal. New York, Norton, 1977; London, Prior, 1978.
Recovering: A Journal 1978-1979. New York, Norton, 1980.
At Seventy: A Journal. New York, Norton, 1984; London, Norton, 1987.
After the Stroke: A Journal. New York, Norton, and London, Women's Press, 1988.
Endgame: A Journal of the Seventy-ninth Year. New York, Norton, 1992; London, Women's Press, 1993.
Encore: A Journal of the Eightieth Year. New York, Norton, and London, Women's Press, 1993.
At Eighty-two: A Journal. New York, Norton, 1995.

For Children

The Fur Person: The Story of a Cat. New York, Rinehart, 1957; London, Muller, 1958.
Punch's Secret. New York, Harper, 1974.
A Walk through the Woods. New York, Harper, 1976.

Other

A World of Light: Portraits and Celebrations. New York, Norton, 1976.
Writings on Writing. Orono, Maine, Puckerbrush Press, 1980.
A Self-Portrait (includes verse), edited by Marita Simpson and Martha Wheelock. New York, Norton, 1986.
Honey in the Hive: Judith Matlack 1898-1982. Boston, Warren, 1988.
Sarton Selected: An Anthology of Novels, Journals, and Poetry, edited by Bradford Dudley Daziel. New York, Norton, 1991.
May Sarton: Among the Usual Days: A Portrait: Unpublished Poems, Letters, Journals, and Photographs, selected and edited by Susan Sherman. New York, Norton, 1993.
From May Sarton's Well: Writings of May Sarton, selected and illustrated by Edith Royce Schade. Watsonville, California, Papier-Mache Press, 1994.

Editor, *Letters to May.* Orono, Maine, Puckerbrush Press, 1986.

Recording: *My Sisters, O My Sisters,* Watershed, 1984.

*

Media Adaptation: *World of Light: A Portrait of May Sarton* (film), 1979.

Bibliography: *May Sarton: A Bibliography* by Lenora P. Blouin, Metuchen, New Jersey, Scarecrow Press, 1978.

Manuscript Collections: Berg Collection, New York Public Library; Houghton Library, Harvard University, Cambridge, Massachusetts; Amherst College, Massachusetts (letters); Westbrook College, Maine.

Critical Studies: *May Sarton* by Agnes Sibley, New York, Twayne, 1972; *May Sarton: Woman and Poet* edited by Constance Hunting, Orono, Maine, National Poetry Foundation, 1982; *World of Light: A Portrait of May Sarton,* New York, Two Lip Art, 1982; interview with Karen Saum, in *Paris Review,* October 1983; *Writing a Woman's Life* by Carolyn Heilbrun, New York, Norton, 1988, London, Women's Press, 1989; *May Sarton Revisited* by Elizabeth Evans, Boston, Twayne, 1989; *That Great Sanity: Critical Essays on May Sarton* edited by Susan Swartzlander and Marilyn R. Mumford, Ann Arbor, University of Michigan Press, 1992; *Celebration....* edited by Constance Hunting, [Maine], Westbrook College Press, 1993; *A House of Gathering: Poets on May Sarton's Poetry*, edited by Marilyn Kallet, Knoxville, University of Tennessee Press, 1993.

* * *

The astonishing thing about May Sarton is that she was not an academic.

She might so easily have become one of those writers who fall easily into lecture schedules, who lend themselves to outlining, whose work is read under compulsion in the pursuit of a degree and then laid aside forever. Her father was George Sarton, the foremost authority on the history of science. He dedicated his life to organizing and recording a vast body of information of interest mainly to scholars; he pursued that aim through everything, including poverty and exile. There was always a universe in the picture. If May had been an average daughter she would either have followed her father's pattern or rejected it consciously.

But May—born Eleanor Marie in 1912, in Wondelgem, Belgium—had a mother who lived a rich emotional life even while she subordinated herself to her husband's exacting schedule. Mabel Elwes had no schooling to speak of, but channelled her rich creativity into a variety of patterns. In Belgium, where she became a member of the *Flinken*—intellectual hippies—she designed beautiful and original furniture. In the United States, without commercial outlet, she worked with fabrics. She made an art of friendship, as her daughter was later to do.

The interweaving of these two rich personalities, acted upon by the happenings of a diverse life, made May into a poet of unusual sensitivity and accuracy. We have no word in English which corresponds to the German *Dichter*—a poet whose prose writings are of the highest quality. May Sarton, poet, novelist, biographer, essayist, was a *Dichter.*

At 17, she decided that she was destined for the stage, and refused to go to college. Her disparate parents not only agreed to this, but scrimped money from their small resources to support her until she could make a start. She went to Parie (obligatory for creative young artists in the Twenties and early Thirties) and then joined Eva La Gallienne's brilliant repertory group. One wonders what would have happened to May if that group had not broken up.

It took her a long time to realize that she was a writer before all else, a longer time to find her readership: publishers, librarians, and college professors like books that are easily classified. How would you categorize *The Single Hound?* Fiction? Biography? A treatise on education? The people who discovered that book knew it to be one of a kind. They became the core of a steadily growing readership, but it was a slow process.

She did some lecturing, some teaching, was eventually poet-in-residence on a few hospitable campuses, an unexpected achievement for a women with no letters after her name. (The letters were to come, a shining array of honorary degrees.) Sarton was into middle age before she was able to earn a living by writing. She wrote potboilers for the women's magazines in hopes that those would be collected and republished (Where are the women who collected *Alternative Alcott?*).

Poetry, of course, never pays. T. S. Eliot was a bank clerk, Hawthorne checked invoices in a customs house. Amy Lowell, independently wealthy, magicked herself into a hundred differently accented voices and so won readers. Sarton's poems are distilled from her own thoughts and emotions, and that there have been so many of them, and that they have found so many readers testifies to the universality of her inner experiences.

Biography is another matter. The journals, finely polished as they are, have to be read as factual—not merely factual, but as fact illuminated by context. And her novels, no two alike, although certain themes run through them, are histories of living persons conceived in her mind and transmitted to paper with great honesty and credibility. If she had done nothing more than create the characters of *Kinds of Love*, she would have a lasting place in literature.

Like her mother, she opened her arms to life and to living people. The range of her friendships includes the Huxleys, Elizabeth Bowen, S. S. Koteliansky (but then "Kot" related to everyone, from babies to sages.) It also included farmers, children, nuns, teachers, the man who did her chores. She kept her friends. More, she shared all of her resources with them, whether she was writing advice to a young poet, going to law to rescue an elderly friend from a dreadful nursing home, or having electricity installed in the home of a hard-pressed village family. She was limited as to money, time, energy, but she shared what she had. And even in the grasp of pain and despair she loved flowers, animals, good food, the changes of the weather, and the books that crossed her desk.

In her late years she found some of the privacy for which she had longed, but she was never isolated. She handled her choices and conflicts judiciously. She lived a lesbian life quietly, until the death of her parents set her free to make a statement, and then she chose to make it in the form of fiction. *Mrs. Stevens Hears the Mermaids Singing* examines many aspects of sexuality, and together with *The Education of Harriet Hatfield* has probably done more for gay rights than all the parades and picket lines.

One of the most poignant messages in the journals is her description of her longtime lovers' final collapse after the gradual breakdown of old age. There is no self pity in it and I doubt that there was any in her dying. Judy no longer knew her, no longer knew anything—that is what happens to people.

Her last years were harassed by ill health. She underwent surgery for cancer, had a stroke which for a while made it impossible to put words together—the ultimate hell for a writer—suffered greatly from colitis, no easy ailment for an epicure to put up with. Old friends died or moved away; those who remained were precious to her. Until her last breath she remained part of the great ongoing stream of human life.

Her work has already become part of the great treasure of human experience. It will last, probably, as long as there are books—or films or whatever alternate media are developed. She sets up a relationship with every reader, and that will last as long as words are used to convey a sense of life.

—Valerie Taylor

SATOKO, Tsushima. *See* **TSUSHIMA, Y ko.**

SCHREINER, Olive (Emilie Albertina)

Pseudonym: Ralph Iron. **Nationality:** South African. **Born:** Wittenbergen Mission Station, Cape of Good Hope, 24 March 1855. **Education:** Self-educated. **Family:** Married Samuel C. Cronwright in 1894. **Career:** Governess to Boer family near Karoo desert, 1874; moved to England, 1881; coorganizer, Men's and Women's Club, London; returned to South Africa, 1889; involved in pacifist work in England, 1912-19. **Died:** 11 December 1920 at Wynberg, Cape Colony; buried at Buffels Kop in the Karoo, next to her infant daughter, husband, and dog.

PUBLICATIONS

Novels

The Story of an African Farm (as Ralph Iron). London, Chapman & Hall, 1883; Boston, Roberts Bros., 1888; with an introduction by Isak Dinesen, Limited Editions Club, 1961.

Trooper Peter Halket of Mashonaland. London, T.F. Unwin, and Boston, Roberts Bros., 1897.

From Man to Man; or Perhaps only.... London, T.F. Unwin, 1926; New York and London, Harper, 1927.

Undine. New York and London, Harper, 1928.

Short Stories

Dreams. 1890; Boston, Roberts Bros., 1891; as *So Here Then Are Dreams,* East Aurora, New York, Roycroft Shop, 1901; expanded as *The Lost Joy and Other Dreams,* Portland, Maine, T.B. Mosher, 1909.

Dream Life and Real Life: A Little African Story. Boston, Roberts Bros., 1893.

Stories, Dreams and Allegories. New York, F. Stokes, 1923.

The Woman's Rose: Stories and Allegories, edited by Cherry Clayton. Johannesburg, Ad Donker, 1986.

Political/Social Theory

The Political Situation [in Cape Colony], with Samuel Cronwright. London, T. F. Unwin, 1896.

The South African Question; by an English South African. Cape Town, South African Newspaper Company, and Chicago, C.H. Sergel, 1899.

An English-South African's View of the Situation: Words in Season. London, Hodder & Stoughton, 1899.

Closer Union: A Letter on the South African Union and the Principles of Government. Cape Town, Constitutional Reform Association, 1908; London, A. C. Fifield, 1909.

Women and Labour. London, T. F. Unwin, and New York, F. Stokes, 1911; selections published as *Women and War,* New York, F. Stokes, 1914.

Thoughts on South Africa. London, T. F. Unwin, 1923.

Other

The Letters of Olive Schreiner, 1876-1920, edited by Samuel Cronwright-Schreiner. London, T. Fisher Unwin, and Boston, Little, Brown, 1924.

The Silver Plume: A Selection from the Writings of Olive Schreiner, edited by Neville Nuttall. Johannesburg, n.p., 1957.

Olive Schreiner: A Selection, edited by Uys Krige. Cape Town and London, Oxford University Press, 1968.

A Track to the Water's Edge: The Olive Schreiner Reader, edited by Howard Thurman. New York, Harper, 1973.

An Olive Schreiner Reader: Writings on Women and South Africa, edited by Carol Barash, afterword by Nadine Gordimer. London, Pandora, 1987.

Olive Schreiner: Letters, edited by Richard M. Rive. New York, Oxford University Press, 1988.

"My Other Self": The Letters of Olive Schreiner and Havelock Ellis, 1884-1920, edited by Yaffa Claire Draznin. New York, P. Lang, 1992.

*

Media Adaptations: *Story of an African Farm* (play), by Merdon Hodge, 1939; *Schreiner: A One-Woman Play,* by Stephen Gray, Cape Town and London, David Philip, 1983.

Bibliography: *Olive Emilie Albertina Schreiner, 1855-1920* by Evelyn Verster, Cape Town, University of Cape Town Libraries, 1946; *Olive Schreiner, 1920-1971: A Bibliography* by Roslyn Davis, Johannesburg, University of the Witwatersrand, Department of Bibliography, Librarianship and Typography, 1972.

Manuscript Collections: Sheffield City Library, Archives Division; Department of Historical Papers, University of the Witwatersrand Library, Johannesburg; Humanities Research Center, University of Texas at Austin; Thomas Pringle Collection for English in Africa, Rhodes University Library, Grahamstown; Olive Schreiner collection, J. W. Jagger Library, University of Cape Town Libraries.

Critical Studies: *The Life of Olive Schreiner* by Samuel C. Cronwright-Schreiner, London, Unwin, 1924; *Not without Honor: The Life and Writings of Olive Schreiner* by Vera Buchanan-Gould, New York, Hutchinson, 1948; *Olive Schreiner: A Study in Latent Meanings*, by Marion V. Friedmann, Johannesburg, Witwatersrand University Press, 1955; *Olive Schreiner: Portrait of a South African Woman* by Johannes Meintjes, Johannesburg, H. Keartland, 1965; *Until the Heart Changes: A Garland for Olive Schreiner* by Zelda Friedlander, Capetown, Tafelberg-Uitgewers, 1967; *Olive Schreiner: Feminist on the Frontier* by Joyce Avrech Berkman, St. Albans, Vermont, Eden Press, 1979; *Olive Schreiner: A Biography* by Ruth First and Ann Scott, New York, Schocken, 1980; *Olive Schreiner* edited by Cherry Clayton, Johannesburg, McGraw-Hill, 1983; *Olive Schreiner and After* edited by Malvern Van Wyke Smith and Don Maclennan, Cape Town, D. Philip, 1983; *The Healing Imagination of Olive Schreiner* by Berkman, Amherst, University of Massachusetts Press, 1989; *Olive Schreiner's Fiction: Landscape and Power* by Gerald Monsman, New Brunswick, New Jersey, Rutgers University Press, 1991; *Fictions of the Female Self: Charlotte Brontë, Olive Schreiner, Katherine Mansfield* by Rugh Parkin-Gounelas, New York, St. Martin's Press, 1991; *The Flawed Diamond: Essays on Olive Schreiner* edited by Itala Vivan, Sydney, New South Wales, Kangaroo Press, 1991; *Difficult Women, Artful Lives: Olive Schreiner and Isak Dinesen, in and out of Africa* by Susan R. Horton, Baltimore, Johns Hopkins University Press, 1995.

* * *

Writer and feminist Olive Schreiner had little regard for prevailing fashions. With her marked disdain for hats, gloves, and restraining undergarments, Schreiner endured the constant disapproval of those who adhered to the rigid code of Victorian decorum. Her apparent disregard for appearances and adoption of the New Woman's reformed dress stemmed from more than a desire for comfort in her native South African climate: it was a deliberate statement on the severely limited boundaries of the woman's sphere. By emphasizing her "strong square figure" in shapeless suits, Schreiner physically asserted the feminist beliefs that formed the basis of her writing.

Olive Emilie Albertina Schreiner was born on 24 March 1855 at a remote Wesleyan mission station, Wittebergen, on the border of Basutoland in Cape Colony, South Africa. The ninth of Gottlieb and Rebecca Lyndall Schreiner's dozen children, Olive was one the seven who survived to adulthood. To supplement his meager salary, her father resorted to private trading, a violation for which he was expelled from the London Missionary Society. Financially unable to provide for his family, Gottlieb Schreiner sent his two youngest children, 11-year-old Olive and her nine-year-old brother Will, to live with their older brother Theo, a school headmaster in Cradock. With her family dispersed, Olive boarded with relatives and friends until 1874, when she began to work as a governess for up-country Boer farming families.

Self-educated and well read, Schreiner took five teaching posts in the Cape Colony over the next seven years. She began writing fiction and saving her wages for a trip abroad, hoping to find a publisher and study medicine. In 1881, at the age of 26, Schreiner travelled to London with three manuscripts, including one she had called *Thorn Kloof* and then *Lyndall* before finally deciding on its title: *The Story of an African Farm.* Writer George Meredith, a reader for the publisher Chapman & Hall, recommended its publication. The novel appeared amid acclaim in January 1883 under the pseudonym Ralph Iron; critics soon charged that the best-selling work had been penned by a woman, making the ideas it espoused all the more controversial.

Set in the landscape of Schreiner's childhood, *The Story of An African Farm* recounts the tale of two orphaned cousins, one a domestic, unimaginative sort, the other the most outspoken feminist to appear until then in British fiction. Lyndall, who becomes pregnant by a lover she refuses to marry, rages against the way "the world makes men and women" out of the "little plastic beings" born into it. "To you," she explains to a man, "it says—*Work!* and to us it says—*Seem!*" In Lyndall, Schreiner had created a New Woman who shocked Victorian readers with her assertions and arguments. "Do you think," she asked, "if Napoleon had been born a woman that he would have been contented to give small tea-parties and talk small scandal?" While Lyndall paid the price for her actions (following her illegitimate infant in death), she nevertheless parted from life with a defiant promise that the world was changing and that "in the future ... perhaps, to be born a woman will not be to be born branded."

Prevented from studying medicine by worsening asthma, Schreiner forged a career as a polemical writer, moving in progressive political and literary circles, planning an edition of Mary Wollstonecraft's *A Vindication of the Rights of Woman*, and agitating for suffrage. Despite her upbringing by missionary parents, she gradually repudiated their traditional religious and social beliefs and formed friendships with free-thinkers like Havelock Ellis, Eleanor Marx, and Karl Pearson.

In 1889 Schreiner returned to South Africa and, five years later, married farmer-politician Samuel C. Cronwright. Defying tradition, she retained her maiden name, while he hyphenated his to Cronwright-Schreiner. Their marriage was intermittently happy, marked by frequent and lengthy separations and marred by the death of their only child soon after her birth in 1895. In 1914 Schreiner again travelled to England, remaining there until just prior to her death; she would die in South Africa in 1920.

Schreiner's other novels, *From Man to Man* (1927) and *Undine* (1929), both had feminist themes and appeared posthumously. During her life she published collections of allegories and stories, articles on South African politics, and her most influential writing on women's lives, *Woman and Labor* (1911). Culling evidence from the animal world and women's history, Schreiner argued that the roles played by men and women were "neither universal nor innate." In the future, she maintained, both sexes would shed outer pretenses and emerge as equal "comrades and co-workers." As a result Schreiner rejected the prevailing Victorian doctrine of separate spheres for the sexes and emerged as an advocate of egalitarian cooperation.

An unconventional woman, Schreiner was a pioneer in her treatment and depiction of women and in her vivid portrayal and use of the African landscape. As a novelist, short-story writer, and political essayist, she was both acclaimed and derided during her lifetime for her pioneering views on the role of women, her rejection of Christian convention, her anti-imperialist stance, and her pacifism during World War I. Schreiner was admired by many for the "bold out-speaking" and "irreligious standpoint" of her work. In a society oriented to a fixed social and political hierarchy, however, she was by and large "a lonely rebel," often unwell, and frequently short of funds. Schreiner feared at times that she was "only a broken and untried possibility" as a writer; citing her literary gifts, her unfinished works, and her difficult private life, fellow writer and feminist Virginia Woolf dubbed her "a diamond marred by a flaw."

Throughout her life, Olive Schreiner worked in spite of ill health and self-doubt to expose and remedy what she called "the desolating *emptiness* and *barrenness* of the majority of middle-class women's lives," paving the way for feminists who followed. Like her heroine in *The Story of An African Farm*, she argued that "the world will never come right, till ... the female element of the race makes its influence felt."

—Jennifer Davis McDaid

SCHÜSSLER FIORENZA, Elisabeth

Nationality: German. **Born:** Tschandad, 17 April 1938; immigrated to the United States in 1970. **Education:** University of Würtzurg, M.Div. 1962, Lic Theol. 1963; University of Münster, Dr.Theol. 1970. **Family:** Married Francis Schüssler Fiorenza in 1967; one daughter. **Career:** Assistant professor, 1970-75, associate professor, 1975-80, professor of theology, 1980-1984, University of Notre Dame, Notre Dame, Indiana; Krister Stendahl Professor of Divinity, Harvard Divinity School, beginning 1984. Harry Emerson Fosdick visiting professor, Union Theological Seminary, New York City, 1974-75. Founder and coeditor, *Journal of Feminist Studies in Religion;* editor, *Religious Studies News* and *Concilium;* contributor to periodicals, including *Concilium, Cross Currents,* and *Horizons.* **Member:** Catholic Biblical Association, Society of Biblical Literature (first woman president), Studiorum Novi Testamenti Societas, American Academy of Religion, College Theology Society. **Address:** Department of Religion, Harvard Divinity School, 45 Francis Ave., Cambridge, Massachusetts 02138-1994, U.S.A.

PUBLICATIONS

Religion/Spirituality

Der vergessene Partner: grundlagen, tatsachen, und möglichkeiten der mitarbeit der frau in der Kirche [The Forgotten Partner: Foundations, Facts, and Possibilities for the Participation of Women in the Church]. Patmos, 1964.

Priester für Gott: studien zum herrschafts—und priestermotiv in der Apokalypse [Priests for God]. Münster, Aschendorff, 1972.

The Apocalypse. Chicago, Franciscan Herald, 1976.

Invitation to the Book of Revelation: A Commentary on the Apocalypse with Complete Text from the Jerusalem Bible. Garden City, New York, Doubleday, 1981; revised as *Revelation: Vision of a Just World,* Minneapolis, Fortress Press, 1991; Edinburgh, T. & T. Clark, 1993.

In Memory of Her: A Feminist Theological Reconstruction of Christian Origins. New York, Crossroad, and London, SCM Press, 1983.

Bread Not Stone: The Challenge of Feminist Biblical Interpretation. Boston, Beacon Press, 1984; Edinburgh, T. & T. Clark, 1990; revised edition, 1995.

The Book of Revelation: Justice and Judgment. Philadelphia, Fortress Press, 1985.

Theological Criteria and Historical Reconstruction: Martha and Mary: Luke 10:38-42, edited by Herman Wätjen. Berkeley, Center for Hermeneutical Studies in Hellenistic and Modern Culture, 1987.

But She Said: Feminist Practices of Biblical Interpretation. Boston, Beacon Press, 1992.

Discipleship of Equals: A Critical Feminist ekkl sia-*ology of Liberation.* New York, Crossroad, and London, SCM Press, 1993.

Jesus: Miriam's Child, Sophia's Prophet: Critical Issues in Feminist Christology. New York, Continuum, 1994; London, SCM Press, 1995.

Searching the Scriptures, with Shelly Matthews. New York, Crossroad, 2 vols., 1993-94; London, SCM Press, 1994-95.

Other

Lent, with Urban T. Holmes (sermons and studies). Philadelphia, Fortress Press, 1981.

Editor, *Aspects of Religious Propaganda in Judaism and Early Christianity.* Notre Dame, Indiana, University of Notre Dame Press, 1976.

Editor, with David Tracy, *The Holocaust as Interruption.* Edinburgh, T. & T. Clark, 1984.

Editor, with Mary Collins, *Women: Invisible in Church and Theology.* Edinburgh, T. & T. Clark, 1985.

Editor, with Anne Carr, *Women, Work, and Poverty.* Edinburgh, T. & T. Clark, 1987.

Editor, with Anne Carr, *Motherhood: Experience, Institution, Theology.* Edinburgh, T. & T. Clark, 1989.

Editor, *The Special Nature of Women?* Trinity Press International, 1991.

Editor, with M. Shawn Copeland, *Violence against Women.* London, SCM Press, and Maryknoll, New York, Orbis, 1994.

Editor, with M. Shawn Copeland, *Feminist Theology in Different Context.* London, SCM Press, and Maryknoll, New York, Orbis, 1996.

*

Critical Studies: "*Women and Early Christianity: Are the Feminist Scholars Right?* by Susanne Heine, London, SCM Press, 1987; "The Limits of the Appeal to Women's Experience" by Sheila Greeve Davaney, in *Shaping New Vision: Gender Values in American Culture,* edited by Clarissa W. Atkinson, Constance H. Buchanan and Margaret Miles, Ann Arbor, UMI Research Press, 1987; "Feminist Perspectives on Bible and Theology: An Introduction to Selected Issues and Literature" by Katherine Doob Sakenfeld, in *Interpretations,* 42(1), January 1988; "Rereading, Reconceiving and Reconstructing Traditions: Feminist Research in Religion" by June O'Connor, in *Women's Studies,* 17(112), 1989; "Some Feminist Methodologies" by Pamela Dickey Young, in *Feminist Theology/Christian Theology: In Search of Method,* Minneapolis, Fortress Press, 1990; *Desperately Seeking Mary: A Feminist Appropriation of a Traditional Religious Symbol* by Els Maeckelberghe, Netherlands, Pharos, 1991; "Woman, Nature and Power: Emancipatory Themes in Critical Theory and Feminist Theology" by Marsha Hewitt, in *Studies in Religion,* 20(3), 1991; Women & Children Last: A Feminist Critique of Liberation Theology" by Barbara Blakely, in *Liberation Theology and Sociopolitical Transformations,* edited by Jorge Garcia Antezana,

Burnaby, British Columbia, Simon Frazer University, 1992; "A Discipleship of Equals: Past, Present, Future" by Joann Wolski Conn, in *Horizons on Catholic Feminist Theology*, edited by Conn and Walter E. Conn, Washington, DC, Georgetown University Press, 1992; "The New Vision of Feminist Theology: Method" by Ann E. Carr, in *Freeing Theology: The Essentials of Theology in Feminist Perspective,* edited by Catherine Mowry LaCugna, San Francisco, HarperSanFrancisco, 1993; "Women and the Bible" by Cullen Murphy, in *Atlantic Monthly,* August 1993; "Constructing a Feminist Liberation Epistemology" by Mary McClintock Fulkerson, in *Changing the Subject: Women's Discourse and Feminist Theology,* Minneapolis, Fortress Press, 1994; "Foundational Hermeneutics" by Francis Martin, in *The Feminist Question: Feminist Theology in the Light of Christian Tradition,* Grand Rapids, Michigan, Eerdmans, 1994; "Memory, Revolution and Redemption: Walter Benjamin and Elisabeth Schüssler Fiorenza" by Marsha Hewitt, in *Critical Theory of Religion: A Feminist Analysis*, Minneapolis, Fortress Press, 1995.

* * *

Elisabeth Schüssler Fiorenza, Christian theologian and exegete, has spent a good portion of her academic career putting women, as subjects, back into biblical texts. When once asked how she, a feminist, could baptize her daughter into the patriarchal Catholic Church, she responded that it was her "vision of Christian lifestyle, responsibility, and community [which] brought [her] to reject the culturally imposed role of women and not vice versa." On the level of institutional commitment she explains: "Christian feminists who still identify with the Catholic tradition and remain within the institutional structures of the Church can do so because we take seriously the Church's self-understanding expressed in Vatican II."

Educated in her native Germany and with several published works on religious topics already to her credit, Schüssler Fiorenza moved to the United States in 1970 where she encountered both an active feminist movement and university theology departments that were open to women. It was at this juncture that, after joining the staff of the theology department at the University of Notre Dame, she began to do theology "as a woman for women."

In her books *In Memory of Her: A Feminist Theological Reconstruction of Christian Origins* (1983), *Bread Not Stone: The Challenge of Feminist Biblical Interpretation* (1984), and *But She Said: Feminist Practices of Biblical Interpretation* (1992), Schüssler Fiorenza articulates her method: a feminist hermeneutics of suspicion, remembrance, proclamation, and liberating vision, all of which place women at the center of the discourse. She deconstructs biblical texts, showing how these texts reflect historical and social perspectives of the time. Having contextualized biblical texts, she then challenges later interpretations of these texts on the basis of their androcentric bias. Intrinsic to her method is the belief that there is no such thing as value-neutral or objective-descriptive history: there is no "history of," only a "history for."

In her pivotal text *In Memory of Her,* Schüssler Fiorenza utilizing the phrase "the Jesus movement," which, she suggests, was an egalitarian movement, an alternative prophetic renewal movement within Israel. Using the four gospels, which she term "paradigmatic remembrances, and not comprehensive accounts of the historical Jesus," Schüssler Fiorenza places women at the center of her discourse, pointing to their activities within this new movement. Her strategy is to shift attention from male activity to female activity. According to Schüssler Fiorenza's feminist methodology, in order to determine the activities of women and other marginal groups within the New Testament one must bring to her/his analysis new kinds of questions. Questions emerging from a feminist perspective are gender reflective: Are there women in this new movement? How are they described, and by whom? When asking questions of biblical texts Schüssler Fiorenza contends that one needs to be aware that the sources are, in themselves, androcentric, if not at times misogynistic. The texts, then, are often silent about women's participation and/or prescriptive (rather than descriptive) when speaking of women.

Schüssler Fiorenza's interpretation of the story of the Syrophoenician or Canaanite woman (Mark 7: 24-30; Matt. 15: 21-28), is an excellent example of a reinterpretation of a New Testament story. In this gospel story a woman heard that Jesus was near her home. She sought him out and appealed to him that he heal her sick daughter. Jesus, however, informed her that: "It is not fair to take the children's bread and throw it to the dogs." The woman responded to Jesus by saying, "Yes Lord, yet even the dogs eat the crumbs that fall from their masters' tables" (Matt 15: 26-27). Upon her reply, Jesus relented, healed the child and commended the woman for her faith.

In Schüssler Fiorenza's interpretation, the woman is not abstracted into a figure whose gender is meaningless. She acknowledges mainstream interpretation of this story that focuses upon the inclusiveness of gentiles into the *basileia* [kingdom] of God, but she also takes up the issue of gender and suggests that this passage can be understood to reflect upon the "historical leadership women had in opening up Jesus' movement and community to the 'gentile sinner.'" She directs attention to the fact that it was a woman who became a major spokesperson for the inclusiveness of gentiles. Schüssler Fiorenza's rereading, reconceiving, and reconstructing of the texts envisions a non-patriarchal Jesus. Instead he is understood to have held an egalitarian perspective, one which was inclusive of women as full human beings. In *But She Said* the Syrophoenician woman—named Justa by Schüssler Fiorenza—is not read as a generic "he," but rather her gender is left intact and used to demonstrate a significant aspect of the story meaningful to Christian women.

When working with Christian texts, Schüssler Fiorenza does not suggest that "different retellings" of the story cancel each other out in an authoritative search for a single, "authentic" version. Instead, she intimates, "like the baptist African-American lining hymn, a rhetorical interpretation does not draw on a single melody in a linear fashion, it amplifies and deepens the individual lines of interpretation.... whereby each telling sheds a different light upon the ongoing debates and conflicts."

Schüssler Fiorenza argues that a retelling and rereading of an androcentric text is necessary when considering women as reading subjects. She points out that reading and thinking in an "androcentric symbol system entices biblical readers to align themselves and to identify with, what is culturally normative, that is, culturally male." Patricinio Schweickart, working in the area of feminist literary criticism, explains in an essay in *Speaking of Gender* that women are taught to identify with the male point of view, to read and think as men, to accept as normal and legitimate a male system of values and in so doing disempower themselves.... it draws her [the reader] into a process that uses her against herself. It solicits her complicity in the elevation of male difference into universality and, accordingly, the denigration of female difference into otherness without reciprocity." By reinterpreting and focusing on women as acting subjects within a patriarchal context in the texts of the New Testament, the Christian woman reader is no longer enticed into, and in collusion with, a patriarchal world view. She is able to challenge current interpretations—ones that exclude women as actors—and reclaim ancient stories that connect her with the past of her tradition.

Elisabeth Schüssler Fiorenza is a daughter of the second generation of Christian women seeking to reread canonical texts within the Christian tradition. Her exegetical work in early Christian origins continues to provide a system of analysis whereby Christian women can reclaim their subjectivity within the texts of Christian mytho-history.

—Darlene M. Juschka

SEMI, Allen. *See* **LARSEN, Nella.**

SEXTON, Anne (Harvey)

Nationality: American. **Born:** Newton, Massachusetts, 9 November 1924. **Education:** Attended Regis College and Fairfield College, 1971. **Family:** Married Alfred M. Sexton in 1948 (divorced 1974); two daughters. **Career:** Worked as a model in Boston; teacher, Wayland High School, Wayland, Massachusetts, 1967-68; lecturer, Boston University, 1969-72, then professor of literature, 1972-74; Crawshaw Professor of literature, Colgate University, Hamilton, New York, 1972. **Awards:** Audience Poetry Prize, 1958-59; Radcliffe Institute for Independent Study scholar, 1961-63; *Poetry* Levinson Prize, 1962; American Academy of Arts and Letters scholar, 1963-64; Ford foundation grant, 1964-65; *First Lit. Magazine* travel award, 1965-66; Pulitzer Prize, 1967, for *Live or Die*; Guggenheim award, 1969; Litt.D.: Tufts University, 1970, Regis College, 1971, and Fairfield University, 1971. **Member:** Phi Beta Kappa (honorary). **Died:** Committed suicide, 4 October 1974.

Publications

Poetry

To Bedlam and Part Way Back. Boston, Houghton, 1960.
All My Pretty Ones. Boston, Houghton, 1962.
Selected Poems. Oxford, Oxford University Press, 1964.
Live or Die. Boston, Houghton, 1966.
Poems, with Thomas Kinsella and Douglas Livingstone. Oxford, Oxford University Press, 1968.
Love Poems. Boston, Houghton, 1969.
The Book of Folly. Boston, Houghton, 1972.
O Ye Tongues. N.p., Rainbow Press, 1973.
The Death Notebooks. Boston, Houghton, 1974.
The Awful Rowing toward God. Boston, Houghton, 1975.
The Heart of Anne Sexton's Poetry. Boston, 3 vols., 1977.
Words for Dr. Y: Uncollected Poems with Three Stories, edited by Linda Gray Sexton. Boston, Houghton, 1978.
The Complete Poems. Boston, Houghton, 1981.
Selected Poems, edited by Diane W. Middlebrook and Diana H. George. Boston, Houghton, 1988.
Love Poems. Boston, Houghton, 1989.

Play

45 Mercy Street (produced New York, 1969), edited by Linda Grey Sexton. Boston, Houghton, 1976.

Short Stories

Transformations. Boston, Houghton, 1971.

For Children

Eggs of Things, with Maxine W. Kumin. New York, Putnam, 1963.
More Eggs of Things, with Maxine W. Kumin. New York, Putnam, 1964.
Joy and the Birthday Present, with Maxine W. Kumin. New York, McGraw, 1971.
The Wizard's Tears, with Maxine W. Kumin. New York, McGraw, 1975.

Other

Anne Sexton: A Self-Portrait in Letters, edited by Linda Gray Sexton and Lois Ames. Boston, Houghton, 1977.
No Evil Star: Selected Essays, Interviews, and Prose, edited by Steven E. Colburn. Ann Arbor, University of Michigan Press, 1985.

*

Bibliography: *Sylvia Plath and Anne Sexton: A Reference Guide* by Cameron Northouse and Thomas P. Walsh, Boston, G. K. Hall, 1974.

Critical Studies: *Anne Sexton: The Artist and Her Critics* edited by J. D. McClatchy, Bloomington, Indiana University Press, 1978; *To Make a Prairie: Essays on Poets, Poetry, and Country Living* by Maxine Kumin, Ann Arbor, University of Michigan Press, 1979; *Oedipus Anne: The Poetry of Anne Sexton* by Diana Hume George, University of Illinois Press, 1987; *Critical Essays on Anne Sexton* edited by Linda Wagner-Martin, n.p., 1989; *Anne Sexton: A Biography* by Diane Wood Middlebrook, Boston, Houghton Mifflin, 1991; *Rossetti to Sexton: Six Women Poets at Texas* edited by Dave Oliphant and Robin Bradford, Austin, University of Texas Press, 1992; "Diane Wood Middlebrook, Alicia Suskin Ostriker, and Diana Hume George Talk about Anne Sexton," in *Poets & Writers,* November/December 1993; *Anne Sexton* by S. L. Berry, Mankato, Minnesota, Creative Education, 1994.

* * *

According to Anne Sexton, "Poetry should be a shock to the senses. It should almost hurt." She made her mark as a poet by writing about the shocking and painful realities of women's lives, but also celebrated the beautiful and redemptive qualities of the female body at a time when it was scandalous to mention such biological realities as menstruation, menopause, or women's sexuality in public.

Sexton was born in Newton, Massachusetts. She did not receive a formal education beyond junior college, but on the recommendation of her psychiatrist attended Robert Lowell's poetry seminars at Boston University, where she began her meteoric rise as a professional poet. Although her career was brief, she achieved exceptional recognition in the field, winning prestigious fellowships as well as the Pulitzer Prize in 1967 for *Live or Die*. She committed suicide on 4 October 1974, a fact that heightens her mystique as a tragic woman artist and tends to overshadow her contribution as an innovator in contemporary American poetry.

Sexton is probably the best known of the poets in a movement in the late 1950s and early 1960s called the "Confessional School," which refers to a group of writers whose literary output involved exploiting the most intimate details of their own lives. It is worth noting that she herself insisted her poetry was as much fabrication as it was confession. Indeed, it is hard to imagine anyone living through even half of what were taken to be the autobiographical events revealed in her poetry. Although her subject matter was intimate, she thought of herself as "an imagist who deals with reality and its hard facts." It may be that her gender has much to do with readers' inability to conceptualize her poetry as more than the journaling of a disturbed, yet brilliant, woman.

Students of Sexton have written that she was not appreciated as a craftsperson because the exhibitionist, performance aspect of her persona tended to eclipse her skills as a writer. In the classes she taught at Boston University she would invite students to vote for or against an image or a poem's preferred ending. This practice is emblematic of Sexton's general attitude toward poetry, that it was something that needed to be made public, to be shared with an audience. Indeed, Sexton took poetry to public venues where it had never before been experienced; at one point, she even shared a stage with the Beatles.

Poet and essayist Maxine Kumin was a close personal friend, and their friendship sustained both women's writing. They had separate phone lines installed in their homes so they could spend hours together talking through their poems. Kumin has said, in response to the adage that we have art in order not to die of the truth, that Sexton's confessional poems not only kept her alive, but nurtured and reached a vast audience. While Sexton had begun to write on the advice of her psychiatrist, psychiatrists around the country began referring their patients to her work for comfort and confirmation.

Transformations, a feminist retelling of Grimm's fairy tales, reflects Sexton's fascination with the cultural power of myth. Given Sexton's bouts with mental illness and the dark nature of some of her work, it may be difficult for the contemporary reader to think of her as having a sense of humor, but this collection in particular showcases her satiric wit.

The poems in *To Bedlam and Back* and *All My Pretty Ones* practically explode off the page with their painful evocation of traumatic events in Sexton's life: her mother's death from cancer, her father's stroke, her own experiences being institutionalized. Often the power of these poems comes as much from her use of form as it does from the subject matter itself, the use of rhyme having forced a certain amount of control from the writer. In later work Sexton abandoned this focus on form and wrote in shorter lines with seemingly random line breaks, a shift that may reflect her need to communicate the urgency of her mental state before her death, a time of "intense, even manic creativity," according to Kumin.

Sexton's poetry is not only emotionally fierce, it is very female, focused on the body in all its filth and glory. And like the body, Sexton is sometimes crude. Her speech is most often colloquial, her poems redemptive of the common, the domestic. A most famous example is the poem "In Celebration of my Uterus." Sexton succeeds where other woman poets celebrating their body parts often bore, because she is outrageously funny; she lets out all the stops. The poet pays obvious homage to Walt Whitman, as she enumerates the many women singing of their healthy uteruses:

> one is in a shoe factory cursing the machine,
> one is at the aquarium tending a seal,
> one is dull at the wheel of her Ford,
> one is at the toll gate collecting,
> one is tying the cord of a calf in Arizona

and on and on. The poem is incantatory, a true binding of the spirit to the flesh.

Sexton has an striking ability to evoke the complications of intimate relationships, the ambiguous strands of love, through her focus on the body. Probably due to both women being suicides, her work has frequently been compared to Sylvia Plath's. While Sexton often echoes Plath's technique of writing from a sense of dissociation from her body in pain, she never manifests the disdain of the latter for the flesh. There is also frequently a sense of redemption in Sexton's work that is virtually absent in Plath's.

Toward the end of her life, Sexton's primary subjects were religious. She was strongly attracted to an absolutism in religion that had not been present in her Protestant upbringing, and sought a God who would be a sure thing, a God who was an authoritarian and yet a forgiving presence. This focus is most clear in *The Awful Rowing toward God*, which Kumin tells us was written "at white heat—two, three, even four poems a day." Although a priest counseled Sexton that she could find God "in her typewriter," she ultimately was unable to overcome her pain, a despair poignantly illustrated by these lines from "Wanting to Die:"

> Death's a sad bone; bruised, you'd say,
> and yet she waits for me, year after year,
> to so delicately undo an old wound,
> to empty my breath from its bad prison.

Poetry had saved Sexton's life in the mid-1950s when she first began writing for therapeutic purposes. But it was ultimately not enough. "She was on loan to poetry," Kumin writes. "We always knew it would end. We just didn't know when or exactly how." Writers have long speculated as to the source of Sexton's mental illness. Diane Wood Middlebrook, author of *Anne Sexton: A Biography* (a book that generated its own controversy because Middlebrook had access to taped sessions between Sexton and her psychiatrist) believes it to have been a biochemical imbalance, which medicine of the time was unable to treat. However, feminist critics have also considered the effect of the social pressures during the 1950s and 1960s, when a white, middle class woman was expected to be a happy housewife and a perfect mother. Perhaps, as Alicia Ostriker has suggested, Sexton had to get sick in order to elude these societal definitions; once identified as imbalanced, she was empowered to say the unsayable, the forbidden truths about the culture and about women's bodies.

—Kate Lynn Hibbard

SHANGE, Ntozake

Name pronounced "*En*-tow-za-key Shan-gay." **Nationality:** American. **Born:** Paulette Williams in Trenton, New Jersey, 18 October 1948; changed name in 1971. **Education:** Barnard College, B.A. (honors) in American studies 1970; University of Southern California, Los Angeles, M.A. 1973. **Family:** Married 2) the musician David Murray in 1977 (divorced); one daughter. **Career:** Writer and performer. Faculty member in women's studies, University of California Extension, 1972-75, Sonoma State University, 1973-75, and Mills College, 1975; artist-in-residence, New Jersey State Council on the Arts; creative writing instructor, City College of New York, 1975; associate professor of drama, University of Houston, beginning 1983; currently instructor in performance and African literature, College of Art, Maryland Institute. Lecturer at institutions, including Douglass College, 1978, Yale University, Howard University, Detroit Art Institute, and New York University. Dancer with Third World Collective, Sounds in Motion, West Coast Dance Works, and *for colored girls who have considered suicide* (Shange's own dance company). Contributor to periodicals, including *Black Scholar, Third World Women, Ms.*, and *Yardbird Reader.* **Member:** Actors Equity, National Academy of Television Arts and Sciences, Dramatists Guild, PEN American Center, Academy of American Poets, Poets & Writers, Inc., Women's Institute for Freedom of the Press, New York Feminist Arts Guild. **Awards:** Obie Award, Outer Critics Circle Award, Audelco Award, *Mademoiselle* Award, and Tony, Grammy, and Emmy award nominations, all 1977, all for *for colored girls who have considered suicide/when the rainbow is enuf;* Frank Silvera Writers' Workshop Award, 1978; *Los Angeles Times* Book Prize, 1981, for *Three Pieces;* Guggenheim fellowship, 1981; Columbia University Medal of Excellence, 1981; Obie Award, 1981, for *Mother Courage and Her Children;* Pushcart Prize; named Taos Poetry Circus World Heavyweight Champion, 1991; Lila Wallace Readers' Digest Award, 1992-95; honored as a "Living Legend" by National Black Theatre Festival, 1993; Pew fellowship in fiction, 1993-94; Lincoln University President's Award, 1994; City of Philadelphia Literature Prize, 1994; Black Theatre Network Winona Fletcher award, 1994. **Address:** Maryland Institute, College of Art, Department of Language and Literature, 1300 West Mount Royal Ave., Baltimore, Maryland 21217, U.S.A.

PUBLICATIONS

Plays

for colored girls who have considered suicide/when the rainbow is enuf: A Choreopoem (produced Berkeley, 1974; produced Off-Broadway, then Broadway, 1976). San Lorenzo, California, Shameless Hussy Press, 1975; revised version, New York, Macmillan, 1976; London, Samuel French, 1981.
A Photograph: A Study of Cruelty (produced Off-Broadway, 1977; revised as *A Photograph: Lovers in Motion,* produced Houston, 1979). In *Three Pieces,* 1981.
Where the Mississippi Meets the Amazon, with Thulani Nkabinde and Jessica Hagedorn (produced New York, 1977).
From Okra to Greens/ A Different Kinda Love Story (produced New York, 1978). London, Samuel French, 1985.
boogie woogie landscapes (produced New York, 1979). New York, St. Martin's Press, 1978.
Spell #7: A Geechee Quick Magic Trance Manual (produced Broadway, 1979). In *Three Pieces,* 1981.
Black and White Two Dimensional Planes (produced New York, 1979).
Mother Courage and Her Children, adapted from the play by Bertoldt Brecht (produced Off-Broadway, 1980).
Three Pieces. London, Samuel French, and New York, St. Martin's Press, 1981.
Mouths (produced 1981).
Carrie (operetta; produced 1981).
Three for a Full Moon [and] *Bocas* (produced Los Angeles, 1982).
Three Views of Mt. Fuji (produced San Francisco, 1987).
Daddy Says (produced New York, 1989).
Plays, One (collection; includes *I Heard Eric Dolphy in His Eyes*). London, Methuen Drama, 1992.
A Sense of Breath, with Jeanne Lee and Mickey Davidson (produced New York, 1993).

Novels

Sassafrass (novelette). San Lorenzo, California, Shameless Hussy Press, 1976.
Melissa & Smith (novelette). N.p., Bookslinger Editions, 1976.
Sassafrass, Cypress & Indigo, New York, St. Martin's Press, 1982; London, Mandarin, 1989.
Betsey Brown. New York, St. Martin's Press, 1985.
Liliane: Resurrection of the Daughter. New York, St. Martin's Press, 1994; London, Methuen, 1995.
Same Song, Same City, with Ifa Bayeza. New York, Random House, 1996.

Poetry

Natural Disasters and Other Festive Occasions. Heirs, 1977.
Nappy Edges. New York, St. Martin's Press, 1978.
Some Men. N.p., 1981.
A Daughter's Geography. New York, St. Martin's Press, 1983.
from okra to greens. Coffee House Press, 1984.
Ridin' the Moon in Texas: Word Paintings. New York, St. Martin's Press, 1987.
The Love Space Demands: A Continuing Saga. New York, St. Martin's Press, 1991.
I Live in Music, paintings by Romare Bearden, edited by Linda Sunshine. New York, Steward Tabori & Chang, 1994.

Essays

See No Evil: Prefaces, Essays and Accounts, 1976-1983. N.p., Momo's Press, 1984.
"'We Are Not Part of Cane Fields,'" in *Modern Maturity,* January/February 1996.

Other

Adapter, *Educating Rita* (play), by Willy Russell (produced Atlanta, 1982).

Recordings: *Beneath the Necessity of Talking* (sound recording) Columbia, Missouri, American Audio Prose Library, 1989.

*

Media Adaptations: *for colored girls who have considered suicide/when the rainbow is enuf* (television film), PBS; *Betsey Brown* (operetta), Joseph Papp's Public Theater, New York City, 1986.

Theatrical Activities:
Director: **Plays:** *The Issue,* 1970; *The Spirit of Sojourner Truth,* 1970; *The Mighty Gents,* 1979; *A Photograph: A Study in Cruelty,* 1979; *Fire's Daughters,* 1993; *The Bridge Party,* 1994. *Flyin' West,* 1995; *Bringin' It All Back Home,* 1996.
Actor: **Plays:** Many of her own plays.

Critical Studies: "For Colored Girls, the Rainbow Is Not Enough" by Michele Wallace, in *Village Voice,* 16 August 1976; *Diving Deep and Surfacing: Women Writers on Spiritual Quest* by Carol P. Christ, Boston, Beacon Press, 1980; "Ntozake Shange: Celebrating Our Creativity" (interview) by Gaye Williams, in *Sojourner,* November 1982; *Black Women Writers at Work* edited by Claudia Tate, New York, Continuum, 1983; *Women Writers and the City: Essays in Feminist Literary Criticism,* edited by Susan Merrill Squier, University of Tennessee Press, 1984; "No More Buried Lives: The Theme of Lesbianism in Lorde, Naylor, Shange, Walker" by Barbara Christian, in *Feminist Issues,* spring 1985; *Interviews with Contemporary Women Playwrights* edited by Kathleen Betsko and Rachel Koenig, n.p., Beech Tree Books, 1987; "'We Are Feeding Our Children the Sun': Talking with Ntozake Shange" by Andrea Stuart, in *Spare Rib: A Women's Liberation Magazine,* May 1987; *Down from the Mountaintop: Black Women's Novels in the Wake of the Civil Rights Movement, 1966-1989* by Melissa Walker, New Haven, Connecticut, Yale University Press, 1991; *Ntozake Shange: A Critical Study of the Plays* by Neal A. Lester, New York, Garland, 1995; *Scars of Conquest/Masks of Resistance: The Invention of Cultural Identities in African, African-American, and Caribbean Drama* by Tejumola Olaniyan, New York, Oxford University Press, 1995.

* * *

Native American poet Awiakta's advice to "Feed your body./Feed your soul./Feed your dream./BUST OUT!!!" serves as an apt introduction to Ntozake Shange's life and work. It is significant too that both of these writers have chosen their own names to match their new *personae,* and each name has in it that attention-getting crack of the whip, the "ak" sound. Until 1971 Paulette Williams, Shange took on this new name from the Zulu and it has been variously translated as "she who comes with her own things" and "she who walks like a lion."

The early life of a prodigy is always subject to mythologizing and the privileged childhood of the then-Paulette Williams is no exception. Michele Wallace has made much of the young girl being a "Jack and Jiller" (a club for the children of the Black elite), but a closer view of how it really felt for her growing up in St. Louis and elsewhere (they moved a lot) can be found in Shange's most autobiographical novel, *Betsey Brown.*

Certainly her psychiatrist social worker mother and her surgeon father must have been a little startled at their carefully brought up daughter's metamorphosis into such a highly visible media figure. Speaking of and to her parents in the rather surprising venue of the AARP magazine, *Modern Maturity,* Shange thanks them for the "magnificent education you both afforded me and paid for," where she encountered:

> some crazy Frenchmen, namely Sartre, Anouilh and Breton, who knew Eurocentrism was irrational, which left me to surmise that I, too, could address this world, act as my own agent and define and design the symbols from Akan sculpture to Chuck Berry that I hold dear ... my tribute to you these past 30 years has been my struggle to make sure we don't disappear in invisibility or in fact.

It was while Shange was working on her M.A. at the University of Southern California that she had one of her many epiphanies. Walking around the stacks of the campus library, looking at books about artists of the past, Shange asked herself, "How can I assign my life to being a secondary source?." She decided from that point on that she would spend life giving and not taking.

Shange's generosity comes then not only from her abundance of energy and talent, but from a principle, again like Awiakta, of "giving to the people." Her teaching was and still is one of the ways she shares her bounty and her discipline, and she takes it seriously. It is, however, in her plays that her social activism reaches the most people, as Neal Lester has analyzed in his full-length study.

In the early '70s, when I first heard Shange speak—in a series on women writers at the San Francisco Public Library—she was already telling us in her inimitable fashion of a) the appallingly high suicide statistics of young black women and b) the imperative for black women and men writers to be free to write out their dreams and fantasies in the face of publishers' demands for realistic (and gritty) accounts of childhood, etc. It was during this era, after all, that poet Al Young had a collection of love poems rejected by his East Coast publisher because they were deemed "not angry enough"!

Shange was angry enough, even then. In her play *for colored girls who have considered suicide/when the rainbow is enuf,* both her anger and her dreams found their artistic outlet, as did her concerns about the suicide rate. Its success stands out as one of the artistic phenomenons of the 1970s. This high-energy music/dance/words/multimedia/cross-genre invention hit the ground running. The seven actresses found in the intense poetry, which hopscotched between the real and the surreal, the ultimate vehicle for their own self-disclosures: "& it waz all I had but bein alive and bein a woman & bein colored is a metaphysical dilemma/i havent conquered yet/do you see the point" (the now famous Shange slant / is a rhythmic marker rather than a signifier of the end of a line of poetry). Crossing borders, violating taboos, stomping out some new ground, it was a memorable theatre experience.

And it still is. During the 20th-anniversary revival of this surprisingly durable piece, I walked through an audience as culturally diverse, hip, and interesting looking as any I have ever seen at our too often class/race/gender-divided cultural events. Everyone was there, seeking an infusion of Shange's poetic, visionary energy and range and sisterhood. A whole lot of women were there for the revival, but there were also a whole lot of men, and no one seemed worried about the bad rap the script had initially garnered for being anti-black male (which Shange always hotly denied while saying simultaneously, of course if the shoe fits...).

In the 20 years that have passed, enough pain has bee disclosed, enough "talk stories" told, to ensure increasing tolerance for truth-telling. After all, we can hear language more shocking than Shange's about women by men and visa versa on the rap music stations daily. The unresolved gender crossfire of communication problems are still an issue, and many of the charges Shange brought against the male figures in her works have been "proven" systematically by linguists like Deborah Tannen and sociologists like Carol Gilligan. However, at the time the backlash was furious and there was even a five-minute film made (by a woman) titled *For Colored Men Who Have Had Enuf.* Interestingly, in the '90s there has been a more grateful response by male writer Keith Antar Mason called *For Colored Boys Who Have Considered Homicide When the Rainbow Wasn't Enough.*

Any "best seller" in the competitive art world brings with it criticism and Shange's success was no exception. As she explained in the *Village Voice* shortly after the opening of *for colored girls,* "I lost a great deal of myself to interviews and audiences and strangers that happen up on me. I never suspected I would do anything besides work in bars, and be a good teacher and a decent poet." Feeling "like an art object instead of a writer" would prompt Shange to move from the over-exposure of New York to Houston a few years later.

Shange is a wonderful "object," with her feathers and furbelows, powerful jewels and cheerful costumes. Sometimes she looks like a little girl dressing up in clothes from trunks in the attic, sometimes she comes out looking like a vamp from Savannah (her daughter's name is Savannah, by the way). From the beginning, when she herself was acting in her play *for colored girls...,* Shange has been willing to take on with her own actual (<u>not</u> virtual) body those theories the french feminists just write about. Shange was doing MTV before there was any such medium. Whether she is the lightning or the lightning rod, I am not sure, but the electricity, the flash, the warmth are all palpable in her presence.

The lightning flash of her language, like her clothing choices, startles and delights:

> ...I am a poet/i write
> poems
> i make words cartwheel and somersault down
> pages
> outta my mouth come visions, distilled like
> bootleg
> whiskey/i am like a radio but i am a channel of
> my own
> i keep saying i do this!

As can be seen from even this small sample, from *Spell #7,* what Shange has done to syntax, to the always dubious status of standardized spellings, and to punctuation is perhaps her most radical act as a feminist writer.

Bernice Reagon, Smithsonian folklorist *emerita* and leader of the singing group Sweet Honey and the Rock, gave a talk at the 1984 Modern Language Association convention on the many languages black women have to learn to survive; Shange has access to them all, plus a few of her own invention. It is as if she had combined the best of Archie Shepp, Andre Breton, Bessie Smith, Bartok, Zora Neale Hurston, and e.e. cummings, along with some really savory street and hearth talk, into a kaleidoscope and turned and turned it to invent an audacious new literary language. She has an unerring ear, the rhythms are right, and people from all English language groups can follow along the fast-paced, free associative, improvisational jazz riffs of her brilliant form/content synthesis, especially when Shange herself performs the poems. Whether her style works as well on the printed page is more problematic (perhaps her experiments should be labelled "DO NOT TRY THIS AT HOME"), but for her they work.

This kind of repossessing and reinterpreting the language of patriarchy connects her as much as does her liberated subject matter with feminist thought. In a marvelous poem from *The Love Space Demands* entitled "M.E.S.L." (which stands, we are told, for male english as a second language), Shange specifies her differences: "there are no umpires/in my game/and no men in lil striped shirts/ usin sign language/deaf women don't understand." She does, however, affirm her belief in "bilingualism," that is, keeping up the dialogue and promises "i do/wanna play wit you," but her game is not to beat or to be beaten:

> when i swim
> i'm not aimin for the other side/
> i'm warm waters/inchin thru coral
> lookin to galavant/on a dolphin's back.
> what's the rush abt?

She is describing a different way of knowing/being.

In another unmistakable feminist statement, Shange confuses or conflates her creativity in having a baby with birthing a poem.

> the baby's refusing to come out/down
> she wants to come out a spoken word
> ...
> i finally figured out what to say
> to this literary die-hard of a child of mine
> "you are an imperative my dear"...
> it is incumbent upon you to present yrself

From the same collection, a poem enacts that obligatory feminist ritual of reclaiming the male godhead: "we need a god who bleeds now/whose wounds are not the end of anything," in short, a god(dess) who menstruates!

Shange makes feminism seem fun, irreverent, sexy, multicultural, inclusive rather than exclusive. White women remain fans even when she takes the occasional side-swipe, as in her *Spell #7:* "oh i know/the first thing a white girl does in the morning is to fling her hair..." Her belief in change, fairness, and in frank disclosure of the complexities of sexuality, all identify her with the best in feminism. Her delightful (and underread) novel *Sassafrass* (originally published by Alta's in-your-face Shameless Hussy Press, after all) was dedicated to "all women in struggle," and included dreams and fabulous recipes, long before the famous food novel *Like Water for Chocolate.*

Her most recent novel, *Liliane,* confirms her politics and her style, though there are more varieties of voice and even some conversations (with the heroines' unclassically gabby psychiatrist) to breat the monologue pattern. It has been called a collage, one of her most playful novels. On this work, as on Shange's long-term literary reputation, the jury is still out, I suppose, but her liberating influence is everywhere: from novelist Terry MacMillan, playwrights Pearl Cleage and Anna Deavere Smith, and even such independent souls as cultural critic bell hooks (note lack of boring initial capital letters). I mention here women of color not to limit Shange's influence to them, but rather to credit her with providing women of color with a model of possibility saying that they can be themselves and be understood and appreciated by a wide audience.

Shange gives new resonance to the term Renaissance Woman, with her amazing ability to combine popular and highbrow cultures into a savory stew. Music is to Shange what flowers were to painter

Georgia O'Keeffe, her subject and her form. Like Zora Neale Hurston, Shange is at home in many worlds, but at base, as she says, she can live anywhere so long as there is room for her to write in, which is, as Virginia Woolf advised, a bottom-line feminist demand. Shange's writing may dazzle and puzzle her readers, and put off so-called serious critics, but as she has made clear many times she is writing for her own sake. As she told Gaye Williams in *Sojourner,* "every time I did any piece of work I learned something else. that's my own private decision about myself.... Writing is something you do by yourself at home, and whether anybody else knows about it or not, it has to be done."

—J. J. Wilson

SHOCKLEY, Ann Allen

Nationality: American. **Born:** Louisville, Kentucky, 21 June 1927. **Education:** Fisk University, Nashville, Tennessee, B.A. 1948; Case Western Reserve University, Cleveland, Ohio, M.S. in library science 1959. **Family:** Married William Shockley in 1949 (divorced); one son and one daughter. **Career:** Assistant librarian, Delaware State College, Dover, 1959-60; assistant librarian, 1960-66, associate librarian, 1966-69, and curator of Negro collection, Maryland State College (now University of Maryland Eastern Shore), Princess Anne; associate librarian and head of special collections, 1969-75, associate librarian for public services, beginning 1975, then associate librarian for special collections, university archivist, and associate professor of library science, Fisk University. Lecturer at University of Maryland, 1968, Jackson State College, 1973, and Vanderbilt University. Contributor to newspapers and periodicals, including *Afro-American, Federalsburg* (Maryland) *Times,* and *Pittsburgh Courier.* **Awards:** American Association of University Women short story award, 1962; Fisk University faculty research grant, 1970; University of Maryland Library Administrators Development Institute fellowship, 1974; American Library Association Black Caucus award, 1975; American Library Association Task Force Book Award nomination, 1980; Hatshepsut Award for literature, 1981; Martin Luther King Jr. Black Author Award, 1982; Susan Koppelman Award, 1988; Outlook Award for pioneering contribution to lesbian and gay writing, 1990; American Library Association Black Caucus Award for professional achievement, 1992. **Agent:** Carole Abel, 160 West 87th Street, 7D, New York, New York 10024, U.S.A. **Address:** Fisk University, 17th Avenue North, Nashville, Tennessee 37203, U.S.A.

PUBLICATIONS

Novels

Loving Her. Indianapolis, Indiana, Bobbs-Merrill, 1974.
Say Jesus and Come to Me. New York, Avon, 1982.

Short Stories

The Black and White of It. Wetherby Lake, Missouri, Naiad Press, 1980.

Uncollected Short Stories

"Abraham and the Spirit," in *Negro Digest,* 8, July 1950.
"The Picture Prize," in *Negro Digest,* 11, October 1962.
"A Far Off Sound," in *Umbra,* 2, December 1963.
"The Funeral," in *Phylon* (Atlanta), 28, spring 1967.
"The President," in *Freedomways,* 10(4), 1970.
"Is She Relevant?," in *Black World,* 20, January 1971.
"Crying for Her Man," in *Liberator,* 11, January/February 1971.
"Her Own Thing," in *Black America,* 2, August 1972.
"Ah: The Young Black Poet," in *New Letters* (Kansas City, Missouri), 41, winter 1974.
"The More Things Change," in *Essence* (New York), 8, October 1977.
"A Case of Telemania," in *Azalea,* 1, fall 1978.
"Women in a Southern Time," in *Feminary,* 11, 1982.

Nonfiction

A History of Public Library Services to Negroes in the South, 1900-1955. Dover, Delaware State College, 1960.
A Handbook for the Administration of Special Negro Collections. Nashville, Fisk University Library, 1970; as *The Administration of Special Black Collections,* 1974.
A Manual for the Black Oral History Program. Nashville, Fisk University Library, 1971.

Uncollected Essays

"Does the Negro College Library Need a Special Negro Collection?," in *Library Journal,* 86, June 1961.
"The Negro Woman in Retrospect: Blueprint for the Future," in *Negro History Bulletin* (Washington, DC), 24, December 1965.
"Tell It Like It Is: A New Criteria for Children's Books in Black and White," in *Southeastern Libraries,* 30, spring 1970.
"Pauline Elizabeth Hopkins: A Biographical Excursion into Obscurity," in *Phylon* (Atlanta), 33, spring 1972.
"American Anti-Slavery Literature: An Overview—1693-1859," in *Negro History Bulletin* (Washington, DC), 37, April-May 1974.
"Black Women Discuss Today's Problems: Men, Families, Societies," with Veronica E. Tucker, in *Southern Voices,* 1, August/September 1974.
"The New Black Feminists," in *Northwest Journal of African and Black American Studies,* 2, winter 1974.
"Black Publishers and Black Librarians: A Necessary Union," in *Black World,* 26, March 1975.
"Joseph S. Cotter Sr.: Biographical Sketch of a Black Louisville Bard," in *College Language Association Journal,* 18, March 1975.
"Oral History: A Research Tool for Black History," in *Negro History Bulletin* (Washington, DC), 41, January-February 1978.
"The Salsa Soul Sisters," in *Off Our Backs,* 11, November 1979.
"The Black Lesbian in American Literature: An Overview," in *Conditions: Five,* 11, autumn 1979; in *Home Girls: A Black Feminist Anthology,* edited by Barbara Smith, New York, Kitchen Table: Women of Color Press, 1983.
"Black Lesbian Biography: Lifting the Veil," in *Other Black Woman,* 1, 1982.

Other

With Sue P. Chandler, *Living Black American Authors: A Biographical Directory.* New York, Bowker, 1973.

Editor, with E.J. Josey, and contributor, *Handbook of Black Librarianship.* Littleton, Colorado, Libraries Unlimited, 1977.

Editor, *Afro-American Women Writers, 1746-1933: An Anthology and Critical Guide.* Boston, G.K. Hall, 1988.

*

Bibliography: *Ann Allen Shockley: An Annotated Primary and Secondary Bibliography* by Rita B. Dandridge, New York, Greenwood Press, 1987, and her "Gathering Pieces: A Selected Bibliography of Ann Allen Shockley," in *Black American Literature Forum,* 21, spring/summer 1987.

Critical Studies: "Comprehensive Oppression: Lesbians and Race in the Work of Ann Allen Shockley" by Evelyn C. White, in *Backbone 3,* 1979; "Ann Allen Shockley" by Helen R. Houston, in *Dictionary of Literary Biography,* Volume 33: *Afro-American Fiction Writers after 1955,* Detroit, Gale, 1984; "Theme and Portraiture in the Fiction of Ann Allen Shockley" (dissertation) by SDiane Bogus, Miami University, 1988, and her "Ann Allen Shockley" in *Gay & Lesbian Literature,* Detroit, St. James Press, 1994.

* * *

A versatile writer, teacher, and feminist activist, Ann Allen Shockley addresses issues such as sexism, racism, and prejudice against lesbians and gays through her articles, short stories, and novels. In her long career as a librarian she has worked to expand the representation of African American writers—particularly women writers—within public libraries; as a writer of fiction Shockley has been equally pioneering. With publication of her novel *Loving Her* in 1974, Shockley earned the distinction of being the first writer to directly confront the strong homophobia prevalent in the black community by making a lesbian of color the main character in a lengthy work of fiction.

Born in Louisville, Kentucky in 1927, Shockley earned her B.A. in library science from Fisk University in 1948, following that with an M.S. from Case Western Reserve University in 1959. She worked as both a journalist and a teacher for ten years before joining her alma mater, Fisk, as an archivist and librarian in their Special Negro Collection, where she continues to work. Through her years within the library system she has combatted the scarcity of material documenting the lives and works of African American writers by publishing *Living Black Authors: A Biographical Directory* (1973) and *Afro-American Women Writers (1746-1933): An Anthology and Critical Guide* (1988). Focussing on writers from colonial America to the Harlem Renaissance, Shockley's work has done much to define and shape the literary tradition that has since inspired and molded the works of new generations of African American woman writers. Her work in this area has been furthered by numerous articles that she has published in such periodicals as *Library Journal, Phylon,* and *Black World.*

Shockley's writing talents have also had a more creative outlet in fiction. Early short stories such as "Abraham and the Spirit" (1950) and "The President" (1970) focus on the devastating effects of racism on black Americans; more recent works have directly confronted the homophobia and sexism that have combined with racism to single out and oppress African American lesbians. In her short story collection *The Black and White of It,* published in 1980, each of the ten stories provide a telling insight into that triple oppression. "A Meeting of the Sapphic Daughters" goes beyond oppression of the individual to cast a light on the racism prevalent in the women's movement of the period, which, though fueled by the civil rights movement of the '50s and '60s, had even deeper roots in the discontent of middle-class, college-educated whites. While Shockley has been criticized for depicting lesbian love affairs within her stories somewhat negatively, those of her characters who act rather than react to the expectations of those around them, both black and white, are eventually rewarded by close, loving relationships.

Loving Her was pathbreaking. The first novel written by an African American woman to feature a black lesbian at its center, it is a realistic portrayal of a lesbian coming of age. Abandoning an abusive and alcoholic husband for Terry, a well-to-do white woman, Renay must deal not only with learning to understand her lesbianism but also with loss of family support, the abandonment of her dreams of a career in the arts, and the death of a child. *Loving Her* also treads openly on the then-taboo territory of interracial love; Renay and Terry's love becomes the medium within which Shockley explores racial and sexual prejudices among diverse segments of society: from straight black males to older women, to the black middle class.

Say Jesus and Come to Me adopts the voice of African American gospel preaching in telling the story of two lesbian women who live within the public spotlight: the manipulative evangelist Myrtle Black and Travis Lee, a singer who through the course of the novel comes to openly accept her own lesbianism. Satirizing the homophobia within the black church, Shockley later told Rita B. Dandridge that *Say Jesus and Come to Me* was also intended to "expose the conservatism and snobbishness of the black middle class and academicians, which I see all the time; black male oppression of women; the superior attitudes and opportunism of some white women towards black women in the women's liberation movement."

Shockley's writing has sometimes been criticized as being too openly didactic, but in light of the black literary tradition that she herself helped to bring to light, that cannot be said to be a fault. She continues on the path of those black women writers who have preceded her; experiencing first hand the oppression surrounding her as both a women of color and a lesbian, Shockley has courageously attempted to counteract that oppression by writing from the heart.

—Lynn MacGregor

SHOWALTER, Elaine

Nationality: American. **Born:** Cambridge, Massachusetts, 21 January 1941. **Family:** Married the professor English Showalter Jr. in 1963; one son, one daughter. **Education:** Bryn Mawr College, B.A. 1962; Brandeis University, M.A. 1964; University of California, Davis, Ph.D. 1970. **Career:** Assistant professor, 1970-74, associate professor of English beginning 1974, Rutgers University, Douglass College, New Brunswick, New Jersey; currently professor and chair, department of English, and Avalon Foundation professor of humanities, Princeton University, Princeton, New Jersey. Visiting professor of English and women's studies, University of Delaware, 1976-77. Editor, *Women's Studies,* beginning 1972, and *Signs: Journal of Women, Culture, and Society,* beginning 1975. **Awards:** Rutgers University Faculty Research fellow, 1972-73; Guggenheim fellow, 1977-78; Rockefeller humanities fellow, 1981-82. **Member:** Modern Language Association of America (member, committee on the status of women, 1971-72), National Organization for Women. **Address:** Department of English, Princeton University, Princeton, New Jersey 08544, U.S.A.

Publications

Literary Criticism

A Literature of Their Own: British Women Novelists from Brontë to Lessing. Princeton, New Jersey, and Guilford, Princeton University Press, 1977; revised, London, Virago, 1982.

Guilt, Authority, and the Shadow of Little Dorrit. N.p., 1979.

Sister's Choice: Traditions and Change in American Women's Writing. Oxford, Clarendon Press, 1991.

History

The Female Malady: Women, Madness, and English Culture, 1830-1980. New York, Pantheon, 1985; London, Virago, 1987.

Sexual Anarchy: Gender and Culture at the Fin-de-Siècle. New York, Viking, 1990; London, Bloomsbury, 1991.

Uncollected Essays

"Hysteria, Feminism, and Gender," in *Beyond Freud,* edited by Sander L. Gilman and others. Berkeley, University of California Press, 1993.

Other

Editor, *Women's Liberation and Literature.* New York, Harcourt, 1971.

Editor, with Carol Ohmann, *Female Studies IV.* N.p., KNOW, 1971.

Editor, *These Modern Women: Autobiographical Essays from the Twenties.* Old Westbury, New York, Feminist Press, 1978.

Editor, *The New Feminist Criticism: Essays on Women, Literature, and Theory.* New York, Pantheon, 1985; London, Virago, 1986.

Editor, *Alternative Alcott.* New Brunswick, New Jersey, and London, Rutgers University Press, 1988.

Editor, *Speaking of Gender.* New York and London, Routledge, 1989.

Editor, *Little Women* by Louisa May Alcott. New York, Penguin, 1989.

Editor, *Daughters of Decadence: Women Writers of the Fin-de-Siècle.* New Brunswick, New Jersey, Rutgers University Press, and London, Virago, 1993.

Editor, with Lea Baechler and A. Walton Litz, *American Women Writers.* New York, Collier, 1993.

Editor, *Maude,* by Christina Rossetti [and] *On Sisterhoods: A Woman's Thoughts about Women,* by Dinah Mulock Craik. New York, New York University Press, 1993.

Editor, *"Where Are You Going, Where Have You Been?"* by Joyce Carol Oates. New Brunswick, New Jersey, Rutgers University Press, 1994.

Recordings: *Women Who Dared to Write,* with others (audio cassette), Washington, DC, National Public Radio, 1978.

*   *   *

Elaine Showalter is a feminist literary critic, cultural historian, and professor of English. She taught English and women's studies at Rutgers University and currently is the chair of the English Department and Avalon Foundation Professor of Humanities at Princeton University. Showalter has written extensively on women writers and on the theories and methods of contemporary feminist literary criticism.

Showalter established herself as part of the vanguard of second-wave, Anglo-American feminist literary scholars with the 1977 publication of her groundbreaking analysis of women writers entitled *A Literature of Their Own: British Women Novelists from Brontë to Lessing.* Along with Patricia Spack's *The Female Imagination* (1975) and Ellen Moers's *Literary Women* (1976), Showalter's study emphasizes the existence of a woman's tradition in literature to challenge the hegemony of the male-dominated literary canon. She describes her book as "an effort to describe the female literary tradition in the English novel from the generation of the Brontës to the present day, and to show how the development of this tradition is similar to the development of any literary subculture." Showalter's thesis retrieves women writers from literary obscurity while arguing that women constitute a "subculture" within the larger framework of society, one which is unified by similar "values, conventions, experiences, and behaviors." She identifies connections among an historical chain of women writers, and, accordingly, divides the history of the female tradition into three distinct stages: Feminine (1840-1880), Feminist (1880-1920), and Female (1920—).

Showalter's first book laid the foundation for her well-known and important theory of "gynocritics," a term coined in her essay "Toward a Feminist Poetics" (1979). Adapted from the French term *la gynocritique,* gynocritics refers to feminist criticism that is concerned with the woman writer "as the producer of textual meaning" and with the "history, themes, genres, and structures of literature by women." With its focus on female culture, gynocritics aims to develop a critical framework appropriate for the specific study of women's literature. According to Showalter, her new feminist methodology is distinguished from "feminist critique" which she claims is "male-oriented" for it relies on masculine theories (such as those proposed by Jacques Lacan or Roland Barthes) and thus limits our understanding of women's feelings and experiences. Not all feminist critics, however, agree with Showalter on this point. In *Sexual/Textual Politics,* Tori Moi, for example, faults Showalter for failing to embrace post-structuralist theory and thus for remaining trapped in outdated ideas about the referentiality of language and the mimetic relationship of literature to life.

In a later essay entitled "Feminist Criticism in the Wilderness" (1981), Showalter elaborates upon the theory of gynocritics, maintaining that it provides a "more complete and satisfying way to talk about the specificity and difference of woman's writing than theories based in biology, linguistics, or psychoanalysis." Here, she sharpens her view of "women's culture" and suggests that women constitute a "muted group, the dominant group." The overlapping and interdependent relationship between the "muted" and "dominant" allows Showalter to argue that women writers are situated inside both male and female literary traditions simultaneously. In this regard, the task of gynocentric criticism is to demarcate the cultural locus of female identity during a given historical period and within a specific social field. Accordingly, singular perspectives on literary history give way to multiple and heterogenous traditions that take into account the impact of gender upon the production of a text.

While Showalter is credited with mapping the theoretical parameters of gynocritics, she has also put these ideas into critical practice. For example, as the editor of *Daughters of Decadence: Women Writers of the Fin-de-Siecle* (1993) she brings together a diverse group of writers who, as a collective, present late 19th-century literary themes from a distinctly female perspective. Moreover, her 1991 study *Sister's Choice: Traditions and Change in American Women's Writing* affirms her ideas of a women's subculture, but this time in the context of American literary history. Moving chronologically from Margaret Fuller's writing to contemporary female gothic, *Sister's Choice* traces how texts in each era are related to previous literary traditions and to women's shared creativity.

Another fundamental assumption of gynocritics involves the archival enterprise, in which previously unfamiliar or unknown women's writing is republished for contemporary audiences. Showalter's *Alternative Alcott* (1988) participates in such an archival project. Here, the dark, sultry, and melodramatic tales attributed to Louisa May Alcott but initially published under her pseudonym A.M. Barnard are compiled, providing an expanded perspective on the well-known author of the children's classic *Little Women*.

While feminist literary criticism is Showalter's forte, she has also written cultural histories that also centralize gender issues. Her study *Sexual Anarchy: Gender and Culture at the Fin de Siecle* (1990), for example, traces the "myths, metaphors, and images of sexual crisis and apocalypse that marked both the late 19th century and our own *fin de siecle*." The book argues that re-definitions of masculinity occurred at the turn-of-the-century, a time characterized by social and cultural upheavals both between and within the sexes. She analyzes the rhetoric of popular periodicals, the vicissitudes of political discourse, and the themes and tensions in literature of the era; in the process, Showalter invents the term "endism" to describe the social and sexual crisis that afflicts both 19th and 20th century *fin de siecle*'s. Subsequently, she draws parallels between syphilis and AIDS, arguing that both are real and symbolic sexual diseases that have "taken on apocalyptic dimensions." With *Sexual Anarchy*, Showalter's contributions to literary, feminist, and cultural criticism and history merge to fortify her status as one of the foremost scholars of gender in the late 20th century.

—Annmarie Pinarski

SHULMAN, Alix Kates

Nationality: American. **Born:** Cleveland, Ohio, 17 August 1932. **Education:** Case Western Reserve University, B.A. 1953; Columbia University, 1953-55; New York University, 1960-62, M.A. 1978. **Family:** Married 1) Marcus Klein in 1953 (divorced); 2) Martin Shulman in 1959 (divorced 1985), one son, one daughter; 3) Scott York in 1989. **Career:** Editor, *Collier's Encyclopedia,* 1957-66, and *Encyclopedia of Philosophy,* 1963-66; early member of Redstockings (radical feminist group); taught writing workshops at New York University, 1976-84, Yale University, 1979-81, University of Southern Maine, 1982-84, and University of Arizona, 1993. Visiting artist, American Academy in Rome, 1982; visiting writer-in-residence, University of Colorado, 1984-86, and Ohio State University, 1987; citizen's chair, University of Hawai'i, 1991-92. Founding member, New York University Faculty Colloquium on Sex and Gender, 1980, and committee for abortion rights and against sterilization abuse. Member of advisory board, New York Feminist Art Institute, 1978-86, International Festival of Women's Films, 1978-80, *Aphra,* 1978-82, *Aurora,* 1979-81, and Westbeth Feminist Theatre. Contributor to periodicals, including *Atlantic Monthly, Feminist Studies, Ms., New York Times, Redbook, Socialist Review,* and *Village Voice.* **Awards:** *New York Times* citation, 1971, for *To the Barricades: The Anarchist Life of Emma Goldman;* MacDowell Colony for the Arts fellow, 1975-77, 1979, 1981; Millay Colony for the Arts fellow, 1978; De Witt Wallace/*Readers Digest* fellow, 1979; *New York Times Book Review* citation, 1981, for *On the Stroll;* Yale University Saybrook College fellow, beginning 1980; National Endowment for the Arts grant, 1983; Golden Key Honor Society, 1992. **Member:** National Writers Union, Women's Ink, Women's Institute for Freedom of the Press, The Women's Salon, Feminist Writer's Guild, New York Institute for the Humanities Seminar on Sex, Gender, and Consumerism. **Agent:** Amanda Urban, ICM Agency, 40 West 57th St., New York, New York 10019, U.S.A.

Publications

Novels

Memoirs of an Ex-Prom Queen. New York, Knopf, 1972.
Burning Questions. New York, Knopf, 1978.
On the Stroll. New York, Knopf, 1981.
In Every Woman's Life.... New York, Knopf, 1987.

Autobiography

Drinking the Rain. New York, Farrar Straus, 1995.

For Children

Bosley on the Number Line, illustrated by Gena. New York, D. McCay, 1970.
To the Barricades: The Anarchist Life of Emma Goldman. New York, Crowell, 1971.
Finders Keepers, illustrated by Emily McCully. Scarsdale, New York, Bradbury Press, 1971.
Awake or Asleep, illustrated by Frank Bozzo. New York, Addison-Wesley, 1971.

Other

Editor, *The Traffic in Women and Other Essays of Feminism,* by Emma Goldman. New York, Times Change Press, 1970.

Editor, *Red Emma Speaks: Selected Writings and Speeches,* by Emma Goldman. New York, Random House, 1972.

*

Critical Studies: "Humanbecoming: Form and Focus in the Neo-Feminist Novel" by Ellen Morgan, in *Images of Women in Fiction: Feminist Perspectives,* edited by Susan Koppelman Cornillon, Bowling Green, Ohio, Bowling Green University Press, 1972; *The Way Women Write* by Mary P. Hiatt, New York, Teachers College Press, 1977; *Feminist Criticism: Essays on Theory, Poetry and Prose* edited by Cherly L. Brown and Karen Olsen, London, Scarecrow Press, 1978; *Between Women: Biographers, Novelists, Critics, Teachers and Artists Write about their Work on Women* edited by Carol Ascher, Louise DeSalvo, and Sara Ruddick, Boston, Beacon Press, 1984; *Daring to Be Bad: Radical Feminism in America: 1967-1975* by Alice Echols, Minneapolis, University of Minnesota Press, 1989; "The 'Taint' of Feminist Fiction" in *Ms.,* December 1991.

* * *

Alix Kates Shulman, whose first novel, *Memoirs of an Ex-Prom Queen,* appeared in 1972, is a feminist pioneer. She is one of the first novelists to emerge directly from the second-wave American feminist movement of the late 1960s and early 1970s. Her work—which includes fiction, biography, children's literature and a memoir—is primarily concerned with the problems facing women in American society and with the political and social implications of the women's liberation movement. Her feminist viewpoint emphasizes the psychological and social constrictions facing women who are brought up to be middle-class housewives and mothers—ornaments and helpmates to men rather than autonomous, fully developed beings.

Born in 1932, Shulman grew up in a fairly conventional, middle-class household in Cleveland, Ohio. Upon graduation from college at age 20, she left for New York City, hoping to escape from the traditional gender roles that were stifling her. Pursuing her intellectual passion for philosophy, she enrolled as a graduate student at Columbia University. She soon found to her disappointment, however, that sexism was as strong in the academic world as anywhere else—that her ideas and her career ambitions were not taken seriously by the faculty or her fellow (mostly male) students. Succumbing to overwhelming social pressures, Shulman married a graduate student, dropped out of school to help support him, divorced, remarried, had two children, and stayed at home to raise them.

Her increasingly constricted life changed dramatically, however, in the late 1960s when she became involved with the fledgling women's movement. As a member of the Redstockings, a militant feminist group committed to political action as well as consciousness-raising, she helped to formulate radical feminist theory. This group not only fought for women's rights in the workplace, but also battled against women's subordination in heterosexual relationships and within the home. Shulman's exciting experiences in the women's movement fueled the beginning of her writing career, giving her not only a subject and an audience, but also the courage to express herself.

Shulman's first two novels, *Memoirs of an Ex-Prom Queen* and 1978's *Burning Questions,* address the problems of growing up female in America during the 1940s and 1950s. The best-selling *Prom Queen,* which catapulted Shulman to fame, recounts with both humor and compassion the story of Sasha Davis's growth from gawky child to beautiful teenager to disillusioned wife and mother. Although Sasha is extremely intelligent, she becomes obsessed with her physical appearance because, as she quickly learns, her beauty is her only asset in a sexist society. Because Sasha must put all her efforts into pleasing men and raising children rather than developing her talents, she becomes psychologically warped and her human potential is stunted. Therefore, although the novel is comic, it makes a serious critique of the damaging effects of sexism. Zane IndiAnna, the heroine of Shulman's next novel, *Burning Questions,* shares with Sasha her demeaning experiences as a sexual plaything and a trivialized housewife/mother. However, Zane has a rebellious nature and, inspired by the example of earlier revolutionary women such as Rosa Luxembourg and Emma Goldman, she struggles to find a way to change her society. She finally finds a productive outlet for her subversiveness within the feminist movement; the power of female bonding and political action gives her life purpose and joy.

Shulman's later books continue her concern with women's issues, although from different perspectives. In *On the Stroll* she departs from her emphasis on middle-class characters and concerns. In this novel she depicts with empathy the stories of two homeless women: a teenage runaway-turned-prostitute and an older "bag lady" who lost her home, children, and position in middle-class society when her husband abandoned her. *In Every Woman's Life* returns to middle-class characters, but focuses on the choices women must face in their emotional lives, especially the question of whether or not to marry. The major themes of this novel concern the conflicts between short-term passion and long-term stability and the pleasures of family life vs. the joys of autonomy. Rather than dogmatically preaching one answer, the novel instead emphasizes the complexity of these issues and the effects of different choices on different characters. Finally, in her memoir *Drinking the Rain,* Shulman switches from political themes to a concern with spiritual development. She describes her discovery, after turning 50, of a new sense of peace and psychological wholeness. The impetus behind this new development is her time spent in solitude on an isolated island off the coast of Maine, where she learns to live a simpler life that is more harmonious with nature.

In addition to her novels and memoir, Shulman's published work includes several children's books and numerous essays on feminist themes. She is also has also written a biography and edited the writings of Emma Goldman (1869-1940), the Russian-born anarchist, feminist, and radical activist. The life of Goldman has been a major inspiration to Shulman's own development as an activist and a political writer. As Shulman writes of Goldman in *Between Women:* "From the time I first began to study her, I have been finding in the rocky pool of her life and work precisely what I've needed to know. I, her biographer, have shaped her life, and she, my subject has shaped mine." Emma Goldman gave Shulman the courage to question all authority and to write with conviction. Although Shulman is most known for her writing, she is also a committed political activist and has taught fiction at various academic institutions, including New York and Yale universities.

—Debra Bielke

SIDHWA, Bapsi

Nationality: Pakistani; exiled; immigrated to United States, 1984. **Born:** Bapsi Bhandara, Karachi, Pakistan, 11 August 1938. **Education:** Kinnaird College for Women, B.A. 1956. **Family:** Married 1) Gustad Kermani, 1957 (died); 2) Noshir R. Sidhwa, 1963; three children. **Career:** Conducted novel writing workshops, Rice University, 1984-86; assistant professor of creative writing, University of Houston, 1985. President, International Women's Club of Lahore, 1975-77. Pakistan's delegate to Asian Women's Congress, 1975. **Agent:** Elizabeth Grossman, Sterling Lord Literary Agency Inc., 1 Madison Ave, New York, New York 10021, U.S.A. **Address:** 1600 Massachusetts Ave., #603, Cambridge, Massachusetts 02138, U.S.A.

Publications

Novels

The Crow Eaters. Lahore, Pakistan, Imani Press, 1978; London, Cape, 1980; New York, St. Martin's Press, 1983.

The Bride. New York, St. Martin's Press, and London, Cape, 1983.

Ice-Candy-Man. London, Heinemann, 1988; as *Cracking India,* Minneapolis, Milkweed Editions, 1991.

An American Brat. Minneapolis, Milkweed Editions, 1993; London, Penguin, 1994.

* * *

Bapsi Sidhwa, Pakistan's leading English-language novelist, was born in the city of Karachi in 1939 and raised in Lahore, where she graduated from Kinnaird College for women. She emigrated to the United States in 1984, and has taught creative writing at Columbia University, Rice University, and the University of Texas at Houston. Her novels—1978's *The Crow Eaters,* 1983's *The Pakistani Bride, Cracking India,* published in 1991 in the United States and in Britain in 1988 as *Ice-Candy-Man,* and 1993's *An American Brat*—are richly detailed and compelling, as they brilliantly interweave themes of nation, gender, history, and fiction. Her characters, often women, are caught up in the historical events surrounding the geographical and social division or "Partition" of India and Pakistan in 1947, and the subsequent development of Pakistan as an independent nation. Recurring themes include coming of age and its attendant disillusionments, human relationships and betrayals, immigration, and cultural hybridity, as well as social and political upheavals. Sidhwa skillfully links gender to community, nationality, religion, and class, demonstrating the ways in which these various aspects of cultural identity and social structure do not merely affect and/or reflect one another, but are inextricably intertwined.

The Pakistani Bride details the events of Partition through the story of Qasim, a Kohistani tribesman, and Zaitoon, a young girl he adopts after witnessing the massacre in which her family was killed. The story chronicles the events leading up to and following the ill-arranged marriage between Zaitoon and a man of Qasim's tribe in the mountains. *The Crow Eaters,* a wonderfully humorous tale, revolves around the lives of the Junglewallas, a Parsee family in turn-of-the-century India. Sidhwa herself is a member of the Parsee community, comprised of followers of Zoroastrianism, the ancient religion of Iran. Most Parsees migrated to South Asia as refugees in the seventh century, and are now dispersed all over the world. In her preface to *The Crow Eaters,* Sidhwa writes that this novel grew out of her affection for her community, as Parsees are now "an endangered species." Today, there are less than 100,000 Parsees in the entire world.

Cracking India tells, or perhaps *double-tells,* the story of Partition through the eyes of the precocious girl-child Lenny. Using the familiar literary device of an unreliable narrator, the novel conveys two (or many) stories in one. Lenny never understands fully the significance of the uprisings taking place in her world, which she describes as "compressed." "There is much disturbing talk," she says. "India is going to be broken. Can one break a country? And what happens if they break it where our house is? Or crack it further up on Warris Road?" Sometimes she misinterprets the events around her. Thus, on the one hand, *Cracking India* is the story of a young girl's coming of age during political tumult. On the other, it is a complex history of the growing divisions among Hindu, Muslim, and Sikh communities at India at this time, as well as a scathing social commentary about the British colonization of India.

Sidhwa's 1993 novel is her first work of fiction to be set outside of South Asia. *An American Brat* is the charming story of 16-year-old Feroza Ginwalla. Alarmed by the rising fundamentalism of Pakistan in the 1970s, Feroza's mother, Zareen, decides to send her to the United States for a brief "holiday." After an initial culture shock, however, Feroza decides to remain in America as a college student, where she falls in love with a young Jewish man and grows increasingly politicized about such issues as gender, imperialism, and global relations. With humor and depth, Sidhwa manages to convey the complexities of identity, loyalty to community, and cultural differences.

—Patricia Duncan

SIMOS, Miriam. *See* **STARHAWK.**

SIMPSON, Harriette. *See* **ARNOW, Harriette Simpson.**

SINGLE, Tom. *See* **ASTELL, Mary.**

SMEDLEY, Agnes

Nationality: American. **Born:** Missouri, 1892. **Education:** Attended Tempe, Arizona Normal School. **Family:** Married Ernest

Brundin in 1912. **Career:** Teacher in rural school, 1908; worked as a journalist for socialist newspapers, beginning 1917; imprisoned for promoting Indian Anticolonialism; imprisoned while campaigning for women's right to birth control with Margaret Sanger; moved to Europe; worked as a journalist in China, 1928-1941; returned to United States and lectured on China until forced to leave country by FBI after being accused of spying for the Soviets, 1949. **Died:** London, England, 6 May 1950.

Publications

Novel

Daughter of Earth (autobiographical novel). New York, Coward-McCann, 1929; revised edition, 1935; foreword by Alice Walker, New York, Feminist Press, 1987.

Nonfiction

Chinese Destinies: Sketches of Present-Day China. New York, Vanguard Press, 1933.
China's Red Army Marches. New York, Vanguard Press, 1934.
China Fights Back: An American Woman with the Eighth Route Army. New York, Vanguard Press, 1938.
Battle Hymn of China. New York, Knopf, 1943; London, Gollancz, 1944.
The Great Road: The Life and Times of Chu Teh. New York, Monthly Review Press, 1956; London, J. Calder, 1958.
Portraits of Chinese Women in Revolution, edited by Janice R. MacKinnon and Steven R. MacKinnon. Old Westbury, New York, Feminist Press, 1976.

*

Media Adaptation: *Daughter of Earth* (play), 1986.

Manuscript Collections: Hayden Library, Arizona State University, Tempe.

Critical Studies: *Agnes Smedley: The Life and Times of an American Radical* by Janice R. MacKinnon and Stephen R. MacKinnon, Berkeley, University of California Press, 1988.

* * *

Agnes Smedley was an American novelist, journalist, biographer, feminist, and champion of the proletariat. Born on a rural farm in northwestern Missouri, Smedley was raised in the squalid coal-mining towns of southern Colorado. Her father was a heavy-drinking, frequent deserter of his family; her mother, who took in laundry to support her family, died of fatigue by the time her daughter was 16. After her mother's death, Smedley left home and worked odd menial jobs throughout the Southwest until she landed a job teaching in a country school in 1908. She supplemented her scant formal education by attending Tempe Normal School in Arizona for one year, and entered an unsuccessful, short-lived marriage with Ernest Brundin in 1912.

The year 1917 marked the beginning of Smedley's active political campaigns against injustice and discrimination around the world. Traveling from California to New York City to Berlin, Smedley encountered and thrived while living among some of the most radical political thinkers of her time. She became deeply involved with the campaign to free India from British colonial rule, as well as with the Berlin Freudians during the 1920s. She published numerous articles in socialist and progressive papers, and participated in many campaigns in support of feminist causes, such as the formation of birth control clinics—for which she would, like Margaret Sanger, be imprisoned—and socialist revolution. During the 1920s Smedley also became involved in a relationship with Virendranath Chattopadhyaya, an exiled leader of the Indian revolution, which ultimately caused her to suffer a nervous breakdown. She wrote her working-class autobiographical novel, *Daughter of Earth,* as a sort of therapy. Published in 1929, the novel portrays the difficult and guilty struggles of a working-class woman whose feminist and socially conscious beliefs force her to face and combat the oppression of patriarchal society.

In 1928 Smedley traveled to China and became closely involved with the Chinese revolution; this experience was to consume most of the rest of her life and her writing talents. By the 1930s she had become an active participant in and reporter of the revolutionary cause, working ceaselessly to procure medical treatment for the soldiers and writing five books and numerous articles detailing her commitment to the Red Army, the proletariat, and the feminist cause. 1933's *Chinese Destinies: Sketches of Present Day China,* her first book about China, examines, through brief narratives and sketches of the lives of individuals—often women—the optimism of the Chinese revolutionaries who hoped to construct a new and better China out of the bitterness and suffering of the old China. Her next book, *China's Red Army Marching,* traces the progress of the Red Army as it moved inland and secured more territory. *China Fights Back: An American Woman with the Eighth Route Army,* published in 1938, tells the amazing and unique story of Smedley's own travels with the Red Army and describes in journal-like fashion what fighting against the Japanese invaders was really like. Vowing in her writing never to "live the life of a cabbage," she embraced the opportunity to challenge the stifling roles that society offered to women.

Smedley's ill health required her to return to the United States in 1942; there, a year later, she published the *Battle Hymn of China* in an attempt to convey to the American reading public all that she had learned and experienced during her years in China. She had expected to be lauded in her native country as an expert on the situation in China, but wartime America rejected her commitment to the Red Army and the Chinese proletariat. Although she was never an official member of the Communist Party, the national hysteria of McCarthyism led to a false accusation that Smedley was in fact a Soviet spy. Hounded by the FBI, Smedley left America in 1949 for the new People's Republic of China; she would never see the outcome of the revolution she had so zealously supported. Smedley died en route, in London, on 6 May 1950, suffering from the complications of an operation. Her ashes were buried in China.

The Great Road: The Life and Times of Chu Teh, Smedley's fifth book about China, was begun in the 1930s and published posthumously in 1956. It tells the story of the author's personal friend Chu Teh, the Chinese peasant who rose to become the leader of the Red Army. *Portraits of Chinese Women in Revolution,* also published posthumously in 1976, offers further examples of Smedley's dedication to exposing the important roles that women play in society.

Agnes Smedley's works were highly acclaimed during her lifetime, but suffered greatly during the anti-Communist agitation of post-World War II America. Her books essentially disappeared from library shelves during the 1950s, not to reappear until interest in them was revived by the relatively recent *Portraits of Chinese Women in Revolution*, and reprints of her novel, *Daughter of Earth.* Her belief in the potential for positive change that existed within the Chinese revolution and her efforts towards improving the female experience in the Western world secures for her an important place in the canon of feminist writers of the mid-20th century.

—Kathleen Drowne

SMITH, Barbara

Nationality: American. **Born:** Cleveland, Ohio, 16 November 1946. **Education:** Mount Holyoke College, South Hadley, Massachusetts, B.A. 1969; University of Pittsburgh, Pennsylvania, M.A. 1971. **Career:** Instructor in women's studies, University of Massachusetts, 1976-81, Barnard College, 1983, New York University, 1985; visiting professor, University of Minnesota, 1986, Hobart William Smith College, 1987, Mount Holyoke College, 1988. Director of Kitchen Table: Women of Color Press, until 1995; member and founder of Combahee River Collective, 1974-80; artist-in-residence, Hambidge Center for the Arts and Sciences, 1983, Millay Colony for the Arts, 1983, Yaddo, 1984, Blue Mountain Center, 1985; member of board of directors, National Coalition of Black Lesbians and Gays, beginning 1985. Contributor of articles to periodicals, including *Gay Community News, The Guardian, Ms., New Statesman & Society, New York Times Book Review, Sojourner,* and *Village Voice.* **Awards:** Outstanding Woman of Color Award, 1982; Women Educator's Curriculum Award, 1983, for *Some of Us Are Brave: Black Women's Studies;* Albany-area NOW Making Waves Award, 1987; National Women's Political Caucus Media Award, 1988; Jessie Bernard Wise Women Award, 1988; Stonewall Award, 1994; recipient of numerous fellowships. **Member:** National Association for the Advancement of Colored Persons. **Address:** 235 Livingston Ave., Albany, New York 12110-2532, U.S.A.

PUBLICATIONS

Literary Criticism

Toward a Black Feminist Criticism (title essay first appeared in *Conditions: 2,* 1977). Brooklyn, New York, Out & Out Books, 1980.

Political/Social Theory

Yours in Struggle: Three Feminist Perspectives on Anti-Semitism and Racism, with Elly Bulkin and Minnie Bruce Pratt. New York, Long Haul Press, 1984; with new introduction, Ithaca, New York, Firebrand, 1988.

Uncollected Essays

"I Am Not Meant to Be Alone and Without You Who Understand: Letters from Black Feminists," with Beverly Smith, in *Conditions: 4,* 1979.

"Racism and Women's Studies," in *Frontiers,* spring 1980.

"Face-to-Face, Day to Day, Racism CR," with Tia Cross, Freada Klein, and Beverly Smith, in *Women's Studies Newsletter,* winter 1980.

"The Other Black Women" (keynote address at first Eastern Black Lesbian conference, New York, January 1981), in *Gay Community News,* February 1981.

"The Truth That Never Hurts: Black Lesbians in Fiction in the 1980s," in *Third World Women and the Politics of Oppression,* edited by Chandra Mohanty and others. Bloomington, Indiana University Press, 1991.

Other

The History of African American Lesbians and Gays. San Francisco, HarperCollins, 1997.

Editor, with Lorraine Bethel, *Conditions: 5* (black women's issue), 1979.

Editor, with Gloria T. Hull and Patricia Bell Scott, *All the Women Are White, All the Blacks Are Men, But Some of Us Are Brave: Black Women's Studies.* New York, Feminist Press, 1981.

Editor, *Home Girls: A Black Feminist Anthology.* New York, Kitchen Table: Women of Color Press, 1983.

*

Critical Studies: "In Their Own Words" by Thulani Davis, in *Nation,* 25 February 1984; "Coming Home" by Gabrielle Daniels, in *Women's Review of Books,* March 1984; *A Day at a Time: The Diary Literature of American Women* edited by Margo Culley, Old Westbury, New York, Feminist Press, 1985.

Barbara Smith comments:

I believe that what has made my work unique is that I not only write as an African American feminist, but also as an out Black lesbian. Very few Black women have been willing to acknowledge their lesbian identities in print. My writing has helped give support to the lives of many persons that the mainstream ignores and vilifies. It has helped to create bridges between people of myriad races, ethnicities, sexual orientations, and genders and I hope it has servee to strengthen the feminist movement and other progressive movements for social change.

* * *

Barbara Smith is a feminist writer, literary critic, and activist who has been committed to the movement of women of color since 1973. she has taught at numerous colleges and universities including the University of Massachusetts and Hobart William Smith College. A frequent contributor to both popular periodicals and scholarly publications as well as the editor of major anthologies of African American women's writing, Smith is also one of the founders of Kitchen Table: Women of Color Press and the Combahee River Collective.

Smith's scholarly and activist endeavors focus on the specific concerns of black feminists that have been neglected by male critics of Afro-American literature and by white feminists of women's writing. In one of the first efforts to delimit the specificity of black women's writing, Smith's groundbreaking 1977 essay entitled "Toward a Black Feminist Criticism" broke the "massive silence" surrounding black women's experiences, existence, and culture. Accordingly, the essay vigorously rebukes all segments of the literary establishment for their lack of attention to the writing of black and other Third World Women and black lesbian writers. One of the main principles driving Smith's approach to black women's writing is the assumption that African American women writers constitute an identifiable literary tradition. Within this tradition, black women writers demonstrate shared thematic, aesthetic, stylistic, and conceptual approaches to the creation of literature. In this regard, one of the tasks of the black feminist critic is to locate "innumerable commonalities" in the works of black women writers.

According to Smith, an African American feminist critic would think and write out of her own identity rather than in ration to the ideas and methodologies of white and/or male literary predecessors. Furthermore, black feminist criticism, when applied to a particular work by a black woman writer, could overturn previous and often misguided assumptions, thus exposing the work's "actual dimensions" or allowing another set of meanings to emerge. Finally, Smith urges black women to verify the existence of black lesbian literature and to create a climate in which black literary history seriously considers the implications of black lesbian images.

Smith elaborate on this last issue in a later and equally important essay entitles "The Truth That Never Hurts: Black Lesbians in Fiction in the 1980s" (1985). Here she challenges the absence of black lesbians as literary subject, a problem also addressed by Ann Allen Shockley in her 1979 essay "The Black Lesbian in American Literature: An Overview." Smith acknowledges that while black women's literature is much more recognized than it was in 1977, far two many nonlesbian black women either ignore or are actively hostile to black lesbians and the literature they create. Smith insists that black feminist critics who are also feminist activists are more likely to challenge and examine homophobia than those who are divorced from the experiences of activism. The essay then addresses the inaccuracies and distortions surrounding interpretations of lesbian representations and, accordingly, proposes "verisimilitude" and "authenticity" as the essential qualities of "truthful" depictions of lesbians in literature.

Smith devotes much of her scholarly writing to the development of appropriate paradigms to study African American women's literature as a whole. The anthologies she has edited are likewise pedagogically inspired endeavors. *Conditions: 5: The Black Woman's Issue* (1979), for example, brings together writing by black women "outside of usual feminist circles." Moreover, along with Gloria T. Hull and Patricia Bell Scott, Smith prepared one of the first reference texts for Black Women's Studies, entitled *All the Women Are White, All the Blacks Are Men, But Some of Us Are Brave.* This anthology provides materials essential to establishing a "frameworks in which Black Women's Studies can be most successfully taught" as well as articles on black women's health, music, and literature. Indeed, this collection has played an essential role in encouraging the acceptance of Black Women's Studies in university curriculums.

Smith's feminist organizing efforts include a founding role in the Combahee River Collective, a group of African American feminists devoted to struggling against racism, sexism, homophobia, and class oppression. furthermore, her involvement in Kitchen Table: Women of Color Press reflects her lifelong commitment to make visible the writing and culture of women of color. According to Smith, the Press began to ensure the autonomy and independence for "multiply disenfranchised women of color" to create and determine their own words and images. Inaugurated in 1981, Kitchen Table is both an activist and literary international publisher as well as a resource center whose target audience is people of color, a constituency often ignored by the mainstream and alternative press alike. Along with Smith's *Home Girls: A Feminist Anthology,* Kitchen Table, under Smith's direction, has published poetry by Audre Lorde and Gloria T. Hull and political theory by Angela Davis. Smith's concurrent scholarship and activism, as well as her lifelong connection to black feminist organizations, places her at the center of 20th-century revolutionary struggle.

—Annmarie Pinarski

SMITH, Lillian

Nationality: American. **Born:** Jasper, Florida, 12 December 1897. **Education:** Attended Piedmont College, Demorest, Georgia, 1915; Peabody Conservatory, Baltimore, 1917, 1919; Columbia Teacher's College, New York, 1928. **Military Service:** Member of Student Nursing Corps, 1918. **Career:** Teacher and head of music department, Virginia Methodist Mission School, Huchow, Chekiang, China, 1922-25; director, with Paula Snelling, and owner, Laurel Falls Camp for Girls, Clayton, Georgia, 1925-49; cofounder, with Snelling, editor, and publisher, *Pseudopodia* (renamed *North Georgia Review,* then *South Today*), 1936-45; travelled to Brazil, 1938; ban on prohibition of first novel, *Strange Fruit,* through the U.S. mails lifted by Eleanor Roosevelt, 1944; teacher of creative writing, University of Indiana and University of Colorado; lecturer, Vassar College, 1955; home destroyed by arson, 1955, 1958. Contributor to periodicals, including *Life, Nation, New Republic, New York Times, Redbook,* and *Saturday Review.* **Awards:** Page One award, 1944, and Constance Skinner Lindsay Award, 1945, both for *Strange Fruit;* Southern Award, 1949, for *Killers of the Dream;* Sidney Hillman award, 1962; National Book Award Committee citation for "distinguished contribution to American letters"; Rosenwald Foundation fellowships. Honorary degrees: Oberlin College, Howard University, Atlanta University. **Member:** American Civil Liberties Union (vice-president; member of national board), Congress for Racial Equality (member of advisory board; resigned 1966), Authors Guild. **Died:** Of cancer, in Atlanta, Georgia, 28 September 1966.

Publications

Novels

Strange Fruit. New York, Reynal, 1944.
One Hour. New York, Harcourt, 1959.

Essays

Now Is the Time. New York, Viking, 1955.
Our Faces, Our Words (pictorial essay). New York, Norton, 1964.

Autobiography

Killers of the Dream. New York, Norton, 1949; revised edition, Garden City, New York, Doubleday, 1963.
The Journey. World Publishing, 1954.
Memory of a Large Christmas. New York, Norton, 1962.

Play

Strange Fruit, with Esther Smith (adapted from her novel; produced Canada; produced New York, 1945).

Other

From the Mountain (originally published in *The South Today*), edited by Helen White and Redding Sugg Jr. N.p., 1972.
The Winner Names the Age: A Collection of Writings by Lillian Smith, edited by Michelle Cliff. New York, Norton, 1978.
Am I to Be Heard? Letters of Lillian Smith, edited by Margaret Rose Gladney. Chapel Hill, University of North Carolina Press, 1993.

*

Bibliography: *A Bibliography of Lillian Smith and Paula Snelling with an Index to The South Today* by Margaret Sullivan, n.p., 1971.

Manuscript Collections: University of Florida, Gainsville; University of Georgia, Athens; Library of Congress, Washington, DC.

Critical Studies: "Lillian Smith: The Public Image and the Personal Vision" by Margaret Sullivan, in *Mad River Review,* summer/fall 1967; "Lillian Smith and the Condition of Women" by Redding Sugg Jr., in *South Atlantic Quarterly,* spring 1972; "Lillian Smith: Reflections on Race and Sex" by Jo Ann Robinson, in *Southern Exposure,* winter 1977; "Lillian Smith: The Southern Liberal as Evangelist" by Morton Sosna, in his *In Search of the Silent South: Southern Liberals and the Race Issue,* New York, Columbia University Press, 1977; "In Re Lillian Smith" by Paula Snelling, in *The Winner Names the Age,* edited by Michelle Cliff, New York, Norton, 1978; *Lillian Smith: A Southerner Confronting the South* by Anne C. Loveland, 1986.

* * *

"Even its children knew that the South was in trouble. No one had to tell them; no words said it aloud." So Lillian Smith opened her controversial memoir, *Killers of the Dream,* a poignant account of the ways that segregation damaged whites as well as blacks in Southern society.

Born to a prosperous middle class family in rural Jasper, Florida, Smith enjoyed a comfortable childhood. Her father ran a profitable naval stores operation and provided his 10 children with the best that money could buy. By her own accounts, theirs was a loving family. Yet her memoir describes wrenching moments created by life in the racially segregated, sexually repressive South: "The mother who taught me what I know of tenderness and love and compassion taught me also the bleak rituals of keeping Negroes in their 'place.' The father who rebuked me for an air of superiority toward schoolmates from the mill and rounded out his rebuke by gravely reminding me that 'all men are brothers,' trained me in the steel-rigid decorum I must demand of every colored male. They who so gravely taught me to split my body from my mind and both from my 'soul,' taught me also to split my conscience from my acts and Christianity from southern tradition." The paradox between her parents' teachings and their actions deeply troubled the child and launched her on a lifelong mission to rouse other Southerners to the hypocrisy inherent in a democratic society which so rigidly proscribed the behaviors of its women and its blacks.

The formative event of Smith's childhood involved this schizophrenic dichotimization of Southern society by race. She describes how her family took in a small white girl found living in a poor home in the black section of Jasper. Whites believed the poor child had been kidnapped by a black family, and the Smith family rescued her, giving her new clothing and treating her as one of their own children. The child, whom they called Janie, was Lillian's age, and the two became fast friends in the few weeks Janie lived with the Smiths. Unfortunately it was soon discovered that Janie was not a white child, as she appeared, but rather a mulatto. Shocked and dismayed, Smith's parents returned Janie to the poor black home where she had been found. In *Killers of the Dream,* Smith describes in heart-rending detail her own confusion and pain at the incident. When she persisted in asking her mother how someone who looked white could be considered black and why black and white people could not live together, her mother told her that she was too young to understand. "I knew my father and mother whom I passionately admired had betrayed something which they held dear," Smith recalled. "And they could not help doing it.... There was something Out There that was stronger than they." This pivotal event shaped Smith's life and her career.

If her own confrontations with the South's racial caste system led Smith to question her own society, a reversal of her father's fortunes propelled her outside the South where she gained the tools to provoke others' questioning. When World War I broke out, the market for naval stores dried up, forcing Smith's father to close his business and move the family to the mountains of northern Georgia. Here he opened a summer hotel and the Laurel Falls Camp for Girls. Smith's education was affected by this financial setback. For a number of years, she seemed to drift, unsure of which path she wanted to take and finding her options restricted by the lack of resources. She attended Piedmont College in Georgia for a year before dropping out to manage her father's new business, a hotel in Daytona Beach, Florida. While there, she met a violinist who urged her to pursue a musical career, so she fled to Baltimore where she enrolled in Peabody Conservatory to study piano. When the United States entered World War I in 1918, she dropped out to join the Student Nursing Corps. After the war, she taught school in a rural Georgia community for a year before returning to Peabody Conservatory. In the end, Smith decided that she was not talented enough to be a concert pianist; she went to Huchow, China, to head the music department at a Methodist mission school.

The three years she spent in China also shaped Smith's thinking about race. She was deeply affected by seeing white missionaries try to force "superior white ideas" on the Chinese. Smith herself saw the Chinese preoccupation with their spiritual lives as being superior to the materialism of the West. In China, she also discovered a passion for educating children and plunged into a study of psychology that was to inform her future work. She came to believe that sexual and social repression were closely linked and were damaging to children.

In 1925 Smith returned to Georgia to take over the running of Laurel Falls Camp from her ailing father. After his death, she continued to run the camp and care for her mother. At the camp, she tried to put her ideas about child psychology to work, particularly encouraging her campers to question the racial caste system in which they lived.

Upon her return to North Georgia, Smith formed one of the most important relationships of her life. She hired a young woman named Paula Snelling to assist her in running Laurel Falls Camp and the two became lifelong companions. Under the direction of the two, Laurel Falls developed a reputation as one of the finest girls camps in the South.

In the winter months when the camp was closed, Smith turned to writing. Her racial and sexual views made her work unique controversial for the day. She understood the intricate relationship between racial oppression and the oppression of white women. She also developed a strong feminist consciousness, writing about the difficulty that women had in establishing independent careers if they were married. Moreover, her work affirmed that women were sexual beings. She dealt explicitly with masturbation, homosexuality, and a healthy sexual attitude.

In 1935, in order to provide an outlet for Smith's work, Smith and Snelling began a small magazine devoted to Southern topics. Initially they called the publication *Pseudopodia,* but it soon became the *North Georgia Review* and eventually *The South Today.* Through articles and editorials in this organ, Smith began to attack segregation and racism, carefully at first, more forcefully as time went on. The magazine also provided a vehicle for young Southern liberals, particularly women, to express their own unorthodox racial views. The magazine grew, achieving a circulation of 10,000 before Smith closed it in 1945.

In addition to her work on *The South Today,* Smith continued to pursue larger fiction and non-fiction projects. Her first novel, published in 1944, was *Strange Fruit,* named for a line from a Billie Holliday song. Taking as its subject an ill-fated interracial love affair, the novel pays close attention to the pathological damage done by the South's constricting racial and sexual expectations. Banned for obscenity in Massachusetts, the book brought Smith considerable notoriety and was the first widespread distribution of her ideas that Southern segregation did irreparable psychological harm to whites as well as blacks. The book also lessened Smith's dependence on the camp for income and enabled her to devote more time to writing and speaking.

Her second book, the 1949 memoir *Killers of the Dream,* went further, openly denouncing segregation. In a foreword to a later edition of the book, Smith noted that she wrote the book as a way of exorcising her own ghosts, of understanding what life in a segregated culture had done to her. She noted that "I realize this is a personal memoir, in one sense; in another sense, it is Every Southerner's memoir.... This haunted childhood belongs to every southerner of my age." Predictably, the book was widely criticized by white Southerners, but it also increased Smith's popularity as a lecturer outside the South. The royalties from the book and her lecture fees made it possible for Smith to close the camp in 1949 and devote all her energies to writing, speaking, and activism in various Southern liberal organizations.

Smith's later works were never as well-marketed or as popular as her earlier books. She also paid a high price for her criticism of segregation. Arsonists set fire to her home in 1955, and again in 1958, destroying unpublished manuscripts and many of her personal papers.

Undeterred by such events, Smith went on to support the non-violent civil rights movement fronted by Dr. Martin Luther King, serving on the board of the Congress of Racial Equality (CORE) until 1966 when the organization adopted a militant black power stance. Smith insisted that a humane world would be free of the alienation preached by black separatists and refused to affiliate with any movement that took such a stand. Her final book, *Our Faces, Our Words* (1964), paid tribute to the non-violent civil rights movement in a photo essay.

In her final days Lillian Smith turned her attention more fully to examining the roles that society allows women to play. When she died of breast cancer in Atlanta in 1966, she left unfinished a novel that, according to Snelling, Smith had hoped would be her major work "on the seductive subject of gender."

—Melissa Walker

SMITH, Rosamond. *See* **OATES, Joyce Carol.**

SMYTH, Dame Ethel Mary

Nationality: British. **Born:** London, 23 April 1858. **Education:** Home-schooled by governesses; studied music at Leipzig Conservatorium, 1878-85. **Career:** Composer of symphonies, choral works, and operas, including *Der Wald* (1902), *The Wreckers* (produced Leipzig, 1906), and *The Boatswain's Mate* (1916). Joined Women's Social and Political Union, 1910; wrote "The March of the Women," 1911; imprisoned for two months but served three weeks in Holloway Gaol, 1912. **Awards:** Created Dame of the British Empire, 1922; honorary degrees: D.Mus. University of Durham, 1910; Mus.Doc., Oxon, 1926; D.Litt., St. Andrews University, 1928. **Died:** 8 May 1944.

Publications

Autobiography

The Memoirs of Ethel Smyth. New York, Viking, 1987.
- *Impressions That Remained.* London and New York, Longmans Green, 2 vols., 1919.
- *As Time Went On.* London and New York, Longmans Green, 1936.
- *What Happened Next.* London and New York, Longmans Green, 1940.

Other

Streaks of Life. London and New York, Longmans Green, 1921.
A Three-Legged Tour in Greece. London, Heinemann, 1927.
A Final Burning of Boats. London and New York, Longmans Green, 1928.

Female Pipings for Eden. London, P. Davies, 1933.
Beecham and Pharoah. London, Chapman & Hall, 1935.
Inordinate(?) Affection. London, Cresset, 1936.
Maurice Baring. London and Toronto, Heinemann, 1938.

*

Manuscript Collections: British Library, London; National Library of Wales; King College Modern Archive Centre, Cambridge University, Cambridge; Herfordshire Record Office; Walter Clinton Jackson Library, University of North Carolina and Greensboro.

Critical Studies: *Ethel Smyth: A Biography* by Christopher St. John, London, Longmans, 1959; "Women, Music, and Ethel Smyth: A Pathway in the Politics of Music" by Elizabeth Wood, in *Massachusetts Review,* 24(1), 1983; *Impetuous Heart: The Story of Ethel Smyth* by Louise Collis, London, William Kimber, 1984.

* * *

In most biographical sourcebooks, such as *Who Was Who* or the *Dictionary of National Biography,* Dame Ethel Smyth is referred to as first a composer and writer and then a feminist. This might be because Smyth embraced feminism in 1910—only after she had first established herself as a composer of considerable repute, both on the continent and in England. Through both her talent and determination, she became the first woman to compose large-scale operas, oratorios, and concertos, achievements for which Smyth was awarded an honorary doctorate in music from the University of Durham in 1910.

Most women's historians remember Smyth for her "March of the Women," the rallying cry for the militant suffrage movement that she wrote in 1911 as part of a welcome ceremony for 21 suffragettes released from prison. "March of the Women" would be followed by two other suffrage songs—"Laggard Dawn," which symbolized a new society bestowed by female enfranchisement, and "1910, A Medley," which described a demonstration.

Smyth was born to Major General John Hall Smyth and Nancy Struth in 1858, the fourth child of eight: six daughters and two sons. She had a stormy relationship with her mother for all of her life, and struggled with her strong-willed father for permission to learn music after she first heard a Beethoven sonata in 1870. Finally, in 1877, 19-year-old Smyth won the battle of wills; her father reluctantly allowed her to go to Leipzig where she studied music for seven years and attached herself to the first of many women she would meet there, Elizabeth "Lisl" Herzongenberg, a friend of Brahms.

It was while she was in Leipzig that Smyth also met Harry Brewster, the wife of Lisl's sister, Julia. Brewster immediately fell in love with Smyth, who resisted entering into a sexual relationship with him until 1895, after his wife had died. Even then Smyth refused to marry Brewster as she was loath to compromise her independence, but agreed that they could become lovers, a relationship that would last until Brewster's death in 1908. Although drawn sexually to Brewster, Smyth was also drawn to physical relationships with women, including the Princesse de Polignac, and the authors Edith Somerville and Virginia Woolf.

According to biographers, Smyth was converted to the women's cause after hearing Emmeline Pankhurst speak at a suffrage meeting in 1910. She originally planned to work for women's suffrage for two years, after which time she would return to writing music. Smyth identified personally with the idea that men repressed and suppressed women in society; she firmly believed that her musical works had not received the attention they deserved because they were written by a woman rather than a man. She was critical of male orchestra members and male conductors for not allowing women to progress in the field of music and composition. The high point of Smyth's years as a suffragist activist occurred in 1912 when she was arrested for throwing a stone through the window of the London home of the anti-suffragist Colonial Secretary, Lewis Harcourt. Smyth was sentenced to two months hard labor, but served only three weeks. She did not participate in the arson campaign that began in 1912 and escalated to the destruction of property; although she did agree with these extreme tactics in principle, she eventually regretted them. The last major political demonstration Smyth took part in was the funeral of Emily Davison in 1913.

World War I virtually ended Smyth's association with the Pankhursts. She began a series of reminiscences in 1919, with *Impressions That Remained,* and in 1922 was created Dame Commander of the Order of the British Empire. She also, tragically, suffered from deafness and hearing distortion; much of the remainder of her life would be spent writing about her earlier years as a noted musician. Smyth died on 8 May 1944.

—Lori Williamson

SOLWOSKA, Mara. *See* **FRENCH, Marilyn.**

SOMERS, Jane. *See* **LESSING, Doris.**

SOMMERS, Christina Hoff

Nationality: American. **Education:** Attended Sorbonne, Paris, 1971; New York University, B.A. in philosophy 1973; Brandeis University, Ph.D. 1979. **Family:** Married the professor Fred Sommers in 1981; two sons. **Career:** Instructor, University of Massachusetts, Boston, 1978-80; assistant professor, 1980-86, then associate professor of philosophy, beginning 1986, Clark University, Worcester, Massachusetts. Visiting lecturer, University of Pittsburgh semester at sea, 1987-88; fellow, Ditchley Foundation, Oxford, 1988. Member, board of advisors, Independent Women's Forum and American Textbook Council; member of advisory committee on Feminism and Philosophy, American Philosophical Association, Eastern division, 1992-95. Contributor to periodicals, including *New Criterion, Partisan Review, Times Literary Supplement, USA Today, Wall Street Journal,* and *Weekly Standard.* **Awards:** Clark University Mellon faculty grant; Higgins Research grant, National Endowment for the Humanities fellow. **Member:**

Phi Beta Kappa. **Address:** Department of Philosophy, Clark University, 950 Main Street, Worcester, Massachusetts 01610-1400, U.S.A.

Publications

Political/Social Theory

Who Stole Feminism? How Women Have Betrayed Women. New York and London, Simon & Schuster, 1994.

Essays

"Ethics without Virtue: Moral Education in America," in *American Scholar,* March 1984.
"Philosophers against the Family," in *Person to Person,* edited by George Graham and Hugh La Follette, Philadelphia, Temple University Press, 1988.
"The Feminist Revelation," in *Ethics, Politics, and Human Nature,* edited by Ellen Paul, Oxford, Basil Blackwell, 1990.
"Do These Feminists Like Women?" in *Journal of Social Philosophy,* spring 1991.
"Pathological Social Science: Carol Gilligan and the Incredible Shrinking Girl," in *The Flight from Science and Reason* (New York Academy of Sciences), June 1996.

Other

Editor, with Robert J. Fogelin, *Vice and Virtue in Everyday Life: Introductory Readings in Ethics.* San Diego, Harcourt Brace, 1984; 4th edition, with Fred Sommers, Fort Worth and London, Harcourt Brace College, 1996.
Editor, with Robert J. Fogelin, *Right and Wrong: Basic Readings in Ethics.* San Diego, Harcourt Brace, 1985.

*

Critical Studies: Special *Who Stole Feminism?* issue of *Democratic Culture,* 3(2), fall 1994; review of *Who Stole Feminism?* by Jean Bethke Elshtain, in *New Republic,* 11 July 1994; "Untainted by Testosterone" by Cathy Young, in *Commentary,* September 1994; "I'm Not a Feminist But I Play One on TV" by Susan Faludi, in *Ms.,* March/April 1995.

* * *

Philosopher and educator Christina Hoff Sommers's principle work, *Who Stole Feminism?,* is an edgy invective against contemporary feminism as the author perceives it. Armed with exaggerations and mistatements of women's vulnerabilities, the "gender feminists" of the 1990s, as Hoff Sommers calls them, "condescend to patronize and pity the benighted females who, because they have been 'socialized' in the sex/gender system, cannot help wanting the wrong things in life." She revisits and finds factual errors in popular feminist "mythologies," including the backlash ("where did Faludi and Wolf get the idea that masses of seemingly free women were being mysteriously manipulated from within?"), the anorexia epidemic, the prevalence of domestic violence and rape ("very little of [male violence] appears to be misogynist.... Rape is just one variety of crime against the person"), and the corrosion of young women's self esteem ("once again we find that the gender feminists' ideological and partisan treatment of a problem ... ends up confusing the issues"). These mythologies and inflated academic theories of patriarchy, she asserts, have reduced women to "victims" instead of the "free creatures" they in fact are.

Hoff Sommers lays blame for the degradation of feminism, ironically, on feminists themselves. She indicts "professional," academic feminists ensconced in the American university, protected by tenure, emboldened by feminism's "bureaucracy of its own," and tied to sources of funding that encourage them to have a professional and economic stake in exaggerating women's oppression.

Despite her lament for contemporary feminism, Hoff Sommers does proclaim herself a feminist who hopes to see a revitalization of classic liberal "equity feminism" in the tradition of Elizabeth Cady Stanton and Betty Friedan. Equity feminism would concern itself with equality and an end to discrimination rather than the all-encompassing, enfeebling views of sexist culture devised by gender feminists.

Although widely criticized by feminists, Hoff Sommers's work does capture a prevalent dissatisfaction among women in the 1980s and 1990s with the conventions and "pc" protocols of some versions of campus feminism. Few who have participated in university politics would deny that some feminists have opted for a tedious, therapeutic style rather than challenging themselves to generate a political agenda or idea. Most academic feminists have attended at least one of the self-absorbed conferences that Hoff Sommers humorously takes exception to and have flinched at its preoccupations with personal "healing" or its intellectual timidity.

Despite her useful, if blunt, attempt to put the brakes on "victim feminism," critics have noted that Hoff Sommers's overstatements and blanket indictments of <u>one</u> version of feminism are based on a simplification of both contemporary feminism and the "equity feminism" she summons from 19th-century "first wave" tradition. Caught in what critic Jean Bethke Elshtain calls "too sharp and severe a contrast " between the "bad new" and the "good old" feminism, Hoff Sommers links a baffling array of disparate feminist ideologies—some of which contradict each other—under the self-fashioned term gender feminism. Those who have dismantled the "sex/gender" concept entirely—poststructuralist feminists—in Hoff Sommers's world share the same ideological ground as the "difference" feminists against whom poststructuralists write. Similarly, those feminists who endorse women-only communities due to "essential" differences between the sexes would find themselves, much to their shock, on the same map by Hoff Sommers's cartography.

Hoff Sommers pairs a misreading of contemporary feminism with a simplification of first wave feminism in order to bolster her "good old" and "bad new" distinction. Heroines Stanton and Friedan, for example, never confined themselves to a bread-and-butter concern with "equality" and an end to discrimination, as Hoff Sommers caricatures their position. Instead, they tackled issues as diverse as, in Stanton's case, dress reform, domestic science, prostitution, and domestic violence and, in Friedan's case, the sublte socialization of men and women in marriage. These manifestations of oppression were no more classically "liberal" concerns than the issues—date rape, anorexia, the "beauty myth"—that preoccupy contemporary feminists.

Perhaps more significantly, however, Hoff Sommers's analysis seems to ask readers to choose between two simplified points of view. The first "gender feminist" point of view, as Hoff Sommers understands it, asserts that women are paralyzed "victims" in the face of subtle sexist practices. The second point of view, one that Hoff Sommers endorses, is that these subtle sexist practices do not really exist—are ridden with factual misstatements—and that women therefore are in fact "free creatures."

Undoubtedly, women's encounters with sexism conform to neither of these simple labels. It is most plausible that women—and all individuals—are simultaneously "free creatures," as Hoff Sommers would put it, and people who are shaped and affected—sometimes negatively—by the sex roles that organize our social relations. Only the crudest feminist—the one that Hoff Sommers uses as a straw man throughout her work—would condescend that women lead joyless lives under the grip of a patriarchy that renders them "helpless." Even the most downtrodden "victim" finds ways to act in the world. Yet only the most embattled feminist critic, by the same token, would deny that women live in a culture with meaningful and powerful, if subtle, prescriptions for how women and men should act, and that these expectations deserve a place in any intelligent cultural analysis, since they have so much to do with our lives. Acknowledging women as "free creatures," in other words, should not require denying the existence of subtly compelling forces such as body image or implied physical violence.

—Pamela Haag

SONG, Cathy

Nationality: American. **Born:** Oahu, Hawai'i, 1955. **Education:** Wellesley College, B.A. 1977; Boston University, M.F.A. 1981. **Family:** Married Douglas Davenport, two children. **Career:** Teaches creative writing at various universities. Contributor to periodicals, including *Asian-Pacific Literature, Hawai'i Review, Poetry,* and *Seneca Review.* **Awards:** Yale Younger Poets Award, 1983, for *Picture Bride;* Shelley Memorial Award; Hawai'i Award for Literature. **Address:** Honolulu, Hawai'i, U.S.A.

Publications

Poetry

Picture Bride. New Haven and London, Yale University Press, 1983.

Frameless Windows, Squares of Light. New York and London, Norton, 1988.

School Pictures. London and Pittsburgh, University of Pittsburgh Press, 1994.

Other

Editor, with Juliet Kono, *Sister Stew: Fiction and Poetry by Women.* Honolulu, Hawai'i, Bamboo Ridge Press, 1991.

*

Critical Studies: "Cathy Song: 'I'm a Poet Who Happens to Be Asian American' by Debbie Murakami Nomaguchi, in *International Examiner* (Seattle, Washington), 2(11), May 2, 1984; "'Third World' as Place and Paradigm in Cathy Song's *Picture Bride*" by Gayle K. Fujita-Sato, *MELUS,* 15(1), 1988; "Divided Loyalties: Literal and Literary in the Poetry of Lorna Dee Cervantes, Cathy Song and Rita Dove" by Patricia Wallace, *MELUS,* 18(3), 1993.

* * *

"I'm a poet who happens to be Asian American," Cathy Song once stated during an interview in the *International Examiner.* Indeed, Song does not wish to be categorized as "Asian American" or "Hawaiian," as is often the tendency of many critics. Instead, she believes that the rich world she creates within her poetry transcends her own ethnic or regional background.

Born in Honolulu, Hawai'i, of both Korean and Chinese ancestry, Song has a background that is as rich and varied as the world she evokes in her writing. Her grandfather emigrated from China to the island of Hawai'i to work as a plantation laborer; her grandmother was his "picture bride," brought from Korea early in the 20th century. Encouraged in her early efforts at writing, Song earned her B.A. from Boston's Wellesley College in 1977 and an M.A. in creative writing from Boston University in 1981.

Song's position in contemporary American poetry has been firmly established with the success of her first three books: *Picture Brides,* published in 1983, *Frameless Windows, Squares of Light,* published five years later, in 1988, and 1994's *School Figures. Picture Bride* won the prestigious Yale Series of Younger Poets competition for 1982 and was nominated for the National Book Critics Circle Award. Other awards for her verse have include the Shelley Memorial Award and the Hawai'i Award for Literature. Song currently resides in Honolulu with her husband and two children, and teaches creative writing at various universities.

Song's poetry concerns the ties binding women to family, to history, and to the land. In the title poem of *Picture Bride,* the poet reminisces about her grandmother: as a picture bride, she left Korea at age 23 to marry a man whom she had never seen in person. They meet and, though her husband's advanced age must have disappointed the young woman, she continues, as she has always done, to endure, accepting her fate. Another poem, "The Youngest Daughter," focuses on a woman who, while bathing her aged mother, reflects on the latter's dedication to her family. And "Lost Sister" advocates women's freedom within a male-dominated Chinese society.

Frameless Windows, Squares of Light continues the theme of family history and relations. The poem "Magic Island" is a recollection of an immigrant family's picnicking in Hawai'i. In "The Tower of Pisa" Song dwells on her father, an airplane pilot whose life was "one of continual repair." "Humble Jar" is written in praise of the poet's Cantonese mother, a seamstress. Song again treats the theme of womanhood in "A Mehinaku Girl in Seclusion," where a tribal girl, after her first menstruation, is removed from society and "married to the earth" for three years.

In *School Figures,* the poet characteristically resumes her family stories. The poems "A Conservative View" and "Journey" explore the lives of Song's parents and in "Sunworshippers" the poet remembers her mother's advice against self-indulgence. The experiences within these poems—coping with the death of a father, listening to the mealtime clatter of relatives, gazing at the upturned face of an infant, and the many hurdles to be overcome in marital relationships—are, through Cathy Song's sensitive, exacting prose, made universal.

—Jae-Nam Han

SOPHIA

A pseudonym. **Other Pseudonyms:** A Gentleman. **Nationality:** British. **Published:** fl. 1739-1741.

Publications

Essays

Beauty's Triumph (includes *Woman Not Inferior to Man, Man Superior to Woman,* and *Woman's Superior Excellence over Man*). London, n.p., 1751; as *Female Restoration,* London, n.p., 1780.

Woman Not Inferior to Man, or A Short and Modest Vindication of the Natural Rights of the Fair-Sex to a Perfect Equality of Power, Dignity, and Esteem, with the Men. London, n.p., 1739.

Man Superior to Woman: or, a Vindication of Man's Natural Right of Sovereign Authority over the Woman (as "A Gentleman"). London, n.p., 1739.

Woman's Superior Excellence over Man. London, J. Hawkin, 1740.

*

Critical Studies: *First Feminists* edited by Moira Ferguson, Bloomington, Indiana University Press, 1985; *The 18th-century Feminist Mind* by Alice Browne, Detroit, Wayne University Press, 1987; "Poulain de la Barre's *The Woman as Good as the Man*" by Michael Seidel, in *Journal of the History of Ideas,* 35(3), 1974; *Women, the Family, and Freedom* edited by Susan Groag Bell and Karen M. Offen, Stanford, Stanford University Press, 1983.

* * *

The identity of the author who published the "Sophia tracts" in 1739 and 1740 is still a mystery. These feminist treatises are thus labeled because they were written by "Sophia, a Person of Quality." Sophia's first essay, *Woman Not Inferior to Man, or A Short and Modest Vindication of the Natural Rights of the Fair-Sex to a Perfect Equality of Power, Dignity, and Esteem with the Men* (1739) incited an anti-feminist response in the popular press later that same year. Sophia then answered the arguments in *Man Superior to Woman: or, a Vindication of Man's Natural Right of Sovereign Authority over the Woman,* which was signed by "a Gentleman," with her *Woman's Superior Excellence over Man* (1740).

With *Woman Not Inferior to Man,* Sophia was answering a piece published in the political journal *Common Sense.* As Sophia describes the purpose of her essay:

> In the course of this little treatise I shall also occasionally examin, whether there be *any essential difference between* the *sexes* which can authorize the *superiority* the *Men* claim over the *Women*; and what are the causes of, and who are accountable for, the seeming difference which makes the sum of their plea. And if, upon mature consideration, it appears that there is no other difference between *Men* and *Us* than what their tyrany has created, it will then appear how unjust they are in excluding us from that power and dignity we have a right to share with them; how ungenerous in denying us the equality of esteem, which is our due; and how little reason they have to triumph in the base possession of an authority, which unnatural violence, and lawless usurpation, put into their Hands.

As Sophia investigates these issues, she determines that the intellectual inequality of the sexes results not from any anatomical difference between men and women, but from the customarily inferior education for women. She insists on commiserate education and greater professional opportunities for women, suggesting that women can succeed in politics, academics and the military.

Sophia's diatribe against "custom," several of her arguments, and the format in *Woman Not Inferior to Man* reveal the influence of Poulain de la Barre, a French author whose treatise on sexual equality was translated as *The Woman as Good as the Man: Or, the Equality of Both Sexes* by "A.L." in 1677. According to Michael A. Seidel, Poulain's "work is a largely ignored seed-bed of feminist thinking, containing in many ways more startling ideas than better known works of more renowned feminists," such as Mary Astell, Mary Wollstonecraft and John Stuart Mill. Although Sophia probably derived many arguments from Poulain and may have reshaped A.L.'s translation, she made *Woman Not Inferior to Man* distinctly British by adding references to British scholars and heroines, such as Alexander Pope and Queen Elizabeth: "*England* has learn'd by repeated experience, how much happier a kingdom is, when under the protection and rule of *a Woman,* than it can hope to be under the government of a *Man.*"

Sophia's debt to Poulain does not conclude with *Woman Not Inferior to Man,* because *Man to Superior to Woman* also follows Poulain's format. Although this essay was signed "a Gentleman," several scholars attribute the piece to Sophia. This stratagem (arguing with herself) she also may have derived from Poulain, who responded to his own book by writing against it himself, thereby indirectly confirming his own arguments. It appears that Sophia also employed this technique, and then responded to her own anti-feminist ploys with her final treatise, *Woman's Superior Excellence over Man.* Thus, Seidel's description of Poulain as arguing "only with himself as a sounding board," but arguing adamantly in the feminist cause seems to apply aptly to Sophia as well.

According to Sophia, *Woman's Superior Excellence over Man* was intended to be a "Reply to the Author of a late Treatise, entitled, *Man Superior to Woman.* In which, the excessive weakness of that Gentleman's Answer to *Woman Not Inferior to Man* is exposed; with a plain Demonstration of Woman's natural Right even to Superiority over the Men in Head and Heart; proving their Minds as much more beautiful than the Men's as their Bodies are, and that, had they the same Advantages of Education, they would excel them as much in Sense as they do in Virtue." This final and longest tract ended Sophia's literary career, because her proposed "parallel History of the most eminent persons of both sexes in past ages" never surfaced, and her true identity was never discovered, although scholars speculate that "Sophia" could have been a pseudonym for Lady Mary Wortley Montagu, Lady Granville, or, perhaps even a man.

—Staci L. Stone

SPARK, Muriel (Sarah)

Nationality: British. **Born:** Muriel Sarah Camberg in Edinburgh, 1 February 1918. **Education:** James Gillespie's School for Girls and Heriot Watt College, both Edinburgh. **Military Service:** Worked in the Foreign Office Political Intelligence Department, 1944. **Family:** Married S.O. Spark in 1937 (marriage ended by 1944); one son. **Career:** Travelled in Rhodesia (now Zimbabwe), 1936-44; general secretary, Poetry Society, and editor, *Poetry Review,* London, 1947-49; founder, *Forum* magazine; converted to Catholicism, 1954. **Awards:** *Observer* story prize, 1951; Italia prize for dramatic radio, 1962, for *The Ballad of Peckenham Rye;* James Tait Black Memorial prize, 1966, for *The Mandelbaum Gate;* F.N.A.C. prize (France), 1987; Bram Stoker award, 1988; Royal Bank of Scotland—Saltire Society award, 1988, for *The Stories of Muriel Spark;* Ingersoll T. S. Eliot award, 1992. D.Litt.: University of Strathclyde, Glasgow, 1971; University of Edinburgh, 1989. Fellow, Royal Society of Literature, 1963; honorary member, American Academy, 1978. O.B.E. (Officer, Order of the British Empire), 1967; Officier de l'Ordre des Arts et des Lettres, 1988; D.B.E. (Dame), 1993. **Agent:** David Higham Associates, Ltd., 5-8 Lower John Street, Golden Square, London W1R 4HA, England.

Publications

Novels

The Comforters. London, Macmillan, and Philadelphia, Lippincott, 1957.
Robinson. London, Macmillan, and Philadelphia, Lippincott, 1958.
Memento Mori. London, Macmillan, and Philadelphia, Lippincott, 1959.
The Ballad of Peckham Rye. London, Macmillan, and Philadelphia, Lippincott, 1960.
The Bachelors. London, Macmillan, 1960; Philadelphia, Lippincott, 1961.
The Prime of Miss Jean Brodie. London, Macmillan, 1961; Philadelphia, Lippincott, 1962.
The Girls of Slender Means. London, Macmillan, and New York, Knopf, 1963.
The Mandelbaum Gate. London, Macmillan, and New York, Knopf, 1965.
The Public Image. London, Macmillan, and New York, Knopf, 1968.
The Driver's Seat. London, Macmillan, and New York, Knopf, 1970.
Not to Disturb. London, Macmillan, 1971; New York, Viking Press, 1972.
The Hothouse by the East River. London, Macmillan, and New York, Viking Press, 1973.
The Abbess of Crewe. London, Macmillan, and New York, Viking Press, 1974.
The Takeover. London, Macmillan, and New York, Viking Press, 1976.
Territorial Rights. London, Macmillan, and New York, Coward McCann, 1979.
Loitering with Intent. London, Bodley Head, and New York, Coward McCann, 1981.
The Only Problem. London, Bodley Head, and New York, Coward McCann, 1984.
A Far Cry from Kensington. London, Constable, and Boston, Houghton Mifflin, 1988.
Symposium. London, Constable, and Boston, Houghton Mifflin, 1990.

Short Stories

The Go-Away Bird and Other Stories. London, Macmillan, 1958; Philadelphia, Lippincott, 1960.
Voices at Play (includes radio plays *The Party through the Wall, The Interview, The Dry River Bed, Danger Zone*). London, Macmillan, 1961; Philadelphia, Lippincott, 1962.
Collected Stories I. London, Macmillan, 1967; New York, Knopf, 1968.
Bang-Bang You're Dead and Other Stories. London, Granada, 1982.
The Stories of Muriel Spark. New York, Dutton, 1985; London, Bodley Head, 1987.

Plays

Doctors of Philosophy (produced London, 1962). London, Macmillan, 1963; New York, Knopf, 1966.

Radio Plays: *The Party through the Wall,* 1957; *The Interview,* 1958; *The Dry River Bed,* 1959; *The Ballad of Peckham Rye,* 1960; *Danger Zone,* 1961.

Poetry

The Fanfarlo and Other Verse. Aldington, Kent, Hand & Flower Press, 1952.
Collected Poems I. London, Macmillan, 1967; New York, Knopf, 1968.
Going Up to Sotheby's and Other Poems. London, Granada, 1982.

Autobiography

Curriculum Vitae. London, Constable, and Boston, Houghton Mifflin, 1992.

Literary Criticism

Child of Light: A Reassessment of Mary Wollstonecraft Shelley. London, Tower Bridge, 1951; revised edition, as *Mary Shelley: A Biography,* New York, Dutton, 1987; London, Constable, 1988.
Emily Brontë: Her Life and Work, with Derek Stanford. London, Owen, 1953.
John Masefield. London, Nevill, 1953; revised edition, London, Hutchinson, 1992.
The Essence of the Brontës. London, Owen, 1993.

For Children

The Very Fine Clock. New York, Knopf, 1968; London, Macmillan, 1969.

The French Window and the Small Telephone. London, Colophon, 1993.

Other

Editor, with David Stanford, *Tribute to Wordsworth.* London, Wingate, 1950.

Editor, *Selected Poems of Emily Brontë.* London, Grey Walls Press, 1952.

Editor, with David Stanford, *My Best Mary: The Letters of Mary Shelley.* London, Wingate, 1953.

Editor, *The Brontë Letters.* London, Nevill, 1954; as *The Letters of the Brontës: A Selection,* Norman, University of Oklahoma Press, 1954.

Editor, with David Stanford, *Letters of John Henry Newman.* London, Owen, 1957.

*

Media Adaptations: *Memento Mori* (play), 1964, televised, BBC, 1992; *The Prime of Miss Jean Brodie* (play), 1966, filmed, 1969, televised, BBC, 1978; *The Girls of Slender Means,* broadcasted on radio, 1964, televised, BBC, 1975; *The Driver's Seat,* filmed, 1974; *The Abbess of Crewe,* filmed, 1977.

Bibliography: *Iris Murdoch and Muriel Spark: A Bibliography* by Thomas T. Tominaga and Wilma Schneidermeyer, Metuchen, New Jersey, Scarecrow Press, 1976.

Critical Studies: *Muriel Spark: A Biographical and Critical Study* by Derek Stanford, Fontwell, Sussex, Centaur Press, 1963; *Muriel Spark* by Karl Malkoff, New York, Columbia University Press, 1968; *Muriel Spark* by Patricia Stubbs, London, Longman, 1973; *Muriel Spark* by Peter Kemp, London, Elek, 1974, New York, Barnes & Noble, 1975; *Muriel Spark* by Allan Massie, Edinburgh, Ramsay Head Press, 1979; *The Faith and Fiction of Muriel Spark* by Ruth Whittaker, London, Macmillan, 1982, New York, St. Martin's Press, 1983; *Comedy and the Woman Writer: Woolf, Spark, and Feminism* by Judy Little, Lincoln, University of Nebraska Press, 1983; *Muriel Spark: An Odd Capacity for Vision* edited by Alan Bold, London, Vision Press, and New York, Barnes & Noble, 1984; *Muriel Spark* by Velma Bourgeois Richmond, New York, Ungar, 1984; *Muriel Spark* by Bold, London, Methuen, 1986; *The Art of the Real: Muriel Spark's Novels* by Joseph Hynes, Rutherford, New Jersey, Fairleigh Dickinson University Press, 1988; *Muriel Spark* by Norman Page, London, Macmillan, 1990; *Vocation and Identity in the Fiction of Muriel Spark* by Rodney Stenning Edgecombe, Columbia, University of Missouri Press, 1990; *Critical Essays on Muriel Spark,* edited by Joseph Hyens, New York, G. K. Hall, 1992; *The Women of Muriel Spark* by Judy Sproxton, New York, St. Martin's Press, 1992.

* * *

Muriel Spark's work can best be described as an attempt to render paradox coherent via the formal constraints of the novel. Born and raised in Edinburgh, Scotland, of Jewish-Italian descent, and a converted Catholic by the age of 36, Spark is intimately familiar with paradox. Professing her conversion to Catholicism, ironically, as an effort to find "my norm ... something to measure from," Spark writes novels in which she meditates upon fiction and its forms as they are metaphorically suggestive of the contemporary human condition. Interrogating life's absurdities through the medium of fiction, Spark deliberately confuses her reader's ability to differentiate fact from fable, reality from illusion.

Spark's fiction, consistently inscribed by her work as a poet in the years prior to 1957, adroitly and self-consciously poses the question of the author's relationship to the characters created, and, in so doing, poses as well the larger metaphysical question of the individual's capacity for free will in a God-centered universe. In novels like 1957's *The Comforters* and *Robinson,* published in 1958, she creates characters who themselves are engaged in the act of writing or reflecting upon fiction. Caroline Rose in *The Comforters* is involved in the process of writing a study on the novel entitled *Form in the Modern Novel* and finds herself having particular difficulty with the chapter on Realism. Unable to escape a sense that her own position has been scripted, Caroline is self-consciously aware of herself as a character in a fiction, while she nevertheless attempts to theorize the status of fiction. Spark's highly self-reflexive prose suggests a powerful relationship between fiction as a form and form as it operates in the world at large and between the world engendered by the novelist and that engendered by God. In the hands of Spark, the paradoxes of modern religion and free will become the paradoxes of modern fiction. Spark's own relationship to Catholicism, ambivalent at best, is acted out in these early novels within which she implies a connection between fiction and reality that highlights the author's role as artificer; a role which she insinuates places perilous demands on her characters.

Spark's application of Realism in her fiction is almost always undermined or complicated by the bizarre and the sinister. In the trio of novels she produced during the early 1970s—*The Driver's Seat, Not to Disturb,* and *The Hothouse by the East River*—Spark's dark comedy simultaneously questions the stability and credibility of many of our most cherished institutions and denies our ability to take comfort in those same institutions. Each of these novels explore the occult not as illusion but, rather, as a powerful extension of the material world. Her portrayal of a world in which the supernatural erupts spontaneously as a natural occurrence links her work to similar explorations in such later works of novelist Henry James as *The Turn of the Screw* or "The House on Jolly Corner."

Her highly poetic approach to the novel leads Spark to develop a fictional aesthetic based on a strict sense of economy. All of her novels, with the exception of 1965's *The Mandelbaum Gate,* rarely run over 150 pages. Thus, in a deliberate move away from the traditional novel, she incisively exposes the fraudulent realistic foundations of fiction with the surrealist tensions evoked by her novels' content and with the lyrical brevity of their prose.

Although Spark's work is not feminist in the sense that she argues for specific rights for women or disparages a society she perceives as oppressing women, her novels explicitly critique reality itself as a fictional construction. Her protagonists are almost exclusively women who struggle for self-definition and agency in a world that seems inherently to deny them both. Thus, while never openly declaring a feminist agenda, her fiction both interrogates a male-centered reality and those responsible for its construction and, in its portrayal of female protagonists who seek some degree of integrity and self-possession, implicitly suggests what it means to be gendered "woman" in the modern world.

—Kimberly Engdahl

SPENCE, Catherine Helen

Nationality: Australian. **Born:** Melrose, Scotland, 1825; immigrated to South Australia, 1839. **Career:** Worked as a governess from 1842; freelance writer and journalist; active in social reform causes from 1879; member, State Children's Council, 1886; lectured on suffrage throughout Great Britain and the United States, addressing conferences at Chicago World's Fair, 1893; cofounder, Effective Voting League of South Australia, 1895, and South Australian branch of National Council of Women; became Australia's first female candidate in a federal election, 1897. Contributor to newspapers and periodicals, including *Cornhill's, Fortnightly,* and *Register.* **Awards:** Honored by naming of Catherine Spence Prize for economics, University of Adelaide, and South Australian social sciences scholarship. **Member:** Women's Suffrage League of South Australia (vice-president, 1891-94). **Died:** 1910.

Publications

Novels

Clara Morison: A Tale of South Australia during the Gold Fever (published anonymously). London, John W. Parker, 1854.

Tender and True: A Colonial Tale (published anonymously). N.p., 1856.

Mr. Hogarth's Will (originally serialized as *Uphill Work,* Adelaide *Weekly Mail,* 1863-64). London, n.p., 3 vols., 1865.

The Author's Daughter (originally serialized as "Hugh Lindsay's Guest" in Adelaide *Observer,* 1867). London, n.p., 1868.

Gathered In (originally serialized in Adelaide *Observer,* 1881-81). Sydney, Sydney University Press, 1977.

Handfasted, edited by Helen Thomson. Harmondsworth, Penguin/ Literature Board of Australian Council, 1984.

A Week in the Future (originally serialized in *Centennial Magazine,* 1888-89). N.p., 1987.

Political/Social Theory

A Plea for Pure Democracy. N.p., 1861.

State Children in Australia: A History of Boarding Out and Its Developments. Adelaide, Vardon & Sons, 1907.

Religion/Spirituality

An Agnostic's Progress from the Known to the Unknown (published anonymously). N.p., 1884.

For Children

The Laws We Live Under: With Some Chapters on Elementary Political Economy and the Duties of Citizens (textbook). Adelaide, Adelaide Education Department, 1880; 2nd edition, 1881.

Autobiography

Catherine Helen Spence: An Autobiography, with Jeanne F. Young. Adelaide, W.K. Thomas, 1910.

Other

Catherine Helen Spence: Selections, edited by Helen Thomas. St. Lucia and London, University of Queensland Press, 1987.

*

Bibliography: *Bibliography of Catherine Helen Spence* by Elizabeth Gunton, Adelaide, Libraries Board of South Australia, 1967.

Critical Studies: *Catherine Helen Spence: A Study and an Appreciation* by Jeanne F. Young, n.p., 1937; *Catherine Spence* by Janet Cooper, Melbourne, Oxford University Press, 1972; *Unbridling the Tongues of Women: A Biography of Catherine Helen Spence* by Susan Magarey, Sydney, Hale & Iremonger, 1985.

* * *

One of 19th-century Australia's major activists on behalf women's suffrage, Catherine Helen Spence used her talent for writing to entertain and educate readers, as well as to support herself as an independent woman. The author of several well-received novels, including the highly praised *Clara Morison,* Spence also published the political tract *A Plea for Pure Democracy,* which argued the cause of proportional representation in elections, as well as numerous articles in newspapers and magazines, many promoting the social reform causes she held so dear.

Born in Scotland in 1824, Spence immigrated to Australia at the age of 15, after her father's speculations in wheat futures wiped out much of the family fortune. Getting a job as a governess two years later, she began to write a novel in her spare time. The anonymous publication of *Clara Morison: A Tale of South Australia during the Gold Fever* in 1854 would make Spence Australia's first notable female novelist when the identity of the popular novel's author became know. A successful journalist during a career that would span over 30 years, Spence became actively involved in social reform work in the 1870s, inspired in part by the work of British philosopher John Stuart Mill. Taking up the cause of homeless children, she aided the efforts of the State Children's Council, an organization that tried to place destitute children with stable families, in addition to opening her home to three separate orphan families. Spence's efforts on behalf of improving children's education—particularly that of teenage girls—included the groundbreaking civics textbook *The Laws We Live Under,* published in 1880 as Australia's first social studies textbook.

Not surprisingly, her work as a social reformer quickly exposed Spence to the glaring realities of the second-class economic and political status endured by women—particularly poor women attempting to raise their children. Becoming a staunch advocate of women's suffrage, she was elected vice-president of South Australia's Women's Suffrage League in 1891; meanwhile, the radical feminism that increasingly imbued her writing caused Spence to fall out of favor with editors of mainstream periodicals like *Cornhill's* and *Fortnightly.*

Spence's two explicitly feminist novels confront several issues of importance to women, including the patriarchy inherent in the image of "real" Australians as rowdy, enterprising bushmen; the conflicts in contemporary religious dogma; and the lack of equal employment opportunities between the sexes. Set in Columbia, a state hidden somewhere in Southern California, Spence's *Handfasted* presents an egalitarian society wherein single mothers are treated with respect rather than as social pariahs. The novel's title refers to a form of trial marriage that would allow each participant the freedom to end the liaison if things proved unsatisfactory. Although completed in 1879, *Handfasted* would not be published until 1984. In *A Week in the Future,* first serialized in 1889, Spence's female protagonist is spirited to the year 1988 via the technology of suspended animation. Upon awakening, she finds herself in the city of London, which has evolved in the space of a century into a Socialist paradise. Like Spence's other feminist work, the novel *Gathered In, A Week in the Future* presented a degree of female autonomy considered threatening during her lifetime; it would not be published book form until 1987.

In 1894, when the fight for the right of women to vote was obtained in South Australia, Spence chose to continue her efforts on behalf of women's suffrage in other countries. Touring the United States and Great Britain as a lecturer for several years, she returned to Australia in 1895 and founded the Effective Voter League. An unsuccessful campaign for the Australian Federal Convention in 1897 would make Catherine Helen Spence the first woman in her country to run for political office.

—Pamela Kester-Shelton

SPENDER, Dale

Nationality: Australian. **Born:** Newcastle, New South Wales, 22 September 1943. **Education:** University of Sydney, B.A. and Dip.Ed.; University of New South Wales, M.A. 1972; University of New England, B.Litt. 1975; University of London, Ph.D. 1981. **Family:** Married (divorced). **Career:** Schoolteacher, New South Wales, Australia, 1960-72; lecturer in English education, James Cook University, Townsville, Queensland, 1973-74; lecturer in English, Institute of Education, University of London, 1976-78; speaker and lecturer at numerous universities worldwide. Founding editor, *Women's Studies International Forum,* London, 1978; co-founder, Pandora Press, London; member of numerous advisory boards; series editor, "Penguin Australian Women's Library." Consultant on education and information technology to schools and colleges, including Macquarie University and University of South Australia. Co-originator, WIKED (international database on women). Contributor to periodicals, including *Courier Mail, Guardian, Listener, New York Times Book Review, Sydney Morning Herald, Times Higher Education Supplement, Women's Review of Books,* and *Australian Author.* **Awards:** Arts Queensland fellowship, 1994. **Member:** Fawcett Society of Fawcett Library (London; executive member and honorary librarian). **Agent:** Tessa Sayle, Literary and Dramatic Agency, 11 Jubilee Place, Chelsea, London SW3 3TE, England. **Address:** 101 Boomerang Road East, St. Lucia 4067, Australia.

Publications

Political/Social Theory

The Spitting Image: Reflections on Language, Education, and Social Class, with Garth Boomer. London, Heinemann, and Upper Montclair, New Jersey, Boynton Cook, 1976.

Man Made Language. London, Routledge & Kegen Paul, 1980; revised, London, Pandora, 1990.

Invisible Women: The Schooling Scandal. London, Writers & Readers, 1982.

There's Always Been a Women's Movement in This Century. London, Pandora Press, 1983.

Time and Tide Wait for No Man. London, Pandora Press, 1984.

Scribbling Sisters, with Lynne Spender. Sydney, Hale & Iremonger, and London, R. Hale, 1984; revised edition, London and Columbia, South Carolina, Camden, 1985.

For the Record: The Making and Meaning of Feminist Knowledge. London, Women's Press, 1985.

Reflecting Men at Twice Their Natural Size, with Sally Cline, cartoons by Rianca Duncan. London, Deutsch, and New York, Seaver, 1987.

Literary Criticism

Women of Ideas and What Men Have Done to Them: From Aphra Benn to Adrienne Rich. London, Routledge & Kegen Paul, 1982.

Mothers of the Novel: 100 Good Women Writers before Jane Austen. London, Pandora Press, 1986.

Writing a New World: Two Centuries of Australian Women Writers. London, Pandora Press, 1988.

The Writing or the Sex? or, Why You Don't Have to Read Women's Writing to Know It's No Good. New York and London, Teachers College Press, 1989.

Other

Nattering on the Net: Women, Power, and Cyberspace. Sydney, Spinifex, 1995.

Editor, with Elizabeth Sarah, *Learning to Lose: Sexism and Education.* London, Women's Press, 1980.

Editor, *Men's Studies Modified: The Impact of Feminism on the Academic Disciplines.* New York and Oxford, Pergamon Press, 1981.

Editor, *Feminist Theorists: Three Centuries of Women's Intellectual Traditions* London, Women's Press, 1983; as *Feminist Theorists: Three Centuries of Key Women Thinkers,* New York, Pantheon, 1983.

Editor, with Lynne Spender, *Gatekeeping: The Denial, Dismissal, and Distortion of Women.* New York, Pergamon Press, 1983.

Editor, with Carole Hayman, *How the Vote Was Won, and Other Suffragette Plays.* London, Methuen, 1985.

Editor, with Renate Duelli Klein and Candida Lacey, *Women's Studies International Forum.* London, Pergamon, 1985.

Editor, *The Education Papers: Women's Quest for Equality in Britain, 1850-1912.* London and New York, Routledge & Kegan Paul, 1987.

Editor, *Penguin Anthology of Australian Women's Writing.* London, Penguin, 1988.

Editor, *The Peaceful Army.* Ringwood, Victoria, Penguin, 1988.

Editor, with Janet Todd, *British Women Writers: An Anthology from the 14th Century to the Present.* London, Pandora Press, 1988; New York, P. Bedrick, 1989.
Editor, *Heroines.* Ringwood, Victoria, Penguin Books Australia, 1991.
Editor, with Cheris Kramarae, *The Knowledge Explosion: Generations of Feminist Scholarship.* New York, Teachers Collge Press, 1992.
Editor, with Patricia Clarke, *Life Lines: Australian Women's Letters and Diaries, 1788-1840.* St. Leonards, New South Wales, Allen & Unwin, 1992.
Editor, *Living by the Pen: Early British Women Writers.* New York, Teachers College Press, 1992.
Editor, *Weddings and Wives.* N.p., n.d.
Editor, *The Diary of Elizabeth Pepys.* N.p., n.d.

* * *

For too long the experiences of women have been trivialized while their voices have not been heard. Much of the work of Dale Spender, an Australian-born feminist, researcher, and writer, has centered on examining why this is so. In her work, Spender examines the lives of women of long ago who voiced many of the same concerns that women continue to face today. She holds that the needs, desires, ideas, and voices from the past are not so very different from those of the present.

In *Women of Ideas* Spender writes: "a patriarchal society depends ... on the experience and values of males being perceived as the *only* valid frame of reference for society, and that it is therefore in patriarchal interest to prevent women from sharing, establishing and asserting their equally real valid and *different* frame of reference, which is the outcome of a different experience." This notion informs much of her thought and research. Time and time again, as she collects the voices and experiences of women, we see this theory at work. The male experience becomes the norm by which the world is described and defined, and it is assumed that this *"partial* experience of the world is all that exists." Spender contends that if patriarchy is to be preserved, then the world as women perceive it must remain invisible, non-existent.

In her search for women's writings, Spender has uncovered a richness in thought and experience in the struggles of our foresisters and shown that the feminist movement of the current age is not a whim, a passing fancy, but a continuation of the work started long ago by such women as Aphra Behn and Mary Wollstonecraft. Spender presents the experiences of Aphra Behn as a case study, in which her literary efforts were considered of little or no value and summarily dismissed by a male-dominated literary establishment which then accused her of plagiarism. They denied her work's popularity as a measure of her artistic ability because she wrote on subjects that made men uncomfortable. Behn recognized that women received inferior educational opportunities and in turn were deemed inferior, both intellectually and creatively. When she wrote about such matters, she was touted as hysterical, her work dismissed as "bawdy" despite the fact that "bawdy" was the style of the age in which she was writing. Spender believes that men have the power to decree how women will be valued in a male-dominated society and to determine how their work will be received.

Just as the literary world worked to silence and erase the works of women, so also has it worked to silence women through the construction of its language. Spender examines this and continues to show how patriarchy shapes and forms the way we speak and how that speech is heard or valued. In *Man Made Language,* she reveals the sexism in language that "relegates women to a secondary or inferior place." Spender studies at the ways in which women are consigned to inferior status by examining how words associated with females acquire negative connotations, dividing our world into a one that associates positive images with masculine values and negative images with feminine values. Even when words designate similar conditions for both genders, such as *spinster* and *bachelor* to indicate unmarried adult status, the "female" term carries negative connotations while the "male" is marked positive. This phenomenon works to construct female inferiority as well as to confirm it.

Spender also explores how women's silence is constructed. The participation of women in the generation of language itself threatens the power structures that men have usurped for themselves and dignified as the norm: the expected way of the world. She explains that while both women and men have the capacity to construct language, women's meanings have not been incorporated into the culture. Women have not had the same opportunities to influence the language because they have been denied access to the public arena as philosophers, orators, linguists, and educators. Because of this, the meanings created by women that are generated on the basis of different experiences and accomplishments are neither assimilated into the culture nor passed on to future generations.

Spender addresses her concerns in regard to the economic plight of women knowing that, while women make up half the world's population, they still control very little of the world's wealth. She contends that as long as women are in need of economic support from men, they cannot be free. At the heart of this is an awareness of a phenomenon of women's work that continues to beleaguer them. Over the past several decades women have been given increasing access to the world of work, often making meaningful contributions in the public domain. Changing social conditions and economic circumstances have turned these opportunities into necessities as women find they *must* work in order to support their families. What has not changed for many however is the delegation of child care and housework responsibilities. In *Scribbling Sisters,* Spender remarks with frustration, "The modern man evidently isn't interested in 'just a housewife' any more but wants a partner (this is someone who will be a partner in earning the money) and so we have the rise of superwoman, who still has children and family to look after, as well as the additional task of money earning." As long as women's work is not perceived as equal to that of men, they will continue to be underpaid, undervalued and overworked.

Spender's interpretation of the female experience is not based solely on her academic pursuits and empirical studies. In *Scribbling Sisters,* written in conjunction with her sister, Lynne Spender, readers come to see that her own life is filled with many of the same struggles as the women whose stories she examines. In a series of written "conversations," the authors explore the continuing difficulties of women in a world that often denies their vision, their reality. They address the difficulties women experience concerning the world of work, child care, education, economics, world peace, and the continuing age old dilemma of being perceived as tainted by the very nature of being woman herself. As Spender shares with her sister her personal struggles, she reflects the same issues found at the heart of every woman's experience.

—Jeanne Grinnan

SPIVAK, Gayatri Chakravorty

Nationality: Indian. **Born:** 1942. **Education:** University of Calcutta, B.A. 1959; Cornell University, M.A. 1962, Ph.D. in comparative literature 1967. **Career:** Professor of English and comparative literature at universities, including University of Iowa, University of Texas; Longstreet Professor of English, Emory University; Andrew K. Mellon Professor of English, University of Pittsburgh; Avalon Foundation Professor in the Humanities, Columbia University, New York, beginning 1991. **Address:** Department of English, Columbia University, 2960 Broadway, New York, New York 10027-6902, U.S.A.

Publications

Essays

In Other Worlds: Essays in Cultural Politics. New York and London, Methuen, 1987.

The Post-Colonial Critic: Interviews, Strategies, Dialogues, edited by Sarah Harasym. New York and London, Routledge, 1990.

Outside in the Teaching Machine. New York and London, Routledge, 1993.

The Spivak Reader, edited by Donna Landry and George McLean. London, Routledge, 1995.

Uncollected Essays

"Displacement and the Discourse of Woman," in *Displacement: Derrida and After.* Bloomington, Indiana University Press, 1983.

"Love me, Love My Ombre, Elle," in *Diacritics: A Review of Contemporary Criticism,* 14(4), 1984.

"Three Women's Texts and a Critique of Imperialism," in *Critical Inquiry,* 12(1), 1985.

"Marx after Derrida," in *Philosophical Approaches to Literature: New Essays on 19th- and 20th-Century Texts,* edited by William E. Cain. Lewisburg, Bucknell University Press, 1984.

"Feminism and Critical Theory," in *For Alma Mater: Theory and Practice in Feminist Scholarship,* edited by Paula Treichler, Cheris Kramarae, and Beth Stafford. Urbana, University of Illinois Press, 1985.

"Imperialism and Sexual Difference," in *Oxford Literary Review,* 8(1-2), 1986.

"Speculation on Reading Marx: After Reading Derrida," in *Post-Structuralism and the Question of History,* edited by Derek Attridge, Robert Young, and Geoff Bennington. Cambridge, Cambridge University Press, 1987.

"Can the Subaltern Speak?" in *Marxism and the Interpretation of Culture,* edited by Cary Nelson and Lawrence Grossberg. London, Macmillan, 1988.

"Who Need the Great Works? A Debate on the Canon, Core Curricula, and Culture," in *Harper's,* 279(1672), September 1989.

"The New Historicism: Political Commitment and the Postmodern Critic," in *The New Historicism,* edited by H. Aram Vesser and Stanley Fish. New York, Routledge, 1989.

"Feminism in Decolonization," with Joan Wallach Scott, in *Differences: A Journal of Feminist Cultural Studies,* 3(3), 1991.

"Theory in the Margin: Coetzee's *Foe* Reading Defoe's *Crusoe/Roxana,*" in *Consequences of Theory,* edited by Jonathan Arac and Barbara Johnson. Baltimore, Johns Hopkins University Press, 1991.

"French Feminism Revisited: Ethics and Politics," in *Feminists Theorize the Political,* edited by Judith Butler and Joan Scott. New York, Routledge, 1992.

"Teaching for the Times," in *Journal of the Midwest Modern Language Association,* 25(1), 1992; revised version in *The Decolonization of the Mind: Culture, Knowledge, and Power,* edited by Jan Nederveen Pieterse and Bhikhu Parekh, London, Zed, 1995.

"Acting Bits/Identity Talk," in *Critical Inquiry,* 18(4), 1992.

"Echo," in *New Literary History: A Journal of Theory and Interpretation,* 24(1), 1993.

"The Burden of English," in *Orientalism and the Postcolonial Predicament: Perspectives on South Asia.* Philadelphia, University of Pennsylvania Press, 1993.

"Responsibility," in *boundary 2,* 21(3), 1994.

"How to Read a 'Culturally Different' Book," in *Colonial Discourse/Postcolonial Theory.* Manchester, Manchester University Press, 1994.

For Children

Myself Must I Remake: The Life and Poetry of W.B. Yeats. New York, Crowell, 1974.

Other

Editor, with Ranajit Guha, *Selected Subaltern Studies.* New York, Oxford University Press, 1988.

Translator, *Of Grammatology,* by Jacques Derrida. Baltimore, Johns Hopkins University Press, 1976.

Translator, *Draupadi,* by Mahasweta Devi, in *Critical Inquiry,* 8(2), 1981; in *In Other Worlds,* 1987.

Translator, *Imaginary Maps,* by Mahasweta Devi, New York, Routledge, 1995.

*

Critical Studies: *White Mythologies* by Robert J. Young, ; "Neo-colonialism and the Secret Agent of Knowledge" (interview), *Oxford Literary Review,* 12(1-2), 1991; "Identity and Alterity" (interview) in *Arena,* 97, 1991; interview by Sara Danius and Stefan Jonsson, in *boundary 2,* 20(2), summer 1993; "Questions of Multiculturalism" in *The Cultural Studies Reader,* edited by Simon During, New York, Routledge, 1993; *Exotic Parodies: Subjectivity in Adorno, Said, and Spivak* by Asha Varadharajan, Minneapolis, University of Minnesota Press, 1995; *Hating Tradition Properly* by Neil Lazarus, forthcoming.

* * *

The feminism of writer/educator Gayatri Chakravorty Spivak is informed by postcolonial thought. Much of her work addresses the importance of her positionality as a writer; she believes that writers need to acknowledge the multiple subject positions or perspectives that influence their work. (For example, I write this entry as Chinese American, female, and privileged, as well as from other subject positions. These perspectives have influenced how I view and write about Spivak.) Spivak's writing embodies this project as she attempts to examine the discontinuities within feminism, Marxism, and deconstruction. Instead of creating a coherent or unitary melding of these perspectives for a single discourse, she believes that these ways of thinking are used together best while embracing the discontinuities and contradictions between them.

Spivak is perhaps most widely known as the translator of Jacques Derrida's *Of Grammatology.* Most recently, she has translated the stories of Indian writer Mahasweta Devi. In her preface to Devi's *Imaginary Maps,* a collection of three stories published in 1995, Spivak discusses the political implications of translating Devi's stories into English for an audience in the United States. She responds to criticisms of her "doorkeeping" of the text for an American audience. acknowledging her position as the person who allows access to Devi's writing and professing her awareness of the distance between the author's language and the academic prose used in the translation. Spivak ends her preface "upon this acknowledgment of prejudice (not derived from the possibility of an unprejudiced translation, even in reading)."

Framing a translation in this manner is characteristic of Spivak. She explains her own relation to the text and then impresses upon the reader that she or he must also do the same. She asks readers to recognize how the writing has been shaped by both the readers' and the translator's prejudice.

While Spivak is one of the most well-known or prominent postcolonial critics, she resists the idea that one voice can represent a way of thinking, particularly when the way of thinking strives to recognize the significance of multiplicity and positionality in the creation of a text. In "Can the Subaltern Speak?," one of her most influential writings, Spivak explores the idea of how the subaltern, or non-elite, finds ways to express its oppression. she argues that the wish of intellectuals to provide a space for this voice becomes problematic because of their respective positions. In the process of speaking about or for the subaltern, the radical intellectual cannot avoid *creating a representation* of the non-elite. This representation does not allow the subaltern to speak and represent itself; rather, the intellectual further colonizes the subaltern by positioning the non-elite as a subject. The subaltern merely becomes a subject of intellectual pursuit instead of a responsive participant in a dialogue. As the intellectual seeks to transform the insurgency of the subaltern into a text that documents its resistance, s/he must consider the politics of representation and how the writing shapes this representation. In an attempt to address this issue, Spivak suggests that intellectuals should acknowledge and understand how their privileged positions can inhibit the possibility of speaking for the subaltern.

The questioning of who speaks for whom is an integral aspect of Spivak's ideas on feminism. She compares how the feminine has been treated in a similar way to the subaltern by pointing to deconstructive criticism and certain types of feminist criticism as spaces where this treatment occurs. She contends that it is because of the colonial production of history and male dominance that women have been silenced through their absence in historiography, not because they have not participated. She points to subaltern historiography as a way to resist this type of representation. Through the use of multiple discourses, Spivak seeks a more global feminism that examines woman's subject position. She believes that a "colonized" feminism with only a limited number of people creating feminist discourse will result unless a more global perspective exists.

In her work, Spivak makes the distinction between anti-sexism and feminism. She marks the differences between the terms because she sees two general approaches to sexism. The term anti-sexism invoked by Spivak refers to responses that are solely reactive to sexism. These types of reactions seek only to mask sexism and patriarchy on a superficial level. She feels that a reactive confrontation of sexism results in a reverse legitimization of sexism. While she acknowledges anti-sexism work—such as battered women's clinics—she asks that people also examine sexual difference and the underlying structures that support and create sexism and patriarchy.

Anti-sexism, then, can be thought of as only treating the symptoms of patriarchy, while feminism examines patriarchy itself. However, Spivak's feminism does not seek to create a dichotomy between feminism and anti-sexism. Rather, she seeks to find ways to integrate feminist theory with practice, and ground practical actions in a more global and theoretical vision. Her intellectual project necessitates confronting the relationship and connections between academic and activist identities.

—Amy Jo-Lan Wan

SPRETNAK, Charlene

Nationality: American. **Born:** Pittsburgh, Pennsylvania, 1946. **Education:** St. Louis University, B.A. (magna cum laude), 1968; University of California, Berkeley, M.A., 1981. **Family:** Married, one daughter. **Career:** Currently visiting professor of philosophy and religion, California Institute of Integral Studies, San Francisco. Founder, Committees of Correspondence (Green political organization). **Awards:** Inducted into Ohio Women's Hall of Fame, 1989. **Address:** Department of Philosophy and Religion, California Institute of Integral Studies, 9 Peter Yorke Way, San Francisco, California, 94109, U.S.A.

Publications

Religion/Spirituality

Lost Goddesses of Early Greece: A Collection of Pre-Helenic Myths. Berkeley, Moon Books, 1978.

Green Politics: The Global Promise, with Fritjof Capra, in collaboration with Rüdiger Lutz. New York, Dutton, 1984; London, Hutchinson, 1985; revised, Santa Fe, New Mexico, Bear, 1986.

The Spiritual Dimension of Green Politics. Santa Fe, New Mexico, Bear, 1986.

States of Grace: The Recovery of Meaning in the Postmodern Age. San Francisco, HarperSanFrancisco, 1991.

The Resurgence of the Real: Body, Nature, and Place in an Age of Fading Ideologies. Boston, Addison-Wesley, 1997.

Other

Editor, *The Politics of Women's Spirituality: Essays on the Rise of Spiritual Power within the Feminist Movement.* New York, Doubleday, 1982; revised, with new introduction, 1994.

*

Critical Studies: Interview with Patrice Wynne, in her *Womanspirit Sourcebook,* San Francisco, Harper & Row, 1988.

Charlene Spretnak comments:

Sometimes people say to me that they cannot see how my books fit together: what could pre-Olympian mythology have to do with Green parties or an ecological post-modernism? They are all explorations of eco-spirituality, a spiritual philosophy that infuses my eco-social thought and activisim, both feminist and Green. An ecological spirituality of the earth body and the personal body should be at the core of our Western cultural heritage, but it was pushed aside and denied. My work contributes to its recovery and the unfolding of its possibilities in our time.

* * *

By her own admission, the roots of Charlene Spretnak's interest in a feminist spirituality that respects the sacred power of both the earth and human bodies lie in her feeling, during her teenage years, that life was empty and meaningless. The path that led her out of this experience of emptiness, though, was not a direct one. Rather, she first lost her feeling of connection with the Catholicism of her parents as an undergraduate. Then, unsatisfied with her initial experiences in graduate school, she traveled in the late 1960s to India, where she began to discover in the Buddhist practice of Vipassana meditation the spiritual rootedness she was seeking. Returning to graduate school at the University of California, Berkeley, she was drawn to the study of the pre-patriarchal mythological heritage of ancient Greece, and at the same time began participating in feminist religious rituals with groups dedicated to honoring the mysteries of creation as revealed in women's bodies and in nature.

These interests are combined in Spretnak's first book, *Lost Goddesses of Early Greece,* in which she attempts to reclaim a religious tradition centered around the Great Goddess, a tradition that she argues was lost when invaders brought with them to pre-Hellenic Greece the worship of the sky God, fragmenting the one Great Goddess into the many subordinate goddesses of classical Hellenism. In her understanding, the ancient worship of the Goddess represents a valuable resource for those feminists who challenge the denial and demonization of the body and the lack of respect for nature that mark much of the Western Judeo-Christian tradition.

Spretnak's view that the patriarchal religions of the West are much in need of a feminist reorientation led her next to edit an anthology of essays entitled *The Politics of Women's Spirituality,* which was reissued in 1994 with a new introduction and updated bibliography. In her introduction to the original edition she argues that, while the Judeo-Christian tradition has been a source of terrible oppression of women, feminists nevertheless need to continue to honor the religious or spiritual elements of life in order to be able to give full expression to the inherent interrelatedness of all living beings, as well as to provide a foundation for an ethics and a politics of mutual respect. In addition, she asserts her belief that the vision of a feminist spirituality, as reflected in *The Politics of Women's Spirituality,* is essential to an adequate recognition of the sacred nature of the earth itself.

As her commitment to the importance of acknowledging the natural world as an expression of the sacred grew, Spretnak became increasingly active in the realm of environmentalist politics. She helped to found the Committees of Correspondence, an organization dedicated to furthering within the United States the political philosophy of West Germany's Green Party. In 1984 she published *Green Politics: The Global Promise,* coauthored with physicist Fritjof Capra, in which she asserts the importance for America of the Green political agenda—an agenda based on nonviolence, respect for the environment, interrelatedness, political and social equality for women, and an ecologically sustainable economy, among other values. Then, in 1986, she followed up on *Green Politics* with *The Spiritual Dimension of Green Politics,* originally presented in 1984 as a lecture to the E.F. Schumacher Society of America. In this volume Spretnak more explicitly claims that the Green sensibility is compatible with and supportive of the kind of feminist spirituality that she envisions as a cure for both the oppression of women and the fundamental spiritual rootlessness of our age.

More recently, Spretnak has issued a direct challenge to that fundamental spiritual rootlessness in *States of Grace: The Recovery of Meaning in the Postmodern Age,* which she published in 1991. In this book she outlines her view that the criticism of modernity that characterizes deconstructive postmodernism has given rise to a widespread sense that spirituality has nothing to offer to contemporary men and women. She then offers as a remedy for this sense of the failure of spiritual values a reading of four of the world's "wisdom traditions"—Buddhism, Native American spirituality, Goddess religion, and the ethical heritage of Judaism, Christianity, and Islam—and argues that the communitarian values that result from honoring the combined wisdom of these traditions contain the healing potential so badly needed by the Postmodern Age. While the explicitly feminist spirituality of her earlier works is not her exclusive concern in this book, Spretnak nevertheless continues to pay homage to her feminist roots in her discussion of the significance of Goddess spirituality, as well as in an appendix in which she sketches a feminist response to deconstructive postmodernism.

Throughout her career as a writer and activist Charlene Spretnak has maintained her commitment to a feminist vision of spirituality in which both bodies and the earth can be recognized and honored as manifestations of divinity, of the cosmic creative force. For her, the importance of Green Party politics lies in its embodiment of the values of feminist spirituality. And it is those same values—which can be located in the particular wisdom traditions of our collective religious heritage—that for Spretnak promise hope of healing in a spiritually troubled world.

—Judith Poxon

STAËL, Germaine de

Also known as Madame de Staël. **Nationality:** French. **Born:** Anne-Louise-Germaine Necker, 22 April 1766. **Education:** Educated by her mother, Suzanne Cochard Necker. **Family:** Married the Swedish ambassador Baron Eric Magnus of Staël-Holstein in 1786 (legally separated, 1800), one daughter; had two children by Narbonne; had one daughter with the writer Benjamin Constant; 2) John Rocca in 1811, one son. **Career:** Attended the literary salon of her mother from childhood; began her own salon in Paris; saved the lives of several aristocratic friends until forced to leave Paris in wake of French Revolution, c. 1793; lived in Coppet,

Geneva; returned to Paris and reopened salon, 1795; exiled by Napoleon Bonaparte, 1795-96; exiled by Directoire, 1799; exiled to within 40 leagues of Paris by Bonaparte after publication of *Delphine*, beginning 1803; traveled in Europe and met Schiller and Goethe; returned to Paris at the invitation of Louis XVIII, 1814. **Died:** 14 July 1817.

Publications

Novels

Sophie ou les sentiments secrets [Sophie or Secret Feelings]. Paris, n.p., 1786.
Jane Gray. Paris, n.p., 1790.
Delphine. Geneva, n.p., 4 vols., 1802; translated, De Kalb, Northern Illinois University Press, 1987.
Corinne ou l'Italie. Paris, n.p., 3 vols., 1807; translated as *Corinne or Italy,* n.p., 1987.

Short Stories

Mirza. Paris, n.p., 1795.
Zulma et trois nouvelles. London, n.p., 1813.

Political/Social Theory

Lettres sur Jean-Jacques Rousseau. Paris, n.p., 1788.
De l'influence des passions sur le bonheur des individus et des nations [The Influence of Passions on the Happiness of Individuals and Nations]. Lausanne, n.p., 1796; edited by Tournier, 1979.
Considérations sur les principaux événements de la Révolution française. Paris, 3 vols., 1818.
Des circonstances actuelles qui peuvent terminer la Révolution et des principes qui doivent fonder la république en France, edited by Lucia Omacina. Geneva, Droz, 1979.

Literary Criticism

Essai sur les fictions. Paris, 1795; edited by Tournier, 1979.
De la littérature considérée dans ses rapports avec les institutions sociales. Geneva, 2 vols., 1800; translated as *A Treatise on Ancient and Modern Literature,* 1803.
De l'Allemagne. Paris, 1810; translated as *On Germany,* London, J. Murray, 1813.

Essays

Réflexions sur le procès de la reine. Paris, n.p., 1793.
Réflexions sur le paix intérieure. Paris, n.p., 1795; edited by C. Cordié, 1945.
Réflexions sur le paix intérieure adressées à M. Pitt et aux Français. Geneva, n.p., 1795.
Réflexions sur le suicide. London, n.p., 1813.
Dix années d'exil. Paris, n.p., 1821; translated as *Ten Years of Exile,* 1972.

Plays

Essais dramatiques: Agar, Geneviève de Brabant, la Sunamite, Sapho, Le Capitaine Kernadec, la Signorina fantastici, le Mannequin. Paris, n.p., 1821.

Other

Recueil de morceaux détachés. Lausanne, n.p., 1795.
Du caractère de M. Necker et de sa vie privée. N.p., 1804.
Oeuvres complètes. Paris, Treuttel & Wurtz, 17 vols., 1820-21.
Oeuvres inédites. Paris, n.p., 3 vols., 1830-36.
Lettres de Mme de Staël à Benjamin Constant, edited by Mme de Nolde. Paris, n.p., 1928.
L'Oeuvre imprimée de Mme Germaine de Staël, edited by F.-C. Lonchamp. Paris, 1949.
Correspondence générale, edited by B. Janinski, Paris, Pauvert, 1960-78.
Mon Journal, edited by S. Balayé in *Cahiers staëliens,* 28, 1980.
An Extraordinary Woman: Selected Writings. New York, Columbia University Press, 1987.

*

Bibliography: By C. Cordié, in *Cultura e Scuola,* 17, January/March 1966.

Critical Studies: *Mistress to an Age: A Life of Mme de Staël* by J.C. Herold, New York, Bobbs-Merrill,1958; *Literary Women: The Great Writers* by Ellen Moers, Garden City, New York, Doubleday, 1976, London, Womens Press, 1977; *Madame de Staël, Novelist* by M. Gutwirth, Urbana, University of Illinois Press, 1978; *Sex and Subterfuge: Women Writers to 1850* by Eva Figes, London, Macmillan, 1982, New York, Persea, 1987; *The Determined Reader: Gender and Culture in the Novel from Napoleon to Victoria* by C.L. Petterson, n.d.; *Mme de Staël* by Renée Winegarten, n.p., 1985; *The Literary Existence of Madame de Staël* by Charlotte Hogsett, Carbondale, Southern Illinois University Press, 1987; *Germaine de Staël: Crossing the Borders* edited by Auriel Goldberger, Madlyn Gutwirth, and Karyna Szmurlo, New Brunswick, New Jersey, Rutgers University Press, 1991.

* * *

An 800-year-old monarchy fell, a revolution came and went, an empire was won and lost, and France, in a wave of nostalgia, brought back the monarchy—this is the background against which the political, social, and literary consciousness of Germaine de Staël took shape.

As the only daughter of the influential banker and finance minister of Louis XVI, Jacques Necker, Germaine knew a privileged childhood, one that included exposure to the literary, political, and economic discussions held in the popular salon of her mother, Suzanne. There, her precocious intelligence neither went unnoticed nor unnourished: by the age of 11 she was composing poetry and by 15 she had produced a commentary on Montesquieu's political treatise *Spirit of the Law.* The wealth and connections of her family also facilitated her marriage at the age of 20 to the Swedish ambassador at the court of France, Eric-Magnus Staël-Holstein, some 18 years her senior. Although she received the title of Baroness as one of the benefits of this match, the two were ill-suited to each other and lived most of their married life apart. In some senses, de Staël's marriage exemplifies the dilemma of France at the dawn of the modern era. When she made her entrance into court society, her bourgeois origins were at first held against her; however, her obvious intelligence and achievements validated the Enlightenment precept of individual merit over birth. Nonetheless, as a woman, de Staël faced criticism for the talents she possessed and the lifestyle she led. Both during her marriage to the Baron and after his death, de Staël would have a number of liaisons, the longest and surely the most famous, with the writer Benjamin Constant. Their stormy but intellectually stimulating relationship lasted from 1794 to 1808.

After her marriage, de Staël established her own salon on the rue du Bac in Paris at a moment when French history was about to be definitively changed. She threw herself into politics, an activity for which she was frequently reproached by her detractors. Despite her family connections to the royal house, her doors were open to writers, politicians, philosophers, and members of the Parisian intelligentsia of all opinions. Her earliest political work, *Lettres sur les écrits et le caractère de J-J Rousseau* (*Letters on the Writings and the Character of J-J Rousseau*, 1788), showed her affinity for the theories of Rousseau. Later, de Staël herself would advocate the model of English democracy as the path for France and soon became allied with the more liberal elements of the Revolutionaries. As the fortunes of that group waned, de Staël abandoned Paris in 1792: first for Coppet in Switzerland, then for England where she joined many of her friends and allies in exile. The pattern of her life was now established: because of her politics or her writings, de Staël would lead a tumultuous existence for nearly three decades. Exiled more than once from the French capital, she would take refuge either at her family estate at Coppet or in travel. It was during a stay at Coppet that she first met Constant, in whom she found not only an emotional partner but also a political ally.

The early years of revolutionary France were trying for de Staël as she spent many of them in exile. However, Robespierre's fall and the end of the Terror in 1795 allowed her free access to Paris. De Staël published many political works during the following years, continuing to work for the revolutionary ideal and helping to bring many of her friends, including Talleyrand, back from exile. This period of de Staël's life coincides with the rise of Napoleon, in whom she saw a potential savior for the Revolution. However, as Napoleon's ambition grew so did de Staël's mistrust and soon her writings were running afoul of Napoleon's pleasure. He quite rightly recognized in her a formidable enemy and finally forced her to leave France in 1802, shortly after the publication of *Delphine,* her first novel. She visited Germany, Italy, settled in at Coppet; then, returned to Germany and at last France, but was again exiled following the publication of *Corinne, ou l'Italie* (*Corinnea, or Italy,* 1807). During this time she saw the death of her father and the Baron de Staël and a rupture with Constant. All the while she continued to try to have her exile revoked. For much of her second marriage to John Rocca, a Swiss officer, she was again on the road, traveling across war-torn Russia, through Scandinavia, and finally England, before returning to Paris in 1814 where she would die three years later. *Dix années d'exil* (*Ten Years of Exile*, 1820) recounts this extraordinary period in her life.

De la littérature (*On Literature*, 1800) and *De l'Allemagne* (*On Germany*, 1810), works of literary history and criticism, fostered the spread of Romanticism among French writers at the turn of the century. *De la littérature* discusses literature in its social and political situation, including the interplay among laws, literature, and social institutions. De Staël also establishes a contrast between Northern and Southern writers, recalling Montesquieu's analysis of climate on national temperament. She also devotes a chapter to the particular paradox of the condition of women: they exert a moral influence and play a civilizing role in society yet have few means of (written) expression and even less access to power. *De l'Allemagne* draws on her experience and encounters with writers such as Goethe and Schiller during her travels, and with Augustus Schlegel whom she invited to Coppet as a tutor for her son. The text not only praises the uniqueness of German temperament and culture but its political message was disturbing enough that Napoleon's police seized and destroyed the book before publication in France. It was only upon her arrival in London in 1813 that de Staël managed to have the work published. Of the two novels written between these major works of literary criticism, *Corinne, ou l'Italie* portrays most fully the perils of the successful woman. The novel treats the life of Corinna, its Anglo-Italian heroine, whose impressive artistic and literary career is nonetheless thwarted by the strictures of a patriarchal system. The novel exerted a major influence throughout the 19th century, most especially on other women writers.

Germaine de Staël led an exceptional life as a writer, literary critic, and political thinker and activist. Although some of her theories today may seem bound to the historical period in which she lived, they do not overshadow her accomplishments, including the development of the study of comparative literature, and the scope of her work that continue to be valued and studied today.

—Edith J. Benkov

STAËL, Madame de. *See* **STAËL, Germaine de.**

STAIRS, Gordon. *See* **AUSTIN, Mary (Hunter).**

STANLEY, Elizabeth. *See* **MANSFIELD, Katherine.**

STANTON, Elizabeth Cady

Nationality: American. **Born:** Jamestown, New York, 12 November 1815. **Education:** Attended Troy Female Seminary, Troy, New York; studied law in her father's office. **Family:** Married abolitionist Henry B. Stanton in 1840; seven children. **Career:** Began agitating for women's suffrage, 1840; aided formation of Female Labor Reform Association, 1845; with Lucretia Mott, initiated first Women's Rights Convention, Seneca Falls, New York, 1848; cofounder, with Susan B. Anthony, National Woman's Loyal League, 1866; ran for United States Congress, 1866; cofounder, with Parker Pillsbury and Anthony, *The Revolution* (suffragist newspaper), 1868; cofounder, with Anthony, and president, National Woman's Suffrage Association, 1869. Contributor of articles to *Lily,* edited by Amelia Bloomer, and *Una.* **Died:** New York, New York, 26 October 1902.

Publications

Political/Social Theory

"Declaration of Rights of the Women of the United States," with Matilda Joslyn Gage. Philadelphia, n.p., 1876.

A History of Woman Suffrage, Volumes 1-3, with Matilda Joslyn Gage and Susan B. Anthony. New York, Fowler & Welles, 4 vols., 1881-88.

Autobiography

Eighty Years and More. New York, European Publishing, and London, T. F. Unwin, 1898.

Other

Elizabeth Cady Stanton, as Revealed in Her Letters, Diary, and Reminiscences, edited by Theodore Stanton and Harriot Stanton Blatch. New York and London, Harper Bros., 2 vols., 1922.

Elizabeth Cady Stanton, Susan B. Anthony: Correspondence, Writings, Speeches, edited by Ellen Carol Dubois. New York, Schocken, 1981.

Editor, *The Woman's Bible.* New York, European Publishing, 2 vols., 1895-98; as *The Woman's Bible: The Original Feminist Attack on the Bible,* introduction by Dale Spender, Edinburgh, Polygon, 1985.

*

Critical Studies: *Created Equal: Elizabeth Cady Stanton, 1815-1902* by Alma Lutz, n.p., 1940; *Elizabeth Cady Stanton* by Mary Ann B. Oakley, Old Westbury, New York, Feminist Press, 1972; *Womanhood in America* by Mary P. Ryan, New Viewpoints, 1975; *Feminism and Suffrage* by Ellen Carol Dubois, Ithaca, New York, Cornell University Press, 1978; *Elizabeth Cady Stanton: A Radical for Woman's Rights* by Lois W. Banner, Boston, Little Brown, 1980; *In Her Own Right: The Life of Elizabeth Cady Stanton* by Elizabeth Griffith, New York, Oxford University Press, 1984.

* * *

Elizabeth Cady Stanton was one of the leading suffragists of 19th-century America. As coorganizer with Susan B. Anthony of the first women's rights convention in the United States, as the author of the first public statement calling for women's suffrage, and as the coauthor of *History of Woman Suffrage,* a massive work documenting the suffragist movement's history in the 19th century, Stanton was a major figure in popularizing the cause of women's rights.

Stanton first became aware of the injustices against women when she was a child visiting her father's law office. Her visits revealed to her the extent of problems faced by women at that time—especially due to their lack of the right to own property—and the little protection afforded them by the law. Stanton later claimed that she was so angered that she wanted to take a pair of scissors to her father's law books and remove the offending portions, but was dissuaded by her father who explained to her that laws were changed through legislative means. Later, Stanton's insight into societal biases against women was reinforced when she attempted to attend Union College and was turned down because of her gender. She was obliged instead to study law at home under her father's guidance, specializing in legal and constitutional history.

In 1839 Stanton met Henry B. Stanton, a leader of the antislavery movement and a popular lecturer and writer on the subject. The couple married the following year and spent their honeymoon at the World Anti-Slavery Convention held in London. Stanton was outraged that female delegates, including Lucretia Mott, were refused permission to participate in the convention's proceedings. The common protest against this action drew the two women together; they were to remain friends and political allies for the next forty years. Mott and Stanton vowed at this time to organize a women's rights convention as soon as they returned to the United States.

Upon her return to Boston, Stanton began a detailed study of the position of women in contemporary society. This six-year period of research led her to the firm conviction that women must be given a legal status the equal of men. In addition to her study and continuing involvement in local reformist circles, Stanton also had the first three of her seven children. In 1847 she and her husband moved their family to Seneca Falls, New York, where Henry, eager to win political office, believed his chances were more favorable than in urban Boston. In the summer of 1848, when Mott and her husband visited the town in conjunction with a Quaker meeting in the area, the two women were united once again and repeated their resolve to hold the women's rights convention they had planned in London eight years earlier. They announced a convention to be held in Seneca Falls in July of 1848 "to discuss the social, civil, and religious condition and rights of women." In her "Declaration of Sentiments," written as a basis for discussion at the convention, Stanton further called for "women of this country to secure to themselves their sacred right to the elective franchise." This demand for women's suffrage is the first such public statement on record. However, her insistence on obtaining the vote—later the women's movement's most important goal—was at first deemed too radical by Mott and Henry, who argued that such a demand would bring general ridicule upon them. Although they initially opposed the idea, Mott and Henry were eventually persuaded by the force of Stanton's argument. The call for a woman's right to vote was also ratified by the convention as a whole. Still, the idea was considered controversial; several of those who signed the convention's resolution later asked to have their names removed from the document. Despite criticism from the popular press and certain church spokespersons, the convention and its ideas had a widespread influence. By 1850 a suffrage organization, with members in seven states, had been formed. By 1860, the group's efforts had pushed fifteen states to grant women property rights and other legal reforms.

In 1851 Stanton met Susan B. Anthony and formed a working partnership that would unite them for the rest of their lives. The two women complimented each others' strengths: Anthony was a strong organizer while Stanton was better at persuasive argument; Anthony could organize the movement's activities while Stanton was a popular writer on its behalf. Unmarried, Anthony had time available to help Stanton with the many demands of her domestic life and large family. She often cared for Stanton's children to give her more time for writing. During the American Civil War, Anthony and Stanton founded the National Woman's Loyal League to work towards the abolition of slavery, the rights of African Americans to vote, and women's suffrage. The woman's suffrage issue had become, with the war raging, by necessity subsumed to the larger issue of abolition; they hoped, however, to tie the two issues together.

After the war and the abolition of slavery, the Republican Party was instrumental in working for the rights of African Americans to vote. Stanton hoped that this would also be the time when women of all races could be granted the same right. In 1865 she petitioned the United States Congress on the issue of woman's suffrage—in vain. Perhaps inspired by this action, she decided in 1866 to run for congress in New York's eighth district. Stanton had found that although women were denied the vote, there was nothing in the law preventing them from running for office. "My creed," she stated in her announcement of candidacy, "is free speech, free press, free men, and free trade—the cardinal points of democracy." Despite her efforts, Stanton received only 24 votes in the election.

In 1866 Stanton, Anthony, and Mott were among the founders of the American Equal Rights Association, a group demanding the vote for both African Americans and women. Republican allies disagreed with the strategy, however, believing that tying the two causes together would be held as unpopular by most voters. When, in 1870, the Republicans passed the Fifteenth Amendment, granting the vote to African American males, Stanton and Anthony felt betrayed. Disillusioned with their former allies among the abolitionists and Republican Party, the two women founded a new independent organization, the National American Woman Suffrage Association, to work for the right of women to vote. For the next twelve years, Stanton toured the nation on behalf of the organization, speaking out for women's suffrage.

Stanton's writings on behalf of the suffragist cause include a longtime column for the periodical *Lily* and articles for *Una,* a monthly magazine on women's issues. In 1868 she and Anthony also founded *The Revolution,* a feminist magazine that was eventually forced for financial reasons to merge with the *Liberal Christian,* a move which the irreligious Stanton observed was a proper "Christian burial." In 1881 Stanton and Anthony, working with Matilda Joslyn Gage, gathered many of their speeches and writings for periodicals and published the first volume of *A History of Woman Suffrage.* The massive work would eventually fill six volumes, the last being published after Stanton's death in 1902. In 1898 Stanton published her most controversial work, the best-selling *The Woman's Bible,* a feminist study of the sexism found in the Judeo-Christian bible. Perhaps nowhere was the book more controversial than among woman suffragists, who were overwhelmingly Christian and whose religious beliefs often motivated their involvement in the movement. Although Anthony tried to dissuade the critics, Stanton lost much of her support in the movement because of *The Woman's Bible* and, by the time of her death, had become a peripheral figure in the cause.

However, Stanton's insistence upon linking social and political reform in working for the voting rights of women rather than waging a lone fight for suffrage would eventually prove insightful. Her energetic and lifelong devotion to the cause of advancing the rights of women, and her progressive views as to the best means of gaining those rights, have, since her death, gained Elizabeth Cady Stanton her rightful place as one of the pivotal leaders of the American feminist movement.

—Denise Wiloch

STARHAWK

Pseudonym of Miriam Simos. **Nationality:** American. **Born:** St. Paul, Minnesota, 17 June 1951. **Education:** University of California, Los Angeles, B.A. in art (cum laude) 1972; Antioch West University, 1980-82, M.A. in feminist therapy 1982. **Family:** Married 1) Edward W. Rahsman in 1977 (divorced); 2) David Miller in 1992. **Career:** Producer of educational programs, Environmental Communications, 1971-72; coordinator, Westside Women's Center, 1972; workshop presenter, 1973-74; adult education teacher, Bay Area Center for Alternative Education, 1975-77; founder, the Compost Coven; minister, elder, and national president, Covenant of the Goddess, 1976-77; freelance scriptwriter, 1978-80; director, teacher, and counselor, Reclaiming: A Center for Feminist Spirituality and Counseling, Berkeley, California, beginning 1980; faculty member, Institute for Culture and Creation Spirituality, Holy Names College, Oakland, California, beginning 1983. Speaker at numerous colleges and universities, including Union Theological Seminary, New York, University of California, San Francisco, American River College, and California State University. Film consultant; contributor to periodicals, including *Anima, Inclination-of-the-Night,* and *Lady-Unique.* **Member:** Media Alliance, Information Film Producers Association, American Academy of Religion. **Address:** Reclaiming: A Center for Feminist Spirituality and Counseling, P.O. Box 14404, San Francisco, California 94114, U.S.A. **Online Address:** (homepage) http://malkuth.sephiroth.org/%7Ecorwin/authors/starhawk/index.html.

PUBLICATIONS

Novels

The Fifth Sacred Thing. New York, Bantam, 1993.
Walking to Mercury. Forthcoming, 1997.

Religion/Spirituality

The Spiral Dance: A Rebirth of the Ancient Religion of the Great Goddess. San Francisco and London, Harper, 1979; 10th anniversary revised edition, New York and London, Harper, 1989.
Dreaming the Dark: Magic, Sex, and Politics. Boston, Beacon Press, 1982; revised edition, 1988; London, Unwin, 1990.
Truth or Dare: Encounters with Power, Authority, and Mystery. San Francisco and London, Harper, 1987.

Plays

The Loss Ritual (five-act; produced San Francisco, 1976).
The Spiral Dance Ritual: In Celebration of the True Halloween (one-act; produced San Francisco, 1979).

Screenplays: *Learning; Managing for Competence; Ground in Motion: Earthquake Engineer; Thinking about the Future: Technology Assessment; The Information Era; Hemophilia; Mary; The Origins of Consciousness in the Breakdown of the Bicameral Mind; Full Circle* (with others), 1996.

Radio Plays: *Winter Solstice,* 1977.

*

Critical Studies: Article in *Vortex: A Journal of New Vision,* spring 1981.

* * *

Starhawk is one of the most recognized practitioners, theoreticians, and teachers of Wicca (feminist witchcraft), a Neo-Pagan belief system that attempts to reclaim pre-patriarchal and non-patriarchal, earth-centered spirituality. According to Starhawk, reclaiming the term "Witch," a derivative of the Anglo-Saxon *wic* (meaning to bend or shape), is important because witchcraft is the practice of shaping reality, changing consciousness, and remaking the world. Most importantly, Starhawk seeks to connect the spiritual and political realms. Although her work has been important to the development of contemporary feminist spirituality, Paganism, and witchcraft, her writing is distinguished from some such traditions by its focus on reclaiming a *feminine* concept of the sacred. "[A]t this moment in history, the mythology and imagery of the Goddess carry special liberating power," she writes in *Truth or Dare.* "They free us from the domination of the all-male God who has so strongly legitimized male rule, and by extension, all systems of domination." Other writers on feminist spirituality who have influenced or been influenced by Starhawk include Carol Christ, Barbara Walker, Zsuszanna Budapest, Dion Fortune, Merlin Stone, Margot Adler, and Silver Ravenwolf.

Born in St. Paul, Minnesota, in 1951, Starhawk dates the beginning of her awareness of earth-based spirituality to the summer of 1968, which she spent hitchhiking along the California coast. She started studying and teaching witchcraft as an independent project for an anthropology course at UCLA, improvising rituals and ultimately meeting and training with "real" Wiccan witches. Starhawk majored in art at UCLA and studied witchcraft with Sara Cunningham and Budapest. Living in Venice, California—a haven for artists and activists—she became active in the feminist movement. She began her writing career shortly after getting her B.A.; as a graduate student in filmmaking she would complete two as-yet-unpublished novels.

After a brief stint in New York, Starhawk moved to San Francisco in 1975 and founded her first coven, the Compost Coven, which she writes about in *The Spiral Dance.* In the Bay Area's active Pagan community, Starhawk was introduced to the Faery tradition by Victor and Cora Anderson. In 1976 she was elected the first officer of the Covenant of the Goddess, a legally recognized church. In 1980 she returned to school, earning an M.A. in women's studies and psychology (feminist therapy) from Antioch West University in 1982. Starhawk became a lecturer on the faculty at the Institute for Culture and Creation Spirituality at Holy Names College, Oakland, since 1983. She has since written several books, served as a consultant to the National Film Board of Canada's "Women's Spirituality" film series, and lectured at a number of colleges and churches in the United States and abroad. A major voice in the growing ecofeminist movement, Starhawk offers workshops in Wiccan spirituality through the Reclaiming collective. And, in keeping with the Wiccan recognition that spiritual is found in the objects and practices of everyday life, Starhawk and her fellow Wiccans are an active presence on the internet.

Starhawk's writings draw upon the social movements of the 1960s and 1970s, including feminism, civil rights, and environmentalism, to produce an earth-based feminist theology of liberation which "values diversity, imposes no dogma, no single name for the sacred, no one path to the center." Starhawk's first and most well-known book, *The Spiral Dance: A Rebirth of the Ancient Religion of the Great Goddess,* sold over 100,000 copies, has been translated into German and Danish, and was republished in a 10th anniversary edition in 1989. *The Spiral Dance* is an introductory "how-to" book on Goddess worship, creative visualization, ritual, and other coven activities. Her latter two books, *Dreaming the Dark* and *Truth or Dare,* are more overtly political, reflecting Starhawk's increasing focus on politics during the right-wing backlash of the Reagan years. These two books represent her continuing quest to wed theory and practice, to marry the magical to the material. In them, she moves outside the boundaries of the single coven to urge contemporary witches to recognize the presence of the spiritual in the body, in matter, and to perform magic (change consciousness and shape energy) through community action. Her first published novel, *The Fifth Sacred Thing,* is set in 21st-century San Francisco and depicts the conflict between an earth-centered culture which values nature and the four sacred elements—earth, air, fire, and water—and a dystopian, authoritarian society whose official religion enforces apartheid and treats women as property. Publication of a prequel, *Walking to Mercury,* is planned for 1997.

In *Truth or Dare,* Starhawk most thoroughly and eloquently elaborates the connections between spirituality and politics. Arguing that is necessary to change the nature of power in order to change the world, she weaves together myth, ritual, and her experiences as a protester at the Livermore Nuclear Weapons Laboratory in England with an analysis of patriarchal forms of domination. She defines three forms of power: 1) "power over" (domination and control); 2) "power from within" (spiritual integrity and personal empowerment); and 3) "power with" (social power to effect change). Starhawk argues that magic, together with a psychology of liberation, is necessary to resist the internally and externally oppressive effects of authority and hierarchy ("power over"). For Starhawk, the magic and ritual are Wiccan tools that can create opportunities for spiritual and social transformation.

—Maria Pramaggiore

STEAD, Christina (Ellen)

Nationality: Australian. **Born:** Rockdale, Sydney, 17 July 1902. **Education:** Teachers' College, Sydney University, teacher certification. **Family:** Married William James Blake in 1952 (died 1968). **Career:** Worked as a public school teacher, special education teacher, and demonstrator in psychology lab, Sydney University; grain company secretary, London, 1928-29; bank clerk, Paris, France, 1930-35; senior writer, Metro-Goldwyn-Mayer,

Hollywood, 1943; workshop instructor, New York University, New York, 1943-44; fellow in creative arts, Australian National University, Canberra, 1969; returned to Australia, 1974. Contributor of short stories to periodicals, including *Kenyon Review, Saturday Evening Post,* and *Southerly.* **Awards:** *Paris Review* Aga Khan Prize, 1966; Arts Council of Great Britain grant, 1967; Patrick White Award, 1974; American Academy and Institute of Arts and Letters honorary member, 1982; Australian Writers Awards Victoria fellowship, 1986, for *An Ocean of Story;* Premier of New South Wales' Award for Literature; several nominations for Nobel Prize. **Died:** 31 March 1983.

Publications

Novels

Seven Poor Men of Sydney. London, Peter Davies, 1934; New York, Appleton-Century, 1935.

The Beauties and Furies. London, Peter Davies, and New York, Appleton-Century, 1936.

House of All Nations. New York, Simon & Schuster, and London, Peter Davies, 1938.

The Man Who Loved Children. New York, Simon & Schuster, 1940; London, Peter Davies, 1941; with an introduction by Randall Jarrell, New York, Holt, 1965.

For Love Alone. New York, Harcourt, 1944; London, Peter Davies, 1945.

Letty Fox: Her Luck. New York, Harcourt, 1946; London, Peter Davies, 1947.

A Little Tea, a Little Chat. New York, Harcourt, 1948; London, Virago, 1981.

The People with the Dogs. Boston, Little Brown, 1952; London, Virago, 1981.

Dark Places of the Heart. New York, Holt, 1966; as *Cotters' England,* London, Secker & Warburg, 1967.

The Little Hotel. Sydney, Angus & Robertson, 1973; New York, Holt, 1975.

Miss Herbert (The Suburban Wife). New York, Random House, 1976; London, Virago, 1982.

I'm Dying Laughing: The Humorist. London, Virago, 1986; New York, Holt, 1987.

Short Stories

The Salzburg Tales. London, Peter Davies, and New York, Appleton-Century, 1934.

The Puzzleheaded Girl (novellas). New York, Holt, 1967; London, Secker & Warburg, 1968.

An Ocean of Story, edited by R. G. Geering. Ringwood, Victoria, Viking Penguin, 1985; New York, Viking, and Harmondsworth, Penguin, 1986.

Other

A Christina Stead Reader, selected by Jean B. Read. New York, Random House, 1978; London and Sydney, Angus & Robertson, 1981.

Christina Stead: Selected Fiction and Nonfiction, edited by R. G. Geering and Anita Segerberg, St. Lucia, Queensland, University of Queensland Press, 1994.

Editor, with William J. Blake, *Modern Women in Love: 60 20th-Century Masterpieces of Fiction.* Hinsdale, New York, Dryden Press, 1946.

Editor, *Great Stories of the South Sea Islands.* London, Muller, 1955.

Translator, *Colour of Asia,* by Fernand Gigon. London, Muller, 1955.

Translator, *The Candid Killer,* by Jean Giltène. London, Muller, 1956.

Translator, *In Balloon and Bathyscaphe,* by August Piccard. London, Cassell, 1956.

*

Critical Studies: *Christina Stead* by R. G. Geering, New York, Twayne, 1969; "Unhappy Families" by Angela Carter, in *London Review of Books,* 3, 16 September 1982; *Christina Stead* by Joan Lidoff, New York, Ungar, 1982; *Christina Stead* by Diana Brydon, London, Macmillan, 1987; *Christina Stead* by Susan Sheridan, New York and London, Harvester Wheatsheaf, 1988; *Writing a Woman's Life* by Carolyn Heilbrun, New York, Norton, 1988, London, Women's Press, 1989; *Christina Stead: A Life of Letters* by Chris Williams, Melbourne, McPhee Gribble, 1989; *Christina Stead: A Biography* by Hazel Rowley, Melbourne, Heinemann, 1993, New York, Holt, 1994, London, Secker & Warburg, 1995; *Christina Stead* by Jennifer Gribble, Melbourne, Oxford University Press, 1994.

* * *

"To open a book, any book, by Christina Stead ... is to be at once aware that one is in the presence of greatness," Angela Carter remarked in the *London Review of Books* in 1982. Stead is without any doubt Australia's greatest woman writer to date, but if she is not as well known as she should be, both in Australia and elsewhere, it is partly because she does not fall easily into any national category. She left Sydney at the age of 26 and spent the next 46 years in the northern hemisphere—mostly in Paris, London, and New York. Since she set all but two of her books in Europe and America, her compatriots, right up until the late 1960s, considered her "un-Australian." Her books were not published in Australia, and were scarcely mentioned in reviews. Still today, much of Stead's work is unknown in Australia because of its northern hemisphere setting and concerns, just as her American and European novels are rarely studied in the northern hemisphere because she is considered Australian. When Virago reissued most of her works in the 1970s and '80s, Stead was recuperated as a major woman writer of international repute. Since then, her status as a "feminist" author has been one of the vexed questions surrounding this brilliant, idiosyncratic writer.

There is considerable anger in Stead's fiction, and as Carolyn Heilbrun points out in *Writing a Woman's Life,* anger, traditionally taboo for women writers, makes readers profoundly uncomfortable. Stead's "gallery of monsters," as her fictional characters are sometimes described, contains a memorable group of emotionally manipulative charmers—both women and men. *The Man Who Loved Children,* Stead's most famous novel, offers a clue as to why she found herself repeatedly attracted and repelled by such figures. This autobiographical novel is based on Stead's own childhood, and the handsome, playful, dominating, egomaniacal Sam Pollit is closely based on Stead's own father.

David Stead was a naturalist and brilliant storyteller who infused in his daughter a deep love of the ancient continent of Australia and a passion for what she called the "ocean of story," but though he appeared to be "the man who loved children," there was something sinister about the way he abused his personal power. Stead's mother died when she was two. David Stead married again when his daughter was six, and Christina's stepmother, who over the years bore six children of her own, disliked Christina. *The Man Who Loved Children* depicts, with an emotional intensity that some readers find almost unbearable, a talented young girl's struggle to assert herself within a patriarchal family structure and against a father whom she both adores and detests. Unfortunately, Stead was virtually compelled by her American publishers to make the setting Baltimore rather than Sydney, for the sake of American readers.

Stead's other autobiographical novel is *For Love Alone.* The only heroic female character in Stead's fiction is Teresa, this novel's central protagonist. Like Stead herself, Teresa is a writer, a passionate young woman who is desperately afraid of being left "on the shelf." (Partly a reflection of the times, this was also, in Stead's case, a result of her father's cruel taunts about her plainness.) Teresa leaves Sydney for London, where she falls in love (as Stead did) with a Marxist businessman, an American, whom she later marries. In a 1982 interview in the Sydney *Morning Herald,* Stead said: "I'm a believer in love. That's really my religion.... I think it has something to do with creativity."

As a lifelong socialist, who believed passionately in love and solidarity between men and women, Stead was impatient with the women's movement of the 1960s and 1970s, which she claimed fostered the separation of the sexes. But the several interviews she gave in the 1970s make her sound unduly defensive, and they rather skew the reality, which is that Stead had always taken a special interest in the situation of women, and this is reflected in several of her fictional works. *For Love Alone* is a vivid (and for its time extremely courageous) portrayal of a young woman's sexual yearnings, as well as her fears of spinsterhood.

Brought up in the repressive Victorian era in which there was a brutally double standard as far as sexual mores were concerned, Stead fervently believed that the sexual liberation of women would help bring about their social equality. She was to be disillusioned. In *Letty Fox,* a novel set mostly in New York in the 1930s and 1940s, we see Letty reach sexual maturity just when the eligible men are being conscripted for World War II. In the race for males, all women are each other's rivals, and Letty's tactics are as dirty as when she tries to secure herself an apartment in New York. Despite her many lovers, she is just as eager for the status and financial security of marriage as Teresa is in *For Love Alone.* As Stead herself pointed out, Letty Fox, for all her libertinage, is "no heroine of feminist freedom."

Eleanor Herbert, in *Miss Herbert (The Suburban Wife),* aspires (like Letty Fox, though differently), to be the clichéd woman of the women's magazines. Miss Herbert is a beautiful English rose who is struggling on the fringes of "Grub Street," the world of London's literary hacks, in the 1940s and 1950s, and juggling her conservatism with her promiscuity.

Stead's collection of four novellas, *The Puzzleheaded Girl,* depicts an array of stray young women who are quite bewildered about their own attitudes to sex, marriage, work, and politics. The offspring of political radicals, this new "lost generation" had grown up in the conservative atmosphere of the Cold War. These portraits of dislocated female drifters, who lack passion and minds of their own, are drawn with the psychological complexity characteristic of Stead's writing. She also has a remarkable talent for capturing voice, and the atmosphere of the times.

Stead's wide range of female characters ar neither heroines nor victims; Stead was not interested in creating morally exemplary characters. Her strength is the way she situates her characters in place and time, showing the ways they are formed by, and participate in, the ideologies and institutions of the society in which they live. As Susan Sheridan writes, Christina Stead's "fictions not only criticize patriarchal capitalist social structures and their ideologies but also insist that women are neither immune from their corruptions nor their passive victims." Stead's women manipulate and play the system—just as her men do.

—Hazel Rowley

STEFAN, Verena

Nationality: Swiss. **Born:** Bern, Switzerland, 1947. **Education:** Trained as a physical therapist. **Career:** Worked as a physical therapist until 1977. Has taught women's studies. Co-founder, Brot Rosen, Berlin, c. 1969. **Awards:** Ehrengabe des Kantons Bern, 1977. **Address:** Munich, Germany.

Publications

Novels

Häutungen. Autobiografische Aufzeichnungen, Gedichte, Träume, Analysen. Munich, Frauenoffensive, 1975; as *Shedding,* New York, Daughters, 1978; with *Literally Dreaming,* "Euphoria," and "Cacophony," New York, Feminist Press, 1994.

Short Stories

Wortgetreu ich träume. Zurich, Arche, 1985; as *Literally Dreaming: Herstories* with *Shedding,* "Euphoria," and "Cacophony," New York, Feminist Press, 1994.

Poetry

mit Füäen mit Flügeln [With Feet with Wings]. Munich, Frauenoffensive, 1980.

Political/Social Theory

Frauenhandbuch Nr. 1, with Brot Rosen. Berlin, Verlag Frauen im Gerhard Verlag, 1972.

Autobiography

Es ist reich gewesen [Times Have Been Good]. Frankfurt am Main, Fischer, 1993.

"Euphoria" [and] "Cacophony," in *Shedding* [and] *Literally Dreaming.* New York, Feminist Press, 1994.

Other

Translator, with Gabriele Meixner, *Lesbische Völker. Ein Wörterbuch (Brouillon pour un dictionnaire des amantes)*, by Monique Wittig and Sande Zweig. Munich, Frauenoffensive, 1983.

Translator, with Gabriele Meixner, *Der Traum einer gemeinsamen Sprache (Dream of a Common Language)*, by Adrienne Rich. Munich, Frauenoffensive, 1982.

*

Critical Studies: "Afterword" by Tobe Levin, in *Shedding* [and] *Literary Dreaming,* New York, Feminist Press, 1994; "Shadowing/Surfacing/Shedding: Contemporary German Writers in Search of a Female *Bildungsroman*" by Sandra Frieden, in *The Voyage In: Fictions of Female Development,* edited by Elizabeth Abel and others, Hanover, University Press of New England, 1983; "Our Language, Our Selves: Verena Stefan's Critique of Patriarchal Language" by Jeannette Clausen, in *Beyond the Feminine: Critical Essays on Women and German Literature,* edited by Susan L. Cocalis and Kay Goodman, Stuttgart, Heinz, 1982; "Fiktiver Brief an Verena Stefan" by Ann Anders, in *Ästhetik und Kommunikation,* 25, September 1976; "Fragen an Verena Stefan" by Gudrun Brug and Saskia Hoffmann-Steltzer, in *alternative,* June-August 1976; *Political Ideology and Aesthetics in Neo-Feminist Fictions: Verena Stefan, Elfriede Jelinek, Margot Schroeder* by Tobe Levin, Ithaca, New York, Cornell University Press, 1979.

* * *

Verena Stefan was born in Switzerland's capital city of Bern in 1947. After moving to Berlin in 1968, she became certified as a physical therapist and co-founded Brot Rosen (Bread Roses), a feminist women's health group. The collective wrote and published a health manual for women in 1972. Inspired by the group, Stefan began working on *Shedding* in 1974. Shortly after the book's publication by a small feminist press in 1975, she left Berlin to live in the countryside of southern Germany, an 18-year-long experiment in living close to nature prompted by, as she wrote, "dreaming of living firsthand." Still active in women's issues, Stefan currently resides in Munich.

The result of an independent publishing effort, *Shedding* is an excellent illustration of how a book can succeed without having access to the traditional publishing network of marketing, major distribution, and press. The initial printing of 3,0000 copies sold out within a month simply through word-of-mouth praise. The continuing grass-roots support finally prompted reviewers to pay serious attention to the book about a year later. To date, *Shedding* has sold more than 300,000 copies in Germany alone, and it has been translated into eight languages. Stefan's politically motivated decision to place the book with a small, underfunded feminist press ultimately paid off: thanks to the surprise bestseller, the publisher was able to create several new jobs for women and expand its catalog of feminist literature.

The slim volume broke ground in other ways, too: it is generally regarded as one of the first works of German feminist literature. Critics called it the "new Bible of the women's movement" and the "Qur'an of the women's movement." After the left-wing, mostly student-led revolution of the 1960s and the consequent social changes, many German women realized that they had not really benefitted from these political efforts. They criticized the fact that many men within the movement remained stuck in patriarchal behavior despite the revolution's intent to redistribute power. "Couples on the Left seemed thoroughly hypocritical to me, their behavior in stark contrast to revolutionary ideals," Stefan writes about that period in her essay "Cacophony." The narrator in *Shedding* expresses what many young (educated) women were feeling. Their efforts having been impeded, they no longer saw the need to cooperate with men and comply with their rules. Instead, women began to look for alternative ways to lead their lives and to trust themselves and their abilities. In her essay "Euphoria," Verena Stefan recalls that

> one of the most important words we taught ourselves in the early 1970s, at least in my view, was *expertin*, the idea of the woman expert. We realized one day that we were assuming ourselves experts, experts on our bodies, our sexuality and the interpretation of our sexuality, our spirit our psyche our dreams and the interpretation of our dreams; we are experts in our creativity and our production.

This confidence may appear self-evident to many women today, but at the time it represented a radical departure from the rules of the male hierarchy that governed German society. Stefan's pioneering achievement consisted in finding a literary expression that paralleled the political criticism of the New Women's Movement since the late 1960s. She not only experimented with new content but also a new literary form. In the afterword to *Shedding,* Stefan describes the act of writing the book as "an experiment which I approached without an apprenticeship, without practical experience, and without professional advice." Corresponding with ideas put forth by French theorists Luce Irigaray and Hélène Cixous, she realized that a new understanding of women's identity could not be achieved using traditional language. Since verbal expression was so thoroughly directed by patriarchy, Stefan decided that she would need a new language to fit her ideas. In her foreword to *Shedding* she names poetry, nature metaphors, and clinical (i.e., neutral) terms for sexual matters as ways to approach this new language. She also rejected most capitalizations (in German all nouns are capitalized) and split up compound nouns and other words. Many critics accused her of falling short of her goal, but she had never intended the book as a complete manual; instead, it was a "rigorous interrogation of patriarchal language," as the feminist scholar Tobe Levin described *Shedding.*

The text is usually regarded as a novel; Sandra Frieden defined it as a "female *Bildungsroman*" (novel of development). Just as it refused to follow many linguistic rules, however, it also rejected the traditional rules of the genre. Stefan subtitled the book "Autobiographical records poems dreams analyses." It describes crucial events in the life of Veruschka, a Swiss woman who moves to Berlin and becomes increasingly politicized. She joins a women's health group with whom she publishes a women's health manual. Dissatisfied with the traditional distribution of gender roles, which extend even to heterosexual relationships between anti-bourgeois, left-wing activists, she finally accepts and celebrates her feelings for the painter Fenna. The protagonist increasingly becomes aware of the relationship between sexuality and power; becoming a lesbian is also a political decision. She criticizes the men in her life for ignoring women's interests and problems or, at best, dismissing them as secondary in the face of larger, global problems. She concludes that "sexism runs deeper than racism than class struggle." Generalizing from her experiences with her black lover Dave, the narrator considers it unlikely that "because of his own oppression, he will treat a woman like a human being. A victim of oppression does not necessarily treat other victims of oppression more humanely."

Veruschka's struggle is literally incorporated in her determination to learn to love her body and thus herself. She realizes the futility of changing and decorating her body just to be accepted by men. By the end of the book, the narrator no longer uses her body and her sexuality to gain security and to end loneliness; she embraces loneliness as a learning process and reaches the point where she is willing to enter into a relationship with Fenna.

"After the shedding comes the identity crisis," Stefan writes in "Cacophony." Her book's success was not a wholly positive experience. She encountered both solidarity and jealousy from members of the feminist community as well as the general public. During a period of what she calls "inner paralysis," she learned to come to terms with outside and personal expectations. Stefan continued to write and also translated books by Adrienne Rich and by Monique Wittig and Sande Zweig, but her popularity rests on the success of *Shedding*. In 1980, she published a book of poems called *mit füâen mit flügeln* [With Feet with Wings]; in 1987 the short story collection *Literally Dreaming,* in which she further explored the theme of life in harmony with nature. Her memoir of her mother, a prolific but unpublished writer, was released in 1993 as *Es ist reich gewesen.*

Shedding inspired German women to write about feminine lives and thus to finally give their gender a history, often through autobiographical texts. Publishers realized the commercial potential of this new *Frauenliteratur* ("women's literature"), and its books continue to appeal to many readers. German feminists have warned, however, that focusing on personal stories without linking them to theory and political activism is ineffective and can reinforce stereotypes about women as powerless victims. However, when Stefan's narrator considers her "private upheaval," she does link the personal with the political. Women's literature in Germany has changed over the past two decades and now often involves female protagonists as strong and professional characters, as well as lesbian or other "new" heroines. To this day, *Shedding* continues to express feelings and experiences many women can relate to. If the book appears dated in some respects, that only confirms its influence: things must have changed for the better since *Shedding* was first published.

—Sabine Schmidt

STEINEM, Gloria

Nationality: American. **Born:** Toledo, Ohio, 25 March 1934. **Education:** Smith College, B.A. (magna cum laude) 1956; graduate study at University of Delhi and University of Calcutta, India, 1957-58. **Career:** Director, Independent Research Service, Cambridge, Massachusetts, and New York, 1959-60; contributing editor, *Glamour* magazine, New York, 1962-69; co-founder and contributing editor, *New York* magazine, 1968-72; co-founder and editor, 1972-87, columnist, 1980-87, consulting editor, 1987, *Ms.* magazine, New York. Contributing correspondent, *Today* show, NBC. Active in civil rights and peace campaigns, including those of United Farm Workers, Vietnam War Tax Protest, and Committee for the Legal Defense of Angela Davis; active in political campaigns of Adlai Stevenson, Robert Kennedy, Eugene McCarthy, Shirley Chisholm, and George McGovern. Editorial consultant to Conde Nast, 1962-69, Curtis Publishing, 1964-65, Random House, beginning 1988, and McCall Publishing. **Member:** National Press Club, Society of Magazine Writers, Authors Guild, Authors League of America, American Federation of Television and Radio Artists, National Organization for Women, Women's Action Alliance (co-founder; chairperson, beginning 1970), National Women's Political Caucus (founding member; member of national advisory committee, beginning 1971), Ms. Foundation for Women (co-founder; member of board, beginning 1972), Coalition of Labor Union Women (founding member), Voters for Choice (co-founder), Phi Beta Kappa. **Awards:** Chester Bowles Asian fellow in India, 1957-58; Penney-Missouri journalism award, 1970, for *New York* article "After Black Power, Women's Liberation"; Ohio Governor's journalism award, 1972; named *McCall's* magazine Woman of the Year, 1972; Doctorate of Human Justice from Simmons College, 1973; American Civil Liberties Union of Southern California Bill of Rights award, 1975; Woodrow Wilson International Center for Scholars fellow, 1977; United Nations Ceres Medal; Front Page Award; Clarion Award. **Address:** c/o *Ms.* Magazine, 230 Park Avenue, New York, New York 10136, U.S.A.

Publications

Political/Social Theory

The Thousand Indias. Government of India, 1957.
The Beach Book. New York, Viking, 1963.
Wonder Woman, with G. Chester. New York, Holt, 1972.
Bedside Book of Self-Esteem. Boston, Little Brown, 1989.
Revolution from Within: A Book of Self-Esteem. Boston, Little Brown, and London, Bloomsbury, 1992.

Essays

Outrageous Acts and Everyday Rebellions. New York, Holt, 1983.
Moving beyond Words. New York, Simon & Schuster, 1993; London, Bloomsbury, 1994.

Other

Marilyn: Norma Jeane. New York, Holt, 1986; London, Golancz, 1987.

Editor, with Wilma Mankiller, Gwendolyn Mink, Marysa Navarro, Barbara Smith, *The Reader's Companion to U.S. Women's History.* Boston, Houghton Mifflin, 1996.

*

Media Adaptations: "I Was a Playboy Bunny" *A Bunny's Tale* (television movie), 1985.

Critical Studies: *The Education of a Woman: The Life of Gloria Steinem* by Carolyn Heilbrun, New York, Dial Press, 1995.

* * *

In her 1994 essay, "Doing Sixty," Gloria Steinem seems to be asking herself what "kind" of movement she helped instigate 30 years earlier: how she became a central voice for that movement, and what her present role in encouraging and sustaining various forms of feminism should be. Her thoughts are reflective, sometimes addressing questions she must have been asked by a parade of invisible interviewers. "I'm not sure feminism should require an adjective," is her response to multiple someones who want her to further define herself.

Some of her comments, which address an early radicalism, seem almost too easy, critics have suggested. Steinem was not part of the suburban housewife reaction triggered by Betty Friedan's *Mystique.* Indeed, her unconventional, sometimes poverty-laden girlhood appears to have provided her with a working-class perspective. Her anger at systemic limitations of women was expressed cleverly; "If Men Could Menstruate," for example, suggests that women's "curse" would become a symbol of power with multiple "show-you" aspects. "I Was a Playboy Bunny," another romp, describes Steinem's "undercover" (no pun intended) foray into Hugh Hefner's Playboy Club in New York City. Concluding that "All women are bunnies," she captures young women's eagerness to become sex objects, complete with plastic bag bust-enhancers, and crude customer expectations. In both these pieces, as in her early interviews of New York politicians, Steinem writes terse, humorous reportage.

As a journalist with a keen talent for spotting the hypocritical feint and a rare ability to write clear, honest prose, Steinem quickly moved into the seemingly glamorous New York magazine world. She was a co-founder of two magazines—*New York* in 1968 and *Ms.* in 1972, publishing successes in supposedly glutted markets. Her more recent examinations of age, race, and economic status delve into similar issues, and to most informed people Steinem's life story follows a path that would have been familiar to feminists of the 19th century, as well. She has been both criticized and deified; even her attempt to teach a feminist cautionary tale by recounting the life of Marilyn Monroe might be best understood as a case of empathy and a desire to explain other possibilities.

Described as an icon by several cultural historians, Steinem has indeed been both symbol and working theorist of the modern women's movement. In addition to her advocacy of women, she has written extensively about the contrast between wealth and poverty. Her activities were not limited to the women's movement; she marched alongside the United Farm Workers, civil-rights activists, and anti-Vietnam War demonstrators as well.

Although Steinem has claimed to have lived her first 50 years externally reacting and being much too nice to many observers, she had been an actor, as well. She grew up in Toledo, Ohio, the second daughter of Leo and Ruth Nuneviller Steinem. Her father might be described as irresponsible but nevertheless provided an emotional anchor. Her mother, who had earned a master's degree in history, had a secret desire to go to New York and be a journalist, and had worked at the *News Bee,* a Toledo paper soon to be bought by the *Blade.* Ruth filled two pages of the paper; a local-events column she prepared was published under the male byline Duncan Mackenzie. Steinem's parents were divorced when she was 10 and she became the custodial guardian of her mother, who was mentally ill. Certainly she found herself reacting to circumstances she felt she had to exercise control over, even as other girls her age were able to enjoy their girlhoods.

Despite the demands upon her, Steinem left home at age 17 to attend Smith College on a scholarship. She has described her Smith life as ideal and has expressed amazement that students would leave this land of books and quiet to get married. Feeling the differences between her low income and the riches of her classmates, she said she used her eclectic wardrobe to underline the differences. About her mother's mental illness, she has been honest. That she doesn't blame her father and continues to appreciate his unconventional life and personal charms is an aspect important to her own philosophy, one that has not pass the "sisterly censor," as Angela Carter has tagged it. Steinem has written of her mother with pride, as well as with despair and confusion. Her biographer Carolyn Heilbrun has written that Steinem's life might challenge us to redefine the functional family; that despite poverty and heavy responsibility, Steinem's childhood produced a passionately engaged and loving human being.

After graduation from Smith, Steinem went to India where she adapted quickly to everything except the strict separation of rich and poor. In fact, she was so affected by rickshaws and other human conveyances that she refused to ride in the back seat of taxicabs when she returned to New York City. In India she wore native dress and traveled to southern India during caste riots there. A social reform that did in time transfer was student politics, according to Heilbrun, who noted that India affected Steinem so profoundly because she came already prepared for its offerings. Despite the cultural differences, it was in India that her talent for writing and advocating became apparent.

Steinem returned to New York in 1958 where she found an unreceptive city at first. Despite several promising interviews, she learned that women weren't hired for major jobs in the publishing world. Instead, she drew upon her experiences in India, which provided a focus for some of her early freelance writing. Steinem's best-known article from her early career came in 1963 when *Show* magazine asked her to cover the opening of the Playboy Club in New York City. For her Bunny piece, Steinem received "training" in the arts related to dressing in scanty Bunny clothes and working to serve the male customers of the club. The Bunny article received raves: It was called "hysterically funny" and powerful. But to Steinem the Bunny experience had been more humiliating than she had expected. Certainly having to undergo a pelvic examination by Playboy Club's doctor would have added to this reaction.

In 1965 Steinem got her first chance to write extensively on politics in *New York Magazine.* Her column "The City Politic" brought her in touch with George McGovern, Martin Luther King Jr., John Lindsay, Nelson Rockefeller, and such visitors to the city as Ho Chi Minh. Co-founder of the publication was Clay Felker, whose lack of professional sexism he credited to the fact that his mother was a competent journalist who had held a job as woman's editor of a St. Louis newspaper. Felker was instrumental boosting Steinem's career by providing a subsidy for the first issue of *Ms.* in January of 1972.

That first issue of *Ms.* would be a turning point for Steinem as she suddenly went from journalist-about-town to editor of a successful monthly magazine. She is quoted in the *Chicago Tribune* as saying that even though she felt that there should be a feminist magazine, she didn't want to start it herself. She wanted to be a freelance person and said she had thought she'd turn the editorship over to someone else as soon as it was on its feet. Seven years later, she had the opportunity to obtain a Woodrow Wilson fellowship and, during her absence, she discovered that her ties to *Ms.* were stronger than she had realized.

Steinem's first collection of essays appeared in 1983 in *Outrageous Acts and Everyday Rebellions.* Here is the Bunny story once again, along with a few other pieces of journalism that Angela Carter calls "far more persuasive ... than are the lay sermons reprinted from *Ms.*" Sketches about her mother and Marilyn Monroe are efforts to advance what feminism or feminist attitudes might have done to alleviate the slavery to attitudes of their times. *Marilyn: Norma Jeane,* a biography accompanied by photographs by George Barris and published three years later, follows the same theme. *Marilyn* received mixed responses from critics. Providing a counterpoint to an earlier piece by Norman Mailer—called by reviewer Julian Barnes the "long, brawling amour he never had with the actress (luckily for her)"—Steinem's biography, by comparison, is an attempt to rescue and understand this "constructed" sex object, this victim of desire.

Revolution from Within: A Book of Self-Esteem (1992) has been dubbed by some critics as "New Age" and too tied up with psychological self-help jargon. But Steinem provides criticism herself of New Age terminology; she notes that support groups include the communal clotheswashing of Pakistani village women. She proposes that men and women unlearn artificial selves and journey back to truer understandings of the self. *Moving beyond Words* (1993), while also on the receiving end of some criticism, is of interest, especially to new or younger readers who may find some of the essays useful in understanding the rationale behind the women's movement. In "The Importance of Un-learning," for example, Steinem sums negative aspects of a sexist educational system. As she puts it, "We need to unlearn some of our respect for education, since it has undermined our respect for ourselves. It's worth taking a little time to demystify it."

—Ann Mauger Colbert

STEPHEN, Virginia. *See* **WOOLF, (Adeline) Virginia.**

STONE, Merlin

Nationality: American. **Born:** New York, New York, 27 September 1931. **Education:** State University of New York at Buffalo, B.S. in art 1957; California College of Arts and Crafts, M.F.A. 1968; Ashmolean Museum, Oxford, England; independent study at museums and libraries worldwide 1971-76. **Career:** Sculptor, 1958-67; teacher at Albright Knox Art Gallery School, 1957-66, State University of New York at Buffalo, 1962, 1966, California College of Arts and Crafts, Oakland, 1968-69, and University of California San Francisco extension, 1969; coordinator, Experiments in Art and Technology (EAT), San Francisco, 1969-70; lecturer throughout the United States, Canada, and Europe. Director of *The Return of the Goddess* (series of four radio programs), CBC, 1986; organizer of Goddess festivals in New York and Toronto. Member of advisory councils, *Women's Studies International Quarterly* and *Woman of Power;* contributor to periodicals, including *Harmonist, Heresies, Spare Rib,* and *Woman of Power.* **Address:** Box 266, 201 Varick St., New York, New York 10014, USA.

Publications

Religion/Spirituality

When God Was a Woman. New York, Dial, 1976; as *The Paradise Papers: The Suppression of Women's Rights,* London, Quartet, 1976.

Ancient Mirrors of Womanhood: Our Goddess and Heroine Heritage. New York, New Sibylline, 1979.

Three Thousand Years of Racism—Recurring Patterns in Racism. New York, New Sibylline, 1981.

Uncollected Short Stories

"The Plasting Project," in *Hear the Silence,* edited by Irene Zahava. Trumansbury, New York, Crossing Press, 1986.

Plays

The Voice of Earth, with Olympia Dukakis (produced Williamstown, Massachusetts, 1990).

*

Media Adaptations: *When God Was a Woman* (13-part radio series), Pacifica Radio, 1978.

* * *

The feminist movement of the 1970s introduced new perspectives involving women's experiences. Women began demanding equality in all aspects of society, from the workplace to the government to religion. The term "feminist spirituality" was first introduced during that decade to encompass all areas of religious thought, particularly from a Judeo-Christian standpoint. Feminist theologians were re-examining Biblical texts, trying to understand the exclusion of women's experience and working towards new forms of spirituality to include women.

Merlin Stone is regarded as one of the key thinkers in the feminist theological movement. Her extremely influential and monumental work, *When God Was a Woman,* falls under the multiple categories of women's studies, religion, and anthropology, due to its extensive historical examination of ancient religions, particularly goddess worship. Stone acknowledges that the cultures of the Upper Paleolithic and the later Neolithic ages worshiped the Goddess, but the evidence is lacking because of their existence prior to the keeping of written records. Stone's evidence is all speculative, but her theories are founded on concrete, tangible evidence that she has interpreted from a feminist perspective.

The two time periods that Stone concentrates on belong to the Stone Age: the Upper Paleolithic—or Old Stone Age—and the Neolithic—or New Stone Age. The Paleolithic is the earliest and longest stage of human cultural development, which lasted from approximately 2.5 million to 10,000 years ago, and is characterized by human's ability to create hand axes, flake and blade tools, and to manufacture stone implements. The Neolithic period followed, improving stone tool manufacturing to include grinding and polishing; agricultural cultivation; domestication of animals; and pottery manufacture. These early developments involving sculpture attracted the attention of Stone, who used her extensive knowledge of both sculpture and anthropology to re-examine these periods for the purpose of gathering an understanding of goddess worship within these ancient cultures. The importance of sculptures of these periods is detailed in the third part of Stone's argument.

The first part of *When God Was a Woman* is an anthropological analogy which explains the beginnings of matrilineal societies. Matrilineal means that the lineage, the family name, is passed from mother to daughter rather than from father to son. Stone explains that in ancient societies, prior to the understanding of conception, women were seen as miraculously giving birth. No connection was made between the father's role and a woman's ability to create new life; women alone were considered the sole parent and producer of the next generation. Stone relies on the theories of anthropologists such as Margaret Mead, who also recognizes the existence of a period prior to the understanding of paternity.

Stone's second body of evidence is the connection between matrilineal societies, religious beliefs, and the beginning of rituals. The source of life is considered through the search for the original source of life. Stone maintains that anthropological and historical evidence prove that the original concepts of religion were manifested in ancestral worship. Since women were seen as the only ones involved in reproducing and since the family name passed from the mother to daughter, the ancestors who were worshiped were women. In the studies of the Paleolithic period there is evidence of burying the dead, a practice that infers that contemporary forms of religion incorporated ancestral worship as one of its beliefs. Stone has examined the graves of these time periods, where women were buried with tools, strewn with red ochre, and separately from men and children.

Stone's final and most tangible evidence comes from her extensive work as a sculptor. She cites the abundance of sculptures of women. These sculptures, also known as *Venus figures*, have been found in the Gravettian-Aurignacian cultures of the Upper Paleolithic Age as far back as 25,000 years ago, in areas as widespread as modern-day Spain, France, Germany, Austria, Czechoslovakia, and Russia. The image that appeared for around 10,000 years is of a woman in various forms; often depicted as pregnant; and made of stone, bone, or clay. All have similar appearances, often with hands to breasts, and shown in three phases of life: a young woman, a mother giving birth, and an old woman. These female figurines are a major connection between the two time periods of the Stone Age, having also been discovered in archeological digs dating from the Neolithic period and located throughout what is now the Near and Middle East. Stone has concluded that such female figurines are, in fact miniature representations of idols of the great mother cult.

Stone has provided much information on goddess worship in ancient societies, which she considers to have been matrilineal. Although mainstream anthropology has yet to fully recognize her arguments as fact, she has provided key information on analyzing and studying the ancient world of goddess worship for great numbers of feminist theologians. Her findings have been used to examine women's current and historical position within the church (particularly their exclusion) by looking at these ancient cultures, studying their transformations and their evolving belief systems. According to Stone, the image of the female deity survived throughout the ancient worlds of Greece and Rome and was not completely repressed until the last Goddess temples were annihilated by Christian emperors around 500 A.D.

Although *When God Was a Woman* is Stone's most notable work, she has written other books on goddesses, as well as exploring other women's issues, and issues of race within her writing. However, *When God Was a Woman* remains one of the best sources of understanding of a time when women were not oppressed; when they were, in fact, leaders of the civilization; when "god" as the primary deity existed in female form.

—Kate Robinson

STOPES, Marie (Charlotte)

Pseudonyms: Erica Fay; Marie Carmichael; G. N. Mortlake. **Nationality:** British. **Born:** Edinburgh, Scotland, 15 October 1880. **Education:** University College, London, B.S. 1902; University of Munich, Ph.D. in botany 1904; University of London, D.Sc. 1905. **Family:** Married 1) the biologist R.R. Gates in 1911 (annulled 1916); 2) the aircraft manufacturer Humphrey Vernon Roe in 1918 (died 1949); one son. **Career:** Lecturer in botany, then paleobotany, Manchester University, beginning 1904; introduced to Margaret Sanger, 1915; founder, Society for Constructive Birth Control and Racial Progress, 1921; cofounder, with H. V. Roe, Mothers' Clinic for Constructive Birth Control, Holloway, North London, 1921; brought libel charges against Dr. Halliday Sutherland, 1923; sued for libel by Sutherland and editor of *Morning Post;* acquires Alexander Moring (small publishing house), 1939. **Died:** Of cancer, Norbury Park, Surrey, 2 October 1958.

Publications

Novels

Love Letters of a Japanese (as G. N. Mortlake). London, S. Paul, 1911.

Love's Creation (as Marie Carmichael). London, Bale & Danielsson, 1928.

Political/Social Theory

Married Love. London, A. C. Fifield, 1918; New York, Critic & Guide Co., 1920.

Wise Parenthood. London, A. C. Fifield, 1918.

A Letter to Working Mothers. Leatherhead, Surrey, privately printed, 1919.

Radiant Motherhood. London, G. P. Putnam, 1920; New York, G.P Putnam, 1921.

Contraception: Its Theory, History, and Practice. London, Bale & Danielsson, 1923.

Sex and the Young. London, Gill, 1926.

Enduring Passion. London, Putnam, 1928; New York, Putnam, 1931.

Roman Catholic Methods of Birth Control. London, P. Davies, 1933.

Birth Control Today, London, Heinemann, 1934.

Marriage in My Time. London, Rich & Cowan, 1935.

Change of Life in Men and Women. London and New York, Putnam, 1936.
Your Baby's First Year. London, Putnam, 1939.
Sleep. London, Hogarth Press, 1956.

Poetry

Man, Other Poems and a Preface. London, Heinemann, 1913.
Love Songs for Young Lovers. London, Heinemann, 1919.
Kings and Heroes (as Erica Fay), New York, Putnam, 1937.
Oriri. London, Heinemann, 1939.
Wartime Harvest. London, A. Moring, 1944.
The Bathe. London, A. Moring, 1946.
Instead of Tears. London, A. Moring, 1947.
We Burn. London, A. Moring, 1951.
Joy and Verity. London, Heinemann, 1952.

Plays

Plays of Old Japan: The No, with Professor J. Sakurai. London, Heinemann, 1913.
Conquest. London, S. French, 1917.
Gold in the Wood and *The Race*, London, A. C. Fifield, 1918.
Our Ostriches. London, Putnam, 1923.
A Banned Play and a Preface on the Censorship. London, Bale & Danielsson, 1926.

For Children

The Road to Fairyland (as Erica Fay). London, Putnam, 1926; New York, Putnam, 1927.

Religion/Spirituality

A New Gospel to All Peoples. London, A.L. Humphreys, 1922.

Nonfiction

Ancient Plants. London, Blackie, 1910.
Dear Dr Stopes (letters), edited by Ruth Hall. London, Deutsche, 1978.

*

Manuscript Collections: British Library, Wellcome Institute.

Critical Studies: *The Authorized Life of Marie Stopes* by Aylmer Maude, London, Williams & Norgate, 1924, revised as *Marie Stopes: Her Work and Play,* London, Putnam, 1933; *Love's Coming of Age* by Edward Carpenter, London, Allen & Unwin, 1930; *Marie Stopes* by Keith Briant, London, Hogarth Press, 1962; *The Trial of Marie Stopes* by Muriel Box, London, Femina, 1967; *Passionate Crusader: The Life of Marie Stopes* by Ruth Hall, London, Deutsch, 1977; *Dangerous Sexualities* by Frank Mort, London and New York, Kegan Paul, 1987; *Marie Stopes and the Sexual Revolution* by June Rose, London, Faber & Faber, 1992; *Dr. Marie Stopes and Press Censorship of Birth Control* by Jack Coldrick, Belfast, Athol, 1992.

* * *

Marie Stopes said she wrote *Married Love,* her seminal work, because "In my first marriage I paid such a terrible price for sex-ignorance that I feel that knowledge gained at such a cost should be placed at the service of humanity.... I hope [this] will save some others years of heartache and blind questioning in the dark." Her work revolutionized the idea of marriage, challenging its basis and redefining its purpose. Stopes led women's fight for equality to its most fundamental level, calling for an equal sexual relationship between husband and wife.

Stopes was born in 1880 in Victorian England, where women were idealized as pure and sexless beings. She inherited her love of science from her father, Henry Stopes, an architect and amateur archaeologist. Her strict mother, Charlotte Carmichael, an intellectual and feminist (when told she had a daughter, Charlotte is said to have exclaimed "Thank the Lord!"), instilled in Stopes her fundamental sense of equality and independence. Initially educated at home by her mother, who attempted to teach her Latin and Greek at age 5, Stopes went to North London Collegiate, a famous progressive girls' school. She raced through university, obtaining a B.S. in botany and geology from the University of London in only two years, and receiving her Ph.D. from Munich University two years later. When she returned to England to become a lecturer in botany at Manchester University, Stopes became the first woman to achieve that position in the science faculty. In 1905 she received her D.Sc. from the University of London, becoming, at age 25, the youngest Doctor of Science in Britain.

Throughout her life, Stopes maintained her unfailing energy, not only in science and in her writing—between 1918-19, for example, she published three sociological works, two plays and a scientific paper—but also when constantly campaigning for various causes. Her academic success was not matched, however, by the personal and romantic fulfillment she so desperately sought after growing up within the cold environment generated by her parents' marriage. After several unhappy affairs, she married the Canadian academic Reginald Ruggles Gates in 1911, but divorced him five years later. It was the sexual unhappiness of this marriage, she claimed, which led her to write *Married Love;* she would maintain that she was a virgin when she wrote it, having obtained an annulment on the grounds of non-consummation.

Described by Stopes as "a book about the plain facts of marriage" and written in blunt, anatomical language, *Married Love* was the result of Stopes's painstaking scientific research. Written from a personal point of view, it was the first instruction manual for sexual technique from the female perspective, claiming women's equal rights to sexual needs and pleasure. Stopes urged husbands to learn how to arouse and satisfy their wives at a time when it was still considered normal for a man to demand his "marital rights" regardless of his wife's feelings, because prevailing attitudes said that "good" women were passive partners, utterly without desires of their own.

Published in 1918, a month after the enfranchisement of women and eight months before the end of World War I, the book responded to changes that were already taking place within society. Because of the war, women's roles had shifted; they had begun to work in jobs to which they had previously been denied access, and had acquired more opportunity to relate to men as peers. This new, fragile freedom led to a desire for more equality within personal relationships. Though obviously shocking to many, *Married Love* was published to instant acclaim, selling two thousand copies in the first two weeks, and ultimately being translated into 12 languages. Stopes became a public figure, seen as an adviser on sexual and emotional problems, and received so many letters that her publishers' offices were overwhelmed.

However, Stopes remained, to a great extent, a product of her age, defending the class system and the inherent superiority of the upper classes. She believed that her work could even enhance existing class structures while it challenged social values. Though she claimed that "there is nothing that helps so much with the economic emancipation of woman as a knowledge of how to control her maternity," Stopes's interest in the subject stemmed not from a feminist viewpoint but from a social one. As she explained in *Radiant Motherhood* (1920), she believed that the lower classes—whose problems, she maintained, were a result of their lesser morality rather than poverty—should be persuaded not to breed, and even be sterilized, so they would not "produce innumerable tens of thousands of warped and inferior infants." Such eugenic ideas now seem untenable, but they were fairly common in Stopes's era.

Combining her reputation as a social reformer with her immense personal energy, Stopes sought constructive and concrete ways to propagate her beliefs. With Humphrey Roe, her second husband, she opened The Mother's Clinic, the first birth control clinic in the British Empire. Staffed entirely by women, much to the dismay of the medical profession, it provided free advice and dispensed low-cost birth control to the poor. They also founded The Society for Constructive Birth Control and Racial Progress, whose name perhaps best exemplifies Stopes's approach. She continued to write prolifically, publishing books such as *Wise Parenthood* (1918), a guide to birth control methods, *Enduring Passion* (1928), a sequel to *Married Love,* and *Birth Control Today,* (1934) a "Practical Handbook."

As the birth control movement grew, Stopes became a prominent publicist for the cause, fighting a series of libel cases and taking the opposition of the Catholic Church extremely personally. However, her egotism and refusal to support others in the movement made her unpopular with many, including Margaret Sanger, her American counterpart. Stopes never obtained for herself the ideal marriage that she had helped inspire in thousands; her marriage to Roe collapsed in the 1930s. Desperately desiring children, she would have only one son, Harry, from whom she deliberately distanced herself after his marriage. Though published and performed, her poetry, fiction, and plays enjoyed very limited success, never earning her the literary recognition she craved. Marie Stopes died of breast cancer in 1958, just prior to her 78th birthday.

—Meredith E. Hyde

SUI SIN FAR

Pseudonym for Edith Maude Eaton. **Nationality:** Canadian. **Born:** Macclesfield, England, 1865; immigrated to Canada c. 1872. **Education:** Attended British and Canadian grade schools; educated at home. **Career:** Worked as a stenographer and journalist, Montréal, Canada, beginning 1883; traveled briefly to Jamaica on assignment, 1897; moved to United States and canvassed newspaper subscriptions, San Francisco's Chinatown, c. 1898; moved to Boston, 1910-12. Contributor of short stories and essays to journals and periodicals. **Died:** Montréal, Canada, 1914.

Publications

Selected Short Stories

"The Gamblers," in *Fly Leaf,* 1896. In *Mrs. Spring Fragrance and Other Writings,* 1995.
"The Story of Iso," in *The Lotus,* 1896. In *Mrs. Spring Fragrance and Other Writings,* 1995.
"The Love Story of the Orient," in *The Lotus,* 1896. In *Mrs. Spring Fragrance and Other Writings,* 1995.
"Ku Yum," in *Land of Sunshine,* 1896. In *Mrs. Spring Fragrance and Other Writings,* 1995.
"A Chinese Feud," in *Land of Sunshine,* 1896. In *Mrs. Spring Fragrance and Other Writings,* 1995.
Mrs. Spring Fragrance. A.C. McClurg & Co., 1912; expanded as *Mrs. Spring Fragrance and Other Writings,* edited by Amy Ling and Annette White-Parks, Urbana, University of Illinois Press, 1995.

Uncollected Short Stories

"Sweet Sin," in *Land of Sunshine,* 1898.
"A Chinese Ishmael," in *Overland,* 1899.
"Ku Yum and the Butterflies," in *Good Housekeeping,* 1909.
"The Kitten-Headed Shoes," in *Delineator,* 1910.
"Bird of Love," in *New England Magazine,* 1910.

Selected Essays

"Leaves from the Mental Portfolio of an Eurasian," in *Independent,* 66(3138), 1909.
"New York as Kept by the Chinese in America," in *The Westerner,* 1909.
"Chinese-American Sunday School," in *The Westerner,* 1909.
"Chinese Food," in *The Westerner,* 1909.
"Americanizing Not Always Christianizing," in *The Westerner,* 1909.

*

Bibliography: In *Sui Sin Far/Edith Maude Eaton: A Literary Biography* by Annette White-Parks, Urbana, University of Illinois Press, 1995.

Critical Studies: "Sui Sin Far/Edith Eaton: First Chinese-American Fictionist" by S.E. Solberg, in *MELUS,* 8, spring 1981, and her "Sui, the Storyteller: Sui Sin Far (Edith Eaton), 1867-1914," in *Turning Shadows into Light: Art and Culture of the Northwest's Early Asian/Pacific Community,* edited by Mayumi Tsutakasa and Alan Chong Lou, Seattle, Young Pine Press, 1982; "Writers with a Cause: Sui Sin Far and Han Suyin" by Amy Ling, in *Women's Studies International Forum,* 9, 1986, and her "Edith Eaton: Pioneer Chinamerican Writer and Feminist," in *American Literary Realism,* 16, autumn 1983; "Defiance or Perpetuation: An Analysis of Characters in *Mrs. Spring Fragrance*" by Lorraine Dong and Marlon K. Hom, in *Chinese America: History and Perspectives,* edited by Him Mark Lai, Ruthanne Lum McCunn, and Judy Yung, San Francisco, Chinese Historical Society of America, 1987; "Revelation and Mask: Autobiographies of the Eaton Sisters" by Ling, in *a/b: Auto/Biography Studies,* 3, summer 1987; "Introduction to 'Wisdom of the New,' by Sui Sin Far" by Annette White-Parks, in *Legacy: A Journal of 19th-Century Women's Literature,* 6, spring 1989; *Between Worlds: Women Writers of Chinese Ancestry* by Ling, New York, Pergamon, 1990; "Between the East and West: Sui Sin Far—The First Chinese American Woman Writer" by Xiao-Huang Yin, in *Arizona Quarterly,* 7, winter 1991; "Audacious Words: Sui Sin Far's *Mrs. Spring Fragrance"* by Elizabeth Ammons, in *Conflicting Stories: American Women Writers at the Turn into the 20th Century,* by Ammons, New York, Oxford University Press, 1991; "Sui Sin Far: Writer on the Chinese-Anglo Borders of North America" (dissertation) by Annette White-Parks, Washington State University, 1991, and her *Sui Sin Far/Edith Maude Eaton: A Literary Biography,* Urbana, University of Illinois Press, 1995.

* * *

Edith Maude Eaton, who writing as Sui Sin Far is considered North America's first Eurasian fiction writer, dedicated her work to defending Chinese immigrants and children of mixed racial heritage. As a hybrid herself—her father was English and her mother Chinese—her presence in print and across a North American landscape provided an alternative to those confining racist and sexist narratives prevalent at the turn of the century. Eaton's journal articles and short stories represented a conscious rewriting of what were once called "yellow peril" narratives: negative fiction about Chinese immigrants written by White authors who intended to arouse anti-Asian sentiments. Additionally, her work resisted prescribed roles for women like herself who were nurtured beneath the shadow of the Victorian cult of true womanhood.

Eaton was born in Macclesfield, England, in 1865, as Edward Eaton's and Lotus Blossom Trefusis's second child, but first daughter. After moving to Canada around 1872 or 1873 when Eaton was about four, the family relocated constantly throughout Montréal, as a growing household which eventually numbered 14, and finally settled in a dirty, unsanitary working-class neighborhood. Since her Asian features were nearly indistinguishable, Eaton and her siblings were able to "pass" as White. However, if somebody learned of their Chinese background, racist comments prompted the children to wonder, as Eaton would later write in "Leaves from the Mental Portfolio of an Eurasian": "Why we are what we are? I and my brothers and sisters. Why did God make us to be hooted and stared at?"

First-hand experiences with racism in numerous North American locations provided material for Eaton's career as a socially conscious journalist and fiction writer. According to Annette White-Parks, in her *Sui Sin Far/Edith Maude Eaton: A Literary Biography* (1995), Eaton drew inspiration from three major locations: Montréal, the West Coast, and Boston. Her writing career began in a Montréal advertising firm whose aim included attracting young women to Canada. Soon after her experiences there, Eaton established herself as a freelance journalist in order to defend Chinese Montréalers. While she often received no byline, articles like "Half-Chinese Children: Those of American Mothers and Chinese Fathers," which appeared in the *Montreal Daily Star* in 1895, and "A Plea for the Chinaman: A Correspondent's Argument in his Favor," a letter to the *Star* editor in 1896 (both of which have been attributed to her), exemplify her defense of Chinese immigrants. Eaton took great pride in her writing goals, once remarking, "I dream dreams of being great and noble. I glory in the idea of dying at the stake and a great genie arising from the flames and declaring to those who have scorned us: 'Behold, how great and glorious and noble are the Chinese people!'" She eventually adopted a Chinese pseudonym to reflect her Asian roots: "Sui Sin Far" translates as "water lily."

On the West Coast, in what White-Parks terms "Pacific Coast Chinatown stories," sketches of San Francisco's Chinese residents began to appear in Eaton's narratives: in her article "Chinatown Boys and Girls" (1903), she presents Chinese children as culturally distinct in their bright clothing, yet since they laugh and play like any group of children, she equates them with those of all ethnicities; in the short story "Lin John" (1899), a woman steals the $400 that her brother has saved in order to buy her out of prostitution, providing grounds for what White-Parks calls a resistance to male-defined authority and morality. In Boston in 1912, Eaton finally achieved her first and only book-length publication, *Mrs. Spring Fragrance,* a collection of short stories that also included 150 pages dedicated to "Tales of Chinese Children."

While Eaton would gain popularity slowly, her sister Winifred enjoyed instant and enormous publishing success under the Japanese-sounding pseudonym "Onoto Watanna," chosen to offset mounting criticism against the Chinese in America. While Winifred knew nothing of Japan—she had never met a Japanese person—she offered the kinds of stories her North American audience wanted to hear: those embellished with "oriental" and "exotic" Japanese settings, according to Amy Ling in *Between Worlds: Women Writers of Chinese Ancestry.* Ling claims that unlike her sister Eaton's stories, Winifred's supported and encouraged social mythology.

Eaton may have dressed her Chinese characters in the "exotic" clothing for which her reading public hungered and by which her sister gained recognition, but beneath these garments lay unexpected strengths and convictions. The character Mrs. Spring Fragrance, for example, contrary to popular contemporary views of the submissive Asian woman in America's "quaint" Chinatowns, is an elegant, spunky, and thoroughly Americanized resident in an upper-middle-class Seattle home. In a subversive gesture, Eaton pleases her audience while also attempting to dismantle preconceived notions of the "Oriental."

As a female Eurasian writer in a White man's publishing market, however, Eaton confronted the very prejudices she battled against: women, especially Eurasian women, were not expected to roam North America as journalists, nor were they encouraged to publish. Eaton declared in "Leaves" that "I am prostrated at times with attacks of nervous sickness ... [because] I know that the cross of the Eurasian bore too heavily upon my childish shoulders"; since she also believed in and experienced a "world ... so cruel and sneering to a single woman," she wrote to highlight these personal and societal wrongs. Despite her contributions toward redefining images of Chinese women at the turn of the century, Eaton was overlooked as an important figure in the realm of cultural studies for more than half a century following her death in 1914, at age 49. Not until the 1970s, and even more so in the 1980s, was she targeted as an important, ethnic literary figure in cultural studies. Her fiction, now more readily accessible, recognizes her defense of Chinese immigrants, especially women, at a time when such a view adopted by a female Eurasian must have incurred an immense measure of stamina and personal integrity. Edith Eaton, praised as a pioneer by Ling, is presently celebrated as an iconoclastic female author who dared to challenge yellow peril stereotypes as well as sexist definitions of "woman."

—Monica Chiu

T

TAN, Amy (Ruth)

Nationality: American. **Born:** Oakland, California, 19 February 1952. **Education:** Attended San Jose City College and University of California at Santa Cruz; San Jose State University, California, B.A. in linguistics and English 1973, M.A. in linguistics 1974; University of California, Berkeley, 1974-76. **Family:** Married Louis M. DeMattei in 1974. **Career:** Specialist in language development, Alameda County Association for Mentally Retarded, Oakland, 1976-80; project director, MORE Project, San Francisco, 1980-81; reporter, managing editor, and associate publisher, *Emergency Room Reports,* 1981-83; technical writer, 1983-87. **Awards:** Commonwealth Club gold award, 1989, and Bay Area Book Reviewers award, 1990, both for *The Joy Luck Club;* Best American Essays award, 1991. Honorary D.H.L.: Dominican College, San Rafael, 1991. **Address:** c/o Random House, Inc., Publicity, 201 East 50th St., 22nd Floor, New York, New York 10022, U.S.A.

Publications

Novels

The Joy Luck Club. New York, Putnam, and London, Heinemann, 1989.
The Kitchen God's Wife. New York, Putnam, and London, Collins, 1991.
The Hundred Secret Senses. New York, Putnam, 1995.

Play

Screenplay: *The Joy Luck Club,* 1993.

For Children

The Moon Lady. New York, Macmillan, 1992.
The Chinese Siamese Cat, illustrated by Gretchen Shields. New York, Macmillan, and London, Hamilton, 1994.

*

Media Adaptation: *The Joy Luck Club* (film), 1993.

Critical Studies: "Amy Tan" by Christina Chiu, in *Lives of Notable Asian Americans: Literature and Education,* New York and Philadelphia, Chelsea, 1996; "Mother-and-Daughter Writing and the Politics of Location in Maxine Hong Kingston's *The Woman Warrior* and Amy Tan's *The Joy Luck Club*" (dissertation) by Wendy Ann Ho, University of Wisconsin—Madison, 1993; "Generation Differences and the Diaspora in *The Joy Luck Club*" by Walter Shear, in *Critique: Studies in Contemporary Fiction,* 34, 1993.

* * *

Novelist Amy Tan was born in 1952, in Oakland, California, to Chinese immigrant parents. Her father, John Tan, emigrated to the United States in 1947 and worked as an engineer before he became a Baptist minister. Tan's mother, Daisy, came to the United States after her first marriage crumbled due to spousal abuse; although she had three children by her former husband, Chinese law at that time would not permit a divorced woman to gain custody of her offspring and Daisy kept her first family a secret from her American-born children for many years. It was only after she lost both her oldest son, Peter, and her husband to brain cancer that Daisy would reveal her past. Still a teen at the time of the death of both her father and brother, Tan grew up with her younger brother in her mother's home, a fact that is reflected in the primacy of mother-daughter relationships within her fiction.

At the age of 15, Tan and her brother followed their mother to live in Europe for three years. After her graduation from high school in Montreux, Switzerland, Tan and her family came back to live in the United States. In 1969 she enrolled at Linfield College in McMinnville, Oregon, intending to study for a medical degree. Soon, however, Tan developed an interest in English literature and gave up her medical career. She transferred to San Jose City College, and then to San Jose State University, where she earned a B.A. with a double major in English and linguistics, followed by an M.A. degree in linguistics. Tan would later attend the University of California at Santa Cruz and the University of California at Berkeley before abandoning her studies in pursuit of additional interests outside academia. These included working with disabled children and working as a reporter, managing editor, and associate publisher for *Emergency Room Reports.* In 1983 she became a freelance writer.

Working as a freelance writer rekindled Tan's interest in fiction writing. Two books particularly sparked her interest: Louise Erdrich's *Love Medicine* and Barbara Kingsolver's *The Bean Trees.* These Native American writers taught Tan how to assert her own unique voice as a writer outside of the fictional mainstream. With encouragement and help from fellow writer Molly Giles, Tan began writing her first novel, *The Joy Luck Club,* which became an instant best-seller upon publication in 1989. She went on to publish two more novels, *The Kitchen God's Wife* and *The Hundred Secret Senses.* Tan is also the author of two children's books, *The Moon Lady* and *The Chinese Siamese Cat.* She currently lives with her husband of over twenty years, Lou DeMattei, in San Francisco and New York.

Tan's works revolve around several themes: mother-daughter relationships, sisterly relationships, cultural conflicts, and gender inequity in old China. *The Joy Luck Club,* which was chosen by the American Library Association as a Best Book for Young Adults, portrays four first-generation Chinese immigrant women and their fully Americanized daughters living in California. The novel consists of 16 stories that reveal not only the generation gap between mothers and daughters, but also their special bonds. In the story "Double Face," the daughter blurts out, "Don't be so old-fashioned, Ma. I'm my own person." The mother is left to wonder, "How can she be her own person? When did I give her up?" In "Magpies," a wealthy merchant's concubine in China commits suicide to procure a better life for her daughter. Because of its popularity with readers, *The Joy Luck Club* was filmed in 1993, produced and written by Tan and fellow writer Ross Bass, and directed by Wayne Wang.

In 1991's *The Kitchen God's Wife,* Tan draws on her own mother's harrowing story of life in pre-communist China. In Tan's fictional version, the Chinese immigrant mother tells her Americanized daughter how she and her Chinese-born children were brutalized by her ill-tempered husband, Wen Fu. Deserted by her own mother, she was forced to marry the abusive Wen Fu, and suffered additional hardships during World War II. The woman finally escapes both China and her husband—just five days before the communist takeover of the country in a novel that is a poignant indictment of a male chauvinist society where women are forced to be silent.

The Hundred Secret Senses relates the life story of Olivia Yee and her half-sister Kwan. Kwan, who came from a small village in China to San Francisco to live with Olivia's family, communicates with ghosts from the yin world of "the hundred secret senses," and Olivia learns to see the yin world too. Although Kwan's un-American behavior is a huge embarrassment to Olivia, the latter learns much about Chinese values and customs through Kwan. Olivia's visit to Changmian, the birthplace of Kwan in China, answers many of her questions about Kwan's childhood and her own life.

In Tan's *The Moon Lady,* adapted from *The Joy Luck Club* and illustrated by Gretchen Shields, the Chinese American Ying-ying tells her three granddaughters about how she, as a seven-year-old girl in China, was granted a secret wish by the Moon Lady. *The Chinese Siamese Cat,* also illustrated by Shields, is a comic story for children about the inadvertent wisdom of a naughty cat named Sagwa. By sheer mistake Sagwa transforms a selfish magistrate into a wise and generous ruler.

Tan's novels have been universally acclaimed by readers and critics alike. *The Joy Luck Club* received both the 1989 Commonwealth Club gold award and the 1990 Bay Area Book Reviewers award. Continuing to explore the many layers of her Chinese-American heritage, through her writing, Tan has also received the 1991 Best American Essays award, as well as an honorary D.H.L. from Dominican College in San Rafael.

—Jae-Nam Han

TAYLOR, Karen. *See* **MALPEDE, Karen.**

TE AWEKOTUKU, Ngahuia

Nationality: New Zealander; tribal affiliation: Te Arawa, Waikato, Tuhoe. **Born:** Ohinemutu, Rotorua. **Education:** Attended Auckland University, Waikato University, and East-West Centre University of Hawa'ii. **Career:** Curator, Waikato Museum of Art & History, 1985-87; lecturer in art history, Auckland University, 1987-1996; professor of Maori studies, Victoria University of Wellington, beginning 1997. Member, Haerewa: Maori Consultant Committee to the Auckland City Art Gallery. **Member:** New Zealand Qualification Authority Art, Craft, and Design Advisory Group, New Zealand Film Archive Trust Board, Auckland Museum Advisory Panel, Council of the National Art Gallery. **Address:** Maori Studies Department, Victoria University of Wellington, P.O. Box 600, Wellington, New Zealand.

Publications

Short Stories

Tahuri. Auckland, New Women's Press, 1989; Toronto, Women's Press, 1991.

Uncollected Short Stories

"He Tiki," in *The Exploding Frangipani,* edited by Cathie Dunsford and Susan Hawthorne. Auckland, New Women's Press, 1990.

"So Easy to Please," in *Spiral Seven,* edited by Marian Evans and Heather McPherson.

"Their Public/Private Passion," in *Landfall,* 183, September 1992.

"Kurangaituku," in *Vital Writing 3: New Zealand Stories and Poems 1991-1992,* edited by Andrew Mason. Godwit Press, 1992.

"Painfully Pink," in *Miscegenation Blues: Voices of Mixed Race Women,* edited by Carole Campter. Toronto, Sister Vision Press, 1994.

"Porutu," in *Below the Surface: Words and Images in Protest at French Testing on Moruroa,* edited by Ambury Hall. Auckland, Random House, 1995.

Essays

Mana Wahine Maori: Selected Writings on Maori Women's Art, Culture, and Politics. Auckland, New Women's Press, 1991.

He Tinkanga Whakaaro: Research Ethics in the Maori Community. Wellington, Ministry of Maori Affairs, 1991.

Uncollected Essays

"Foreigners in Our Own Land," with Marilyn Waring, in *Sisterhood Is Powerful,* edited by Robin Morgan. New York, Anchor Press, 1984.

"Kia Mau, Kia Manawanui—We Will Never Go Away," in *Feminist Voices: Women's Studies Texts for Aotearoa, New Zealand,* edited by Rosemary Du Plessis, Kathie Irwin, Alison Laurie, and Sue Middleton. Oxford University Press, 1992.

"Lesbian Organising," with Alison Laurie, Julie Glamuzina, and Shirley Tamihana, and "Nga Roopu Wahine Maorie: Maori Women's Organisations," with Tania Rei and Geraldine McDonald, in *Women Together: A History of Women's Organisations in New Zealand,* edited by Anne Else. International Affairs/Daphne Brasell, 1993.

"He Puna Roimata mo Te Pa Harakeke," in *Nga Nui o Te Ra: Teaching, Nurturing ,Developments of Maori Women's Weaving.* Auckland, Aotearoa, Moananui a Kiwa Weavers, 1993.

"Some Ideas for Maori Women," in *The Vote, the Pill, and the Demon Drink: A History of Feminist Writing,* edited by Charlotte Macdonald. Wellington, Bridget Williams Books, 1993.

"He Ngangahua," in *Mana Wahine: Women Who Show the Way,* edited by Amy Brown. Auckland, Reed, 1994.

*

Critical Studies: Interview in *Convent Girls: New Zealand Women Talk to Jane Tolerton,* Auckland, Penguin, 1994.

* * *

Ngahuia Te Awekotuku, recently appointed professor of Maori studies at Victoria University, Wellington, has a history as a spokeswoman on feminist, lesbian, and Maori issues in Aotearoa (New Zealand). In 1971, when a student at Auckland University, she was involved in the beginning of the women's liberation movement, taking part in marches and protests, but always aware of being "the only lesbian." Offered a Student Leadership scholarship to the United States she was refused a visa as a "known sexual deviant." As a result of speaking about this at Auckland University, the first gay liberation group in New Zealand was set up in March 1972. In April 1972 Te Awekotuku was funded by the Students' Association to tour New Zealand campuses promoting Gay Liberation. In late 1972 she became involved in Nga Tamatoa, the emergent Maori Rights group. In *Mana Wahine Maori* she writes:

> *And woman suffers, while the warrior snarls within her.*
> *I am one such woman*
> Maori-lesbian-feminist. Born into a colonized tribal patriarchy in the thermal districts of Aotearoa, I discovered my lesbianism relatively early, though I certainly did not survive the stormy years of late adolescence a maiden intact. Years of study at University fashioned a cosmopolitan exterior, and the galloping madness of antipodean hippiedom and antiwar actions soon sharpened my political edge, making me aware and verbal in the white middle-class world. Particularly on issues I felt affected me directly: class, and deeper still, colour. Despite a lightish skin—my people's delight—and an educated accent, I was still visibly, boldly, Maori. Nothing could ever change that—it was/is as permanent, wonderful, and as inexorable as my femaleness.

In 1974 Te Awekotuku completed an M.A. in English with a thesis on New Zealand novelist Janet Frame and in 1975 went to the East-West Centre in Hawaii on a joint doctoral project with Waikato University, New Zealand, resulting in a thesis on the socio-cultural impact of tourism on the Te Arawa people of Rotorua, her hometown. From 1985-1987 she was curator of Ethnology at the Waikato Museum, where she was responsible for the restoration of Te Winika, a carved war canoe, with a team of five women and one man. "Originally regarded as men's work, best done by men only, this project gently but irrevocably changed many of the restrictions regarding work of this nature," she would note. Since 1987 she has been on numerous government boards and committees concerned with cultural conservation and Maori Arts.

Both Te Awekotuku's books were published by New Women's Press, a small women-only publishing house, now defunct, that also published the reprint of *The Old Time Maori* by Makereti, a Maori woman who studied at Oxford in the 1920s, for which Te Awekotuku wrote the introduction. In *Mana Wahine Maori: Selected Writings on Maori Women's Art, Culture and Politics* (1991) she weaves together the strands of her identity as feminist, lesbian, academic, and Moria in a collection of essays whose title translates as *The Power of Maori Women.*

> As a Maori lesbian, I am often compelled to consider the colliding urgencies of my life. I have risked the brand of 'house nigger', for I have defended the middle-class white rape victim before the disadvantaged and deprived brown rapist—for his act violates all women, and welds the manacles of sexist oppression more fixedly than before.

Her first short story, "Tahuri: The Runaway" was published in a New Women's Press collection of New Zealand women's short stories in 1987. This story is included in *Tahuri* (1989), a collection of stories about a young Maori girl growing up in Te Awekotuku's own life. They are clear, concise, and movingly powerful stories, which suggest that lesbianism is cross culture and ahistorical, and has always existed in Polynesian society. The young girl encounters gang rape and brotherly incest but finds role models and refuge amongst older lesbian women in the Maori community. Pakeha (white New Zealanders) are peripheral in the stories, which give a vivid sense of Maori women watching one another, revelling in one another, loving and supporting one another. Rather than being the marginalised other, Maori women and particularly lesbian Maori women become central in these stories. As she writes in *Mana Wahine Maori:*

> Throughout my life I have never doubted that women are stronger, braver and more resourceful—regardless of men's rules, men's games, and men's petty triumphs. My role models—of the fierce women fighters, shamans and poets of Maori legend and myth; of the resilient, courageous women of my own extended family—demonstrate this to me. For as much as colonial and contemporary ethnography and tribal record attempt to annihilate the relevance and radiance of their achievements, it is my responsibility to them as their inheritor, to ensure their stories are not lost in a mawkishly romantic muddle of male-translated history.

—Aorewa Pohutukawa McLeod

THOMAS, Martha Carey

Nationality: American. **Born:** Baltimore, Maryland, 2 January 1857. **Education:** Cornell University, A.B. 1877; postgraduate work at Johns Hopkins University, 1877-78, University of Leipzig, 1879-82, and the Sorbonne; University of Zurich, Ph.D. (summa cum laude) 1882. **Career:** Dean of Faculties and professor of English, from 1884, president, 1895-1922, Bryn Mawr College for Women; founder, Bryn Mawr School for Girls, 1895; president, National College Women's Equal Suffrage League, 1908; founder, school of social work, 1915, and Bryn Mawr Summer School for Women in Industry, 1921. **Awards:** L.L.D., Western University of Pennsylvania, 1896. **Member:** Association of College Alumni, League to Enforce Peace. **Died:** 1949.

Publications

Essay

The Higher Education of Women. Albany, New York, J. B. Lyon, 1900.

Literary Criticism

Sir Gawain and the Green Knight: A Comparison with the French Perceval. Zurich, n.p., 1883.

Autobiography

Memoir of Martha Carey Thomas, Late of Baltimore. London, n.p., 1846.

Other

The Educated Woman in America: Selected Writings of Catharine Beecher, Margaret Fuller, and Martha Carey Thomas, edited by Barbara M. Cross, New York, Teachers College Press, 1965.

The Making of a Feminist: Early Journals and Letters of M. Carey Thomas, edited by Marjorie Houspian Dobkin, Kent, Ohio, Kent State University Press, 1979.

*

Critical Studies: *Carey Thomas of Bryn Mawr* by Edith Finch, n.p., 1947; *Alma Mater: Design and Experience in the Women's Colleges from Their Nineteenth-Century Beginnings to the 1930s* by Helen Lefkowitz Horowitz, New York, Knopf, 1984.

* * *

Martha Carey Thomas, president of Bryn Mawr College from 1894 to 1922, advanced women's education in America by building an institution based on the premise that women possess the same intellectual capabilities as men. In shaping Bryn Mawr, Thomas did not endeavor to transplant such established women's colleges as Smith, Vassar or Wellesley to Philadelphia; instead she sought to establish a women's college that offered its students the challenges and advantages of the world's finest research universities.

Born in 1857 to James and Mary Thomas, Martha Carey Thomas expressed an early desire for intellectual stimulation within communities of women. A Baltimore Quaker family of comfortable, although declining, financial means, the Thomases sent their first born child to the local Friends school and then to Howlanad Institute, a Quaker boarding school in Ithaca, New York. By age 15, Thomas began dreaming of a life of the mind for herself. Together with her cousin and best friend, Bessie King, she planned to attend Vassar and become a scholar. As she wrote in her journal, she and Bessie "would live loving each other and urging each other on to every high and noble deed or action and all who passed should say 'their example arouses me, their books ennoble me, their ideas inspire me and behold they are women.'" Thomas's adult life developed largely as she had imagined, albeit with some alteration in the details. Instead of going to Vassar, she became part of Cornell University's first class of female students. And although she and her cousin did not live together as adults, Thomas, who never married, sustained long-term relationships with women, first with friend Mary Gwinn and later with Mary Garrett, with whom she would share her home.

After graduating from Cornell in 1877, Thomas spent an unsuccessful year at Johns Hopkins University where she was not permitted to attend classes. She subsequently convinced her father to allow her to study abroad, in Germany. But because no university in Germany would grant her a Ph.D., Thomas transferred to the University of Zurich where she received her doctoral degree in 1882, graduating summa cum laude.

In the following year, Thomas wrote to the trustees then in the process of establishing Bryn Mawr College—a group that included her father—and asked to be named president. Although her initial request was denied, Thomas was appointed dean of the college and professor of English. Her interest in becoming president did not wane and by 1892 Thomas was president in all but name. Following the retirement of the college's first president two years later, Thomas reached her goal, becoming Bryn Mawr's second president.

As president, Thomas managed to steer Bryn Mawr away from the founders' original vision: creating a "female Haverford"—in essence, the sister school of a nearby liberal arts college for men—and towards her goal of building a women's college that upheld the standards set by research universities, Johns Hopkins University in particular. To this end she instituted an entrance exam as difficult as that administered at Harvard; she designed a demanding curriculum similar to that offered at Johns Hopkins; she hired a faculty composed of recent graduates from German universities—mostly men—who were expected to conduct original research; and she added a graduate school to keep her scholarly faculty engaged.

In addition to transforming the young Bryn Mawr into one of the nation's premier women's colleges, Thomas also involved herself in various reform activities of benefit to women. In 1908 she became the first president of the National College Women's Equal Suffrage League. After the passage of the suffrage amendment, Thomas allied herself with the National Woman's Party, a group that took an uncompromising stand on women's equality. In 1921 she helped establish the Bryn Mawr Summer School for Women in Industry, bringing young working women to the college for eight weeks of classes in the liberal arts. Through her enormous energy, dedication, and conviction to the belief that women were intellectually the equal of their male counterparts, Thomas fulfilled her childhood dream, becoming a woman whose example and ideas inspired generations of young women to reach new intellectual heights.

—Anne Lewis Osler

THOMPSON, Dorothy

Nationality: American. **Born:** Lancaster, New York, 9 July 1893. **Education:** Syracuse University, B.A. 1914. **Family:** Married 1) Josef Bard in 1922 (divorced 1927); 2) the writer Sinclair Lewis in 1928 (divorced 1942), one son; 3) the painter Maxim Kopf (died 1958). **Career:** Publicist and lecturer for women's suffrage movement, Buffalo, New York, c. 1915; publicity director, Social Unit (New York-based philanthropic reform organization), Cincinnati, Ohio; freelance journalist and publicist for American Red Cross, c. 1920; overseas correspondent, then bureau chief, *Philadelphia Public Ledger* and *New York Evening Post,* 1923-28; first correspondent ordered to leave Berlin, Germany, on orders from Hitler, 1934; author of syndicated column "On the Record"; broadcaster, NBC Radio, New York. Cofounder, American Friends of the Middle East, 1951. Contributor to numerous periodicals, including *Commentary, Cosmopolitan, Foreign Affairs, Ladies' Home Journal, New York Herald Tribune,* and *Saturday Evening Post.* **Awards:** American Woman's Association Achievement award, 1938. **Died:** Lisbon, Portugal, 30 January 1961.

Publications

Political/Social Theory

The New Russia. New York, Holt, 1928; London, Cape, 1929.
I Saw Hitler! New York, Farrar & Rinehart, 1932.
Dorothy Thompson's Political Guide: A Study of American Liberalism and Its Relationship to Modern Totalitarian States. New York, Stackpole, 1938.
Refugees: Anarchy or Organization? New York, Random House, 1938.
Christian Ethics and Western Civilization. New York, Town Hall, 1940.
A Call to Action. New York, Ring of Freedom, 1941.
Our Lives, Fortunes, and Sacred Honor. San Francisco, Windsor, 1941.
To Whom Does the Earth Belong? London, Jewish Agency for Palestine, 1944.
I Speak Again as a Christian. New York, Christian Council on Palestine and American Palestine Committee, 1945.
Let the Promise Be Fulfilled: A Christian View of Palestine. New York, American Christian Palestine Committee, 1946.
The Developments of Our Times. De Land, Florida, John B. Stetson University Press, 1948.
The Truth about Communism. Washington, Public Affairs Press, 1948.
The Crisis of the West. Toronto, University of Toronto Press, 1955.

Essays

Concerning Vermont. Brattleboro, Vermont, Hindreth, 1937.
Once on Christmas. London and New York, Oxford University Press, 1938.
Let the Record Speak (columns). Boston, Houghton Mifflin, and London, Hamish Hamilton, 1939.
Listen, Hans. Boston, Houghton Mifflin, 1942.
The Courage to Be Happy. Boston, Houghton Mifflin, 1957.

Uncollected Essays

"Refugees: A World Problem," in *Foreign Affairs,* 16, April 1938.
"How I Was Duped by a Communist," in *Saturday Evening Post,* 221, 16 April 1949.
"America Demands a Single Loyalty," in *Commentary,* 9, March 1950.
"My First Job," in *Ladies' Home Journal,* 74, April 1957.
"I'm the Child of a King," in *Ladies' Home Journal,* 76, November 1959.

Other

Translator, *Job: The Story of a Simple Man,* by Joseph Roth. New York, Viking, 1931.

*

Manuscript Collection: Syracuse University Library, Syracuse, New York.

Critical Studies: *Dorothy and Red* by Vincent Sheean, Boston, Houghton Mifflin, 1963; *Dorothy Thompson: A Legend in Her Time* by Marion K. Sanders, Boston, Houghton Mifflin, 1973; *Brilliant Bylines: A Biographical Anthology of Notably Newspaperwomen in America* by Barbara Belford, New York, Columbia University Press, 1986; *American Cassandra: The Life of Dorothy Thompson* by Peter Kurth, n.p., 1990.

* * *

Once hailed by *Time* magazine as the most influential woman next to Eleanor Roosevelt, journalist Dorothy Thompson has the knack for getting the interviews that others could not. Covering world events during the international crisis years between World Wars I and II, Thompson often encountered danger but met it head on. A highly visible journalist in the United States, she lectured and appeared on radio programs to air her political views. Thompson's syndicated column "On The Record" was printed in nearly 200 newspapers and read by seven million readers.

The adventurous side of Thompson emerged when she was just a child and never left her. She had the habit of running away from home but always returned to the father she adored, Reverend Peter Thompson, a Methodist minister. Continually punished for minor infractions, Dorothy's discipline consisted of memorizing books, poems and psalms from her father's collection. Her love of literature grew as did her fantasy world wherein she traveled to foreign places. Thompson's daydreams ended when her mother died during a miscarriage and her father remarried a woman who was not fond of children. She became a defiant teenager and was sent to Chicago where she lived with an aunt.

Although an English teacher told Thompson that her only talents would be "in the kitchen," she attended Syracuse Methodist University and, after graduating in 1914, decided to become a writer. Thompson's first job though was giving speeches to help raise money for the campaign for women's suffrage in Buffalo, New York. Her flair for drawing attention got her a promotion to organizer. Finally, in 1917 the New York State legislators passed the 19th Amendment, a step on the way to national ratification of the amendment awarding women the vote.

Thompson's daydreams of sailing to Europe and visiting foreign countries came true in 1920. A chance interview with Terence MacSwiney, an Irish independence leader, enabled her to sign on with the International News Service (INS) and her fate as a journalist covering European events was sealed. Covering such stories as a metal workers' lockout in Italy, human dramas of refugee noblemen fleeing the Russian Revolution, and dodging machine-gun fire in the Balkans and Poland, Thompson freelanced and sold articles to the American Red Cross, the Associated Press, the *London Star*, and the *Philadelphia Public Ledger*. Nicknamed the "blue-eyed tornado," she was acclaimed as the "best journalist" of her generation.

Thompson tried for seven years to see Adolph Hitler and finally succeeded in 1931. The interview and subsequent article, first published in *Cosmopolitan* magazine, later became a book titled *I Saw Hitler!* Thompson wrote that within "fifty seconds" of their meeting she believed Hitler incapable of becoming the dictator of Germany. She called him "insignificant" and the "prototype of the Little Man." Although her assessment of his powerful rise proved wrong, her book contained a good analysis of the rise of the Nazi movement and provided many photographs. Thompson's subsequent denouncements of Hitler led to her expulsion from Nazi Germany in 1934. Thereafter her battle against fascism continued and her career rose, her articles gaining worldwide recognition.

In 1927 Thompson married her second husband, the novelist Sinclair Lewis, with whom she bore a son, Michael. Although Lewis had pursued her across the European continent prior to their marriage, the relationship would not stand the strain of both writers' careers. Lewis never enjoyed the same exciting lifestyle as his wife did nor did he share her interest in politics. In addition, he drank to excess, which inflamed his jealousy of his wife. Lewis's career declined after he won a Nobel Prize for literature in 1930 while Thompson's as a foreign correspondent soared. During the last years of their marriage Thompson had a relationship with the German writer Christa Winsloe, author of the lesbian novel *Mädchen in Uniform,* which eventually became America's first film with a lesbian theme. Thompson never professed to be a lesbian but believed she should be able to have "the right to love where my mind and heart admire." She married again in 1943, this time to the Austrian artist Maxim Kopf.

Thompson felt that the best of her writing came following 1935, when she began interpreting events rather than just recording them. At home she wrote about political events like the New Deal. She became a columnist for the *Ladies' Home Journal;* meanwhile "On the Record" appeared three times a week, and a collection of these columns was published in book form in 1939 as *Let the Record Speak.* Many issues gained public attention through Thompson's writing. In 1938, for example, her article "Refugees, A World Program" helped to initiate an international refugee conference in France. Thompson urged that the United States coordinate a global program for refugees, drawing from her own experience in aiding European friends in need of a visa and shelter in the United States. Following World War II, the focus of Thompson's politics changed to a pro-Arab stance regarding the situation in the Middle East, leading to a decline in her popularity.

Initially Thompson's clear, concise writing was geared toward involving women in reading and understanding current events without relying on their husbands' input, but as time progressed more and more men joined her readership. A daring and liberated woman, Thompson ventured into areas where few others would go and expressed her ever-changing views regardless of what others thought. Even when married to Sinclair Lewis and drawn into his fame by association, she refused to allow the loss of her own independence, identity, or writing talents. In addition to inspiring a new generation of female journalists, Dorothy Thompson accomplished several female "firsts," which included becoming one of two women to head the European news bureau and being the first woman to cover a national political convention for a radio network. She felt her audiences should always be told the truth; they, in turn, respected her candid, well-researched reporting and her short, easy-to-understand sentences. Thompson's life and personality were reflected by her writing style, punctuated with exclamation marks.

—Marilyn Elizabeth Perry

TING LING. *See* **DING LING.**

TRABA, Marta

Nationality: Colombian. **Born:** Buenos Aires, Argentina, 25 January 1930. **Education:** Graduated from the National University in Buenos Aires in 1950. **Family:** Married 1) Alberto Zalamea in 1950 (divorced 1967), two sons; 2) the literary critic Angel Rama in 1969. **Career:** Art critic and writer in Colombia; professor of art history, University of Andes 56-66; founder and editor of the art criticism journal *Prisma,* 1957; founder and director of the Museum of Modern Art, Bogota, 1963-68; professor of art, University of Puerto Rico, Rio Piedras, 1970-71; professor of Latin American art, Caracas Teacher's College, Caracas, Venezuela, 1977-79; lecturer in art at Harvard University, University of Massachusetts, Oberlin College, University of Maryland, and Middlebury College, 1980-81. **Awards:** Casa de las Americas Prize, 1966, for *Las ceremonias del verano;* Guggenheim fellowship, 1968. **Died:** In a plane crash, with her husband, near Madrid, Spain, 27 November 1983.

Publications

Novels

Las ceremonias del verano. 1966.
Los laberintos insolados [The Insolate Labyrinths]. Madrid, n.p., 1967.
La jugada del sexto día [The Play of the Sixth Day]. 1969.
Homérica latina [A Latin American Epic]. 1979.
Conversacións al sur. 1981; translated as *Mothers and Shadows,* New York, Readers International, 1989.
En cualquier lugar [In Any Place]. 1984.
Casa sin fin [Endless House] 1984.

Short Stories

Pasó así [So It Was]. 1969.

Other

El museo vacío [The Empty Museum]. 1952.
Arte en America. Washington, D.C., Pan American Union, 1959.
La pintura nueva en Latino Américo. 1961.
El Arte Bizantino. 1965.
La rebelíon de los santos. 1971.
Propuesta polémica sobre el arte puertorriqueño. 1971.

En el humbral del arte moderno [On the Threshold of Modern Art]. 1972.
Dos décadas vulnerables en las arte plásticas latinoamericanas, 1950-1970 [Two Vulnerable Decades of Latin American Art, 1950-1970]. 1973.
Mirar en Caracas [Looking in Caracas]. 1974.
La Zona del silencio. 1975.
Hombre americano a todo color. 1975.
Guide to 20th-Century Latin American Art. 1982.

*

Critical Studies: *Women's Voices From Latin America* by Evelyn Picon Garfield, Detroit, Wayne State University Press, 1985; *Women Writers of Latin America: Intimate Histories* by Magdalena Garcia Pinto, Austin, University of Texas Press, 1988; "Subversions of Authority: Feminist Literary Culture in the River Plate Region" by Francine Masiello, in *Chasqui: Revista de la literatura latinoamericana,* 21(1), May 1992; "The Silent Zone: Marta Traba" by Elia Goeffrey Kantaris, in *Modern Language Review,* 87(1), January 1992; "Marta Traba: A Life of Images and Words" by Gloria Bautista Gutiérrez, in *A Dream of Light and Shadow. Portraits of Latin American Women Writers,* edited by Marjorie Agosín, Albuquerque, University of New Mexico Press, 1995.

* * *

Marta Traba lived energetically and worked relentlessly to revitalize Latin American art and promote it, both throughout the continent of its origin and around the world. Born in 1930 in Buenos Aires, Argentina, she was a voracious reader as a child, and lost herself in the literature of Latin American authors, as well as in the books of European and Russian writers. During her childhood, Traba would come into contact with two tiers of Argentine society: because of the poverty that her family suffered, she was familiar with evictions and constant relocations; due to the Bohemian lifestyle of her father, she became familiar with the world of literature and the arts. A precocious child, Traba entered this world as an active participant. While still a teenager she earned a scholarship to study art history in Chile first, and then in Paris.

Traba married in 1950, and with her husband Alberto Zalamea lived in Paris and in Italy. After their stay in Europe, she and Zalamea emigrated to Bogota, Colombia in 1954, where her energy was immediately channelled into the service of Latin American Art. She founded *Prisma,* a journal of art criticism, as well as directing and appearing in a public television program about art in Latin America. Traba viewed television as an extremely useful medium for the dissemination of new ideas about art, and for exposing new and exciting artists whose work broke with traditional and safe practices in the art world. Only when she was already firmly established as an art critic, did she then began to write novels.

At the urging of her good friend Antonia Palacios, Traba wrote *Las ceremonias del verano,* which deals with the kind of life she led as a young mother in Italy. She sent the book Cuba in 1966, to compete for the coveted Casa de las Americas prize; much to her surprise Traba became that year's winner. With the backing of the Casa Prize jury, she plunged headlong into the world of fiction while maintaining her position as professor of art history at the University of the Andes. In 1967, however, her boldness was challenged by the government of Colombia after her televised comments against the vandalism by government troops of the University campus earned her a decree of exile. Traba recalled in later interviews that thousands of telephone calls, telegraphs, and motions of protest forced the government to relent. In public, the president granted her leniency because she had two sons who were Colombian citizens. 1967 would be a year of multiple crises for the critic and author; it was the year in which she also divorced her first husband.

Never one to succumb to obstacles, Traba saw her only volume of short stories published in 1967, and began to arrange support toward the receipt of a Guggenheim fellowship which would take her to the United States in 1968. She was married again in 1969, to the Uruguayan literary critic Angel Rama, and together they took up residence in Puerto Rico for two years starting in 1970. There they both lectured at the University of Puerto Rico in Rio Piedras. Their joint careers led the couple to the United States again in 1979, where they were denied permanent residency in 1982. From there Traba and Rama moved to Paris, their official residence at the time of the plane accident that took their lives in 1983.

It is hard not to be impressed with the pace and scope of Traba's life work, and to wonder what she may have continued to achieve had she lived. Her constant travel and wide recognition in the world of Latin American art history pose an interesting counterpoint to her work as a writer of fiction, in which she declares to be an "avowed Proustian." Indeed, her absorption with details and recollection of events in dreamlike conversations that have a decidedly more tranquil pace than her biography of constant travel reveals that Traba was also an extremely thoughtful passenger.

Though *Ceremonias del verano* was the winner of a prestigious prize, her best-known novel is probably *Conversacións al sur* (1981), translated as *Mothers and Shadows.* In it, Irene and Dolores, two Argentine women, recall through conversations what the repressive regimes in both Argentina and Chile have meant to them and to their lives, as a disruption and an invasion of the sense of self. By recalling their horrible experiences—forced miscarriage, imprisonment and torture, bearing witness to the protests by the Mother of the Plaza de Mayo in Buenos Aires—each woman can then put her nightmares to rest.

In an interview with Evelyn Picon Garfield, Traba discussed her concept of "feminine" writing. Although she herself disavowed being a "feminist, I believe in feminine literature, in a tender regard for detail that is not perceived by men. I find this tendency in Carson McCullers, Sylvia Plath, Katherine Mansfield,... I believe that women perceive reality more keenly than men. They grasp what lies in between the cracks. Man encompasses more and possesses a well-ordered, organized intellect. But women behold what is interstitial; it is a very specific, tender, feminine view, and one that I share."

Traba's denial that she was a feminist is most likely due to the fact that she endeavored to create a portrayal of fairness and justice that would encompass both men and women. Her affirmation that women have a greater fascination with and ability to relate details is an interesting assessment of her own writing and that of other writers from Latin America. With it, she carves a special place for the feminine voice and its unique quality as the subconsciousness of her continent. The novels of Marta Traba reveal a continent plagued by injustice, one that might perhaps begin to be healed by the attention to the details of everyday life and their transformation into an art form.

—Helena Cochrane

TRIBLE, Phyllis

Nationality: American. **Born:** Richmond, Virginia, 25 October 1932. **Education:** Meredith College, Raleigh, North Carolina, B.A. (magna cum laude) 1954; Union Theological Seminary, New York, 1954-56; Columbia University, Ph.D. 1963. **Career:** Teacher, Masters School, Dobbs Ferry, New York, 1960-63; assistant, then associate professor of religion, Wake Forest University, Winston-Salem, North Carolina, 1963-71; associate professor, then professor of Old Testament, Andover Newton Theological School, Newton Centre, Massachusetts, 1975-79; professor of Old Testament, 1979-81, then Baldwin Professor of Sacred Literature, beginning 1981, Union Theological Seminary, New York. Visiting professor at schools, including Seinan Gakuin University, Fukuoka, Japan, University of Virginia, Boston University, Vancouver School of Theology, Brown University, Saint John's University, University of Notre Dame, and Iliff School of Theology, Denver, Colorado; lecturer at numerous colleges and universities worldwide. **Awards:** National Endowment for the Humanities Younger Humanist fellowship 1974-75; Meredith College Alumna Award, 1977; honorary degrees from Franklin College, 1985, and Lehigh University, 1994. **Member:** Society of Biblical Literature (president, 1994). **Address:** Union Theological Seminary, 3041 Broadway, New York, New York 10027-5710, U.S.A.

Publications

Religion/Spirituality

God and the Rhetoric of Sexuality. Philadelphia, Fortress Press, 1978.

Texts of Terror: Literary-Feminist Readings of Biblical Narratives. Philadelphia, Fortress Press, 1984.

Rhetorical Criticism: Context, Method, and the Book of Jonah. Minneapolis, Fortress Press, 1994.

Essays

"Eve and Adam: Genesis 2-3 Reread," in *Andover Newton Quarterly,* March 1973; in *Womanspirit Rising,* edited by Carol P. Christ and Judith Plaskow. San Francisco, Harper & Row, 1979.

"Depatriarchalizing in Biblical Interpretation," in *Journal of the American Academy of Religion,* 1973; in *The Jewish Woman,* edited by Elizabeth Koltun. New York, Schocken, 1976.

"Feminist Hermeneutics and Biblical Studies," in *The Christian Century,* 10 February 1982; in *Feminist Theology: A Reader,* edited by Ann Loades. Louisville, Kentucky, Westminster/John Knox Press, 1990.

"The Pilgrim Bible on a Feminist Journey," in *The Auburn News,* spring 1988.

"Bringing Miriam out of the Shadows," in *Bible Review,* February 1989; in *A Feminist Companion to Exodus to Deuteronomy,* edited by Athalya Brenner. Sheffield, Sheffield Academic Press, 1994.

"Five Loaves and Two Fishes: Feminist Hermeneutics and Biblical Theology," in *Theological Studies,* 50, 1989; enlarged in *The Promise and Practice of Biblical Theology,* edited by John Reumann. Minneapolis, Fortress Press, 1991.

"Exegesis for Storytellers and Other Strangers," in *Journal of Biblical Literature,* March 1995.

*

Critical Studies: "Women and the Bible" by Cullen Murphy, *Atlantic Monthly,* August 1993.

* * *

In the work of theologian Phyllis Trible storytelling holds central importance. Central to her scholarship is how biblical stories inform us about our pasts, the status of women's lives and, more powerfully, how at times the misappropriation of such stories has justified women's lesser status in society. Trible's written work, informed by feminism, examines Hebrew stories from biblical sources. With a uniquely innovative twist she reveals language's structural parameters and metaphor, as well as presenting interpretations that highlight, in particular, the lives of women. In her retelling of the story of Abraham and Sarah, for example, the servant Hagar is Trible's main preoccupation. Through her retelling—worked out via a complex examination of the story's structure—she represents the injustices Hagar suffers at the hands of Sarah and the god YHWH. This new interpretation of the character of Hagar is a primary example of Trible's work as she searches for hidden secrets that may exist on the margins of the central story; secrets that add, or even transform, the story's theological implications.

The passion with which Trible engages in her work stems from a experience in her first-year doctoral class at Union Theological Seminary in New York. Under the mentorship of Dr. James Muilenburg, she learned the use of rhetorical criticism in bringing biblical passages to dramatic life. Rhetorical criticism is a highly complex but instructive form of literary criticism. It moves beyond linguistic studies by reaching out into other disciplines that might add interpretative understanding to the times, places, culture, and certainly the language. The work that best profiles this method is Trible's *Rhetorical Criticism: Context, Method and the Book of Jonah.* The book is meant to function as a teaching tool, helping others to understand how rhetorical criticism functions in a history that dates back to ancient Greece. At that time, as Trible claims, rhetoric was part of a program of skillful discourse; through time it has grown into a more complex form of communication. Rhetorical criticism has lost none of the complexity that artful communication brings to it; as such, a fundamental component of Trible's work is discerning the intentionality of the storyteller.

Trible's work requires immersion in the meaning of words in their Hebrew contexts: how those words have been used in other contexts, when titles and proper names are interchanged, and how metaphors are used to recall other functions from earlier sources. At all times feminist theory calls attention to what women are doing in these stories: their position in the family, in society, and their relationship to the world in general. By focusing on specifics, as in the story of Hagar, the complexity of life and its meaning for women are highlighted.

Trible herself asserts that there are two primary features in her work meant to instruct theological interpretations. Her first intent is to demonstrate how language and its rhetorical features function to create meaning. This work necessarily entails examining the original Hebrew rather than relying on questionable translations. Indeed, it is through Trible's extensive knowledge of Hebrew, syntax, and culture that new and dramatic meaning is extracted from the text, meaning that has often been missed or hidden in the telling of stories through the centuries. Her retelling often sits as an uncomfortable antithesis to orthodox interpretations that have at times functioned to justify injustices.

A second intent in Trible's work—one that has sometimes been met with derision by biblical scholars—is her firm commitment to eliminate sexist language. In theology, the replacement of exclusive language with nongendered terms imposes new and vastly different conceptions on such fundamental tenets as the deity itself. As Trible admits, this commitment has not been undertaken without problems both in accomplishing the task and its reception.

Trible sees herself as not rooted to any particular interpretative structure, allowing her a flexibility in interpretation, unbound by the constraints placed on most theologians by institutional requirements of belief. Her disconnectedness, which belies the profound scholarship involved, yields her an openness to feminist theory and permits her to expose injustice and empowerment wherever she encounters them. She examines the structural components of the stories but includes, as well, her knowledge of the cultural traditions and pressures of the time. In *God and the Rhetoric of Sexuality* and *Texts of Terror: Literary-Feminist Readings of Biblical Narratives,* Trible uses biblical stories to uncover the complexity of women's lives in all their dimensions.

Trible, through her reworking of stories, demonstrates to what extent translations have created meanings contrary to what the original may have intended. As an example, in her work on the creation stories of Eve and Adam she finds little evidence to support the contention that men have been given special attributes that allow them greater authority. When examined in detail (noting there are actually two creation stories) Trible finds, in fact, that the stories can be read in such a fashion as to prove that Eve and Adam are equal creatures in both their conception and their downfall. The first creation story—often passed over or ignored entirely—established the birth of humanity rather than a hierarchy of genders. In this case the Hebrew *adham* means humanity, not a specific gender. The version of rather dubious fame is the story that constructs Eve's birth from Adam's rib and their eating of the forbidden fruit. Trible artfully illustrates that Eve's creation from Adam's rib is based on utility rather than Eve's lesser status, and that when compared to Adam's creation from dust neither birth can claim to be more esteemed.

Trible allows for an openendedness in her work, so that new interpretative insights might be added as scholarship increases. She acknowledges this flexibility as a condition of dealing with stories stemming from ancient times and inundated with dense theological meaning that alters, as individuals and groups come to new understandings.

—Helen-May Eaton

TRINH T. MIN-HA

Nationality: Vietnamese; immigrated to United States in 1970. **Born:** Vietnam, 1952. **Education:** Attended schools in Vietnam, the Philippines, France, and the United States. **Career:** Currently Chancellor's Distinguished Professor of Women's Studies, University of California, Berkeley, and associate professor of cinema, San Francisco State University. Guest editor, *Discourse: Journal for Theoretical Studies in Media and Culture;* contributor of articles to periodicals, including *Aperture, City Lights Review,* and *Motion Picture.* **Address:** Department of Women's Studies, University of California, Berkeley, Berkeley, California 94720-0001, U.S.A.

Publications

Political/Social Theory

Women, Native, Other: Writing Postcoloniality and Feminism. N.p., 1989.

When the Moon Waxes Red: Representation, Gender, and Cultural Politics. London, Routledge, 1991.

Framer Framed: Film Scripts and Interviews. New York and London, Routledge, 1992.

Poetry

En miniscules. N.p., 1987.

Plays

Screenplays: *Reassemblage,* 1982; *Naked Spaces—Living Is Round,* 1985; *Surname Viet Given Name Nam,* 1989; *Shoot for the Contents,* 1991.

Other

Un Art sans oeuvre. N.p., 1981.

African Spaces: Designs for Living in Upper Volta, with Jean-Paul Bourdier. N.p., 1985.

Editor, with Russell Ferguson, Martha Gever, and Cornel West, *Out There: Marginalization in Contemporary Culture.* N.p., 1990.

*

Critical Studies: Interview with Harriet A. Hirshorn, in *Heresies,* 6(2), 1987; "Deconstruction's other: Trinh T. Min-ha and Jacques Derrida" by Herman Rapaport, in *Diacritics,* 25, summer 1995.

* * *

Trinh T. Minh-ha was born in Vietnam, and immigrated to the United States in 1970 at the age of 17. She was educated in Vietnam, the Philippines, France, and the United States. A well-known scholar, theorist, writer, poet, artist, composer, and filmmaker, Trinh has had a long commitment to post-colonial and feminist writing and ideas. Her work is often experimental, postmodern, and even poetic. In many of her writings and films she pushes and challenges disciplinary boundaries and theoretical paradigms. In fact, she suggests a re-thinking of feminism itself, as well as a critical stance in relation to the feminist movement for women of color and Third World women. For example, in an interview with Pratibha Parmar (published in *Framer Framed*) she says: "[While]

I readily acknowledge my debt to the movement in all the reflections advanced on the oppression of women of color ... I also feel that a critical space of differentiation needs to be maintained since issues specifically raised by Third World women have less to do with questions of cultural difference than with a different notion of feminism itself—how it is lived and how it is practiced."

Trinh is currently Chancellor's Distinguished Professor in Women's Studies at the University of California, Berkeley, as well as associate professor of cinema at San Francisco State University. She is the author of several books, including *Woman, Native, Other: Writing Postcoloniality and Feminism* (1989) and *When the Moon Waxes Red: Representation, Gender, and Cultural Politics* (1991), as well as the 1990 anthology *Out There: Marginalization in Contemporary Culture,* which she edited with Russell Ferguson, Martha Gever, and Cornel West. In addition, she has edited special issues of *Discourse: Journal for Theoretical Studies in Media and Culture,* including *(Un)Naming Cultures* (11.2), and *She, the Inappropriate/d Other* (8). Her articles have appeared in anthologies including *Dia-Art Discussions* and *Making Face, Making Soul/ Haciendo Caras: Creative and Critical Perspectives by Women of Color,* and Her poetry has appeared in *Poesie 1; Aperture;* and *City Lights Review.* A creative writer and filmmaker as well, Trinh has written numerous poems; her films include *Reassemblage* (Senegal, 1982); *Naked Spaces—Living Is Round* (West Africa, 1985); *Surname Viet, Given Name Nam* (1989); and *Shoot for the Contents* (1991). Her *Framer Framed: Film Scripts and Interviews,* published in 1992, includes the scripts for three of her films.

Trinh's work is especially notable for its consistent questioning of existing contemporary categories, its critical view of both documentary form and the field of anthropology, and its ability to problematize the relationships between truth and fiction, theory and poetry. For example, her beautifully filmed and lyrical *Surname Viet, Given Name Nam* offers a layering and multiplicity of voices, identities, nations, and forms. In the film Trinh problematizes language, translation, speaking, and silence, as well as the notion of an "authentic" Vietnamese identity. By casting Vietnamese American women (who, incidentally, are not professional actors) to play the roles of Vietnamese women in what at first appears to be a documentary or an "authentic" filmic portrayal, Trinh disrupts stereotypes of Vietnamese and Vietnamese American women, as well as viewers' expectations of these women, Vietnam, war, and representation. A critical shift occurs halfway through the film, when we, the viewers, discover the "truth" about the identities of these women. They are playing roles—they are *acting.* Suddenly, any possibility of "true" identities is shattered, and we can only question our own assumptions and ideologies.

Similarly, in her text *Woman, Native, Other: Writing Postcoloniality and Feminism,* Trinh questions the notion of authenticity. She problematizes any idea of a true self, suggesting instead that the "I" of identity consists of infinite layers and represents categories that always "leak." Meanwhile the *real* is nothing more than a "code of representation." It is never "really real." Thus, Trinh not only suggests a re-thinking of authentic selves, she creates a space for multiple selves, for hybrid and hyphenated identities and realities, and, more specifically, for the Third World woman writer. For writing, she tells us, is essential, and stories must be told. Whether or not these stories could be classified as "truth" is perhaps not always the most relevant question. In fact, as Trinh says, "[truth] exceeds measure."

In an interview with Judith Mayne (also in *Framer Framed*), Trinh says, "I am always working at the borderlines of several shifting categories, stretching out to the limits of things, learning about my own limits and how to modify them." Indeed, Trinh's films and texts demonstrate the viability of this kind of "border work." Her work is not simply located at the intersections of many disciplines (e.g., women's studies, literary criticism, anthropology, etc.). Rather, by re-figuring how we conceptualize such fields of study, she undoes the notion of disciplinary boundaries altogether. Trinh brilliantly demonstrates how we, too, may undo such boundaries and regimes, in order to decenter certain paradigms of domination. Trinh suggests not only new ways to think, but also new ways to live.

—Patti Duncan

TRISTAN, Flora

Nationality: French. **Born:** Paris, 7 April 1803. **Education: Family:** Married the painter André Chazal in 1821 (separated 1824); two sons and one daughter. **Career:** Worked as a governess and traveling companion in England, 1826-30; traveled to Peru to attempt to claim inheritance, 1833; moved to Paris, 1834; introduced to socialists, including reformer Robert Owen, 1837; wounded during murder attempt by estranged husband, 1838; traveled extensively in England; attempted to organize French workers into prototypical labor union, c. 1840. **Died:** Bordeaux, France, 14 November 1844.

Publications

Novel

Méphis, ou le Prolétaire. Paris, Ladvocat, 2 vols., 1838.

Political/Social Theory

L'Union Ouvrière. Paris, Prevot, 1843; as *The Worker's Union,* Urbana and London, University of Illinois Press, 1983.

L'Emancipation de la femme ou le testament de la Paria. Paris, Guarin, 1846.

Flora Tristan: vie, oeuvres mêlées, annotated by Dominique Desanti. Paris, Union generale, 1973.

Autobiography

Pérégrinations d'une paria. Paris, A. Bertrand, 2 vols., 1838; as *Peregrinations of a Pariah, 1833-34,* London, Virago, 1986.

Promenades dans Londres. Paris, H-L Delloye, 1840; as *Promenades dans Londres; ou, L'aristocracie et les proletaires angalis,* Paris, R. Bocquet, 1842; translated as *London Walks,* London, W. Jeffs, 1842; as *Flora Tristan's London Journal,* Boston, Charles River, and London, Prior, 1980.

Other

Nécessité de faire un bon accueil aux femmes étrangèrs (On the Need to Provide Good Hospitality to Foreign Women). Paris, Delaunay, 1835.

Lettres: Flora Tristan, edited by Stéphane Michaud. Paris, Seuil, 1980.

Flora Tristan, Utopian Feminist: Her Travel Diaries and Personal Crusade, edited and translated by Doris and Paul Beik, Bloomington, Indiana University Press, 1993.

*

Critical Studies: *Seven Women against the World* by Margaret Goldsmith, London, Methuen, 1935; *Gaughin's Astonishing Grandmother; The Biography of Flora Tristan* by C. N. Gattey, London, Femina, 1970; *A Woman in Revolt: A Biography of Flora Tristan* by Dominique Desanti, translated by Elizabeth Zelvin, New York, Crown, 1976; *Flora Tristan: Feminism in the Age of George Sand* by Sandra Dijkstra, London, Pluto Press, 1984; *The Odyssey of Flora Tristan* by Laura S. Strumingher, New York, P. Lang, 1988; *The Feminism of Flora Tristan* by Máire Cross and Tim Gray, Oxford and Providence, Rhode Island, Berg, 1992.

* * *

Forgotten for many years amid such contemporary feminist heroines as the writer George Sand, Flora Tristan's fame was more often reflected in the notoriety of her artist grandson, Paul Gauguin. Born to a French women and a Peruvian Spanish colonel, Flora might have grown up amid wealth, had her father not died and left his family impoverished. Unable to obtain a formal education, Tristan instead spent her life in a state of energetic restlessness, ambitious to improve her lot in life through her own efforts, yet faced with hardships due to both her lack of learning and the fact of her gender.

Living in France with her mother, Tristan married her employer, Andre Chazal, in 1821, but left him three years later, leaving her three children in the hands of her mother. Without a husband she had no social status and without an occupation life was difficult. Evading Chazal, who would stalk her for 15 years, abduct their children, and at one point even attempt to shoot her, Tristan changed her name and even left France for several years in order to evade him. Chazal's pursuit heightened as his wife's increasing success in supporting herself through her writing made her more independent. His attempt to murder her resulted in his being sentenced to prison for 20 years, leaving Tristan greater peace of mind but with the difficulty of escaping the scandalous incident.

In 1833 Tristan went to Peru, hoping to secure monetary aid from relatives of her father; she received a meager allowance and a healthy dose of disapprobation for being a woman traveling alone. This led to Tristan's first published pamphlet, 1835's *L'Emancipation de la femme ou le testament de la Paria* (On the Need to Provide Good Hospitality for Foreign Women), which lobbied for the creation of an international organization to help single women alone in foreign countries. In other pamphlets she addressed the concern that French women be allowed to obtain a divorce, a right that had been denied since 1818. In 1837 Tristan would petition the government to have the right to divorce reinstated.

Her feminist instincts rising, Tristan took on the cause of the French women of the lower classes, who worked 18 hours a day for low wages. Anticipating Karl Marx's communist ideology, she published *L'Union Ouvrière (The Worker's Union)* in 1843, ignoring common reform theories that called for societal changes and urging the French working class to unite and form an economic organization capable of empowering each worker to help improve his or her own future.

Tristan's vision of women's rights continued to broaden to include equal rights as men, including suffrage, economic rights, and a singular standard for morals. In 1838 she achieved literary success with both the publication of her autobiographical work *Pérégrinations d'une paria (Peregrinations of a Pariah)* and a novel entitled *Méphis, ou le Prolétaire,* a tale of two lovers that held an underlying social message on acceptance of women in a competitive society. Her popular *Promenades dans Londres (London Walks),* published in 1840, offered the reader a social critique of English working conditions, which she had investigated by traveling to industrial districts, asking questions and gathering statistics. Called an "apostle in petticoats" Tristan included prostitution, insanity and prison conditions in her studies.

Flora Tristan's knowledge of the world around her and her perception of the consequences of industrialization and revolution put her ahead of her time. A woman familiar with the currents of Utopianism, Socialism, and unionism, she focused her extraordinary energies to her desire "to free womankind from man's slavery, the poor from the slavery of the rich, and the soul from the slavery of sin." Had that life not been cut short in 1844, perhaps the restless Tristan might have accomplished what she so wished for; justice and social equality for all women.

—Marilyn Elizabeth Perry

TRUTH, Sojourner

Nationality: American. **Born:** Isabella, into slavery, in Hurley, Ulster County, New York, 1797; changed name to Sojourner Truth, 1843. **Family:** Bore 13 children. **Career:** Ran away from owner in New Paltz, New York, 1827; emancipated by state decree, 1828; gained custody of a child illegally sold into slavery in Alabama, 1828; moved to New York and worked as a domestic servant, c. 1829; joined abolitionist Northampton Association, Northampton, Massachusetts; gave speech "Ain't *I* a Woman?" in Akron, Ohio, 1851; aided slave refuges, beginning 1865; petitioned Congress to designate federal Western lands for former slaves. Speaker on abolition, women's rights, and religion. **Died:** Battle Creek, Michigan, 26 November 1883.

Publications

Essays

"Ain't *I* a Woman?" (speech), edited by Frances Dana Gage. [Akron, Ohio], n.p., c. 1852; reprinted in *History of Woman Suffrage,* Vol. 1, by Elizabeth Cady Stanton, Matilda Joslyn Gage, and Susan B. Anthony, New York, Fowler & Welles, 1881.

Autobiography

The Narrative of Sojourner Truth, transcribed by Olive Gilbert. Boston, *Liberator,* 1850; enlarged by Frances Titus, n.p., 1875-87.

*

Critical Studies: Sojourner Truth, the Libyan Sibyl" by Harriet Beecher Stowe, in *Atlantic Monthly,* 1863; *Journey toward Freedom: The Story of Sojourner Truth* by Jacqueline Bernard, 1967, second edition, New York, Feminist Press, 1990; *Sojourner Truth: God's Faithful Pilgrim* by Arthur Fauset, New York, Russell, 1971; "Sojourner Truth in Life and Memory: Writing the Biography of an American Exotic" by Nell Irvin Painter, in *Gender and History,* 2(1), spring 1990; "Sojourner Truth in Feminist Abolitionism: Difference, Slavery, and Memory" by Nell Irvin Painter, in *An Untrodden Path: Antislavery and Women's Political Culture,* edited by Jean Fagan Yellin and John C. Van Horne, 1993.

* * *

Born into slavery in Ulster County, New York, the young woman known to her fellow slaves only by the name of Isabella would one day be known to the world as Sojourner Truth. A courageous woman, Truth not only spoke out against the racial oppression that she had endured throughout her childhood but acted on her beliefs, inspiring men and women of all races with her personal strength, wisdom, and social activism.

Truth's early years would be documented for posterity in *The Narrative of Sojourner Truth,* which she published in 1850 and which became popular abolitionist reading after Harriet Beecher Stowe publicized it in an article for *Atlantic Monthly.* Unable to read or write herself, Truth had dictated her memories of slavery to a neighbor, Olive Gilbert, and then printed and sold copies in order to earn money to support herself. The property of one Charles Hardenbergh, Truth had been sold to a series of masters before being acquired by the family of John Dumont of New Paltz when she was 13. For the next seventeen years she would remain in their service, giving birth to several children who were most often taken from her and then sold upon reaching a suitable age.

In 1827 Truth fled Dumont's farm and became a runaway. Protected on her journey by Northern abolitionists, she eventually arrived in New York City two years later; meanwhile, the state of New York had decreed the emancipation of slaves, enabling Truth to cease hiding and openly sue her former owner for illegally selling her son Paul into slavery in Alabama several years earlier. Now in New York, she worked as a servant, while also becoming heavily involved in a succession of religious movements. In 1843, inspired by preacher William Miller's prediction of the imminent second coming of Christ, she renamed herself Sojourner Truth.

A charismatic speaker, Truth became an itinerant preacher, travelling around New England spreading the gospel of Jesus, abolition, and, eventually, women's rights. By 1851 she was active in the suffrage movement and a featured speaker that May at a woman suffrage convention in Akron, Ohio. A local clergyman began heckling the speakers—which included notable suffragists Elizabeth Cady Stanton, Susan B. Anthony, and Lucy Stone—as unworthy of the vote because they were merely "the weaker sex." Truth angrily stepped to the podium and made what has become her most famous pronouncement on behalf of women's rights:

> That man over there says that women need to be helped into carriages, and lifted over ditches, and to have the best place everywhere. Nobody ever helps me into carriages, or over mud-puddles, or gives me any best place! And ain't I a woman? Look at me! I have ploughed and planted, and gathered into barns, and no man could head me! Ain't I a woman?.... I have borne 13 children, and seen almost all of them sold off into slavery, and when I cried out with my mother's grief, no one but Jesus heard me. And ain't I a woman?

After the Emancipation Proclamation was signed into law in 1863, Truth continued to support her people, aiding refugee slaves in the greater Washington, D.C. area. Acting on her theory that there should be land made available to former slaves in the unclaimed areas in the West, she circulated a petition to Congress, but it was never acted upon. Retiring to Battle Creek, Michigan, in the mid-1850s, Truth died on 26 November 1883.

—Lynn MacGregor

TSUSHIMA Yūko

Pseudonym for Tsushima Satoko. **Nationality:** Japanese. **Born:** Tokyo, 30 March 1947. **Education:** Shirayuri Women's University, B.A. in English, 1969; Meiji University Graduate School, 1969-71. **Family:** Married in 1970 (divorced, 1976); one daughter, one son. **Career:** Writer. Lecturer in Japanese literature, Institute of Occidental Languages, University of Paris, 1991-92. Contributor of short stories and essays to periodicals, including *Mita Bungaku, Bungei, Gunzo, Umi,* and *Bungakukai.* **Awards:** Kawabata Yasunari Prize, 1974, for *Danmari Ichi;* Tamura Toshiko Prize, 1975, for *Mugura no Haha;* Izumi Kyoka Prize, 1977, for *Kusa no Fushido;* Women's Literature Prize, 1978, for *Choji;* Noma Bungei New Writer Prize, 1979, for *Hikari no Ryobun;* Yomiuri Prize, 1986, for *Yoru no Hikari ni Owarete;* Hirabahashi Taiko Prize, 1989, for *Mhiru e;* Ito Sei Prize, 1995, for *Kaze yo, Sora Kakeru Kaze yo.* **Member:** Nihon Bungei Kyokai (Japanese literary association). **Agent:** Tatemi Sakai, Orion Press, 1-58, Kanda-Jimboco, Chiyoda-ku, Tokyo, Japan. **Address:** 6-15-16-602, Honkomagome, Bunkyo-ku, Tokyo, Japan, 113.

Publications

Novels

Doji no Kage [The Shadow of a Child]. Tokyo, Kawaide Shobo, 1973.

Ikimono no Atsumaru Ie [House Appointed to All Living]. Tokyo, Shinchosha, 1973.

Choji [Child of Fortune]. Tokyo, Kawaide Shobo, 1978; translated, New York, Kodansha International, 1983.

Hikari no Ryobun [Realm of Light]. Tokyo, Kodansha, 1979

Moeru Kaze [Burning Wind]. Tokyo, Chuokoronsha, 1980.

Yama o Hashiru Onna [Woman Running in the Mountains]. Tokyo, Kodansha, 1980.

Hi no Kawa no Hotori de [By the River of Fire]. Tokyo, Kodansha, 1983.

Yoru no Hikari ni Owarete [The Light of Night Runs after Me]. Tokyo, Kodansha, 1986.

Mahiru e [To High Noon]. Tokyo, Shinchosha, 1988.

Kaze yo, Sora Kakeru Kaze yo [Wind, Wind That Runs through the Sky]. Tokyo, n.p., 1995.

Short Stories

"Rekuiemu—Inu to Otona no Tame ni" [Requiem—For Dog and Adult], in *Mita Bungaku,* 1969.
Shanikusai [Carnival]. Tokyo, Kawaide Shobo, 1971.
Danmari Ichi [Silent Traders]. Tokyo, Kodansha, 1974.
Waga Chichitachi [My Fathers]. Tokyo, Kodansha, 1975.
Mugura no Haha. Tokyo, Kawaide Shobo, 1975; title story translated as "The Mother in the House of Grass," in *Literary Review,* 30, winter 1987.
Kusa no Fushido. Tokyo, Kodansha, 1977; title story translated as "A Bed of Grass," in *This Kind of Woman: 10 Stories by Japanese Women, 1960-1976,* edited by Yukiko Tanaka and Elizabeth Hanson, Stanford, Stanford University Press, 1982.
Yorokobi no Shima [Island of Joy]. Tokyo, Chuokoronsha, 1978.
Saigo no Shuryo [The Last Hunting]. Tokyo, Sakuhinsha, 1979.
Hyogen [Ice Fields]. Tokyo, Sakuhinsha, 1979.
Suifu [Water City]. Tokyo, Kawaide Shobo, 1982.
Oma Monogatari [Phantom Stories]. Tokyo, Kodansha, 1984.
Yume no Kiroku [Records of Dreams]. Tokyo, Bungeishunju, 1988.
The Shooting Gallery. London, Women's Press, 1986; New York, Pantheon, 1988.
"The Marsh," in *Unmapped Territories: New Women's Fiction from Japan,* edited by Yukiko Tanaka. N.p., Women in Translation, 1991.
Oi naru Yume yo, Hikari yo [My Great Dream, My Light]. Tokyo, n.p., n.d.

Essays

Yoru no Tii Paati [The Evening Tea Party]. Kyoto, Jinbunshoin, 1979.
Tomei Kukan ga Mieru Toki [When One Can See the Transparent Space]. Tokyo, Seidosha, 1977.
Nani ga Seikaku o Tsukuruka [What Makes Personality]. Tokyo, Asahi Shuppan, 1979.
Yoru to Asa no Tegami [Letters from Night and Morning]. Tokyo, Kairyusha, 1980.
Watashi no Jikan [My Time]. Kyoto, Jinbunshoin, 1982.
Shosetsu no Naka no Fukei [Landscape in the Novel]. Tokyo, Chuokoronsha, 1982.
Osanaki Hibi e [To the Childhood Day]. Tokyo, Kodansha, 1986.
Hon no Naka no Shojotachi [Girls in Books]. Tokyo, Chuokoronsha, 1989.
"The Possibility of Imagination in These Islands," in *boundary 2,* 21, 1994.

*

Critical Studies: Essay by Van C. Gessel in *Japan Quarterly,* 35(4), 1988; essay by Rebecca L. Copeland, in *Japan Quarterly,* 39(1), 1992.

* * *

Tsushima Yūko is one of the most important women writers of contemporary Japan whose fiction challenges established social customs, especially regarding women's sexuality and family relationships, and proposes alternatives to stifling conventions. As do other highly praised contemporary women writers such as Kono Taeko and Oba Minako, Tsushima explores sociocultural taboos like incest and violent expressions of human sexuality. Tsushima's insightful descriptions of everyday details, combined with her tactful allusions to mythological landscape and use of dreams, brings home the "reality" of her characters' lives, sensations, and emotions.

Born in post-World War II Tokyo as second daughter to renowned writer Dazai Osamu, Tsushima grew up with virtually no memory of her father, who committed double suicide with his lover when Tsushima was only one year old. She attended a Catholic girls' school for her middle and high school and university education, earning a bachelor's degree in English. In 1969 Tsushima enrolled in graduate school at Meiji University, but her attendance was sporadic and she never finished her studies, partly due to the student strikes that overtook many Japanese university campuses at that time.

While in college Tsushima kept herself busy with numerous extracurricular activities, which all represented her search for a means of self-discovery and self-expression: she initiated student-designed seminars, founded a folk song group that mainly sang protest songs, and traveled frequently. An ideal venue seems to have been finally provided by writing, as she started a hand-printed journal for creative writing and simultaneously joined another, more established group of aspiring young writers in 1966. During this formative period, she was an avid reader of both Japanese and western writers, including Tanizaki Junichiro, Okamoto Kanoko, Izumi Kyoka, Feodor Mikhailovich Dostoyevsky, James Joyce, Virginia Woolf, William Faulkner, and Edgar Allan Poe. Tsushima began her career as professional writer relatively early with her fiction, "Requiem—For Dog and Adult," published in *Mita Bungaku* to critical acclaim in 1969.

The haunting spiritual and literary presence of her untimely deceased novelist father, along with her experience of growing up with a brother who had been born with Down Syndrome, has been a major source of inspiration for Tsushima's fiction. She started reading her father's works at a precociously young age, in an effort to understand her absentee parent, and much of her writing recreated father-daughter relationships that never existed in real life. For example, in the short story "Water City" the father, who like Tsushima's own has drowned himself, is living in an underwater world, which allows the daughter to have an ongoing relationship with the deceased parent. In contrast to such surrealistic existence that her fiction often assigns to father fixtures, Tsushima's memory of her older brother is that of a person of substantial presence who could not count or walk normally but who could genuinely love others without taint of envy or resentment, a person who embodied the joy of living and "wisdom of love." He reappears as the mentally and physically handicapped brother of the protagonist Koko in *Child of Fortune.* Koko's memory of this dead brother, who loved her deeply and protected her fiercely whenever he sensed danger, continues to support her in her unorthodox choice of lifestyle that includes affairs with married or otherwise non-committal men while raising a daughter from a previous marriage. In contrast, her conservative sister relentlessly criticizes Koko's "immoral" behavior, a rejection by a family member that symbolizes the protagonist's ostracized position in Japanese society at large. Tsushima's novel purposefully contrasts the late brother's unconditional acceptance of Koko with her sister's overt disapproval.

True to the tradition of the "private" or autobiographical novel (*shi-shosetsu*) that has long been the central genre of Japanese literature (in which her father also excelled), Tsushima's fiction reflects the author's other life experiences, such as marriage and motherhood. A fatherless daughter, Tsushima herself became a single mother of two when she divorced her husband in the same year she gave birth to an illegitimate son. This experience of being an unmarried mother informs many of her short stories and novels. For instance, *Woman Running in the Mountains* (1980) and *The Light of Night Runs After Me* (1986) both feature an unwed mother, and *By the River of Fire* (1983) portrays the life of an illegitimate daughter.

What these works do, in focusing on the lives of socially marginalized women characters, is to dissect existing human/family relationships and to challenge conventional social expectations and moral beliefs. Tsushima openly defies the norm of monogamous marriage with her portrayal of women who raise children without the help of the biological fathers. Pregnancy, child bearing, and child rearing, for Tsushima, is a fundamentally natural process that ensures continuation of the species and does not need to be sustained by social customs and mundane moral codes. In this basic cycle of life and death, men are given neither social nor familial roles to play, much like the situation of most animals, domestic or wild. Tsushima's use of animal imagery, of dogs and cats, for example, is a fictional device to highlight the radical meaning of motherhood that is untrammelled by social conventions. In several of the stories collected in *Phantom Stories,* boundaries between humans and animals are blurred, and in an extreme case ("Princess Fuse"), the protagonist dreams that she has given birth to six children at once, some human and others puppies (as happens in the mystical legend after which the story is titled), and is nursing all of them on her six nipples. Women and women's bodies, in Tsushima's fiction, are viewed as a source of all life, and the sense of the body, of such immediate physicality as exemplified by pregnancy and childbirth, dominates much of her prose.

In creating women characters who are forced to, or choose to, embrace marginalized existence, Tsushima successfully points out the deficiencies of rigid social strictures that cripple people's ability to connect to each other and to live true to themselves. At the same time she draws attention to women's energy and powers that are deeply rooted in their sexual and physical existence, while never neglecting the sense of desolation and loneliness that inevitably accompanies the life of a woman who elects to lead a life of her own.

—Tomoko Kuribayashi

TURNER, Sheila. *See* **ROWBOTHAM, Sheila.**

TYNAN, Katharine

Nationality: British. **Born:** Clondalkin, County Dublin, 23 January 1861. **Education:** Attended Catholic convent school, Drogheda, Ireland. **Family:** Married H.A. Hinkson in 1893 (died 1919); children. **Career:** Lived in England, 1894-1911; travelled Europe as a journalist, beginning 1919; contributor to periodicals. **Died:** 2 April 1931.

Publications

Novels

The Way of a Maid. London, Lawrence & Bullen, 1895.
Oh! What a Plague is Love. London, Black, 1896.
She Walks in Beauty. London, Smith Elder, 1899.
Lord Edward: A Study in Romance. London, Smith Elder, 1916.
Love of Brothers. London, Constable, 1919.
Denys the Dreamer. New York, Benzinger, 1920.
The House in the Forest. London, Ward Lock, 1928.
A Fine Gentleman. London, Ward Lock, 1929.
The Admirable Simmons. London, Ward Lock, 1930.

Short Stories

An Isle of Water. London, A. & C. Black, 1895.

Poetry

Louise de la Vallière and Other Poems. London, Kegan Paul, 1885.
Shamrocks. London, Kegan Paul, 1887.
Ballads and Lyrics. London, Kegan Paul, 1890.
Cuckoo Songs. London, Mathews & Lane, 1894.
Lover's Breast Knot. London, Mathews & Lane, 1896.
Poems. London, Lawrence & Bullen, 1901.
Innocencies: A Book of Verse. London, Bullen, 1905.
Irish Poems. New York, Benziger, 1914.
The Holy War. London, Sidgwick & Jackson, 1916.
Herb O'Grace: Poems in War-Time. London, Sidgwick & Jackson, 1918.
Collected Poems. London, Macmillan, 1930.
The Poems of Katharine Tynan. Dublin, Allen Figgis, 1963.

Play

Miracle Plays: Our Lord's Coming and Childhood. London, J. Lane, 1895.

Autobiography

Twenty-Five Years: Reminiscences. London, Smith Elder, 1913.
The Years of the Shadow. Boston, Houghton Mifflin, 1919.
Memories. London, Nash & Grayson, 1924.

Other

A Nun, Her Friends, and the Order (biography). London, Kegan Paul, 1891.
The Wind in the Trees. London, Richards, 1898.

*

Critical Studies: *Ireland's Literary Renaissance* by Ernest Boyd, New York, Knopf, 1922; "Katherine [sic] Tynan and Her Stories" in *Some Catholic Novelists: Their Art and Outlook* by Patrick Braybrooke, Freeport, New York, Books for Libraries, 1966; *Let-*

ters to Katharine Tynan by W.B. Yeats, Clonmore & Reynolds, 1953; *Katharine Tynan* by Marilyn Gaddis Rose, Cranbury, New Jersey, Bucknell University Press, 1974; *Katharine Tynan* by Anne Connerton Fallon, Boston, Twayne, 1979; "The Little Red Fox, Emblem of the Irish Peasant in Poems by Yeats, Tynan, and Ní Dhomhnaill" by Linda L. Revie, in *Learning the Trade: Essays on W.B. Yeats and Contemporary Poetry,* West Cornwall, Connecticut, Locust Hill, 1993; "Katharine Tynan" by Katherine Sutherland, in *Dictionary of Literary Biography,* Volume 153: *Late-Victorian and Edwardian British Novelists,* Detroit, Gale, 1995.

* * *

The Irish poet, AE (George Russell), once said of Katharine Tynan that she was "the earliest singer in that awakening of our imagination which has been spoken of as the Irish Renaissance." Cast as an engendering force in this important literary movement, Tynan fulfills a role she believed was crucial to her existence, that of mother. She wrote sensational fiction in order to support her family, and she wrote poetry that expressed her belief that it was as a daughter, a wife, and a mother that she truly understood her womanhood. Her feminism is often revealed more in her actions that in her writing; yet these actions were frequently atypical and even rebellious by the standards of the Catholic and Victorian society into which she was born and in which she lived for her first 40 years.

Tynan was born in Dublin into a comfortably situated albeit not wealthy family. She loved Whitehall, the family home in Clandalkin, not only for its pastoral surroundings, but for the study her father established there for her use. Tynan often writes fondly of this room in her autobiographical works; here she was able to write, read, and entertain guests such as W.B. Yeats, AE, and Douglas Hyde, who would later become first president of the newly established Irish Rebublic. Katherine Sutherland remarks that this room "clearly came to symbolize an intellectual haven for Tynan, presaging by more than forty years Virginia Woolf's notorious comment that 'a woman must have money and a room of her own'" in order to be able to write. Both because of and in spite of her lack of formal education, Tynan was, as she wrote, "starved for poetry," and eagerly read the works of Swinburne, Morris, and Christina and D.G. Rossetti, works assuredly unconventional for a young Irish Catholic woman. Tynan published poetry in Irish and English periodicals while in her early 20s. Her first book, *Louise de la Vallière,* a collection of this poetry, appeared in 1885 and was an immediate critical and commercial success in both Ireland and England.

Although the majority of the poems in this volume arise from the beloved Catholicism to which she would return in her later verse again and again, three poems concern Irish nationalist themes, thereby establishing her, along with Yeats, as a forerunner of the Irish Literary Revival. Known also as the Celtic Revival, the Celtic Renaissance, and the Irish Renaissance, the proponents of this movement, defined by its first historian, Ernest Boyd, as the rise of "a literature whose patriotism had its roots in the rich soil of the Gaelic tradition, and was only incidentally concerned with the political passions of nationalism," felt called upon to preserve Irish traditions of folk culture and song after English replaced Gaelic as the national language of Ireland. Despite co-founder Yeats's later eclipse of Tynan's literary reputation, her impressive debut in *Louise de la Vallière* brought significant attention to a movement that would later influence Irish writers such as Lady Gregory, Dora Sigerson, James Joyce, and J.M. Synge. In addition, Tynan, along with Yeats and Hyde, contributed poetry to *The Poems and Ballads of Young Ireland,* which, as Boyd notes, "in 1888 announced the co-operative, concerted nature of the effort of the younger generation to give a new impulse to Irish poetry." "The Children of Lir," from the collection *Shamrocks* and one of Tynan's best known poems reappeared in this first collective effort of the Irish Literary Revivalists; she continued to explore Celtic folk tales in *Ballads and Lyrics,* which Yeats considered her best volume of poetry. Tynan rarely spoke of her gender nor wrote of feminism in the early years of her career; her simple expectation that she could and would be instrumental in an important literary movement, that she would be asked to and could both edit and write elegant introductions for the massive collections, *The Cabinet of Irish Literature* and *The Wild Harp: A Selection from Irish Lyrical Poetry* bespeak her subconscious awareness that a woman, even a sheltered, uneducated woman, was capable of contributing meaningful and distinguished poetry and prose to an appreciative audience.

While after 1893 Tynan took great delight in her new roles as wife and especially mother, neither did she lay aside her continual striving in her literary career. While writing more frequently in her poetry on nature and religious faith, she also increasingly addressed specifically feminine, if not feminist, issues such as the importance of providing domestic harmony in poems such as "Any Woman" and "Any Wife," and in poems such as "The Senses," "The Sick Child," and "The Mother's Hour," of the challenges and joys of unconditional mother love. She continued to contribute widely to the British periodicals of the day, as well as published her first novel, *The Way of a Maid,* shortly after her marriage. This romantic novel laid a foundation for her later Gothic fiction and what she referred to in her autobiography, *The Middle Years,* as "novels for boiling the pot." She notes, however, that the writing of sensational fiction "might even be called a Holy War, the struggle to keep the fire on the hearth for the children and the securities and sanctities of home about them." Tynan took great pride in her ability to sustain her family through her writing; her husband, Henry Hinkson, seems to have been an ineffective provider. Furthermore, Tynan continued to deepen her unwavering awareness of society's special challenges to women as the new century brought a World War that robbed them of their sons and difficult working conditions that robbed them of their health. Marilyn Gaddis Rose points out that at the end of her life, Tynan wrote moving editorials in the *Irish Statesman* of the plight of Irish schoolchildren and unwed mothers, views in which "she moves far beyond the accepted moral confines of her class." Despite her conventional Irish Catholic upbringing and fulfillment of social expectations of wifehood and motherhood, Tynan continued to assert her right to speak up for those who had no voice—women and children.

Suthlerland suggests that Tynan is "perhaps best described as a woman of her time, and in this context she may be seen as a more socially and politically radical figure than she would be by today's standards." Indeed, Katharine Tynan was a woman who wrote both within and outside of her cultural boundaries, perhaps best illustrating her feminism through an unstated and uncomplicated belief in her entitlement to choose a life and career of her own determination.

—Siobhan Craft Brownson

U-V

UNDSET, Sigrid

Nationality: Norwegian. **Born:** Kalundborg, Denmark, 20 May 1882. **Education:** Christiania Commercial College, secretarial certificate, c. 1898. **Family:** Married the artist Anders C. Svarstad in 1912 (marriage annulled 1924); two sons, one daughter. **Career:** Secretary, German Electric Company, Christiania (now Oslo), Norway, c. 1898-1908; full-time writer, beginning 1908; fled Norway and worked as a researcher for U.S. government during World War II. Translator of various Icelandic tales. Contributor to periodicals. **Awards:** Nobel Prize, 1928, for *Kristin Lavransdatter* and *Olav Audunssøn;* presented Grand Cross of the Order of Saint Olav by King Haakon VII, 1947. Honorary degrees: Rolins College, 1942; Smith College, 1943. **Died:** Lillehammer, Norway, 10 June 1949.

Publications

Novels

Fru Marta Oulie [Mrs. Marta Oulie]. Kristiania, Aschehoug, 1907.

Fortellingen om Viga-Ljot og Vigdis [and] *Sankt Halvards liv, dod og jaertgen.* Kristiania, Aschehoug, 1909; translation of the former as *Gunnar's Daughter,* New York, Knopf, 1936.

Jenny. Kristiania, Aschehoug, 1911; translated, New York, Knopf, 1921.

Vaaren [Spring]. Kristiania, Aschehoug, 1914.

Gymnadenia. Olso, Aschehoug, 1929; translated as *The Wild Orchid,* New York, Knopf, 1931.

Den brennende busk. Olso, Aschehoug, 1930; translated as *The Burning Bush,* New York, Knopf, 1932.

Ida Elisabeth. Olso, Aschehoug, 1932; translated, New York, Knopf, 1933.

Den trofaste hustru. Oslo, Aschehoug, 1936, translated as *The Faithful Wife,* New York, Knopf, 1937.

Kristin Lavransdatter. Oslo, Aschehoug 3 vols, 1920-22; Nobel Prize edition translated as *Kristin Lavransdatter,* New York, Knopf, 1929.

Kransen. Kristiania, Aschehoug, 1920; translated as *The Bridal Wreath,* New York, Knopf, 1923; translated as *The Garland,* London, Knopf, 1930.

Husfrue. Kristiania, Aschehoug, 1921; translated as *The Mistress of Husaby.* New York, Knopf, 1925.

Korset. Kristiania, Aschehoug, 1922; translated as *The Cross,* New York, Knopf, 1927.

The Master of Hestviken. Nobel Prize edition, New York, Knopf, 1934.

Olav Audunssøn i Hestviken. Oslo, Aschehoug, 2 vols., 1925; translated as *The Axe* [and] *The Snake Pit,* 2 vols., New York, Knopf, 1928-29.

Olav Audunssøn og hans börn. Oslo, Aschehoug, 2 vols., 1927; translated as *In the Wilderness* [and] *The Son Avenger,* New York, Knopf, 1929-30.

Madame Dorthea. Oslo, Aschehoug, 1939; translated, New York, Knopf, 1940.

Middelalder-romaner [Medieval Novels] (collection). Oslo, Aschehoug, 10 vols., 1949; as *Middelalder-verker,* 8 vols., 1982.

Romaner og fortaellinger fra nutiden (collection). Oslo, Aschehoug, 10 vols., 1964-65; as *Natidsverker,* 12 vols., 1983.

Short Stories

Den lykkelige alder [The Happy Age]. Kristiania, Aschehoug, 1908.

Fattige skjebner [Poor Fortunes]. Kristiania, Aschehoug, 1912; selections translated in *Four Stories,* 1959.

De kloge jomfruer [The Wise Virgins]. Kristiania, Aschehoug, 1918; selections translated in *Four Stories,* 1959.

Four Stories (contains "Thjodolf," "Selma Broter," "Simonsen," "Miss Smith-Tellefsen"), translated by Naomi Walford. New York, Knopf, 1959.

Play

In the Gray Light of Dawn. N.d.

For Children

Die saga von Vilmund Vidutan und seinen Gefaehrten. Hausen Verlagagesellschaft, 1931; translated as *Sigurd and His Brave Companions: A Tale of Medieval Norway,* illustrated by Gunvor Bull Teilman, New York, Knopf, 1943.

Essays

Et kvindesynspunkt. Kristiana, Aschehoug, 1919.

Etapper: Ny rakke. Oslo, Aschehoug, 1933; translated as *Stages on the Road,* New York, Knopf, 1934.

Norske helgener. Oslo, Aschehoug, 1937; translated as *Saga of Saints,* Longmans Green, 1934.

Selvportretter og landskapsbilleder. Oslo, Aschehoug, 1938; translated as *Men, Women, and Places,* New York, Knopf, 1939.

Kirke og klosterliv: Tre essays fro norsk middelalder. Olso, Cappelen, 1963.

Kritikk og tro: Tekster, edited by Liv Bliksrud. Stavanger, St. Olav, 1982.

Autobiography

Elleve aar. Olso, Aschehoug, 1934; translated as *The Longest Years,* New York, Knopf, 1935.

Return to the Future, translated by Henrietta C.K. Naeseth. New York, Knopf, 1942; as *Tilbake til fremtiden,* Oslo, Aschehoug, 1949.

Happy Times in Norway, New York, Knopf, 1942; as *Lykkelige dager.* Oslo, Aschehoug, 1947.

Other

Fortaellinger om Kong Artur og ridderne av det Runde bord (adapted from the stories of Thomas Mallory). Kristiania, Aschehoug, 1915.

Splinten av troldspeilet (contains Fra Hjeld and Fra Waage). Kristiania, Aschehoug, 1917; translation of *Fra Hjeld* as *Images in a Mirror,* New York, Knopf, 1938.

Caterina av Siena (biography). Olso, Aschehoug, 1951; translated as *Catherine of Siena,* New York, Sheed & Ward, 1954.

Artikler og taler fra krigstiden, edited by A. H. Winsnes. Olso, Aschehoug, 1952.

Djaere dea (letters), edited with foreword by Christianne Undset Svarstad. Oslo, Cappelen, 1979.

Sigrid Undset skriver hjem: En vandring gjennom enigrantarene i Amerika (letters), edited by Arne Skouen. Oslo, Aschehoug, 1982.

Editor, *True and Untrue, and Other Norse Tales* (based on original stories from Asbjoernsen and Moe's *Folkeeventyr*), illustrations by Frederick T. Chapman. New York, Knopf, 1945.

*

Bibliography: *Sigrid Undset bibliografi* by I. Packness, Bergen, n.p., 1963.

Manuscript Collections: Rutgers University, Rutgers, New Jersey (letters).

Critical Studies: *Sigrid Undset: A Nordic Moralist* by Victor Vinde, translated by Babette Hughes and Glenn Hughes, University of Washington Book Store, 1930; *The Twentieth Century Novel: Studies in Technique* by Joseph Warren Beach, New York, Appleton-Century-Crofts, 1932; *Three Ways of Modern Man* by Harry Slochower, International, 1937; *Six Scandinavian Novelists* by Alrick Gustafson, New Brunswick, New Jersey, Princeton University Press, 1940; *The Novel and Society: A Critical Study of the Modern Novel* by N. Elizabeth Monroe, Chapel Hill, University of North Carolina Press, 1941; *Sigrid Undset: A Study in Christian Realism* by A.H. Winsnes, translated by P.G. Foote, London, Sheed & Ward, 1953; *Ibsen and the Temper of Norwegian Literature* by James Walter McFarlane, Oxford, Oxford University Press, 1960; "Sigrid Undset's Letters to Hope Emily Allen" by Marlene Ciklamini, in *Journal of the Rutgers University Library,* 33, 1969; "An Appendix to the Sigrids Saga" by C.A. Brady, in *Thought,* 40, 1973; *Sigrid Undset* by Carl F. Bayerschmidt, New York, Twayne, 1970; "Sigrid Undset: Revaluations and Recollections" by A. Saether, in *Scandinavica,* 23, 1984; "Religion as Fulfillment in the Novels of Sigrid Undset" by J.C. Whitehouse, in *Renascence,* 38, 1985; *Sigrid Undset* by M. Brundale, New York, St. Martin's Press, 1988; *Kristin: A Reading* by Andrew Lytle, Columbia and London, University of Missouri Press, 1992; *Redefining Integrity: The Portrayal of Women in the Contemporary Novels of Sigrid Undset* by Elisabeth Solbakken, Frankfurt am Main, P. Lang, 1992; *Paradigms and Paradoxes in the Life and Letters of Sigrid Undset* by Sister Margaret Dunn, Lanham, Maryland, University Press of America, 1994.

* * *

Sigrid Undset's epic trilogy *Kristin Lavransdatter* and her own favorite work, *The Master of Hestviken,* assured the author an honored place in world literature, but she was also the author of three volumes of memoirs, several books of short stories and a book of Norse tales for children as well as a play. One of Norway's best-known authors, she received the Nobel Prize in 1928, and she was considered so important to the people of Norway that during World War II she was spirited out of the country lest she be forced to be a propagandist. Safely in the United States, Undset became a spokesperson against the occupation and the Nazis retaliated by burning her books and hacking apart her desk, a gesture that had resonance for her readers. Her heroine Kristin endured many trials and had lost her home—Undset's own life is echoed in the medieval epic, but perhaps their greatest likeness was in a spiritual quest that lasted throughout life. Undset, a convert to Catholicism in 1924, is known as a Catholic writer of great importance, but with a critical revival of interest in her work after a long period of neglect, she is now seen in a feminist context. Her career has an all-too familiar arc for a woman author: significant promise and hard work combined with burdensome personal obligations are overcome and the work wins out. Honor follows, and the work suffers an interruption when the writer's life changes drastically. Even if the war years silenced Undset as a novelist, her corpus of work is remarkable. Undset is certainly a woman whose life and work merit study and appreciation.

The novelist was born into a privileged, cultured existence in Kalundborg, Denmark on 20 May 1882. Her father, Ingevald, was a famous archaeologist, and her mother, Anna Charlotte, was a well-educated and independent-minded woman who was both a full partner in her husband's work and a mother who, with her husband, helped shape her daughter's imagination. The family moved to Oslo in Undset's second year, and she grew up a happy and precocious child. A voracious reader, particularly of the Norse sagas and of history, she was intellectually challenged by both her parents. Undset gave the credit for her intellectual development to her adored father, but revisionist assessments have noted her mother's considerable influence as well as the strong similarity in the two women's temperaments.

The young girl was greatly affected by her father's death at age 11, and even in reduced circumstances her mother found the means to educate her children in excellent schools. To her daughter Anna Charlotte also transmitted her somewhat radical ideas: she dressed her daughters in pants as well as skirts and above all taught them to think for themselves. Always iconoclastic, Sigrid decided against the university and instead trained as a secretary. Undset worked in an office for ten years; her higher education was reading classic world literature and in 1907, after many setbacks, her first novel, *Fru Marta Oulie,* was published. In 1909 she began to travel abroad and in Rome she met and married the artist Anders Castus Svarstad in 1912. For Undset, marriage to a divorcee with three children proved a formidable test. She herself had three children; one, a daughter, was retarded, further taxing her energy. The marriage was annulled in 1924, and Undset, a devoted mother, worked tirelessly to support her family and further her career. An early novel, *Jenny* (1911), enjoyed success and was typical of her first efforts—but modern themes suited her less well than her work on the Middle Ages, and her writing began to reflect her great love of folk tales and her new religiosity.

With *Kristin Lavransdatter,* these two strands were joined brilliantly: an extraordinary, vibrant woman is the focus of a tale of love, tragedy, and redemption. Praising Undset's creation, critic Maura Boland wrote: "She is ... one of the great romantic heroines—but one with a difference.... Kristin does what few romantic heroines are allowed to do: she lives on, grows old, and concerns herself with the fate of her soul." In the first book, *The Bridal Wreath,* she is betrothed to one man chosen by her father, yet is seduced by another, Erlend. Their stormy yet devoted relationship is darkened by their sin—ultimately it divides the two and Kristin withdraws to a convent to live out her days. Like Undset, Kristin is the true support of her family—in *The Mistress of Husaby,* she is the one who rebuilds their fortunes, and she is the mother of sons who are the future. Erlend, a complex and riveting figure, loves Kristin but his transgressions cost the family all she has worked for—he loses his lands and goes to prison. The final book, *The Cross,* finds Kristin a widow who takes the veil when she is no longer needed by her sons and who dies after contracting the plague from a corpse she had carried to consecrated ground. Kristin's willful nature is both her strength and her greatest fault—the novel affirms her life and struggle as a life well lived and a soul saved.

The Master of Hestviken, Undset's second Norse medieval epic, also involves a couple—Olav and Ingunn are introduced as childhood playmates and then as sweethearts forced apart by family greed. Their efforts to remain together and the consequences of their love and subsequent repentance are the main focus of the novel, considered by many as a lesser effort.

Overall, however, Undset's research yielded books that were praised for their verisimilitude, and as a realist, her world view is consistent and her characters are complex psychologically. Her years away from Norway were difficult but she enjoyed the friendship of the Catholic activist Dorothy Day, and authors Willa Cather and Marjorie Kinnan Rawlings. When she returned to Norway in 1945, she spent the rest of her life at her home in Lillehammer, where she died in 1949. Her last work, a spiritual biography of Catherine of Siena, was published in 1952.

—Mary A. Hess

VALENZUELA, Luisa

Nationality: Argentinian. **Born:** Buenos Aires, 26 November 1938. **Education:** Attended University of Buenos Aires. **Family:** Married in 1958; one daughter. **Career:** Moved to Paris, 1958; program writer, Radio Difusion Français, Paris; returned to Buenos Aires, 1961; assistant editor, *La Nación* Sunday supplement, until 1972; editor, *Crisis,* beginning 1974; reporter, *Gente* magazine; moved to the United States, 1979; writer-in-residence, Columbia University, 1979, and New York University, 1985-90; returned to Buenos Aires, 1989. Conductor of numerous writing workshops. Contributor to periodicals, including *Atlántida, El Hogar, Esto Es, New York Times, New York Review of Books,* and *Village Voice.* **Awards:** Premio Kraft award, 1965; Fulbright grant, 1969-70; National Arts Foundation Grant, 1972-73; Instituto Nacional de Cinematografia award, 1973, for *Clara* (film script); Guggenheim fellowship, 1983. **Member:** Amnesty International, New York Institute for the Humanities (fellow), PEN Freedom to Write committee. **Address:** Buenos Aires, Argentina.

Publications

Novels

Hay que sonreír. Buenos Aires, Américalee, 1966; translated as *Clara,* in *Clara: 13 Short Stories and a Novel,* 1976.

El gato eficaz. Mexico City, Mortiz, 1972; as *Cat-O-Nine-Deaths,* n.p., n.d.

Como en la guerra. Buenos Aires, Sudamericana, 1977; translated as *He Who Searches,* Elmwood Park, New Jersey, Dalkey Archive, 1987.

Cola de lagartija. Buenos Aires, Bruguera, 1983; translated as *The Lizard's Tail,* New York, Farrar Straus, 1983; London, Serpent's Tale, 1987.

Novela negra con argentinos. Hanover, New Hampshire, Ediciones del Norte, 1990; translated as *Black Novel with Argentines,* New York, Simon & Schuster, 1992.

Short Stories

Los heréticos. Buenos Aires, Paidós, 1967; translated in *Clara: 13 Short Stories and a Novel.*

Aquí pasan cosas raras. Buenos Aires, Flor, 1975; translated as *Strange Things Happen Here,* New York, Harcourt Brace, 1979.

Cambio de armas. Hanover, New Hampshire, Ediciones del Norte, 1982; translated as *Other Weapons,* 1985.

Donde viven las águilas. Buenos Aires, Celtia, 1983; as *Up among the Eagles,* in *Open Door,* San Francisco, North Point, 1988.

Realidad nacional desde la cama. Buenos Aires, Grupo Editor Latinoamericano, 1990; translated as *Bedside Manners,* London, Serpent's Tail, 1995.

Simetrías. Buenos Aires, Sudamericana, 1993.

Open Door. San Francisco, North Point Press, 1988; London, Serpent's Tail, 1992.

Plays

Screenplays: *Clara,* 1972.

Other

Clara: 13 Short Stories and a Novel. New York, Harcourt Brace, 1976; selections published as *The Censors,* Willimantic, Connecticut, Curbstone Press, 1992.

Libro que no muerde. Mexico City, UNAM, 1980.

*

Bibliography: *Spanish American Woman Authors: A Bio-bibliographical Source Book* edited by Diane E. Marting, Westport, Connecticut, Greenwood Press, 1990.

Critical Studies: "Luisa Valenzuela: From *Hay que sonreír* to *Cambio de armas*" by Sharon Magnarelli, in *World Literature Today,* 58, 1984; special Valenzuela issue of *Review of Contemporary Fiction,* 6, fall 1986; *Review of Contemporary Fiction,* 6(3), fall 1986; *Reflections/Refractions: Reading Luisa Valenzuela* by Magnarelli, New York, P. Lang, 1988; interview with Magdalena Garcia Pinto, in her *Women Writers of Latin America;* "An Interview with Luisa Valenzuela" by Robert C. Dash, in *Chasqui: Revista de literatura latinoamericana,* 21-22, 1992-93.

* * *

One of the most significant writers to emerge from Argentina in the second half of the 20th century, Luisa Valenzuela is probably also the most widely translated woman of her continent. Born in 1928 in Buenos Aires, she is the daughter of a mother well-imbued with the literary tradition. Valenzuela sought artistic expression first as a painter, but realized by the time she was 18 years old that her skills as a writer far outstripped her painting abilities. Her first short story, "Ciudad ajena," was published in 1956 and would be included in the collection *Los hereticos,* which was translated into English in *Clara: 13 Short Stories and a Novel* in 1967.

Valenzuela had an early start and has not slowed down in her advocacy of both literature and human rights throughout the world. Her novels and short stories are remarkable in their fusion of the issues mentioned with a unique treatment of language as a form of liberation from oppression. In addition, the author's portrayal of female sexuality as a target for masculine abuse serves as an allegory of political repression, most specifically in her native Argentina, where the 1970s and the early 1980s were witness to repression, abuse, and torture on a massive scale. After a stay of three years in Paris from 1958-61—a period during which she confesses she felt great nostalgia for her native city of Buenos Aires—Valenzuela returned to Argentina, and remained as a journalist until 1979. During that period she was awarded numerous grants and foundation awards that facilitated her writing, and brought her into contact with authors in North America as well. In 1979 Valenzuela moved to New York, where she lived for ten years, though she returned once more to Argentinian 1989, which now remains her home base, though she continues to travel in order to lecture and participate in writers' workshops.

Valenzuela has written two collections of short stories that raise particular questions about patriarchy and about methods of oppression, including a portrayal of sexual perversion that is central to the hunger for power as Valenzuela sees it acted out in the Southern Cone of South America. 1972's "Other Weapons" and 1985's "Strange Things Happen Here" seem on the surface to be about strained and perverse relations between men and women when, in fact, they deal with the flaws inherent in a society where brute strength is equal to power. 1983's *The Lizard's Tale* is a parody of the power exercised by one of Juan Peron's ministers, Juan Lopez Rega, and his bizarre and maniacal grip on Argentina during the mid-1970s.

Another salient feature of Valenzuela's style is her approach to language as not only the means of conveying a theme, but also as the object of the story. Language is supple and malleable, its purpose can be different for different people, and the denial of access to its multiple ranges of applications is seen as another form of oppression. Valenzuela contends that, as a writer, she is always discovering new meanings to words and that she hopes to unlock their secrets each time she endeavors to write something new. Particularly in her story "Other Weapons," language and its referential function are underlined. The main character, Laura, is an amnesiac who is kept closed up in a beautiful apartment with beautiful clothing, perfect furnishings, and meals prepared for her by her maid. As the story progresses, Laura attempts to decipher the signs around her that point to a healthy life, but have no genuine meaning for her, because she has no memory of having fallen in love with her husband/captor, a military man who comes and goes, leaving her alone under the watchful eye of the maid and two bodyguards outside the door. Her home, her clothing, her meals, even her sexual relationship with her husband, do not belong in any world outside themselves, that is , they represent an isolation of word from their meaning, effects from their causes, people from their needs and wills, and reflect the helplessness of a people condemned to silence by terror, oppression, or censorship.

Valenzuela does engage in play with language through parody and metaphor. In her novel *The Lizard's Tale,* as well as in *Black Novel with Argentines,* the language she uses to relate her story has every bit of the weight that the plot might carry. In the first, she says, she carries the literal meaning of the rhetoric of a military dictatorship to its extreme, and comes up with a main character called "The Sorcerer," who possesses extraordinary genitalia, and whose evil promotion of terror is a fusion of sexual and linguistic perversion. In the second, Valenzuela's detective novel about two Argentine writers who are also lovers living in New York, their heightened awareness of the power of metaphors leads them to unravel the mystery of the motive for a murder.

Luisa Valenzuela could be place into the post-boom generation of Latin American writers, following on the heals of the explosion of popularity of authors who enjoyed a widely translated readership in Europe and North America. She is emphatic, however, that the Latin American boom was a sexist phenomenon, since all the writers recognized within that group were men, and since women whose writing was of comparable quality were virtually ignored. While much progress has been made since the mid-1970s in the promotion of literature by women in Latin America, Valenzuela still believes that men enjoy greater privileges in the publishing world, and see their work in print more readily. To combat that tendency, Valenzuela continues her prolific pace of writing, and encourages women to appropriate dominant language in Latin American society, and to create their own unique voices. Her own writing is a continuous examination of the language of dominance, and a subversion of the ones who possess it.

—Helena Antolin Cochrane

W

WALKER, Alice (Malsenior)

Nationality: American. **Born:** Eatonton, Georgia, 9 February 1944. **Education:** Spelman College, Atlanta, 1961-63; Sarah Lawrence College, Bronxville, New York, B.A. 1965. **Family:** Married Melvyn Rosenman Leventhal in 1967 (divorced 1976); one daughter. **Career:** Worked as a voter registration worker in Georgia, a worker in Head Start program in Mississippi, and on staff of New York City welfare department; co-founder and publisher, Wild Trees Press, Navarro, California, 1984-88. Writer-in-residence and teacher of black studies at Jackson State College, 1968-69, and Tougaloo College, 1970-71; lecturer in literature, Wellesley College and University of Massachusetts—Boston, both 1972-73; distinguished writer in Afro-American studies department, University of California, Berkeley, 1982; Fannie Hurst Professor of Literature, Brandeis University, Waltham, Massachusetts, 1982. Lecturer and reader of own poetry at universities and conferences. Member of board of trustees of Sarah Lawrence College. Consultant on black history to Friends of the Children of Mississippi, 1967. Contributing editor, *Southern Voices, Freedomways,* and *Ms.* **Awards:** Bread Loaf Writer's Conference scholar, 1966; American Scholar essay prize, 1967; Merrill writing fellowship, 1967; McDowell Colony fellowship, 1967, 1977-78; National Endowment for the Arts grant, 1969, 1977; Radcliffe Institute fellowship, 1971-73; honorary Ph.D., Russell Sage College, 1972; Southern Regional Council Lillian Smith Award, 1973, for *Revolutionary Petunias;* American Academy Rosenthal Foundation Award, 1974, for *In Love and Trouble;* Guggenheim grant, 1977-78; Pulitzer Prize and American Book Award, both 1983, both for *The Color Purple;* O. Henry Award, 1986, for "Kindred Spirits." D.H.L.: University of Massachusetts, 1983. **Address:** c/o Harcourt Brace Jovanovich, 1250 Sixth Ave, San Diego, California 92101, U.S.A.

Publications

Novels

The Third Life of Grange Copeland. New York, Harcourt Brace, 1970; London, Women's Press, 1985.
Meridian. New York, Harcourt Brace, and London, Deutsch, 1976.
The Color Purple. New York, Harcourt Brace, 1982; London, Women's Press, 1983.
The Temple of My Familiar. New York, Harcourt Brace, and London, Women's Press, 1989.
Possessing the Secret of Joy. New York, Harcourt Brace, and London, J. Cape, 1992.

Short Stories

In Love and Trouble: Stories of Black Women. New York, Harcourt Brace, 1973; London, Women's Press, 1984.
You Can't Keep a Good Woman Down. New York, Harcourt Brace, 1981; London, Women's Press, 1982.
The Complete Stories. London, Women's Press, 1994.
Everyday Use, edited by Barbara T. Christian. New Brunswick, New Jersey, Rutgers University Press, 1994.

Uncollected Short Stories

"Cuddling," in *Essence* (New York), July 1985.
"Kindred Spirits," in *Prize Stories 1986,* edited by William Abrahams. Garden City, New York, Doubleday, 1986.

For Children

Langston Hughes: American Poet. New York, Crowell, 1973.
To Hell with Dying, illustrations by Catherine Deeter. New York, Harcourt Brace, 1988; London, Hodder & Stoughton, 1991.
Finding the Green Stone, illustrations by Catherine Deeter. New York, Harcourt Brace, and London, Hodder & Stoughton, 1991.

Poetry

Once: Poems. New York, Harcourt Brace, 1968; London, Women's Press, 1986.
Five Poems. Detroit, Broadside Press, 1972.
Revolutionary Petunias and Other Poems. New York, Harcourt Brace, 1973; London, Women's Press, 1988.
Goodnight, Willie Lee, I'll See You in the Morning. New York, Dial Press, 1979; London, Women's Press, 1987.
Horses Make a Landscape Look More Beautiful. New York, Harcourt Brace, 1984; London, Women's Press, 1985.
Her Blue Body Everything We Know: Earthling Poems, 1965-1990. New York, Harcourt Brace, and London, Women's Press, 1991.

Other

In Search of Our Mothers' Gardens: Womanist Prose. New York, Harcourt Brace, 1983; London, Women's Press 1984.
Living by the Word: Selected Writings, 1973-1987. New York, Harcourt Brace, and London, Women's Press, 1988.
Warrior Marks: Female Genital Mutilation and the Sexual Blinding of Women, with Pratibha Parmar. New York, Harcourt Brace, 1993.
The Same River Twice: Honoring the Difficult. New York, Scribner, 1996.

Editor, *I Love Myself When I'm Laughing ... and Then Again When I Am Looking Mean and Impressive: A Zora Neale Hurston Reader,* introduction by Mary Helen Washington. Old Westbury, New York, Feminist Press, 1979.

*

Media Adaptations: *The Color Purple* (film), 1985.

Bibliography: *Alice Malsenior Walker: An Annotated Bibliography 1968-1986* by Louis H. Pratt and Darnell D. Pratt, Westport, Connecticut, Meckler, 1988; *Alice Walker: An Annotated Bibliography 1968-1986* by Erma Davis Banks and Keith Byerman, New York and London, Garland, 1989.

Critical Studies: *Interviews with Black Writers* by John O'Brien, New York, Liveright, 1973; *Black Women Writers (1950-1980): A Critical Evaluation* edited by Mari Evans, New York, Anchor, 1984; "Alice Walker" by Barbara Christian, in *Dictionary of Literary Biography,* Volume 33: *Afro-American Writers after 1955,* Detroit, Gale, 1984; *Alice Walker* edited by Harold Bloom, New York, Chelsea House Press, 1989; *Race, Gender, and Desire: Narrative Strategies in the Fiction of Toni Cade Bambara, Toni Morrison, and Alice Walker* by Elliott Butler-Evans, Philadelphia, Temple University Press, 1989; *Down from the Mountaintop: Black Women's Novels in the Wake of the Civil Rights Movement, 1966-1989* by Melissa Walker, New Haven, Connecticut, Yale University Press, 1991; *The Other Side of the Story: Structures and Strategies of Contemporary Feminist Narrative* by Molly Hite, Ithaca, New York, Cornell University Press, 1989; *Alice Walker* by Donna Haisty Winchell, New York, Twayne, 1992; *Alice Walker: Critical Perspectives Past and Present* edited by Henry Louis Gates Jr. and K.A. Appiah, New York, Amistad, 1993; *Alice Walker and Zora Neale Hurston: The Common Bond* edited by Lillie P. Howard, Westport, Connecticut, Greenwood Press, 1993; "Claiming the Bittersweet Matrix: Alice Walker, Sandra Cisneros, and Adrienne Rich" by Nancy Corson Carter, in *Critique,* 35(4), summer 1994; *Womanist and Feminist Aesthetics: A Comparative Review* by Tuzyline Jita Allan, Athens, Ohio University Press, 1995; *The Voices of African American Women: The Use of Narrative and Authorial Voice in the Works of Harriet Jacobs, Zora Neale Hurston, And Alice Walker* by Yvonne Johnson, New York, P. Lang, 1995.

* * *

Alice Walker calls herself a womanist, her term for a feminist of color. She outlines her definition of a womanist as a preface to her collection of essays, *In Search of Our Mothers' Gardens.* A womanist, she explains, is a responsible, adult woman who often wants "to know more and in greater depth than is considered 'good' for one." Womanism, however, involves more than intellectual curiosity; Walker also uses the term to describe women who love other women and who at the same time dedicate themselves to the "survival and wholeness of entire people, male *and* female." A womanist, according to Walker, loves "the Folk" and above all, herself. This womanist philosophy has both been shaped by and done much to shape Walker's life and, above all, her writing. Indeed, the threads of womanism wind through all of her work, which includes novels and short stories, poetry and essays, children's books and academic collections.

Walker's life story, like many of her novels, is set against the backdrop of the South. She was born the last of eight children in Eatonton, Georgia in 1944. Walker's parents, Willie Lee and Minnie Lou Grant Walker, worked as sharecroppers and struggled to carve out a home for their children in spite of the political, economic, and social injustices that characterized life for black people in the segregated South. As the critic Barbara Christian explains in the *Dictionary of Literary Biography,* that oppression fosters a sustaining spirit that appears in Walker's writing: "Her works confront the pain and struggle of black people's history, which for her has resulted in a deeply spiritual tradition."

Walker's view of herself and her world was profoundly altered by an incident that took place when she was eight years old. A game of "cowboys and Indians" ended tragically when one of Walker's older brothers shot her in the eye with a BB gun. The family's isolation and poverty meant that the injured girl did not visit a doctor until a week later. By that time a cataract had already formed, leaving her blind in one eye.

For the next few years, Walker felt horribly ugly and feared losing her sight in the other eye. Even after an operation at age fourteen removed the scar tissue that had formed where the BB struck her eye, Walker's self-consciousness about what she regarded as her deformity stayed with her until much later. At the same time, however, living with partial blindness meant that Walker began to pay more attention to the things and people around her, and to record those observations. Looking back on her blindness in the essay "Beauty: When the Other Dancer Is the Self," Walker writes: "I realize that I have dashed about the world madly, looking at this, looking at that, storing up images against the fading of the light."

Walker turns those sharp observation skills on the life of a sharecropping family in her first novel, *The Third Life of Grange Copeland.* Here she explores the effects of racism and poverty on Southern black family life. The text traces three generations of the Copeland's lives and the violence the family's women experience at the hands of their husbands and lovers. Walker's next novel, *Meridian,* is similarly set in the South and covers the period from the 1960s civil rights movement to the years following it. Like the characters in *The Third Life of Grange Copeland, Meridian*'s title character feels the weight of racism pressing down on her so completely that it almost destroys her. A student activist who leaves the movement because she cannot convince herself that using violence is the way to end oppression, Meridian Hill becomes a lone crusader for equality. At the same time, Meridian grapples with issues of particular concern to black women: she struggles to maintain her self-confidence when her black lover leaves her for a white woman and must ultimately strike a balance between black people's need for survival and her own.

Events in *Meridian* mirror some of the events in Walker's own life. Like the novel's protagonist, going to college in Atlanta led her to become actively involved in the civil rights movement. Walker attended the black women's college, Spelman, for two years but became frustrated with the school's efforts to turn out Southern black 'ladies' that stood in stark contrast to her mother's and aunts' experiences. Still, the activist's spirit that grew in Walker during her time at Spelman would have a lasting influence on her life and writing.

Walker finished her education at the predominantly white women's school, Sarah Lawrence College, in Bronxville, New York. During her last year at there, Walker learned she was pregnant. Some of the turmoil, isolation, and despair that knowledge aroused in her appear in her first collection of poetry, *Once: Poems.* The pregnancy and subsequent abortion gave Walker a new sense of herself as a woman. She explains that she "began to understand how alone woman is, because of her body." Walker's second volume of poetry, *Revolutionary Petunias and Other Poems,* similarly translates personal experience into creative expression as Walker recalls her years in Mississippi working as a civil rights activist. *Goodnight, Willie Lee, I'll See You in the Morning* centers on the poet's relationships with family and friends, and suggests that love between men and women may offer a source for social change. Walker's most recent volume of poetry, *Her Blue Body Everything We Know: Earthling Poems,* contains the complete texts of Walker's earlier books of poetry along with new poems, some focused on environmental issues.

Though Walker has produced a steady stream of creative work, it was not until the publication of *The Color Purple*, which won the both the Pulitzer Prize and the American Book Award in 1983, that her writing gained widespread national attention. The novel was almost universally praised for its author's skillful and dignified use of the black folk idiom to tell the story of Celie, a poor black woman who, in spite of repeated sexual and emotional abuse, discovers her own self-worth. That discovery comes by way of writing letters to God and to her sister, Nettie, and by way of forming a healing sexual and emotional relationship with another woman, Shug Avery. Walker based the character Celie in part on her great-grandmother's experiences, who was raped when she was a girl of twelve.

However, both the novel and Steven Spielberg's film adaptation were criticized, primarily by black male scholars, for what they regarded as Walker's stereotypical portrayals of violent, animalistic black male characters. Such critics ignored or made light of the redemptive transformation that Celie's husband, Albert, undergoes once he begins to see his wife as a human being with needs and feelings. The movie generated so much controversy that Walker has attempted to put the matter to rest by writing about it. Her most recent book, *The Same River Twice: Honoring the Difficult,* contains journal entries, letters, and the script for her unused screenplay in an effort to document her thoughts about the film.

The survival, and even the triumph, of female characters like Celie and Sarah Davis, the protagonist in Walker's short story "A Sudden Trip Home in the Spring," reveal her faith in black women's strength and creative powers. Indeed, Walker suggests that making art—in the form of Celie's letters or Sarah's sculptures—provides a crucial means of self-preservation for black women. However, Walker also celebrates the more transitory art forms black women have produced. Art, she suggests, appeared in the note of a song carrying over a hot field and in the kaleidoscope of color that was her mother's garden. These artist figures also find their way into Walker's texts, like Mem in *The Third Life of Grange Copeland,* who decorates her house with flowers.

Walker seeks not only to create art herself and to imagine artistic characters in her writing, but also to preserve it. While doing research on voodoo practices among rural Southern blacks for a short story, "The Revenge of Hannah Kemhuff," she discovered a book by the writer Zora Neale Hurston. Her delight in Hurston's prose style and her recognition of herself in the people who populated Hurston's texts drove Walker to rescue the author from being a mere footnote to the mostly male list of "great" black writers. Indeed, she has been instrumental in attracting new readers and scholars to Hurston's work. Walker records her efforts to find and mark Hurston's grave in Florida in the essay "Looking for Zora" and has edited a collection of her works entitled, I Love Myself When I'm Laughing ... and Then Again When I Am Looking Mean and Impressive. And of the now-celebrated Hurston novel, *Their Eyes Were Watching God,* Walker remarks, "There is no book more important to me than this one." Walker's crusade to rescue Hurston from anonymity stemmed both from a need to acknowledge and preserve the work of her literary foremother and from the recognition that her work, too, might just as easily be consigned to obscurity.

Walker's womanist sensibility and creative endeavors have most recently stretched beyond portraying the geography and people of the South and even the United States to include the land and people of Africa. Part of *The Color Purple* takes place in the Olinkan village where Nettie goes to work as a missionary. Similarly, sections of *The Temple of My Familiar,* a richly woven tapestry of stories that span time and space, take place in Africa and offer an alternative view of human history. However, Walker is careful not to romanticize Africa; *Possessing the Secret of Joy* explores the impact that the female circumcision ritual performed in some African countries has on one character's life.

Alice Walker's writing pays homage to the complexity of human experience; it illustrates the pain and violence that has marked so many black people's lives even as it offers hope for personal transformation and renewal. Such changes become most possible, Walker's womanist writing suggests, when black men and women stand shoulder to shoulder working to end oppression both in their relationships and in the world.

—Allison Kimmich

WALKER, Margaret

Nationality: American. **Born:** Birmingham, Alabama, 7 July 1915. **Education:** Northwestern University, B.A. 1935; University of Iowa, M.A. 1940, Ph.D. 1965. **Family:** Married Firnist James Alexander in 1943 (deceased); children: two daughters, two sons. **Career:** Joined Federal Writers Project, Chicago, 1935; worked as a social worker, newspaper reporter, and magazine editor; member of faculty, 1941-41, and professor of English, 1945-46, Livingstone College, Salisbury, North Carolina; instructor in English, West Virginia State College, Institute, 1942-43; professor of English 1949-79, director of Institute for the Study of the History, Life, and Culture of Black Peoples, beginning 1968, Jackson State College, Jackson, Mississippi. Lecturer, National Concert and Artists Corp. Lecture Bureau, 1943-48; visiting professor in creative writing, Northwestern University, 1969. Staff member, Cape Cod Writers Conference, Craigville, Massachusetts, 1967 and 1969; participant, Library of Congress Conference on the Teaching of Creative Writing, 1973. Contributor to *Negro Digest, Opportunity, Phylon, Poetry, Saturday Review, Virginia Quarterly,* and *Yale Review.* **Awards:** Yale Series of Younger Poets Award, 1942, for *For My People;* named to New York Public Library Honor Roll of Race Relations, 1942; Rosenwald fellowship, 1944; Ford fellowship for study at Yale University, 1954; Houghton Mifflin Literary fellowship, 1966; Fulbright fellowship, 1971; National Endowment for the Humanities fellowship, 1972; D.Lit., Northwestern University, 1974; D.Lett., Rust College, 1974; D.F.A., Dennison University, 1974; D.H.L., Morgan State University, 1976. **Member:** National Council of Teachers of English, Modern Language Association, Poetry Society of America, American Association of University Professors, National Education Association, Alpha Kappa Alpha. **Address:** c/o Department of English, Jackson State College, Jackson, Mississippi 39217, U.S.A.

Publications

Novel

Jubilee. Boston, Houghton Mifflin, 1965; London, Hodder & Stoughton, 1967.

Poetry

For My People. New Haven, Connecticut, Yale University Press, 1942; as *Margaret Walker's "For My People": A Tribute,* photographs by Roland L. Freeman, Jackson, University of Mississippi Press, 1992.
Ballad of the Free. Detroit, Broadside Press, 1966.
Prophets for a New Day. Detroit, Broadside Press, 1970.
October Journey. Detroit, Broadside Press, 1973.
This Is My Century: New and Collected Poems. University of Georgia Press, 1989.

Essays

"Black Studies: Some Personal Observations," in *Afro-American Studies,* 1970.
How I Wrote "Jubilee." Chicago, Third World Press, 1972; expanded as *How I Wrote Jubilee and Other Essays on Life and Literature,* edited by Maryemma Graham. New York, Feminist Press, 1990.
"Some Aspects of the Black Aesthetic," in *Freedomways,* 16, winter 1976.
"On Being Female, Black, and Free," in *The Writer on Her Work,* edited by Janet Sternburg. New York, Norton, 1980.

Other

A Poetic Equation: Conversations between Nikki Giovanni and Margaret Walker, with Nikki Giovanni. Washington, D.C., Howard University Press, 1974; with new postscript, 1983.
Richard Wright, Daemonic Genius: A Portrait of the Man, A Critical Look at His Work. New York, Dodd Mead, 1987.
God Touched My Life: The Inspiring Autobiography of the Nun Who Brought Song, Celebration, and Soul to the World, with Sister Thea Bowman. San Francisco, Harper, 1992.

Recordings: *Margaret Walker Reads Jubilee,* Columbia, Missouri, American Audio Prose Library, 1991.

*

Manuscript Collections: Millsaps-Wilson Library, Millsaps College, Jackson, Mississippi; Jackson State University.

Critical Studies: "'Oh Freedom': Women and History in Margaret Walker's *Jubilee*" by Phyllis R. Klotman, in *Black American Literature Forum,* 11, winter 1977; interview with John Griffith Jones in *Mississippi Writers Talking,* Vol. 2, Jackson, University of Mississippi Press, 1983; interview with Claudia Tate in *Black Women Writers at Work,* edited by Tate, New York, Continuum, 1983; "Fields Watered with Blood: Myth and Ritual in the Poetry of Margaret Walker" by Eugenia Collier, in *Black Women Writers (1950-1980),* edited by Mari Evans, n.p., 1984; *Conjuring: Black Women, Fiction, and Literary Tradition* edited by Marjorie Pryse and Hortense J. Spillers, Bloomington, Indiana University Press, 1985; "Black Women's Literature and the Task of Feminist Theology" by Delores S. Williams, in *Immaculate and Powerful: The Female in Sacred Image and Social Reality,* edited by Clarissa W. Atkinson, Constance H. Buchanan, and Margaret Ruth Miles, Boston, Beacon Press, 1985; *Black and White Women of the Old South: The Peculiar Sisterhood in American Literature* by Minrose C. Gwin, Knoxville, University of Tennessee Press, 1985; "'Somebody Forgot to Tell Somebody Something': African-American Women's Historical Novels" by Barbara Christian, in *Wild Women in the Whirlwind: Afra-American Culture and the Contemporary Literary Renaissance,* edited by Joanne M. Braxton and Andree Nicola McLaughlin, New Brunswick, New Jersey, Rutgers University Press, 1990.

* * *

When Margaret Walker won the Yale Younger Poets Series Award in 1942 for *For My People,* she became not only one of the United States' youngest published African American poets but also the first black woman in North America to receive such a prestigious honor. And *Jubilee,* the novel for which she is perhaps best known is considered by many to be the first historically factual black American novel. It was also the first work by an African American to directly address the oppression of black women. As cornerstones of a growing body of literature that affirms both the folk roots of black culture and the unique problems faced by African American women, Walker's books are visionary in their ability to prefigure the cultural unity of African Americans that would be constructed on their foundation.

In *For My People* Walker celebrates colorful black characters such as the New Orleans sorceress Molly Means; Kissie Lee, a tough young woman who dies "with her boots on switching blades"; and the legendary Stagolee, who kills a white officer but eludes a lynch mob. More than a collection of individual portraits, *For My People* urges action, demands sweeping changes for blacks, and cogently notes that such changes may one day come about through a "bloody peace." "[Using] the language of the grass-roots people, Walker spins yarns of folk heroes and heroines," notes Eugenia Collier in *Black Women Writers (1950-1980): A Critical Evaluation:* "those who, faced with the terrible obstacles which haunt Black people's very existence, not only survive but prevail—with style."

The title poem of Walker's first collection lyrically paints the black historic experience in America—from the rural folk culture, spirituality, and worklife of Southern plantations to the alienation and squalor of the Northern cities—culminating with an awakening whereby African Americans rise and take control of their future, creating a fresh beginning. Other poems in *For My People* are narrated by a voice rebelling against black provincialism and romanticism, a voice that senses that the decades of black complacency are coming to an end. Walker's other collections of verse continue to celebrate both African American history and culture, as well as focus on the strong matrilineal legacy epitomized so well in the traditional figure of the powerful black "conjure woman" that Walker portrays in "Molly Means."

1966's *Jubilee,* the novel on which Walker's literary reputation solidly rests, is the story of a slave family during and after the civil war. The novel took her 30 years to write; as she explains in *How I Wrote "Jubilee,"* Walker first heard about the "slavery time" in stories told by her maternal grandmother, Elvira Ware Dozier. When mature enough to realize the value of her family history, she drew more details from her grandmother, promising in return to write down the story that took shape in her imagination. Extensive research would follow, on everything from obscure birth records to information on the history of tin cans. "Most of my life I have been involved with writing this story about my great-grandmother," Walker adds, "and even if *Jubilee* were never considered an artistic or commercial success I would still be happy just to have finished it."

The life story of Vyry, a young black woman, *Jubilee* comprises three sections: the antebellum years spent in slavery on a Georgia plantation, the chaos of the Civil War years, and the aftershocks of the Reconstruction era. Against this historic backdrop, Vyry grows from a small child into womanhood. In the first section the black woman is enslaved; she matures, marries, and ultimately separates from her husband. Vyry's attempt to escape from Dutton's plantation with her two children is met with violence in the form of a flogging. The second section depicts the destruction of war and the resulting social upheaval for both slaveowner and slaves. The novel ends as Vyry, now free amid the rubble of the Old South, searches for a place to call home. Notable for both her realistic portrayal of daily life in a black slave community and her depiction of a strong, indomitable female character, Walker also emphasizes the importance of folkways, prefacing each chapter of *Jubilee* with proverbs or lines taken from traditional spirituals. She weaves her narrative with verses of songs sung by women, lines from sermons, the rhymes of slave children.

Characteristic of much of Walker's writing, *Jubilee* owes little to her academic life and much to a rich Southern homelife, where the rich heritage of African American culture was highly valued. A Jamaican native, Walker's father was a scholar and methodist minister who instilled in his daughter a love of both the written word and the sounds of spoken language; her mother's love of music and poetry supplemented this. It was clear to Walker, even as a child, that writing was her destiny.

As a senior at Northwestern in 1934 she began a fruitful association with the Federal Writers Project located in Chicago. One of her most rewarding friendships during this period was with Richard Wright; the liaison, while it lasted, was valuable to both fledgling writers. Walker recalls her three-year friendship with Wright as a "rare and once-in-a-lifetime association ... rather uncommon in its completely literary nature." During those years both Walker and Wright worked diligently to get their works published in national periodicals. Walker was successful: her poems "For My People" (1937), "We Have Been Believers" (1938), and "The Struggle Staggers Us" (1939) were published in *Poetry.* Wright would leave Chicago in 1937; their friendship abruptly ended two years later as the result of a misunderstanding that was never resolved.

Meanwhile, aware that she would need a paying vocation in order to pursue her writing, Walker obtained her M.A. degree and worked as a professor of English from the early 1940s until her retirement in 1979. Because of her race and gender, her career as an academic was characterized by opposition and difficulty. "I'm a third-generation college graduate," Walker explained in an interview with Claudia Tate in *Black Women Writers at Work.* "Society doesn't want to recognize that there's this kind of black writer. I'm the Ph.D. black woman. That's horrible. That is to be despised. I didn't know how bad it was until I went back to school [in order to teach] and found out." In the early 1960s, with the older of her four children nearing college age, Walker decided to take a leave from her position in the English department at Jackson State University, planning to earn her Ph.D. under the assumption that she would then qualify for a raise in pay to enable her to cover her children's education costs. When she returned in 1965, she found herself slighted by the administration. Persevering in the face of such treatment, Walker went on to develop the school's black studies program, thereby attaining personal, if not financial, fulfillment in her last years as an educator. "My birth certificate reads female," she wrote in her inspiring essay "On Being Female, Black, and Free." "Call it fate or circumstance, this is my condition.... I like being a woman. I have a proud black heritage, and I have learned from the difficult exigencies of life that freedom is a philosophical state of mind and existence.... In my mind I am absolutely free."

Margaret Walker, poet, novelist, educator, and essayist. Throughout a career that has spanned over half a century, the themes and images underlying her writing—a balanced historical perspective and a forward-thinking humanism—have remained relevant despite the racial and gender-related fluctuations in attitudes and focuses within American society. "To choose the life of a writer," Walker believes, "a black female must arm herself with a fool's courage, foolhardiness, and serious purpose and dedication to the art of writing, strength of will and integrity, because the odds are always against her. The cards are stacked. Once the die is cast, however, there is no turning back." Walker's own example continues to serve as a reminder that such dedication, commitment, and optimism in the face of adversity can transcend many barriers.

—Pamela Kester-Shelton

WALKER, Rebecca

Nationality: American. **Born:** Jackson, Mississippi, 11 November 1970; daughter of writer Alice Walker. **Education:** Yale University, B.A. (cum laude) in 1992. **Family:** Companion of Angel Williams. **Career:** Contributing editor, *Ms.,* beginning 1989; co-founder, Third Wave Direct Action Corporation, New York, 1992; owner, Kokobar, Brooklyn, New York, 1996. **Awards:** "Paz y Justicia" award, Vanguard Foundation; California Abortion Rights Action League Champion of Choice award; Fund for Feminist Majority Feminist of the Year award; Kingsborough Community College Woman of Distinction award; Yale University Pickens Prize for excellence in African-American scholarship, 1992. **Address:** Brooklyn, New York, U.S.A. **Online Address:** minnie@nyo.com

Publications

Political/Social Theory

To Be Real: Telling the Truth and Changing the Face of Feminism. New York, Anchor, 1995.

Essays

"Lusting for Freedom," in *Listen Up: Voices from the Next Feminist Generation,* edited by Barbara Findlen. Seattle, Washington, Seal Press, 1995.

"The Fight Is Far from Over," in *Black Scholar,* 1992.

*

Critical Studies: "Rebecca Walker Steps Out" (interview) by Retha Powers, in *Girlfriends,* May/June 1996.

* * *

Rebecca Walker is becoming a rallying voice for young feminists. But rather than always speaking for them, she is working to create a forum where young women can speak for themselves and voice their own ideas. As a new generation of feminist thinkers and activists tries to define themselves and their lives, Walker's suggestion that "feminism" is an individual's to create is a welcome and much-needed one. In 1994 *Time* magazine named Walker as one of the 50 future leaders in the United States. Indeed, she is a leader in the next generation's feminist movement.

Born in 1970 in Jackson, Mississippi, Walker grew up in New York City and San Francisco. She attended Yale University where she graduated cum laude in 1992. Angry at women's social condition, she decided to chose a life of social activism. Upon graduation she co-founded, with Shannon Liss, Third Wave Direct Action Corporation, a national, non-profit organization designed to inspire leadership and activism among young women. Third Wave's first endeavor was to register 20,000 new voters, mostly young women in inner cities, in time for the 1992 U.S. presidential elections. For their "Freedom Ride," as they called their registration campaign, Walker won the Feminist of the Year award from the Fund for Feminist Majority. Her other Third Wave projects include fighting young women's illiteracy levels by educating young women about technology, so that they are not left behind on the information superhighway. And in 1996 she opened a cybercafe and bookstore, Kokobar, with her partner Angel Williams, bringing the Internet into a multi-cultural, inner-city community.

In addition to her activism, Walker has been a contributing editor to *Ms.* magazine since 1989. She has also written for the *New York Daily News, SPIN, Harpers, Sassy,* and *Black Scholar.* In perhaps her most powerful essay, "The Fight Is Far from Over," which appeared in *Black Scholar* in 1992, she writes of the 1991 Anita Hill/Clarence Thomas congressional hearings. Walker calls upon her peers to become angry, and then turn that anger into power. Anger can change the politics as usual. Her other writings encompass topics like domestic violence, reproductive freedom, sexuality, and, of course, feminism.

In "Lusting for Freedom," an essay for fellow *Ms.* editor, Barbara Findlen's, anthology *Listen Up: Voices from the Next Generation,* Walker writes about the power of female sexuality. She explores how self-knowledge, desire, and self-exploration of her body have made her a powerfully sexual being, as well as how her sexuality has, in turn, empowered her. She writes about the need to give women a safe place to find their sexuality, to be comfortable with it because without knowledge and comfort, there is no pleasure. Building a bridge between the act of sex and personal sexuality is important, she says. With knowledge, there is power. Walker argues that women need a place to love their bodies and create their own boundaries. She wants other young women to have the same kinds of experiences as she did—ones that will create healthy sexuality. She calls on women to rejoice in the power of choice. With that perspective, her readers see power in their own lives.

In her first book, *To Be Real: Telling the Truth and Changing the Face of Feminism,* published in 1995, Walker recruited young writers to discuss their battles with "traditional" feminist ideologies. Walker asks: Is there more than one way to be a feminist? The essayists answer a collective and resounding, "Yes!" Feminism "isn't about putting on an ideological straitjacket," notes Walker.

In "Brideland," *To Be Real* contributor Naomi Wolf struggles with how she can make her wedding feminist and progressive yet traditional, with all the trimmings: lace, veils, romance. Wolf finds that to make her wedding hers, she has made it right. In an interview with super-model Veronica Webb, Walker and Webb discuss the seeming contradictions of modeling and feminism. Webb argues that her modeling career gives her economic power and control over her life that most women do not experience. Each author in *To Be Real,* like its readers, lives in a world with seemingly strict feminist ideologies. Walker realizes the restrictions of this kind of world, and creates a place for people to build their own feminism.

To Be Real also explores the reasons for separation at the "third generation" feminist movement. She says that young feminists are alienated by the media, with its stereotype of feminism, and even perhaps maligned by older generations of feminists. Young women lack basic knowledge of women's history and achievements, Walker says, and it leads to a lack of pride within the movement. Walker suggests that instead of finding a niche in the feminist movement, most people leave it altogether. The writers in *To Be Real* live in an imperfect world, but Walker maintains that they tell the truth about their world. Their honesty will help a generation of young feminists to place themselves within the movement. Perhaps more young women will become activists in their communities, an ultimate goal of Walker's.

Walker's ideas about feminism are like an open window in a ideological room that is at risk of losing its next generation of leaders; her ideas have the potential to inspire a new era of activism. She will undoubtedly continue in her leadership role as she works on her next project—an anthology about bisexuality. Controversial, like *To Be Real,* this new project will bring attention to Rebecca Walker as she continues to give a strong voice to what seems a muted movement.

—Barbara Stretchberry

WALLACE, Michele

Nationality: American. **Born:** New York, New York, 4 January 1952; daughter of the artist Faith Ringgold. **Education:** City College of the City University of New York, B.A. 1974, M.A. 1984; attended Yale University, 1980. **Career:** Book review researcher, *Newsweek,* New York City, 1974-75; instructor in journalism, New York University, New York, beginning 1976; currently assistant professor of English, City College of the City University of New York. Contributor of articles and poetry to numerous periodicals, including *Esquire, Ms., Village Voice,* and *Women's Review of Books.* **Member:** National Black Feminist Organization (founding member), Art without Walls (president 1974). **Address:** New York, New York, U.S.A.

PUBLICATIONS

Political/Social Theory

Black Macho and the Myth of the Superwoman. New York, Dial Press, 1976.

Invisibility Blues: From Pop to Theory. New York and London, Verso, 1991.

*

Critical Studies: Review of *Black Macho and the Myth of the Superwoman* in *Black Scholar,* March 1979; "Loving Themselves Fiercely 20 Years Later" (interview) by Lisa Jones, in *Village Voice,* 11 July 1995.

* * *

Upon publication of *Black Macho and the Myth of the Superwoman* in 1979, *Ms.* magazine hailed it as "the book that will shape the 1980s," no small accomplishment for its author, then 26-year-old Michele Wallace. Wallace, who based her arguments about black women's second-class status both in and outside of the Civil Rights movement largely on her own experiences, maintained that her decision to continue to proclaim feminist beliefs, especially in the fall-out of *Black Macho,* has never been easy. "People didn't become feminists to have fun," she told Lisa Jones. "We became feminists out of a sense of duty and obligation. It's an ethical system, a politics, and a philosophy, but its not really a life for most of us. A life involves relationships, and being a feminist doesn't necessarily provide you with the most satisfying relationships."

Black Macho is composed of two essays: an analysis of the Black Power Movement of the late 1960s and early 1970s and the situation of black women within that movement. In her book, Wallace maintained that during the fight for racial equality the black male began to perceive himself as a power figure only in sexual terms: "Black Macho allowed for only the most primitive notions of women—women as possessions, women as the spoils of war, leaving black women with no resale value. As a possession, the black woman was a symbol of defeat, and therefore of little use to the revolution except as the performer of drudgery (not unlike her role in slavery)." For black men, who were motivated largely by a hidden desire for revenge, the only way to enter the white power structure was by exercising sexual prowess over white women, and whites had once done to black women.

The myth of the "Superwoman"—black woman who successfully carry the burden of working and keeping a home and raising the family when her demoralized man can't find a job—was perpetuated, Wallace believes, by a report written in 1965 by Senator Daniel Moynihan that underscored to many African Americans the stereotype of the black women as strong enough, matriarchal enough, to exist and thrive independent of men. Balanced with the myth of the street-smart black macho male, the superwoman mythos put black women at odds with the feminist movement. Condescended to by whites—feminists as well as non—black women determined that their racial oppression was a more pressing problem than their sexual inequality. Believing in their powers as "superwoman," black women simply opted out of the feminist movement in the hopes that once racial equality was achieved, they would rise alongside African American men to an equal footing with whites.

In openly challenging the status quo of the sexual order within the black community, *Black Macho* not surprisingly caused a stir. While revered by some black women for her courage, Wallace was also reviled by many others—both men and women—who condemned her efforts to divide an already fragmented community. Criticized as well by white feminists and academics for relying on a limited personal history and second-hand sources rather than a deep well of knowledge, *Black Macho* left its author intellectually isolated. While Wallace would later admit that her perspective on the problem of the oppression of black women has altered as she has learned more, she notes in the introduction to the 1990 edition of the book, that "It is impossible for me to look back at this book without the conviction that the significance of black women as a distinct category is routinely erased by the way in which the Women's Movement and the Black Movement choose to set their goals and recollect their histories."

In her 1991 book, *Invisibility Blues: From Pop to Theory,* Wallace continues to maintain that sexism is an active—and destructive—sociocultural force within the African American community. This time addressing the realm of cultural production, she posits the belief in what she calls the "Harlem effect." For any black woman who comes of age with the desire to engage with society on an intellectual or creative level, "there is ... a Harlem of the mind that may set the parameters of her endeavors.... the idea that the black community has little need for certain levels of intellectual activity." Drawing again on her own experience, as well as that of her mother, noted artist Faith Ringgold, and of the lives and works of other black writers, filmmakers, and entertainers, Wallace once more raises a feminist voice, once more out of duty, full in the knowledge that, indeed, feminism is not fun.

—Nancy Raye Tarcher

WARNER, Sylvia Townsend

Nationality: British. **Born:** Harrow, Middlesex, 6 December 1893. **Education:** Educated privately. **Family:** Companion of poet Valentine Ackland (died 1969). **Career:** Editor, *Tudor Church Music,* London, 1923-29; supporter of British Communist Party until the 1940s; regular contributor to *New Yorker,* 1936-78; contributor to periodicals, including *Blackwood's Magazine, Countryman, Eve, Left Review, London Mercury, New Statesman and Nation, Our Time,* and *Time and Tide.* Composer of musical scores and librettos. **Member:** Royal Society of Literature (fellow), American Academy of Arts and Letters (honorary member). **Died:** 1 May 1978.

Publications

Novels

Lolly Willowes, or, The Loving Huntsman. London, Chatto & Windus, and New York, Viking, 1926; with introduction by Anita Miller, Academy Chicago, 1979.

Mr. Fortune's Maggot. London, Chatto & Windus, and New York, Viking, 1927.

The True Heart. London, Chatto & Windus, and New York, Viking, 1929.

Summer Will Show. London, Chatto & Windus, and New York, Viking, 1936.

After the Death of Don Juan. London, Chatto & Windus, 1938; New York, Viking, 1939.

The Cat's Cradle-Book. New York, Viking, 1940; London, Chatto & Windus, 1960.
The Corner That Held Them. London, Chatto & Windus, and New York, Viking, 1948.
The Flint Anchor. London, Chatto & Windus, and New York, Viking, 1954; as *The Barnards of Loseby,* New York, Popular Library, 1974.

Short Stories

The Maze: A Story to Be Read Aloud. London, Cresset, 1928.
Elinor Barley. London, Cresset, 1930.
A Moral Ending and Other Stories. London, Jackson 1931; enlarged as *The Salutation,* London, Chatto & Windus, and New York, Viking, 1932.
More Joy in Heaven and Other Stories. London, Cresset, 1935.
24 Short Stories, with Graham Green and James Laver. London, Cresset, 1939.
A Garland of Straw and Other Stories. London, Chatto & Windus, and New York, Viking, 1943.
The Museum of Cheats. London, Chatto & Windus, and New York, Viking, 1947.
Winter in the Air and Other Stories. London, Chatto & Windus, 1955; New York, Viking, 1956.
A Spirit Rises. London, Chatto & Windus, and New York, Viking, 1962.
A Stranger with a Bag and Other Stories. London, Chatto & Windus, 1966; as *Swans on an Autumn River,* New York, Viking, 1966.
The Innocent and the Guilty. London, Chatto & Windus, and New York, Viking, 1971.
The Kingdoms of Elfin. London, Chatto & Windus, and New York, Viking, 1977.
One Thing Leading to Another and Other Stories, edited by Susanna Pinney. London, Chatto & Windus, and New York, Viking, 1984.
Selected Stories of Sylvia Townsend Warner. London, Chatto & Windus, and New York, Viking, 1988.

Poetry

The Espalier. London, Chatto & Windus, and New York, Dial Press, 1925.
Time Importuned. London, Chatto & Windus, and New York, Viking, 1928.
Some World Far from Ours; and "Stay, Corydon, Thou Swain." London, Mathews & Marrot, 1929.
Opus 7. London, Chatto & Windus, and New York, Viking, 1931.
Rainbow. New York, Knopf, 1932.
Whether a Dove or a Seagull, with Valentine Ackland. New York, Viking, 1933; London, Chatto & Windus, 1934.
Two Poems. Derby, England, Hopkins, 1945.
Boxwood, with Reynolds Stone. London, privately printed, 1957; enlarged, London, Chatto & Windus, 1960.
King Duffus and Other Poems. Wells, England, Clare, 1968.
Azrael and Other Poems. Newbury, Libanus, 1978; as *12 Poems,* London, Chatto & Windus, 1980.
Collected Poems, edited by Claire Harman. Manchester, Carcanet, and New York, Viking, 1983.
Selected Poems, edited by Claire Harman. Manchester, Carcanet, 1985.

Autobiography

Scenes of Childhood. London, Chatto & Windus, 1981; New York, Viking, 1982.

Other

This Our Brother. London, Cambridge, 1930.
The People Have No Generals. London, Newport, 1941.
Somerset. London, Elek, 1949.
Jane Austen: 1775-1817. London and New York, Longmans Green, 1951; revised, 1957.
Sketches from Nature. Wells, England, and London, Clare, 1963.
T. H. White: A Biography. London, Cape, 1967; New York, Viking, 1968.
Letters, edited by William Maxwell. London, Chatto & Windus, 1982; New York, Viking, 1983.

Editor, *The Weekend Dickens.* London, Machelose, and New York, Lorring & Mussey, 1932.
Editor, *The Portrait of a Tortoise: Extracted from the Journals of Gilbert White.* London, Chatto & Windus, and Toronto, Oxford University Press, 1946.

Translator, *By Way of Saint-Breve,* by Marcel Proust. London, Chatto & Windus, 1958; as *On Art and Literature: 1896-1917,* New York, Dell, 1964.
Translator, *A Place of Shipwreck,* by Jean René Huguenin. London, Chatto & Windus, 1963.

*

Manuscript Collections: Dorset County Museum, Dorchester, England; Beinecke Rare Book and Manuscript Library, Yale University, New Haven, Connecticut (letters); Harry Ransom Humanities Research Center, University of Texas at Austin (letters).

Critical Studies: "A Wilderness of One's Own: Feminist Fantasy Novels of the Twenties, Rebecca West and Sylvia Townsend Warner" by Jane Marcus, in *Women Writers and the City,* edited by Susan Merrill Squier, Knoxville, University of Tennessee Press, 1984; *For Sylvia: An Honest Account* by Valentine Ackland, New York and London, Norton, 1985; *This Narrow Place: Sylvia Townsend Warner and Valentine Ackland: Life, Letters, and Politics, 1930-1951* by Wendy Mulford, London, Pandora Press, 1988; *Sylvia Townsend Warner: A Biography* by Claire Harmon, London, Chatto & Windus, and New York, Viking, 1989; "Exiled to Home: The Poetry of Sylvia Townsend Warner and Valentine Ackland" by Gillian Spraggs, in *Lesbian and Gay Writing: An Anthology of Critical Essays,* edited by Mark Lilly, Philadelphia, Temple University Press, 1990; "Sylvia Townsend Warner and the Counterplot of Lesbian Fiction" by Terry Castle, in *Sexual Sameness: Textual Differences in Lesbian and Gay Writing,* edited by Joseph Bristow, London, Routledge, 1992.

* * *

Sylvia Townsend Warner was an intellectual, writer, and activist whose extraordinary imagination and expansive vision were juxtaposed with a profound understanding of human and animal behavior. Her writing life spanned more than 50 years. She published seven novels, five books of poetry (including one joint book with her lover and life-time companion Valentine Ackland, *Whether a Dove or a Seagull*), 12 collections of short stories, a translation of Marcel Proust, a celebrated biography of T. H. White, and a multitude of articles, stories, and poems in various periodicals, pamphlets, and anthologies. Popular with the Book-of-the-Month-Club and a 40-year contributor to the prestigious magazine *The New Yorker*, Warner was well-loved and highly esteemed in her day and yet has been almost entirely forgotten by today's modern scholars. Unlike her contemporaries James Joyce, Virginia Woolf, and T. S. Eliot, she did not cast herself as a visible participant in, or forger of, literary Modernism. Instead, Warner lived life in the trenches. Her art reflects not only her deep and abiding faith in humanity but also her intense belief that life necessitates active and conscious engagement.

Warner may also have been neglected by Modernist scholars for so long due to the fact that they have found it difficult to categorize her work efficiently. Her fiction skirts genres as widely diverse as fairy tale, the fantastic, realism, and what one may refer to as the historical novel, while never settling distinctively into any single classification. Warner's novels often place the reader in a historical period or context where the boundaries of reality may initially appear to be stable. However, reality, in the world of Warner's fictions, is hardly stable, as fairies, witches, and various other fantastic characters often share the same universe as the radical or the revolutionary. Warner deliberately challenges her readers' complacency with all that may be perceived as familiar and, in so doing, refuses their ability to categorize either perceptions or experiences by means of stable and coherent definitions.

Warner was born in 1893, nine years prior to the end of Queen Victoria's reign. Her immediate contemporaries included writers like Edith Sitwell and Ivy Compton-Burnett and she was only a few years younger than D. H. Lawrence and T. S. Eliot. While her mother, Nora Townsend Warner, was a distant and highly critical presence in Sylvia's life, her father was intimately involved in her educational process. Deemed a disruptive and incorrigible member of her kindergarten class, Warner found herself delivered from a formal education into the hands of her loving and erudite father at an early age. George Townsend Warner was House Master and distinguished professor of history at Harrow, as well as the author of several highly respected books. He immersed his daughter in history, music, and English poetry, while actively encouraging her natural vitality and irrepressible curiosity about the world around her.

As a young adult, Warner had every intention of going to Vienna to study musical composition with Arnold Schönberg. However, the outbreak of World War I thwarted her intentions and she found herself instead working in a munitions factory. Her passion for music was nevertheless followed through on in her role as editor of *Tudor Church Music.* The year 1916 was a crucial turning point for Warner: her beloved father and teacher died, some said as a consequence of the severe grief provoked by the death of so many of his young students in World War I, and she published her first article in *Blackwood's Magazine* based on her experiences working as a "relief munitions worker" during the war. Warner continued for the next ten years as editor of *Tudor Church Music,* while simultaneously instigating the beginnings of her own literary career. 1925 saw the publication of her first collection of poems, *The Espalier*, which was rapidly followed in 1926 by her first novel, *Lolly Willowes. Lolly Willowes,* the story of a 28-year-old spinster-turned-witch, gained wide popular acclaim and was chosen as the first Book-of-the-Month-Club selection. Combining the contemporary with the fantastic, Warner's first novel details the life of Laura/Lolly who, following the death of her father, moves in with her brother Henry's family in London. In her brother's household she all too quickly becomes the ever dependable, self-sacrificing "Aunt Lolly." Passionately in love with the countryside, Laura eventually finds herself heeding a mysterious call to relocate to the rural area called Great Mop. The novel charts Lolly's gradual awakening to the fact that she must have a life she can call her own. Surprisingly, this involves making a pact with the devil, whose "undesiring and unjudging gaze ... and his satisfied but profoundly indifferent ownership" leave her to herself. Towards the end of the novel, Lolly's final declaration of independence entails her full identification with witchcraft, "That's why we become witches: to show our scorn of pretending life's a safe business, to satisfy our passion for adventure ... to have a life of one's own, not an existence doled out to you by others, charitable refuse of their thoughts." Borrowing upon the tradition of pastoral romance as sketched in the novels of late 19th-century writers like Thomas Hardy, Warner creates a supernatural tale that aggressively questions gendered values. Lolly's pursuit of a rural lifestyle mirrors Warner's own lifetime commitment to living in rural as opposed to urban communities.

While *Lolly Willowes* is perhaps the finest example of Warner's tendency towards the supernatural or the fantastic, her 1936 novel *Summer Will Show* illustrates her use of the genre of the historical novel as a means of exploring the personal as political. Warner's own long-term relationship with lover and companion Valentine Ackland is implicitly explored in this novel about a conventional Victorian woman, Sophia, who ultimately journeys to Paris where she befriends the radical Minna and becomes inadvertently involved in the 1848 revolution. Warner and Ackland, united in their resistance of European Fascism, joined the Communist Party in 1930 and left for Spain where they would become actively involved in the Spanish Civil War. *Summer Will Show* begins by suggesting that Victorian mores and conventions are stale. The young men in the novel, like the character Damian, are enervated in comparison to women like Sophia who represent the dawning of the New Woman and the necessity for a new social structure. England, suggests Warner, does not yet offer such a new structure, and, in order for Sophia to liberate herself from the stays of Victorian morality, she must journey to revolutionary Paris. Estranged from her husband Frederick, Sophia makes the trip across the English Channel where, confronted by the terrors and uncertainties of revolution as well as her love for her husband's mistress Minna, she finds herself able to re-imagine herself beyond the rigid parameters of 19th-century Victorian England. The historical and political context of revolutionary Paris becomes a powerful backdrop for Sophia's personal revolution.

Warner continued to explore these themes in later novels, increasingly merging the fantastic and the historical to create often bizarre but nonetheless astute explorations of alternative realities. In 1940's *The Cat's Cradle-Book* Warner tells the story of a young man's search for the origins of narrative. Believing he has found the source in the feline species, the male narrator collects, colonizes, and interrogates the felines in an effort to understand their language, an ethnographic project that ultimately ends up destroying the felines. In a provocative blurring of the borders between human and animal, Warner explores the appropriation of the female body for male storytelling. By figuring females as felines, she tries to imagine mothers not only as the metaphorical bearers of narrative but as cultural speakers, tellers of tales. While the young man, in purchasing the feline's narratives, destroys them, he nevertheless cannot own the tales they tell for they are not text-bound. Warner expresses a deep nostalgia for an oral tradition of storytelling which, historically, was predominantly female.

In addition to experimenting with merging the historical and the fantastic, Warner explored deviating from the linearity of conventional narrative structure. Her 1948 novel *The Corner That Held Them* endeavors to account for the daily life of a group of nuns over a period of approximately 30 years. Shifting inadvertently between characters, the novel explores the quotidian existence of these nuns in prose that replicates the strained discipline of their days and the insipid familiarity of their environment. There is only one incident that incites a lapse into linearity yielding suspense and climax and it has absurd resonance in this otherwise torpid world. Rather than being about the individual characters which it chronicles, this novel, in which the author views her landscape as a vast expanse within which individual lives fail to dominate, is a panoramic exploration of time. While it could be deemed one of Warner's more pessimistic inquiries into humanity, *The Corner That Held Them* is important for its deliberate stylistic assertions against conventional narrative structure.

Towards the end of her career, Warner, then age 80, had a tremendous and final burst of creativity in which she wrote a large number of fairy tales that friend and *New Yorker*-editor William Maxwell referred to as almost uncannily based on first-hand information. The final and most celebrated of these, *The Kingdom of Elfin,* was praised in a contemporary review by *Time* as prose that "duplicates the iridescent beauty of elfin life. Her descriptions are brushed with an unsettling magic." This "unsettling magic" permeates Warner's entire oeuvre. When asked by Maxwell why she had left off composing music, Warner responded that she had come to the conclusion that she didn't do it authentically enough, "whereas when I turned to writing I never have a doubt of what I mean to say." Sylvia Townsend Warner has left us prose that shimmers with magic but that, in the lucidity of its vision, also challenges us to think about the ways in which history makes meaning and meaning, in turn, makes history.

—Kimberly Engdahl

WASSERSTEIN, Wendy

Nationality: American. **Born:** Brooklyn, New York, 18 October 1950. **Education:** Mount Holyoke College, South Hadley, Massachusetts, B.A. 1971; City College of the City University of New York, M.A. 1973; Yale University, M.F.A., 1976. **Career:** Playwright. Teacher, Columbia University, New York, New York; actress in plays, including *The Hotel Play,* 1981. Member of artistic board of Playwrights Horizons. Contributor of articles to periodicals, including *Esquire, New York Times,* and *New York Woman.* **Member:** Dramatists Guild (member of steering committee and women's committee), Dramatists Guild for Young Playwrights. **Awards:** Joseph Jefferson Award, *Dramalogue* Award, and Inner Boston Critics Award, all for *Uncommon Women and Others;* Playwrights Commissioning Program of Phoenix Theater grant, c. 1970s; Hale Mathews Foundation Award; Guggenheim fellowship, 1983; British-American Arts Association grant; American Playwrights Project grant, 1988; Pulitzer Prize for drama, Antoinette Perry Award, for best play from League of American Theatres and Producers, New York Drama Critics' Circle award, and Susan Smith Blackburn Prize, all 1989, all for *The Heidi Chronicles.* **Agent:** International Creative Management, 40 West 57th St., New York, New York 10019, U.S.A.

Publications

Plays

Any Woman Can't (produced Off-Broadway, 1973).

Happy Birthday, Montpelier Pizz-zazz (produced New Haven, Connecticut, 1974).

When Dinah Shore Ruled the Earth, with Christopher Durang (produced New Haven, Connecticut, 1975).

Uncommon Women and Others (one-act; produced New Haven, Connecticut, 1975; revised and enlarged two-act version produced Off-Broadway, 1977). New York, Dramatists Play Service, 1978.

Isn't It Romantic (produced Off-Broadway, 1981; revised version produced Off-Broadway, 1983). Garden City, New York, Doubleday, 1984.

Tender Offer (one-act; produced Off-Off Broadway, 1983).

The Man in a Case (one-act; adapted from short story by Anton Chekhov), in *Orchards* (anthology of seven one-act plays adapted from stories by Chekhov; produced Off-Broadway, 1986). New York, Knopf, 1986.

Miami (musical; produced Off-Broadway, 1986).

The Heidi Chronicles (produced Off-Broadway, 1988; produced Broadway, 1989). New York, Dramatists Play Service, 1990; as *The Heidi Chronicles and Other Plays* (includes *Uncommon Women and Others* and *Isn't It Romantic*), San Diego, Harcourt Brace, 1990; Harmondsworth, Penguin, 1991.

The Sisters Rosensweig (produced 1992). New York, Harcourt Brace, 1993.

Sunset at Camp O'Henry (stage conception, with Gerald Gutierrez). N.P., n.d.

Television Plays: *Uncommon Women and Others,* from her own play, 1978; *The Sorrows of Gin,* from the short story by John Cheever, 1979; *Drive,* n.d.; *She Said,* n.d.; *Comedy Zone,* 1984. *The Heidi Chronicles,* from her own play, 1991.

Essays

Bachelor Girls. New York, Knopf, 1990.

*

Critical Studies: "Uncommon Woman: An Interview with Wendy Wasserstein" by Esther Cohen, in *Women's Studies: An Interdisciplinary Journal,* 15(1-3), 1988; "Comic Textures and Female Communities 1937 and 1977: Clare Boothe and Wendy Wasserstein" by Susan L. Carlson, in *Modern Drama,* 27, December 1984; *Modern American Drama: the Female Canon,* edited by June Schlueter, Rutherford, New Jersey, Fairleigh Dickinson University Press, 1990; "Feminism, Postfeminism, and *The Heidi Chronicles*" by Bette Mandl, in *Studies in the Humanities,* 17(2), December 1990; "Drama and the Dialogic Imagination: *The Heidi Chronicles* and

Fefu and Her Friends" by Helene Keyssar, in *Modern Drama,* 34(1), March 1991.

* * *

Born in New York City in 1950, Wendy Wasserstein attended several prestigious girl's schools, most notably the conservative Mount Holyoke College. At Mount Holyoke, Wasserstein cultivated her sometimes wry sense of humor. Surveying prospects for a career in either business or in law after completion of her Master's Degree at City University, the future Pulitzer Prize winner ultimately opted for the greater attraction of writing plays. She entered Yale Drama School. There she became friends with Christopher Durang, a fellow classmate who encouraged her play writing and with whom she later collaborated. Under the leadership of Robert Brustein, of Yale's elite drama school, the young playwright flourished and developed great discipline. She became engrossed in the plays of 19th-century Russian author Anton Chekhov, one of the forefathers of modern drama, and scrutinized the elder playwright's work intensely—Chekhov's influence unmistakably surfaces in Wasserstein's own later dramas, especially in her subtle portrayal of emotions.

Devoid of bombast, Wasserstein's plays—especially her situation comedies—adopt an emotional tenor of reservedness. In 1983's serious one-act drama, *Tender Offer,* for example, little action occurs. No one screams, storms out of a room, or gets killed; nonetheless, enormous changes occur in the characters. The theme itself, subtly conveyed, underscores the need for empathetic communication between a father, Paul, and his daughter, Lisa, as Wasserstein demonstrates that the special ingredient of effective communication is contingent upon mutual understanding. By the play's end, Paul and his daughter learn to respect one another's language and perspective. The absent father and the rebellious, truculent daughter unite, as underscored by their "harmony" of song and dance. Thus, Wasserstein's play "tenders" a kind of romance, one in which both characters learn to forgive, to respect, and to appreciate one another. Most importantly, father and daughter again participate in one another's lives, a prerequisite to the healing of old wounds.

Similar to *Tender Offer,* the Chekhovian-like comedy *The Sisters Rosensweig* offers little action; yet, overnight, the sisters change positively. A kind of Jewish version of the McGrath sisters of Beth Henley's *Crimes of the Heart,* the Rosensweig sisters find unity, love, and strength in each other, in a sense of community—despite their old irritations, fears, and reservations. Indeed, they are marked by their humanity and compassion—also similar to the McGraths—for they demonstrate an ability to reach beyond themselves and to embrace others, even to discover new love.

Uncommon Women and Others, a comedy, also chooses as its focus the world of women. Critic Susan L. Carlson likens the "play's superstructure of five main characters playing out social roles against a backdrop of clearly typed characters" to Clare Boothe's *The Women* (1937). Here, Wasserstein introduces a collection of various kinds of women: from the traditional wife, who chooses the role of reflecting light from her husband's "star," to the female who boasts a professional career or who proclaims radical feminist notions. Again, Wasserstein highlights female community and friendship, even amidst the tension ignited by woman's trying to "fit in" to prescribed social roles, yet simultaneously, attempting to "define herself."

Wasserstein's most acclaimed play and winner of the 1989 Pulitzer Prize, *The Heidi Chronicles* tracks its heroine for over 25 years, from her days of high school social activism in the 1960s, through the rise of the feminist movement and a developing "feminist consciousness" in the 1970s, to her professional career and partial disillusionment in the 1980s. Choosing a career as an art historian, Wasserstein's protagonist often lectures about the absence of women artists in history books. The play appeals to feminists especially because they identify with the protagonist's struggle for change and search for her own identity. At times, self-effacing, but at other times, powerful and wise beyond her years, Heidi makes audiences believe in her. Her struggle is, in many ways, our own.

—Linda Rohrer Paige

WATKINS, Gloria. *See* **hooks, bell.**

WEBB, (Martha) Beatrice

Nationality: British. **Born:** Standish, Gloucestershire, 22 January 1858. **Education:** Educated privately. **Family:** Married the economist Sidney Webb in 1892. **Career:** Social worker and assistant to Charles Booth; cofounder, with Sidney Webb, London School of Economics, 1895; member, Royal Commission on Poor Law and Unemployment, 1905-09; member, government committees, including Grants in Aid of Distress in London, 1914-14, Statutory War Pensions Committee, 1916-17, Reconstruction Committee, and Committee on National Registration, both 1917-18, Committee on the Machinery of Government, 1918-19, War Cabinet Committee on Women in Industry, 1918-19, and Lord Chancellor's Advisory Committee for Women Justices, 1919-20; cofounder, with husband, *The New Statesman,* 1913; justice of the peace, London, 1919-27. **Awards:** D.Litt.: University of Manchester; LL.D.: University of Edinburgh; D. in political economy, University of Munich. Fellow, British Academy, 1931. **Member:** Fabian Society. **Died:** 30 April 1943.

SELECTED PUBLICATIONS

Political/Social Theory

The Co-operative Movement in Great Britain. London, Sonnenschein, and New York, Scribner, 1891.

How Best to Do Away with the Sweating System. Manchester, Co-operative Union, 1892.

A History of Trade Unionism, with Sidney Webb. London and New York, Longmans, 1894; revised edition, 1920.

Women and the Factory Acts. London, Fabian Society, 1896.

Industrial Democracy, with Sidney Webb. London and New York, Longmans, 2 vols., 1897; revised, 1920.

Problems of Modern Industry. London and New York, Longmans, 1898.
English Local Government, with Sidney Webb. London and New York, Longmans, 11 vols., 1903-11.
The New Crusade against Destitution. Manchester, National Labour Press, 1910.
The State and the Doctor. London and New York, Longmans, 1910.
A Woman's Appeal: ... Personal Expenditures in Wartimes. London, National War Savings committee, 1916.
The Abolition of the Poor Law. London, Fabian Society, 1918.
The Wages of Men and Women: Should They Be Equal? London, Fabian Society, 1919.
The Decay of Capitalist Civilisation, with Sidney Webb. London, Fabian Society, and New York, Harcourt Brace, 1923.
A New Reform Bill. London, Fabian Society, 1931.

Essays

The Relationship between Co-operation and Trade Unionism (lecture). Manchester, Co-operative Union, 1892.

Uncollected Essays

"The Dock Life of East London," in *Nineteenth Century,* 11, 1887.
"East London Labour," in *Nineteen Century,* 24, 1888.
"Pages from a Working-Girl's Diary," in *Nineteenth Century,* 24, 1888.
"The Lords and the Sweating System," in *Nineteenth Century,* 27, 1890.
"The Failure of the Labour Commission," in *Nineteenth Century,* 36, 1894.
"Law and the Laundry," with Helen Bosanquet and Louise Creighton, *Nineteenth Century,* 41, 1897.

Autobiography

My Apprenticeship. London and New York, Longmans, 1926.
Our Partnership, edited by Barbara Drake and Margaret I. Cole. London and New York, Longmans, 1948.
Diaries, 1912-1932, edited by Margaret I Cole. London and New York, Longmans, 2 vols., 1952-56.
American Diary, 1898, edited by David A. Shannon. Madison, University of Wisconsin Press, 1963.
The Diary of Beatrice Webb, edited by Norman and Jeanne MacKenzie. London, Virago/London School of Economics, 4 vols., 1982.

Other

The Letters of Sidney and Beatrice Webb, edited by Norman MacKenzie. London, Oxford University Press, 3 vols., 1978.

Editor, *The Case for the Factory Acts.* London, Richards, and New York, Dutton, 1901.

*

Bibliography: *Publications of Sidney and Beatrice Webb: An Interim Checklist,* London, British Library of Political and Economic Science, 1973.

Manuscript Collections: British Library of Political and Economic Science, London; Bodleian Library, Oxford; British Library, London; National Library of Scotland; Sheffield University Library; National Library of Wales; Cambridge University; Internationaal Instituut voor Social Geschiedenis, Amsterdam; Plunkett Foundation for Co-operative Studies, Oxford; McMaster University, Hamilton, Ontario; House of Lords Record Office, London; National Museum of Labour History, Manchester, England; Sussex University Library, Sussex, England; Nuffield College Library, Oxford University.

Critical Studies: *Sidney and Beatrice Webb* by Mary A. Hamilton, London, Sampson Low, 1933; *Beatrice Webb* by Margaret Cole, London, Longmans, 1945, New York, Harcourt Brace, 1946; *The Pursuit of Certainty: David Hume, Jeremy Bentham, John Stuart Mill, Beatrice Webb* by Shirley R. Letwin, Cambridge, Cambridge University Press, 1967; *The Life of Beatrice Webb* by K. Muggeridge and R. Adam, London, n.p., 1968; *A Victorian Courtship: The Story of Beatrice Potter and Sidney Webb* by Jeanne MacKenzie, London, Weidenfeld & Nicolson, 1979; *The Apprenticeship of Beatrice Webb* by Deborah Epstein Nord, Amherst, University of Massachusetts Press, 1985; *Beatrice Webb: A Life* by Carole Seymour-Jones, Chicago, I. R. Dee, 1992.

* * *

Beatrice Webb was born in 1858 near Gloucester, the eighth of nine daughters. Her father, Richard Potter, was a financier, and in her autobiography, *My Apprenticeship,* published in 1926, she recollected that "he was the only man I ever knew who genuinely believed that women were superior to men, and acted as if he did; the paradoxical result being that all his nine daughters started life as anti-feminists!"

Although Webb was not directly involved in any woman's rights campaign she did address the issue of women's wages and their working conditions in such publications as *The Wages of Men and Women: Should They Be Equal?* However, she refused to focus her attention on the plight of women only because to do so would be to adopt a gender-exclusive and -inclusive interpretation of social and economic problems. Webb's importance within the feminist movement, therefore, was as an illustration of an educated woman's ambivalence. Although she signed the 1889 anti-suffrage petition which had been drafted by Mrs. Humphrey Ward, Webb later referred to her support of Ward's efforts as "a false step" motivated by the narrow outlook of women's suffrage, which focused on the vote for single, propertied women, as well as by her own inability to directly identify with the plight of most women because she had never experienced personally the "disabilities" associated with having been born female.

If Webb can, in any way, be considered a feminist, then, it would be as a "different" feminist. She was acutely aware of the differences between men and women and believed that the sexes had been created for different roles in life. She shared the Positivist view that women possessed innate characteristics that channelled them towards domesticity. She regarded child rearing, teaching and fostering spirituality as the *raison d'etre* of all women, yet by 1906, as the militant women's suffrage campaign got underway, she understood that these areas were also the concern of the state, and that women should be given the obligation, for she did not believe in arbitrarily assigned rights to participate directly in the workings of government. For Webb this meant suffrage for all women, married or propertied or not.

In 1908 Webb was a founder member of the Fabian Women's Group, established to study women's economic situation and to advance the concept of economic equality with men. Ten years later she was appointed to the War Cabinet Committee on Women in Industry and in 1919 to the Lord Chancellor's Advisory Committee for Women Justices. She is perhaps best known for her partnership, both professional and personal, with Sidney Webb, for being a Fabian, and for her investigations into late-19th and early-20th century social and industrial conditions. She worked for the Charity Organisation Society for five years beginning in 1882, and contributed to Charles Booth's Life and Labour of the People. In the years up to World War I, Webb also served on numerous Royal Commissions and Committees, including the Royal Commission on the Poor Law, the Government Committee upon Grants in Aid of Distress in London, and the Statutory War Pensions Committee. She collaborated with her husband on a number of projects including *The History of Trade Unionism, Industrial Democracy,* and a multi-volume study entitled *English Local Government.* Together the Webbs helped found the London School of Economics in 1895 and *The New Statesman* in 1913. Beatrice Webb became Lady Passfield in 1929 and died in 1943.

—Lori Williamson

WEBB, Mary (Gladys)

Nationality: British. **Born:** Mary Meredith, Leighton-under-the-Wrekin, Shropshire, 25 March 1881. **Education:** Educated at home and for two years at a private school in Lancashire. **Family:** Married Henry Bertram Law in 1912. **Career:** Contracted Graves' disease (hyperthyroidism) in 1901; market gardener in Weston-super-Mare, Somerset, and Lyth Hill, Shropshire, 1915-20; lived in London from 1921; reviewer for periodicals, including *Bookman.* **Awards:** Femina-Vie Heureuse prize, 1926, for *Precious Bane.* **Died:** 8 October 1927.

Publications

Novels

The Golden Arrow. London, Constable, 1916.
Gone to Earth. London, Constable, and New York, Dutton, 1917.
The House in Dormer Forest. London, Hutchinson, 1920; New York, Doran, 1921.
Seven for a Secret: A Love Story. London, Hutchinson, 1922; New York, Doran, 1923.
Precious Bane. London, Cape, and New York, Dutton, 1924.
Armour Wherein He Trusted: A Novel and Some Stories. London, Cape, 1928; New York Dutton, 1929.

Short Stories

The Chinese Lion. London, B. Rota, 1937.

Essays

The Spring of Joy: A Little Book of Healing. London, Dent, and New York Dutton, 1917.

Poetry

Poems, and The Spring of Joy. London, n.p., 1928; New York, Dutton, 1929.
Fifty-one Poems. London, Cape, 1946; New York, Dutton, 1947.

Other

The Spring of Joy: Poems, Some Prose Pieces, and the Unfinished Novel Armour Wherein He Trusted. London, Cape, and New York, Dutton, 1937.
Collected Prose and Poems, edited by Gladys Mary Coles. Shrewsbury, Wildings, 1977.
A Mary Webb Anthology, edited by H. B. L. Webb. London, Cape, 1939; New York, Dutton, 1940.

*

Media Adaptation: *Precious Bane* (play), 1932.

Bibliography: *Mary Webb: A Narrative Bibliography of Her Life and Works* by Gordon Dickins, 1981.

Critical Studies: *Mary Webb: A Short Study of Her Life and Work* by Hilda Addison, n.p., 1931; *Goodbye to Morning: A Biographical Study of Mary Webb* by Dorothy P. H. Wrenn, n.p., 1964; *The Flower of Light: A Biography of Mary Webb* by Gladys Mary Coles, London, Duckworth, 1978; *Daughters and Lovers: The Life and Writing of Mary Webb* by Michèle Aina Barale, Middletown, Connecticut, Wesleyan University Press, 1986; *Mary Webb* by Coles, Bridgend, Mid Glamorgan, Seren, 1990.

* * *

Mary Webb was born and raised in the Shropshire region of England. As a child, she reveled in Shropshire's lush, natural terrain and as an adult it is this terrain that consistently inspired her fiction. However, the fiction is not merely a meditation on the natural environment Webb grew to know and love so well. Rather, it is a sophisticated look at the transition from the Edenic world of childhood to the more complicated world of adulthood. Webb was painfully familiar with this transition. At the young age of 20 she contracted Graves' disease and forever left the untainted world of her childhood behind her. However, she never lost contact with the natural world that had so sustained her as a child. Instead, that world literally becomes a character within her fictions, sustaining her protagonists against the brutality and chaos of the unnatural social world.

Webb's novels, most of which are love stories, repeatedly explore a process of awakening in her female protagonists who must move from a stage of animal innocence—in which all actions are intuitive and spontaneous—to the chaos that ensues as a result of a passionate encounter with another human being. Leaving behind the relative safety and natural logic of the animal kingdom, Webb's heroines experience the suffering that inevitably commences with adult sexuality. Her characters, all of whom have a deep connection with nature, are forced to exchange their previous Edenic bliss for a temporal love in which human mortality, duality, death, and decay cannot be denied. While she has often been dismissed by critics as a sentimentalist and an idealist, such readings fail to account for the astute insight Webb had into the female condition.

In each novel she wrote, she struggled to find a definition of female happiness. Most often, her definition of complete happiness entailed total immersion in nature and thus isolation from the social world. However, realistically, Webb knew that life cannot be lived in such isolation. Thus, her novels are an attempt to bridge the gap between the isolated self and society.

For women in the late 19th and 20th century this attempt is particularly charged because entry into society essentially entailed self-renunciation. While Webb's heroines ultimately marry, thereby entering into a socially sanctioned institution—and hence society—the actual marital act is really inconsequential. For each of her female protagonists marry, not for social or moral approval, but instead freely choose their desired partner regardless of the ramifications. Thus, Webb's romantic conclusions are enacted by two individuals who, while they perform the socially prescribed ceremony of marriage, nevertheless refuse to choose a partner according to the dictates of their society. Webb figures this repudiation again and again in an effort to contend with her own fear of complete social isolation.

The two novels that best enact the tension between the natural and the social world are *Gone to Earth,* published in 1917, and *Precious Bane,* published in 1926. In the former, the inability to reconcile the two worlds results in a brutal and tragic ending, while in the latter, the possibility of a creative union between the two is imagined. Hazel Woodus, the female protagonist in *Gone to Earth,* longs only to continue her life in the woods with her animal companion "Foxy," free from any social or moral constraints. The story Webb weaves, however, implies that life in its essence demands growth and for women such growth entails marriage and children. Hazel's options, as she is tied to a woman's body, are either to marry or to die. Webb's implication is that no woman can escape the destiny ascribed to her by her vulnerable female body. Hence, in spite of her efforts to refuse the social and moral demands of society, Hazel is raped, impregnated, and ultimately cruelly murdered by her ravager's hunting dogs as she runs, heavy with child, in an attempt to save "Foxy" from his demise. While Webb suggests women's inability to escape the social world due to the vulnerability of her female body, she also provides us with a story of courage and a woman's refusal to be constrained, even if that refusal means death, by the life society wills she must lead.

Precious Bane, perhaps Webb's most celebrated novel, is most certainly a direct expression of her own experience with physical deformity due to Graves' disease. Prue Sarn, the heroine of *Precious Bane* is born with a harelip, which the country folk believe to be the sign of a witch. Alienated as a result of her deformity, that deformity is nevertheless Prue's "precious bane" for it enables her to follow a different pattern than that allotted to other women in her village, namely the roles of wife and mother. While Prue initially mourns the feminine life she had seen herself as desiring, she soon learns to delight in and profit from her autonomy. Unable to marry due to her deformity, she agrees to labor as "a prentice, a wife, and a dog" for her brother Gideon who promises her, in return for her labor, a house and furniture as well as china and gowns. Although Gideon's assumption of their farm following their mother's death and his consequent greed force Prue into a life of cruel servitude, she nevertheless gains the benefit of learning to read and write. As a result of this knowledge, she begins writing letters to Kester Woodseaves, a weaver who she has for so long loved and admired. Kester is successfully wooed and marries Prue in spite of her harelip, thus enabling her to escape from the merciless Gideon. While Prue's escape is indeed dependent on another man, Webb quite deliberately insists on the agency allotted to her due to her ability to read and write. As Michèle Aina Barale suggests in her book *Daughters and Lovers: The Life and Writing of Mary Webb, Precious Bane* can be read as an "allegory" of the authoring woman whose "needs and talents set her apart, label her as 'witch' and as 'unnatural', ally her with the world of men and power rather than home and hearth, but who finds her literary 'curse' the means by which she can alleviate her own unhappiness."

Mary Webb has often been cited as a Regionalist writer, a category that has proven to be a means of dismissing the accomplishments of such women writers as the Americans Sarah Orne Jewett and Mary Wilkins Freeman. While Webb powerfully chronicles the lives and environment inherent to the Shropshire region, her heroines, as they struggle to reconcile their status as women with their desire both for love and self-actualization, speak to an audience that is by no means limited to the rural confines of England's Shropshire.

—Kimberly Engdahl

WEIL, Simone (Adolphine)

Pseudonym: Émile Novis. **Nationality:** French. **Born:** Paris, 3 February 1909. **Education:** Lycée Henri IV, Paris, agrégation 1931. **Military Service:** Served briefly in the Spanish Republican Army, 1936. **Career:** Taught philosophy at lycées in Le Puy, Auxerre, Roanne, Bourges, and Saint-Quentin, 1931-37; factory worker, 1934-35, and farm worker in Marsailles, 1941; left France to join the Free French Forces in London, 1942. **Died:** Of self-starvation, Ashford, Kent, 24 August 1943.

Publications

Political/Social Theory

L'Enracinement: Prelude à une déclaracion des devoirs envers l'être humain. Paris, Gallimard, 1949; as *The Need for Roots,* London, Kegan Paul, 1952; New York, Putnam, 1953.

Oppression et Liberté. Paris, Gallimard, 1955; as *Oppression and Liberty,* London, Routledge, 1958.

Écrits historiques et politiques [Historical and Political Writing]. Paris, Gallimard, 1960.

Philosophy

Leçons de philosophie (Roanne 1933-1934), edited by Anne Reynaud. Paris, Plon, 1959; as *Lectures on Philosophy,* London, Cambridge University Press, 1978.

Simone Weil's Philosophy of Culture: Readings towards a Divine Humanity, edited by Richard Bell. Cambridge, Cambridge University Press, 1993.

Religion/Spirituality

Attente de Dieu. Paris, La Colombe, 1950; as *Waiting for God,* London, Kegan Paul, and New York, Putnam, 1951.

Lettre à un religieux. Paris, Gallimard, 1951; as *Letter to a Priest,* London, Routledge, 1953; New York, Putnam, 1954.

Intuitions pré-chrétiennes. Paris, La Colombe, 1951; as *Intimations of Christianity,* London, Routledge, 1957; Boston, Beacon Press, 1958.
La Source grecque. Paris, Gallimard, 1953; selections in *Intimations of Christianity,* 1957.
Pensées sans ordre concernant l'amour de Dieu [Random Thoughts concerning the Love of God]. Paris, Gallimard, 1962.

Essays

La Condition ouvrière. Paris, Gallimard, 1951.
Selected Essays. London, Oxford University Press, 1962.
On Science, Necessity, and the Love of God, edited by Richard Rees. London and New York, Oxford University Press, 1967.
Formative Writings, 1929-1941, edited by Dorothy Tuck McFarland and Wilhelmina Van Ness. Amherst, University of Massachusetts Press, 1987.

Poetry

"L'Iliade; ou, Le Poème de la force" (as Émile Novis), in *Le Cahiers du Sud* (Marseilles) 26, 1947; translated by Mary McCarthy as *The Iliad; or, The Poem of Force,* n.p., Politics Pamphlets, 1947; Wallingford, Pennsylvania, Pendle Hill Pamphlets, 1956.
Poèmes, suivis de Venis sauvée. Paris, Gallimard, 1968.

Play

Venise sauvée: Tragédie en trois actes. Paris, Gallimard, 1955.

Autobiography

Cahiers. Paris, Plon, 3 vols., 1951-56; as *The Notebooks of Simone Weil,* London, Kegan Paul, and New York, Putnam, 2 vols., 1956.

Other

La Pesanteur et la Grâce. Paris, Plon, 1947; as *Gravity and Grace,* London, Routledge, 1952.
La Connaissance surnaturelle. Paris, Gallimard, 1950.
Écrits de Londres et dernières lettres. Paris, Gallimard, 1957.
The Simone Weil Reader, edited by George A. Panichas. New York, McKay, 1977.
Simone Weil: An Anthology, edited by Sian Miles. New York, Weidenfeld & Nicolson, 1986.
Seventy Letters, edited by Richard Rees. London and New York, Oxford University Press, 1965.

*

Media Adaptations: *The Panel* (play) by Dorothy Bryant, 1992.

Bibliography: In *Simone Weil: A Fellowship in Love* by Jacques Cabaud, New York, Channel Press, 1964.

Critical Studies: *Simone Weil as We Knew Her* by J.M. Perrin and Gustave Thibon, London, Routledge, 1952; *Simone Weil* by E. W. F. Tomlin, Cambridge, Bowes & Bowes, and New Haven, Connecticut, Yale University Press, 1954; *Simone Weil: A Fellowship in Love* by Jacques Cabaud, New York, Channel Press, 1964; *Juicios sumarios* [Summary Judgements] by Rosario Castellanos, Jalapa, Mexico, Universidad Veracruzana, 1966; *Simone Weil: A Life* by Simone Pétrement, New York, Pantheon, 1976, London, Mowbrays, 1977; *Simone Weil: Interpretations of a Life* edited by George Abbott White, Amherst, University of Massachusetts Press, 1981; *Simone Weil: An Introduction to Her Thought* by John Hellman, Waterloo, Ontario, Wilfrid Laurier University Press, 1982; *Three Outsider: Pascal, Kierkegaard, Simone Weil* by Diogenes Allen, Cambridge, Massachusetts, Cowley, 1983; *Christus Mediator: Platonic Mediation in the Thought of Simone Weil* by Eric O. Springsted, Chico, California, Scholars, 1983; *Simone Weil* by Dorothy Tuck McFarland, New York, F. Ungar, 1983; *Simone Weil* by John M. Dunaway, Boston, Twayne, 1984; "Sister/Outsider: Some Thoughts on Simone Weil" by Michelle Cliff, in *Between Women: Biographers, NOvelists, Critics, Teachers, adn Artists Write about Their Works on Women,* edited by Carol Ascher, Louise DeSalvo, and Sara Ruddick, Boston, Beacon Press, 1984; *A Sketch for a Portrait* by Richard Rees, n.p., n.d.; *Simone Weil: "The Just Balance"* by Peter Winch, Cambridge, Cambridge University Press, 1989; *Looking for Heroes in Postwar France: Albert Camus, Max Jacob, and Simone Weil* by Neil Oxenhandler, Dartmouth, University Press of New England, 1995.

* * *

Dubbed "the saint of all outsiders" by writer Andre Gidé, Simone Weil was an innovative contributor to 20th-century thought whose writings have gained serious recognition from scholars and students of literature. Her diverse talents led her into a wide range of disciplines, including philosophy, political ideology, social criticism, religious and spiritual discourse, poetry, and drama. Her steadfast dedication to her political beliefs, along with her emphasis on self-sacrifice and humility, enhanced her literary efforts, giving her various texts an admirable sense of honesty and authenticity. Weil was a zealous advocate of political reform, and her compassion for the lower classes and democratic sensibilities make her work accessible to present-day readers. Sadly, it was this very sympathy and rigid adherence to the principle of self-denial that led to her death in 1943 at the age of 34.

Weil was born in Paris, France, on 3 February 1909. After graduating from the Lycee Henri IV in Paris in 1931, she taught philosophy at lycées in Le Puy, Auxerre, Roanne, Bourges, and Saint-Quentin until 1937. During this time, devoted to self-sacrifice and hoping to acquire a greater empathy for the working classes, Weil served in the Spanish Republican Army for a brief period in 1936 and worked as a factory worker from 1934 to 1935. In 1941 she worked as a farm laborer in Marsailles. The outbreak of World War II signified a turning point in her life and career. In 1942, during the Nazi occupation of France, Weil went to London to work at the Headquarters of the Provisional French Government. There she aligned her efforts with the Free French Forces, an active resistance organization. Her health weakened by years of self-denial and poor eating (some would term her anorexic), she entered the Middlesex hospital in 1943, where doctors discovered that she was suffering from tuberculosis. After being sent to a sanitorium in Ashford, Kent, Weil continued her practice of self-sacrifice, eating only small amounts of food out of sympathy for the conditions of the working classes in occupied France. She told attendants at the sanitorium that she would only eat as much food as she believed Hitler allotted to the average working man or woman in her native country. A month after arriving at the sanitorium, Weil died; the doctors who examined her ruled her death a suicide.

As a literary figure, Weil exemplified the modernist emphasis on the search for identity and spiritual truths in an environment characterized by chaos, political turmoil, and religious doubt. While working as teacher, army volunteer, factory worker, and farm laborer in the 1930s and early 1940s, she began writing essays that addressed her awakening political sensibilities. In these early writings, she promoted pacifism, libertarian social reform, and democratic unionism, while expressing her genuine concern for the plight of the lower classes. Translated versions of these essays were published posthumously as *The Need for Roots* in 1952 and *Oppression and Liberty* in 1958. Others were published in Paris in 1960 in the collection *Écrits historiques et politiques.* Weil's lectures at the lycée at Roanne were published in translation in 1978 in *Lectures on Philosophy.* This collection provides fascinating insight into her developing philosophical perspective during these formative years.

Besides political theory, social criticism, and philosophy, Weil was an influential writer in the area of religion and spirituality. Refusing to ally herself to any church, several mystical experiences in the 1930s prompted her to embrace self-deprivation as a means by which to achieve spiritual insight. Weil thus adapted the "imitation of Christ" concept to her own thinking regarding spiritual inquiry. This preoccupation with self-abnegation and sacrifice intensified her sympathies for the working classes and the under-privileged. In her renowned work, *Attente de Dieu* (*Waiting for God*), published in 1950, Weil endorses the strategy of deliberately removing oneself from the materialistic aspects of the world to achieve spiritual bliss. Her other religious writings, all published posthumously, include *Lettre à un religieux* (*Letter to a Priest*) (1951), *Intuitions pré-chrétiennes* (*Intimations of Christianity*) (1951), and *Pensées sans ordre concernant l'amour de Dieu* (1962). Students of 20th-century literature, readers of French literature, and Weil scholars have also identified religious themes and her emphasis on the immediacy of spiritual experiences in essays translated in such collections as *Selected Essays* (1962) and *On Science, Necessity, and the Love of God* (1967). Critics have compared her religious writings to the work of Blaise Pascal and Ludwig Wittgenstein, praising her philosophical insight and her literary prowess.

Weil's extraordinary literary talents found many outlets. Writing under the pseudonym Émile Novis, she wrote "L'Iliade; ou, Le Poème de la force," which was translated by Mary McCarthy in 1947 as *The Iliad; or, The Poem of Force.* A play, *Venise sauvée: Tragédie en trois actes,* was published in 1955. Translations of Weil's extensive notebooks were published in a two-volume set in 1956. Throughout her works, notebooks, and letters, Simone Weil's dedication to political and social reform, as well as her democratic sympathy for working men and women and the under-privileged, can be seen as a provocative and influential feature of her literary expression.

—Richard Williamson

WELDON, Fay

Nationality: British. **Born:** Fay Birkinshaw in Alvechurch, Worcestershire, 22 September 1931; raised in New Zealand. **Education:** Attended Girls' High School, Christchurch, and Hampstead Girls' High School, London; University of St. Andrews, Fife, M.A. in economics and psychology 1952. **Family:** Married Ronald Weldon in 1960; four sons. **Career:** Writer for the Foreign Office and *Daily Mirror,* both London, late 1950s; later worked as an advertising copywriter. **Awards:** Writers Guild award, 1973, for radio play; Giles Cooper award, 1978, for radio play; Society of Authors traveling scholarship, 1981; Los Angeles *Times* award for fiction, 1989. D.Litt.: University of Bath, 1988; University of St. Andrews, 1992. **Agent:** Sheilhand Associates, 43 Doughty Street, London WC1N 2LF, England.

Publications

Novels

The Fat Woman's Joke. London, MacGibbon & Kee, 1967; as *. . . and the Wife Ran Away,* New York, McKay, 1968.

Down among the Women. London, Heinemann, 1971; New York, St. Martin's Press, 1972.

Female Friends. London, Heinemann, and New York, St. Martin's Press, 1975.

Remember Me. London, Hodder & Stoughton, and New York, Random House, 1976.

Words of Advice. New York, Random House, 1977; as *Little Sisters,* London, Hodder & Stoughton, 1978.

Praxis. London, Hodder & Stoughton, and New York, Summit, 1978.

Puffball. London, Hodder & Stoughton, and New York, Summit, 1980.

The President's Child. London, Hodder & Stoughton, 1982; Garden City, New York, Doubleday, 1983.

The Life and Loves of a She-Devil. London, Hodder & Stoughton, 1983; New York, Pantheon, 1984.

The Shrapnel Academy. London, Hodder & Stoughton, 1986; New York, Viking, 1987.

The Heart of the Country. London, Hutchinson, 1987; New York, Viking, 1988.

The Hearts and Lives of Men. London, Heinemann, 1987; New York, Viking, 1988.

Leader of the Band. London, Hodder & Stoughton, 1988; New York, Viking, 1989.

The Cloning of Joanna May. London, Collins, 1989; New York, Viking, 1990.

Darcy's Utopia. London, Collins, 1990; New York, Viking, 1991.

Life Force. London, Collins, and New York, Viking, 1992.

Affliction. London, Collins, 1994; as *Trouble,* New York, Viking, 1994.

Splitting. New York, Atlantic Monthly Press, 1994.

Short Stories

Watching Me, Watching You. London, Hodder & Stoughton, and New York, Summit, 1981.

Polaris and Other Stories. London, Hodder & Stoughton, 1985; New York, Penguin, 1989.

The Rules of Life (novella). London, Hutchinson, and New York, Harper, 1987.

Moon over Minneapolis. London, HarperCollins, 1991.

Wicked Women. London, HarperCollins, 1995.

Uncollected Short Story

"Ind Aff; or, Out of Love in Sarajevo," in *Best Short Stories 1989,* edited by Giles Gordon and David Hughes. London, Heinemann, 1989; as *The Best English Short Stories 1989,* New York, Norton, 1989.

Plays

Permanence, in *We Who Are about to . . .* , later called *Mixed Doubles* (produced London, 1969). London, Methuen, 1970.
Time Hurries On, in *Scene Scripts,* edited by Michael Marland. London, Longman, 1972.
Words of Advice (produced London, 1974). London, French, 1974.
Friends (produced Richmond, Surrey, 1975).
Moving House (produced Farnham, Surrey, 1976).
Mr. Director (produced Richmond, Surrey, 1978).
Polaris (broadcast 1978). In *Best Radio Plays of 1978,* London, Eyre Methuen, 1979.
Action Replay (produced Birmingham, 1978; as *Love among the Women,* produced Vancouver, 1982). London, French, 1980.
I Love My Love (broadcast 1981; produced Richmond, Surrey, 1982). London, French, 1984.
After the Prize (produced New York, 1981; as *Word Worm,* produced Newbury, Berkshire, 1984).
Jane Eyre, adaptation of the novel by Charlotte Brontë (produced Birmingham, 1986).
The Hole in the Top of the World (produced Richmond, Surrey, 1987).
Someone like You, music by Petula Clark and Dee Shipman (produced London, 1990).

Radio Plays: *Spider,* 1973; *Housebreaker,* 1973; *Mr. Fox and Mr. First,* 1974; *The Doctor's Wife,* 1975; *Polaris,* 1978; *Weekend,* 1979; *All the Bells of Paradise,* 1979; *I Love My Love,* 1981; *The Hole in the Top of the World,* 1993.

Television Plays: *Wife in a Blonde Wig,* 1966; *A Catching Complaint,* 1966; *The Fat Woman's Tale,* 1966; *What about Me,* 1967; *Dr. De Waldon's Therapy,* 1967; *Goodnight Mrs. Dill,* 1967; *The 45th Unmarried Mother,* 1967; *Fall of the Goat,* 1967; *Ruined Houses,* 1968; *Venus Rising,* 1968; *The Three Wives of Felix Hull,* 1968; *Hippy Hippy Who Cares,* 1968; *£13083,* 1968; *The Loophole,* 1969; *Smokescreen,* 1969; *Poor Mother,* 1970; *Office Party,* 1970; "On Trial" (*Upstairs, Downstairs* series), 1971; *Old Man's Hat,* 1972; *A Splinter of Ice,* 1972; *Hands,* 1972; *The Lament of an Unmarried Father,* 1972; *A Nice Rest,* 1972; *Comfortable Words,* 1973; *Desirous of Change,* 1973; *In Memoriam,* 1974; *Poor Baby,* 1975; *The Terrible Tale of Timothy Bagshott,* 1975; *Aunt Tatty,* from the story by Elizabeth Bowen, 1975; *Act of Rape,* 1977; "Married Love" (*Six Women* series), 1977; "Act of Hypocrisy" (*Jubilee* series), 1977; "Chickabiddy" (*Send in the Girls* series), 1978; *Pride and Prejudice,* from the novel by Jane Austen, 1980; *Honey Ann,* 1980; *Life for Christine,* 1980; "Watching Me, Watching You" (*Leap in the Dark* series), 1980; *Little Mrs. Perkins,* from a story by Penelope Mortimer, 1982; *Redundant! or, The Wife's Revenge,* 1983; *Out of the Undertow,* 1984; "Bright Smiles" (*Time for Murder* series), 1985; "Zoe's Fever" (*Ladies in Charge* series), 1986; "A Dangerous Kind of Love" (*Mountain Men* series), 1986; episodes of *Heart of the Country* series, 1987.

For Children

Wolf the Mechanical Dog. London, Collins, 1988.
Party Puddle. London, Collins, 1989.

Other

Simple Steps to Public Life, with Pamela Anderson and Mary Stott. London, Virago Press, 1980.
Letters to Alice: On First Reading Jane Austen. London, Joseph, 1984; New York, Taplinger, 1985.
Rebecca West. London and New York, Viking, 1985.
Sacred Cows. London, Chatto & Windus, 1989.
Lady Is a Tramp: Portraits of Catherine Bailey, with David Bailey. London, Thames & Hudson, 1995.

Editor, with Elaine Feinstein, *New Stories 4.* London, Hutchinson, 1979.

*

Media Adaptations: *She-Devil* (film), 1989.

Critical Studies: *Fay Weldon* by W. Brandmark, N.p., n.d.; *Women Noveilists Today* by Olga Kenyon, New York, St. Martin's Press, 1988, and her *Women Novelists Talk* (interviews), New York, Carroll & Graf, 1989; *Fay Weldon's Wicked Fictions* edited by Regina Barreca, Hanover, New Hampshire, University Press of New England, 1994.

* * *

Fay Weldon is a novelist, playwright, and essayist whose "wicked" writing has won her acclaim worldwide. Born in 1931 to Margaret Jepson and Frank Birkinshaw in Alvechurch, Worcestershire, Weldon grew up in all-female households and New Zealand following her parents' divorce when she was five years old. Educated at Hampstead Girl's School and St. Andrews University, Fife, Weldon earned an M.A. in economics and psychology. After a brief marriage in her early 20s, she became a single mother of a son, working various odd jobs and eventually succeeding as an advertising copywriter. In 1960 she married Ron Weldon (with whom she has three sons) and moved from writing advertising copy to writing for television to finally writing fiction and nonfiction for wide audiences.

Weldon is prolific in several genres and media. To date, her numerous works of fiction have been translated into more than a dozen languages. Moreover, she has completed television and radio drama and stage plays, as well as nonfictional studies of Jane Austen and Rebecca West. Weldon's writing has circulated widely, appearing in publications ranging from the *New York Times* "Op-Ed" pages to conventional women's magazines such as *Cosmopolitan* and *Allure.* Literary critic Regina Barreca (who is Weldon's official biographer) speculates that Weldon's popularity and success with both mainstream and academic audiences can be attributed to her unique signature style, for which the term "Weldonesque" has been coined. Barreca defines a classic Weldonesque moment as "one in which all the forces in the universe seem to converge in the most unlikely of ways." To this extent, ironic understatement and satiric wit figure prominently into Weldon's literary vision.

While Weldon's writings provide an astute understanding of women's experiences in a male-dominated world, her feminist perspective is linked to specific structures of power that embattle both sexes. The narrator of *Praxis* (1978) explains that "it is not a matter of male or female after all; it never was: merely of power." At the same time, Weldon's fictional and non-fictional subject matter corresponds with contemporary feminist concerns about female friendship, the institution of motherhood, the limitations of heterosexual relationships, and the social construction of femininity and beauty. Indeed, she states that she is "preoccupied with women's state in the world" and thus will not "run out of things to say." Far from utopic, however, the feminist perspective in Weldon's work exposes the myths that keep women in their place but rarely suggests alternative sot the historical conditions that perpetuate patriarchal attitudes. Specifically, her novels are cautionary tales that offer negative critiques of women's roles as wives, mothers, and mistresses. Yet, through irony and satire, her writing maintains a comic edge, targeting and exaggerating traditions and attitudes that affirm the status quo.

Weldon's first novel, *The Fat Woman's Joke* (1967), presents a theme central to her oeuvre as it bemoans Western assumptions about the female body that limit women's potentiality. Esther Sussman, the heroine, complains: "Look around you. All the women are nicely groomed and attractive and good looking, and the men no better than fat slugs, for the most part, or skinny runts.... They get away with everything, men." As her marriage is falling apart, Esther pessimistically concludes that "All women are animals. They have no control over themselves. They feel compelled to have children.... it is a blind instinct."

The lack of control that many women feel about their married lives is explored again in perhaps her most well-known novel, *The Lives and Loves of a She-Devil* (1984). Here, Weldon presents an extreme case of a wife who entirely restructures her fact and body through plastic surgery in the image of her husband's glamorous mistress to win him back and to regain the pretense of normalcy. Ruth, the "she-devil" of the title, literally transforms herself into the other woman and; in the process, the novel scathingly comments on the negative effects of love and marriage for women. A sanitized Hollywood film version of the novel, which leaves out the plastic surgery, stars Roseanne Barr as Ruth and Meryl Streep as Mary Fischer.

The devastating consequences of the "war between the sexes" is a consistent theme in Weldon's work. While women are often positioned as morally superior to men, Weldon depicts both sexes as equally culpable and complicit in shaping their miserable circumstances. *Trouble* (1993), for example, lays most of the blame for a failing marriage on the husband who allows himself to fall prey to a manipulative therapist. However, the wife in this novel is far from blameless; Weldon depicts her as a victim of both her husband's psychological machinations and her own emotional weaknesses. Although *Trouble* holds men and women as individuals accountable for their venal behaviors, Weldon treats traditional bastions of male power, like the medical profession, most severely. In *The Cloning of Joanna May* (1989), for instance, Weldon exposes the horrors of the medical profession and critiques the restrictions placed on women's reproductive rights. Here, Carl May exerts his medical power and exacts revenge on his adulterous wife by cloning her, hoping to "create the perfect woman." His plan backfires when the clones refuse to or are unable to reproduce. More polemical than *The Cloning,* an earlier novel, *The Shrapnel Academy* (1986), castigates another institution of male power, the military, presenting an apocalyptic fable about the potential global destruction of the arms race.

Weldon uses ironic understatement and caustic humor deftly, creating memorable and usually irreverent characters and situations. Yet, it is her astute and complex treatment of women's myriad experiences that informs Weldon's feminism. From her personal favorite novel, *Puffball* (1980), which, in her own words, "captures some of the extraordinary feelings and emotions of pregnancy" to the devastating *Splitting* (1995), which chronicles a wife's disintegration into multiple, competing personalities, Fay Weldon provides layered narratives, replete with the contradictory attitudes that characterize contemporary culture.

—Annmarie Pinarski

WEST, Rebecca

Pseudonym of Cicely Isabel Fairfield. **Other Pseudonym:** Lynx. **Nationality:** British. **Born:** London, 21 December 1892; adopted name Rebecca West c. 1912. **Education:** Graduated from George Watson's Ladies' College, Edinburgh, Scotland; attended Royal Academy of Dramatic Art, London. **Family:** Married Henry Maxwell Andrews in 1930 (died 1968); one son, with H.G. Wells. **Career:** Reviewer for *Freewoman,* beginning 1911; political writer, *Clarion,* 1912; began ten-year affair with H.G. Wells, 1913; active in the Fabian Society; regular reviewer, *Sunday Telegraph* (London), beginning 1931; supervised British Broadcasting Corp. (BBC) talks to Yugoslavia during World War II; covered postwar treason trials of William Joyce (Lord Haw-Haw) and others, for the *New Yorker;* made cameo appearance in *Reds* (film), 1981. Contributor to periodicals, including *Harper's, New Republic, New Statesman, New York Herald Tribune, New Yorker, Vogue,* and *Times* (London). **Awards:** Order of St. Sava, 1937; Women's Press Club Award for journalism, 1948; named commander of the British Empire, 1949; Chevalier of the Legion of Honor, 1957; named Dame Commander of the British Empire, 1959; Royal Society of Literature Benson Medal, 1966; *Yorkshire Post* Book of the Year Award, 1966, for *The Birds Fall Down;* D. Litt.: New York University, 1965; Edinburgh University, 1980. **Member:** Royal Society of Literature (fellow), American Academy of Arts and Sciences, (honorary member), Oxford and Cambridge Club, Lansdowne Club. **Died:** Of pneumonia, London, 15 March 1983.

Publications

Novels

The Return of the Soldier. London, Nisbet & Co., and New York, Century, 1918.

The Judge. London, Hutchinson, and New York, Doran, 1922.

Harriet Hume: A London Fantasy. London, Hutchinson, and New York, Doubleday, 1929.

War Nurse (anonymously). New York, Cosmopolitan Book Corporation, 1930.

The Harsh Voice: Four Short Novels (includes *Life Sentence, There Is No Conversation, The Salt of the Earth,* and *The Abiding Vision*). London, J. Cape, and New York, Doubleday, 1935.

The Thinking Reed. London, Hutchinson, and New York, Viking, 1936.

The Fountain Overflows. New York, Viking, 1956; London, Macmillan, 1957.

The Birds Fall Down. London, Macmillan, and New York, Viking, 1966.

This Real Night (sequel to *The Fountain Overflows*). London, Macmillan, 1984, and New York, Viking, 1985.

Cousin Rosamund (unfinished). London, Macmillan, 1985; New York, Viking, 1986.

Sunflower. London, Virago, 1986; New York, Viking, 1987.

Political/Social Theory

The Meaning of Treason. New York, Viking, 1947; London, Macmillan, 1949; revised as *The New Meaning of Treason,* 1964.

A Train of Powder. London, Macmillan, and New York, Viking, 1955.

History

1900. London, Weidenfeld & Nicolson, 1982; New York, Viking, 1983.

Literary Criticism

Ending in Earnest: A Literary Log. New York, Doubleday, 1931.

The Court and the Castle: Some Treatments of a Recurrent Theme. New Haven, Connecticut, Yale University Press, 1957; as *The Court and the Castle: A Study of the Interactions of Political and Religious Ideas in Imaginative Literature,* London, Macmillan, 1958.

McLuhan and the Future of Literature. Oxford, Oxford University Press, 1969.

Essays

"The Life of Emily Davidson," in *Clarion,* 20 June 1913.

"Mr Chesterton in Hysterics," in *Clarion,* 14 November 1913.

"On a Form of Nagging," in *Time and Tide,* 31 October 1923.

The Strange Necessity: Essays and Reviews. New York, Doubleday, 1928.

Arnold Bennett Himself (monograph). London, John Day, 1931.

A Letter to a Grandfather (monograph). London, Hogarth, 1933.

The Young Rebecca: Writings of Rebecca West, 1911-1917, edited by Jane Marcus. New York, Viking, 1982.

Autobiography

Family Memories. London, Virago, 1987.

Other

Henry James. London, Nisbet & Co., and New York, Holt, 1916.

Lions and Lambs (as Lynx), illustrated by David Low. New York, Harcourt, 1929.

D.H. Lawrence. London, Martin Secker, 1930; as *Elegy,* London, Phoenix Book Shop, 1930.

St. Augustine. London, Peter Davies, and New York, Appleton, 1933.

The Modern "Rake's Progress," illustrated by David Low. London, Hutchinson, 1934.

Black Lamb and Grey Falcon: The Record of a Journey through Yugoslavia. New York, Viking, 1941; London, Macmillan, 1942.

Rebecca West: A Celebration, introduction by Samuel Hynes. London, Macmillan, 2 vols, 1942; New York, Viking, 1977.

The Only Poet and Short Stories. London, Virago, 1992.

Editor, *Selected Poems,* by Carl Sandburg. New York, Harcourt, 1926.

*

Media Adaptations: *The Return of the Soldier* (play), adapted for the stage by John van Druten, 1928, (film), 1985; *The Birds Fall Down* (radio play), BBC, n.d.

Bibliography: *A Preliminary List of the Writings of Rebecca West, 1912-1951* by G. Evelyn Hutchinson, Yale University Press, 1957.

Critical Studies: *The Itinerant Ivory Tower* by G. Evelyn Hutchinson, New Haven, Connecticut, Yale University Press, 1953; *Persona Grata* by Cecil Beaton and Kenneth Tynan, New York, Putnam, 1954; *The Novels of Rebecca West: A Complex Unity* by Sister Mary Margarita Orlich, University Microfilms, 1967; *Rebecca West: Artist and Thinker* by Peter Wolfe, Southern Illinois University Press, 1971; *Rebecca West: Master of Reality* by Tony Redd, University of South Carolina Press, 1972; *H.G. Wells and Rebecca West* by Gordon N. Ray, New Haven, Connecticut, Yale University Press, 1974; *Rebecca West* by Motley F. Deakin, New York, Twayne, 1980; *The Young Rebecca* by Jane Marcus, New York, Viking, 1982; *Rebecca West* by Fay Weldon, London and New York, Viking, 1985; *Rebecca West: A Life* by Victoria Glendinning, London, Weidenfeld & Nicolson, 1987.

* * *

Rebecca West was the pseudonym of Cicily Isabel Fairfield, born in London in 1892. Although she harbored an early ambition to be an actress, she only attended the Royal Academy of Dramatic Art in London for three terms before deciding it was not the profession for her. She remained there long enough, however, to play the role of Rebecca West in Ibsen's *Romersholm,* and the first published piece bearing this pen-name appeared in *The Freewoman* in February 1912.

West always made light of her decision to launch a literary career: "at home," she said, "we all wrote and thought nothing of it." If this is true, it makes the immediacy of her success all the more startling. Her articles for *The Freewoman,* a feminist weekly established in 1911, soon attracted the attention of a number of prominent writers, among them H.G. Wells, who was struck by her review of his novel *Marriage,* published in September 1912.

This marked the beginning of a ten-year relationship between Wells and West—an affair that has tended to eclipse West's own success. It was as a book reviewer and journalist that she initially established her reputation, writing for a growing number of prominent publications, including *The Freewoman, The New Freewoman, Clarion,* and *New Statesman* in Britain, and the *New York Herald Tribune* and *Vanity Fair* in the United States.

Many of West's early pieces were written in support of the women's suffrage movement. For example, "The Life of Emily Davison" is an angry and moving essay on the suffragette who threw herself in front of the King's horse at Ascot. Here, West vehemently attacks the system that drove women to such desperate lengths to obtain the vote: "She was imprisoned eight times; she hunger-struck seven times; she was forcibly fed forty-nine times. That is the kind of life to which we dedicate our best and kindest and wittiest women."

Although, as the above quotation demonstrates, West had the ability to write passionate polemical prose, she was also adept at the acerbic aside, a technique she employed to devastating effect in her literary reviews. Although she claimed in her essay "Mr Chesterton in Hysterics" that "I myself have never been able to find out what Feminism is; I only know that people call me a Feminist whenever I express sentiments that differentiate me from a doormat or a prostitute," her adherence to a broadly feminist point of view is clear. The target of many of her reviews is the male literary establishment, in which she quietly but effectively pokes critical fun at some of the most prominent authors of the period. One of her best-known pieces in this vein is "Uncle Bennett," in which she characterizes the "Big Four" literary figures of turn-of-the-century letters—Bennett, Wells, Galsworthy and Shaw—as avuncular "visiting uncles." While she does not belittle her artistic indebtedness to these writers, she is not at all in awe of them. "Uncle" Wells, for example, is accused of writing "passages where his prose suddenly loses its firmness and begins to shake like blanc-mange," while "Uncle" Bennett is condemned as "one of the most unequal writers who ever attained to eminence."

West's first book was a extended example of the same kind of exercise—a study of the American writer Henry James, published in 1916. In retrospect, it can be regarded as an early work of feminist literary criticism, in which West condemned James for portraying women only as "failed sexual beings," and accuses him of lacking intellectual passion. While it also shows West to be a great admirer of James, the book came in for criticism from those who regarded it unseemly for a 23-year-old woman to criticize the work of such an esteemed writer.

West's first work of fiction was *The Return of the Soldier*, published in 1918. It is a moving novel that deals with the topic of the First World War from the perspective of the women waiting at home "wishing for the return of a soldier." It is not, however, a romantic piece, but a narrative that combines Freudian psychoanalysis with a critique of the disruptive effects of the war on the British class system. As with her journalism, West served no period of apprenticeship in the writing of fiction but achieved immediate praise and recognition. *The Return of the Soldier* went into a second printing within a month; and when her second novel, *The Judge*, was published in 1922 it inspired Somerset Maugham to write "I do not think there is anyone writing now who can hold a candle to you."

However, after the publication of her fifth novel, *The Thinking Reed*, in 1957, West wrote no more fiction for nearly 20 years, producing instead her monumental work on Yugoslavia, *Black Lamb and Grey Falcon* (1942), and *The Meaning of Treason* (1947), a book that grew out of her coverage of the Neurenberg war crime trials for the *New Yorker*. She was to publish only two more novels before her death in 1983. *The Fountain Overflows* (1957) is a semi-autobiographical evocation of West's Edinburgh childhood. It was the first part of an intended trilogy, the second two books of which, *This Real Night* and *Cousin Rosamund*, were published posthumously. *The Birds Fall Down*, which appeared in 1966, was described by West as a study of treachery and can, perhaps, be seen as the working out in fictional form of themes that appeared in *The Meaning of Treason*.

Rebecca West's career spanned over 70 years, and her literary output is so large and varied that it is difficult to summarize. As a reviewer, journalist, historian, and novelist, her achievement was immense, and the position she occupied in her last years as (in the words of Fay Weldon) the "formidable elder stateswoman of English literature" was certainly justified.

—Sarah Gamble

WILKINS, Mary. *See* **FREEMAN, Mary F. Wilkins.**

WILLARD, Emma Hart

Nationality: American. **Born:** Berlin, Connecticut, 23 February 1787. **Education:** Attended schools in Worthington, Berlin, and Hartford, Connecticut. **Family:** Married 1) physician John Willard in 1809 (died 1825), one son; 2) physician Christopher C. Yates in 1838 (divorced 1843). **Career:** Teacher at academies in Berlin, Connecticut, Westfield, Massachusetts, and Middlebury, Vermont, 1804-09; founder, Middlebury Female Seminary, Middlebury, Vermont, 1814-19; founder, Troy Female Seminary (later the Emma Willard School), Troy, New York, 1821-38; toured Europe, 1830; aided in founding a girl's school in Athens, Greece, 1831; founder, Willard Association for the Mutual Improvement of Female Teachers, 1837; superintendent of schools, Kensington, Connecticut, 1840-41; delegate to World's Educational Convention, 1854. **Died:** Troy, New York, 15 April 1870.

Publications

Essay

A Plan for Improving Female Education. Middlebury, Vermont, Middlebury College, 1818; 2nd edition, 1819.

History

History of the United States. New York, White Gallaher, 1828; 5th edition, 1837; subtitled as *Continued to the Close of the Mexican War,* 1849.

Universal History in Perspective. Philadelphia, A.S. Barnes, 1837; 2nd edition, 1845; revised, New York, A.S. Barnes, 1882.

Abridgement of the History of the United States; or Republic of America. New York, White Gallaher, 1831; as *Abridged History of the United States; or, Republic of America,* New York, Pratt Wooford, 1844; enlarged edition, New York, A.S. Barnes & Burr, 1869.

Last Leaves of American History: Comprising Histories of the Mexican War and California. New York, A.S. Barnes, 1849; subtitled as *Comprising a Separate History of California,* 1853.

Willard's Historic Guide: Guide to the Temple of Time; and Universal History for Schools. New York, A.S. Barnes, 1849.

Late American History: Containing a Full Account of the Courage, Conduct, and Successes of John C. Fremont. New York, A.S. Barnes, 1856.

Poetry

Rocked in the Cradle of the Deep. N.p., 1830.
The Fulfillment of a Promise. New York, White Gallaher, 1831.

Other

The Woodbridge and Willard Geographies and Atlases. N.p., 1823.
Geography for Beginners; or, The Instructor's Assistant. Hartford, Connecticut, O.D. Cooke, 1826.
Ancient Geography. Hartford, Connecticut, O.D. Cooke, 1827.
Journals and Letters from France and Great Britain. Troy, New York, N. Tuttle, 1833.
A Treatise on the Motive Powers Which Produce the Circulation of the Blood. New York and London, Wiley Putnam, 1846.
Willard's English Chronographer. New York, A.S. Barnes, 1849.
Respiration and Its Effects. New York, Huntington & Savage, 1849.
Astronomy. Troy, Merriam Moore, 1854.
Morals for the Young. New York, A.S. Barnes, 1857.

*

Media Adaptations: "Rocked in the Cradle of the Deep" (hymn), music composed by Joseph P. Knight, n.p., 1841.

Critical Studies: *Mrs. Willard's Life and Work in Middlebury* by Ezra Brainerd, Middlebury, Vermont, 1918; *Emma Willard: Daughter of Democracy* by Alma Lutz, Boston, Houghton Mifflin, 1929, and her *Emma Willard: Pioneer Educator of American Women,* Boston, Beacon Press, 1964; *Pioneers of Women's Education in the United States* by Willystine Goodsell, New York, London, McGraw-Hill, 1931; "The Ever Widening Circle: The Diffusion of Feminist Values from the Troy Female Seminary" by Anne Firor Scott, in *History of Education Quarterly* 19, spring 1979; "Women and the Republic: Emma Willard's Rhetoric of History" by Nina Baym, in *American Quarterly,* 43(1), March 1991; "Emma Hart Willard" by Sister Sharon Dei, in *Women Public Speakers in the United States, 1800-1925,* edited by Karlyn Kohrs Campbell, Westport, Connecticut, Greenwood Press, 1993.

* * *

In 1800, when Emma Hart Willard was 12 years old, she spent long winter evenings teaching herself geometry, one of many subjects then considered incomprehensible to the female brain. As Willard matured, her delighted fascination for self-education turned to frustration and resentment as she came face to face with society's prejudices concerning women's intellectual abilities. This anger fueled her determination to change society's views toward education for women. During the course of her career in education, she was the first to introduce science and mathematics courses to women and was among the first to establish a school of higher education for women. One of the first women lobbyists, Willard also devoted her energies to publicly persuading the male political establishment of the nation's critical need for well-educated women.

Born 23 February 1787 in Berlin, Connecticut, Emma Hart received much of her education at home, attended one of the first academies in Connecticut, and became a teacher at age 17. Three years later, reports of her effective teaching methods led to her being accepted for a top leadership position in a female academy in Middlebury, Vermont. After her marriage in 1809 to Dr. John Willard, a physician-turned-politician, Willard ceased teaching, had a child, and pursued her self-education in physiology, medicine, geometry, and philosophy. When her husband experienced a financial reversal in 1814, Willard established her own boarding school in Middlebury. For the next five years she perfected her teaching methods and expanded the traditional curriculum by adding courses in mathematics, geography, and philosophy. She also began writing a proposal to convince legislators of the necessity of higher education for women.

In 1819, a supporter conveyed her document "A Plan for Improving Female Education" to De Witt Clinton, then governor of New York. He praised the proposal and exhorted the legislature to take action to improve women's education. In preparation for presenting this plan to the legislature, Emma and John Willard self-published 1,000 copies of the proposal to assist them in their lobbying effort. Although the legislators received her address enthusiastically, concerns that education would harm women's health, create intellectual competition between the sexes, and disturb the social order led them to refuse appropriations for women's education.

Although Willard's "A Plan for Improving Female Education" did not achieve its principal goal, its influence as a landmark document in the promotion of women's education reached far beyond New York. In the proposal, she skillfully combined an acute awareness of her all-male middle-class audience while simultaneously articulating the needs and sentiments of American women born in the first decades of the new nation. In the plan's description of the ideal women's seminary, Willard emphasized that women's education would help ensure the survival of the republic. She argued that without well-educated mothers, it would be impossible to create a base of educated citizens capable of preserving, building, and defending the fragile new nation. Although this concept of republican motherhood was not new, the plan gave the ideal immediacy and converted it into a practical design. Key to the document's strategic success were reassurances to her male audience that education for women would not alter traditional gender roles or threaten the status quo of female subservience in society and in the home.

The citizens of Troy, New York, urged Willard to establish a school in their community. With the opening of the Troy Female Seminary in 1821, she finally had the opportunity to institute the ideas outlined in her plan. Although moral education received a primary emphasis (as in the men's colleges) and domestic subjects were not neglected, she also instructed students in natural philosophy (science) and mathematics. Ever mindful of the need to publicize the successes of women's education, she invited members of the community, legislators, and other educators to observe the school's final examinations.

During her years in Troy, Willard innovated new teaching methods, trained over 200 teachers, and wrote numerous textbooks. Her history and geography textbooks were enormously successful and brought her wealth and national acclaim. 1828's *History of the United States* (later reprinted as *Republic of America*), a bestseller, was typical of her history writing in its goal to propagate republican patriotism. Willard remarried in 1838 (John died in 1825), leaving the administration of Troy to her son and daughter-in-law. When this second marriage failed, she returned to Connecticut and became the first woman superintendent of schools in Kensington. In 1844 she returned to Troy and, for the rest of her life, remained involved in the activities of the school she had founded and in the national movement for female teacher education.

Although Emma Willard has been long criticized for her refusal to become actively involved in the feminist movement, her accomplishments and writings attest powerfully to her feminism, especially her unwavering belief in the intellectual equality of the sexes. For Willard, however, the republic's need for educated women superseded the needs of women to gain their individual rights. Although she believed passionately in the power of education to uplift women, she always framed this imperative in terms of the country's urgent need for an educated citizenry.

—Judith E. Harper

WILLIAMS, Patricia J.

Nationality: American. **Born:** Boston, Massachusetts, in 1951. **Education:** Wellesley College, Wellesley, Massachusetts, B.A. 1972; Harvard University Law School, J.D. 1975. **Career:** Associate professor of law, Golden Gate University, 1980-84, City University of New York at Queens, 1984-88, and the University of Wisconsin, 1988-91; professor of law, Columbia University, New York, beginning 1991. Contributor to newspapers and periodicals, including *Christian Science Monitor, Harvard Law Review, Ms., Nation, New Yorker, Washington Post.* **Address:** c/o School of Law, Columbia University, 435 West 116th St., New York, New York 10027-7201, U.S.A.

Publications

Political/Social Theory

The Alchemy of Race and Rights: Diary of a Law Professor. Cambridge, Harvard University Press, 1991; London, Virago, 1993.

The Rooster's Egg: On the Persistence of Prejudice. Cambridge, Harvard University Press, 1995.

Essays

"On Being the Object of Property," in *Signs,* autumn 1988; in *Beacon Book of Essays by Contemporary American Women,* edited by Wendy Martin. Boston, Beacon Press, 1996.

"Blockbusting the Canon," in *Ms.,* September 1992.

"Clarence X, Man of the People," in *Malcolm X: In Our Own Image,* edited by Joe Wood. New York, St. Martin's Press, 1992.

"Alchemical Notes: Reconstructing Ideals from Deconstructed Rights," in *Harvard Civil Rights/Civil Liberties Legal Review,* 22(401), 1987; in *Constitutional Law,* edited by Mark V. Tushnet. New York, New York University Press, 1992.

"Refusing to Be Silenced," in *Ms.,* January 1992.

"The Rules of the Game," in *Village Voice,* 12 May 1992; in *Reading Rodney King: Reading Urban Uprising,* edited by Robert Gooding-Williams, New York, Routledge, 1993.

"A Rare Case Study of Muleheadedness and Men," in *Race-ing Justice, En-gendering Power: Essays on Anita Hill, Clarence Thomas, and the Construction of Social Reality,* edited by Toni Morrison. New York, Pantheon, 1992.

"Among Moses' Bridge-Builders," in *Nation,* 23 May 1994.

"The Death of the Profane: A Commentary on the Genre of Legal Writing," in *Feminism and Community,* edited by Penny A. Weiss and Marilyn Friedman. Philadelphia, Temple University Press, 1995.

"America and the Simpson Trial," in *Nation,* 13 March 1995.

"Meditations on Masculinity," in *Constructing Masculinity,* edited by Maurice Berger, Brian Wallis, and Simon Watson. New York, Routledge, 1995.

*

Bibliography: *African-American Women in the Legal Academy: Selected Bibliography of Patricia R. Harris, Lani Guinier, Patricia J. Williams, Emma Coleman Jordan, and Eleanor Holmes Norton* by Cheryl Smith Cheatham, Cleveland, Case Western Reserve Law Library, 1994.

Critical Studies: *Writing Selves: Contemporary Feminist Autobiography* by Jeanne Perrealut, Minneapolis, University of Minnesota Press, 1995.

* * *

Watch the television, listen to the radio, or glance at a newspaper in any U.S. city and you will find evidence of one of the major issues crippling America today—racism. While many would like the problem to solve itself, dissappear if it is ignored long enough, some brave souls are willing to confront it head on. Patricia J. Williams, a professor of law at Columbia University, is one such person. As tensions build and the United States appears to continues taking backward strides in terms of civil rights and gender equality, Williams's increasing popularity within the mainstream media speaks to the concerns of many.

Williams was born in Boston in 1951. Rather than a Baby Boomer, she considers herself a "Little Rocker," growing up as she did in the shadow of the Little Rock Nine, who integrated the first schools in Arkansas during the 1950s. Attending Wellesley College, from which she earned her B.A. in 1972, Williams would be among the first class of Affirmative Action candidates to begin the process of racially integrating American businesses, law courts, government agencies, and universities. After Wellesley, she went on to Harvard University Law School, where she earned her J.D. in 1975. Her experience at Harvard was less that pleasant; as she writes in *The Alchemy of Race and Rights,* "My abiding recollection of being a student at Harvard Law School is the sense of being invisible. I spent three years wandering in a murk of unreality.... [observing] mostly male bodies assert themselves against one another like football players caught in the gauzy mist of intellectual slow motion." Williams makes a point of saying that things have not changed dramatically for black women at Harvard over the years. As late as 1990, she noted that Harvard could not find "one black woman on the entire planet who is good enough to teach there."

Williams is a prolific writer. In addition to her two books, *The Alchemy of Race and Rights* (1991) and *The Rooster's Egg* (1995), she has published articles in numerous journals and newspapers, including the *Boston Globe, Harvard Law Review, The Nation, Village Voice,* and the *Washington Post.* In 1995 she would make a television appearance on the "Charlie Rose" program alongside fellow feminist Gloria Steinem to speak out about the O.J. Simpson Trial and her reaction to the verdict.

Her writing style—which has been the subject of much controversy—can be considered autobiographical, or what is now called personal criticism. Williams works in a space wherein she combines both political and social theory, integrating her own personal experience to inform the arguments that she makes. Her work is connected to her racial and gendered self; her work is specifically projected through her personal world-view. Because of this, many critics have complained that Williams goes too far; that she violates too many academic practices. Many feminists and critical theorists, meanwhile, have lauded her writing style, praising her for her honest, fresh approach.

In *The Alchemy of Race and Rights* Williams deals with race, how it combines with class to affect the law, and how the resulting law reflects personal rights. "In the law," she notes, "rights are islands of empowerment. To be unrighted is to be disempowered, and the line between rights and no-rights is most often the line between dominators and oppressors." Thus, those in positions of power are fully assured of their rights, while others, for reasons of race, class, or gender, are at risk of being on the side of "no-rights."

Inside this paradigm of rights and empowerment, Williams focuses on issues of particular significance to African Americans. Cornell West, a professor at Harvard and a prominent thinker in the area of racial issues, has discussed the plight of black in the United States. His term "problem people" to talk about a people with problems is a good way of describing Williams's approach to the subject. While acknowledging that African Americans have many problems due to their disenfranchisement throughout history, she makes it very clear, as West does, that whites have been conditioned to see African Americans as the problem itself, rather than a people suffering with the problems of racism, hopelessness, poverty, and violence. She argues that when people are disenfranchised, their ability to defend, or even to state, their rights is disabled. What cannot be defended may technically be lost.

To further illustrate her point, Williams focuses on specific instances of racial violence: the 1984 shooting of a 67-year-old black woman by a white New York City Police officer during an eviction; the 1986 attack and assault of three black youths in the white community of Howard Beach; the 1986 subway shooting of four young black men by Bernhard Goetz. In each of these examples she analyzes the ways in which the media and the law each viewed these cases, and the role that race played in the public's response to each.

In *The Rooster's Egg,* Williams delves into more recent issues of social concern: the Clarence Thomas hearings; the 1992 Republican National Convention; Hillary Rodham Clinton and her relationship to the media; sexual harassment; young women's relationship to the feminist movement; and the wave of talk-show fever that swept American during the early 1990s. Williams examined how welfare and those that benefit from the current system had changed from people who were down on their luck to an "image of women who prey upon their children, leaving the children to fend for themselves and steal in turn from society." Responsibility for this revolving vision of welfare and its recipients is racism, contends Williams, who claims that much of what is currently being said about the welfare system stems from the fact that "we as a nation have continued to underestimate the complicated and multiple forms of prejudice at work in the United States."

This same attitude has transformed the perception of affirmative action from a program designed to give all a fair chance into a construct of quotas and method by which the "undeserving" minorities can displace the "deserving" majority. As Williams so clearly states, "[a]s integration became synonymous with assimilation into whiteness, affirmative action became synonymous with pushing out more qualified whites." The events surrounding Lani Guinier's appointment as director of the Civil Rights division of the Justice Department are further evidence that she employs to illustrate how the meanings and purposes of affirmative action and its supporters have been distorted and misconstrued.

In the midst of the controversy surrounding welfare and affirmative action programs, Williams discusses the increasing popularity of those she dubs "Radio Hoods": people like Rush Limbaugh and Howard Stern, who "[b]laring the battle hymn of the First Amendment ... enshrine a crude demagoguery that makes me heartsick." She contends that radio personalities like Stern and Limbaugh use the First Amendment to spew their own versions of racism and sexism forth over the airwaves, giving voice to a large segment of white America whose thoughts are broadcast through the medium of talk radio. "What does it mean," she posits, "that a manic, penis-obsessed adolescent named Howard Stern is number one among radio listeners, that Rush Limbaugh's wittily smooth sadism has gone the way of prime-time television, and that these men's books tie for the number one slot on all the best seller lists?"

In *The Rooster's Egg, The Alchemy of Race and Rights,* and in her many published essays, Williams has dared to ask the kinds of questions that have gotten her labeled a radical and a troublemaker. Indeed, as she herself remarks, in each job she has held there has "been some moment when I have protested what I perceived to be some thoughtless or intentional form of bias. And my reputation for either remarkable insight or radical troublemaking has grown accordingly." With this kind of bravery and fresh vision, Patricia J. Williams continues to be one of the foremost political voices of our time. She discusses with cogent argument and astonishing insight about the issues and controversies that confront contemporary America. It is no wonder that her work continues to be well received and popular among those concerned with equality and dignity for all in the United States.

—Jennifer Kohout

WILLY. *See* **COLETTE, (Sidonie-Gabrielle).**

WILLY, Colette. *See* **COLETTE, (Sidonie-Gabrielle).**

WILSON, Barbara (Ellen)

Nationality: American. **Born:** Long Beach, California, 17 October 1950. **Career:** Writer. Publisher, Seal Press, Seattle, Washington, 1982-94. Contributor of articles and short fiction to periodicals, including *Zyzzva.* **Awards:** Columbia Translation Prize; British Crime Writers award, and Lambda Literary award, both 1991, both for *Gaudi Afternoon..* **Address:** c/o Seal Press, 3131 Western Avenue, Suite 410, Seattle, Washington 98121, U.S.A. **Online Address:** wilcarz@aol.com.

Publications

Novels

Ambitious Women. New York, Spinsters, 1982; London, Women's Press, 1983.
Murder in the Collective. Seattle, Seal Press, and London, Women's Press, 1984.
Sisters of the Road. Seattle, Seal Press, 1986; London, Women's Press, 1987.
Cows and Horses. Portland, Oregon, Eighth Mountain Press, 1988; London, Virago Press, 1989.
Dog Collar Murders. Seattle, Seal Press, and London, Virago Press, 1989.
Gaudi Afternoon. Seattle, Seal Press, 1990; London, Virago Press, 1991.
Trouble in Transylvania. Seattle, Seal Press, and London, Virago Press, 1993.
If You Had a Family. Seattle, Seal Press, 1996.

Short Stories

Talk and Contact. Seattle, Seal Press, 1978.
Thin Ice. Seattle, Seal Press, 1981.
Walking on the Moon: Six Stories and a Novella. Seattle, Seal Press, 1983; London, Women's Press, 1986.
Miss Venezuela (includes selections from *Thin Ice* and *Walking on the Moon*). Seattle, Seal Press, 1988.

Uncollected Short Stories

"Murder at the International Feminist Book Fair," in *Reader I Murdered Him,* edited by Jen Green. London, Women's Press, 1989; New York, St. Martin's Press, 1990.
"We Didn't See It," in *Lesbian Love Stories,* edited by Irene Zahava. Watsonville, California, Crossing Press, 1989.
"The Theft of the Poet," in *A Woman's Eye,* edited by Sara Paretsky and Martin H. Greenberg. New York, Delacorte, 1990.
"Is This Enough for You?," in *Lesbian Love Stories,* Vol. 2, edited by Irene Zahava. Watsonville, California, Crossing Press, 1991.
"The Death of a Much-Travelled Woman," in *The Fourth Woman Sleuth Anthology,* edited by Irene Zahava. Watsonville, California, Crossing Press, 1991.
"Belladonna," in *A Woman's Eye II,* edited by Sara Paretsky. New York, Delacorte, 1996.

Uncollected Essays

"The Erotic Life of Fictional Characters," in *An Intimate Wilderness: Lesbian Writers on Sexuality,* edited by Judith Barrington. Portland, Oregon, Eighth Mountain Press, 1991.
"My Work," in *In/Versions: Writing by Dykes, Queers, and Lesbians,* edited by Betsy Warland. Vancouver, British Columbia, Press Gang Publishers, 1991.
"The Outside Edge: Lesbian Mysteries," in *Daring to Dissent: Lesbian Culture from Margin to Mainstream,* edited by Liz Gibbs. London, Cassell, 1994.
"A Glacier Summer," in *Another Wilderness: Women Writing about the Outdoors,* edited by Susan Fox Rogers. Seattle, Seal Press, 1994.

For Children

The Geography Lesson, illustrations by Gregory MacDonald. Seattle, Seal Press, 1977.

Other

Editor, with Faith Conlon and Rachel de Silva, *The Things That Divide Us.* Seattle, Seal Press, 1985; London, Sheba, 1986.

Translator, *Cora Sandel: Collected Short Stories.* Seattle, Seal Press, 1985.
Translator, *Nothing Happened* by Ebba Haslund. Seattle, Seal Press, 1987.
Translator, with Katherine Hanson, *Backstreets,* by Liv Finstad and Cecelie Høigard. Philadelphia, Temple University Press, 1992.

*

Critical Sources: *The Safe Sea of Women: Lesbian Fiction, 1969-1989* by Bonnie Zimmerman, Boston, Beacon Press, 1991, London, Onlywomen Press, 1992; "The Feminist Counter-Tradition in Crime: Cross, Grafton, Paretsky, and Wilson" by Maureen T. Reddy, in *The Cunning Craft: Original Essays on Detective Fiction and Contemporary Literary Theory,* edited by Ronald G. Walker, Macomb, Western Illinois University, 1990.

* * *

A writer, translator, and publisher, Barbara Wilson infuses her fictional works with her politics. Confronting society's patriarchal determination of "appropriate" female behavior, she presents realistic female characters drawn from a broad spectrum of society. This diversity—of age, race, sexual orientation, intellect, vocation, and physical attributes—allows Wilson to posit new ways of viewing and structuring politics and society, with a deftness of touch and a sense of humor that engages her readers on several levels.

Born in Long Beach, California, in 1950, Wilson was not taught to read until relatively late in her childhood. Attending college briefly in the late 1960s, she left academia to learn about life first-hand. Travelling around the world over the next few years, her natural aptitude for language allowed Wilson to teach herself Spanish, German, and Norwegian, an undertaking that she would later put to use in translating the works of several Scandinavian woman writers, including Cora Sandel and Ebba Haslund. In the mid-1970s Wilson settled in the Seattle area and worked for several years as an investigative journalist. In 1976 she cofounded Seal Press, a publisher of lesbian fiction.

While she does not consider herself a "mystery writer," Wilson has utilized the traditional male genre of the detective novel to engage in political and social commentary. Using greater Seattle and the West Coast area as her primary setting, she has written a series of novels featuring the leftist, lesbian-feminist detective Pam Nilsen. In *Murder in the Collective,* published in 1984, Nilsen must confront both racism and homophobia by relying on her own wherewithal rather than male support; *Sisters of the Road* (1986) find the resourceful Nilsen grappling with the effects of prostitution, while *Dog Collar Murders* (1989)directly and humorously addresses the inter-feminist debates over pornography, lesbian sadomasochism, and other violence against women.

In a second series of mysteries beginning with *Gaudi Afternoon* (1991),Wilson introduces a more self-assured sleuth named Cassandra Reilly. Following the killer's path means more than following a trail of physical evidence; amidst such women-centered social issues as parenthood and child custody, Wilson's protagonist, also a translator, becomes the vehicle through which both sexuality and gender are explored in this many-layered work of detective fiction. Indeed, Reilly, who appears again in *Trouble in Transylvania* (1993) as well as several of Wilson's short stories, can be seen as a more strongly developed version of Nilsen. As in all of Barbara Wilson's novels, "feminism is the source of each detective's authority and therefore of her power," according to Maureen T. Reddy, "while each murderer's corrupt definition and destructive use of power is rooted in patriarchal, capitalist ideology, which is seen finally to lack legitimate authority."

—Pamela Kester-Shelton

WINTERSON, Jeanette

Nationality: British. **Born:** Lancashire, 27 August 1959. **Education:** St. Catherine's College, Oxford, B.A. 1981. **Family:** Companion of Dr. M. Reynolds. **Career:** Held a variety of jobs including ice-cream van driver, make-up artist in a funeral parlor, and domestic assistant in a mental hospital. **Awards:** Publishing for People Award, 1985; Whitbread Award and Booksellers Association of Great Britain & Ireland Award, both 1985, for *Oranges Are Not the Only Fruit;* John Llewellyn Rhys Memorial prize, 1987; American Academy of Arts and Letters E.M. Forster Award, 1989; British Association of Film and Television Arts Award, 1991; Prix Italia, 1991; FIPA d'Argent (Cannes), 1991; Ace Award, 1991. **Agent:** International Creative Management, 40 West 57th Street, New York, New York 10019, USA. **Address:** c/o Jonathan Cape, 20 Vauxhall Bridge Road, London SW1V 2SA, England.

Publications

Novels

Oranges Are Not the Only Fruit. London, Pandora Press, 1985; New York, Atlantic Monthly Press, 1987.
The Passion. London, Bloomsbury, 1987; New York, Atlantic Monthly Press, 1988.
Sexing the Cherry. London, Bloomsbury, 1989; New York, Atlantic Monthly Press, 1990.
Written on the Body. London, Cape, 1992; New York, Knopf, 1993.
Art and Lies: A Piece for Three Voices and a Bawd. London, Cape, 1994; New York, Knopf, 1995.

Uncollected Short Stories

"Psalms," in *New Statesman,* 26 April 1985.
"Only the Best for the Lord," in *New Statesman,* 19-26 December 1986.
"Stories and Histories," in *Harper's,* September 1987.
"Orion," in *Winter's Tales 4* (new series), edited by Robin Baird-Smith. London, Constable, and New York, St. Martin's Press, 1988.
"The World and Other Places," in *Grand Street,* summer 1990.
"The Poetics of Sex," in *Lesbian Short Stories,* edited by Margaret Reynolds. Harmondsworth, Penguin, 1993; New York, Penguin, 1994.
"The Lives of Saints," in *Paris Review,* fall 1993.
"The Green Man," in *New Yorker,* 26 June-3 July 1995.

Plays

Oranges Are Not the Only Fruit (adaptation of her novel). London, Vintage, 1990.
Great Moments in Aviation. London, BBC Enterprises/Miramax, 1993.

Screenplays: *Oranges are Not the Only Fruit,* 1990; *Great Moments in Aviation,* 1993;

Essays

Art Objects: Essays on Ecstasy and Effrontery. London, Cape, 1995; New York, Knopf, 1996.

Other

Fit for the Future: The Guide for Women Who Want to Live Well. London, Pandora Press, 1980.
Boating for Beginners, illustrations by Paula Youens. London, Methuen, 1985.

Editor, *Passion Fruit: Romantic Fiction with a Twist.* London, Pandora Press, 1986.

*

Media Adaptations: *Oranges Are Not the Only Fruit* (film), BBC-TV, 1990; *Great Moments in Aviation* (film), London, BBC Enterprises/Miramax, 1993.

Critical Studies: "Into the Mystic: Jeanette Winterson's Fable Manners," by Carol Anshaw, in *Voice Literary Supplement,* June 1990; "Mothers and the Avant-Garde: A Case of Mistaken Identity" by Susan Rubin Suleiman, in *Femmes Frauen Women,* edited by Guyon Francoise van Rossum, Amsterdam, Rodopi, 1990; *The Safe Sea of Women: Lesbian Fiction, 1969-1989* by Bonnie Zimmerman, Boston, Beacon Press, 1990; "Fingers in the Fruit Basket: A Feminist Reading of *Oranges Are Not the Only Fruit*" by Rebecca O'Rourke, in *Feminist Criticism: Theory and Practice,* edited by Susan Sellers, Toronto, University of Toronto Press, 1991; "*Oranges Are Not the Only Fruit*: Reaching Audiences Other

Lesbian Texts Cannot Reach" by Hilary Hinds, in *New Lesbian Criticism: Literary and Cultural Readings*, edited by Sally Munt, New York, Columbia University Press, 1992; "Hubris and the Young Author: The Problem of the Introduction to *Oranges Are Not the Only Fruit*" by G.P. Lainsbury, in *Notes on Contemporary Literature*, 22(4), September 1992; "Models for Female Loyalty: The Biblical Ruth in Jeanette Winterson's *Oranges Are Not the Only Fruit*" by Laurel Bollinger, in *Tulsa Studies in Women's Literature,* 13(2), fall 1994; "Jeanette Winterson's Sexing the Postmodern" by Laura Doan, in *The Lesbian Postmodern*, edited by Doan, New York, Columbia University Press, 1994; "The Cartography of Passion: Cixous, Wittig and Winterson" by Daphne Kutzer, in *Re-naming the Landscape*, edited by Bruce A. Butterfield and Jurgen Kleist, New York, P. Lang, 1994.

* * *

Jeanette Winterson, now one of England's most critically acclaimed writers, rose to prominence in 1985 with the publication of her first novel, *Oranges Are Not the Only Fruit.* Winner of the Whitbread Prize for a First Novel, this first-person narrative about an adopted girl growing up in a strict, religious family in a northern town quite clearly reflects the early life of the author. As was the case with Winterson, the narrator is named Jeanette, is adopted into a family of Pentecostal Evangelists, and learns in her teenage years that she is sexually attracted to women. Since the precocious preacher has been raised to believe that she is a perfect child of God, Jeanette cannot understand the church community's expressions of horror and disgust when her relationship with a recently converted girl, which she sees as a thing of beauty, is cruelly revealed to her congregation. Jeanette's inability to comprehend these reactions is compounded by the fact that most of the women around her—who feel that she should "see boys"—are generally dissatisfied with their own relationships with men, whom they regard as drunkards, wastrels, or adulterers. When it becomes clear that the religious zealots' attempts to change the girl's ways are hopeless, they oust her from the community and her home.

Winterson was similarly obliged to leave home at a young age and take a variety of jobs, from working in a funeral parlor to driving an ice-cream van, to support herself while studying at Accrington College of Further Education. Eventually, like her semi-autobiographical namesake, Winterson was accepted to St. Catherine's College, Oxford, where she studied English. After graduating in 1981 she worked for a short time at the Roundhouse Theatre before starting a career in publishing. She would leave publishing in 1987 in order to write full-time.

In much of her fiction Winterson deals with issues of gender identity, sexuality, and religious hypocrisy, but in her later work she leaves behind the realism of *Oranges Are Not the Only Fruit*—interrupted, though it is, with retellings of fairy tales—in favor of magical, historical locations. In her second work, *Boating for Beginners*, sometimes labeled a novel, sometimes a "comic book," Winterson rewrites the Book of Genesis from a feminist perspective both comical and critical. In the ancient city of Ur, Noah, a thriving capitalist, accidentally creates "God" out of a piece of cake and a giant toaster and has protagonist Gloria Munde gather pairs of animals in readiness for a deluge. The flood is the ideal solution to many problems, thinks the "God" who is "fed up with this world and its whingeing, scrounging pop-art people." While *Boating for Beginners* is perhaps not Winterson's best work, its feminist attacks on everything from patriarchal zealots and contemporary writers of both "substance" and romance to arbitrary notions of female beauty make it an amusing read.

Winterson's next work, *The Passion*, which won the John Llewellyn Rhys Memorial Prize in 1987, combines historical fiction with magical realism in a tale about Henri, Napoleon's faithful cook, and Villanelle, the webbed-footed daughter of a Venetian boatman. Romantic love and obsession are the themes of this novel, which follows the incredible adventures of the two protagonists from Russia to Venice, where ultimately Villanelle asks Henri to retrieve her heart from the married woman who has literally captured it. The *Passion* won much praise from critics on both sides of the Atlantic and was the work that would lead Gore Vidal to call Winterson "the most interesting writer I have read in twenty years."

Two years after the success of *The Passion*, Winterson confirmed her talent with the mythical, historical novel *Sexing the Cherry*. Set in a pestilential London during the reign of Charles II, the work tells the story of Jordan, a Moses-like character who is found floating down the Thames River and subsequently adopted by the brutish and grotesque giantess Dog-Woman, who lives in squalid poverty with her many canine companions. Jordan grows up to be an explorer of both worldly and magical realms. From around the globe he returns with exotic plants and fruits, and from one of the otherworldly locations he returns in love with a flying princess. While Jordan is seeking beauty elsewhere, Dog-Woman remains in London, fighting oppressive military and religious forces. Although the story's competing narratives seem to comment on the fortitude of women who traditionally have been denied the social and geographical mobility afforded to men, they also allow Winterson a space in which to air her concerns about religious persecution, the environment, and even the writing of history. Nevertheless, the emphasis on the significance of gender identity in both *Sexing the Cherry* and *The Passion*, which are at times reminiscent of Virginia Woolf's *Orlando*, should not be underestimated.

While gender identity shifts in Woolf's *Orlando*, in Winterson's next novel, *Written on the Body*, it goes undetermined for much of the story. The narrator, whose gender is initially ambiguous, is in love with Louise, a victim of leukemia who has recently left her mean-spirited husband. However, the cancer specialist husband is the only one who can get Louise access to the treatment she needs and will only do so if the narrator renounces the relationship with his wife. The narrator reluctantly does so, and the rest of the story deals with her (we eventually discover) move away and philosophizing over the whole affair. She is ultimately reunited with Louise, but the strength of the work comes during the time of separation, during which the narrator, sometimes precisely, sometimes impressionistically, reminisces over their time together.

Winterson experiments with narrative technique once more in the 1994 novel *Art and Lies: A Piece for Three Voices and a Bawd.* The work is essentially a three-way conversation about philosophy, music, art, and sexuality—along with the more mundane aspects of modern life—that takes place between Handel, Picasso, and Sappho. Handel is a doctor who bemoans the banality of contemporary life; Picasso is a young girl whose family objects to her painting; and Sappho is a "sexualist" who, among other things, gives out advice on double standards in heterosexual relationships.

In much of her fiction, and in the pages of her essay collection *Art Objects: Essays on Ecstasy and Effrontery,* Winterson forces us to look for the beautiful—whether it be real or imaginative.

Not a great lover of television (despite having had *Oranges Are Not the Only Fruit* successfully adapted to the screen), she makes us question the reality that has been shaped around us and understand that it can be reshaped. Perhaps her most important contribution to feminist studies, however, is her fictional treatment of gender identity, which reaffirms the theories of many contemporary feminists who see gender as an unstable social construction.

As well as writing novels and essays, Jeannette Winterson has written plays for the screen and edited a book of short stories, *Passion Fruit: Romantic Fiction with a Twist*, which has been praised by fellow writer Dorothy Allison. She is currently at work on another novel and is a regular contributor of fiction and essays to a number of publications, including *Sight and Sound, New Statesman and Society*, and *The New Yorker*.

—Jonathan Morrow

WITTIG, Monique

Nationality: French. **Born:** Haut Rhin, Alsace, 1935; has lived in the United States since 1976. **Education:** Studied Oriental languages, literature, history, and philosophy, Sorbonne, University of Paris, Ph.D. in literary language 1986. **Career:** Visiting professor, University of California (Berkeley), University of Southern California, (Los Angeles), Duke University, Vassar College, and New York University; currently professor of French literature, University of Arizona, Tucson; co-founder, MLF (Mouvement de libération des femmes); active member of the "Féministes Révolutionnaires" beginning 1970, and the "Gouines rouges" ("Red Dykes"), beginning 1971; member of editorial collective of *Questions Féministes,* Paris, 1977-80; advisory editor, *Feminist Issues* (Berkeley, CA), 1980-91. **Awards:** Prix Médicis, 1964, for *L'Opoponax.* **Address:** c/o Éditions de Minuit, 7 rue Bernard-Palissy, 75006 Paris, France.

PUBLICATIONS

Works of Fiction

L'Opoponax. Paris, Minuit, 1964; translated by Helen Weaver as *The Opoponax,* New York, Simon & Schuster, and London, P. Owen, 1966.

Les Guérillères. Paris, Minuit, 1969; translated by David LeVay as *The Guérillères,* New York, Viking, and London, P. Owen, 1971.

Le Corps lesbien. Paris, Minuit, 1973; translated by David LeVay as *The Lesbian Body,* New York, Morrow, and London, P. Owen, 1975.

Brouillon pour un dictionnaire des amantes, with Sande Zeig. Paris, Grasset & Fasquelle, 1976.

Lesbian Peoples: Material for a Dictionary, with Sande Zeig. New York, Avon, 1979; London, Virago, 1980.

Virgile, non. Paris, Minuit, 1985; translated by David LeVay and Margaret Crosland as *Across the Acheron,* London, P. Owen, 1987.

Uncollected Short Stories

"Banlieues", in *Le Nouveau Commerce* (Paris), 5, spring/summer 1965.

"Yallankoro", in *Nouvelle Revue Française* (Paris), 30(167), July/September 1967.

"Une Partie de campagne", in *Le Nouveau Commerce* (Paris), 26, fall 1973.

"Un Jour mon prince viendra", in *Questions Féministes* (Paris), 2, February 1978.

"Les Tchiches et les Tchouches", in *Le Genre Humain* (Paris), 6, 1983.

"Paris-la-Politique", in *Vlasta* (Paris), 4, June 1985.

Essays

The Straight Mind and Other Essays (many originally appeared in *Feminist Issues* [Berkeley, California]). Boston, Beacon Press, 1992.

Uncollected Essays and Author's Notes

"Bouvard et Pécuchet", in *Cahiers Renaud-Barrault* (Paris), 59, 1967.

"Combat pour la libération de la femme" with Gille Wittig, Marcia Rothenburg, and Margaret Stephenson, in *L'Idiot International* (Paris), 6, 1970.

"Author's Note" to *The Lesbian Body,* New York, Morrow, 1975.

"Paradigm", translated by George Stambolian, in *Homosexualties and French Literature,* edited by Elaine Marks and George Stambolian. Ithaca, New York, Cornell University Press, 1979.

"La Pensée straight", in *Questions Féministes* (Paris), 7, February 1980; translated in *Feminist Issues* (Berkeley, California), 1(1), 1980.

"On ne naît pas femme", in *Questions Féministes* (Paris), 8, May 1980; translated in *Feminist Issues* (Berkeley, California, 4(1), 1985.

"Avant-note" to *La Passion* by Djuna Barnes, Paris, Flammarion, 1982.

"Les Questions féministes ne sont pas des questions lesbiennes", in *Amazones d'hier, Lesbiennes d'aujourd'hui* (Montréal), 2(1), 1983.

"Le Lieu de l'action", in *Digraphe* (Paris), 32, 1984.

"Le Voyage sans fin", in the Programme of the Compagnie Renaud-Barrault Production, Paris, 1985; translated by Barbara Godard in "*The Constant Journey:* An Introduction," in *Modern Drama* (Toronto), 39(1), spring 1996.

"Avant-Note" to *Le Voyage sans fin,* supplement to *Vlasta* (Paris), 4, June 1985; translated by Barbara Godard in "*The Constant Journey:* A Prefatory Note," in *Modern Drama* (Toronto), 39(1), spring 1996.

"Quelques Remarques sur *Les Guérillères,*" in *L'Esprit Créateur,* (Lexington, Kentucky), 34(4), winter 1994.

Plays

L'Amant vert (produced Bolivia, 1969).

The Constant Journey with Sande Zeig (produced Goddard College, 1984; as *Le Voyage sans fin,* produced Paris, 1985), in supplement to *Vlasta* (Paris), 4, June 1985.

Radio Plays: *Le Grand Cric-Jules, Récréation, Dialogue pour les deux frères et la soeur,* broadcast in Germany, Stockholm, London, and Paris. n.d.

Translations

Translator, with Herbert Mancuse, *L'Homme Unidimensionnel,* by Marcuse. Paris, Minuit, 1968.

Translator, with Vera Alves da Nobrega and Evelyne le Garrec, *Nouvelles Lettres portugaises,* by the "Three Marias": Maria Isabel Barreno, Maria Teresa Horta, and Maria Fatima Velho da Costa. Paris, Seuil, 1974.

Translator, with Djuna Barnes, *La Passion* (translation of *Spillway*), by Barnes. Paris, Flammarion, 1982.

Translator, "Le Cheval de Troie," by Marthe Rosenfeld, in *Vlasta* (Paris), 4, 1985.

*

Bibliography: In *French Feminist Criticism: Women, Language, and Literature: An Annotated Bibliography* edited by Elissa Gelfland and Virginia Hules, New York and London, Garland, 1985; "Bibliographie" in *Vlasta* (Paris), 4, 1985; in "Monique Wittig" by Diane Griffin Crowder, in *French Women Writers: A Bio-Bibliographical Source Book,* edited by Eva Martin Sartori and Dorothy Wynne Zimmerman, Wesport, Connecticut, Greenwood Press, 1991.

Critical Studies: "Everybody's Childhood" by Mary McCarthy, in *The Writing on the Wall and Other Literary Essays,* New York, Harcourt, 1970; Monique Wittig et les lesbiennes barbues: entretien avec Monique Wittig", in *Actuel* (Paris), 38, January 1974; "A Cosmogony of O: Wittig's *Les Guérillères*" by Erika Ostrovsky, in *Twentieth-Century French Fiction: Essays for Germaine Brée,* edited by George Stambolian, New Brunswick, Rutgers University Press, 1975; " The Two-Breasted Amazon" by Margaret Crosland, in her *Women of Iron and Velvet,* London, Constable, 1976; "Nouvelle Nouvelle Autobiographie: Monique Wittig's *Le Corps lesbien"* by Lynn Higgins, in *Sub-Stance: A Review of Theory and Literary Criticism* (Madison, Wisconsin), 14, 1976; "Myth and Ms.: Entrapment and Liberation in Monique Wittig's *Les Guérillères"* by Mary Pringle Spraggins, in *International Fiction Review* (Fredericton, New Brunswick), 3(1), January 1976; "Lesbian Intertextuality" by Elaine Marks, in *Homosexualities and French Literature: Cultural Contexts/Critical Texts,* edited by Marks and George Stambolian, Ithaca, Cornell University Press, 1979; "A Mythology for Women: Monique Wittig's *Les Guérillères"* by Marcelle Thiébaux, in *The Analysis of Literary Texts: Current Trends in Methodology,* edited by Randolph D. Pope, Ypsilanti, Michigan, Bilingual Press, 1980; "Pre-Texts for the Transatlantic Feminist" by Alice Jardine, in *Yale French Studies,* 62, 1981; "Language and the Vision of a Lesbian-Feminist Utopia in Wittig's *Les Guérillères"* by Marthe Rosenfeld, in *Frontiers: A Journal of Women Studies* (Boulder), spring/summer 1981; "The Text As Body/Politics: An Appreciation of Monique Wittig's Writings in Context" by Hélène Vivienne Wenzel, in *Feminist Studies* (College Park, Maryland), summer 1981; "The Semiotic Functions of Ideology in Literary Discourse" by Diane Griffin Crowder, in *Bucknell Review,* 27(1), 1982, and her "Amazons and Mothers? Monique Wittig, Hélène Cixous and Theories of Women's Writing," in *Contemporary Literature,* 24(2), summer 1983; "Displacing the Phallic Subject: Wittig's Lesbian Writing" by Namascar Shaktini, in *Signs* (Chicago), 8(1), autumn 1982; "Language and Childhood: *L'Opoponax* by Monique Wittig" by Jean H. Duffy, in *Forum for Modern Language Studies* (St. Andrews, Scotland), 19(4), October 1983, and her "Women and Language in *Les Guérillères* by Monique Wittig," in *Stanford French Review,* 7(3), winter 1983; "The Dream Is the Bridge: In Search of Lesbian Theatre" by Harriet Ellenberger, in *Trivia* (Amherst), 5, fall 1984; "The Linguistic Aspect of Sexual Conflict: Monique Wittig's *Le Corps lesbien*" by Marthe Rosenfeld, in *Mosaic: A Journal for the Comparative Study of Literature* (Winnipeg, Manitoba), 17(2), spring 1984; "Un Nom pour tout le monde: *L'Opoponax* de Monique Wittig" by Susanna Stampanoni, in *Vlasta* (Paris) 4, June 1985; "La Passion selon Wittig" by Christine Delphy, in *Nouvelles Questions Féministes* (Paris), 1-2, winter 1985; "Body/Language: French Feminist Utopias" by Cecile Lindsay, in *French Review* (Champaign, Illinois), 60(1), October 1986; "Monique Wittig: The Lesbian" by Martha Noel Evans, in her *Masks of Transition: Women and the Politics of Writing in 20th-Century France,* Ithaca, Cornell University Press, 1987; "Speaking in Lesbian Tongues: Monique Wittig and the Universal Point of View" by Julia Creet, in *Resources for Feminist Research* (Toronto), 16(4), December 1987; "By Myriad Constellations: Monique Wittig and the Writing of Women's Experience" by Winnie Woodhull and Patricia S. Yaeger, in *Power, Gender, Values,* edited by Judith Genova, Edmonton, Manitoba, Academic, 1987; "Poetic Politics: How the Amazons Took the Acropolis" by Jeffner Allen, in *Hypatia,* 3(2), 1988; "Writing and Reading the Body: Female Sexuality and Recent Female Fiction" by Molly Hite, in *Feminist Studies,* 14, 1988; "Sexual Indifference and Lesbian Representation" by Teresa de Lauretis, in *Theatre Journal* (Baltimore, 40(2), May 1988; "The Ontology of Language in a Post-Structuralist Feminist Perspective: Explosive Discourse in Monique Wittig" by Lois Oppenheim, in *Poetics of the Elements in the Human Condition,* Vol. II: *The Airy Elements in Poetic Imagination,* edited by Anna-Teresa Tymieniecka, Dordrecht, Netherlands, Kluwer, 1988; "Exploding the Issue: "French" "Women" "Writers" and "The Canon"?" (interview) by Alice A. Jardine and Anne M. Menke, in *Yale French Studies* (New Haven), 75, 1988; "Experimental Novels? Yes, But Perhaps 'Otherwise': Nathalie Sarraute, Monique Wittig" by Germaine Brée, in *Breaking the Sequence: Women's Experimental Fiction,* edited by Ellen G. Friedman, Princeton, Princeton University Press, 1989; "Monique Wittig's Anti-Essential Materialism" by Diana Fuss, in her *Essentially Speaking: Feminism, Nature, and Difference,* New York, Routledge, 1989; "Is There a Lesbian in this Text? Derrida, Wittig, and the Politics of the Three Women" by Heather Findlay, in *Coming to Terms: Feminism, Theory, Politics,* edited by Elizabeth Weed, New York, Routledge, 1989; "Writing Feminism: Myth, Epic and Utopia in Monique Wittig's *Les Guérillères*" by Lawrence M. Porter, in *L'Esprit Créateur* (Lexington, Kentucky), 29(3), fall 1989, and his "Feminist Fantasy and Open Structure in Monique Wittig's *Les Guérillères,"* in *The Celebration of the Fantastic: Selected Papers from the 10th Anniversary International Conference on the Fantastic in the Arts,* edited by Donald E. Morse, Marshall B. Tymn, and Csilla Bertha, Westport, Connecticut, Greenwood Press, 1992; "Lifting Belly Is a Language": The Postmodern Lesbian Subject" by Penelope J. Englebrecht, in *Feminist Studies,* 16(1), spring 1990; "Monique Wittig: Bodily Disintegration and Fictive Sex" by Judith Butler, in her *Gender Trouble: Feminism and the Subversion of Identity,* New York, Routledge, 1990; "The Trojan Horse of Universalism: Language as "War Machine" in the Writings of Monique Wittig" by Linda Zerilli, in *Social Text* (Durham, North Carolina), 8-9, 1990; "Figuring Circulation: Claude Lévi-Strauss and Monique Wittig" by Namascar Shaktini, in *Contemporary French Fiction* *by Women: Feminist Perspectives,* edited by Margaret Atack and Phil Powrie, Manchester, Manchester University Press, 1990, and her "A Revolutionary Signifier: The Lesbian Body," in *Lesbian Texts and Contexts: Radical Revisions,* edited by Karla Jay and Joanne Glasgow, New York, New York University Press, 1990; "Enfance en archipels: *L'Opoponax* de Monique Wittig" by Marcelle Marini, in *Revue des Sciences Humaines* (Paris) 96,(2), 1991; "Plastic Actions: Linguistic Strategies in *Le Corps lesbien*" by Karin Cope, in *Hypatia,* 6(3), fall 1991; *A Constant Journey: The Fiction of Monique Wittig* by Erika Ostrovsky, Carbondale and Edwardsville, Southern Illinois University Press, 1991; "Rememoration or War? French Feminist Narrative and the Politics of Self-Representation" by Linda M.G. Zerilli, in *differences: A Journal of Feminist Cultural Studies* (Providence, Rhode Island), 3(1), spring 1991; "Encyclopedic Dictionary as Utopian Genre: Two Feminist Ventures" by Kristine Anderson, in *Utopian Studies: Journal of the Society for Utopian Studies,* 2(1-2), 1991; "Violence against Violence against Women: An Avant-Garde for the Time" by Dianne Chisholm, in *Atlantis: A Woman's Studies Journal/Revue d'Etudes sur les Femmes* (Halifax, Nova Scotia), 17(2), spring-summer 1992; "The Communal Self: Re-Membering Female Identity in the Works of Christa Wolf and Monique Wittig" by Kathleen L. Komar, in *Comparative Literature* (Eugene, Oregon), 44(1), 1992;"*Elles* and the Ladies of Orange: Monique Wittig's Deconstructive Use of Epic" by Namascar Shaktini, in *Romance Languages Annual,* 4, 1992; "Deleuzian Bodies: Not Thinking Straight in *Capitalism and Schizophrinia"* by Shelton Waldrep, in *Pre-Text: A Journal of Rhetorical Theory,* 13(3-4), 1992; "Lesbianizing Love's Body: Interventionist Imag(in)ings of Monique Wittig" by Dianne Chisholm, in *ReImagining Women: Representation of Women in Culture,* edited by Shirley Neuman and Glennis Stephenson, Toronto, University of Toronto Press, 1993; "Separatism and Feminist Utopian Fiction" by Crowder, in *Sexual Practice, Textual Theory: Lesbian Cultural Criticism,* edited by Susan J. Wolfe and Julia Penelope, Cambridge, Massachusetts, Blackwell, 1993; "Masochism, Sadism, and Women's Writing: The Examples of Marguerite Duras and Monique Wittig" by Owen Heathcote, in *Nottingham French Studies,* 32(2), 1993; "Lesbianizing English: Wittig and Zeig Translate Utopia" by Kristine J. Anderson, in *L'Esprit Créateur,* 34(4), winter 1994; "Des Mythes en éclats dans *Le Corps lesbien* de Wittig" by Dominique Bourque, in *Mythes dans la littérature d'expression française,* edited by Metka Zupancic, Ottawa, Le Nordir, 1994; "The United States in Contemporary French Fiction: A Geography of the Fantastic" by Ingeborg M. Kohn, in *Contours of the Fantastic: Selected Essays from the 8th Conference on the Fantastic in the Arts,* edited by Michele K. Langford, New York, Greenwood Press, 1994; "The Cartography of Passion: Cixous, Wittig, and Winterson" by Daphne M. Kutzer, in *Re-Naming the Landscape,* edited by Jurgen Kleist and Bruce A. Butterfield, New York, P. Lang, 1994; "Postmodernism Meets the Great Beyond: *Les Guérillères* and *Le Corps lesbien"* by Catherine Nelson-McDermott, in *Canadian Review of Comparative Literature/Revue Canadienne de Littératue Comparée* (Edmonton, Alberta), 21(3), September 1994; "Lesbians and Lyotard: Legitimation and the Politics of the Name" by Judith Roof, in *The Lesbian Postmodern,* edited by Laura Doan, New York, Columbia University Press, 1994; "Escaping the Categories of Sex: Mobility and Lesbian Writing" by Lindsay Tucker, in *Textual Escap(e)ades: Mobility, Maternity, and Textuality in Contemporary Fiction by Women,* Wesport, Connecticut, Greenwood Press, 1994; *Heterosexual Plots and Lesbian Narratives* by Marilyn R. Farwell, New York, New York University Press, 1996; "Lesbians on the French Stage: From Homosexuality to Monique Wittig's Lesbianization of the Theatre" by Jeannelle Laillou Savona, in *Modern Drama* (Toronto), 39(1), spring 1996.

* * *

Monique Wittig was born and educated in France where she graduated from the Sorbonne with a solid grounding in history, philosophy, and foreign languages. In the late 1950s and 1960 she was shaped by the rebellious and creative spirit of a time when French left-wing intellectuals, fired by Mao Zedong's "little red book," Bertolt Brecht's epic theatre, and Roland Barthes's sarcastic essays on "bourgeois" values, were strongly opposed to France's colonial wars in Viet Nam and Algeria. In 1964 Wittig published her first fiction, *The Opoponax,* which was immediately recognized as a work of great originality and awarded the Prix Médicis. Later on, she shared in the euphoria of the May 1968 revolution—uniting students and workers against bureaucratic institutions—which partly inspired *Les Guérillères* (1969), her second fiction. Around 1970 she became actively involved in various groups that contributed to the development of the MLF (Mouvement de Libération des Femmes). Wittig's materialist feminism gained theoretical support and nourishment when she joined the radical lesbians who formed the *Questions Féministes* collective in 1977. These women, who published important sociological or anthropological works on such issues as race, gender, domestic work, and women's awareness of domination, had all been deeply influenced by Marxism, from which they borrowed the notions of class struggle, ideology, and oppression. Wittig moved to the United States in 1976, but the essays she wrote in French in the 1970s, and in English during the 1980s, remain faithful to the political project of the Journal, although they definitely bear the mark of her own personal thinking.

The boldness of Wittig's philosophical vision appears clearly in *The Straight Mind* (1992), a collection of most of her essays written between 1976 and 1990. Wittig considers heterosexuality as the main source of women's oppression, since it serves to maintain two "categories of sex" establishing one sex as possessing all universal values and all social power, and the other as playing only a complementary and submissive role. She redefines heterosexuality as a tacit, unquestioned, and "forced" "social contract" (the notion is borrowed from Rousseau). Based on the false notion of "sexual difference," which conceals a political relation of oppression from one class over another, this contract, or "political regime", heterosexualizes women into "sexual beings meaningful only through their reproductive activities." Like racism, founded on a mythology of "race," heterosexuality, founded on a mythology of "nature," is supported by invasive ideologies underlying all mental categories and social structures. Wittig names these ideologies "the straight mind" and denounces some of their post-structuralist manifestations (such as the notion of the Lacanian Unconscious), for ignoring the historical and material conditions of oppressed groups: women, lesbians, and gays. Heterosexuality must therefore be abolished both philosophically and politically: philosophically, through an "epistemological revolution" that will eradicate the categories of sex and create truly universal mental structures, and politically, through socio-political changes that will give women the power to stop their own personal and collective appropriation by men and negotiate a new social contract. But in her most recent essays, including 1990's "Homo Sum," Wittig has become bitterly aware that her political project goes against the contemporary prevailing philosophies of "difference," which, after the failure of Hegelian dialectics and socialist revolutions, have invaded pseudo-feminist theories with such ahistorical (and mainly psychoanalytical) concepts as "the mind of the Other," "the Feminine brain," or "the Symbolic order."

Wittig's attack on heterosexuality appears much deeper than Adrienne Rich's eloquent analysis in "Compulsory Heterosexuality and Lesbian Existence" (1980). For Wittig, a productive alliance between women cannot be based on "woman identification" or such common female experiences as the mother-daughter bond. It must start with individual acts of escape from heterosexual relations, leading to the formation of "voluntary associations." Lesbians who, according to Wittig, are not women since they have broken the heterosexual contract by refusing to depend on men, stand very high in her project of liberation. When used by Wittig, the term "lesbian" often designates a process of change and revision, a "constant journey" towards a space that has to be conquered both within oneself, through a "subjective cognitive practice," and in the "here and now" of new communities. Whether this prestigious concept of "lesbian" can be claimed by feminists who have removed themselves from heterosexuality without being practising homosexuals, or by gay men who are involved in fighting sexism and heterosexual hegemony, is not absolutely clear. But the verb "to lesbianize," coined by Wittig, denotes a violent process of degenderization through language and subversive representation, which aims at universality.

Wittig first began to write at the age of 12, when she fell in love with another young girl, not unlike Catherine Legrand, the main character of *The Opoponax,* who invents the word "opoponax" in order to express the merging of her first homosexual feelings with her need for writing, as she cannot find any other suitable word to translate her new experience into language. This anecdote and its literary representation are emblematic of Wittig's literary undertaking to create innovative forms capable of re-creating the uniqueness of oppressed subjectivities (female children, revolutionary women, lesbian heroes). In her works of fiction, Wittig was first greatly influenced by the writers of the *Nouveau Roman:* Sarraute, Beckett, Butor, Pinget, Ollier, and Robbe-Grillet, with whom she shares an interest in the material forms of books (graphics, typography, etc.), a frequent use of self-reflexive strategies calling attention to the process of writing, a rejection of narrative linearity, and a distanced type of narration focused on objects, actions, and gestures that recalls cinematic techniques. Like the *Nouveaux Romanciers,* she wants to revolutionize traditional narrative forms, but unlike them, she combines this ambition with a political aim: that of a lesbian feminist agenda. The main challenge, for Wittig, is to attempt to annihilate the category of sex through inherited forms of language and literature, which are marked by grammatical gender and (hetero)sexist lexical connotations. In the original French versions of all her literary works, Wittig either avoids heavily genderized terms, like "woman" or "mother", or she "lesbianizes" the lexicon by using feminine words or coining others which, through consistent repetition, will (hopefully) enter the realm of the universal. She also makes use of "on" ("one"), "elles" ("they"), or "j/e" (translated as "*I*") as narrative pronouns. Although some of her literary strategies happen to overlap those of Hélène Cixous, her purpose is definitely in conflict with "écriture féminine," since she wants to abolish the very notion of "feminine."

In all of Wittig's creative works, images of "voluntary associations" and collective rebellions prevail, whether her female heroes are iconoclastic school girls resisting the corporal and mental discipline of their teachers (*The Opoponax*), or groups of strong Amazon fighters who either recreate a new society (*Les Guérillères*), or take their well-deserved place in a new History of Humankind where women are autonomous and powerful (*Lesbian Peoples: Material for a Dictionary*). Her heroes often appear in couples who fight side by side against men and the ideologies of the social contract, as they do in *Lesbian Peoples, The Constant Journey, Across the Acheron,* and to a certain extent, *The Lesbian Body,* where the two protagonists devote themselves to various destructive and reconstructive bodily acts in order to replace "the feminine body" and its conventional, domesticated forms of eroticism with the free and shockingly violent passions of "the lesbian body," an alternative and complex poetic construction, a new decentred locus of desire and pleasure.

Feminist critics have focused on the positive impact of Wittig's utopian fictions, which project an empowering image of a new space and a new time—past and future—in which women can invent their own destinies collectively. Wittig's writings make ample use of historical documents on the Ancient Amazons, Latin, Greek and medieval history, an international assortment of mythologies, and her own vivid imagination, to give life to an exhilarating world of power and courage. *Les Guérillères,* her best-known fiction, has inspired almost three decades of feminist readers who have borrowed from it the courage to unite with other women and speak up on their behalf. *Lesbian Peoples,* a mock dictionary written with Sande Zeig, completes *Les Guérillères* through its fantastic rewriting of women's histories. In its evocation of Amazonian cultures, the book records a striking historical clash between Amazons and Mothers that appears like a humorous attack on motherhood, viewed as an institution. But this clash also refers to the gap that often exists between lesbians and heterosexual women. In both *Across the Acheron* and *The Constant Journey,* Wittig's more recent literary works, this gap has become an almost impassable chasm. The support of young men and the sympathetic evocation of a loving heterosexual couple in *Les Guérillères* have given way to an entirely negative depiction of heterosexual relations as Hell-on-Earth in *Across the Acheron* (a re-writing of Dante's *The Divine Comedy*), and to a half-comical, half-tragic epic of lesbian feminist heroism in *The Constant Journey* (a play based on Cervantes's *Don Quixote*). In the Hell of *Across the Acheron,* the extreme violence of men and the horrible conditions of women's lives are accepted by the "damned souls" (heterosexual women) themselves; limbo, the lesbian space, is confined to poolrooms and bars, and paradise appears but a remote, beautiful, but purely metaphoric place. Wittig, the character, and Manastabal, her guide, two fictive projections of Monique Wittig the writer, are often trying to protect women with a laser beam or various other weapons, but they find absolutely no support in the "damned souls," who all either ignore, or fear, or despise lesbians. Feminist rebellions are totally absent from this nightmarish world. In *The Constant Journey,* Quixote and Sancha, two lesbians enthused by ancient Amazonian epics, are also in search of a better world, but their attempts at improving women's lives meet with failure or betrayal. Although Wittig's recent works are imbued with both irony and humour, they express a profound bitterness concerning heterosexual women and feminism's accomplishments. This may explain why they have been comparatively neglected by feminist critics despite the originality of their literary and theatrical features.

Monique Wittig's overall contribution to both literature and feminist theories is undoubtedly one of the greatest importance. Her creative writings exert a deep fascination through the clarity and concision of their style, which conveys innovative images and beautifully coloured vignettes. They first appeal to the eyes and imagination of the reader/spectator who, haunted by Wittig's vision and unusual formal experimentation, feels compelled to assemble their somewhat jagged, fragmented pieces into a meaningful whole. But Wittig's books constitute so many different open-ended *oeuvres* whose polysemy resist any narrow interpretations. Yet there seems to be a profound unity between all her fictive works and her feminist lesbian philosophy, a unity critics have not yet fully investigated.

—Jeannelle Laillou Savona

WOLF, Christa

Nationality: German. **Born:** Landsberg an der Warthe (now Gorzow Wielkopolski, Poland), 18 March 1929. **Education:** Attended University of Jena and University of Leipzig, 1949-53. **Family:** Married the writer Gerhard Wolf in 1951; two daughters. **Career:** Technical assistant, East German Writers Union; reader, Neues Leben (publisher), East Berlin; editor, *Neue Deutsche Literatur* (magazine); reader, Mitteldeutscher Verlag (publisher), Halle, East Germany, 1959-62; full-time writer beginning 1962. Guest lecturer at universities. **Awards:** City of Halle literary prize, 1961; German Academy Heinrich Mann Prize, 1963, for *Der geteilte Himmel;* German Democratic Republic Prize for Art and Literature, 1964; Fontane Prize, 1972; Bremen Literature Prize, 1978; Georg Büchner Prize, 1980; City of Graz' Franz Nable Prize, 1983; Schiller Memorial Prize, 1983; Austrian National Prize for European literature, 1985; Sibling Scholl Prize, 1987; National Prize of the First Class of the GDR, 1987; Premio Modello, 1990, Officier des arts et des lettres Medal (Paris), 1990; Erich Fried honor, 1992; honorary member of American Academy and Institute of Arts and Letters, 1993. **Member:** Socialist Unified Party (SED; member of Central Committee, 1989).

PUBLICATIONS

Novels

Moskauer Novelle. Darmstadt, Luchterhand, 1961.
Der geteilte Himmel. Darmstadt, Luchterhand, 1963; translated as *Divided Heaven: A Novel of Germany Today,* Seven-Seas Press, 1965; Adler's Foreign Books, 1976.
Nachdenken über Christa T. Darmstadt, Luchterhand, 1968; translated as *The Search for Christa T.,* New York, Farrar Straus, 1971.
Kindheitsmuster. Darmstadt, Luchterhand, 1976; translated as *A Model Childhood,* New York, Farrar Straus, 1980; as *Patterns of Childhood,* 1984.
Kein Ort, Nirgends. Berlin, Aufbau, 1979; as *No Place on Earth,* New York, Farrar, Straus, 1980.
Kassandra: Vier Vorlesungen; eine Erzählung (includes essays). Darmstadt, Luchterhand, 1983; as *Cassandra: A Novel and Four Essays,* New York, Farrar, Straus, 1984.
Störfall. Darmstadt, Luchterhand, 1987; translated as *Accidents: A Day's News,* New York, Farrar, Straus, 1989.
Sommerstück. Darmstadt, Luchterhand, 1989.
Was bleibt. Darmstadt, Luchterhand, 1989; translated in *What Remains and Other Stories,* New York Farrar Straus, 1994.
Medea. Stimmen. Darmstadt, Luchterhand, 1996.

Short Stories

Unter den Linden: Drei unwahrscheinliche Geschichten [Under the Linden Tree: Three Improbable Stories]. Berlin, Aufbau, 1974.
"Selbstversuch" [Self-Experiment], in *Geschlechtertausch. Sarah Kirsche, Irmtraud Morgner und Christa Wolf.* Darmstadt, Luchterhand, 1980.
Gesammelte Erzählungen. Darmstadt, Luchterhand, 1980.
Neue Lebensansichten eines Katers; Juninachmittag. Reclam, 1981.

Essays

Lesen und Schreiben: Aufsätze und Betrachtungen. Darmstadt, Luchterhand, 1972; as *Lesen und Schreiben: Aufsätze und Prosastücke.* Luchterhand, 1972; translated as *The Reader and the Writer: Essays, Sketches, Memories.* New York, Signet, 1977.
J'ecris sur ce qui m'inquiete: debats dans Sinn un Form sur son dernier roman. Paris, Centre d'etudes et de recherches marxistes, 1977.
Fortgesetzter Versuch: Aufsätze, Gespräche, Essays. Reclam, 1979.
Voraussetzungen einer Erzählung: Kassandra [Genesis of a Story: Kassandra] (lectures). Luchterhand, 1983.
Die Dimension des Autors: Essays und Aufsätze, Reden und Gespräche 1959-1986. Luchterhand, 1987.
Ansprachen. Luchterhand, 1989.
Reden im Herbst. Berlin, Aufbau, 1990.
Auf dem Weg nach Tabou. Texte 1990-1994. Köln, Kiepenheuer & Witsche, 1994.

Other

Editor, *In diesen Jahren: Deutsche Erzähler der Gegenwart* [In These Years: Contemporary German Short Story Writers]. Reclam, 1957.
Editor, with Gerhard Wolf, *Wir, unsere Zeit* [We, in Our Time]. Berlin, Aufbau, 1959.
Editor, *Proben junger Erzähler: Ausgewählte deutsche Prosa* [A Sampler of Work by Young Short Story Writers]. Reclam, 1959.
Editor, *Der Schatten eines Traumes,* by Karoline von Günderode. Der Morgen, 1979.
Editor, *Historischer Verein für Hessen, 1934-1983: Vorträge, Exkursionen, Publikationen.* Verlag des Historischen Vereins für Hessen, 1983.
Editor, *Ausgewählte Erzählungen,* by Anna Seghers. Luchterhand, 1983.

*

Media Adaptations: *Divided Heaven* (film), 1964; *Selbstversuch* (film), 1990.

Bibliography: *Christa Wolf* by Alexander Stephan, Amsterdam, Rodopi, 1980.

Critical Studies: *Women Writers: The Divided Self; Analysis of Novels by Christa Wolf, Ingeborg Bachmann, Doris Lessing, and Others* by Inta Ezergailis, Grundmann, 1982; *The Death of Socialist Realism in the Novels of Christa Wolf* by George Buehler, London, P. Lang, 1984; *Christa Wolf's Utopian Vision: From Marxism to Feminism* by Anna K. Kuhn, Cambridge, Cambridge University Press, 1988; "The Transsexual as Anders in Christa Wolf's 'Self-Experiment'" by Ann Herrman, in *Genders,* 3, fall 1988, and her *The Dialogic and Difference,* New York, Columbia University Press, 1989; *Responses to Christa Wolf: Critical Essays* edited by Marilyn Sibley Fries, Detroit, Wayne State University Press, 1989; *The Fourth Dimension: Interviews with Christa Wolf* translated by Hilary Pilington, London, n.p., 1990.

* * *

Although she has recently become the focus of great controversy, Christa Wolf is one of the most highly regarded German writers. In 1990, after German unification, a great debate erupted over her alleged participation more than 30 years ago in spy activities in the former East Germany (GDR) and over the publication in 1979 of her book *Was bleibt.* This novel had originally been written in 1979 and chronicles the events of a day in the life of an East German women writer who is being observed by the secret police, the "Stasi." Because Wolf did not publish this story until after the demise of the GDR regime, critics accused her of stylizing herself as a victim of an oppressive government after the fact while instead holding a privileged and secure position.

From the beginning of the GDR in 1949 to its demise in 1990, Wolf had been an active participant and an ardent believer in the socialist state, and she has always been as interested in literature as she has been in political affairs. Her first novel, *Divided Heaven,* published in 1963 and situated against the background of the building of the Berlin Wall in 1961, exhibited the enthusiasm of the beginning years of the socialist state. With her second novel, *The Quest for Christa T.* in 1968, however, Wolf started to scrutinize and openly question the social and political development within the GDR and its "male" principle of reality (by which she means not a critique of gender but rather of a certain male-defined value system) that fosters a society based on instrumental reason, scientific objectivity, and human alienation to the exclusion of exclusion of values usually associated with the realm of women, such as emotionality, nurturing, and community.

Although all her works are clearly all informed by a feminist sensibility, Wolf, like many German women writers, is reluctant to be labeled a "feminist" author. Yet she thematized the problems of "subjectivity" and "female authenticity" long before these became terms with which to describe the experience of women's lives in a patriarchally defined society. This led Wolf's friend and critic Sonja Hilzinger to define Wolf's style as "a female aesthetic of resistance."

Among her most significant contributions to feminist literature are her novels *The Quest for Christa T., No Place on Earth* (1979), *Cassandra: A Novel and Four Essays* (1983), *Accidents: A Day's News* (1987) and her latest novel, *Medea* (1996). In all of her novels, but more so in these particular works, Wolf explores personal issues of female identity and combines them with a critique of patriarchal western society.

In *The Quest for Christa T.* Wolf examines the life of a women who, like herself, at first eagerly embraced the hope of the new, socialist state, but who quickly realizes that she cannot adjust as readily as her friends. The novel begins with the epitaph "This coming to oneself—what is it?," a quotation by Johannes R. Becher, cultural minister of the GDR, that already summarizes the theme of the novel: the question of individual (female) self-actualization (realization) within a socialist state or "the difficulty of saying 'I'" in a society insisting upon a collective "we." In 1980 Wolf's overriding concern as a long-time member of the peace and environmental movement faced with the impending installation of American cruise missiles on West German soil, was the survival of a Europe that seemed to move dangerously close toward a possible nuclear war. During the same time, after having re-read the Iliad and having been struck by the absence of women's voices from the historical record in favor of an emphasis on hero worship and war activities, Wolf began research on her new novel *Cassandra,* in which she rewrites the history of the Trojan War from the viewpoint of Cassandra, the Trojan princess/prophetess who had the gift of foretelling the future, yet was cursed with never being believed. In writing *Cassandra,* Wolf's aim was to resurrect the "vox feminae"—the voice of women—back into history in order to provide a glimpse of hope for the future, for increasingly, Wolf looks to women and the values associated with them for answers to the survival of the human species. Therefore, her critique of patriarchy and out-of-control technology intensifies from novel to novel, perhaps culminating in *Accident: News of a Day,* a novel in which she attempts to discover the reasons behind the nuclear catastrophe at Chernobyl in 1986. In *Medea* Wolf retraces—much in the same way as she did in *Cassandra*—the steps of the mythical figure accused of killing her own children, and tries to reclaim her from a patriarchy history.

Besides being a respected novelist, Wolf is also a prolific essayist and literary critic. She has published volumes of essays on the role of the writer in society, on the art of writing itself, on other writers, as well as on political and feminist issues. In her latest collection of texts, *Auf dem Weg nach Tabou* [On the Way to Taboo] (1994), she chronicles the crucial political events in Germany between 1990 and 1994 with essays, speeches, letters, and diary notes. And it is here in her many theoretical writings, foremost among them the four essays published alongside with *Cassandra,* that her feminist stance is most clearly pronounced. For although Wolf aims at female autonomy for her heroines in her novels, in the end they are not able to transcend their restrictive societies. But in her critical writings, Wolf succeeds in articulating an empancipatory female consciousness as an alternative to the reified rational discourse of western civilization.

Although Christa Wolf's works were usually met with resistance when first published, they have since been reprinted numerous times and translated into many different languages, attesting to the fact that she is considered one of the most important writers of the GDR and now of united Germany. Her novels not only give an invaluable insight into GDR life but also raise important issues about women's roles, and the balance of responsibility between the individual and society.

—Karin U. Herrmann

WOLF, Naomi

Nationality: American. **Born:** San Francisco, California, 12 November 1962. **Education:** Yale University, B.A. in English literature 1984; attended New College, Oxford. **Family:** Married David Shipley in 1993. **Career:** Journalist and lecturer. Contributor to periodicals, including *Glamour, Ms., New Republic, New York Times, Wall Street Journal,* and *Wall Street Journal.* Founder, Culture Babes, New York. **Awards:** Rhodes scholar, 1986; Academy of American Poets prize, twice. **Agent:** c/o Royce Carleton, 866 UN Plaza, New York, New York 10017, USA.

Publications

Political/Social Theory

The Beauty Myth: How Images of Beauty Are Used against Women. London, Chatto & Windus, 1990; New York, Morrow, 1991.

Fire with Fire: The New Female Power and How It Will Change the 21st Century. New York, Random House, and London, Chatto & Windus, 1993.

* * *

Since the publication of *The Beauty Myth: How Images of Beauty Are Used against Women,* Naomi Wolf has become a important voice in the feminist movement. This book takes a critical look at the feminist movement and the "backlash" that Wolf sees associated with it in the 1990s. As Wolf states in *The Beauty Myth,* "we [women] are in the midst of a violent backlash against feminism that uses images of female beauty as a political weapon against women's advancement: the beauty myth." Wolf argues that the modern-day obsession with beauty has negated much of the advances associated with the feminist movement. The beauty myth, according to Wolf, is responsible for the rise in eating disorders and cosmetic surgery and the general decline in self-esteem in women. As Wolf argues, "in terms of how we feel about ourselves physically, we may actually be worse off than our unliberated grandmothers." Aside from the successes women have achieved in terms of gaining equality in society, Wolf notes that the beauty myth has threatened these improvements.

Although she has been criticized for fabricating numbers for her figures concerning women's health issues (the figures on eating disorders for example), Wolf has made some important observations about the role of feminism in society. Her examination of the beauty myth encompasses the beginnings of the myth and its development. Wolf also includes the political implications of the beauty myth. Reading at times like a social history, *The Beauty Myth* details the ways in which the beauty myth has remained, through centuries, one of the fundamental ways for men to secure patriarchal dominance within a society. The beauty myth, as Wolf states, is "undermining—slowly, imperceptibly, without our being aware of the real forces of erosion—the ground women have gained through the long hard, honorable struggle." Whether it is the cosmetics industry or the diet industry, Wolf sees that modern culture's perpetuation of the beauty myth is "destroying women physically and depleting [them] psychologically."

Following *The Beauty Myth,* Wolf published *Fire with Fire: The New Female Power and How It Will Change the 21st Century.* Appealing to women who saw themselves far removed from the early origins of the feminist movement, this book offered further exploration of the modern-day role of feminism in society, as well as an opportunity for an older generation to reevaluate the movement. This book again reveals Wolf's criticism of the feminist movement as well as her challenge to women to forge ahead and create their own modern version of feminism. Wolf challenges the feminists of today to join together. She notes that feminism has divided into two strands which she names "victim feminism" and "power feminism." Urging women to move away from "victim feminism" which centers itself on the position of women as eternal victims of male dominance, Wolf advocates a "power feminism" that recognizes the advantages that women have such as being a part of the majority of the population in the United States.

While many young women interested in feminism may feel detached from the women's movement as it existed in the late 1960s and early 1970s, Wolf offers an alternative way of looking at feminism. She challenges women to take a stand in defining the future of the feminist movement. This is part of the appeal of *Fire with Fire;* it is a challenge to make a change. Wolf encourages women to take control of their lives and to live in the present rather than focusing on past events.

Despite her departure from the beginnings of the feminist movement, Naomi Wolf remains a powerful voice in feminist criticism. At a time when women seem to be under attack by American culture at large through the images seen in the media, Wolf offers a distinct view of the role of the woman today. She challenges women to look ahead in order to begin to heal the wounds of the past. Perhaps most importantly, Wolf's work reminds us that feminism has come a long way but has a longer way to go.

—Melissa L. Evans

WOLLSTONECRAFT, Mary

Also wrote as Mary Wollstonecraft Godwin. **Pseudonym:** Mr. Cresswick. **Nationality:** British. **Born:** Hoxton, England, 27 April 1759. **Education:** Self-educated. **Family:** Companion of Captain Gilbert Imlay beginning 1792; one daughter; married William Godwin in 1797; one daughter, the author Mary Shelley. **Career:** Lived in Beverly, Yorkshire, 1768-73, London, 1774-75, and 1777, and Laugharne, Wales, 1776; paid companion to Mrs. Dawson, Bath, England, 1778-80; cared for her invalid mother, 1780-82; with sisters and friend Fanny Blood, started a school in Islington, then Newington Green, 1784-86; governess to family of Lord Kingsborough, Mitchelstown, County Cork, Ireland, 1786-87; reader, writer, and translator for Joseph Johnson (publisher), and editorial assistant for his journal *Analytical Review,* London, 1787-92, and 1797; met Thomas Paine and Henry Fuseli; lived in Paris with American soldier Gilbert Imlay, beginning 1792; reported on the French Revolution, 1792-95; travelled with Imlay in Scandinavia, 1795; attempted suicide, 1795. **Died:** 10 September 1797.

Publications

Essays

Thoughts on the Education of Daughters: with Reflections on Female Conduct, in the More Important Duties of Life. London, J. Johnson, 1787.

A Vindication of the Rights of Men, in a Letter to the Right Honorable Edmund Burke. London, J. Johnson, 1790; revised, 1790.

A Vindication of the Rights of Women: with Strictures on Political and Moral Subjects. London, J. Johnson, and Boston, Thomas & Andrews, 1792; second edition, London, J. Johnson, 1792.

An Historical and Moral View of the Progress of the French Revolution, and the Effect It Has Produced in Europe. London, J. Johnson, 1794.

Letters Written during a Short Residence in Sweden, Norway, and Denmark. London and Wilmington, Delaware, J. Johnson, 1796.

Novels

Mary: A Fiction. London, n.p., 1788; in *Mary, and The Wrongs of Woman,* edited by James Kinsley and Gary Kelly, Oxford, Oxford University Press, 1976; published separately, New York, Garland, 1974.

Maria; or, The Wrongs of Woman (as Mary Wollstonecraft Godwin). In *Posthumous Works,* 1798; Philadephia, J. Carey, 1799.

For Children

Original Stories from Real Life; with Conversations, Calculated to Regulate the Affections and Form the Mind to Truth and Goodness, illustrated by William Blake. London, J. Johnson, 1791.

Other

Posthumous Works of the Author of A Vindication of the Rights of Woman, edited by William Godwin. London, J. Johnson, 4 vols., 1798.

Letters to Imlay. London, Kegan Paul, 1879; New York, Haskell House, 1971.

The Love Letters of Mary Wollstonecraft to Gilbert Imlay. London, Hutchinson, and Philadelphia, Lippincott, 1908.

Four New Letters of Mary Wollstonecraft and Helen M. Williams, edited by Benjamin P. Kurtz and Carrie C. Autrey. Berkeley, University of California Press, 1937.

Godwin and Mary: Letters of William Godwin and Wollstonecraft, edited by Ralph Wardle. Lawrence, University of Kansas Press, 1966.

A Wollstonecraft Anthology, edited by Janet Todd. Bloomington, Indiana University Press, 1977; Cambridge, Polity Press, 1989.

Collected Letters, edited by Ralph M. Wardle. Ithaca, New York, and London, Cornell University Press, 1979.

A Wollstonecraft Reader, edited by Barbara H. Solomon and Paula S. Berggren. New York, New American Library, 1983.

The Collected Works of Mary Wollstonecraft, edited by Marilyn Butler, Janet Todd, and Emma Rees-Mogg. London, Pickering & Chatto, 7 vols., 1989.

Political Writings, edited by Janet Todd. London, W. Pickering, and Toronto, University of Toronto Press, 1993.

Editor (as Mr. Cresswick), *The Female Reader.* London, J. Johnson, 1789; Delmar, New York, Scholars Facsimiles, 1980.

Translator, *Of the Importance of Religious Opinions,* by Jacques Necker. London, J. Johnson, 1788.

Translator, *Young Grandison: A Series of Letters from Young Persons to Their Friends,* by Maria Geertrudia van de Werken de Cambon. London, J. Johnson, 2 vols., 1790.

Translator, *Elements of Morality, for the Use of Children,* by Christian Gotthilf Salzmann. London, J. Johnson, 2 vols., 1790.

*

Bibliography: *Wollstonecraft: An Annotated Bibliography* by Janet Todd, London and New York, Garland, 1976; *Mary Wollstonecraft (Godwin): A Bibliography of Her Writings, 1787-1982* by J. R. Windle, Los Angeles, J. Windle, 1988.

Manuscript Collections: Bodleian Library, Oxford University; Carl H. Pforzheimer Collection, New York Public Library.

Critical Studies: *Memoirs of the Author of A Vindication of the Rights of Women* by William Godwin, J. Johnson, 1788, New York, Garland, 1974; *A Study of Mary Wollstonecraft and the Rights of Woman* by Emma Rauschenbusch Clough, London and New York, Longmans Green, 1898; *Mary Wollstonecraft* by Madeline Linford, Boston, Small Maynard, 1924; *Mary Wollstonecraft: A Sketch* by Henry R. James, London, Oxford University Press, 1932; "Mary Wollstonecraft" by Virginia Woolf, in her *The Second Common Reader,* New York, Harcourt, 1932; *Wollstonecraft: A Critical Biography* by Ralph Wardle, Lawrence, University of Kansas Press, 1951; *One Woman's Situation: A Study of Mary Wollstonecraft* by Margaret George, Urbana, University of Illinois Press, 1970; *Wollstonecraft: Her Life and Times* by Edna Nixon, London, Dent, 1971; *Mary Wollstonecraft: A Biography* by Eleanor Flexner, New York, Coward McCann, 1972; *The Life and Death of Mary Wollstonecraft* by Clair Tomalin, London, Weidenfeld & Nicholson, and New York, Harcourt Brace, 1974, revised, London, Penguin, 1992; *A Different Face: The Life of Mary Wollstonecraft* by Emily W. Sunstein, New York, Harper, 1975; *A Most Extraordinary Pair: Mary Wollstonecraft and William Godwin* by Jean Detre, Garden City, New York, Doubleday, 1975; *Mary Wollstonecraft and the Beginnings of Female Emancipation in France and England* by Jacob Bouten, Philadelphia, Porcupine Press, 1975; *Wollstonecraft: A Social Pioneer* by Margaret Tims, London, Millington, 1976; "Radical Politics in Mary Wollstonecraft's *A Vindication of the Rights of Woman*" by Elissa Guralnick, in *Studies in Burke and His Time,* 18, autumn 1977; *Mary Wollstonecraft* by Moira Fergusen and Janet Todd, Boston, Twayne, 1984; *The Proper Lady and the Woman Writer: Ideology as Style in the Works of Mary Wollstonecraft, Mary Shelley, and Jane Austen* by Mary Poovey, Chicago, University of Chicago Press, 1984; "Impeccable Governesses, Rational Dames, and Moral Mothers: Mary Wollstonecraft and the Female Tradition in Georgian Children's Books" by Mitzi Myers, in *Children's Literature,* 14, 1986; *The Eighteenth-Century Feminist Mind* by Alice Browne, Detroit, Wayne University Press, 1987; *Women in Romanticism: Mary Wollstonecraft, Dorothy Wordsworth, and Mary Shelley* by Meena Alexander, London, Macmillan, 1989; *The Godwins and the Shelleys: The Biography of a Family* by William St. Clair, London, Faber, and New York, Norton, 1989; "Revolution in Bounds: Wollstonecraft, Women, and Reason" by Timothy J. Reiss, in *Genre and Theory: Dialogues of Feminist Criticism,* edited by Linda Kaufmann, Oxford, Blackwell, 1989; *Mary Wollstonecraft: The Making of a Radical Feminist* by Jennifer Lorch, Oxford, Berg, 1990; *Revolutionary Feminism: The Mind and Career of Mary Wollstonecraft* by Gary Kelly, London, Macmillan, 1991, New York, St. Martin's Press, 1992; *A Vindication of Political Virtue: The Political Theory of Mary Wollstonecraft* by Virginia Shapiro,

Chicago, University of Chicago Press, 1992; *Mary Wollstonecraft and the Language of Sensibility* by Syndy McMillen Conger, Rutherford, New Jersey, Farleigh Dickinson University Press, 1994; *Equivocal Beings: Politics, Gender, and Sentimentality in the 1790s: Wollstonecraft, Radcliffe, Burney, Austen* by Claudia L. Johnson, Chicago, University of Chicago Press, 1995; *Feminist Interpretations of Mary Wollstonecraft* edited by Maria J. Falco, University Park, Pennsylvania, Pennsylvania State University Press, 1996.

* * *

Nearly two centuries after her death in 1797 from complications following the birth of her famous daughter, Mary Shelley, Mary Wollstonecraft occupies an important place in feminist literary studies. During her life, the popular press attacked her "radical" views; after her death, Wollstonecraft served as an example to women of the 19th century, either as an "unsex'd female" or, to an important few, as a model author in the male-dominated world of letters. The 20th century has witnessed Wollstonecraft's emergence as a seminal figure in feminist writing.

Wollstonecraft's early life exercised an important influence on the books she would write and predisposed her to find the radical politics of the 1780s and 1790s appealing. From her family experience as the second of seven children born to an abusive father, she learned first-hand the limits of her gendered social position. The young Wollstonecraft attempted all of the respectable employment options for unmarried middle-class women: she worked as a paid companion in the fashionable resort of Bath, as a governess in an aristocratic family, and as the proprietor of a school. She witnessed the failure of contemporary education for girls and young women, as well as the powerless position of women in unhappy marriages. During the mid-1780s, she met Dr. Richard Price and his circle of Dissenters in Newington Green, and her conversations with them introduced her to authors who helped shape her political and social thinking, as well as to an important resource for her career change, liberal publisher Joseph Johnson.

Her first publication, *Thoughts on the Education of Daughters* (1787), may seem conventional to modern readers, but it argued against many accepted child-rearing and educational practices of the 18th century. With this conduct book—written to satisfy the growing appetite of an emerging middle class—Wollstonecraft worked within an accepted genre for women writers. Still, in this collection of essays on forming the moral character of girls, she also applies the lessons of her self-education, drawing on the ideas of Locke, Rousseau, and other liberal writers. Her moralistic pronouncements on the proper education for daughters clearly anticipate her later critique of the condescending social construction of gender for girls and women.

Wollstonecraft again remains very clearly within the female tradition of authorship with her 1788 novel, *Mary: A Fiction*. Published by Johnson (like all her books), the novel fuses autobiographical elements with an assessment of the self-defeating effects of morbid sentimentalism. A third-person account of a woman dissatisfied with her arranged marriage and overcome with affection for another man, Mary's story admits of only one outcome—her death from a fever after she accepts the hopelessness of her life. The novel concludes with its heroine "hastening to that world *where there is neither marrying*, nor giving in marriage."

Also published in 1788, *Original Stories, from Real Life* intensifies her earlier critique of the inadequacies of contemporary education for females, in this case two sisters, the vain Caroline and the hypercritical Mary. Suffering from the neglect of wealthy, fashionable parents who have relegated the important matter of their education to servants, the sisters listen to the "moral conversations and stories" of a female relative—the wise and virtuous Mrs. Mason, chosen by their father to provide a much needed corrective to the girls' moral training. Selections ranging from animal parables to allegorical warnings in the accounts of such figures as Mrs. Trueman, Mr. Lofty, and Jane Fretful, echo Wollstonecraft's own conviction that reason is God's gift to all humans, whatever their gender. Reasoned Christian virtue can guide every aspect of human life from the treatment of animals to the design of clothing for females.

In London, Wollstonecraft's friendship with Johnson and her success as a professional writer brought her into association with some of the leading radical and dissenting minds of the time at dinners the publisher hosted. Along with such figures as artist and poet William Blake, she became friends with Thomas Christie, Johnson's partner in launching his new periodical, *The New Analytical Review*. Wollstonecraft's self-confidence no doubt benefited from her new friendships as she entered the traditionally male domain of authorship. During the early years of the French Revolution, she would contribute reviews on subjects ranging from poetry to medicine to *The New Analytical Review,* as well as translating philosophical works from German and French, both languages she learned on her own.

In 1789 Wollstonecraft assumed the pseudonym "Mr. Cresswick, Teacher of Elocution" for her *The Female Reader,* a collection of instructional prose and verse "selected from the best writers." Along with excerpts from the Bible and Shakespeare, Wollstonecraft includes "A Conversation on Truth" from her own *Original Stories* and an admonition on the vanity of dress signed "M. Wollstonecraft." Under her pseudonym, she prefaces *The Female Reader* with an essay on female education based on the development of reason and virtue—"the improvement of her [every young woman's] mind and heart ... the business of her whole life."

Johnson, who would later be imprisoned for selling Thomas Paine's *Rights of Man,* encouraged the radicals among his authors, and he supported Wollstonecraft when she responded to an attack on the ideals of the French Revolution by one of England's leading political figures, Edmund Burke. In his *Reflections on the Revolution in France,* published in November 1790, Burke set the tone for reactionary opposition and inspired a series of responses from liberal and radical authors. Burke's personal attacks on her friend and mentor, Richard Price, his complacency over social and economic injustices, and his style and reasoning, which she attacked as "effeminate" and "sentimental," deeply offended Wollstonecraft. Her *Vindication of the Rights of Man* was published anonymously by Johnson the following month, a second edition appearing shortly afterwards bearing her name on the title page.

Unlike the women who had attacked the slave trade two years earlier in poems with sentimental appeal, Wollstonecraft chose argumentative prose and responded by reasoning from immutable principles. Although she attacks Burke, the individual, as well as his conservative, "organic" notions of political development, and employs sarcasm as a weapon, she emphasizes reason, individual merit, and moral virtue in her argument. She was not the first woman to enter the male-dominated domain of political discourse, but she was clearly the most visible and least diffident female to challenge publicly such an eminent male politician and rhetorician. A hostile notice of the second edition in the *Critical Review* bears testament to just how unconventional her work was considered.

Early in 1792 Wollstonecraft made the connection which few others would make between the rights of men and the situation of women. By far her best known book—and the one on which her reputation as an early feminist rests—Wollstonecraft's *Vindication of the Rights of Woman* stimulated a new debate on sexual injustice and earned her the moral condemnation of conservative men and women alike. Her appeal opens with a dedication to Tallyrand, one of the principle figures behind reform of education in revolutionary France; it then assaults Rousseau's sexist notions of female education in his otherwise enlightened *Émile.* In this protest against social inequality, Wollstonecraft combines her early dissatisfaction with the education of girls with a heightened political awareness to produce one of the first revolutionary feminist statements.

Although acknowledging certain differences between men and women from the outset, *Vindication of the Rights of Woman* bases its argument on the spiritual equality of all human beings. From this first principle, she ridicules the contemporary gender construction of females as weak and modest, attractive and shallow playthings for men, reinforced by an education based in sentiment and focused on luring a suitable mate, however deceptively. Wollstonecraft reasons that if women are indeed capable of being moral beings, then their education should be designed to help them achieve a moral and intellectual development equal (or very nearly so) to men's. In marriage, she maintains, women should be the equal partners of their husbands, not merely attractive and desirable objects of male passion. As the basis of relations between the sexes, education, as Wollstonecraft envisions it, can become an agent for a change in power relations within the family and society at large. The implications of considering women as "human creatures," Wollstonecraft clearly understands, include a challenge to the double standard of sexual behavior and artificial social distinctions. If her book is not explicitly subversive in political terms, reactions to her thinking leave little doubt that conservatives, from Horace Walpole and Hannah More to Richard Polwhele, considered it nothing less than revolutionary.

After publication of *Vindication of the Rights of Woman,* Wollstonecraft decided to travel to Paris for the express purpose of writing a history of the revolution. Her experiences in France during the terror softened her views on the revolution, a change reflected in the sole volume of her series, *An Historical and Moral View of the French Revolution, and the Effect it Has Produced in Europe.* Wollstonecraft's *French Revolution* continues her attack on injustice in France and the social construction of gender, but as history it suffers from her lack of understanding of the nation and the limited scope of the only volume completed. She wrote under considerable pressure and with the awareness that, like her friend Helen Maria Williams, she could become a victim of the current hysteria. Her personal distractions—a relationship with Gilbert Imlay, the first real love of her life, and the birth of their daughter Fanny in 1794—were not conducive to writing something so different from her previous work.

After her relationship with Imlay soured, Wollstonecraft left France with Fanny to tour Scandinavia as his business agent. During these months, she kept up a personal correspondence with Imlay, chronicling the manners of the people she observed during her travels. These letters, returned by her estranged lover, formed the bulk of *Letters Written during a Short Residence in Sweden, Norway, and Denmark,* the book Godwin later claimed led him to fall in love with its author. The work is generally regarded as stylistically her best writing.

Wollstonecraft's last important work, the unfinished novel, *Maria, or the Wrongs of Woman,* appeared posthumously in Godwin's candid *Memoirs of the Author of the Vindication of the Rights of Woman* (1798), which inspired scores of attacks on her moral character and radical politics. In the novel, Wollstonecraft confronts legal injustices perpetrated against women in regard to property, child custody, sexual and reproductive freedom, extralegal incarceration, and divorce. The heroine, Maria, "bastiled" in a mental institution by her husband, consummates a "natural" marriage with a fellow inmate and eventually escapes with him. During a subsequent trial for adultery, Maria delivers an impassioned argument against British law and legal system and extends the scope of Wollstonecraft's social and political criticism.

Maria's keeper and later confidante, Jemima, relates her own story of sexual oppression, rape, abortion, and prostitution during the course of the novel. By including a laboring class women in this final protest against sexual oppression, Wollstonecraft offers a broader critique of patriarchy. In contrast to her earlier focus on the bourgeois woman—and a sometimes disdainful attitude toward the lower orders—*Maria* depicts sympathetically the plight of a plebeian woman oppressed by class as well as gender. Education, the primary concern of Wollstonecraft's social and political commentary from the beginning, plays a secondary role in the world of Maria and Jemima, a world in which the tyranny of the status quo imprisons women at every turn. This final comment on the status of women tantalizes with its hints of the possible direction of Mary Wollstonecraft's feminist thinking had she survived the medical practices of her day.

—R. Edward Ball

WOOLF, (Adeline) Virginia

Also wrote as Virginia Stephen. **Nationality:** British. **Born:** London, 25 January 1882; daughter of the writer Sir Leslie Stephen. **Education:** Self-educated. **Family:** Married Leonard Woolf in 1912. **Career:** Moved to Bloomsbury, London 1904; instructor in English, Morley College, London, 1905; reviewer, *Times Literary Supplement,* from 1905; co-founder and operator, with Leonard Woolf, Hogarth Press, Richmond, Surrey, then London, 1917-41. **Awards:** *Femina-Vie Heureuse* Prize, 1928. **Died:** Committed suicide by drowning in the Ouse River, Lewes, Sussex, 28 March 1941.

Publications

Novels

The Voyage Out. London, Duckworth, 1915; revised, New York, Doran, 1920; earlier version as *Melymbrosia: An Early Version of "The Voyage Out,"* edited by Louise A. DeSalvo, New York, New York Public Library, 1982.

Night and Day. London, Duckworth, 1919; New York, Doran, 1920.

Jacob's Room. Richmond, Hogarth Press, 1922; New York, Harcourt, 1923.
Mrs. Dalloway. London, Hogarth Press, and New York, Harcourt, 1925; selection published as *Mrs. Dalloway's Party: A Short Sequence,* edited by Stella McNichol, London, Hogarth Press, 1973; New York, Harcourt, 1975.
To the Lighthouse. London, Hogarth Press, and New York, Harcourt, 1927.
Orlando: A Biography. London, Hogarth Press, and New York, Crosby Gaige, 1928; early version as *Orlando: The Original Holograph Draft,* edited by Stuart Nelson Clarke, London, S.N. Clarke, 1993.
The Waves. London, Hogarth Press, and New York, Harcourt, 1931; early version as *The Waves: The Two Holograph Drafts,* transcribed and edited by John W. Graham, Toronto and Buffalo, University of Toronto Press, 1976.
Flush, A Biography. London, Hogarth Press, and New York, Harcourt, 1933.
The Years. London, Hogarth Press, and New York, Harcourt, 1937; selections published as *The Pargiters: The Novel-Essay Portion of "The Years,"* edited by Mitchell A. Leaska, New York, New York Public Library, 1977.
Between the Acts. London, Hogarth Press, and New York, Harcourt, 1941.

Short Stories

Two Stories Written and Printed by Virginia Woolf and L.S. Woolf. Richmond, Hogarth Press, 1917; story by Virginia Woolf published separately as *The Mark on the Wall,* Richmond, Hogarth Press, 1919.
Kew Gardens. Richmond, Hogarth Press, 1919; Folcroft, Pennsylvania, Folcroft Press, 1969.
Monday or Tuesday. London, Duckworth, 1919; New York, Doran, 1920.
A Haunted House and Other Short Stories. London, Hogarth Press, 1943; New York, Harcourt, 1944.
The Complete Shorter Fiction of Virginia Woolf, edited by Susan Dick. New York, Harcourt, 1985.
Selected Short Stories of Virginia Woolf, edited by Sandra Kemp. London, Penguin, 1993.

Essays

A Room of One's Own. London, Hogarth Press, and New York, Harcourt, 1929.
On Being Ill. London, Hogarth Press, 1930.
A Letter to a Young Poet. London, Hogarth Press, 1932; Folcroft, Pennsylvania, Folcroft Press, 1975.
Three Guineas. London, Hogarth Press, and New York, Harcourt, 1938.
The Death of the Moth and Other Essays. New York, Harcourt, 1941; London, Hogarth Press, 1942.
The Moment and Other Essays. London, Hogarth Press, 1947; New York, Harcourt, 1948.
The Captain's Death Bed and Other Essays. London, Hogarth Press, and New York, Harcourt, 1950.
Granite and Rainbow. London, Hogarth Press, and New York, Harcourt, 1958.
Collected Essays. London, Hogarth Press, 4 vols., 1966-67; New York, Harcourt, 1967.
The London Scene: Five Essays. New York, F. Hallman, 1975.
The Essays of Virginia Woolf, edited by Andrew McNeillie. New York, Harcourt, and London, Hogarth Press, 4 vols., 1986-94.
A Woman's Essays, edited by Rachel Bowlby. Harmondsworth, Penguin, 2 vols., 1993.

Literary Criticism

Mr. Bennett and Mrs. Brown. London, Hogarth Press, 1924; Folcroft, Pennsylvania, Folcroft Press, 1977.
The Common Reader. London, Hogarth Press, and New York, Harcourt, 1925.
The Common Reader, Second Series. London, Hogarth Press, 1932; as *The Second Common Reader,* New York, Harcourt, 1932.
Contemporary Writers. London, Hogarth Press, 1965; New York, Harcourt, 1966.
Books and Portraits: Some Further Selections from the Literary and Biographical Writings of Virginia Woolf, edited by Mary Lyon. London, Hogarth Press, 1977; New York, Harcourt, 1978.
Women and Writing, edited by Michèle Barrett. London, Women's Press, 1979; New York, Harcourt, 1980.

Play

Freshwater: A Comedy, edited by Lucio P. Ruotolo. New York, Harcourt, 1976.

For Children

Nurse Lugton's Golden Thimble. London, Hogarth Press, 1966.
Nurse Lugton's Curtain. San Diego, Harcourt, 1991.

Autobiography

A Writer's Diary: Being Extracts from the Diary of Virginia Woolf, edited by Leonard Woolf. London, Hogarth Press, 1953; New York, Harcourt, 1954.
Moments of Being, edited by Jeanne Schulkind. London, Chatto & Windus, 1976; New York, Harcourt, 1978.
The Diary of Virginia Woolf, 1915-1919 ([1920-1924], [1925-1930], [1931-1935]), edited by Anne Olivier Bell. London, Hogarth Press, 4 vols., 1977-82; New York, Harcourt, 4 vols., 1979-82.
Virginia Woolf's Reading Notebooks, edited by Brenda R. Silver. Princeton, New Jersey, and Guildford, Surrey, Princeton University Press, 1982.
A Passionate Apprentice: The Early Journals of Virginia Woolf, 1897-1909, edited by Mitchell A. Leaska. London, Hogarth Press, and San Diego, Harcourt, 1990.

Other

Street Haunting. San Francisco, Westgate Press, 1930.
Beau Brummell. New York, Rimington & Hooper, 1930.
Walter Sickert: A Conversation. London, Hogarth Press, 1934; Folcroft, Pennsylvania, Folcroft Press, 1970.
Reviewing. London, Hogarth Press, 1939; Folcroft, Pennsylvania, Folcroft Press, 1969.
Roger Fry: A Biography. London, Hogarth Press, and New York, Harcourt, 1940.

Virginia Woolf and Lytton Strachey: Letters, edited by Leonard Woolf and James Strachey. New York, Harcourt, 1956.
Hours in a Library. New York, Harcourt, 1958.
A Cockney's Farming Experience, edited by Suzanne Dick. New York, Harcourt, 1972.
The Letters of Virginia Woolf; abridged as *Congenial Spirits: The Selected Letters of Virginia Woolf,* edited by Joanne Trautmann Banks. New York, Harcourt, and London, Hogarth Press, 1989.
The Flight of the Mind, 1888-1912, edited by Nigel Nicolson and Joanne Trautmann. London, Hogarth Press, 1975; as *The Letters of Virginia Woolf, Volume 1: 1888-1912,* New York, Harcourt, 1975.
The Question of Things Happening, 1912-1922, edited by Nigel Nicolson and Joan Trautmann. London, Hogarth Press, 1976; as *The Letters of Virginia Woolf, Volume 2: 1912-1922,* New York, Harcourt, 1976.
A Change of Perspective, 1923-28, edited by Nigel Nicolson and Joan Trautmann. London, Hogarth Press, 1977; as *The Letters of Virginia Woolf, Volume 3: 1923-1928,* New York, Harcourt, 1978.
A Reflection of the Other Person, 1929-1931, edited by Nigel Nicolson and Joan Trautmann. London, Hogarth Press, 1978; as *The Letters of Virginia Woolf, Volume 4: 1929-1931,* New York, Harcourt, 1979.
The Sickle Side of the Moon, 1932-1935, edited by Nigel Nicolson and Joan Trautmann. London, Hogarth Press, 1979; as *The Letters of Virginia Woolf, Volume 5: 1932-1935,* New York, Harcourt, 1979.
Leave the Letters Till We're Dead, 1936-1941, edited by Nigel Nicolson and Joan Trautmann. London, Hogarth Press, 1980; as *The Letters of Virginia Woolf, Volume 6: 1936-1941,* New York, Harcourt, 1980.
Rupert Brooke. Burford, England, Cygnet Press, 1978.
The Virginia Woolf Reader, edited by Mitchell A. Leaska. San Diego, Harcourt, 1984.
The Hogarth Letters. London, Chatto & Windus, 1985.
Paper Darts. London, Collins & Brown, 1991.
Travels with Virginia Woolf, edited by Jan Morris. London, Hogarth Press, 1993.

Translator, with S. S. Koteliansky, *Stavogrin's Confession,* by Feodor Dostoevsky. N.p., 1922.
Translator, with S. S. Koteliansky, *Tolstoi's Love Letters.* N.p., 1923.
Translator, with S. S. Koleliansky, *Talks with Tolstoy,* by A.D. Goldenveizer. N.p., 1923.

*

Media Adaptations: *Orlando* (film), 1994.

Manuscript Collections: Henry W. and Albert A. Berg Collection of English and American Literature, New York Public Library; Charleston Papers, King's College, Cambridge; Monk's House Papers, University of Sussex Library; Washington State University's Library at Pullman, Washington; University of Texas at Austin.

Bibliography: *Virginia Woolf: An Annotated Bibliography of Criticism* by Robin Majumdar, New York and London, Garland, 1976; *A Bibliography of Virginia Woolf* by B.J. Kirkpatrick, Oxford, Clarendon Press, 1980.

Critical Studies: *The Well of Loneliness* by Radclyffe Hall, New York, Covici-Friede, 1928; *Mimesis: The Representation of Reality in Western Literature* by Erich Auerbach, translation by Willard R. Trask, Princeton, Princeton University Press, 1953; *Feminism and Art: A Study of Woolf* by Herbert Marder, n.p., 1968; *Modern Fiction Studies,* autumn, 1972 (Virginia Woolf issue); *Virginia Woolf: A Biography* by Quentin Bell, New York, Harcourt, 1972; *The Jessamyn Brides: The Friendship of Virginia Woolf and Vita Sackville West* by Joan Trautmann, University Park, Pennsylvania, Pennsylvania State Studies, 1973; *Virginia Woolf: A Personal Debt* by Margaret Drabble, New York, Aloe, 1973; *Virginia Woolf and the Androgynous Vision* by Nancy Topping Bazin, New Brunswick, New Jersey, Rutgers University Press, 1973; *Toward a Recognition of Androgyny* by Carol G. Heilbrun, New York, Knopf, 1973; *Portrait of a Marriage* by Nigel Nicholson, New York, Antheneum, 1973; *Virginia Woolf: A Critical Reading* by Avrom Fleishman, Baltimore, Johns Hopkins University Press, 1975; *Virginia Woolf and Her World* by John Lehmann, New York, Harcourt, 1975; *The Bloomsbury Group: A Collection of Memoirs, Commentary, and Criticism* by S.P. Rosenbaum, Toronto, University of Toronto Press, 1975; *Bulletin of the New York Library,* winter 1977; *Virginia Woolf: Sources of Madness and Art* by Jean O. Love, Berkeley and London, University of California Press, 1977; *A Marriage of the Minds* by George Spater and Ian Parsons, New York, Harcourt, 1977; *Woman of Letters: A Life of Virginia Woolf,* New York, Oxford University Press, 1978; *Bloomsbury: A House of Lions* by Leon Edel, Philadelphia and New York, Lippincott, 1979; *Continuing Presences: Virginia Woolf's Use of Literary Allusion* by Beverly Ann Schlack, University Park, Pennsylvania State University Press, 1979; *Virginia Woolf: Revaluation and Continuity,* edited by Ralph Freedman, Berkeley and London, University of California Press, 1980; *The Absent Father: Virginia Woolf and Walter Pater* by Perry Meisel, New Haven and London, Yale University Press, 1980; *New Feminist Essays on Virginia Woolf* edited by Jane Marcus, Lincoln, University of Nebraska Press, 1981; *All That Summer She Was Mad* by Stephen Trombley, New York, Continuum, 1982; *Virginia Woolf's Literary Sources and Allusions: A Guide to the Essays* by Elizabeth Steele, New York and London, Garland, 1983; *Virginia Woolf: A Guide to Research* by Thomas Jackson Rice, New York and London, Garland, 1984; *Virginia Woolf: A Writer's Life* by Lyndall Gordon, Oxford, Oxford University Press, 1984; *Virginia Woolf and the Languages of Patriarchy* by Jane Marcus, Bloomington, Indiana University Press, 1987; "'If I Saw You Would You Kiss Me?': Sapphism and the Subversiveness of Virginia Woolf's *Orlando*" by Sherron E. Knopp, in *PMLA,* January 1988; *Virginia Woolf: Life and London; A Biography of Place* by Jean Moorcroft Wilson, New York, Norton, 1988; *Who Killed Virginia Woolf? A Psychobiography* by Alma Halbert Bond, Human Sciences Press, 1989; *Virginia Woolf: The Impact of Childhood Sexual Abuse on Her Life and Work* by Louise A. DeSalvo, Boston, Beacon Press, 1989, and her *Conceived with Malice: Literature as Revenge,* New York, Penguin, 1995; "Sexual Identity and *A Room of One's Own:* 'Secret Economies' in Virginia Woolf's Feminist Discourse" by Ellen Bayuk Rosenman, in *Signs: Journal of Women in Culture and Society,* spring 1989; *Woolf and the Fictions of Psychoanalysis* by Elizabeth Abel, n.p., 1990; *The Reading of Silence: Woolf in the English Tradition* by Patricia Ondek Laurence, n.p., 1991; *Virginia Woolf* by Clare Hanson, New York, St. Martin's Press, 1994; *Aesthetic Autobiography: From Life to Art* by Suzanne Nalbantian, New York, St. Martin's Press, 1994;

Woolf and Lessing: Breaking the Mold edited by Ruth Saxton and Jean Tobin, New York, St. Martin's Press, 1994; *Anglo-Feminist Challenges to the Rhetorical Traditions: Virginia Woolf, Mary Daly, and Adrienne Rich* by Krista Ratcliffe, Carbondale, Southern Illinois University Press, 1995; *Womanist and Feminist Aesthetics: A Comparative Review* by Tuzyline Jita Allan, Athens, Ohio University Press, 1995; *Virginia Woolf and Samuel Johnson: Common Readers* by Beth Carole Rosenberg, New York, St. Martin's Press, 1995.

* * *

Virginia Woolf (née Stephen) was born in London and is considered by many to be the mother of 20th-century feminist literary criticism. In addition to her novels and feminist treatises, she wrote volumes of essays and reviews. Her father, Leslie Stephen, was a literary critic and biographer. Believing that women should not be sent to college, he taught Woolf at home and had a significant influence on her intellectual development. Stephen's presence in the household was tyrannical, dark, and brooding, and when his wife Julia Jackson Duckworth died, he was prone to irrational, emotional outbursts. Reflecting on the anniversary of Stephen's death, Woolf wrote that had he lived there would be "no writing, no books—inconceivable." Woolf's mother represented the typical Victorian "angel in the house," who dedicated her life to Stephen, their children, and charities outside the home. Woolf believed that her mother died prematurely from exhaustion. Woolf's characters, Mrs. Ramsay (*To the Lighthouse*) and Clarissa Dalloway (*Mrs. Dalloway*), are said to be modeled on Julia, while Leslie Stephen shares qualities with the character Mr. Ramsay.

Woolf and her older sister, the painter Vanessa Bell, moved to a house in Bloomsbury after their father's death in 1904. Their new home would become central to activities of the intellectual Bloomsbury group, which included Woolf's brothers, Thoby and Adrian Stephen, painters Clive Bell and Duncan Grant, critics Roger Fry and Desmond MacCarthy, biographer Lytton Strachey, economist Maynard Keynes, and political theorist Leonard Woolf. In 1912, Virginia married Leonard Woolf, with whom she established the Hogarth Press in 1917.

Leonard and Virginia had an unconventional marriage—neither was interested in a sexual relationship though they were deeply engaged in an intellectual one. The Platonic nature of their relationship, and Woolf's later lesbian alliances, have been explained as Virginia's reaction to the sexual abuse she suffered from her step-brother, Gerald Duckworth. In many ways, Leonard was Woolf's caretaker; he worked to create an environment where she could pursue her writing. He took care of the practicalities of their lives while also reading and commenting on her manuscripts. Woolf had suffered a nervous breakdown in 1895 after her mother's death, and then had two others during her lifetime which Leonard helped to nurse her through. As London was being bombed by Germany during World War II, Woolf felt the symptoms of another breakdown. Her diary tells us that she believed she would not recover from this one and felt she could not sentence Leonard to taking care of her for the rest of his life. In 1941, after rewriting drafts of her suicide note, she put rocks in her pockets and drowned herself in the River Ouse.

Woolf's concern with questions of women's subjugation and women and writing are the dominant themes of *Orlando* (1928), *A Room of One's Own* (1929), and *Three Guineas* (1938). *Orlando* was dedicated to and based on the family history of the aristocratic Vita Sackville-West, with whom Woolf had a long and serious love affair from 1923 to 1928. The novel, subtitled *A Biography,* is a historical fantasy that parodies a number of literary texts as well as satirizing academic historical writing. Written as a biography, an anonymous narrator tells the life of Orlando, a young man from an aristocratic background who wishes to write poetry. Orlando begins in the Renaissance, moves through three hundred years of history, transforms his sex along the way, and ends up as woman in the 20th century. *Orlando* analyzes the way gender determines the individual's relationship to property and art at different moments in history. The novel also introduces the concept of androgyny as a way to understand gender.

A Room of One's Own also investigates the issue of androgyny. A classic in Anglo-feminist literary theory, Woolf's work discusses the androgynous mind, a mind that transcends gender and that is necessary for any writer, male or female, to be great. Written in the form of a lecture, the premise of *A Room of One's Own* is to discuss "women and fiction." She offers the opinion that a woman must have money and a room of her own if she is to write fiction. The essay becomes an analysis of women's relationship to economic, social, and educational structures. In addition to the concept of androgyny and women's economic status, the essay discusses the possibility of creating a female literary history. Woolf states that "we think back through our mothers if we are women" and argues for a matrilineal literary tradition. The reason there are no great women writers of Shakespeare's status is because women writers have not had a long tradition to draw upon. What women know about themselves has been told to them by men, and so "women [are] as looking-glasses ... reflecting the figure of man at twice its natural size." For women to understand themselves they must understand the role patriarchy plays in their self-definition. Woolf's argument also includes a discussion of the "female sentence" and proposes a definite connection between sexual difference and language.

The most famous and widely cited invention from Woolf's *A Room* is that of Judith Shakespeare. Woolf develops a myth of what might have happened if William Shakespeare had a sister. According to Woolf, Judith, William's "wonderfully gifted" sister who is denied the education her brother receives, is beaten by her father when she says the marriage he has arranged is hateful to her, and runs away to London at the age of 16 to pursue her dream of being a playwright. Rebuffed and laughed at by the theater men, Judith is eventually seduced by the theater manager Nick Greene and, finding herself pregnant, kills herself. Judith Shakespeare has become a powerful trope of the silenced woman artist. Like other tropes from *A Room,* "Shakespeare's sister" has influenced feminist writers in fields other than the literary.

Three Guineas (1938) is the second of Woolf's major non-fiction works, conceived as a sequel to *A Room.* It has established Woolf as significant voice in the cause of pacifism and feminism. The work is in the form of a letter written to a barrister who has asked Woolf how war might be prevented. In her response, Woolf incorporates letters and drafts of letters to other correspondents who have written for aid. The essay was initially conceived as a talk given to the London/National Society for Women's Service and is intimately linked with the conception and development of her novel, *The Years* (1937). *Three Guineas* looks at the enforced development of a "society of outsiders," emphasizes the importance of economic independence for the daughters of educated men, and questions the nature of women's education. She assesses here the notion of woman as scapegoat of history and argues the necessity for women and other marginalized groups, particularly the working classes, to make a claim for their own history and literature.

Woolf is best known as one of the great experimental novelists during the modernist period. Her earliest novels, *The Voyage Out* (1915) and *Night and Day* (1917), contain traditional, linear narratives, and reflect the Victorian notion of form that Woolf eventually breaks from. *The Voyage Out* reflects Woolf's own struggle with issues of engagement and marriage, with relations between men and women in patriarchal society, and the effects of premature death of people she loved. *Night and Day* is a comic novel of manners concerning five young people struggling with issues of love and work, engagement and marriage, in London in the early years of the 20th century. The five protagonists are part of the Edwardian generation, which Woolf herself belonged to, that sought to escape the social and moral strictures of their parents' Victorian world.

Woolf began her narrative experimentation with the novel *Jacob's Room* (1922). However, the new narrative form that Woolf helped to develop, the "stream-of-consciousness technique," found a more complete expression in *Mrs. Dalloway* (1925) and *To the Lighthouse* (1927). *Mrs. Dalloway* is told through the consciousness of Clarissa Dalloway and relies heavily on memory and psychology for its structure. The novel investigates the world of upper-class London, the sterility of its conventions and manners, its definitions of identity, its impositions of gender and class, and its inheritance of Victorian gender ideologies. *To the Lighthouse* picks up the themes of *Mrs. Dalloway.* It develops the stream-of-consciousness technique through its layering of subjective perceptions. The novel takes place at the summer home of the Ramsay family and is broken into three sections; the final section picks up the narrative many years after the first section. This helps to dramatize the effects of World War I on the Ramsays, who represent upper-class British society. Mr. and Mrs. Ramsay are modelled on Woolf's parents, and she saw the writing of the novel as a kind of catharsis that allowed her to put the memory of her parents to rest. The Ramsay's family friend, Lily Briscoe, is an artist, and her conflicts are reflection of Woolf's concern with form in the novel. Discussions of Lily and Mrs. Ramsay have focused on issues of women's sexuality, creativity, and subjectivity, and how the world is perceived by women.

Woolf's experimental narrative finds its fullest form in her novels *The Waves* (1931) and *Between the Acts* (1941). *The Waves* is probably Woolf's most aesthetic novel, with its focus on form and language. It is usually omitted from political considerations of Woolf, although some have argued that its assault on the traditional novel is part of Woolf's general subversion of patriarchal ideology. The composition of the novel caused Woolf more concern than any of her novels because she was struggling to find a more encompassing form. *The Waves* contains nine poetic interludes that alternate with nine episodes; each episode contains a soliloquy by one of the main characters. In an attempt to articulate the structure of the novel, Woolf called it a gigantic conversation. She also felt that it was structured to a rhythm not to a plot. *Between the Acts* is Woolf's last novel, completed just before her suicide. It is set on a June day and is structured as a series of scenes separated by page breaks. It is a novel concerned with public and private histories: a satirical version of the history of England is told in a pageant and is represented by both the villagers who act in it and by those who watch it. The history of the individuals is represented by the major characters' memories. The troubling and fragmented nature of the novel reflects Woolf's own state of mind during her last days.

—Beth Carole Rosenberg

WOOTEN, Mr. *See* **ASTELL, Mary.**

Y-Z

YEZIERSKA, Anzia

Nationality: Polish. **Born:** Plinsk, Russian Poland, early 1880s; immigrated to United States, c. 1890, naturalized citizen, 1912. **Education:** Columbia University Teacher's College, New York, 1904. **Family:** Married 1) Jacob Gordon in 1910 (marriage annulled 1910); 2) Arnold Levitas in 1911 (divorced 1916), one daughter. **Career:** Worked as a seamstress, in a factory, and as a domestic and cook for a wealthy family, New York, c. 1900-03; teacher of domestic science in an elementary school, c. 1908-10; translator for project for Polish immigrants sponsored by Columbia University, Philadelphia, 1917-18; screenwriter, Hollywood, 1922; cataloger of trees in Central Park for Work Project Administration (WPA), New York, c. 1933; writer, 1915-69. Contributor of reviews and short fiction to periodicals, including *Chicago Jewish Forum, Forum,* and *New York Times.* **Awards:** Edward J. O'Brien prize, 1919, for "The Fat of the Land." **Died:** Ontario, California, 21 November 1970.

PUBLICATIONS

Novels

Salome of the Tenements. New York, Boni & Liveright, 1922.
All I Could Never Be. New York, Putnam, 1932.
Bread Givers: A Struggle between a Father of the Old World and a Daughter of the New. New York, Doubleday, 1925; with introduction by Alice Kessler Harris, New York, Persea, 1975.
Arrogant Beggar. New York, Doubleday, 1927.
Red Ribbon on a White Horse, introduction by W. H. Auden. New York, Scribner's, 1950.

Short Stories

Hungry Hearts (contains "The Fat of the Land" and "How I Found America"). Boston, Houghton Mifflin, 1920; enlarged as *Hungry Hearts and Other Stories,* New York, Persea, 1985.
Children of Loneliness. New York, Funk & Wagnalls, 1923.
Collected Stories of Anzia Yezierska, edited by Louise Levitas Henriksen, New York, Persea, 1991.
How I Found America: Collected Stories of Anzia Yezierska (contains *Hungry Hearts, Children of Loneliness,* and seven uncollected stories). New York, Persea, 1991.

Plays

Screenplays: *Hungry Hearts,* 1922; *Salome of the Tenements,* 1926.

Other

The Open Cage: An Anzia Yezierska Collection, edited by Alice Kessler Harris. New York, Persea, 1979.

*

Manuscript Collection: Mugar Memorial Library, Boston, University.

Critical Studies: *Anzia Yezierska* by Carol B. Shoen, Boston, G.K. Hall, 1982; *Love in the Promised Land: The Story of Anzia Yezierska and John Dewey* by Mary V. Dearborn, New York, Free Press, 1988, and her "Anzia Yezierska and the Making of an Ethnic American Self," in *The Invention of Ethnicity,* edited by Werner Sollors, New York, Oxford University Press, 1989; *Anzia Yezierska* by her daughter, Louise Levitas Henriksen, New Brunswick, Rutgers University Press, 1988; "Cultural Mediation and the Immigrant's Daughter: Anzia Yezierska's *Bread Givers*" by Gay Wilentz, in *MELUS,* 17(3), fall 1991-92; "'Working Ourselves Up': Middle-Class Realism and the Reproduction of Patriarchy in *Bread Givers,*" in *Ethnic Passages: Literary Immigrants in 20th-Century America,* by Thomas J. Ferraro, Chicago, Chicago University Press, 1994; "Looking at Yezierska" by Laura Wexler, in *Women of the Word: Jewish Women and Jewish Writing,* edited by Judith R. Baskin, Detroit, Wayne State University Press, 1994.

* * *

In a story in *Hungry Hearts,* a husband says to his wife longing to leave the poverty and persecution of Russia, "Empty hands—empty pockets—yet it dreams itself in you America." In Yiddish-inflected English, Anzia Yezierska brings to word the intense passion that characterized her life and writing: the quest for a woman's place in the America that dreamed itself in her.

Born in the early 1880s in Russian Poland, Yezierska arrived in New York's Lower East Side Jewish ghetto in the early 1890s with her large family. Her life resembles the core of many of her stories. The youngest of many children, Anzia was the boldest and most rebellious against the hardship and squalor. After breaking away from her parents at age 17, she put herself through night school and college, became exposed to socialism and feminism, and had a love affair with the eminent philosopher John Dewey (whose love poems to her have been recently discovered). Twice married, she found herself unsuited to the traditional wife's role. Having changed her name back from the Americanized Hattie Mayer, she published her first story in 1915. Four years later, she won the prestigious Edward J. O'Brien award for best short story. When *Hungry Hearts,* a collection of her stories, was published in 1920 and attracted studio owner Samuel Goldwyn's attention, she was catapulted into fame. A contract, a Hollywood scriptwriting stint, and the film version of the book followed. The Hollywood publicity machine squeezed dry a sensational version of her life, billing her as the "sweatshop Cinderella" and making her famous through Sunday-supplement articles. But dissatisfied with Hollywood, Yezierska turned down a permanent job offer from Goldwyn and returned to the East Coast. She published most of her work in the 1920s and early '30s, then strangely disappeared from the literary world until 1950, when her fictionalized autobiography, *Red Ribbon on a White Horse,* appeared. After the 1930s she faced poverty again and the pain of being a forgotten author. The resuscitation of her work came after her death, with second-wave feminism in the 1970s, when Yezierska was once again "discovered."

Yezierska's writing stands at the vital confluence of the immigrant experience and feminist consciousness. Mostly centered around Jewish immigrant women characters, her fiction details the pain of displacement, poverty, and the search for an America of one's own through stories about daughters defying Old *and* New World patriarchy, immigrant mothers spurned by assimilated children, young, working-class women's yearnings for education, and ardent newcomers' love for aloof, upper-class, Anglo-Saxon men. The expression of woe and desire is always at a high pitch, at times lachrymose and sentimental but mostly wrenching and powerful.

Written in both immigrant and standard English, the fiction debunks myths of easy and grateful assimilation of Jews into America depicted in works such as Mary Antin's 1912 *The Promised Land.* There is no picturesque poverty nor silent suffering in Yezierska. Her heroines grasp, fight, and refuse. Without ever alluding to feminism, they demand the right to self-actualize, and they challenge the rules of the game. In *Bread Givers,* Yezierska's best novel, Sara runs away from home and away from a father who tells her "It says in the Torah, only through a man has a woman an existence." But it is not only the Jewish father, "a picture out of the Bible," that stands in her way. American-style patriarchal domesticity is also inimical to Yezierska's protagonists. The hunger (a key Yezierska word) to "become a person" and not only wife, or daughter, or laborer defines them. In "America and I" (*Children of Loneliness*), the narrator dreams: "in America, I'd cease to be a slave of the belly. I'd be a creator, a giver, a human being!" But when the deadening jobs at starvation wages push her to desperation, she exclaims, "Who am I? What am I? Where is America? Is there an America? What is this wilderness in which I'm lost?"

For the uncompromisingly independent women in Yezierska's works, Americanization was a goal, but it did not mean integration into a ready-made, perfect setting. America was an incomplete project that needed help from the very immigrant who was thought to only require help. Yezierska's protagonists defy the straitjacket of a future that philanthropy offers to young women. *Salome of the Tenements* is in part a critique of the kind of charity work that imposed itself on "the other half" at the turn of the century. In "How I Found America" (*Hungry Hearts*), the protagonist appeals to a benefactress of a school for immigrants: "'I'm crazy to learn!' I gasped breathlessly." When the woman suggests training to be a servant, the disappointed narrator says, "I got ideas how to make America better, only I don't know how to say it out. Ain't there a place I can learn? ... Here I got all those grand things in me, and America won't let me give nothing." The rich woman perceives this need to take from *and* give to America as ingratitude and audacity. Yezierska's heroines refuse to be what the author called a "hand" (cheap manual labor) for America—they want to contribute to its soul and mind. As women and immigrants, the desire seems doubly impossible to fulfill, and for Yezierska, doubly necessary.

Much of the dilemma of the peculiar, in-between status of the young, ambitious immigrant woman, belonging neither in the Jewish ghetto nor in the Anglo-Saxon world, is dramatized though depictions of impossible love between the women and the sons of long-established, privileged American families in *Salome of the Tenements, The Arrogant Beggar,* and *All I Could Never Be.* The gulf between the lovers is not only economic and social—the fiery immigrant and the reserved Protestant cannot find emotional common ground, and the relationship comes to a sorrowful end. Another frequent theme, intergenerational conflict, also presents the young protagonists as caught between conflicting ideals. At home neither with her parents nor native-born Americans, the immigrant woman is at a constant struggle to define her independent identity.

In her life and in her writing, Anzia Yezierska sought to expand the idea of both womanhood and American identity. A pioneer in women-centric Jewish-American literature, Yezierska found America in only writing about the ghetto and the astonishing, determined, soulful women she created in her fiction.

—Dalia Kandiyoti

ZETKIN, Clara

Nationality: German. **Born:** Wiederau, 1857. **Education:** Leipzig Teacher's College for Women. **Family:** Common-law marriage with Osip Zetkin from 1882 until his death, c. 1890; two children. **Career:** Joined German Social Democratic Party, 1881-1917; lived in Paris and Switzerland; returned to Germany, 1889; delegate to Second Socialist International, 1889; founder, social democratic women's movement, Germany; editor, *Die Gleicheit* [Equality] (newspaper), 1892-1916; founder, International Socialist Women's Congress, 1907; credited with proposal of International Women's Day, to be celebrated on the anniversary of the March 8, 1908, women garment workers strike in New York City, 1910; jailed for pacifism, 1914; with Rosa Luxemburg, helped organize peace conference, Berne, Switzerland, 1915; co-founder, radical Spartacus League, 1916; Independent Social Democratic Party, 1917; and German Communist Party, 1918; member of Executive Committee and head of International Women's Secretariat, Communist International, 1921; member of Reichstag until she formally denounced Adolf Hitler, 1920-32; spent final years in U.S.S.R. **Died:** Moscow, Union of Soviet Socialist Republics, 1933.

Publications

Nonfiction

Erinnerungen an Lenin. 1925; as *My Recollections of Lenin,* in *The Emancipation of Lenin,* New York, International Publishers, 1966.

Clara Zetkin, Selected Writings, edited by Philip Foner. New York, International Publishers, 1984.

*

Critical Studies: "Clara Zetkin: A Socialist Approach to the Problems of Women's Oppression" by Karen Honeycut, in *European Women on the Left,* edited by J. Slaughter and R. Kern, n.p., 1981; "Clara Eissner Zetkin," by Norma C. Noonan, in *Modern Encyclopedia of Russian and Soviet History,* Vol. 46, Florida, n.p., 1987.

* * *

An essayist and editorialist, Clara Zetkin is remembered as an advocate on behalf of women more than as a writer. Zetkin promoted women's issues within the constraints of the international Marxist movement. For most Marxists, the fate of the overall revolutionary movement was more important than advocacy of improved rights for women or any other group. Zetkin's views on women were derived principally from the later writings of Frederich Engels and those of August Bebel. According to fellow revolutionary Angela Davis, Zetkin, together with Engels and Bebel, can be considered one of the pioneering theorists of women's status within a capitalist society. Zetkin's prominence in the international communist movement should not be underestimated. She was acquainted with Engels, Bebel, Laura LaFargue (Karl Marx's daughter) and later knew Lenin and his wife, Nadezhda Krupskaya.

Zetkin's feminism differed from that of traditional feminists of her day, whom Marxists described as "bourgeois feminists." Although Zetkin shared with feminists advocacy of women's suffrage and other rights, she was critical of the feminist movement's limited reformist goals. Zetkin believed only revolution could liberate all workers. She organized the first congress of socialist women, and despite criticism from prominent Marxists persisted in advocating women's issues.

The editor of a socialist women's newspaper, *Die Gleichheit* [Equality] from 1892 to 1917, she maintained a high profile as an advocate for women; Philip Foner reveals Zetkin wrote at least 30 articles on women during her years as editor. Zetkin expressed her ideas on women boldly and directly, trying to fight for women within the German Socialist Party (SPD) and to persuade women that their future lay with the socialist movement and party. Her views on women were often at odds with the views of the leadership of the SPD. Her strong advocacy of women and her opposition to World War I may have contributed to her loss of the editorship of *Die Gleichheit.*

Zetkin had a rather untraditional upbringing for a German girl of her era. Her mother was a progressive woman who insured that her daughter received a good education. Clara studied with August Schmidt. When she began to associate with Russian and German Social Democrats in Leipzig, her family and Schmidt objected, resulting in alienation from her family. Clara became involved with Osip Zetkin, a native of the Russian Empire. Later Zetkin would become her common-law husband and the father of her two sons. Although their association lasted only a decade prior to his death, she took his name and devoted herself to him, especially during the late 1880s when he was dying of tuberculosis.

Clara's association with Zetkin gave her an entree into the Russian Marxist movement. After the Bolshevik Revolution, she participated in the highly radical Spartacus League and the German Communist Party, but was soon called to Moscow to work for the newly created Communist International or Comintern. In the last decade of her life she lived principally in Moscow, although she never gave up her German citizenship and was elected to the Reichstag in 1932.

A German communist who made Soviet Russia her second homeland, by the late 20th century, Clara Zetkin's work as an activist had largely overshadowed her writing. She is perhaps best remembered for her role in advocating the establishment of an international women's day. March 8, the day selected, marked the anniversary of the 1908 women garment workers' strike. Initially celebrated only by socialists and communists, March 8th would later be adopted by the international women's movement as a day to recognize women worldwide.

—Norma C. Noonan

NATIONALITY INDEX

Below is the list of entrants divided by nationality. The nationalities were chosen largely from information supplied by the entrants. A small number of entrants submitted two nationalities (e.g., American and British) and thus are listed under both. It should be noted that "British" was used for all English entrants and for any other British entrant who chose that designation over a more specific one, such as "Scottish."

American

Edith Abbott
Jane Addams
Louisa May Alcott
Meena Alexander
Paula Gunn Allen
Dorothy Allison
Susan B. Anthony
Gloria Anzaldúa
June Arnold
Harriette Simpson Arnow
Mary Austin
Marilou Awiakta
Sandra Bartky
Mary Ritter Beard
Jessie Bernard
Harriot Stanton Blatch
Marion Zimmer Bradley
Anne Bradstreet
Charles Brockden Brown
Rita Mae Brown
Susan Brownmiller
Dorothy Bryant
Charlotte Bunch
Judith Butler
Rachel Carson
Ana Castillo
Carrie Chapman Catt
Denise Chávez
Phyllis Chesler
Nancy Chodorow
Kate Chopin
Barbara Christian
Sandra Cisneros
Michelle Cliff
Patricia Hill Collins
Anna Julia Haywood Cooper
Nancy F. Cott
Caroline Wells Healey Dall
Mary Daly
Angela Davis
Rebecca Harding Davis
Barbara Deming
Frederick Douglass
Alice Moore Dunbar-Nelson
Andrea Dworkin
Barbara Ehrenreich
Carol Emshwiller
Lillian Faderman
Susan Faludi
Jessie Redmon Fauset
Elizabeth Fox-Genovese
Mary E. Wilkins Freeman
Marilyn French
Betty Friedan
Marilyn Frye
Margaret Fuller
Matilda Joslyn Gage
Sally Miller Gearhart
Sandra M. Gilbert
Carol Gilligan
Charlotte Perkins Gilman
Jewelle Gomez
Linda Gordon
Mary Gordon
Sue Grafton
Susan Griffin
Sarah Moore Grimké
Susan Gubar
Marilyn Hacker
Lorraine Hansberry
Sandra G. Harding
H.D.
Carolyn G. Heilbrun
Lillian Hellman
Beth Henley
bell hooks
Julia Ward Howe
Susan Howe
Fannie Hurst
Zora Neale Hurston
Harriet Ann Jacobs
Sarah Orne Jewett
Jill Johnston
Erica Jong
Adrienne Kennedy
Maxine Hong Kingston
Nella Larsen
Ursula K. Le Guin
Gerda Lerner
Denise Levertov
Audre Lorde
Maud Hart Lovelace
Catharine A. MacKinnon
Karen Malpede
Del Martin
Mary McCarthy
Carson McCullers
Margaret Mead
Jean Baker Miller
Kate Millett
Valerie Miner
Ellen Moers
Cherríe Moraga
Robin Morgan
Toni Morrison
Lucretia Mott
Bharati Mukherjee

SUBJECT AND GENRE INDEX INDEX

Below is the list of entrants categorized by the primary literary genres in which they wrote or subject areas relevant to the study of feminism covered in their works.

17th-Century Voices
Mary Astell
Aphra Behniii
Anne Bradstreet
Marie le Jars de Gournay
Sor Juana Inés de la Cruz

18th-Century Voices
Mary Astell
Charles Brockden Brown
Elizabeth Montagu
Mary Robinson
Sophia
Germaine de Staël
Flora Tristan
Mary Wollstonecraft

19th-Century Voices
Jane Addams
Louisa May Alcott
Susan B. Anthony
Dorothea Beale
August Bebel
Charles Brockden Brown
Carrie Chapman Catt
Kate Chopin
Frances Power Cobbe
Anna Julia Haywood Cooper
Caroline Wells Healey Dall
Rebecca Harding Davis
Frederick Douglass
Alice Moore Dunbar-Nelson
Maria Edgeworth
Emily Faithfull
Mary E. Wilkins Freeman
Margaret Fuller
Matilda Joslyn Gage
Charlotte Perkins Gilman
Sarah Moore Grimké and Angelina Grimké Weld
Julia Ward Howe
Harriet Ann Jacobs
Sarah Orne Jewett
Harriet Martineau
Harriet Taylor Mill and John Stuart Mill
Lucretia Mott
John Neal
Christabel Pankhurst
Emilia Pardo Bazán
Elizabeth Stuart Phelps
George Sand
Olive Schreiner
Catherine Helen Spence
Elizabeth Cady Stanton
Sui Sin Far
Martha Carey Thomas
Sojourner Truth
Beatrice Webb
Mary Webb
Emma Hart Willard

20th-Century Voices
Edith Abbott
Fleur Adcock
Jane Addams
Etel Adnan
Ama Ata Aidoo
Meena Alexander
Paula Gunn Allen
Isabel Allende
Dorothy Allison
Nawal al'Sadaawi
Susan B. Anthony
Gloria Anzaldúa
June Arnold
Harriette Simpson Arnow
Margaret Atwood
Mary Austin
Marilou Awiakta
Enid Bagnold
Sandra Bartky
Mary Ritter Beard
Patricia Beer
Jessie Bernard
Marie-Claire Blais
Harriot Stanton Blatch
Karen Blixen
Eavan Boland
Elizabeth Dorothea Cole Bowen
Marion Zimmer Bradley
Beth Brant
Vera Brittain
Nicole Brossard
Rita Mae Brown
Susan Brownmiller
Dorothy Bryant
Charlotte Bunch
Katharine Burdekin
Judith P. Butler
Marie Cardinal
Emily Carr
Rachel Carson
Angela Carter
Rosario Castellanos
Ana Castillo
Carrie Chapman Catt
Denise Chávez
Phyllis Chesler
Nancy Chodorow

Growing Up Female

Health and Well-being

Historical Fiction

Humor & Satire

Jewish-American Voices

Marxism/Socialism

Philosophy

Poetry

Political Theory

Pornography

Pre-17th-Century Writers

Psychology/Psychiatry

Racism

Radical Feminist Voices

Religion & Spirituality

Science Fiction

Science & Technology

Sexism

Sexuality & Courtship

Short Fiction

Slavery & Oppression

Translations

Travel Writing

Violence & Brutality

War & Military Aggression

TITLE INDEX

The following index includes all major works listed in the "Publications" sections of the entries. The name in parenthesis is meant to direct the user to the appropriate entry, where full publication information is given. The term "series" indicate a recurring distinctive word or phrase (or name) in the titles of the entrant's books.

Coast of Illyria (Parker), 1949
Cobbler's Rune (Le Guin), 1983
Cockatoos: A Story of Youth and Exodists (Franklin), 1954
Cold (Rodriguez), 1992
Cold Spring and Other Poems (Levertov), 1969
Collected Earlier Poems, 1940-1960 (Levertov), 1979
Collected Early Poems, 1950-1970 (Rich), 1992
Collected Essays (Woolf), 1966-67
Collected Impressions (Bowen), 1950
Collected Poems (Hewett), 1995
Collected Poems (Tynan), 1930
Collected Poems (Warner), 1983
Collected Poems 1912-1944 (H.D.), 1983
Collected Poems 1930-1973 (Sarton), 1974
Collected Poems, 1930-1993 (Sarton), 1993
Collected Poems 1949-1984 (Duffy), 1985
Collected Poems I (Spark), 1967
Collected Poems of H.D (H.D.), 1925
Collected Poems of Muriel Rukeyser (Rukeyser), 1978
Collected Poems: The Two Seasons (Livesay), 1972
Collected Poetry of Dorothy Parker (Parker), 1944
Collected Short Stories and the Novel, The Ballad of the Sad Cafe (McCullers), 1955
Collected Stories (Lessing), 1978
Collected Stories (Paley), 1994
Collected Stories I (Spark), 1967
Collected Stories of Elizabeth Bowen (Bowen), 1981
Collected Works of John Stuart Mill (Mill), 1963-92
Collector of Treasures and Other Botswana Village Tales (Head), 1977
College, the Market, and the Court; or, Woman's Relations to Education, Labor, and Law (Dall), 1867
Color Purple (Walker, A.), 1982
Color Struck (Hurston), 1926
Colors of Space (Bradley), 1963
Colors of the Day (Rukeyser), 1961
Colossus (Plath), 1960
Colour of God's Face (Livesay), 1964
Colours of Space (Bradley), 1989
Come Back, Paul (Rukeyser), 1955
Come unto These Yellow Sands (Carter), 1984
Comedy: American Style (Fauset), 1933
Comfort Pease and Her Gold Ring (Freeman), 1895
Comforters (Spark), 1957
Comic Dramas in Three Acts (Edgeworth), 1817
Comic Tragedies Written by Jo and Meg and Acted by the Little Women (Alcott), 1893
"Coming Book" (Kingston), 1980
Coming into Eighty (Sarton), 1994
Coming of Age in Samoa: A Psychological Study of Primitive Youth for Western Civilization (Mead), 1928
"Coming of Lilith" (Plaskow), 1974
"Coming of Night" (Davis, R.), 1909
Coming to Writing and Other Essays (Cixous), 1991
Common Reader (Woolf), 1925
Common Reader, Second Series (Woolf), 1932
Commons Debate on Women Suffrage with a Reply (Pankhurst), 1908
Communism and the Family (Kollontai), 1918
Companion of the Tour of France (Sand), 1847
Company of Women (Gordon, M.), 1981
Company She Keeps (McCarthy), 1942
Compass Rose (Le Guin), 1982
Competition: A Feminist Taboo? (Miner), 1987
"Complaint of the Ladies" (de Gournay), 1987
Complete Poems (Sexton), 1981
Complete Stories (Walker, A.), 1994
Compulsory Heterosexuality and Lesbian Existence (Rich), 1981
Compulsory Option (Pollock), 1972
Concerning Children (Gilman), 1900
Concerning Vermont (Thompson), 1937
Confessions of a Wife (Phelps, as Adams), 1902
Confessions of Madame Psyche (Bryant), 1986
"Confrontation: Black/White" (Allison), 1981
Congratulatory Poem to Her Sacred Majesty Queen Mary (Behn), 1689
Connections, Disconnections, and Violations (Miller), n.d.
Conquest (Stopes), 1917
Conquest of the School at Madhubaï (Cixous), 1986
Considerations on Representative Government (Mill), 1861
Constant Husband (Hamilton), 1912
Constant Journey (Wittig), 1984
Constant Reader (Parker), 1970
"Constructed Body" (Guillaumin), 1993
Consuelo: A Romance of Venice (Sand), 1851
Contemporary Roman Catholicism: Crises and Challenges (Ruether), 1987
Contemporary Writers (Woolf), 1965
"Contest Winner" (Sarton), 1946
Continuation of Early Lessons (Edgeworth), 1814
Continuities in Cultural Evolution (Mead), 1964
"Continuous Performance: The Film Gone Male" (Richardson), 1932
Contraception: Its Theory, History, and Practice (Stopes), 1923
Contract with the World (Rule), 1980
Contraries (Oates), 1981
"Contribution to the Critique of the Political Economy of Sex and Gender" (Rubin), 1974
Control Freaks (Henley), 1992
Conversations of Cow (Namjoshi), 1985
Cook and the Carpenter (Arnold, as Carpenter), 1973
Cooperation and Competition among Primitive Societies (Mead), 1937
Copy-Cat and Other Stories (Freeman), 1914
Corinne or Italy (Staël), 1987
Corner That Held Them (Warner), 1948
Corporate Tradition and National Rights: Local Dues on Shipping (Martineau), 1857
Cossack Rebellions: Social Turmoil in the 16th-Century Ukraine (Gordon, L.), 1983
Cotters' England (Stead), 1967
Countess of Rudolstadt (Sand), 1891
Country By-Ways (Jewett), 1881
Country Doctor (Jewett), 1884
Country Girls Trilogy from 1960
Country of the Pointed Firs (Jewett), 1896
Country of the Pointed Firs and Other Stories (Jewett), 1982
Courage to Be Happy (Thompson), 1957
Court and the Castle: A Study of the Interactions of Political and Religious Ideas in Imaginative Literature (West), 1958
Court and the Castle: Some Treatments of a Recurrent Theme (West), 1957

"Dusty Distance" (Namjoshi), 1991
Dutch Lover (Behn), 1673
Duties of Women. A Course of Lectures (Cobbe), 1881
"Dying Year" (Drabble), 1987
Dynamics of European Nuclear Disarmament (Myrdal), 1981
"Dynastic Encounter" (Piercy), 1970

"E" Is for Evidence (Grafton), 1988
Each His Own Wilderness (Lessing), 1959
Eagle and the Chickens and Other Stories (Aidoo), 1986
Early Candlelight (Lovelace), 1929
Early Draft of John Stuart Mill's Autobiography (Mill), 1961
Early Poems of Enid Bagnold (Bagnold), 1987
Early Stories: Encounters and Ann Lee's (Bowen), 1951
Earth Horizon (Austin), 1932
"Earthen Pitchers" (Davis, R.), 1873
Earthly Paradise (Colette), 1966
Earthsea series (Le Guin), from 1968
"East London Labour" (Webb, B.), 1888
Easy Death (Churchill), 1962
"Echo" (Spivak), 1993
Eclipse (Oates), 1990
Edgar Huntley; or, Memoirs of a Sleep-Walker (Brown, C.), 1799
Edge of the Sea (Carson), 1955
Edgewater People (Freeman), 1918
Edible Woman (Atwood), 1969
Education of Harriet Hatfield (Sarton), 1989
Education of the Masses (Pankhurst), 1924
Education of Women, and How It Would Be Affected by University Examinations (Cobbe), 1862
"Effects of Modernization on the Male-Female Dynamics in a Muslim Society" (Mernissi), 1991
Egg (Pollock), 1988
Eggs of Things (Sexton), 1963
Eglantina (Freeman), 1910
Egotists (Fallaci), 1968
Egypt's Place in History (Dall), 1868
Eight Chambers of the Heart (Piercy), 1995
Eight Cousins; or, The Aunt-Hill (Alcott), 1875
Eighty Years and More (Stanton), 1898
"El Paisano Is a Bird of Good Omen" (Anzaldúa), 1983
El Salvador: Requiem and Invocation (Levertov), 1984
El Santero de Cordova (Chávez), 1981
Electra (Kennedy), 1980
Elegiac Verses to a Young Lady on the Death of Her Brother (Robinson), 1776
Elegies (Rukeyser), 1949
Elemental Passions (Irigaray), 1992
Elevators (Chávez), 1977
Elinor Barley (Warner), 1930
Elizabeth Bowen's Irish Stories (Bowen), 1978
"Elizabeth's Thanksgiving" (Davis, R.), 1893
Ella Price's Journal (Bryant), 1972
"Ellen" (Davis, R.), 1863
Ellen's Idol (Phelps), 1864
Embroideries (Levertov), 1969
"Emily Brontë and Wuthering Heights" (Freeman), 1901
Emily Brontë: Her Life and Work (Spark), 1953
Emily of Deep Valley (Lovelace), 1950
"Emmy" (Fauset), 1912
Emperor of the Moon (Behn), 1688
Empty House and Other Stories (Phelps), 1910
Empty Purse: A Christmas Story (Jewett), 1905
En miniscules (Trinh), 1987
"Enchantress" (Enchi), 1958
Encore (Sarton), 1993
Encounter in April (Sarton), 1937
Encounters (Bowen), 1923
Encounters with the Element Man (Atwood), 1982
End of My Career (Franklin), 1981
End of This Day's Business (Burdekin), 1990
End of War (Malpede), 1977
"End to Technology: A Modest Proposal" (Gearhart), 1984
Endgame (Sarton), 1992
Ending in Earnest: A Literary Log (West), 1931
Endless Universe (Bradley), 1979
Endless Voyage (Bradley), 1975
Enduring Passion (Stopes), 1928
Enfranchisement of Women (Mill), 1851
England's Hour (Brittain), 1941
English Diaries and Journals (O'Brien, K.), 1943
English Local Government, 11 vols. (Webb, B.), 1903-11
English Novelists (Bowen), 1942
English-South African's View of the Situation: Words in Season (Schreiner), 1899
Enid Bagnold's Autobiography (Bagnold), 1969
Enormous Changes at the Last Minute (Paley), 1974
Enough Rope (Parker), 1926
Enquiry after Wit (Astell), 1722
"Entering In: The Immigrant Imagination" (Marlatt), 1984
Enterprise of England (Beer), 1979
Epistle to the Clergy of the Southern States (Grimké), 1836
"Equal to Whom?" (Irigaray), 1989
Equality of Races and the Democratic Movement (Cooper), 1945
Equinox (Figes), 1966
"Eritrea on the Eve; the Past and Future of Italy's First-Born" Colony, Ethiopia's Ancient Sea Province (Pankhurst), 1952
Eros of Everyday Live: Essays on Ecology, Gender and Society (Griffin), 1995
"Erotic Life of Fictional Characters" (Wilson), 1991
Erotic World of Faery (Duffy), 1972
Errata; or, The Works of Will Adams (Neal), 1823
Espalier (Warner), 1925
Essay on Intuitive Morals, Being an Attempt to Popularize Ethical Science (Cobbe), 1859
Essay on the Writings and Genius of Shakespeare, Compared with the Greek and French Dramatic Poets (Montagu), 1769
Essays and Sketches (Dall), 1849
Essays of Virginia Woolf (Woolf), 1986-94
Essays on Irish Bulls (Edgeworth), 1802
Essays on Literature and Society (Mill), 1965
Essays on Professional Education (Edgeworth), 1809
Essays on Sex Equality (Mill), 1970
Essays on Some Unsettled Questions of Political Economy (Mill), 1844
Essays on the Pursuits of Women (Cobbe), 1863
Essays on Women, Medicine and Health (Oakley), 1993
Essence of the Brontës (Spark), 1993
Essential Faith of the Universal Church Deduced from the Sacred Records (Martineau), 1831
Estuary (Beer), 1971
Ethics of Ambiguity (de Beauvoir), 1948

Fourteen to One (Phelps), 1891
Foxfire: Confessions of a Girl Gang (Oates), 1993
"Fra Lippi and Me" (Arnow), 1979
Frameless Windows, Squares of Light (Song), 1988
Framer Framed: Film Scripts and Interviews (Trinh), 1992
Frances Waldeaux (Davis, R.), 1897
Francis! (Chávez), 1983
François the Waif (Sand), 1889
Frank (Edgeworth), 1822
Franz into April (Gems), 1977
Freaks of Genius (Alcott), 1991
Frederick Douglass on Women's Rights (Douglass), 1976
Free Enterprise (Cliff), 1993
Free Love (Kollontai), 1932
"Freedom" (Larsen, as Semi), 1926
Freeing of the Dust (Levertov), 1975
Freischütz (Jellicoe), 1963
"French Feminism Revisited: Ethics and Politics" (Spivak), 1992
French Kiss (étreinte-exploration) (Brossard), 1974
French Window and the Small Telephone (Spark), 1993
Freshwater: A Comedy (Woolf), 1976
"Freud on Women" (Chodorow), 1991
"Freud's Mnemonic: Women, Screen Memory, and Feminist Nostalgia" (Jacobus), 1987
Friend of Heraclitus (Beer), 1993
Friendless Girls and How to Help Them: Being an Account of the Preventive Mission at Bristol (Cobbe), 1861
Friends (Weldon), 1975
Friends and Heroes (Manning), 1965
Friends and Relations (Bowen), 1931
Friends from the Other Side—Amigos del otra lado (Anzaldúa), 1993
Friends: A Duet (Phelps), 1881
from okra to greens (Shange), 1984
From a Land Where Other People Live (Lorde), 1973
From A to Z (Adnan), 1982
From Elfland to Poughkeepsie (Le Guin), 1973
From Here to Maternity (Oakley), 1981
From Jo March's Attic (Alcott), 1993
From Man to Man; or Perhaps only... (Schreiner), 1926
From Okra to Greens/ A Different Kinda Love Story (Shange), 1985
From Relief to Social Security: The Development of the New Public Welfare Services (Abbott), 1941
"From Separate Spheres to Dangerous Streets: Postmodernist Feminism and the Problem of Order" (Fox-Genovese), 1993
From Sunset Ridge (Howe, J.), 1899
From the Bedside Book of Nightmares (Namjoshi), 1984
"From the Country of Regrets" (Jong), 1973
From the Inside Out: Afro-American Women's Literary Tradition and the State (Christian), 1987
"From the Scene of the Unconscious to the Scene of History" (Cixous), 1988
From the South Seas (Mead), 1939
Frozen Earth and Other Poems (Holtby), 1935
Fruits & Vegetables (Jong), 1971
Fruits of Merchant Capital: Slavery and Bourgeois Property in the Rise and Expansion of Capitalism (Fox-Genovese), 1983
Fugitive (Blais), 1978
Fulfillment of a Promise (Willard), 1831
Full Stop (Hamilton), 1931
"Funeral" (Shockley), 1967
Funland (Oates), 1983
Funnyhouse of a Negro (Kennedy), 1964
Fur Person (Sarton), 1957
Future of Marriage (Bernard), 1972
Future of Motherhood (Bernard), 1974
Future of Parenthood (Bernard), 1975
"Future—If There Is One—Is Female" (Gearhart), 1982
"Futures in Feminist Fiction" (Maitland), 1989

"G" Is for Gumshoe (Grafton), 1990
Gallant Lords of Bois-Doré (Sand), 1890
"Galle Face" (Hewett), 1973
"Gamblers" (Sui Sin Far), 1896
Game of Disarmament: How the United States and Russia Run the Arms Race (Myrdal), 1977
Games at Twilight and Other Stories (Desai), 1978
Garden of Earthly Delights (Oates), 1967
Garden of Eros (Bryant), 1979
Garden Party and Other Stories (Mansfield), 1922
Garland (Undset), 1930
Garland for Girls (Alcott), 1887
Garland of Straw and Other Stories (Warner), 1943
Garnett Family (Heilbrun), 1961
Garrick Year (Drabble), 1964
Gaslight Sonatas (Hurst), 1918
Gates (Rukeyser), 1976
Gates Ajar (Phelps), 1868
Gates Between (Phelps), 1887
Gates of Ivory (Drabble), 1991
Gathered In (Spence), 1977
Gathering (O'Brien, E.), 1974
Gaudi Afternoon (Wilson), 1990
"Gender as a Personal and Cultural Construction" (Chodorow), 1995
"Gender, Relation, and Difference in Psychoanalytic Perspective" (Chodorow), 1990
Gender Trouble: Feminism and the Subversion of Identity (Butler), 1990
"Genealogy of 'Dependency': Tracing a Key Word of the U.S. Welfare State" (Gordon, L.), 1993
Generations (Pollock), 1981
Gentle Libertine (Colette, as Willy), 1931
Gentlemen at Gyang Gyang: A Tale of the Jumbuck Pads on the Summer Runs (Franklin, as Brent of Bin Bin), 1956
Gentlemen from England (Lovelace), 1937
Geography Lesson (Wilson), 1977
"George Eliot: A Moralizing Fabulist" (O'Brien, K.), 1935
"George Elliot" (Phelps), 1881
George Sand (Sand), 1985
Gertie (Bagnold), 1952
Getting It Straight (Pollock), 1992
Getting Out (Norman), 1977
"GHANA: To Be a Woman" (Aidoo), 1982
Ghostlight (Bradley), 1995
Ghosts (Figes), 1988
Gia and God: An Ecofeminist Theology of Earth Healing (Ruether), 1992
Gift (H.D.), 1982
"Gift of Laughter" (Fauset), 1925
"Gifts of War" (Drabble), 1970

Gigi (Colette), 1953
Gilda Stories (Gomez), 1991
Giles Corey, Yeoman (Freeman), 1893
Girl (Oates), 1974
"Girl Who Wants to Write: Things to Do and Avoid" (Freeman), 1913
Girl with Green Eyes (O'Brien, E.), 1964
Girl's Journey (Bagnold), 1954
Girls in Their Married Bliss (O'Brien, E.), 1964
Girls of Slender Means (Spark), 1963
Giveaway (Jellicoe), 1970
"Giveaway: Native Lesbian Writers" (Brant), 1993
Givers (Freeman), 1904
"'Giving Character to Our Whole Civil Polity': Marriage and State Authority in the Late 19th Century" (Cott), 1995
Giving Up the Ghost: Teatro in Two Acts (Moraga), 1984
"Glacier Summer" (Wilson), 1994
Glassy Sea (Engel), 1978
Glimpses of Louisa (Alcott), 1968
"Global Violence against Women: The Challenge to Human Rights and Development" (Bunch), 1994
Gnostic Gospels (Pagels), 1979
Gnostic Jesus and Early Christian Politics (Pagels), 1981
Gnostic Paul: Gnostic Exegesis of the Pauline Letters (Pagels), 1975
Go-Away Bird and Other Stories (Spark), 1958
Go West, Young Woman (Gems), 1974
God and the Nations (Ruether), 1995
God and the Rhetoric of Sexuality (Trible), 1978
God Dies by the Nile (al'Sadaawi), 1985
God Must Be Sad (Hurst), 1961
Godded and Codded (O'Faolain), 1970
Goddess and Other Women (Oates), 1974
"God's Blood" (Piercy), 1974
Going Back to the River (Hacker), 1990
Going down Fast (Piercy), 1969
Going out with Peacocks and Other Poems (Le Guin), 1994
Going to Iran (Millett), 1981
Going Too Far: The Personal Chronicle of a Feminist (Morgan), 1977
Going Up to Sotheby's and Other Poems (Spark), 1982
Gold in the Wood (Stopes), 1918
Golden Arrow (Webb, M.), 1916
Golden Notebook (Lessing), 1962
Golden Oldies (Hewett), 1981
Golden Valley: Song of the Seals (Hewett), 1985
Golden Wedge: Indian Legends of South America (Lovelace), 1942
Gone to Earth (Webb, M.), 1917
Gone to Soldiers (Piercy), 1987
Good Bones (Atwood), 1992
Good Bones and Simple Murders (Atwood), 1994
Good Boys and Dead Girls and Other Essays (Gordon, M.), 1991
"Good Red Road: Native Women's Journey of Writing" (Brant), 1993
Good Terrorist (Lessing), 1985
Good Thing or a Bad Thing (Jellicoe), 1975
Good Tiger (Bowen), 1965
"Good Wits, Pen and Paper" (Freeman), 1899
Goodness of St. Rocque and Other Stories (Dunbar-Nelson), 1899
Goodnight, Willie Lee, I'll See You in the Morning (Walker, A.), 1979
Goody Two-Shoes and Other Famous Nursery Tales (Freeman), 1883
Gor Saga (Duffy), 1981
Grain of Mustard Seed (Sarton), 1971
"Grandmothers" (Awiakta), 1995
Granite and Rainbow (Woolf), 1958
Grass Is Singing (Lessing), 1950
"Gray Woman of Appalachia" (Arnow), 1970
Great Day (Hurston), 1932
Great Drag Race, or Smoked, Choked, and Croaked (Pollock), 1974
Great Fortune (Manning), 1960
Great Laughter (Hurst), 1936
Great Love (Kollontai), 1923
Great Moments in Aviation (Winterson), 1993
Great Road: The Life and Times of Chu Teh (Smedley), 1956
Great Scourge and How to End It (Pankhurst), 1913
Great Wave and Other Stories (Lavin), 1961
Green Bough (Austin), 1913
Green Door (Freeman), 1910
Green Madonna (Chávez), 1982
"Green Man" (Winterson), 1995
Green Pitcher (Livesay), 1928
Green Politics: The Global Promise (Spretnak), 1984
Green Wave (Rukeyser), 1948
Greenhouse (Hewett), 1979
Gregory of Nazianzus, Rhetor and Philosopher (Ruether), 1969
Grimké Sisters from South Carolina: Rebels against Slavery (Lerner), 1967
Grounding of Modern Feminism (Cott), 1987
Group (McCarthy), 1963
Groves of Academe (McCarthy), 1952
Growing Pains: The Autobiography of Emily Carr (Carr), 1946
Growing Up (Manning), 1948
Growing Up in New Guinea (Mead), 1930
"Growing Up to Be a Woman Writer in Lebanon" (Adnan), 1990
Growth and Culture: A Photographic Study of Balinese Childhood (Mead), 1951
Guérillères (Wittig), 1971
Guilt, Authority, and the Shadow of Little Dorrit (Showalter), 1979
Guinevere (Gems), 1976
Gullibles Travels (Johnston), 1974
Gunnar's Daughter (Undset), 1936
Gwendolen (Emecheta), 1989
Gwilan's Harp (Le Guin), 1981
Gyn/Ecology: The Metaethics of Radical Feminism (Daly), 1978
Gypsy Breynton (Phelps), 1866
Gypsy's Cousin Joy (Phelps), 1866
Gypsy's Sowing and Reaping (Phelps), 1866
Gypsy's Year at the Golden Crescent (Phelps), 1868

H.D. (H.D.), 1926
"H" Is for Homicide (Grafton), 1991
Habit of Loving (Lessing), 1957
Hairs = Pelitos (Cisneros), 1994
Halcyon, or the Future of Monogamy (Brittain), 1929
Half-Lives (Jong), 1973
Halfway to Silence (Sarton), 1980
Hallelujah (Hurst), 1944
Hamlet's Mother and Other Women: Feminist Essays on Literature (Heilbrun), 1990
Hamlets (Martineau), 1836

Hampdens: A Historiette (Martineau), 1880
Hand that Cradles the Rock (Brown, R.), 1971
Handbook for the Administration of Special Negro Collections (Shockley), 1970
Handfasted (Spence), 1984
Handmaid's Tale (Atwood), 1985
Hands of Veronica (Hurst), 1947
Hang-Glider's Daughter (Hacker), 1990
Hanoi (McCarthy), 1968
"Happiest Day of a Woman's Life" (Piercy), 1972
Happiness and Other Stories (Lavin), 1969
Happiness in Marriage (Sanger), 1926
Happy Birthday, Montpelier Pizz-zazz (Wasserstein), 1974
Happy Foreigner (Bagnold), 1920
Happy Prince (Pollock), 1974
Happy Times in Norway (Undset), 1942
Hard Loving (Piercy), 1969
Hard Words and Other Poems (Le Guin), 1981
"Hardy's Magian Retrospect" (Jacobus), 1982
Harriet Beecher Stowe and American Literature (Moers), 1978
Harriet Hume: A London Fantasy (West), 1929
Harriet Martineau's Autobiography, with Memorials by Maria Weston Chapman (Martineau), 1877
Harrington (Edgeworth), 1817
Harry and Lucy (Edgeworth), 1825
Harsh Voice (West), 1935
Hassan's Tower (Drabble), 1980
Haunted (Oates), 1994
Haunted House and Other Short Stories (Woolf), 1943
Haunted Pool (Sand), 1890
Having a Wonderful Time (Churchill), 1960
Hawai'i One Summer (Kingston), 1987
Hawkmistress! (Bradley), 1982
He and She (Sand), 1902
"He Ngangahua" (Te Awekotuku), 1994
"He Puna Roimata mo Te Pa Harakeke" (Te Awekotuku), 1993
He, She and It (Piercy), 1991
"He Tiki" (Te Awekotuku), 1990
He Tinkanga Whakaaro (Te Awekotuku), 1991
He Who Searches (Valenzuela), 1987
Head above Water (Emecheta), 1986
Heart Is a Lonely Hunter (McCullers), 1940
Heart of a Peacock (Carr), 1953
Heart of a Stranger (Laurence), 1976
Heart of Anne Sexton's Poetry (Sexton), 1977
Heart of Britain (Das), 1983
Heart of the Country (Weldon), 1987
Hearts and Lives of Men (Weldon), 1987
Heart's Highway: A Romance of Virginia in the 17th Century (Freeman), 1900
Hearts of Men: American Dreams and the Flight from Commitment (Ehrenreich), 1983
Heat and Other Stories (Oates), 1991
Heat of the Day (Bowen), 1949
Hecho en México (Chávez), 1983
Hedged In (Phelps), 1870
Hedgehog (H.D.), 1936
Hedylus (H.D.), 1928
"Heidegger and the Modes of World-Disclosure" (Bartky), 1979
"Heidegger's Philosophy of Art" (Bartky), 1969
Heidi Chronicles (Wasserstein), 1988
Heirs of Hammerfell (Bradley), 1989
Helen (Edgeworth), 1834
Helen in Egypt (H.D.), 1961
Hélène Cixous, Rootprints (Cixous), 1996
Heliodora and Other Poems (H.D.), 1924
Her (H.D.), 1984
Her Blue Body Everything We Know (Walker, A.), 1991
"Her Body, Mine, and His" (Allison), 1991
Her Mother's Daughter (French), 1987
"Her Name Is Helen" (Brant), 1991
"Her Own Thing" (Shockley), 1972
Her Own Woman (Miner), 1975
Herb O'Grace: Poems in War-Time (Tynan), 1918
Here and Now (Levertov), 1957
Here and There (Marlatt), 1981
"Here and There in the South" (Davis, R.), 1887
Here Comes and Other Poems (Jong), 1975
Here Lies (Parker), 1939
Here She Is! (Oates), 1995
Heritage of Hastur (Bradley), 1975
Herland (Gilman), 1915
Hermetic Definition (H.D.), 1972
HERmione (H.D.), 1981
Heroes and Saints and Other Plays (Moraga), 1994
Heroes and Villains (Carter), 1969
Heroes of their Own Lives: The Politics and History of Family Violence, Boston 1880-1960 (Gordon, L.), 1988
Heroic Slave, in The Classic African-American Novels (Douglass), 1990
Herstories (Stefan), 1994
"Heterosexuality as a Compromise Formation" (Chodorow), 1992
"Hey Diddle Diddle, (Namjoshi), 1994
Hidden Face of Eve: Women in the Arab World (al'Sadaawi), 1980
Hidden From History: Rediscovering Women in History From the 17th Century to the Present (Rowbotham), 1973
Hidden Journey (Hewett), 1968
Hidden Side of the Moon (Russ), 1987
High Cost of Living (Piercy), 1978
High Hearts (Brown, R.), 1986
High Road (O'Brien, E.), 1988
High Tide in the Garden (Adcock), 1971
Higher Education of Women (Thomas), 1900
"Highs and the Lows of Black Feminist Criticism: A Speak Peace" (Christian), 1990
Highway Sandwiches (Hacker), 1970
Hinge Picture (Howe, S.), 1974
Hippolytus (Howe, J.), 1941
Hippolytus Temporizes (H.D.), 1927
His Religion and Hers: A Study of the Faith of Our Fathers and the Work of Our Mothers (Gilman), 1923
Historical and Moral View of the Progress of the French Revolution, and the Effect It Has Produced in Europe (Wollstonecraft), 1794
"Historical and Textual Analysis of the Relationship between Futurism and Eschatology in the Apocalyptic Texts of the Intertestament period (Ruether), Historical Perspectives: The Equal Rights Amendment in the 1920s" (Cott), 1990
Historical Pictures Retouched (Dall), 1860
"Historical Roots of Domestic Violence" (Martin), 1987
History of England during the 30 Years' Peace 1816-46 (Martineau), 1849

"Let Us Now Praise Unknown Women and Our Mothers Who Begat Us" (Maitland), 1986
Letter to a Child Never Born (Fallaci), 1976
Letter to a Grandfather (West), 1933
Letter to a Priest (Weil), 1953
Letter to a Young Poet (Woolf), 1932
Letter to Catherine Beecher, in Reply to An Essay on Slavery and Abolitionism (Grimké), 1838
"Letter to My Students" (Kennedy), 1993
Letter to the Women of England, on the Injustice of Mental Subordination (Robinson, as Randall), 1799
Letter to Working Mothers (Stopes), 1919
Letters concerning the Love of God (Astell), 1695
Letters for Literary Ladies, to Which Is Added an Essay on the Noble Science of Self-Justification (Edgeworth), 1795
Letters from a War Zone: 1976-1987 (Dworkin), 1988
"Letters from Emily Carr" (Carr), 1972
Letters from Maine (Sarton), 1984
Letters from the Field, 1925-1975 (Mead), 1977
Letters on Mesmerism (Martineau), 1845
Letters on the Equality of the Sexes and the Condition of Women (Grimké), 1838
Letters on the Laws of Man's Nature and Development (Martineau), 1851
Letters Written during a Short Residence in Sweden, Norway, and Denmark (Wollstonecraft), 1796
Letty Fox: Her Luck (Stead), 1946
Levant Trilogy from (Manning), 1977
Liberation Theology: Human Hope Confronts Christian History and American Power (Ruether), 1972
Liberties (Howe, S.), 1980
Liberty Bell (Dall), 1847
Licking the Bed Clean (Roberts), 1978
Lie of the Land (Beer), 1983
Life and Death (Dworkin), 1966
Life and Loves of a She-Devil (Weldon), 1983
Life and Times of Frederick Douglass, Written by Himself (Douglass), 1881
Life before Man (Atwood), 1979
Life Errant (Hamilton), 1935
Life Force (Weldon), 1992
Life in the Forest (Levertov), 1978
"Life in the Iron Mills" (Davis, R.), 1866
Life in the Iron Mills and Other Stories (Davis, R.), 1972
Life in the Sick-Room (Martineau), 1844
"Life Line" (Anzaldúa), 1989
Life of Brown (Brown, C.), 1815
Life of Dr. Anadabai Joshee, a Kinswoman of the Pundita Ramabai (Dall), 1888
Life of Dr. Marie Zakrzewska (Dall), 1860
"Life of Emily Davidson" (West), 1913
Life of Emmeline Pankhurst (Pankhurst), 1935
Life of Frances Power Cobbe. By Herself (Cobbe), 1894
Life of Nancy (Jewett), 1895
Life of the Finnish Workers (Kollontai), 1903
Life Sentence (West), 1935
Life under the Sea (Carson), 1968
Life Without and Life Within (Fuller), 1859
Light (Figes), 1983
Light Shining in Buckinghamshire (Churchill), 1978
Light Up the Cave (Levertov), 1981
"Like a Great Door Closing Suddenly" (Piercy), 1974
Like the Iris of an Eye (Griffin), 1976
Likely Story (Lavin), 1957
Liliane: Resurrection of the Daughter (Shange), 1994
Lillian Hellman (Hellman), 1972
Limelighters (Fallaci), 1967
Linden Hills (Naylor), 1985
Lindy (Rodriguez), 1992
Lion and the Rose (Sarton), 1948
Lipstick Papers (Gomez), 1980
"List" (Rule), 1969
Listen, Hans (Thompson), 1942
Literally Dreaming (Stefan), 1994
Literary Affair (Blais), 1979
Literary Essays and Reviews (Brown, C.), 1992
Literary Studies of Poems, New and Old (Beale), 1902
Literary Women (Moers), 1976
Literature and Art (Fuller), 1853
"Literature, Feminism, and the African Woman Today" (Aidoo), 1996
Literature of Their Own: British Women Novelists from Brontë to Lessing (Showalter), 1977
Little Disturbances of Man: Stories of Men and Women in Love (Paley), 1959
Little Eden: A Child at War (Figes), 1978
Little Fadette (Sand), 1928
Little Foxes (Hellman), 1939
Little Girl and Other Stories (Mansfield), 1924
Little Girls (Bowen), 1964
Little Hotel (Stead), 1973
Little Idiot (Bagnold), 1953
Little Men (Alcott), 1871
Little Mocassin; or, Along the Madawaska (Neal), 1866
"Little Mother" (Dunbar-Nelson), 1900
Little Plays for Children (Edgeworth), 1827
"Little Purse" (Sarton), 1949
"Little Sister, Cat and Mouse" (Piercy), 1973
Little Sisters (Weldon), 1978
Little Tea, a Little Chat (Stead), 1948
Little Women (Alcott), 1869
Little Women and Good Wives (Alcott), 1895
Little Women Married (Alcott), 1873
Little Women Wedded (Alcott), 1872
Live or Die (Sexton), 1966
"Lives of Saints" (Winterson), 1993
Lives of the Great Poisoners (Churchill), 1993
Lives of the Twins (Oates, as Smith), 1987
Living in the Open (Piercy), 1976
Living My Life (Goldman), 1931
Living of Charlotte Perkins Gilman (Gilman), 1935
"Living with Other Women" (Brown, R.), 1975
Lizard's Tail (Valenzuela), 1983
Lloyd George Takes the Mask Off (Pankhurst), 1920
Logan: A Family History (Neal), 1822
Loitering with Intent (Spark), 1981
Lolly Willowes, or, The Loving Huntsman (Warner), 1926
Lolly-Madonna War (Grafton), 1969
London Observed (Lessing), 1992
London Scene (Woolf), 1975
London Walks (Tristan), 1842
Londoners (Duffy), 1983

Manual for the Black Oral History Program (Shockley), 1971
Manuscripts of Pauline Archange (Blais), 1970
March Moonlight (Richardson), 1967
Margaret Atwood's Poems 1965-1975 (Atwood), 1991
"Margaret Bronson" (Phelps), 1865
Margaret Sanger: An Autobiography (Sanger), 1938
"Margaret Walker's For My People" (Walker, M.), 1992
Margret Howth (Davis, R.), 1862
Maria; or, The Wrongs of Woman (Wollstonecraft), 1798
Marigold from North Vietnam (Levertov), 1968
"Marigolds and Mules" (Arnow), 1935
Marine Lover of Friedrich Nietzsche (Irigaray), 1991
Mark on the Wall (Woolf), 1919
Marmalade Me (Johnston), 1971
Marquis de Villemer (Sand), 1871
Marriage and Family among Negroes (Bernard), 1966
Marriage as a Trade (Hamilton), 1909
Marriage in My Time (Stopes), 1935
"Marriage Is a Matter of Give and Take" (Piercy), 1973
Marriages and Infidelities (Oates), 1972
Marriages between Zones Three, Four, and Five (Lessing), 1980
Married Love (Stopes), 1918
Married Lover (Colette), 1935
Mars and Her Children (Piercy), 1992
Marsh, Hawk (Atwood), 1977
Marsh Island (Jewett), 1885
"Marsh" (Tsushima), 1991
Maru (Head), 1971
"Marx after Derrida" (Spivak), 1984
Mary Austin Reader (Austin), 1996
Mary Lavelle (O'Brien, K.), 1936
Mary Lavin (Lavin), 1981
Mary O'Grady (Lavin), 1950
Mary Shelley: A Biography (Spark), 1987
Mary, The Feminine Face of the Church (Ruether), 1977
Mary: A Fiction (Wollstonecraft), 1788
Marya: A Life (Oates), 1986
Mask of November (Chávez), 1975
Mask of State: Watergate Portraits (McCarthy), 1974
Masks (Enchi), 1983
Masque of Henry Purcell (Duffy), 1995
Massacre by Bombing (Brittain), 1981
Massacre of the Dreamers: Essays on Xicanisma (Castillo), 1994
Master Bellringers (Sand), n.d.
Master of Hestviken series (Undset), from 1925
Mate of the Daylight, and Friends Ashore (Jewett), 1884
Matilda's Mistake (Oakley), 1990
Matter of Gravity (Bagnold), 1970
Matter of Money (Hamilton), 1916
Mauve (Brossard), 1985
Mauve (Marlatt), 1985
Mauve Desert (Brossard), 1990
Maybe: A Story (Hellman), 1980
Maze: A Story to Be Read Aloud (Warner), 1928
Mazes (Rukeyser), 1970
McLuhan and the Future of Literature (West), 1969
Meadow Blossoms (Alcott), 1879
Mean Season (Ehrenreich), 1987
Meaning of Treason (West), 1947
Medieval English Nunneries c. 1275-1535 (Power), 1922
Medieval People (Power), 1924
Medieval Women (Power), 1975
Medina (McCarthy), 1972
Meditation on the Threshold (Castellanos), 1988
"Meditations on Masculinity" (Williams), 1995
Mediterranean (Rukeyser), 1938
Meeting at the Crossroads (Gilligan), 1992
Meeting the Comet (Adcock), 1988
Melancholy Baby and Other Stories (O'Faolain), 1978
Melissa & Smith (Shange), 1976
"Melymbrosia: An Early Version of The Voyage Out" (Woolf), 1982
Member of the Wedding (McCullers), 1946
Memento Mori (Spark), 1959
Memoir of Martha Carey Thomas, Late of Baltimore (Thomas), 1846
Memoirs (Fuller), 1852
Memoirs from the Women's Prison (al'Sadaawi), 1986
Memoirs of a Survivor (Lessing), 1974
Memoirs of a Woman Doctor (al'Sadaawi), 1988
Memoirs of an Ex-Prom Queen (Shulman), 1972
Memoirs of Carwin the Biloquist (Brown, C.), 1991
Memoirs of the Late Mrs. Robinson, Written by Herself. With Some Posthumous Pieces (Robinson), 1801
Memorials of the Quick and the Dead (Duffy), 1979
Memories (Tynan), 1924
Memories of a Catholic Girlhood (McCarthy), 1957
Memories of a Dutiful Daughter (de Beauvoir), 1959
Memory and Other Stories (Lavin), 1972
Memory Board (Rule), 1987
"Memory, Creation, and Writing" (Morrison), 1984
Memory of a Large Christmas (Smith, L.), 1962
"Men against Patriarchy" (Moi), 1989
Men and Angels (Gordon, M.), 1985
Men, Women, and Ghosts (Phelps), 1869
Men, Women, and Places (Undset), 1939
Menaced World (Levertov), 1984
Men's Room (Oakley), 1988
Mer-Child: A Legend for Children and Other Adults (Morgan), 1991
Mercy (Dworkin), 1990
Mercy Gliddon's Work (Phelps), 1866
Meridian (Walker, A.), 1976
"Mess of Pork" (Arnow), 1935
"Metaphors in the Tradition of the Shaman" (Anzaldúa), 1990
Miami (Wasserstein), 1986
Microcosm (Duffy), 1966
Midday Sun (Churchill), 1984
"Middle-Aged Woman" (Davis, R.), 1875
Middle-Class Education (Oates), 1980
Middle Ground (Drabble), 1980
Middle of the Air (Rukeyser), 1945
Middleman and Other Stories (Mukherjee), 1988
Midsummer Madness (Pardo Bazán), 1907
Mild Attack of Locusts (Lessing), 1977
Militant Methods of the NWSPU (Pankhurst), 1908
Miller of Angibault (Sand), 1871
Million Dollar Month (Plath), 1971
Millstone (Drabble), 1965
"Miracle in the Museum" (Sarton), 1948
"Miracle of Lesbianism" (Gearhart), 1974
Miracle Play (Oates), 1974

Miracle Plays: Our Lord's Coming and Childhood (Tynan), 1895
Mirror of the Mother (Roberts), 1985
Miscellany (Behn), 1685
"Misguided, Dangerous, and Wrong: An Analysis of Anti-Pornography Politics" (Rubin), 1993
Miss Firecracker Contest (Henley), 1980
Miss Giardino (Bryant), 1978
Miss Herbert (The Suburban Wife) (Stead), 1976
Miss Hewitt's Shenanigans (Hewett), 1975
Miss Pickthorn and Mr. Hare (Sarton), 1966
Miss Sophie's Diary, Beijing, Panda Books (Ding Ling), 1985
Miss Venezuela (Wilson), 1988
Miss Z, The Dark Young Lady (Carter), 1970
Mistress of Husaby (Undset), 1925
Mists of Avalon (Bradley), 1982
Mitsou; or, How Girls Grow Wise (Colette), 1930
Mixquiahuala Letters (Castillo), 1986
Mobilizing Woman-Power (Blatch), 1918
Model Childhood (Wolf), 1980
Moderation Truly Stated (Astell, as Single), 1704
Modern Griselda (Edgeworth), 1805
Modern Manners, a Poem. In Two Cantos (Robinson, as Juvenal), 1792
Modern Mephistopheles (Alcott), 1877
Modern Rack. Papers on Vivisection (Cobbe), 1889
Modulations for Solo Voice (Levertov), 1977
Mohawk Trail (Brant), 1985
Moment and Other Essays (Woolf), 1947
Moments of Being (Woolf), 1976
Monday or Tuesday (Woolf), 1919
Monodromos (Engel), 1973
Monody to the Memory of Sir Joshua Reynolds (Robinson), 1792
Monody to the Memory of the Late Queen of France, Marie Antoinette (Robinson), 1793
Monster (Morgan), 1972
Monster Has Stolen the Sun (Malpede), 1987
Month of Saturdays (Parker), 1971
Montserrat (Hellman), 1950
Moods (Alcott), 1865
Moon Is Always Female (Piercy), 1980
Moon Lady (Tan), 1992
Moon over Minneapolis (Weldon), 1991
Moonlight Bride (Emecheta), 1981
Moon's Ottery (Beer), 1978
Moonshadow (Carter), 1982
Moonshots (Adnan), 1966
Moose-Hunter; or, Life in the Maine Woods (Neal), 1864
Moral Aspects of Vivisection (Cobbe), 1875
Moral Ending and Other Stories (Warner), 1931
Moral Tales for Young People (Edgeworth), 1801
More Eggs of Things (Sexton), 1964
More Joy in Heaven and Other Stories (Warner), 1935
More Leaves from Lantern Lane (McClung), 1937
More Night (Rukeyser), 1981
More Tales I Tell My Mother (Maitland), 1987
More Tales I Tell My Mother (Miner), 1987
More Tales I Tell My Mother (Roberts), 1987
"More Things Change" (Shockley), 1977
Morning Glory (Colette), 1932
Morning Hair (Dworkin), 1968
Morning in the Burned House (Atwood), 1995
Morning-Glories, and Other Stories (Alcott), 1868
Moses, Man of the Mountain (Hurston), 1939
Most Unfortunate Day of My Life (Edgeworth), 1931
Mother Courage and Her Children (Shange), 1980
"Mother in the House of Grass" (Tsushima), 1987
Mother of Claudine (Colette), 1937
Motherhood in Bondage (Sanger), 1928
"Mothering, Object-Relations, and the Female Oedipal Configuration" (Chodorow), 1978
Mothers and Shadows (Traba), 1989
Mothers of Maya Diip (Namjoshi), 1989
Mothers of the Novel (Spender), 1986
Mothers on Trial: The Battle for Children and Custody (Chesler), 1986
Mountain Arapesh (Mead), 1968-71
Mountain Path (Arnow, as Simpson), 1936
Mouthful of Birds (Churchill), 1987
Mouths (Shange), 1981
Movement (Miner), 1982
Movie Star Has to Star in Black and White (Kennedy), 1984
Moving beyond Words (Steinem), 1993
Moving Clocks Go Slow (Churchill), 1975
Moving House (Weldon), 1976
"Moving On" (Rule), 1968
Moving the Mountain (Gilman), 1911
"Mr Chesterton in Hysterics" (West), 1913
Mr. Bennett and Mrs. Brown (Woolf), 1924
Mr. Director (Weldon), 1978
Mr. Dollinger (Lessing), 1958
Mr. Fortune's Maggot (Warner), 1927
Mr. Hogarth's Will (Spence), 1865
"Mr. Pomeroy's Battle" (Sarton), 1948
Mrs. Armstrong's Admirer (Hamilton), 1920
Mrs. Beer's House (Beer), 1968
"Mrs. Christiansen's Harvest" (Sarton), 1947
Mrs. Dalloway (Woolf), 1925
Mrs. Frampton (Gems), 1989
Mrs. Noah and the Minoan Queen (Rodriguez), 1983
Mrs. Porter and the Angel (Hewett), 1970
Mrs. Reinhardt and Other Stories (O'Brien, E.), 1978
Mrs. Spring Fragrance Co. (Sui Sin Far), 1912
Mrs. Stevens Hears the Mermaids Singing (Sarton), 1965
Mrs. Vance (Hamilton), 1907
"Ms. Right, My Soul Mate" (Anzaldúa), 1991
Mudcrab at Gambaro's (Rodriguez), 1980
Mule Bone: A Comedy of Negro Life (Hurston), 1964
Mules and Men (Hurston), 1935
Murder at Monticello, or, Old Sins (Brown, R.), 1994
"Murder at the International Feminist Book Fair" (Wilson), 1989
"Murder between the Sheets" (Grafton), 1986
Murder in the Collective (Wilson), 1984
Murder in the Dark (Atwood), 1983
Murder in the English Department (Miner), 1982
"Murder of the Glenn Ross" (Davis, R.), 1861
Muriel Rukeyser Reader (Rukeyser), 1994
Museum of Cheats (Warner), 1947
Music-hall Sidelights (Colette), 1957
"Musing with Mothertongue" (Marlatt), 1987
Must We Burn Sade? (de Beauvoir), 1953
My Apprenticeship (Webb, B.), 1926
My Apprenticeships (Colette), 1957

Paradise Papers: The Suppression of Women's Rights (Stone), 1976
Paradox Players (Duffy), 1967
"Parasitism and Civilized Vice" (Gilman), 1931
Parent's Assistant, or, Stories for Children (Edgeworth), 1796
"Pargiters: The Novel-Essay Portion of The Years" (Woolf), 1977
"Paris Hat" (Sarton), 1948
"Parker Shotgun" (Grafton), 1986
Parliamentary Vote for Women (Pankhurst), 1896
Parting of Arwen (Bradley), 1974
Party Puddle (Weldon), 1989
Passing (Larsen), 1929
Passion (Winterson), 1987
Passion according to G.H. (Lispector), 1988
Passion Flowers (Howe, J.), 1854
Passion of New Eve (Carter), 1977
Passionaria (Gems), 1985
Passionate Apprentice (Woolf), 1990
Passionate Politics: Feminist Theory in Action: Essays, 1968-1986 (Bunch), 1987
Passionate Shepherdess (Duffy), 1977
"Passionlessness: An Interpretation of Anglo-American Sexual Ideology, 1790-1840" (Cott), 1978
Past Is before Us: Feminism in Action from the Late 1960s (Rowbotham), 1989
"Pathological Social Science: Carol Gilligan and the Incredible Shrinking Girl" (Sommers), 1996
Patriarchal Attitudes: Women in Society (Figes), 1970
"Patriarchal Thought and the Drive for Knowledge" (Moi), 1989
Patriarchy: Notes of an Expert Witness (Chesler), 1994
Patriot Sun and Other Stories (Lavin), 1956
Patriotism: A Menace to Liberty (Goldman), 1908
Patronage (Edgeworth), 1814
Patterns of Childhood (Wolf), 1984
Patty Gray's Journey to the Cotton Islands (Dall), 1869-70
"Paul Blecker" (Davis, R.), 1863
"Pauline Elizabeth Hopkins: A Biographical Excursion into Obscurity" (Shockley), 1972
Pause: A Sketch Book (Carr), 1953
Pavements at Anderby: Tales of 'South Riding' and Other Regions (Holtby), 1937
"Paw Paw Hunt" (Davis, R.), 1871
Pay Dirt;, or Adventures at Ash Lawn (Brown, R.), 1996
Paycockes of Coggshall (Power), 1920
Peace and Bread in Time of War (Addams), 1922
Peacock Garden (Desai), n.d.
Peak in Darien, with Some Other Inquiries Touching Concerns of the Soul and the Body (Cobbe), 1882
"Pearl of Great Price" (Davis, R.), 1868
"Peasant Life and Rural Conditions (c. 1100 to c. 1500)" (Power), 1932
Pembroke (Freeman), 1894
Penelope at War (Fallaci), 1966
Penguin Modern Poets 9 (Levertov), 1967
Peninsula (Hewett), 1994
Pentimiento (Hellman), 1973
People and Places (Mead), 1959
"People of Color in Louisiana" (Dunbar-Nelson), 1916
People of Our Neighborhood (Freeman), 1898
People Who Led to My Plays (Kennedy), 1987
People with the Dogs (Stead), 1952
"Pepper-Pot Woman" (Davis, R.), 1874
Perfectionist (Oates), 1995
Perfectionist and Other Plays (Oates), 1995
Permanence (Weldon), 1970
Personal Collections of the Grimké Family and the Life and Writings of Charlotte Forten Grimké (Cooper), 1951
"Perspectives on the Use of Case Studies: All It Takes Is One" (Chodorow), 1993
"Peter Bell the First" (Jacobus), 1974
Petticoat Court (Lovelace), 1930
Phases of Love: Adolescence, 1925-1928 (Livesay), 1980
Philanthropy and Social Progress (Addams), 1893
Philip Stanley; or, The Enthusiasms of Love (Brown, C.), 1807
"Philosophers against the Family" (Sommers), 1988
Philosophy and Feminism (Bartky), 1977
Philosophy and Women (Bartky), 1979
Phoenix Again (Sarton), 1987
Photograph: A Study of Cruelty (Shange), 1981
Phyl (Hamilton), 1913
Piaf (Gems), 1979
Piano Player (Jelinek), 1988
Picnic on Paradise (Russ), 1968
Pictorial History of St. Martin-in-the-Fields (Brittain), 1962
Picture Bride (Song), 1983
"Picture Prize" (Shockley), 1962
Picture Theory (Brossard), 1982
"Pictures" (Rule), 1976
Pictures and Conversations (Bowen), 1975
Piece of the Night (Roberts), 1978
Pieces (Rich), 1977
Pierre, or The Spring War (Blais), 1991
Pig Dreams: Scenes from the Life of Sylvia (Levertov), 1981
"Pilgrim Bible on a Feminist Journey" (Trible), 1988
Pilgrimage (Richardson), 1938
Pindarick on the Death of Our Late Sovereign (Behn), 1685
Pindarick Poem on the Happy Coronation of His ... Majesty James II and His Illustrious Consort Queen Mary (Behn), 1685
Pioneers on Parade (Franklin), 1939
"Pit Bull Opportunity" (Gearhart), 1994
Pitied but Not Entitled: Single Mothers and the History of Welfare 1890-1935 (Gordon, L.), 1994
Pivot of Civilization (Sanger), 1922
"Placing Women's History in History" (Fox-Genovese), 1982
Plagiarized Material (Oates, as Fernandes/Oates), 1974
Plague-Time (Chávez), 1985
Plain Brown Rapper (Brown, R.), 1976
Plain Facts about a Great Evil (Pankhurst), 1913
Plainsongs (Livesay), 1969
Plan for Improving Female Education (Willard), 1818
Planet of Exile (Le Guin), 1966
Planet Savers (Bradley), 1962
Plant Dreaming Deep (Sarton), 1968
"Plasting Project" (Stone), 1986
Play Days: A Book of Stories for Children (Jewett), 1878
Play Room (Manning), 1969
Play with a Tiger (Lessing), 1962
Players Come Again (Heilbrun, as Cross), 1990
Playfellow (Martineau), 1841-43
Playing in the Dark: Whiteness and the Literary Imagination (Morrison), 1992
Plays of Old Japan: The No (Stopes), 1913

Shadow of a Man (Sarton), 1950
Shadow on Glass (Rodriguez), 1978
Shadows on the Grass (Blixen), 1961
Shakers (Norman), 1983
Shakespeare (Greer), 1986
Shakespeare's Division of Experience (French), 1981
Shamrocks (Tynan), 1887
Sharra's Exile (Bradley), 1981
Shattered Chain (Bradley), 1976
She Came to Stay (de Beauvoir), 1949
"She Came to Stay" (Moi), 1986
"She Didn't Come Home" (Grafton), 1986
She Has No Place in Paradise (al'Sadaawi), 1987
She Talks (Kennedy), 1991
She Walks in Beauty (Tynan), 1899
Shedding, New York, Daughters (Stefan), 1978
Shelley; or The Idealist (Jellicoe), 1966
"Shifting the Center" (Collins), 1994
"Shipwreck" (Davis, R.), 1876
Shirley Chisholm: A Biography (Brownmiller), 1970
Shoot the Works (Parker), 1931
Short History of the American Labor Movement (Beard), 1920
Shorter Novels and Stories of Carson McCullers (McCullers), 1972
Shoulders of Atlas (Freeman), 1908
Shower of Summer Days (Sarton), 1952
Shrapnel Academy (Weldon), 1986
Shrine and Other Stories (Lavin), 1977
Sí, Hay Posada (Chávez), 1981
Sicilian Lover. A Tragedy in Five Acts (Robinson), 1796
Sick in Workhouses (Cobbe), 1861
Sido (Colette), 1953
Sight, the Cavern of Woe, and Solitude (Robinson), 1793
Sign in Sidney Brustein's Window (Hansberry), 1964
Signpost (Livesay), 1932
Sigurd and His Brave Companions: A Tale of Medieval Norway (Undset), 1943
Silence and Other Stories (Freeman), 1898
Silence Between: Moeraki Conversations (Hulme), 1982
Silence Now (Sarton), 1988
Silence Wager Stories (Howe, S.), 1992
Silent Partner (Phelps), 1871
Silent Peter (Jellicoe), 1975
Silent Spring (Carson), 1962
Silent Spring Revisited (Carson), 1987
Silhouettes of American Life (Davis, R.), 1892
Silk Room (Duffy), 1966
Silver Pitchers (Alcott), 1876
"Simone de Beauvoir and The Second Sex" (Hansberry), 1957
"Simone de Beauvoir's L'Invité: An Existentialist Melodrama" (Moi), 1991
Simone Weil's Philosophy of Culture: Readings towards a Divine Humanity (Weil), 1993
Singing Door (Lessing), 1973
Singing Steel (Hurston), 1934
Single Eye (Duffy), 1964
Single Hound (Sarton), 1938
Single Lady and Other Stories (Lavin), 1951
"Single Parenthood in 1900" (Gordon, L.), 1991
Singular Life (Phelps), 1895
Singularities (Howe, S.), 1990
Sink (Griffin), 1973
Sir Gawain and the Green Knight: A Comparison with the French Perceval (Thomas), 1883
Sir Patient Fancy (Behn), 1678
"Siren song" (Maitland), 1994
Sirian Experiments: The Report by Ambien II, of the Five (Lessing), 1981
Sister Act (Hurst), 1941
Sister Gin (Arnold), 1975
Sister Outsider (Lorde), 1984
Sister's Choice: Traditions and Change in American Women's Writing (Showalter), 1991
Sisters of the Road (Wilson), 1986
Sisters of the Yam: Black Women and Self-Recovery (hooks), 1993
Sisters Rosensweig (Wasserstein), 1992
Sita (Millett), 1977
Sitt Marie Rose (Adnan), 1978
Six Darn Cows (Laurence), 1979
Six of One (Brown, R.), 1978
Six Trees (Freeman), 1903
Sixth Commandment (Hamilton), 1906
"Skeletons of Men" (Enchi), 1988
Skin: Talking about Sex, Class and Literature (Allison), 1994
Skins and Bones (Allen), 1988
Skriker (Churchill), 1994
Slave Girl (Emecheta), 1977
Slavery and the French Revolutionists (1788-1805) (Cooper), 1988
Slavery in America (Grimké), 1837
Sleep (Stopes), 1956
"Sleeper Wakes" (Fauset), 1920
Sleeping Beauty and Other Favourite Fairy Tales (Carter), 1982
Slip-Shod Sibyls: Recognition, Rejection and the Woman Poet (Greer), 1995
"Slow Walk of Trees Hopeless" (Morrison), 1976
Small Changes (Piercy), 1973
Small Conference: An Innovation in Communication (Mead), 1966
Small Personal Voice (Lessing), 1974
Small Room (Sarton), 1961
"Small Town Girl Makes Dyke" (Gearhart), 1994
Smile, Smile, Smile, Smile (Roberts), 1980
Smiling John (Jellicoe), 1975
Snake Eyes (Oates, as Smith), 1992
Snake Pit (Undset), 1929
Snake Poems (Atwood), 1983
Snapshots of a Daughter-in-Law (Rich), 1963
Snarling Citizen (Ehrenreich), 1995
Snowfall (Oates), 1978
"So Easy to Please" (Te Awekotuku), 1992
So Far from God (Castillo), 1993
So Here Then Are Dreams (Schreiner), 1901
"Social Construction of Black Feminist Thought" (Collins), 1989
"Social Darwinism" (Gilman), 1907
Social Organization of Manua (Mead), 1930
Social Problems at Midcentury: Role, Status, and Stress in a Context of Abundance (Bernard), 1957
Social Settlement (Cooper), 1913
Social Significance of the Modern Drama (Goldman), 1914
Social Welfare and Professional Education (Abbott), 1931
Socialism and the New Life: The Personal and Sexual Politics of Edward Carpenter and Havelock Ellis (Rowbotham), 1977
Society and Maternity (Kollontai), 1916

Truth or Dare: Encounters with Power, Authority, and Mystery (Starhawk), 1987
Truth-Teller (Oates), 1995
"Truth That Never Hurts: Black Lesbians in Fiction in the 1980s" (Smith, B.), 1991
Tune Is in the Tree (Lovelace), 1950
Tunnel (Richardson), 1919
Turn of a Pang (Brossard), 1976
Turn Out; or, Patience the Best Policy (Martineau), 1829
Turning Wind (Rukeyser), 1939
"Turtle Gal" (Brant), 1990
Twelve Plays (Oates), 1991
Twentieth-Century Faith: Hope and Survival (Mead), 1972
"Twenty Years after The Feminine Mystique" (Friedan), 1983
Twenty Years at Hull-House, with Autobiographical Notes (Addams), 1910
Twenty-Five Years: Reminiscences (Tynan), 1913
Twenty-one Love Poems (Rich), 1977
Twilight Lovers (Bradley, as Gardner), 1964
"Two Brave Boys" (Davis, R.), 1910
Two Congratulatory Poems to Their Most Sacred Majesties (Behn), 1688
Two Dreisers (Moers), 1969
"Two Hunters" (Arnow), 1942
Two Letters on Cow-Keeping, Addressed to the Governor of the Guiltcross Union Workhouse (Martineau), 1850
Two of Them (Russ), 1978
Two or Three Things I Know for Sure (Allison), 1995
Two Poems (Warner), 1945
Two to Conquer (Bradley), 1980
"Two Ways of Telling" (Paley), 1990
Two Women in One (al'Sadaawi), 1985
Two-Headed Poems (Atwood), 1978

U.S. 1 (Rukeyser), 1938
Uncle Vanya (Gems), 1979
Uncollected Short Stories of Sarah Orne Jewett (Jewett), 1971
Uncollected Verse of Aphra Behn (Behn), 1989
Uncommon Women and Others (Wasserstein), 1975
Uncurtained Future (Pankhurst), 1940
"Under 40: A Symposium of American Literature and the Younger Generation of American Jews" (Rukeyser), 1949
Under My Skin: Volume 1 of My Autobiography, to 1949 (Lessing), 1994
Under the Lilacs (Alcott), 1878
Under the Sea-Wind: A Naturalist's Picture of Ocean Life (Carson), 1941
Underground River (Sarton), 1947
Undersong (Lorde), 1992
Understudies (Freeman), 1901
Undine (Schreiner), 1928
Undiscovered Country: The New Zealand Stories of Katherine Mansfield (Mansfield), 1974
Unearthing Suite (Atwood), 1983
Unfinished Woman (Hellman), 1969
Unholy Loves (Oates), 1979
Unicorn (Carter), 1966
Universal History in Perspective (Willard), 1837
Unlocking the Air and Other Stories (Le Guin), 1996
Unquiet Bed (Livesay), 1967
Unremembered Country (Griffin), 1987
Unshackled. The Story of How We Won the Vote (Pankhurst), 1959
"Unwelcome Pals and Decorative Slaves—or Glimpses of Women as Writers and Characters in Contemporary African Literature" (Aidoo), 1981
Up among the Eagles (Valenzuela), 1988
Up Hill; or, Life in the Factory (Phelps), 1865
Up in Sweden (Gems), 1975
Up in the Tree (Atwood), 1978
Up the Country: A Saga of Pioneering Days (Franklin), 1987
Up the Country: A Tale of the Early Australian Squattocracy (Franklin, as Brent of Bin Bin), 1928
Upon the Sweeping Flood and Other Stories (Oates), 1966
Upstairs in the Garden (Morgan), 1990
Urewera Notebook (Mansfield), 1978
Us (Malpede), 1992
Uscoque: A Venitian Story (Sand), 1850
Useless Sex, Voyage around the Woman (Fallaci), 1964
Usual Star (H.D.), 1934
Utilitarianism (Mill), 1863

V.V.; or, Plots and Counterplots (Alcott, as Barnard), 1870
Vagabond (Colette), 1954
Valentine Box (Lovelace), 1966
Vamps and Tramps (Paglia), 1994
Vancenza; or, The Dangers of Credulity (Robinson), 1792
Vancouver Poems (Marlatt), 1972
Veil and the Male Elite: A Feminist Interpretation of Women's Right in Islam (Mernissi), 1991
Veiled Countries/Lives (Blais), 1984
"Veiled Lips" (Irigaray), 1983
Venus Envy (Brown, R.), 1993
Venus in Scorpio: A Romance of Versailles 1770-1793 (Burdekin), 1940
Venus Rising (Emshwiller), 1992
Venus Touch (Duffy), 1971
Verbatim Report of Mrs. Pankhurst's Speech Delivered 13 November 1913 (Pankhurst), 1913
Verging on the Pertinent (Emshwiller), 1989
Verses (Jewett), 1916
Verses of a V.A.D (Brittain), 1918
Vertical City (Hurst), 1922
Very Easy Death (de Beauvoir), 1972
Very Far Away from Anywhere Else (Le Guin), 1976
Very Fine Clock (Spark), 1968
Very Long Way from Anywhere Else (Le Guin), 1976
Vida (Piercy), 1980
Vietnam (McCarthy), 1967
(Vietnam) Variations (Dworkin), n.d.
Village by the Sea (Desai), 1982
"Villette's Buried Letter" (Jacobus), 1978
Vindication of the Rights of Men, in a Letter to the Right Honorable Edmund Burke (Wollstonecraft), 1790
Vindication of the Rights of Women: with Strictures on Political and Moral Subjects (Wollstonecraft), 1792
Vinegar Tom (Churchill), 1978
Violets and Other Tales (Dunbar-Nelson, as Moore), 1895
Virgin Territory (Maitland), 1984
Virginia (O'Brien, E.), 1981
Virginia Woolf, A Critical Study (Holtby), 1932
Virginia Woolf's Reading Notebooks (Woolf), 1982

"Vision" (Gordon, M.), 1989
Vision on Fire (Goldman), 1983
Visionary: The Life Story of Flicker of the Serpentine of Telina-Na (Le Guin), 1984
Visit from Dr. Katz (Le Guin), 1988
Visitation (Roberts), 1978
Vocation and A Voice (Chopin), 1991
Voice from the South by a Black Woman of the South (Cooper), 1892
Voice of Earth (Stone), 1990
Voices (Griffin), 1975
Voices at Play (Spark), 1961
Voices in the City (Desai), 1965
"Voluntary Motherhood" (Gordon, L.), 1973
Voodoo Gods: An Inquiry into Native Myths and Magic in Jamaica and Haiti (Hurston), 1939
Voyage Out (Woolf), 1915
"Voyage to Cythera" (Drabble), 1967

Wage-Earning Woman and the State (Abbott), n.d.
Wages of Men and Women: Should They Be Equal? (Webb, B.), 1919
Wages of Unskilled Labor in the United States, 1850-1900 (Abbott), 1905
Wagon and the Star: A Study of American Community Initiative (Mead), 1966
Waiting for God (Weil), 1951
Waiting for the Verdict (Davis, R.), 1867
Waiting Years (Enchi), 1971
Wake Island (Rukeyser), 1942
Wake of Jamey Foster (Henley), 1985
Waking (Figes), 1981
Walk through the Woods (Sarton), 1976
"Walking Fire: Finding Cordelia's Voice as Working-Class Hero" (Miner), 1992
Walking on the Moon (Wilson), 1983
Walking to Mercury (Starhawk), 1997
Walled In (Phelps), 1909
Walls Do Not Fall (H.D.), 1944
Walsh (Pollock), 1973
Walsingham: or, The Pupil of Nature (Robinson), 1797
Wanderer's Daysong (Levertov), 1981
Wanderground: Stories of the Hill Women (Gearhart), 1978
Wandering Recollections of a Somewhat Busy Life (Neal), 1869
War (Pankhurst), 1914
War against Women (French), 1992
War Horse (Boland), 1975
War Nurse (West), 1930
War of Dreams (Carter), 1974
Warrior Woman (Bradley), 1985
Wars, Weapons, and Everyday Violence (Myrdal), 1977
Wartime Harvest (Stopes), 1944
Wash Us and Comb Us (Deming), 1972
"Washerwoman's Day" (Arnow), 1936
"Waste of Private Housekeeping" (Gilman), 1913
Watch on the Rhine (Hellman), 1941
Watching Me, Watching You (Weldon), 1981
Water Cresses (Alcott), 1879
Water Is Wide (Le Guin), 1976
Water Life (Rodriguez), 1976
Waterfall (Drabble), 1969
Waterlily Fire (Rukeyser), 1962
Waverly Place (Brownmiller), 1989
Waves (Woolf), 1931
Way of a Maid (Tynan), 1895
Way of Seeing (Mead), 1970
We Are All Part of One Another (Deming), 1984
"We Are Also Your Sisters: The Development of Women's Studies in Religion" (Plaskow), 1993
"We Are Not Part of Cane Fields" (Shange), 1996
We Are Ten (Hurst), 1937
We Burn (Stopes), 1951
We Cannot Live Without Our Lives (Deming), 1974
"We Didn't See It" (Wilson), 1989
We Might See Sights! and Other Stories (O'Faolain), 1968
We Who Are About To. . . (Russ), 1977
Web of Darkness (Bradley), 1984
Web of Light (Bradley), 1983
Websters' First New Intergalactic WICKEDARY of the English Language (Daly), 1987
Wedding Trip (Pardo Bazán), 1891
Weddings and Funerals (Maitland), 1984
Weedkiller's Daughter (Arnow), 1970
Week in the Future (Spence), 1987
Western Borders (Howe, S.), 1976
Western Trails (Austin), 1987
What about the People! (Hewett), 1962
What Cabrillo Found (Lovelace), 1958
"What Can Be Had" (Piercy), 1977
What Diantha Did (Gilman), 1910
What Do I Love? (H.D.), 1950
"What Europe Thought of the Pan-African Congress" (Fauset), 1921
What Every Boy and Girl Should Know (Sanger), 1927
What Every Girl Should Know (Sanger), 1913
What Every Mother Should Know; or, How Six Little Children Were Taught the Truth (Sanger), 1914
What Happened Next (Smyth), 1940
"What Has the Church to Offer the Men of Today?" (Dunbar-Nelson), 1913
What I Lived For (Oates), 1994
What Is Found There: Notebooks on Poetry and Politics (Rich), 1994
"What Is Lesbian Literature?: Creating a Historical Canon" (Faderman), 1995
"What Is the Relation between Psychoanalytic Feminism and the Psychoanalytic Psychology of Women?" (Chodorow), 1989
"What Is Women's History?" (Gordon, L.), 1985
"What Keeps a Woman Captive in a Violent Relationship? The Social Context of Battering" (Martin), 1979
What Remains and Other Stories (Wolf), 1994
"What Should Women's Historians Do: Politics, Social Theory, and Women's History" (Gordon, L.), 1978
"What the Black Woman Thinks about Women's Lib" (Morrison), 1971
What Use Are Flowers? (Hansberry), 1972
What We Really Know about Shakespeare (Dall), 1885
"What's in a Name? The Limits of Social Feminism or, Expanding the Vocabulary of Women's History" (Cott), 1989
"What's in a Name? Womanism, Black Feminism, and Beyond" (Collins), 1996
Wheel of Love and Other Stories (Oates), 1970

NOTES ON ADVISERS AND CONTRIBUTORS

AKINS, Frances. Doctoral student in political science, University of Georgia, Athens, Georgia. Author of papers about gender and the welfare state, the representation of women in political parties and legislatures, and the role of informal groups in Congress. **Essay:** Linda Gordon.

ARNOLD, Ellen. Ph.D. candidate in 19th-century British literature and Women's Studies at University of South Carolina; Columbia, South Carolina. **Essay:** Harriet Taylor Mill and John Stuart Mill.

BALL, R. Edward. Visiting assistant professor of literature and language, University of North Carolina, Asheville. Author of "Mary Shelley" in *Dictionary of Literary Biography,* Vol. 158: *British Writers of Short Fiction, 1800-1880.* **Essay:** Mary Wollstonecraft.

BARRY, Naomi M. Student, Mount Holyoke College, South Hadley, Massachusetts. Harry S. Truman Scholar, Woodrow Wilson Fellow. **Essays:** Margaret Mead; Denise Chavez; Cherríe Moraga.

BEILKE, Debra. Doctoral candidate, University of Wisconsin--Madison. Has presented papers on writers, including Zora Neale Hurston, Jean Rhys, Margaret Atwood, and Leslie Marmon Silko. **Essays:** Dorothy Parker; Alix Kates Schulman.

BELGRADE, Sandia. Writer and teacher of English as a Second Language and Computer Literacy, Santa Cruz Adult School, Santa Cruz, California. Author of *Sor Juana: The Libretto,* 1996, *Guess Who's Coming for Dinner,* 1992, *Turtle Island,* 1991, and *Children of the Second Birth,* 1980; translator, *At the Sweet Hour of Hand in Hand* by Renee Vivien, Naiad Press, 1979; poetry has appeared in the anthology *The Persistent Desire* and in periodicals, including *Sinister Wisdom* and *Plains Review.* **Essay:** Sor Juana de la Cruz.

BENKOV, Edith J. Professor of French, San Diego University. Associate editor, *Concerns: The Journal of the Womens' Caucus of the Modern Language Association.* Articles, essays, and reviews in *Encyclopedia of Continental Women Writers, Symposium, Moyen Français, Romance Philology, Classical and Modern Literature, 16th-Century Journal,* among others. **Essays:** Marie de Gournay; Germaine de Staël.

BILY, Cynthia. Instructor, Adrian College, Adrian, Michigan. Author of articles about women writers in various reference works. **Essay:** Eavan Boland.

BLEND, Benay. Instructor, Louisiana School for Math, Science, and the Arts, Natchitoches. Formerly instructor, College of Eastern Utah, Prince. Author of articles about women writers and minority and environmental issues in various journals. **Essay:** Mary Austin.

BOUFIS, Christina. Affiliated scholar, Stanford Institute for Research on Women and Gender, Stanford University. Co-editor, with Victoria C. Olsen, *On the Market: Ph.D.'s Tell Their Stories of the Academic Job Search,* forthcoming 1997. Author of articles on 19th-century literature, culture, and feminism. **Essays:** Dorothea Beale; Carol Gilligan.

BRANTLEY, Jennifer. English department, University of Wisconsin--River Falls. Article on Anne Ellis in *Women's Life-Writing;* sections on Southern women writers in *Chronology of Women Worldwide: People, Places, and Events that Shaped World History,* 1996. **Essays:** Kate Chopin; Carson McCullers.

BRESNAHAN, Eileen. Assistant professor of political science and women's studies, University of Utah, Salt Lake City. Formerly, collective member (editor and writer), *Big Mama Rag Feminist Newsjournal,* Denver; collective member (editor, writer, and announcer), "Women Everywhere" Radio Collective, Denver; founding member, Denver Feminist Organizing Committee; founding member and member of board of directors, University of South Florida Women's Center, Tampa. **Essays:** Mary Daly; Shulamith Firestone; Catharine MacKinnon.

BROWNSON, Siobhan Craft. Ph.D. candidate and teaching assistant, University of South Carolina, Columbia. Formerly assistant professor of English, Community College of Allegheny County, Pittsburgh, Pennsylvania. Articles about James Barrie and Lord Dunsany in *Dictionary of Literary Biography, Book of Wonder,* and *Magill's Encyclopedia of the Essay.* **Essays:** Karen Blixen; Katharine Tynan.

CAIAZZA, Amy. Doctoral candidate, Department of Political Science, Indiana University. Author of an upcoming article about feminism and political science in *Southeastern Political Review.* **Essay:** Visakha Kumari Jayawardena.

CHERRY, Caroline Lockett. Chair, Department of English, Eastern College, St. Davids, Pennsylvania. Associate editor of *Quaker History;* author of *The Most Unvalued'st Purchase: Women in the Plays of Thomas* Middleton (1973), and articles about Renaissance literature and women's literature in various journals. **Essay:** Patricia Beer.

CHICK, Nancy. Ph.D. candidate in English and teaching assistant in the area of multicultural literature, University of Georgia, Athens. Author of articles about Jamaica Kincaid and Marita Bonner in *CLA Journal* and *Langston Hughes Review,* and Judith Ortiz Cofer and Phillis Wheatley in *Issues and Identity in Literature.* **Essay:** Tony Morrison.

CHIU, Monica. Assistant professor of English, University of Wisconsin--Eau Clair. Ph.D. in English in May 1996 from Emory University, Atlanta, Georgia. **Essay:** Sui Sin Far.

CLARK, Tracy. Doctoral student, Southern Illinois University. Author of several biographical/critical essays for *Contemporary Popular Writers,* 1996. **Essays:** Michele Roberts; Vera Brittain.

COCHRANE, Helena Antolin. Assistant professor of Spanish language and literature, Widener University, Pennsylvania. Author of book reviews and criticism on Latin American women's literature. **Essays:** Emilia Pardo Bazán; Rosario Castellanos; Clarice Lispector; Marta Traba.

COCKIN, Katharine. Research Associate in Women's Studies, Nene College, Northampton, England. Freelance writer for *New Dictionary of National Biography* (Oxford University Press). Formerly part-time tutor at Leicester University, Loughborough University and De Montfort University. Author of *Edith Craig: Dramatic Lives,* 1997, *The Pioneer Players (1911-25): From Women's Suffrage to Art Theatre,* 1998, and articles about Edith Craig, The Pioneer Players, women's suffrage drama, and women's writing. **Essay:** Cicely Hamilton.

COLBERT, Ann Mauger. Journalism coordinator, Indiana Purdue University, Fort Wayne. Formerly publications coordinator, Indiana University Foundation, Bloomington; congressional press secretary, Washington, D.C.; reporter and copyeditor. Recipient of two writing awards. **Essays:** Susan B. Anthony; Mary Ritter Beard; Harriot Stanton Blatch; Emily Faithfull; Susan Faludi; Margaret Sanger; Gloria Steinem.

COPELAND, Rebecca L. Assistant professor of Japanese language and literature, Washington University in St. Louis, Missouri. Author of *The Sound of the Wind: The Life and Works of Uno Chiyo,* 1992, and articles about modern Japanese women writers in *Japan Quarterly, Journal of the Association of Teachers of Japanese,* and other journals. Translator of *The Story of a Single Woman,* by Uno Chiyo, 1992. **Essay:** Fumiko Enchi.

CORNELL, Sarah. Research associate, Centre d'Études Féminines, University of Paris VIII. Author of articles about "feminine writing." Translator, with Ann Liddle, *Vivre l'Orange/To Live the Orange,* by Hélène Cixous, 1980; with Liddle, Deborah Jenson, and Susan Sellers, *Coming to Writing and Other Essays* by Cixous, 1991; and, with Sellers, *Three Steps on the Ladder of Writing,* by Cixous, 1993. **Essay:** Hélène Cixous.

CURB, Rosemary Keefe. Head of English, Southwest Missouri State University, Springfield. Formerly director of women's studies, Rollins College, Florida. Author of articles about African-American and Australian feminist playwrights in *Hypatia: A Journal of Feminist Philosophy, Theatre Journal, MELUS, Chrysalis, Kentucky Folklore Record, Women in American Theatre, Making a Spectacle: Feminist Essays on Contemporary Women's Theatre, Radical Revisions: Lesbian Texts and Contexts,* and *Intersecting Boundaries: The Theatre of Adrienne Kennedy.* Editor of *Lesbian Nuns: Breaking Silence,* 1985, and *Amazon All Stars: 13 Lesbian Plays,* 1996. Advisor, *Feminist Writers.* **Essay:** Dorothy Hewett.

CURRY, Renee R. Associate professor of literature and writing, California State University San Marcos. Author of feminist essays on literary and cinema figures, including as Woody Allen, Elizabeth Bishop, Julie Dash, Hanif Kureishi, and May Sarton. Editor, *States of Rage: Emotional Eruption, Violence, and Social Change,* 1996, and *Perspectives on Woody Allen,* 1996. **Essays:** Susan Griffin; Marilyn Hacker; Kate Millett.

DALLAS, Phyllis Surrency. Assistant professor, Georgia Southern University, Statesboro, Georgia. Author of articles on Emersonian philosophy in Gloria Naylor's *Mama Day,* Henry James's Prefaces as autobiography, and Myra Jehlen as a feminist critic. **Essays:** Mary McCarthy; Gloria Naylor.

DAVIDIS, Maria M. Ph.D. in English literature, Princeton University, Princeton, New Jersey. **Essay:** Kate O'Brien.

DONOHUE, Stacey. Assistant professor of English, Central Oregon Community College, Bend. **Essay:** Mary Lavin.

DROWNE, Kathleen. Freelance writer and doctoral candidate in American literature, University of North Carolina, Chapel Hill. Co-author of *Encyclopedia of Allegorical Literature,* 1996, and essays in *The Storytelling Encyclopedia,* 1997. **Essays:** Marilyn French; Robin Morgan; Agnes Smedley.

DUNCAN, Patricia. Ph.D. candidate, Emory University, Atlanta, Georgia. Author of articles about women of color and sexual identities, Asian/Pacific Islander lesbians, and Asian/Pacific Islander women's writing, published in anthologies of lesbian/gay/bisexual studies, and Asian American Studies. **Essays:** Lillian Faderman; Gayle Rubin; Bapsi Sidhwa; Trinh T. Minh-ha.

DUFFY, P. A. Doctoral student in sociology, University of Georgia, Athens, Georgia. Author of papers about public perceptions of welfare recipients and the impact of the Industrial Revolution on black families in the United States. **Essay:** Alva Myrdal.

EATON, Helen-May. Ph.D. candidate at the Centre for the Study of Religion, University of Toronto, Ontario. Author of *The Political Voice of Archbishop Romero,* 1994. Essays include: "Citizenship, Identity, Community: Feminists (Re) Present the Political," "The Eclipsed Presence of Women in Latin American Liberation Theology," "The Recovery of Oppressed Voices of Latin American Women: A Critical Examination," and "The testimonial Writing of Latin American Women." **Essays:** Judith Plaskow; Phyllis Tribble.

ENGDAHL, Kimberly. Doctoral candidate, University of Utah. **Essays:** Dorothy Richardson; Muriel Spark; Sylvia Townsend Warner; Mary Webb.

EVANS, Deborah. Ph.D. candidate, University of North Carolina at Chapel Hill. Author of articles on Sarah Orne Jewett, Alice and Phoebe Cary, and Hedda Hopper for various journals. **Essays:** Mary E. Wilkins Freeman; Margaret Fuller; Charlotte Perkins Gilman.

EVANS, Melissa. M.A. in English, Indiana State University, 1996. Formerly, instructor of Freshman Composition, Indiana State University. Has published critical essays on Oscar Hujuelos and Leslie Marmon Silko in *Contemporary Popular Writers,* St. James Press. **Essays:** bell hooks; Naomi Wolf.

FULTON, Keith Louise. Associate professor of English, University of Winnipeg, Winnipeg, Manitoba, Canada. Formerly Margaret Laurence Chair of Women's Studies, University of Manitoba and University of Winnipeg. Past editor of *Contemporary Verse 2: a feminist poetry journal, Herizons,* and *Canadian Research Institute for the Advancement of Women Paper Series.* Author of articles in various journals about women's studies, women and literature, women and journal assignments in university courses, and homophobia. **Essay:** Jane Rule.

GAMBLE, Sarah. Lecturer in English studies, University of Sunderland, England. Author of *Angela Carter: Writing from the Front Line,* Edinburgh University Press, forthcoming 1997, and articles on women's fiction in various journals. **Essays:** Winifred Holtby; Marge Piercy; Rebecca West.

GARAY, Kathleen E. Assistant professor, history and women's studies, McMaster University, Hamilton, Canada. **Essay:** Marie de France.

GARDNER, Janet E. Assistant professor, Department of English, University of Massachusetts--Dartmouth, North Dartmouth, Massachusetts. Author of articles and book reviews about contemporary drama in various journals, including *Theatre InSight* and *New Theatre Quarterly.* **Essays:** Caryl Churchill; Pam Gems.

GHAZNAVI, Mahnaz. Doctoral candidate in literature, University of California--San Diego, La Jolla. **Essays:** Ama Ata Aidoo; 'Molara Ogundipe-Leslie; Sheila Rowbotham.

GIUNTA, Edvige. Assistant professor of English, Jersey City State College. Formerly visiting assistant professor of English at Union College, N.Y. Editor of a special issue of *VIA: Voices in Italian Americana* devoted to women (1996). Author of the Afterword for the reprint of Tina De Rosa's *Paper Fish* by the Feminist Press (1996) and articles and reviews in various journals. **Essays:** Ana Castillo; Maria Rosa Cutrufelli.

GODARD, Barbara. Associate professor of English, women's studies, and social and political thought, York University, Canada. Author of books, including *Talking about Ourselves: The Cultural Productions of Canadian Native Women,* 1985, and *Audrey Thomas: Her Life and Work,* 1989, and numerous essays on Canadian and Quebec writers and feminist theory; coauthor, with Coomi Vevaina, *Intersections: Issues of Gender and Race in Canadian Women's Writing,* forthcoming. Translations include Nicole Brossard's *These Our Mothers,* 1983, and *Picture Theory,* 1991; editor of *Gynocritics/Cynocritiques: Feminist Approaches to the Writing of Canadian and Quebec Women,* 1987. Advisor, *Feminist Writers.* **Essays:** Margaret Atwood; Nicole Brossard.

GREEN, Amy S. Bosler Assistant Professor of American Women's History, Denison University, Granville, Ohio. **Essay:** Harriet Arnow.

GREEN, Ann E. Doctoral candidate, SUNY Albany, Albany, New York. Currently editing 19th-century American women's diaries and researching working-class women writers. **Essay:** Louisa May Alcott.

GREENBLAT, Ellen. Catalog editor, State University of New York at Buffalo. Formerly, head, Romance Languages Cataloging Team, Princeton University. Former chairman, American Library Association Gay, Lesbian, and Bisexual Book Awards Committee. Co-editor, *Gay and Lesbian Library Service* (1990) and author of articles on lesbian and gay librarianship. Listowner of internet discussion groups QSTUDY-L (Queer Studies) and LEZBRIAN (Lesbian and Bisexual Women Library Workers). Advisor, *Feminist Writers.*

GREWAL, Gurleen. Assistant professor in women's studies, University of Southern Florida, Tampa. Book on Toni Morrison is forthcoming, 1997. **Essays:** Jamaica Kincaid; Joy Kogawa.

GRINNAN, Jeanne. Composition coordinator, SUNY Brockport, Brockport, New York. **Essay:** Dale Spender.

HAAG, Pamela. Independent writer and scholar; received Ph.D. from Yale University. Currently at work on a popular history of the idea of the sexual revolution in postwar America. **Essays:** Camile Paglia; Christine Hoff Sommers.

HAEDICKE, Janet V. Assistant professor, Northeast Louisiana University, Monroe, Louisiana. Author of articles about feminism and modern American drama in such journals as *Modern Drama, Journal of Dramatic Theory and Criticism,* and *Illinois English Bulletin.* **Essay:** Lillian Hellman.

HAN, Jae-Nam. Doctoral candidate and instructor of English, University of Nebraska-Lincoln; completing a Ph.D. dissertation on T. S. Eliot and Flannery O'Connor. **Essays:** Maxine Hong Kingston; Cathy Song; Amy Tan.

HARPER, Judith E. Freelance writer and independent scholar, Greater Boston. Area of expertise: 19th-century American social and literary history. Currently working on an cultural biography of Sarah Orne Jewett, Annie Adams Field, and the large community of women writers, artists, and scholars in late 19th-century Boston. Member, National Coalition of Independent Scholars. **Essays:** Sarah Orne Jewett; Emma Willard.

HENDERSON, Jennifer. Ph.D. candidate, York University, Toronto. Editor of *Tessera,* a Canadian journal of experimental feminist writing. Author of articles about poststructuralist narrative, and gender in Canadian literary criticism, in the journals *Open Letter, Room of One's Own,* and *Studies in Canadian Literature.* **Essay:** Dorothy Livesay.

HENN, Martha. Reference librarian for arts and humanities, Mervyn H. Sterne Library, University of Alabama at Birmingham. **Essays:** Elisabeth Bowen; Katherine Mansfield.

HERRMANN, Karin U. Assistant professor of German, University of Arkansas, Fayetteville. Has published on Christa Wolf and Elfriede Jelinek, as well as translated for *Dimension2.* **Essays:** Elfriede Jelinek; Christa Wolf.

HESS, Mary. Ph.D. student in American history, Michigan State University, East Lansing. Formerly on teh Cultural Heritage staff of the Turner House, East Lansing. **Essays:** Phyllis Chesler; Angela Davis; Miles Franklin; Mary Gordon; Ellen Moer; Sigrid Undset.

HIBBARD, Kate Lynn. Teaching fellow, Department of English, University of Oregon, Eugene, Oregon. Author of poems published in *Calyx: A Women's Journal of Art and Literature,* 1993, *Garden Variety Dykes,* 1994, *The Seattle Review,* forthcoming, and *New Letters,* forthcoming. **Essays:** Erica Jong; Adrienne Rich; Anne Sexton.

HOENESS-KRUPSAW, Susanna. Assistant professor of English, University of Southern Indiana, Evansville. Dissertation on *The Role of the Family in the Novels of E. L. Doctorow,* 1992; author of "Rereading Jack Keroac's *On the Road:* Another American Hero in Search of a Family," in *Southern Indiana Review,* 2, 1995. **Essays:** Simone de Beauvoir; Collete.

HOOGESTRAAT, Jane. Associate professor in English, Southwest Missouri State University, Springfield. Essays on Ezra Pound, Robert Penn Warren, Richard Wilbur, Adrienne Rich, and Mona Van Duyn. Poetry has appeared in *Poetry, Southern Review, High Plains Literary Review,* and *DoubleTake.* **Essay:** Susan Howe.

HYDE, Meredith. Freelance lecturer, London, England. Formerly a lecturer at Oxford University, The American University, and M.I.T. Holds a B.A. with distinction in English literature from Yale University and an M.Phil. in Victorian literature from Oxford University. **Essays:** Fleur Adcock; Olivia Manning; Marie Stopes.

JACOBS, Heidi L. M. Doctoral student, University of Nebraska--Lincoln. Coeditor, *American Women Prose Writers, 1879-1920,* forthcoming. **Essay:** Nellie L. McClung.

JENSEN, Sophie Anna. Retired journalist, formerly lifestyle editor, Santa Rosa *Press Democrat,* instructor in Introduction to Journalism, Sonoma State University, Rohnert Park, California. **Essay:** Carolyn Heilbrun.

JESSER, Nancy. Doctoral candidate, University of North Carolina, Chapel Hill. **Essays:** Marion Zimmer Bradley; Sally Gearhart; Ursula K. Le Guin.

JUSHKA, Darlene. Ph.D. candidate, Centre for the Study of Religion, University of Toronto. Editor, *Method and Theory in the Study of Religion* (journal). **Essays:** Elisabeth Schüssler Fiorenza; Rosemary Radford Ruether.

KANDIYOTI, Dalia. Doctoral candidate, Department of Comparative Literature, New York University. Author of articles about French author J. K. H. Huysmans and the city in *Nineteenth-Century French Studies* (forthcoming); Tunisian-Jewish author Albert Memmi in *European Legacies;* Roland Barthes and Pierre Loti in *History of European Ideas;* and Zora Neale Hurston's *Mules and Men,* forthcoming. Translator of short stories from the Turkish. **Essay:** Anzia Yezierska.

KAUFMAN, Janet E. Assistant visiting professor of English and English education, University of Utah, Salt Lake City. Has taught middle school and high school. **Essay:** Muriel Rukeyser.

KENNELLY, Ivy. Doctoral student in sociology, University of Georgia, Athens, Georgia. Author of articles about gender and race in organizations, images of women, and urban poverty. **Essay:** Barbara Ehrenreich.

KIMMICH, Allison. Ph.D. student in women's studies, Emory University, Atlanta, Georgia. **Essays:** Harriet Jacobs; Audre Lorde; Alice Walker.

KOHOUT, Jennifer. Doctoral candidate in English, University of Toledo. Co-editor, *The Mark: A Literary Journal.* Currently at work on dissertation dealing with the politics of whiteness. **Essay:** Patricia J. Williams.

KOOCHEK, Stacie J. Graduate student, Department of English, East Carolina University, Greenville, North Carolina. Area of concentration: literary theory. **Essay:** Toril Moi.

KRAVER, Jeraldine R. Assistant professor of English, Texas A & M International University, Laredo. Most recent work, "Revolution *Through* Poetic Language: Bilingualism in Latina Poetry from *la frontera,*" forthcoming in *Lit;* has written on Anzia Yezierska and Katherine Anne Porter. **Essay:** Tillie Olsen.

KUDA, Marie. Independent scholar, historian, archivist, writer and lecturer who has been an activist for over 25 years. Author of *Women Loving Women: A Select and Annotated Bibliography of Women Loving Women in Literature,* 1995; contributor of reviews to periodicals, including *Booklist.* Advisor, *Feminist Writers.*

KURIBAYASHI, Tomoko. Assistant professor of English, Humanities Department, Trinity College of Vermont, Burlington. Author of articles on Sandra Cisneros' fiction and editor of *Creating Safe Space: Violence and Women's Writing,* 1997. Author of creative writing pieces in *Hudson Valley Echoes, Métis,* and *Black Buzzard Review.* **Essays:** Marian Engel; Daphne Marlatt; Yūko Tsushima.

LAILLOU SAVONA, Jeannelle. Professor Emerita of French, Trinity College, University of Toronto. On the Editorial Board of *Modern Drama,* 1976-93. Author of *Le Juif dans le roman américain contemporain,* 1974, *Jean Genet,* 1983, and many articles on contemporary French theatre, French women authors, and feminist and lesbian theories in *Littérature, Études littéraires, Revue des lettres modernes, Australian Journal of French Studies, French Forum, Resources for Feminist Research, Atlantis, Canadian Review of Comparative Literature, Voix et Images, Modern Drama,* and several books of collected essays. Editor, *Etudes littéraires,* 13(3), 1981; co-editor, *Modern Drama,* 15(1), 1982, *Théâtralité, écriture et mise en scène,* 1985, and *Modern Drama,* 32(1), 1989. **Essay:** Monique Wittig.

LARIMORE, Victoria. Award-winning independent filmmaker and writer with an interest in gender and cultural issues. Works include films *The Amish: Not to Be Modern* (1985) and *Saying Kaddish* (1992; nominated for an Emmy award); and screenplays *Manhattan Meat* (1987), *The Bluest Eye* (1989; based on the novel by Toni Morrison), *Beyond the Veil* (1992), *Animal Behavior* (1994), and *The Lager* (1996). Contributor of articles and essays to various magazines. **Essay:** Karen Horney.

LINDEN, Julie. Scholar, University of Connecticut, Storrs. M.A. thesis: "From Woman to Human: A Radical Feminist Reading of Joanna Russ's *The Female Man* and *Extra(Ordinary) People.*" Editor, unofficial Joanna Russ homepage on the World Wide Web: http://www.lib.uconn.edu/~jlinden/russ.htm. **Essay:** Joanna Russ.

LOOSER, Devoney. Assistant professor of English and women's studies, Indiana State University, Terre Haute. Author of articles about feminist theory, 18th-century British women, Jane Austen, American popular film, and Sylvia Plath in various journals. Editor, *Jane Austen and Discourses of Feminism* (1995). **Essay:** Sylvia Plath.

LOUTZENHEISER, Lisa. Master's/Ph.D. candidate, educational policy studies, University of Wisconsin-Madison. Previously a teacher of sexuality, computers, and social studies at an alternative high school in California. **Essays:** Jessie Bernard; Ann Oakley.

LYLE, Teresa. Doctoral candidate in English, Miami University, Oxford, Ohio. **Essay:** Mary Astell.

MacGREGOR, Lynn. Independent scholar and freelance writer. Author of numerous articles in periodicals. **Essays:** Charlotte

Bunche; Barbara Christian; Christine de Pisan; Marilyn Frye; Sandra G. Harding; Julia Ward Howe; Luce Irigaray; Karen Malpede; Juliet Mitchell; Sappho; Ann Allen Shockley; Sojourner Truth.

MARIE, Jacqueline. Reference/Women's Services coordinator, University of California, Santa Cruz. Formerly head of Women's Center Library, University of California, Berkeley. Has written articles and essays about international women's studies, women's literature, women's libraries and archives, women's history, and women and the Internet in various publications, including *Women Library Workers Journal, Women's Studies, Gay & Lesbian Literature,* 1994, and *Women, Information, and the Future.* **Essays:** Kamala Das; Suniti Namjoshi.

MARTINEZ, Theresa A. Assistant professor of sociology, University of Utah, Salt Lake City. Formerly a research and teaching associate, University of New Mexico, Albuquerque. Recent work includes "Toward a Chicana Feminist Epistemological Standpoint: Theory at the Intersection of Race, Class, and Gender," in *Race, Gender, and Class: An Interdisciplinary Journal;* "Where Popular Culture Meets Deviant Behavior: Classroom Experiences with Music," and "Popular Music in the Classroom: Teaching Race, Class and Gender with Popular Culture," both in *Teaching Sociology;* "Recognizing the Enemy: Rap Music in the Wake of the Los Angeles Riots," in *Explorations in Ethnic Studies,* and "Embracing the Outlaw: Deviance at the Intersection of Race, Class, and Gender," in the *Utah Law Review.* Interests include the intersection of race, class, and gender, the sociology of deviance, and the sociology of culture. **Essays:** Gloria Anzaldúa; Sandra Cisneros.

MATHUR, Suchitra. Ph.D. candidate, Department of English, Wayne State University, Detroit, Michigan. Received B.A. and M.A. degrees from Delhi University, India. Co-editor, *Reading with a Difference: Gender, Race, and Cultural Identity.* **Essays:** Anita Desai; Bharati Mukherjee.

MAY, Gita. Professor of French, Columbia University, New York. Author of *Diderot et Baudelaire, critiqes d'art,* 1957; *De Jean-Jacques Rousseau à Madame Roland,* 1964; *Madame Roland and the Age of Revolution,* 1970; *Stendhal and the Age of Napoleon,* 1977; and numerous articles on French Enlightenment, aesthetics, post-revolutionary era, and women in literature, history and art in various journals and *festschrifts.* Has published essays on such notable women as Germaine de Stäel, Julie de Lespinasse, Elisabeth Vigée Le Brun, George Sand, Simone de Beauvoir, Rebecca West, and Anita Brookner. Coeditor, *Diderot Studies III,* 1961; contributor of critical editions of Diderot's writings on art for the *Oeuvres complètes,* 1984, 1995. General editor, "The Age of Revolution and Romanticism" series, 1991--. **Essay:** Georges Sand.

MAY, Vivian. Ph.D., Institute for Women's Studies, Emory University, Atlanta, 1996. Contributor to *New Critical Essays on James Baldwin's "Go Tell It on the Mountain"* (1995), and *Oxford Companion to African American Literature* (1996). **Essays:** Patricia Hill Collins; Anna Julia Cooper; Margaret Laurence.

McCAFFREY, Barbara Lesch. Director of Affirmative Action and Faculty Affairs, instructor in English, and instructor at Hutchins School of Liberal Arts, Sonoma State University, Rohnert Park, California. Has written on Adnan's work and presented a paper on Adnan at the National Women's Studies Association Conference, Minneapolis, 1988. **Essays:** Etel Adnan; Nawal al'Sadaawi.

McCLENDON, Jacquelyn. Associate professor of English, College of William and Mary, Williamsburg, Virginia. Author of *The Politics of Color in the Fiction of Jessie Fauset and Nella Larsen,* 1995, and articles about African American women writers. **Advisor,** *Feminist Writers.* **Essays:** Jessie Fauset; Nella Larsen.

McDAID, Jennifer Davis. Archival assistant, Library of Virginia, Richmond. Author of essays on the history of Southern women, including "'Living on a Frontier Part': Virginia Women among the Indians, 1622-1794," *Virginia Cavalcade* (winter 1993) and "From Municipal Housekeeping to Political Equality: The Virginia Woman Suffrage Movement, 1870-1920" (exhibit pamphlet), Library of Virginia, 1995; contributing author, *Chronology of Women's History, Historical Dictionary of Women's Education,* and *Dictionary of Virginia Biography.* **Essay:** Olive Schreiner.

McHUGH, Nancy. Ph.D. candidate, Temple University, Philadelphia. **Essay:** Sandra Bartky.

McLEOD, Aorewa Pohutukawa. Senior lecturer, English Department, University of Auckland, New Zealand. **Essays:** Keri Hulme; Ngahuia Te Awekotuku.

McLEOD, Laura. Ph.D. candidate in anthropology and at the Center for Advanced Feminist Studies, University of Minnesota, Minneapolis. Academic interests include economic anthropology, indigenous land rights, and feminist enthnography. Co-author of a history of the Minnesota Indian Women's Resource Center; research associate, White Earth Land Recovery Project. **Essay:** Zora Neale Hurston.

McNENNY, Gerri. Assistant professor and Director of Composition, University of Houston--Downtown, Houston, Texas. Author of articles concerning feminist epistemology and theory, collaboration, and writing instruction appearing in *Dialogue, Rhetoric Review,* and the *Encyclopedia of Rhetoric and Composition,* 1995. **Essay:** Nancy Chodorow.

MEEM, Deborah T. Professor of English and women's studies, University of Cincinnati, Cincinnati, Ohio. Co-editor of *Variant.* Author of articles on lesbian studies, feminist pedagogy, 19th-century literature, and composition in various journals. **Essays:** Dorothy Allison; Rita Mae Brown.

MISRA, Joya. Assistant professor of sociology, University of Georgia, Athens, Georgia. Author of articles about family policy, welfare spending, union strength, and the consolidation of the welfare state in various journals, including *American Sociological Review* and *American Journal of Sociology.* **Essays:** Barbara Ehrenreich; Linda Gordon; Alva Myrdal.

MONTELARO, Janet J. Research assistant and professor of women's studies, University of Pittsburgh, Pennsylvania. Author of *Producing a Womanist Text: The Maternal as Signifier in Alice Walker's "The Color Purple,"* in *English Literary Studies* monograph series, 1996. **Essays:** Isabel Allende; Buchi Emechetta; Joyce Carol Oates.

MORRIS, Bonnie. Visiting assistant professor of women's studies, George Washington University, Washington, D.C. Formerly assistant professor of women's history at St. Lawrence University, 1992-94, and visiting research associate in women's studies and religion at Harvard Divinity School, 1990-91. Author of articles on lesbian identity in *HOT WIRE, Sojourner, off our backs, National Women's Studies Association Journal,* and essays in anthologies of lesbian writing, including *Sportsdykes, Out of the Class Closet, Sister/Stranger, Amazon All-Stars,* and *My Lover Is a Woman.* **Essays:** Andrea Dworkin; Jill Johnson.

MORRISON, Lucy. Ph.D. candidate in English literature, University of South Carolina, Columbia, South Carolina. Co-Author of *A Mary Shelley Encyclopedia,* forthcoming 1997, and articles about Keats and Chatterton in *Keats-Shelley Review* and Rebecca Harding Davis in *Studies in Short Fiction.* **Essays:** Rebecca Harding Davis; H.D. (Hilda Doolittle).

MORROW, Jonathan. Doctoral candidate, English Department, West Virginia University, Morgantown. Co-editor (with Anna Elfenbein) and author of afterward of reprinting of Olive Tilford Dargan's *From My Highest Hill* (1941), forthcoming 1997. Contributor to *Encyclopedia of Novel into Film,* 1996. **Essay:** Jeanette Winterson.

NOONAN, Norma C. Professor of political science, Augsburg College, Minneapolis. Co-editor and contributor to *Russian Women in Politics and Society,* 1996. Numerous articles for scholarly journals, encyclopedias, and reference works, including *Modern Encyclopedia of Russian and Soviet History, Dictionary of Russian Women Writers, Gorbachev Encyclopedia, The Soviet Union: A Biographical Dictionary, Women and Politics,* and other publications. **Essays:** Maude Hart Lovelace; Clara Zetkin.

NULL, David. Head research librarian, Memorial Library, University of Wisconsin--Madison. **Advisor,** *Feminist Writers.*

O'GRADY, Kathleen A. Doctoral student, Trinity College, University of Cambridge, England. Author of *Julia Kristeva: A Bibliography of Primary and Secondary Sources,* forthcoming 1997; "The Pun or the Eucharist? Eco and Kristeva on the Consummate Model for the Metaphoric Process," *Literature and Theology,* 1997; co-moderator, french-feminism@jefferson.village.virginia.edu **Essay:** Julia Kristeva.

OSLER, Anne. Scholar and writer; Ph.D. University of Wisconsin--Madison. **Essays:** Charles Brockdon Brown; Carrie Chapman Catt; the Grimke sisters; Martha Carey Thomas.

PAIGE, Linda Rohrer. Associate professor, Department of English and Philosophy, Georgia Southern University, Statesboro. Author of articles on women and literature, theater, film, and popular culture. **Essays:** Beth Henley; Marsha Norman; Wendy Wasserstein.

PAPADOPOULOS, Yiota. Doctoral candidate in counseling psychology, Teachers College, Columbia University, New York. **Essay:** Jean Baker Miller.

PEACOCK, Sandra. Assistant professor of history, Georgia Southern University, Statesboro. Author of *Jane Ellen Harrison: The Mask and the Self,* 1988. **Essay:** Eileen Power.

PERRY, Marilyn Elizabeth. Graduate student, Roosevelt University, Chicago. Author of "Elizabeth Christman" and "Virginia Payne" in *Historical Encyclopedia of Chicago Women;* contributor to *Ready Reference: Women's Issues.* **Essays:** Edith Abbott; Caroline Dall; Betty Friedan; Emma Goldman; Aleksandra Kollontai; Dorothy Thompson; Flora Tristan.

PINARSKI, Annmarie. Instructor of English, Bowling Green University. Author of doctoral dissertation "Parodic Imagination: Women/Writing/History." **Essays:** Ellen Showalter; Barbara Smith; Fay Weldon.

POXON, Judith. Ph.D. candidate, Syracuse University, Syracuse, New York. **Essays:** Elaine Pagels; Charlene Spretnak.

PRAMAGGIORE, Maria. Assistant professor, Department of English, North Carolina State University, Raleigh. Coeditor of *RePresenting Bisexualities: Subjects and Cultures of Fluid Desire,* 1996; author of articles about feminist performance art and avant garde film in *Theatre Journal* and *Cinema Journal.* **Essay:** Starhawk.

PRENOWITZ, Eric. Research associate and doctoral candidate, Centre d'Études Féminine, University of Paris VIII. Translator, *Hélène Cixous: Rootprints,* by Cixous and Mireille Calle-Gruber, 1996; and *Archive Fever* by Jacques Derrida, 1996. **Essay:** Hélène Cixous.

PULTAR, Gönül. Member of the Department of English Language and Literature, Bilkent University, Ankara, Turkey. Editor of *JAST: Journal of American Studies of Turkey.* Author of *Technique and Tradition in Beckett's Trilogy of Novels,* 1996; *Dünya Bir Atl'kar'nca* [The World Is a Merry-Go-Round] (novel), 1979; *Ellerimden Su 'çsinler* [Let Them Drink from My Hands] (novel), forthcoming; and articles about women writers, modern fiction, and ex-Soviet cultures. **Essay:** Fatima Mernissi.

RAYMOND, Maria Elena. Student of women's literature at University of California at Davis and 20-year television and print news journalist. Co-editor, *American Women Speak: Voices of American Women in Public Life,* 1996. Currently compiling a bibliography on writings by and about African Americans post-Civil War. **Essays:** Barbara Deming; Ding Ling; Oriana Fallaci; Elizabeth Fox Genovese; Germaine Greer; Doris Lessing.

RENFRO, Elizabeth. Instructor of English and women's studies, California State University, Chico. Author of *Basic Writing,* 1985; *The Shasta Indians of California,* 1992; and articles about women writers and activists in various anthologies. **Essay:** Susan Brownmiller.

ROBINSON, Daniel. Ph.D. candidate, University of South Carolina, Columbia. Author of articles about women Romantic poets and the 18th-century sonnet revival, Mary Robinson, Samuel Taylor Coleridge, Mary Wollstonecraft, Anna Seward, and William Hazlitt in various journals. **Essays:** Elizabeth Montagu; Mary Robinson.

ROBINSON, Kate. Freelance writer and web designer in New York City. B.A. in interdisciplinary studies, Appalachian State University, Boone, North Carolina, 1993; M.A. in women and religion, New York University, 1996. **Essay:** Merlin Stone.

ROCHE, John. Independent scholar. Formerly, assistant professor of American thought and language, Michigan State University, East Lansing. Reviewer for *Choice: Current Reviews for College Libraries.* N.E.H. fellow, University of Chicago, summer 1996. **Essay:** Katharine Burdekin.

ROGERS, Lori. Visiting lecturer, Tufts University, Boston. Formerly instructor, State University of New York at Stony Brook. Author of articles about contemporary Ango-Irish novelists in *Society for the Philosophic Study of the Contemporary Visual Arts Journal* and *Critique: Studies in Modern Fiction;* author of "Feminine Nation: Gender and Resistance," in *A Vanishing Border: Feminist Remappings of Modern Anglo-Irish Literature,* and "'That's everybody's song': Violence and Masculine Ethnicity in Neil Jordan's *Angel,*" in *Irish Cinema,* both forthcoming. **Essay:** Julia O'Faolain.

ROMEYN, Sara. Ph.D. candidate, American Civilization program, The George Washington University, Washington, D.C. **Essay:** Nancy Cott.

ROSENBERG, Beth Carole. Assistant professor, University of Nevada, Las Vegas. Associate editor, *Woolf Studies Annual.* Author of *Virginia Woolf and Samuel Johnson: Common Readers,* 1995, and articles about Woolf in various journals. **Essays:** Sandra M. Gilbert and Susan Gubar; Virginia Woolf.

ROSNER, Victoria. Ph.D. candidate, Columbia University, New York. **Essay:** Marie Cardinal.

ROWLEY, Hazel. Senior lecturer in literary studies, Deakin University, Melbourne, Australia. Author of *Christina Stead: A Biography,* 1993 (winner of Australia's National Book Council Award in 1994), and articles about Stead in *Contemporary Literature* (University of Wisconsin), *Meridian,* and *Westerly.* **Essay:** Christina Stead.

SAINT-MARTIN, Lori. Associate professor, Université du Québec à Montréal, Montréal, Québec, Canada. Author of *Malaise et révolte dans l'écriture des femmes au Québec depuis 1945,* 1989, *Lettre imaginaire à la femme de mon amant,* 1991, *Contre-voix. Essais de critique au féminin,* 1996, *le Nom de la Mère. Maternité et textualité dans l'oeuvre des femmes québécoises,* forthcoming, and articles about feminist theory and women's writing, particularly in Québec, in various Canadian and American journals, as well as a number of short stories. Editor, *l'Autre Lecture. La critique au féminin et les textes québécois,* 2 vols., 1992, 1994. Translator, with Paul Gagné, of *Ana Historic* by Daphne Marlatt (*Ana historique,* 1992), and *The Case of Emily V.* by Keith Oatley (*le Cas d'Emily V.,* 1996). **Essay:** Marie-Clair Blais.

SARKER, Sonita. Assistant professor, Macalester College, Saint Paul, Minnesota. Formerly assistant editor, M.P. Birla Encyclopedia Project, Calcutta; fiction editor, *Jacaranda Review,* University of California at Los Angeles. Author of "'The Woods Are Burning': Arthur Miller's *Death of a Salesman*" in *Thoughts on American Literature,* 1988. Editor, *Gender and Space in South and South-East Asia* (forthcoming). **Essay:** Bessie Head.

SCHABERG, Jane. Professor of religious studies and women's studies, University of Detroit-Mercy, Detroit, Michigan. Author of *The Father, the Son, and the Holy Spirit: Matt 28:19,* 1982; *The Illegitimacy of Jesus,* 1990; commentary on Luke in *The Women's Bible Commentary,* 1994, and on Proto-James in *Searching the Scriptures,* 1994; and articles in journals including *Feminist Studies in Religion, Journal of Jewish Studies, New Testament Studies,* and *Semeia.* **Advisor,** *Feminist Writers.*

SCHMIDT, Sabine. Instructor in German, Rhodes College, Memphis. Formerly editor-in-chief, *Downtown News,* Hamburg, Germany; editor, *Around Hollywood* (CD-ROM), 1995. Author of articles about American and German literature, music, film in various journals. Translator of *Weight* by Henry Rollins, 1994, (with H. Raykowski and M. Hannes) *Tobermory und noch ein paar Geschichten* by Saki, 1982, and fiction by Milena Moser, Rose Ausländer, Günter Herburger, Paul S. Beatty, and Iceberg Slim. **Essay:** Verena Stefan.

SKOLNIK, Leslie-Anne. Independent writer, editor, and project manager, Mount Vernon, New York. Cornell University, B.A. English; Radcliffe Publishing Procedures course. Contributor, *Principles of Medical Assisting,* 1996. Editor, *The Journey of Your Soul,* 1995, *The Legal Side of Quality,* 1996. Project editor, *Encyclopedia of Bioethics,* 1995. **Essays:** Enid Bagnold; Lorraine Hansberry; Ann Jellicoe.

SIMPSON, Megan. Ph.D. candidate and teaching assistant, University of New Mexico, Albuquerque. Author of articles about experimental poetry by American women in *North Carolina Literary Review, Blue Mesa Review,* and forthcoming in *Contemporary Literature.* **Essay:** Mary Jacobus.

SIMMONS, James R. Ph.D. candidate, University of South Carolina, Columbia. Author of articles and reviews about Charles Dickens, the Brontës, Amelia Opie, Stanley J. Weyman, G. K. Chesterton, Anne Radcliffe, Joanna Baillie, William Shakespeare, Gertrude Stein, and others, in *The Dickensian, English Language Notes, Brontë Society Transactions, Victorian Studies, 19th-Century Prose, Literature/Film Quarterly, Dictionary of Literary Biography, Reference Guide to American Literature,* and other journals and reference works. **Essay:** Harriet Martineau.

SPILLERS, Hortense. Professor of English, Cornell University, Ithaca, New York. Formerly, professor of English and women's studies, Emory University, Atlanta. Editor, with Marjory Pryse, *Women, Fiction, and Literary Traditions* (1985); editor, *Comparative American Ideologies: Race, Sex, and Nationality in the Modern Text* (1991). Author of numerous articles on the African American literary tradition; author of guest forward, "Feminist Writings: At Century's End," for *Feminist Writers.*

SPINELLI, Michelle A. Freelance writer and assistant to the dean, Sarah Lawrence College, New York. Author of "'Neither a Personal nor a Private Enterprise': The College Settlements Association, 1887-1917" (M.A. thesis), Sarah Lawrence College, 1995. **Essay:** Jane Addams.

STONE, Staci L. M.A. candidate, University of South Carolina, Columbia. Author of "Maria Edgeworth" in *Encyclopedia of the Essay,* forthcoming, and coauthor of *A Mary Shelley Encyclopedia,* forthcoming. **Essays:** Maria Edgeworth; Sophia.

STOVEL, Nora Foster. Associate professor, University of Alberta, Edmonton. Author of monographs *Margaret Drabble:*

Symbolic Moralist, Rachel's Children: Margaret Laurence's A JEST OF GOD, 1992, and *Stacey's Choice: Margaret Laurence's FIRE-DWELLERS,* 1993, as well as articles on 20th-century writers, including D. H. Lawrence, Margaret Drabble, Margaret Atwood, and Margaret Laurence, in various scholarly journals, such as *D. H. Lawrence Review, Literature in Transition,* and *English Studies in Canada,* as well as in *festschriften* on D.H. Lawrence and Margaret Laurence. **Essay:** Margaret Drabble.

STRETCHBERRY, Barbara. Writer and managing editor, *New Moon: The Magazine for Girls and Their Dreams,* Duluth, Minnesota. **Essay:** Rebecca Walker.

TARCHER, Nancy Rae. Ph.D., Wayne State University. Independent scholar in the area of African American social history. **Essays:** Barbara Christian; Michele Wallace.

TAYLOR, Valerie. Poet. **Essays:** Denise Levertov; May Sarton.

THOMPSON, Helen. Ph.D., Hattiesburg, Mississippi. Former graduate assistant, University of Southern Mississippi. Recipient of the National Women's Studies Association Illinois Book Manuscript Award, 1996, for her work on Edna O'Brien. **Essay:** Edna O'Brien.

VAN DYKE, Annette. Assistant professor of interdisciplinary studies and woman's studies, University of Illinois at Springfield. Author of *The Search for a Woman-Centered Spirituality,* 1992, and articles on Paula Gunn Allen, S. Alice Callahan, Louise Erdrich, and Leslie Marmon Silko. **Essays:** Paula Gunn Allen; June Arnold; Beth Brant.

VAN GESSEL, Nina. Lecturer, McMaster University, Hamilton, Ontario. Author of "The Forgotten Mother Tongues of Modernism: Autobiographies of Interwar Women Editors and Publishers," in *Postscript,* forthcoming. **Essay:** Sharon Pollock.

WALKER, Melissa. Assistant professor of history, Converse College, Spartanburg, South Carolina. Author of articles about home extension work, Southern rural and farm women, and portrayals of women in popular press advertising in *Agricultural History, Historical Dictionary of Women's Education, Research Reports from the Rockefeller Archive Center, Southern Historian,* and *Popular Culture Review.* **Essay:** Lillian Smith.

WALKER, Stephanie Kirkwood. Assistant professor, Department of Religion and Culture, Wilfrid Laurier University, Waterloo, Ontario, Canada. Author of *This Woman in Particular: Contexts for the Biographical Image of Emily Carr,* 1996, and scholarly articles on biography; director of *An Attentive Life: Conversations with Edna Staebler* (video), 1995. **Essay:** Emily Carr.

WAN, Amy Jo-Lan. Graduate student, Binghamton University, Binghamton, New York. **Essay:** Gayatri Spivak.

WHITE-PARKS, Annette. Member, Department of Minority Studies, University of Wisconsin, La Crosse. Author of *Sui Sin Far/ Edith Maude Eaton: A Literary Biography* (1995). Advisor, *Feminist Writers.*

WILLIAMSON, Lori. Lecturer in modern British social history, Oxford Brookes University, Oxford. Completing biography of Frances Power Cobbe. **Essays:** Frances Power Cobbe; the Pankhursts; Ethel Smythe; Beatrice Webb.

WILLIAMSON, Richard. Assistant professor of English, Muskingum College, New Concord, Ohio. **Essay:** Simone Weil.

WILOCH, Denise. Freelance writer and editor. **Essays:** Meena Alexander, Angela Carter; Maureen Duffy; Carol Emshwiller; Eva Figes; Sue Grafton; Adrienne Kennedy; John Neal; Grace Paley; Judith Rodriguez; Elizabeth Cady Stanton.

WILSON, J. J. Professor of English, Sonoma State University, Rohnert Park, California. Coeditor, *Virginia Woolf Miscellany;* author of numerous articles on Woolf. Author of an essay on Carrington, reprinted in *Between Women,* edited by Ascher, Carol, Louise De Salvo, and Sara Ruddick (1984). Coauthor, with Karen Peterson, of *Women Artists: Recognition and Reappraisal,* 1976. Advisor, *Feminist Writers.* **Essays:** Marilu Awiakta; Dorothy Bryant; Ntozake Shange.

WINTER, Bronwyn. Member of faculty, Departments of French Studies and Women's Studies, University of Sydney. **Essay:** Colette Guillaumin.

YOUNG, Elizabeth V. Associate professor of English and associate director of the Center for Faculty Development, California State University, Long Beach. Author of "Aphra Behn, Gender and Pastoral," *Studies in English Literature,* 33(3), 1993; "Images of Women in England and America, 1688-1800," with Patricia Cleary, in *Teaching the 18th Century: Three Courses,* American Society for 18th-Century Studies, 1995; "Aphra Behn's Elegies," forthcoming in *Genre;* "Eve" (poem), forthcoming in *Phoebe;* "Some Current Publications," forthcoming in *Restoration.* **Essays:** Aphra Behn; Anne Bradstreet.

ADDITIONAL FEMINIST WRITERS NOT COVERED IN THIS VOLUME

ACKER, Kathy (American; 1948-) Novelist and playwright whose satirical, postmodernist works challenge the social, political, and linguistic structures that have excluded women. Novels include *Hello, I'm Erica Jong* (1982), *Empire of the Senseless* (1988), and *My Mother: Demonology* (1993).

ADAMS, Abigail (American; 1744-1818) Wife of President John Adams and mother of President Samuel Adams, she herself never received a formal education. Through her collected letters to her husband, she can be seen attempting to right this injustice, gently encouraging John to "remember the ladies and be more generous and favorable to them than their ancestors."

AGOSIN, Marjorie (Chilean; 1955-) Poet and fiction writer whose *Conchalí* (1980) draws sensitive and sometimes humorous comparisons between the lot of women in South America and the United States. Her bilingual *Hogueras/Bonfires* was published in 1992.

AI (American; 1947-) A poet whose verses reflect her own battle in establishing a racial identity due to her mixed-race heritage; her dramatic monologues directly confront the virulent and violent aspects of both society and sexuality.

ALMOG, Ruth (Israeli; 1936-) Novelist and journalist; she writes for a leading Israeli newspaper and has authored several novels, including *Death in the Rain* (1993), that portray women trapped between naive expectations of marriage and society and their desire for personal liberation.

ALONI, Shulamit (Israeli; 131-) Israeli government official who founded the Israeli Civil Rights party in 1973; author of *The Rights of the Child in Israel* and *Woman as a Human Being.*

AL-SA' D, Amina (Egyptian; 1914-) Raised by educated parents, she was one of the first women to graduate from Cairo University; the editor of *Haw* (women's magazine), she has written and lectured on emancipation of Arab women throughout the world.

ALTA (American; 1942-) Author who uses her irreverent attitude and skill as a writer to speak out against racism, sexism, homophobia, war, and ageism; her work moves from her own personal experiences as a white, middle-class housewife to address political, social, and psychological oppression in the United States. Works include *No Visible Means of Support* (1971) and *The Shameless Hussy* (1980).

ALTHER, Lisa (American; 1944-) Sometimes called a regionalist writer for her portraits of southerners who live within the limitations of both gender and social standing; *Original Sins* (1981) depicts an extended southern family driven apart by race, ambition, and gender.

ANGELOU, Maya (American; 1928-) Poet, playwright, and autobiographer; her five-part autobiography, which began with the critically acclaimed *I Know Why the Caged Bird Sings* (1970), reflects concerns with racism, cultural conflicts, and woman's oppression.

ANGER, Jane (English; 16th c.) Author of *Her Protection for Women* (1589), the first known book written in English in defense of woman's intrinsic nature and worth to society.

APTHEKER, Bettina (American; 1944-) Sociologist and activist in feminism and civil rights; affiliated with women's studies program at University of California during the 1960s and with American Institute for Marxist Studies; the daughter of Marxist historian Herbert Aptheker, she collaborated with her father on *Racism and Reaction in the United States* and with black activist Angela Davis on *If They Come in the Morning: Voices of Resistance* (1971).

ARLEN, Michael (British; 1895-1956) Born in Bulgaria, Arlen reinvented himself as an Englishman and made a reputation as a writer with the novel *The Green Hat* (1924) and *The Romantic Lady* (1921), a collection of short fiction.

AUERBACH, Nina (American; 1943-) Educator and 19th- and 20th-century literary critic; author of *Communities of Women: An Idea in Fiction* (1978), *Romantic Imprisonment: Women and Other Glorified Outcasts* (1985), and *Forbidden Journeys: Fairy Tales and Fantasies by Victorian Woman Writers* (1992).

BA, Miriama (West African; 1929-1981) Senegalese novelist and feminist activist who worked as a teacher until forced to leave the profession due to ill health; her *So Long a Letter* (1981) was awarded the Noma Award.

BACA-ZINN, Maxine (American; 1942-) Sociologist, educator, and author of numerous articles reevaluating the role of Chicana women; her editorship, with Bonnie Thorston Dill, of *Women of Color in U.S. Society* (1993) added a new dimension to the modern feminist movement.

BALLARD, George (English; 1706-1755) Antiquarian who published *Memoirs of Several Ladies of Great Britain Who Have Been Celebrated for Their Writing or Skill in the Learned Languages, Arts, and Sciences* (1752).

BARNES, Djuna (American; 1892-1982) Author of fiction, poetry, and drama who was noted for ignoring creative, political, and sexual conventions in both her life and her writing. Moving to Paris in 1919 she was an integral part of the Paris literary scene; works like *Ladies' Almanack* (1928) and *Nightwood* (1936) focus on an exploration of female sexuality groundbreaking for their time.

BARRETT, Michèle (British; 1949-) Marxist political and social theorist and author of *Women's Oppression Today: The Marxist/ Feminist Encounter* (revised, 1988); editor of several anthologies of feminist thought, including *The Politics of Diversity: Feminism, Marxism, and Nationalism* (with Roberta Hamilton; 1986) and *Destabilizing Theory: Contemporary Feminist Debates* (with Anne Phillips; 1992).

BAYM, Nina (American; 1936-) Educator and literary critic; author of *Women's Fiction: A Guide to Novels by and about Women in America 1820-1870* (1978), an early effort to restore forgotten 19th century writers to the American literary canon.

BEAL, M. F. (American; 1937-) Novelist and essayist; author of *Angel Dance* (1977), the first detective thriller to feature an outwardly lesbian--not to mention Latina--protagonist.

BLAIR, Emily (American; 1877-1951) Suffragist and journalist who helped found the League of Women Voters before becoming the first vice-president of the Democratic National Committee in 1924; author of numerous articles and short stories, as well as a novel, *A Woman of Courage* (1933).

BLOOMER, Amelia Jenks (American; 1818-1894) Suffragist and advocate of women's dress reform. Founder of the first feminist newspaper, *The Lily* (1849-55), through which she publicized women's issues and advanced the wearing of her own version of men's trousers, which were dubbed "bloomers."

BLUME, Judy (American; 1938-) Novelist and author of fiction for young teens; noted for her up-front and realistic portrayal of the problems undergone by pre-adolescent girls, her books (which have sometimes been subject to censorship) include *Are You There, God, It's Me, Margaret* (1970) and *Otherwise Know as Sheila the Great* (1972); author of adult novels including *Smart Women* (1984).

BODICHON, Barbara Leigh Smith (English; 1827-1891) Artist and activist on behalf of women's suffrage; author of *A Brief Summary in Plain Language of the Most Important Laws Concerning Women* (1854), which was highly influential.

BOMBAL, María Luisa (Chilean; 1910-1980) Novelist and short story writer; her novels, which include *The House of Mist* (1947) and *The Shrouded Woman* (1948), are poetic renderings of women's psychology. She won the Nobel Prize for Literature in 1945, the first Latin American author to do so.

BORSON, Roo (Canadian; 1952-) Poet whose works reflect a subtle feminist spirit between their lushly literate lines; author of *Night Walk* (1981) and *Intent, or The Weight of the World* (1989).

BOSTON WOMEN'S HEALTH BOOK COLLECTIVE Author of the groundbreaking sourcebook *Our Bodies; Our Selves* (1973; revised 1985).

BOUCHERETT, Jessie (English; 1825-1905) Suffragist and founder of the Society for Promoting the Employment of Women in 1860; editor of *Englishwoman's Review,* 1866-71, and author, with Helen Blackbury, of *The Condition of Working Women* (1896).

BRENNER, Athalya (British) Educator and feminist theologian; author/editor of "Feminist Companion to the Bible" series (1993-95) and *On Gendering Texts: Female and Male Voices in the Hebrew Bible,* 1993.

BRONNER, E. M. (American; 1930-) Novelist, playwright, and author of short fiction; typical of her works, *A Weave of Women* (1978) features a group of Jewish women celebrating the rediscovery of their religious and historic heritage.

BURNEY, Fanny (English; 1752-1850) Novelist and playwright; through Samuel Johnson she became a member of Elizabeth Montagu's "Bluestockings"; author of *Evelina* (1778), which describes a young woman's entry into London society.

BUTLER, Octavia (American; 1947-) Science-fiction novelist whose novels feature women of color fighting both sexism and racism in a futuristic setting; novels include her "Patternist" series: *Patternmaster* (1976), *Mind of My Mind* (1977), and *Wild Seed* (1980).

CAIRD, Mona (English; 1858-1932) Novelist and author of *The Morality of Marriage and Other Essays* (1897), wherein she argues for the reform of marriage and increased educational opportunities for women; novels, which were considered examples of "New Woman" fiction, include *The Daughters of Danaus* (1894).

CARBY, Hazel (British; 1948-) Educator and literary critic; author of *Reconstructing Womanhood: The Emergence of the Afro-American Woman Novelist* (1987), a groundbreaking work in black feminist 19th-century literary criticism.

CHARNAS, Suzie McKee (American; 1939-) Science-fiction novelist whose *Walk to the End of the World* (1974) sets the tone for her controversial novels--it features a post-nuclear holocaust world called "Holdfast" that has become a patriarchal paradise; white males have complete control and women--inferior beings called "fems" have been burdened with the guilt for the earth's destruction.

CHUDLEIGH, Mary (1656-1710) Poet, essayist and author of *The Ladies' Defense* (1703), written as a response to a misogynistic sermon on conjugal duty made by a noted clergyman.

CLAFFIN, Tennessee (American; 1846-1923) Journalist and radical suffragist; with sister Victoria Woodhull, she published the *Woodhull & Claffin's Weekly,* a socialist/feminist newspaper that featured Claffin's colorful editorials on such radical topics as female sexual freedom, venereal disease, abortion, and the efforts of workingwomen to make a better life for themselves. Drawing on her friendship with Cornelius Vanderbilt, Claffin gained backing for a successful brokerage firm in New York, making the two women the first female stockbrokers on Wall Street.

COLLETT, Camilla (Norwegian; 1813-1895) Novelist and essayist whose *The Governor's Daughter* (1854-55), with its portrayal of marriage as a stifling institution for women, is her country's first feminist novel. An activist, she is credited with starting the women's suffrage movement in Norway.

CONDORCET, Marie Jean (French; 1742-1794) Mathematician and leading philosopher of the Enlightenment, who proposed the extension of voting rights to women in his *Progress of the Human Spirit* (1794).

CROCKER, Hannah Mather (American; 1752-1829) Puritan essayist and advocate of social reform; in her *Observations of the Real Right so Women, with Their Appropriate Duties, Agreeable to Scripture, Reason, and Common Sense* (1818) she maintains that women's role in holding together the family is essential for the health of the nation. Crocker was the granddaughter of New England preacher Cotton Mather.

CROOK, Margaret Brackenbury (English; 1886-?) Unitarian minister and educator; a professor of religion at Smith college since 1921, she is the author of *Women and Religion* (1964), of numerous articles on the role of women within organized religion.

CROTHERS, Rachel (American; 1870-1958) Playwright whose *The Three of Us* (1906) features a strong and independent female protagonist. Later works include *Mary the Third* (1923) and *When Ladies Meet* (1932), each introducing themes of women's search for self-expression within a masculine-dominated world.

CRUIKSHANK, Margaret (American; 1940-) Educator and author/editor of anthologies that showcase the emerging lesbian literary oeuvre; her *Gay and Lesbian Liberation Movement* (1992) is a history of the movement's political and social roots.

DAS, Mahadai (Caribbean; 20th c.) Poet, who writes on feminist, nationalistic, and racial themes; works include *I Want to Be a Poetess of My People* (1976) and *Bones* (1989).

DAVIES, Emily (English; 1830-1921) Suffragist and educational reformer; founder of the London Schoolmistresses' Association, 1886, and opened a satellite women's college in association with Cambridge University that was incorporated as Girton College in 1874. Author of *Thought on Some Questions Relating to Women, 1860-1908,* which expresses her feminist viewpoint.

DELPHY, Christine (French; 1941-) Writer and researcher; cofounder, with Simone de Beauvoir, of radical socialist feminist journal *Nouvelles questions féministes* (1977); her materialist feminism is further explored in *The Main Enemy* (1974) and *Close to Home* (1984).

DESHPANDE, Shashi (Indian; 1938-) Novelist and author of short fiction; her works, which include *The Dark Holds No Terrors* (1980) and *Roots and Shadows* (1983), are noted for their feminist themes.

DIDEROT, Denis (French; 1713-1784) Leading philosopher of the Enlightenment whose novel *La Religieuse* (1760) argued against the forced internment of young women in religious convents due to that lifestyle's detrimental psychological and physical effects.

DRAKULIC, Slavenka (Croatian; 1949-) Journalist and fiction-writer whose essay collection *How We Survived Communism and Even Laughed* was followed by the semi-autobiographical first novel, *Holograms of Fear* (1992). Drakulic is East European correspondent for *Ms.* magazine.

DRINKER, Sophie (American; 1888-1967) Musicologist, choral director, and writer whose *Music and Women* (1948) was groundbreaking in its examination of women's musical activities throughout history. A lecturer on women's importance in musical history, she also authored numerous articles to promote women's choruses.

DURAS, Marguerite (French: 1914-1996) Novelist, playwright, and author of screenplays; many of her works, which focus on love and sexuality, draw from her early years living in French Indochina. Books include *Les Impudents* (1943), *The Lover* (1984), and the screenplay *Hiroshima, Mon Amour* (1959).

EASTMAN, Crystal (American; 1881-1928) Social reformer, labor attorney, and activist for world peace, Eastman was active in numerous pacifist organizations, as well as suffrage activities. Cofounder of the Congregational Union for Woman Suffrage and a delegate to the International Woman Suffrage Congress in 1913, she was editor of *The Liberator* and author of numerous articles promoting women's rights; works have been collected by Blanche Wiesen Cook as *Crystal Eastman on Women and Revolution* (1978).

ELGIN, Suzette Haden (American; 1936) Science fiction novelist and linguist; her novels, which include *At the Seventh Level* (1972) and *The Judas Rose* (1988), are noted for their focus on communication in many forms, including telepathy, for strong female characters, and for the weak men who get in their way.

ELLET, Elizabeth (American; 1818-1877) Novelist, poet, and historian, she promoted the contributions of women throughout history in such works as *Women of the American Revolution* (1851) and *Women Artists in All Ages and Countries* (1861).

ELLMANN, Mary Literary critic; her *Thinking about Women* (1968) was the first published work of feminist literary criticism.

ENGELS, Friedrich (German; 1820-1895) The coauthor of *the Communist Manifesto,* Engels based his exploration of the origins of the family on the work of American anthropologist Lewis H. Morgan. "The modern individual family is founded on the open or concealed domestic slavery of the wife," he would write in *The Origin of Family, Private Property, and the State* (1884), "and modern society is a mass composed of these individual families as its molecules."

ESTÉS, Clarisa Pinkola (American; 1943-) Jungian psychoanalyst and author of *Women Who Run with the Wolves: Myths and Stories of the Wild Woman Archetype* (1992), a bestselling work that encouraged women to explore their transformative inner "wild" nature.

FAIRBAIRNS, Zöe (British; 1928-) Novelist and author of short fiction; works include *Study War No More* 1974) and *Closing* (1988); coauthor, with others, of short-story anthology *Tales I Tell My Mother* (1978).

FAIRSTEIN, Linda (American; 1948-) New York City district attorney whose *Sexual Violence: Our War against Rape* (1993) has been instrumental in making the public aware of the injustice done to rape victims by the U.S. legal system.

FETTERLY, Judith (American; 1938-) Educator and literary critic; her study of 19th-century U.S. writers resulted in *The Resisting Reader: Feminist Approaches to American Fiction* (1978), which suggests that women's experience of literature is different than that of their male counterparts.

FORCHÉ, Carolyn (American; 1950-) Poet and historian; her works, which include *The Country between Us* (1981) and *The Angel of History* (1994) reflect the social and political concerns that she gained while living in El Salvador.

FORD, Ford Madox (English; 1873-1939) Prolific novelist and fiction-writer; his novel *The Good Soldier: A Tale of Passion* (1915) is a compelling look at the sexual pressures of four upper-middle class characters, whose rigid moral codes prevent them from dealing with the psychological side-effects of marital infidelity. He was the grandson of noted preraphaelite artist Ford Madox Brown.

FORNÉS, María Irene (Cuban-American; 1930-) Playwright and director; author of the award-winning *Fefu and Her Friends* (1977).

FOX, Margaret Fell (English; 1614-1702) Quaker essayist; her *Women's Speaking Justified* (1666) argued for women's right to preach as they were "sent by Christs own command."

FRIDAY, Nancy (American; 1937-) Psychologist; her *My Mother/ Myself* (1977) showcased the intricate, emotional relationship between generations through personal interviews with more than 300 women.

FUSS, Diana (American; 1960-) Educator and literary critic; author of *Essentially Speaking: Feminism, Nature and Difference* (1989) and *Identification Papers* (1995).

GALANT, Mavis (Canadian; 1922-) Novelist and author of short fiction; works include *The End of the World and Other Stories* (1974) and *Home Truths* (1981), which won the Governor General's Award for her quasi-autobiographical portrayal of an independent-minded woman.

GALE, Zona (American; 1874-1938) Midwest regionalist novelist and activist on behalf of pacifism and women's suffrage; her *A Daughter of the Morning* (1917) condemns women's working conditions while *Miss Lulu Bett* (1920) is her Pulitzer Prize-winning exploration of a young woman's rejection of traditional family customs.

GILLMORE, Inez Haynes (American; 1873-1970) Novelist, short story writer, and suffragist, her *Story of the Woman's Party* (1921) provides an engaging account of the formation of the party by Alice Paul and Lucy Burns; the novel *The Lady of Kingdoms* (1917) also contains a feminist perspective.

GOLDEN, Marita (American; 1950-) Novelist, poet, journalist, and educator; the importance of social relationships between women as affirming and supportive are a characteristic theme of her novels, which include *A Woman's Place* (1986) and *Long Distance Life* (1989); she is a founding member of the African American Writers' Guild.

GOM, Leona (Canadian; 1946-) Poet, novelist, and playwright; her novel *Private Properties* (1986) portrays women's powerlessness in the face of the negative demands of society, while *Zero Avenue* (1989) focuses on an incest victim's attempts to resolve her relationship with a mother who was aware of her abuse.

GRAHN, Judy (American; 1940-) Poet, novelist, and playwright; author of poetry collections *A Woman Is Talking to Death* (1974) and *The Queen of Swords* (1987), and of *Blood, Bread, and Roses: How Menstruation Created the World* (1993).

GRAND, Sarah (Irish; 1854-1943) Novelist who is credited with coining the term "New Woman" in 1894. Her bestselling novel *The Heavenly Twins* (1893) was notable for its shocking confrontation of the inequity of marriage and promotion of women's suffrage.

GRAY, Francine du Plessix (American; 1930-) Journalist, educator, and writer; her feminist-inspired biographies include *Rage and Fire: A Life of Louise Colet, Pioneer Feminist* (1994) and *Soviet Women: Walking the Tightrope* (1990).

GRIMKÉ, Charlotte Forten (American; 1837-1914) Abolitionist, poet, educator, and diarist; her journals (1854-1864) are important to the formation of a tradition of African American women's writing as the portrait of a woman of color who is dedicated to proving, by both word and example, the equality of her race.

HAWES, Elizabeth (American; 1903-1971) Fashion designer and journalist, her best-selling book *Fashion Is Spinach* (1938) attacked the fashion industry's manipulation of women; *Anything but Love* (1948) is a satire on the rules of appropriate female behavior as depicted by the media.

HAYS, Mary (English; 1760-1843). Novelist and historian; author of *Appeal to the Men of Great Britain in Behalf of Women* (1798) and *Female Biography; or, Memoirs of Illustrious and Celebrated Women of All Ages and Countries* (1803).

HENRY, Sherrye (American) Radio talk-show host, whose failed bid for the New York state senate prompted *The Deep Divide* (1994), her examination of why women fail to support feminist political candidates.

HIGGINSON, Thomas Wentworth (American; 1823-1911) Essayist whose biography of Margaret Fuller (1890) and *Women and Men* (1887) helped to popularize the concept of women's social and intellectual equality.

HITE, Shere (American; 1942-) Cultural historian; author of *Sexual Honesty: By Women for Women* (1974) and *The Hite Report* (1981).

HOLLANDER, Nicole (American) Cartoonist and author of popular, feminist-inspired and partly autobiographical "Sylvia" syndicated comic strip.

HOLLEY, Marietta (American; 1836-1926) Essayist and humorist who promoted both temperance and women's suffrage in such works as *Josiah Allen on the Women Question* (1914) and *My Wayward Pardner; or, My Trials with Josiah, America, the Widow Bump, and Etcetery.* (1901), using the fictitious Josiah Allen as her foil.

IBSEN, Henrik (Norwegian; 1828-1906) Playwright and poet; his character Nora from *A Doll's House* (1879) embodies the dilemma of women of her era: how to be an engaging, feminine woman, a responsible parent and home manager, and an independent person.

IVINS, Molly (American; 1944-) Political commentator and journalist, whose satirical essays on "good old boy" politics as usual have been collected in *Molly Ivins Can't Say That, Can She* (1991) and *Nothin' But Good Times Ahead* (1993).

JANEWAY, Elizabeth (American; 1913-) Critic, novelist, and lecturer; author of *Man's World--Woman's Place; A Study in Social Mythology* (1971) and *Between Myth and Morning; Women Awakening* (1974).

JOHNSON, Sonia (American; 1936-) Author and social activist; her excommunication from the Mormon church for her support of the Equal Rights Amendment is recalled in *From House-*

wife to Heretic (1981); other books include *Going out of Our Minds: The Metaphysics of Liberation* (1987) and *The Ship That Sailed into the Living Room: Sex and Intimacy Reconsidered* (1991).

JORDAN, June (American; 1936-) Educator, poet, and author of books for children; her womanist and politically inspired works include *New Days: Poems of Exile and Return* (1973) and *Naming Our Destiny: New and Selected Poems* (1979).

KELLER, Evelyn Fox (American; 1936-) Educator and scientist; her works, including *Reflections on Gender and Science* (1985) and *Body/Politics: Women and the Discourses of Science* (1990) examine the psychological underpinnings of women's relationship with scientific knowledge.

KEY, Ellen (Swedish; 1840-1926) Educator and writer, whose *The Century of the Child* (1900) and *The Renaissance of Motherhood* (1914) argued that, as the superior parent, mothers should stay at home with their children, while women without children should become politically and socially committed; her teaching theories were widely followed in Scandinavia.

KHOURI, Callie (American) Scriptwriter; author of screenplay for film *Thelma and Louise* (1991).

KLEIN, Viola (English) Psychoanalyst and author of *The Feminine Character* (1946); coauthor, with Alva Myrdal, of *Women's Two Roles* (1956), which argued that husbands should be made more than just "visitors" in the home.

KRAEMER, Ross Shepard (English; 1943-) Author of *Her Share of the Blessings,* a wide-ranging exploration of the role of women in biblical times.

LAGERLÖFF, Selma (Swedish; 1858-1940) Novelist and author of short stories and books for children; winner of the Nobel Prize in 1909, her works, which consistently feature strong female characters, include *The Wonderful Adventures of Nils* (1907) and *The Ring of Löwenskölds* (1925-28).

LARCOM, Lucy (American; 1824-1893) Poet and autobiographer, whose memories of working alongside other "mill girls" in the Lowell, Massachusetts, textile mills are contained in *A New England Girlhood* (1889).

LAWSON, Louisa (Australian; 1848-1902) Journalist; a radical feminist, she edited the feminist newspaper *The Dawn* for 17 years, printing it with an all-female staff despite the protest of unionized typesetters; she also founded the Darlinghurst Hostel for Working Girls.

LEFKOWITZ, Mary Rosenthal (American; 1935-) Educator and historian; author of *Women in Greek Myth* (1992) and editor, with Maureen B. Fant, of *Women in Greece and Rome* (1977).

LEWALD, Fanny (German; 1811-1889) Novelist and author of short fiction; her novels deal with the inequities of marriage and social injustice, and argue for increasing educational opportunities for women; works include *Hulda; or, The Deliverer* (1874) and *The Mask of Beauty* (1894).

LURIE, Alison (American; 1926-) Educator and novelist; her works, which include *The War between the Tates* (1974) and *Foreign Affairs* (1984) often examine adultery and point up the dilemmas facing women in their middle age; nonfiction works include *Fabulous Beasts* (1981 and *The Language of Clothes* (1982).

MARKS, Elaine (American; 1930-) Educator and French literary critic; author of *Simone de Beauvoir: Encounters with Death* (1973), *Colette* (1960), and *Marrano as Metaphor: The Jewish Presence in French Writing* (1996); editor of *New French Feminisms: An Anthology* (1980) and, with George Stambolian, *Homosexualities and French Literature: Cultural Contexts, Critical Texts* (1979)

MARSON, Una (Jamaican; 1905-1965) Poet, playwright, and journalist; she was the first Caribbean author to directly address feminist issues in her examination of the unique inner nature of women of color; works include *Heights and Depths* (1932) and *The Moth and the Star* (1937).

MARTÍN GAITE, Carmen (Spanish; 1925-) Novelist and author of books for children; her works for adults, which include *Behind the Curtains* (1958; trans. 1990), feature female protagonists of many generations who exemplify the social and psychological oppressions of women during the Franco regime.

MARTINAC, Paula (American; 1954-) Novelist and author of short fiction that features predominately lesbian protagonists; her novels, which include *Out of Time* (1990) and *Home Movies* (1993) are praised for their examination of the intricacies of women's inner lives as well as their relationships with family and friends.

McCAFFERTY, Nell (Irish; 1944-) Journalist whose essays on feminist and civil rights concerns have been collected in *The Best of Nell* (1983) and *Goodnight Sister* (1987). Nonfiction works include *The Armagh Women* (1981) and *Peggy Deery: A Derry Family at War* (1988).

McCLARY, Susan (American; 1946-) Musicologist and educator, whose *Feminine Endings: Music, Gender, and Sexuality* (1990) provides a feminist approach to Western musical theory.

McINTYRE, Vonda N. (American; 1948-) Science fiction writer; her novels, which include *Dreamsnake* (1978) and *The Entropy Effect* (1981) features a future world where biologically altered humans are engaged in sex roles that have evolved beyond the traditional monogamous heterosexual pairing.

MEYER, Annie Nathan (American; 1867-1951) Educator, journalist, and writer; highly educated, she dedicated her life to increasing educational opportunities for women and founded Barnard College in 1893; books include *Women's Work in America* (1891) and the novel *Helen Brent, M.D.* (1892), in which she argues women should not give up their profession after marriage.

MEYERS, Carol (American) Educator, theologian, and archeologist; books include *Discovering Eve: Ancient Israelite Women in Context* (1988).

MILLAY, Edna St. Vincent (American; 1892-1950) Poet and playwright active in socialist and feminist concerns whose verses, collected in volumes such as *A Few Figs from Thistles* (1920) and *Wine from These Grapes* (1934) reflect a passionate, intellectual, and unconventional female voice.

MIRIKITANI, Janice (Japanese-American) Poet whose works include *Shedding Silence* (1987) and *We, the Dangerous: New and Selected Poems* (1995).

MITCHISON, Naomi (Scottish; 1897-) Novelist, playwright, and author of short fiction and essays; a prolific writer, her novel *Solution Three* (1975) is considered a classic of feminist science fiction.

MONTAGU, Ashley (English-American; 1905-) Anthropologist whose writings, which include *Man's Most Dangerous Myth: The Fallacy of Race* (1964), *On Being Human* (1966), and *The Natural Superiority of Women* (1962), argue against the genetic determination of cultural phenomenon.

MONTERO, Rosa (Spanish; 1951-) Novelist and journalist whose works include *Chronicles of Falling Out of Love* (1979), an autobiographical work that focuses on such feminist issues as abortion, single parenting, and homosexuality.

MOURNING DOVE (Okanogan Indian; 1888-1936) Folklorist and writer; her *Cogawea the Half-Blood: A Depiction of the Great Montana Cattle Range* (1927) combines tribal legends with elements of the Western romance genre in what is hailed as the first novel by a Native American woman.

MULLER, Mary (New Zealand; 1820-1902) Suffragist who, under the penname "Femina" due to the disapproval of her husband, wrote emotional articles in favor of women's gaining the right to vote, and published *An Appeal to the Men of New Zealand* (1869). New Zealand was the first country to grant women the suffrage, which they did in 1894.

MURRAY, Judith Sargent (American; 1751-1820) Poet and essayist; her "Desultory Thoughts upon the Utility of Encouraging a Degree of Self-Complacency, Especially in Female Bosoms" (1779) was the first feminist work to be published in North America.

NESTLE, Joan (American; 1940-) Journalist and lesbian feminist activist; co-founder of the Lesbian Herstory Archives (1973), her works include *Sister & Brother: Lesbians and Gay Men Write about Their Lives* (1994), edited with John Preston.

NEWLAND, Kathleen (American; 1951-) Social researcher and writer; works include *The Sisterhood of Man* (1979) and *Global Employment and Economic Justice* (1979).

NEWMAN, Frances (American; 1883-1928) Librarian and author, whose first novel, *The Hard-Boiled Virgin* (1926) proved so shocking in both title and content--a young woman strives for sexual emancipation--that it was banned in Boston; her second novel, *Dead Lovers Are Faithful Lovers* (1928) did nothing to improve her literary reputation.

NIGHTINGALE, Florence (English; 1820-1910) Nurse and social reformer in the field of public health, she expressed her frustration in the lack of intellectual opportunities open to women in *Cassandra* (1852).

NIN, Anais (French; 1903-1977) Diarist and novelist; her unconventional life is recorded in her *Diaries* (1966-1980; revised 1992-95) while novels such as *House of Incest* (1936) and *The Four-Chambered Heart* (1950) explore the sensual lives of women.

NOCHLIN, Linda (American; 1931-) Art historian and educator; works include *Women Artists: 1550-1950* (1976), written with Ann Sunderland Harris, and *Women, Art, and Power and Other Essays* (1988).

OLDS, Sharon (American; 1942-) Poet, whose verse deals with human sexuality in a graphic and confrontational manner; works include *Powers of Desire* (1983).

OPIE, Amelia (English; 1769-1853) Novelist, poet, and journalist; her *Adeline Mowbray* (1804) is a novelization of the life of Mary Wollstonecraft.

PAINE, Thomas (American; 1737-1809) Journalist and political theorist, his early essays for *Pennsylvania Magazine,* which he began editing in 1775, advanced the cause of women's rights and the end of slavery; his most famous work, *Common Sense* (1776) is addressed "to the inhabitants of America."

PARETSKY, Sara (America; 1947-) Mystery writer whose detective novels feature the independent P.I. V.I. Warshawski in her battles against the Christian Right, environmental villains, and corrupt politicians; titles include *Killing Orders* (1985), *Bitter Medicine* (1987), and *Guardian Angel* (1992).

PARREN, Kalliroe (Greek; 1861-1940) Novelist and playwright; a feminist activist, her *Women's Newspaper* became the first journal to be written, produced, and addressed exclusively to women upon its initial
publication in 1888.

POULAIN DE LA BARRÉ, François (French; 17th c.) Philosopher and writer; in his *De l'excellence des hommes contre l'egalité de deux sexes* (1675) he argues that custom and prejudice, rather than natural abilities, prevent women from attaining education and social status.

PUTNAM, Emily Jane. (American; 1865-1944) A member of Bryn Mawr's first graduating class, she became the first dean of Barnard College in 1894. In *The Lady* (1910), her study of the evolution of upper-class women in society, she would deem them an anachronistic and "somewhat dangerous type": "In the age-long war between men and women, [the lady] is a hostage in the enemy's camp. Her fortunes do not rise and fall with those of women but with those of men."

RADWAY, Janice (American; 1949-) Historian and educator; in *Reading the Romance: Women, Patriarchy and Popular Literature* (1984) she argues that romance novels can be viewed as a method of protesting a patriarchal society.

RAMABAI, Pandita (Indian; 1858-1922) Social reform and women's rights activist; her *High-Caste Hindu Woman* (1888) alerted westerners to the social conditions of Indian woman. Esteemed as an international lecturer on the plight of women in her native land, she founded the Sharada Sadan, a home for widowed women, in 1882.

RANDALL, Margaret (American) Activist, poet, and essayist; a critic of U.S. foreign policy, she is the author of *Gathering Rage: The Failure of 20th-Century Revolutions to Develop a Feminist Agenda* (1992).

RANDALL, Marta (American; 1948-) Science-fiction writer; novels like *Dangerous Games* (1980), *The Sword of Winter* (1983), and *Those Who Favor Fire* (1984) feature strong female protagonists and examine sexual taboos and alternative sexual lifestyles.

RICE, Anne (American; 1941-) Novelist whose popular horror fiction, which includes the three-volume *The Vampire Chronicles* (1976-89) feature intelligent female protagonists who are strengthened by their alienation from society, whether it be polite society or human society altogether; she is also the author of erotic fiction under the name A.N. Roquelaure.

RICHARDS, Janet Radcliffe (1944-) Educator and author of *The Skeptical Feminist* (1983).

RIIS, Sharon (Canadian; 1947-) Novelist and scriptwriter; her novel *The True Story of Ida Johnson* (1976), which concerns a woman who murders her husband and children, has become a classic of Canadian feminist literature.

RILEY, Denise (English; 1948-) Poet, feminist theoretician, and activist in the women's movement; her verse, collected in books such as *Marxism for Infants* (1977) and *Dry Air* (1985), is intricate; she is also the author of *War in the Nursery: Theories of the Child and Mother* (1983) and *"Am I That Name?": Feminism and the Category of "Women" in History* (1988).

ROBINSON, Harriet Hanson (American; 1825-1911) Abolitionist and writer; she was fortunate to rise above her early employment in a Lowell, Massachusetts, textile mill and describe the poor working conditions, unfair wages, and long hours endured by New England "mill girls" in *Loom and Spindle* (1898).

ROIPHE, Katie (American) Author of *The Morning After: Sex, Fear, and Feminism on Campus.* The daughter of author Anne Roiphe, she addressed the concerns of the younger members of the feminist movement, particularly taking case with male bashing.

ROY, Gabrielle (French Canadian; 1909-1983) Novelist; novels, which include *The Tin Flute* (1945) and *Children of My Heart* (1977), contain realistic portrayals of women transcending emotional and physical boundaries.

RYLANT, Cynthia (American; 1954-) Children's author; her sensitive and perceptive fiction for young children and pre-teen readers includes *When I Was Young in the Mountains* (1982) and *A Blue-eyed Daisy* (1985).

SALMONSON, Jessica Amanda (American; 1950-) Science-fiction writer; her novels, which feature strong female warriors as protagonists, include *The Swordswoman* (1982) and *Ou Lu Khen and the Beautiful Madwoman* (1985).

SARGENT, Pamela (American; 1948-) Novelist and author of short fiction; in addition to her groundbreaking work in the feminist science-fiction genre she has edited the two-volume anthology *Women of Wonder: Science Fiction by Women* (1995).

SCHNEIDERMAN, Rose (American; 1882-1972) Activist on behalf of labor reform and women's rights; her early efforts as a union organizer on behalf of the Women's Trade Union League and as secretary of the New York State Department of Labor are recounted in *All for One* (1967).

SHAW, George Bernard (Irish; 1856-1950) Playwright, journalist, and socialist essayist; the author of numerous plays that satirize the role of women in 19th-century civilization; his *The Intelligent Women's Guide to Socialism and Capitalism* (1923) is considered by many to be one of the most astute explanations of economic theory ever published.

SHEEHY, Gail (American; 1937-) Journalist and author of *Passages: Predictable Crises of Adult Life* (1976) and *The Silent Passage: Menopause* (1992).

SHEPPARD, Kate (New Zealander; 1848-1934) Social former who was active in both physically and legally emancipating women; her many pamphlets, which include *Ten Reasons Why the Women of New Zealand Should Vote* (c. 1886), and her lectures and political lobbying on behalf of the Women's Christian Temperance Union helped women acquire the vote in 1894.

SINCLAIR, Mary Amelia St. Clair (English; 1865-1946) Suffragist and novelist; her works, which include *The Three Sisters* (1914) and *Mary Olivier* (1919), were among the first to use stream-of-consciousness as a literary technique. Her novels redefined appropriate subject matter by transcending repressive Victorian morality.

SMITH, Elizabeth Oakes (American; 1806-1893) Journalist, novelist, poet, and memoirist; she lectured on feminist topics and contributed the column "Women and Her Needs" to the New York *Tribune* from 1850-51, bringing to a large audience the positions of the nascent Women's Rights movement. She was nominated for president of the 3rd Seneca Falls convention.

SMITH, Stevie (English; 1902-1971) Poet and novelist; the oppression of suburban life figures in much of her work, which includes *Novel on Yellow Paper* (1936), *The Holiday* (1949), and the poetry collection *Not Waving but Drowning* (1957).

SMITH-ROSENBERG, Caroll (American; 20th c.) Historian and educator; her essay "The Female World of Love and Ritual; Relations between Women in 19th-Century America," first published in *Signs* in 1975, was groundbreaking in its examination of class and gender from a political perspective. Other works include *Disorderly Conduct: Visions of Gender in Victorian America* (1985)

SNOWDON, Ethel (English; 20th c.) Writer and socialist activist; the wife of socialist MP Phillip Snowdon, she wrote *The Woman Socialist* (1907) and *The Feminist Movement* (1913), as well as several political pamphlets.

SPENCER, Anna Garlin (American; 1851-1931) An educator, minister, and journalist, she set forth the contributions of women throughout history in *Women's Share in Social Culture* (1912). Supporting the right of gifted women to extend themselves beyond the home into the realms of industry, education, and the arts, she would write: "[W]hen her biographer says of an Italian woman poet, 'during some years her Muse was intermitted,' we do not wonder at the fact when he casually mentions her ten children."

STONE, Lucy (American; 1818-1893) Lecturing on behalf of Anti-Slavery societies led her to the cause of women's suffrage, which she further supported by publishing, with her husband, Henry Blackwell, the *Woman's Journal,* from 1879.

STONE, Ruth (American; 1915-) Poet and educator; her verses resonate with a multifaceted female voice in their reactions to marriage, family, and landscape; collections include *Second-Hand Coat* (1987) and *Simplicity* (1995).

STREET, Jessie (Australian; 1889-1970) Feminist socialist activist and writer; founder of United Associations of Women and cofounder, Australian League of Nations; author of *Truth or Repose* (1966).

TENNANT, Emma (English; 1937-) Novelist; she has expanded classical works of literature from a feminist perspective in *Two Women of London: The Strange Case of Ms Jekyll and Mrs Hyde* (1989) and *Pemberly: A Sequel to Pride and Prejudice* (1993); science-fiction novels include *The Bad Sister* (1978) and *Faustine* (1992).

TEPPER, Sheri S. (American; 1929-) Novelist; her separatist works of science-fiction and fantasy include *the Gate to Women's Country* (1988), a controversial portrayal of a human race that has split into opposing matriarchal and patriarchal societies.

THOMAS, Audrey (Canadian; 1935-) Novelist and author of short fiction; in works such as *Mrs. Blood* (1970) and *Intertidal Life* (1984) she portrays the woman-centered concerns of pregnancy and marriage through her deft use of language and style.

THOMPSON, William (Irish; 1775-1833) Socialist reformer and political economist; his *Appeal of One Half of the Human Race, Women, against the Pretensions of the Other Half, Men, to Retain Them in Political, and thence in Civil and Domestic Slavery* (1825) was pioneering in its advancement of sexual equality.

TIPTREE, James (American; 1915-1987) Science-fiction writer; when it was announced that the author of short story collections that included *Star Songs of an Old Primate* (1978) and *The Girl Who Was Plugged In* (1989) was actually a woman named Alice Sheldon, Charles Platt would note in his *Dream Makers* that "merely by having existed unchallenged for years, 'Tiptree' has shot the stuffing out of male stereotypes of women writers."

TREMAIN, Rose (English; 1943-) Novelist and author of short fiction, nonfiction, and books for children; her *The Fight for Freedom for Women* (1973) provides a detailed history of the British and U.S. suffrage movements.

TUTTLE, Lisa (American; 1952-) Short story writer; her feminist science fiction uses the element of horror to make its point; works include *A Nest of Nightmares* (1986); *A Spaceship Built of Stone and Other Stories* (1987); and *Memories of the Body: Tales of Desire and Transformation* (1992).

VEBLEN, Thorsten (American; 1857-1929) A social theorist whose *Theory of the Leisure Class* (1899) revolutionized the concept of conspicuous consumption and conspicuous leisure. "The leisure rendered by the wife ... is ... not a simple manifestation of idleness or indolence," he writes. "It almost invariable occurs disguised under some form of work or household duties or social amenities, which ... serve little or no ulterior end beyond showing that she does not and need not occupy herself with anything that is gainful or that is of substantial use."

VIVIEN, Renée (English-French; 1877-1909) Poet and author of short fiction; she lived an openly lesbian life in Paris, where she composed love poetry inspired by historic styles; works include *At The Sweet Hour of Hand in Hand* (1979) and *The Muse of Violets* (1910).

VONARBURG, Élisabeth (French Canadian; 1947-) Novelist; her science fiction works, which feature androgynous protagonists that cause readers to examine bisexuality as a means to bridge the gender gap, include *The Silent City* (1981) and *The Mareland Chronicles* (1993).

WALKER, Barbara G. (American; 1930-) Novelist and feminist theologian; author of *The Women's Encyclopedia of Myths and Secrets* (1983), *The Crone: Woman of Age, Wisdom and Power* (1985), and *The Skeptical Feminist; Discovering the Virgin, Mother and Crone* (1987).

WALTERS, Joseph J. (Liberian; 19th c.) Novelist, whose *Guanya Pau: A Story of an African Princess* (1891) reflected its author's view that "woman is as good and great as man, and intended to be his equal."

WANDOR, Michelene (English; 1940) Playwright, poet, and author of short fiction and literary criticism; her plays, which include *Spilt Milk* (1973) and *Aid Thy Neighbor* (1978) are heavily influenced by her feminist outlook; her nonfiction works include *Carry on, Understudies: Theatre and Sexual Politics* (1981) and *Look Back in Gender* (1987).

WARING, Marilyn J. Economist; author of *If Women Counted: A New Feminist Economics* (1988).

WARNER, Marina (English; 1946-) Novelist and social historian; her examinations of woman-centered mythology include *From the Beast to the Blonde* (1994) and *Six Myths of Our Time* (1995).

WARREN, Mercy Otis (American; 1728-1814) Playwright, poet, and essayist; well educated for her time, she became one of North America's most respected political writers; her play *The Ladies of Castille* (1790) is notable for its forward-thinking protagonist, who states "I ne'er will yield,/ Nor own myself a slave."

WEST, Jessamyn (American; 1902-1984) Novelist and playwright; in her many novels she attempted to create realistic female characters well grounded in reason, integrity, and maturity. Works include *The Friendly Persuasion* (1945); *South of the Angels* (1960); and *The Life I Really Lived* (1979).

WILHELM, Kate (American; 1928-) Novelist and author of short fiction; her books in the mystery and science-fiction genres are praised for their emotional realism; works include *The Clewison Test* (1976), which depicts the isolation felt by many women, and the short-story collection *Naming the Flowers* (1992).

WILLARD, Frances (American; 1839-1898). Social reformer, writer, and advocate of woman's suffrage; president of the National Woman's Christian Temperance Union, who declared, in a speech, women to be "the less tainted half of the race." Author of *Woman and Temperance* (1883).

WOODHULL, Victoria (American; 1838-1927) Journalist who, with her sister Tennessee Claffin, published the radical newspaper *Woodhull & Claffin's Weekly* from 1870. An outspoken proponent of "free love," she also lectured on behalf of women's suffrage, becoming the first woman to address the House Judiciary Committee. Woodhull's meteoric rise in the suffrage movement as a protegé of Elizabeth Cady Stanton would be cut short by Susan B. Anthony, who expelled Woodhull and her associates from the 1873 suffrage convention.

WRIGHT, Frances (American; 1795-1852) Born in Scotland, Wright immigrated to the United States as a travelling companion of General Lafayette. In addition to publishing the New York *Free Enquirer,* a liberal newspaper, she lectured on feminist topics such as birth control and equal education, remarking in 1829 that "until women assume the place in society which good sense and good feeling assign to them, human improvement must advance but feebly."

SOURCES FOR MORE INFORMATION ON FEMINIST WRITERS

Bibliographies and Encyclopedic References

African Women: A General Bibliography, 1976-1985, by Davis Bullwinkle. New York, Greenwood Press, 1989.

American Women's Magazines: An Annotated Historical Guide, by Nancy K. Humphreys. New York, Garland, 1989.

American Women Writers: An Annotated Bibliography of Criticism, by Barbara A. White. New York, Garland, 1977.

The Annotated Bibliography of Canada's Major Authors, edited by Robert Lecker and Jack David. Downsview, Ontario, ECW, 1979--.

Biographical Dictionary of British Feminists, edited by Olive Banks. Brighton, Wheatsheaf, and New York, New York University Press, 1985.

Bloomsbury Guide to Women's Literature, edited by Claire Buck. New York, Prentice-Hall, 1992.

British Women Poets of the Romantic Era, 1770-1840, edited by Paula R. Feldman. Baltimore, Johns Hopkins University Press, 1996.

Dictionary of Feminist Theory, by Maggie Humm. Columbus, Ohio State University Press, 1990.

A Dictionary of British and American Women Writers, 1660-1800, edited by Janet Todd. Totawa, New Jersey, Rowman & Albrheld, 1985.

The Equal Rights Amendment: An Annotated Bibliography of the Issues, 1976-1985, by Renee Feinberg. New York, Greenwood Press, 1986.

Encyclopedia of Feminism, by Lisa Tuttle. New York, Facts on File, 1986.

Encyclopedia of Women's History in America, by Kathryn Cullen-DuPont. New York, Facts on File, 1996.

The Feminist Companion to Literature in English: Women Writers from the Middle Ages to the Present, edited by Virginia Blain, Patricia Clements, and Isobel Grundy. New Haven, Connecticut, Yale University Press, 1990.

A Feminist Dictionary, by Cheris Kramarae and Paula A. Treichler. London and Boston, Pandora Press, 1985.

Feminist Issues in Literary Scholarship, by Shari Benstock. Bloomington, Indiana University Press, 1987.

Feminist Literary Criticism: A Bibliography of Journal Articles, 1975-1987, by Wendy Frost and Michele Valquette. New York, Garland, 1988.

Feminist Literary Theory: A Dictionary, edited by Beth Kowaleski-Wallace. New York, Garland, 1996.

The Feminist Papers: From Adams to De Beauvoir, edited by Alice S. Rossi. New York, Bantam, 1974.

Feminist Theorists: Three Centuries of Women's Intellectual Traditions, edited by Dale Spender. London, Women's Press, 1983; as *Feminist Theorists: Three Centuries of Key Women Thinkers,* New York, Pantheon, 1983.

French Feminist Criticism: Women, Language, and Literature: An Annotated Bibliography, by Elissa D. Gelfand and Virginia Thorndike Hules. New York, Garland, 1985.

The Lesbian in Literature: A Bibliography, by Gene Damon and Lee Stuart. San Francisco, The Ladder, 1967; second edition, 1975.

New Feminist Scholarship: A Guide to Bibliographies, edited by Jane Williamson. Old Westbury, New York, Feminist Press, 1979.

Norton Anthology of Literature by Women: The Tradition in English, edited by Sandra M. Gilbert and Susan Gubar. New York, Norton, 1985; 2nd edition, 1996.

Oxford Companion to Women's Writing in the United States, edited by Linda Wagner-Martin and Cathy N. Davidson. New York, Oxford University Press, 1995.

The Reader's Companion to U.S. Women's History, edited by Wilma Mankiller, Gwendolyn Mink, Marysa Navarro, Barbara Smith, and Gloria Steinem. Boston, Houghton Mifflin, 1996.

Romantic Poetry by Women: A Bibliography, 1770-1835, by J. R. de Jackson. Oxford, Clarendon, and New York, Oxford University Press, 1993.

Third World Women's Literature: A Dictionary and Guide to Material in English, by Barb Fisher. Westport, Connecticut, and London, Greenwood Press, 1995.

Toward a Feminist Tradition: An Annotated Bibliography of Novels in English by Women, 1891-1920, by Diva Daimes and Janet Grimes. New York, Garland, 1981.

The Womanspirit Sourcebook, by Patrice Wynne. San Francisco, Harper & Row, 1988.

Women: A Bibliography of Bibliographies, by Patricia K. Ballou. Boston, G. K. Hall, 1980.

Women and Society: A Critical View of the Literature with a Selected Annotated Bibliography, by Marie Barovic Rosenberg and Len V. Bergstrom. Beverly Hills, Sage, 1975; supplement, 1978.

Women Are History: A Bibliography in the History of American Women, edited by Gerda Lerner. New York, Sarah Lawrence College, 1975; 4th edition, with Marie Laberge, Madison, University of Wisconsin Press, 1986.

Women in Ireland: An Annotated Bibliography, by Anna Brady. New York, Greenwood Press, 1988.

Women in the Third World: A Historical Bibliography, by Pamela R. Byrne. Santa Barbara, ABC-Clio, 1986.

Women Loving Women: A Select and Annotated Bibliography of Women Loving Women in Literature, by Marie J. Kuda. Chicago, Lavender Press, 1974.

Women's Encyclopedia of Myths and Secrets, by Barbara G. Walker. San Francisco, Harper & Row, 1983.

The Women's Movement in the Seventies: An International English-Language Bibliography, by Albert Krichmar. Metuchen, New Jersey, Scarecrow Press, 1977.

Women's Studies: A Recommended Core Bibliography, by Esther Stineman and Catherine Loeb. Libraries Unlimited, 1979; revised edition, 1987.

Women's Studies Encyclopedia, edited by Helen Tierney. New York, Greenwood Press, 2 vols., 1989-90.

Women's Words: The Columbia Book of Quotations by Women, edited by Mary Biggs. New York, Columbia University Press, 1996.

Women Writers in the United States: A Timeline of Literary, Cultural, and Social History, by Cynthia J. Davis and Kathryn West. New York, Oxford University Press, 1996.

Overviews and General Resources

An Alchemy of Genres: Cross-Genre Writing by American Feminist Poet-Critics, by Diane P. Freedman. Charlottesville, University Press of Virginia, 1992.

Alien to Femininity: Speculative Fiction and Feminist Theory, by Marleen S. Barr. Westport, Connecticut, Greenwood Press, 1987.

American Women's Autobiography: Fea(s)ts of Memory, by Margo Culley. Madison, University of Wisconsin Press, 1992.

Arms and the Woman: War, Gender, and Literary Representation, by Helen M. Cooper, Adrienne Auslander Munich, and Susan Merrill Squier. Chapel Hill, University of North Carolina Press, 1989.

Black Women Novelists: The Development of a Tradition, 1892-1976, by Barbara Christian. Westport, Connecticut, Greenwood Press, 1981.

Breaking Barriers: The Feminist Revolution from Susan B. Anthony to Margaret Sanger to Betty Friedan, by Jules Archer. New York, Viking, 1991.

British Women Writers: An Anthology from the 14th Century to the Present, edited by Dale Spender and Janet Todd. London, Pandora Press, and New York, Bendrick Books, 1989.

The Cause, History of the Women's Movement, by Ray Strachey. London, Virago, 1978.

Century of Struggle: The Woman's Rights Movement in the United States, by Elinor Flexner and Ellen Fitzpatrick. Cambridge, Harvard University Press, enlarged edition, 1996.

Changing the Story: Feminist Fiction and Tradition, by Gayle Green. Bloomington, Indiana University Press, 1992.

Communities of Women: An Idea in Fiction, by Nina Auerbach. Cambridge, Harvard University Press, 1978.

Contemporary French Fiction by Women: Feminist Perspectives, edited by Margaret Atack and Phil Powrie. Manchester, Manchester University Press, 1990.

Decolonizing Feminisms: Race, Gender, and Empire Building, by Laura E. Donaldson. Chapel Hill, University of North Carolina Press, 1992.

Diving Deep and Surfacing: Women Writers on Spiritual Quests, by Carol P. Christ. Boston, Beacon Press, 1980.

Ecological Feminist Philosophies, edited by Karen J. Warren. Bloomington, Indiana University Press, 1996.

Feminism and Poetry: Language, Experience, Identity in Women's Writing, by Jan Montefiore. New York and London, Pandora, 1987.

Feminism in France, by Clair Duchen. London, Routledge & Kegan Paul, 1986.

Feminist Alternatives: Irony and Fantasy in the Contemporary Novel by Women, by Nancy A. Walker. Jackson, University Press of Mississippi, 1990.

Feminist Criticism: Women as Contemporary Critics, by Maggie Humm. Brighton, Harvester, 1986.

Feminist Drama: Definition and Critical Analysis, by Janet Brown. Metuchen and London, Scarecrow Press, 1979.

Feminist Epistemologies, edited by Linda Alcoff and Elizabeth Potter. New York and London, Routledge, 1993.

Feminist Fabulations: Space/Postmodern Fiction, by Marleen S. Barr. Iowa City, University of Iowa Press, 1992.

Feminist Fiction: Feminist Uses of Generic Fiction, by Anne Cranny-Francis. New York, St. Martin's Press, 1990.

Feminist Perspectives on Biblical Scholarship, edited by Adela Yarbro Collins. Atlanta, Georgia, Scholar's Press, 1985.

Feminist Theatre: A Study in Persuasion, by Elizabeth J. Natalle. Metuchen, New Jersey, Scarecrow Press, 1985.

Feminist Theatre Groups, by Dinah Luise Leavitt. Jefferson, North Carolina, McFarland, 1980.

Feminist Theory by Josephine Donovan. New York, Continuum, 1992.

Feminist Thought: A Comprehensive Introduction, by Rosemarie Tong. Boulder and San Francisco, Westview Press, 1989.

Feminist Utopias, by Frances Bartkowski. Lincoln, University of Nebraska Press, 1989.

The Feminization of Quest-Romance: Radical Departures, by Dana A. Heller. Austin, University of Texas Press, 1990.

The Fight for Freedom for Women, by Rose Tremain. New York, Balantine, 1973.

Forever There: Race and Gender in Contemporary Native American Fiction, by Elizabeth I. Hanson. New York, P. Lang, 1989.

From Margin to Mainstream: Feminism and Fictional Modes in Italian Women's Writing, 1968-1990 by Carol Lazzaro-Weis. Philadelphia, University of Pennsylvania Press, 1993.

From the Hearth to the Open Road: A Feminist Study of Aging in Contemporary Literature, by Barbara Frey Waxman. Westport, Connecticut, Greenwood Press, 1990.

The Grounding of Modern Feminism, by Nancy F. Cott. New Haven, Connecticut, and London, Yale University Press, 1987.

Growing Up Female: Adolescent Girlhood in American Fiction, by Barbara A. White. Westport, Connecticut, Greenwood Press, 1985.

Gynocritics: Feminist Approaches to Canadian and Quebec Women's Writing, edited by Barbara Godard. Toronto, ECW Press, 1987.

Hypatia's Daughters: 1500 Years of Women Philosophers, edited by Linda Lopez McAlister. Bloomington, Indiana University Press, 1996.

In Our Own Voices: Four Centuries of American Women's Religious Writing, edited by Rosemary Radford Ruether and Rosemary Skinner Keller. San Francisco, HarperSanFrancisco, 1995.

In the Chinks of the World Machine: Feminism and Science Fiction, by Sarah Lefanu. London, Women's Press, 1988.

Liberating Literature: Feminist Fiction in America, by Maria Lauret. New York, Routledge, 1994.

Literary Women: The Great Writers, by Ellen Moers. New York, Doubleday, 1976; London, Women's Press, 1977.

A Literature of Their Own: British Women Novelists from Brontë to Lessing, by Elaine Showalter. Princeton, Princeton University Press, 1977.

The Mother/Daughter Plot: Narrative, Psychanalysis, Feminism, by Marianne Hirsch. Bloomington, Indiana University Press, 1989.

My Life a Loaded Gun: Female Creativity and Feminist Poetics, by Paula Bennett. Boston, Beacon Press, 1986.

No Man's Land: The Place of the Woman Writer in the 20th Century, by Sandra M. Gilbert and Susan Gubar. New Haven, Connecticut, Yale University Press, 1988.

The Other Side of the Story: Structures and Strategies of Contemporary Feminist Narrative by Molly Hite. Ithaca, New York, Cornell University Press, 1989.

Penguin Anthology of Australian Women's Writing, edited by Dale Spender. London, Penguin, 1988.

Philosophy and Feminism at the Border, by Andrea Nye. New York, Twayne, 1995.

Reading the Romance: Women, Patriarchy, and Popular Literature, by Janice Radway. Chapel Hill, University of North Carolina Press, 1984.

Reconstructing Womanhood: The Emergence of the Afro-American Woman Novelist, by Hazel Carby. Cambridge and New York, Oxford University Press, 1987.

The Resisting Reader: Feminist Approaches to American Fiction, by Judith Fetterley. Bloomington and London, Indiana University Press, 1978.

Sex Variant Women in Literature, by Jeannette H. Foster. Tallahassee, Florida, Naiad Press, 1985.

She Who Is: The Mystery of God in Feminist Discourse, by Elizabeth A. Johnson. New York, Crossroad, 1995.
Significant Sisters: The Grassroots of Active Feminism, 1839-1939, by Margaret Forster. New York, Knopf, 1985.
The Sisterhood: The Inside Story of the Women's Movement and the Leaders Who Made It Happen, edited by Marcia Cohen. N.p., 1988.
Suffrage and Beyond: International Feminist Perspectives, edited by Caroline Daley and Melanie Nolan. New York, New York University Press, 1994.
Taking Center Stage: Feminism in Contemporary U.S. Drama, by Janet Brown. Metuchen, New Jersey, Scarecrow Press, 1979.
Women in Hispanic Literature: Icons and Fallen Idols, edited by Beth Miller. Berkeley, University of California Press, 1983.
Women in Political Theory: From Ancient Misogyny to Contemporary Feminism, by Diana H. Coole. Sussex, Wheatsheaf, and Boulder, Colorado, Reiner, 1988.
Women of Ideas and What Men Have Done to Them: From Aphra Benn to Adrienne Rich, by Dale Spender. London, Routledge & Kegen Paul, 1982.
Women Writers in Black Africa, by Lloyd W. Brown. Westport, Connecticut, Greenwood Press, 1981.
Writing a New World: Two Centuries of Australian Women Writers, by Dale Spender. London, Pandora Press, 1988.
Writing Selves: Contemporary Feminist Autography, by Jeanne Perreault. Minneapolis and London, University of Minnesota Press, 1995.

Anthologies and Criticism: By Decade

Before 1900

Literary Criticism

Burdens of History: British Feminists, Indian Women, and Imperial Culture, 1865-1915, by Antoinette Burton. Chapel Hill, University of North Carolina Press, 1995.
A Dictionary of British and American Women Writers, 1660-1800, edited by Janet Todd. Totawa, New Jersey, Rowman & Albrheld, 1985.
Doing Literary Business: American Women Writers in the 19th Century, by Susan Coultrap-McQuin. Chapel Hill, University of North Carolina Press, 1990.
The 18th-Century Feminist Mind, by Alice Browne. Detroit, Wayne State University Press, 1987.
Femininity to Feminism: Women and Literature in the 19th Century, by Susan R. Gorsky. New York, Macmillan, 1992.
Feminism in 18th-Century England, by Katharine M. Rogers. Urbana, University of Illinois Press, 1982.
First Feminists: British Women Writers, 1578-1799, by Moira Ferguson. Bloomington, Indiana University Press, 1985.
Honey-Mad Women: Emancipatory Strategies in Women's Writing, by Patricia Yaeger. New York, Columbia University Press, 1988.
The Madwoman in the Attic: The Woman Writer and the 19th-Century Literary Imagination, by Sandra M. Gilbert and Susan Gubar. New Haven, Connecticut, Yale University Press, 1979.
New Women, New Novels, by Ann Ardis. New Brunswick, New Jersey, Rutgers University Press, 1990.
Only Paradoxes to Offer: French Feminists and the Rights of Man, by Joan Wallach Scott. Cambridge, Harvard University Press, 1996.
The Origins of Modern Feminism: Women in Britain, France, and the United States, 1780-1869, by Jane Rendall. Basingstoke, Macmillan, 1985.
Sex and Subterfuge: Women Writers to 1850, by Eva Figes. London, Macmillan, 1980; New York, Persea Press, 1988.
Significant Sisters: The Grassroots of Active Feminism, 1839-1939, by Margaret Forster. New York, Knopf, 1985.
Victorian Feminists, by Barbara Caine. Oxford, Oxford University Press, 1992.
Unlikely Heroines: 19th-Century American Women Writers and the Woman Question, by Ann R. Shapiro. Westport, Connecticut, Greenwood Press, 1987.
Woman's Cause: The Jewish Woman's Movement in England and the United States, 1881-1944, by Linda Kuzmack. N.p., n.d.
Women and Sisters: The Anti-Slavery Feminists in American Culture, by Jean Fagan Yellin. New Haven, Connecticut, Yale University Press, 1989.

Anthologies

Before Their Time: Six Women Writer of the 18th Century, edited by Katharine M. Rogers. New York, Ungar, 1979.
Daring to Dream: Utopian Stories by United States Women, 1836-1919, edited by Carol Farley Kessler. Boston, Pandora Press, 1984.
Feminism: The Essential Historical Writings, edited by Miriam Schneir. New York, Random House, 1972.
The Feminist Papers: From Adams to De Beauvoir, edited by Alice S. Rossi. New York, Bantam, 1974.
Feminist Poems from the Middle Ages to the Present: Four Bilingual Anthologies, edited by Angel Flores and Kate Flores. Old Westbury, New York, Feminist Press, 1985.
Feminist Theorists: Three Centuries of Women's Intellectual Traditions, edited by Dale Spender. London, Women's Press, 1983; as *Feminist Theorists: Three Centuries of Key Women Thinkers,* New York, Pantheon, 1983.
History of Women in the United States: Historical Articles on Women's Lives and Activities, edited by Nancy F. Cott. New Haven, Connecticut, and Munich, K. G. Saur, 20 vols., 1992-94.
Strong-Minded Women and Other Lost Voices from 19th-Century England, edited by Janet Murray. Harmondsworth, Penguin, 1984.
The Women's Sharp Revenge: Women Pamphleteers in the Renaissance, edited by Simon Shepherd. London, Fourth Estate, 1985.

1900-1959

Literary Criticism

Honey-Mad Women: Emancipatory Strategies in Women's Writing, by Patricia Yaeger. New York, Columbia University Press, 1988.
The New Women and the Old Men, by Ruth Brandon. London, Flamingo, 1991.
Woman and the Republic: A Survey of the Woman Suffrage Movement in the United States and a Discussion of the Claims and Arguments of Its Foremost Advocates, by Helen Kendrick Johnson. New York, Guidon Club, 1913.
Women of the Left Bank: Paris, 1900-1940, by Shari Benstock. Austin, University of Texas Press, 1987.

Anthologies

Daring to Dream: Utopian Stories by United States Women, 1836-1919, edited by Carol Farley Kessler. Boston, Pandora Press, 1984.

Feminism: The Essential Historical Writings, edited by Miriam Schneir. New York, Random House, 1972.

The Feminist Papers: From Adams to De Beauvoir, edited by Alice S. Rossi. New York, Bantam, 1974.

These Modern Women: Autobiographical Essays from the Twenties, edited by Elaine Showalter. Old Westbury, New York, Feminist Press, 1978.

1960s

Literary Criticism

Daring to Be Bad: Radical Feminism in American 1967-1975, by Alice Echols. Minneapolis, University of Minnesota Press, 1989. <tit>*Thinking about Women,* by Mary Ellman. New York, Harcourt, 1968.

Anthologies

Radical Feminism, edited by A. Koedt, E. Levine, and A. Rapone. New York, Quadrangle, 1973.

1970s

Literary Criticism

The Authority of Experience: Essays in Feminist Criticism, edited by Arlyn Diamond and Lee R. Edwards. Amherst, University of Massachusetts Press, 1977.

Between Myth and Morning: Women Awakening, by Elizabeth Janeway. New York, Morrow, 1974.

Communities of Women: An Idea in Fiction, by Nina Auerbach. Cambridge, Harvard University Press, 1978.

Daring to Be Bad: Radical Feminism in American 1967-1975, by Alice Echols. Minneapolis, University of Minnesota Press, 1989.

The Female Eunuch, by Germaine Greer. London, MacGibbon & Key, 1970; New York, McGraw Hill, 1971.

Feminist Criticism: Essays on Theory, Poetry, and Prose, edited by Cheryl L. Brown and Karen Olson. Metuchen, New Jersey, and London, Scarecrow Press, 1978.

Feminist Literary Criticism: Explorations in Theory, edited by Josephine Donovan. Lexington, University of Kentucky Press, 1975.

Images of Women in Fiction: Feminist Perspectives, edited by Susan Koppelman Cornillon. Bowling Green, Ohio, Bowling Green University Press, 1972.

Patriarchal Attitudes: Women in Society, by Eva Figes. London, Faber, and New York, Stein & Day, 1970.

Portrayal of Women in British and American Literature, edited by M. Springer. Princeton, New Jersey, Princeton University Press, 1975.

Sexual Politics, by Kate Millet. Garden City, New York, Doubleday, 1970.

Shakespeare's Sisters: Feminist Essays on Women Poets, edited by Sandra M. Gilbert and Susan Gubar. Bloomington, University of Indiana Press, 1979.

Toward a Recognition of Androgyny: Aspects of Male and Female in Literature, by Carolyn Heilbrun. New York, Knopf, and London, Gollancz, 1973.

Women's Liberation and Literature, edited by Elaine Showalter. New York, Harcourt, 1971.

Anthologies

Capitalist Patriarchy and the Case for Socialist Feminism, edited by Zillah R. Eisenstein. New York, Monthly Review Press, 1978.

Class and Feminism: A Collection of Essays from The Furies, edited by Charlotte Bunch and Nancy Myron. Oakland, California, Diana Press, 1974.

Liberation NOW! Writings from the Women's Liberation Movement, edited by Deborah Babcox and Madeline Belkin. New York, Dell, 1971.

The New Woman: A Motive Anthology on Women's Liberation, edited by Charlotte Bunch-Weeks, Robin Morgan, and Joanne Cooke. New York, Bobbs-Merrill, 1970.

Sisterhood Is Powerful: An Anthology of Writings from the Women's Liberation Movement, edited by Robin Morgan. New York, Random House, 1970.

Tearing the Veil: Essays on Femininity, edited by Susan Lipshitz. London, Routledge, and Boston, Kegan Paul, 1978.

Voices from Women's Liberation, edited by Leslie Tanner. New York, Signet, 1970.

Womanspirit Rising: A Feminist Reader in Religion, edited by Judith Plaskow and Carol P. Christ. San Francisco, Harper & Row, 1979; revised, 1992.

1980s

Literary Criticism

American Novelists Revisited: Essays in Feminist Criticism, edited by Fritz Fleishmann. Boston, G. K. Hall, 1982.

Black Feminist Criticism: Perspectives on Black Women Writers, edited by Barbara Christian. New York, Pergamon Press, 1985.

Carry on, Understudies: Theatre and Sexual Politics, by Michelene Wandor. London and New York, Routledge, 1981; revised, 1986.

The Difference Within: Feminism and Critical Theory, edited by Elizabeth Meese and Alice Parker. Philadelphia, John Benjamins, 1988.

Essentially Speaking: Feminism, Nature, and Difference, by Diana Fuss. New York and London, Routledge, 1989.

The Feminine Eye (science fiction), edited by Tom Staicar. New York, F. Ungar, 1982.

Feminine Focus: The New Women Playwrights, edited by Enoch Brater. New York, Oxford University Press, 1989.

Feminist Criticism and Social Change: Sex, Class, and Race in Literature and Culture, edited by Judith Newton and Deborah Rosenfelt. New York, Methuen, 1985.

Feminist Criticism: Women as Contemporary Writers, by Maggie Humm. London, Harvester, 1986.

Feminist Readings: French Texts/American Contexts, edited by Colette Gaudin, and others, in *Yale French Studies* (New Haven, Connecticut), 62, 1981.

Feminist Theory: A Critique of Ideology, edited by Nanerl O. Keohane, Michelle Z. Rosaldo, and Barbara C. Gelpi. Chicago, University of Chicago Press, 1982.

Gender and Literary Voice, edited by Janet M. Todd. New York, Holmes & Meier, 1980.

Gender and Theory: Dialogues on Feminist Criticism, edited Linda Kauffman. Oxford, Basil Blackwell, 1989.

Gender, Politics, and Fiction, edited by Carole Ferrier. N.p., 1985.

Look Back in Gender: Sexuality and the Family in Post-War British Drama, by Michelene Wandor. London, n.p., 1987.

Making a Difference: Feminist Literary Criticism, edited by Gayle Green and Coppélia Kahn. London and New York, Methuen, 1985.

The New Feminist Criticism: Essays on Women, Literature, and Theory, edited by Elaine Showalter. New York, Pantheon, 1985; London, Virago, 1978.

The Politics of the Feminist Novel, by Judi M. Roller. Westport, Connecticut, Greenwood Press, 1986.

Reading Woman: Essays in Feminist Criticism, by Mary Jacobus. New York, Columbia University Press, 1986.

Sexual/Textual Politics, by Toril Moi. New York, Methuen, 1985.

Towards a Black Feminist Criticism, by Barbara Smith. Brooklyn, New York, Out & Out Books, 1980.

Women and Utopia: Critical Interpretations, edited by Marleen S. Barr and Nicolas D. Smith. Lanham, Maryland, University Press of America, 1983.

Women Writers and the City: Essays in Feminist Literary Criticism, edited by Susan Merrill Squier. Knoxville, University of Tennessee Press, 1984.

Women's Oppression Today: Problems in Marxist Feminist Analysis, by Michele Barrett. London, NLB, 1980; revised, London, Verso, 1988.

Anthologies

All the Women Are White, All the Blacks Are Men, But Some of Us Are Brave: Black Women's Studies, edited by Barbara Smith and Gloria T. Hull. New York, Feminist Press, 1981.

American Feminist Thought, 1982-1992, edited by Linda Kauffman. Oxford, Basil Blackwell, 1992.

Breaking Boundaries: Latina Writing and Critical Readings, edited by Asunción Horno-Delgado, Eliana Ortega, Nina M. Scott, and Nancy Saporta Sternbach. Amherst, University of Massachusetts Press, 1989.

Coming to Terms: Feminism, Theory, Politics, edited by Elizabeth Weed. London, Routledge, 1989.

Discovering Reality: Feminist Perspectives on Epistemology, Metaphysics, Methodology, and Philosophy of Science, edited by Sandra G. Harding and Merrill Hintikka. N.p., D. Reidel, 1983.

Face to Face: Fathers, Mothers, Masters, Monsters--Essays for a Nonsexist Future, edited by Meg McGavran Murray. Westport, Connecticut, Greenwood Press, 1983.

Feminism, Culture, and Politics, edited by Rosalind Brunt and Caroline Rowan. London, Lawrence & Wishart, 1982.

For Alma Mater: Theory and Practice in Feminist Scholarship, edited by Paula A. Treichler, Cheris Kramarae, and Beth Stafford. Urbana, University of Illinois Press, 1985.

A Gathering of Spirit: A Collection by North American Indian Women, edited by Beth Brant. Sinister Wisdom, 1984, expanded edition, Ithaca, New York, Firebrand, 1988.

Home Girls: A Black Feminist Anthology, edited by Barbara Smith. New York, Kitchen Table: Women of Color Press, 1983.

Learning Our Way: Essays in Feminist Education, edited by Charlotte Weeks and Sandra Pollack. Freedom, California, Crossing Press, 1983.

Making a Spectacle: Feminist Essays on Contemporary Women's Theater, edited by Lynda Hart. Ann Arbor, University of Michigan Press, 1989.

Making Face, Making Soul--Hacienda Caras: Creative and Critical Perspectives by Feminists of Color, edited by Gloria Anzaldúa. San Francisco, Aunt Lute Books, 1990.

Mapping the Moral Domain: A Contribution of Women's Thinking to Psychological Theory and Education, edited by Carol Gilligan, Janie Victoria Ward, Jill McClean Taylor, and Betty Bardige. Cambridge, Harvard University Press, 1989.

A Mazing Space: Writing Canadian Women Writing, edited by Shirley Neuman and Smaro Kamboureli. Edmonton, Longspoon-NeWest Press, 1987.

The (M)other Tongue: Essays in Feminist Psychoanalytic Interpretation, edited by Shirley Nelson Garner, Claire Kahane, and Madelon Sprengnether. Ithaca, New York, Cornell University Press, 1985.

New French Feminisms: An Anthology, edited by Elaine Marks and Isabelle de Courtivron. Amherst, University of Massachusetts Press, 1980.

Personally Speaking: Women's Thoughts on Women's Issues, edited by Liz Steiner Scott. Dublin, Attic Press, 1985.

The Politics of Women's Spirituality: Essays on the Rise of Spiritual Power within the Feminist Movement, edited by Charlene Spretnak. New York, Doubleday, 1982.

Seductions: Studies in Reading and Culture, by Jane Miller. Cambridge, Harvard University Press, 1984.

Sisterhood Is Global: The International Women's Movement Anthology, edited by Robin Morgan. Garden City, New York, Doubleday, 1984; Harmondsworth, Penguin, 1985.

Speaking of Faith: Global Perspectives on Women, Religion, and Social Change, edited by Diana L. Eck and Devaki Jain, foreward by Rosemary Radford Ruether. Santa Cruz, California, New Society, 1987.

Speaking of Gender, edited by Elaine Showalter. New York and London, Routledge, 1989.

Take Back the Night: Women on Pornography, edited by Laura Lederer. New York, Morrow, 1980.

Talking Back: Thinking Feminist, Thinking Black, by bell hooks. Boston, South End Press, 1989.

This Bridge Called My Back: Writings by Radical Women of Color, edited by Gloria Anzaldúa and Cherríe Moraga. Watertown, Massachusetts, Persephone Press, 1981; 2nd edition, Kitchen Table, Women of Color Press, 1983.

Weaving the Visions: New Patterns in Feminist Spirituality, edited by Judith Plaskow and Carol P. Christ. San Francisco, Harper & Row, 1989.

What Is Feminism? edited by Juliet Mitchell and Ann Oakley. New York, Pantheon, and Oxford, Basil Blackwell, 1986.

Women and Language in Literature and Society, edited by Sally McGonnell-Ginet, Ruth Borker, and Nelly Furman. New York, Praeger, 1980.

Women and Russia: Feminist Writings from the Soviet Union, edited by Tatyana Mamonova, foreword by Robin Morgan. Oxford, Blackwell, 1984.

Women Writing and Writing about Women, edited by Elizabeth Abel. London, Harvester, 1982.

The Writer on Her Work, edited by Janet Sternburg. New York, Norton, 2 vols., 1980-91.

Writing and Sexual Difference, edited by Elizabeth Abel. Chicago, University of Chicago Press, 1982.

1990s

Literary Criticism

By, For, About: Feminists Re-Present Literary Theory, edited by Wendy Waring. Toronto, Women's Press, 1991.

By, For & About: Feminist Cultural Politics, edited by Wendy Waring. Toronto, Women's Press, 1994.

De/Colonizing the Subject: The Politics of Gender in Women's Autobiography, edited by Sidonie Smith and Julia Watson. Minneapolis, University of Minnesota Press, 1992.

Female Traditions in Southern Literature, edited by Carol Manning. Urbana, University of Illinois Press, 1993.

Hamlet's Mother and Other Women: Feminist Essays on Literature, by Carolyn Heilbrun. New York, Columbia University Press; London, Women's Press, 1991.

Liberating Literature: Feminist Fiction in America, by Maria Lauret. New York, Routledge, 1994.

Revaluaing French Feminism: Critical Essays on Difference, Agency, and Culture, edited by Sandra Bartky and Nancy Fraser. Bloomington, Indiana University Press, 1992.

Sexual Personae: Art and Decadence from Nefertiti to Emily Dickinson, by Camille Paglia. New Haven, Connecticut, Yale University Press, 1990.

Sister's Choice: Traditions and Change in American Women's Writing, by Elaine Showalter. Oxford, Clarendon Press, 1991.

Anthologies

American Feminist Thought, 1982-1992, edited by Linda Kauffman, Oxford, Basil Blackwell, 1992.

And Still We Rise: Canadian Feminists Organizing for Change, edited by Linda Carty. Toronto, Women's Press, 1993.

Antifeminism in the Academy, edited by Shirley Nelson Garens, Ketu Kalrak, VeVee Clark, and Margaret Higgonet. New York, Routledge, 1996.

Beacon Book of Essays by Contemporary American Women, edited by Wendy Martin. Boston, Beacon Press, 1996.

Body/Politic: Women and the Discourses of Science, edited by Mary Jacobus, Evelyn Fox Keller, and Sally Shuttleworth. New York and London, Routledge, 1990.

Collaboration on the Feminine: Writings on Women and Culture from Tessera. Toronto, Second Story Press, 1994.

Comparative American Identities: Race, Sex, and Nationality in the Modern Text, edited by Hortense Spillers. New York, Routledge, 1991.

Feminism and American Literary History: Essays, by Nina Baym. New Brunswick, New Jersey, Rutgers University Press, 1992.

Feminism 3: The Third Generation in Fiction, edited by Irene Zahava. Freedom, California, Crossing Press, 1994.

Feminist Generations: The Persistence of the Radical Feminist Movement, by Nancy Whitter. Philadelphia, Temple University Press, 1995.

Feminist Theology: A Reader, edited by Ann Loades. Louisville, Kentucky, Westminster/John Knox Press, 1990.

Illegitimate Positions: Women and Language. Toronto, Feminist Caucus of the League of Canadian Poets, 1992.

Listen Up: Voices from the Next Feminist Generation, edited by Barbara Finden. Seattle, Washington, Seal Press, 1995.

Modern Feminisms: Political, Literary, Cultural, edited by Maggie Humm. New York, Columbia University Press, 1992.

Norton Book of Women's Lives, edited by Phyllis Rose. New York, Norton, 1993.

Race, Class, and Gender: An Anthology, edited by Patricia Hill Collins and Margaret Anderson. Belmont, California, Wadsworth, 1992; 2nd edition, 1994.

A Reader in Feminist Knowledge, edited by Sneja Gunew. New York and London, Routledge, 1991.

Reading Black, Reading Feminist: A Critical Anthology, edited by Henry Louis Gates Jr. New York, Meridian Books, 1990.

Reconstructing Womanhood, Reconstructing Feminism: Writings on Black Women, edited by Delia Jarrett-Macauley. London and New York, Routledge, 1996.

Theorizing Black Feminisms, edited by Stanlie James and Abena Busia. London and New York, Routledge, 1993.

To Be Real: Telling the Truth and Changing the Face of Feminism, edited by Rebecca Walker. New York, Anchor, 1995.

Writer to the Heart: Wit and Wisdom of Women Writers, edited by Amber Cloverdale Sumral. Freedom, California, Crossing Press, 1992.

ADDITIONAL RESOURCES FOR THE STUDY OF FEMINIST WRITING

Research Sites:

The following are major guides to library and archival collections:

Subject Collections, 7th edition, compiled by Lee Ash. New York, Bowker, 1993. See especially headings "Women's Studies" and "Women's Liberation Movement."

Directory of Archives and Manuscript Repositories in the United States, 2nd edition. Phoenix, Oryx, 1988. See headings starting with "Women."

Directory of Repositories Collecting Records of Women's Organizations, compiled by Mary Lee Tom. Cambridge, Massachusetts, Arthur and Elizabeth Schlesinger Library on the History of Women in America, 1994.

Women's History Sources: A Guide to Archives and Manuscript Collections in the United States, edited by Andrea Hinding. New York, Bowker, 1979.

See also: *Special Collections,* spring/summer 1986. See heading "Women's Collections: Libraries, Archives, and Consciousness."

Organizations:

American Association of University Women
1111 Sixteenth Street NW
Washington, D.C. 20036
PHONE: (202)785-7700 FAX (202) 872-1425
http://www.aauw.org

Center for the Study of Women in Society
340 Hendricks Hall
University of Oregon
Eugene, Oregon 97403
PHONE: (541) 346-5015 FAX: (541) 346-2040

Latin American Women's Organization
P.O. Box 4142
Charlotte, North Carolina 28226
PHONE: (704)333-5447

League of Women Voters of the United States
1730 M Street NW
Washington, D.C. 20016
PHONE: (202)429-1965 FAX: (202)429-0854
http://www.electriciti.com/~lwvus/

Ms. Foundation for Women
120 Wall Street, 33rd Floor
New York, New York 10005
PHONE: (212) 742-2300 FAX (212) 742-1653
http://www.ms.foundation.org/msinfopg.html

National Organization for Women
1000 16h St. NW, Ste. 700
Washington, D.C. 20036
PHONE (202) 331-0066 FAX (202) 785-8576
http://www.now.org

National Women's History Project
7738 Bell Road
Windsor, California 95492-8518
PHONE: (707) 838-6000 FAX: (707) 838-0478
E-MAIL NWHP@aol.com
http://www.nwhp.org

National Women's Studies Association
c/o Loretta Younger
7100 Baltimore Ave., Ste. 301
College Park, Maryland 20740
PHONE: (301) 403-0525 FAX: (301) 403-4137

See also the following specific directories:

Encyclopedia of Women's Associations Worldwide, edited by Jacqueline K. Barrett. Detroit, Gale Research International, 1993.

Minority Organizations: A National Directory, 4th edition, Garrett Park, Maryland, Garrett Park Press, 1992.

National Women of Color Organizations: A Report to the Ford Foundation, prepared by Aileen C. Hernandez. New York, Ford Foundation, 1991.

U.S. Women's Interest Groups: Institutional Profiles, edited by Sarah Slavin. Westport, Connecticut, Greenwood Press, 1995.

Also, look under keywords, e.g. women, feminist, feminism, etc. in current editions of *Encyclopedia of Associations,* Detroit, Gale, and *Research Centers Directory,* Detroit, Gale.

Periodicals:

Listed below are a few of the many feminist periodicals available. For a complete listing of those currently published, see the list of periodicals included in *Feminist Periodicals: A Current Listing of Contents.* Madison, Wisconsin, Office of the University of Wisconsin System Women's Studies Librarian, 1981 to date.

Feminist Review
65 Manor Road
London N16, England

Ms.
119 West 40th Street
New York, New York 10018, U.S.A.

Off Our Backs
2423 18th Street NW
Washington, D.C. 20009, U.S.A.

Signs: Journal of Women in Culture and Society.
University of Chicago Press
5720 South Woodlawn Avenue
Chicago, Illinois 60637, U.S.A.

Sinister Wisdom.
P.O. Box 3252

Berkeley, California 94703, U.S.A.
PHONE: (510) 534-2335

Tessera.
350 Stong College
York University
4700 Keele Street
North York, Canada ONT M3J 1P3

Women's History Review
Department of History
University of Southern California-Los Angeles
Los Angeles, California 90089-0034, U.S.A.
PHONE: (213) 740-1670 FAX: (213) 740-6999

Women's Review of Books.
Wellesley Center for Research on Women
Wellesley, Massachusetts 02181, U.S.A.
PHONE: (617) 431-1453 FAX: (617) 239-1150

Women's Studies Quarterly
Feminist Press at the City University of New York
311 East 94th Street
New York, New York 10128, U.S.A.
PHONE: (212) 360-5794 FAX: (212) 348-1241

Feminist Presses:

Aunt Lute Books
P.O. Box 410687
San Francisco, California 94141, U.S.A.
PHONE: (415) 826-1300 FAX: (415) 826-8300

Chicory Blue Press
795 East Street North
Goshen, Connecticut 06756, U.S.A.
PHONE: (860) 491-2271 FAX: (860) 491-8619

Crossing Press
P.O. Box 1048
Freedom, California 95019-1048, U.S.A.
PHONE: (408) 722-0711 FAX: (408) 722-2749

The Feminist Press at the City University of New York
311 East 94th Street
New York, New York 10128, U.S.A.
PHONE: (212) 360-5790 FAX: (212) 348-1241

Firebrand Books
141 The Commons
Ithaca, New York 14850, U.S.A.
PHONE: (607) 272-0000

The Free Press
203 East Broad Street
Columbus, Ohio 43215-3701, U.S.A.

Kitchen Table: Women of Color Press
P.O. Box 40-4920
Brooklyn, New York 11240-4920 U.S.A.
PHONE: (718) 935-1082 FAX: (718) 935-1107

National Council for Research on Women
530 Broadway, 10th Floor
New York, New York 10012-0627, U.S.A.
PHONE: (212) 274-0730 FAX: (212) 274-0821
EMAIL: denny@is.nyu.edu

Naiad Press
P.O. Box 10543
Tallahasee, Florida 32302, U.S.A.
PHONE (904) 539-5965 FAX (904) 539-9731

Press Gang Publishers
101-225 East 17th Avenue
Vancouver, British Columbia V5V 1A6
Canada
PHONE: (604) 876-7787 FAX: (604) 876-7892

Seal Press
3131 Western Avenue, Suite 410
Seattle, Washington 98121-1028, U.S.A.
PHONE: (206) 283-7844 FAX: (206) 385-9410

Sister Vision Books
390 Dufferin Street
P.O. Box 217, Stn. E
Toronto, Ontario M6H 4E2
Canada
PHONE: (416) 533-2184 FAX: (416) 533-2736

Spinifex Press
504 Queensberry St.
North Melbourne 3051, Victoria
Australia
PHONE: (03) 9320 6088 FAX: (03) 9329 9238

Spinsters Ink
P.O. Box 410687
San Francisco, California 94141, U.S.A.
E-MAIL: http:/www.lesbian.org/spinsters-ink

Third Side Press
2250 West Farragut
Chicago, Illionis 60625, U.S.A.
PHONE: (312) 271-3029 FAX: (312) 271-0459

Third Woman Press
University of California, Ethnic Studies
508A Barrow Hall
Berkeley, California 94720, U.S.A.
PHONE: (510) 525-7935 FAX: (510) 525-8236

Virago Press
20 Vauxhall Bridge R.
London SW1V 2SA
England
PHONE: 0171 93 9750 FAX: 1071 233 6123

Women's Press (Canada)
517 College St., Ste. 233
Toronto, Ontario M6G 4A2
Canada
PHONE: (416) 921-2425 FAX: (416) 921-4428

The Women's Press (London)
34 Great Sutton St.
London EC1V 0DX
England
PHONE: 0171 251 3007 FAX: 0171 608 1938

Internet Discussion Groups*

A good directory for discussion groups is:

Gender-related Electronic Forums, by Joan Korenman: http://www-unix.umbc.edu/~korenman/wmst/forums.html

Some major lists are:

FIST: Feminism in/and Science and Technology. Subscribe to FIST-REQUEST@niestu.com

H-WOMEN: A forum for scholars and teachers of women's history. Subscribe to LISTSERV@MSU>EDU

SWIP-L: A forum for members of Society for Women in Philosophy and others interested in Feminist philosophy. Subscribe to LISTSERV@CFRVM.CFR.USF.EDU

WMST-L: An academic forum for discussion of the teaching of Women's Studies, with subscribers from over 40 different countries. Subscribe to LI STSERV@UMDD.UMD.EDU

WOMEN-L: A forum for women interested in furthering imput into internet culture. Subscribe to MAJORDOMO@HELIX.NET

FEM-ALERT: An informational mailing list established by the Feminist Majority. Subscribe to MAJORDOMO@FEMINIST.ORG

Worldwide Web Sites:

There are many feminist and women's web sites. Some good general indexes to web sites are:

FeMiNa: http://www.femina.com

Vandergrift's Feminist Websites:
http://scils.rutgers.edu/special/kay/femsites.html

WWWomen: http://www.wwwomen.com

Yahoo:Social Science:Women's Studes:
http://www.yahoo.com/Social_Science/Women_s_Studies/

Some other major web sites are:

Carnegie Mellon University:
http://English-www.hs.cmu.edu/feminism.html

Feminist Majority Online:
http://www.feminist.org/

19th-Century American Women Writers Web:
http:/clever.net/19cwww/

University of Maryland Women's Studies Resources:
http://www.inform.umd.edu:8080/EdRes/Topic/WomensStudies/

University of Wisconsin Library System Women's Studies Office:
http://www.library.wisc.edu/libraries/WomensStudies/

*(Note: URLs change frequently and the ones listed may not always be accurate.)